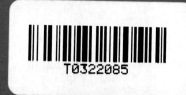

SPANISH ENGLISH

ILLUSTRATED DICTIONARY

FREE
AUDIO APP

Author

Thomas Booth worked for 10 years as an English teacher in Poland, Romania, and Russia. He now lives in England, where he works as an editor and English-language materials writer. He has contributed to a number of books in the *English for Everyone* series.

SPANISH ENGLISH
ILLUSTRATED DICTIONARY

DK

PRODUCED BY
Author / Editor Thomas Booth
Senior Art Editor Sunita Gahir
Art Editors Ali Jayne Scrivens, Samantha Richiardi
Illustrators Edward Byrne, Gus Scott
Project Manager Sunita Gahir / bigmetalfish design

DK UK
Senior Editors Amelia Petersen, Christine Stroyan
Senior Designers Clare Shedden, Vicky Read
Managing Art Editor Anna Hall
Managing Editor Carine Tracanelli
Jacket Editors Stephanie Cheng Hui Tan, Juhi Sheth
Jacket Development Manager Sophia MTT
Production Editors Gillian Reid, Robert Dunn, Jacqueline Street
Production Controller Sian Cheung
Publisher Andrew Macintyre
Art Director Karen Self
Publishing Director Jonathan Metcalf

Translation Andiamo! Language Services Ltd

DK INDIA
Desk Editors Joicy John, Tanya Lohan
DTP Designers Anurag Trivedi, Satish Gaur, Jaypal Chauhan, Bimlesh Tiwary, Rakesh Kumar
DTP Coordinator Pushpak Tyagi
Jacket Designer Vidushi Chaudhry
Senior Jackets Coordinator Priyanka Sharma Saddi
Managing Editor Saloni Talwar
Creative Head Malavika Talukder

First published in Great Britain in 2023 by
Dorling Kindersley Limited
DK, One Embassy Gardens, 8 Viaduct Gardens,
London, SW11 7BW

The authorized representative in the EEA is
Dorling Kindersley Verlag GmbH. Arnulfstr. 124,
80636 Munich, Germany

10 9 8 7 6 5 4
007–329227–Jun/2023

A CIP catalogue record for this book is available from the British Library
ISBN: 978-0-2415-6618-3

Printed and bound in China

For the curious
www.dk.com

MIX
Paper | Supporting responsible forestry
FSC™ C018179

This book was made with Forest Stewardship Council™ certified paper - one small step in DK's commitment to a sustainable future.
For more information go to www.dk.com/our-green-pledge

Contents

How to use this book 10

LAS PERSONAS PEOPLE

01 Las partes del cuerpo / Parts of the body 12
02 Las manos y los pies / Hands and feet 14
03 Los músculos y el esqueleto / Muscles and skeleton 16
04 Los órganos internos / Internal organs 18
05 La familia / Family 20
06 Los estados de ánimo / Feelings and moods 22
07 Los acontecimientos de la vida / Life events 24
08 El embarazo y la infancia / Pregnancy and childhood 26
09 Las rutinas diarias / Daily routines 28
10 Los rasgos de personalidad / Personality traits 30
11 Las habilidades y las acciones / Abilities and actions 32

LA APARIENCIA APPEARANCE

12 La apariencia y el cabello / Appearance and hair 34
13 La ropa / Clothes 36
14 La ropa (continuación) / Clothes continued 38
15 La ropa (continuación) / Clothes continued 40
16 Los accesorios / Accessories 42
17 El calzado / Shoes 44
18 La belleza / Beauty 46

LA SALUD HEALTH

19 Las enfermedades y lesiones / Illness and injury 48
20 La visita al médico / Visiting the doctor 50
21 El hospital / The hospital 52
22 El dentista y el oculista / The dentist and optician 54
23 La dieta y la nutrición / Diet and nutrition 56
24 Cuerpo sano, mente sana / Healthy body, healthy mind 58

EL HOGAR HOME

25 Un lugar donde vivir / A place to live 60
26 El salón y el comedor / Living room and dining room 62
27 La cocina y la vajilla / Kitchen and tableware 64
28 El menaje de cocina / Kitchenware 66
29 La cocina / Cooking 68
30 El dormitorio / Bedroom 70
31 El cuarto de baño / Bathroom 72
32 La casa y el hogar / House and home 74
33 La electricidad y la fontanería / Electrics and plumbing 76
34 Las tareas domésticas / Household chores 78
35 El bricolaje / Home improvements 80
36 Las herramientas / Tools 82
37 La decoración / Decorating 84
38 Las plantas de interior y de jardín / Garden plants and houseplants 86

39 La jardinería — Practical gardening — 88

40 Las herramientas de jardinería — Garden tools — 90

41 Los elementos del jardín — Garden features — 92

LA VIDA EN LA CIUDAD CITY LIFE

42 La ciudad — In town — 94

43 La ciudad (continuación) — In town continued — 96

44 Los edificios y la arquitectura — Buildings and architecture — 98

45 El banco y la oficina de correos — The bank and post office — 100

46 Las compras — Shopping — 102

47 El centro comercial — The shopping mall — 104

48 El supermercado — The supermarket — 106

49 La farmacia — The pharmacy — 108

50 Los servicios de emergencias — Emergency services — 110

51 La energía y el suministro eléctrico — Energy and power supply — 112

LOS ALIMENTOS FOOD

52 Beber y comer — Drinking and eating — 114

53 La carne — Meat — 116

54 El pescado y el marisco — Fish and seafood — 118

55 La verdura — Vegetables — 120

56 La verdura (continuación) — Vegetables continued — 122

57 La fruta — Fruit — 124

58 La fruta y los frutos secos — Fruit and nuts — 126

59 Las hierbas y las especias — Herbs and spices — 128

60 La despensa — In the pantry — 130

61 Los productos lácteos — Dairy produce — 132

62 La panadería — The bakery — 134

63 La panadería (continuación) — The bakery continued — 136

64 La delicatessen — The delicatessen — 138

65 En la cafetería — At the café — 140

66 En la cafetería (continuación) — At the café continued — 142

67 Las golosinas — Sweets — 143

68 En el bar — At the bar — 144

69 En el restaurante — At the restaurant — 146

70 La comida rápida — Fast food — 148

71 El desayuno — Breakfast — 150

72 El almuerzo y la cena — Lunch and dinner — 152

LOS ESTUDIOS STUDY

73 En la escuela — At school — 154

74 Las matemáticas — Mathematics — 156

75 La física — Physics — 158

76 La química — Chemistry — 160

77 La biología — Biology — 162

78 La tabla periódica — The periodic table — 164

79 La historia — History — 166

80 En la universidad At college 168

EL TRABAJO WORK

81 En el trabajo At work 170

82 En la oficina In the office 172

83 Los ordenadores y la tecnología Computers and technology 174

84 Los medios de comunicación Media 176

85 El derecho Law 178

86 La agricultura Farming 180

87 La construcción Construction 182

88 El Ejército Military 184

89 Los trabajos Jobs 186

90 Los trabajos (continuación) Jobs continued 188

91 Las industrias y los departamentos Industries and departments 190

92 Presentarse para un puesto de trabajo Applying for a job 192

93 Las competencias laborales Workplace skills 194

94 El dinero y las finanzas Money and finance 196

95 Reuniéndose y presentando Meeting and presenting 198

DESPLAZARSE GETTING AROUND

96 Las carreteras Roads 200

97 Los coches Cars 202

98 Los coches (continuación) Cars continued 204

99 Los coches y los autobuses Cars and buses 206

100 Las motocicletas Motorcycles 208

101 El ciclismo Cycling 210

102 Los trenes Trains 212

103 El avión Aircraft 214

104 En el aeropuerto At the airport 216

105 Los buques Sea vessels 218

106 El puerto The port 220

LOS DEPORTES SPORTS

107 El fútbol americano American football 222

108 El rugby Rugby 224

109 El fútbol Football 226

110 El hockey y el lacrosse Hockey and lacrosse 228

111 El críquet Cricket 230

112 El baloncesto y el voleibol Basketball and volleyball 232

113 El béisbol Baseball 234

114 El tenis Tennis 236

115 El golf Golf 238

116 El atletismo Athletics 240

117 Los deportes de combate Combat sports 242

118 La natación Swimming 244

119 La navegación y los deportes acuáticos Sailing and watersports 246

120 La equitación Horse riding 248

121 La pesca 250
Fishing

122 Los deportes de invierno 252
Winter sports

123 Los deportes de motor 254
Motorsports

124 En el gimnasio 256
At the gym

125 Otros deportes 258
Other sports

EL TIEMPO LIBRE LEISURE

126 Sobre el escenario 260
On stage

127 Las películas 262
Films

128 La música 264
Music

129 La música (continuación) 266
Music continued

130 Los museos y las galerías 268
Museums and galleries

131 El viaje y el alojamiento 270
Travel and accommodation

132 La visita turística 272
Sightseeing

133 Las actividades al aire libre 274
Outdoor activities

134 En la playa 276
On the beach

135 La acampada 278
Camping

136 El ocio en el hogar 280
Home entertainment

137 La televisión 282
Television

138 Los libros y la lectura 284
Books and reading

139 La fantasía y los mitos 286
Fantasy and myth

140 Los juegos 288
Games

141 Las manualidades 290
Arts and crafts

142 Las manualidades (continuación) 292
Arts and crafts continued

EL ENTORNO ENVIRONMENT

143 El espacio 294
Space

144 El espacio (continuación) 296
Space continued

145 El planeta Tierra 298
Planet Earth

146 La geografía 300
Geography

147 La geografía (continuación) 302
Geography continued

148 Los mapas y las indicaciones 304
Maps and directions

149 Los países 306
Countries

150 Los países (continuación) 308
Countries continued

151 Los países (continuación) 310
Countries continued

152 Las nacionalidades 312
Nationalities

153 Las nacionalidades (continuación) 314
Nationalities continued

154 El tiempo 316
Weather

155 El clima y el medio ambiente 318
Climate and the environment

156 Las rocas y los minerales 320
Rocks and minerals

EL MUNDO NATURAL NATURAL WORLD

157 La historia natural 322
Natural history

158 Los mamíferos 324
Mammals

159 Los mamíferos (continuación) 326
Mammals continued

160 Las aves 328
Birds

161 Las aves (continuación) 330
Birds continued

LAS REFERENCIAS REFERENCE

¡Aprendamos algunos nombres de bichos!
Let's learn some words for bugs!

¡He leído más de 10 000 palabras!
I have read more than 10,000 words!

How to use this book

This *Spanish English Illustrated Dictionary* will help you to understand and remember more than 10,000 of the most useful words and phrases in Spanish. The Spanish given in this book is the language spoken in Spain and Europe. Each of the 180 units in the dictionary covers a practical or everyday topic (such as health, food, or the natural world), and words are shown in a visual context to fix them in your memory along with their English equivalent. Using the audio app that accompanies the dictionary will help you learn and remember the new vocabulary.

Unit number The book is divided into units. The unit number helps you to find the unit easily when searching through the contents page.

Illustrated scenes Many units include illustrated scenes that make vocabulary easy to understand and remember.

English words The English translation is provided for each word.

Module numbers Most units are broken down into modules. Every module is identified with a unique number, so you can locate the audio on the app.

Illustrations All the entries in the dictionary are illustrated, helping you to understand and memorize new vocabulary.

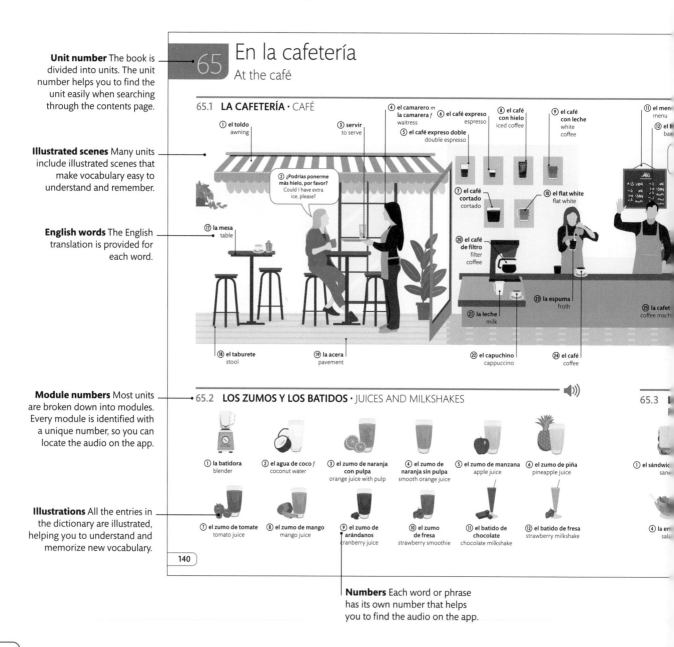

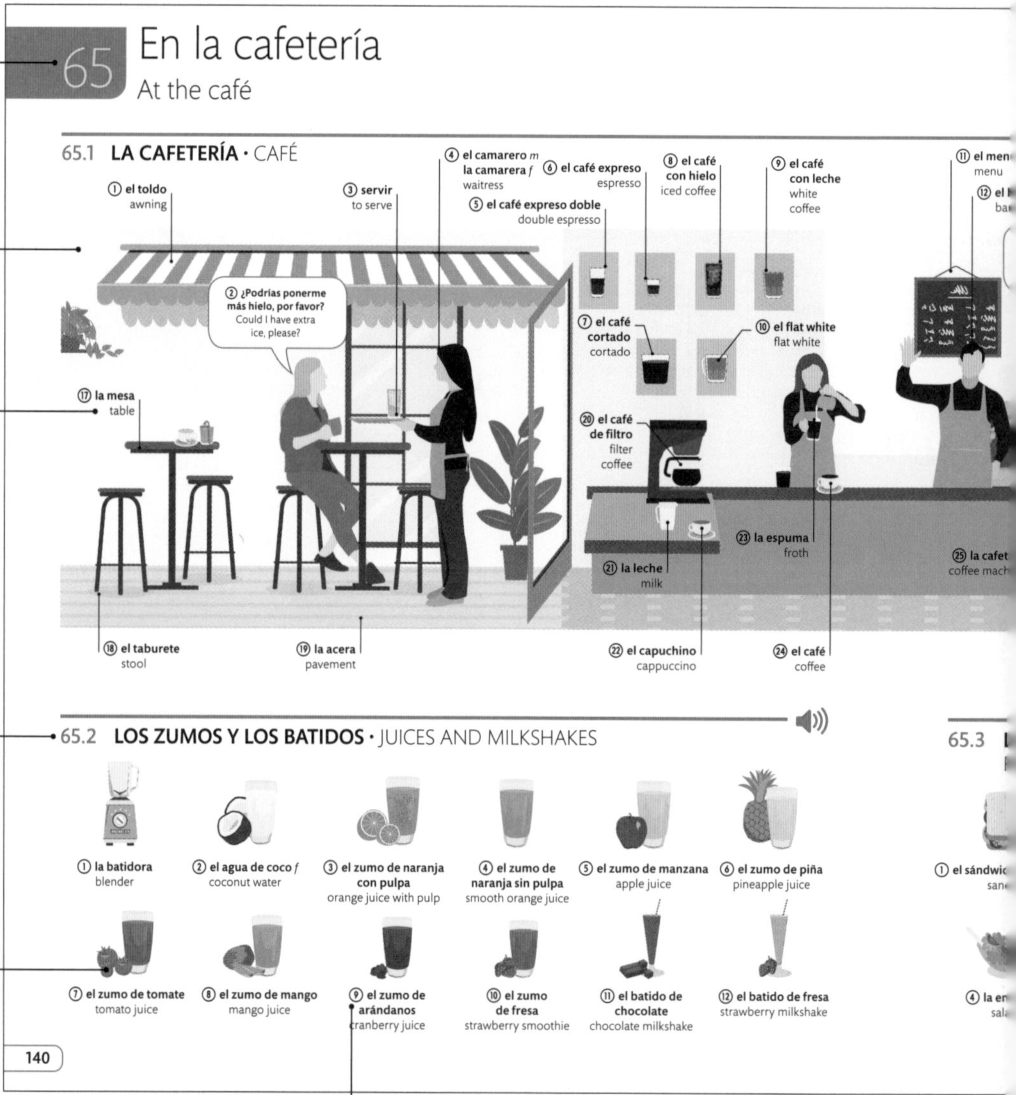
65
En la cafetería
At the café
65.1 LA CAFETERÍA · CAFÉ
① el toldo
awning
② ¿Podrías ponerme más hielo, por favor?
Could I have extra ice, please?
③ servir
to serve
④ el camarero m
la camarera f
waitress
⑤ el café expreso doble
double espresso
⑥ el café expreso
espresso
⑦ el café cortado
cortado
⑧ el café con hielo
iced coffee
⑨ el café con leche
white coffee
⑩ el flat white
flat white
⑪ menu
⑰ la mesa
table
⑱ el taburete
stool
⑲ la acera
pavement
⑳ el café de filtro
filter coffee
㉑ la leche
milk
㉒ el capuchino
cappuccino
㉓ la espuma
froth
㉔ el café
coffee
65.2 LOS ZUMOS Y LOS BATIDOS · JUICES AND MILKSHAKES
① la batidora
blender
② el agua de coco f
coconut water
③ el zumo de naranja con pulpa
orange juice with pulp
④ el zumo de naranja sin pulpa
smooth orange juice
⑤ el zumo de manzana
apple juice
⑥ el zumo de piña
pineapple juice
⑦ el zumo de tomate
tomato juice
⑧ el zumo de mango
mango juice
⑨ el zumo de arándanos
cranberry juice
⑩ el zumo de fresa
strawberry smoothie
⑪ el batido de chocolate
chocolate milkshake
⑫ el batido de fresa
strawberry milkshake
65.3
140

Numbers Each word or phrase has its own number that helps you to find the audio on the app.

See also Each unit has a "see also" box that directs you to other units with useful or related vocabulary.

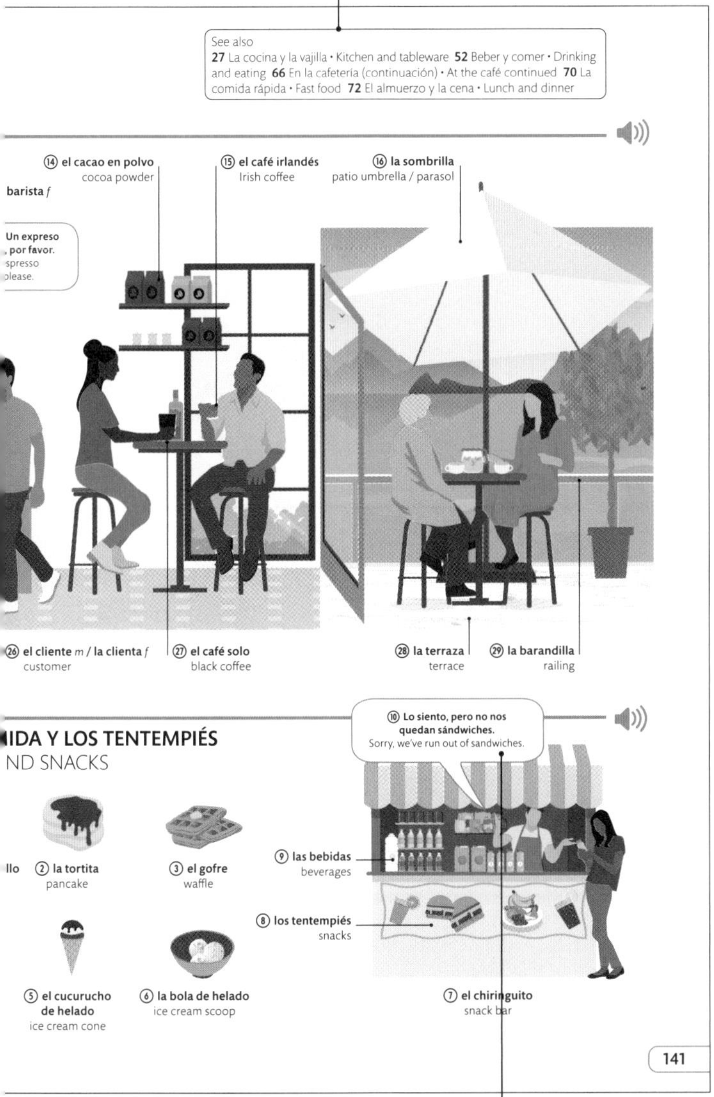

Speech bubbles Useful expressions and examples of real-life Spanish appear in speech bubbles throughout the book.

Gender and articles

All nouns in the dictionary are preceded by the definite article ("the"). In Spanish, nouns are masculine or feminine, and the definite article is "el" or "la" respectively ("los" or "las" for plurals). When a feminine singular noun starts with a stressed "a" or "ha", the masculine article "el" is used, and the gender is indicated with *f*.

el menú
menu

la mesa
table

el agua *f*
water

los cacahuetes
peanuts

las aceitunas
olives

Word lists

The Spanish and English word lists at the back of the book contain every entry from the dictionary. All the vocabulary is listed in alphabetical order, and each entry is followed by the unit number or numbers in which it is found, enabling you to look up any word in either Spanish or English. The Spanish words are listed without their articles, so that you can search for words alphabetically. The English word list also provides information about the part of speech (for example noun, verb, or adjective) of each word.

Audio app

The *Spanish English Illustrated Dictionary* is supported by a free audio app containing every Spanish word and phrase in the book. Listen to the audio and repeat the words and phrases out loud, until you are confident you understand and can pronounce what has been said. The app can be found by searching for "DK Illustrated Dictionary" in the App Store or Google Play. When prompted, choose the Castilian Spanish option to download the audio for this book.

FREE AUDIO APP

01 Las partes del cuerpo
Parts of the body

1.1 EL CUERPO HUMANO • THE HUMAN BODY

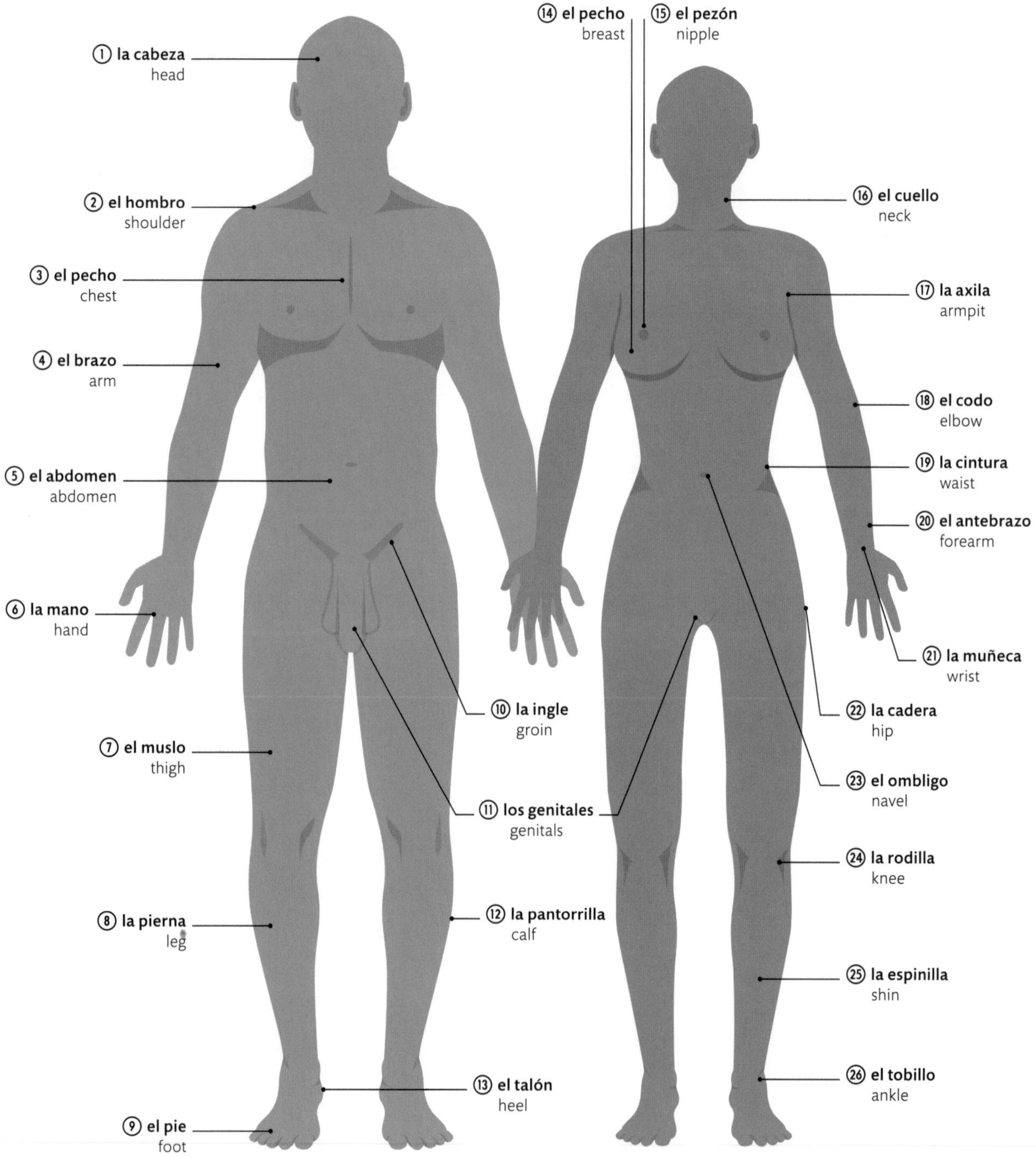

See also
02 Las manos y los pies • Hands and feet **03** Los músculos y el esqueleto • Muscles and skeleton
04 Los músculos y el esqueleto • Internal organs **19** Las enfermedades y lesiones • Illness and injury
20 La visita al médico • Visiting the doctor **22** El dentista y el oculista • The dentist and optician

1.2 EL ROSTRO • FACE

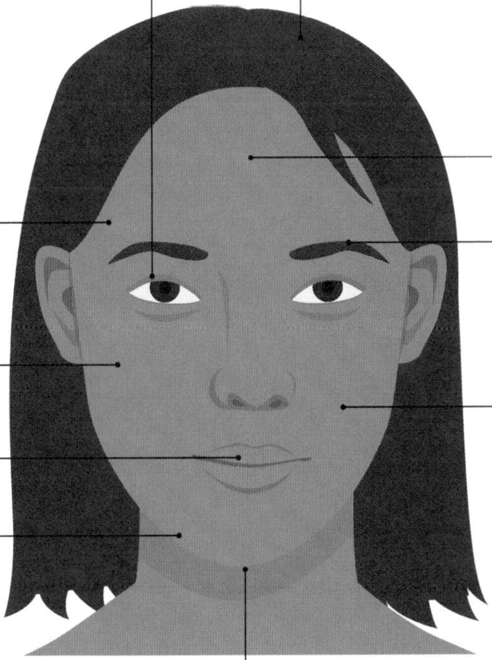

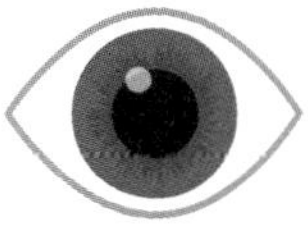

⑪ **el ojo**
eye

⑫ **la oreja**
ear

⑬ **la nariz**
nose

⑭ **las fosas nasales**
nostrils

⑮ **la boca**
mouth

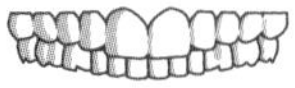

⑯ **los dientes**
teeth

1.3 LOS OJOS • EYES

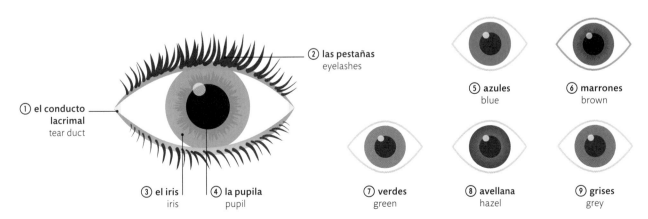

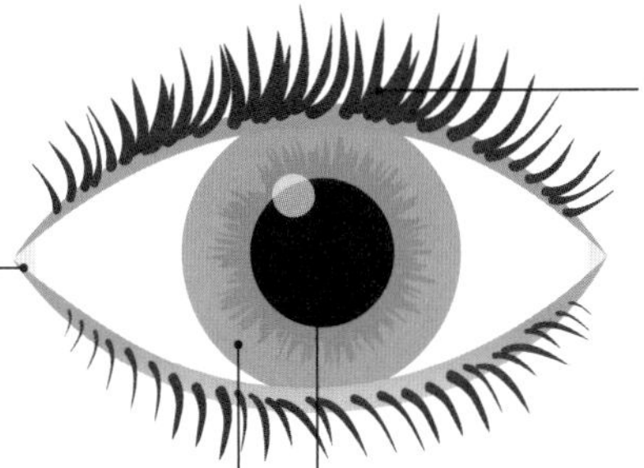

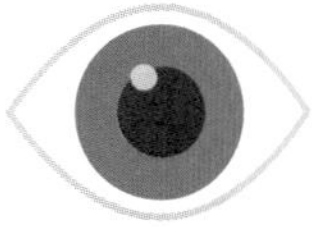

⑤ **azules**
blue

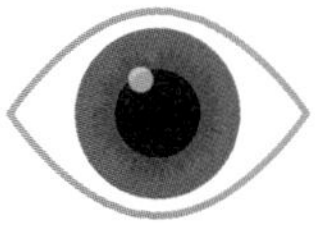

⑥ **marrones**
brown

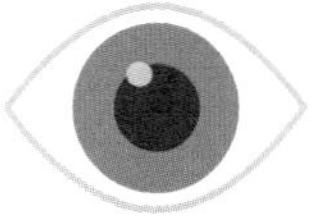

⑦ **verdes**
green

⑧ **avellana**
hazel

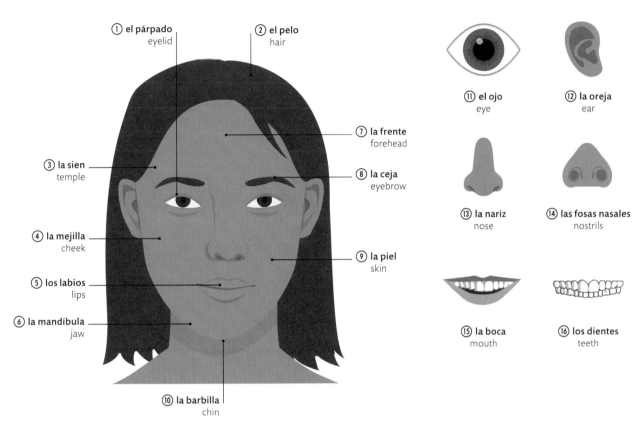

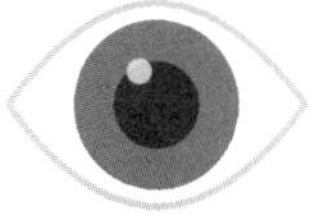

⑨ **grises**
grey

02 Las manos y los pies

Hands and feet

2.1 LAS MANOS · HANDS

① **la palma**
palm

② **el pulgar**
thumb

③ **el índice**
index finger

④ **el dedo corazón**
middle finger

⑤ **el anular**
ring finger

⑥ **el meñique**
little finger

⑦ **la muñeca**
wrist

⑧ **la uña**
fingernail

⑨ **la cutícula**
cuticle

⑩ **el nudillo**
knuckle

⑪ **el puño**
fist

2.2 LOS VERBOS DEL CUERPO · BODY VERBS

① **sonreír**
to smile

② **sonreír de oreja a oreja**
to grin

③ **fruncir el ceño**
to frown

④ **guiñar**
to wink

⑤ **parpadear**
to blink

⑥ **ruborizarse**
to blush

⑦ **bostezar**
to yawn

⑧ **roncar**
to snore

⑨ **lamer**
to lick

⑩ **sorber**
to suck

⑪ **respirar**
to breathe

⑫ **aguantar la respiración**
to hold your breath

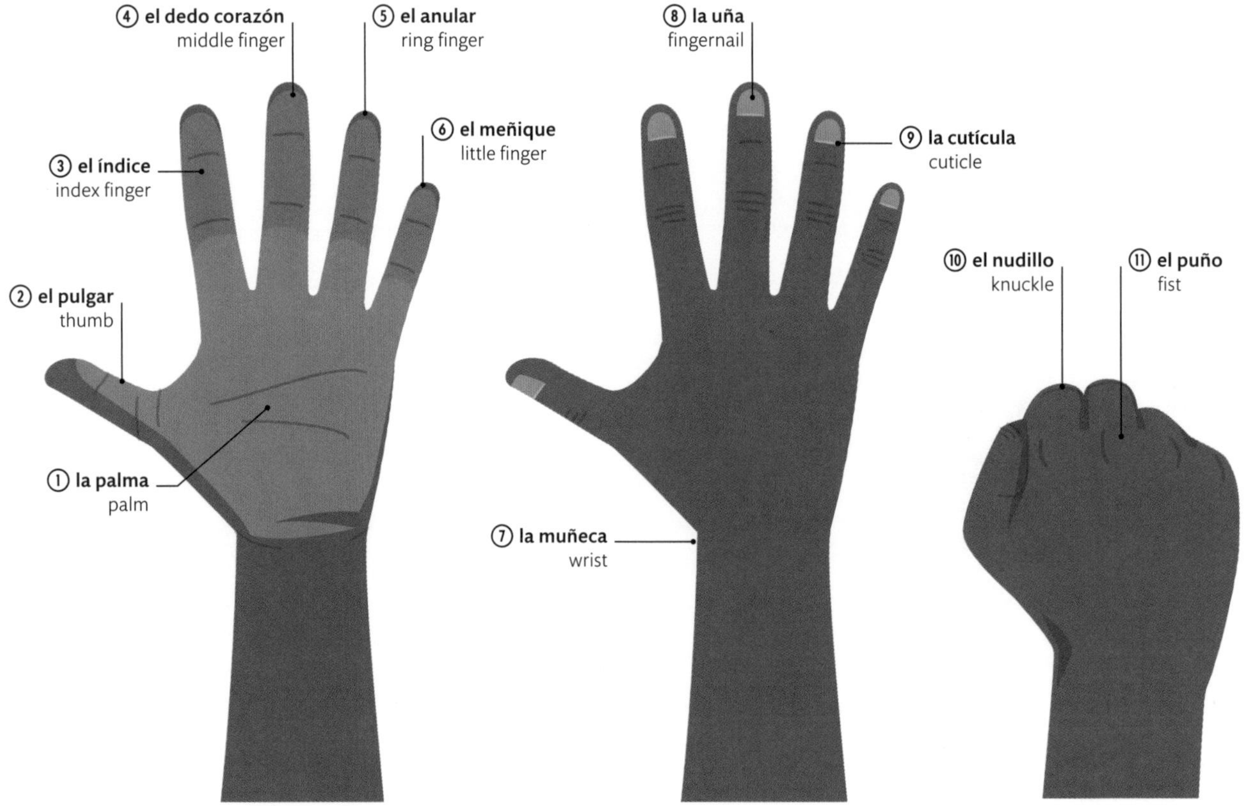

See also
01 Las partes del cuerpo • Parts of the body **03** Los músculos y el esqueleto
Muscles and skeleton **19** Las enfermedades y lesiones • Illness and injury

2.3 **LOS PIES** • FEET

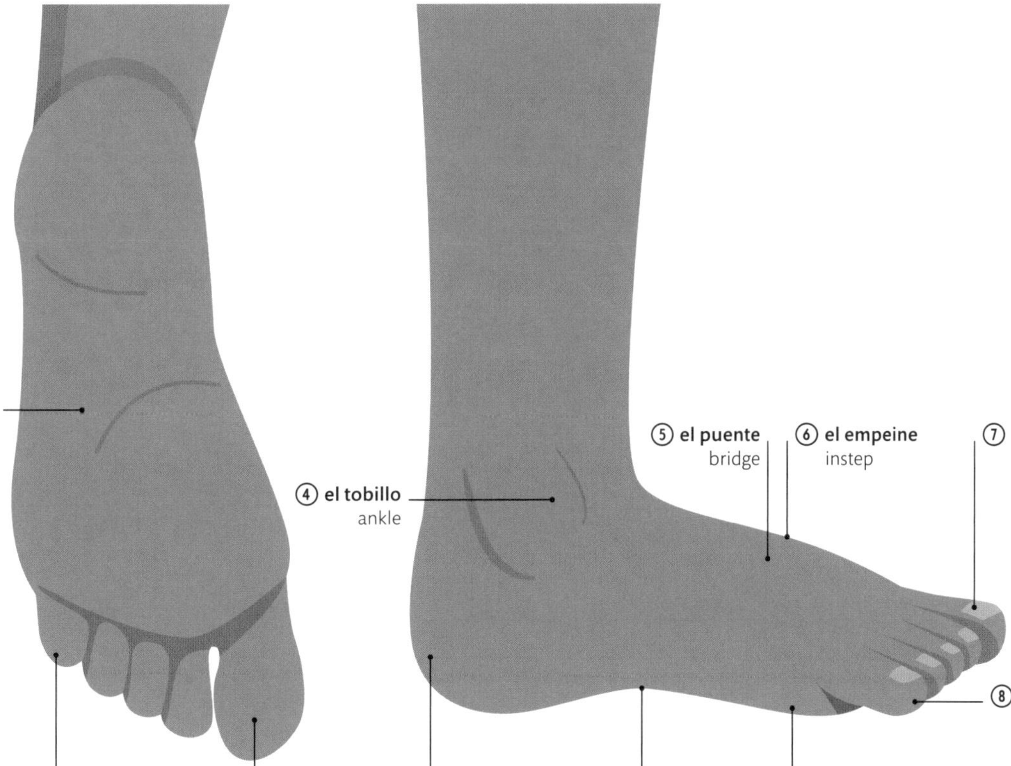

⑬ **reír**
to laugh

⑭ **llorar**
to cry

⑮ **suspirar**
to sigh

⑯ **saludar**
to wave

⑰ **encogerse de hombros**
to shrug

⑱ **hacer una reverencia**
to bow

⑲ **aplaudir**
to clap

⑳ **sudar**
to sweat / to perspire

㉑ **tiritar**
to shiver

㉒ **estornudar**
to sneeze

㉓ **negar**
to shake your head

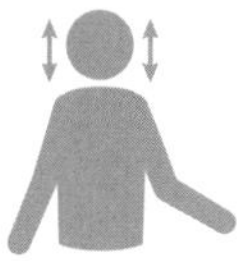
㉔ **asentir**
to nod

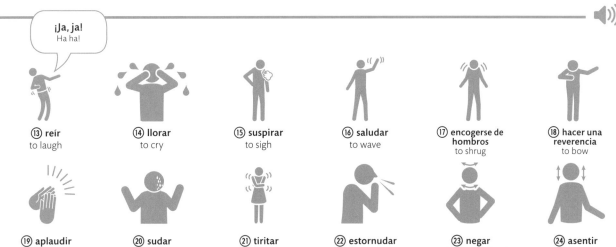

03 Los músculos y el esqueleto
Muscles and skeleton

3.1 LOS MÚSCULOS
MUSCLES

① **el frontal**
frontal

② **el pectoral**
pectoral

③ **los músculos intercostales**
intercostal

④ **el bíceps**
biceps

⑤ **los oblicuos**
obliques

⑥ **los abdominales**
abdominals

⑦ **el cuádriceps**
quadriceps

⑧ **delante**
front

⑨ **el deltoide**
deltoid

⑩ **el trapecio**
trapezius

⑪ **el tríceps**
triceps

⑫ **el dorsal ancho**
latissimus dorsi

⑬ **el glúteo**
buttock / gluteus maximus

⑭ **los isquiotibiales**
hamstring

⑮ **el gemelo**
calf

⑯ **el tendón de Aquiles**
Achilles tendon

⑰ **detrás**
back

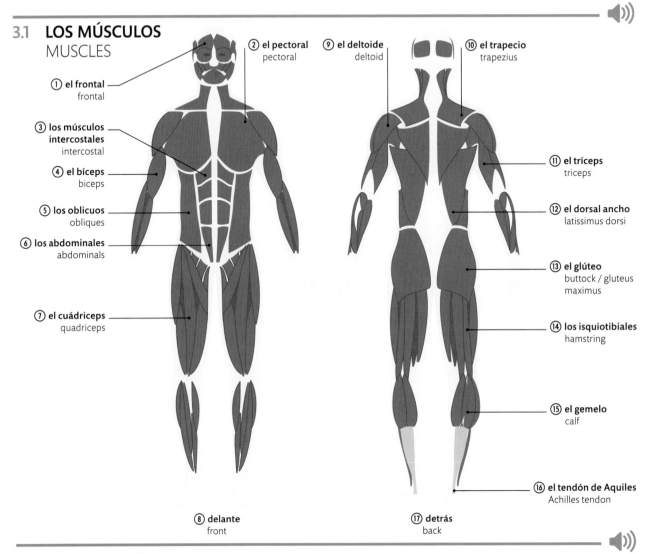

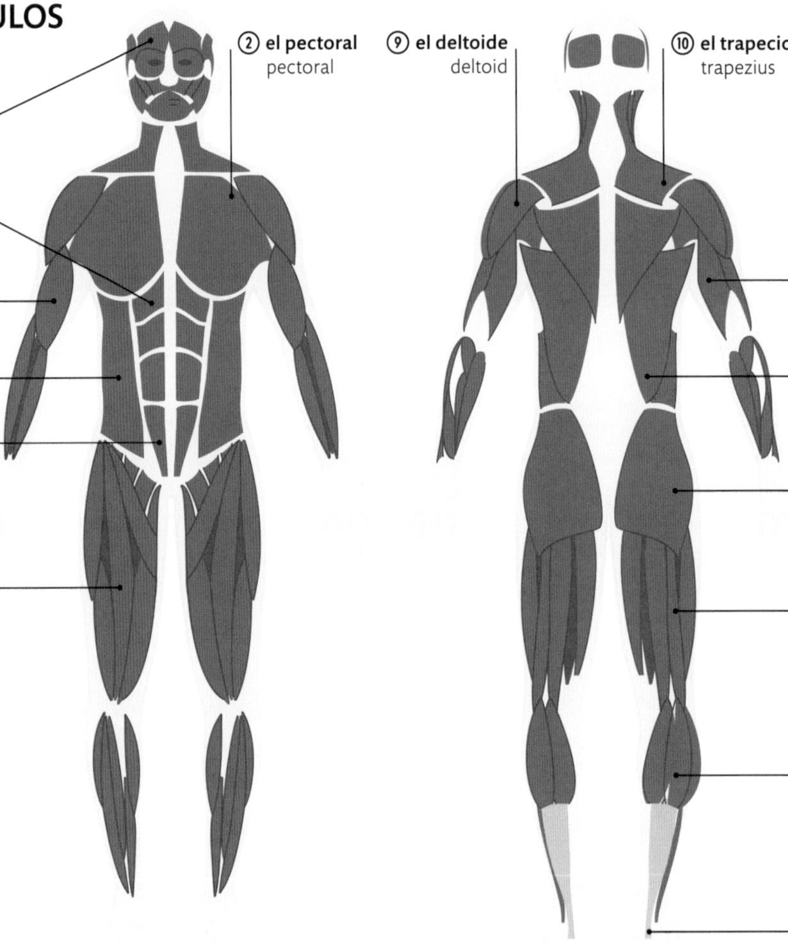

3.2 LOS DIENTES · TEETH

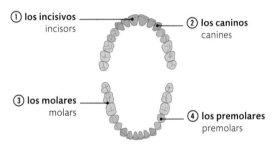

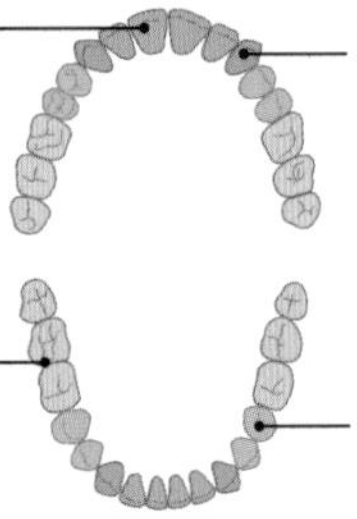

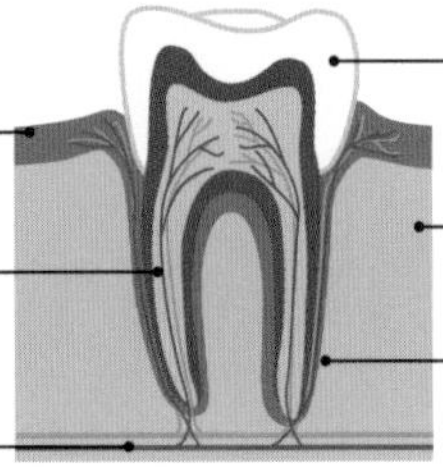

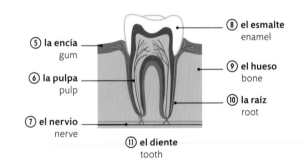

See also
01 Las partes del cuerpo • Parts of the body **02** Las manos y los pies • Hands and feet
04 Los órganos internos • Internal organs **19** Las enfermedades y lesiones • Illness and injury
20 La visita al médico • Visiting the doctor **21** El hospital • The hospital

3.3 EL ESQUELETO • SKELETON

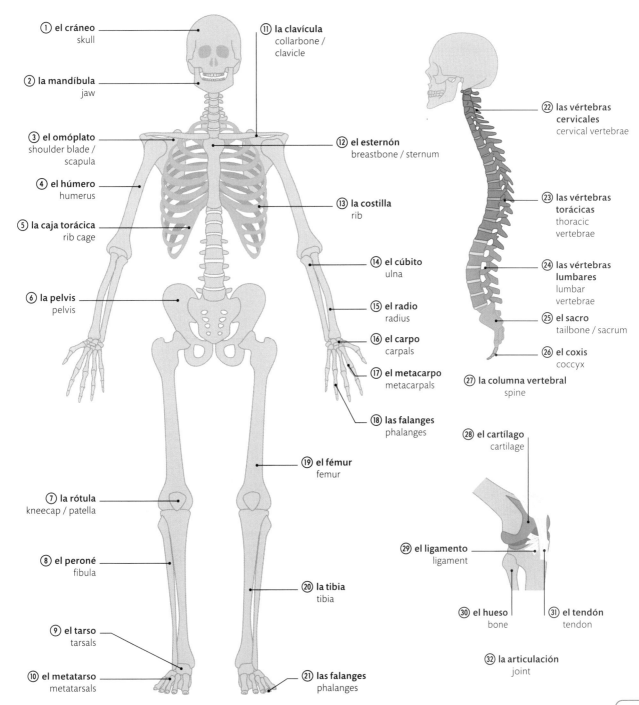

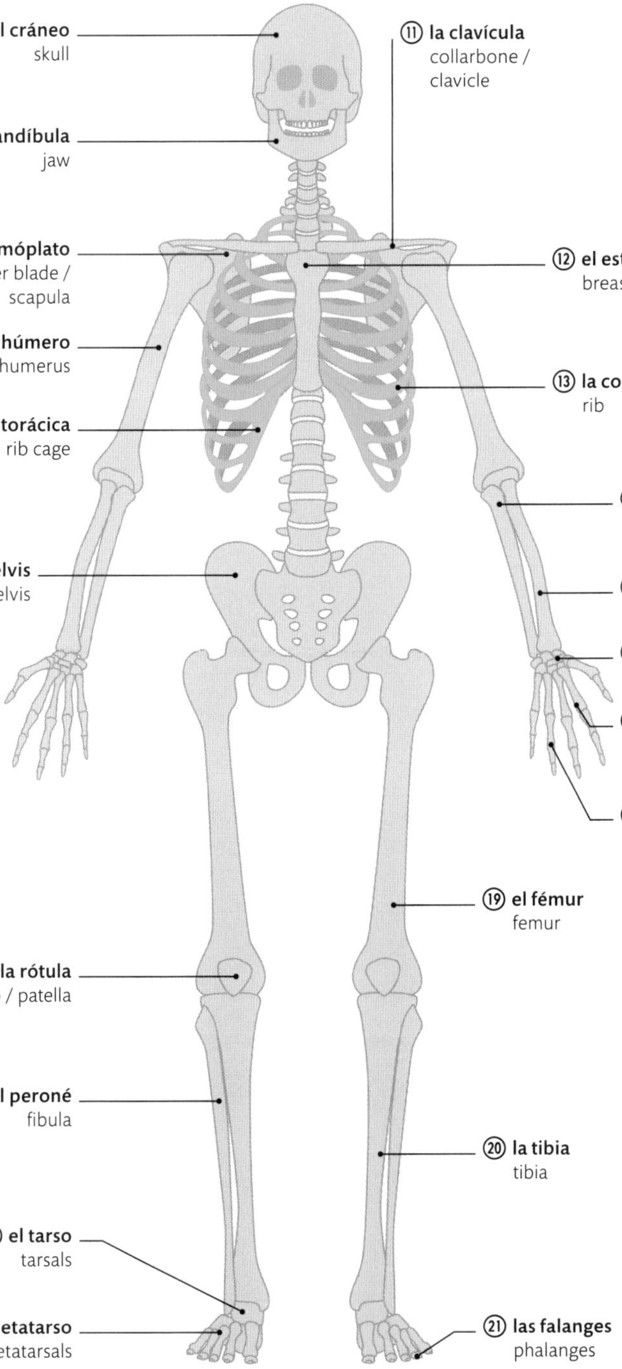

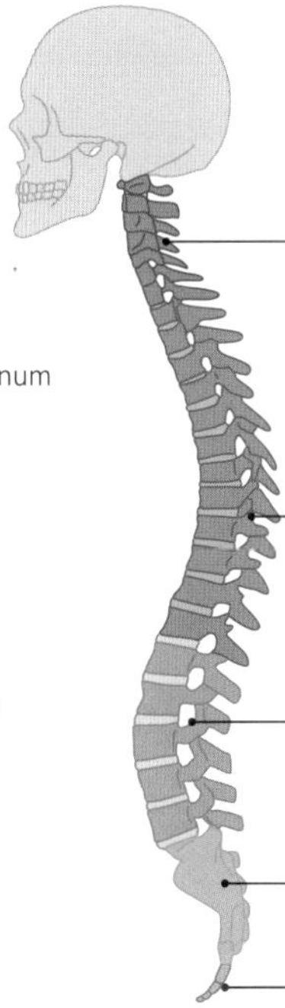

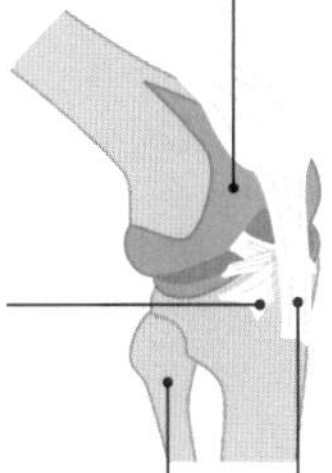

04 Los órganos internos
Internal organs

4.1 LOS ÓRGANOS INTERNOS · INTERNAL ORGANS

1. **la tráquea** trachea
2. **el pulmón** lung
3. **el hígado** liver
4. **la vesícula biliar** gall bladder
5. **la glándula suprarrenal** adrenal gland
6. **el riñón** kidney
7. **el apéndice** appendix
8. **el tiroides** thyroid gland
9. **el corazón** heart
10. **el estómago** stomach
11. **el bazo** spleen
12. **el páncreas** pancreas
13. **el intestino delgado** small intestine
14. **el intestino grueso** large intestine

4.2 LOS SISTEMAS CORPORALES · BODY SYSTEMS

④ **urinario** urinary

⑤ **endocrino** endocrine

⑥ **linfático** lymphatic

⑦ **reproductor** reproductive

⑧ **cardiovascular** cardiovascular

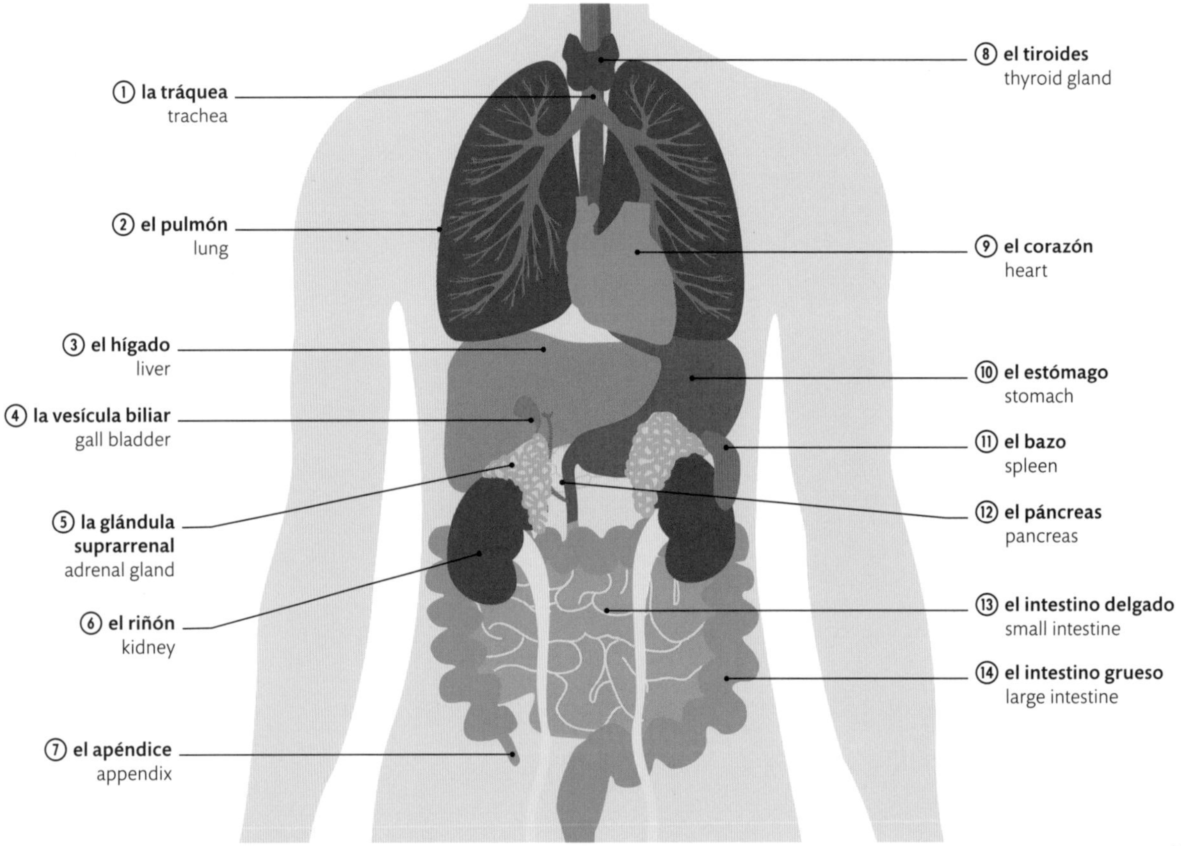

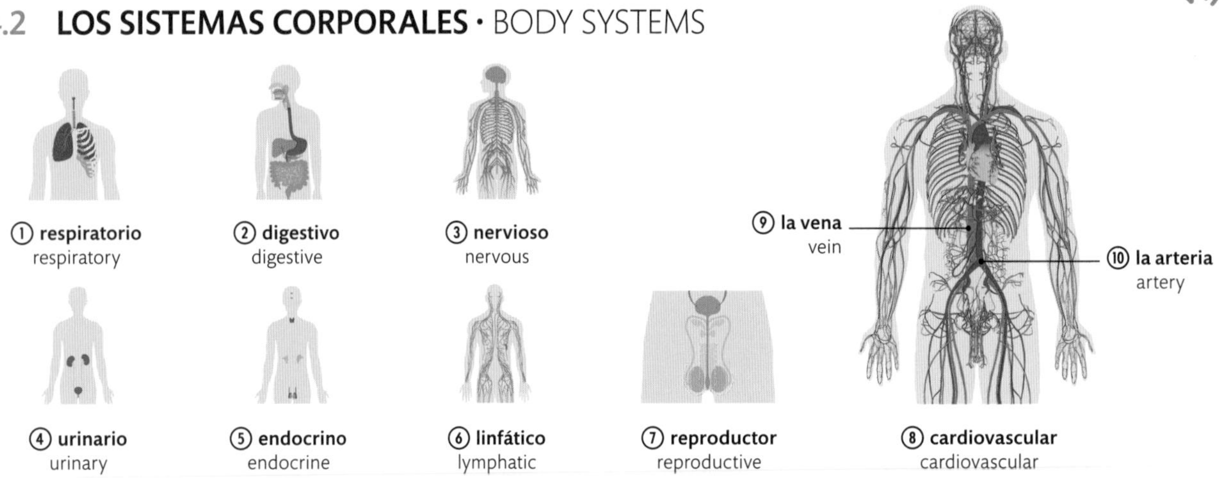

See also
01 Las partes del cuerpo • Parts of the body **03** Los músculos y el esqueleto • Muscles and skeleton **19** Las enfermedades y lesiones • Illness and injury **20** La visita al médico • Visiting the doctor **21** El hospital • The hospital

4.3 LA CABEZA • HEAD

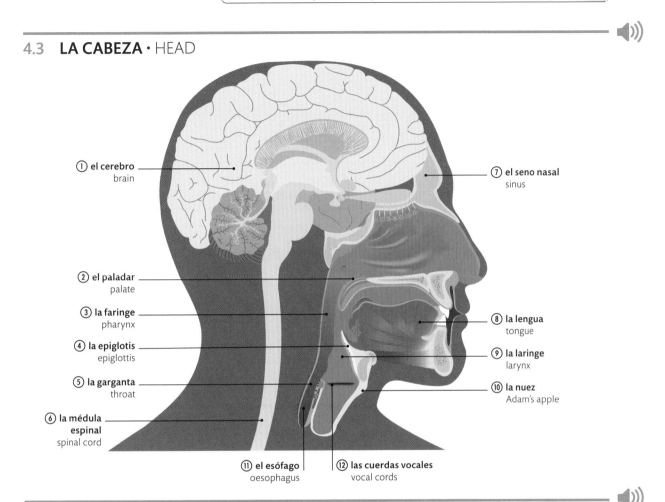

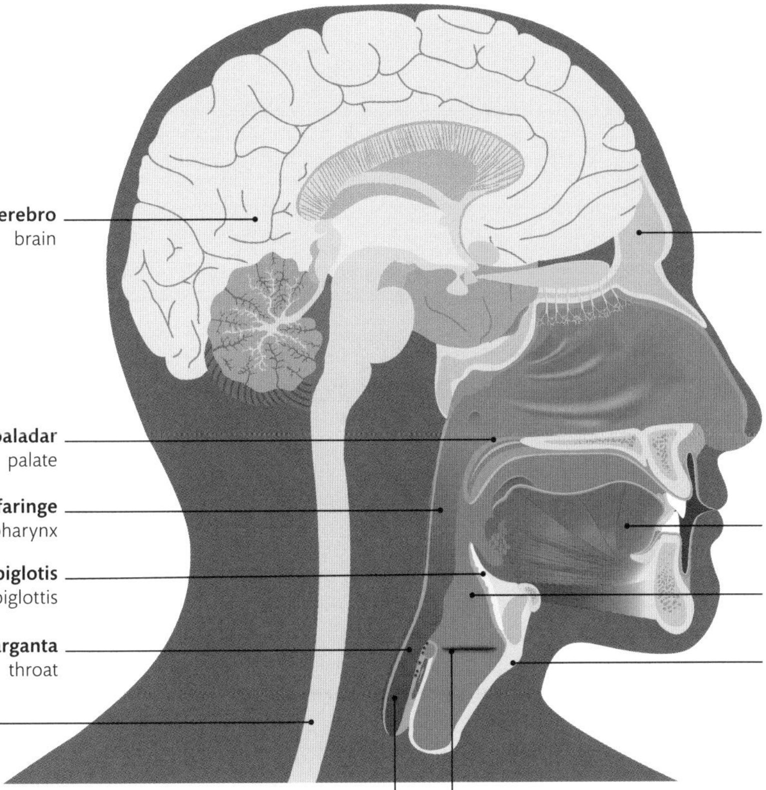

4.4 LOS ÓRGANOS REPRODUCTORES • REPRODUCTIVE ORGANS

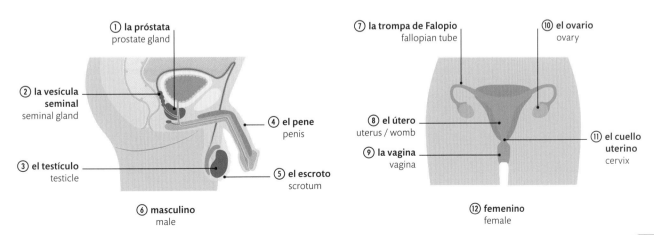

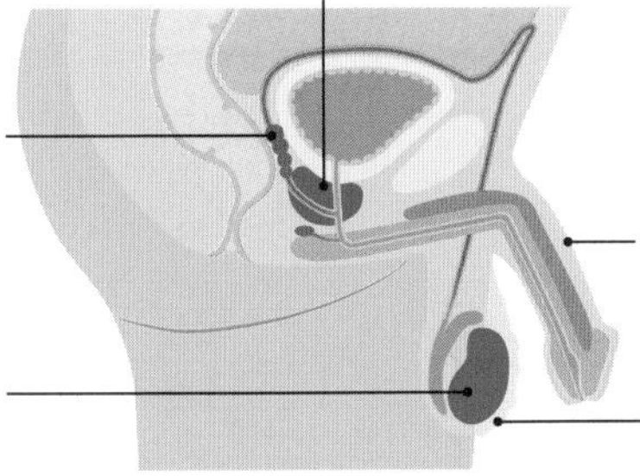

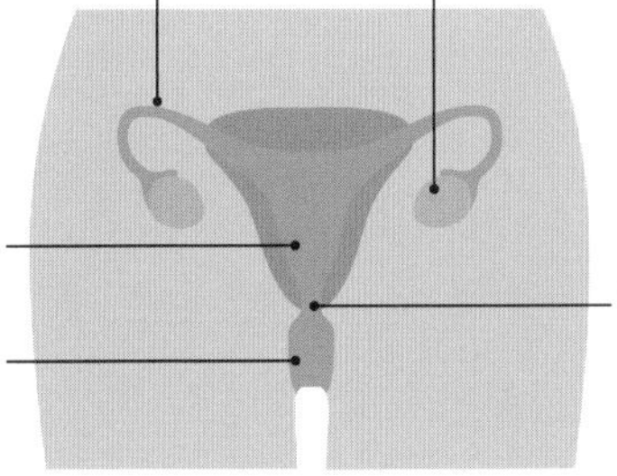

05 La familia
Family

5.1 LA FAMILIA DE CARLOS · CARLOS'S FAMILY

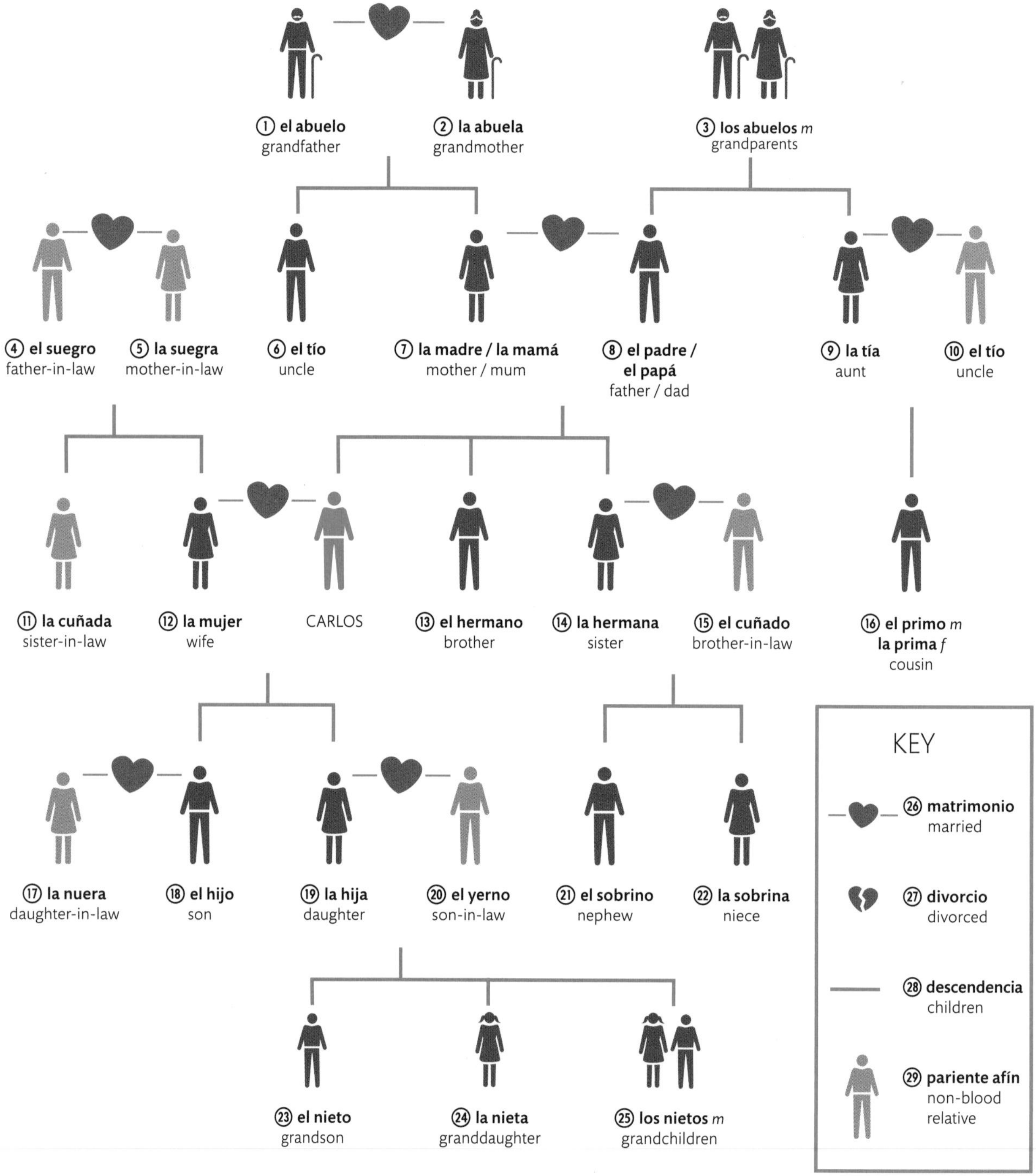

See also
07 Los acontecimientos de la vida • Life events
08 El embarazo y la infancia • Pregnancy and childhood

5.2 LA FAMILIA DE SARA
SARA'S FAMILY

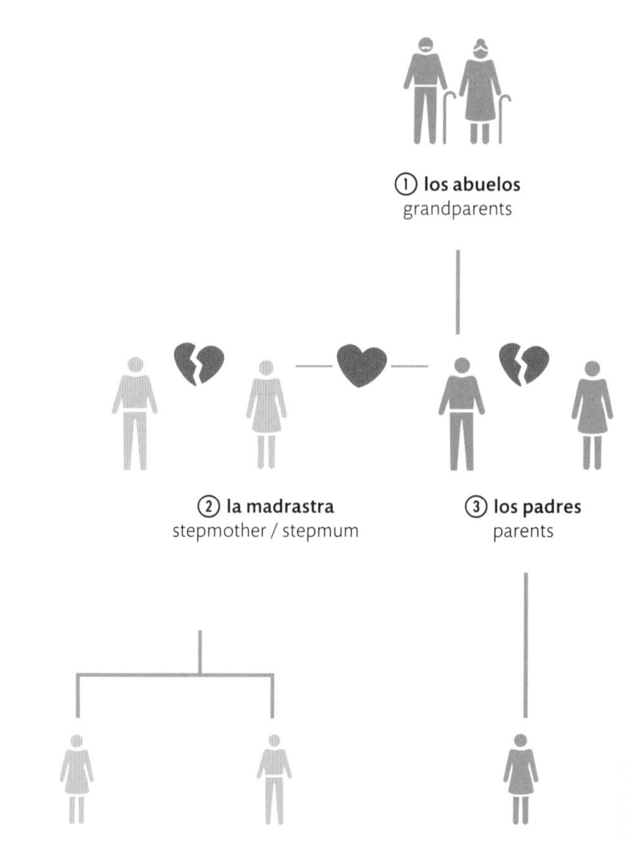

① **los abuelos**
grandparents

② **la madrastra**
stepmother / stepmum

③ **los padres**
parents

④ **la hermanastra**
stepsister

⑤ **el hermanastro**
stepbrother

SARA

5.3 LAS RELACIONES • RELATIONSHIPS

① **el novio** *m*
la novia *f*
boyfriend and girlfriend

② **la pareja**
partner

③ **el padre soltero** *m*
la madre soltera *f*
single parent

④ **la viuda** *f*
widow

⑤ **casados**
married

⑥ **el marido**
husband

⑦ **la mujer**
wife

⑧ **divorciados**
divorced

⑨ **la exmujer**
ex-wife

⑩ **el exmarido**
ex-husband

⑪ **los hermanos** *m*
siblings

⑫ **los gemelos** *m*
las gemelas *f*
twins

⑬ **los trillizos** *m*
las trillizas *f*
triplets

⑭ **el hijo único** *m*
la hija única *f*
only child

5.4 EL CRECIMIENTO • GROWING UP

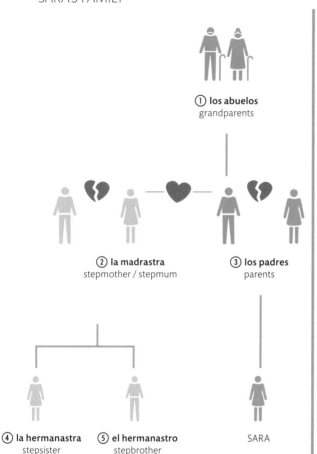

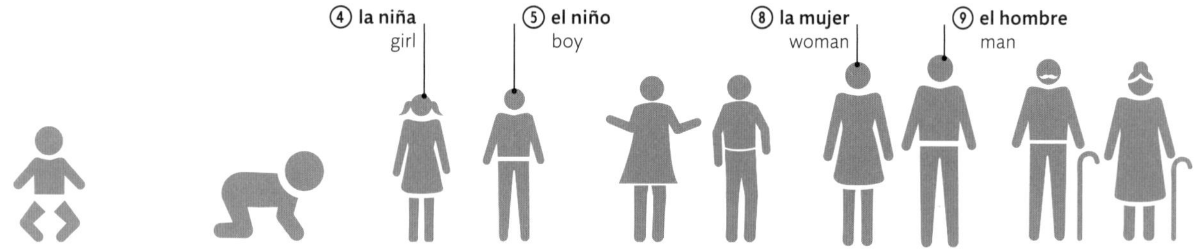

① **el bebé**
baby

② **el niño pequeño** *m*
la niña pequeña *f*
toddler

③ **los niños** *m*
las niñas *f*
child

④ **la niña**
girl

⑤ **el niño**
boy

⑥ **los adolescentes**
teenagers

⑦ **los adultos**
adults

⑧ **la mujer**
woman

⑨ **el hombre**
man

⑩ **el anciano** *m*
la anciana *f*
elderly

06 Los estados de ánimo
Feelings and moods

6.1 LOS ESTADOS DE ÁNIMO • FEELINGS AND MOODS

① **contento** *m*
contenta *f*
pleased

② **alegre**
cheerful

③ **feliz**
happy

④ **encantado** *m*
encantada *f*
delighted

⑤ **eufórico** *m*
eufórica *f*
ecstatic

⑥ **divertido** *m*
divertida *f*
amused

⑦ **agradecido** *m*
agradecida *f*
grateful

⑧ **afortunado** *m*
afortunada *f*
lucky

⑨ **interesado** *m*
interesada *f*
interested

⑩ **curioso** *m*
curiosa *f*
curious

⑪ **intrigado** *m*
intrigada *f*
intrigued

⑫ **asombrado** *m*
asombrada *f*
amazed

⑬ **sorprendido** *m*
sorprendida *f*
surprised

⑭ **orgulloso** *m*
orgullosa *f*
proud

⑮ **emocionado** *m*
emocionada *f*
excited

⑯ **entusiasmado** *m*
entusiasmada *f*
thrilled

⑰ **calmado** *m*
calmada *f*
calm

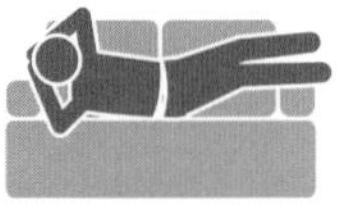
⑱ **relajado** *m*
relajada *f*
relaxed

⑳ **Me ha encantado la comida. Gracias.**
Thank you. I really enjoyed the meal.

⑲ **apreciativo** *m* / **apreciativa** *f*
appreciative

㉑ **seguro** *m* / **segura** *f*
confident

㉒ **optimista**
hopeful

㉓ **compasivo** *m* / **compasiva** *f*
sympathetic

㉔ **molesto** *m*
molesta *f*
annoyed

㉕ **celoso** *m* / **celosa** *f*
jealous

㉖ **avergonzado** *m*
avergonzada *f*
embarrassed

See also
10 Los rasgos de personalidad • Personality traits
24 Cuerpo sano, mente sana • Healthy body, healthy mind
93 Las competencias laborales • Workplace skills

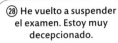

㉘ **He vuelto a suspender el examen. Estoy muy decepcionado.**
I failed the exam again. I'm very disappointed.

㉗ **decepcionado** *m* / **decepcionada** *f*
disappointed

㉙ **preocupado** *m* **preocupada** *f*
worried

㉚ **ansioso** *m* / **ansiosa** *f*
anxious

㉛ **nervioso** *m* **nerviosa** *f*
nervous

㉜ **asustado** *m* / **asustada** *f*
frightened

㉝ **atemorizado** *m* **atemorizada** *f*
scared

㉞ **aterrado** *m* / **aterrada** *f*
terrified

㉟ **triste**
sad

㊱ **infeliz**
unhappy

㊲ **lloroso** *m* / **llorosa** *f*
tearful

㊳ **abatido** *m* / **abatida** *f*
miserable

㊴ **deprimido** *m* **deprimida** *f*
depressed

㊵ **solitario** *m* / **solitaria** *f*
lonely

㊶ **irritado** *m* / **irritada** *f*
irritated

㊷ **frustrado** *m* **frustrada** *f*
frustrated

㊸ **enfadado** *m* / **enfadada** *f*
angry

㊹ **furioso** *m* **furiosa** *f*
furious

㊺ **asqueado** *m* / **asqueada** *f*
disgusted

㊻ **desganado** *m* **desganada** *f*
unenthusiastic

㊼ **cansado** *m* **cansada** *f*
tired

㊽ **exhausto** *m* / **exhausta** *f*
exhausted

㊾ **confundido** *m* **confundida** *f*
confused

㊿ **aburrido** *m* / **aburrida** *f*
bored

(51) **distraído** *m* **distraída** *f*
distracted

(52) **serio** *m* / **seria** *f*
serious

(53) **indiferente**
indifferent

(54) **estresado** *m* / **estresada** *f*
stressed

(55) **culpable**
guilty

(56) **poco impresionado** *m* **poco impresionada** *f*
unimpressed

(57) **disgustado** *m***disgustada** *f*
upset

(58) **impactado** *m* **impactada** *f*
shocked

07 Los acontecimientos de la vida
Life events

7.1 LAS RELACIONES · RELATIONSHIPS

① **el vecino** *m*
la vecina *f*
neighbour

② **el amigo** *m*
la amiga *f*
friend

③ **el conocido** *m*
la conocida *f*
acquaintance

④ **el compañero de trabajo** *m* / **la compañera de trabajo** *f*
colleague

⑤ **el amigo por correspondencia** *m*
la amiga por correspondencia *f*
pen pal

⑥ **la pareja**
couple

⑦ **el mejor amigo** *m*
la mejor amiga *f*
best friend

⑧ **el cónyuge** *m*
la cónyuge *f*
partner

⑨ **¿Quieres casarte conmigo?**
Will you marry me?

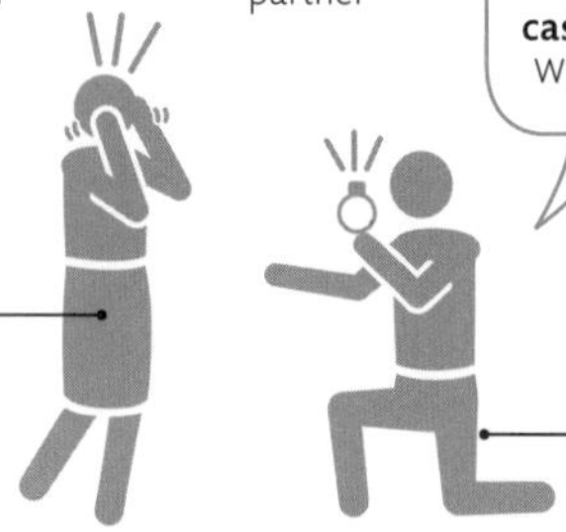

⑩ **la prometida**
fiancée

⑪ **el prometido**
fiancé

⑫ **la pareja comprometida**
engaged couple

⑬ **la novia**
bride

⑭ **el novio**
groom

⑮ **el matrimonio**
married couple

7.2 ACONTECIMIENTOS DE LA VIDA · LIFE EVENTS

① **nacer**
to be born

② **el certificado de nacimiento**
birth certificate

③ **ir a la guardería**
to go to nursery

④ **ir a la escuela**
to start school

⑤ **hacer amigos**
to make friends

⑥ **ganar un premio**
to win a prize

⑦ **graduarse**
to graduate

⑧ **emigrar**
to emigrate

⑨ **encontrar trabajo**
to get a job

⑩ **enamorarse**
to fall in love

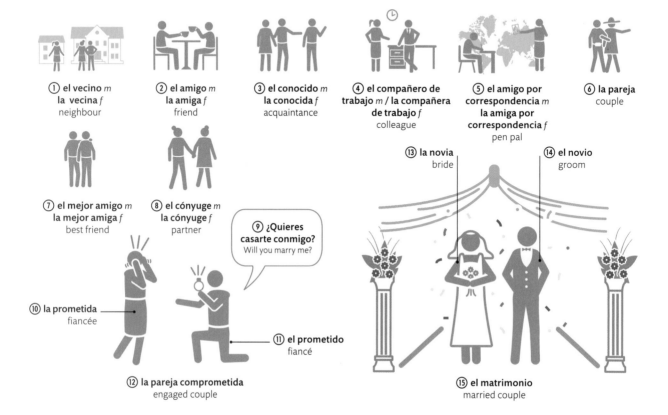

⑪ **casarse**
to get married

See also
05 La familia • Family **08** El embarazo y la infancia • Pregnancy and childhood **19** Las enfermedades y lesiones • Illness and injury **73** En la escuela • At school **80** En la universidad • At college **92** Presentarse para un puesto de trabajo • Applying for a job **131** El viaje y el alojamiento • Travel and accommodation

7.3 LAS FIESTAS Y LAS CELEBRACIONES • FESTIVALS AND CELEBRATIONS

① **el cumpleaños**
birthday

② **el regalo**
present

③ **la tarjeta de cumpleaños**
birthday card

④ **la Navidad**
Christmas

⑤ **el Año Nuevo**
New Year

⑥ **el carnaval**
carnival

⑦ **el Día de Acción de Gracias**
Thanksgiving

⑧ **la Semana Santa**
Easter

⑨ **Halloween**
Halloween

⑩ **el Kwanzaa**
Kwanzaa

⑪ **la Pascua judía**
Passover

⑫ **el Diwali**
Diwali

⑬ **el Día de los Muertos**
Day of the Dead

⑭ **el Eid al-Fitr / la Fiesta del Fin del Ayuno**
Eid al-Fitr

⑮ **el Holi**
Holi

⑯ **la Janucá**
Hanukkah

⑰ **el Baisakhi / Vaisakhi**
Baisakhi / Vaisakhi

⑫ **la boda**
wedding

⑬ **la luna de miel**
honeymoon

⑭ **el aniversario**
anniversary

⑮ **tener un bebé**
to have a baby

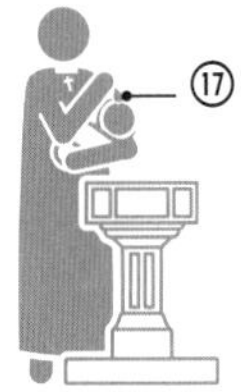
⑰ **el agua bendita** *f*
holy water

⑯ **el bautismo**
christening / baptism

⑱ **el bar mitzvá** *m*
el bat mitzvá *f*
bar mitzvah / bat mitzvah

⑲ **el Hajj / peregrinar a La Meca**
to go on Hajj

⑳ **jubilarse**
to retire

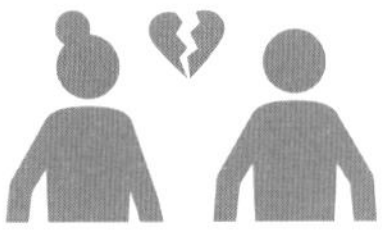
㉑ **divorciarse**
divorce

㉒ **hacer testamento**
to make a will

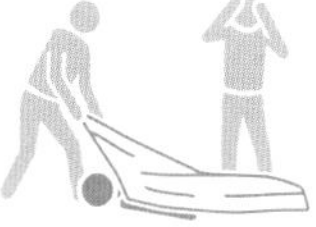
㉓ **morirse**
to die

㉔ **el funeral**
funeral

08 El embarazo y la infancia
Pregnancy and childhood

8.1 **EL EMBARAZO Y EL PARTO** · PREGNANCY AND CHILDBIRTH

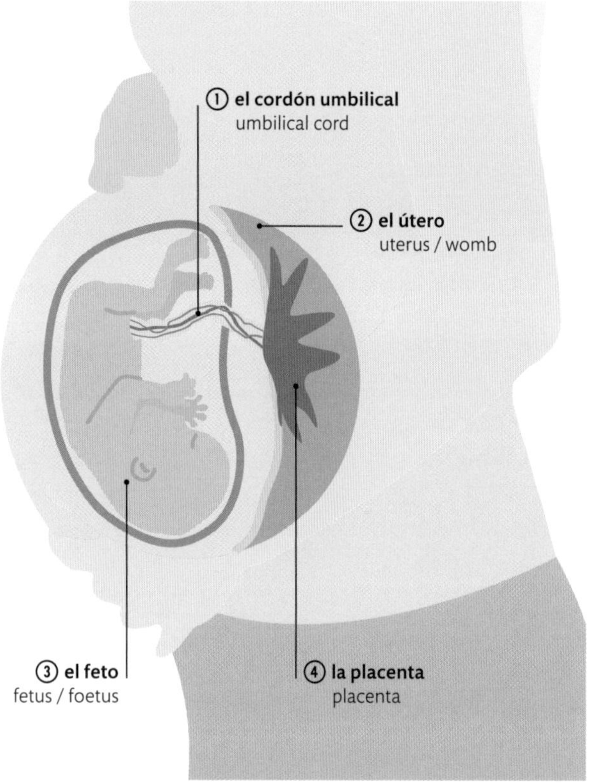

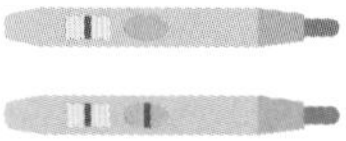

5 **el test de embarazo**
pregnancy test

6 **la embarazada**
pregnant

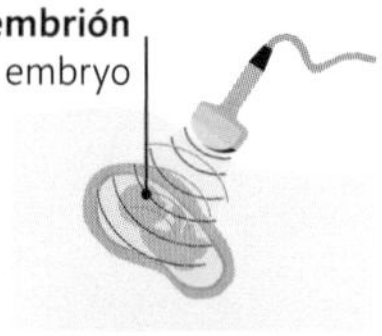

7 **la ecografía**
ultrasound

9 **la fecha de parto**
due date

10 **el matrón** *m*
la matrona *f*
midwife

11 **el obstetra** *m*
la obstetra *f*
obstetrician

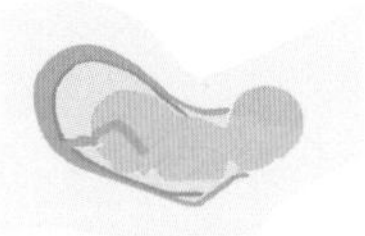

12 **el parto**
birth

13 **el recién nacido** *m*
la recién nacida *f*
newborn baby

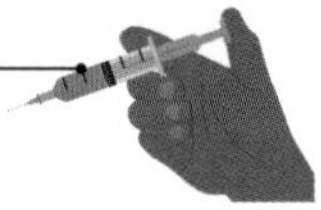

14 **la vacuna**
vaccination

15 **la incubadora**
incubator

8.2 **LOS JUEGOS Y LOS JUGUETES** · TOYS AND GAMES

1 **la muñeca**
doll

2 **la casa de muñecas**
doll's house

3 **el oso de peluche**
soft toy

4 **el juego de mesa**
board game

5 **los bloques de construcción**
building blocks / building bricks

6 **la pelota**
ball

7 **la peonza**
spinning top

8 **el yoyó**
yo-yo

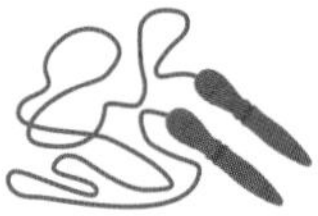

9 **la comba**
skipping rope

10 **la cama elástica**
trampoline

11 **el rompecabezas**
jigsaw puzzle

12 **el tren de juguete**
train set

See also
05 La familia • Family **13** La ropa • Clothes **20** La visita al médico • Visiting the doctor **21** El hospital • The hospital **30** El dormitorio • Bedroom

8.3 LA INFANCIA • CHILDHOOD

① **la silla de paseo**
buggy

② **el carro de bebé**
pram

③ **la trona**
high chair

④ **el chupete**
dummy

⑤ **el sonajero**
rattle

⑥ **el vigilabebés**
baby monitor

⑦ **la barrera de seguridad**
stair gate

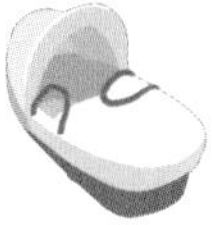
⑧ **el moisés**
Moses basket

⑨ **la bañera para bebés**
baby bath

⑩ **el orinal**
potty

⑪ **las toallitas**
wet wipe

⑫ **el niño pequeño** *m*
la niña pequeña *f*
toddler

⑬ **la crema de pañal**
nappy rash cream

⑭ **el pañal**
nappy

⑮ **el bolso cambiador**
changing bag

⑯ **el parque para bebés**
playpen

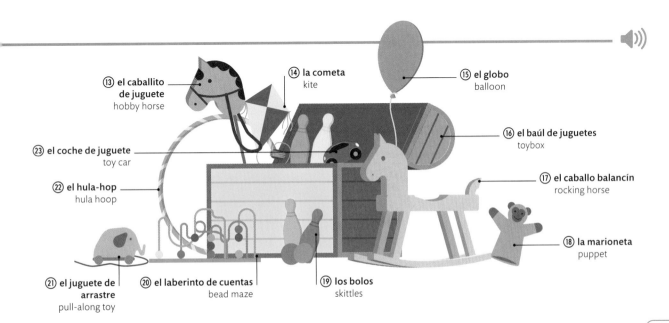

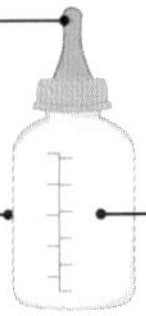

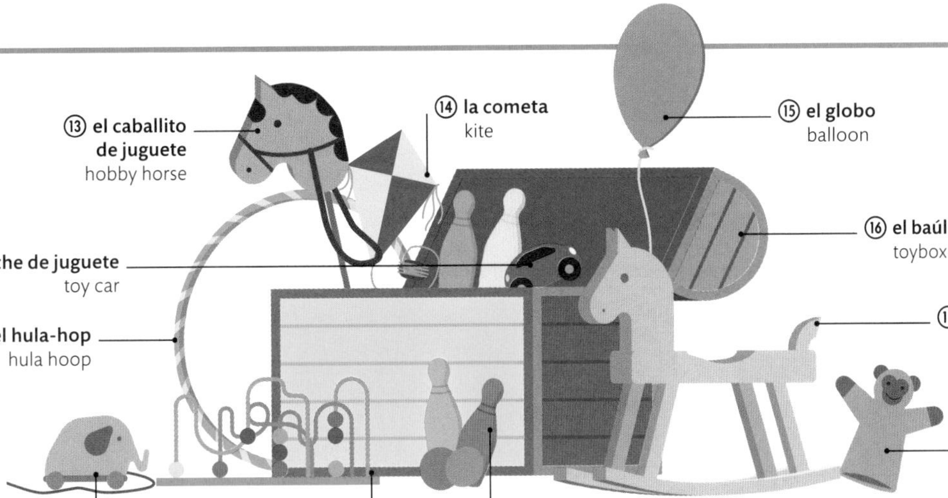

Las rutinas diarias

Daily routines

9.1 POR LA MAÑANA Y POR LA TARDE · MORNING AND AFTERNOON

① **apagar el despertador**
alarm goes off

② **despertarse**
to wake up

③ **levantarse**
to get up

④ **ducharse**
to take (or have) a shower

⑤ **bañarse**
to take (or have) a bath

⑥ **maquillarse**
to put on makeup

⑦ **afeitarse**
to shave

⑧ **lavarse el pelo**
to wash your hair

⑨ **secarse el pelo**
to dry your hair

⑩ **planchar una camisa**
to iron a shirt

⑪ **vestirse**
to get dressed

⑫ **cepillarse los dientes**
to brush your teeth

⑬ **lavarse la cara**
to wash your face

⑭ **cepillarse el pelo**
to brush your hair

⑮ **hacer la cama**
to make the bed

⑯ **desayunar**
to have (or eat) breakfast

⑰ **preparar el almuerzo**
to pack your lunch

⑱ **salir de casa**
to leave the house

⑲ **ir a trabajar**
to go to work

⑳ **ir a la escuela**
to go to school

㉑ **conducir**
to drive

㉒ **coger el autobús**
to catch the bus

㉓ **coger el tren**
to catch the train

㉔ **leer el periódico**
to read a newspaper

㉕ **llegar**
to arrive

㉖ **llegar temprano**
to arrive early

㉗ **llegar a tiempo**
to arrive on time

㉘ **almorzar**
to have (or eat) lunch

㉙ **leer el correo electrónico**
to check your emails

㉚ **hacer una pausa**
to have a break

㉜ Siento llegar tarde otra vez.
I'm sorry I'm late again.

㉛ **llegar tarde**
to arrive late / to be late

See also
11 Las habilidades y las acciones • Abilities and actions **29** La cocina • Cooking
81 En el trabajo • At work **82** En la oficina • In the office **171** El tiempo • Time
178 Los verbos compuestos comunes • Common phrasal verbs

9.2 POR LA NOCHE • EVENING

① **terminar el trabajo**
to finish work

④ **¡Como en casa en ningún sitio!**
There's no place like home!

② **salir del trabajo**
to leave work

③ **trabajar horas extras**
to work overtime

⑤ **llegar a casa**
to arrive home

⑥ **hacer la cena**
to cook dinner

⑦ **cenar**
to have (or eat) dinner

⑧ **recoger la mesa**
to clear the table

⑨ **lavar los platos**
to wash up

⑩ **escuchar la radio**
to listen to the radio

⑪ **ver la tele**
to watch TV

⑫ **beber té o café**
to drink tea or coffee

⑬ **sacar la basura**
to take out the rubbish

⑭ **acostar a los niños**
to put the children to bed

⑮ **irse a la cama**
to go to bed

⑯ **poner la alarma**
to set the alarm

⑰ **irse a dormir**
to go to sleep

9.3 OTRAS ACTIVIDADES
OTHER ACTIVITIES

① **hacer los deberes**
to do homework

② **sacar al perro**
to walk the dog

③ **dar de comer al perro / al gato**
to feed the dog / cat

④ **hacer la compra**
to buy groceries

⑤ **salir con amigos**
to go out with friends

⑥ **tomar un café**
to go to a café

⑦ **llamar a un amigo / a un familiar**
to call a friend / to call your family

⑧ **cortar el césped**
to mow the lawn

⑨ **hacer ejercicio**
to exercise

⑩ **jugar con tus hijos**
to play with your kids

⑪ **pagar las facturas**
to pay the bills

⑫ **dormir la siesta**
to take a nap

⑬ **lavar el coche**
to clean the car

⑭ **tocar un instrumento**
to play a musical instrument

⑮ **charlar con amigos**
to chat with friends

⑯ **chatear en línea**
to chat online

⑰ **regar las plantas**
to water the plants

⑱ **enviar un paquete**
to send a package / parcel

10 Los rasgos de personalidad
Personality traits

10.1 DESCRIBIR LA PERSONALIDAD • DESCRIBING PERSONALITIES

① **amistoso** *m*
amistosa *f*
friendly

② **antipático** *m*
antipática *f*
unfriendly

③ **hablador** *m*
habladora *f*
talkative

④ **entusiasta**
enthusiastic

⑤ **serio** *m* / **seria** *f*
serious

⑥ **asertivo** *m*
asertiva *f*
assertive

⑦ **crítico** *m*
crítica *f*
critical

⑧ **bondadoso** *m*
bondadosa *f*
caring

⑨ **sensible**
sensitive

⑩ **insensible**
insensitive

⑪ **razonable**
reasonable

⑫ **irracional**
unreasonable

⑬ **amable**
kind

⑭ **desagradable**
unkind

⑮ **reservado** *m*
reservada *f*
secretive

⑯ **maduro** *m*
madura *f*
mature

⑰ **inmaduro** *m*
inmadura *f*
immature

⑱ **cauteloso** *m*
cautelosa *f*
cautious

⑲ **generoso** *m*
generosa *f*
generous

⑳ **valiente**
brave

㉑ **gracioso** *m*
graciosa *f*
funny

㉒ **mezquino** *m*
mezquina *f*
mean

㉓ **paciente**
patient

㉔ **impaciente**
impatient

㉕ **vago** *m* / **vaga** *f*
lazy

㉖ **optimista**
optimistic

㉗ **sociable**
outgoing

㉘ **apasionado** *m*
apasionada *f*
passionate

㉙ **educado** *m*
educada *f*
polite

㉚ **maleducado** *m*
maleducada *f*
rude

㉛ **tímido** *m*
tímida *f*
shy

㉜ **inteligente**
intelligent

㉝ **nervioso** *m*
nerviosa *f*
nervous

㉞ **seguro** *m*
segura *f*
confident

㉟ **tonto** *m* / **tonta** *f*
silly

㊱ **egoísta**
selfish

See also
05 La familia • Family **06** Los estados de ánimo • Feelings and moods **11** Las habilidades y las acciones • Abilities and actions **93** Las competencias laborales • Workplace skills

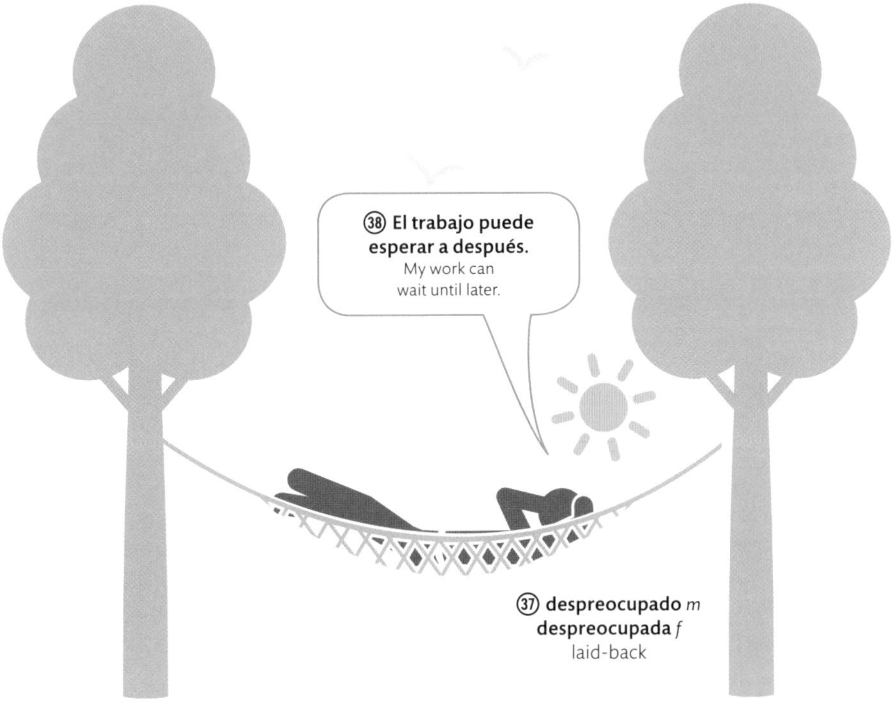
㊳ **El trabajo puede esperar a después.**
My work can wait until later.

㊲ **despreocupado** *m*
despreocupada *f*
laid-back

㊴ **ambicioso** *m*
ambiciosa *f*
ambitious

㊵ **espontáneo** *m*
espontánea *f*
spontaneous

㊶ **romántico** *m*
romántica *f*
romantic

㊷ **calmado** *m*
calmada *f*
calm

㊸ **excéntrico** *m*
excéntrica *f*
eccentric

㊹ **honrado** *m*
honrada *f*
honest

㊺ **mentiroso** *m*
mentirosa *f*
dishonest

㊻ **alentador** *m*
alentadora *f*
supportive

㊼ **impulsivo** *m*
impulsiva *f*
impulsive

㊽ **formal**
reliable

㊾ **informal**
unreliable

㊿ **talentoso** *m*
talentosa *f*
talented

51 **arrogante**
arrogant

52 **considerado** *m*
considerada *f*
considerate

53 **aventurero** *m*
aventurera *f*
adventurous

54 **tratable**
approachable

55 **intratable**
unapproachable

56 **decidido** *m*
decidida *f*
decisive

57 **meticuloso** *m*
meticulosa *f*
meticulous

58 **torpe**
clumsy

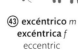

59 **desconsiderado** *m*
desconsiderada *f*
thoughtless

11 Las habilidades y las acciones

Abilities and actions

11.1 DESCRIBIR LAS HABILIDADES Y LAS ACCIONES

DESCRIBING ABILITIES AND ACTIONS

① **ver**
to see

② **saborear**
to taste

③ **oler**
to smell

④ **gatear**
to crawl

⑩ **Me encanta bailar.**
I love to dance.
⑪ **¡A mí también!**
Me too!

⑨ **bailar**
to dance

⑤ **golpear**
to hit

⑥ **jugar**
to play

⑦ **patear**
to kick

⑧ **lanzar**
to throw

⑫ **atrapar**
to catch

⑬ **correr**
to run

⑭ **brincar**
to hop

⑮ **saltar**
to jump

⑯ **moverse sigilosamente**
to creep

⑰ **agitar**
to shake

⑱ **trabajar horas extras**
to work

⑲ **soplar**
to blow

⑳ **hacer (un muñeco de nieve)**
to make (a snowman)

㉑ **deletrear**
to spell

㉒ **hacer (los deberes)**
to do (homework)

㉓ **copiar**
to copy

㉔ **construir**
to build

㉕ **cavar**
to dig

㉖ **reparar**
to repair

㉗ **arreglar**
to fix

㉘ **sentarse**
to sit down

㉙ **levantarse**
to stand up

㉚ **entender**
to understand

㉛ **caerse**
to fall

㉜ **levantar**
to lift

㉝ **sumar**
to add

㉞ **restar**
to subtract

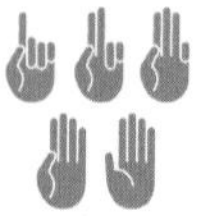

㉟ **contar**
to count

See also
09 Las rutinas diarias • Daily routines **93** Las competencias laborales • Workplace skills **178** Los verbos compuestos comunes • Common phrasal verbs

(36) **escuchar**
to listen

(37) **hablar**
to talk

(38) **decir**
to speak

(39) **gritar**
to shout

(40) **cantar**
to sing

(41) **actuar**
to act

(42) **susurrar**
to whisper

(43) **pensar**
to think

(44) **decidir**
to decide

(45) **recordar**
to remember

(46) **olvidar**
to forget

(47) **ayudar**
to help

(48) **señalar**
to point

(49) **empaquetar**
to pack

(50) **desempaquetar**
to unpack

(51) **volar**
to fly

(52) **montar**
to ride

(53) **escalar**
to climb

(54) **lamer**
to lick

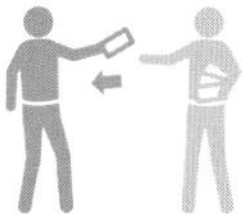

(55) **coger**
to take

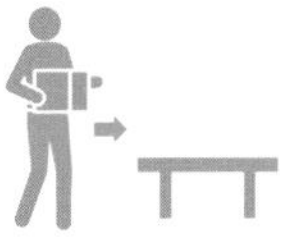

(56) **traer**
to bring

(57) **recoger**
to pick up / to collect

(58) **entrar**
to enter

(59) **salir**
to exit

(60) **ganar**
to win

(61) **alzar**
to raise

(62) **cargar**
to carry

(63) **hacer malabares**
to juggle

(64) **sujetar**
to hold

(65) **mover**
to move

(66) **empujar**
to push

(67) **tirar**
to pull

12 La apariencia y el cabello
Appearance and hair

12.1 LA APARIENCIA GENERAL
GENERAL APPEARANCE

① **estatura media**
medium height

② **alto** *m*
alta *f*
tall

③ **bajo** *m*
baja *f*
short

④ **guapa** *f*
beautiful

⑤ **apuesto** *m*
handsome

⑥ **joven**
young

⑦ **de mediana edad**
middle-aged

⑧ **viejo** *m* / **vieja** *f*
old

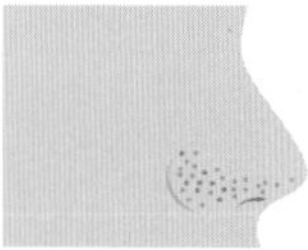

⑨ **los poros**
pores

⑩ **las pecas**
freckles

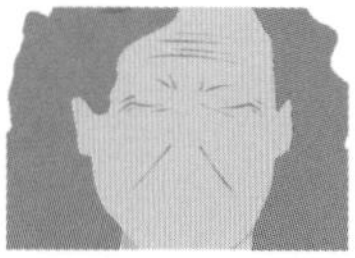

⑪ **las arrugas**
wrinkles

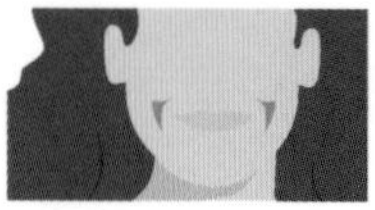

⑫ **los hoyuelos**
dimples

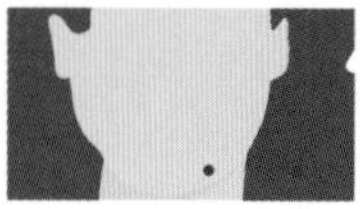

⑬ **el lunar**
mole

12.2 EL PELO · HAIR

① **peinarse**
to style your hair

② **lavarse el pelo**
to wash your hair

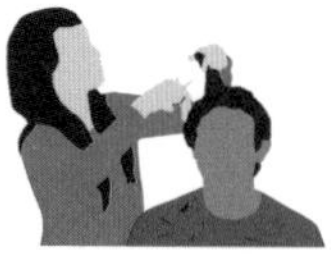

③ **cortarse el pelo**
to have (or get) your hair cut

④ **recogerse el pelo**
to tie your hair back

⑤ **dejarse crecer el pelo**
to grow your hair

⑥ **afeitarse**
to shave

⑦ **el pelo largo**
long hair

⑧ **el pelo corto**
short hair

⑨ **la media melena**
shoulder-length hair

⑩ **la raya al lado**
side parting

⑪ **la raya en medio**
centre parting

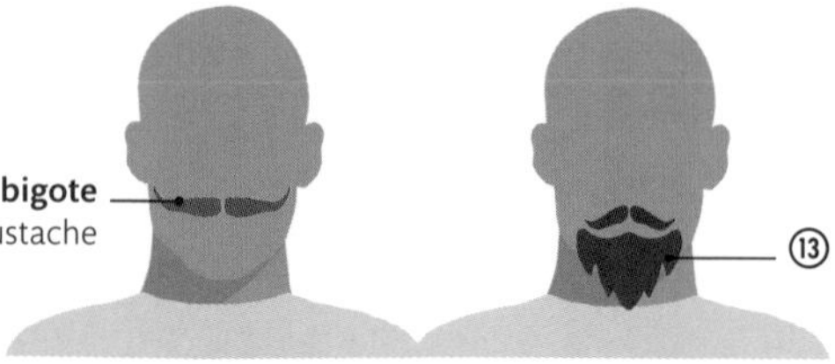

⑫ **el bigote**
moustache

⑬ **la perilla**
goatee

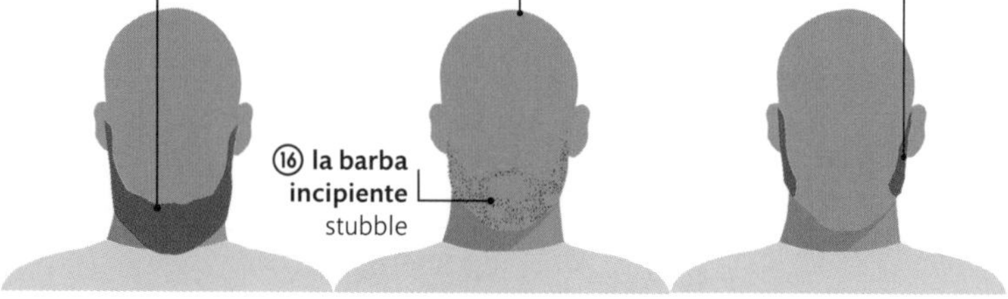

⑭ **la barba**
beard

⑮ **la cabeza rapada**
shaved head

⑯ **la barba incipiente**
stubble

⑰ **las patillas**
sideburns

⑱ **el vello facial**
facial hair

See also
13-15 La ropa • Clothes **16** Los accesorios • Accessories
17 El calzado • Shoes **18** La belleza • Beauty

19 **el corte de pelo militar**
crew cut

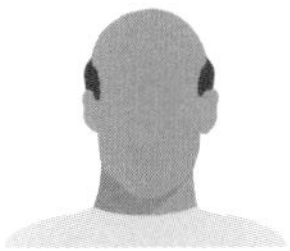

20 **la calvicie**
bald

21 **el pelo liso**
straight hair

22 **el pelo ondulado**
wavy hair

23 **el pelo rizado**
curly hair

24 **el pelo encrespado**
frizzy hair

25 **la coleta**
ponytail

26 **la trenza**
plait

27 **las coletas**
pigtails

28 **el corte bob**
bob

29 **el pelo muy corto**
crop

30 **la peluca**
wig

31 **la trenza francesa**
French plait

32 **el moño**
bun

33 **las mechas**
highlights

34 **el pelo afro**
Afro

35 **las trenzas africanas**
braids

36 **las trenzas apretadas**
cornrows

37 **el cabello normal**
normal hair

38 **el cabello graso**
greasy hair

39 **el cabello seco**
dry hair

40 **la caspa**
dandruff

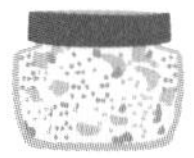

41 **el gel para el cabello**
hair gel

42 **la laca**
hair spray

43 **el pelo negro**
black hair

44 **el pelo castaño**
brown hair

45 **el pelo rubio**
blond / blonde hair

46 **el pelo pelirrojo**
red hair

47 **el pelo cobrizo**
auburn hair

48 **el pelo canoso**
grey hair

49 **la plancha**
hair straightener

50 **el rizador de pelo**
hair curler

51 **el cepillo**
hairbrush

52 **el peine**
comb

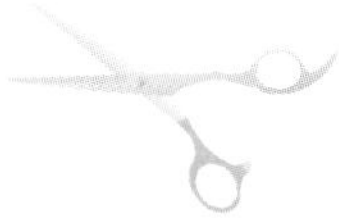

53 **las tijeras de peluquería**
hair scissors

54 **el secador de pelo**
hair dryer

13 La ropa
Clothes

13.1 DESCRIBIR LA ROPA · DESCRIBING CLOTHES

① **el cuero**
leather

② **el algodón**
cotton

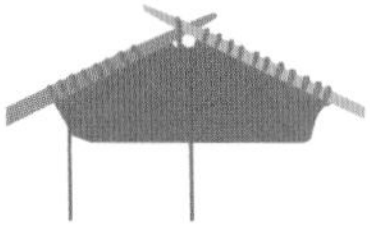
③ **la lana**
woollen

④ **la seda**
silk

⑤ **la fibra sintética**
synthetic

⑥ **la tela vaquera**
denim

⑦ **liso**
plain

⑧ **a rayas**
striped

⑨ **de cuadros**
checked

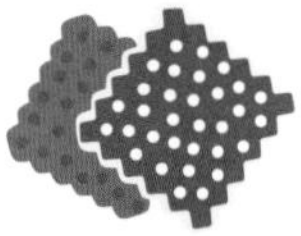
⑩ **de lunares**
spotted

⑪ **de cachemir**
paisley

⑫ **de cuadros escoceses**
plaid

⑬ **holgado** *m*
holgada *f*
loose / baggy

⑭ **ajustado** *m*
ajustada *f*
fitted

⑮ **entallado** *m*
entallada *f*
tight

⑯ **arrugado** *m*
arrugada *f*
crumpled

⑰ **corto** *m* / **corta** *f*
cropped

⑱ **clásico** *m* / **clásica** *f*
vintage

13.2 EL UNIFORME DE TRABAJO · WORK CLOTHES AND UNIFORMS

③ **el uniforme de cocinero**
chef's uniform

④ **el delantal**
apron

⑤ **la bata**
lab coat

⑥ **el uniforme de bombero**
firefighter's uniform

⑦ **el mono de trabajo**
overalls

See also
12 La apariencia y el cabello • Appearance and hair
14-15 La ropa (continuación) • Clothes continued
16 Los accesorios • Accessories **17** El calzado • Shoes

13.3 LA ROPA DE BEBÉ Y DE NIÑO • KIDS' AND BABIES' CLOTHES

① **la capucha**
hood

② **las manoplas**
mittens

③ **el traje de invierno**
snowsuit

④ **el babero**
bib

⑤ **el peto**
dungarees

⑥ **el pelele**
babygro

⑦ **los botones de presión**
popper

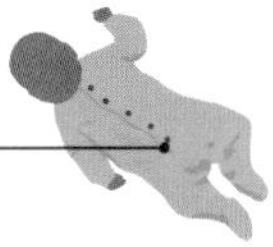

⑧ **el pijama de bebé**
sleepsuit

⑨ **el mono largo**
play suit

⑩ **el mono corto**
romper suit

⑪ **el onesie**
onesie

⑫ **el disfraz**
costume

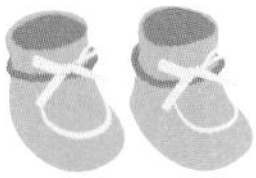

⑬ **los patucos**
booties

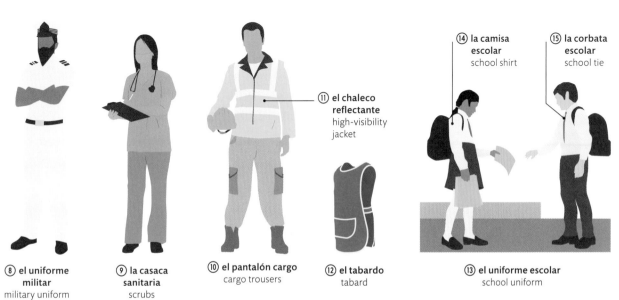

⑧ **el uniforme militar**
military uniform

⑨ **la casaca sanitaria**
scrubs

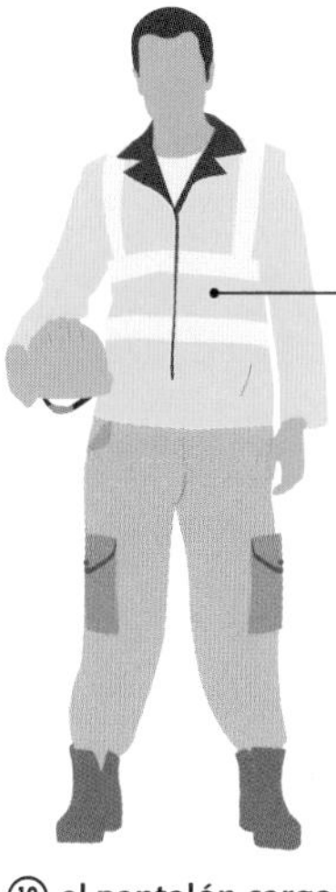

⑪ **el chaleco reflectante**
high-visibility jacket

⑩ **el pantalón cargo**
cargo trousers

⑫ **el tabardo**
tabard

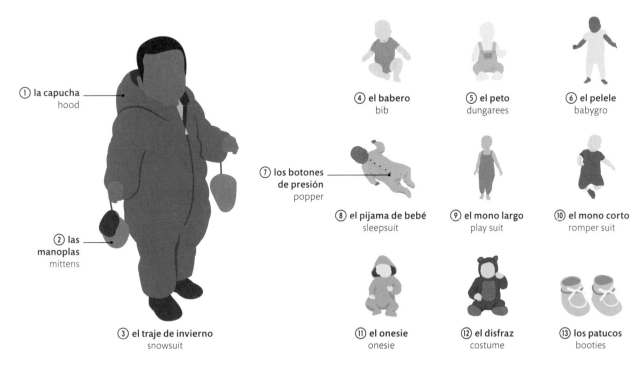

⑭ **la camisa escolar**
school shirt

⑮ **la corbata escolar**
school tie

⑬ **el uniforme escolar**
school uniform

14 La ropa (continuación)
Clothes continued

14.1 LA ROPA INFORMAL · CASUAL CLOTHES

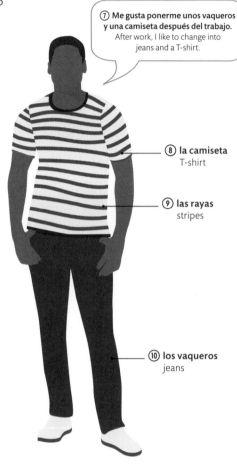

① **Prefiero este conjunto informal a mi ropa de trabajo formal.**
I prefer this casual outfit to my formal work clothes.
② **la blusa** blouse
③ **el jersey** sweater / jumper
④ **la falda** skirt
⑤ **el pliegue** pleat
⑥ **el bajo** hem
⑦ **Me gusta ponerme unos vaqueros y una camiseta después del trabajo.**
After work, I like to change into jeans and a T-shirt.
⑧ **la camiseta** T-shirt
⑨ **las rayas** stripes
⑩ **los vaqueros** jeans

⑪ **la sudadera** sweatshirt

⑫ **los pantalones cortos** shorts

⑬ **las bermudas** bermuda shorts

⑭ **la rebeca** cardigan

⑮ **la camiseta de tirantes** tank top

⑯ **el vestido** dress

⑰ **las mallas** leggings

⑱ **la camisa de manga corta** short-sleeved shirt

⑲ **el polo** polo shirt

⑳ **el sombrero** sun hat

㉑ **el cuello de pico** V-neck

㉒ **el cuello redondo** round neck

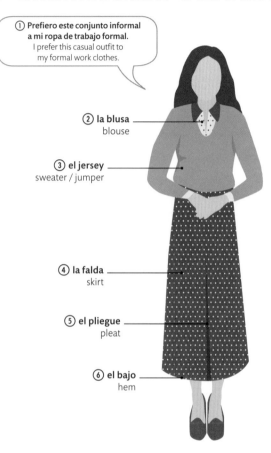

See also
12 La apariencia y el cabello • Appearance and hair **15** La ropa (continuación) Clothes continued **16** Los accesorios • Accessories **17** El calzado • Shoes

14.2 LA ROPA DE DORMIR • NIGHTWEAR

① **la camisola**
camisole

② **las pantuflas**
slippers

③ **el antifaz**
eye mask

④ **el pijama**
pyjamas

⑤ **el camisón**
nightgown / nightie

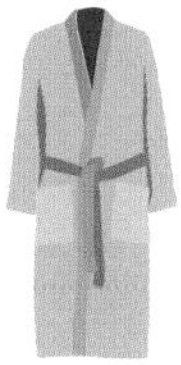

⑥ **el batín**
dressing gown

14.3 LA ROPA INTERIOR • UNDERWEAR

① **las braguitas**
knickers

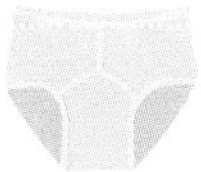

② **los calzoncillos**
pants

③ **los bóxers**
boxer shorts

④ **los calcetines**
socks

⑤ **el sujetador**
bra

⑥ **la combinación**
slip dress

⑦ **la camiseta interior**
vest

⑧ **los pantis**
tights

⑨ **las medias**
stockings

⑩ **el corsé**
basque

⑪ **la liga**
garter

⑫ **el liguero**
suspenders

14.4 LOS VERBOS PARA LA ROPA • VERBS FOR CLOTHES

① **llevar**
to wear

② **ajustar**
to fit

③ **ponerse**
to put on

④ **quitarse**
to take off

⑤ **atar**
to fasten

⑥ **desatar**
to unfasten

⑦ **quedar bien (a alguien)**
to suit (someone)

⑧ **cambiarse**
to change / to get changed

⑨ **colgar**
to hang up

⑩ **doblar**
to fold

⑪ **remangar**
to turn up

⑫ **probarse**
to try something on

15 La ropa (continuación)

Clothes continued

15.1 LA ROPA FORMAL · FORMAL WEAR

① **con hombros descubiertos** off the shoulder
② **la manga de casquillo** cap sleeve
③ **la falda con abertura** slit skirt
④ **largo hasta el suelo** floor length
⑤ **el vestido de noche** evening dress
⑥ **el cuello** collar
⑦ **la corbata** tie
⑧ **la chaqueta** jacket
⑨ **los puños** cuff
⑩ **los pantalones** trousers
⑪ **las hombreras** shoulder pad
⑫ **la camisa** shirt
⑬ **la manga** sleeve
⑭ **el botón** button
⑮ **a medida** tailored
⑯ **el traje** suit

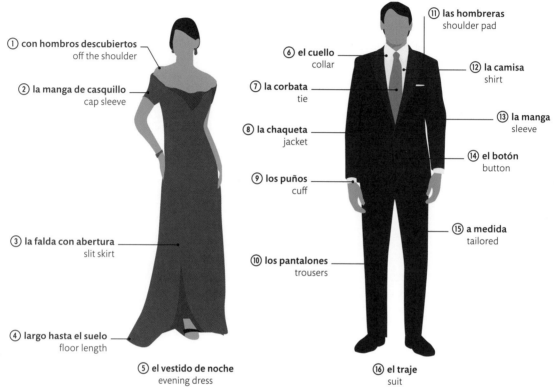

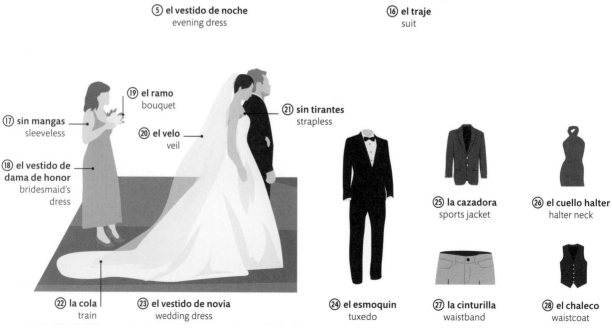

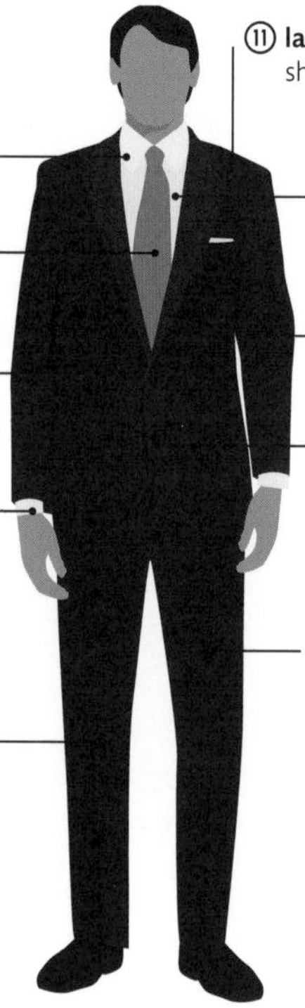

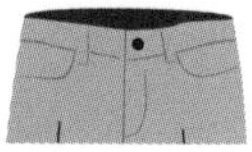

See also
12 La apariencia y el cabello • Appearance and hair
16 Los accesorios • Accessories **17** El calzado • Shoes

15.2 LOS ABRIGOS • COATS

① **el chubasquero**
raincoat

② **la capucha**
hood

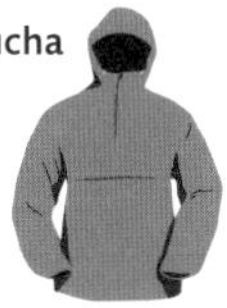

③ **el anorak**
anorak

④ **la trenca**
duffle coat

⑤ **el poncho**
poncho

⑥ **la chaqueta vaquera**
denim jacket

⑦ **la chaqueta acolchada**
quilted jacket

⑧ **la chaqueta bomber**
bomber jacket

⑨ **la capa**
cloak

⑩ **la gabardina**
trench coat

⑪ **el forro**
lining

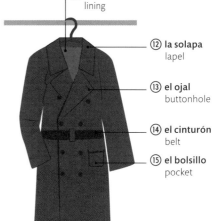

⑫ **la solapa**
lapel

⑬ **el ojal**
buttonhole

⑭ **el cinturón**
belt

⑮ **el bolsillo**
pocket

15.3 LA ROPA DEPORTIVA
SPORTSWEAR

① **el chándal**
tracksuit

② **el sujetador deportivo**
sports bra

③ **los pantalones de gimnasia**
sweatpants

④ **el leotardo**
leotard

⑤ **la camiseta de fútbol**
football shirt

⑥ **el esnórquel y las gafas de buceo**
snorkel and mask

⑦ **las aletas**
fins / flippers

⑧ **el bañador**
swimsuit

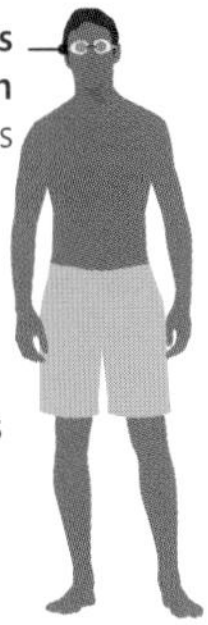

⑨ **las gafas de natación**
goggles

⑩ **el bañador de hombre**
swimming trunks

15.4 LA ROPA TRADICIONAL
TRADITIONAL CLOTHES

① **la agbada**
agbada

② **el vestido de flamenca**
flamenco dress

③ **el lederhosen**
lederhosen

④ **el kimono**
kimono

⑤ **el thawb**
thawb

⑥ **el sari**
sari

⑦ **el kilt**
kilt

⑧ **el sarong**
sarong

⑨ **la blusa tradicional**
folk blouse

16 Los accesorios

Accessories

16.1 LOS ACCESORIOS DE MODA · FASHION ACCESSORIES

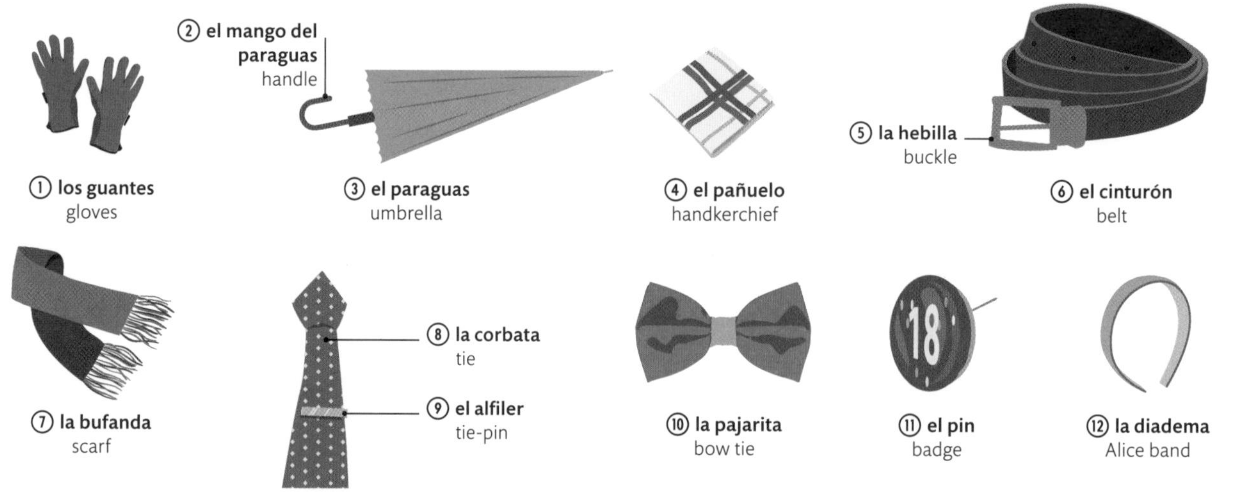

16.2 LA JOYERÍA · JEWELLERY

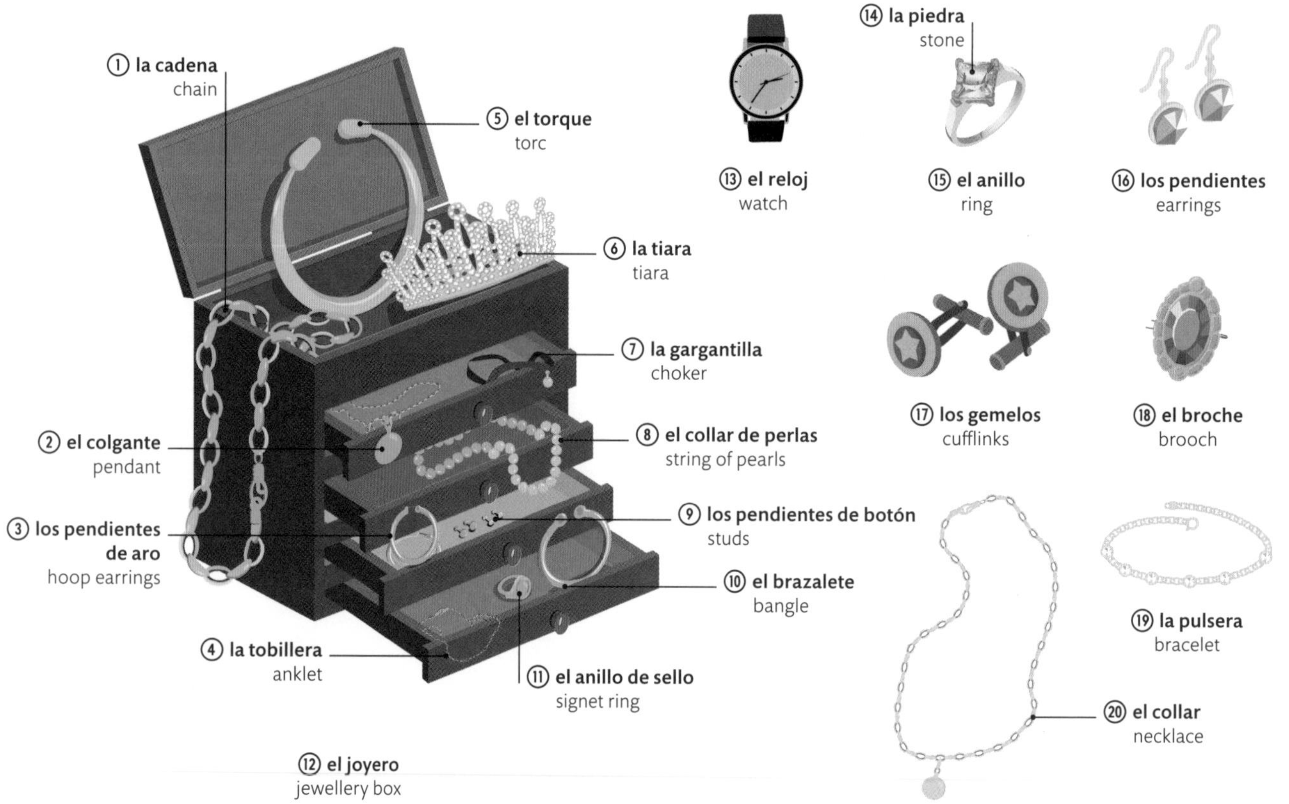

① la cadena
chain

② el colgante
pendant

③ los pendientes de aro
hoop earrings

④ la tobillera
anklet

⑤ el torque
torc

⑥ la tiara
tiara

⑦ la gargantilla
choker

⑧ el collar de perlas
string of pearls

⑨ los pendientes de botón
studs

⑩ el brazalete
bangle

⑪ el anillo de sello
signet ring

⑫ el joyero
jewellery box

⑬ el reloj
watch

⑭ la piedra
stone

⑮ el anillo
ring

⑯ los pendientes
earrings

⑰ los gemelos
cufflinks

⑱ el broche
brooch

⑲ la pulsera
bracelet

⑳ el collar
necklace

See also
12 La apariencia y el cabello • Appearance and hair
13-15 La ropa • Clothes **17** El calzado • Shoes

16.3 LOS SOMBREROS • HEADWEAR

① **la gorra inglesa**
flat cap

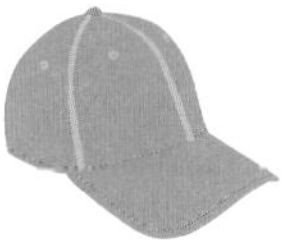

② **la gorra de béisbol**
baseball cap

③ **el gorro con pompón**
bobble hat

④ **el hijab**
hijab

⑤ **la kipá**
yarmulke

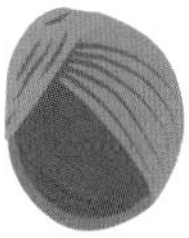

⑥ **el turbante**
turban

⑦ **la boina**
beret

⑧ **el sombrero de fieltro**
fedora

⑨ **la gorra de cazador**
deerstalker

⑩ **el fez**
fez

⑪ **el sombrero de vaquero**
cowboy hat

⑫ **el sombrero mexicano**
sombrero

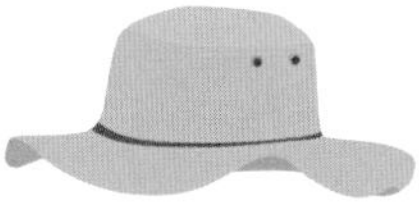

⑬ **la pamela**
sun hat

⑭ **la gorra de repartidor de periódicos**
newsboy cap

⑮ **el sombrero de Panamá**
panama

⑯ **el canotier**
boater

⑰ **el gorro de punto**
beanie

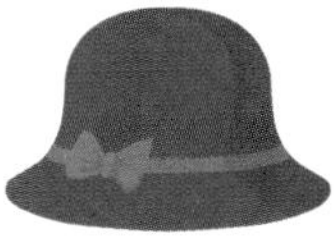

⑱ **el sombrero de campana**
cloche

16.4 LOS BOLSOS • BAGS

① **el maletín**
briefcase

② **la mochila**
backpack / rucksack

③ **la cartera**
purse

④ **la bolsa de viaje**
holdall

⑤ **el bolso de mano**
handbag

⑥ **la maleta**
suitcase

⑩ **el bolso de hombro**
shoulder bag

El calzado
Shoes

17.1 **EL CALZADO Y LOS ACCESORIOS** · SHOES AND ACCESSORIES

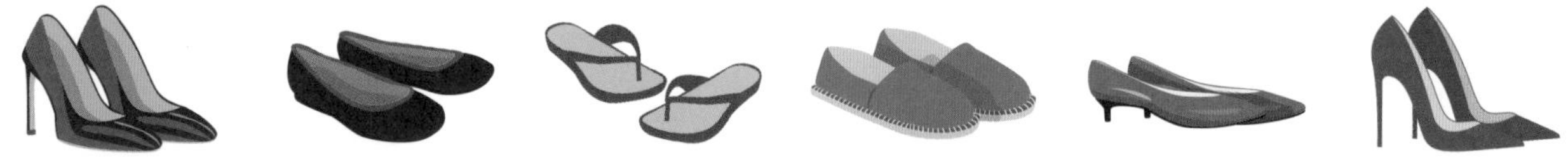

① **los tacones** high-heeled shoes
② **los zapatos planos** flats
③ **las chanclas** flip-flops
④ **las alpargatas** espadrilles
⑤ **los tacones bajos** kitten heels
⑥ **los tacones de aguja** stilettos

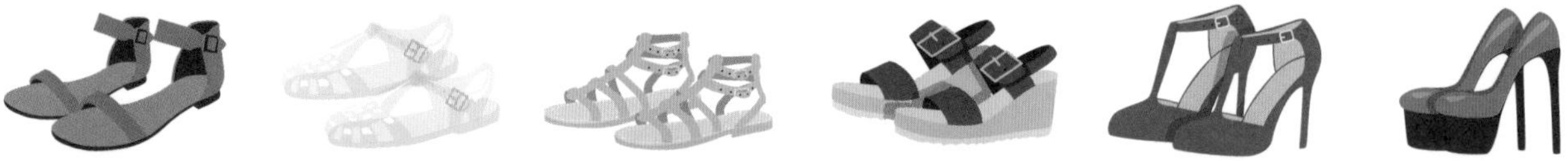

⑦ **las sandalias** sandals
⑧ **las cangrejeras** jelly sandals
⑨ **las sandalias gladiadoras** gladiator sandals
⑩ **las sandalias con cuña** wedge sandals
⑪ **los tacones con tira en T** T-strap heels
⑫ **los zapatos con plataforma** platforms

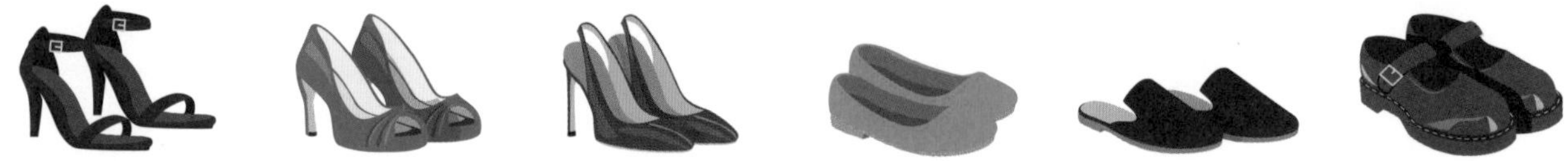

⑬ **los tacones con tira tobillera** ankle strap heels
⑭ **los tacones con puntera abierta** peep toes
⑮ **los tacones con tira talonera** slingback heels
⑯ **las bailarinas** ballet flats
⑰ **las chinelas** mules
⑱ **las merceditas** Mary Janes

17.2 **LAS BOTAS** · BOOTS

① **las botas de trabajo** work boots
② **las botas Chelsea** Chelsea boots
③ **las botas de montaña** hiking boots
④ **los botines** ankle boots
⑤ **la bota por encima de la rodilla** thigh-high boot
⑦ **las botas safari** chukka boots / desert boots

⑫ **las botas de cordones** lace-up boots

⑬ **las botas hasta el muslo** knee-high boots
⑭ **las botas de lluvia** wellington boots
⑮ **las botas vaqueras** cowboy boots

See also
12 La apariencia y el cabello • Appearance and hair **13-15** La ropa • Clothes
16 Los accesorios • Accessories **40** Las herramientas de jardinería • Garden tools

⑲ los zapatos Oxford
Oxfords

⑳ los zapatos Derby
Derby shoes

㉑ los zapatos sin cierres
slip-ons

㉒ los mocasines indios
moccasins

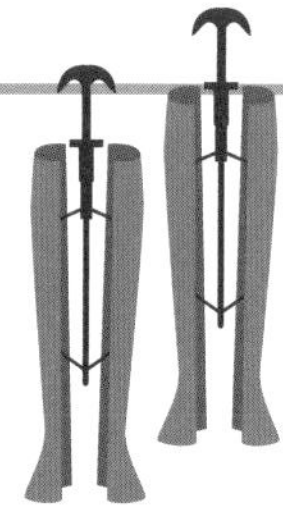

㉓ las hormas para botas
boot shapers

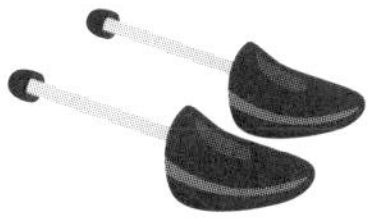

㉔ las hormas para zapatos
shoe trees

㉕ los zuecos
clogs

㉖ los zapatos con hebilla
buckled shoes

㉗ las chanclas
slides

㉘ las pantuflas
slippers

㉙ los cordones
shoelaces

㉚ las plantillas
insoles

㉛ los mocasines con bridón
loafers

㉜ los náuticos
boat shoes

㉝ los zapatos de niño
kids' shoes

㉞ los brogues
brogues

㉟ el betún
shoe polish

㊱ el cepillo para zapatos
shoe brush

17.3 EL CALZADO DEPORTIVO • SPORTS SHOES

① las zapatillas de clavos
running spikes

② los tacos de béisbol
baseball cleats

③ las zapatillas para correr
running shoes

④ los zapatos abotinados
high-tops

⑤ los zapatos de golf
golf shoes

⑦ la lengüeta
tongue

⑥ la zapatilla deportiva
trainer

⑧ la zapatilla de ciclismo
cycling shoe

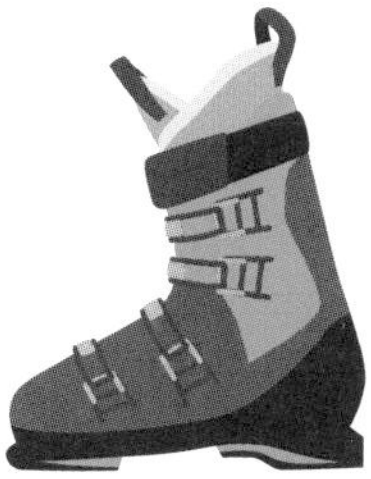

⑨ la bota de esquí
ski boot

⑩ los escarpines
water shoes

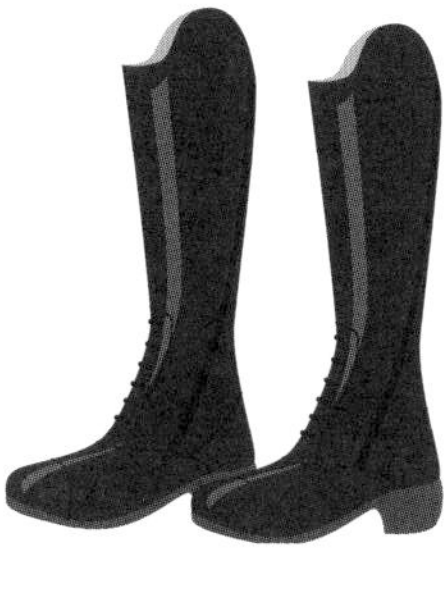

⑪ las botas de montar
riding boots

⑫ los tabi
tabi boots

⑬ las botas de fútbol
football boots

18 La belleza
Beauty

18.1 EL MAQUILLAJE · MAKEUP

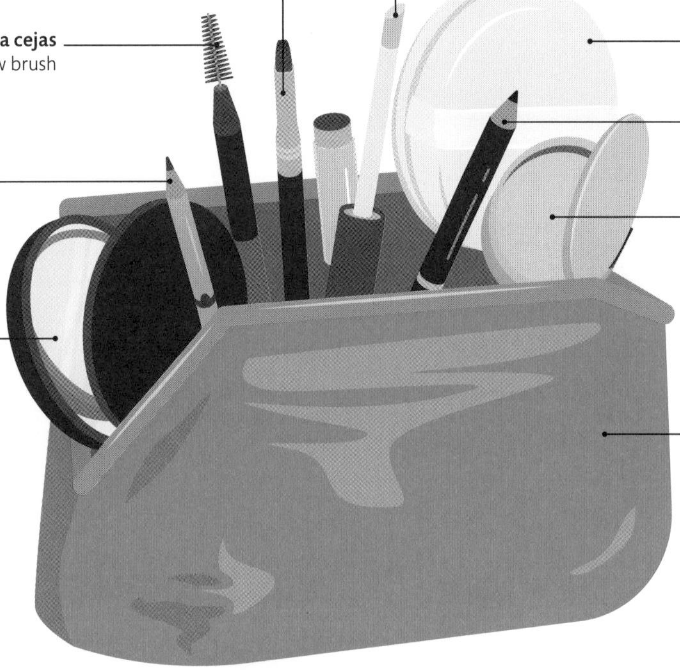

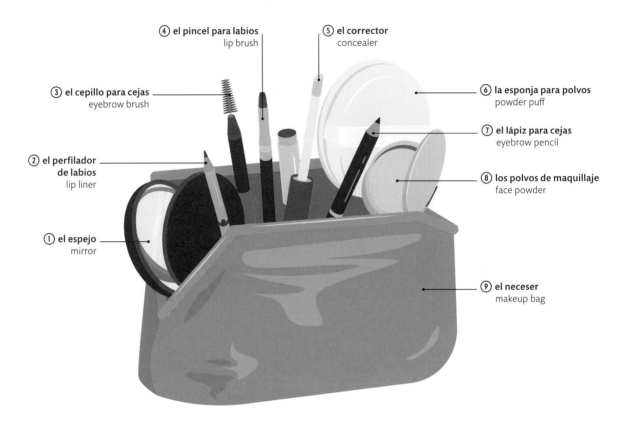

④ **el pincel para labios**
lip brush

⑤ **el corrector**
concealer

③ **el cepillo para cejas**
eyebrow brush

⑥ **la esponja para polvos**
powder puff

⑦ **el lápiz para cejas**
eyebrow pencil

② **el perfilador de labios**
lip liner

⑧ **los polvos de maquillaje**
face powder

① **el espejo**
mirror

⑨ **el neceser**
makeup bag

⑩ **la brocha**
blusher

⑪ **el lápiz de ojos**
eyeliner

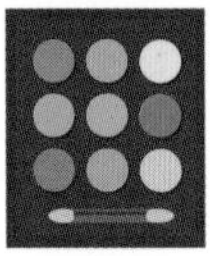

⑫ **la sombra de ojos**
eyeshadow

⑬ **la base de maquillaje**
foundation

⑭ **el rímel**
mascara

⑮ **la barra de labios**
lipstick

18.2 LOS TIPOS DE PIEL · SKIN TYPE

① **normal**
normal

② **seca**
dry

③ **grasa**
oily

④ **sensible**
sensitive

⑤ **mixta**
combination

See also
12 La apariencia y el cabello • Appearance and hair **13-15** La ropa • Clothes **16** Los accesorios • Accessories **17** El calzado • Shoes **31** El cuarto de baño • Bathroom

18.3 **LA MANICURA** • MANICURE

① **las tijeras de uñas**
nail scissors

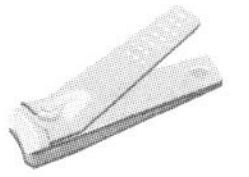

② **el cortaúñas**
nail clippers

③ **el pintaúñas**
nail polish / nail varnish

④ **el quitaesmalte**
nail polish remover

⑤ **la lima**
nail file

⑥ **la crema de manos**
hand cream

18.4 **LA COSMÉTICA Y LOS TRATAMIENTOS DE BELLEZA** • TOILETRIES AND BEAUTY TREATMENTS

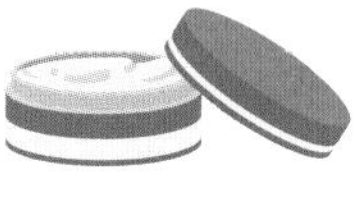

① **la crema hidratante**
moisturizer

② **el tónico**
toner

③ **el jabón facial**
face wash

④ **el limpiador**
cleanser

⑤ **el perfume**
perfume

⑥ **la loción de afeitar**
aftershave

⑦ **el bálsamo labial**
lip balm

⑧ **la espuma de baño**
bubble bath

⑨ **las bolas de algodón**
cotton balls

⑩ **el tinte de pelo**
hair dye

⑪ **las pinzas**
tweezers

⑫ **la cera**
wax

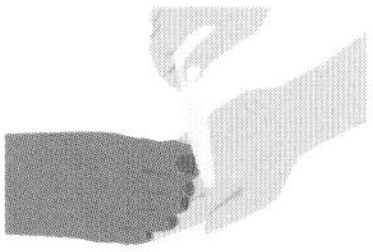

⑬ **la pedicura**
pedicure

⑭ **la crema bronceadora**
self-tanning lotion

⑮ **el guante autobronceador**
tanning mitt

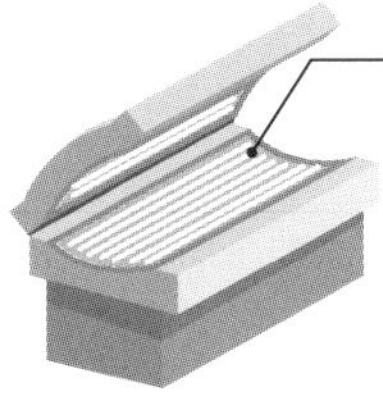

⑰ **los tubos de rayos UVA**
UV tubes

⑯ **la cabina de bronceado**
sun bed

⑱ **las gafas de bronceado**
tanning goggles

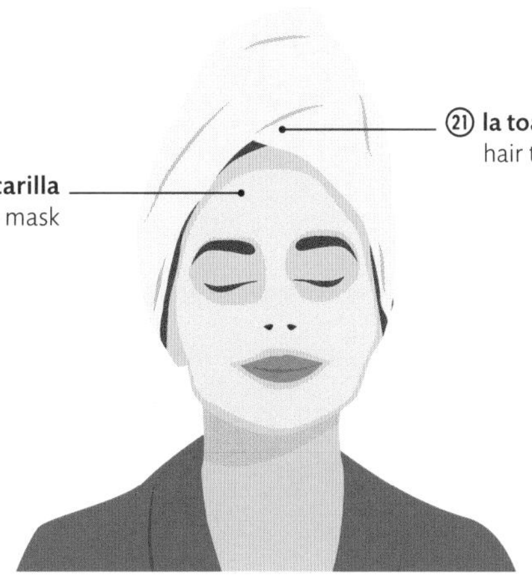

⑳ **la mascarilla**
face mask

㉑ **la toalla del pelo**
hair towel wrap

⑲ **el tratamiento facial**
facial

19 Las enfermedades y lesiones

Illness and injury

19.1 LAS ENFERMEDADES · ILLNESS

1 **la gripe**
flu

2 **el resfriado**
cold

3 **la tos**
cough

4 **el moqueo**
runny nose

5 **el virus**
virus

6 **la fiebre**
fever

7 **los escalofríos**
chill

8 **el dolor de garganta**
sore throat

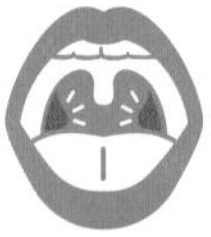
9 **la amigdalitis**
tonsillitis

10 **el dolor de cabeza**
headache

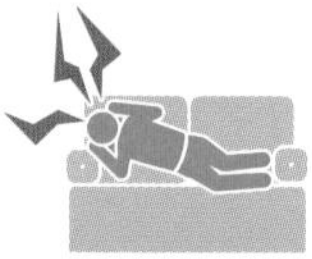
11 **la migraña**
migraine

12 **el mareo**
dizzy

13 **la intoxicación alimenticia**
food poisoning

14 **el envenenamiento**
poisoning

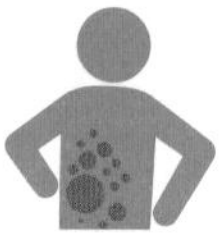
15 **el sarpullido**
rash

16 **la varicela**
chickenpox

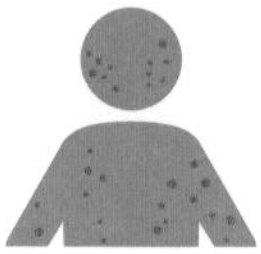
17 **el sarampión**
measles

18 **las paperas**
mumps

19 **el eczema**
eczema

20 **el asma** *f*
asthma

21 **la alergia**
allergy

22 **la alergia al polen**
hay fever

23 **la infección**
infection

24 **la diabetes**
diabetes

25 **el estrés**
stress

26 **la hemorragia nasal**
nosebleed

27 **las náuseas**
nausea

28 **la apendicitis**
appendicitis

29 **la hipertensión**
high blood pressure

30 **los síntomas**
symptoms

31 **el calambre**
cramp

32 **el dolor de espalda**
backache

33 **el dolor**
pain

34 **el dolor de estómago**
stomach ache

35 **el insomnio**
insomnia

36 **la diarrea**
diarrhoea

See also
01 Las partes del cuerpo • Parts of the body **03** Los músculos y el esqueleto Muscles and skeleton **04** Los órganos internos • Internal organs
20 La visita al médico • Visiting the doctor **21** El hospital • The hospital

19.2 LAS LESIONES • INJURY

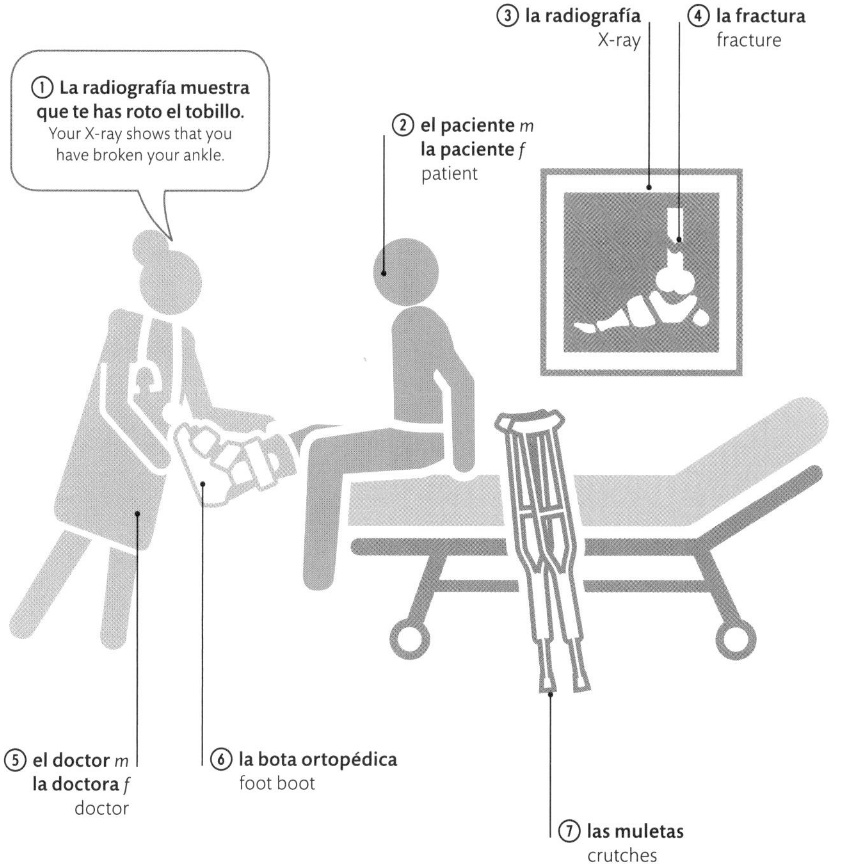
① **La radiografía muestra que te has roto el tobillo.**
Your X-ray shows that you have broken your ankle.
② **el paciente** *m*
la paciente *f*
patient
③ **la radiografía**
X-ray
④ **la fractura**
fracture
⑤ **el doctor** *m*
la doctora *f*
doctor
⑥ **la bota ortopédica**
foot boot
⑦ **las muletas**
crutches

⑧ **el esguince**
sprain

⑨ **el hueso roto**
broken bone

⑩ **el cabestrillo**
sling

⑪ **el latigazo cervical**
whiplash

⑫ **el collarín cervical**
neck brace

⑬ **el corte**
cut

⑭ **el rasguño**
graze

⑮ **el moratón**
bruise

⑯ **la astilla**
splinter

⑰ **la quemadura solar**
sunburn

⑱ **la quemadura**
burn

⑲ **el mordisco**
bite

⑳ **la picadura**
sting

㉑ **el accidente**
accident

㉒ **la herida**
wound

㉓ **la hemorragia**
haemorrhage

㉔ **la ampolla**
blister

㉕ **la conmoción cerebral**
concussion

㉖ **la herida en a cabeza**
head injury

㉗ **la descarga eléctrica**
electric shock

20 La visita al médico
Visiting the doctor

20.1 EL TRATAMIENTO • TREATMENT

① **No me encuentro bien.**
I'm not feeling well.

② **Voy a tomarte la tensión.**
I'm going to take your blood pressure.

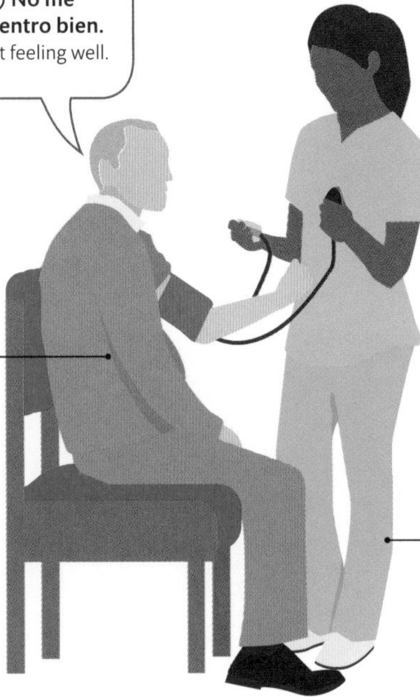

③ **el paciente** *m*
la paciente *f*
patient

④ **la enfermera** *m*
el enfermero *f*
nurse

⑤ **la tensión arterial**
blood pressure

⑥ **el doctor** *m*
la doctora *f*
doctor

⑦ **el ambulatorio**
doctor's surgery

⑧ **la sala de espera**
waiting room

⑨ **la cita médica**
appointment

⑩ **el examen médico**
medical examination

⑪ **la vacuna**
inoculation / vaccination

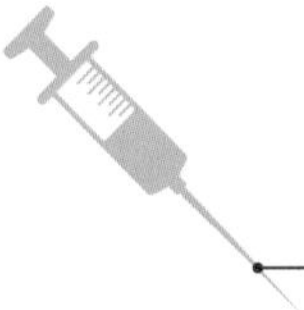

⑫ **la jeringuilla**
syringe

⑬ **la aguja**
needle

⑭ **el análisis de sangre**
blood test

⑮ **los resultados**
test results

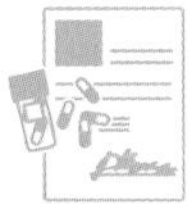

⑯ **la receta**
prescription

⑰ **la medicación**
medicine / medication

⑱ **las pastillas**
pills / tablets

⑲ **la báscula**
scales

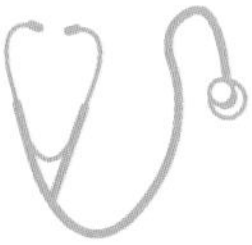

⑳ **el estetoscopio**
stethoscope

㉑ **el inhalador**
inhaler

㉒ **el espray nasal**
nasal spray

㉓ **la mascarilla**
face mask

㉔ **el cabestrillo**
sling

㉕ **el vendaje**
dressing

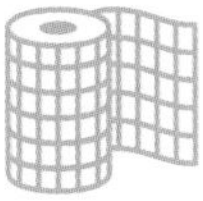

㉖ **la gasa**
gauze

㉗ **el esparadrapo**
tape

㉘ **el termómetro**
thermometer

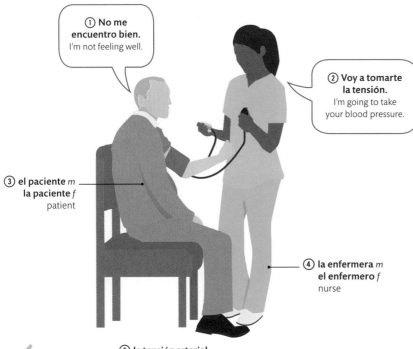

㉙ **el termómetro de oído**
ear thermometer

See also
01 Las partes del cuerpo • Parts of the body **02** Las manos y los pies • Hands and feet **03** Los músculos y el esqueleto • Muscles and skeleton **04** Los órganos internos • Internal organs **19** Las enfermedades y lesiones • Illness and injury **21** El hospital • The hospital

20.2 EL BOTIQUÍN DE PRIMEROS AUXILIOS • FIRST-AID KIT

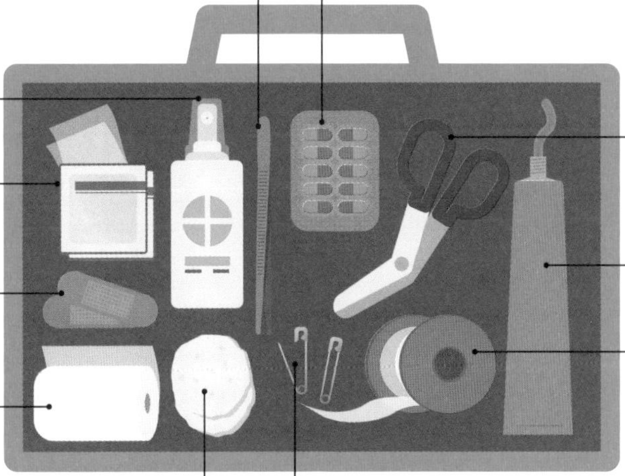

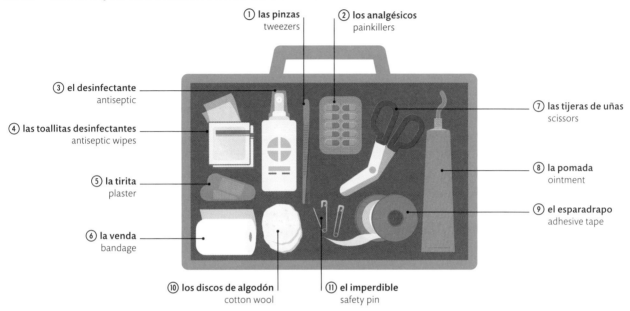

① **las pinzas** tweezers
② **los analgésicos** painkillers
③ **el desinfectante** antiseptic
④ **las toallitas desinfectantes** antiseptic wipes
⑤ **la tirita** plaster
⑥ **la venda** bandage
⑦ **las tijeras de uñas** scissors
⑧ **la pomada** ointment
⑨ **el esparadrapo** adhesive tape
⑩ **los discos de algodón** cotton wool
⑪ **el imperdible** safety pin

20.3 LOS VERBOS PARA DESCRIBIR LAS ENFERMEDADES • VERBS TO DESCRIBE ILLNESS

① **vomitar** to vomit

② **estornudar** to sneeze

③ **toser** to cough

④ **doler** to hurt / to ache

⑤ **sangrar** to bleed

⑥ **desmayarse** to faint

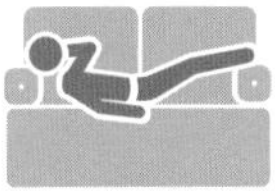

⑦ **tumbarse** to lie down

⑧ **descansar** to rest

⑨ **perder peso** to lose weight

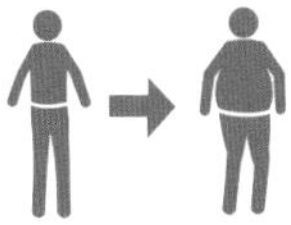

⑩ **ganar peso** to gain weight

⑪ **beber agua** to drink water

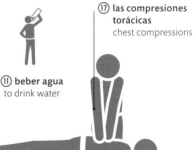

⑫ **hacer ejercicio** to exercise

⑬ **curar** to heal

⑭ **recuperarse** to recover

⑮ **sentirse mejor** to feel better

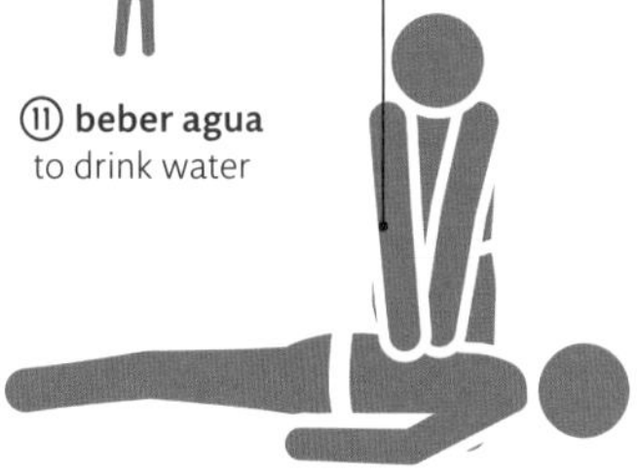

⑯ **reanimar** to resuscitate
⑰ **las compresiones torácicas** chest compressions

21 El hospital
The hospital

21.1 EN EL HOSPITAL • AT THE HOSPITAL

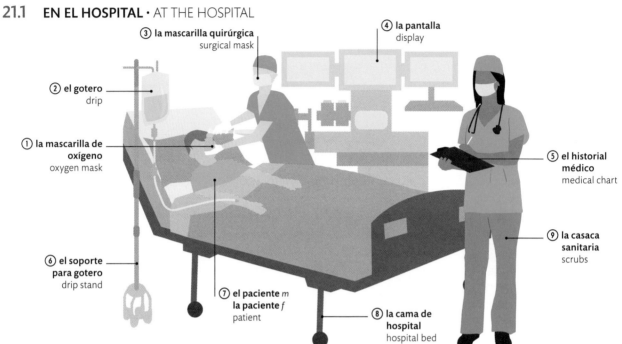

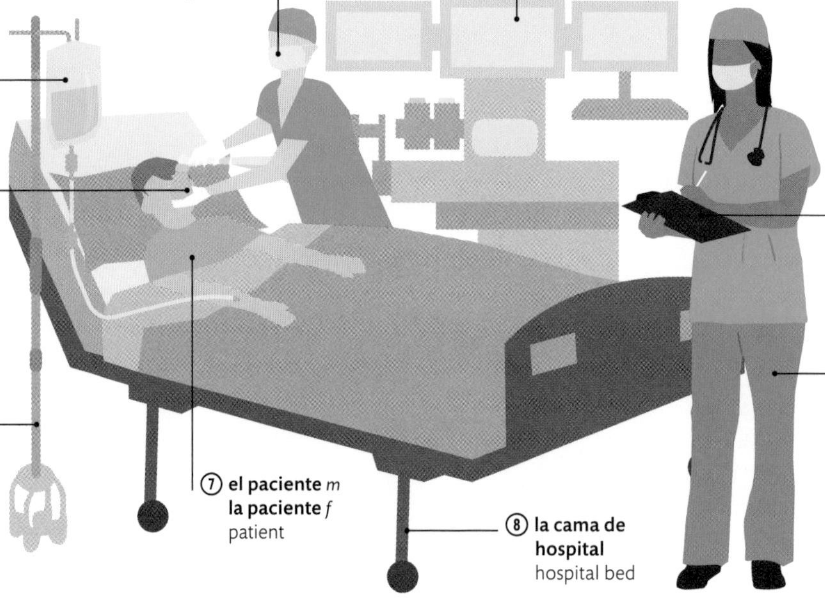

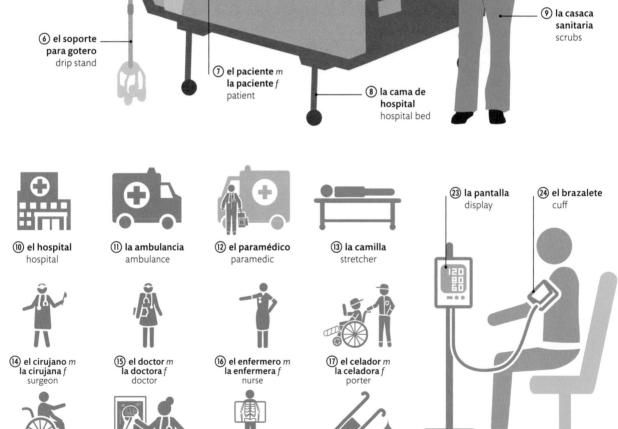

⑩ **el hospital**
hospital

⑪ **la ambulancia**
ambulance

⑫ **el paramédico**
paramedic

⑬ **la camilla**
stretcher

⑭ **el cirujano** *m*
la cirujana *f*
surgeon

⑮ **el doctor** *m*
la doctora *f*
doctor

⑯ **el enfermero** *m*
la enfermera *f*
nurse

⑰ **el celador** *m*
la celadora *f*
porter

⑱ **la silla de ruedas**
wheelchair

⑲ **el escáner**
scan

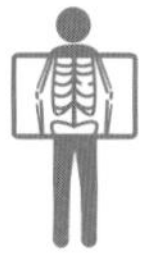
⑳ **la radiografía**
X-ray

㉑ **el análisis de sangre**
blood test

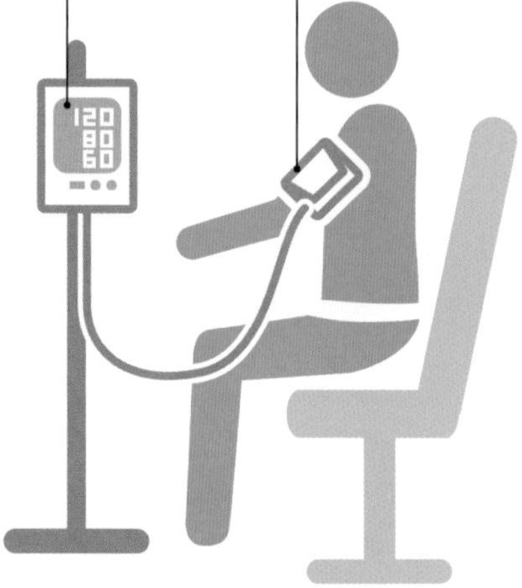

㉒ **el tensiómetro**
blood pressure monitor

See also
01 Las partes del cuerpo • Parts of the body **03** Los músculos y el esqueleto • Muscles and skeleton **04** Los órganos internos • Internal organs **19** Las enfermedades y lesiones • Illness and injury **20** La visita al médico • Visiting the doctor

㉕ **el bisturí**
scalpel

㉖ **los puntos**
stitches

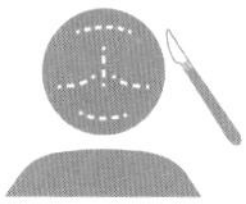

㉗ **la cirugía plástica**
plastic surgery

㉘ **el tratamiento**
treatment

㉙ **la operación**
operation

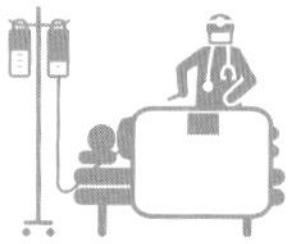

㉚ **la mesa de operaciones**
operating table

㉛ **el quirófano**
theatre

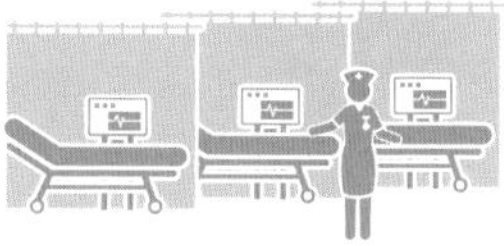

㉜ **la sala de urgencias**
A&E

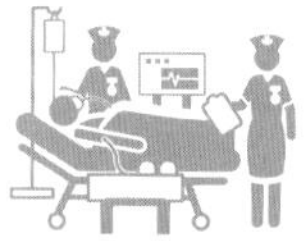

㉝ **la unidad de cuidados intensivos**
intensive care unit

㉞ **la sala de reanimación**
recovery room

㉟ **la habitación privada**
private room

㊱ **la sala de hospital**
ward

㊲ **la sala de pediatría**
children's ward

㊳ **la sala de maternidad**
maternity ward

㊴ **ingresar**
to admit

㊵ **dar de alta**
to discharge

㊶ **el paciente externo**
outpatient

21.2 LOS DEPARTAMENTOS
DEPARTMENTS

① **otorrinolaringología** *f*
ENT (ear, nose, and throat)

② **cardiología** *f*
cardiology

③ **traumatología** *f*
orthopaedics

④ **neurología** *f*
neurology

⑤ **radiología** *f*
radiology

⑥ **patología** *f*
pathology

⑦ **pediatría** *f*
paediatrics

⑧ **dermatología** *f*
dermatology

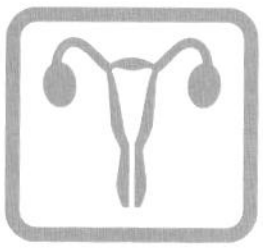

⑨ **ginecología** *f*
gynaecology

⑩ **cirugía** *f*
surgery

⑪ **rehabilitación** *f*
physiotherapy

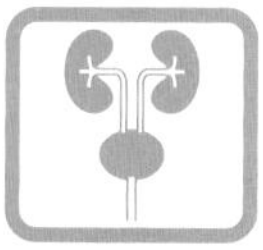

⑫ **urología** *f*
urology

⑬ **maternidad** *f*
maternity

⑭ **psiquiatría** *f*
psychiatry

⑮ **oftalmología** *f*
ophthalmology

⑯ **endocrinología** *f*
endocrinology

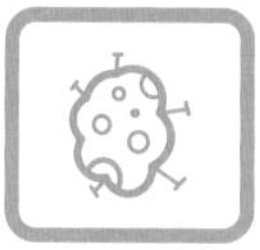

⑰ **oncología** *f*
oncology

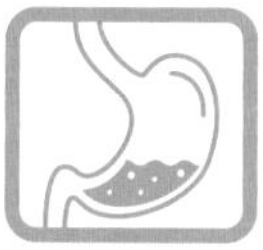

⑱ **gastroenterología** *f*
gastroenterology

22 El dentista y el oculista

The dentist and optician

22.1 LA CLÍNICA DENTAL • DENTAL SURGERY

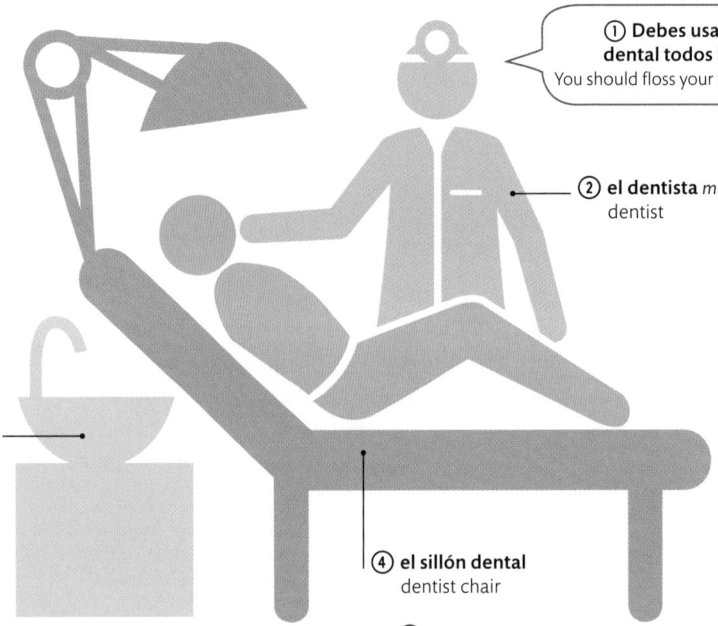
① **Debes usar el hilo dental todos los días.**
You should floss your teeth every day.

② **el dentista** *m* / **la dentista** *f*
dentist

③ **la escupidera**
basin

④ **el sillón dental**
dentist chair

⑤ **la revisión**
check-up

⑥ **el dolor de muelas**
toothache

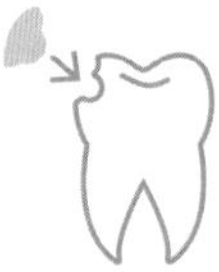

⑦ **el empaste**
filling

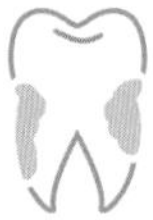

⑧ **el sarro**
plaque

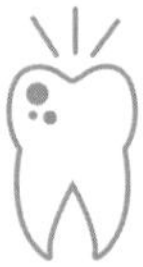

⑨ **la caries**
decay

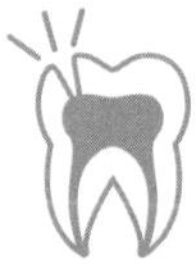

⑩ **la cavidad**
cavity

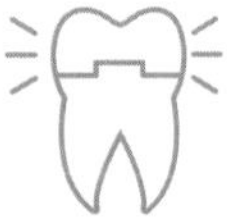

⑪ **la corona**
crown

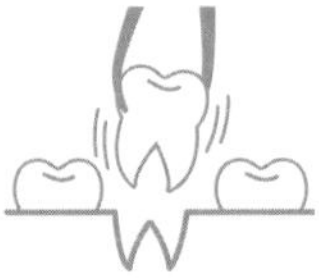

⑫ **la extracción**
extraction

⑬ **los dientes de leche**
milk teeth

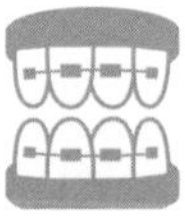

⑭ **la ortodoncia**
braces

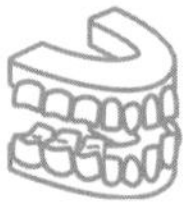

⑮ **la dentadura postiza**
dentures / false teeth

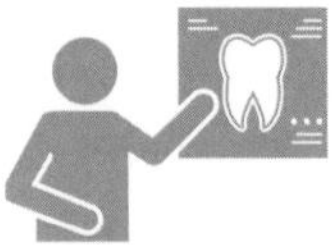

⑯ **la radiografía dental**
dental X-ray

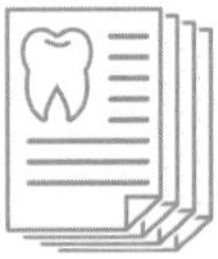

⑰ **el historial dental**
dental history

⑱ **la fresa**
drill

⑲ **el espejo**
dental mirror

⑳ **la sonda**
probe

㉑ **el cepillo interdental**
interdental brush

㉒ **el blanqueamiento dental**
whitening

㉓ **el higienista dental** *m*
la higienista dental *f*
dental hygienist

㉔ **el hilo dental**
dental floss

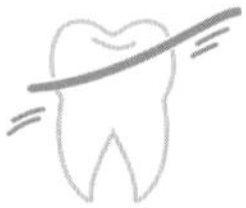

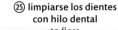

㉕ **limpiarse los dientes con hilo dental**
to floss

㉖ **cepillarse los dientes**
to brush

㉗ **enjuagarse**
to rinse

See also
01 Las partes del cuerpo • Parts of the body **03** Los músculos y el esqueleto • Muscles and skeleton **20** La visita al médico • Visiting the doctor **21** El hospital • The hospital **31** El cuarto de baño • Bathroom

22.2 **EL OCULISTA** • OPTICIAN

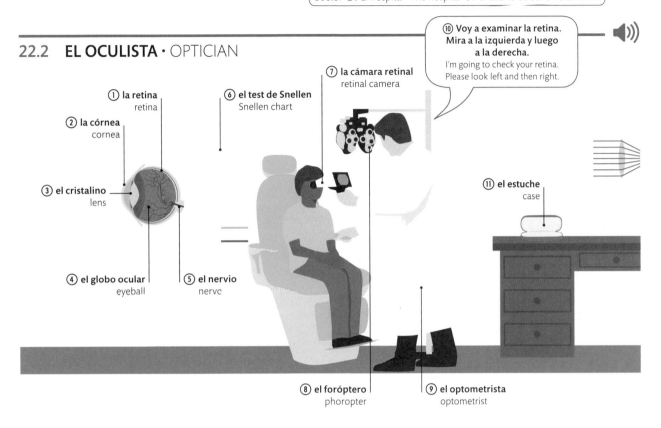

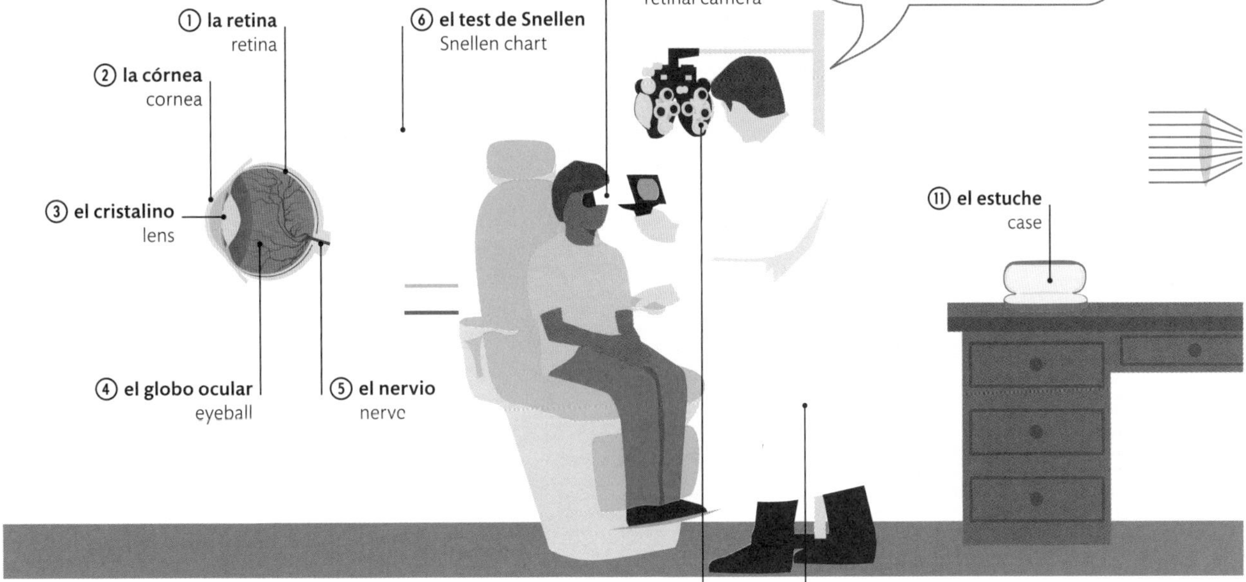
⑩ **Voy a examinar la retina. Mira a la izquierda y luego a la derecha.**
I'm going to check your retina. Please look left and then right.
① **la retina**
retina
② **la córnea**
cornea
③ **el cristalino**
lens
④ **el globo ocular**
eyeball
⑤ **el nervio**
nerve
⑥ **el test de Snellen**
Snellen chart
⑦ **la cámara retinal**
retinal camera
⑧ **el foróptero**
phoropter
⑨ **el optometrista**
optometrist
⑪ **el estuche**
case

⑫ **la visión**
vision

⑬ **la hipermetropía**
long-sighted

⑭ **la miopía**
short-sighted

⑮ **la lágrima**
tear

⑯ **la catarata**
cataract

⑰ **el astigmatismo**
astigmatism

㉓ **las lentes bifocales**
lens

⑱ **las gafas de lectura**
reading glasses

⑲ **las lentes bifocales**
bifocal

⑳ **el monóculo**
monocle

㉑ **los prismáticos de ópera**
opera glasses

㉒ **las gafas de lectura**
glasses

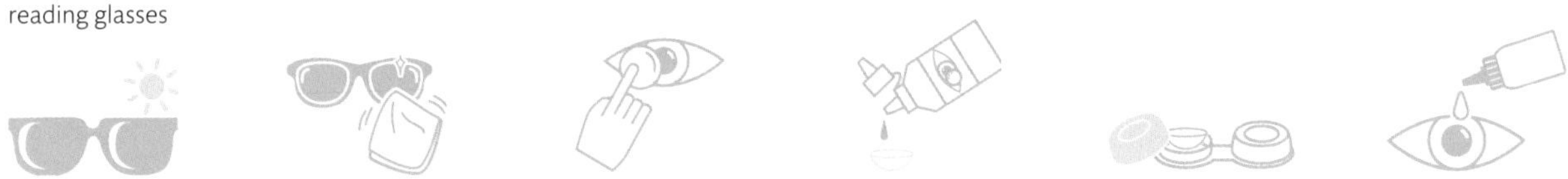

㉔ **las gafas de sol**
sunglasses

㉕ **la gamuza para gafas**
lens cleaning cloth

㉖ **las lentillas**
contact lenses

㉗ **el líquido de lentillas**
contact lens solution

㉘ **el estuche de lentillas**
lens case

㉙ **el colirio**
eye drops

23 La dieta y la nutrición
Diet and nutrition

23.1 LA VIDA SANA · HEALTHY LIVING

① **las proteínas**
protein

② **los carbohidratos**
carbohydrates

③ **la fibra**
fibre

④ **los lácteos**
dairy

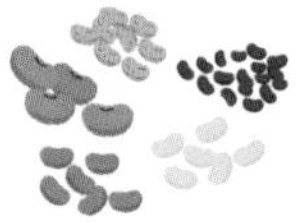

⑤ **las legumbres**
pulses

⑥ **el azúcar**
sugar

⑦ **la sal**
salt

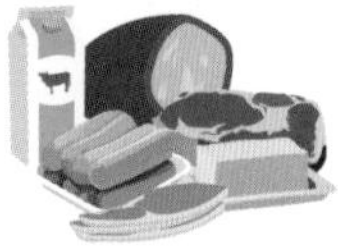

⑧ **las grasas saturadas**
saturated fat

⑨ **las grasas insaturadas**
unsaturated fat

⑩ **las calorías**
calories / energy

A
C
E
D

⑪ **las vitaminas**
vitamins

Ca
Zn
P
Fe
Co
Mn

⑫ **los minerales**
minerals

⑬ **el calcio**
calcium

⑭ **el hierro**
iron

⑮ **el colesterol**
cholesterol

⑯ **la dieta detox**
detox

⑰ **la dieta equilibrada**
balanced diet

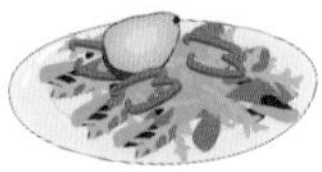

⑱ **la dieta baja en calorías**
calorie-controlled diet

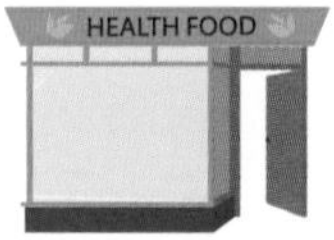
HEALTH FOOD

⑲ **la tienda ecológica**
health food shop

⑳ **los alimentos ecológicos**
organic food section

㉑ **los productos locales**
local produce

㉒ Me gusta comprar frutas y verduras ecológicas.
I like to buy organic fruit and vegetables.

㉓ **el mercadillo agrícola**
farmers' market

See also
03 Los músculos y el esqueleto • Muscles and skeleton **19** Las enfermedades y lesiones • Illness and injury **24** Cuerpo sano, mente sana • Healthy body, healthy mind **29** La cocina • Cooking **48** El supermercado • The supermarket **52-72** Los alimentos • Food

㉔ **los alimentos procesados** processed food

㉕ **los superalimentos** superfoods

㉖ **orgánico** *m* **orgánica** *f* organic

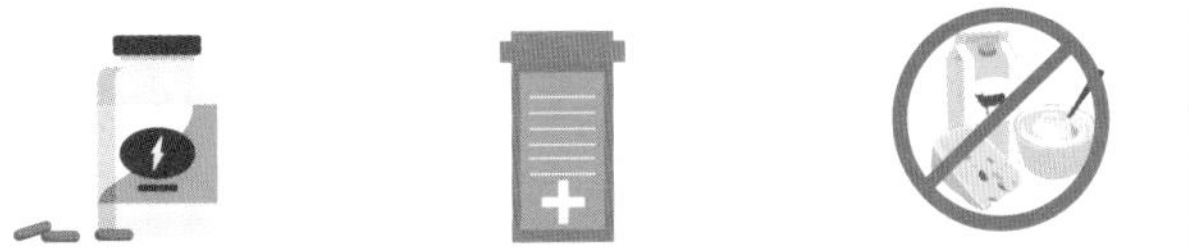

㉗ **los suplementos** supplement

㉘ **los aditivos** additives

㉙ **sin lactosa** dairy-free

㉚ **vegetariano** vegetarian

㉛ **vegano** vegan

㉜ **pescetariano** pescatarian

㉝ **sin gluten** gluten-free

㉞ **perder peso** to lose weight

㉟ **los alimentos precocinados** convenience food

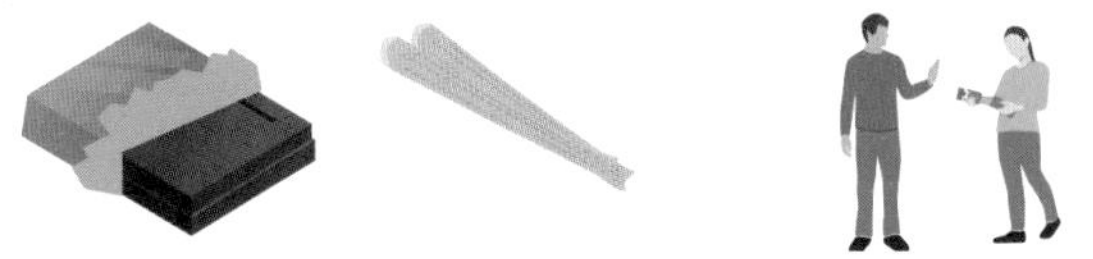

㊱ **rico en calorías** high-calorie

㊲ **bajo en calorías** low-calorie

㊳ **reducir el consumo** to cut down on

㊴ **dejar de tomar** to give up

㊵ **ponerse a dieta** to go on a diet

㊶ **atracarse** to overeat

23.2 LAS ALERGIAS ALIMENTARIAS
FOOD ALLERGIES

① **la alergia a los frutos secos** nut allergy

② **la alergia a los cacahuetes** peanut allergy

③ **la alergia al marisco** seafood allergy

④ **la intolerancia a la lactosa** lactose intolerant

⑤ **la celiaquía** gluten intolerant

⑥ **la alergia a la leche** dairy allergy

⑦ **la alergia al trigo** wheat allergy

⑧ **la alergia al huevo** egg allergy

⑨ **la alergia al sésamo** sesame allergy

⑩ **la alergia a la soja** soya allergy

⑪ **la alergia al apio** celery allergy

⑫ **la alergia al sulfito** sulphite allergy

⑭ **la alergia a la mostaza** mustard allergy

⑬ **alérgico** *m* **alérgica** *f* allergic

⑮ **intolerante** intolerant

24 Cuerpo sano, mente sana
Healthy body, healthy mind

24.1 EL YOGA · YOGA

① **las mallas de yoga**
yoga pants

② **la esterilla**
mat

③ **la parada de cabeza**
headstand

④ **la clase de yoga**
yoga class

⑤ **Inspira profundamente y luego espira.**
Take a deep breath in, and then breathe out.

⑥ **el niño**
child's pose

⑦ **la cobra**
cobra pose

⑧ **el guerrero**
warrior pose

⑨ **la media torsión sentada**
seated twist

⑩ **el triángulo**
triangle pose

⑪ **la pinza**
seated forward fold

⑫ **el cadáver**
corpse pose

⑬ **el cuervo**
crow pose

⑭ **la silla**
chair pose

⑮ **la montaña**
mountain pose

⑯ **el puente**
bridge pose

⑰ **la plancha**
plank pose

⑱ **el arco**
bow pose

⑲ **la paloma**
pigeon pose

⑳ **el árbol**
tree pose

㉑ **el perro boca abajo**
downward dog

㉒ **el loto**
bound ankle pose

㉓ **el camello**
camel pose

㉔ **la rueda**
wheel pose

㉕ **la media luna**
half moon pose

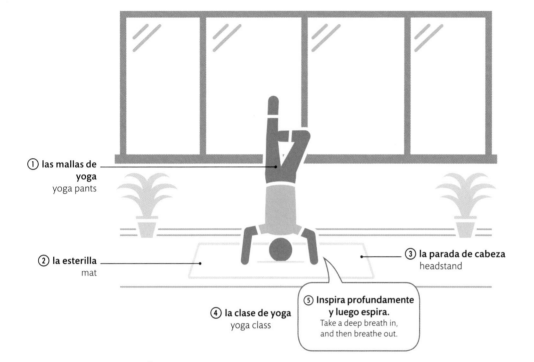

㉖ **el delfín**
dolphin pose

See also
03 Los músculos y el esqueleto • Muscles and skeleton **04** Los órganos internos • Internal organs
19 Las enfermedades y lesiones • Illness and injury **20** La visita al médico • Visiting the doctor
21 El hospital • The hospital **23** La dieta y la nutrición • Diet and nutrition **29** La cocina • Cooking

24.2 **LOS TRATAMIENTOS Y LAS TERAPIAS** • TREATMENTS AND THERAPY

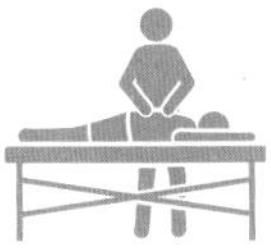
① **el masaje**
massage

② **el shiatsu**
shiatsu

③ **la quiropráctica**
chiropractic

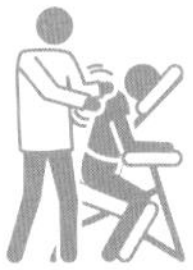
④ **la osteopatía**
osteopathy

⑤ **la reflexología**
reflexology

⑥ **la meditación**
meditation

⑦ **el reiki**
reiki

⑧ **la acupuntura**
acupuncture

⑨ **el ayurveda**
ayurveda

⑩ **la hipnoterapia**
hypnotherapy

⑪ **la hidroterapia**
hydrotherapy

⑫ **la aromaterapia**
aromatherapy

⑬ **la herbología**
herbalism

⑭ **los aceites esenciales**
essential oils

⑮ **la homeopatía**
homeopathy

⑯ **la acupresión**
acupressure

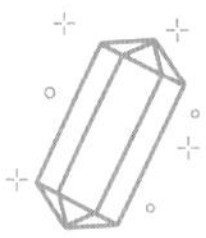
⑰ **la sanación con cristales**
crystal healing

⑱ **la naturopatía**
naturopathy

⑲ **el feng shui**
feng shui

⑳ **la poesía terapéutica**
poetry therapy

㉑ **la arteterapia**
art therapy

㉒ **la terapia asistida con animales**
pet therapy

㉓ **la ecoterapia**
nature therapy

㉔ **la musicoterapia**
music therapy

㉕ **la relajación**
relaxation

㉖ **la atención plena**
mindfulness

㉗ **el orientador** *m* **la orientadora** *f*
counsellor

㉘ **la psicoterapia**
psychotherapy

㉚ **Hoy hablaremos sobre el estrés en el trabajo.**
Today, we're talking about stress at work.

㉙ **la terapia de grupo**
group therapy

25 Un lugar donde vivir
A place to live

25.1 LA VIVIENDA • HOUSES

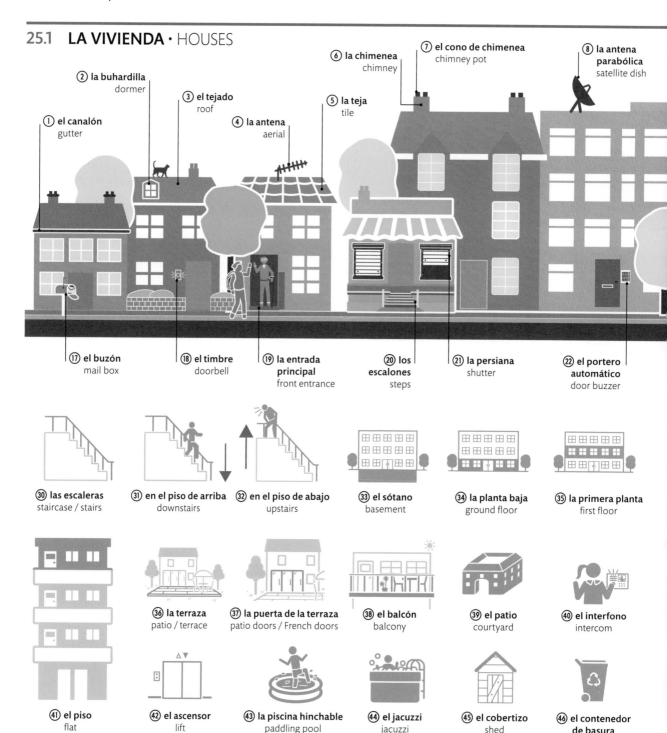

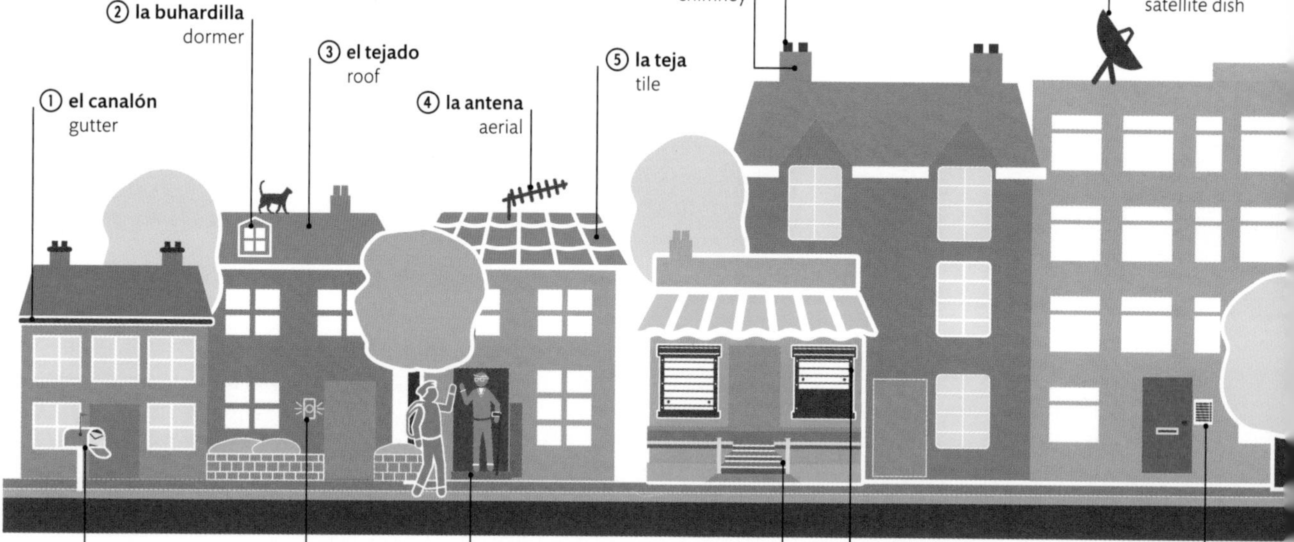

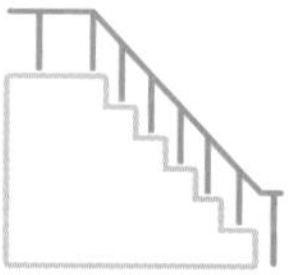

㉚ **las escaleras**
staircase / stairs

㉛ **en el piso de arriba**
downstairs

㉜ **en el piso de abajo**
upstairs

㉝ **el sótano**
basement

㉞ **la planta baja**
ground floor

㉟ **la primera planta**
first floor

㊱ **la terraza**
patio / terrace

㊲ **la puerta de la terraza**
patio doors / French doors

㊳ **el balcón**
balcony

㊴ **el patio**
courtyard

㊵ **el interfono**
intercom

㊶ **el piso**
flat

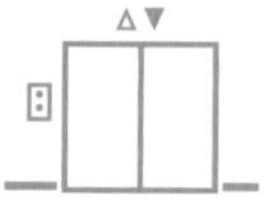

㊷ **el ascensor**
lift

㊸ **la piscina hinchable**
paddling pool

㊹ **el jacuzzi**
jacuzzi

㊺ **el cobertizo**
shed

㊻ **el contenedor de basura**
wheelie bin

See also
32 La casa y el hogar • House and home **34** Las tareas domésticas • Household chores **37** La decoración • Decorating **42-43** La ciudad • In town **44** Los edificios y la arquitectura • Buildings and architecture

⑨ **el bloque de pisos**
block of flats

⑩ **la ventana**
window

⑪ **la luz del porche**
porch light

⑫ **la parada de autobús**
bus stop

⑬ **la farola**
streetlight

⑭ **la ventana de guillotina**
sash window

⑮ **el ático**
attic

⑯ **la alarma antirrobo**
burglar alarm

㉓ **el césped**
grass

㉔ **el porche**
porch

㉕ **el cubo de basura**
dustbin

㉖ **la acera**
pavement

㉗ **el escaparate**
shop window

㉘ **la ventana mirador**
bay window

㉙ **el garaje**
garage

25.2 EL RELLANO • HALLWAY

① **la ranura del correo**
letterbox

② **la llave**
key

③ **el cerrojo**
bolt

④ **la puerta principal**
front door

⑤ **el pomo de la puerta**
door handle / knob

⑥ **el felpudo**
doormat

⑦ **el ojo de la cerradura**
keyhole

⑧ **el rellano**
hallway

⑨ **el pasamanos**
handrail

⑩ **la barandilla**
banister

⑪ **la pared**
wall

⑫ **el suelo**
floor

⑬ **la aldaba**
door knocker

⑭ **la cadena de la puerta**
door chain

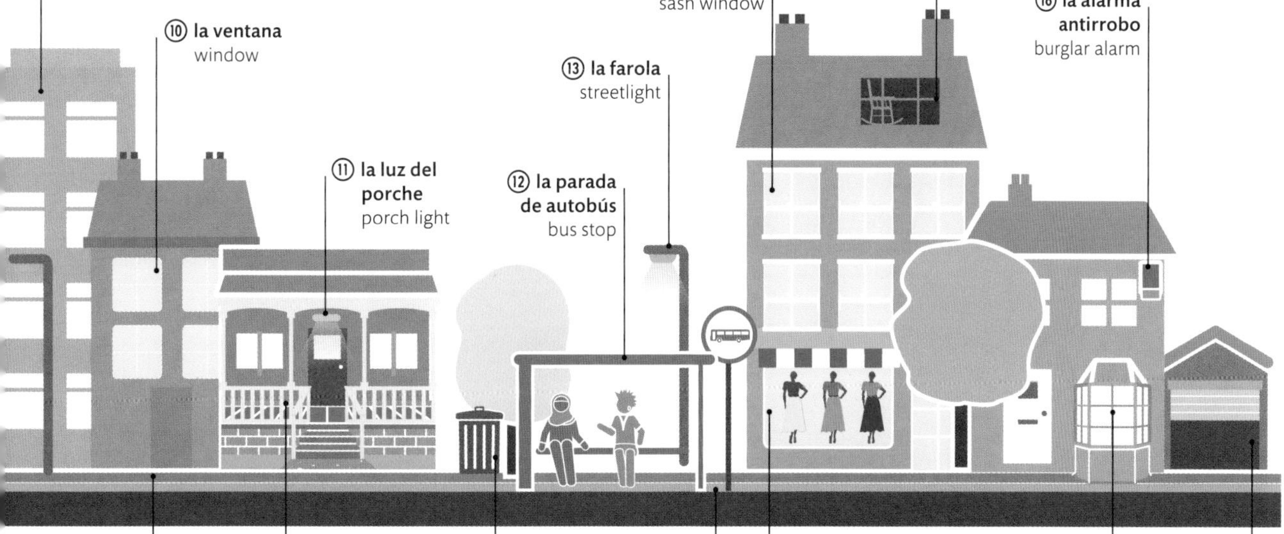

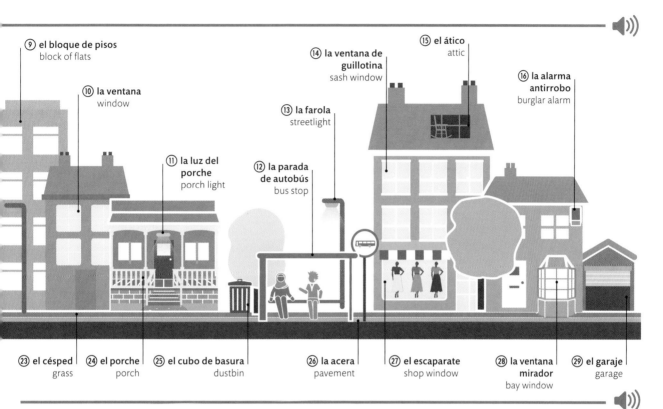

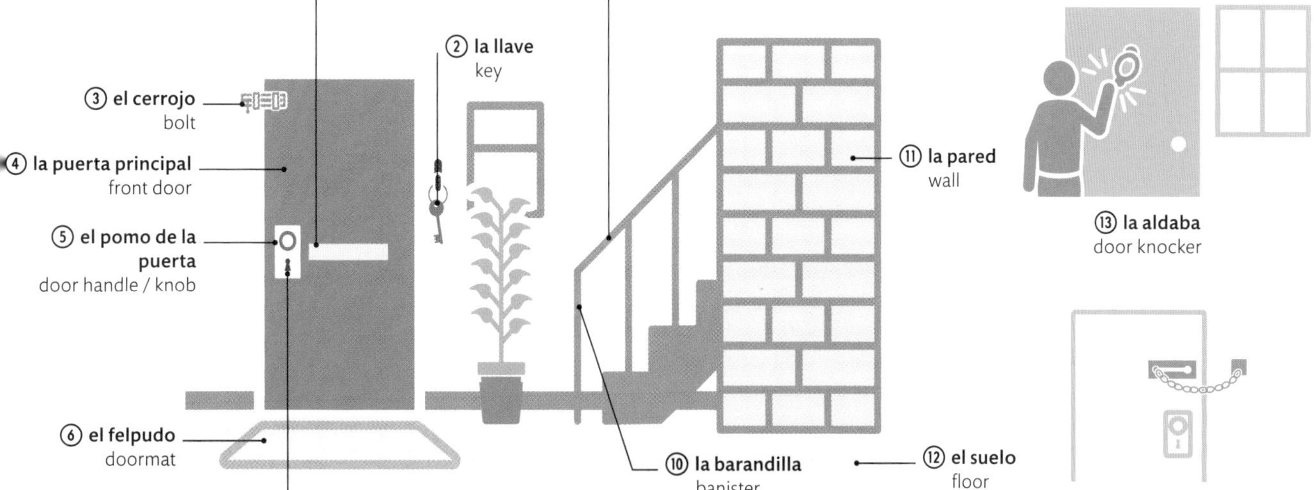

26 El salón y el comedor
Living room and dining room

26.1 EL SALÓN • LIVING ROOM

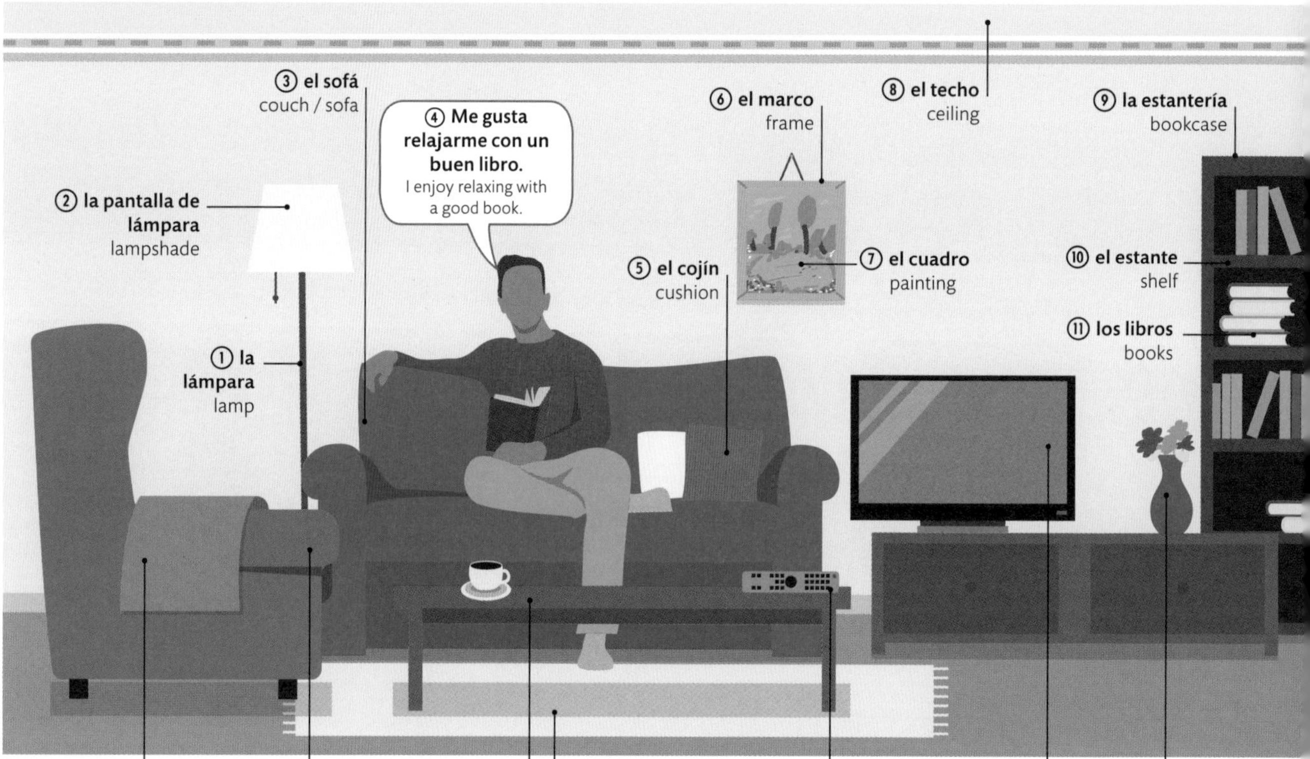

③ el sofá
couch / sofa
④ Me gusta relajarme con un buen libro.
I enjoy relaxing with a good book.
⑥ el marco
frame
⑧ el techo
ceiling
⑨ la estantería
bookcase
② la pantalla de lámpara
lampshade
⑤ el cojín
cushion
⑦ el cuadro
painting
⑩ el estante
shelf
⑪ los libros
books
① la lámpara
lamp
⑫ la manta
throw
⑬ el sillón
armchair
⑭ la mesa de centro
coffee table
⑮ la alfombra
rug
⑯ el mando a distancia
remote control
⑰ la televisión / la TV
television / TV
⑱ el jarrón
vase

⑲ **la chimenea**
fireplace

⑳ **la repisa**
mantlepiece

㉑ **la persiana veneciana**
Venetian blinds

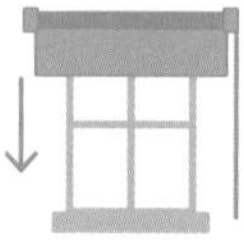

㉒ **la persiana enrollable**
roller blind

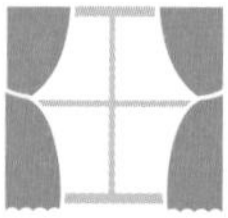

㉓ **las cortinas**
curtains

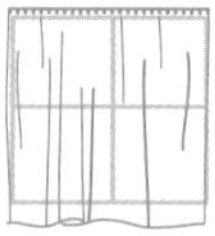

㉔ **el visillo**
net curtain

㉕ **el sofá cama**
sofa bed

㉖ **la mecedora**
rocking chair

㉗ **el reposapiés**
foot stool

㉘ **el aplique**
wall light

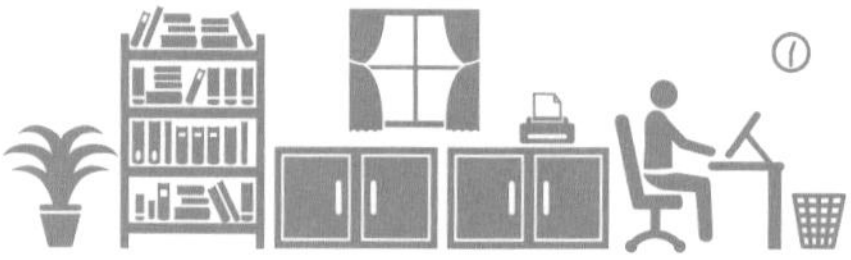

㉙ **el despacho**
study

See also
25 Un lugar donde vivir • A place to live **27** La cocina y la vajilla • Kitchen and tableware **34** Las tareas domésticas • Household chores **71** El desayuno • Breakfast **72** El almuerzo y la cena • Lunch and dinner **136** El ocio en el hogar • Home entertainment

26.2 **EL COMEDOR** • DINING ROOM

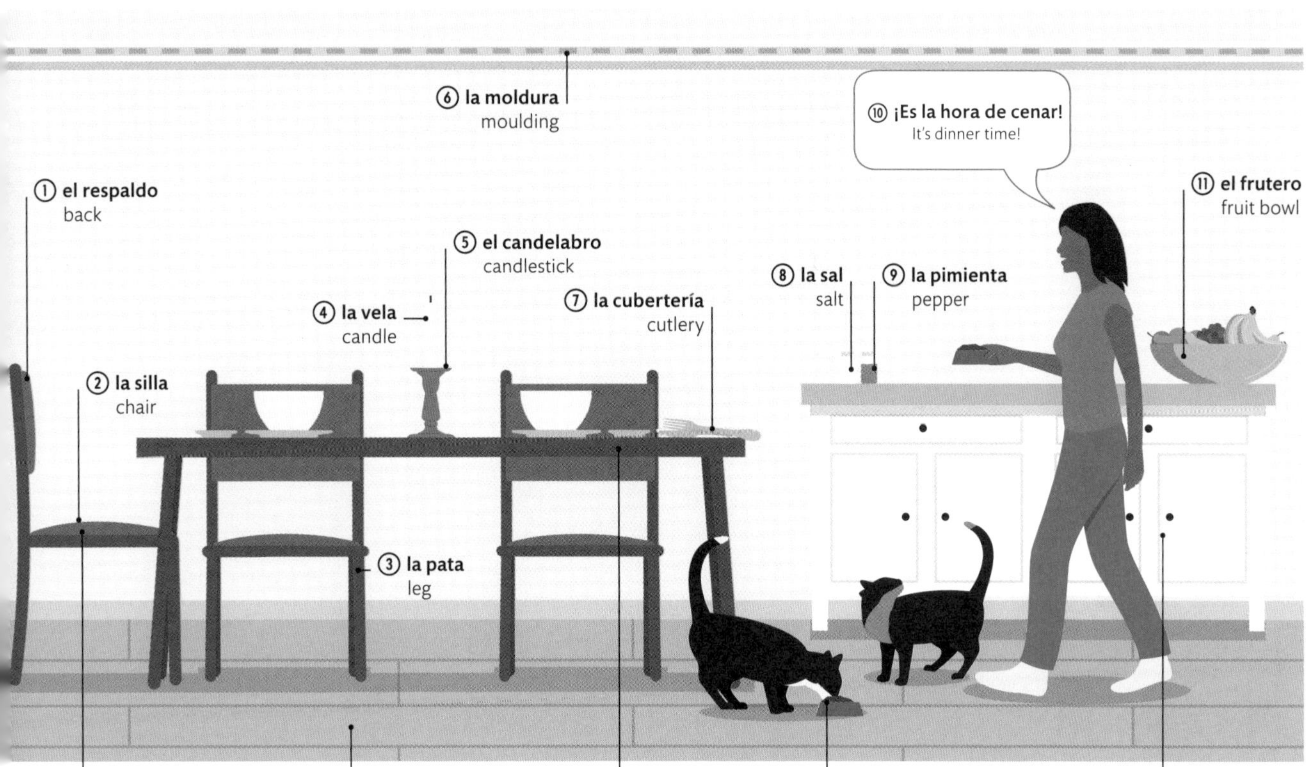

⑰ poner la mesa
to set the table

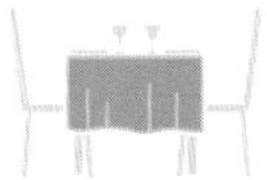

⑱ el mantel
tablecloth

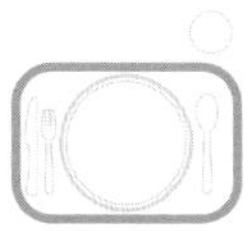

⑲ el salvamanteles
place mat

⑳ el desayuno
breakfast

㉑ el almuerzo
lunch

㉒ la cena
dinner

㉓ el anfitrión *m*
la anfitriona *f*
host / hostess

㉔ tener hambre
hungry

㉕ estar lleno *m*
estar llena *f*
full

㉖ la porción
portion

㉗ el banquete
dinner party

27 La cocina y la vajilla

Kitchen and tableware

27.1 LOS ELECTRODOMÉSTICOS · KITCHEN APPLIANCES

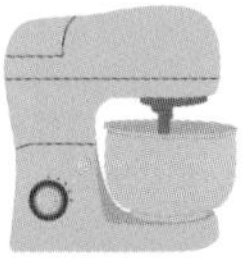

① **la batidora**
mixer

② **la tostadora**
toaster

③ **la licuadora**
blender / food processor

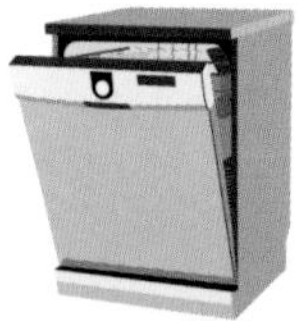

④ **el lavavajillas**
dishwasher

⑤ **el hervidor eléctrico**
electric kettle

⑥ **la olla arrocera**
rice cooker

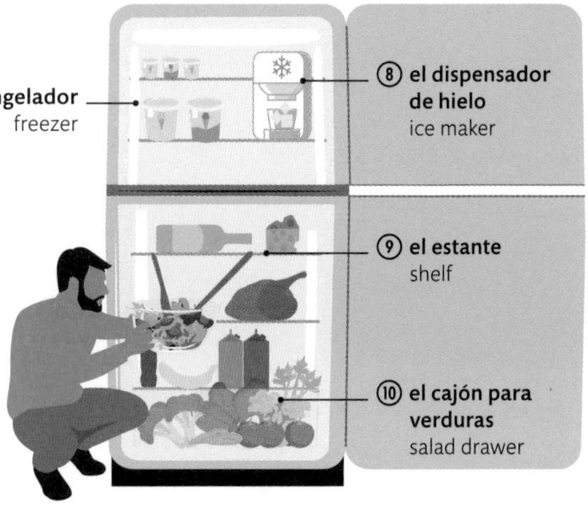

⑪ **la nevera / el frigorífico**
fridge / refrigerator

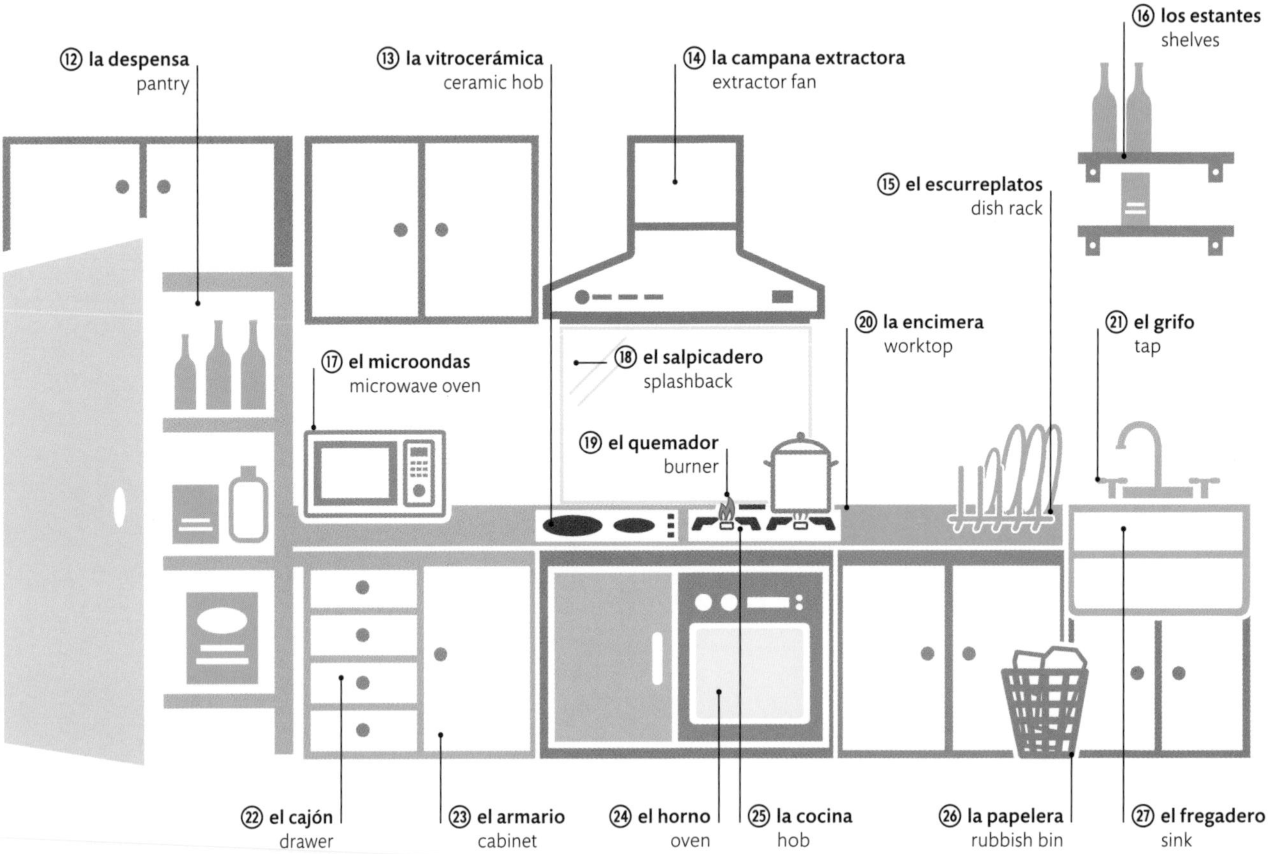

See also
28 El menaje de cocina • Kitchenware **29** La cocina • Cooking **59** Las hierbas y las especias • Herbs and spices **60** La despensa • In the pantry **71** El desayuno • Breakfast
72 El almuerzo y la cena • Lunch and dinner

27.2 LA VAJILLA • TABLEWARE

① **el tenedor**
fork

② **el cuchillo**
knife

③ **la cuchara**
tablespoon

④ **la cucharilla**
teaspoon

⑤ **la cuchara sopera**
soup spoon

⑥ **la cuchara de servir**
serving spoon

⑦ **los cubiertos**
cutlery

⑧ **el cuchillo para la mantequilla**
butter knife

⑨ **los palillos**
chopsticks

⑩ **el cucharón**
ladle

⑪ **el plato llano**
dinner plate

⑫ **el plato de postre**
side plate

⑬ **la vajilla**
crockery

⑭ **la taza de café**
coffee cup

⑮ **la taza de té**
teacup

⑯ **la taza**
mug

⑰ **la cafetera**
espresso maker

⑱ **la tetera**
teapot

⑲ **la disposición de la mesa**
place setting

⑳ **la servilleta**
napkin

㉑ **el servilletero**
napkin ring

㉒ **el bol**
bowl

㉓ **el bol de sopa**
soup bowl

㉔ **el bol de arroz**
rice bowl

㉕ **la huevera**
egg cup

㉖ **la vajilla de sushi**
sushi set

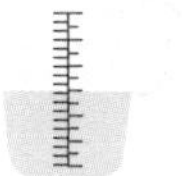
㉗ **la jarra medidora**
measuring jug

㉘ **el vaso de whisky**
tumbler

㉙ **la copa de vino**
wineglass

㉚ **el vaso de pinta**
pint glass

㉛ **las copas**
stemware

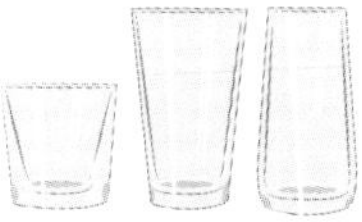
㉜ **la cristalería**
glasses / glassware

㉝ **el frasco**
jar

㉞ **vaso con boquilla**
beaker

㉟ **el vaso de sake**
sake cup

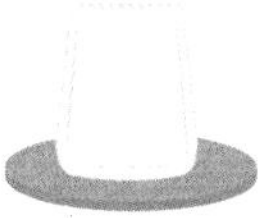
㊱ **el posavasos**
coaster

28 El menaje de cocina
Kitchenware

28.1 LOS UTENSILIOS DE COCINA · KITCHEN EQUIPMENT

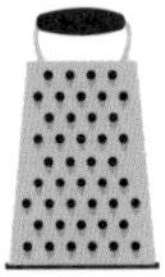

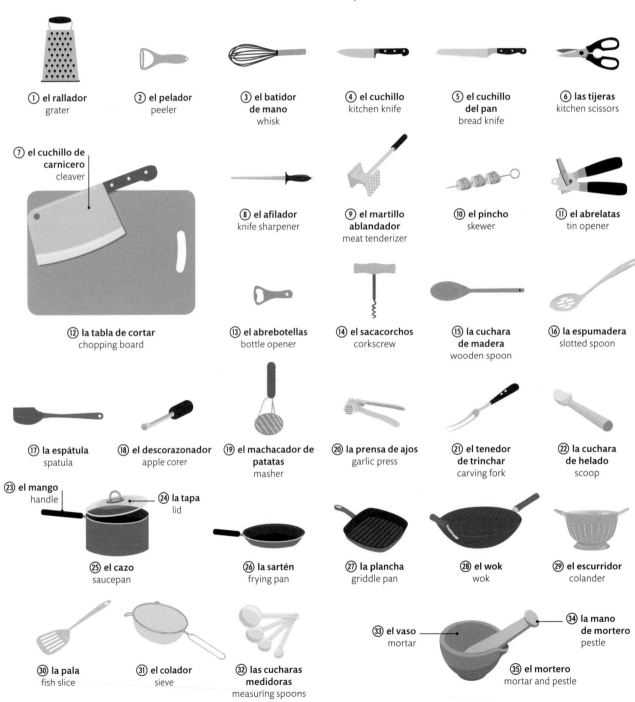

① **el rallador**
grater

② **el pelador**
peeler

③ **el batidor de mano**
whisk

④ **el cuchillo**
kitchen knife

⑤ **el cuchillo del pan**
bread knife

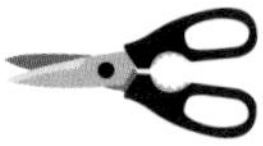

⑥ **las tijeras**
kitchen scissors

⑦ **el cuchillo de carnicero**
cleaver

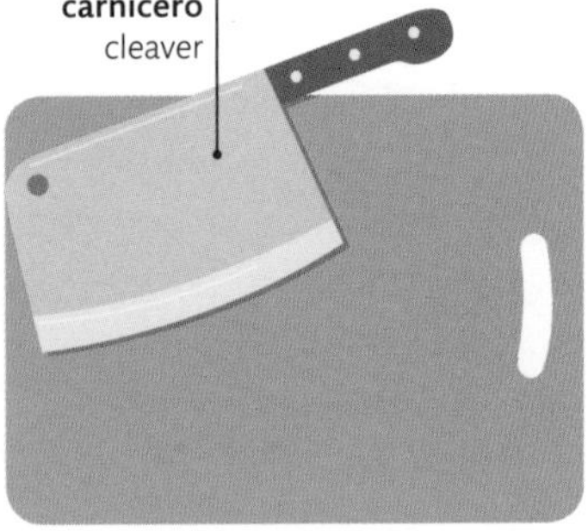

⑫ **la tabla de cortar**
chopping board

⑧ **el afilador**
knife sharpener

⑨ **el martillo ablandador**
meat tenderizer

⑩ **el pincho**
skewer

⑪ **el abrelatas**
tin opener

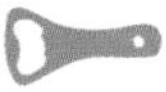

⑬ **el abrebotellas**
bottle opener

⑭ **el sacacorchos**
corkscrew

⑮ **la cuchara de madera**
wooden spoon

⑯ **la espumadera**
slotted spoon

⑰ **la espátula**
spatula

⑱ **el descorazonador**
apple corer

⑲ **el machacador de patatas**
masher

⑳ **la prensa de ajos**
garlic press

㉑ **el tenedor de trinchar**
carving fork

㉒ **la cuchara de helado**
scoop

㉓ **el mango**
handle

㉔ **la tapa**
lid

㉕ **el cazo**
saucepan

㉖ **la sartén**
frying pan

㉗ **la plancha**
griddle pan

㉘ **el wok**
wok

㉙ **el escurridor**
colander

㉚ **la pala**
fish slice

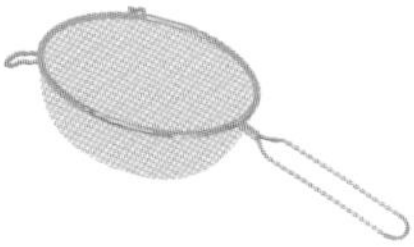

㉛ **el colador**
sieve

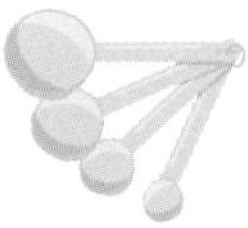

㉜ **las cucharas medidoras**
measuring spoons

㉝ **el vaso**
mortar

㉞ **la mano de mortero**
pestle

㉟ **el mortero**
mortar and pestle

See also
27 La cocina y la vajilla • Kitchen and tableware **29** La cocina • Cooking
59 Las hierbas y las especias • Herbs and spices **60** La despensa • In the pantry
71 El desayuno • Breakfast **72** El almuerzo y la cena • Lunch and dinner

36 **el tayín**
tagine

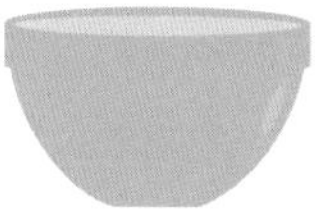
37 **el bol**
mixing bowl

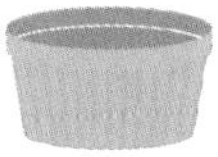
38 **el molde de suflé**
soufflé dish

39 **el molde individual**
ramekin

40 **la cazuela**
casserole dish

41 **la cesta freidora**
frying basket

42 **la mantequera**
butter dish

43 **el reloj de cocina**
timer

44 **el temporizador**
egg timer

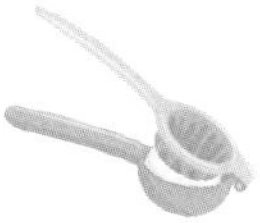
45 **el exprimidor de limones**
lemon squeezer

46 **la cafetera francesa**
coffee press / cafetière

47 **el termómetro de carne**
meat thermometer

48 las jarras medidoras
measuring jugs
49 el molde para bizcochos
cake tin
60 Vamos a picar unas hierbas frescas.
Let's chop up some fresh herbs.
50 la sartén de hierro fundido
skillet
51 la fuente de vidrio
glass baking dish
52 las pinzas
tongs
53 el colador
strainer
55 el soporte para cuchillos
knife stand
54 la mandolina
mandolin
56 el cortador de pizza
pizza cutter
57 el paño de cocina
tea towel
58 el cortahuevos
egg slicer
59 la olla a presión
pressure cooker

29 La cocina
Cooking

29.1 LOS VERBOS PARA COCINAR • COOKING VERBS

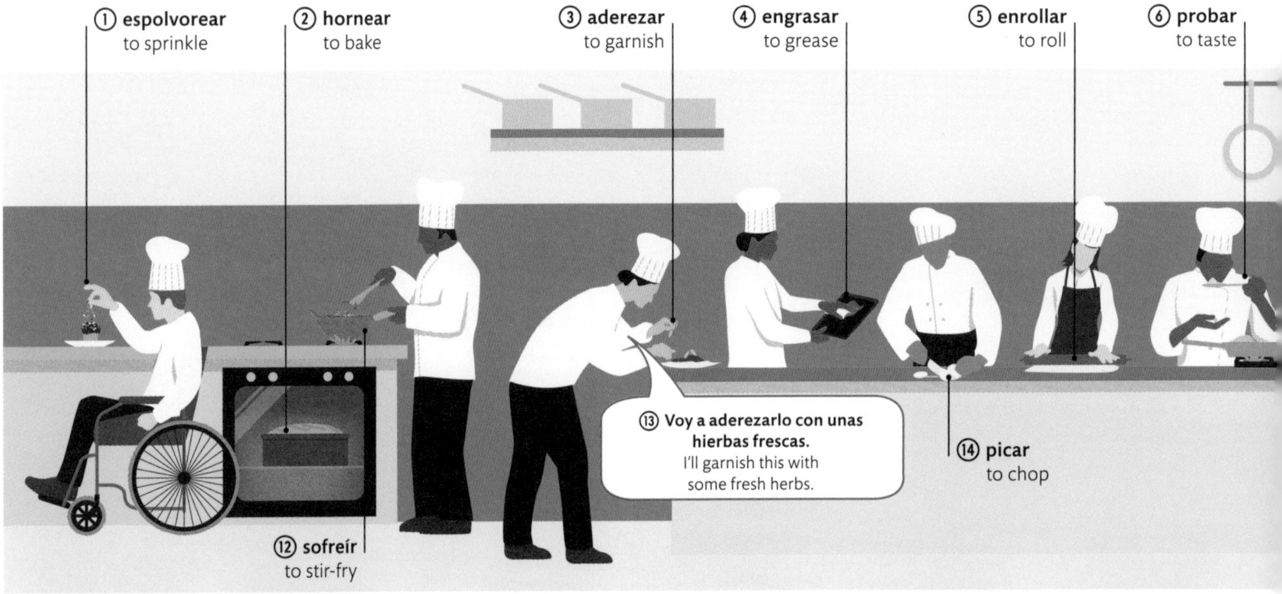

① espolvorear
to sprinkle
② hornear
to bake
③ aderezar
to garnish
④ engrasar
to grease
⑤ enrollar
to roll
⑥ probar
to taste
⑬ Voy a aderezarlo con unas hierbas frescas.
I'll garnish this with some fresh herbs.
⑭ picar
to chop
⑫ sofreír
to stir-fry

⑳ **asar a la parrilla**
to grill

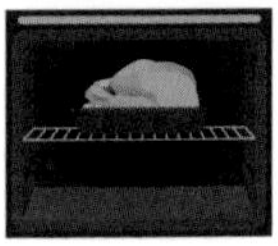
㉑ **asar**
to roast

㉒ **freír**
to fry

㉓ **pochar**
to poach

㉔ **cocer a fuego lento**
to simmer

㉕ **hervir**
to boil

㉖ **congelar**
to freeze

㉗ **añadir**
to add

㉘ **mezclar**
to mix

㉙ **remover**
to stir

㉚ **batir huevos**
to whisk

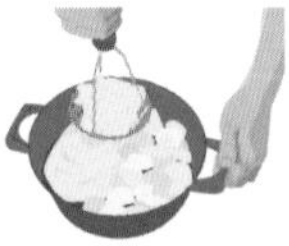
㉛ **machacar**
to mash

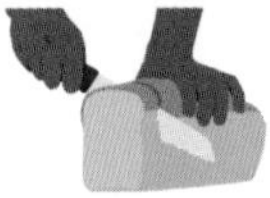
㉜ **rebanar**
to slice

㉝ **una pizca**
a pinch

㉞ **un chorro**
a dash

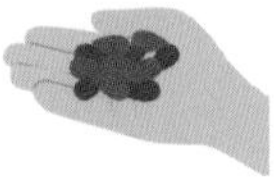
㉟ **un puñado**
a handful

㊱ **picar carne**
to mince

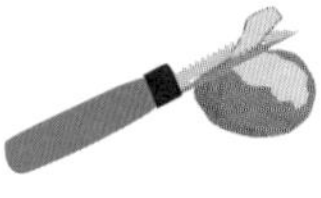
㊲ **pelar**
to peel

㊳ **cortar**
to cut

㊴ **rallar**
to grate

㊵ **verter**
to pour

See also
27 La cocina y la vajilla • Kitchen and tableware **28** El menaje de cocina • Kitchenware **59** Las hierbas y las especias • Herbs and spices **60** La despensa • In the pantry **62-63** La panadería • The bakery **71** El desayuno • Breakfast **72** El almuerzo y la cena • Lunch and dinner

⑦ **cocinar al vapor**
to steam

⑧ **¿Puedes cortar una zanahoria en dados?**
Can you dice a carrot for me, please?

⑨ **batir huevos**
to beat eggs

⑩ **Se me han quemado las cebollas. ¡Ahora ya no sirven!**
I've burned the onions. They are ruined!

⑪ **calentar en el microondas**
to microwave

⑮ **derretir la mantequilla**
to melt butter

⑯ **trinchar**
to carve

⑰ **cortar en dados**
to dice

⑱ **quemar**
to burn

⑲ **saltear**
to sauté

29.2 HORNEAR • BAKING

① **el delantal**
apron

② **las manoplas**
oven glove

③ **el molde para bizcochos**
cake tin

④ **el molde para tartaletas**
flan tin

⑤ **el molde de hornear**
pie dish

⑥ **el pincel de cocina**
pastry brush

⑦ **el rodillo**
rolling pin

⑧ **la bandeja de horno**
baking tray

⑨ **el molde de magdalenas**
muffin tray

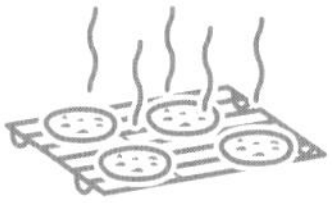
⑩ **la rejilla**
cooling rack

⑪ **el glaseado**
icing

⑫ **la manga pastelera**
piping bag

⑬ **la balanza**
scales

⑭ **la taza medidora**
measuring jug

⑮ **decorar**
to decorate

El dormitorio
Bedroom

30.1 EL DORMITORIO · BEDROOM

㉗ **la cama individual**
single bed

㉘ **la cama de matrimonio**
double bed

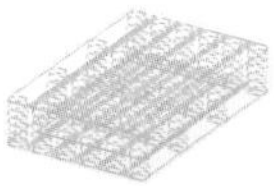

㉙ **el somier de muelles**
bedspring

㉚ **la otomana**
Ottoman

㉛ **el baúl**
linen chest

㉜ **la manta**
throw

㉝ **la colcha**
quilt

㉞ **la manta**
blanket

㉟ **la manta eléctrica**
electric blanket

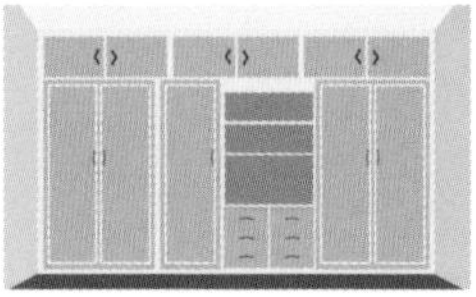

㊱ **el armario empotrado**
built-in wardrobe

㊲ **la bolsa de agua caliente**
hot-water bottle

See also
08 El embarazo y la infancia • Pregnancy and childhood **13-15** La ropa • Clothes
25 Un lugar donde vivir • A place to live **32** La casa y el hogar • House and home

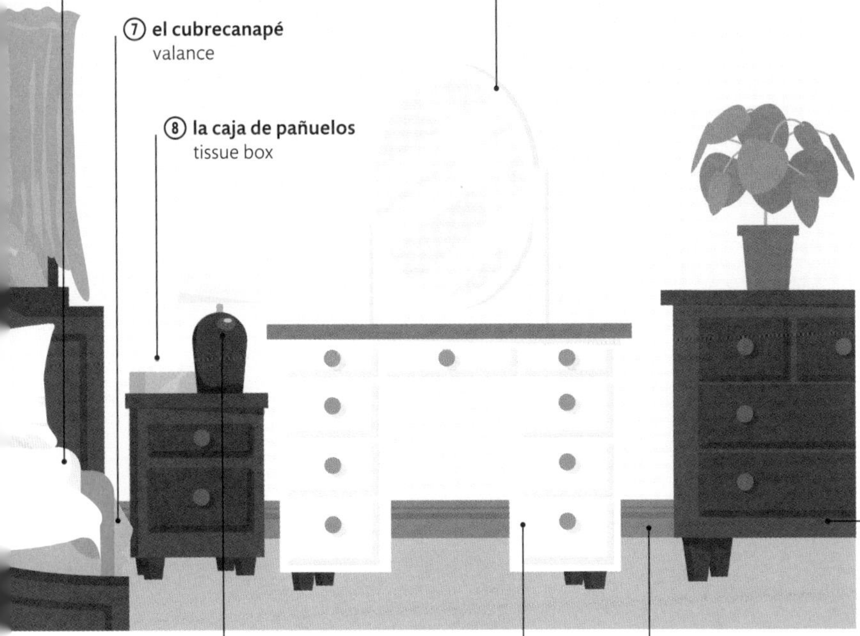

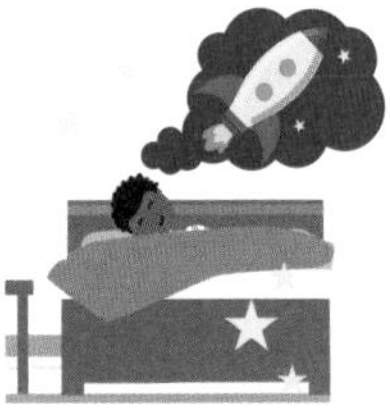
⑩ **el sueño**
dream

⑪ **la pesadilla**
nightmare

⑫ **el insomnio**
insomnia

⑬ **roncar**
to snore

30.2 LA HABITACIÓN DEL BEBÉ • NURSERY

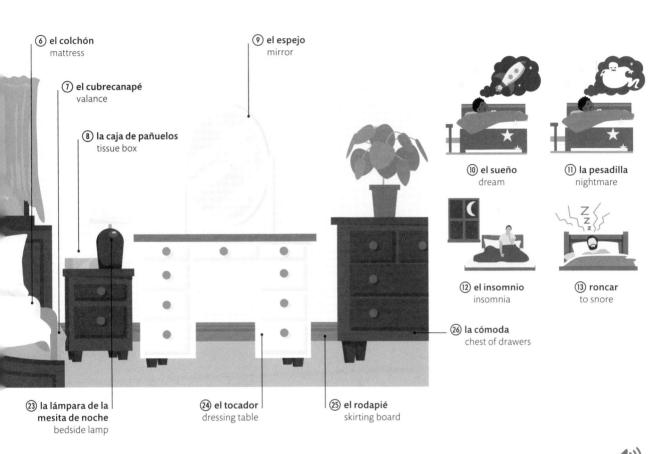

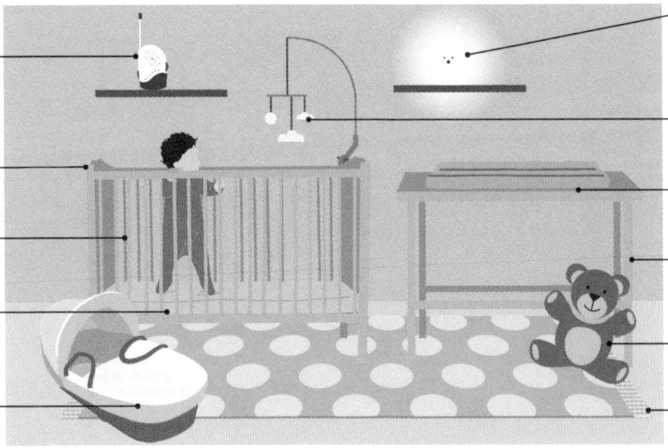

31 El cuarto de baño

Bathroom

31.1 EN EL CUARTO DE BAÑO · IN THE BATHROOM

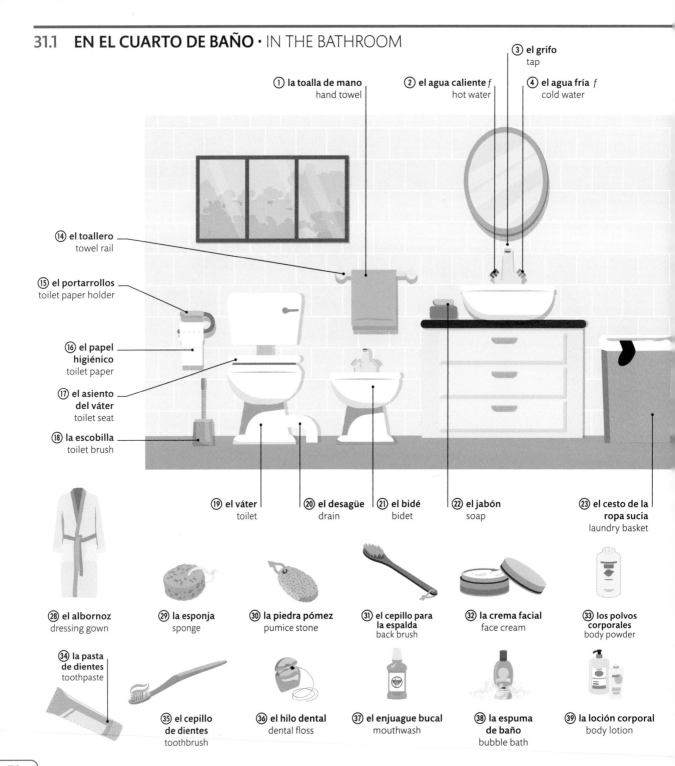

1 **la toalla de mano** hand towel

2 **el agua caliente** *f* hot water

3 **el grifo** tap

4 **el agua fría** *f* cold water

14 **el toallero** towel rail

15 **el portarrollos** toilet paper holder

16 **el papel higiénico** toilet paper

17 **el asiento del váter** toilet seat

18 **la escobilla** toilet brush

19 **el váter** toilet

20 **el desagüe** drain

21 **el bidé** bidet

22 **el jabón** soap

23 **el cesto de la ropa sucia** laundry basket

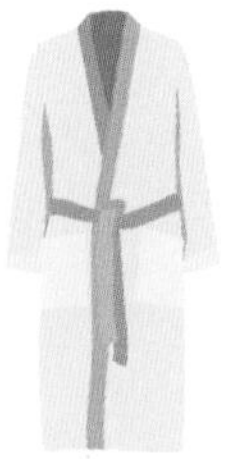

28 **el albornoz** dressing gown

29 **la esponja** sponge

30 **la piedra pómez** pumice stone

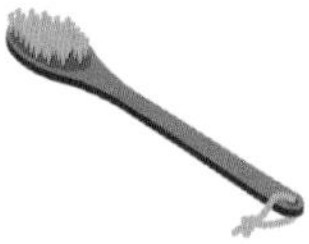

31 **el cepillo para la espalda** back brush

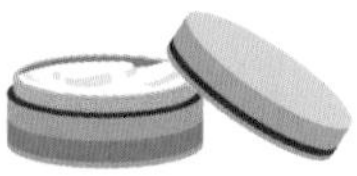

32 **la crema facial** face cream

33 **los polvos corporales** body powder

34 **la pasta de dientes** toothpaste

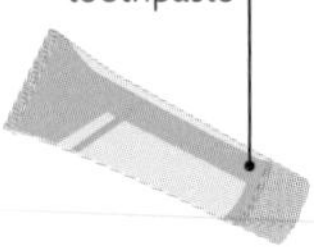

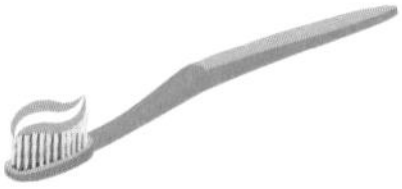

35 **el cepillo de dientes** toothbrush

36 **el hilo dental** dental floss

37 **el enjuague bucal** mouthwash

38 **la espuma de baño** bubble bath

39 **la loción corporal** body lotion

See also
18 La belleza • Beauty **25** Un lugar donde vivir • A place to live **32** La casa y el hogar • House and home **33** La electricidad y la fontanería • Electrics and plumbing

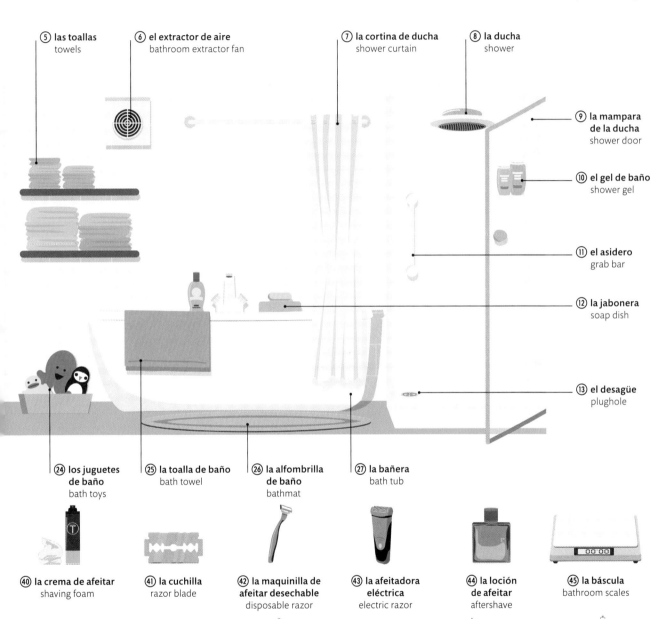

⑤ **las toallas**
towels

⑥ **el extractor de aire**
bathroom extractor fan

⑦ **la cortina de ducha**
shower curtain

⑧ **la ducha**
shower

⑨ **la mampara de la ducha**
shower door

⑩ **el gel de baño**
shower gel

⑪ **el asidero**
grab bar

⑫ **la jabonera**
soap dish

⑬ **el desagüe**
plughole

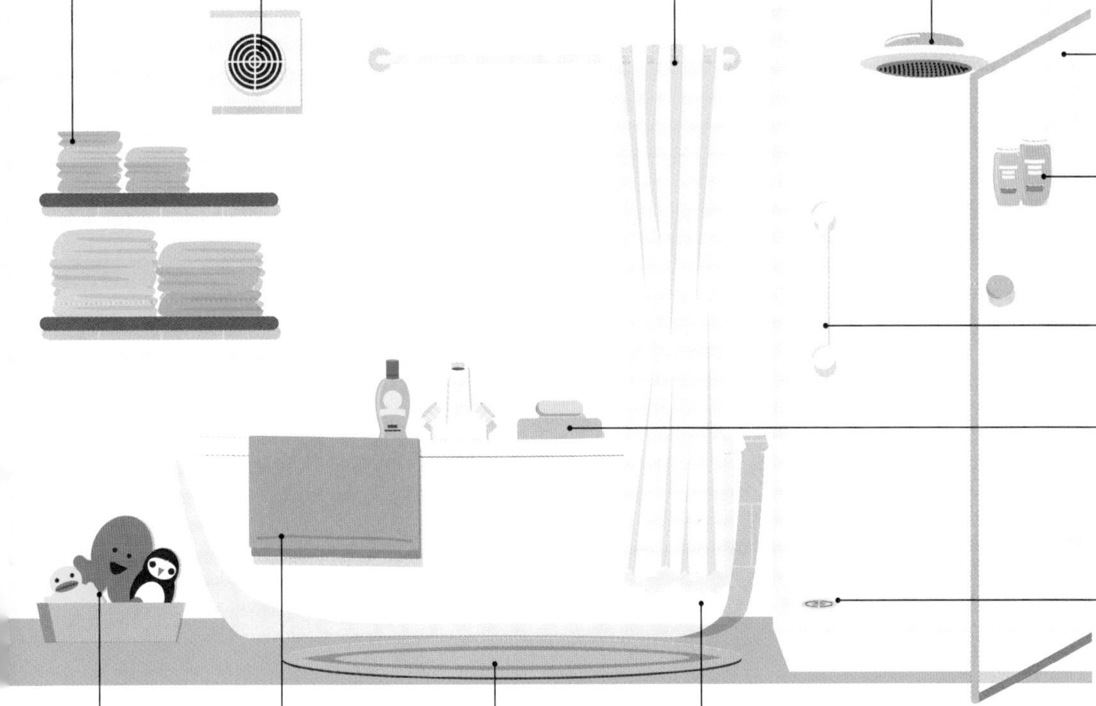

㉔ **los juguetes de baño**
bath toys

㉕ **la toalla de baño**
bath towel

㉖ **la alfombrilla de baño**
bathmat

㉗ **la bañera**
bath tub

㊵ **la crema de afeitar**
shaving foam

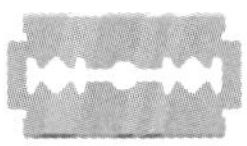

㊶ **la cuchilla**
razor blade

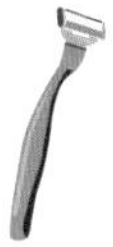

㊷ **la maquinilla de afeitar desechable**
disposable razor

㊸ **la afeitadora eléctrica**
electric razor

㊹ **la loción de afeitar**
aftershave

㊺ **la báscula**
bathroom scales

㊻ **el desatascador**
plunger

㊼ **el tapón**
plug

㊽ **secarse**
to dry yourself

㊾ **afeitarse**
to shave

㊿ **ducharse**
to take (or have) a shower

(51) **bañarse**
to take (or have) a bath

32 La casa y el hogar
House and home

32.1 LOS TIPOS DE CASAS · TYPES OF HOUSES

① **la casa unifamiliar**
detached house

② **la casa pareada**
semi-detached

③ **la casa adosada**
terraced house

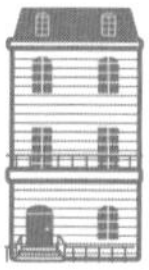
④ **la vivienda urbana**
town house

⑤ **la casa de campo**
cottage

⑥ **la villa**
villa

⑦ **el bungalow**
bungalow

⑧ **la mansión**
mansion

⑨ **la caravana**
caravan

⑩ **la cabaña**
cabin

⑪ **la casa del árbol**
tree house

⑫ **el chalet**
chalet

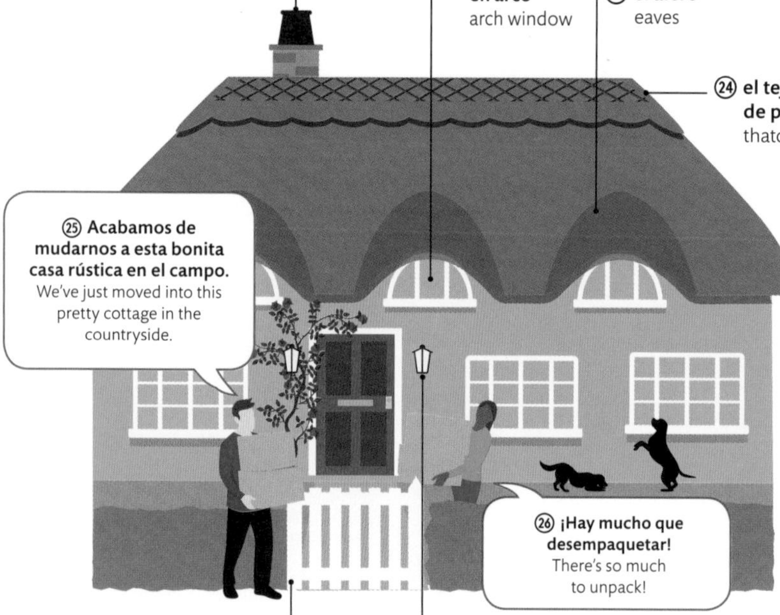
㉕ Acabamos de mudarnos a esta bonita casa rústica en el campo.
We've just moved into this pretty cottage in the countryside.
㉖ ¡Hay mucho que desempaquetar!
There's so much to unpack!

㉑ **la chimenea**
chimney

㉒ **la ventana en arco**
arch window

㉓ **el alero**
eaves

㉔ **el tejado de paja**
thatched roof

㉘ **la verja**
gate

㉗ **la luz**
light

㉙ **la casa rústica con tejado de paja**
thatched cottage

⑬ **la yurta**
yurt

⑭ **la choza**
hut

⑮ **la tienda india**
wigwam

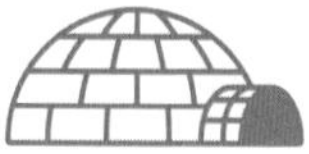
⑯ **el iglú**
igloo

⑰ **el tipi**
teepee

⑱ **la casa flotante**
houseboat

⑲ **la casa prefabricada**
prefab house

⑳ **el palafito**
stilt house

See also
25 Un lugar donde vivir • A place to live **33** La electricidad y la fontanería • Electrics and plumbing **35** El bricolaje • Home improvements **37** La decoración • Decorating **42-43** La ciudad • In town **44** Los edificios y la arquitectura • Buildings and architecture

32.2 LA COMPRA Y EL ALQUILER DE UNA CASA • BUYING AND RENTING A HOUSE

① **el agente inmobiliario** *m* / **la agente inmobiliaria** *f*
estate agent

② **la inmobiliaria**
property

③ **visitar una casa**
to view a house

④ **amueblado** *m* **amueblada** *f*
furnished

⑤ **sin amueblar**
unfurnished

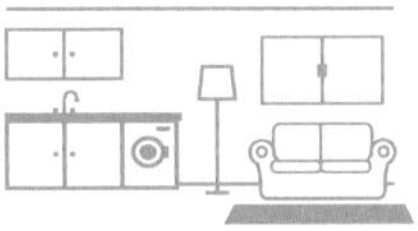

⑥ **de planta abierta**
open-plan

⑦ **la plaza de garaje**
parking space

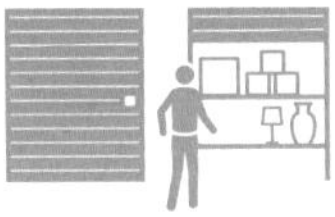

⑧ **el trastero**
storage

⑨ **ahorrar**
to save up

⑩ **comprar**
to buy

⑪ **tener en propiedad**
to own

⑫ **las cajas**
boxes

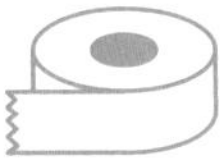

⑬ **la cinta**
tape

⑭ **las llaves**
keys

⑮ **empaquetar**
to pack

⑯ **el camión de la mudanza**
removal van

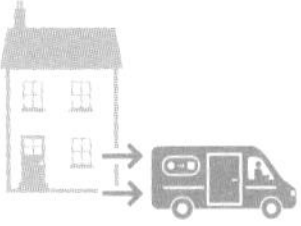

⑰ **mudarse de**
to move out

⑱ **mudarse a**
to move in

⑲ **desempaquetar**
to unpack

⑳ **alquilar**
to rent out

㉑ **pagar el alquiler**
to rent

㉒ **el contrato de alquiler**
lease / tenancy agreement

㉓ **el inquilino** *m* **la inquilina** *f*
tenant

㉔ **el propietario** *m* **la propietaria** *f*
landlord

㉕ **el depósito**
deposit

㉖ **dar aviso**
to give notice

㉗ **la hipoteca**
mortgage

㉘ **las facturas**
bills

㉙ **el inquilino** *m* **la inquilina** *f*
lodger

㉚ **el compañero de piso** *m* **la compañera de piso** *f*
housemate

㉛ **el área residencial** *f*
residential area

33 La electricidad y la fontanería
Electrics and plumbing

33.1 LA ELECTRICIDAD · ELECTRICITY

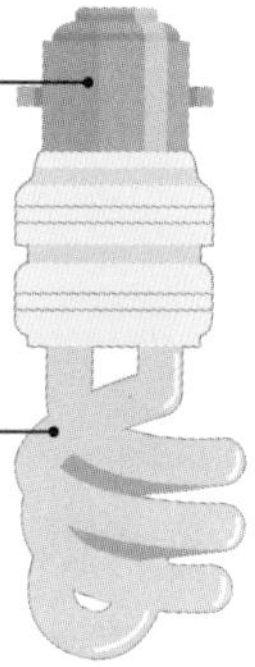

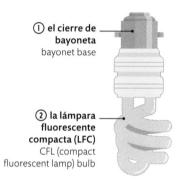

① **el cierre de bayoneta**
bayonet base

② **la lámpara fluorescente compacta (LFC)**
CFL (compact fluorescent lamp) bulb

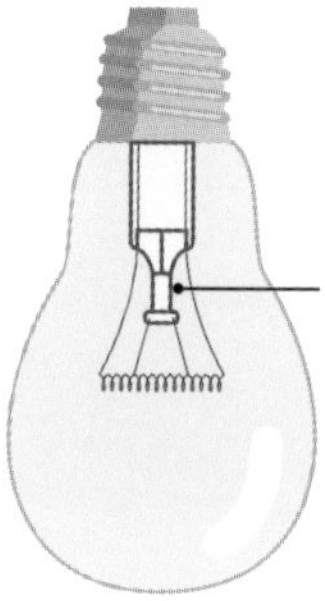

③ **la bombilla incandescente**
incandescent bulb

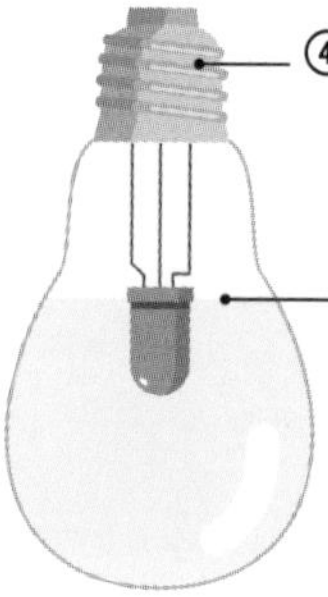

④ **el casquillo**
screw base

⑤ **la bombilla LED**
LED (light emitting diode) bulb

⑥ **las bombillas**
light bulbs

⑦ **el enchufe**
socket

⑧ **el interruptor**
light switch

⑨ **la corriente continua**
direct current

⑩ **la corriente alterna**
alternating current

⑪ **el generador**
generator

⑫ **la estufa de gas**
gas space heater

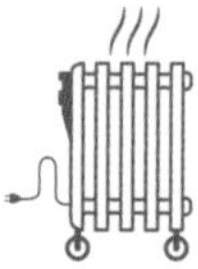

⑬ **el radiador de aceite**
oil-filled radiator

⑭ **el ventilador calefactor**
fan space heater

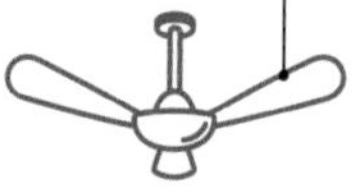

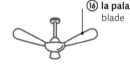

⑯ **la pala**
blade

⑮ **el ventilador de techo**
ceiling fan

⑰ **el ventilador**
fan

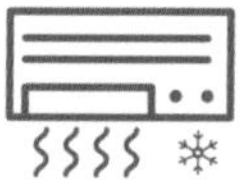

⑱ **el aire acondicionado**
air conditioning

⑲ **la energía**
power

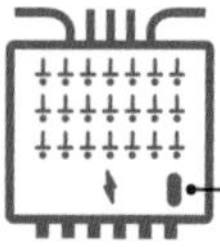

㉑ **el interruptor de fusibles**
trip switch

⑳ **la caja de fusibles**
fuse box

㉒ **el amperio**
amp

㉓ **la fase**
live

㉔ **el neutro**
neutral

㉕ **los cables**
wires

㉖ **la toma de tierra**
earthing

㉗ **el voltaje**
voltage

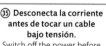

㉘ **la clavija**
plug

㉙ **el pin**
pin

㉟ **Desconecta la corriente antes de tocar un cable bajo tensión.**
Switch off the power before touching a live wire.

㉞ **el cableado**
wiring

㉚ **el contador de la luz**
electricity meter

㉛ **el transformador**
transformer

㉜ **el corte de luz**
power cut

㉝ **la red eléctrica**
mains supply

See also
31 El cuarto de baño • Bathroom **35** El bricolaje • Home improvements **36** Las herramientas • Tools **37** La decoración • Decorating **87** La construcción • Construction

33.2 **LA FONTANERÍA** • PLUMBING

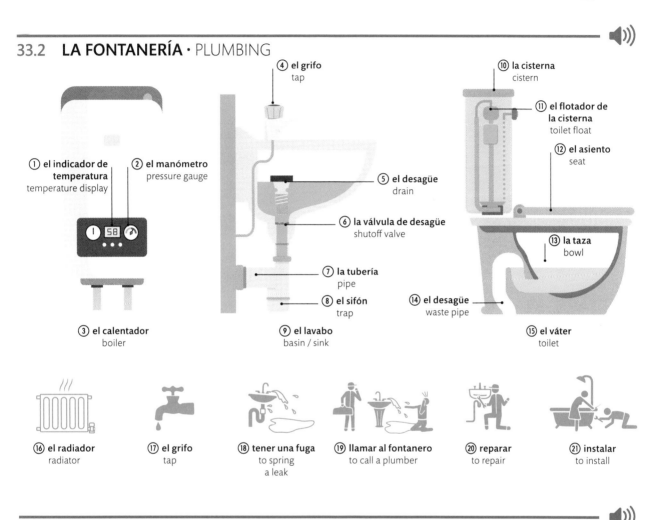

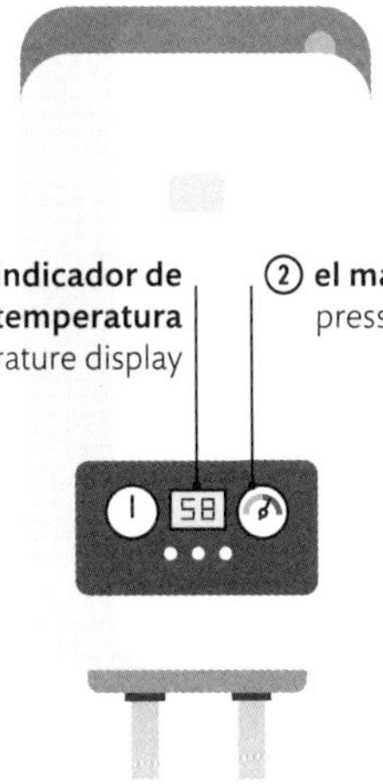

① **el indicador de temperatura**
temperature display

② **el manómetro**
pressure gauge

③ **el calentador**
boiler

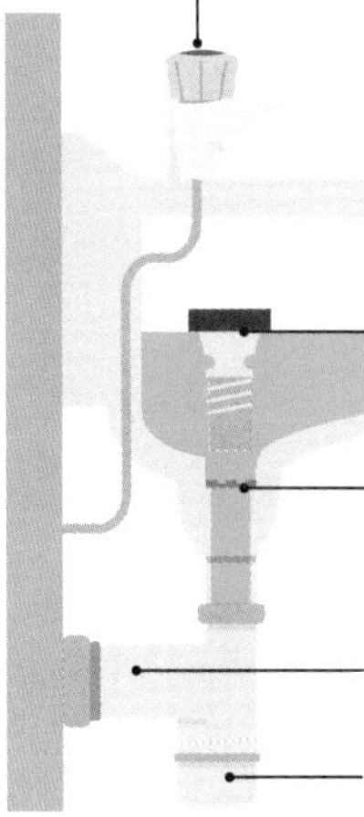

④ **el grifo**
tap

⑤ **el desagüe**
drain

⑥ **la válvula de desagüe**
shutoff valve

⑦ **la tubería**
pipe

⑧ **el sifón**
trap

⑨ **el lavabo**
basin / sink

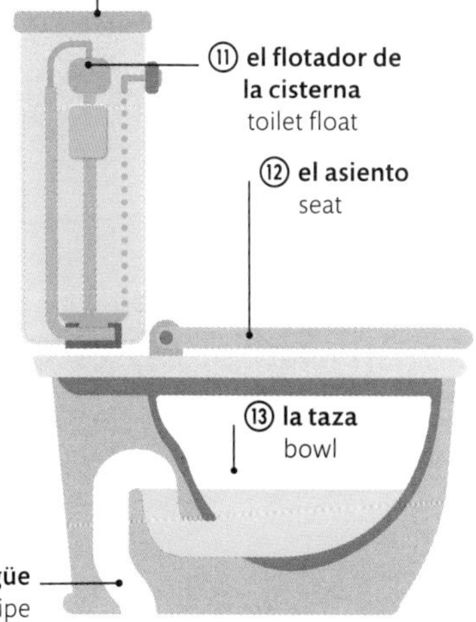

⑩ **la cisterna**
cistern

⑪ **el flotador de la cisterna**
toilet float

⑫ **el asiento**
seat

⑬ **la taza**
bowl

⑭ **el desagüe**
waste pipe

⑮ **el váter**
toilet

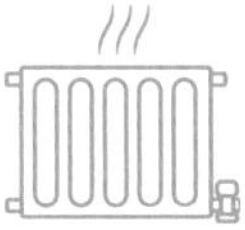

⑯ **el radiador**
radiator

⑰ **el grifo**
tap

⑱ **tener una fuga**
to spring a leak

⑲ **llamar al fontanero**
to call a plumber

⑳ **reparar**
to repair

㉑ **instalar**
to install

33.3 **LOS RESIDUOS** • WASTE

① **la papelera**
rubbish bin

② **la papelera de reciclaje**
recycling bin

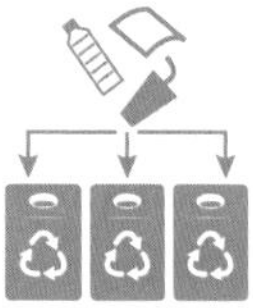

③ **el sistema de clasificación de basura**
sorting unit

④ **el compostador**
food compost bin

⑤ **la bolsa de basura**
bin liner

⑥ **los residuos biodegradables**
biodegradable waste

⑦ **los residuos tóxicos**
hazardous waste

⑧ **los residuos electrónicos**
electrical waste

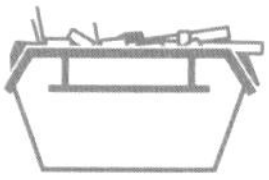

⑨ **los escombros**
construction waste

34 Las tareas domésticas
Household chores

34.1 LAS TAREAS DE CASA · HOUSEHOLD TASKS

① **cambiar las sábanas**
to change the sheets

② **hacer la cama**
to make the bed

③ **alimentar a las mascotas**
to feed the pets

④ **regar las plantas**
to water the plants

⑤ **lavar el coche**
to wash the car

⑥ **barrer**
to sweep the floor

⑦ **fregar el suelo**
to scrub the floor

⑧ **limpiar el horno**
to clean the oven

⑨ **limpiar las ventanas**
to clean the windows

⑩ **descongelar el congelador**
to defrost the freezer

⑪ **aspirar la moqueta**
to vacuum the carpet

⑫ **quitar el polvo**
to dust

⑬ **limpiar el baño**
to clean the bathroom

⑭ **recoger**
to tidy

⑮ **hacer la compra**
to buy groceries

⑯ **lavar la ropa**
to do the laundry

⑰ **tender la ropa**
to hang out clothes

⑱ **planchar**
to do the ironing

⑳ **Suelo hacer las tareas de casa por la tarde.**
I usually do the housework in the evening.

⑲ **fregar**
to mop the floor

㉑ **doblar la ropa**
to fold clothes

㉒ **poner la mesa**
to set the table

㉓ **retirar la mesa**
to clear the table

㉔ **llenar el lavavajillas**
to load the dishwasher

㉕ **vaciar el lavavajillas**
to unload the dishwasher

㉖ **limpiar las superficies**
to wipe the surfaces

㉗ **lavar los platos**
to do the dishes

㉘ **secar los platos**
to dry the dishes

㉙ **sacar la basura**
to take out the rubbish

See also
09 Las rutinas diarias • Daily routines **25** Un lugar donde vivir • A place to live
33 La electricidad y la fontanería • Electrics and plumbing **35** El bricolaje • Home improvements **37** La decoración • Decorating **39** La jardinería • Practical gardening

34.2 **LA COLADA Y LA LIMPIEZA** • LAUNDRY AND CLEANING

① **el estropajo**
scouring pad

② **la esponja**
sponge

③ **el paño**
cloth

④ **el trapo del polvo**
duster

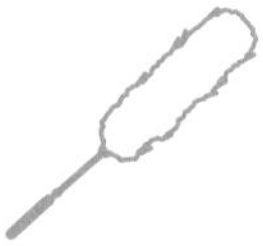

⑤ **el plumero**
feather duster

⑥ **la escobilla limpiacristales**
squeegee

⑦ **el cubo**
bucket

⑧ **la fregona**
mop

⑨ **el cepillo de fregar**
scrubbing brush

⑩ **el recogedor**
dustpan

⑪ **la escobilla**
brush

⑫ **la escoba**
broom

⑬ **el cubo de reciclaje**
recycling bin

⑭ **la bolsa de basura**
bin liner

⑮ **el abrillantador**
polish

⑯ **el limpiador de superficies**
surface cleaner

⑰ **el limpiador de baños**
toilet cleaner

⑱ **el desinfectante de váter**
toilet block

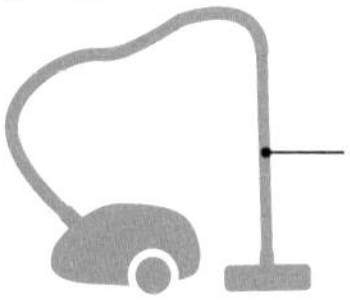

⑳ **la manguera de succión**
suction hose

⑲ **la aspiradora**
vacuum cleaner

㉑ **los guantes de goma**
rubber gloves

㉒ **el vinagre blanco**
white vinegar

㉓ **la ropa sucia**
dirty washing

㉔ **la cesta de la ropa**
laundry basket

㉕ **la lavadora**
washing machine

㉖ **la secadora**
tumble dryer

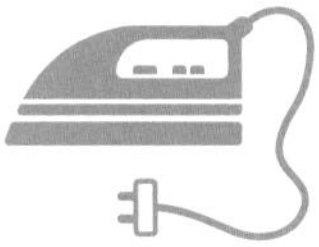

㉗ **la plancha**
iron

㉘ **la tabla de planchar**
ironing board

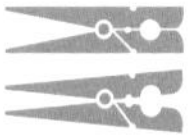

㉙ **las pinzas**
clothes peg

㉚ **el tendedero**
clothesline / washing line

㉛ **el detergente de ropa**
laundry detergent

㉜ **el suavizante de ropa**
fabric softener

㉝ **el lavavajillas**
dishwasher

㉞ **la pastilla de lavavajillas**
dishwasher tablets

㉟ **el líquido de lavavajillas**
washing-up liquid

㊱ **la lejía**
bleach

El bricolaje

Home improvements

35.1 LAS HERRAMIENTAS Y LOS APARATOS · TOOLS AND DIY EQUIPMENT

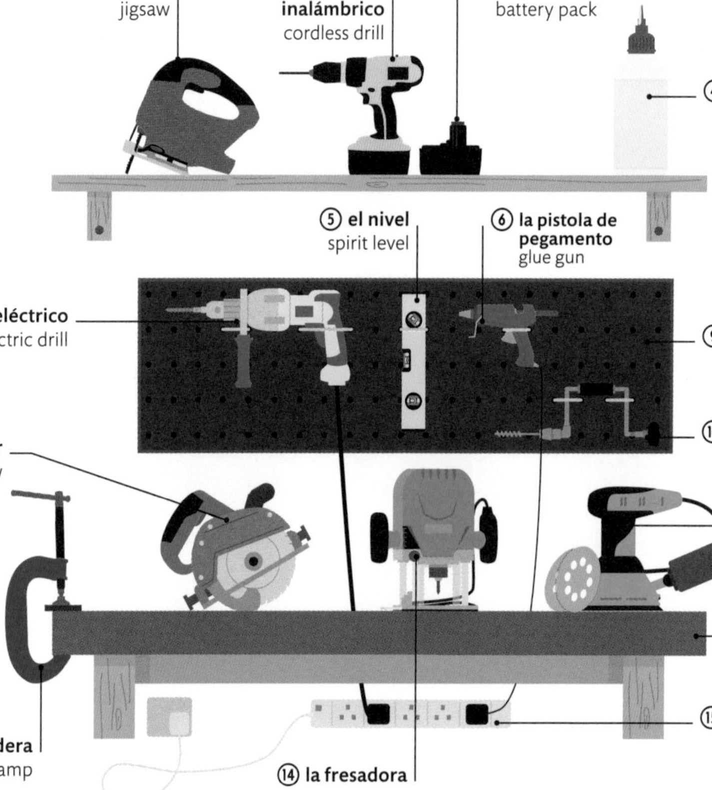

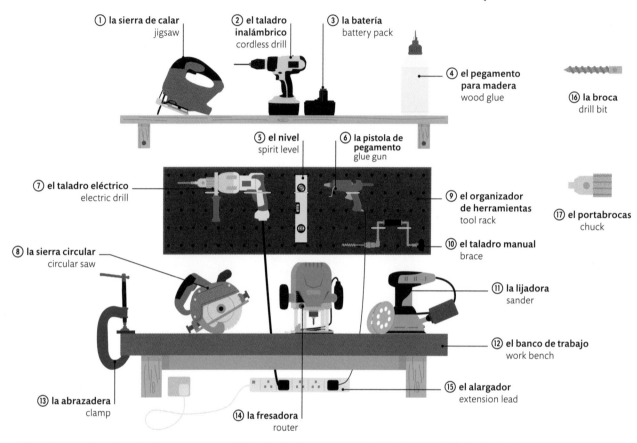

① **la sierra de calar**
jigsaw

② **el taladro inalámbrico**
cordless drill

③ **la batería**
battery pack

④ **el pegamento para madera**
wood glue

⑤ **el nivel**
spirit level

⑥ **la pistola de pegamento**
glue gun

⑦ **el taladro eléctrico**
electric drill

⑧ **la sierra circular**
circular saw

⑨ **el organizador de herramientas**
tool rack

⑩ **el taladro manual**
brace

⑪ **la lijadora**
sander

⑫ **el banco de trabajo**
work bench

⑬ **la abrazadera**
clamp

⑭ **la fresadora**
router

⑮ **el alargador**
extension lead

⑯ **la broca**
drill bit

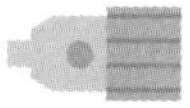

⑰ **el portabrocas**
chuck

35.2 LOS VERBOS DE BRICOLAJE · DIY VERBS

① **cortar**
to cut

② **serrar**
to saw

③ **taladrar**
to drill

④ **martillear**
to hammer

⑤ **alisar**
to plane

⑥ **tornear**
to turn

⑦ **tallar**
to carve

⑧ **alicatar**
to tile

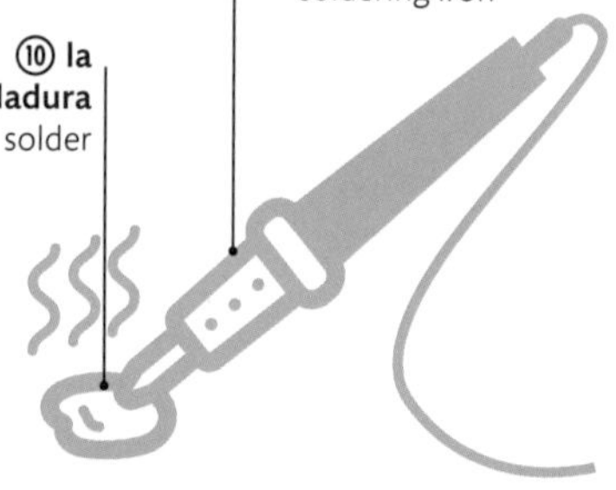

⑩ **la soldadura**
solder

⑪ **el soldador**
soldering iron

⑨ **soldar**
to solder

See also
33 La electricidad y la fontanería • Electrics and plumbing **36** Las herramientas • Tools
37 La decoración • Decorating **87** La construcción • Construction

35.3 **LOS MATERIALES** • MATERIALS

① **la madera**
wood

② **la madera dura**
hardwood

③ **la madera blanda**
softwood

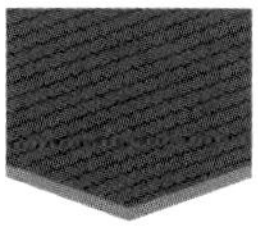
④ **la chapa de madera**
hardboard

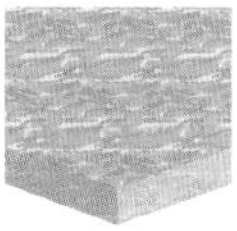
⑤ **el aglomerado**
chipboard

⑥ **el contrachapado**
plywood

⑦ **el tablero MDF**
MDF

⑧ **los azulejos**
tiles

⑨ **el hormigón**
concrete

⑩ **el metal**
metal

⑪ **el alambre**
wire

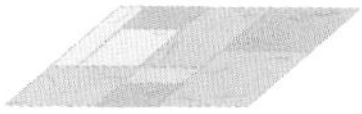
⑫ **la losa**
flagstone

⑬ **el aislamiento**
insulation

⑭ **la arena**
sand

⑮ **la grava**
gravel

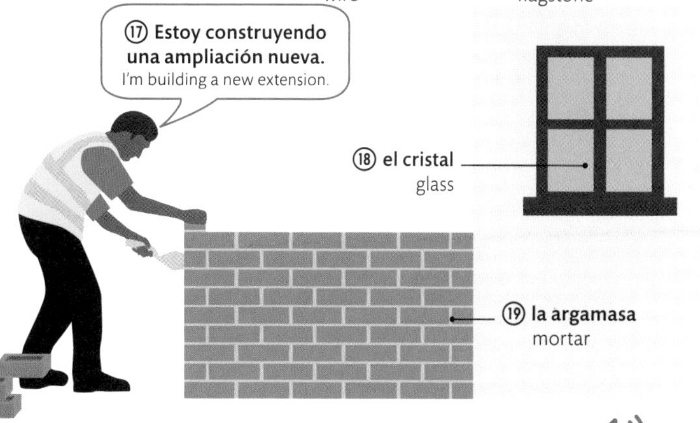
⑰ Estoy construyendo una ampliación nueva.
I'm building a new extension.
⑱ el cristal
glass
⑲ la argamasa
mortar
⑯ los ladrillos
bricks

⑫ **poner una moqueta**
to fit a carpet

⑬ **desatascar el lavabo**
to unblock the sink

⑭ **cambiar la instalación eléctrica**
to rewire the house

⑮ **levantar un muro de ladrillos**
to lay bricks

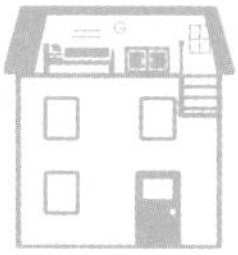
⑯ **reformar el ático**
to convert the attic / loft

⑰ **hacer unas cortinas**
to make curtains

⑱ **colgar una estantería**
to put up shelves

⑲ **cambiar una bombilla**
to change a light bulb

⑳ **desatascar el váter**
to unblock the toilet

㉑ **derribar una pared**
to knock down a wall

㉒ **pintar una pared**
to paint a wall

㉓ **reparar una valla**
to fix a fence

36 Las herramientas
Tools

36.1 LA CAJA DE HERRAMIENTAS · TOOLBOX

36.2 LAS BROCAS · DRILL BITS

① **la broca para metal**
metal bit

② **la broca para hormigón**
masonry bit

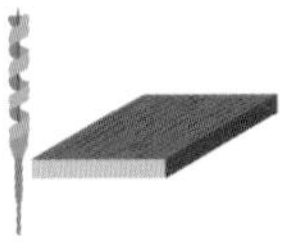

③ **la broca para madera**
carpentry bit

④ **la broca plana para madera**
flat wood bit

⑤ **la broca de seguridad**
security bit

⑥ **el escariador**
reamer

See also
33 La electricidad y la fontanería • Electrics and plumbing **35** El bricolaje • Home improvements **37** La decoración • Decorating **87** La construcción • Construction

36.3 LAS HERRAMIENTAS • TOOLS

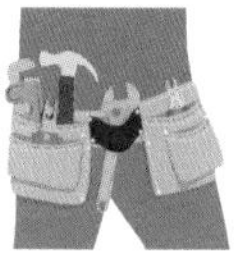
① **el cinturón de herramientas**
tool belt

② **el clavo**
nail

③ **el tornillo**
screw

④ **el perno**
bolt

⑤ **la arandela**
washer

⑥ **la tuerca**
nut

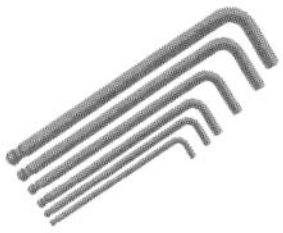
⑦ **la llave Alen**
hex keys / Allen keys

⑧ **la cinta métrica**
tape measure

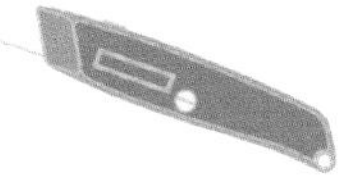
⑨ **el cúter**
utility knife

⑩ **la sierra de arco**
hacksaw

⑪ **el serrucho**
tenon saw

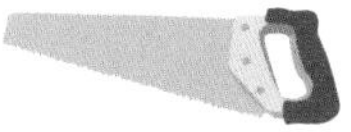
⑫ **la sierra de mano**
handsaw

⑬ **el cepillo**
plane

⑭ **el taladro de mano**
hand drill

⑮ **la llave fija**
spanner

⑯ **el cincel**
chisel

⑰ **la lima**
file

⑱ **la piedra de afilar**
sharpening stone

⑳ **el peldaño**
rung

⑲ **la escalera**
ladder

㉑ **el pelacables**
wire strippers

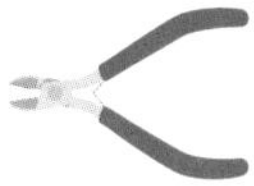
㉒ **el cortaalambres**
wire cutters

㉓ **la cinta aislante**
insulating tape

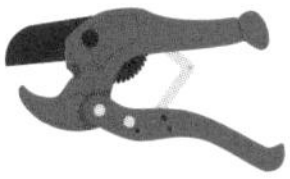
㉔ **el cortatubos**
pipe cutter

㉕ **el desatascador**
plunger

㉖ **el mazo**
mallet

㉗ **el hacha** *f*
axe

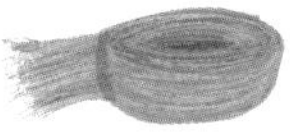
㉘ **el estropajo de aluminio**
wire wool

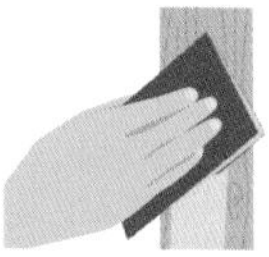
㉙ **el papel de lija**
sandpaper

㉚ **las gafas de seguridad**
safety goggles

㉛ **el soldador**
soldering iron

㉜ **la soldadura**
solder

㉝ **la burbuja**
vial

㉞ **el nivel**
spirit level

37 La decoración
Decorating

37.1 LAS REFORMAS • HOUSEHOLD RENOVATION

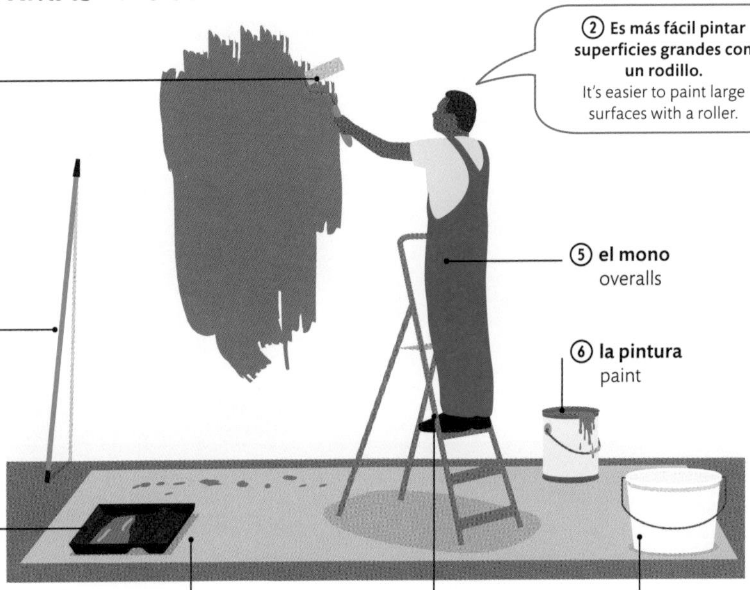

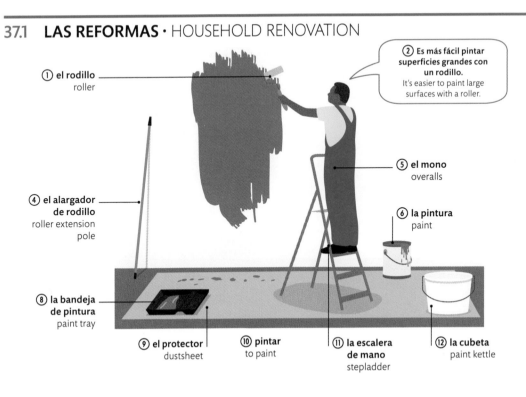

① **el rodillo**
roller

② **Es más fácil pintar superficies grandes con un rodillo.**
It's easier to paint large surfaces with a roller.

③ **la brocha**
paintbrush

④ **el alargador de rodillo**
roller extension pole

⑤ **el mono**
overalls

⑥ **la pintura**
paint

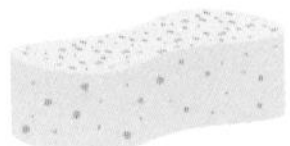

⑦ **la esponja**
sponge

⑧ **la bandeja de pintura**
paint tray

⑨ **el protector**
dustsheet

⑩ **pintar**
to paint

⑪ **la escalera de mano**
stepladder

⑫ **la cubeta**
paint kettle

⑬ **la cinta de carrocero**
masking tape

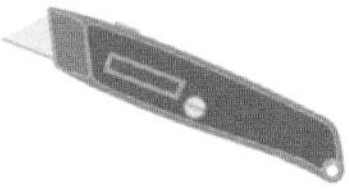

⑭ **el cúter**
craft knife

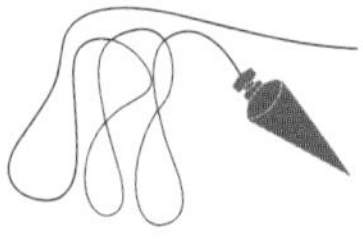

⑮ **la plomada**
plumb line

⑯ **el papel de lija**
sandpaper

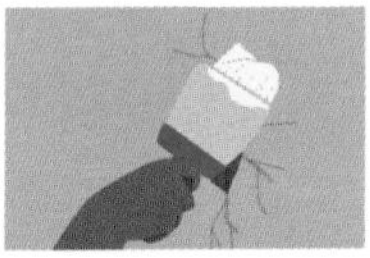

⑰ **la masilla**
filler

⑱ **el aguarrás mineral**
white spirit

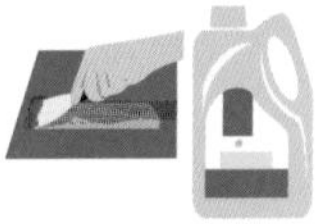

⑲ **el decapante**
paint stripper

⑳ **el yeso**
plaster

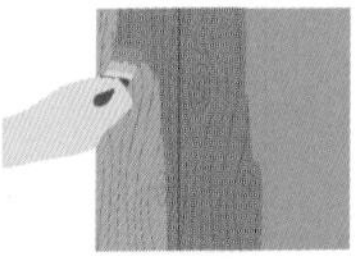

㉑ **la imprimación**
primer

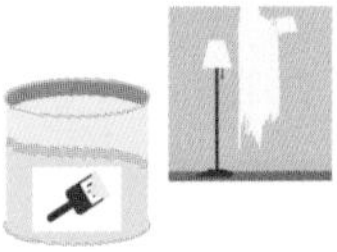

㉒ **la primera mano**
undercoat

㉓ **la pintura de emulsión**
emulsion

㉔ **mate**
matte

㉕ **brillante**
gloss

㉖ **la plantilla**
stencil

㉗ **el disolvente**
solvent

㉘ **el sellador**
sealant / caulk

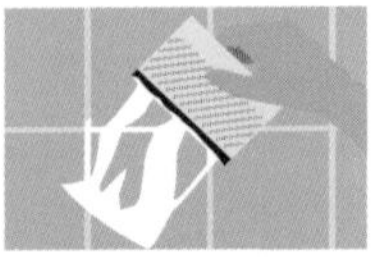

㉙ **la lechada**
grout

㉚ **el conservante de madera**
wood preserver

㉛ **el barniz**
varnish

See also
32 La casa y el hogar • House and home **33** La electricidad y la fontanería • Electrics and plumbing **34** Las tareas domésticas • Household chores **35** El bricolaje • Home improvements

㉜ **las tijeras**
scissors

㉝ **el revestimiento de papel**
lining paper

㉞ **el desprendedor de papel pintado**
wallpaper stripper

㉟ **el raspador**
scraper

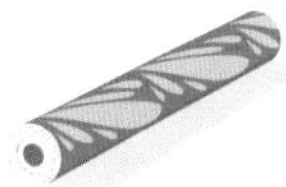

㊱ **el rollo de papel pintado**
wallpaper roll

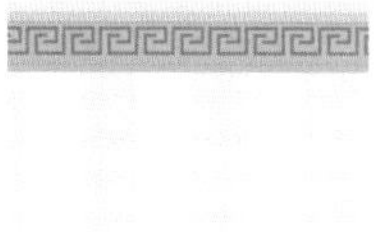

㊲ **la cenefa**
wallpaper border

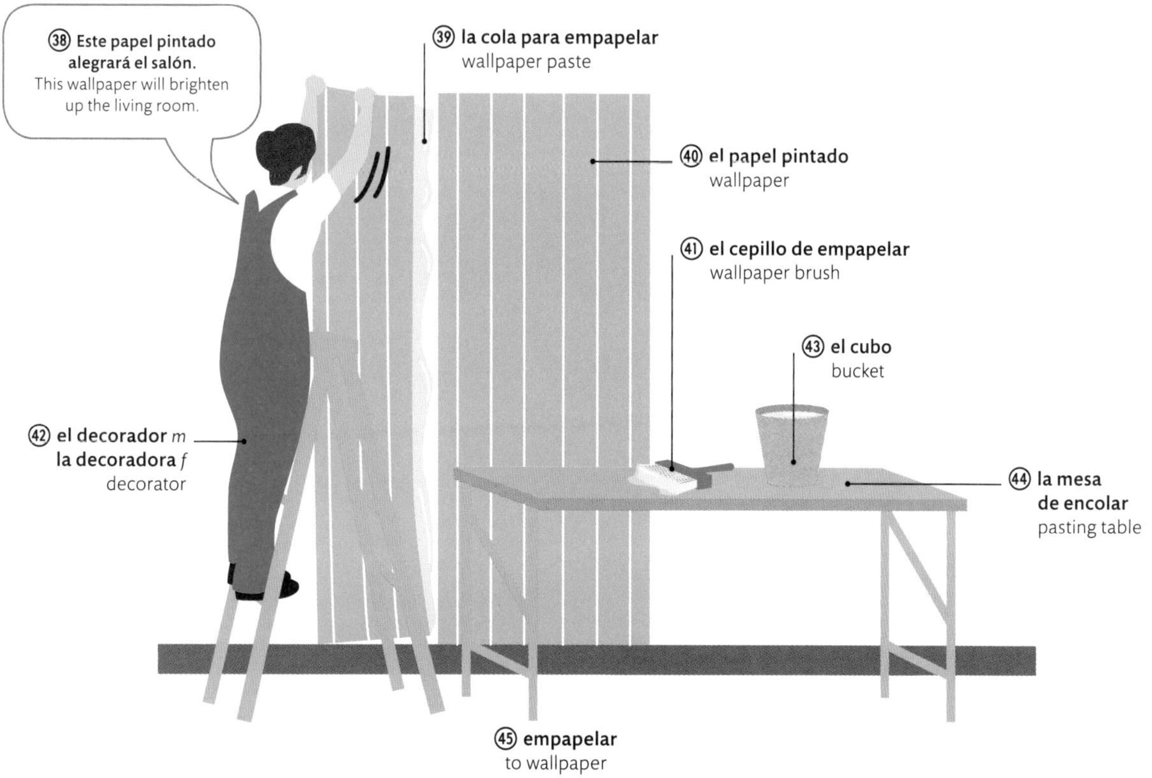

37.2 VERBOS DE DECORACIÓN • VERBS FOR DECORATING

① **quitar**
to strip

② **rellenar**
to fill

③ **lijar**
to sand

④ **enyesar**
to plaster

⑤ **colgar**
to hang

⑥ **alicatar**
to tile

38 Las plantas de interior y de jardín

Garden plants and houseplants

38.1 LAS PLANTAS DE JARDÍN Y LAS FLORES · GARDEN PLANTS AND FLOWERS

① **el diente de león**
dandelion

② **la onagra**
evening primrose

③ **el cardo**
thistle

④ **el tulipán**
tulip

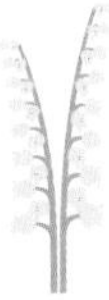
⑤ **el lirio de los valles**
lily of the valley

⑥ **el clavel**
carnation

⑧ **la margarita**
daisy

⑨ **el ranúnculo**
buttercup

⑩ **la amapola**
poppy

⑪ **el pensamiento**
pansy

⑫ **el geranio**
geranium

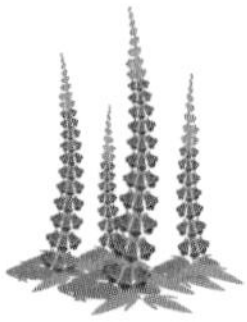
⑬ **la dedalera**
foxglove

⑮ **el altramuz**
lupin

⑯ **la rosa**
rose

⑰ **el girasol**
sunflower

⑱ **la orquídea**
orchid

⑲ **la begonia**
begonia

⑳ **el lirio**
lily

㉒ **la violeta**
violet

㉓ **el azafrán**
crocus

㉔ **el narciso**
daffodil

㉕ **la lila**
lilac

㉖ **la gardenia**
gardenia

㉗ **la lavanda**
lavender

㉙ **la caléndula**
marigold

㉚ **la azalea**
azalea

㉛ **el crisantemo**
chrysanthemum

㉜ **el rododendro**
rhododendron

㉝ **el hibisco**
rose of Sharon / hibiscus

㉟ **la madreselva**
honeysuckle

㊱ **el iris**
iris

㊲ **el loto**
lotus

㊳ **la glicinia**
wisteria

㊴ **la margarita africana**
African daisy

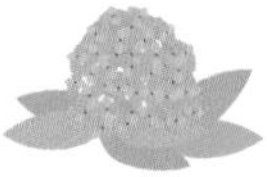
㊵ **la hortensia**
hydrangea

See also
39 La jardinería • Practical gardening **40** Las herramientas de jardinería • Garden tools
41 Los elementos del jardín • Garden features **167-169** Las plantas y los árboles • Plants and trees

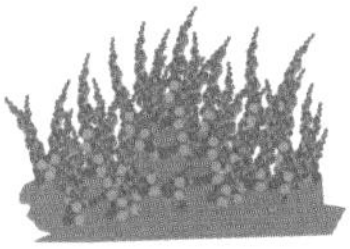
⑦ **el brezo**
heather

⑭ **la camelia**
camellia

㉑ **la cortadera**
pampas grass

㉘ **la protea**
protea

㉞ **el romero**
rosemary

㊶ **el laurel**
bay tree

38.2 LAS PLANTAS DE INTERIOR • HOUSEPLANTS

① **el lirio de la paz**
peace lily

② **la planta serpiente**
snake plant

③ **la planta araña**
spider plant

④ **la yuca**
yucca

⑤ **la drácena**
dragon tree

⑥ **el bonsái**
bonsai tree

⑦ **la monstera**
Swiss cheese plant

⑧ **las suculentas**
succulents

⑨ **la planta del dinero china**
Chinese money plant

⑩ **el ficus**
rubber plant

⑪ **la cheflera**
umbrella plant

⑫ **la hoja de sangre**
polka dot plant

⑬ **la reina de mármol**
marble queen

⑭ **el poto**
jade pothos

38.3 LA ANATOMÍA DE LA FLOR
FLOWER ANATOMY

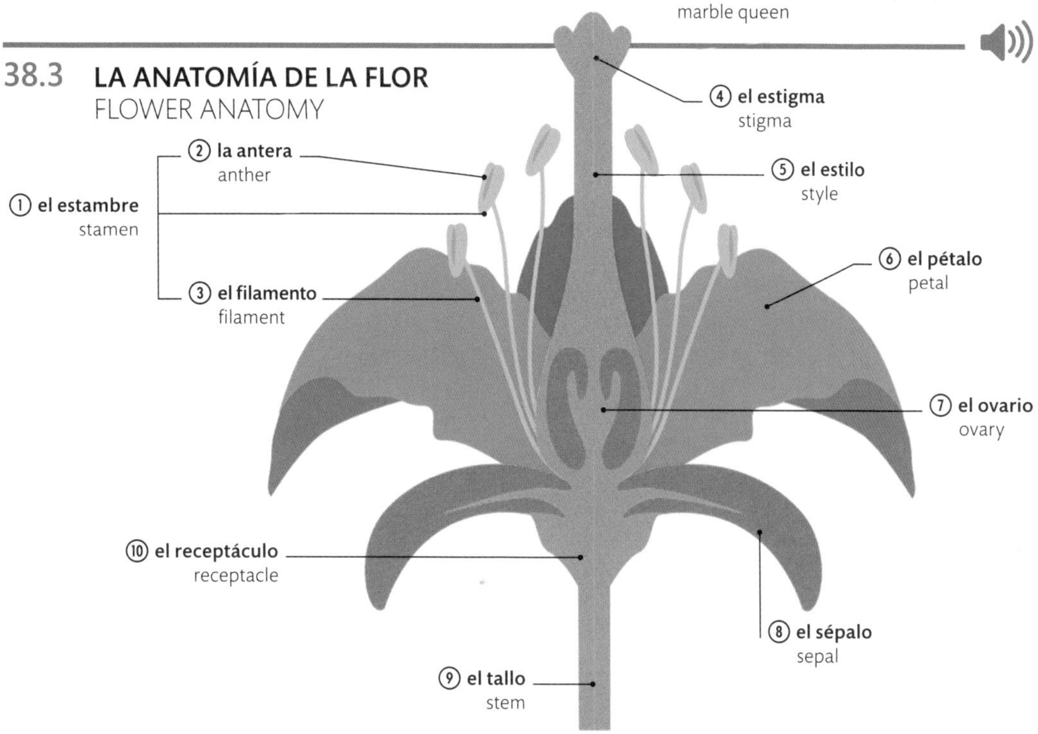

39 La jardinería
Practical gardening

39.1 LOS VERBOS DE JARDINERÍA · GARDENING VERBS

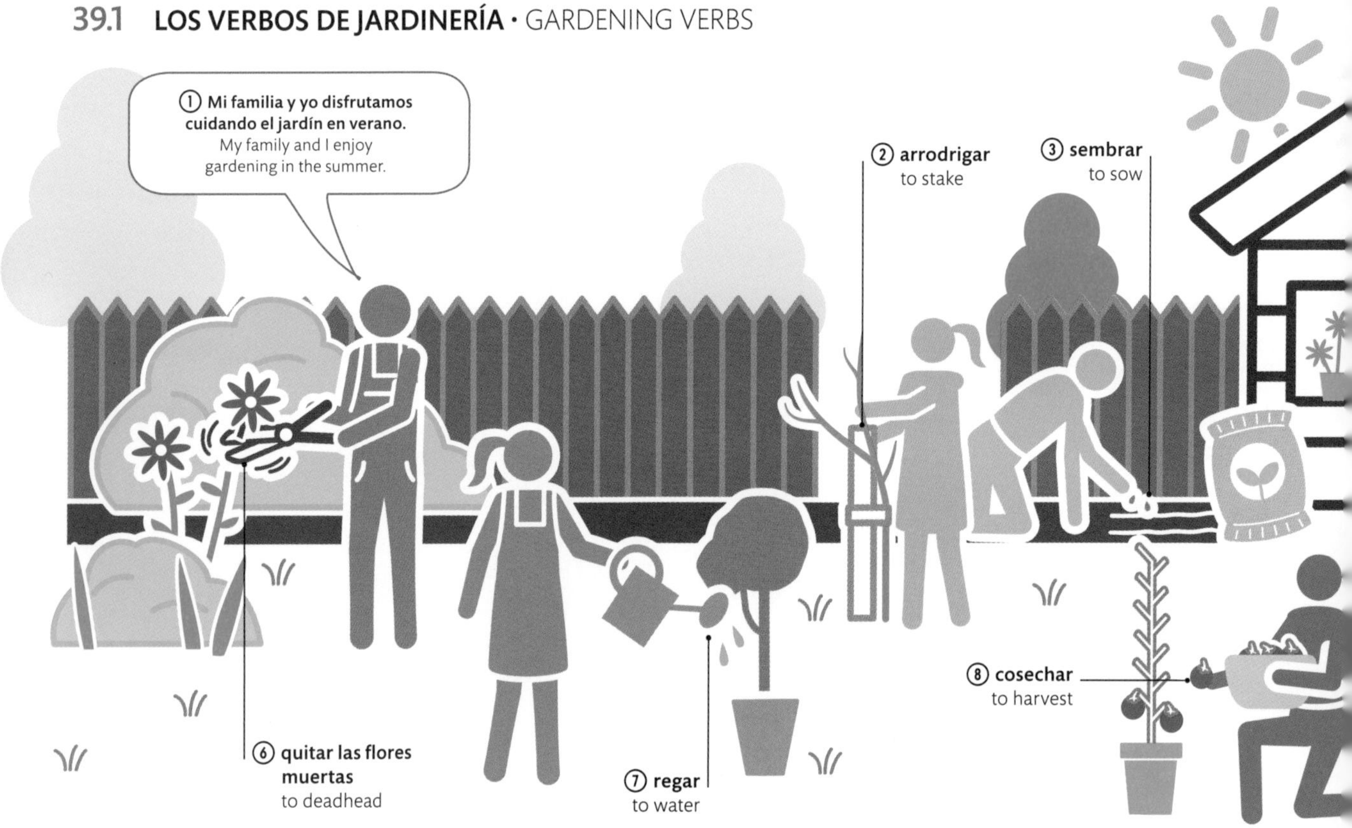

⑮ cortar el césped
to mow the lawn

⑯ instalar el césped artificial
to lay turf

⑰ rastrillar
to rake (soil)

⑱ rastrillar las hojas
to rake (leaves)

⑲ airear
to aerate

⑳ la cajonera
cold frame

㉔ injertar
to graft

㉕ propagar
to propagate

㉖ plantar
to plant

㉗ cubrir la tierra
to mulch

㉘ escardar
to do the weeding

㉙ trasplantar
to transplant

㉞ cultivar
to cultivate

㉟ recortar
to trim

㊱ podar
to prune

㊲ talar
to chop

㊳ cribar
to sieve

㊴ diseñar el jardín
to landscape

See also
38 Las plantas de interior y de jardín • Garden plants and houseplants
40 Las herramientas de jardinería • Garden tools **41** Los elementos del jardín
Garden features **167-169** Las plantas y los árboles • Plants and trees

④ **el cobertizo de jardín**
potting shed

⑤ **cavar**
to dig

⑨ **plantar en una maceta**
to pot up

⑩ **la harina de huesos**
bone meal

⑪ **el esqueje**
plant cutting

⑫ **el invernadero**
greenhouse

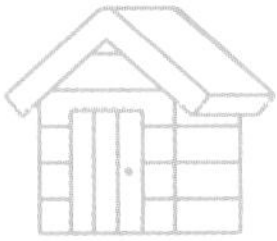

⑬ **el cobertizo**
shed

⑭ **el drenaje**
drainage

㉑ **abonar**
to top dress

㉒ **cuidar**
to tend

㉓ **guiar**
to train

㉚ **rociar**
to spray

㉛ **el suplemento para plantas**
plant food

㉜ **orgánico**
organic

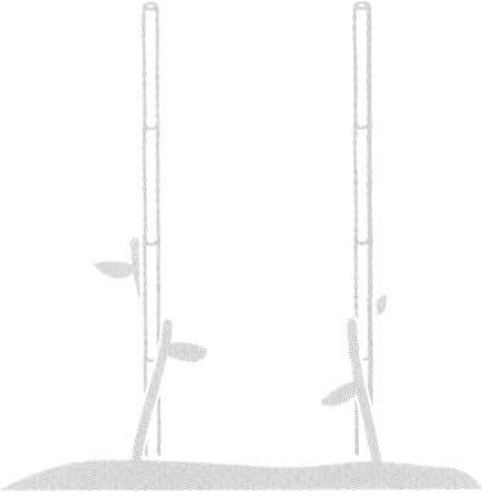

㉝ **el tutor**
training / support cane

㊵ **el fertilizante**
fertilizer

㊶ **fertilizar**
to fertilize

㊷ **el herbicida**
weedkiller

39.2 LOS TIPOS DE SUELO
TYPES OF SOIL

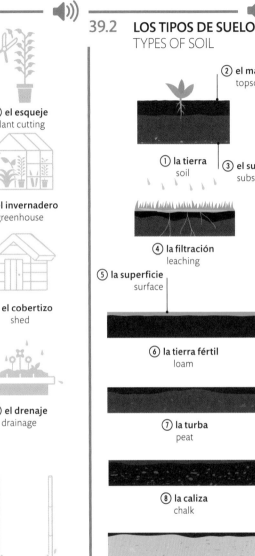

② **el mantillo**
topsoil

① **la tierra**
soil

③ **el subsuelo**
subsoil

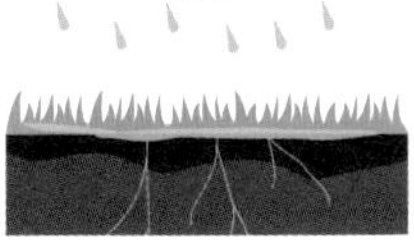

④ **la filtración**
leaching

⑤ **la superficie**
surface

⑥ **la tierra fértil**
loam

⑦ **la turba**
peat

⑧ **la caliza**
chalk

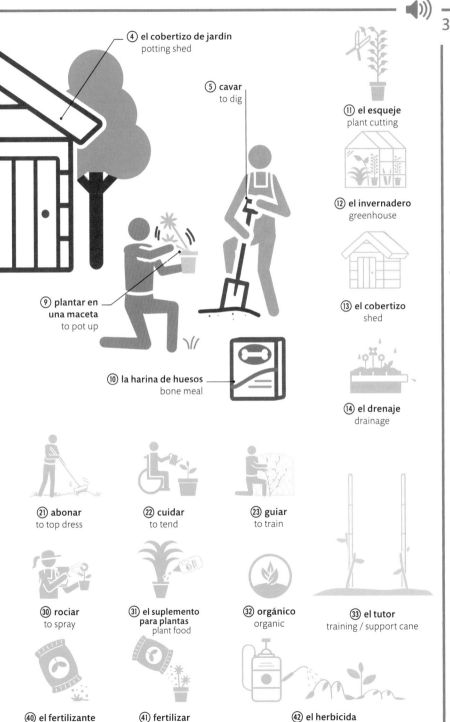

⑨ **la arena**
sand

⑩ **el cieno**
silt

⑪ **la arcilla**
clay

40 Las herramientas de jardinería
Garden tools

40.1 LOS ÚTILES DE JARDINERÍA · GARDENING EQUIPMENT

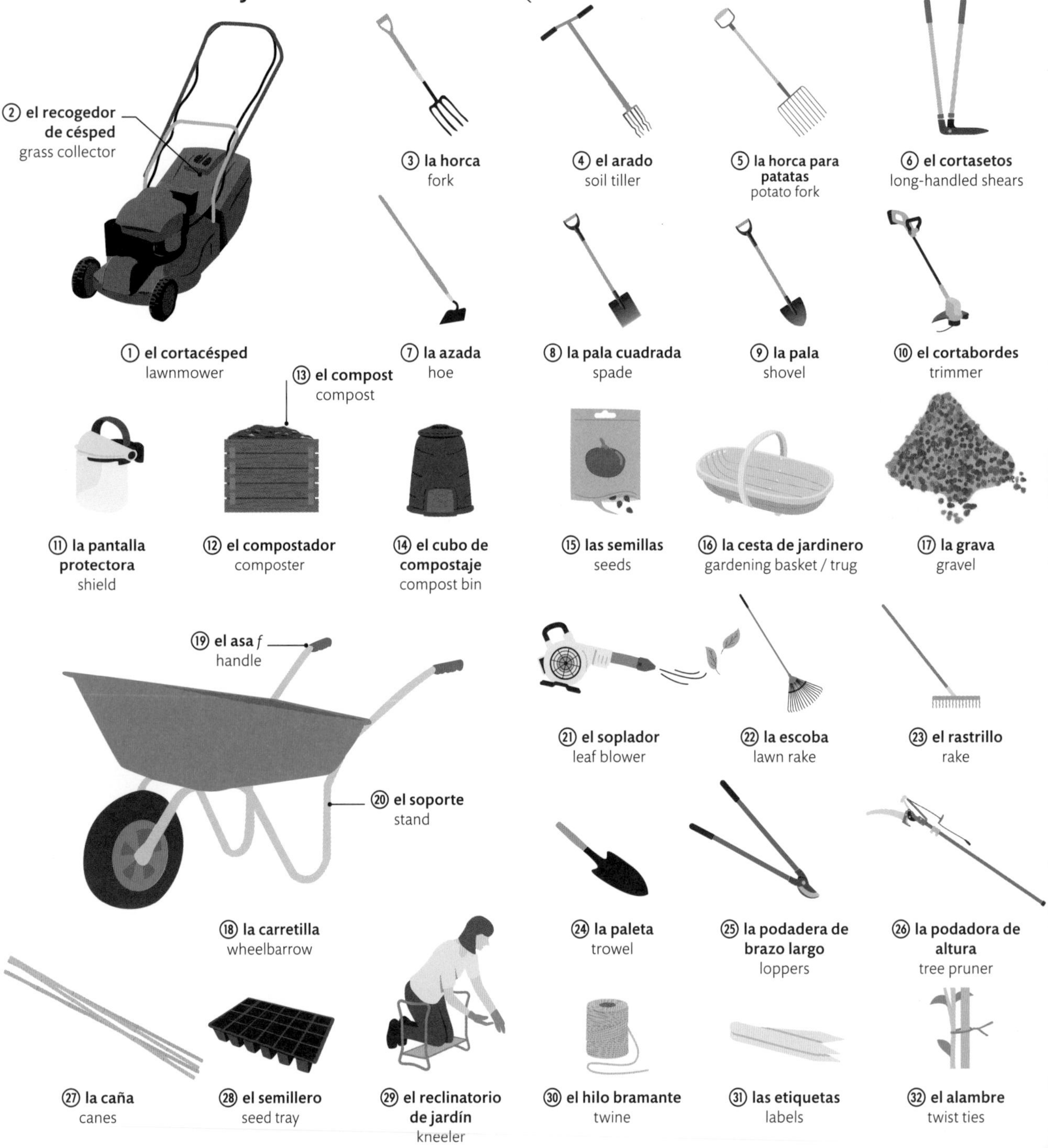
① el cortacésped
lawnmower
② el recogedor de césped
grass collector
③ la horca
fork
④ el arado
soil tiller
⑤ la horca para patatas
potato fork
⑥ el cortasetos
long-handled shears
⑦ la azada
hoe
⑧ la pala cuadrada
spade
⑨ la pala
shovel
⑩ el cortabordes
trimmer
⑪ la pantalla protectora
shield
⑫ el compostador
composter
⑬ el compost
compost
⑭ el cubo de compostaje
compost bin
⑮ las semillas
seeds
⑯ la cesta de jardinero
gardening basket / trug
⑰ la grava
gravel
⑱ la carretilla
wheelbarrow
⑲ el asa *f*
handle
⑳ el soporte
stand
㉑ el soplador
leaf blower
㉒ la escoba
lawn rake
㉓ el rastrillo
rake
㉔ la paleta
trowel
㉕ la podadera de brazo largo
loppers
㉖ la podadora de altura
tree pruner
㉗ la caña
canes
㉘ el semillero
seed tray
㉙ el reclinatorio de jardín
kneeler
㉚ el hilo bramante
twine
㉛ las etiquetas
labels
㉜ el alambre
twist ties

See also
38 Las plantas de interior y de jardín • Garden plants and houseplants **39** La jardinería • Practical gardening
41 Los elementos del jardín • Garden features **167-169** Las plantas y los árboles • Plants and trees

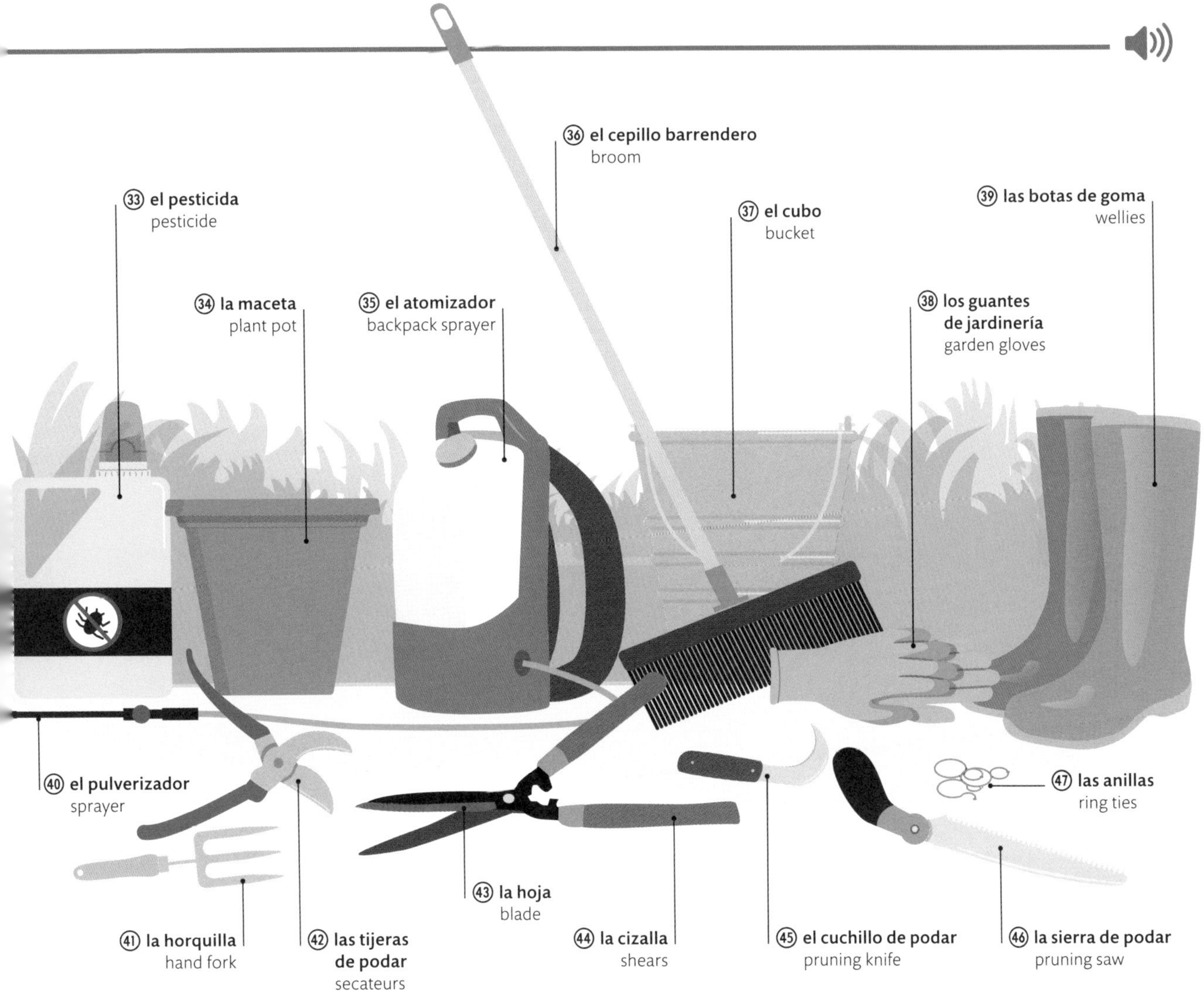

40.2 EL RIEGO • WATERING

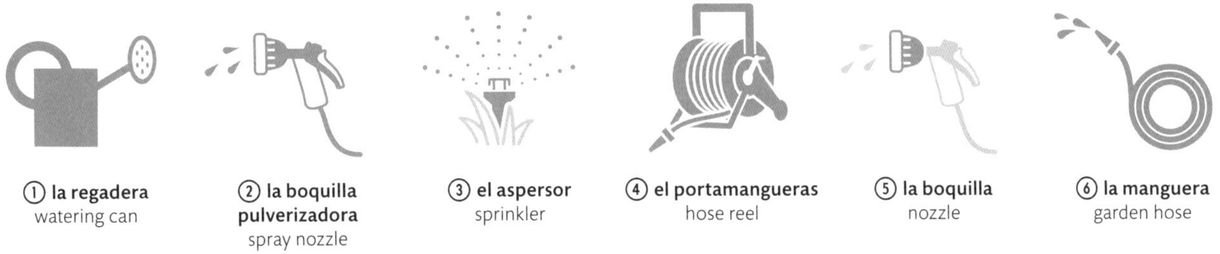

41 Los elementos del jardín
Garden features

41.1 LOS ESTILOS Y ADORNOS DE JARDÍN · GARDEN TYPES AND FEATURES

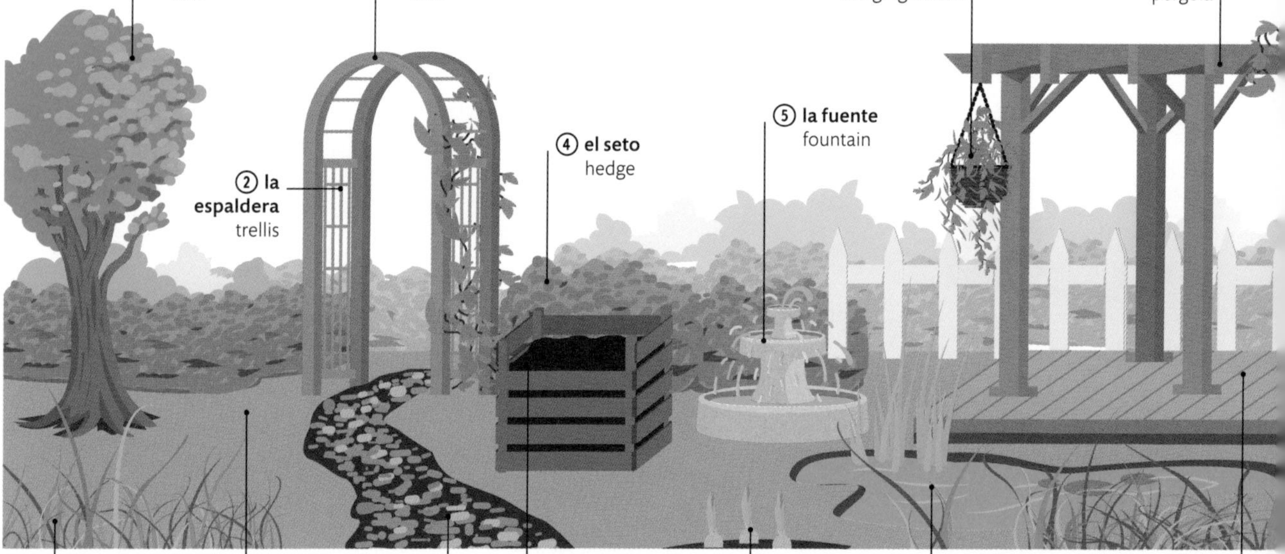

① **el árbol** tree

② **la espaldera** trellis

③ **el arco** arch

④ **el seto** hedge

⑤ **la fuente** fountain

⑥ **la cesta colgante** hanging basket

⑦ **la pérgola** pergola

⑮ **la hierba** grass

⑯ **el césped** lawn

⑰ **el camino** path

⑱ **el montón de compost** compost heap

⑲ **el bulbo** bulb

⑳ **el estanque** pond

㉑ **el entarimado** decking

㉖ **la terraza ajardinada** patio garden

㉗ **el jardín de la azotea** roof garden

㉘ **la rocalla** rock garden

㉙ **el jardín clásico** formal garden

41.2 LOS TIPOS DE PLANTAS · TYPES OF PLANTS

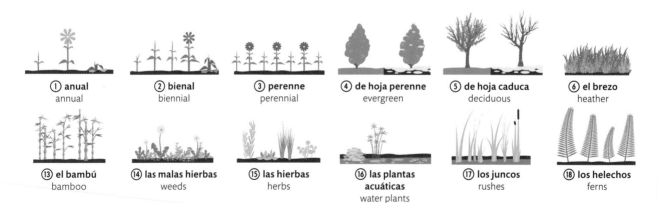

① **anual** annual

② **bienal** biennial

③ **perenne** perennial

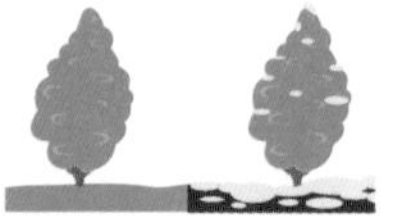

④ **de hoja perenne** evergreen

⑤ **de hoja caduca** deciduous

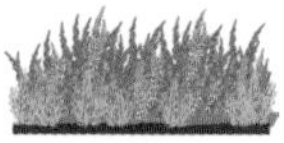

⑥ **el brezo** heather

⑬ **el bambú** bamboo

⑭ **las malas hierbas** weeds

⑮ **las hierbas** herbs

⑯ **las plantas acuáticas** water plants

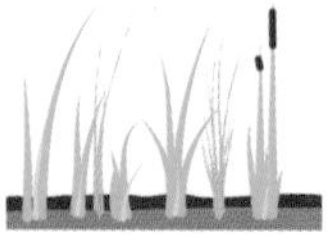

⑰ **los juncos** rushes

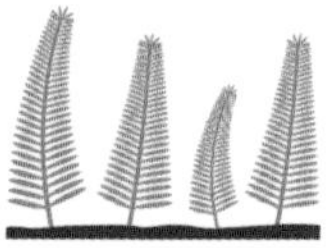

⑱ **los helechos** ferns

See also
38 Las plantas de interior y de jardín • Garden plants and houseplants **39** La jardinería • Practical gardening
40 Las herramientas de jardinería • Garden tools **167-169** Las plantas y los árboles • Plants and trees

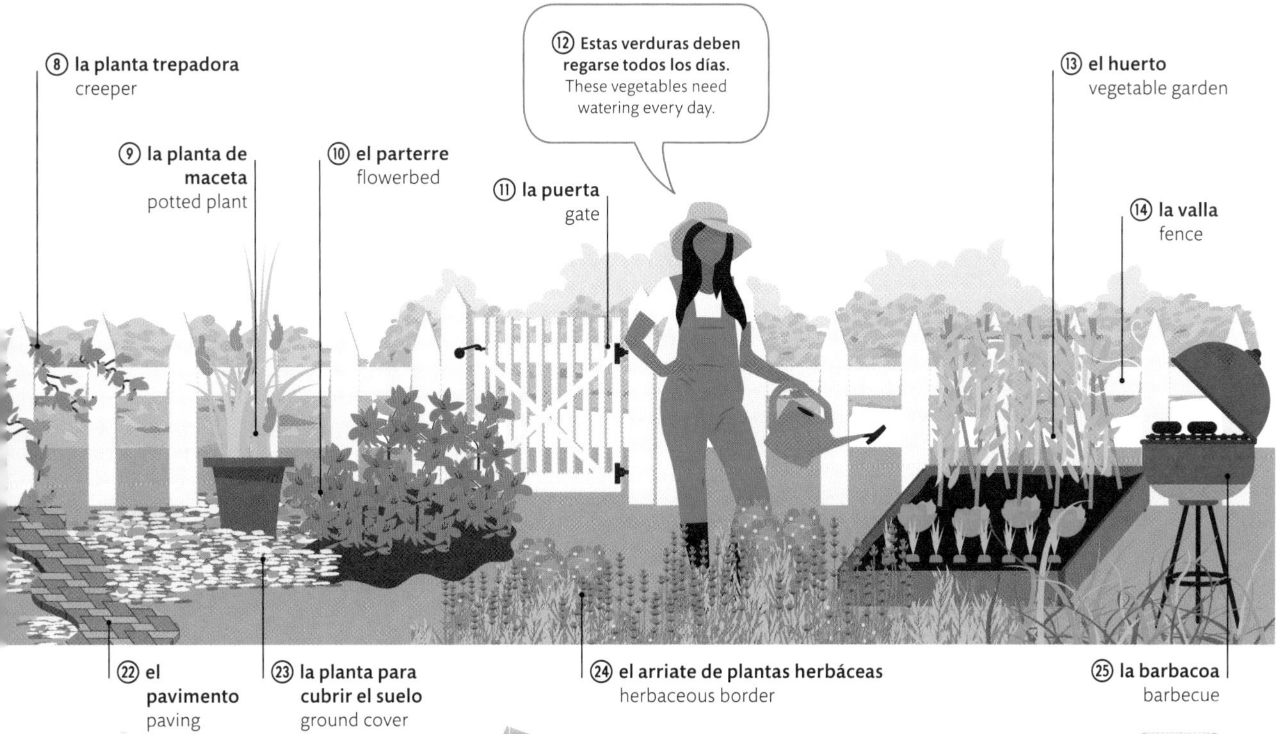
⑧ **la planta trepadora**
creeper
⑨ **la planta de maceta**
potted plant
⑩ **el parterre**
flowerbed
⑪ **la puerta**
gate
⑫ **Estas verduras deben regarse todos los días.**
These vegetables need watering every day.
⑬ **el huerto**
vegetable garden
⑭ **la valla**
fence
㉒ **el pavimento**
paving
㉓ **la planta para cubrir el suelo**
ground cover
㉔ **el arriate de plantas herbáceas**
herbaceous border
㉕ **la barbacoa**
barbecue

㉚ **el jardín de plantas herbáceas**
herb garden

㉛ **el jardín acuático**
water garden

㉜ **el jardín campestre**
cottage garden

㉝ **el patio**
courtyard

⑦ **las palmeras**
palms

⑧ **las coníferas**
conifers

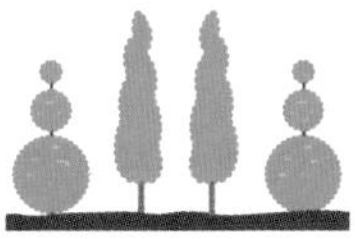

⑨ **los topiarios**
topiary

⑩ **la planta trepadora**
climber

⑪ **las plantas ornamentales**
ornamental plants

⑫ **las plantas de sombra**
shade plants

⑲ **las plantas alpinas**
alpine plants

⑳ **las suculentas**
succulents

㉑ **los cactus**
cacti

㉒ **los arbustos**
shrubs

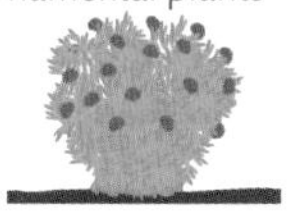

㉓ **el arbusto de flor**
flowering shrub

㉔ **el césped**
grasses

42 La ciudad

In town

42.1 LOS EDIFICIOS Y OTROS ELEMENTOS
BUILDINGS AND OTHER FEATURES

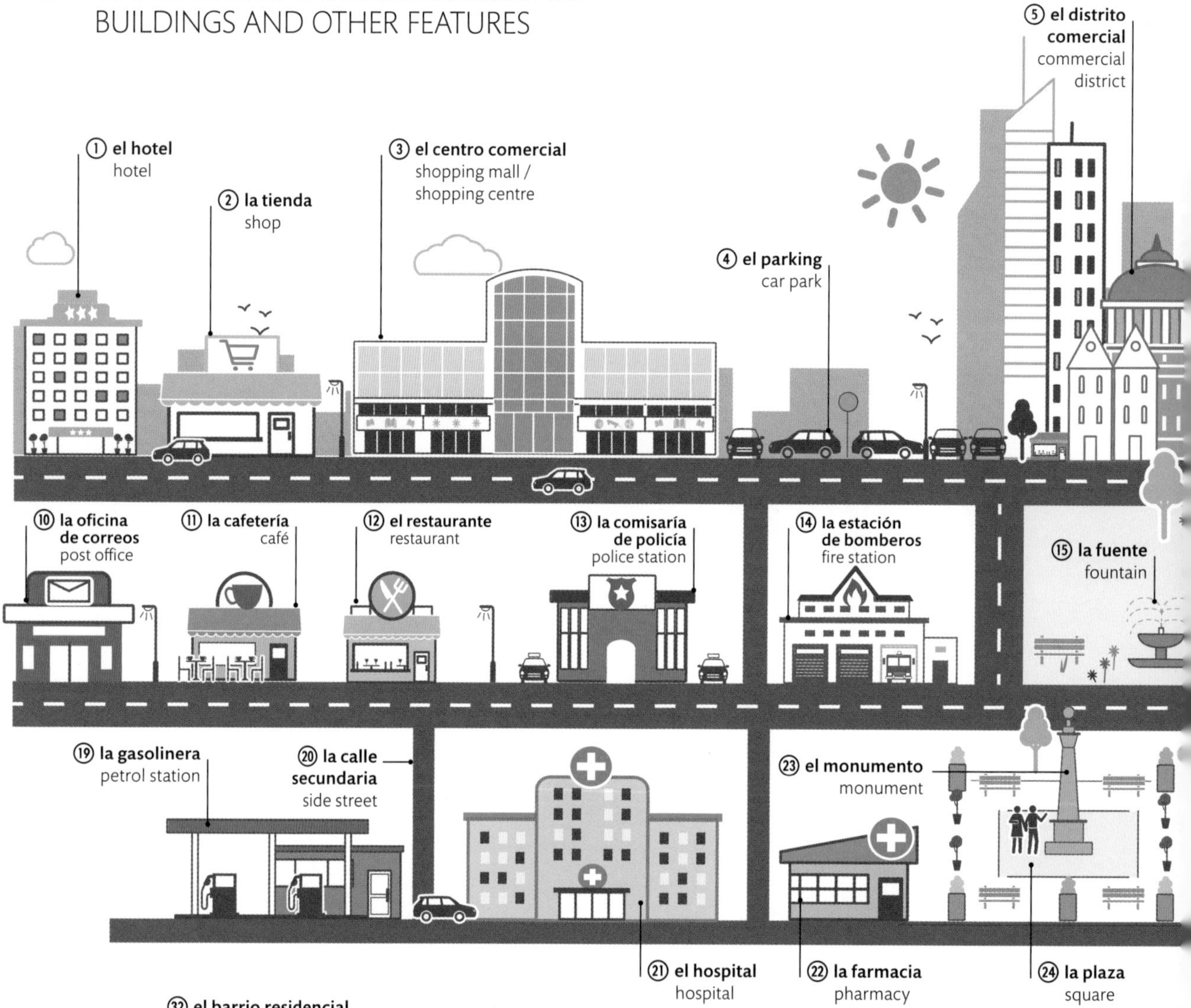

㉚ **los barrios**
districts

㉛ **el centro**
city centre

㉝ **las afueras**
suburb

㉞ **la zona peatonal**
pedestrian zone

See also
25 Un lugar donde vivir • A place to live **43** La ciudad (continuación) • In town continued **44** Los edificios y la arquitectura • Buildings and architecture **46** Las compras • Shopping **47** El centro comercial • The shopping mall **102** Los trenes • Trains **104** En el aeropuerto • At the airport **106** El puerto • The port

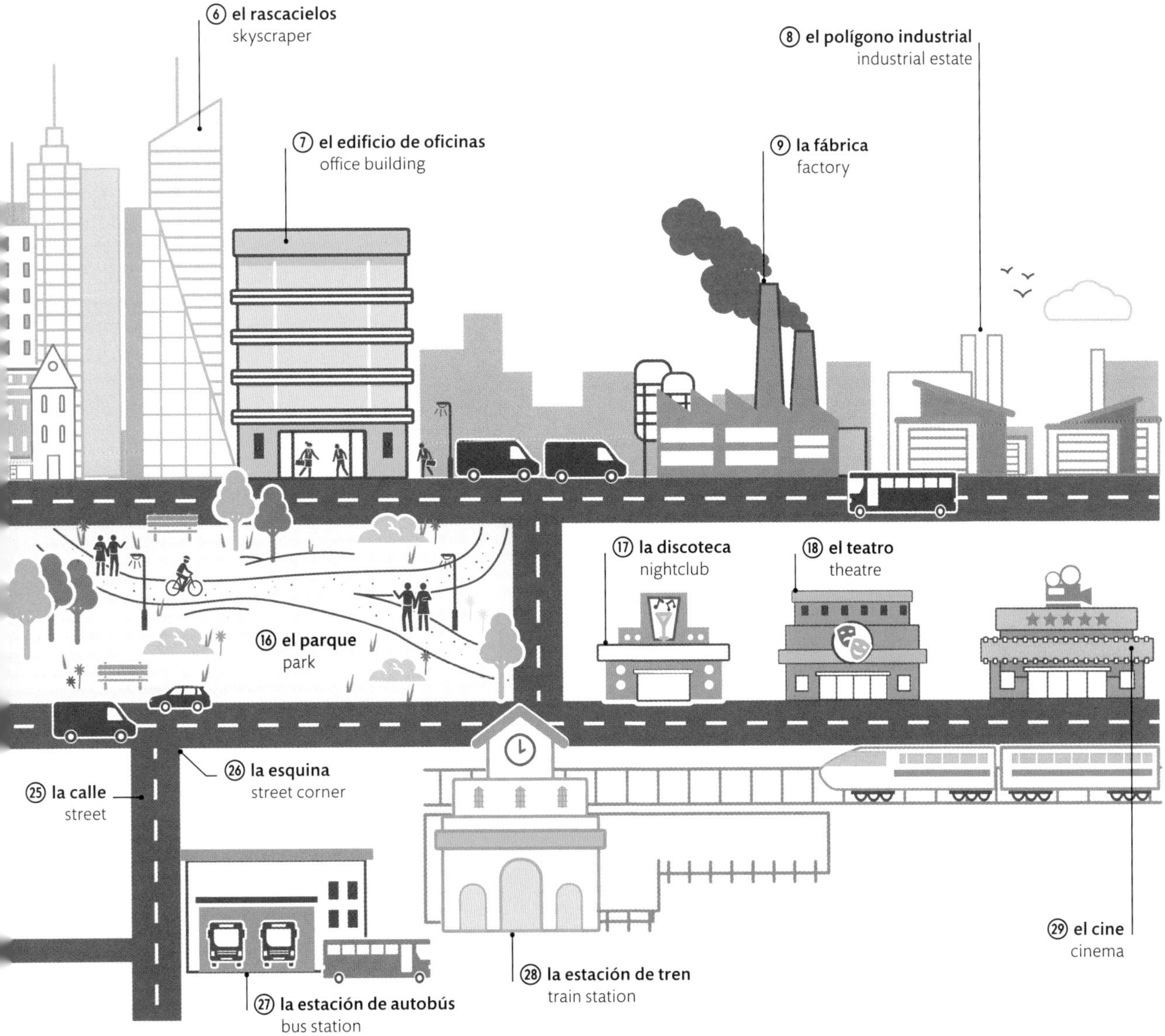

㉟ el callejón
alley

㊱ la hora punta
rush hour

㊲ la vía de un solo sentido
one-way system

㊳ la oficina de turismo
tourist information

La ciudad (continuación)
In town continued

43.1 LOS EDIFICIOS Y OTROS ELEMENTOS · BUILDINGS AND OTHER FEATURES

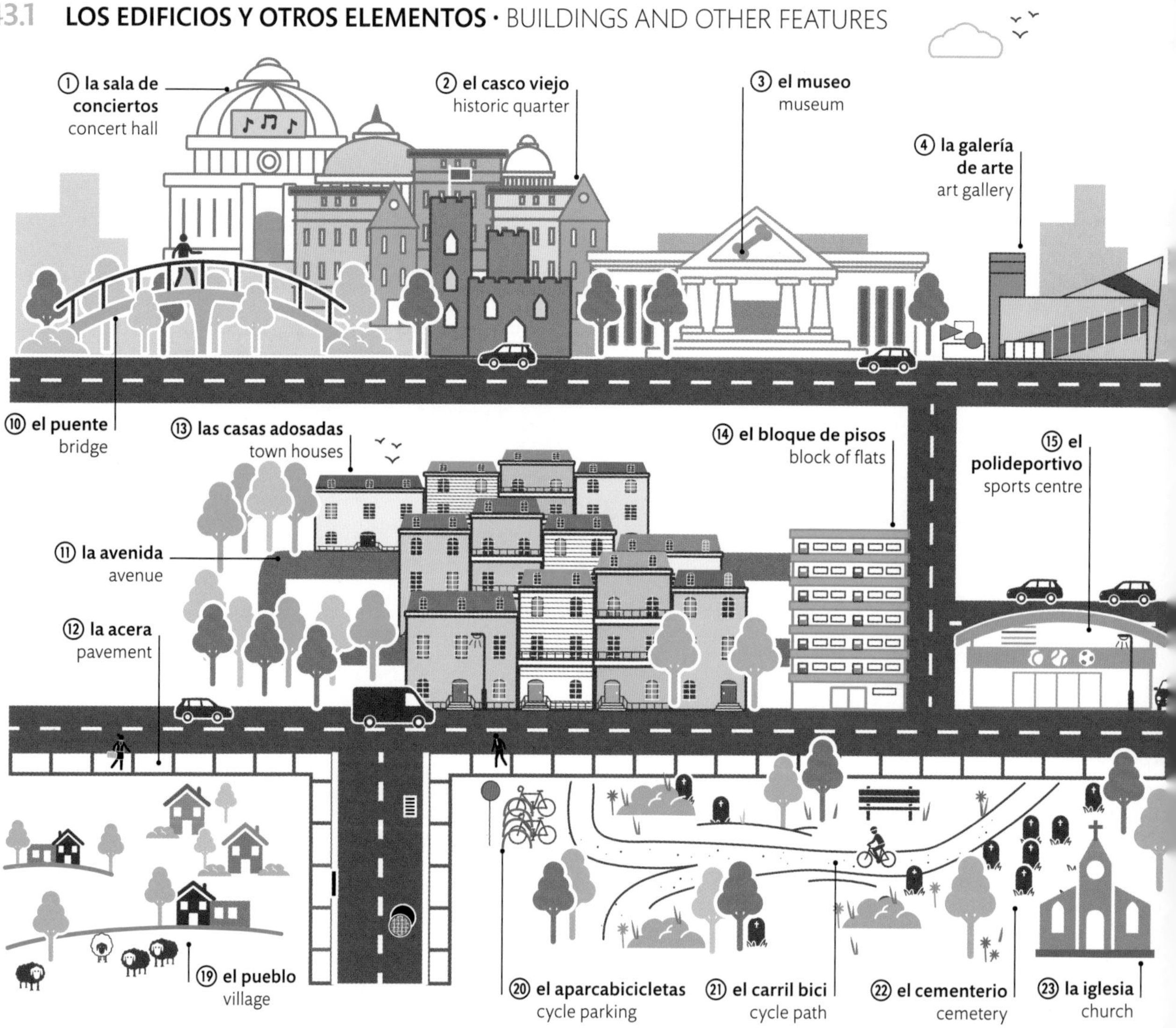

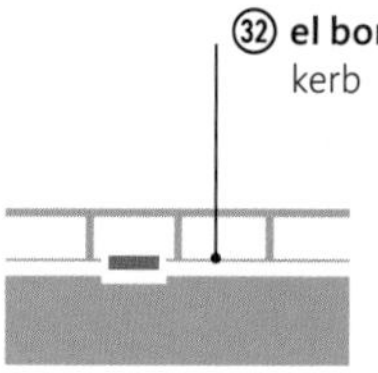

See also
25 Un lugar donde vivir • A place to live **44** Los edificios y la arquitectura • Buildings and architecture **46** Las compras • Shopping **47** El centro comercial • The shopping mall **102** Los trenes • Trains **104** En el aeropuerto • At the airport **106** El puerto • The port

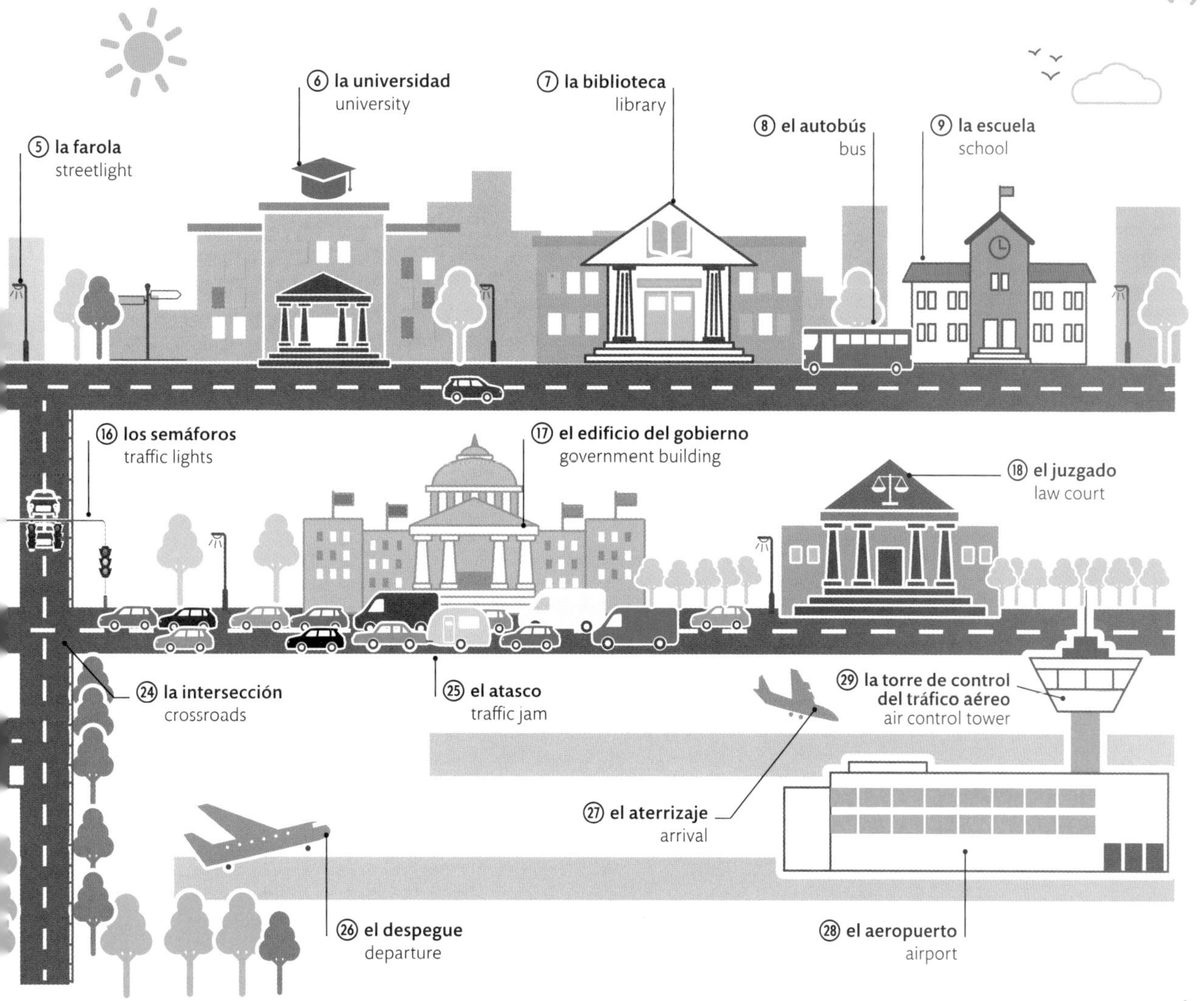
⑤ la farola
streetlight
⑥ la universidad
university
⑦ la biblioteca
library
⑧ el autobús
bus
⑨ la escuela
school
⑯ los semáforos
traffic lights
⑰ el edificio del gobierno
government building
⑱ el juzgado
law court
㉔ la intersección
crossroads
㉕ el atasco
traffic jam
㉙ la torre de control del tráfico aéreo
air control tower
㉗ el aterrizaje
arrival
㉖ el despegue
departure
㉘ el aeropuerto
airport

43.2 EL PARQUE INFANTIL • PLAYGROUND

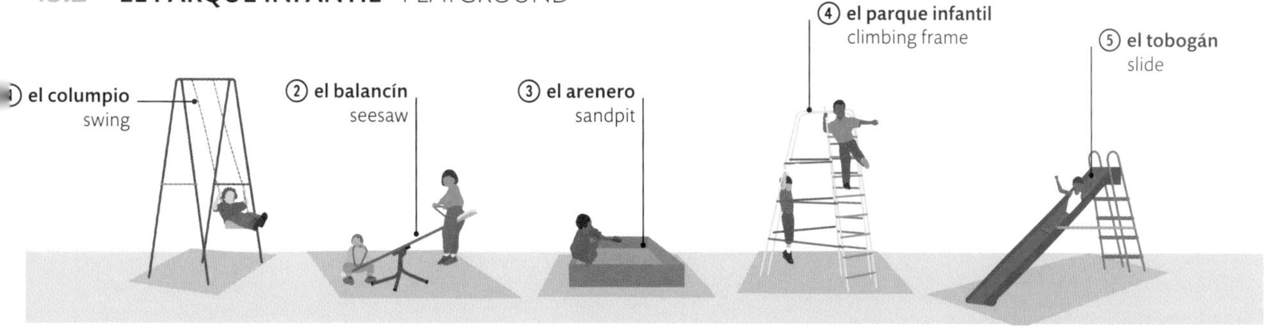
el columpio
swing
② el balancín
seesaw
③ el arenero
sandpit
④ el parque infantil
climbing frame
⑤ el tobogán
slide

44 Los edificios y la arquitectura

Buildings and architecture

44.1 LOS TIPOS DE EDIFICIOS · TYPES OF BUILDINGS

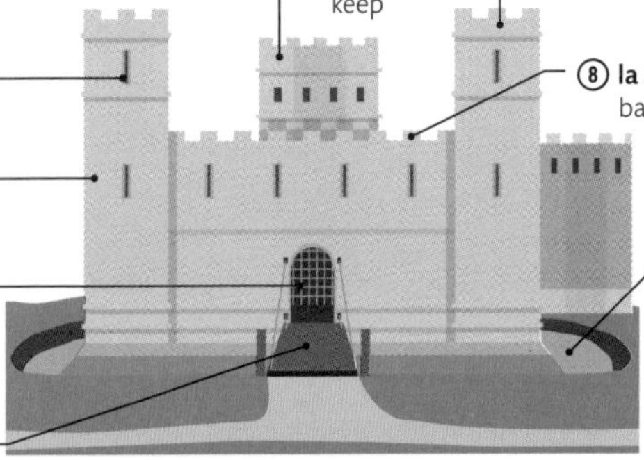

② el puente levadizo
drawbridge
③ el rastrillo
portcullis
④ el muro
wall
⑤ la tronera
arrow slit
⑥ la torre del homenaje
keep
⑦ el torreón
turret
⑧ la almena
battlement
⑨ el foso
moat

① **el castillo**
castle

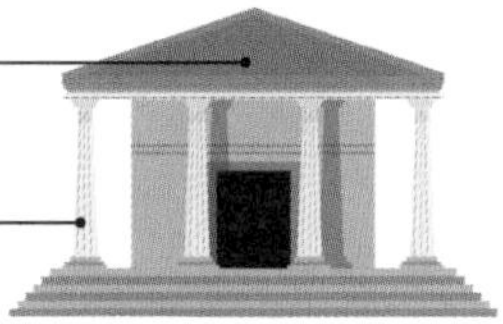

⑪ el frontón
pediment
⑫ la columna
column

⑩ **el templo griego**
Ancient Greek temple

⑭ la vidriera
stained glass window
⑮ el campanario
bell tower

⑬ **la iglesia**
church

⑯ **el zigurat**
ziggurat

⑰ **el molino**
windmill

⑱ **el almacén**
warehouse

⑲ **el refugio**
shelter

⑳ **el monasterio**
monastery

㉑ **las ruinas**
ancient ruins

㉒ **el edificio abandonado**
derelict building

㉓ **el faro**
lighthouse

㉔ **la central eléctrica**
power station

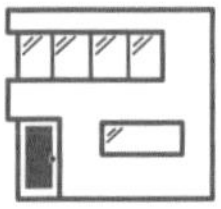

㉕ **el edificio moderno**
modern building

㉖ **el edificio histórico**
historic building

㉗ **el edificio de viviendas**
residential buildings

㉙ la cúpula
dome
㉚ el minarete
minaret

㉘ **la mezquita**
mosque

㉜ la cúpula bulbosa
onion dome

㉛ **la iglesia ortodoxa**
Orthodox church

㉞ el alero
overhanging eaves

㉝ **el templo**
temple

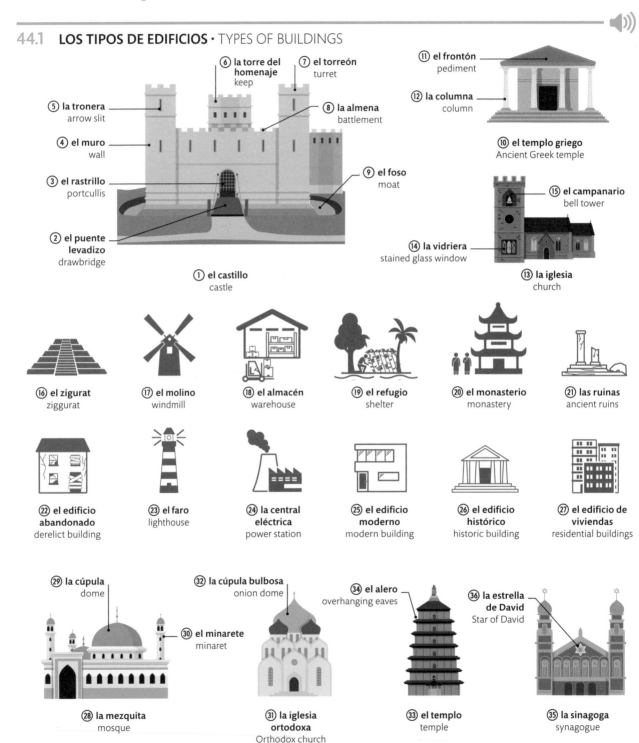

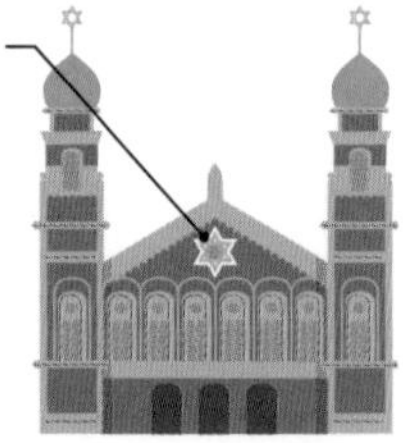

㉟ **la sinagoga**
synagogue

See also
25 Un lugar donde vivir • A place to live **32** La casa y el hogar • House and home **42-43** La ciudad • In town **132** La visita turística • Sightseeing

44.2 LOS EDIFICIOS Y LOS MONUMENTOS FAMOSOS • FAMOUS BUILDINGS AND MONUMENTS

② **el arco**
arch

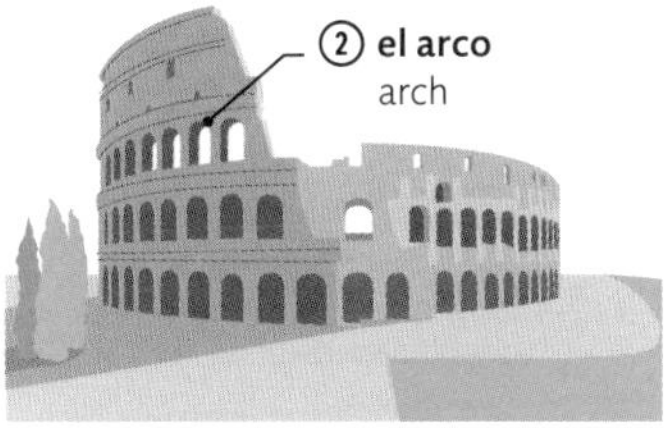

① **el Coliseo**
the Colosseum

③ **las pirámides de Guiza**
the pyramids of Giza

⑤ **la quibla**
qibla prayer wall

⑥ **la torre**
tower

④ **la Gran Mezquita de Djenné**
the Great Mosque of Djenné

⑦ **la Casa Blanca**
the White House

⑧ **el Taj Mahal**
the Taj Mahal

⑨ **la Ciudad Prohibida**
the Forbidden City

⑩ **la Catedral de San Basilio**
St. Basil's cathedral

⑪ **la Ópera de Sídney**
Sydney Opera House

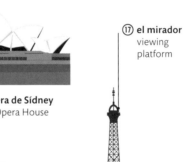

⑫ **el Castillo Himeji**
Himeji Castle

⑭ **el reloj**
clock

⑬ **el Big Ben**
Big Ben

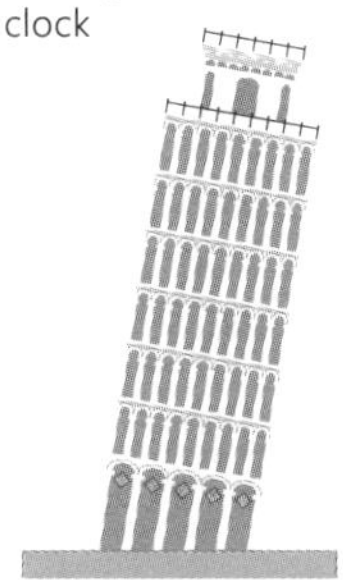

⑮ **la Torre de Pisa**
the Leaning Tower of Pisa

⑰ **el mirador**
viewing platform

⑯ **la Torre Eiffel**
the Eiffel Tower

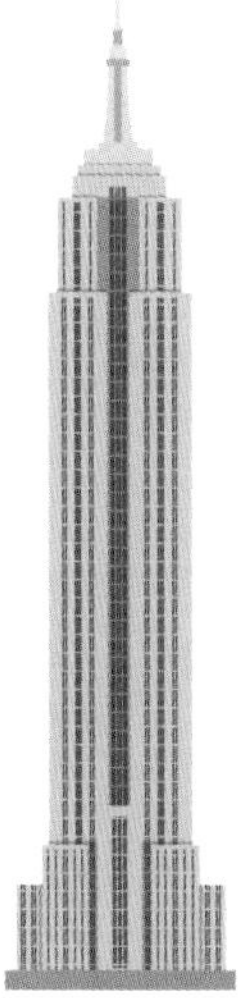

⑱ **el Empire State Building**
the Empire State Building

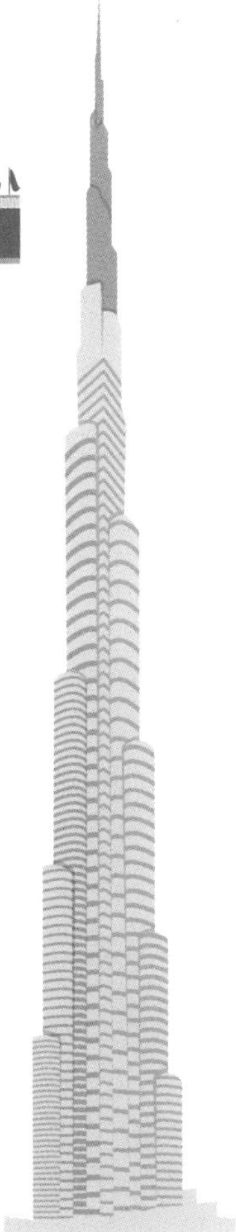

⑲ **el Burj Khalifa**
Burj Khalifa

45 El banco y la oficina de correos
The bank and post office

45.1 EL BANCO • BANK

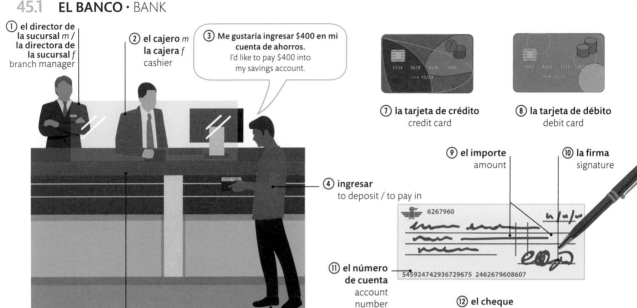

① **el director de la sucursal** *m* / **la directora de la sucursal** *f*
branch manager

② **el cajero** *m* **la cajera** *f*
cashier

③ **Me gustaría ingresar $400 en mi cuenta de ahorros.**
I'd like to pay $400 into my savings account.

④ **ingresar**
to deposit / to pay in

⑤ **el mostrador**
counter

⑥ **el cliente** *m* / **la clienta** *f*
customer

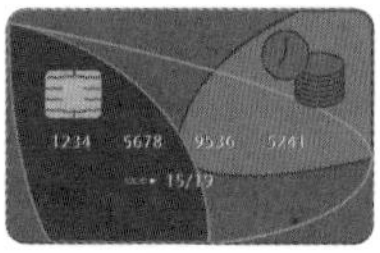

⑦ **la tarjeta de crédito**
credit card

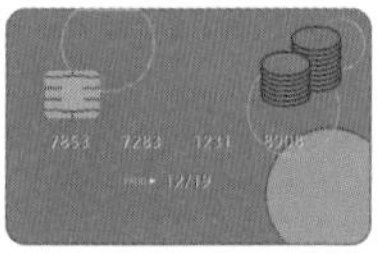

⑧ **la tarjeta de débito**
debit card

⑨ **el importe**
amount

⑩ **la firma**
signature

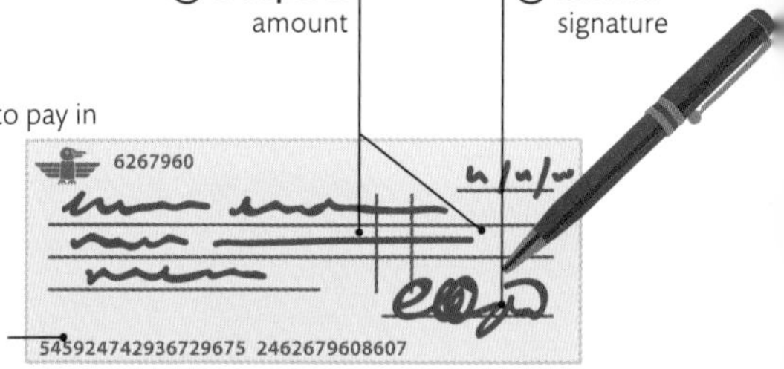

⑪ **el número de cuenta**
account number

⑫ **el cheque**
cheque

⑬ **la cuenta de ahorros**
savings account

⑭ **los ahorros**
savings

⑮ **la cuenta corriente**
current account

⑯ **la domiciliación bancaria**
direct debit

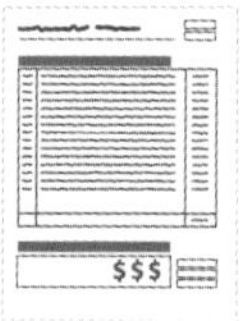

⑰ **el extracto**
bank statement

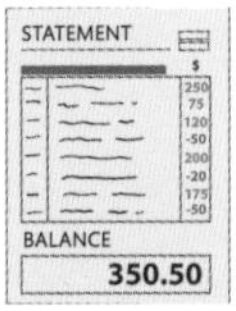

⑱ **el saldo positivo**
in the black / in credit

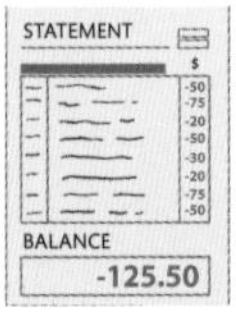

⑲ **en números rojos**
in the red / in debt

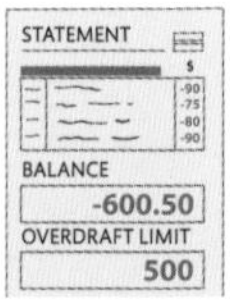

⑳ **el descubierto bancario**
overdraft

㉑ **la banca digital**
online banking

㉒ **la tasa de interés**
interest rate

㉓ **el préstamo**
bank loan

㉔ **la hipoteca**
mortgage

㉕ **sacar dinero**
to withdraw money

㉖ **enviar dinero**
to transfer money

See also
94 El dinero y las finanzas • Money and finance
131 El viaje y el alojamiento • Travel and accommodation

45.2 EL DINERO • MONEY

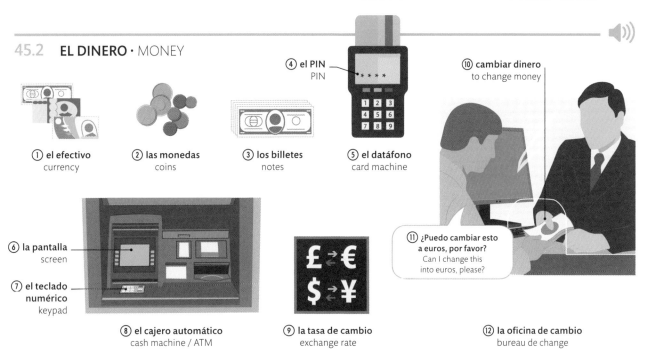

① **el efectivo**
currency

② **las monedas**
coins

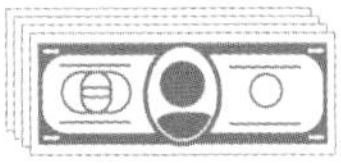

③ **los billetes**
notes

④ **el PIN**
PIN

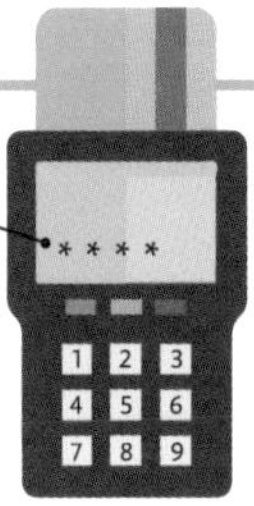

⑤ **el datáfono**
card machine

⑥ **la pantalla**
screen

⑦ **el teclado numérico**
keypad

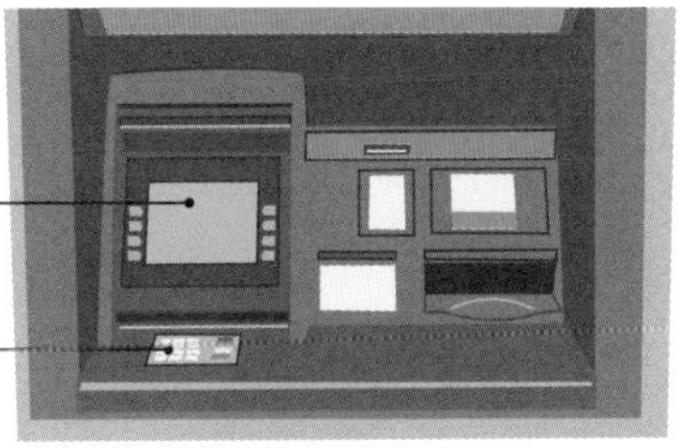

⑧ **el cajero automático**
cash machine / ATM

⑨ **la tasa de cambio**
exchange rate

⑩ **cambiar dinero**
to change money

⑪ **¿Puedo cambiar esto a euros, por favor?**
Can I change this into euros, please?

⑫ **la oficina de cambio**
bureau de change

45.3 LA OFICINA DE CORREOS • POST OFFICE

① **el empleado de correos** *m* **/ la empleada de correos** *f*
postal worker

② **la báscula**
scales

③ **la carta**
letter

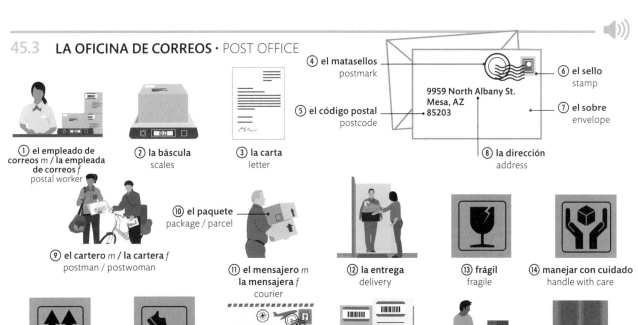

④ **el matasellos**
postmark

⑤ **el código postal**
postcode

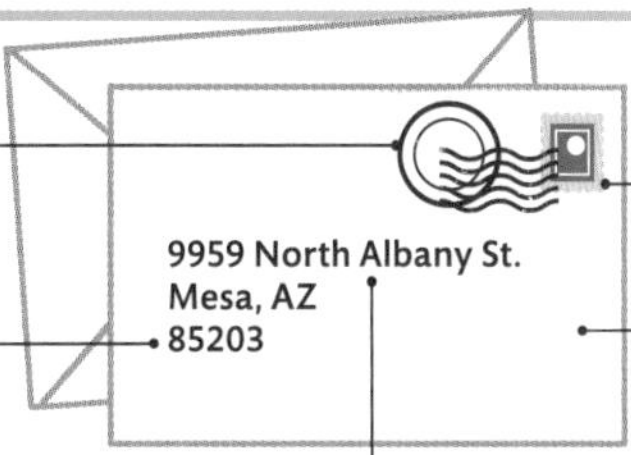

⑥ **el sello**
stamp

⑦ **el sobre**
envelope

⑧ **la dirección**
address

⑨ **el cartero** *m* **/ la cartera** *f*
postman / postwoman

⑩ **el paquete**
package / parcel

⑪ **el mensajero** *m*
la mensajera *f*
courier

⑫ **la entrega**
delivery

⑬ **frágil**
fragile

⑭ **manejar con cuidado**
handle with care

⑮ **este lado hacia arriba**
this way up

⑯ **no doblar**
do not bend

⑰ **el correo aéreo**
airmail

⑱ **el correo certificado**
registered post

⑲ **el buzón**
postbox

⑳ **la ranura del correo**
letterbox

Las compras
Shopping

46.1 EN LA CALLE PRINCIPAL · ON THE HIGH STREET

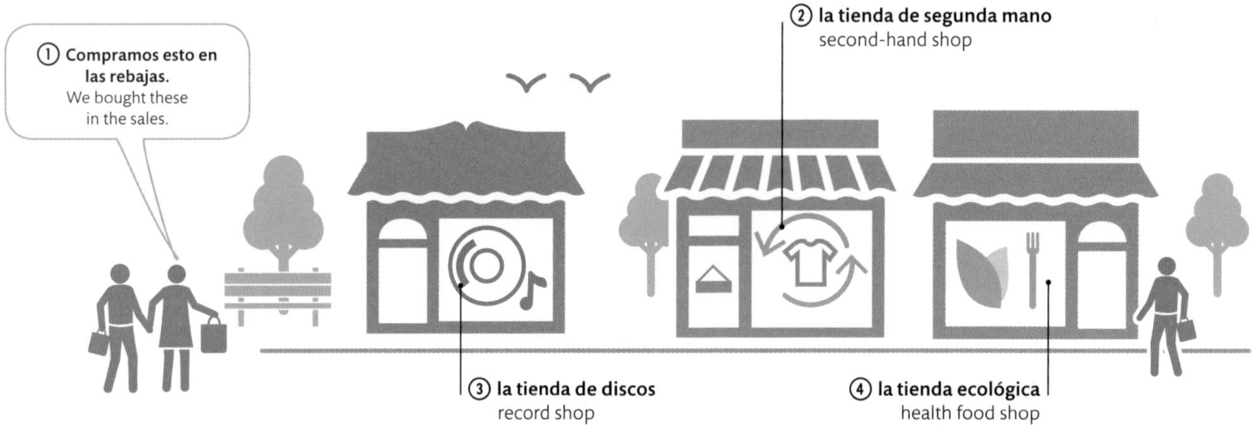

⑤ **la tienda de regalos**
gift shop

⑥ **la tienda de moda**
boutique

⑦ **la joyería**
jeweller's

⑧ **la tienda de arte**
art shop

⑨ **la tienda de antigüedades**
antiques shop

⑩ **la juguetería**
toy shop

⑪ **la óptica**
optician

⑫ **la ferretería**
hardware store

⑬ **la cerrajería**
key cutting shop

⑭ **la tienda de electrónica**
electronics store

⑮ **la tienda de mascotas**
pet shop

⑯ **la agencia de viajes**
travel agent

⑰ **el mercadillo**
street market

⑱ **la pescadería**
fishmonger

⑲ **la carnicería**
butcher

⑳ **la panadería**
bakery

㉑ **la verdulería / la frutería**
greengrocer

㉒ **la delicatessen**
delicatessen

㉓ **la pastelería**
cake shop

㉔ **la cafetería**
café / coffee shop

㉕ **la licorería**
off licence

㉖ **el kiosco**
newsstand / kiosk

㉗ **la librería**
bookshop

㉘ **la zapatería**
shoe shop

See also
42-43 La ciudad • In town **47** El centro comercial • The shopping mall
48 El supermercado • The supermarket

㉙ el vivero
garden centre

㉚ la floristería
florist

㉛ la sastrería
tailor

㉜ el fotomatón
photo booth

㉝ la lavandería
launderette

㉞ la tintorería
dry cleaner's

㉟ ir de compras
shopping spree

㊱ mirar escaparates
window shopping

㊲ Me olvidé de apuntar la leche en la lista de la compra.
I forgot to put milk on my shopping list.

㊳ la lista de la compra
shopping list

46.2 LOS VERBOS DE COMPRAS • SHOPPING VERBS

① elegir
to choose

② vender
to sell

③ comprar
to buy

④ querer
to want

⑤ quedar bien
to fit

⑥ pagar
to pay

⑦ probarse
to try on

⑧ regatear
to haggle

⑨ reclamar
to complain

⑩ cambiar
to exchange

⑪ reembolsar
to refund

⑫ devolver
to return

46.3 LAS COMPRAS EN LÍNEA • ORDERING ONLINE

① añadir al carrito
to add to the cart

② añadir a la lista de deseos
to add to wishlist

③ tramitar el pedido
to proceed to checkout

④ pedir
to order

⑤ hacer el seguimiento del pedido
to track your order

47 El centro comercial
The shopping centre

47.1 EL CENTRO COMERCIAL · SHOPPING CENTRE

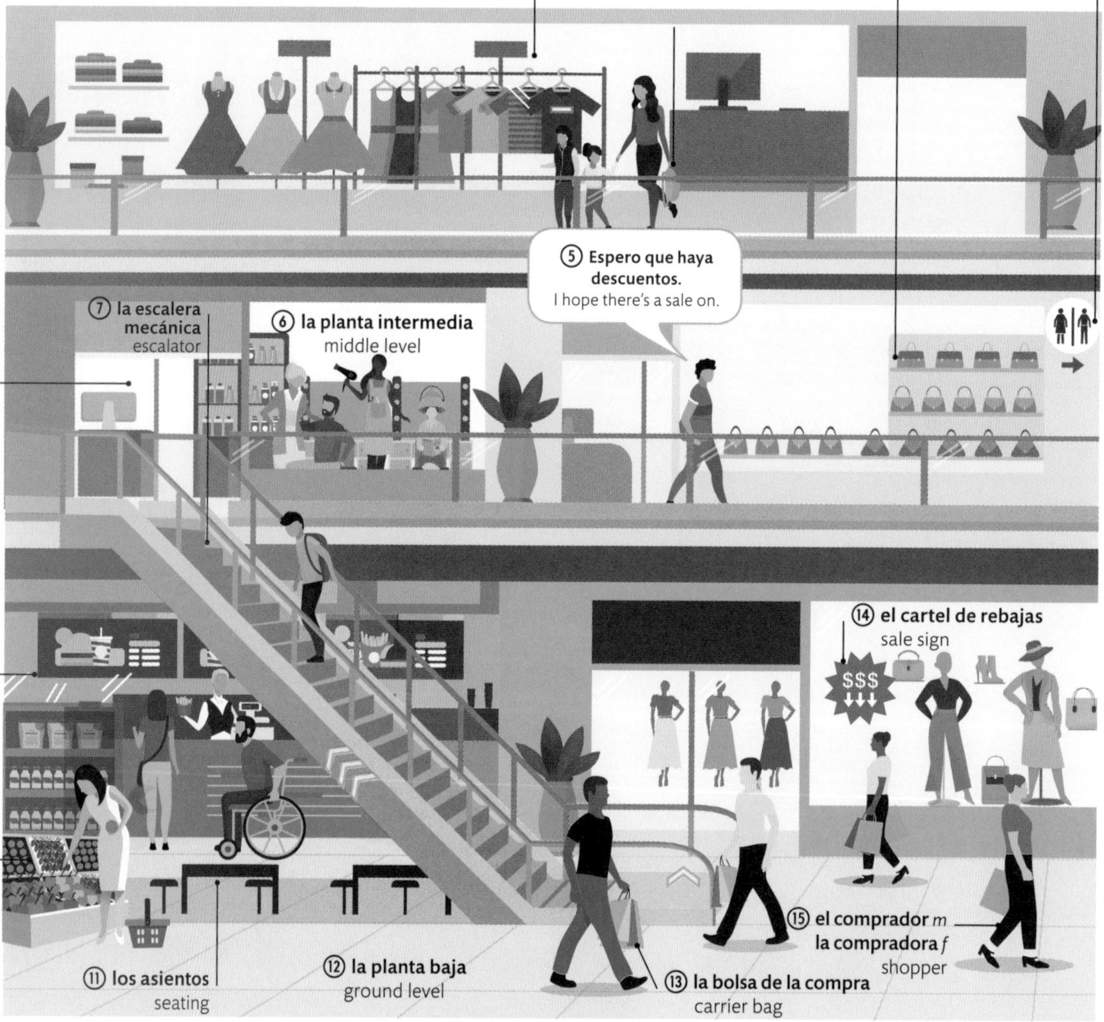

① la planta alta
upper level
② la tienda de ropa
fashion store
③ la tienda de bolsos
bag store
④ los aseos
toilets
⑤ Espero que haya descuentos.
I hope there's a sale on.
⑥ la planta intermedia
middle level
⑦ la escalera mecánica
escalator
⑧ la peluquería
hair salon
⑨ la comida rápida
fast food
⑩ la tienda ecológica
health food store
⑪ los asientos
seating
⑫ la planta baja
ground level
⑬ la bolsa de la compra
carrier bag
⑭ el cartel de rebajas
sale sign
$$$
⑮ el comprador *m*
la compradora *f*
shopper

⑯ **el centro comercial**
shopping centre

⑰ la planta baja
ground floor
⑱ la primera planta
first floor
⑲ el parking subterráneo
basement parking

⑳ **los grandes almacenes**
department store

㉑ **el ascensor**
lift

㉒ **de alta gama**
upmarket

㉓ **la garantía**
guarantee

See also
13-15 La ropa • Clothes **16** Los accesorios • Accessories **17** El calzado • Shoes
18 La belleza • Beauty **42-43** La ciudad • In town **46** Las compras • Shopping

㉔ los probadores
changing rooms

㉕ la ropa de mujer
womenswear

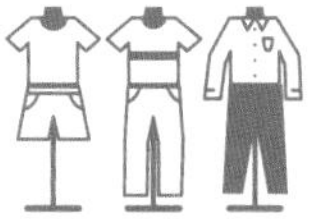

㉖ la ropa de hombre
menswear

㉗ el cambiador de bebés
baby changing facilities

㉘ el departamento infantil
children's department

㉙ las marcas de diseño
designer labels

㉚ la rebaja
sale

㉛ la lencería
lingerie

㉜ el mobiliario
home furnishings

㉝ la etiqueta del precio
price tag

㉞ la iluminación
lighting

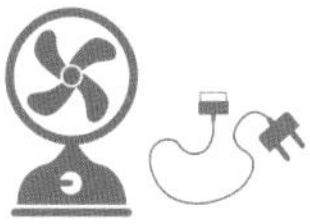

㉟ los aparatos electrónicos
electrical appliances

㊱ la tarjeta de fidelización
loyalty card

㊲ el bricolaje
DIY (do it yourself)

㊳ los productos de belleza
beauty

㊴ la atención al cliente
customer service

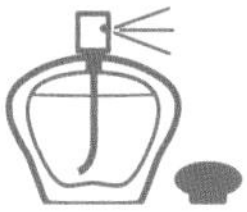

㊵ la perfumería
perfumery

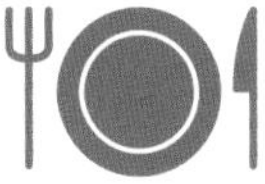

㊶ la zona de restaurantes
food court

47.2 EL PUESTO DE FLORES · FLOWER STALL

48 El supermercado
The supermarket

48.1 EL SUPERMERCADO · SUPERMARKET

① **abierto**
open

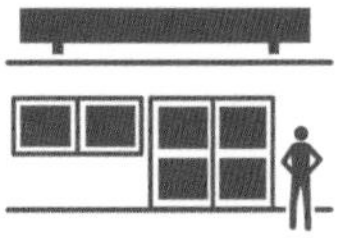
② **cerrado**
closed

③ **el cliente** *m*
la clienta *f*
customer

④ **el recibo**
receipt

⑤ **la oferta especial**
special offer

⑥ **el chollo**
bargain

⑦ **una gran variedad**
wide range

⑧ **la cola**
queue

⑨ **el datáfono**
card machine

⑩ **la compra en línea**
online shopping

⑪ **el repartidor**
delivery man

⑫ **la entrega a domicilio**
home delivery

48.2 LA CAJA · CHECKOUT

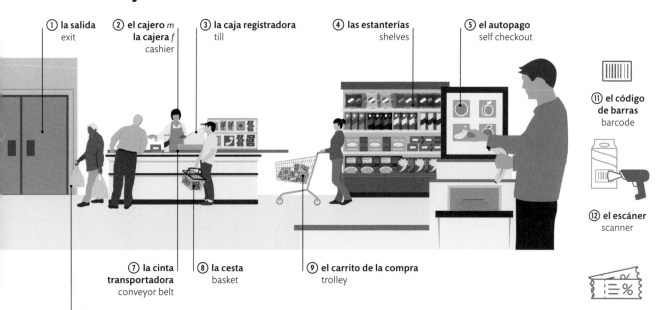

① **la salida**
exit

② **el cajero** *m*
la cajera *f*
cashier

③ **la caja registradora**
till

④ **las estanterías**
shelves

⑤ **el autopago**
self checkout

⑦ **la cinta transportadora**
conveyor belt

⑧ **la cesta**
basket

⑨ **el carrito de la compra**
trolley

⑥ **la bolsa de la compra**
carrier bag

⑩ **la caja**
checkout

⑪ **el código de barras**
barcode

⑫ **el escáner**
scanner

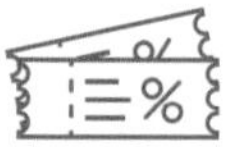

⑬ **el cupón**
discount voucher

See also
46 Las compras • Shopping **53** La carne • Meat **54** El pescado y el marisco • Fish and seafood **55-56** La verdura • Vegetables **57** La fruta • Fruit **58** La fruta y los frutos secos Fruit and nuts **59** Las hierbas y las especias • Herbs and spices **60** La despensa • In the pantry **61** Los productos lácteos • Dairy produce **62-63** La panadería • The bakery

48.3 LOS PASILLOS / LAS SECCIONES • AISLES / SECTIONS

① **la panadería**
bakery

② **los lácteos**
dairy

③ **los cereales**
breakfast cereals

④ **las conservas**
tinned food

⑤ **las golosinas**
confectionery

⑥ **la verdura**
vegetables

⑦ **la fruta**
fruit

⑧ **la carnicería**
meat and poultry

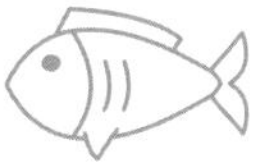
⑨ **la pescadería**
fish

⑩ **la charcutería**
deli

⑪ **los congelados**
frozen food

⑫ **la comida precocinada**
convenience food

⑬ **las bebidas**
drinks

⑭ **los productos de limpieza**
household products

⑮ **los artículos de aseo**
toiletries

⑯ **los artículos para el bebé**
baby products

⑰ **los electrodomésticos**
electrical goods

⑱ **la comida para mascotas**
pet food

48.4 EL KIOSCO • NEWSSTAND / KIOSK

① **el periódico**
newspaper

② **la revista**
magazine

③ **el cómic**
comic

④ **la postal**
postcard

⑤ **el mapa**
tourist map

⑥ **los sellos**
stamps

⑦ **la tarjeta de transporte**
travel card

⑧ **la tarjeta SIM**
sim card

⑨ **la barrita**
snack bar

⑩ **las patatas fritas**
crisps

⑪ **el agua** *f*
water

49 La farmacia
The pharmacy

49.1 LA FARMACIA · PHARMACY

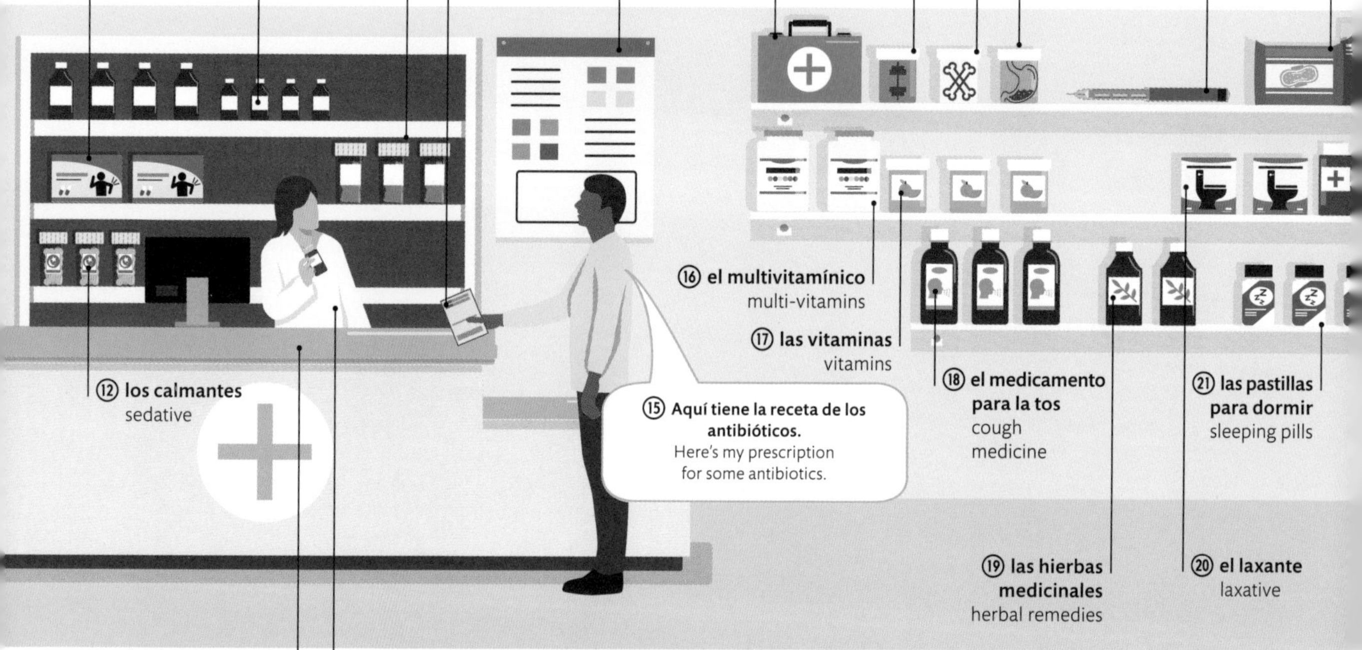

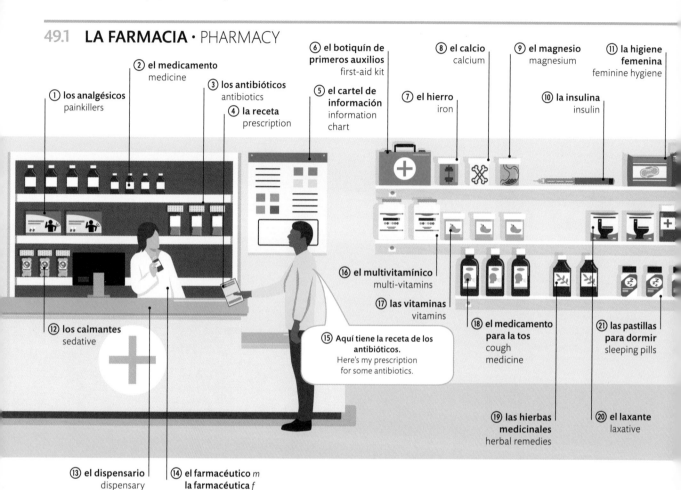

① **los analgésicos** painkillers
② **el medicamento** medicine
③ **los antibióticos** antibiotics
④ **la receta** prescription
⑤ **el cartel de información** information chart
⑥ **el botiquín de primeros auxilios** first-aid kit
⑦ **el hierro** iron
⑧ **el calcio** calcium
⑨ **el magnesio** magnesium
⑩ **la insulina** insulin
⑪ **la higiene femenina** feminine hygiene
⑫ **los calmantes** sedative
⑬ **el dispensario** dispensary
⑭ **el farmacéutico** *m* **la farmacéutica** *f* pharmacist
⑮ **Aquí tiene la receta de los antibióticos.** Here's my prescription for some antibiotics.
⑯ **el multivitamínico** multi-vitamins
⑰ **las vitaminas** vitamins
⑱ **el medicamento para la tos** cough medicine
⑲ **las hierbas medicinales** herbal remedies
⑳ **el laxante** laxative
㉑ **las pastillas para dormir** sleeping pills

㉒ **los efectos secundarios** side effects

㉓ **la medicación** medication

㉔ **las cápsulas** capsules

㉕ **las pastillas** pills / tablets

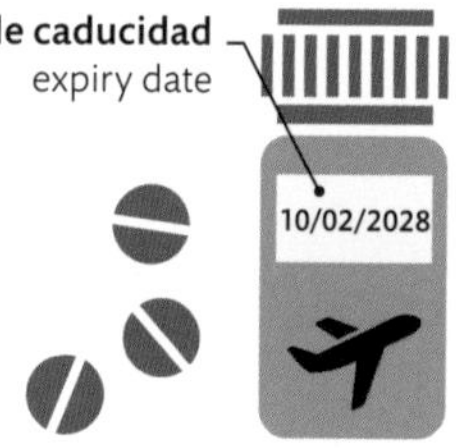

㉛ **la fecha de caducidad** expiry date

㉚ **las pastillas para el mareo** travel-sickness pills

㉖ **la dosis** dosage

㉗ **el antiinflamatorio** anti-inflammatory

㉘ **los medicamentos sin receta** over-the-counter drugs

㉙ **la pastilla para la garganta** throat lozenge

See also
19 Las enfermedades y lesiones • Illness and injury **20** La visita al médico • Visiting the doctor
21 El hospital • The hospital **46** Las compras • Shopping

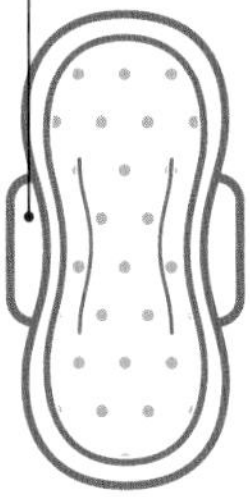

33 las alas
wings

32 la compresa
sanitary towel

34 el tampón
tampon

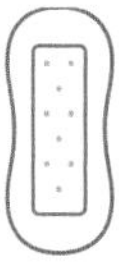

35 el protegeslip
panty liner

36 la ropa interior absorbente
incontinence pads

37 el supositorio
suppository

38 el desodorante
deodorant

39 el cuidado de la piel
skin care

40 el protector solar
sun cream

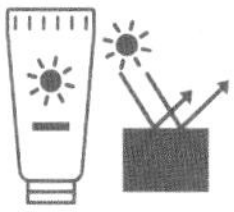

41 el bloqueador solar
sunblock

42 la venda
bandage

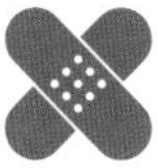

43 la tirita
plaster

44 la salud dental
dental care

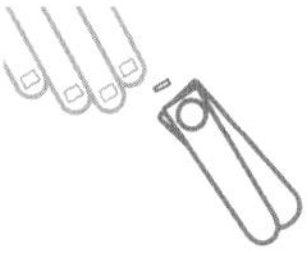

45 el cortaúñas
nail clippers

46 las toallitas
wet wipes

47 el pañuelo
tissue

48 las plantillas
insoles

49 las gafas de lectura
reading glasses

50 el repelente de insectos
insect repellent

51 las lentillas
contact lens

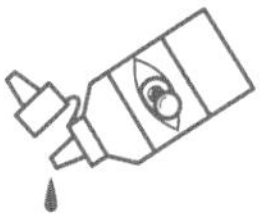

52 el líquido de lentillas
lens solution

53 la jeringuilla
syringe

54 el inhalador
inhaler

55 las gotas
drops

56 el suplemento
supplement

57 efervescente
soluble

58 la pomada
ointment

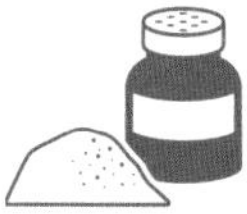

59 los polvos
powder

60 el espray
spray

61 el gel
gel

62 la crema
cream

64 la cuchara medidora
measuring spoon

63 el jarabe
syrup

50 Los servicios de emergencias
Emergency services

50.1 **LOS ACCIDENTES Y LAS EMERGENCIAS** · ACCIDENT AND EMERGENCY

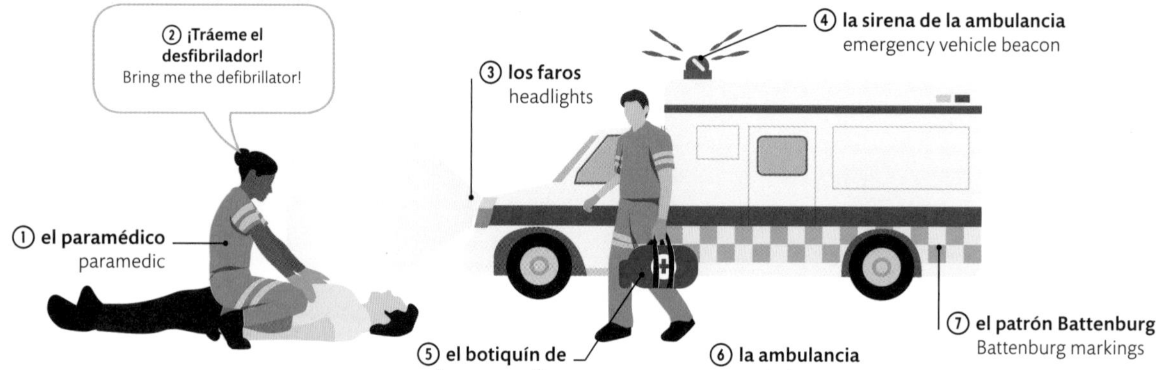

⑧ **la ambulancia aérea**
air ambulance

⑨ **la camilla de ambulancia**
ambulance stretcher

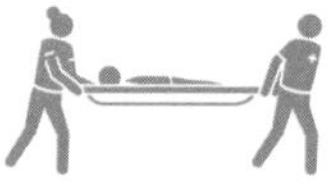

⑩ **la camilla de lona**
pole stretcher

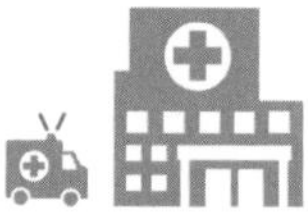

⑪ **el servicio de urgencias**
emergency department / A&E

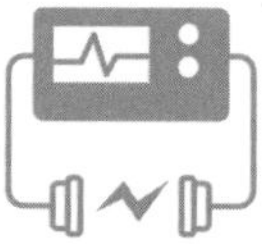

⑫ **el desfibrilador**
defibrillator

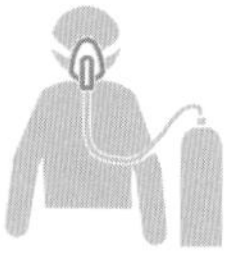

⑬ **la mascarilla de oxígeno**
oxygen mask

50.2 **EL CUERPO DE BOMBEROS** · FIRE BRIGADE

① **el detector de humo**
smoke alarm

② **la alarma de incendios**
fire alarm

③ **la escalera de incendios**
fire escape

④ **la estación de bomberos**
fire station

⑤ **la botella de aire comprimido**
compressed-air cylinder

⑥ **el extintor**
fire extinguisher

See also
19 Las enfermedades y lesiones • Illness and injury
21 El hospital • The hospital **85** El derecho • Law

50.3 LA POLICÍA • POLICE

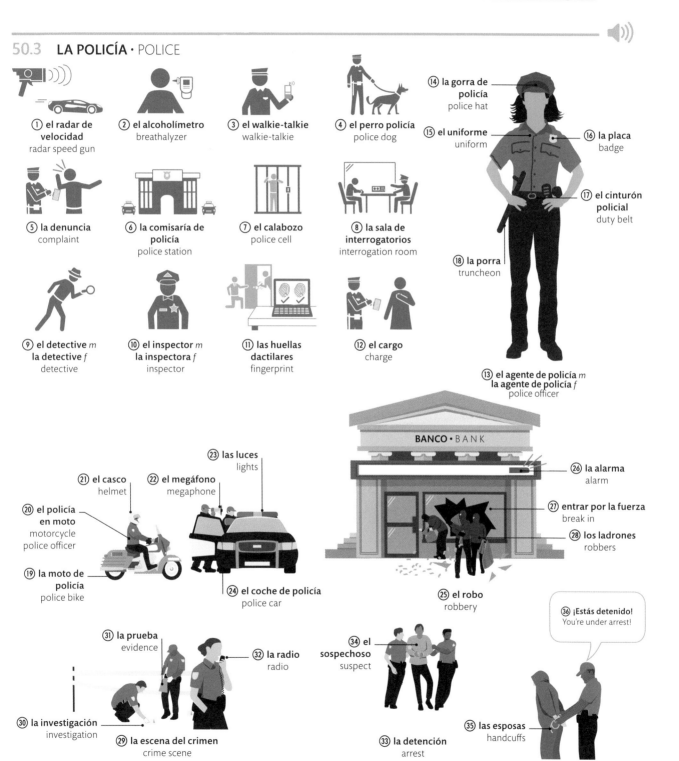

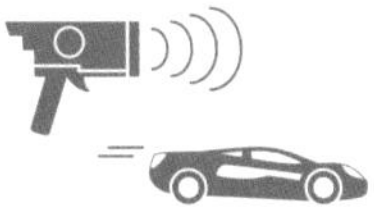
① **el radar de velocidad**
radar speed gun

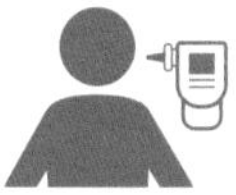
② **el alcoholímetro**
breathalyzer

③ **el walkie-talkie**
walkie-talkie

④ **el perro policía**
police dog

⑤ **la denuncia**
complaint

⑥ **la comisaría de policía**
police station

⑦ **el calabozo**
police cell

⑧ **la sala de interrogatorios**
interrogation room

⑨ **el detective** *m*
la detective *f*
detective

⑩ **el inspector** *m*
la inspectora *f*
inspector

⑪ **las huellas dactilares**
fingerprint

⑫ **el cargo**
charge

⑬ **el agente de policía** *m*
la agente de policía *f*
police officer

⑭ **la gorra de policía**
police hat

⑮ **el uniforme**
uniform

⑯ **la placa**
badge

⑰ **el cinturón policial**
duty belt

⑱ **la porra**
truncheon

⑲ **la moto de policía**
police bike

⑳ **el policía en moto**
motorcycle police officer

㉑ **el casco**
helmet

㉒ **el megáfono**
megaphone

㉓ **las luces**
lights

㉔ **el coche de policía**
police car

㉕ **el robo**
robbery

㉖ **la alarma**
alarm

㉗ **entrar por la fuerza**
break in

㉘ **los ladrones**
robbers

㉙ **la escena del crimen**
crime scene

㉚ **la investigación**
investigation

㉛ **la prueba**
evidence

㉜ **la radio**
radio

㉝ **la detención**
arrest

㉞ **el sospechoso**
suspect

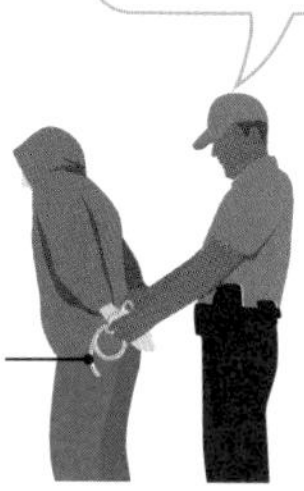
㉟ **las esposas**
handcuffs

㊱ **¡Estás detenido!**
You're under arrest!

51 La energía y el suministro eléctrico

Energy and power supply

51.1 LA ENERGÍA NUCLEAR Y LOS COMBUSTIBLES FÓSILES · NUCLEAR ENERGY AND FOSSIL FUELS

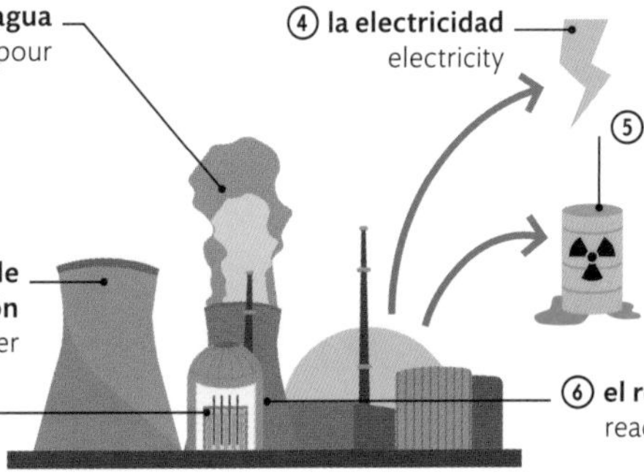

⑦ **la central nuclear** nuclear station

⑪ **los combustibles fósiles** fossil fuels

⑫ **la mina a cielo abierto** open-cast mining

⑭ **el campo petrolífero** oil field

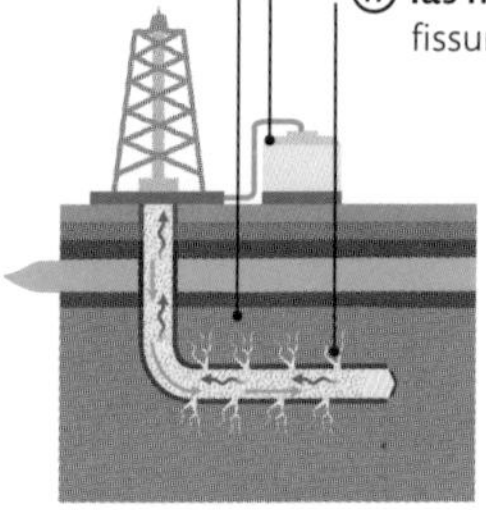

⑱ **la fracturación hidráulica** fracking

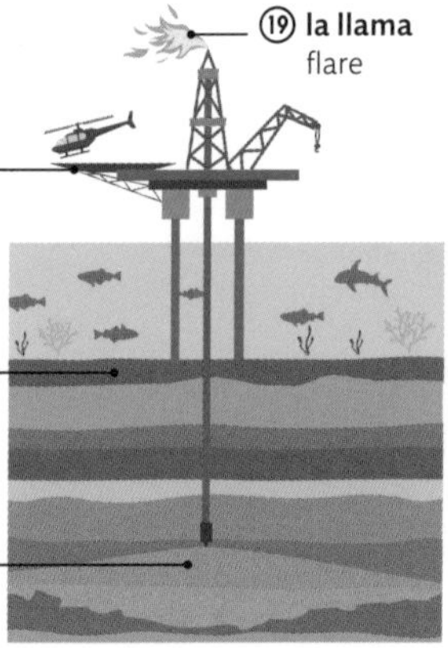

㉓ **la plataforma petrolífera** drilling rig

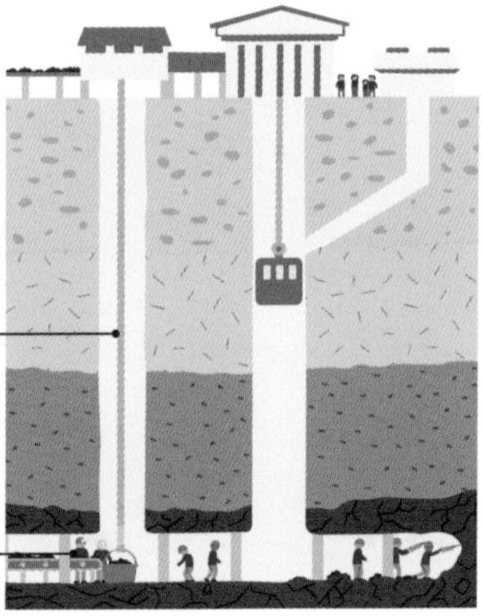

㉖ **la mina de carbón** coal mine

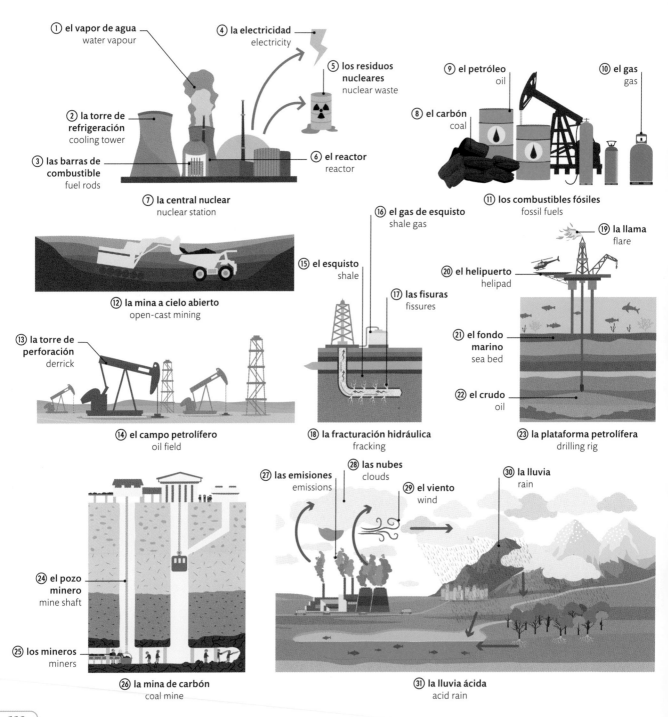

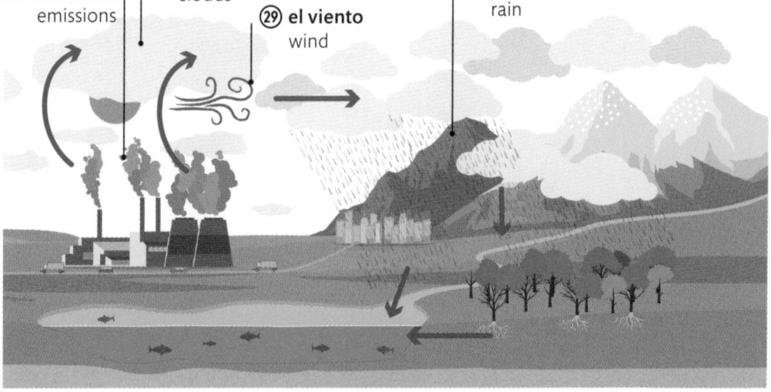

㉛ **la lluvia ácida** acid rain

See also
33 La electricidad y la fontanería • Electrics and plumbing **42-43** La ciudad • In town **145** El planeta Tierra • Planet Earth **155** El clima y el medio ambiente • Climate and the environment

51.2 LA ENERGÍA RENOVABLE • RENEWABLE ENERGY

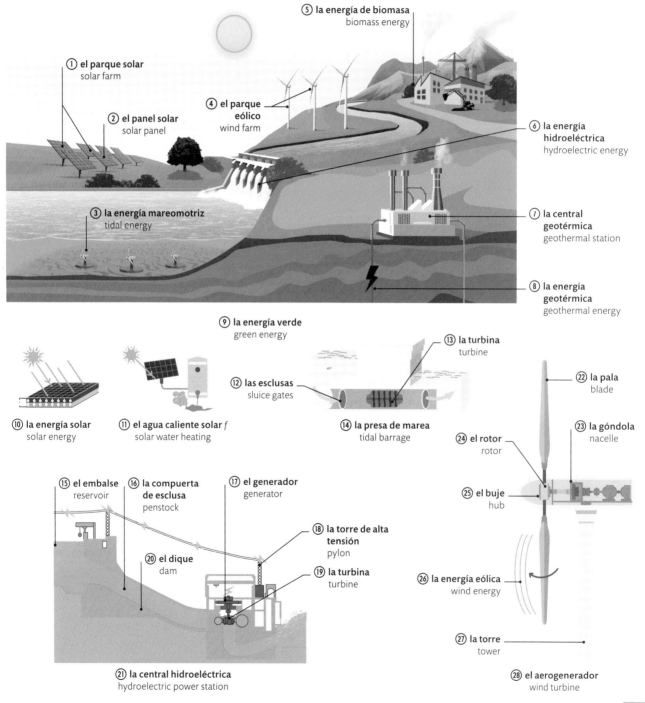

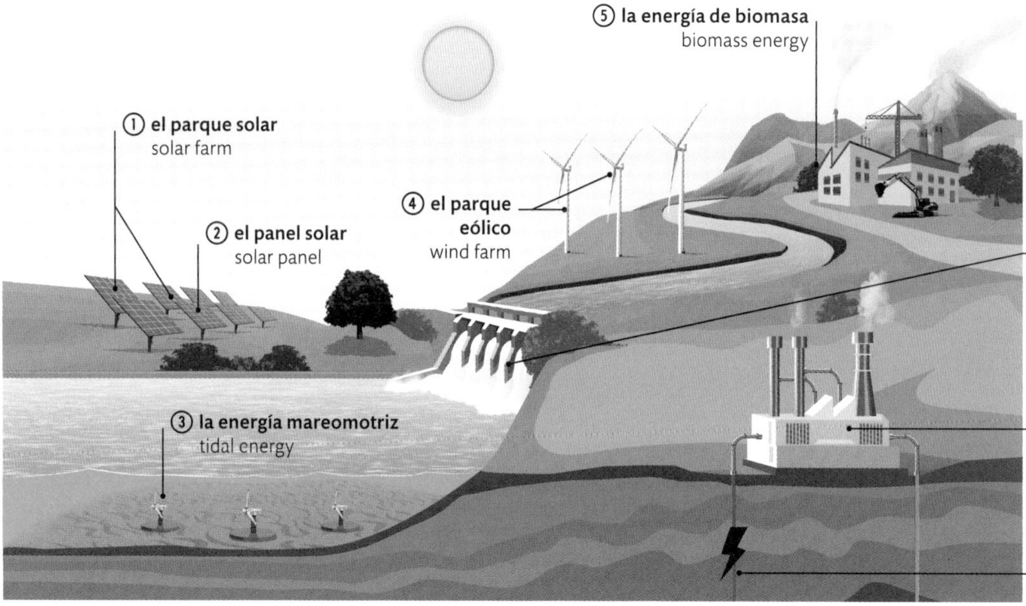

① **el parque solar**
solar farm

② **el panel solar**
solar panel

③ **la energía mareomotriz**
tidal energy

④ **el parque eólico**
wind farm

⑤ **la energía de biomasa**
biomass energy

⑥ **la energía hidroeléctrica**
hydroelectric energy

⑦ **la central geotérmica**
geothermal station

⑧ **la energía geotérmica**
geothermal energy

⑨ **la energía verde**
green energy

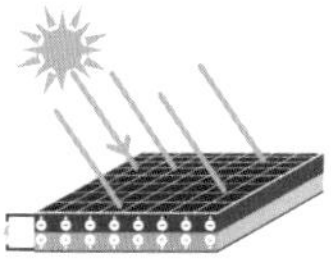

⑩ **la energía solar**
solar energy

⑪ **el agua caliente solar** *f*
solar water heating

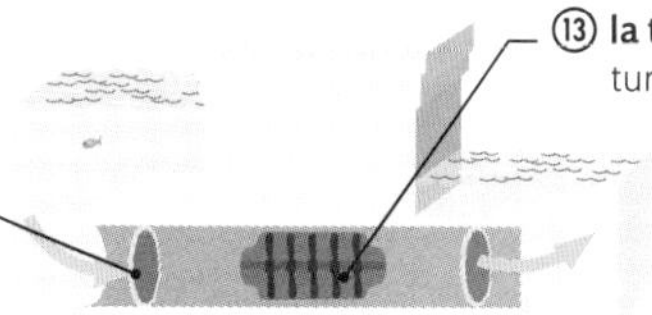

⑫ **las esclusas**
sluice gates

⑬ **la turbina**
turbine

⑭ **la presa de marea**
tidal barrage

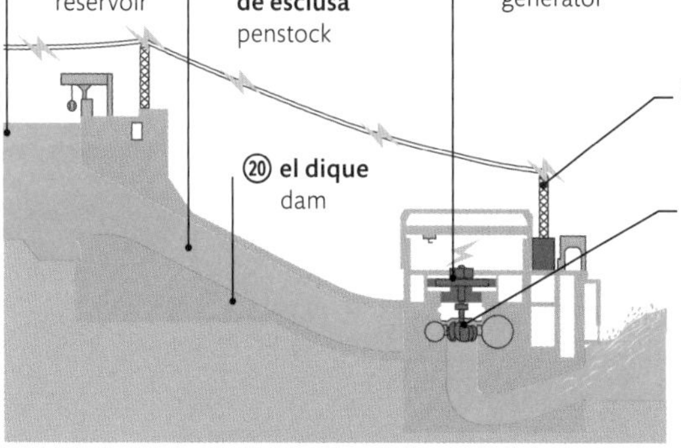

⑮ **el embalse**
reservoir

⑯ **la compuerta de esclusa**
penstock

⑰ **el generador**
generator

⑱ **la torre de alta tensión**
pylon

⑲ **la turbina**
turbine

⑳ **el dique**
dam

㉑ **la central hidroeléctrica**
hydroelectric power station

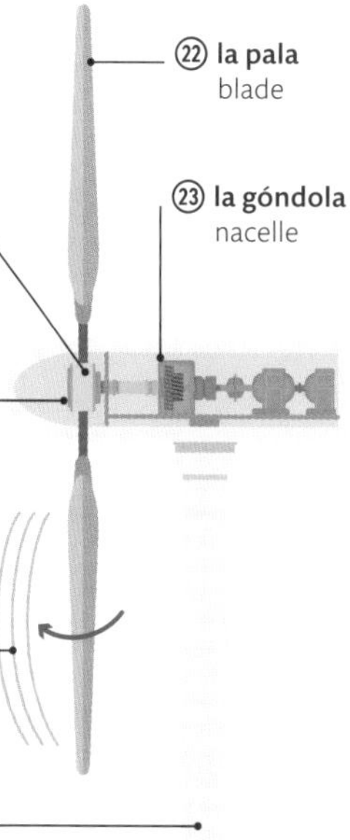

㉒ **la pala**
blade

㉓ **la góndola**
nacelle

㉔ **el rotor**
rotor

㉕ **el buje**
hub

㉖ **la energía eólica**
wind energy

㉗ **la torre**
tower

㉘ **el aerogenerador**
wind turbine

52 Beber y comer
Drinking and eating

52.1 LAS BEBIDAS · DRINKS

① **el café**
coffee

② **el té**
tea

③ **el chocolate caliente**
hot chocolate

④ **la infusión**
herbal tea

⑤ **el té helado**
iced tea

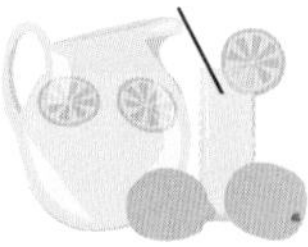
⑥ **la limonada**
lemonade

⑦ **el zumo**
juice

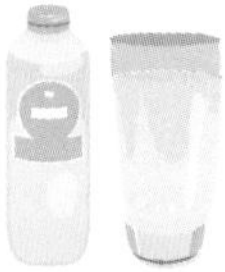
⑧ **el agua mineral** *f*
mineral water

⑨ **el agua del grifo** *f*
tap water

⑩ **el smoothie**
smoothie

⑪ **la naranjada**
orangeade

⑫ **el refresco de cola**
cola

⑬ **el batido**
milkshake

⑭ **la bebida energética**
sports drink / energy drink

⑮ **el vino tinto**
red wine

⑯ **el vino blanco**
white wine

⑰ **el vino rosado**
rosé wine

⑱ **la cerveza**
beer

52.2 LOS RECIPIENTES · CONTAINERS

① **la botella**
bottle

② **el vaso**
glass

③ **el cartón**
carton

④ **el frasco**
jar

⑤ **la bolsa**
bag

⑥ **el paquete**
packet

⑦ **la caja**
box

⑧ **la lata**
tin

⑨ **el termo**
flask

⑩ **el bol**
bowl

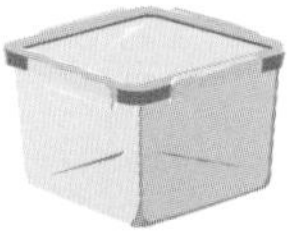
⑪ **el recipiente hermético**
airtight container

⑫ **el tarro**
Mason jar

See also
27 La cocina y la vajilla • Kitchen and tableware **28** El menaje de cocina
Kitchenware **29** La cocina • Cooking **52-72** Los alimentos • Food

52.3 LOS ADJETIVOS • ADJECTIVES

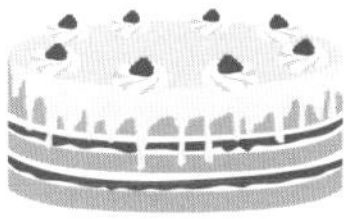
① **dulce**
sweet

② **salado** *m* / **salada** *f*
savoury

③ **agrio** *m* / **agria** *f*
sour

④ **salado** *m* / **salada** *f*
salty

⑤ **amargo** *m* / **amarga** *f*
bitter

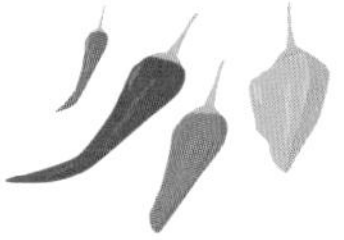
⑥ **picante**
spicy / hot

⑦ **fresco** *m* / **fresca** *f*
fresh

⑧ **pasado** *m* / **pasada** *f*
off

⑨ **fuerte**
strong

⑩ **frío** *m* / **fría** *f*
iced / chilled

⑪ **con gas**
carbonated / sparkling

⑫ **sin gas**
non-carbonated / still

⑬ **pesado** *m*
pesada *f*
rich

⑭ **jugoso** *m* / **jugosa** *f*
juicy

⑮ **crujiente**
crunchy

⑯ **delicioso** *m*
deliciosa *f*
delicious

⑰ **asqueroso** *m*
asquerosa *f*
disgusting

⑱ **sabroso** *m*
sabrosa *f*
tasty

52.4 LOS VERBOS PARA BEBER Y COMER
DRINKING AND EATING VERBS

① **comer**
to eat

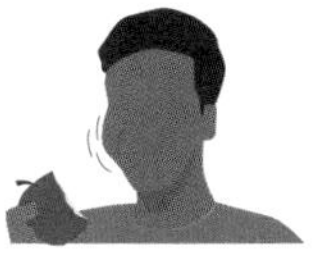
② **masticar**
to chew

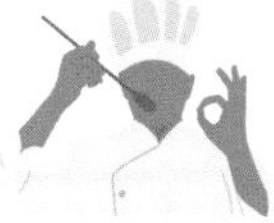
③ **probar**
to taste

⑤ **cenar**
to dine

⑥ **mordisquear**
to nibble

⑦ **morder**
to bite

⑧ **tragar**
to swallow

⑨ **sorber**
to sip

⑩ **beber**
to drink

⑪ **dar un trago**
to gulp

53 La carne
Meat

53.1 EL CARNICERO · THE BUTCHER

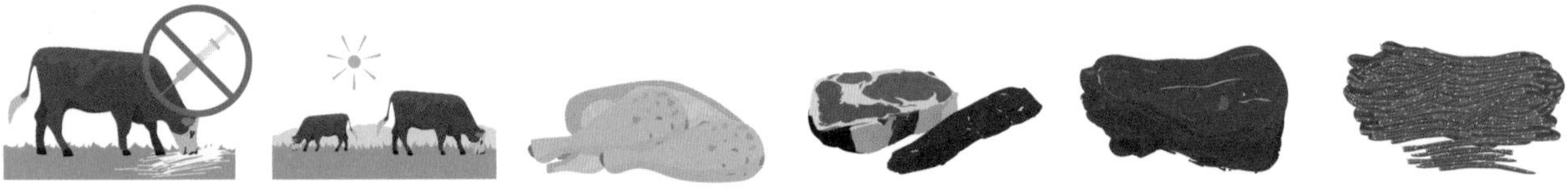

① **orgánico** *m* **orgánica** *f*
organic

② **de granja**
free-range

③ **la carne blanca**
white meat

④ **la carne roja**
red meat

⑤ **la carne magra**
lean meat

⑥ **la carne picada**
mince

⑦ **el salami**
salami

⑧ **el chorizo**
chorizo

⑨ **el jamón**
ham

⑩ **el hígado**
liver

⑪ **la chuleta**
chop

⑫ **el gancho**
meat hook

⑬ **el filete de cadera**
rump steak

⑭ **el carnicero** *m* **la carnicera** *f*
butcher

⑮ **el conejo**
rabbit

⑯ **las salchichas**
sausages

⑰ **la carne de caza**
game

⑱ **el beicon**
streaky bacon

⑲ **la cinta de lomo**
back bacon

⑳ **el filete de solomillo**
sirloin steak

See also
29 La cocina • Cooking **52** Beber y comer • Drinking and eating **54** El pescado y el marisco • Fish and seafood **69** En el restaurante • At the restaurant **72** El almuerzo y la cena • Lunch and dinner **165** Los animales de granja • Farm animals

53.2 LOS TIPOS DE CARNE • TYPES OF MEAT

① **el cordero**
lamb

② **el cerdo**
pork

③ **el vacuno**
beef

④ **la ternera**
veal

⑤ **el venado**
venison

⑥ **la cabra**
goat

⑦ **la liebre**
rabbit

⑧ **el jabalí**
wild boar

⑨ **la carne cocinada**
cooked meat

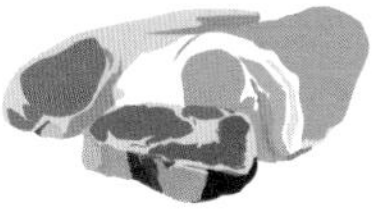
⑩ **la carne cruda**
raw meat

⑪ **la carne curada**
cured meat

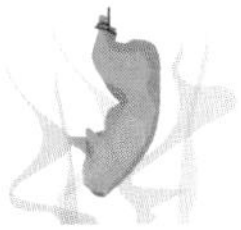
⑫ **la carne ahumada**
smoked meat

53.3 LA CARNE DE AVE • POULTRY

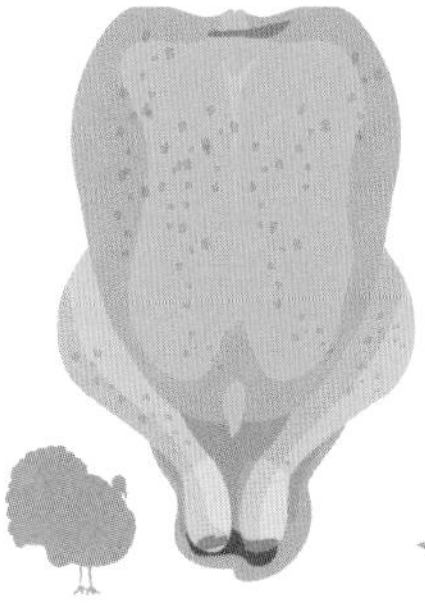
① **el pavo**
turkey

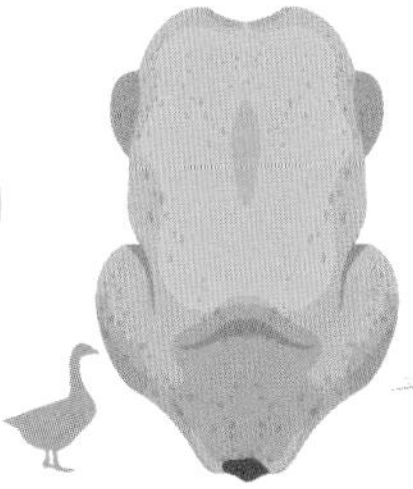
② **el ganso**
goose

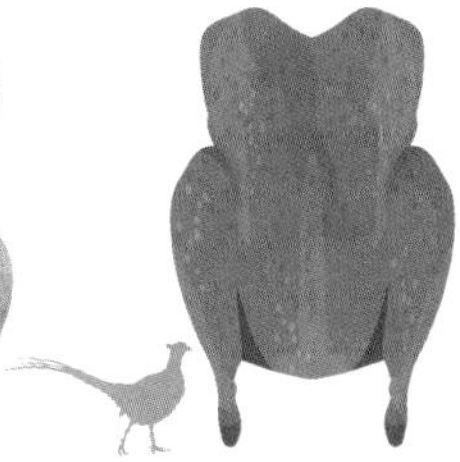
③ **el faisán**
pheasant

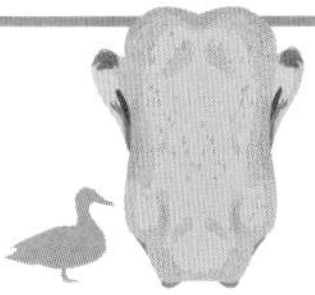
④ **el pato**
duck

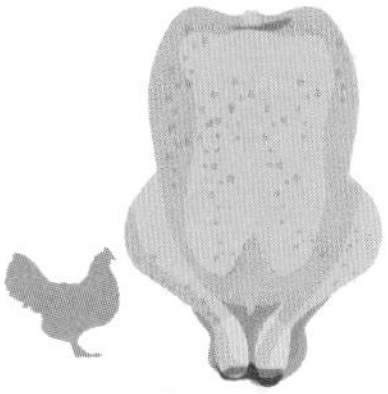
⑤ **el pollo**
chicken

⑥ **la codorniz**
quail

⑦ **¿Este pollo es de corral?**
Is this chicken free-range?

⑧ **Sí, es de origen local.**
Yes, it's locally sourced.

53.4 LOS CORTES DE CARNE • CUTS OF MEAT

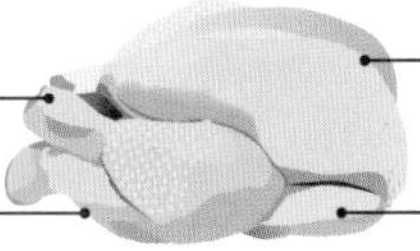
① **la pierna**
leg

② **el muslo**
thigh

③ **la pechuga**
breast

④ **el ala** *f*
wing

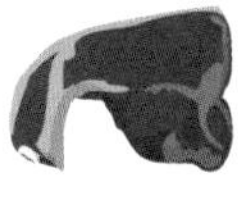
⑤ **la costilla**
rib

⑥ **el filete**
fillet

⑦ **los cortes**
cuts

⑧ **la pieza**
joint

⑨ **la rodaja**
slice

⑩ **el corazón**
heart

⑪ **la lengua**
tongue

⑫ **el riñón**
kidney

⑬ **las vísceras**
offal

54 El pescado y el marisco
Fish and seafood

54.1 EL PESCADO · FISH

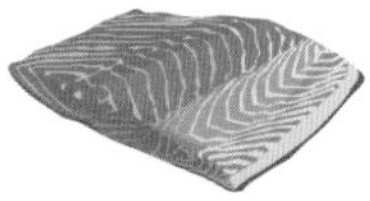
① **el filete de salmón**
salmon fillet

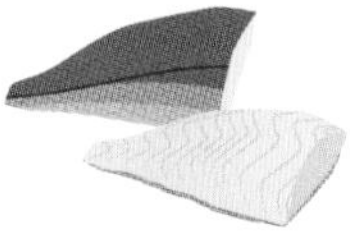
② **la cola de abadejo**
haddock tail

③ **las alas de raya**
skate wing

④ **el filete de bacalao**
cod fillet

⑤ **las sardinas**
sardines

⑥ **el salmonete**
red mullet

⑧ **la caballa**
mackerel

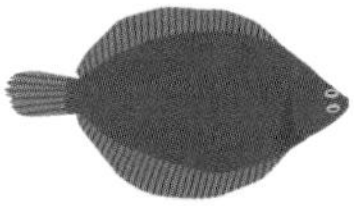
⑨ **el lenguado**
sole

⑩ **el pargo**
sea bream

⑪ **el rape**
monkfish

⑫ **la lubina**
sea bass

⑬ **el barbo**
catfish

㉖ el pez espada
swordfish
㉗ el atún
tuna
㉘ el pescadero m / la pescadera f
fishmonger
㉕ la trucha
trout
㉔ ¿Me pones cuatro filetes de trucha, por favor?
Can I have four trout fillets, please?
㉙ la platija
plaice
㉓ la carpa
carp
㉚ el abadejo
pollock
㉛ el filete
fillet
㉜ la caja de pescado
fish box

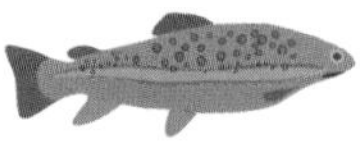
⑮ **la trucha arco iris**
rainbow trout

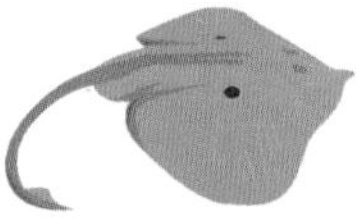
⑰ **la raya**
skate

⑲ **el arenque**
herring

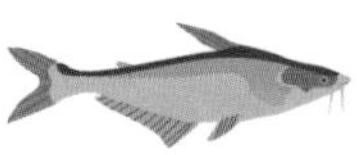
㉑ **la panga**
basa

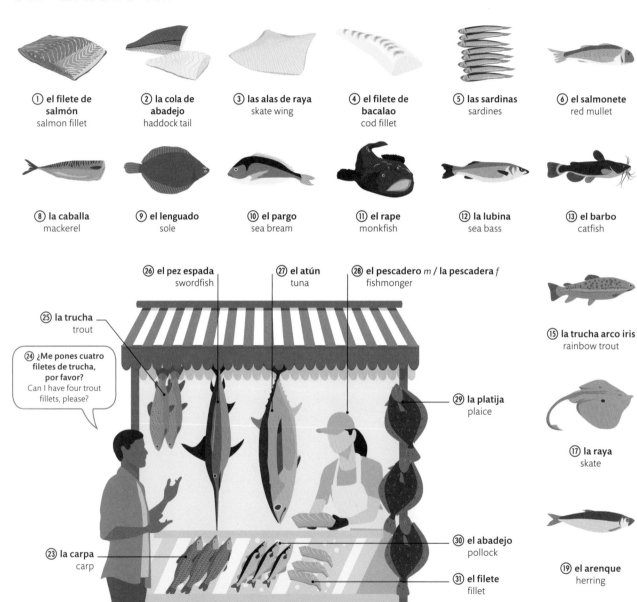

See also
29 La cocina • Cooking **52** Beber y comer • Drinking and eating **55-56** La verdura • Vegetables **69** En el restaurante • At the restaurant **72** El almuerzo y la cena • Lunch and dinner **166** La vida oceánica • Ocean life

⑰ **la pescadilla**
whiting

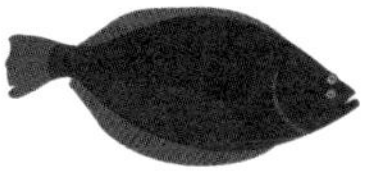

⑭ **el fletán**
halibut

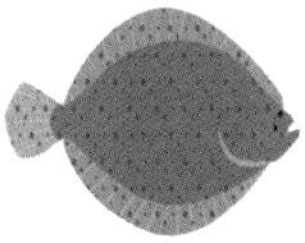

⑯ **el rodaballo**
turbot

⑱ **la anguila**
eel

⑳ **la perca**
perch

㉒ **la lucioperca**
pike perch

54.2 EL MARISCO • SEAFOOD

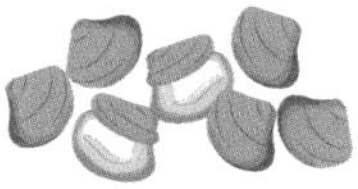

① **la almeja**
clam

② **el pulpo**
octopus

③ **la langosta**
lobster

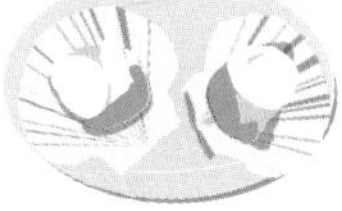

④ **la vieira**
scallop

⑤ **la cigala**
crayfish

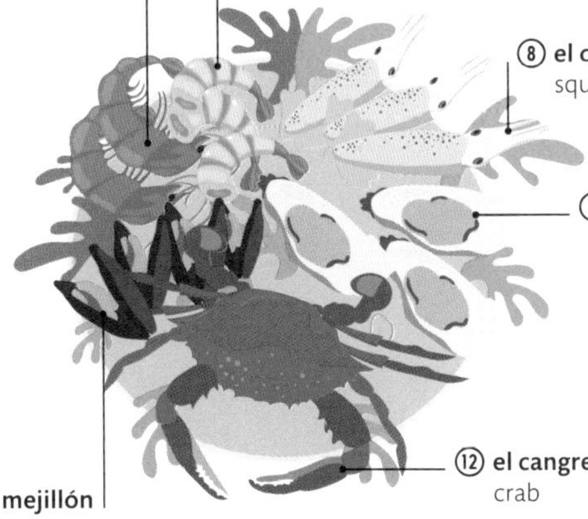

⑥ **la gamba sin pelar**
unpeeled prawn

⑦ **la gamba pelada**
peeled prawn

⑧ **el calamar**
squid

⑨ **la ostra**
oyster

⑩ **el mejillón**
mussel

⑪ **la mariscada**
seafood platter

⑫ **el cangrejo**
crab

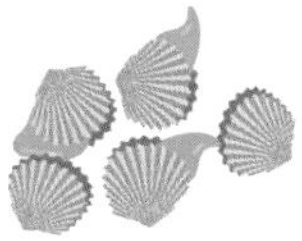

⑬ **el berberecho**
cockle

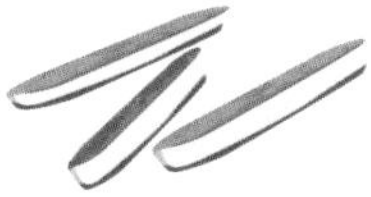

⑭ **la navaja**
razor-shell

⑮ **las rabas**
calamari

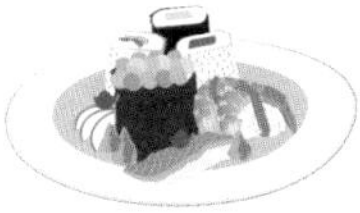

⑯ **el sushi**
sushi

54.3 LA PREPARACIÓN • PREPARATION

① **la escama**
scale

② **fresco** *m* / **fresca** *f*
fresh

③ **la cola**
tail

④ **congelado** *m*
congelada *f*
frozen

⑤ **ahumado** *m*
ahumada *f*
smoked

⑥ **en sal**
salted

⑦ **descamado** *m*
descamada *f*
descaled

⑧ **limpio** *m* / **limpia** *f*
cleaned

⑨ **sin espinas**
boned

⑩ **el lomo**
loin

55 La verdura
Vegetables

55.1 LA VERDURA · VEGETABLES

① **las habas**
broad beans

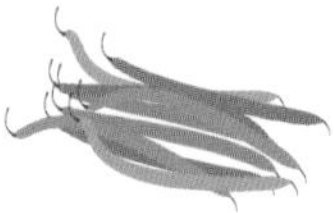

② **las judías planas**
runner beans

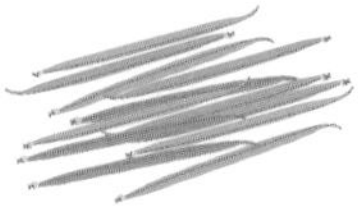

③ **las judías verdes**
green beans / French beans

④ **las judías secas**
dried beans

⑤ **el apio**
celery

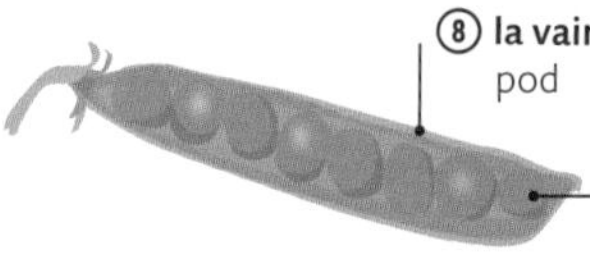

⑦ **los guisantes**
garden peas

⑩ **el tirabeque**
mangetout

⑪ **la okra**
okra

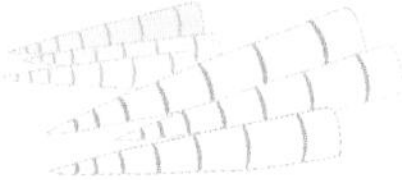

⑫ **el bambú**
bamboo

⑬ **los brotes de soja**
bean sprouts

⑮ **la achicoria**
chicory

⑯ **el hinojo**
fennel

⑰ **los palmitos**
palm hearts

⑱ **las mazorquitas**
baby sweetcorn

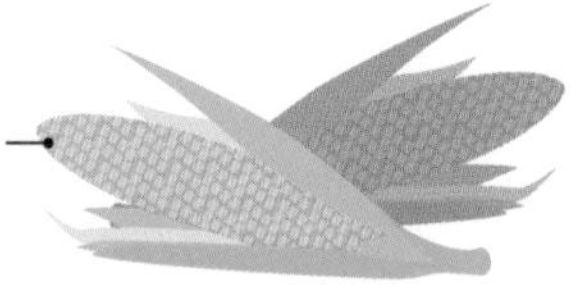

⑳ **la mazorca**
corn / sweetcorn

㉓ **la endivia**
endive

㉔ **el diente de león**
dandelion

㉕ **la acelga suiza roja**
Swiss chard

㉖ **la col rizada**
kale

㉗ **la acedera**
sorrel

㉘ **la espinaca**
spinach

㉛ **la acelga china**
pak-choi

㉜ **el colinabo**
kohlrabi

㉝ **las coles de Bruselas**
Brussels sprouts

㉞ **los tallos**
spring greens

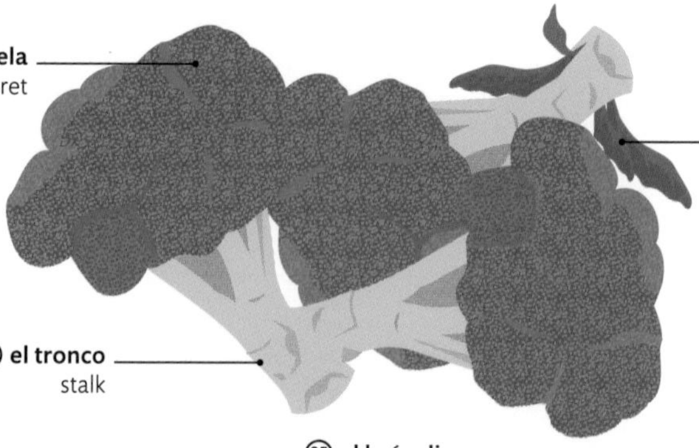

㉟ **el brócoli**
broccoli

See also
29 La cocina • Cooking **52** Beber y comer • Drinking and eating **56** La verdura (continuación) • Vegetables continued **57** La fruta • Fruit **58** La fruta y los frutos secos • Fruit and nuts **59** Las hierbas y las especias Herbs and spices **69** En el restaurante • At the restaurant **72** El almuerzo y la cena • Lunch and dinner

⑥ **la berza**
collards

⑭ **la col de Saboya**
savoy cabbage

㉑ **la col**
cabbage

㉒ **la col lombarda**
red cabbage

㉙ **la col negra**
cavolo nero

㉚ **las hojas de remolacha**
beet leaves

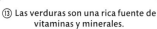

㊵ **los pesticidas**
pesticides

㊴ **las verduras orgánicas**
organic vegetables

55.2 LAS VERDURAS PARA ENSALADA
SALAD VEGETABLES

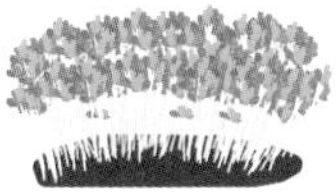

① **el berro**
cress

② **la rúcula**
rocket

③ **la lechuga iceberg**
iceberg lettuce

④ **la lechuga romana**
romaine lettuce

⑤ **el cogollo**
little gem

⑥ **la cebolleta**
spring onion

⑦ **los tomates cherry**
cherry tomatoes

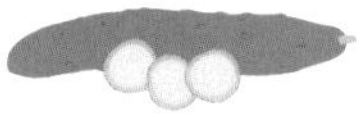

⑧ **el pepino**
cucumber

⑨ **la escarola**
frisée

⑩ **el berro de agua**
watercress

⑪ **la achicoria roja**
radicchio

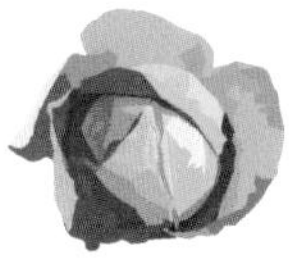

⑫ **la lechuga**
lettuce

⑬ **Las verduras son una rica fuente de vitaminas y minerales.**
Vegetables are a great source of vitamins and minerals.

⑭ **la ensalada**
salad

56 La verdura (continuación)
Vegetables continued

56.1 EN LA VERDULERÍA · AT THE GREENGROCERS

① **el nabo**
turnip

② **el rábano**
radish

③ **la chirivía**
parsnip

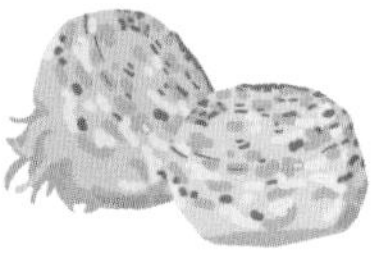
④ **la raíz de apio**
celeriac

⑤ **la mandioca**
cassava

⑥ **la patata**
potato

⑦ **la castaña de agua**
water chestnut

⑧ **el boniato**
yam

⑨ **la remolacha**
beetroot

⑩ **la rutabaga**
swede

⑪ **el tupinambo**
Jerusalem artichoke

⑫ **la raíz de taro**
taro root

⑬ **el rábano picante**
horseradish

⑭ **el frutipán**
breadfruit

⑮ **la chalota**
shallot

⑯ **el chile**
chilli

⑰ **el tomate pera**
plum tomato

⑱ **los espárragos trigueros**
asparagus tip

⑲ **el corazón de alcachofa**
artichoke heart

⑳ **la seta ostra**
oyster mushroom

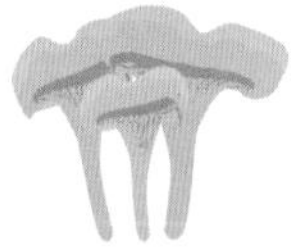
㉑ **el rebozuelo**
chanterelle

㉒ **el shiitake**
shiitake mushroom

㉓ **la trufa**
truffle

㉔ **el enoki**
enoki mushroom

㉕ **el calabacín**
marrow

㉖ **la calabaza violín**
butternut squash

㉗ **la calabaza bellota**
button acorn squash

㉘ **la calabaza**
pumpkin

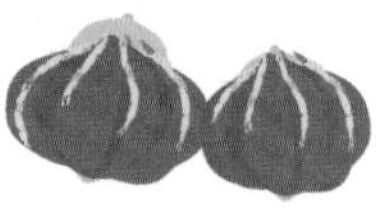
㉙ **la calabaza de invierno**
buttercup squash

㉚ **la calabaza bonetera**
patty pan

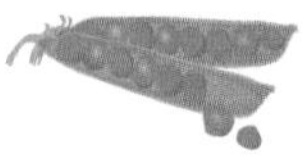
㉛ **fresco** *m* / **fresca** *f*
fresh

㉜ **congelado** *m* **congelada** *f*
frozen

㉝ **enlatado** *m* **enlatada** *f*
tinned

㉞ **crudo** *m* / **cruda** *f*
raw

㉟ **cocinado** *m* **cocinada** *f*
cooked

㊱ **picante**
hot / spicy

See also
29 La cocina • Cooking **52** Beber y comer • Drinking and eating **57** La fruta • Fruit
58 La fruta y los frutos secos • Fruit and nuts **69** En el restaurante • At the restaurant
72 El almuerzo y la cena • Lunch and dinner

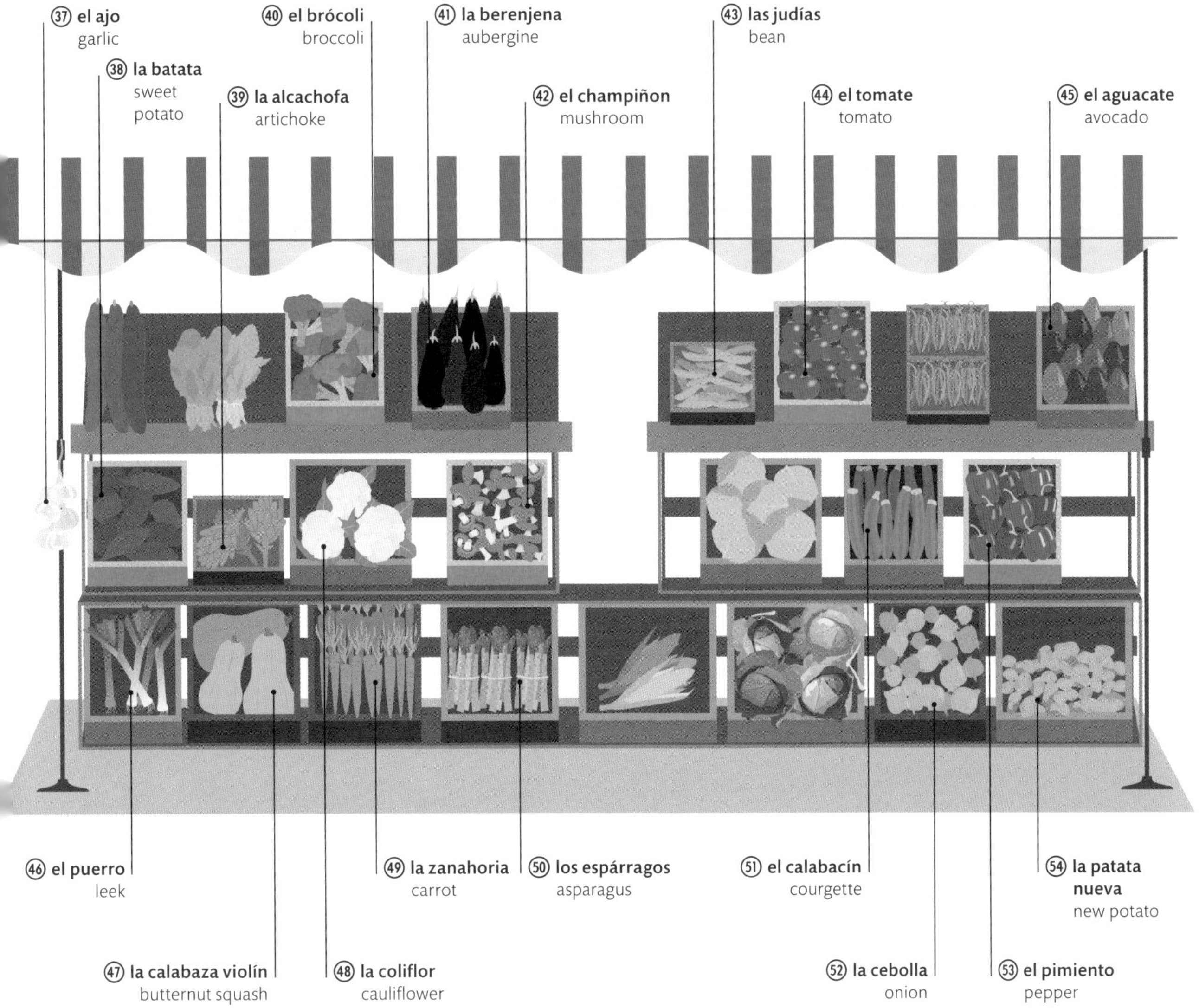

55 **dulce**
sweet

56 **crujiente**
crunchy

57 **amargo** *m*
amarga *f*
bitter

58 **de hoja**
leafy

57 La fruta
Fruit

57.1 LOS CÍTRICOS · CITRUS FRUIT

① **la naranja**
orange

② **la naranja sanguina**
blood orange

③ **el ugli**
ugli fruit

④ **el pomelo**
pomelo

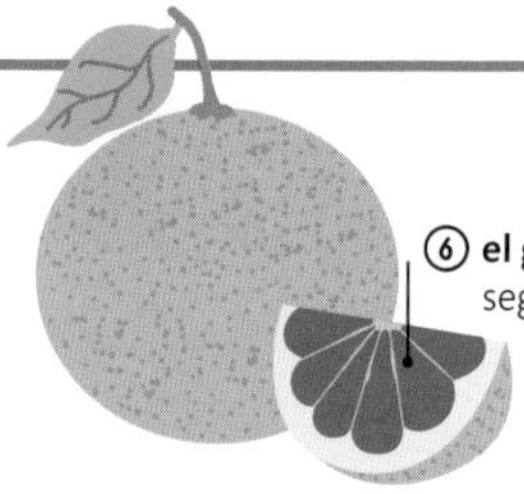

⑥ **el gajo**
segment

⑤ **la toronja**
grapefruit

⑦ **la clementina**
clementine

⑧ **la satsuma**
satsuma

⑨ **el kumquat**
kumquat

⑩ **la lima**
lime

⑪ **el limón**
lemon

⑫ **la ralladura**
zest

57.2 DESCRIBIR LA FRUTA · DESCRIBING FRUIT

① **la cáscara de coco**
coconut shell

② **duro** *m* / **dura** *f*
hard

③ **suave**
soft

④ **sin semillas**
seedless

⑤ **Estas peras ya están maduras y listas para recolectar.**
These pears are ripe and ready to pick.

⑥ **recolectar**
to pick

⑦ **de primavera**
spring

⑧ **de verano**
summer

⑪ **dulce**
sweet

⑫ **agrio** *m* / **agria** *f*
sour

⑬ **maduro** *m* / **madura** *f*
ripe

⑭ **podrido** *m* **podrida** *f*
rotten

⑨ **de otoño**
autumn

⑩ **la fruta de temporada**
seasonal fruit

⑮ **fresco** *m* / **fresca** *f*
crisp

⑯ **el corazón**
core

⑰ **la fibra**
fibre

⑱ **la pulpa**
pulp

See also
29 La cocina • Cooking **52** Beber y comer • Drinking and eating **55-56** La verdura • Vegetables
58 La fruta y los frutos secos • Fruit and nuts **65-66** En la cafetería • At the café **69** En el restaurante
At the restaurant **71** El desayuno • Breakfast **72** El almuerzo y la cena • Lunch and dinner

57.3 LAS BAYAS Y LAS FRUTAS CON HUESO • BERRIES AND STONE FRUIT

① **la frambuesa**
raspberry

② **la grosella negra**
blackcurrant

③ **la mora**
blackberry

④ **la grosella blanca**
white currant

⑤ **la fresa**
strawberry

⑥ **la cesta de frutas**
basket of fruit

⑦ **el arándano rojo**
cranberry

⑧ **el arándano azul**
blueberry

⑨ **la mora roja**
loganberry

⑩ **la uchuva**
cape gooseberry

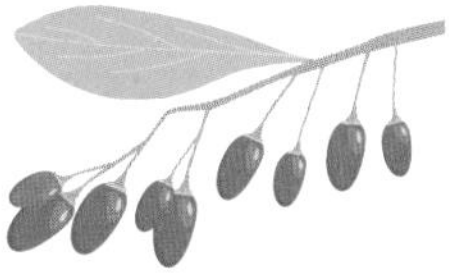

⑪ **la baya goji**
goji berry

⑫ **la uva espina**
gooseberry

⑬ **la grosella roja**
redcurrant

⑭ **el mirtilo**
bilberry

⑮ **la baya del saúco**
elderberry

⑯ **las uvas**
grapes

⑰ **la mora**
mulberry

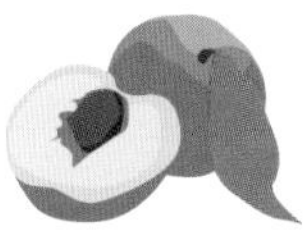

⑱ **el melocotón**
peach

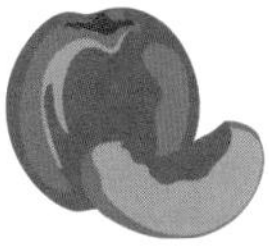

⑲ **la nectarina**
nectarine

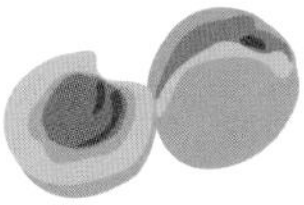

⑳ **el albaricoque**
apricot

㉑ **el mango**
mango

㉒ **la ciruela**
plum

㉓ **la cereza**
cherry

㉔ **el dátil**
date

㉕ **el lichi**
lychee

58 La fruta y los frutos secos
Fruit and nuts

58.1 LOS MELONES · MELONS

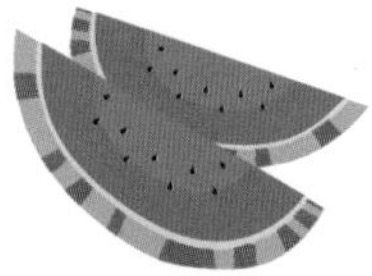

① **la sandía**
watermelon

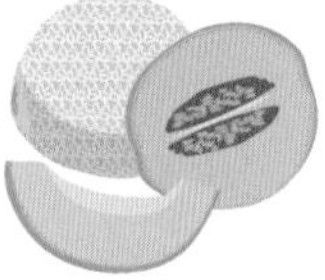

② **el melón cantalupo**
cantaloupe

③ **el melón verde**
honeydew melon

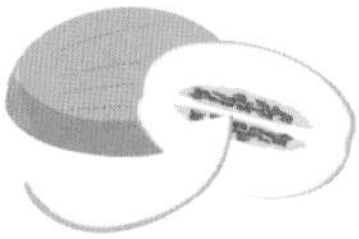

④ **el melón amarillo**
Canary melon

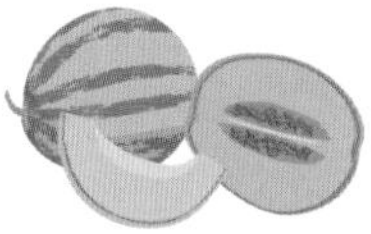

⑤ **el melón Charentais**
charentais

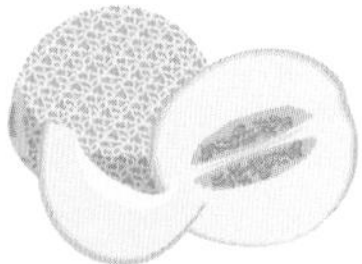

⑥ **el melón Galia**
galia

58.2 OTRAS FRUTAS · OTHER FRUIT

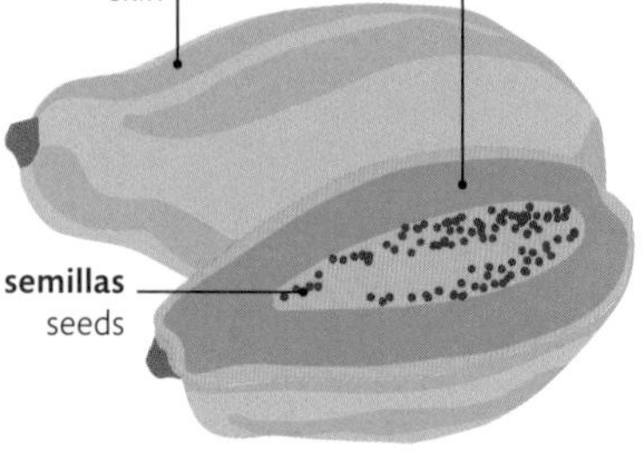

① **la papaya**
papaya

⑤ **el membrillo**
quince

⑥ **la fruta de la pasión**
passion fruit

⑦ **la guayaba**
guava

⑧ **la carambola**
starfruit

⑨ **el caqui**
persimmon

⑩ **la feijoa**
feijoa

⑪ **la piña**
pineapple

⑫ **el higo chumbo**
prickly pear

⑬ **el tamarillo**
tamarillo

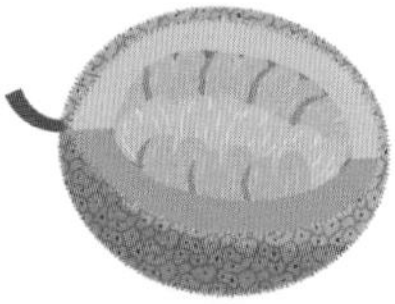

⑭ **la jaca**
jackfruit

⑮ **el mangostino**
mangosteen

⑯ **la granada**
pomegranate

⑰ **el plátano**
banana

⑱ **el kiwi**
kiwi fruit

⑲ **la manzana**
apple

⑳ **la manzana silvestre**
crab apples

㉑ **la pera**
pear

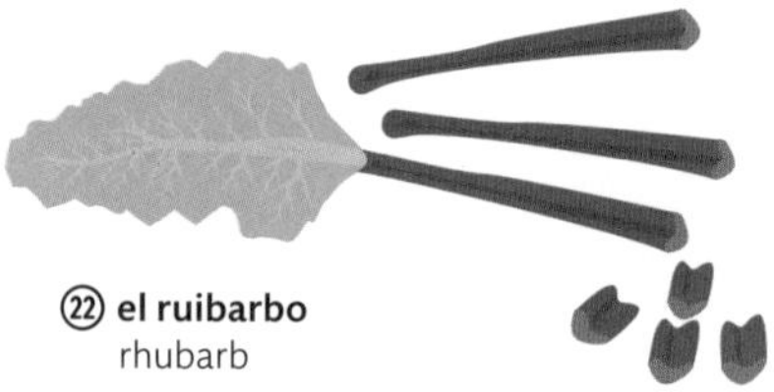

㉒ **el ruibarbo**
rhubarb

See also
29 La cocina • Cooking **52** Beber y comer • Drinking and eating **55-56** La verdura
Vegetables **57** La fruta • Fruit **65-66** En la cafetería • At the café **69** En el restaurante
At the restaurant **71** El desayuno • Breakfast **72** El almuerzo y la cena • Lunch and dinner

58.3 LOS FRUTOS SECOS Y LA FRUTA DESHIDRATADA • NUTS AND DRIED FRUIT

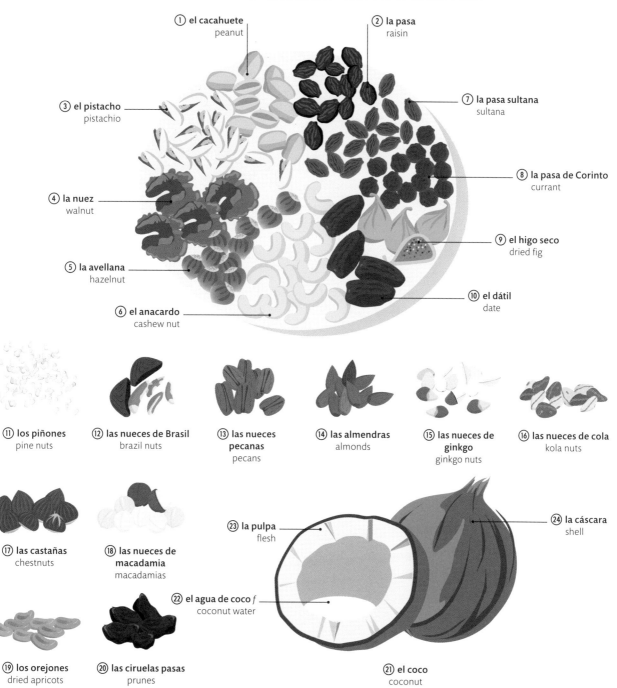

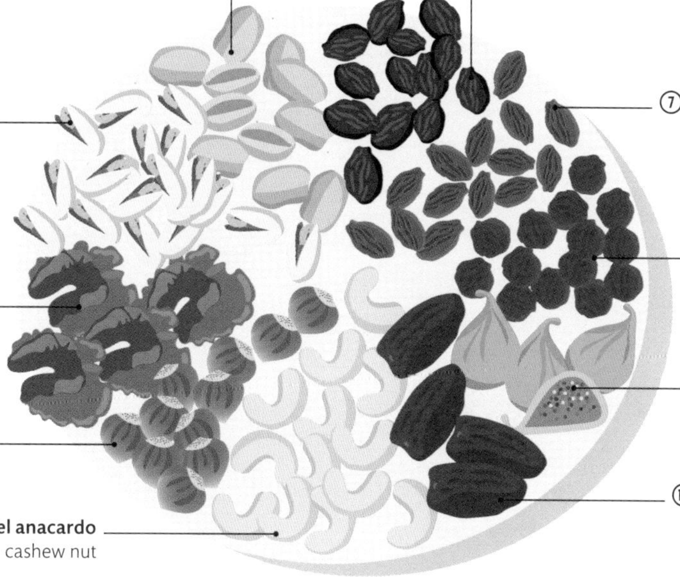

⑪ **los piñones**
pine nuts

⑫ **las nueces de Brasil**
brazil nuts

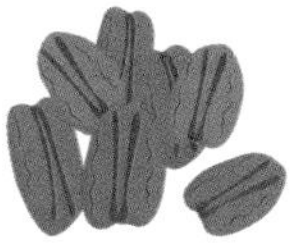

⑬ **las nueces pecanas**
pecans

⑭ **las almendras**
almonds

⑮ **las nueces de ginkgo**
ginkgo nuts

⑯ **las nueces de cola**
kola nuts

⑰ **las castañas**
chestnuts

⑱ **las nueces de macadamia**
macadamias

⑲ **los orejones**
dried apricots

⑳ **las ciruelas pasas**
prunes

㉑ **el coco**
coconut

59 Las hierbas y las especias
Herbs and spices

59.1 LAS ESPECIAS · SPICES

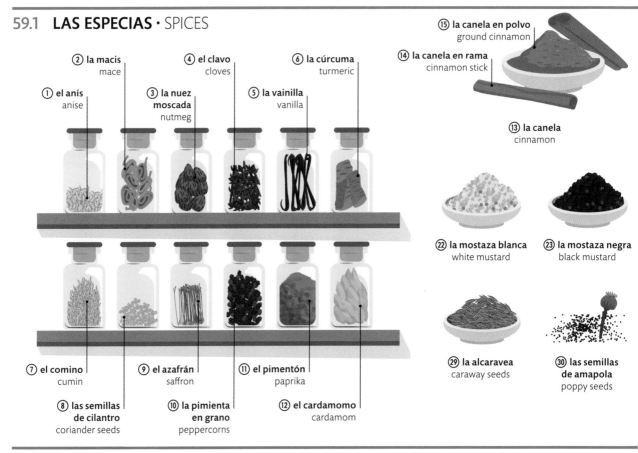

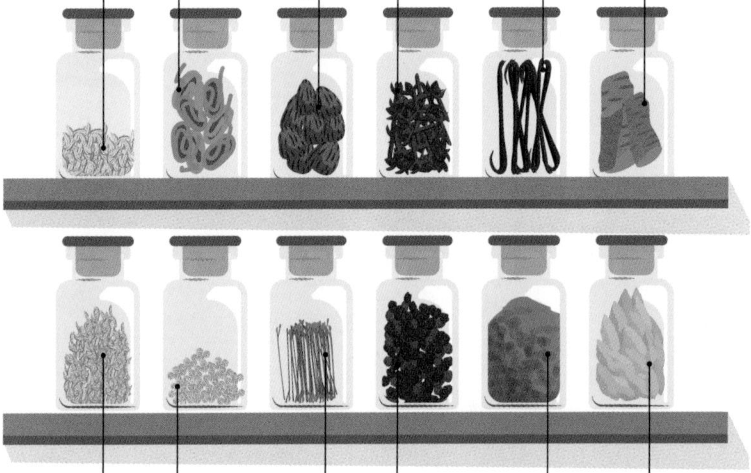

① **el anís** anise
② **la macis** mace
③ **la nuez moscada** nutmeg
④ **el clavo** cloves
⑤ **la vainilla** vanilla
⑥ **la cúrcuma** turmeric
⑦ **el comino** cumin
⑧ **las semillas de cilantro** coriander seeds
⑨ **el azafrán** saffron
⑩ **la pimienta en grano** peppercorns
⑪ **el pimentón** paprika
⑫ **el cardamomo** cardamom

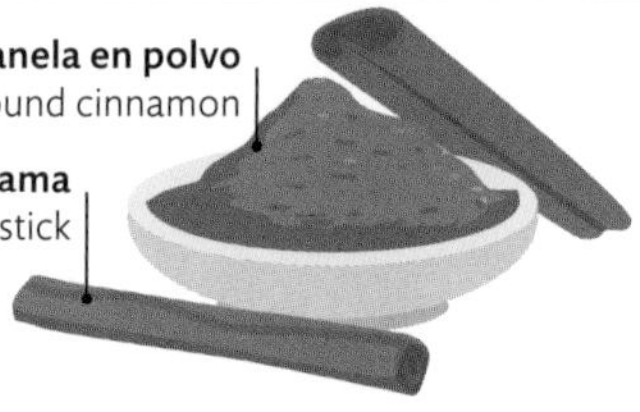

⑮ **la canela en polvo** ground cinnamon
⑭ **la canela en rama** cinnamon stick
⑬ **la canela** cinnamon

㉒ **la mostaza blanca** white mustard

㉓ **la mostaza negra** black mustard

㉙ **la alcaravea** caraway seeds

㉚ **las semillas de amapola** poppy seeds

59.2 LAS HIERBAS · HERBS

① **el hinojo** fennel

② **el laurel** bay leaf

③ **el perejil** parsley

④ **el cebollino** chives

⑤ **la menta** mint

⑥ **el cilantro** coriander

⑬ **el tomillo** thyme

⑭ **la salvia** sage

⑮ **el estragón** tarragon

⑯ **la mejorana** marjoram

⑰ **la albahaca** basil

⑱ **el orégano** oregano

See also
29 La cocina • Cooking **52** Beber y comer • Drinking and eating **53** La carne Meat **55-56** La verdura • Vegetables **60** La despensa • In the pantry

⑯ **el anís estrellado**
star anise

⑰ **el zumaque**
sumac

⑱ **el polvo de cinco especias**
five spice

⑲ **el ras el hanout**
ras el hanout

⑳ **la pimienta de Jamaica**
allspice

㉑ **el curry en polvo**
curry powder

㉔ **el jengibre**
ginger

㉕ **la cayena**
cayenne pepper

㉖ **el jalapeño**
jalapeños

㉗ **el chile ojo de pájaro**
bird's eye chillies

㉘ **el chile en polvo**
ground chilli

㉛ **las semillas de hinojo**
fennel seeds

㉜ **las semillas de nigella**
nigella seeds

㉝ **el chile**
fresh chillies

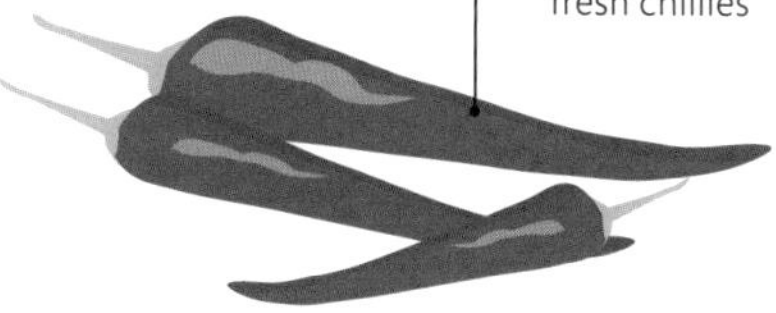

㉞ **los copos de chile**
chilli flakes

⑦ **el hisopo**
hyssop

⑧ **el eneldo**
dill

⑨ **el romero**
rosemary

⑩ **el perifollo**
chervil

⑪ **el apio del monte**
lovage

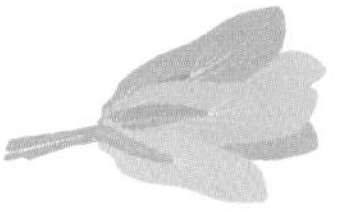
⑫ **la acedera**
sorrel

⑲ **el lemongrass**
lemongrass

⑳ **la melisa**
lemon balm

㉑ **la borraja**
borage

㉒ **el fenogreco**
fenugreek leaves

㉓ **el bouquet garni**
bouquet garni

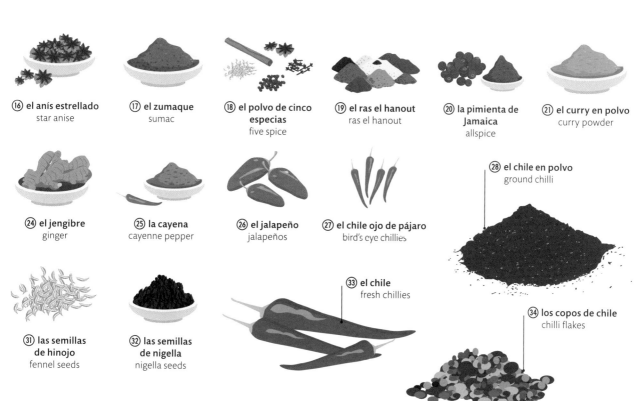

60 La despensa

In the pantry

60.1 LAS BOTELLAS DE ACEITE · BOTTLED OILS

① **el aceite**
oil

② **el aceite de palma**
palm oil

③ **el aceite de girasol**
sunflower oil

④ **el aceite de colza**
canola / rapeseed oil

⑤ **el aceite de maíz**
corn oil

⑥ **el aceite de soja**
soybean oil

⑦ **el aceite de cacahuete**
groundnut oil

⑧ **el aceite de avellana**
hazelnut oil

⑨ **el aceite de coco**
coconut oil

⑩ **el aceite aromatizado**
flavoured oil

⑬ **el aceite de sésamo**
sesame seed oil

⑭ **el aceite de almendras**
almond oil

⑮ **el aceite de nuez**
walnut oil

⑯ **el aceite de semilla de uva**
grapeseed oil

⑰ **el aceite de oliva**
olive oil

60.2 LAS CONFITURAS · SWEET SPREADS

① **la crema de limón**
lemon curd

② **la mermelada de frambuesa**
raspberry jam

③ **la mermelada de fresa**
strawberry jam

⑤ **la miel pura**
set honey

⑥ **la miel**
honey

⑨ **la mermelada / la confitura**
marmalade

⑩ **el sirope de arce**
maple syrup

⑪ **la mantequilla de cacahuete**
peanut butter

⑫ **la crema de chocolate**
chocolate spread

⑬ **el tarro de conservas**
preserving jar

See also
27 La cocina y la vajilla • Kitchen and tableware **29** La cocina • Cooking **52** Beber y comer • Drinking and eating **53** La carne • Meat **55-56** La verdura • Vegetables **65-66** En la cafetería • At the café **69** En el restaurante • At the restaurant

60.3 LAS SALSAS Y LOS CONDIMENTOS • SAUCES AND CONDIMENTS

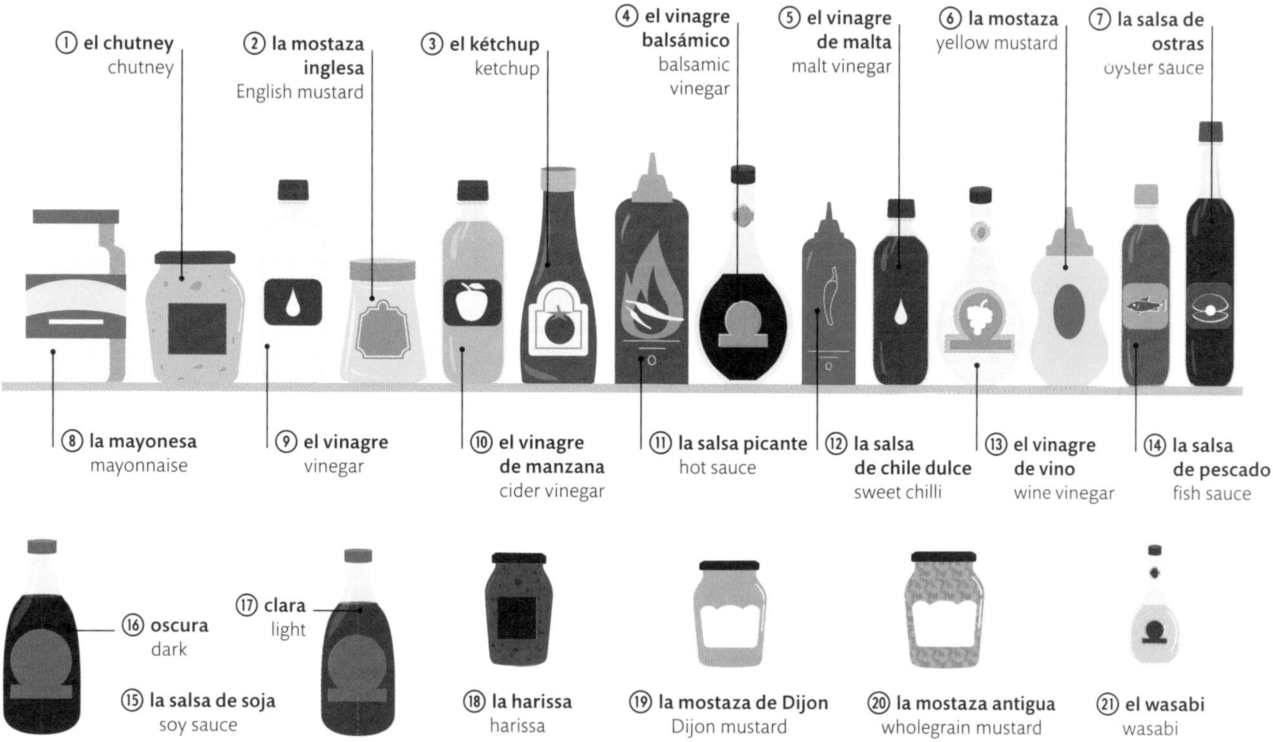

60.4 LOS ENCURTIDOS • PICKLES

61 Los productos lácteos
Dairy produce

61.1 EL QUESO · CHEESE

① **el queso curado**
hard cheese

② **el queso semicurado**
semi-hard cheese

③ **el queso cremoso semicurado**
semi-soft cheese

④ **el queso cremoso**
soft cheese

⑤ **el queso de oveja**
sheep's milk cheese

⑥ **el queso de cabra**
goat's cheese

⑦ **el queso azul**
blue cheese

⑧ **la corteza**
rind

⑨ **el queso rallado**
grated cheese

⑩ **el queso fresco**
fresh cheese

⑪ **el queso cottage**
cottage cheese

⑫ **el queso de untar**
cream cheese

61.2 LOS HUEVOS · EGGS

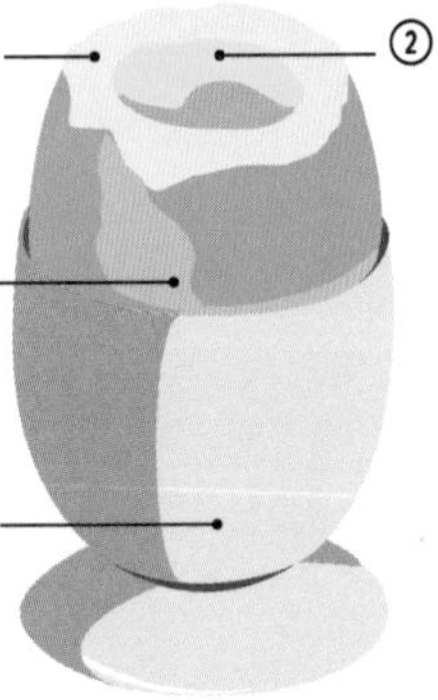
① **la clara**
egg white

② **la yema**
yolk

③ **la cáscara**
shell

④ **la huevera**
egg cup

⑤ **el huevo cocido**
boiled egg

⑥ **el huevo frito**
fried egg

⑦ **los huevos revueltos**
scrambled eggs

⑧ **el huevo escalfado**
poached egg

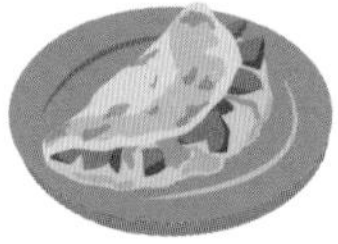
⑨ **la tortilla**
omelette

⑩ **el huevo de ganso**
goose egg

⑪ **el huevo de pato**
duck egg

⑫ **el huevo de gallina**
hen's egg

⑬ **el huevo de codorniz**
quail egg

61.3 LA LECHE · MILK

① **pasteurizada**
pasteurized

② **cruda**
unpasteurized

③ **sin lactosa**
lactose free

④ **homogeneizada**
homogenized

⑤ **desnatada**
fat free

⑥ **en polvo**
powdered milk

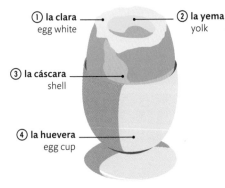

See also
29 La cocina • Cooking **52** Beber y comer • Drinking and eating **65-66** En la cafetería • At the café **69** En el restaurante • At the restaurant **71** El desayuno • Breakfast

61.4 LOS PRODUCTOS LÁCTEOS • MILK PRODUCTS

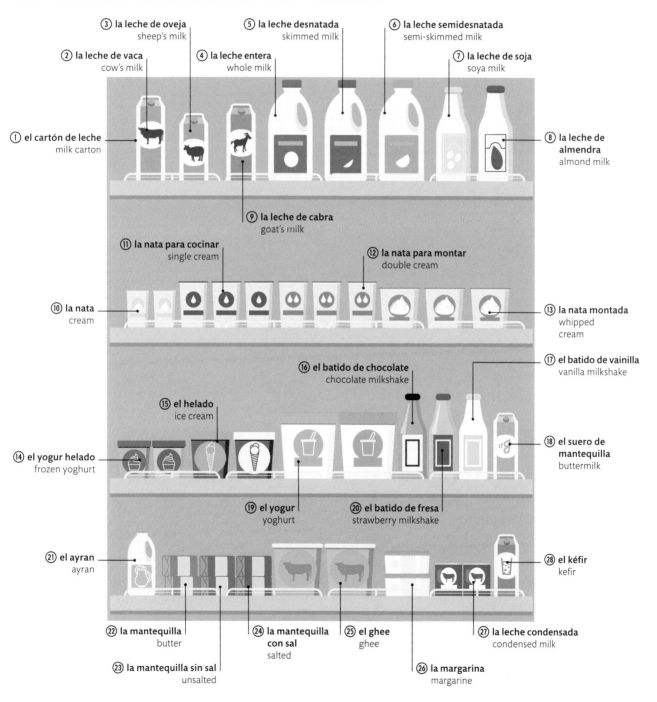

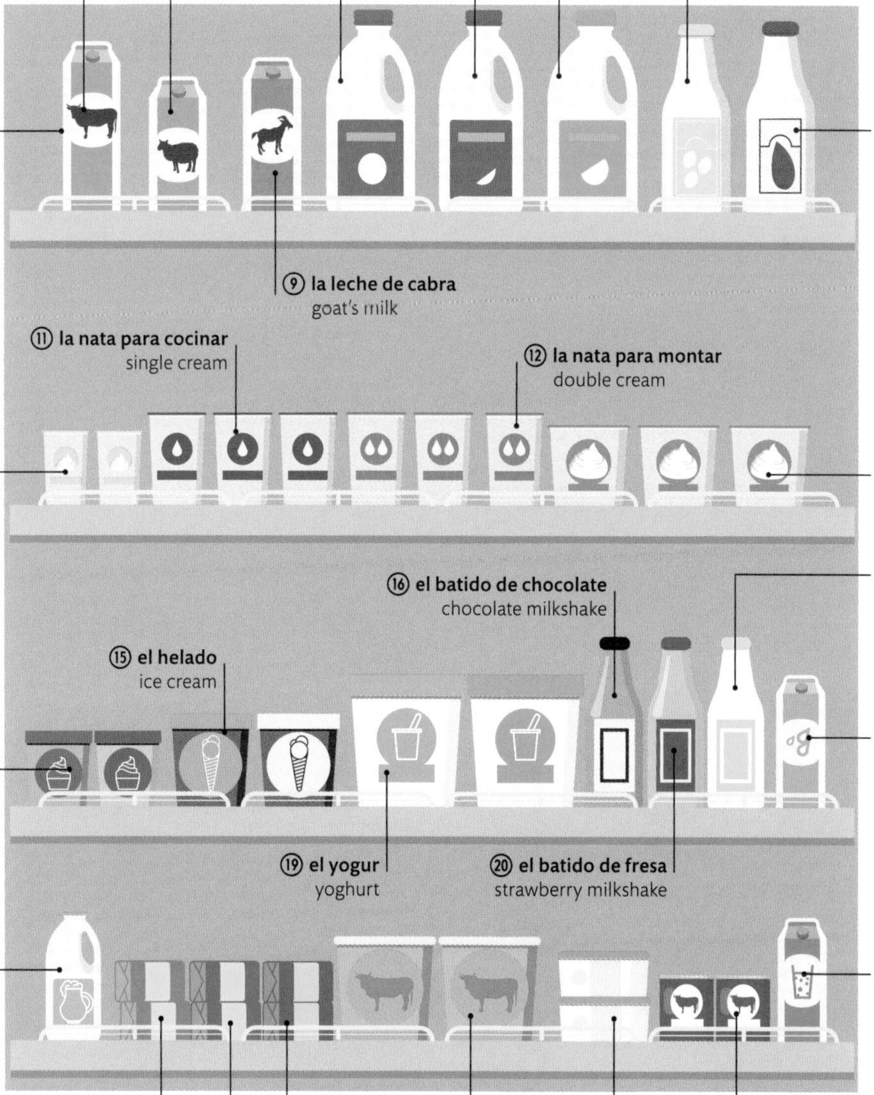

62 La panadería
The bakery

62.1 **LOS PANES Y LAS HARINAS** · BREADS AND FLOURS

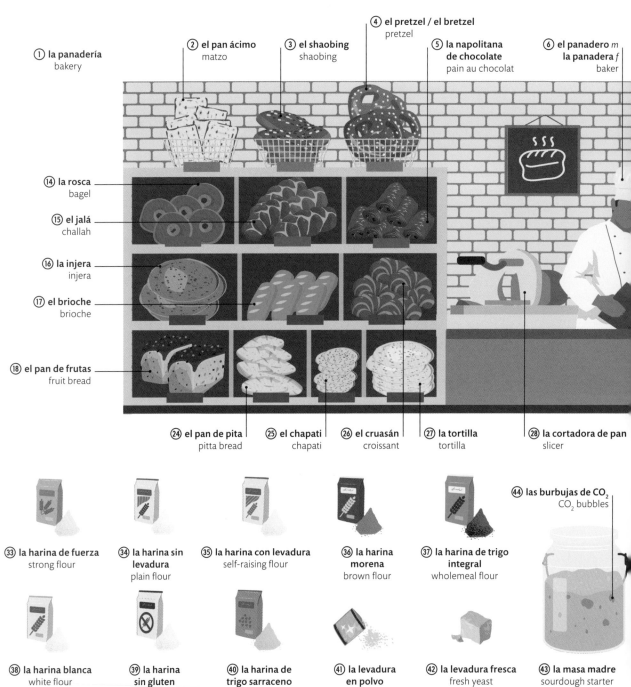

㉝ **la harina de fuerza**
strong flour

㉞ **la harina sin levadura**
plain flour

㉟ **la harina con levadura**
self-raising flour

㊱ **la harina morena**
brown flour

㊲ **la harina de trigo integral**
wholemeal flour

㊳ **la harina blanca**
white flour

㊴ **la harina sin gluten**
gluten-free flour

㊵ **la harina de trigo sarraceno**
buckwheat flour

㊶ **la levadura en polvo**
dried yeast

㊷ **la levadura fresca**
fresh yeast

㊸ **la masa madre**
sourdough starter

See also
29 La cocina • Cooking **52** Beber y comer • Drinking and eating
63 La panadería (continuación) • The bakery continued **65-66** En la cafetería
At the café **69** En el restaurante • At the restaurant **71** El desayuno • Breakfast

㊺ **cribar** to sift
㊻ **mezclar** to mix
㊼ **subir** to rise
㊽ **leudar** to prove
㊾ **la masa madre** dough
㊿ **glasear** to glaze
(51) **hornear** to bake
(52) **rebanar** to slice
(53) **amasar** to knead

63 La panadería (continuación)
The bakery continued

63.1 **LAS TARTAS Y LOS POSTRES** · CAKES AND DESSERTS

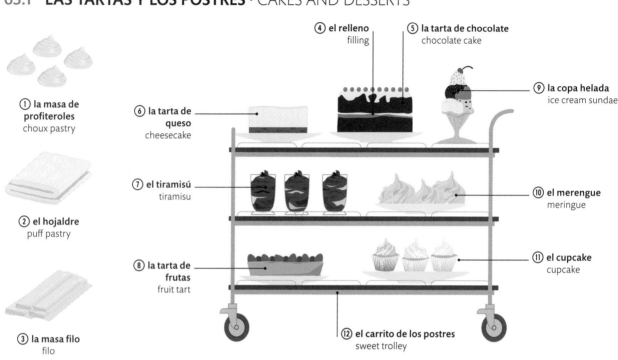

① **la masa de profiteroles**
choux pastry

② **el hojaldre**
puff pastry

③ **la masa filo**
filo

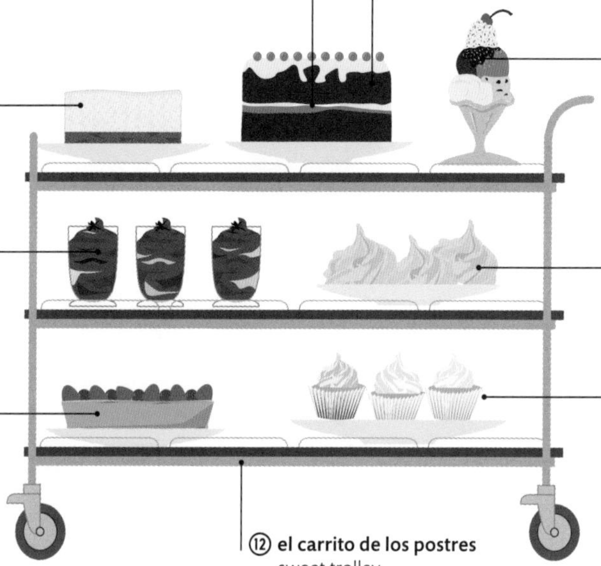

④ **el relleno**
filling

⑤ **la tarta de chocolate**
chocolate cake

⑥ **la tarta de queso**
cheesecake

⑦ **el tiramisú**
tiramisu

⑧ **la tarta de frutas**
fruit tart

⑨ **la copa helada**
ice cream sundae

⑩ **el merengue**
meringue

⑪ **el cupcake**
cupcake

⑫ **el carrito de los postres**
sweet trolley

⑬ **la crema pastelera**
crème pâtissière

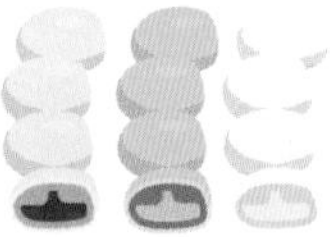

⑭ **el mochi**
mochi

⑮ **el dónut**
doughnut

⑯ **el dónut relleno de mermelada**
jam doughnut

⑰ **el dónut de chocolate**
chocolate doughnut

⑱ **la magdalena**
muffin

⑲ **el baklava**
baklava

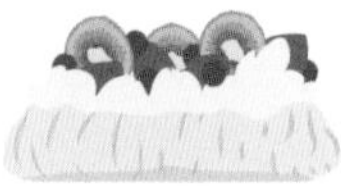

⑳ **la pavlova**
pavlova

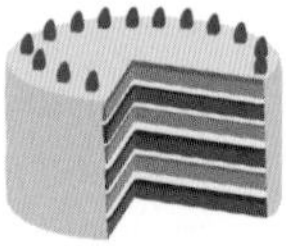

㉑ **la tarta rellena**
layer cake

㉒ **el bizcocho**
sponge cake

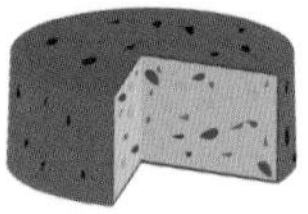

㉓ **la tarta de frutas**
fruitcake

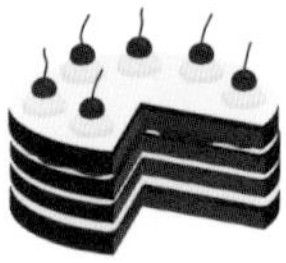

㉔ **el pastel**
gateau

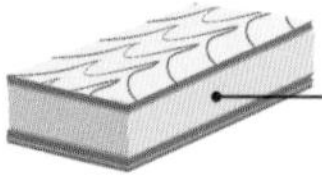

㉖ **la crema**
custard

㉕ **el milhojas**
custard slice

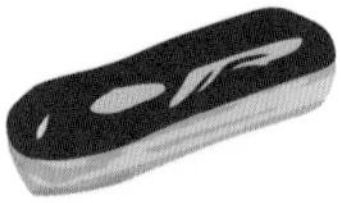

㉗ **el petisú de chocolate**
éclair

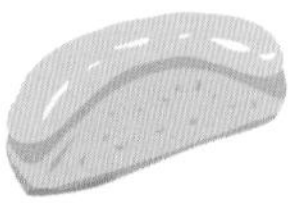

㉘ **el petisú de crema**
iced bun

㉙ **la pasta**
pastry

㉚ **el arroz con leche**
rice pudding

See also
29 La cocina • Cooking **52** Beber y comer • Drinking and eating
67 Las golosinas • Sweets **71** El desayuno • Breakfast

63.2 LAS GALLETAS • COOKIES AND BISCUITS

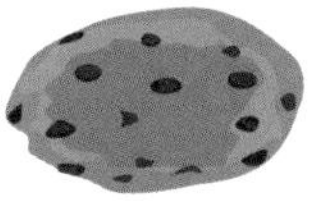

① **la galleta con trocitos de chocolate**
chocolate chip cookie

② **la galleta florentina**
Florentine

③ **la galleta de mantequilla**
shortbread

④ **el macarrón**
macaron

⑤ **el hombre de jengibre**
gingerbread man

⑥ **la galleta de la suerte**
fortune cookies

63.3 LAS TARTAS PARA CELEBRACIONES • CELEBRATION CAKES

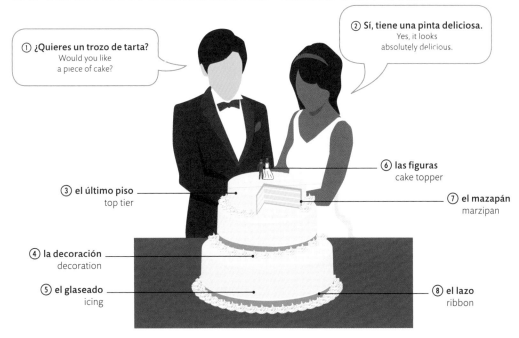

⑨ **la tarta de boda**
wedding cake

⑩ **glasear**
to glaze

⑪ **hornear**
to bake

⑫ **decorar**
to decorate

64 La delicatessen

The delicatessen

64.1 LAS DELICATESSEN · DELICATESSEN

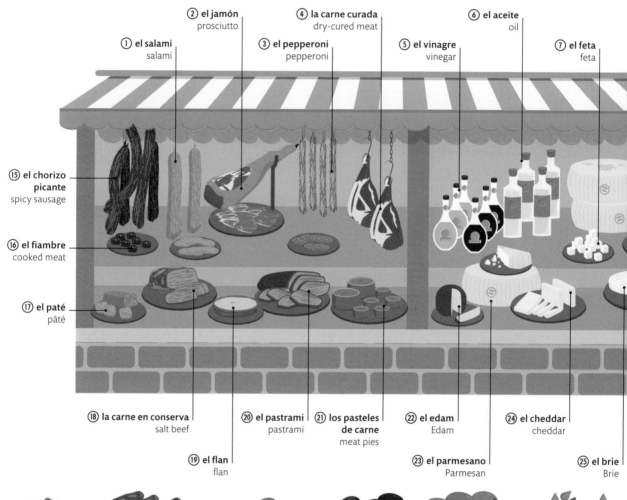

㉗ **el chile**
chillies

㉘ **las hojas de parra rellenas**
stuffed vine leaves

㉙ **las aceitunas verdes**
green olives

㉚ **las aceitunas negras**
black olives

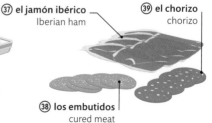

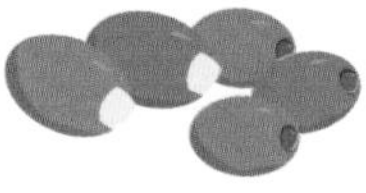
㉛ **las aceitunas rellenas**
stuffed olives

㉜ **las alcaparras**
capers

㉝ **en aceite**
in oil

㉞ **las salsas**
sauces

㉟ **marinado** *m* **marinada** *f*
marinated

㊱ **sazonado** *m* **sazonada** *f*
salted

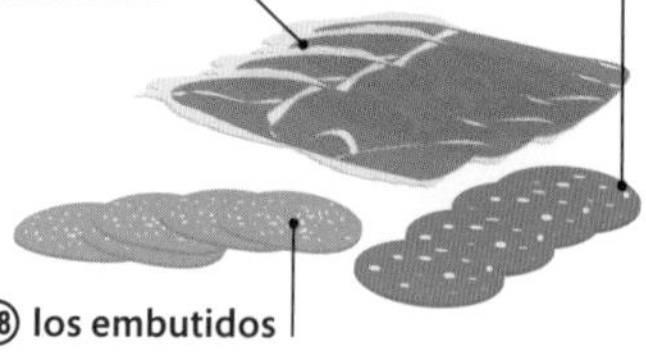

See also
29 La cocina • Cooking **52** Beber y comer • Drinking and eating **53** La carne • Meat **60** La despensa • In the pantry
61 Los productos lácteos • Dairy produce **65-66** En la cafetería • At the café **69** En el restaurante • At the restaurant
71 El desayuno • Breakfast **72** El almuerzo y la cena • Lunch and dinner

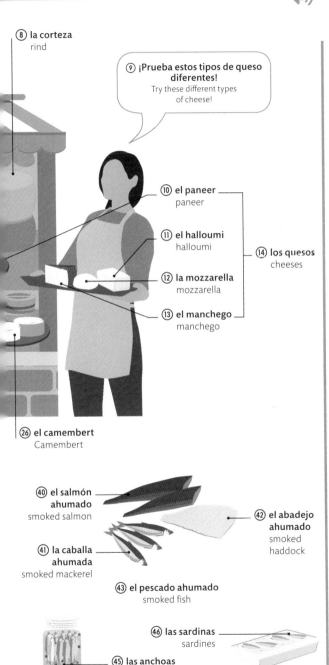

⑧ **la corteza**
rind

⑨ **¡Prueba estos tipos de queso diferentes!**
Try these different types of cheese!

⑩ **el paneer**
paneer

⑪ **el halloumi**
halloumi

⑫ **la mozzarella**
mozzarella

⑬ **el manchego**
manchego

⑭ **los quesos**
cheeses

㉖ **el camembert**
Camembert

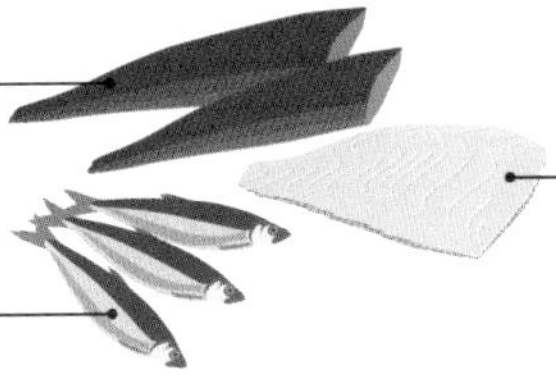

㊵ **el salmón ahumado**
smoked salmon

㊷ **el abadejo ahumado**
smoked haddock

㊶ **la caballa ahumada**
smoked mackerel

㊸ **el pescado ahumado**
smoked fish

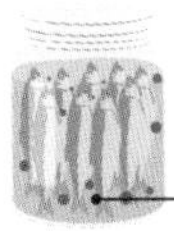

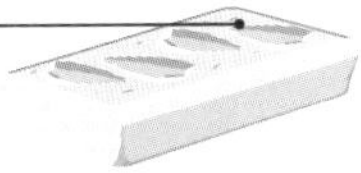

㊻ **las sardinas**
sardines

㊺ **las anchoas**
anchovies

㊹ **en escabeche**
in brine

㊼ **el pescado marinado**
marinated fish

64.2 LA PASTA Y LOS FIDEOS
PASTA AND NOODLES

① **la lasaña**
lasagne

② **los conchiglie**
conchiglie / shells

③ **los fusilli**
fusilli

④ **los macarrones**
macaroni

⑤ **los ñoquis**
gnocchi

⑥ **los macarrones penne**
penne

⑦ **los canelones**
cannelloni

⑧ **los tortellini**
tortellini

⑨ **los fideos**
noodles

⑩ **los fideos de arroz**
rice noodles

⑪ **el ramen**
ramen

⑫ **el udon**
udon

⑬ **los espaguetis**
spaghetti

⑭ **la salsa boloñesa**
Bolognese sauce

65 En la cafetería
At the café

65.1 **LA CAFETERÍA** · CAFÉ

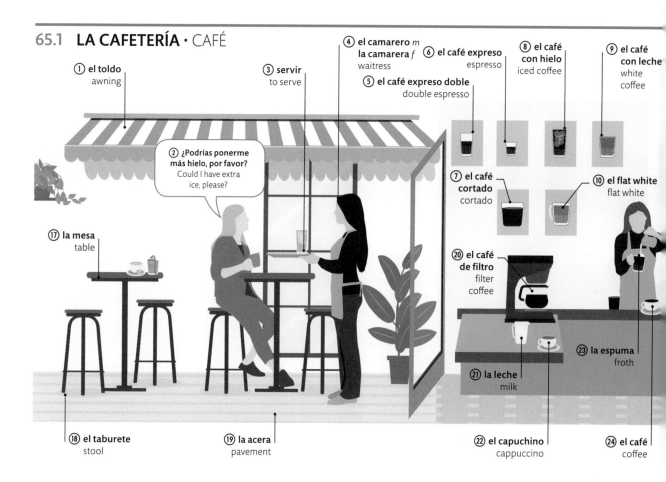

② ¿Podrías ponerme más hielo, por favor?
Could I have extra ice, please?

① **el toldo**
awning

② **¿Podrías ponerme más hielo, por favor?**
Could I have extra ice, please?

③ **servir**
to serve

④ **el camarero** *m* **la camarera** *f*
waitress

⑤ **el café expreso doble**
double espresso

⑥ **el café expreso**
espresso

⑦ **el café cortado**
cortado

⑧ **el café con hielo**
iced coffee

⑨ **el café con leche**
white coffee

⑩ **el flat white**
flat white

⑰ **la mesa**
table

⑱ **el taburete**
stool

⑲ **la acera**
pavement

⑳ **el café de filtro**
filter coffee

㉑ **la leche**
milk

㉒ **el capuchino**
cappuccino

㉓ **la espuma**
froth

㉔ **el café**
coffee

65.2 **LOS ZUMOS Y LOS BATIDOS** · JUICES AND MILKSHAKES

① **la batidora**
blender

② **el agua de coco** *f*
coconut water

③ **el zumo de naranja con pulpa**
orange juice with pulp

④ **el zumo de naranja sin pulpa**
smooth orange juice

⑤ **el zumo de manzana**
apple juice

⑥ **el zumo de piña**
pineapple juice

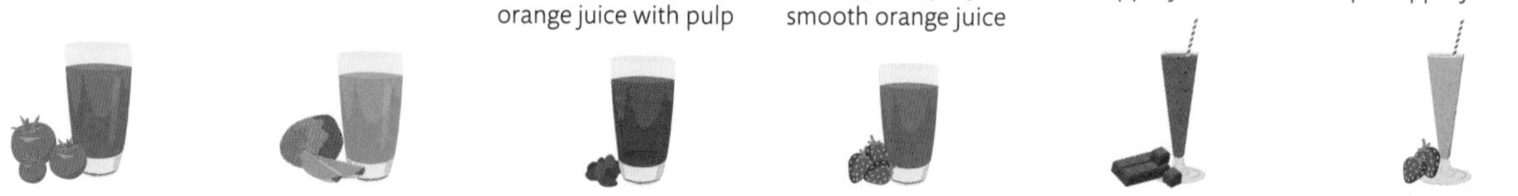

⑦ **el zumo de tomate**
tomato juice

⑧ **el zumo de mango**
mango juice

⑨ **el zumo de arándanos**
cranberry juice

⑩ **el zumo de fresa**
strawberry smoothie

⑪ **el batido de chocolate**
chocolate milkshake

⑫ **el batido de fresa**
strawberry milkshake

See also
27 La cocina y la vajilla • Kitchen and tableware **52** Beber y comer • Drinking and eating **66** En la cafetería (continuación) • At the café continued **70** La comida rápida • Fast food **72** El almuerzo y la cena • Lunch and dinner

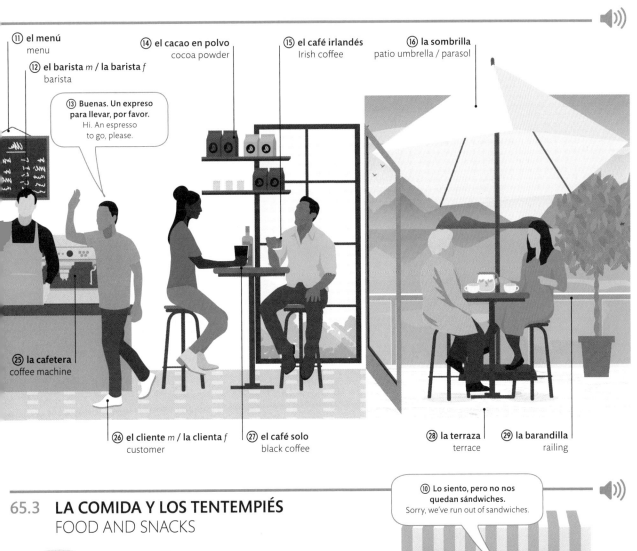

⑪ **el menú**
menu
⑫ **el barista** *m* / **la barista** *f*
barista
⑬ **Buenas. Un expreso para llevar, por favor.**
Hi. An espresso to go, please.
⑭ **el cacao en polvo**
cocoa powder
⑮ **el café irlandés**
Irish coffee
⑯ **la sombrilla**
patio umbrella / parasol
㉕ **la cafetera**
coffee machine
㉖ **el cliente** *m* / **la clienta** *f*
customer
㉗ **el café solo**
black coffee
㉘ **la terraza**
terrace
㉙ **la barandilla**
railing

65.3 LA COMIDA Y LOS TENTEMPIÉS
FOOD AND SNACKS

① **el sándwich / el bocadillo**
sandwich

② **la tortita**
pancake

③ **el gofre**
waffle

④ **la ensalada**
salad

⑤ **el cucurucho de helado**
ice cream cone

⑥ **la bola de helado**
ice cream scoop

⑩ **Lo siento, pero no nos quedan sándwiches.**
Sorry, we've run out of sandwiches.
⑨ **las bebidas**
beverages
⑧ **los tentempiés**
snacks

⑦ **el chiringuito**
snack bar

66 En la cafetería (continuación)
At the café continued

See also
27 La cocina y la vajilla • Kitchen and tableware
52 Beber y comer • Drinking and eating
72 El almuerzo y la cena • Lunch and dinner

66.1 **EL TÉ** • TEA

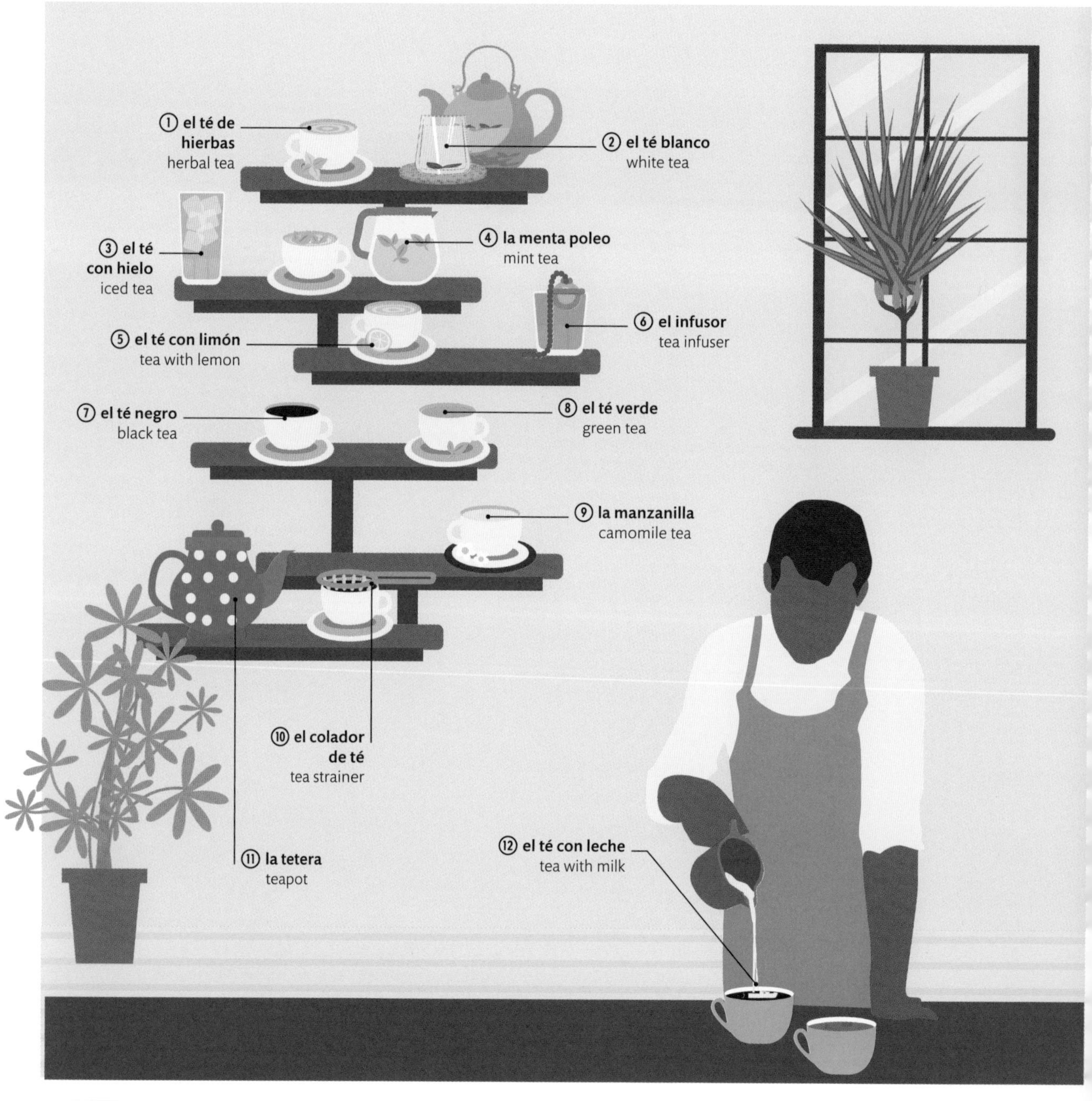

Las golosinas
Sweets

See also
48 El supermercado • The supermarket
62-63 La panadería • The bakery

67.1 LA TIENDA DE GOLOSINAS • SWEET SHOP

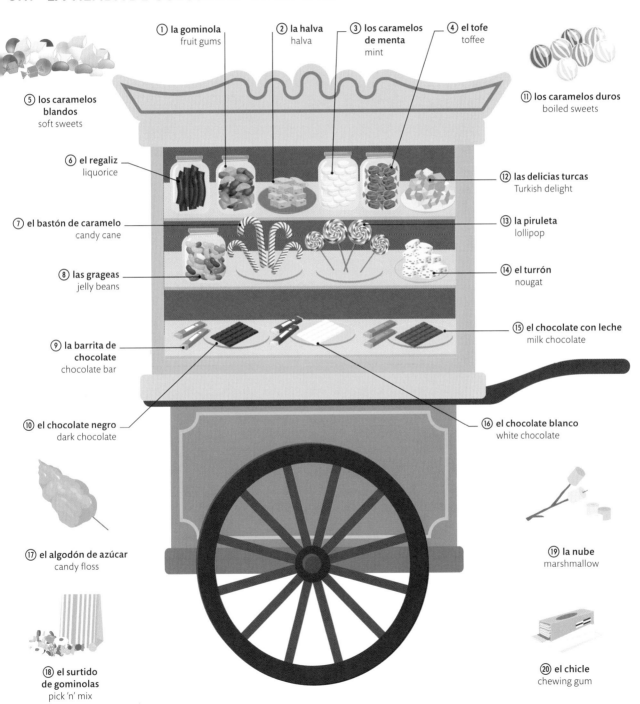

⑤ **los caramelos blandos**
soft sweets

⑪ **los caramelos duros**
boiled sweets

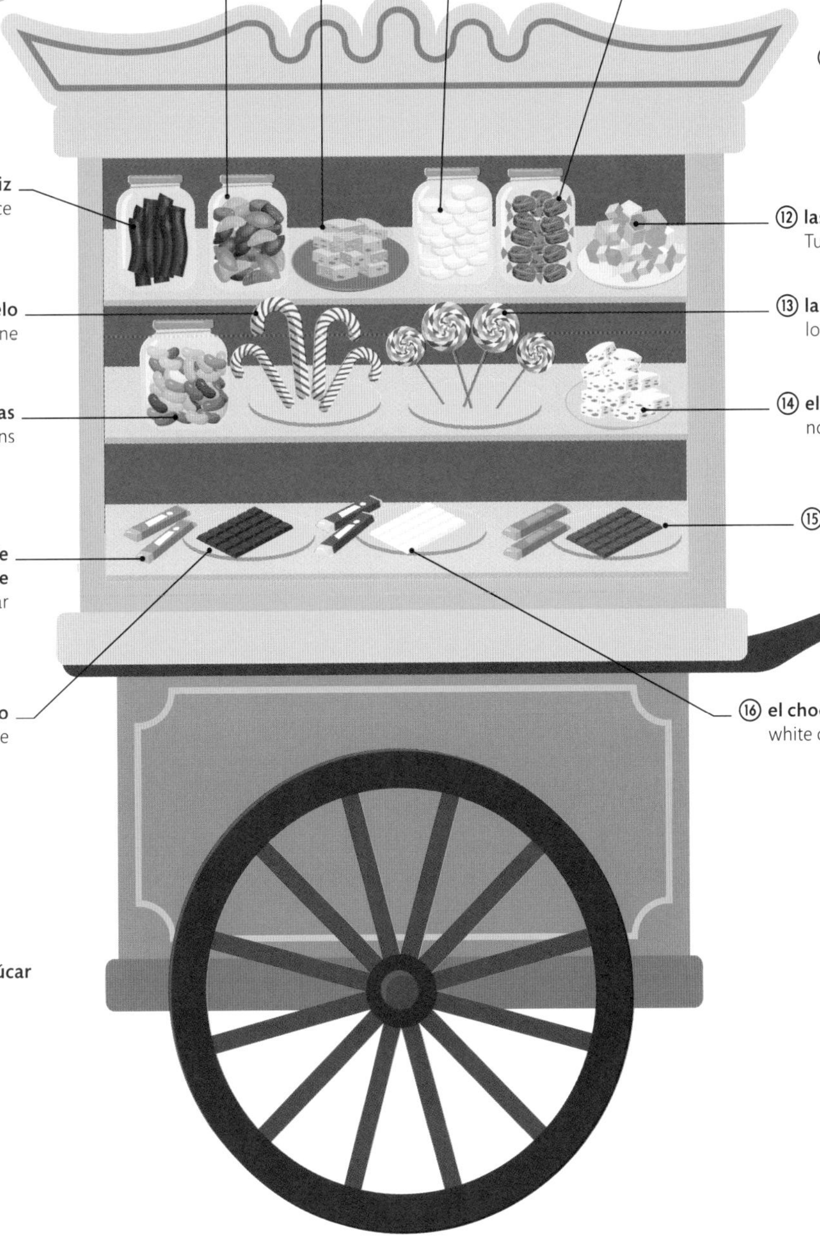

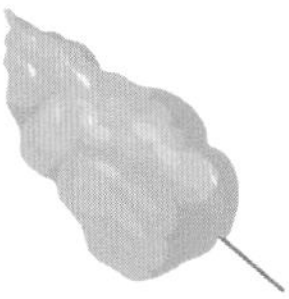
⑰ **el algodón de azúcar**
candy floss

⑲ **la nube**
marshmallow

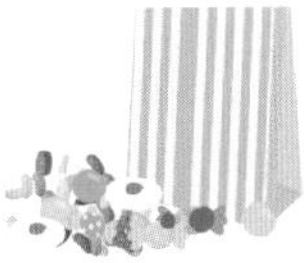
⑱ **el surtido de gominolas**
pick 'n' mix

⑳ **el chicle**
chewing gum

68 En el bar
At the bar

68.1 EL BAR · BAR

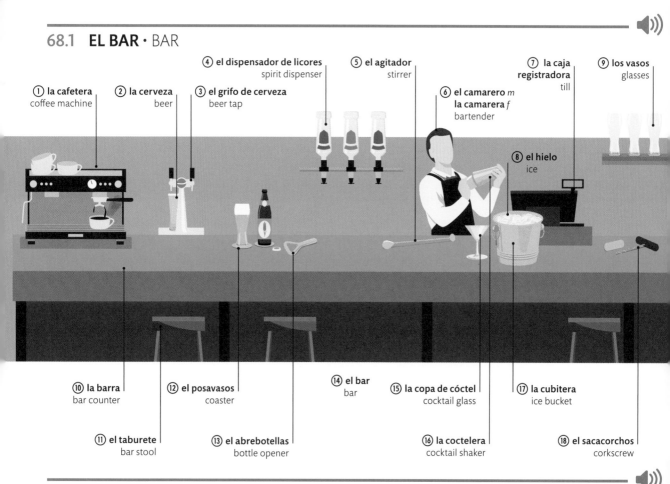

① la cafetera — coffee machine
② la cerveza — beer
③ el grifo de cerveza — beer tap
④ el dispensador de licores — spirit dispenser
⑤ el agitador — stirrer
⑥ el camarero *m* / la camarera *f* — bartender
⑦ la caja registradora — till
⑧ el hielo — ice
⑨ los vasos — glasses
⑩ la barra — bar counter
⑪ el taburete — bar stool
⑫ el posavasos — coaster
⑬ el abrebotellas — bottle opener
⑭ el bar — bar
⑮ la copa de cóctel — cocktail glass
⑯ la coctelera — cocktail shaker
⑰ la cubitera — ice bucket
⑱ el sacacorchos — corkscrew

68.2 LA CERVEZA Y EL VINO · BEER AND WINE

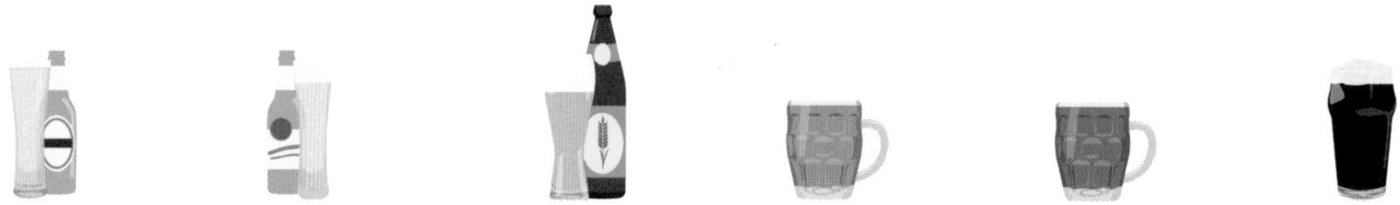

① la cerveza lager — lager
② la cerveza pilsener — Pilsner
③ la cerveza de trigo — wheat beer
④ la cerveza IPA — Indian pale ale (IPA)
⑤ la cerveza ale — ale
⑥ la cerveza negra — stout

⑦ la cerveza sin alcohol — alcohol-free beer
⑧ el vino tinto — red wine
⑨ el vino blanco — white wine
⑩ el vino rosado — rosé
⑪ el vino espumoso — sparkling wine
⑫ el champán — Champagne

See also
52 Beber y comer • Drinking and eating **69** En el restaurante At the restaurant **72** El almuerzo y la cena • Lunch and dinner

68.3 LAS BEBIDAS • DRINKS

① **el agua mineral** *f*
mineral water

② **la sidra**
cider

③ **el ron**
rum

④ **el ron con cola**
rum and cola

⑤ **el vodka**
vodka

⑥ **el vodka con naranja**
vodka and orange

⑦ **el gin-tonic**
gin and tonic

⑧ **el martini**
Martini

⑨ **el cóctel**
cocktail

⑩ **el cóctel sin alcohol**
mocktail

⑪ **el jerez**
sherry

⑫ **el oporto**
port

⑬ **el whisky**
whisky

⑭ **el whisky escocés con agua**
Scotch and water

⑮ **el brandy**
brandy

⑯ **el licor**
liqueur

⑰ **con hielo**
with ice

⑱ **sin hielo**
without ice

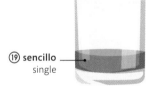

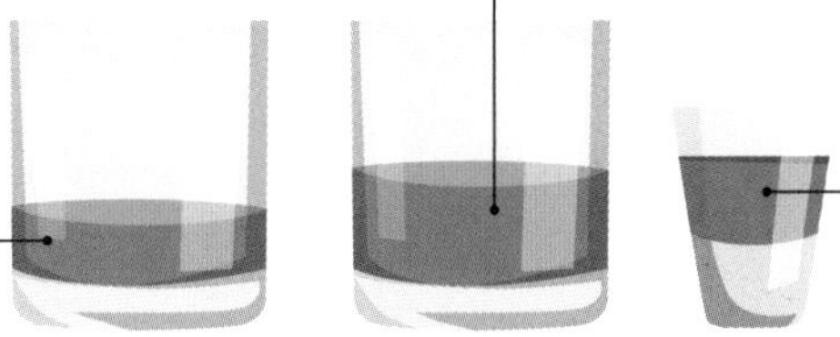

⑲ **sencillo**
single

⑳ **doble**
double

㉑ **el chupito**
shot

㉒ **la medida**
measure

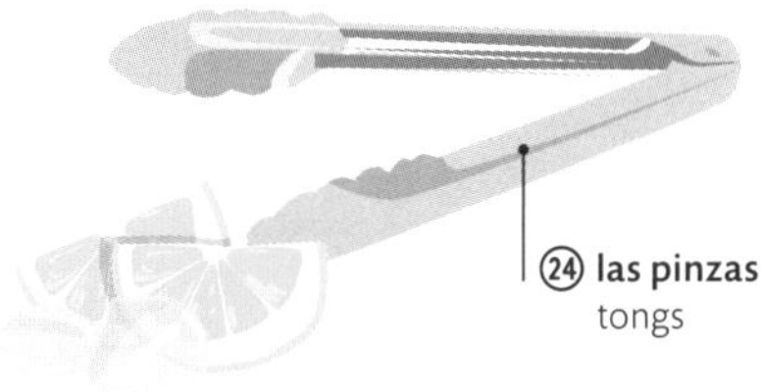

㉔ **las pinzas**
tongs

㉓ **el hielo y el limón**
ice and lemon

68.4 LOS APERITIVOS • BAR SNACKS

① **las patatas fritas**
crisps

② **los frutos secos**
nuts

③ **las almendras**
almonds

④ **los anacardos**
cashew nuts

⑤ **los cacahuetes**
peanuts

⑥ **las aceitunas**
olives

69 En el restaurante
At the restaurant

69.1 **EL RESTAURANTE** · RESTAURANT

⑱ **el menú del día**
set menu

⑲ **el brunch**
brunch

⑳ **el almuerzo**
lunch menu

㉑ **el menú a la carta**
à la carte menu

㉒ **los platos del día**
specials

㉓ **el menú infantil**
child's meal

㉔ **el bufét**
buffet

㉕ **la comida de tres platos**
three-course meal

㉖ **la sopa**
soup

㉗ **el entrante**
starter

㉘ **el plato principal**
main course

㉙ **la guarnición**
side / side order

㉚ **la tabla de quesos**
cheese platter

㉛ **el postre**
dessert / pudding

㉜ **la bebida**
beverage

㉝ **el café**
coffee

㉞ **el digestivo**
digestif

See also
27 La cocina y la vajilla • Kitchen and tableware **52** Beber y comer • Drinking and eating **53** La carne • Meat **54** El pescado y el marisco • Fish and seafood **55-56** La verdura • Vegetables **72** El almuerzo y la cena • Lunch and dinner

㉟ **el sumiller**
sommelier

㊱ **comer fuera**
to eat out

㊲ **reservar**
to make a reservation

㊳ **cancelar**
to cancel

㊴ **pedir**
to order

㊵ **la cuenta**
bill

㊶ **pagar por separado**
to pay separately

㊷ **pagar a medias**
to split the bill

㊸ **el servicio**
service charge

㊹ **servicio incluido**
service included

㊺ **servicio no incluido**
service not included

㊻ **la propina**
tip

㊼ **el recibo**
receipt

㊽ **el bistró**
bistro

70 La comida rápida
Fast food

70.1 EN EL RESTAURANTE DE COMIDA RÁPIDA
IN A FAST-FOOD RESTAURANT

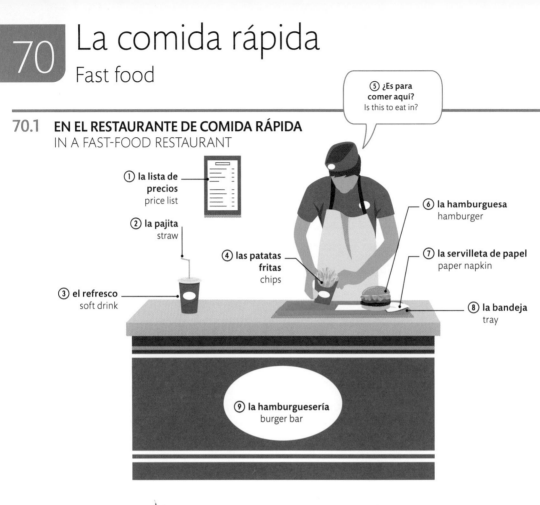

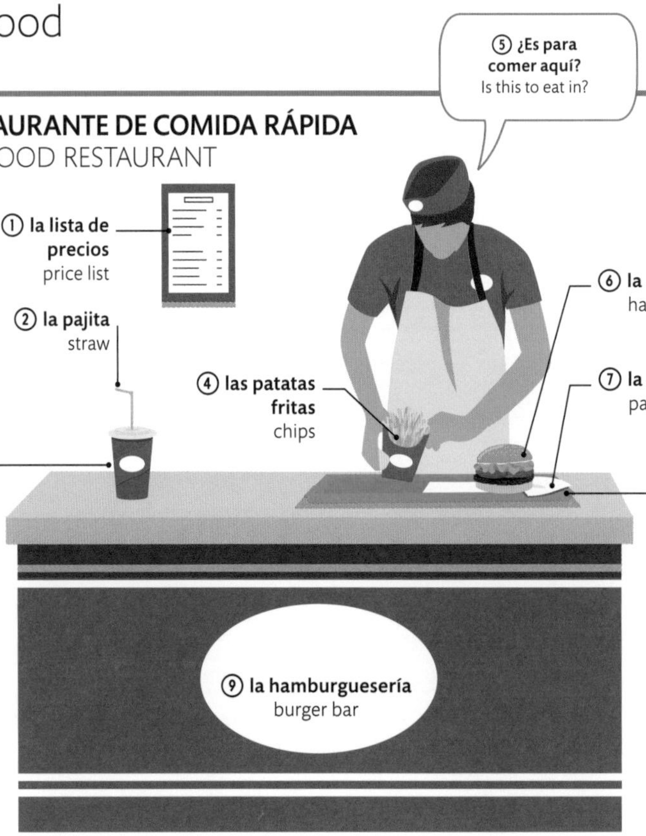

⑩ **comer en el local**
to eat in

⑪ **para llevar**
take-away

⑫ **a domicilio**
home delivery

⑭ **el menú**
menu

⑮ **el batido**
milkshake

⑯ **la bebida en lata**
canned drink

⑰ **el refresco**
fizzy drink

⑬ **el puesto callejero**
street stall

⑱ **el combo**
meal deal

⑲ **el vaso reutilizable**
reusable cup

⑳ **la salsa**
sauce

㉑ **la furgoneta de comida / el food truck**
food van

㉒ **el gofre**
waffle

㉓ **el helado**
ice cream

㉔ **la magdalena**
muffin

㉕ **el dónut**
doughnut

㉖ **el repartidor de comida a domicilio**
food delivery driver

See also
52 Beber y comer • Drinking and eating **60** La despensa • In the pantry
65 En la cafetería • At the café **67** Las golosinas • Sweets

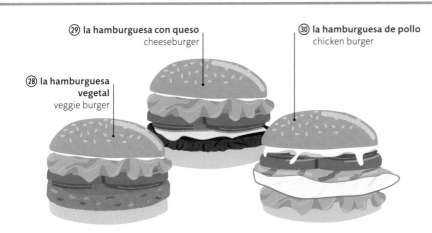

㉙ **la hamburguesa con queso**
cheeseburger

㉚ **la hamburguesa de pollo**
chicken burger

㉘ **la hamburguesa vegetal**
veggie burger

㉛ **la hamburguesa**
burger

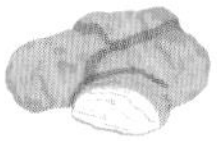

㉜ **los nuggets de pollo**
chicken nuggets

㉝ **el pollo frito**
fried chicken

㉞ **las tortitas de patata**
hash browns

㉟ **el pescado frito con patatas**
fish and chips

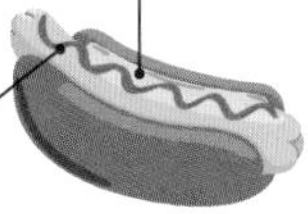

㊳ **la mostaza**
mustard

㊲ **el kétchup**
ketchup

㊱ **el perrito caliente**
hot dog

㊴ **el kebab**
kebab

㊵ **las costillas**
ribs

㊶ **los fideos**
noodles

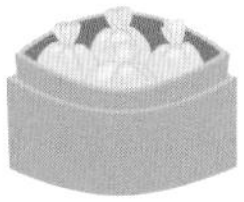

㊷ **los dumplings**
dumplings

㊸ **la empanada**
empanada

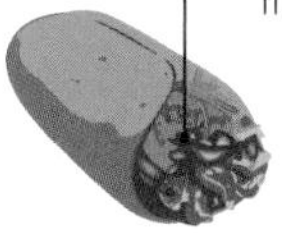

㊺ **el relleno**
filling

㊹ **el wrap**
wrap

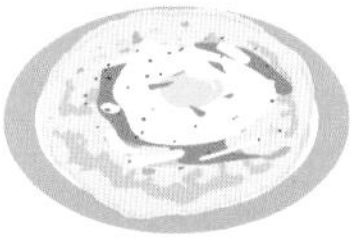

㊻ **la crep**
crêpe

㊼ **el taco**
taco

㊽ **el falafel**
falafel

㊾ **los nachos**
nachos

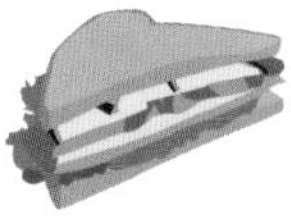

㊿ **el sándwich / el bocadillo**
sandwich

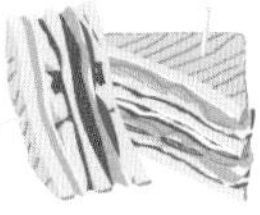

(51) **el sándwich club**
club sandwich

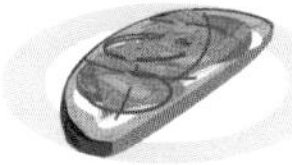

(52) **la tosta**
open sandwich

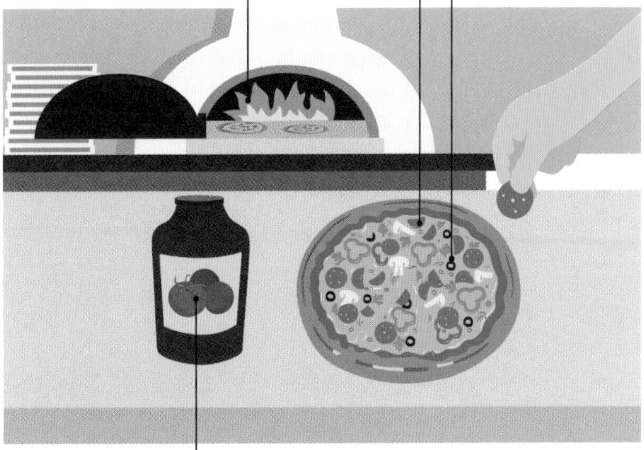

(53) **el horno de pizza**
pizza oven

(54) **la pizza**
pizza

(55) **los ingredientes**
topping

(56) **la salsa de tomate**
tomato sauce

(57) **la pizzería**
pizzeria

71 El desayuno
Breakfast

71.1 EL BUFÉT DE DESAYUNO · BREAKFAST BUFFET

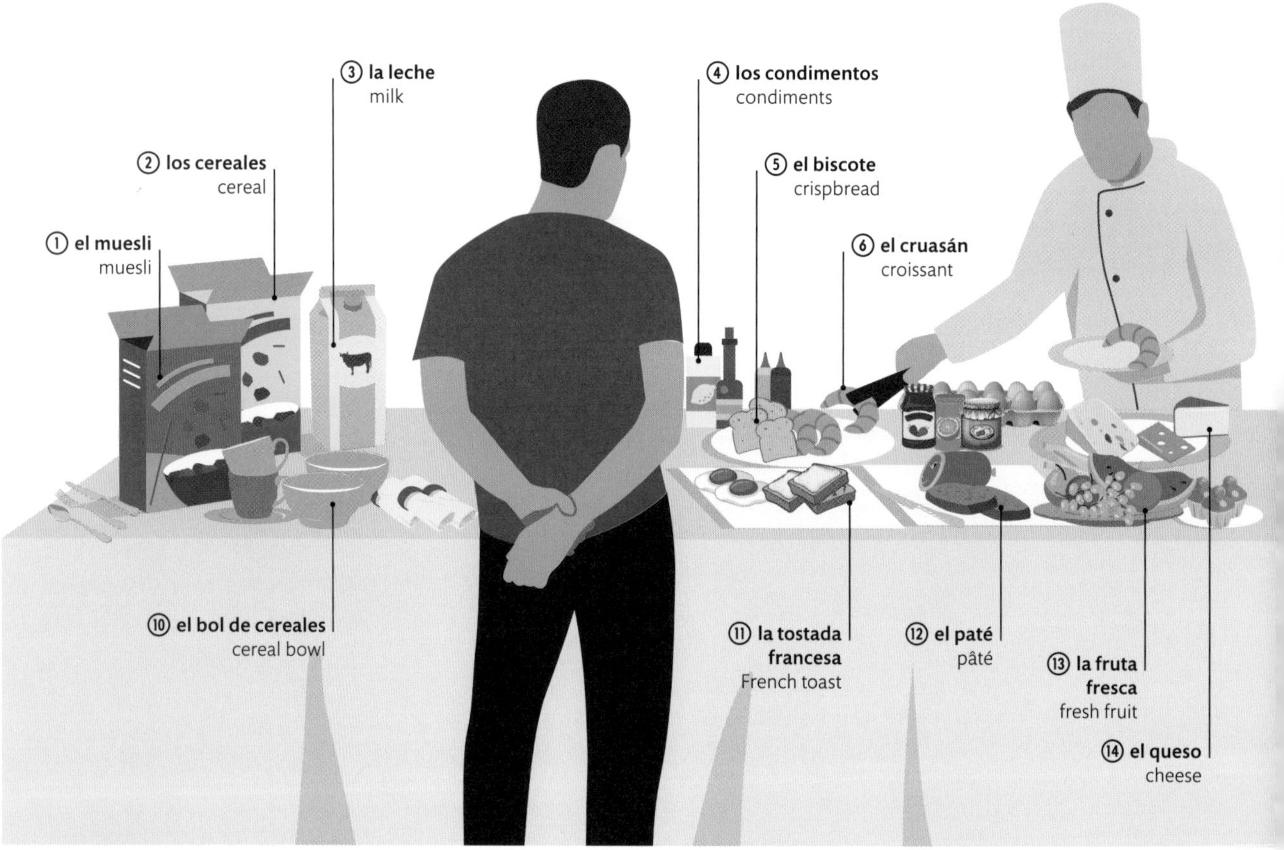

⑰ **el jamón**
ham

⑱ **el sándwich tostado**
toasted sandwich

⑲ **la tortilla**
omelette

⑳ **la tostada con aguacate**
avocado toast

㉑ **la rosca**
bagel

㉒ **los rollos de canela**
cinnamon rolls

㉕ **la mermelada**
jam

㉖ **la mermelada de cítricos**
marmalade

㉗ **la miel**
honey

㉘ **el té**
tea

㉙ **el café**
coffee

㉚ **el zumo de fruta**
fruit juice

See also
29 La cocina • Cooking **52** Beber y comer • Drinking and eating **53** La carne • Meat
57 La fruta • Fruit **57** La fruta y los frutos secos • Fruit and nuts **61** Los productos lácteos
Dairy produce **64** Las delicatessen • The delicatessen **65-66** En la cafetería • At the café

⑨ **la cesta de pan**
bread basket

⑦ **el fiambre**
cold meats

⑧ **el brioche**
brioche

⑯ **el pan**
bread

⑮ **la mantequilla**
butter

㉓ **los gofres**
waffles

㉔ **la nata**
cream

㉛ **la fruta deshidratada**
dried fruit

㉜ **el yogur de frutas**
fruit yoghurt

71.2 EL DESAYUNO COCINADO • COOKED BREAKFAST

① **la salchicha**
sausage

② **la hamburguesa de salchicha**
sausage patties

③ **el beicon**
bacon

④ **el arenque ahumado**
kippers

⑤ **el salmón ahumado**
smoked salmon

⑥ **la caballa ahumada**
smoked mackerel

⑦ **la morcilla**
black pudding / blood sausage

⑧ **los riñones**
kidneys

⑨ **los huevos revueltos**
scrambled eggs

⑩ **el huevo escalfado**
poached egg

⑪ **el huevo cocido**
boiled egg

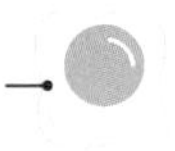

⑫ **la clara**
egg white

⑬ **la yema**
yolk

⑭ **el huevo frito**
fried egg

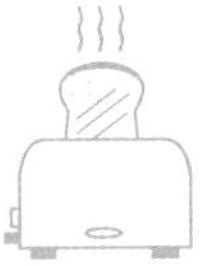

⑮ **la tostada**
toast

⑯ **los champiñones salteados**
fried mushrooms

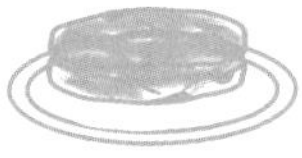

⑰ **las tortitas de patata**
hash browns

⑱ **el tomate a la parrilla**
grilled tomato

⑲ **el tomate en conserva**
tinned tomato

⑳ **las alubias con tomate**
baked beans

㉑ **el panecillo de desayuno**
breakfast roll

㉒ **el burrito de desayuno**
breakfast burrito

㉓ **los pastelitos de patata**
potato cakes

㉔ **las tortitas**
pancakes

㉕ **las gachas**
porridge

72 El almuerzo y la cena
Lunch and dinner

72.1 LAS COMIDAS Y LOS PLATOS · MEALS AND DISHES

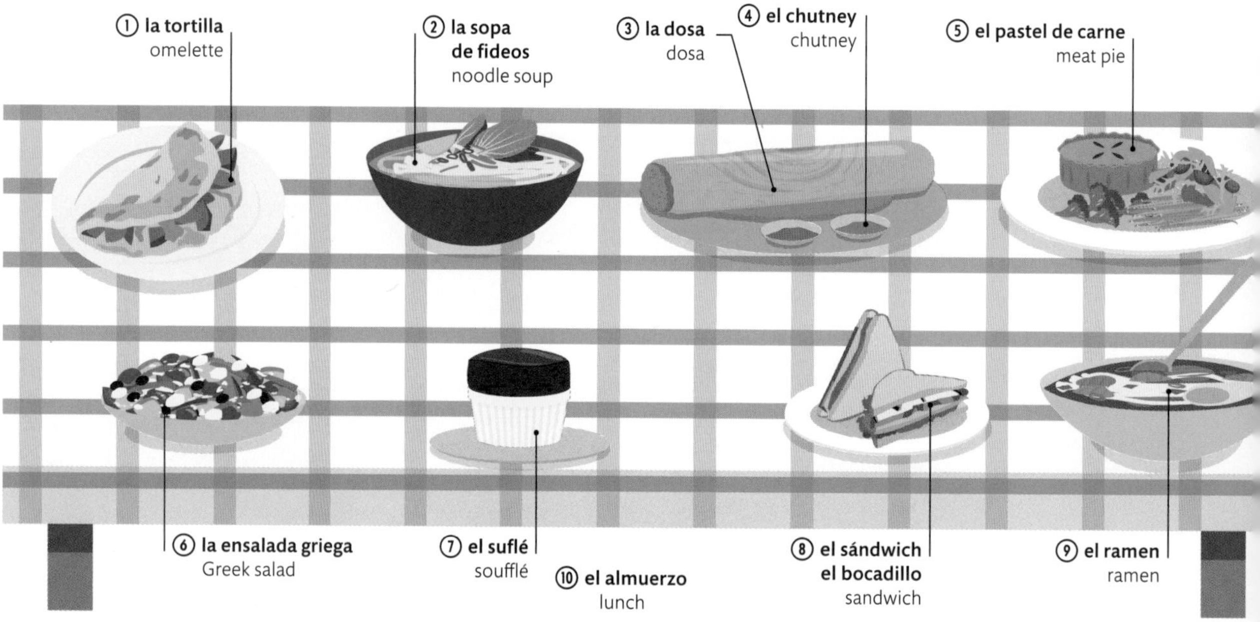

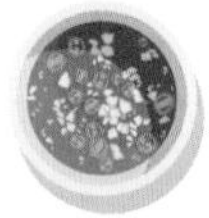

⑪ **la sopa**
soup

⑫ **las verduras cocidas**
cooked vegetables

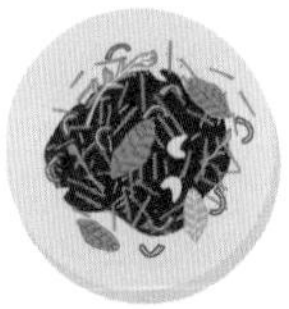

⑭ **el salteado**
stir-fry

⑮ **el rollo de verano**
summer roll

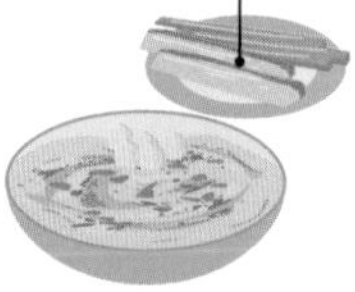

⑰ **el hummus**
hummus

⑲ **el pan de pita**
pitta bread

⑳ **el arroz**
rice

㉑ **el risotto**
risotto

㉒ **la paella**
paella

㉓ **la pasta**
pasta

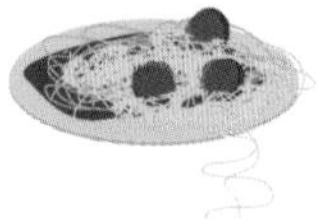

㉔ **las albóndigas**
meatballs

㉕ **los fideos**
noodles

㉖ **la guarnición**
side dishes

㉗ **los rollitos de primavera**
spring roll

㉘ **la ensalada picada**
chopped salad

㉙ **el aliño**
dressing

㉚ **los encurtidos**
pickles

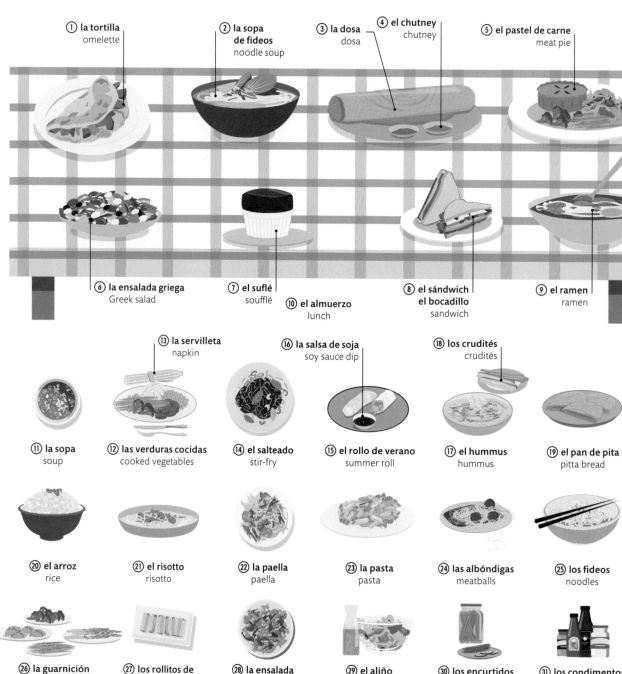

㉛ **los condimentos**
condiments

See also
27 La cocina y la vajilla • Kitchen and tableware **29** La cocina • Cooking **52** Beber y comer • Drinking and eating **53** La carne • Meat **55-56** La verdura • Vegetables **65-66** En la cafetería • At the café **69** En el restaurante • At the restaurant

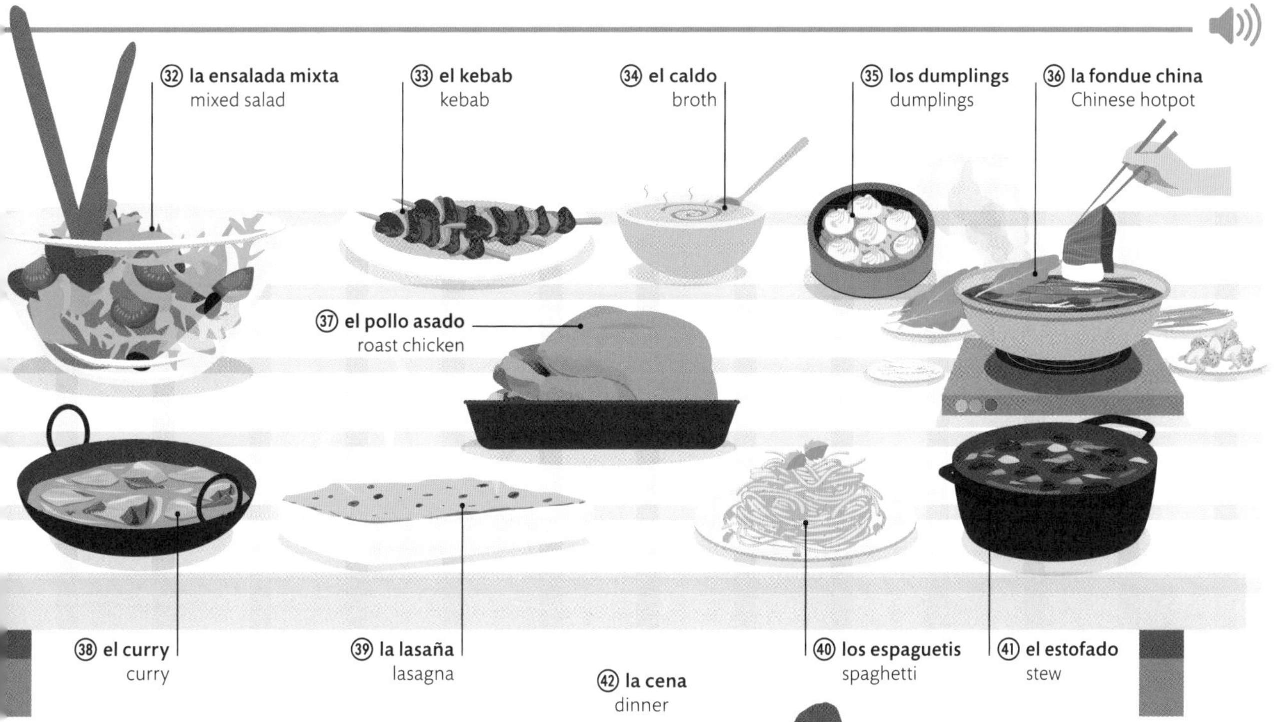

72.2 LA PREPARACIÓN DE LOS ALIMENTOS
FOOD PREPARATION

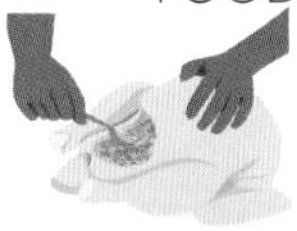

① **relleno** *m* **rellena f** stuffed

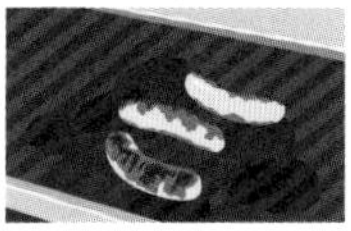

② **a la parrilla** grilled

③ **marinado** *m* **marinada** *f* marinated

④ **en salsa** in sauce

⑤ **escalfado** *m* **escalfada** *f* poached

⑥ **hervido** *m* **hervida** *f* boiled

⑦ **horneado** *m* **horneada** *f* baked

⑧ **salteado** *m* / **salteada** *f* stir-fried

⑨ **frito** *m* / **frita** *f* fried

⑩ **frito con mucho aceite** deep-fried

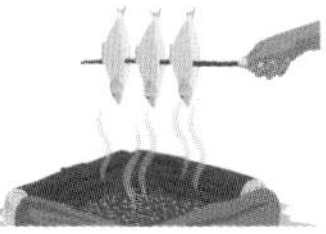

⑪ **ahumado** *m* **ahumada** *f* smoked

⑫ **al vapor** steamed

⑬ **machacado** *m* **machacada** *f* mashed

⑭ **aliñado** *m* **aliñada** *f* dressed

⑮ **curado** *m* **curada** *f* cured

⑯ **en vinagre** pickled

⑰ **kosher** kosher

⑱ **halal** halal

73 En la escuela
At school

73.1 LA ESCUELA Y LOS ESTUDIOS · SCHOOL AND STUDY

① **la escuela**
school

② **el aula** *f*
classroom

③ **la clase**
class

④ **el profesor** *m*
la profesora *f*
teacher

⑤ **la pizarra**
whiteboard

⑥ **el alumno** *m*
la alumna *f*
pupil

⑦ **el escritorio**
desk

⑧ **los estudiantes**
school students

⑨ **la mochila**
school bag

⑩ **la literatura**
literature

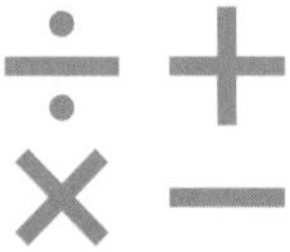
⑪ **las matemáticas**
maths

⑫ **la geografía**
geography

⑬ **la historia**
history

⑭ **la ciencia**
science

⑮ **la química**
chemistry

⑯ **la física**
physics

⑰ **la biología**
biology

⑱ **el inglés**
English

⑲ **los idiomas**
languages

⑳ **el diseño y la tecnología**
design and technology

㉑ **la informática**
information technology

㉒ **el arte**
art

㉓ **la música**
music

㉔ **el teatro**
drama

㉕ **la educación física**
physical education

㉖ **el director** *m*
la directora *f*
head teacher /principal

㉗ **los deberes**
homework

㉘ **la lección**
lesson

㉙ **el examen**
exam

㉚ **la redacción**
essay

㉛ **la nota**
grade

㉜ **la enciclopedia**
encyclopedia

㉝ **el diccionario**
dictionary

㉞ **el atlas**
atlas

㉟ **el examen**
test

See also
74 Las matemáticas • Mathematics **75** La física • Physics **76** La química • Chemistry
77 La biología • Biology **79** La historia • History **80** En la universidad • At college
83 Los ordenadores y la tecnología • Computers and technology

73.2 LOS VERBOS DE LA ESCUELA
SCHOOL VERBS

① **leer**
to read

② **escribir**
to write

③ **preguntar**
to question

④ **hacer un examen**
to take an exam

⑤ **aprender**
to learn

⑥ **dibujar**
to draw

⑦ **responder**
to answer

⑧ **deletrear**
to spell

⑨ **repasar**
to revise

⑩ **repetir**
to resit

⑪ **tomar apuntes**
to take notes

⑫ **discutir**
to discuss

⑬ **suspender**
to fail

⑭ **aprobar**
to pass

⑮ **He aprobado el examen.**
I've passed my test.

73.3 EL MATERIAL ESCOLAR
EQUIPMENT

① **el lápiz**
pencil

② **el sacapuntas**
pencil sharpener

③ **el bolígrafo**
pen

④ **el plumín**
nib

⑤ **la goma de borrar**
rubber

⑥ **los lápices de colores**
coloured pencils

⑦ **el estuche**
pencil case

⑧ **la regla**
ruler

⑨ **el cartabón**
set square

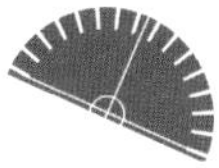
⑩ **el transportador**
protractor

⑪ **la calculadora**
calculator

⑫ **el compás**
compass

⑬ **el libro de texto**
textbook

⑭ **la libreta**
notebook / exercise book

⑮ **el proyector digital**
digital projector

⑯ **el subrayador**
highlighter

⑰ **el clip**
paper clip

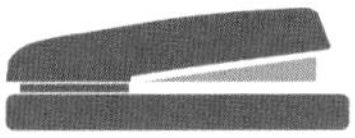
⑱ **la grapadora**
stapler

74 Las matemáticas
Mathematics

74.1 LAS FORMAS · SHAPES

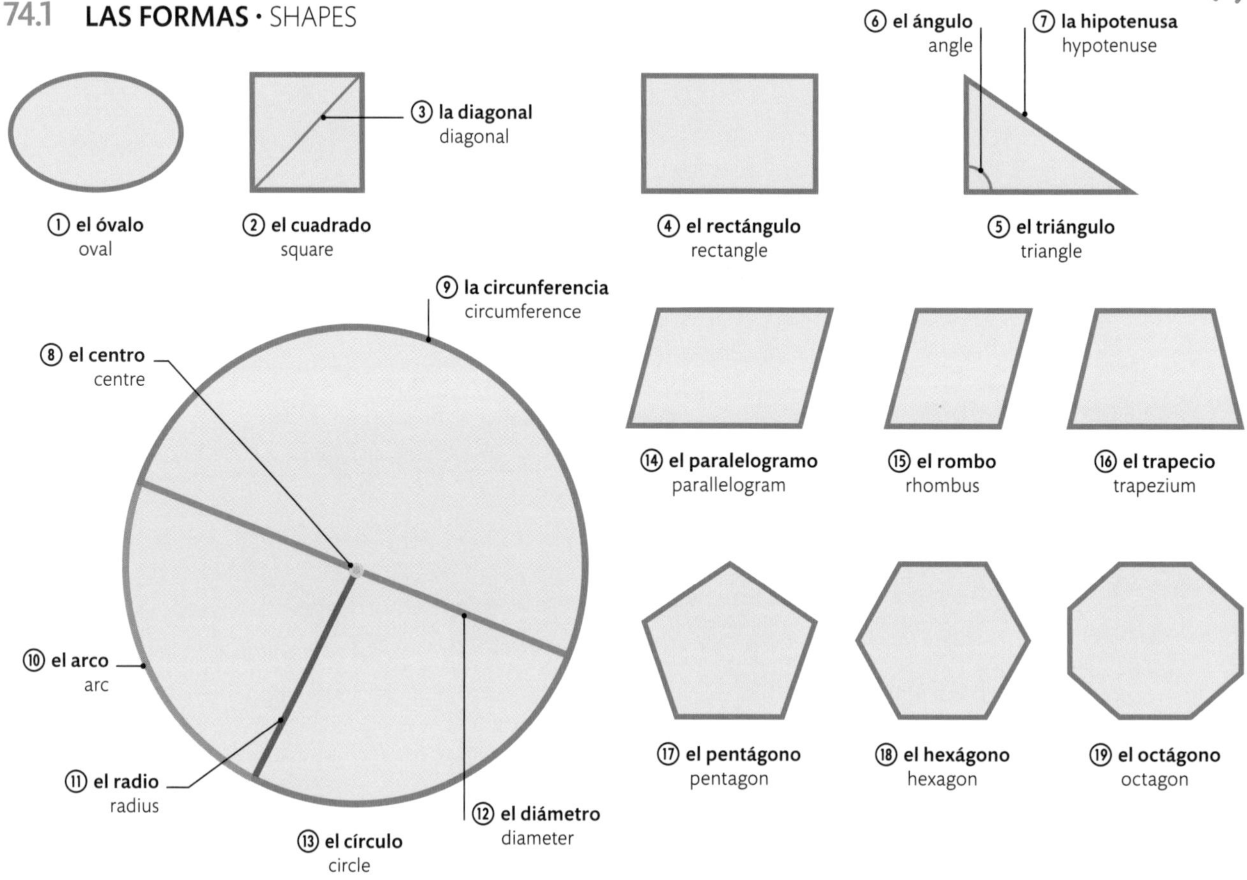

74.2 LAS FIGURAS ESPACIALES · SOLIDS

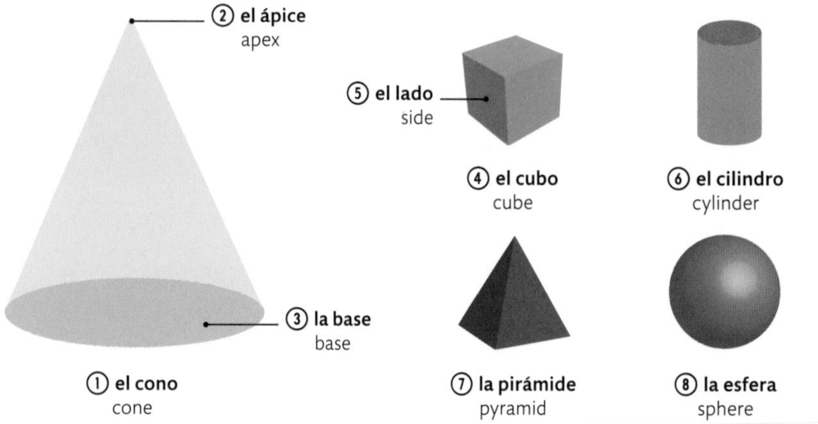

74.3 LAS LÍNEAS · LINES

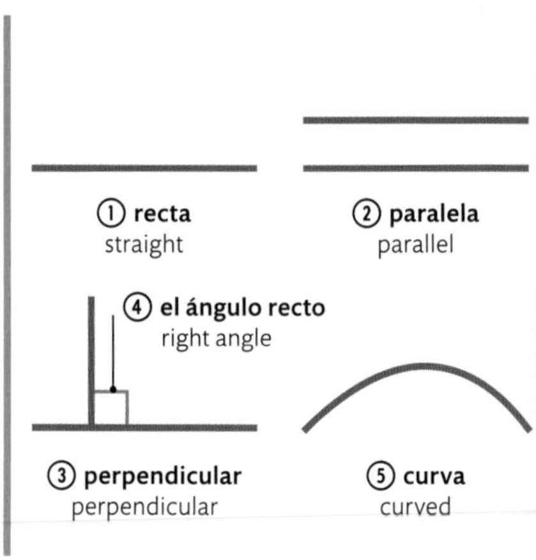

See also
73 En la escuela • At school **94** El dinero y las finanzas • Money and finance
173 Los números • Numbers **174** Los pesos y las medidas • Weights and measures

74.4 LAS UNIDADES DE MEDIDA • MEASUREMENTS

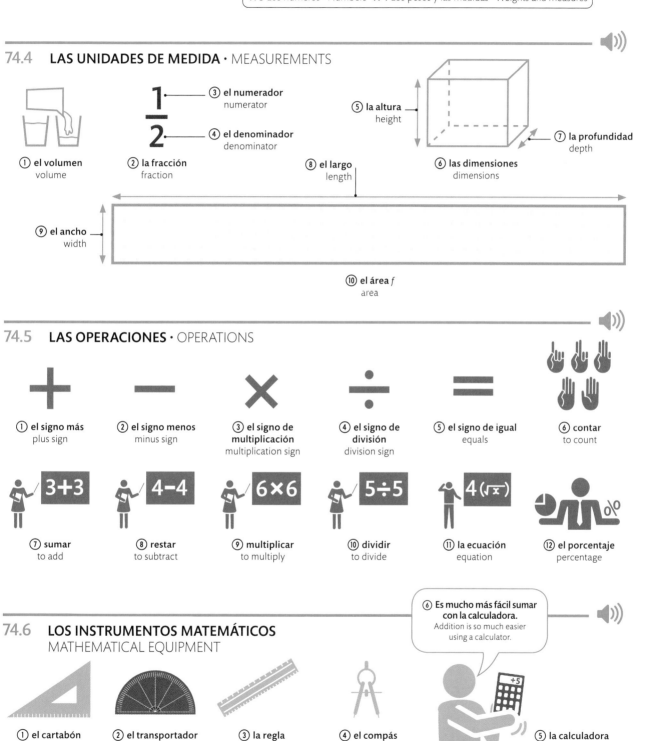

① **el volumen**
volume

$\frac{1}{2}$

② **la fracción**
fraction

③ **el numerador**
numerator

④ **el denominador**
denominator

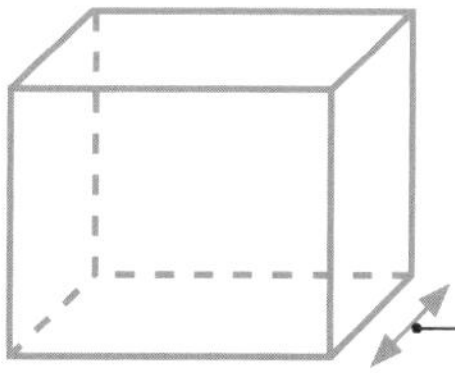

⑤ **la altura**
height

⑥ **las dimensiones**
dimensions

⑦ **la profundidad**
depth

⑧ **el largo**
length

⑨ **el ancho**
width

⑩ **el área** *f*
area

74.5 LAS OPERACIONES • OPERATIONS

$+$

① **el signo más**
plus sign

$-$

② **el signo menos**
minus sign

$\times$

③ **el signo de multiplicación**
multiplication sign

$\div$

④ **el signo de división**
division sign

$=$

⑤ **el signo de igual**
equals

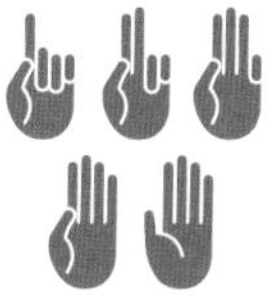

⑥ **contar**
to count

⑦ **sumar**
to add

⑧ **restar**
to subtract

⑨ **multiplicar**
to multiply

⑩ **dividir**
to divide

⑪ **la ecuación**
equation

⑫ **el porcentaje**
percentage

74.6 LOS INSTRUMENTOS MATEMÁTICOS
MATHEMATICAL EQUIPMENT

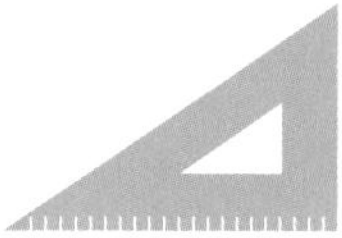

① **el cartabón**
set square

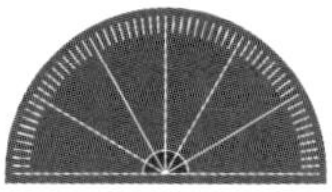

② **el transportador**
protractor

③ **la regla**
ruler

④ **el compás**
compass

⑥ **Es mucho más fácil sumar con la calculadora.**
Addition is so much easier using a calculator.

⑤ **la calculadora**
calculator

75 La física
Physics

75.1 LA FÍSICA · PHYSICS

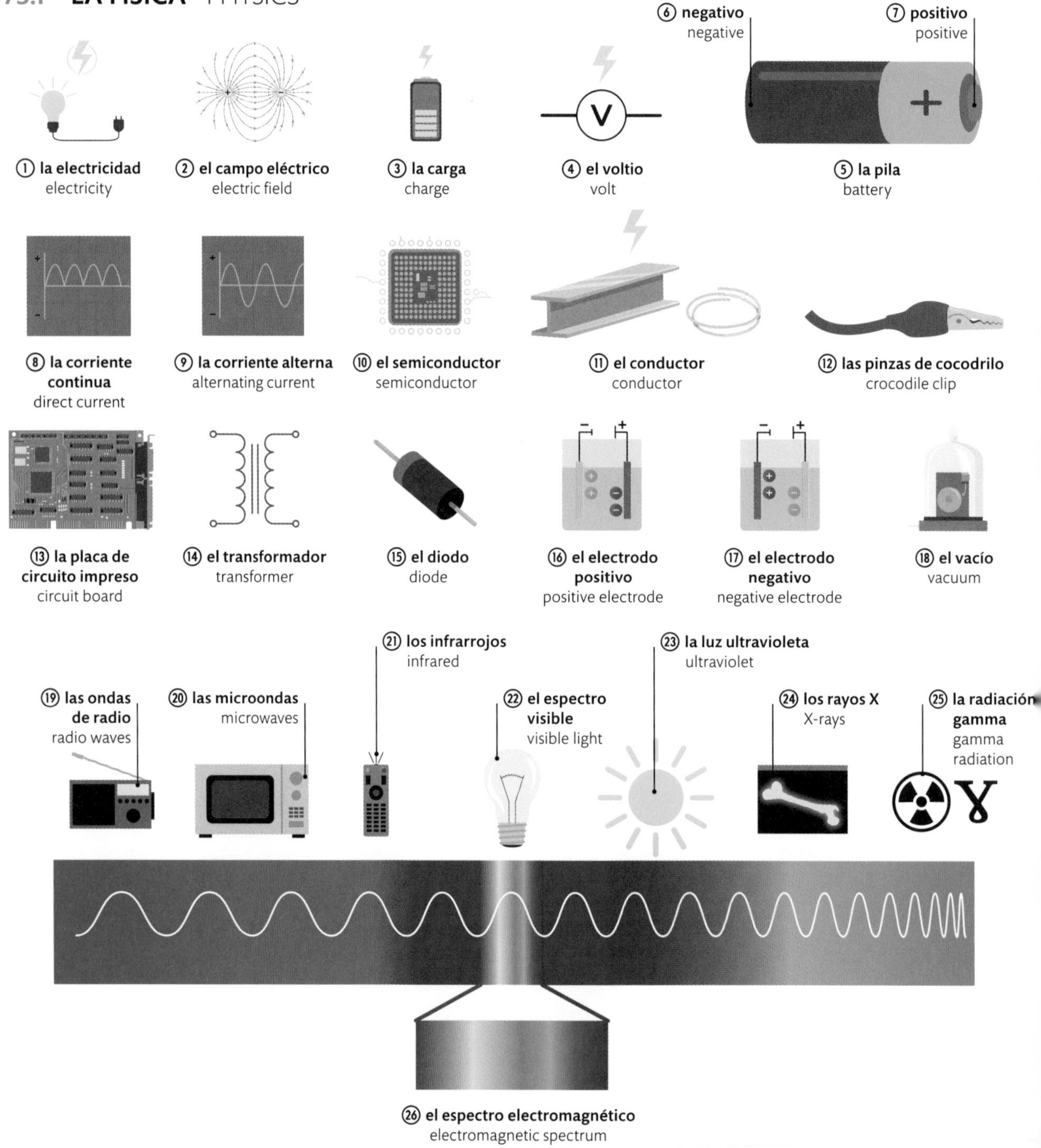

See also
73 En la escuela • At school **74** Las matemáticas • Mathematics **76** La química • Chemistry **77** La biología • Biology **78** La tabla periódica • The periodic table

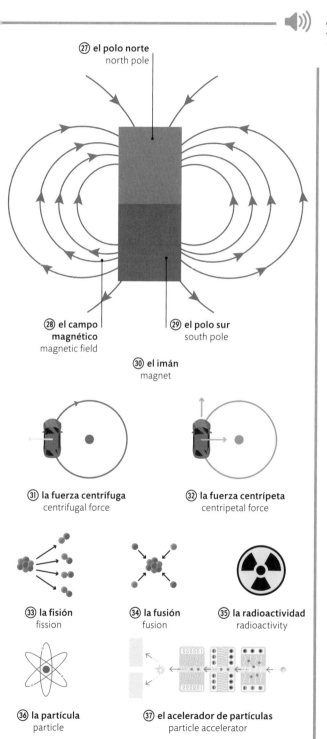

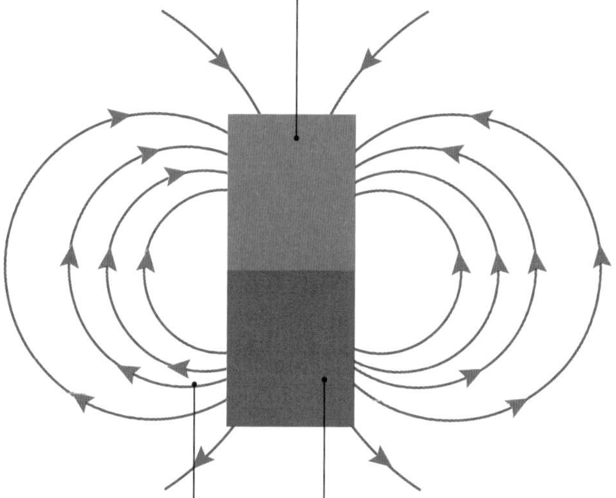

(27) **el polo norte**
north pole

(28) **el campo magnético**
magnetic field

(29) **el polo sur**
south pole

(30) **el imán**
magnet

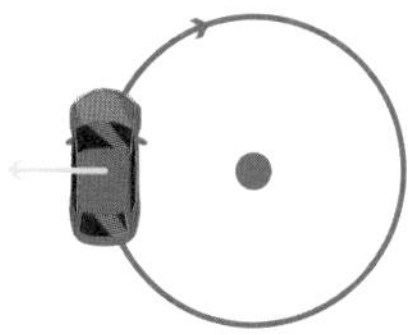

(31) **la fuerza centrífuga**
centrifugal force

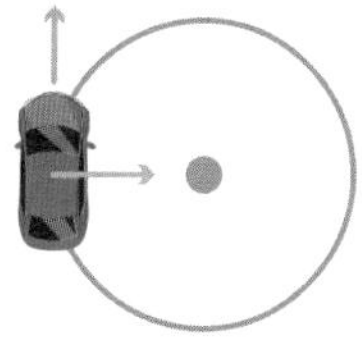

(32) **la fuerza centrípeta**
centripetal force

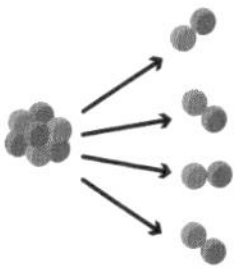

(33) **la fisión**
fission

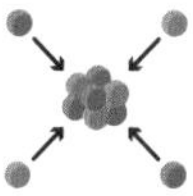

(34) **la fusión**
fusion

(35) **la radioactividad**
radioactivity

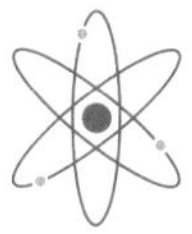

(36) **la partícula**
particle

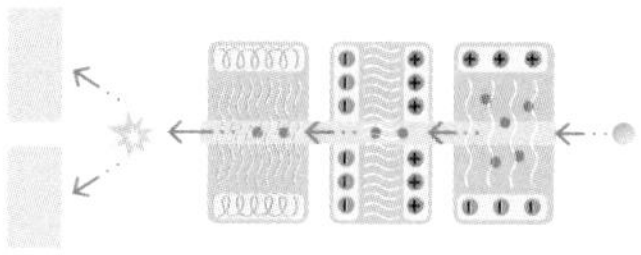

(37) **el acelerador de partículas**
particle accelerator

75.2 LA ÓPTICA • OPTICS

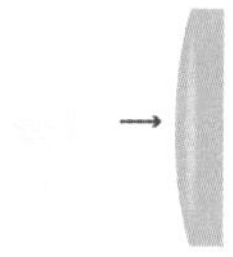

(1) **la lente**
lens

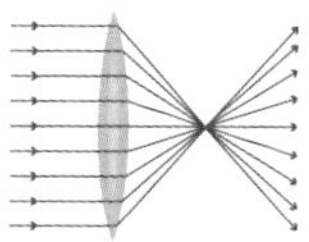

(2) **la lente convexa**
convex lens

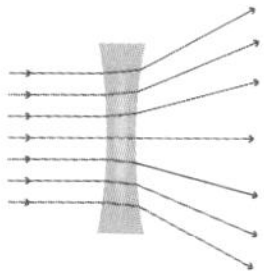

(3) **la lente cóncava**
concave lens

(4) **el láser**
laser

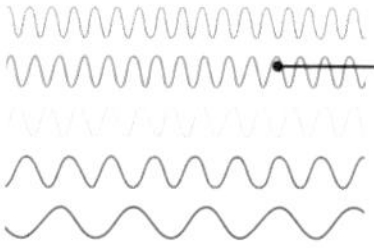

(5) **la onda**
wave

(6) **la longitud de onda**
wavelength

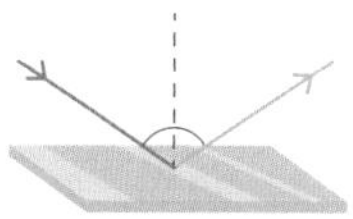

(7) **la reflexión**
reflection

(8) **la refracción**
refraction

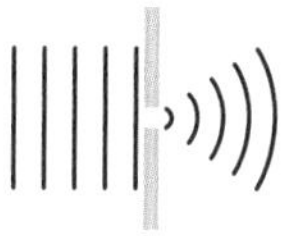

(9) **la difracción**
diffraction

(10) **el prisma**
prism

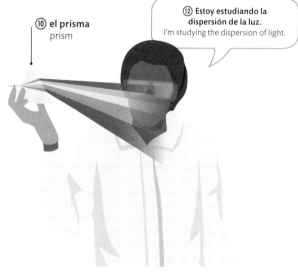

(12) **Estoy estudiando la dispersión de la luz.**
I'm studying the dispersion of light.

(11) **la dispersión**
dispersion

76 La química
Chemistry

76.1 EN EL LABORATORIO · IN THE LABORATORY

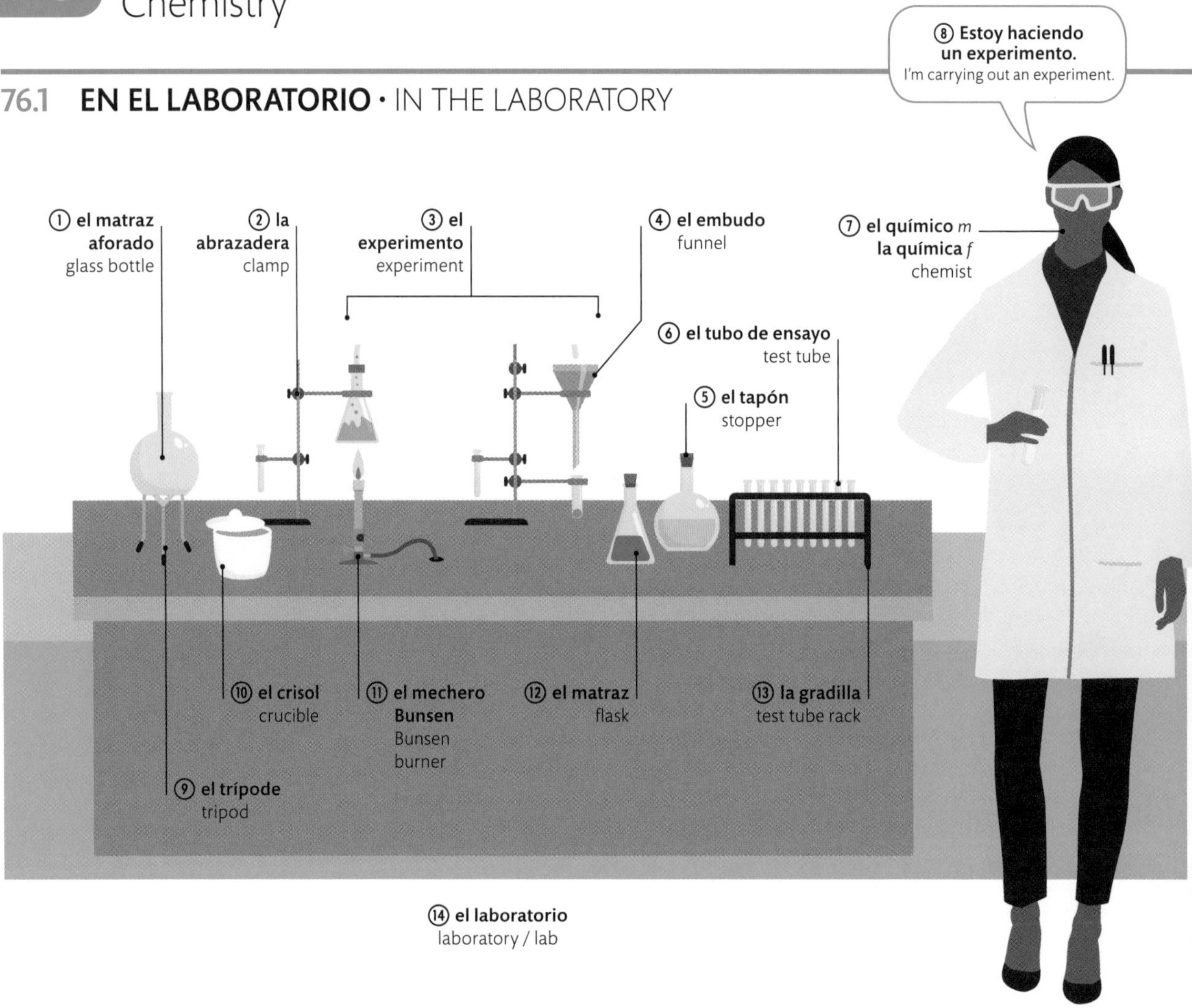

⑭ **el laboratorio**
laboratory / lab

⑮ **la balanza**
scales

⑯ **el temporizador**
timer

⑰ **el termómetro**
thermometer

⑱ **las pinzas**
tongs

⑲ **la espátula**
spatula

㉑ **el mortero**
mortar

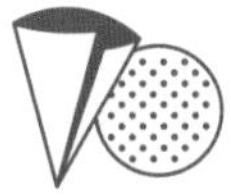

㉒ **el papel de filtro**
filter paper

㉓ **el cuentagotas**
dropper

㉔ **la pipeta**
pipette

㉕ **el vaso de precipitado**
beaker

㉖ **la varilla de vidrio**
glass rod

㉗ **las gafas de seguridad**
safety goggles

See also
73 En la escuela · At school **74** Las matemáticas · Mathematics **75** La física
Physics **77** La biología · Biology **78** La tabla periódica · The periodic table

2 moléculas de hidrógeno
2 hydrogen molecules

1 molécula de oxígeno
1 oxygen molecule

2 moléculas de agua
2 water molecules

32 **el protón**
proton

33 **el electrón**
electron

34 **el núcleo**
nucleus

35 **el neutrón**
neutron

31 **el átomo**
atom

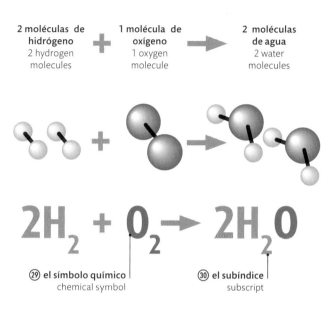

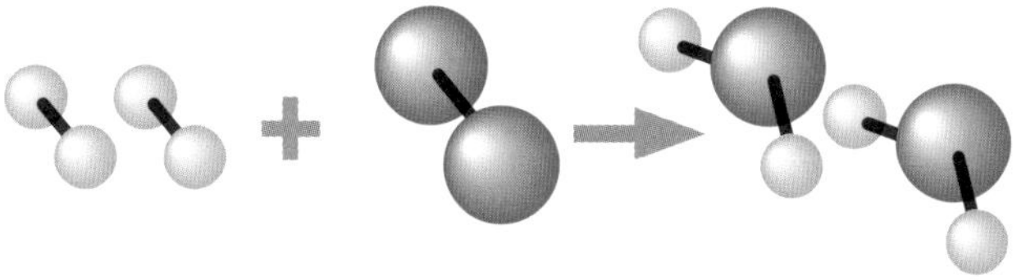

$$2H_2 + O_2 \rightarrow 2H_2O$$

29 **el símbolo químico**
chemical symbol

30 **el subíndice**
subscript

28 **la ecuación química**
chemical equation

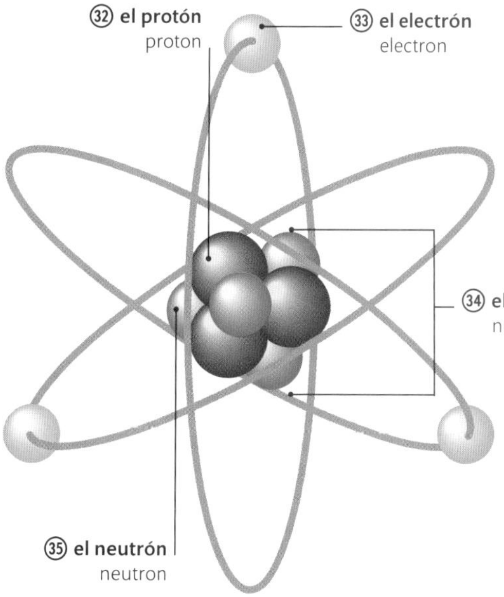

H_2O

36 **la fórmula química**
chemical formula

37 **los elementos**
elements

38 **la molécula**
molecule

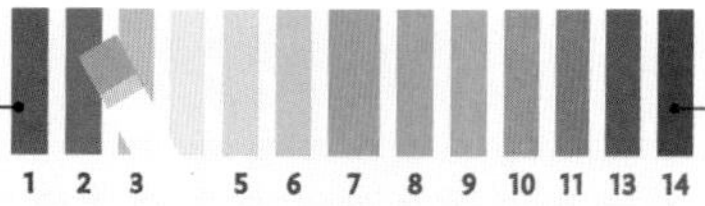

40 **el ácido**
acid

41 **el álcali**
alkali

1 2 3 5 6 7 8 9 10 11 13 14

39 **la escala de pH**
pH level

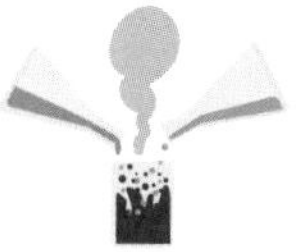

42 **la reacción**
reaction

Q<K

43 **la dirección de la reacción**
reaction direction

Q⇌K

44 **la reacción reversible**
reversible direction

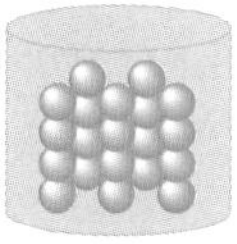

45 **el sólido**
solid

46 **el líquido**
liquid

47 **el gas**
gas

48 **el compuesto**
compound

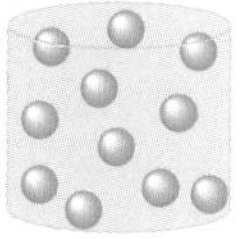

49 **la base**
base

50 **la difusión**
diffusion

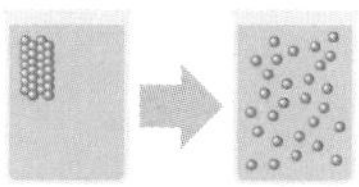

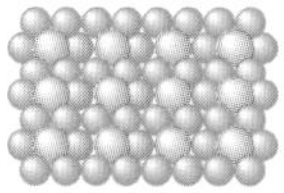

51 **la aleación**
alloy

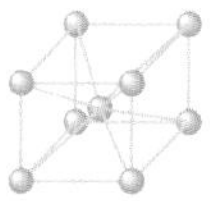

52 **el cristal**
crystal

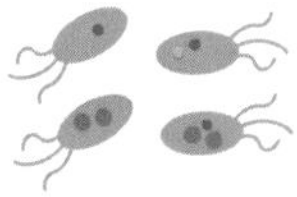

53 **la bioquímica**
biochemistry

77 La biología
Biology

77.1 LA BIOLOGÍA · BIOLOGY

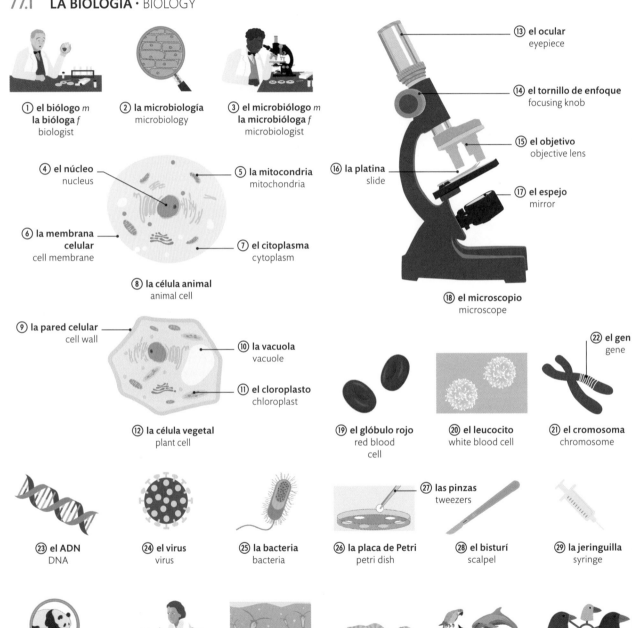

① **el biólogo** *m* **la bióloga** *f*
biologist

② **la microbiología**
microbiology

③ **el microbiólogo** *m* **la microbióloga** *f*
microbiologist

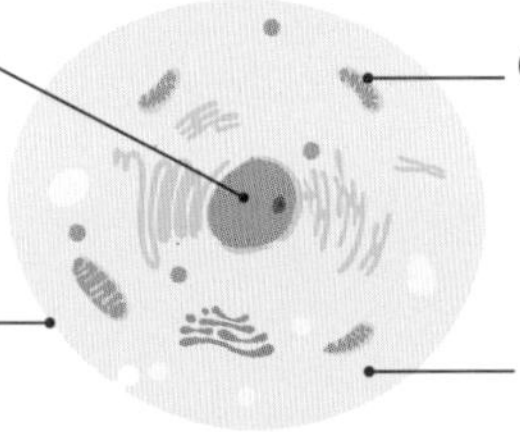

④ **el núcleo**
nucleus

⑤ **la mitocondria**
mitochondria

⑥ **la membrana celular**
cell membrane

⑦ **el citoplasma**
cytoplasm

⑧ **la célula animal**
animal cell

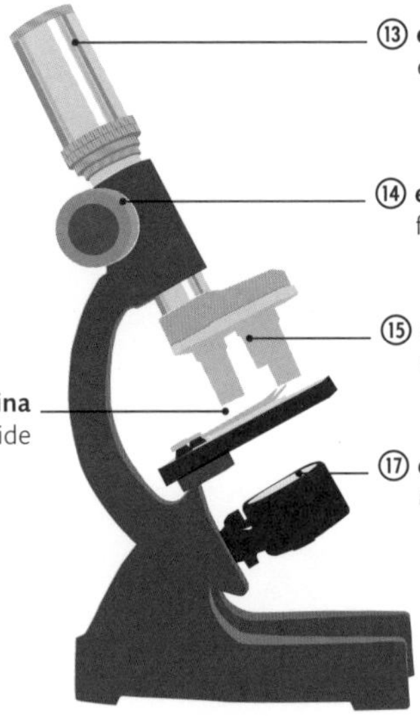

⑬ **el ocular**
eyepiece

⑭ **el tornillo de enfoque**
focusing knob

⑮ **el objetivo**
objective lens

⑯ **la platina**
slide

⑰ **el espejo**
mirror

⑱ **el microscopio**
microscope

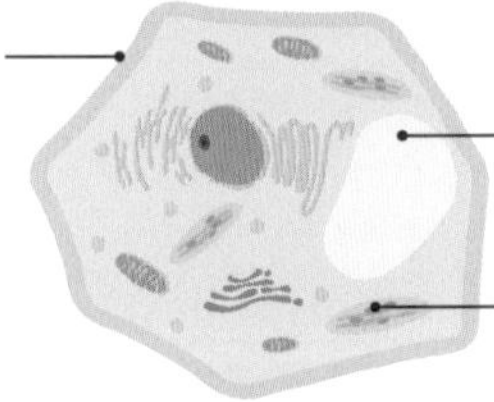

⑨ **la pared celular**
cell wall

⑩ **la vacuola**
vacuole

⑪ **el cloroplasto**
chloroplast

⑫ **la célula vegetal**
plant cell

⑲ **el glóbulo rojo**
red blood cell

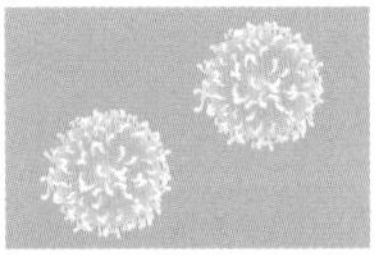

⑳ **el leucocito**
white blood cell

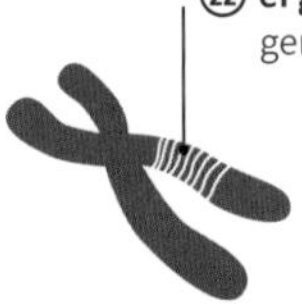

㉒ **el gen**
gene

㉑ **el cromosoma**
chromosome

㉓ **el ADN**
DNA

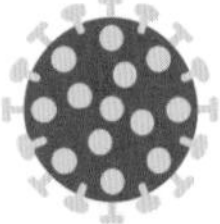

㉔ **el virus**
virus

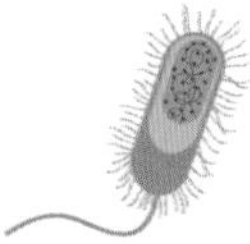

㉕ **la bacteria**
bacteria

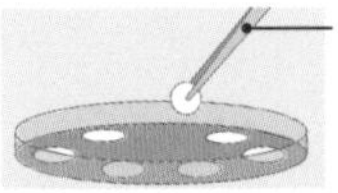

㉗ **las pinzas**
tweezers

㉖ **la placa de Petri**
petri dish

㉘ **el bisturí**
scalpel

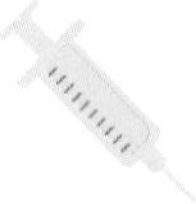

㉙ **la jeringuilla**
syringe

㉚ **la zoología**
zoology

㉛ **el zoólogo** *m* **la zoóloga** *f*
zoologist

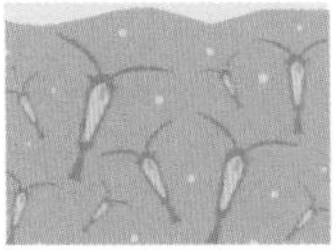

㉜ **el plancton**
plankton

㉝ **los invertebrados**
invertebrate

㉞ **los vertebrados**
vertebrate

㉟ **las especies**
species

See also
157 La historia natural • Natural history **158-159** Los mamíferos • Mammals **160-161** Las aves • Birds
162 Los insectos y los bichos • Insects and bugs **163** Los anfibios y los reptiles • Reptiles and amphibians
166 La vida oceánica • Ocean life **167-169** Las plantas y los árboles • Plants and trees **170** Los hongos • Fungi

(36) **el ecosistema**
ecosystem

(37) **el exoesqueleto**
exoskeleton

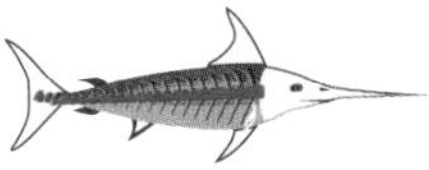

(38) **el endoesqueleto**
endoskeleton

(39) **la reproducción**
reproduction

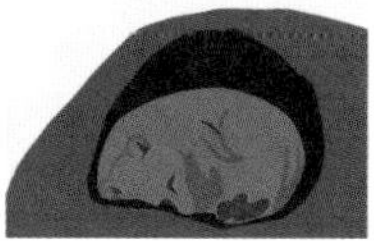

(40) **la hibernación**
hibernation

(41) **la botánica**
botany

(42) **el botánico** *m*
la botánica *f*
botanist

(43) **la planta**
plant

(44) **los hongos**
fungi

(45) **la fotosíntesis**
photosynthesis

(46) **el paleontólogo** *m*
la paleontóloga *f*
paleontologist

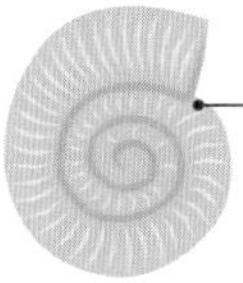

(47) **el fósil**
fossil

(48) **la evolución**
evolution

77.2 LA METAMORFOSIS • METAMORPHOSIS

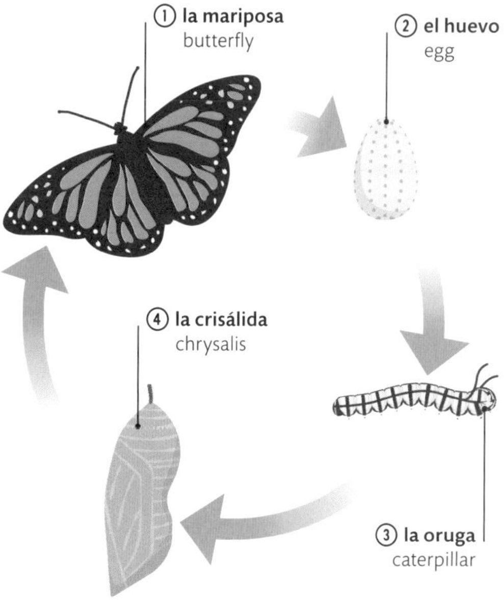

(1) **la mariposa**
butterfly

(2) **el huevo**
egg

(3) **la oruga**
caterpillar

(4) **la crisálida**
chrysalis

(5) **el ciclo de vida de la mariposa**
life cycle of a butterfly

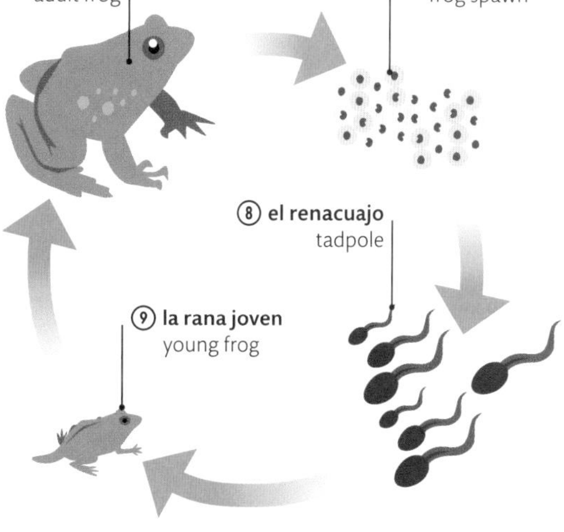

(6) **la rana adulta**
adult frog

(7) **las huevas de rana**
frog spawn

(8) **el renacuajo**
tadpole

(9) **la rana joven**
young frog

(10) **el ciclo de vida de la rana**
life cycle of a frog

78 La tabla periódica
The periodic table

78.1 LA TABLA PERIÓDICA · THE PERIODIC TABLE

- 119 **los metales alcalinos** alkali metals
- 120 **los metales alcalinotérreos** alkaline earth metals
- 121 **los metales de transición** transition metals
- 122 **los lantánidos** lanthanide series
- 124 **otros metales** *m, pl* other metals
- 125 **los metaloides** semi-metals
- 126 **los no metales** non-metals
- 127 **los halógenos** halogens

1 **H** **hidrógeno** *m* hydrogen								
3 **Li** **litio** *m* lithium	4 **Be** **berilio** *m* beryllium							
11 **Na** **sodio** *m* sodium	12 **Mg** **magnesio** *m* magnesium							
19 **K** **potasio** *m* potassium	20 **Ca** **calcio** *m* calcium	21 **Sc** **escandio** *m* scandium	22 **Ti** **titanio** *m* titanium	23 **V** **vanadio** *m* vanadium	24 **Cr** **cromo** *m* chromium	25 **Mn** **manganeso** *m* manganese	26 **Fe** **hierro** *m* iron	27 **Co** **cobalto** *m* cobalt
37 **Rb** **rubidio** *m* rubidium	38 **Sr** **estroncio** *m* strontium	39 **Y** **itrio** *m* yttrium	40 **Zr** **circonio** *m* zirconium	41 **Nb** **niobio** *m* niobium	42 **Mo** **molibdeno** *m* molybdenum	43 **Tc** **tecnecio** *m* technetium	44 **Ru** **rutenio** *m* ruthenium	45 **Rh** **rodio** *m* rhodium
55 **Cs** **cesio** *m* caesium	56 **Ba** **bario** *m* barium	**La-Lu**	72 **Hf** **hafnio** *m* hafnium	73 **Ta** **tántalo** *m* tantalum	74 **W** **tungsteno** *m* tungsten	75 **Re** **renio** *m* rhenium	76 **Os** **osmio** *m* osmium	77 **Ir** **iridio** *m* iridium
87 **Fr** **francio** *m* francium	88 **Ra** **radio** *m* radium	**Ac-Lr**	104 **Rf** **rutherfordio** *m* rutherfordium	105 **Db** **dubnio** *m* dubnium	106 **Sg** **seaborgio** *m* seaborgium	107 **Bh** **bohrio** *m* bohrium	108 **Hs** **hasio** *m* hassium	109 **Mt** **meitnerio** *m* meitnerium

57 **La** **lantano** *m* lanthanum	58 **Ce** **cerio** *m* cerium	59 **Pr** **praseodimio** *m* praseodymium	60 **Nd** **neodimio** *m* neodymium	61 **Pm** **prometio** *m* promethium	62 **Sm** **samario** *m* samarium
89 **Ac** **actinio** *m* actinium	90 **Th** **torio** *m* Thorium	91 **Pa** **protactinio** *m* Protactinium	92 **U** **uranio** *m* Uranium	93 **Np** **neptunio** *m* neptunium	94 **Pu** **plutonio** *m* plutonium

130 **Los elementos son sustancias puras.** Elements are pure substances.

See also
73 En la escuela • At school **75** La física • Physics **76** La química
Chemistry **156** Las rocas y los minerales • Rocks and minerals

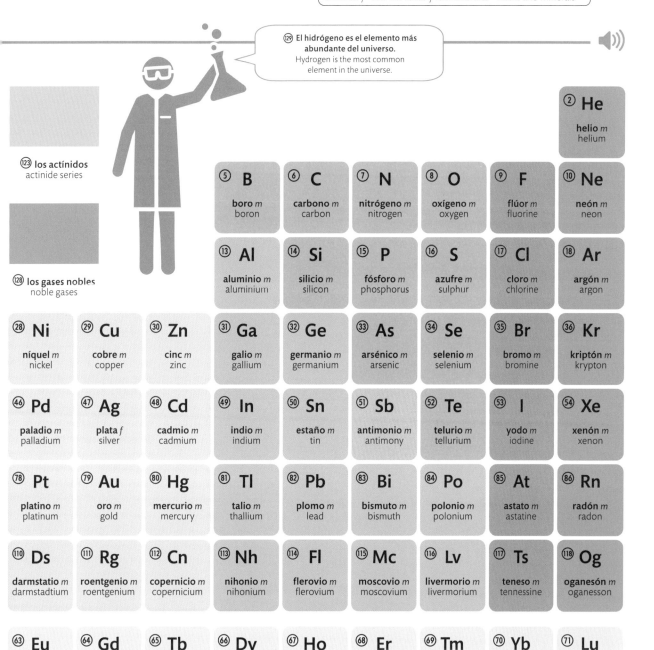

(129) **El hidrógeno es el elemento más abundante del universo.**
Hydrogen is the most common element in the universe.

(123) **los actínidos**
actinide series

(128) **los gases nobles**
noble gases

								2 He **helio** *m* helium
			5 B **boro** *m* boron	6 C **carbono** *m* carbon	7 N **nitrógeno** *m* nitrogen	8 O **oxígeno** *m* oxygen	9 F **flúor** *m* fluorine	10 Ne **neón** *m* neon
			13 Al **aluminio** *m* aluminium	14 Si **silicio** *m* silicon	15 P **fósforo** *m* phosphorus	16 S **azufre** *m* sulphur	17 Cl **cloro** *m* chlorine	18 Ar **argón** *m* argon
28 Ni **níquel** *m* nickel	29 Cu **cobre** *m* copper	30 Zn **cinc** *m* zinc	31 Ga **galio** *m* gallium	32 Ge **germanio** *m* germanium	33 As **arsénico** *m* arsenic	34 Se **selenio** *m* selenium	35 Br **bromo** *m* bromine	36 Kr **kriptón** *m* krypton
46 Pd **paladio** *m* palladium	47 Ag **plata** *f* silver	48 Cd **cadmio** *m* cadmium	49 In **indio** *m* indium	50 Sn **estaño** *m* tin	51 Sb **antimonio** *m* antimony	52 Te **telurio** *m* tellurium	53 I **yodo** *m* iodine	54 Xe **xenón** *m* xenon
78 Pt **platino** *m* platinum	79 Au **oro** *m* gold	80 Hg **mercurio** *m* mercury	81 Tl **talio** *m* thallium	82 Pb **plomo** *m* lead	83 Bi **bismuto** *m* bismuth	84 Po **polonio** *m* polonium	85 At **astato** *m* astatine	86 Rn **radón** *m* radon
110 Ds **darmstatio** *m* darmstadtium	111 Rg **roentgenio** *m* roentgenium	112 Cn **copernicio** *m* copernicium	113 Nh **nihonio** *m* nihonium	114 Fl **flerovio** *m* flerovium	115 Mc **moscovio** *m* moscovium	116 Lv **livermorio** *m* livermorium	117 Ts **teneso** *m* tennessine	118 Og **oganesón** *m* oganesson

63 Eu **europio** *m* europium	64 Gd **gadolinio** *m* gadolinium	65 Tb **terbio** *m* terbium	66 Dy **disprosio** *m* dysprosium	67 Ho **holmio** *m* holmium	68 Er **erbio** *m* erbium	69 Tm **tulio** *m* thulium	70 Yb **iterbio** *m* ytterbium	71 Lu **lutecio** *m* lutetium
95 Am **americio** *m* americium	96 Cm **curio** *m* curium	97 Bk **berkelio** *m* berkelium	98 Cf **californio** *m* californium	99 Es **einstenio** *m* einsteinium	100 Fm **fermio** *m* fermium	101 Md **mendelevio** *m* mendelevium	102 No **nobelio** *m* nobelium	103 Lr **laurencio** *m* lawrencium

79 La historia
History

79.1 LA GUERRA Y LAS ARMAS · WAR AND WEAPONS

① la cuadriga
chariot
② el arco
bow
③ la flecha
arrow
⑤ la gada
gada / mace
⑥ la cimitarra
scimitar
⑦ la guerra
warfare
⑧ el hacha *f*
axe
⑨ el escudo
shield
⑩ la espada
sword

79.2 LAS PERSONAS A TRAVÉS DEL TIEMPO · PEOPLE THROUGH TIME

② las herramientas de sílex
flint tools
① la Edad de Piedra
the Stone Age
③ la Edad de Bronce
the Bronze Age
④ la Edad de Hierro
the Iron Age
⑤ el granjero *m*
la granjera *f*
farmer
⑥ el comerciante *m*
la comerciante *f*
merchant
⑦ el artesano *m*
la artesana *f*
artisan
⑫ el emperador
emperor
⑬ la emperatriz
empress
⑭ el rey
king
⑮ la reina
queen
⑯ el príncipe *m* / la princesa *f*
prince / princess
⑰ los nobles
nobles
㉒ la Edad de Oro islámica
the Islamic Golden Age
㉔ la Ilustración
the Enlightenment
㉓ el filósofo
philosopher
㉕ la Revolución Industrial
the Industrial Revolution

See also
44 Los edificios y la arquitectura • Buildings and architecture **73** En la escuela • At school **80** En la universidad • At college **88** El ejército • Military

④ **la lanza**
spear

⑪ **el caballo de guerra**
warhorse

⑫ **el elefante de guerra**
war elephant

⑬ **la batalla**
battle

⑭ **el cañón**
cannon

⑮ **la catapulta**
catapult

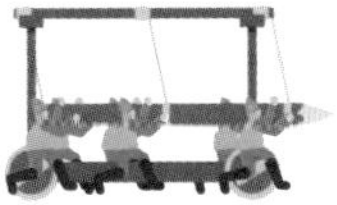

⑯ **el ariete**
battering ram

⑰ **el caballero**
knight

⑱ **la armadura**
armour

⑲ **el guerrero**
warrior

⑧ **el herrero** *m* / **la herrera** *f*
blacksmith

⑨ **los campesinos**
peasants

⑩ **el reino**
kingdom

⑪ **el imperio**
empire

⑱ **el señor** *m*
la señora *f*
lord / lady

⑲ **el trovador**
minstrel

⑳ **el bufón**
jester

㉑ **el escriba** *m* / **la escriba** *f*
scribe

㉖ **la Revolución Tecnológica**
the Technological Revolution

㉗ **la Era de la Información**
the Information Age

79.3 ESTUDIANDO EL PASADO
STUDYING THE PAST

① **el historiador** *m*
la historiadora *f*
historian

② **el archivo**
archive

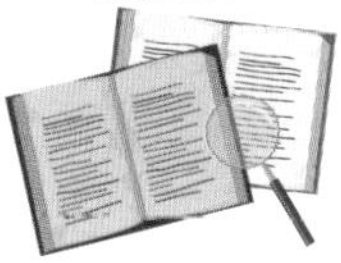

③ **las fuentes**
sources

④ **el pergamino**
scroll

⑤ **el documento**
document

⑥ **la arqueología**
archaeology

⑦ **el arqueólogo** *m*
la arqueóloga *f*
archaeologist

⑧ **la excavación**
dig / excavation

⑩ **la turbera**
peat bog

⑨ **los restos**
remains

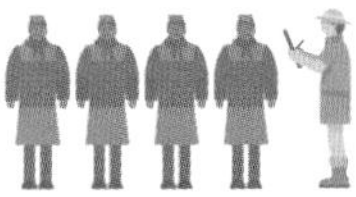

⑪ **el descubrimiento**
finds

⑫ **la tumba**
tomb

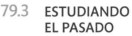

⑬ **el lugar histórico**
historical site

80 En la universidad
At college

80.1 LA UNIVERSIDAD • UNIVERSITY

① **el campus**
campus

② **el auditorio**
lecture theatre

③ **el profesor** *m* / **la profesora** *f*
lecturer

④ **el campo deportivo**
sports field

⑤ **el comedor**
refectory

⑥ **la residencia de estudiantes**
halls of residence

⑦ **la beca**
scholarship

⑧ **la oficina de acceso**
admissions

⑨ **el estudiante de grado** *m*
la estudiante de grado *f*
undergraduate

⑩ **el título**
diploma

⑪ **la disertación**
dissertation

⑫ **el grado**
degree

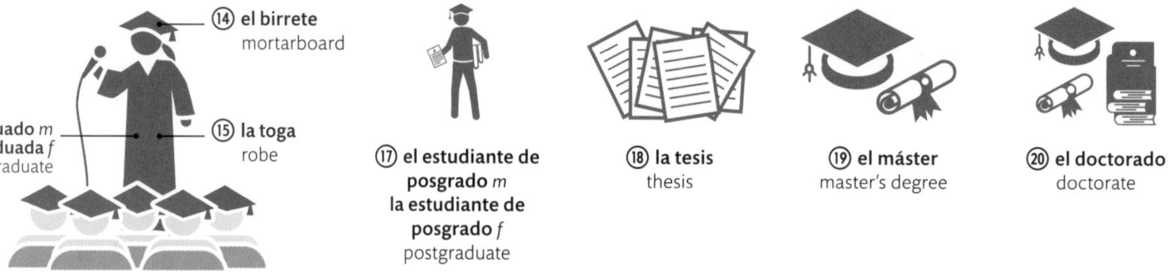

⑬ **el graduado** *m*
la graduada *f*
graduate

⑭ **el birrete**
mortarboard

⑮ **la toga**
robe

⑯ **la ceremonia de graduación**
graduation ceremony

⑰ **el estudiante de posgrado** *m*
la estudiante de posgrado *f*
postgraduate

⑱ **la tesis**
thesis

⑲ **el máster**
master's degree

⑳ **el doctorado**
doctorate

80.2 LOS DEPARTAMENTOS Y LAS FACULTADES • DEPARTMENTS AND SCHOOLS

① **las humanidades**
humanities

② **la política**
politics

③ **la literatura**
literature

④ **los idiomas**
languages

⑤ **la economía**
economics

⑥ **la filosofía**
philosophy

⑦ **la historia**
history

⑧ **las ciencias sociales**
social sciences

⑨ **la sociología**
sociology

⑩ **el derecho**
law

⑪ **la medicina**
medicine

⑫ **la enfermería**
nursing

See also
73 En la escuela • At school **74** Las matemáticas • Mathematics **75** La física • Physics **76** La química • Chemistry **77** La biología • Biology **79** La historia • History **85** El derecho • Law **138** Los libros y la lectura • Books and reading

80.3 **LA BIBLIOTECA** • LIBRARY

① **la sala de lectura**
reading room

② **la lista de lectura**
reading list

③ **sacar en préstamo**
to borrow

④ **renovar**
to renew

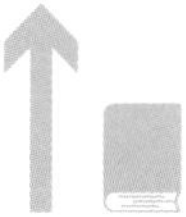

⑤ **devolver**
to return

⑥ **reservar**
to reserve

⑦ **el pasillo**
aisle

⑧ **la estantería**
bookshelf

⑨ **el bibliotecario** *m*
la bibliotecaria *f*
librarian

⑩ **el carnet de biblioteca**
library card

⑪ **la revista**
periodical / journal

⑫ **el libro**
book

⑬ **la biblioteca**
library

⑭ **el mostrador de préstamos**
loans desk

⑭ **Me han concedido una beca de investigación científica.**
I received a grant to do scientific research.

⑬ **las ciencias**
sciences

⑮ **la química**
chemistry

⑯ **la física**
physics

⑰ **la biología**
biology

⑱ **la ingeniería**
engineering

⑲ **la zoología**
zoology

⑳ **el conservatorio**
music school

㉑ **la escuela de danza**
dance school

㉒ **la escuela de arte**
art college / school

81 En el trabajo
At work

81.1 EL TRABAJO DE OFICINA · OFFICE WORK

① **la empresa**
company

② **la sucursal**
branch

③ **el empleo**
employment

④ **ganar**
to earn

⑤ **fijo** *m* / **fija** *f*
permanent

⑥ **temporal**
temporary

⑩ **el trabajo de nueve a cinco**
nine-to-five job

⑪ **trabajar a media jornada**
to work part-time

⑫ **trabajar a turnos**
to work shifts

⑬ **las vacaciones**
annual leave

⑭ **tener un día libre**
to have a day off

⑮ **coger la baja por maternidad**
to go on maternity leave

⑲ **ausentarse por enfermedad**
to call in sick

⑳ **dar el preaviso de baja voluntaria**
to hand in your notice

㉑ **ser despedido** *m*
ser despedida *f*
to get fired

㉒ **ser cesado** *m*
ser cesada *f*
to be laid off

㉓ **estar desempleado** *m*
estar desempleada *f*
to be unemployed

㉔ **la prestación por desempleo**
unemployment benefit

㉞ **el empresario**
businessman

㊴ **el gerente** *m*
la gerente *f*
manager

㉙ **la oficina central**
headquarters

㉚ **el recepcionista** *m*
la recepcionista *f*
receptionist

㉝ **el director** *m*
la directora *f*
CEO (chief executive officer)

㊳ **el aprendiz** *m*
la aprendiz *f*
apprentice

㊵ **el asistente personal** *m*
la asistenta personal *f*
PA (personal assistant)

㊶ **el líder / la líder**
leader

㉛ **la zona de espera**
waiting area

㉟ **el acuerdo comercial**
business deal

㊱ **la empresaria**
businesswoman

㊷ **los clientes**
clients

㉘ **la recepción de la oficina**
office reception

㉜ **la oficina del director** *m* / **la oficina de la directora** *f*
CEO's office

㊲ **la reunión**
meeting

See also
82 En la oficina • In the office **89-90** Los trabajos • Jobs **91** Las industrias y los departamentos • Industries and departments **92** Presentarse para un puesto de trabajo • Applying for a job **93** Las competencias laborales • Workplace skills **95** Reuniéndose y presentando • Meeting and presenting

⑦ **el horario flexible**
flexitime

⑧ **trabajar desde casa**
to work from home

⑨ **trabajar a jornada completa**
to work full-time

⑯ **ascender**
to be promoted

⑰ **dimitir**
to resign

⑱ **jubilarse**
to retire

㉕ **el viaje de trabajo**
business trip

㉖ **la cita**
appointment

㉗ **la comida de negocios**
business lunch

81.2 EL SALARIO • PAY

① **el salario por hora**
hourly rate

② **las horas extra**
overtime

③ **el salario fijo**
salary

④ **el salario variable**
wages

⑤ **la nómina**
pay slip

⑥ **la bonificación**
bonus

⑦ **las prestaciones**
benefits

⑧ **el aumento salarial**
raise

⑨ **el recorte salarial**
pay cut

㊹ **el entrevistador** *m*
la entrevistadora *f*
interviewer

㊺ **el candidato** *m*
la candidata *f*
applicant

㊽ **el trabajador** *m*
la trabajadora *f*
worker

㊾ **el compañero de trabajo** *m*
la compañera de trabajo *f*
co-worker / colleague

㊿ **el empleado** *m*
la empleada *f*
employee

(51) **el supervisor m**
la supervisora f
supervisor

(52) **el becario** *m*
la becaria *f*
intern

㊻ **el empleador** *m* / **la empleadora** *f*
employer

㊸ **la entrevista**
interview

㊼ **el personal**
staff

(53) **el jefe de personal** *m*
la jefa de personal *f*
office manager

82 En la oficina

In the office

82.1 LA OFICINA · OFFICE

① **el tablón de anuncios** notice board
② **las carpetas** files / folders
③ **la lámpara** lamp
④ **el ordenador** computer
⑤ **la papelera** bin
⑥ **el papel** paper
⑦ **el bloc de notas** notepad
⑧ **las notas adhesivas** sticky notes
⑨ **las bandejas** trays
⑩ **el dispensador de agua** water cooler

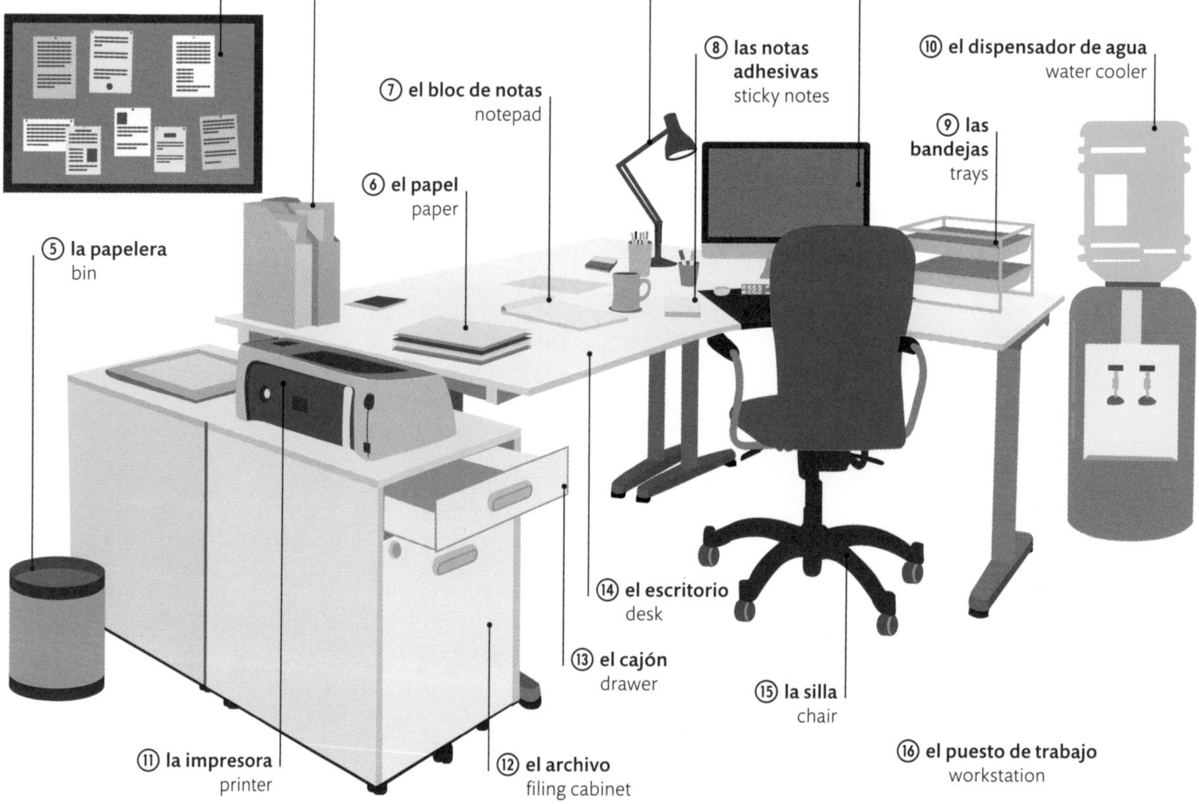

⑪ **la impresora** printer
⑫ **el archivo** filing cabinet
⑬ **el cajón** drawer
⑭ **el escritorio** desk
⑮ **la silla** chair
⑯ **el puesto de trabajo** workstation

82.2 EL EQUIPO DE LA SALA DE REUNIONES · MEETING-ROOM EQUIPMENT

① **la presentación** presentation
② **la propuesta** proposal
③ **el informe** report

④ **el proyector digital** digital projector
⑤ **la reunión** meeting

⑥ **el rota** flip cha
⑦ **el caba** easel

See also
81 En el trabajo • At work **83** Los ordenadores y la tecnología • Computers and technology **91** Las industrias y los departamentos • Industries and departments **92** Presentarse para un puesto de trabajo • Applying for a job **93** Las competencias laborales • Workplace skills **95** Reuniéndose y presentando• Meeting and presenting

82.3 LOS MATERIALES DE OFICINA • OFFICE EQUIPMENT

① **la fotocopiadora**
photocopier

② **el escáner**
scanner

③ **el teléfono**
telephone / phone

④ **el ordenador portátil**
laptop

⑤ **el proyector**
projector

⑥ **los cascos**
headset

⑦ **la trituradora de papeles**
shredder

⑧ **el teléfono móvil**
mobile phone

⑨ **el reposapiés**
footrest

⑩ **la silla de rodillas**
kneeling chair

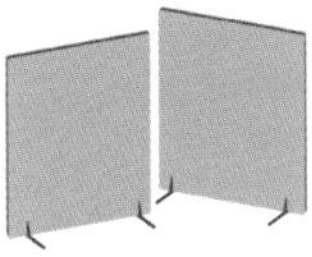
⑪ **el panel móvil**
movable panel

⑫ **el material de papelería**
stationery

⑬ **la carta**
letter

⑭ **el sobre**
envelope

⑮ **el calendario**
calendar

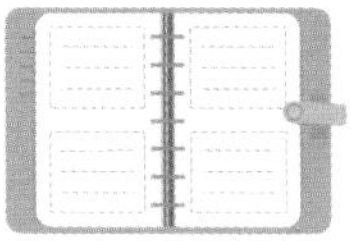
⑯ **la agenda**
diary

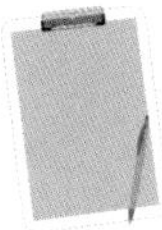
⑰ **el sujetapapeles**
clipboard

⑱ **la perforadora**
hole punch

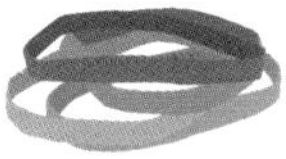
⑲ **las bandas elásticas**
rubber bands

⑳ **la pinza sujetapapeles**
binder clip

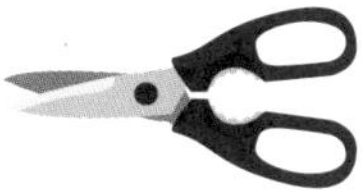
㉑ **las tijeras**
scissors

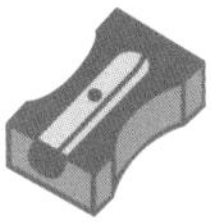
㉒ **el sacapuntas**
pencil sharpener

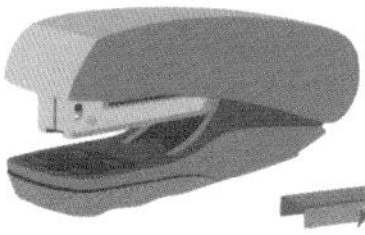
㉓ **la grapadora**
stapler

㉔ **las grapas**
staples

㉕ **el líquido corrector**
correction fluid

㉖ **el acta** *f*
minutes

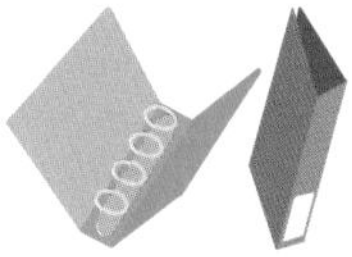
㉗ **el clasificador**
ring binder

㉘ **el subrayador**
highlighter

㉙ **el pegamento**
glue

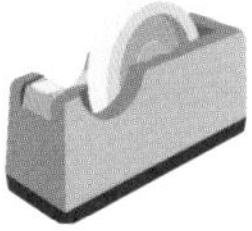
㉚ **la cinta adhesiva**
tape

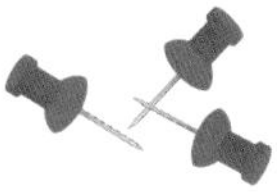
㉛ **la chincheta**
drawing pin

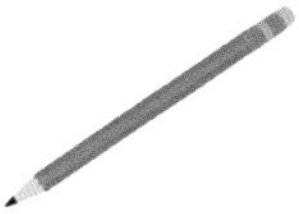
㉜ **el lápiz**
pencil

㉝ **el bolígrafo**
pen

㉞ **los clips**
paper clips

㉟ **la goma de borrar**
rubber

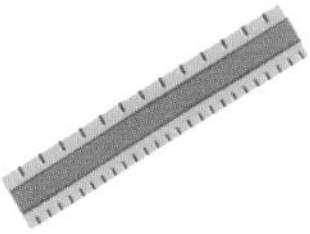
㊱ **la regla**
ruler

83 Los ordenadores y la tecnología
Computers and technology

83.1 LOS DISPOSITIVOS Y LA TECNOLOGÍA · GADGETS AND TECHNOLOGY

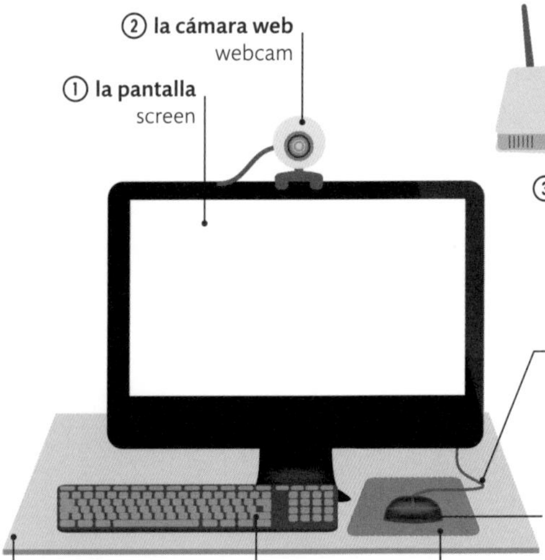

① **la pantalla**
screen

② **la cámara web**
webcam

⑦ **el cable**
wire

⑧ **el ratón**
mouse

⑨ **la mesa de ordenador**
computer desk

⑩ **el teclado**
keyboard

⑪ **la alfombrilla para el ratón**
mouse mat

⑫ **el ordenador de sobremesa**
desktop computer

③ **el router**
router

④ **el wifi**
Wi-Fi

⑤ **el libro electrónico**
e-reader

⑥ **la tableta**
tablet

⑬ **el ordenador portátil**
laptop

⑭ **la cámara**
camera

⑮ **el reloj inteligente**
smartwatch

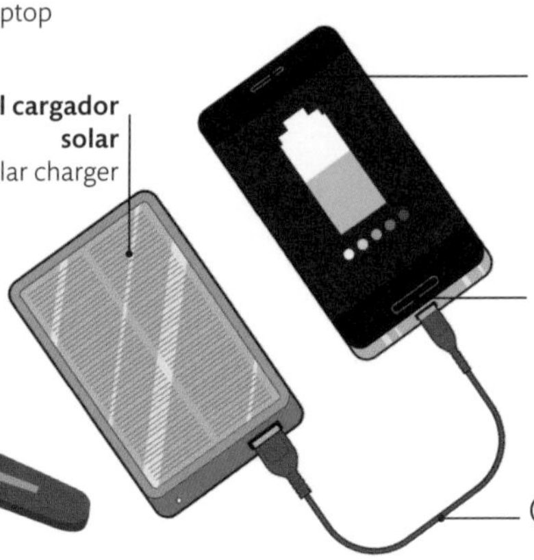

⑯ **el cargador solar**
solar charger

⑰ **el teléfono inteligente**
smartphone

⑱ **el botón de inicio**
home button

⑲ **el cable de carga**
charging cabl

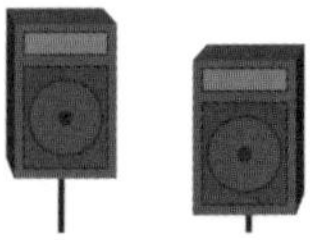

⑳ **los altavoces**
speakers

㉑ **la cámara de vídeo**
camcorder

㉒ **la conexión inalámbrica**
wireless

㉓ **el auricular Bluetooth**
Bluetooth headset

㉔ **la pila**
battery

㉕ **la unidad USB**
USB drive

㉖ **la grabadora de voz**
voice recorder

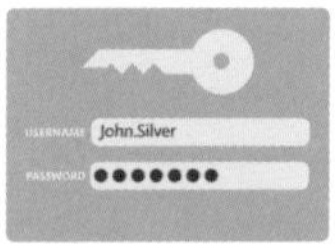

㉗ **la contraseña**
password

㉘ **la tarjeta de memoria**
memory card

㉙ **el disco duro**
hard drive

㉚ **la clavija**
plug

㉛ **el cable de alimentación**
power lead

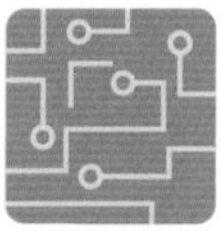

㉜ **el circuito**
circuit

㉝ **el mando a distancia**
remote control

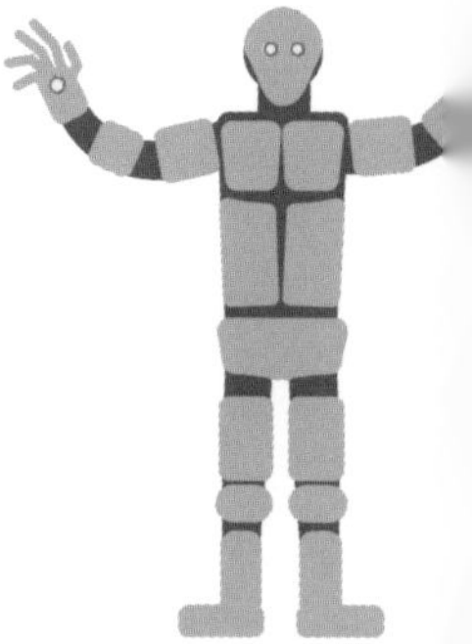

㉞ **la inteligencia artificial**
artificial intelligence

See also
73 En la escuela • At school **80** En la universidad • At college **81** En el trabajo • At work **82** En la oficina • In the office **95** Reuniéndose y presentando • Meeting and presenting **140** Los juegos • Games

83.2 LA COMUNICACIÓN EN LÍNEA • ONLINE COMMUNICATION

① **encender**
to turn on

② **apagar**
to turn off

③ **iniciar sesión**
to log in

④ **cerrar sesión**
to log out

⑤ **descargar**
to download

⑥ **subir**
to upload

⑦ **hacer una copia de seguridad**
to back up

⑧ **hacer clic**
to click

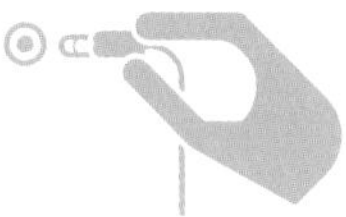
⑨ **enchufar**
to plug in

⑩ **eliminar**
to delete

⑪ **imprimir**
to print

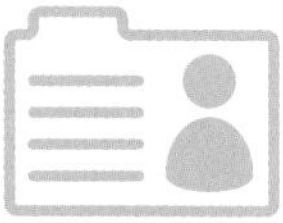
⑫ **el contacto**
contact

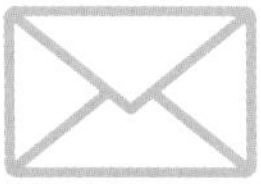
⑬ **el correo electrónico**
email

⑭ **responder**
to reply

⑮ **responder a todos**
to reply to all

⑯ **enviar**
to send

⑰ **reenviar**
to forward

⑱ **el borrador**
draft

⑲ **la bandeja de entrada**
inbox

⑳ **la bandeja de salida**
outbox

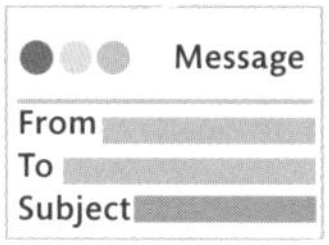

㉑ **el asunto**
subject

㉒ **el spam**
junk mail / spam

㉓ **la papelera**
trash

㉔ **el documento adjunto**
attachment

㉕ **el chat**
chat

㉖ **la videollamada**
video chat

㉗ **la firma**
signature

㉘ **el hashtag**
hashtag

㉙ **la arroba**
at sign /
at symbol

㉚ **Tienes que activar el micrófono, Liz.**
You need to turn on your microphone, Liz.

㉛ **la videoconferencia**
video conference

84 Los medios de comunicación
Media

84.1 EL ESTUDIO DE TELEVISIÓN · TELEVISION STUDIO

① **la iluminación**
light

② **la pértiga para micrófono**
sound boom

③ **el presentador** *m*
la presentadora *f*
presenter

④ **la cámara**
camera

⑤ **la grúa de la cámara**
camera crane

⑥ **el cámara** *m*
la cámara *f*
camera operator

⑦ **Entramos en directo dentro de 5 segundos.**
We're going live in 5 seconds.

⑧ **el director** *m*
la directora *f*
director

⑨ **la claqueta**
clapper board

⑩ **el estudio de televisión**
television studio

⑪ **el teleprompter**
teleprompter / autocue

⑫ **la silla del director**
director's chair

84.2 LA RADIO · RADIO

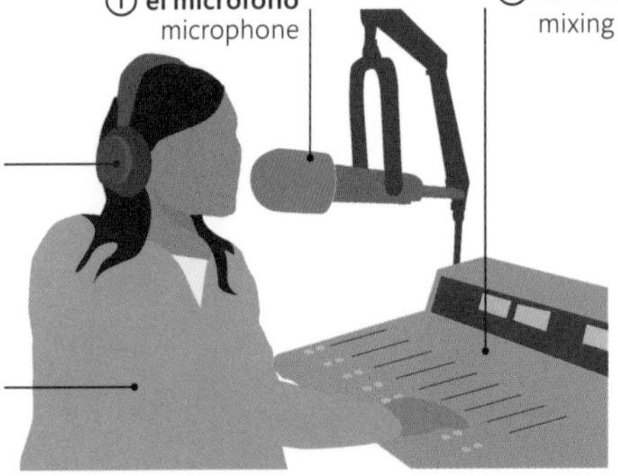

① **el micrófono**
microphone

② **la mesa de mezclas**
mixing desk

③ **los cascos**
headphones

④ **el DJ** *m* / **la DJ** *f*
DJ

⑤ **el estudio de grabación**
recording studio

⑥ **el técnico de sonido** *m*
la técnica de sonido *f*
sound technician

⑦ **la emisora de radio**
radio station

⑧ **emitir**
to broadcast

⑨ **digital**
digital

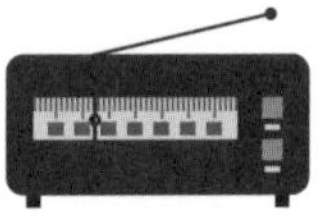

⑩ **FM**
FM

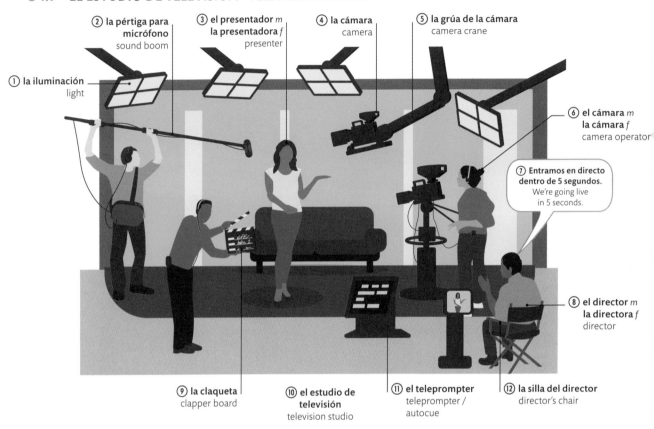

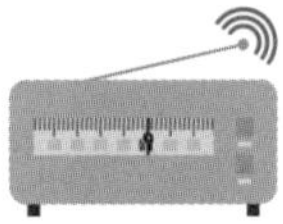

⑪ **la frecuencia**
frequency

See also
83 Los ordenadores y la tecnología • Computers and technology **128-129** La música • Music **136** El ocio en el hogar • Home entertainment **137** La televisión • Television

84.3 LOS MEDIOS EN LÍNEA Y LAS REDES SOCIALES
SOCIAL AND ONLINE MEDIA

① **seguir**
to follow

② **dar a me gusta**
to like

③ **hacerse viral**
to go viral

④ **ser tendencia**
to trend

⑤ **el avatar**
avatar

⑥ **el vlog**
vlog

⑦ **el vlogger** *m*
la vlogger *f*
vlogger

⑧ **el blog**
blog

⑨ **Mi blog tiene más de 500 seguidores.**
My blog has over 500 followers.

⑩ **el blogger** *m*
la blogger *f*
blogger

⑪ **compartir**
to share

⑫ **bloquear**
to block

⑬ **publicar**
to post

⑭ **enviar un MD**
to DM someone

⑮ **el influencer** *m*
la influencer *f*
influencer

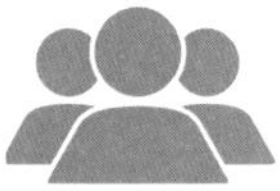
⑯ **el seguidor** *m*
la seguidora *f*
follower

⑰ **el pódcast**
podcast

⑱ **el emoji**
emoji

⑲ **el hashtag**
hashtag

⑳ **el hilo**
thread

㉑ **la cronología**
newsfeed

㉒ **la actualización de estado**
status update

㉓ **el CMS (sistema de gestión de contenidos)**
CMS (content management system)

㉔ **la plataforma**
platform

㉕ **las cookies**
cookie

㉖ **la ventana emergente**
pop-up

㉗ **la web de noticias**
news website

㉘ **la revista en línea**
magazine website

㉙ **la web comunitaria**
community website

㉚ **trolear**
trolling

85 El derecho
Law

85.1 EL SISTEMA JUDICIAL · THE LEGAL SYSTEM

⑯ **el taquígrafo** *m* **la taquígrafa** *f* stenographer

⑰ **el funcionario judicial** *m* **la funcionaria judicial** *f* court official

⑱ **el bufete de abogados** lawyer's office

⑲ **la citación** summons

⑳ **el cliente** *m* **la clienta** *f* client

㉑ **la resolución judicial** warrant

㉒ **la orden judicial** writ

㉓ **el cargo** charge

㉔ **la asesoría legal** legal advice

㉕ **la declaración** statement

㉖ **la fecha del juicio** court date

㉗ **el juicio** court case

㉘ **el veredicto** verdict

㉙ **condenar** to sentence

㉚ **la deliberación del jurado** jury deliberation

See also
50 Los servicios de emergencias • Emergency services **91** Las industrias y los departamentos • Industries and departments

(33) **el retrato robot**
photofit

(34) **la prueba**
evidence

(35) **el sospechoso** *m*
la sospechosa *f*
suspect

(36) **los antecedentes penales**
criminal record

(37) **el criminal** *m*
la criminal *f*
criminal

(38) **el acusado** *m*
la acusada *f*
accused

(39) **abogar**
to plead

(40) **inocente**
innocent

(41) **culpable**
guilty

(42) **apelar**
to appeal

(43) **los presos** *m*
las presas *f*
prisoners

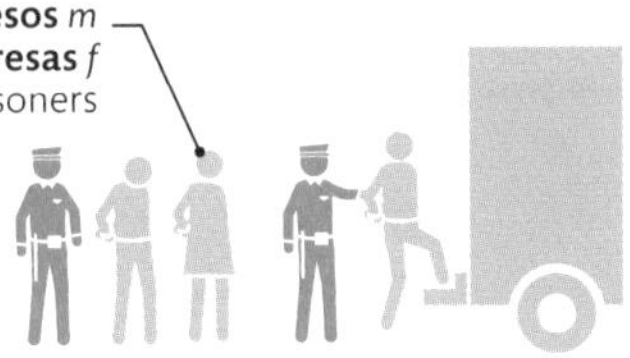
(44) **los carceleros** *m*
las carceleras *f*
prison guards

(45) **la prisión**
prison

(46) **la celda**
cell

(47) **la fianza**
bail

(48) **la libertad condicional**
parole

(49) **la multa**
fine

(50) **ser absuelto** *m*
ser absuelta *f*
to be acquitted

85.2 EL CRIMEN • CRIME

(1) **el atraco**
robbery / burglary

(2) **el robo**
mugging

(3) **el robo de vehículos**
car theft

(4) **el gamberrismo**
hooliganism

(5) **el vandalismo**
vandalism

(6) **el contrabando**
smuggling

(7) **el fraude**
fraud

(8) **la piratería informática**
hacking

(9) **el carterismo**
pickpocketing

(10) **el soborno**
bribery

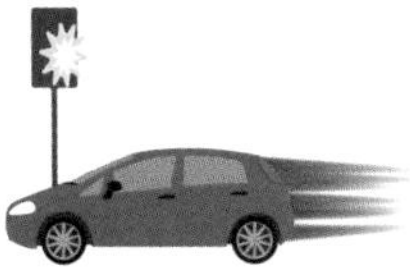
(11) **el exceso de velocidad**
speeding

(12) **el tráfico de drogas**
drug dealing

(13) **el grafiti**
graffiti

(14) **el robo en una tienda**
shoplifting

86 La agricultura
Farming

86.1 EN LA GRANJA • ON THE FARM

① **el seto** hedge
② **el granero** barn
③ **el tractor** tractor
④ **las tierras de cultivo** farmland
⑤ **el silo** silo
⑥ **el espantapájaros** scarecrow
⑦ **la cosechadora** combine harvester
⑧ **la casa de labranza** farmhouse
⑨ **el establo** stable
⑩ **el estanque** pond
⑪ **la valla** fence
⑫ **el gallinero** chicken coop
⑬ **el pasto** pasture
⑭ **el corral** farmyard
⑮ **la colmena** beehive
⑯ **la pocilga** pigpen
⑰ **el granjero** *m* **la granjera** *f* farmer
⑱ **la verja** gate

86.2 LOS VERBOS DE LA GRANJA • FARMING VERBS

① **arar** to plough

② **sembrar** to sow

③ **ordeñar** to milk

④ **dar de comer** to feed

⑤ **plantar** to plant

⑥ **cosechar** to harvest

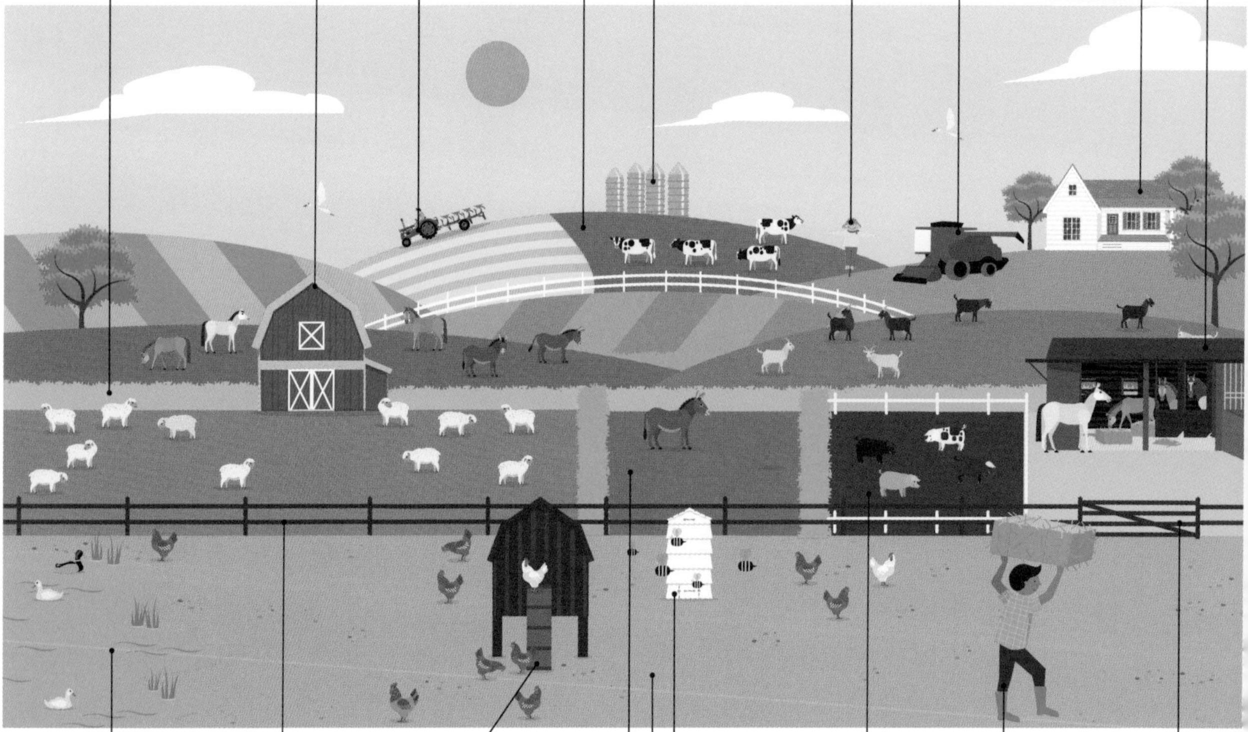

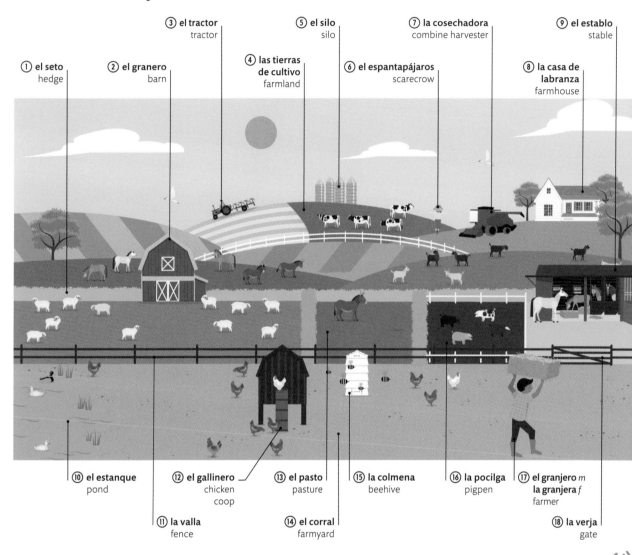

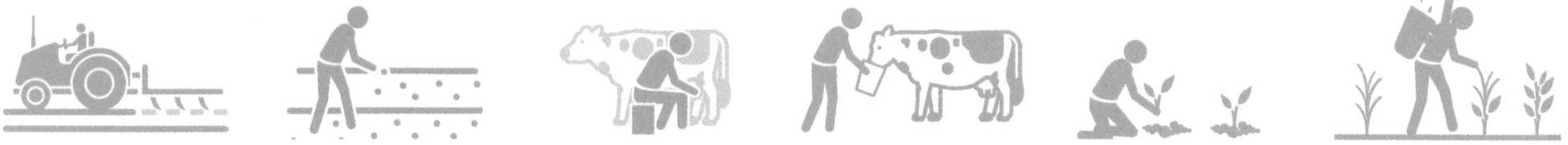

See also
53 La carne • Meat **55-56** La verdura • Vegetables **57** La fruta • Fruit **58** La fruta y los frutos secos • Fruit and nuts **61** Los productos lácteos • Dairy produce **165** Los animales de granja • Farm animals

86.3 EL VOCABULARIO DE LA GRANJA • FARMING TERMS

① **la agricultura**
arable farm

② **la granja lechera**
dairy farm

③ **la granja ovina**
sheep farm

④ **la granja avícola**
sheep farm

⑤ **la granja porcina**
pig farm

⑥ **la piscifactoría**
fish farm

⑦ **el rebaño**
herd

⑧ **la granja frutícola**
fruit farm

⑨ **el viñedo**
vineyard

⑩ **el huerto**
vegetable garden / vegetable plot

⑪ **el herbicida**
herbicide

⑫ **el pesticida**
pesticide

86.4 LOS CULTIVOS • CROPS

① **el trigo**
wheat

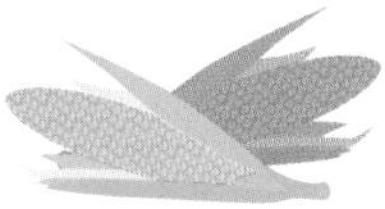

② **el maíz**
maize

③ **la cebada**
barley

④ **la colza**
rapeseed

⑤ **los girasoles**
sunflowers

⑥ **el heno**
hay

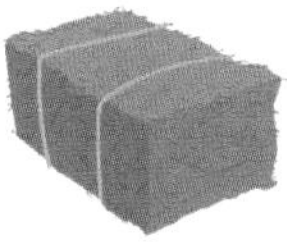

⑦ **la alfalfa**
alfalfa

⑧ **el tabaco**
tobacco

⑨ **el arroz**
rice

⑩ **el té**
tea

⑪ **el café**
coffee

⑫ **la caña de azúcar**
sugar cane

⑬ **el lino**
flax

⑭ **el algodón**
cotton

⑮ **las patatas**
potatoes

⑯ **la batata**
yams

⑰ **el mijo**
millet

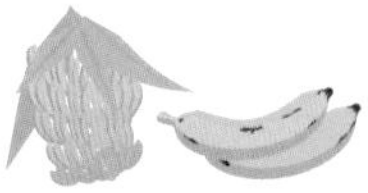

⑱ **el plátano**
plantains

87 La construcción

Construction

87.1 **LA OBRA** · BUILDING SITE

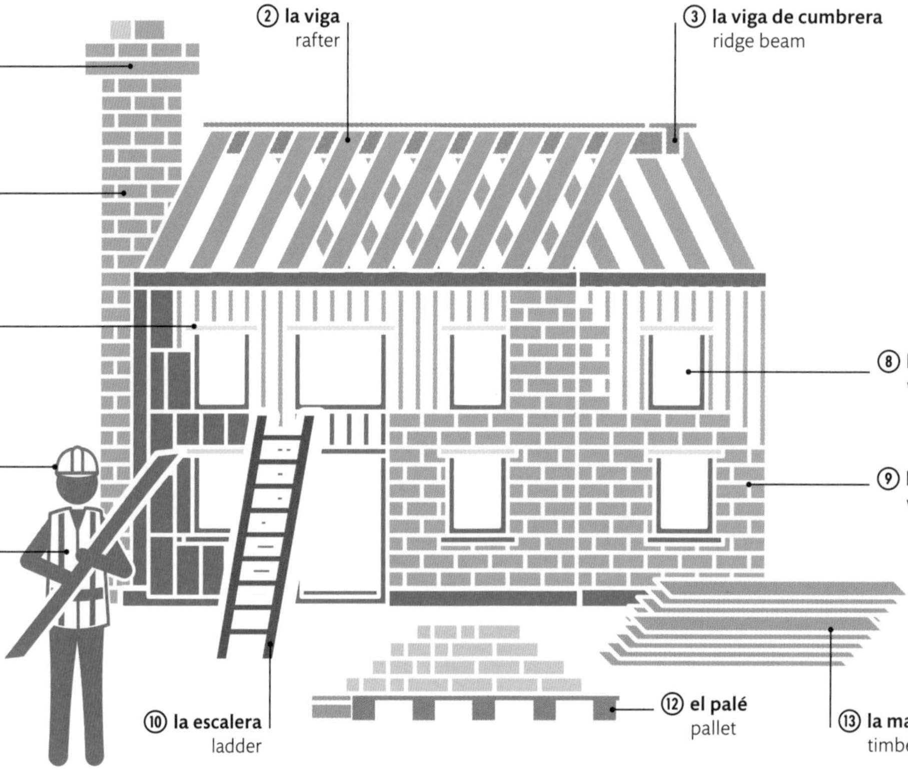

① **la chimenea**
chimney

② **la viga**
rafter

③ **la viga de cumbrera**
ridge beam

④ **el ladrillo**
brick

⑤ **el dintel**
lintel

⑥ **el casco**
hard hat

⑦ **el obrero** *m*
la obrera *f*
builder

⑧ **la ventana**
window

⑨ **la pared**
wall

⑩ **la escalera**
ladder

⑫ **el palé**
pallet

⑬ **la madera**
timber

⑪ **la obra**
building site

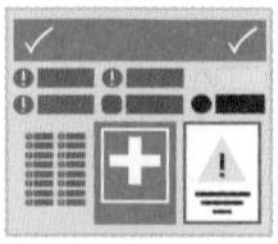

⑭ **el cartel de seguridad**
safety notice board

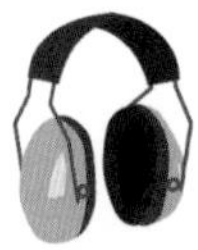

⑮ **las orejeras**
ear protectors / ear muffs

⑯ **el chaleco reflectante**
high-visibility vest

⑰ **los guantes de seguridad**
safety gloves

⑱ **las gafas de seguridad**
safety glasses

⑲ **el cinturón de herramientas**
tool belt

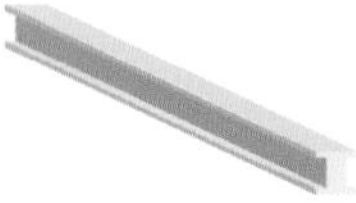

⑳ **la viga maestra**
girder

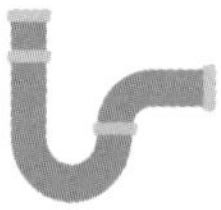

㉑ **la tubería**
pipe

㉒ **el cemento**
cement / mortar

㉓ **el bloque de hormigón**
breeze block

㉔ **las tejas**
roof tiles

㉕ **construir**
to build

See also
25 Un lugar donde vivir • A place to live **32** La casa y el hogar • House and home **33** La electricidad y la fontanería • Electrics and plumbing **35** El bricolaje • Home improvements **36** Las herramientas • Tools **37** La decoración • Decorating

87.2 LA MAQUINARIA • MACHINERY

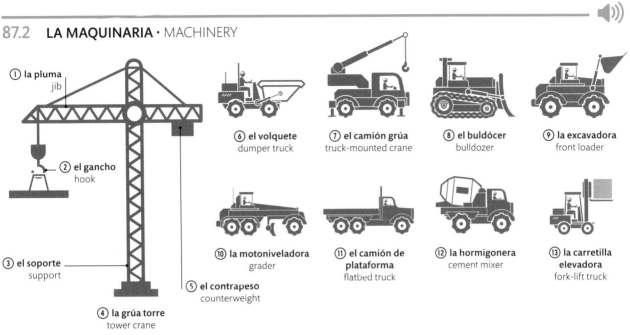

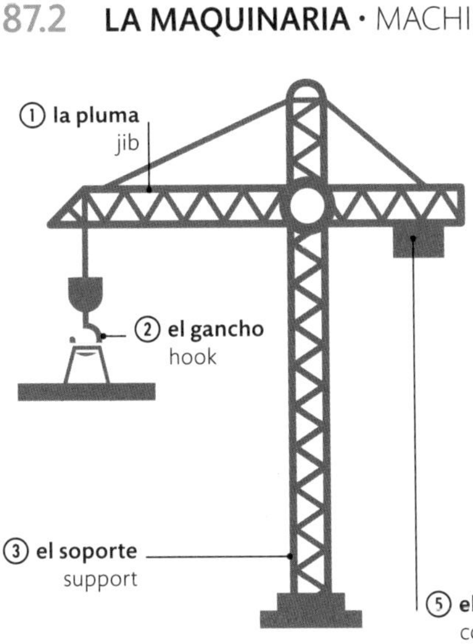
① **la pluma** jib
② **el gancho** hook
③ **el soporte** support
④ **la grúa torre** tower crane
⑤ **el contrapeso** counterweight

⑥ **el volquete** dumper truck
⑦ **el camión grúa** truck-mounted crane
⑧ **el buldócer** bulldozer
⑨ **la excavadora** front loader
⑩ **la motoniveladora** grader
⑪ **el camión de plataforma** flatbed truck
⑫ **la hormigonera** cement mixer
⑬ **la carretilla elevadora** fork-lift truck

87.3 LAS HERRAMIENTAS Y LAS OBRAS EN LA CARRETERA • TOOLS AND ROADWORKS

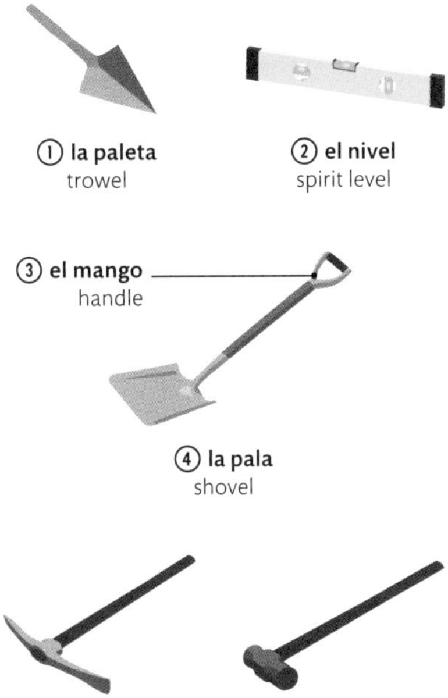
① **la paleta** trowel
② **el nivel** spirit level
③ **el mango** handle
④ **la pala** shovel
⑤ **el pico** pickaxe
⑥ **el mazo** sledgehammer

⑦ **la excavadora** excavator / digger
⑧ **Debes llevar el casco cuando estés en la obra.** You must wear a hard hat while you're on the site.
⑨ **la apisonadora** roller
⑩ **el cono** cone
⑪ **la repavimentación** resurfacing
⑫ **el martillo neumático** pneumatic drill
⑬ **las obras en la carretera** roadworks

88 El ejército
Military

88.1 LAS FUERZAS ARMADAS
ARMED FORCES

① **el ejército**
army

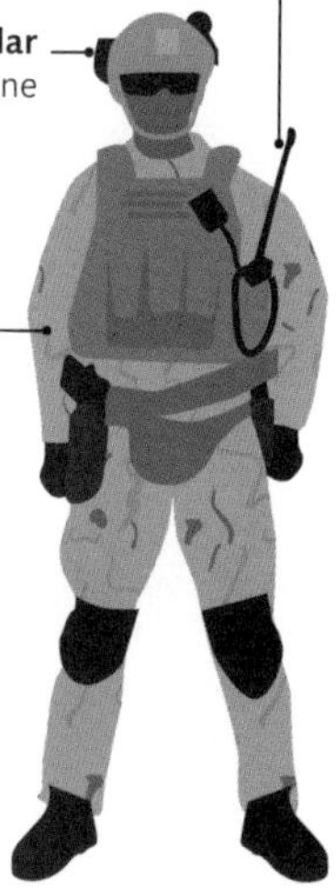

⑤ **la radio**
radio

⑥ **el auricular**
ear phone

⑦ **el camuflaje**
camouflage

④ **el soldado** *m*
la soldado *f*
soldier

② **el soldado de marina** *m* / **la soldado de marina** *f*
marine

③ **la armada**
navy

⑧ **los marineros** *m* / **las marineras** *f*
sailors

⑨ **el general** *m*
la general *f*
general

⑩ **el almirante** *m*
la almirante *f*
admiral

⑫ **el piloto** *m*
la piloto *f*
airman

⑬ **el uniforme**
uniform

⑪ **la fuerza aérea**
airforce

⑮ **la medalla**
medal

⑭ **el veterano** *m*
la veterana *f*
veteran

88.2 LOS VEHÍCULOS MILITARES
MILITARY VEHICLES

③ **el tanque**
tank

① **el cañón**
gun

② **el vehículo blindado**
armoured vehicle

④ **el camión militar**
military truck

⑤ **el vehículo anfibio**
amphibious vehicle

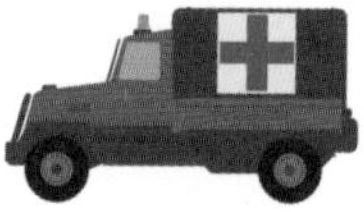

⑥ **la ambulancia militar**
military ambulance

⑦ **el vehículo de exploración**
reconnaissance vehicle

88.3 LOS BUQUES DE LA ARMADA
NAVY VESSELS

② **la isla**
island

① **el portaviones**
aircraft carrier

③ **el destructor**
destroyer

④ **el crucero**
cruiser

⑤ **la fragata**
frigate

⑥ **el submarino**
submarine

See also
79 La historia • History **148** Los mapas y las indicaciones
Maps and directions **149-151** Los países • Countries

88.4 LOS AVIONES DE COMBATE • COMBAT AIRCRAFT

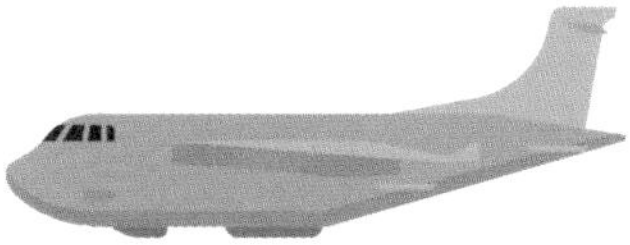

① **el avión de transporte militar**
military transport aircraft

② **el bombardero**
bomber

③ **el helicóptero de ataque**
attack helicopter

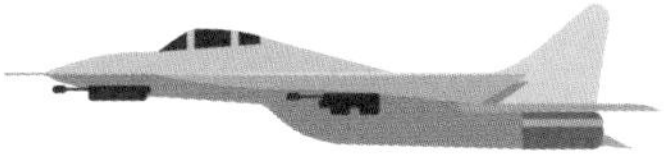

④ **el caza**
fighter

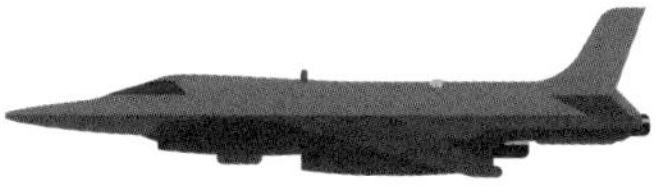

⑤ **el avión de reconocimiento**
reconnaissance aircraft

⑥ **el helicóptero de transporte**
transport helicopter

88.5 LA GUERRA Y LAS ARMAS • WAR AND WEAPONS

① **la batalla**
battle

② **el frente**
front

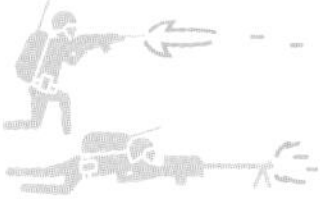

③ **los disparos**
gunfire

④ **la baja**
casualty

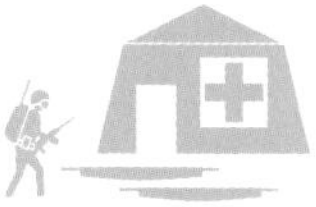

⑤ **el hospital de campaña**
field hospital

⑥ **el comedor**
mess

⑦ **las armas**
guns

⑧ **la ametralladora**
machine gun

⑨ **la pistola**
pistol

⑩ **la escopeta**
shotgun

⑪ **el rifle**
rifle

⑬ **la granada**
grenade

⑫ **el lanzagranadas**
grenade launcher

⑭ **el misil antiaéreo**
surface-to-air missile

⑮ **el misil balístico**
ballistic missile

⑯ **el lanzamisiles portátil**
shoulder-launched missile

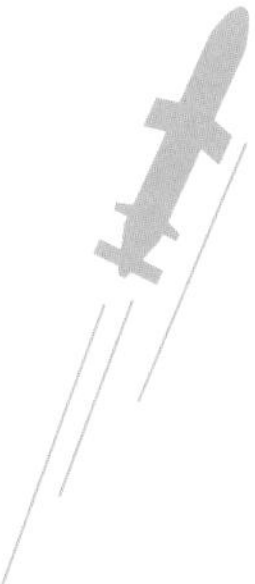

⑰ **el misil teledirigido**
cruise missile

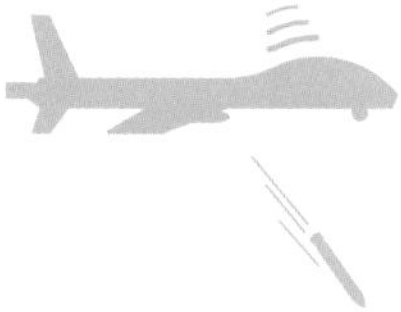

⑱ **el dron armado**
armed drone

89 Los trabajos
Jobs

89.1 LAS PROFESIONES · OCCUPATIONS

① **el actor** *m*
la actriz *f*
actor

② **el sociólogo** *m*
la socióloga *f*
sociologist

③ **el barbero**
barber

④ **el editor** *m*
la editora *f*
editor

⑤ **el barman** *m*
la barman *f*
bartender

⑥ **el pescador** *m*
la pescadora *f*
fisherman

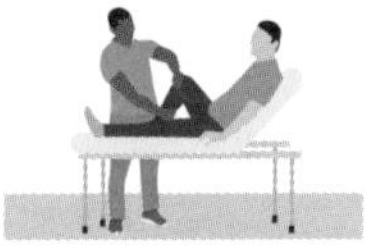

⑦ **el fisioterapeuta** *m*
la fisioterapeuta *f*
physical therapist / physiotherapist

⑧ **el óptico** *m*
la óptica *f*
optician

⑩ **Esta tubería tiene una fuga.**
This pipe has sprung a leak.

⑨ **el fontanero** *m* / **la fontanera** *f*
plumber

⑪ **el carpintero** *m*
la carpintera *f*
carpenter

⑫ **el capitán** *m*
la capitana *f*
ship's captain

⑬ **el profesor** *m*
la profesora *f*
lecturer

⑭ **el cómico** *m*
la cómica *f*
comedian

⑮ **el bailarín** *m*
la bailarina *f*
dancer

⑯ **el payaso** *m*
la payasa *f*
clown

⑰ **el limpiador** *m*
la limpiadora *f*
cleaner

⑱ **el doctor** *m*
la doctora *f*
doctor

⑲ **el profesor de autoescuela** *m* / **la profesora de autoescuela** *f*
driving instructor

⑳ **el pintor** *m*
la pintora *f*
painter

㉑ **el electricista** *m*
la electricista *f*
electrician

㉒ **el diseñador** *m*
la diseñadora *f*
designer

㉓ **el barista** *m*
la barista *f*
barista

㉔ **el bombero** *m*
la bombera *f*
firefighter

㉕ **el desarrollador de aplicaciones** *m*
la desarrolladora de aplicaciones *f*
app developer

㉖ **el espía** *m*
la espía *f*
spy

㉗ **el florista** *m*
la florista *f*
florist

㉘ **el encargado de mantenimiento** *m*
la encargada de mantenimiento *f*
ground maintenance

㉙ **el jardinero** *m*
la jardinera *f*
gardener

㉚ **el verdulero** *m*
la verdulera *f*
greengrocer

㉛ **el minero** *m*
la minera *f*
miner

㉜ **el informático** *m*
la informática *f*
IT manager

㉝ **el joyero** *m*
la joyera *f*
jeweller

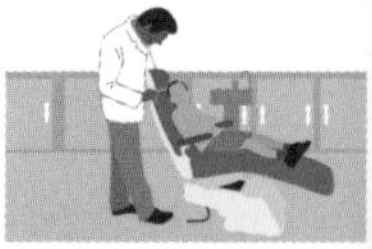

㉞ **el dentista** *m*
la dentista *f*
dentist

See also
81 En el trabajo • At work **82** En la oficina • In the office **90** Los trabajos (continuación) Jobs continued **91** Las industrias y los departamentos • Industries and departments **92** Presentarse para un puesto de trabajo • Applying for a job **93** Las competencias laborales • Workplace skills **95** Reuniéndose y presentando • Meeting and presenting

(35) **la empleada doméstica** *m* **/ el empleado doméstico** *f*
maid / housekeeper

(36) **el peluquero** *m* **la peluquera** *f*
hairdresser / stylist

(37) **el mecánico** *m* **la mecánica** *f*
mechanic

(38) **el intérprete** *m* **la intérprete** *f*
interpreter

(39) **el conservador del museo** *m* **la conservadora del museo** *f*
museum curator

(40) **el detective privado** *m* **la detective privada** *f*
private investigator

(41) **el jefe de obra** *m* **la jefa de obra** *f*
site manager

(42) **el ortodoncista** *m* **la ortodoncista** *f*
orthodontist

(43) **el presentador** *m* **la presentadora** *f*
newsreader

(44) **el farmacéutico** *m* **la farmacéutica** *f*
pharmacist

(45) **el carnicero** *m* **la carnicera** *f*
butcher

(46) **el fotógrafo** *m* **la fotógrafa** *f*
photographer

(47) **el policía** *m* **la policía** *f*
police officer

(48) **el enfermero** *m* **la enfermera** *f*
nurse

(49) **el marinero** *m* **la marinera** *f*
sailor

(50) **el dependiente** *m* **la dependienta** *f*
sales assistant

(51) **la camarera**
waitress

(52) **el camarero**
waiter

(53) **el escultor** *m* **la escultora** *f*
sculptor

(54) **el guardia de seguridad** *m* **la guardia de seguridad** *f*
security guard

(55) **el sastre** *m* **la modista** *f*
tailor

(56) **el instructor de esquí** *m* **/ la instructora de esquí** *f*
ski instructor

(57) **el soldado** *m* **la soldado** *f*
soldier

(58) **el granjero** *m* **la granjera** *f*
farmer

(59) **el deportista** *m* **la deportista** *f*
sportsperson

(60) **el pescadero** *m* **la pescadera** *f*
fishmonger

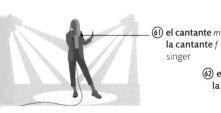

(61) **el cantante** *m* **la cantante** *f*
singer

(62) **el agente inmobiliario** *m* **la agente inmobiliaria** *f*
estate agent

(63) **el investigador de mercado** *m* **la investigadora de mercado** *f*
market researcher

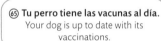

(65) **Tu perro tiene las vacunas al día.**
Your dog is up to date with its vaccinations.

(64) **el veterinario** *m* **/ la veterinaria** *f*
vet

Los trabajos (continuación)
Jobs continued

90.1 **LAS PROFESIONES** · OCCUPATIONS

① **el guardia de seguridad** *m* / **la guardia de seguridad** *f*
security guard

② **el limpiador de cristales** *m* / **la limpiadora de cristales** *f*
window cleaner

③ **el artista** *m*
la artista *f*
artist

④ **el guardaespalda** *m*
la guardaespaldas *f*
bodyguard

⑤ **el psicólogo** *m*
la psicóloga *f*
psychologist

⑥ **el empresario**
businessman

⑦ **la empresaria**
businesswoman

⑧ **el contable** *m*
la contable *f*
accountant

⑨ **el chef** *m* / **la chef** *f*
chef

⑩ **el obrero** *m*
la obrera *f*
builder

⑪ **el DJ de radio** *m*
la DJ de radio *f*
radio DJ

⑫ **el ingeniero** *m*
la ingeniera *f*
engineer

⑬ **el diseñador de moda** *m* / **la diseñadora de moda** *f*
fashion designer

⑭ **la estrella del rock** *m* / *f*
rock star

⑮ **el instructor de vuelo** *m* / **la instructora de vuelo** *f*
flight instructor

⑯ **el conserje** *m*
la conserje *f*
janitor

⑰ **el guía turístico** *m*
la guía turística *f*
tour guide

⑱ **el cartero** *m*
la cartera *f*
postman, postwoman

⑲ **el asistente personal** *m* / **la asistenta personal** *f*
personal assistant (PA)

⑳ **el bibliotecario** *m*
la bibliotecaria *f*
librarian

㉑ **el cerrajero** *m*
la cerrajera *f*
locksmith

㉒ **el paramédico** *m*
la paramédica *f*
paramedic

㉓ **el profesor de música** *m* / **la profesora de música** *f*
music teacher

㉔ **el niñero** *m*
la niñera *f*
childcare provider

㉕ **el montador de cocinas** *m* / **la montadora de cocinas** *f*
kitchen installer / fitter

㉖ **el taxista** *m*
la taxista *f*
taxi driver

㉗ **el guardián del zoo** *m*
la guardiana del zoo *f*
zookeeper

㉙ **Antes de ser juez, debes adquirir experiencia en los tribunales.**
You should have a lot of courtroom experience before you become a judge.

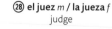

㉘ **el juez** *m* / **la jueza** *f*
judge

See also
81 En el trabajo • At work **82** En la oficina • In the office **91** Las industrias y los departamentos Industries and departments **92** Presentarse para un puesto de trabajo • Applying for a job **93** Las competencias laborales • Workplace skills **95** Reuniéndose y presentando • Meeting and presenting

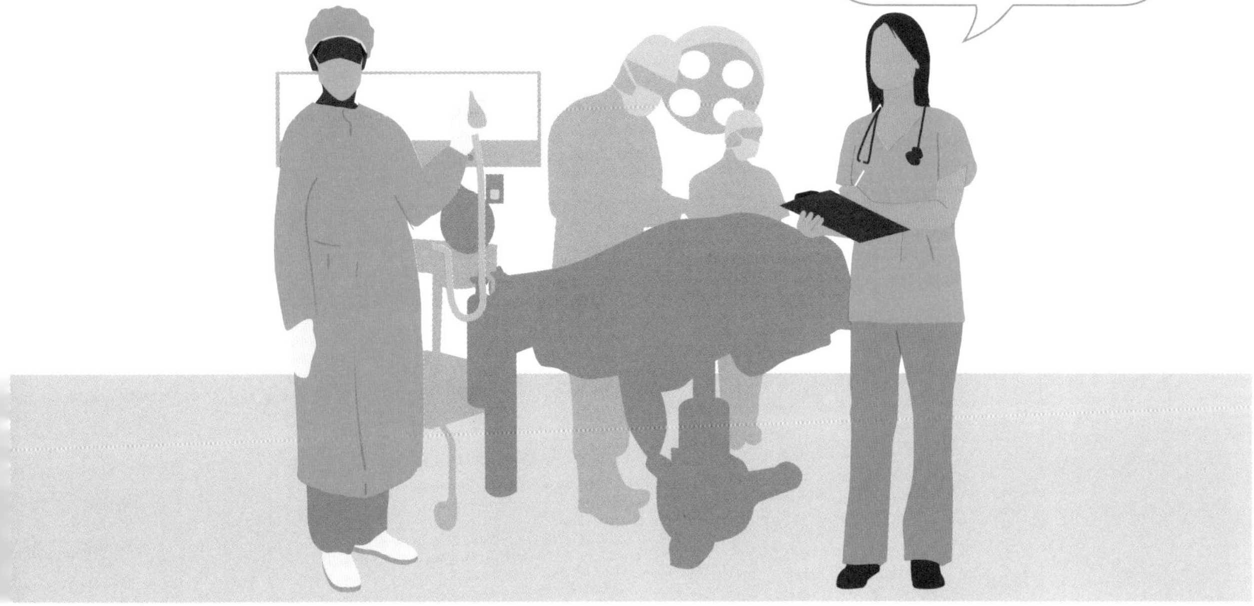

㉜ Mi turno empezó a las 8 de la mañana.
My shift started at 8 o'clock this morning.

㉚ el anestesista *m* **/ la anestesista** *f*
anaesthetist

㉛ el cirujano *m* **/ la cirujana** *f*
surgeon

㉝ el conductor *m*
la conductora *f*
driver

㉞ el secretario *m*
la secretaria *f*
secretary

㉟ el recepcionista *m*
la recepcionista *f*
receptionist

㊱ el azafato *m*
la azafata *f*
flight attendant

㊲ el científico *m*
la científica *f*
scientist

㊳ el conductor de autobús *m* **/ la conductora de autobús** *f*
bus driver

㊴ el músico *m*
la música *f*
musician

㊵ el topógrafo *m*
la topógrafa *f*
surveyor

㊶ el abogado *m*
la abogada *f*
lawyer

㊷ el profesor *m*
la profesora *f*
teacher

㊸ el periodista *m*
la periodista *f*
journalist

㊹ el maquinista *m*
la maquinista *f*
train driver

㊺ el agente de viajes *m*
la agente de viajes *f*
travel agent

㊻ el camionero *m*
la camionera *f*
lorry driver

㊼ el arquitecto *m*
la arquitecta *f*
architect

㊽ el escritor *m*
la escritora *f*
writer

㊾ el profesor de yoga *m*
la profesora de yoga *f*
yoga teacher

㊿ el piloto *m*
la piloto *f*
pilot

91 Las industrias y los departamentos
Industries and departments

91.1 LAS INDUSTRIAS · INDUSTRIES

1 **la publicidad**
advertising

2 **los servicios personales**
personal services

3 **la agricultura**
agriculture / farming

4 **las fuerzas armadas**
military

5 **el mercado inmobiliario**
property

6 **la industria automovilística**
automotive industry

10 **la banca**
banking

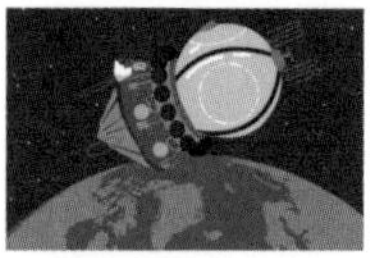

11 **la industria aeroespacial**
aerospace

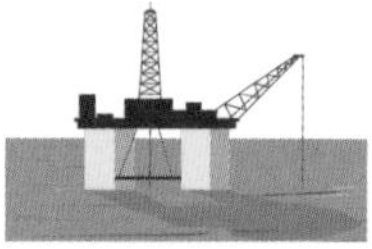

12 **la ingeniería petrolífera**
petroleum engineering

13 **la industria química**
chemical industry

14 **las artes**
arts

15 **la educación**
education

19 **los videojuegos**
gaming

20 **la energía**
energy

21 **la investigación**
research

22 **la moda**
fashion

23 **el reciclaje**
recycling

24 **el entretenimiento**
entertainment

28 **el transporte marítimo**
shipping

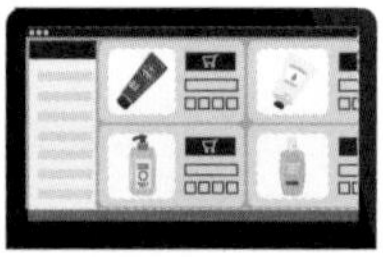

29 **el comercio en línea**
online retail

30 **el periodismo**
journalism

31 **la industria textil**
textiles

32 **los medios**
media

33 **la industria hotelera**
hospitality

37 **la entrega a domicilio**
online delivery

38 **la industria del agua**
water

39 **las artes escénicas**
performing arts

40 **la biotecnología**
biotechnology

42 Nuestras acciones han caído en picado.
Our stocks have fallen dramatically.

41 **las finanzas**
finance

See also
81 En el trabajo • At work **82** En la oficina • In the office **89-90** Los trabajos • Jobs **92** Presentarse para un puesto de trabajo • Applying for a job **93** Las competencias laborales • Workplace skills

⑧ **Este es uno de nuestros edificios más emblemáticos.**
This is one of our most famous buildings.

⑦ **el turismo**
tourism

⑨ **los servicios veterinarios**
pet services

⑯ **el catering**
catering / food

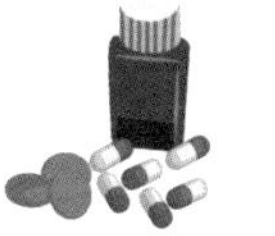

⑰ **la industria farmacéutica**
pharmaceuticals

⑱ **la construcción**
construction

㉕ **la pesca**
fishing

㉖ **la electrónica**
electronics

㉗ **el comercio**
retail

㉞ **la sanidad**
healthcare

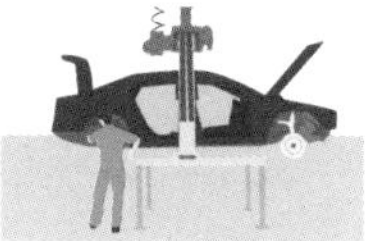

㉟ **la manufactura**
manufacturing

㊱ **la minería**
mining

㊸ **el transporte**
transport

91.2 LOS DEPARTAMENTOS
DEPARTMENTS

① **el departamento financiero**
accounts / finance

② **el departamento de producción**
production

CONTRACT

③ **el departamento jurídico**
legal

④ **el departamento de marketing**
marketing

⑤ **el departamento informático**
information technology (IT)

⑥ **el departamento de mantenimiento**
facilities / office services

⑦ **el departamento de ventas**
sales

⑧ **el departamento de administración**
administration

⑨ **el departamento de relaciones públicas**
public relations (PR)

⑩ **el departamento de compras**
purchasing

⑪ **el departamento de recursos humanos**
human resources (HR)

⑬ **Me encantan las ideas para el nuevo proyecto.**
I love these ideas for the new project.

⑫ **el departamento de investigación y desarrollo (I+D)**
research and development (R&D)

92 Presentarse para un puesto de trabajo
Applying for a job

92.1 LA SOLICITUD DE EMPLEO · JOB APPLICATIONS

① **las ofertas de empleo**
job ads

② **el formulario de solicitud**
application form

③ **la carta de presentación**
cover letter

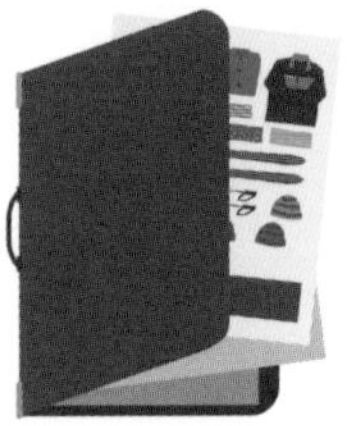

④ **el portafolio**
portfolio

⑤ **el currículum**
CV

⑧ ¿Qué tipo de trabajo estás buscando?
What kind of work are you looking for?

⑦ **rellenar un formulario**
to fill out a form

⑥ **la empresa de selección de personal**
recruitment agency

92.2 PRESENTARSE PARA UN PUESTO DE TRABAJO · APPLYING FOR A JOB

② **la vacante**
vacancies

① **presentarse para un puesto de trabajo**
to apply for a job

④ ¿Qué te hace ser la candidata perfecta para el puesto?
What makes you the perfect candidate for this job?
⑤ Soy muy aplicada y trabajo bien en equipo.
I'm hardworking and I'm a team player.

③ **hacer una entrevista**
to have an interview

See also
81 En el trabajo • At work **89-90** Los trabajos • Jobs **91** Las industrias y los departamentos • Industries and departments **93** Las competencias laborales Workplace skills **95** Reuniéndose y presentando • Meeting and presenting

92.3 EL TRABAJO EN EQUIPO
TEAMWORK

① **colaborar**
to collaborate

② **coordinar**
to coordinate

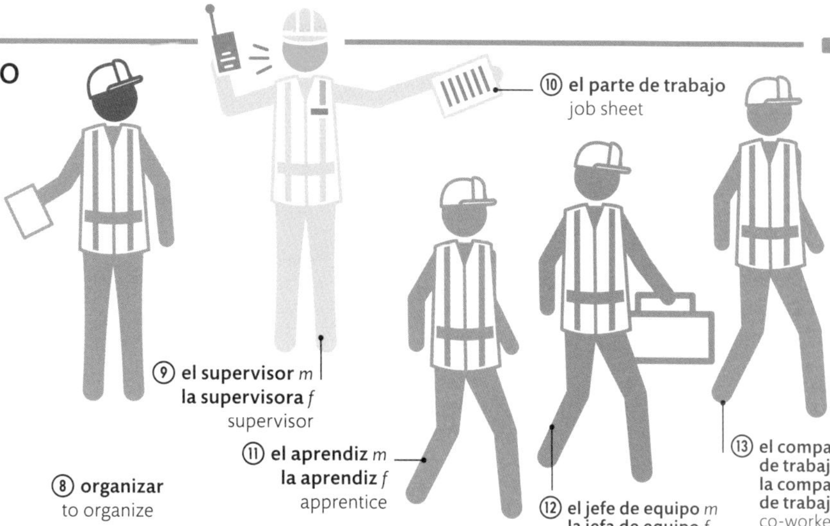
⑩ **el parte de trabajo**
job sheet
⑨ **el supervisor** *m*
la supervisora *f*
supervisor
⑪ **el aprendiz** *m*
la aprendiz *f*
apprentice
⑫ **el jefe de equipo** *m*
la jefa de equipo *f*
team leader
⑬ **el compañero de trabajo** *m*
la compañera de trabajo *f*
co-worker / colleague

⑧ **organizar**
to organize

③ **negociar**
to negotiate

④ **ofrecerse voluntario** *m*
ofrecerse voluntaria *f*
to volunteer

⑤ **supervisar**
to supervise

⑥ **dirigir**
to manage

⑦ **cumplir el plazo de entrega**
to meet a deadline

⑧ **Bienvenida a la empresa. Estamos deseando trabajar contigo.**
Welcome to the company. We are looking forward to working with you.
⑦ **dar la mano**
to shake hands

⑥ **conseguir el empleo**
to get the job

⑪ **Tengo muchas ganas de empezar.**
I can't wait to get started.
⑩ **el contrato**
contract

⑨ **firmar un contrato**
to sign a contract

93 Las competencias laborales
Workplace skills

93.1 LOS ATRIBUTOS PROFESIONALES • PROFESSIONAL ATTRIBUTES

① **organizado** *m*
organizada *f*
organized

② **paciente** *m / f*
patient

③ **creativo** *m*
creativa *f*
creative

④ **honrado** *m*
honrada *f*
honest

⑤ **práctico** *m*
práctica *f*
practical

⑥ **profesional**
professional

⑦ **adaptable**
adaptable

⑧ **ambicioso** *m*
ambiciosa *f*
ambitious

⑨ **calmado** *m*
calmada *f*
calm

⑩ **seguro** *m*
segura *f*
confident

⑪ **puntual**
punctual

⑫ **fidedigno** *m*
fidedigna *f*
reliable

⑬ **orientado al cliente** *m*
orientada al cliente *f*
customer-focused

⑭ **independiente**
independent

⑮ **eficiente**
efficient

⑯ **colaborador** *m*
colaboradora *f*
team player

⑰ **responsable**
responsible

⑱ **innovador** *m*
innovadora *f*
innovative

⑲ **motivado** *m*
motivada *f*
motivated

⑳ **resuelto** *m* / **resuelta** *f*
determined

㉑ **energético** *m*
energética *f*
energetic

㉓ Carlos es el chef más aplicado que he conocido.
Carlo is the hardest-working chef I've ever met.

㉒ **aplicado** *m*
aplicada *f*
hard-working

㉔ **competitivo** *m*
competitiva *f*
competitive

㉕ **asertivo** *m* / **asertiva** *f*
assertive

㉖ **imaginativo** *m*
imaginativa *f*
imaginative

㉗ **curioso** *m* / **curios**
curious

㉘ **original**
original

㉙ **preciso** *m*
precisa *f*
accurate

㉚ **que sabe escuchar**
good listener

㉛ **flexible**
flexible

See also
10 Los rasgos de personalidad • Personality traits
11 Las habilidades y las acciones • Abilities and actions
81 En el trabajo • At work **82** En la oficina • In the office

93.2 LAS HABILIDADES PROFESIONALES • PROFESSIONAL EXPERTISE

① **la organización**
organization

② **la alfabetización informática**
computer literacy

③ **la informática**
computing

④ **la resolución de problemas**
problem-solving

⑤ **la analítica**
analytics

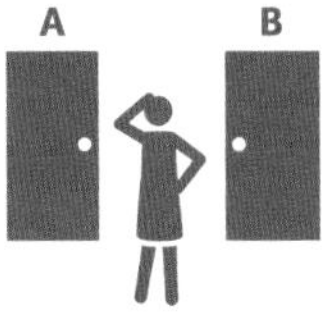

⑥ **la toma de decisiones**
decision-making

⑦ **el trabajo en equipo**
teamwork

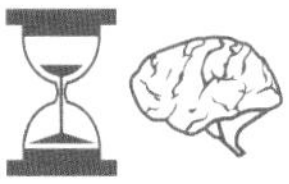

⑧ **el aprendizaje rápido**
being a fast learner

⑨ **la atención a los detalles**
paying attention to detail

⑩ **la atención al cliente**
customer service

⑪ **el liderazgo**
leadership

⑫ **la investigación**
research

⑬ **el dominio de los idiomas**
fluent in languages

⑭ **la alfabetización tecnológica**
technology literate

⑮ **la oratoria**
public speaking

⑯ **la negociación**
negotiating

⑰ **la comunicación escrita**
written communication

⑱ **la iniciativa**
initiative

⑲ **los modales por teléfono**
telephone manner

⑳ **la capacidad de trabajo bajo presión**
working well under pressure

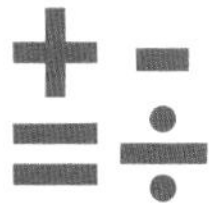

㉑ **las habilidades numéricas**
numeracy

㉒ **la capacidad para conducir**
ability to drive

㉓ **bien cualificado** *m* **bien cualificada** *f*
well-qualified

㉔ **la autogestión**
self management

㉕ **servicial**
service focused

㉖ **influyente**
influencer

㉜ **¡Tienes que mejorar en la gestión del tiempo! Este informe llega tarde.**
You must improve your time management! This report is late.

㉗ **la actitud profesional**
businesslike attitude

㉘ **las habilidades interpersonales**
interpersonal skills

㉙ **la gestión de proyectos**
project management

㉚ **la administración**
administration

㉛ **la gestión del tiempo**
time management

94 El dinero y las finanzas

Money and finance

94.1 EL DINERO · MONEY

① **el valor** denomination
② **la marca de agua** watermark
③ **las monedas** coins
④ **la tarjeta de crédito** credit card
⑤ **la tarjeta de débito** debit card
⑥ **la cartera** wallet
⑦ **el monedero** purse
⑧ **el dinero falso** counterfeit money
⑨ **el dinero** money
⑩ **los billetes** notes

⑪ **la billetera digital** digital wallet

⑫ **la moneda digital** digital currency

⑬ **el banco** bank

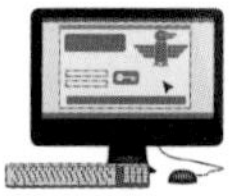

⑭ **la banca digital** online banking

⑮ **la banca móvil** mobile banking

⑯ **la banca telefónica** telephone banking

⑰ **el recibo** receipt

⑱ **la divisa** currency

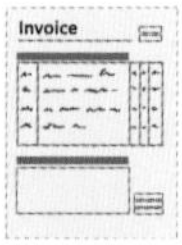

⑲ **la factura** invoice

⑳ **el cheque** cheque

㉑ **la caja registradora** till

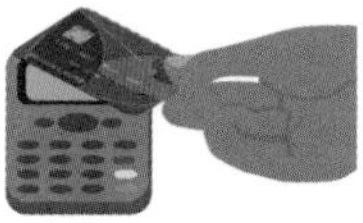

㉒ **pagar con tarjeta** to pay by card

㉔ **¿Se puede pagar en efectivo?** Do you accept cash here?

㉓ **pagar en efectivo** to pay with cash

See also
45 El banco y la oficina de correos • The bank and post office
91 Las industrias y los departamentos • Industries and departments

94.2 **LAS FINANZAS** • FINANCE

① **el agente de bolsa** *m*
la agente de bolsa *f*
stockbroker

② **el mercado de valores** *m*
la bolsa de valores *f*
stock exchange

③ **las acciones**
shares

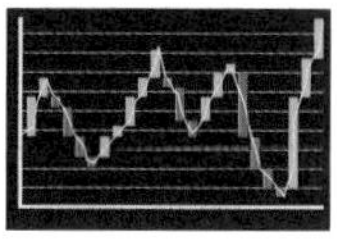

④ **la cotización**
share price

⑤ **los dividendos**
dividends

⑥ **la comisión**
commission

⑦ **el patrimonio neto**
equity

⑧ **la inversión**
investment

⑨ **la cartera de valores**
portfolio

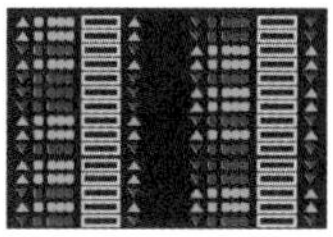

⑩ **las acciones**
stocks

⑪ **la tasa de cambio**
exchange rate

⑫ **los ingresos**
income

⑬ **el presupuesto**
budget

⑭ **endeudarse**
to get into debt

⑮ **obtener beneficios**
to make a profit

⑯ **tener pérdidas**
to make a loss

⑰ **cubrir pérdidas**
to break even

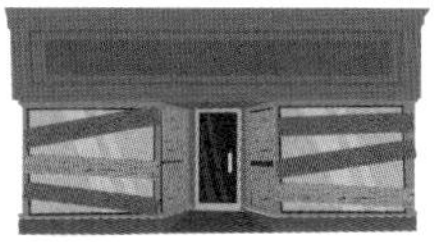

⑱ **quebrar**
to go out of business

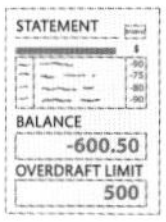

⑲ **el descubierto**
overdraft

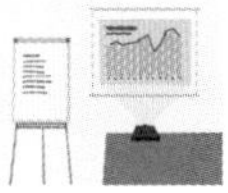

⑳ **el gasto**
expenditure / outlay

㉑ **la recesión**
economic downturn

㉒ **el contable** *m*
la contable *f*
accountant

㉔ **Puedo aconsejarte dónde invertir tu dinero.**
I can advise you where to invest your money.

㉓ **el asesor financiero** *m*
la asesora financiera *f*
financial advisor

95 Reuniéndose y presentando
Meeting and presenting

95.1 REUNIÉNDOSE · MEETING

② **¿Cuál es el orden del día hoy, María?**
What's on the agenda today, Maria?

③ **Vamos a debatir las presentaciones para la próxima semana.**
We're discussing the presentations for next week.

① **asistir a una reunión**
to attend a meeting

④ **hacer una teleconferencia**
to have a conference call

⑤ **redactar el acta**
to take minutes

⑥ **responder preguntas**
to take questions

⑦ **ausentarse**
to be absent

⑧ **interrumpir**
to interrupt

⑨ **llegar a un consenso**
to reach a consensus

⑩ **el voto unánime**
unanimous vote

⑪ **los puntos de acción**
action points

⑫ **la votación a mano alzada**
show of hands

⑬ **otros asuntos**
any other business

⑭ **la sala de juntas**
boardroom

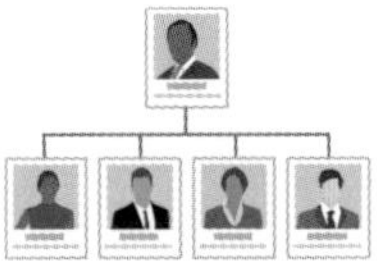

⑮ **la junta directiva**
board of directors

⑯ **llegar a un acuerd**
to reach an agreement

⑰ **la asamblea general anual**
annual general meeting (AGM)

⑱ **concluir la reunión**
to wrap up the meeting

⑲ **la pizarra**
whiteboard

⑳ **la libreta**
notebook

㉑ **el orden del día**
agenda

See also
81 En el trabajo • At work **82** En la oficina • In the office
83 Los ordenadores y la tecnología • Computers and technology **84** Los medios de comunicación • Media

95.2 **PRESENTANDO** • PRESENTING

① **comenzar**
to commence

② **resumir**
to sum up

③ **quedarse sin tiempo**
to run out of time

④ **la diapositiva**
slide

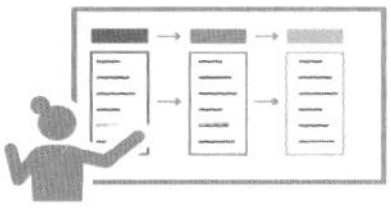

⑤ **la hoja de ruta**
roadmap

⑥ **dar una presentación**
to give a presentation

⑦ **el proyector**
projector

⑧ **el temporizador**
timer

⑨ **el cable HDMI**
HDMI cable

⑩ **los altavoces portátiles**
portable speakers

⑪ **los folletos**
handouts

⑫ **las notas**
notes

⑬ **el puntero láser**
smartpen

⑭ **el micrófono**
microphone

⑮ **los cascos**
headphones

⑯ **el rotafolio**
flip chart

⑰ **compartir la pantalla**
to share your screen

⑱ **el mando para presentaciones**
presenter remote

⑲ **la conferencia**
conference

⑳ **el ponente invitado** *m*
la ponente invitada *f*
guest speaker

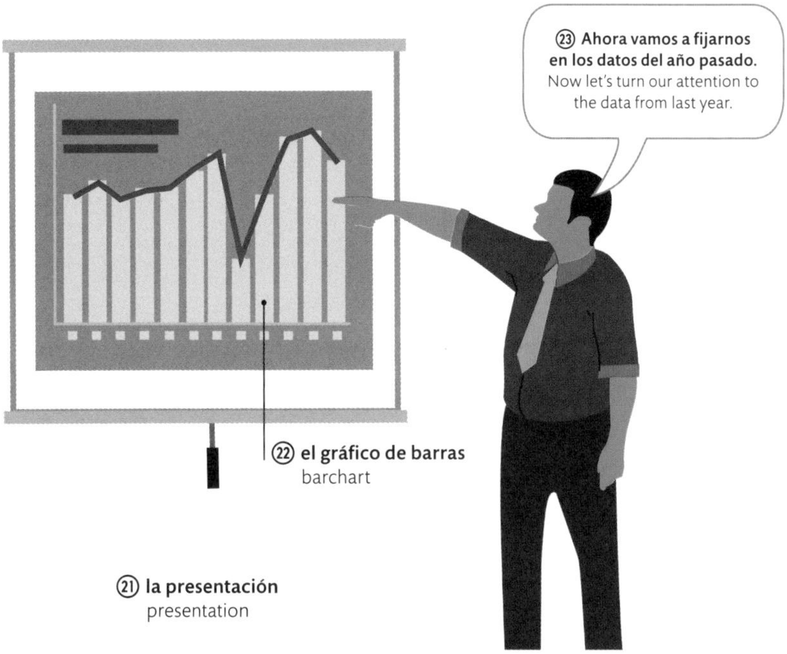

㉓ **Ahora vamos a fijarnos en los datos del año pasado.**
Now let's turn our attention to the data from last year.

㉒ **el gráfico de barras**
barchart

㉑ **la presentación**
presentation

96 Las carreteras
Roads

96.1 POR LA CARRETERA · ON THE ROAD

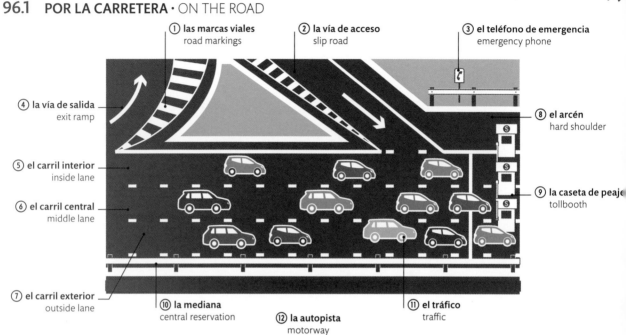

① **las marcas viales**
road markings

② **la vía de acceso**
slip road

③ **el teléfono de emergencia**
emergency phone

④ **la vía de salida**
exit ramp

⑤ **el carril interior**
inside lane

⑥ **el carril central**
middle lane

⑦ **el carril exterior**
outside lane

⑧ **el arcén**
hard shoulder

⑨ **la caseta de peaje**
tollbooth

⑩ **la mediana**
central reservation

⑪ **el tráfico**
traffic

⑫ **la autopista**
motorway

⑭ **la línea divisoria**
divider

⑬ **la autovía**
dual carriageway

⑮ **el cruce**
junction

⑯ **la rotonda**
roundabout

⑰ **el paso elevado**
flyover

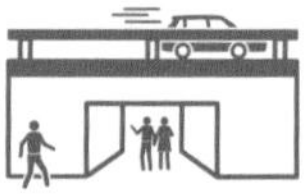

⑱ **el paso subterráneo**
underpass

⑲ **la barrera de tráfico**
crash barrier

⑳ **el desvío**
diversion

㉑ **el radar de velocidad**
speed camera

㉒ **la luz roja**
traffic light

㉓ **el atasco**
traffic jam

㉔ **la vía de un solo sentido**
one-way street

㉕ **el paso de peatones**
pedestrian crossing

㉖ **las obras en la carretera**
roadworks

㉗ **el parking para minusválidos**
disabled parking

㉘ **el guardacoches** *m*
la guardacoches *f*
parking attendant

㉙ **el parquímetro**
parking meter

See also
42-43 La ciudad • In town **97-98** Los coches • Cars **99** Los coches y los autobuses • Cars and buses **100** Las motocicletas • Motorcycles **101** El ciclismo • Cycling **123** Los deportes de motor • Motorsports **148** Los mapas y las indicaciones • Maps and directions

96.2 LAS SEÑALES DE TRÁFICO • ROAD SIGNS

① **prohibido el paso**
no entry

② **el límite de velocidad**
speed limit

③ **peligro** *m*
hazard

④ **no girar a la derecha**
no right turn

⑤ **prohibido cambiar de sentido**
no U-turn

⑥ **curva peligrosa hacia la derecha**
right bend

⑦ **el ceda el paso** *m*
give way

⑧ **la señal de prioridad**
priority traffic

⑨ **prohibido el adelantamiento**
no overtaking

⑩ **la zona escolar**
school zone

⑪ **los baches**
bumps

⑫ **paso de animales salvajes**
deer crossing

⑬ **el sentido obligatorio**
direction to follow

⑭ **las obras**
roadworks ahead

⑮ **el peligro por semáforos**
traffic light ahead

⑯ **el fin de la vía para ciclistas**
closed to bicycles

⑰ **la entrada prohibida a peatones**
closed to pedestrians

96.3 LOS VERBOS DE CONDUCCIÓN • VERBS FOR DRIVING

① **conducir**
to drive

② **dar marcha atrás**
to reverse

③ **parar**
to stop

⑤ **el guardia de tráfico** *m*
la guardia de tráfico *f*
traffic warden

④ **remolcar**
to tow away

⑥ **girar hacia la izquierda**
to turn left

⑦ **girar hacia la derecha**
to turn right

⑧ **seguir recto**
to go straight ahead / to go straight on

⑨ **girar en la primera calle a la izquierda**
to take the first left

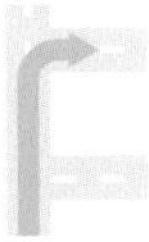
⑩ **girar en la segunda calle a la derecha**
to take the second right

Los coches
Cars

97.1 EL EXTERIOR DEL COCHE · CAR EXTERIOR

⑪ **el parabrisas**
windscreen

⑫ **el limpiaparabrisas**
wiper

⑬ **el retrovisor**
wing mirror

⑭ **el faro**
headlight

⑮ **el intermitente**
indicator

⑯ **la matrícula**
licence plate

⑰ **la vista frontal**
front view

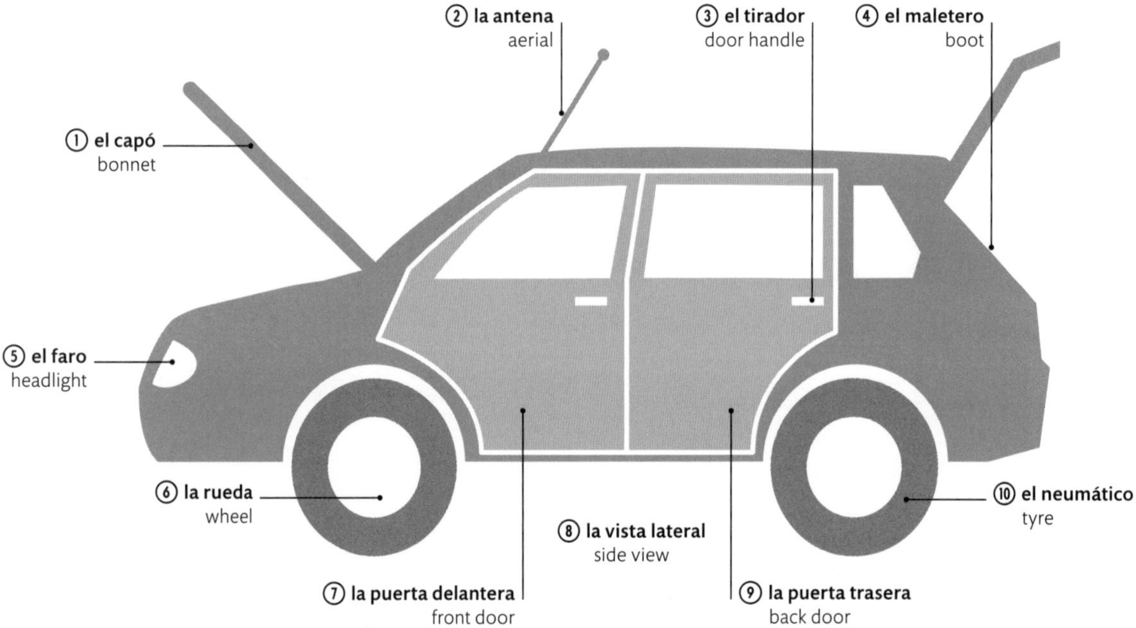

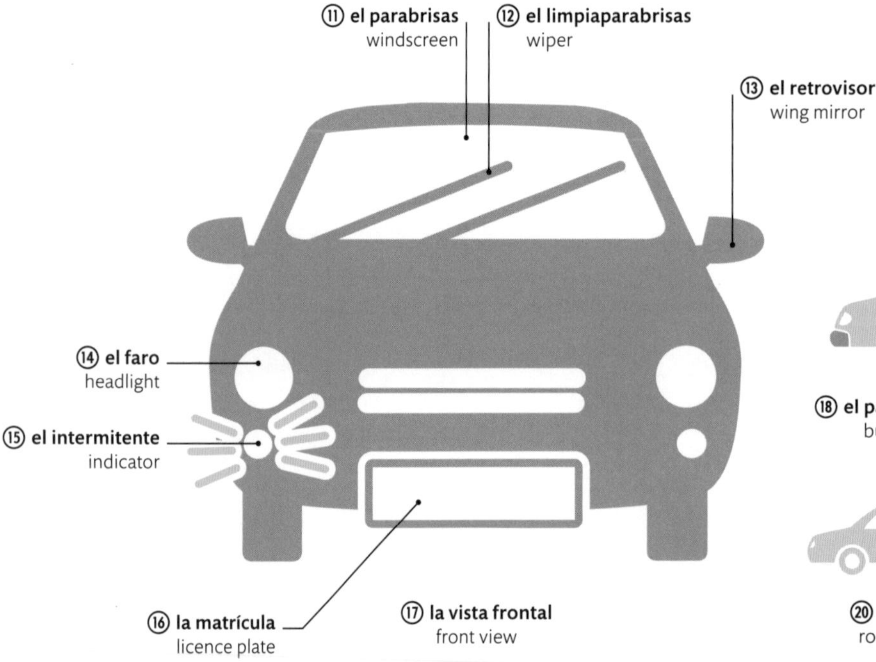

⑱ **el parachoques**
bumper

⑲ **los neumáticos de invierno**
snow tyres

⑳ **la baca**
roof rack

㉑ **la puerta del maletero**
tailgate

See also
42-43 La ciudad • In town **96** Las carreteras • Roads **98** Los coches • Cars **99** Los coches y los autobuses • Cars and buses **100** Las motocicletas • Motorcycles **123** Los deportes de motor • Motorsports

97.2 LOS TIPOS DE COCHES • TYPES OF CARS

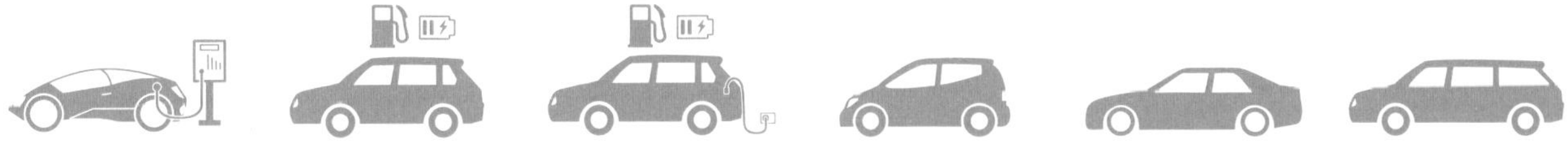

① **el coche eléctrico**
electric car

② **el coche híbrido**
hybrid

③ **el coche híbrido enchufable**
plug-in hybrid

④ **el coche de cinco puertas**
hatchback

⑤ **el sedán**
saloon

⑥ **la ranchera**
estate

⑦ **el todoterreno**
four-wheel drive

⑧ **la minifurgoneta**
people carrier

⑨ **la limusina**
limousine

⑪ **el alerón**
spoiler

⑩ **el coche deportivo**
sports car

⑮ **la barra antivuelco**
roller bar

⑫ **el descapotable**
convertible

⑬ **el coche de época**
vintage

⑭ **el buggy**
beach buggy

⑱ **el alerón trasero**
rear wing

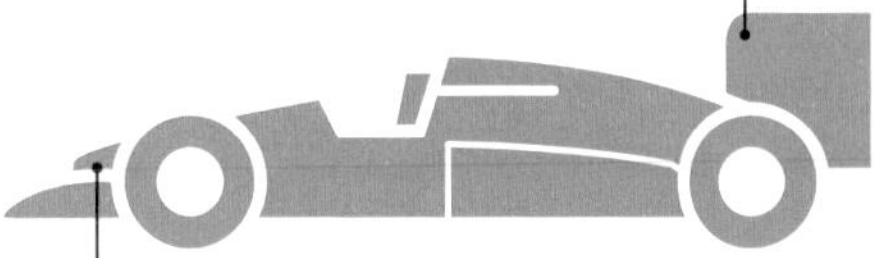

⑰ **el alerón delantero**
front wing

⑯ **el coche de carreras**
racing car

97.3 LA GASOLINERA • PETROL STATION

① **el surtidor**
petrol pump

② **la zona de abastecimiento**
forecourt

③ **el punto de recarga**
electric charge point

④ **el líquido limpiaparabrisas**
screen wash

⑤ **el anticongelante**
antifreeze

⑥ **la gasolina**
petrol

⑦ **sin plomo**
unleaded

⑧ **con plomo**
leaded

⑨ **diésel**
diesel

⑩ **el aceite**
oil

⑪ **el lavadero de coches**
car wash

Los coches (continuación)
Cars continued

98.1 LA ASISTENCIA EN CARRETERA · BREAKDOWN ASSISTANCE

98.2 LA MECÁNICA · MECHANICS

① **la correa del ventilador** fan belt
② **el filtro de aire** air filter
③ **el radiador** radiator
④ **la bujía** spark plug
⑤ **la caja de fusibles** fuse box
⑥ **el distribuidor** distributor
⑦ **el techo corredizo** sunroof
⑧ **el techo** roof
⑨ **el tubo de escape** exhaust pipe
⑩ **el sistema de refrigeración** cooling system
⑪ **el motor** engine
⑫ **la caja de cambios** gearbox
⑬ **la transmisión** transmission
⑭ **la suspensión** suspension
⑮ **el eje de transmisión** driveshaft
⑯ **el tapacubos** hubcap
⑰ **el silenciador** silencer

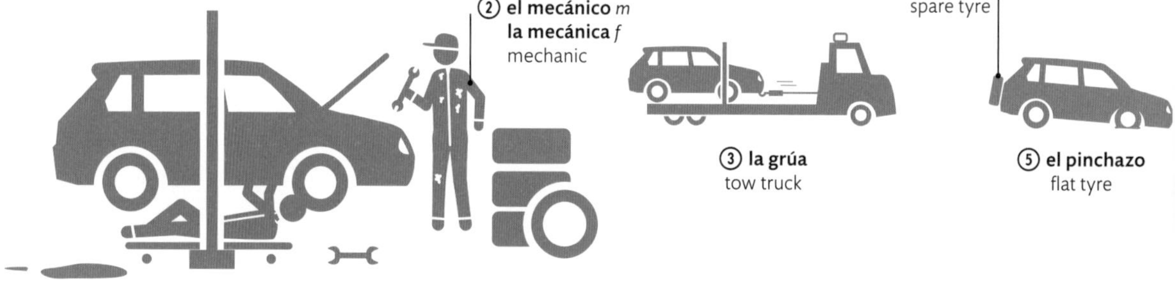

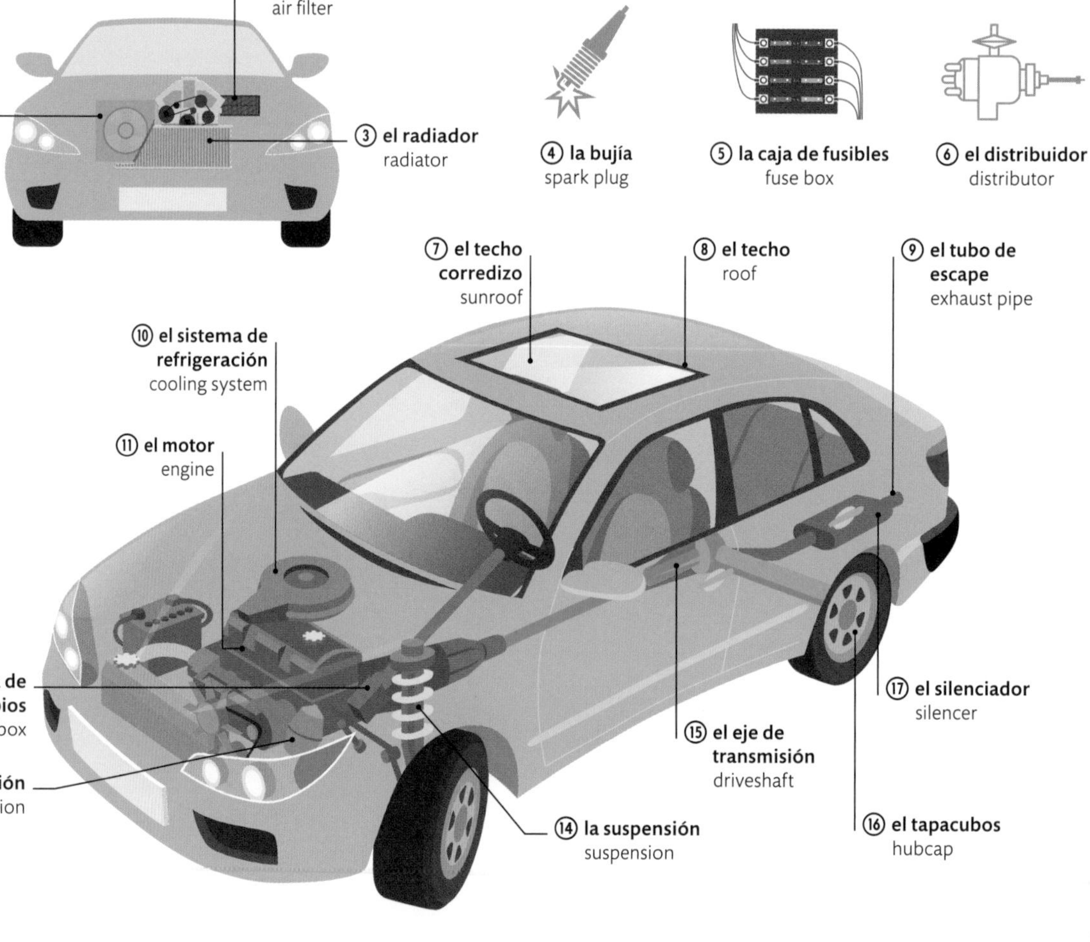

See also
42-43 La ciudad • In town **96** Las carreteras • Roads **99** Los coches y los autobuses • Cars and buses **100** Las motocicletas • Motorcycles **123** Los deportes de motor • Motorsports

6 la llave fija
wrench

7 las tuercas de llanta
wheel nuts

8 el gato hidráulico
jack

18 el depósito del líquido limpiaparabrisas
screen wash reservoir

19 el capó
bonnet

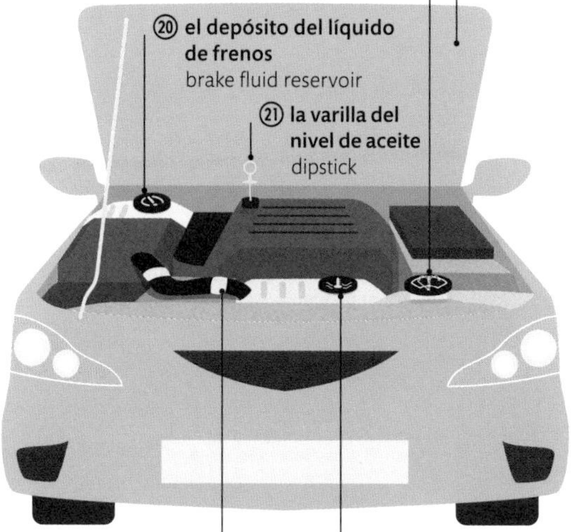

20 el depósito del líquido de frenos
brake fluid reservoir

21 la varilla del nivel de aceite
dipstick

22 el tubo
pipe

23 el depósito del líquido refrigerante
coolant reservoir

24 la batería
battery

25 la carrocería
bodywork

26 la culata
cylinder head

98.3 LOS VERBOS DE CONDUCCIÓN
VERBS FOR DRIVING

1 repostar
to fill up

2 comprobar el nivel de aceite
to check the oil

3 comprobar los neumáticos
to check the tyres

4 pasar la revisión al coche
to service the car

5 aparcar
to park

6 irse
to set off

7 poner el intermitente
to indicate

8 frenar
to brake

9 reducir la velocidad
to slow down

10 acelerar
to speed up

11 recoger a alguien
to pick someone up

12 dejar a alguien
to drop someone off

13 tener un accidente de coche
to have a car accident

14 averiarse
to break down

15 adelantar
to overtake

99 Los coches y los autobuses
Cars and buses

99.1 EL INTERIOR DEL COCHE · CAR INTERIOR

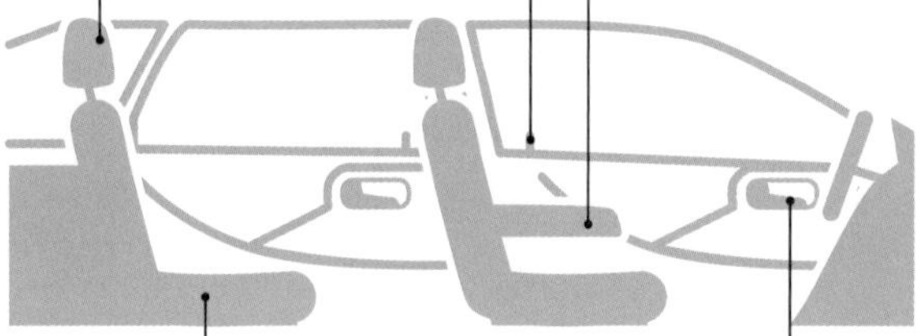

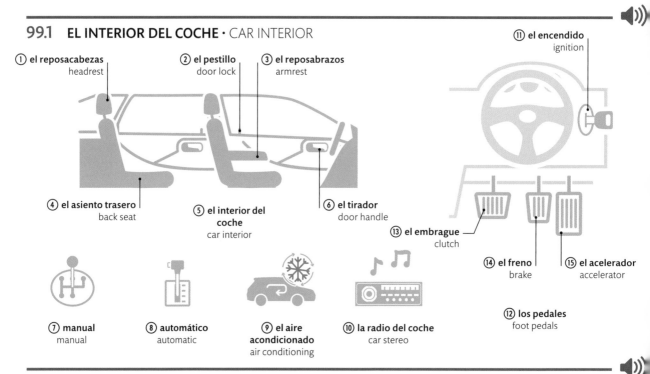

① **el reposacabezas**
headrest

② **el pestillo**
door lock

③ **el reposabrazos**
armrest

④ **el asiento trasero**
back seat

⑤ **el interior del coche**
car interior

⑥ **el tirador**
door handle

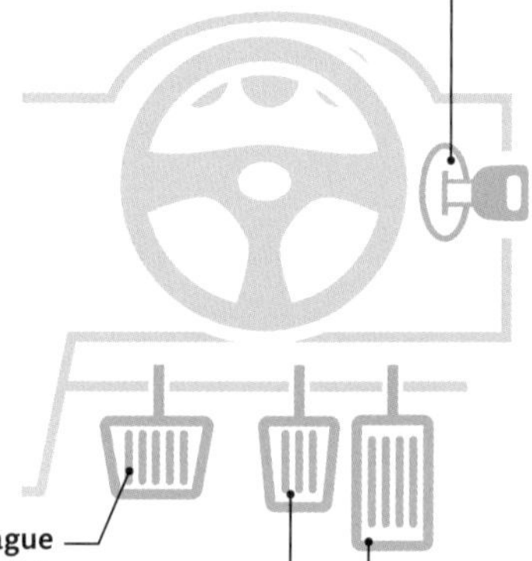

⑪ **el encendido**
ignition

⑬ **el embrague**
clutch

⑭ **el freno**
brake

⑮ **el acelerador**
accelerator

⑫ **los pedales**
foot pedals

⑦ **manual**
manual

⑧ **automático**
automatic

⑨ **el aire acondicionado**
air conditioning

⑩ **la radio del coche**
car stereo

99.2 EL SALPICADERO Y LOS CONTROLES · DASHBOARD AND CONTROLS

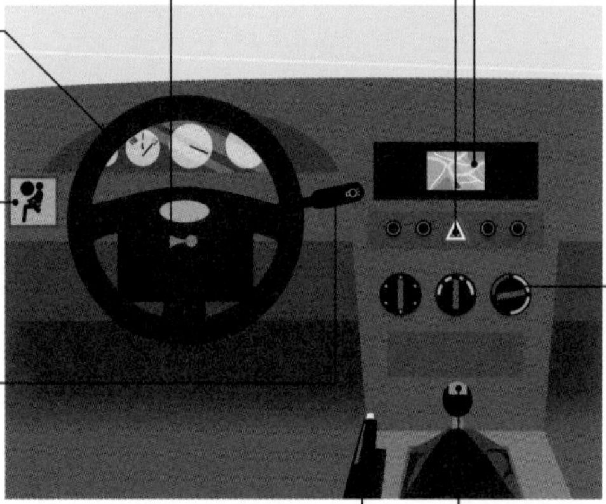

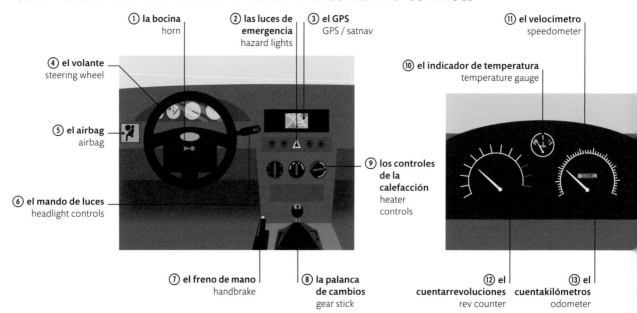

① **la bocina**
horn

② **las luces de emergencia**
hazard lights

③ **el GPS**
GPS / satnav

④ **el volante**
steering wheel

⑤ **el airbag**
airbag

⑥ **el mando de luces**
headlight controls

⑦ **el freno de mano**
handbrake

⑧ **la palanca de cambios**
gear stick

⑨ **los controles de la calefacción**
heater controls

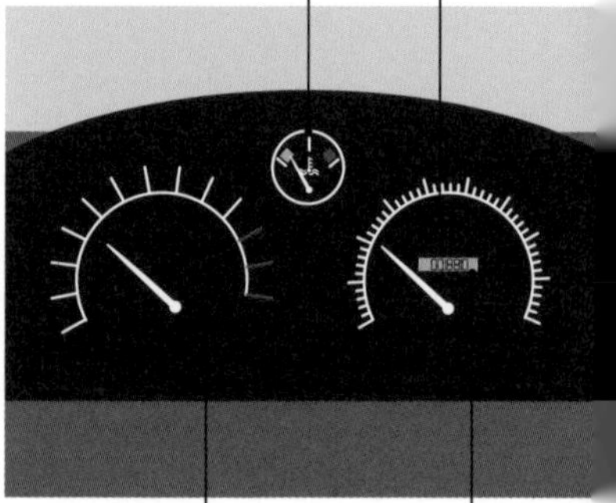

⑪ **el velocímetro**
speedometer

⑩ **el indicador de temperatura**
temperature gauge

⑫ **el cuentarrevoluciones**
rev counter

⑬ **el cuentakilómetros**
odometer

See also
42-43 La ciudad • In town **96** Las carreteras • Roads **97-98** Los coches • Cars
100 Las motocicletas • Motorcycles **123** Los deportes de motor • Motorsports

99.3 EL AUTOBÚS • BUS

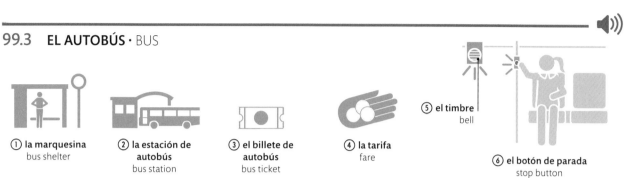

① **la marquesina**
bus shelter

② **la estación de autobús**
bus station

③ **el billete de autobús**
bus ticket

④ **la tarifa**
fare

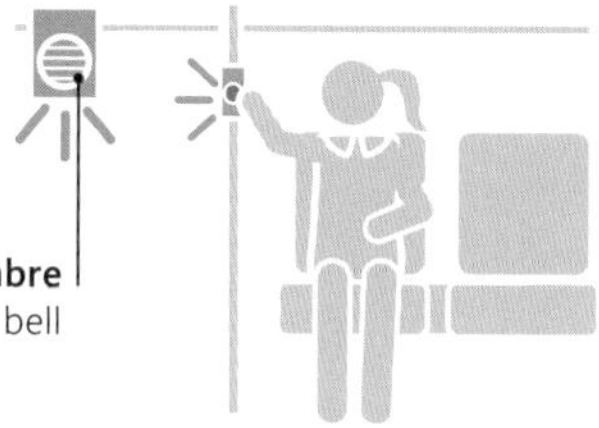

⑤ **el timbre**
bell

⑥ **el botón de parada**
stop button

⑦ **el asiento del conductor**
driver's seat

⑧ **la barandilla**
handrail

⑨ **la ventana**
window

⑩ **la puerta**
door

⑪ **la rueda trasera**
rear wheel

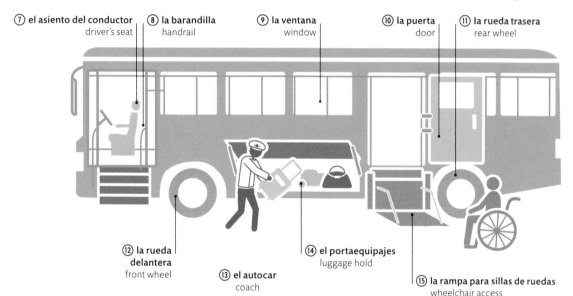

⑫ **la rueda delantera**
front wheel

⑬ **el autocar**
coach

⑭ **el portaequipajes**
luggage hold

⑮ **la rampa para sillas de ruedas**
wheelchair access

99.4 LOS TIPOS DE AUTOBUSES • TYPES OF BUSES

② **el piso superior**
upper deck

③ **el piso inferior**
lower deck

④ **el conductor**
driver

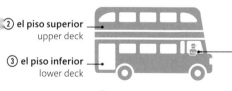

① **el autobús de dos pisos**
double-decker bus

⑥ **la visita turística**
sightseeing

⑤ **el autobús turístico**
tourist bus

⑦ **el número de ruta**
route number

⑧ **el autobús escolar**
school bus

⑨ **el minibús**
minibus

⑩ **el autobús articulado**
articulated bus

⑪ **el autobús de transbordo**
shuttle bus

⑫ **el trolebús**
trolley bus

⑬ **el tranvía**
tram

100 Las motocicletas
Motorcycles

100.1 LA MOTO · MOTORBIKE

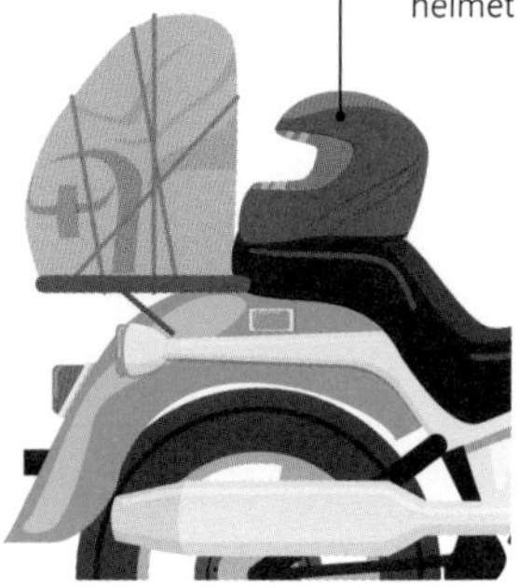

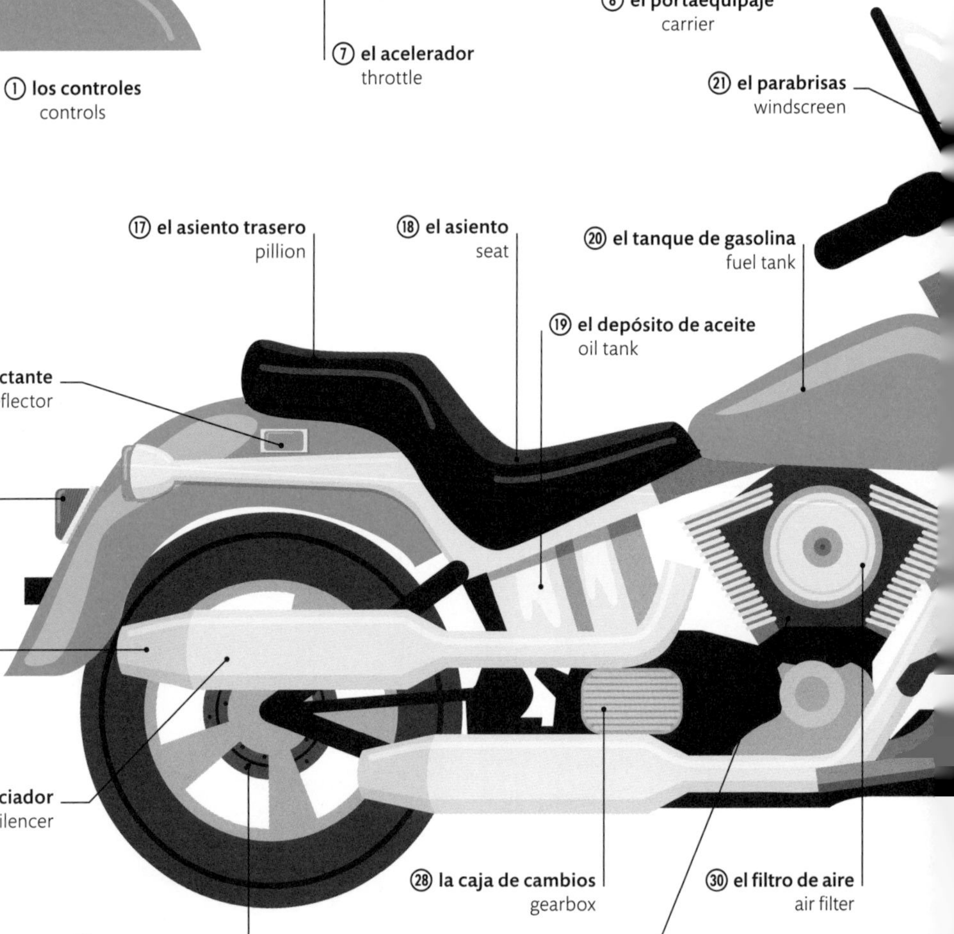

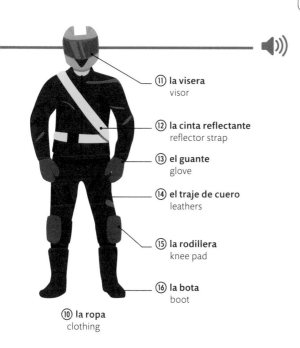

See also
42-43 La ciudad • In town **96** Las carreteras • Roads
97-98 Los coches • Cars **123** Los deportes de motor • Motorsports

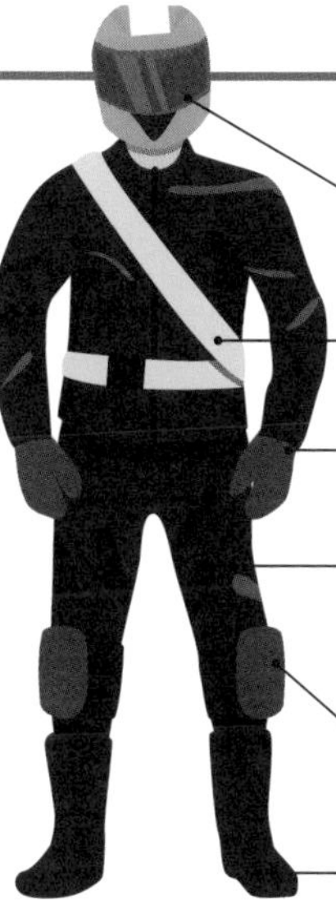

⑪ **la visera**
visor

⑫ **la cinta reflectante**
reflector strap

⑬ **el guante**
glove

⑭ **el traje de cuero**
leathers

⑮ **la rodillera**
knee pad

⑯ **la bota**
boot

⑩ **la ropa**
clothing

㉒ **el faro**
headlight

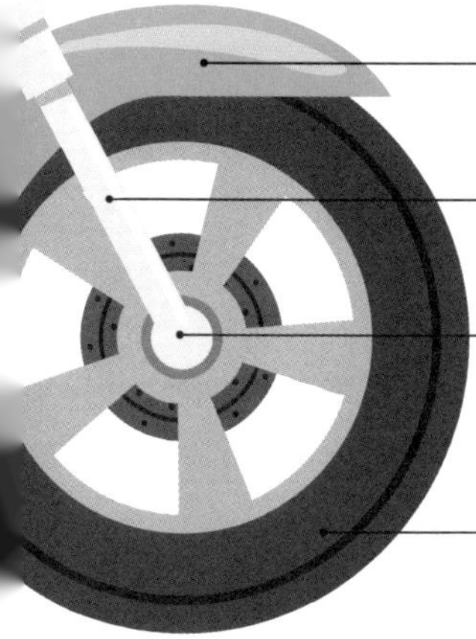

㉜ **el guardabarros**
mudguard

㉝ **la suspensión**
suspension

㉞ **el eje**
axle

㉟ **el neumático**
tyre

100.2 LOS TIPOS DE MOTOS
TYPES OF MOTORCYCLES

② **el guardabarros alto**
raised mudguard

③ **el número de corredor**
race number

④ **el neumático con dibujo profundo**
deep-tread tyre

① **la moto todoterreno**
off-road motorcycle

⑤ **la moto de carreras**
racing bike

⑥ **la moto de turismo**
tourer

⑦ **el quad**
all-terrain vehicle / quad bike

⑧ **el sidecar**
side car

⑨ **la moto eléctrica**
electric motorcycle

⑩ **el patinete eléctrico**
electric scooter

⑪ **el scooter de tres ruedas**
three-wheeler

⑫ **el scooter**
motor scooter

⑬ **el motorista** *m*
la motorista *f*
rider

⑭ **ir de pasajero**
to ride pillion

⑮ **subirse**
to get on / mount

⑯ **bajarse**
to get off / dismount

El ciclismo
Cycling

101.1 LA BICICLETA · BICYCLE

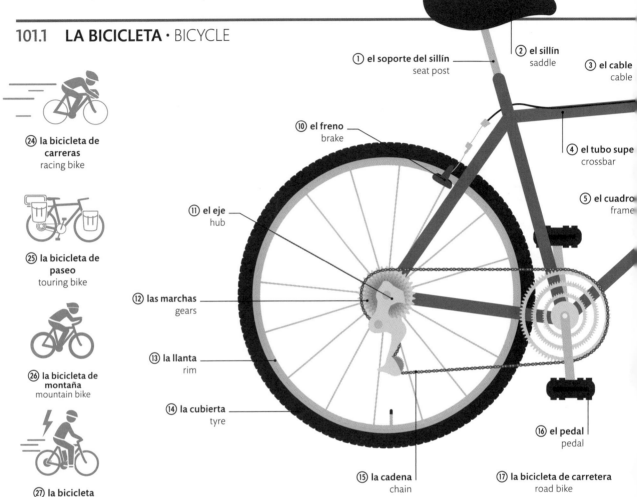

(24) **la bicicleta de carreras**
racing bike

(25) **la bicicleta de paseo**
touring bike

(26) **la bicicleta de montaña**
mountain bike

(27) **la bicicleta eléctrica**
electric bike

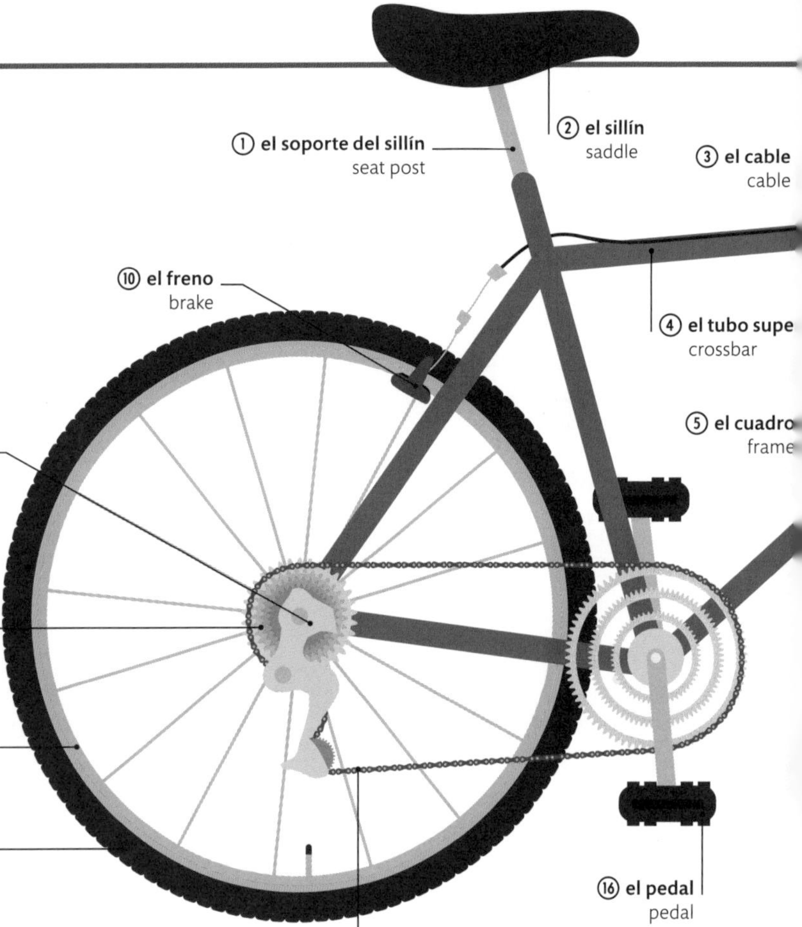

(17) **la bicicleta de carretera**
road bike

(28) **el tándem**
tandem

(29) **la cesta**
basket

(30) **la silla de niños**
child seat

(31) **el caballete**
kickstand

(32) **la pastilla de frenos**
brake pad

(33) **las ruedas de ape**
stabilizers

(34) **el monociclo**
unicycle

(35) **el calapiés**
toe clip

(36) **la correa del calapiés**
toe strap

(37) **la luz**
lamp

(38) **el faro trasero**
rear light

(39) **la cámara**
inner tube

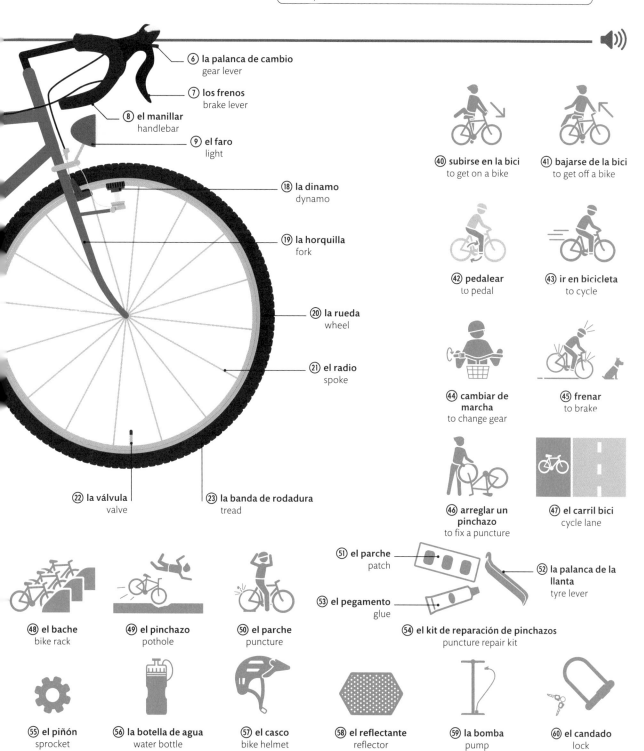

See also
42-43 La ciudad • In town **96** Las carreteras • Roads **100** Las motocicletas
Motorcycles **133** Las actividades al aire libre • Outdoor activities

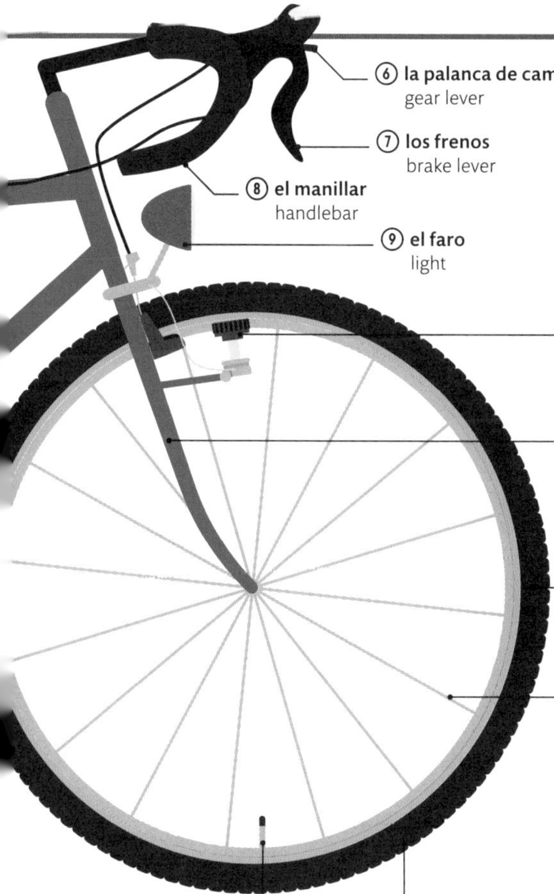

⑥ **la palanca de cambio**
gear lever

⑦ **los frenos**
brake lever

⑧ **el manillar**
handlebar

⑨ **el faro**
light

⑱ **la dinamo**
dynamo

⑲ **la horquilla**
fork

⑳ **la rueda**
wheel

㉑ **el radio**
spoke

㉒ **la válvula**
valve

㉓ **la banda de rodadura**
tread

㊵ **subirse en la bici**
to get on a bike

㊶ **bajarse de la bici**
to get off a bike

㊷ **pedalear**
to pedal

㊸ **ir en bicicleta**
to cycle

㊹ **cambiar de marcha**
to change gear

㊺ **frenar**
to brake

㊻ **arreglar un pinchazo**
to fix a puncture

㊼ **el carril bici**
cycle lane

㊽ **el bache**
bike rack

㊾ **el pinchazo**
pothole

㊿ **el parche**
puncture

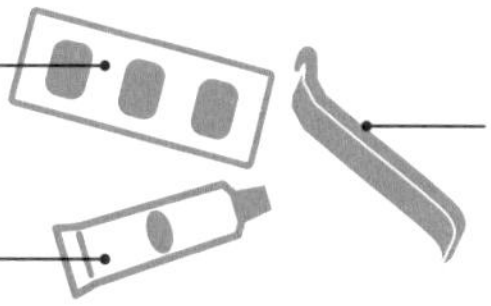

(51) **el parche**
patch

(52) **la palanca de la llanta**
tyre lever

(53) **el pegamento**
glue

(54) **el kit de reparación de pinchazos**
puncture repair kit

(55) **el piñón**
sprocket

(56) **la botella de agua**
water bottle

(57) **el casco**
bike helmet

(58) **el reflectante**
reflector

(59) **la bomba**
pump

(60) **el candado**
lock

102 Los trenes
Trains

102.1 LA ESTACIÓN DE TREN · TRAIN STATION

⑩ la oficina de objetos perdidos
lost property office

⑪ el billete
ticket

⑫ la tarifa
fare

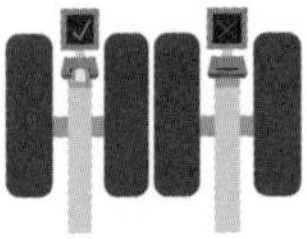

⑬ la barrera
ticket barrier

⑭ el vestíbulo
concourse

⑰ la red ferroviaria
rail network

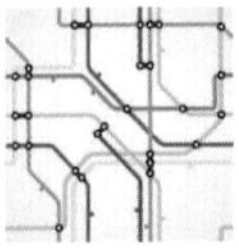

⑱ el mapa del metro
underground map

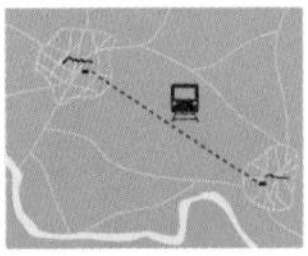

⑲ el tren de cercanías
intercity train

⑳ el retraso
delay

㉑ la hora punta
rush hour

㉓ coger el tren
to catch a train

See also
42-43 La ciudad • In town **131** El viaje y el alojamiento • Travel and accommodation

㉔ **perder el tren**
to miss a train

㉕ **cambiar de tren**
to change trains

㉗ **el raíl electrificado**
live rail

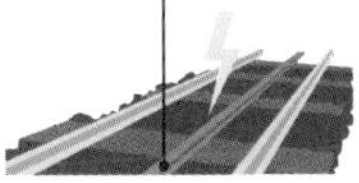

㉖ **la vía**
track

㉘ **la catenaria**
electric lines

㉙ **el paso subterráneo**
underpass

㉚ **el paso elevado**
overpass

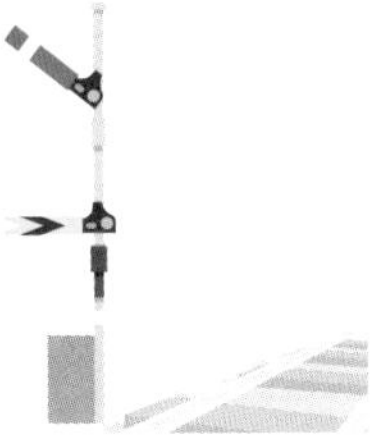

㉛ **la señal**
signal

㉝ **el portaequipajes**
luggage rack

㉞ **la ventana**
window

㉟ **la puerta**
door

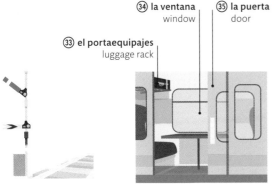

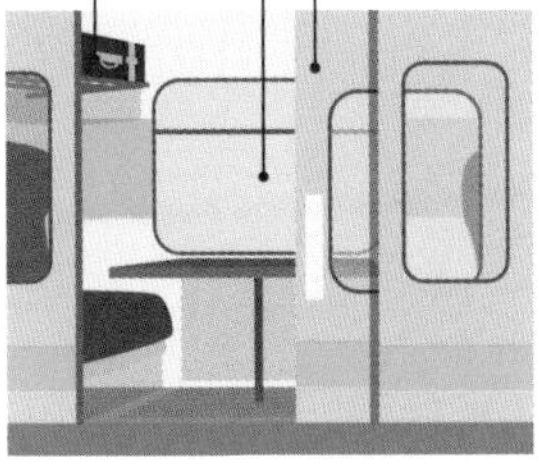

㉜ **el compartimento**
compartment

㊱ **el vagón**
carriage

㊲ **el vagón restaurante**
dining car

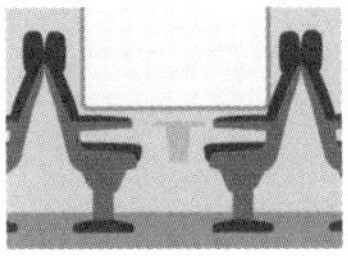

㊳ **el asiento**
seat

㊴ **el coche cama**
sleeping compartment

㊵ **el revisor** *m*
la revisora *f*
ticket inspector

㊶ **la palanca de emergencia**
emergency lever

102.2 LOS TIPOS DE TREN • TYPES OF TRAINS

① **el domo de vapor**
steam dome

② **el tope**
buffer

③ **la biela de acoplamiento**
coupling rod

④ **el tren de vapor**
steam train

⑤ **el quitapiedras**
cowcatcher

⑥ **el pantógrafo**
pantograph

⑦ **el tren eléctrico**
electric train

⑧ **la cabina del conductor**
driver's cab

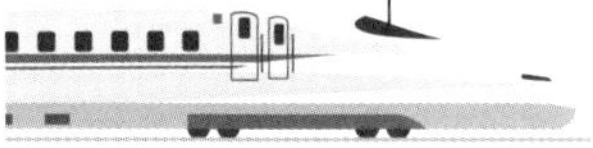

⑨ **el tren bala**
bullet train

⑩ **el tren de alta velocidad**
high-speed train

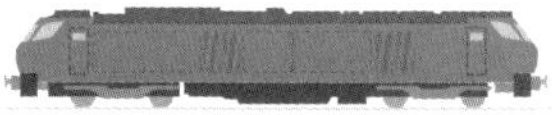

⑪ **el tren diésel**
diesel train

⑫ **el tren de mercancías**
cargo

⑬ **el cargamento**
freight train

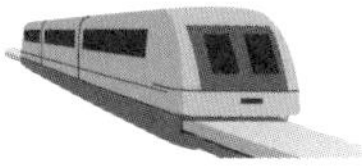

⑭ **el tren de levitación magnética**
maglev

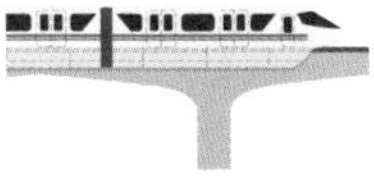

⑮ **el monorraíl**
monorail

⑯ **el metro**
underground train

⑰ **el tranvía**
tram

103 El avión
Aircraft

103.1 EL AVIÓN DE PASAJEROS · AEROPLANE

① **el copiloto** *m* / **la copiloto** *f*
co-pilot

② **el piloto** *m* / **la piloto** *f*
pilot

③ **el azafato** *m* / **la azafata** *f*
flight attendant

④ **la clase turista**
business class

⑤ **la clase ejecutiva**
economy class

⑥ **el alerón**
aileron

⑦ **la ventanilla**
window

⑬ **la cabina del piloto**
cockpit

⑭ **el morro**
nose

⑮ **el tren delantero**
nosewheel

⑯ **¿Sabes cuánto dura el vuelo?**
Do you know how long the flight takes?

⑰ **el equipaje de mano**
hand luggage

⑱ **el Boeing 747**
jumbo jet

⑲ **el motor**
engine

⑳ **el tren de aterrizaje**
landing gear

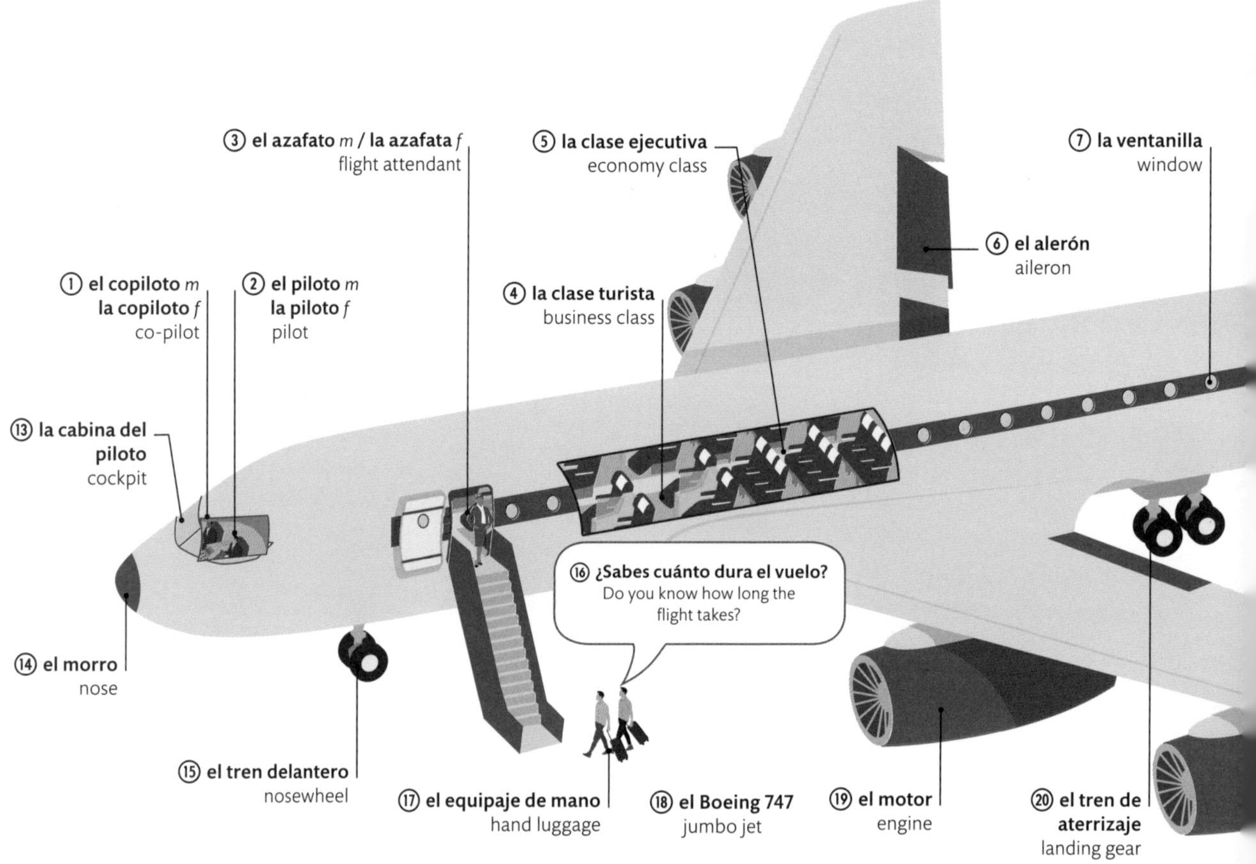

103.3 LOS TIPOS DE AVIÓN · TYPES OF AIRCRAFT

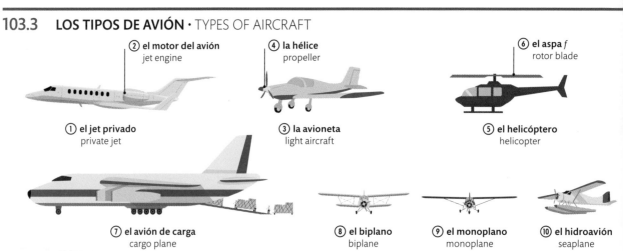

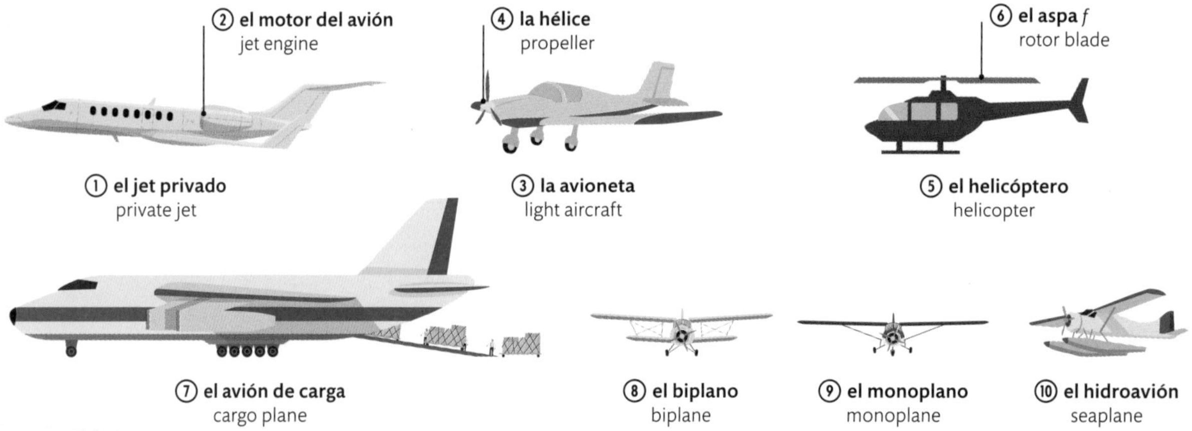

See also
42-43 La ciudad • In town **104** En el aeropuerto • At the airport
131 El viaje y el alojamiento • Travel and accommodation

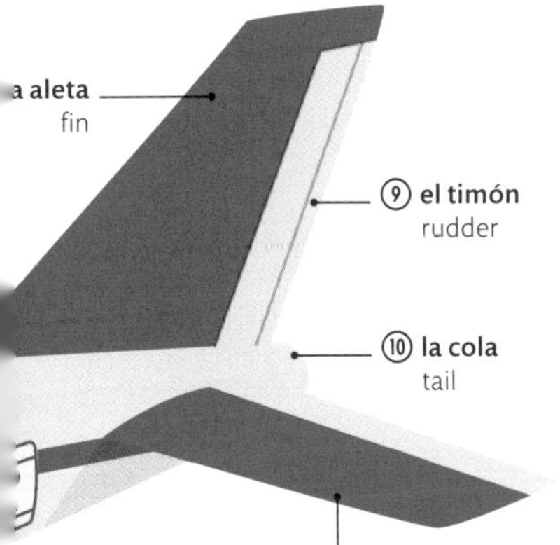

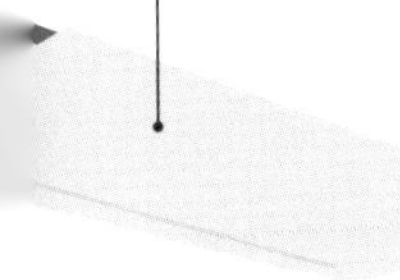

103.2 LA CABINA • CABIN

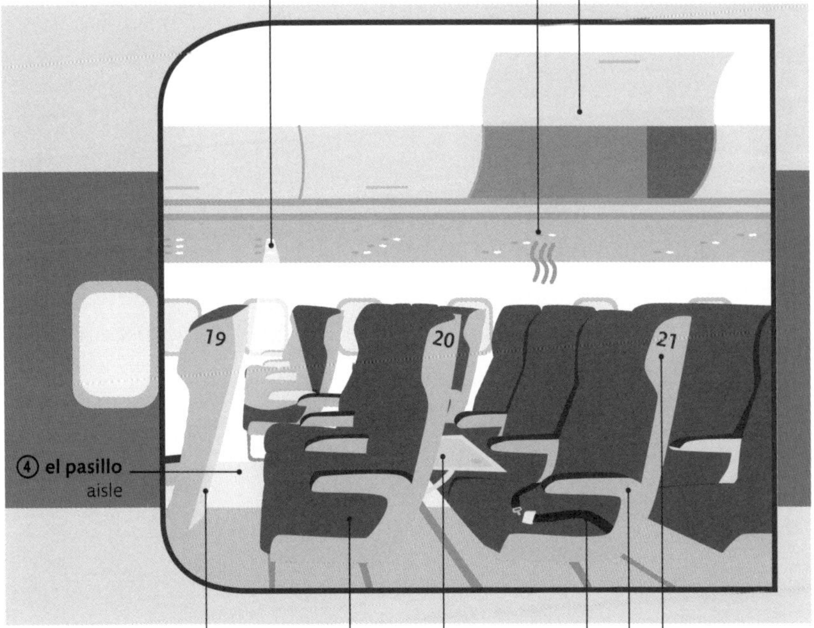

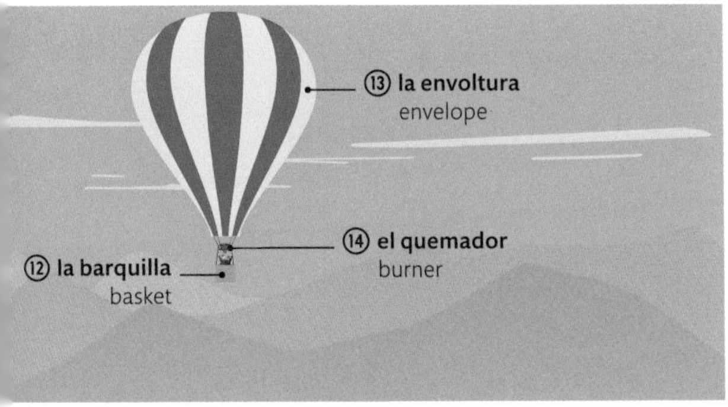

⑪ **el globo aerostático**
hot-air balloon

⑮ **el dirigible**
airship

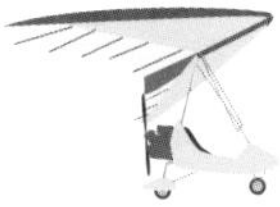

⑯ **el ultraligero**
microlight

⑲ **el paramotor**
paramotor

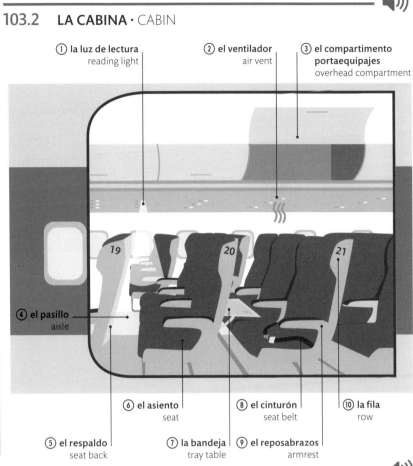

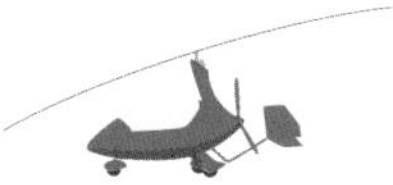

⑰ **el autogiro**
gyrocopter

⑱ **el planeador**
glider

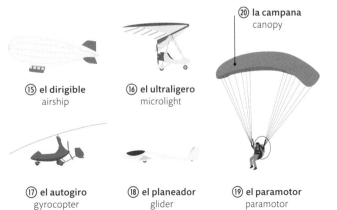

104 En el aeropuerto
At the airport

104.1 EN LA TERMINAL · AT THE TERMINAL

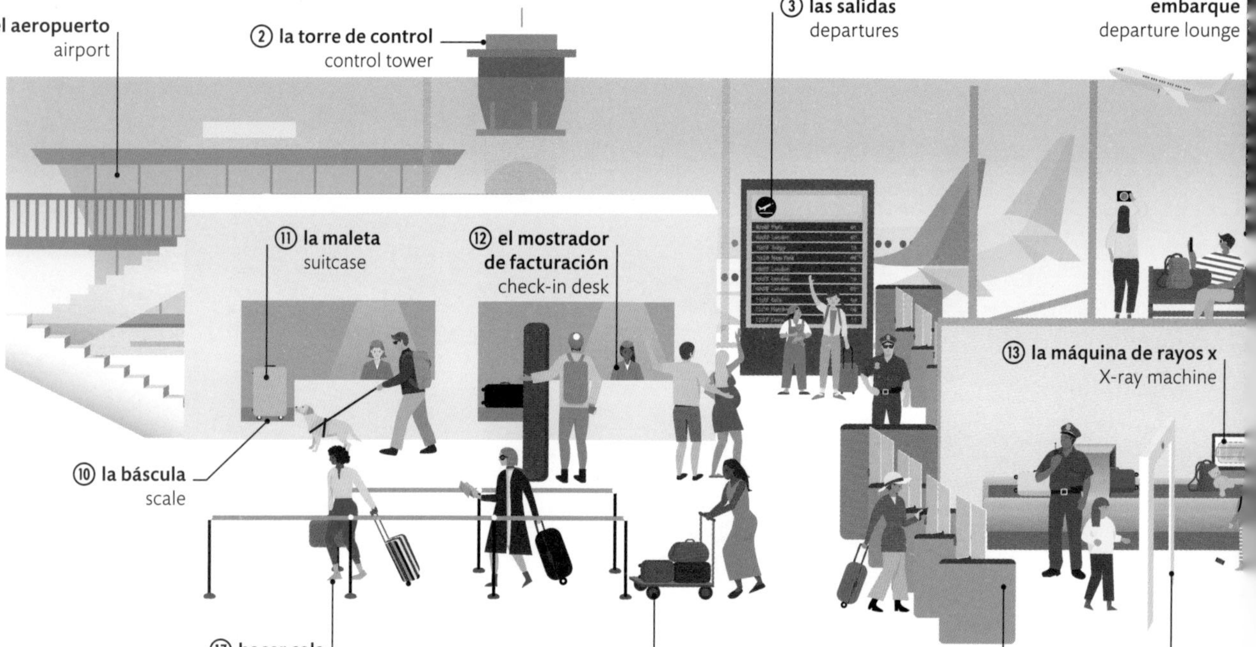

① el aeropuerto
airport
② la torre de control
control tower
③ las salidas
departures
④ la sala de embarque
departure lounge
⑪ la maleta
suitcase
⑫ el mostrador de facturación
check-in desk
⑬ la máquina de rayos x
X-ray machine
⑩ la báscula
scale
⑰ hacer cola
to queue
⑱ la terminal
terminal
⑲ el carrito
trolley
⑳ la seguridad
security
㉑ el escáner
scanner

㉘ **el pasaporte**
passport

㉙ **el pasaporte biométrico**
biometric passport

㉚ **el visado**
visa

㉛ **el billete**
ticket

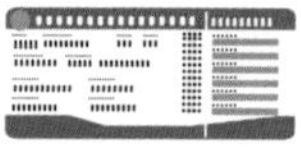
㉜ **la tarjeta de embarque**
boarding pass

㉝ **la facturación en línea**
online check-in

㊵ **las vacaciones**
holiday

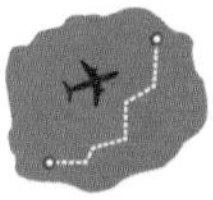
㊶ **el vuelo nacional**
domestic flight

㊷ **el vuelo internacional**
international flight

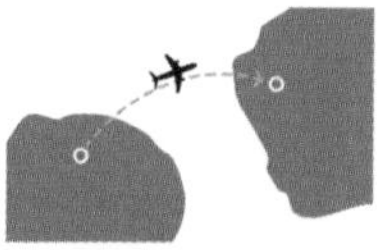
㊸ **viajar al extranjero**
to go abroad

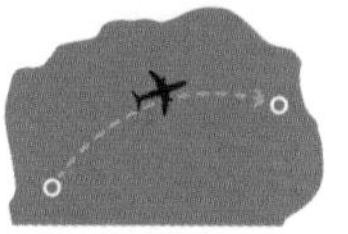
㊹ **el vuelo directo**
direct flight

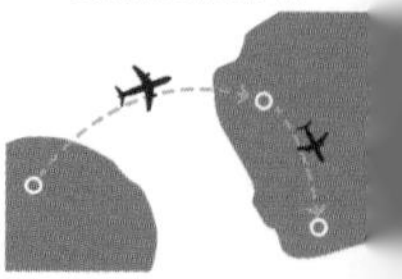
㊺ **la escala**
connection

51 **el exceso de equipaje**
excess baggage

52 **el control de pasaportes**
passport control

53 **el cambio de divisa**
currency exchange

54 **la tienda libre de impuestos**
duty-free shop

55 **la oficina de objetos perdidos**
lost and found

56 **retrasarse**
to be delayed

See also
103 El avión • Aircraft **131** El viaje y el alojamiento • Travel and accommodation **149-151** Los países • Countries

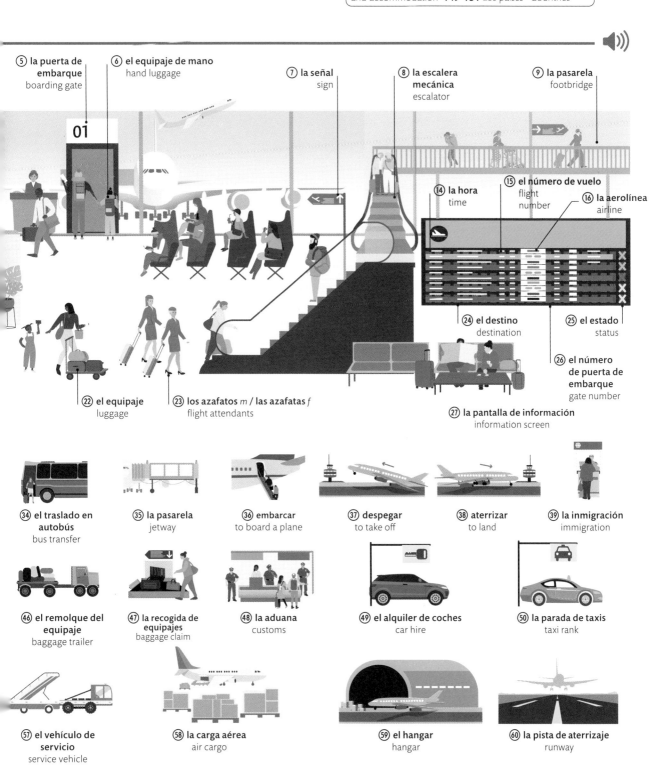

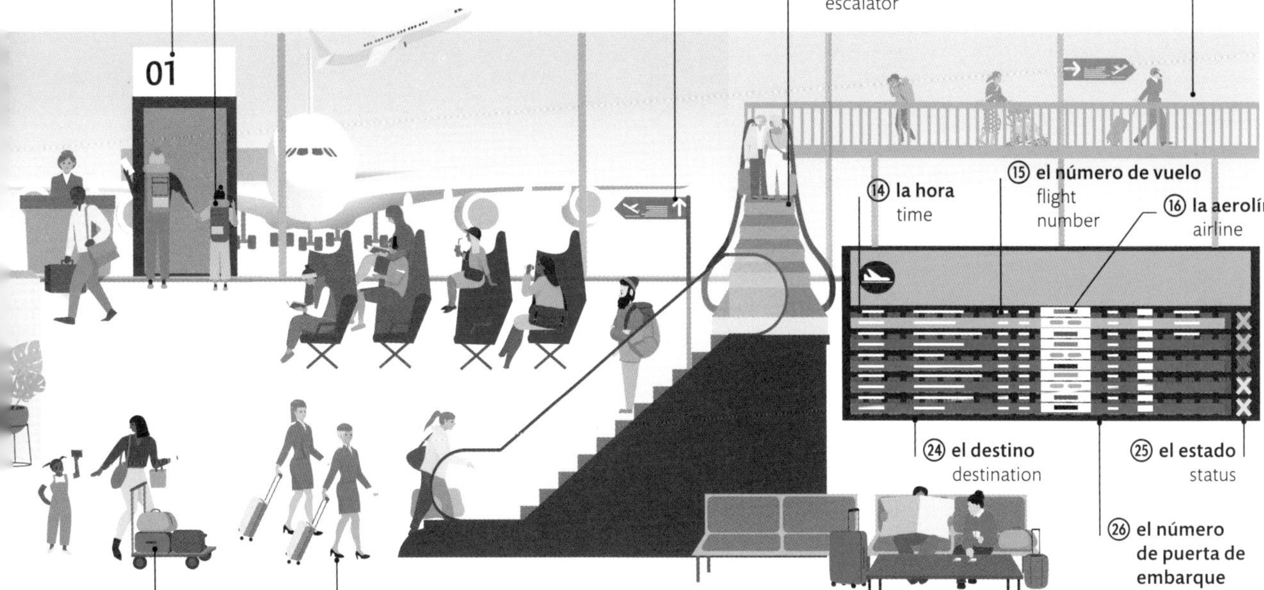
⑤ **la puerta de embarque**
boarding gate
01
⑥ **el equipaje de mano**
hand luggage
⑦ **la señal**
sign
⑧ **la escalera mecánica**
escalator
⑨ **la pasarela**
footbridge
⑭ **la hora**
time
⑮ **el número de vuelo**
flight number
⑯ **la aerolínea**
airline
㉔ **el destino**
destination
㉕ **el estado**
status
㉖ **el número de puerta de embarque**
gate number
㉗ **la pantalla de información**
information screen
㉒ **el equipaje**
luggage
㉓ **los azafatos** *m* / **las azafatas** *f*
flight attendants

㉞ **el traslado en autobús**
bus transfer

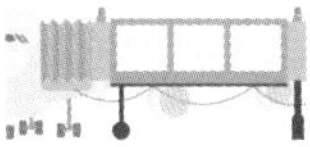
㉟ **la pasarela**
jetway

㊱ **embarcar**
to board a plane

㊲ **despegar**
to take off

㊳ **aterrizar**
to land

㊴ **la inmigración**
immigration

㊻ **el remolque del equipaje**
baggage trailer

㊼ **la recogida de equipajes**
baggage claim

㊽ **la aduana**
customs

㊾ **el alquiler de coches**
car hire

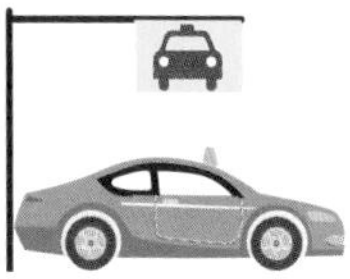
㊿ **la parada de taxis**
taxi rank

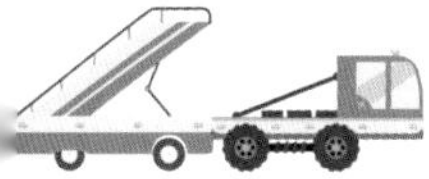
57 **el vehículo de servicio**
service vehicle

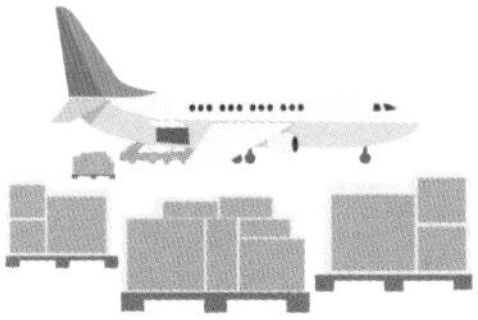
58 **la carga aérea**
air cargo

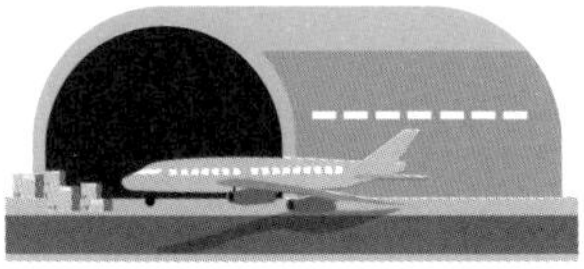
59 **el hangar**
hangar

60 **la pista de aterrizaje**
runway

105 Los buques
Sea vessels

105.1 EL BUQUE · SHIP

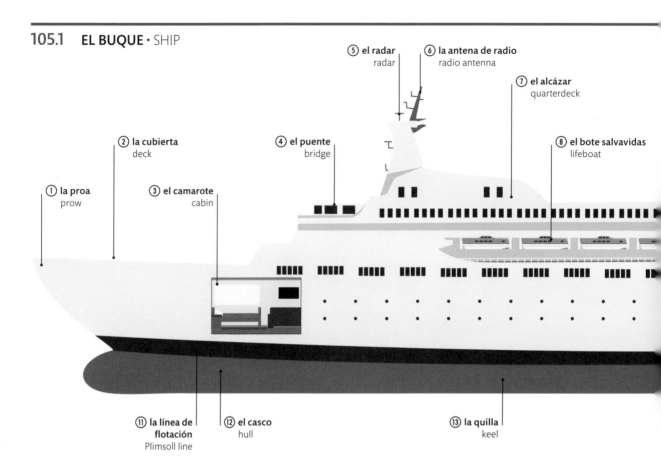

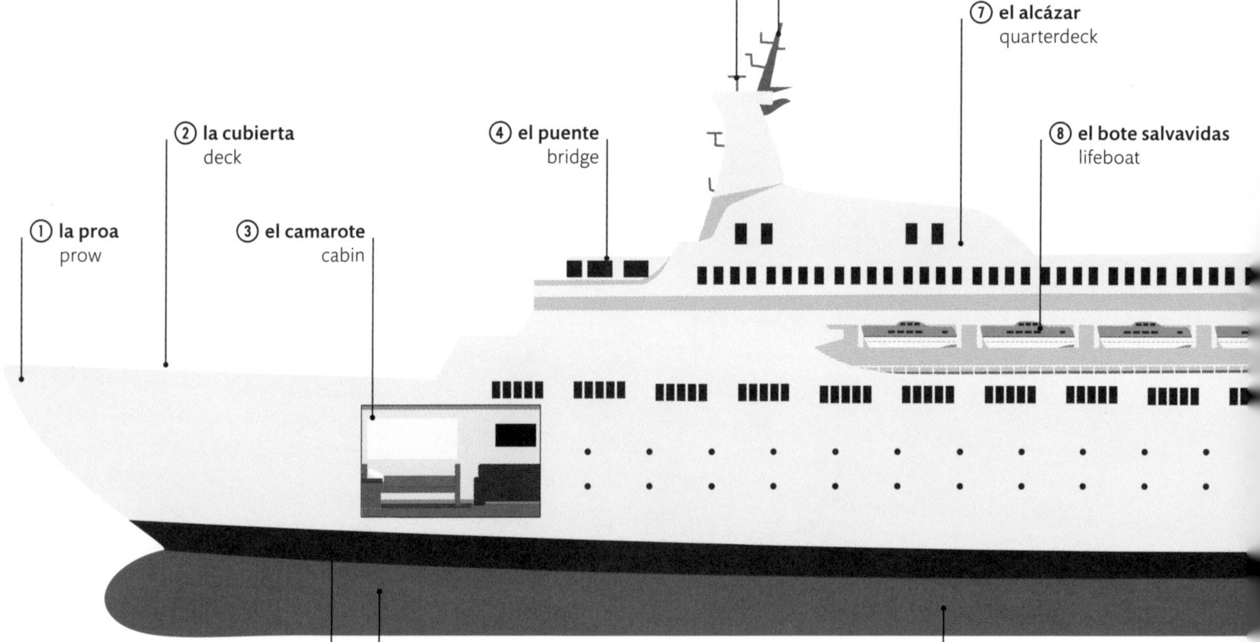

105.2 OTROS BARCOS Y BUQUES · OTHER BOATS AND SHIPS

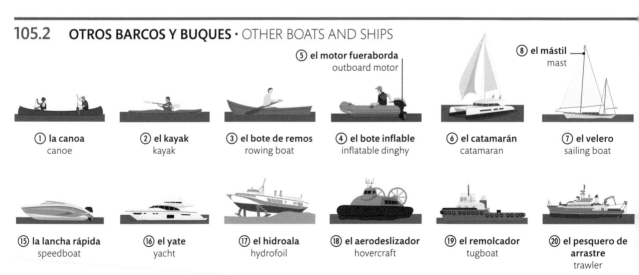

① **la canoa**
canoe

② **el kayak**
kayak

③ **el bote de remos**
rowing boat

④ **el bote inflable**
inflatable dinghy

⑥ **el catamarán**
catamaran

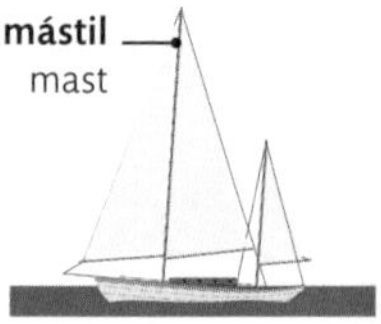

⑦ **el velero**
sailing boat

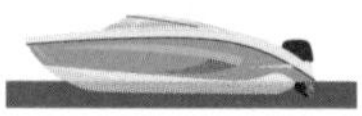
⑮ **la lancha rápida**
speedboat

⑯ **el yate**
yacht

⑰ **el hidroala**
hydrofoil

⑱ **el aerodeslizador**
hovercraft

⑲ **el remolcador**
tugboat

⑳ **el pesquero de arrastre**
trawler

See also
106 El puerto • The port **119** La navegación y los deportes acuáticos • Sailing and watersports **131** El viaje y el alojamiento • Travel and accommodation

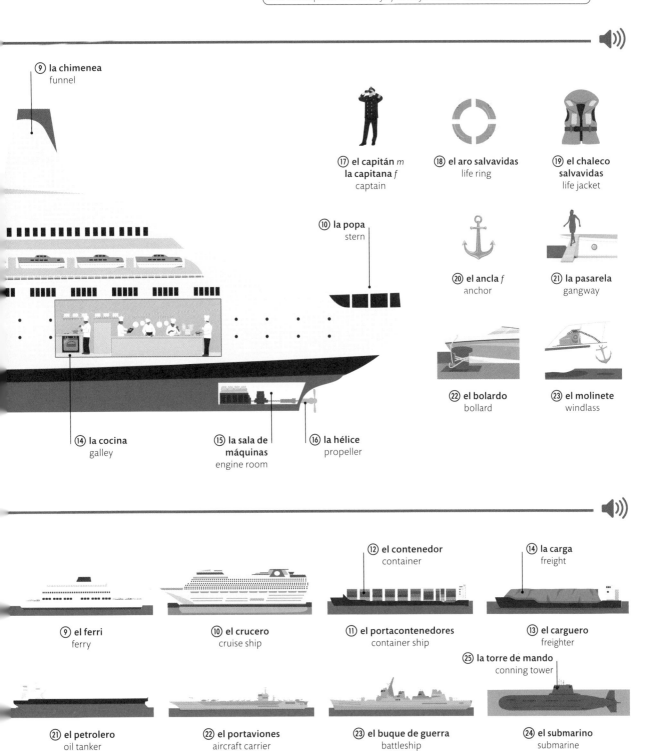

⑨ **la chimenea**
funnel

⑩ **la popa**
stern

⑭ **la cocina**
galley

⑮ **la sala de máquinas**
engine room

⑯ **la hélice**
propeller

⑰ **el capitán** *m*
la capitana *f*
captain

⑱ **el aro salvavidas**
life ring

⑲ **el chaleco salvavidas**
life jacket

⑳ **el ancla** *f*
anchor

㉑ **la pasarela**
gangway

㉒ **el bolardo**
bollard

㉓ **el molinete**
windlass

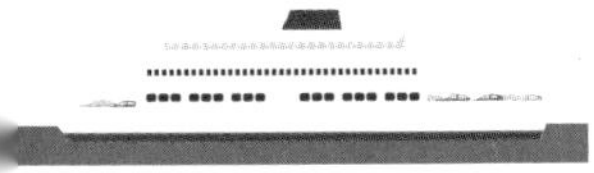

⑨ **el ferri**
ferry

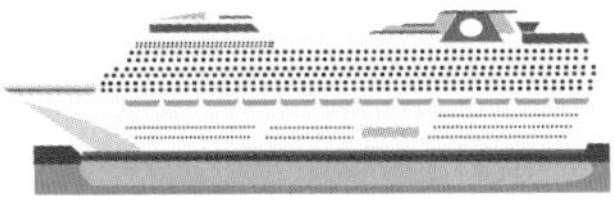

⑩ **el crucero**
cruise ship

⑫ **el contenedor**
container

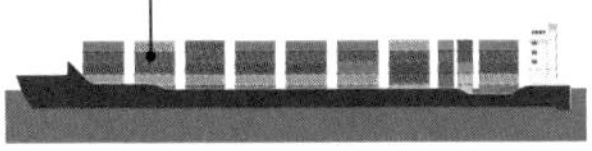

⑪ **el portacontenedores**
container ship

⑭ **la carga**
freight

⑬ **el carguero**
freighter

㉑ **el petrolero**
oil tanker

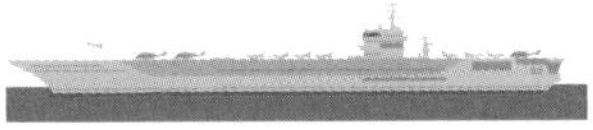

㉒ **el portaviones**
aircraft carrier

㉓ **el buque de guerra**
battleship

㉕ **la torre de mando**
conning tower

㉔ **el submarino**
submarine

106 El puerto
The port

106.1 EN EL MUELLE • AT THE DOCKS

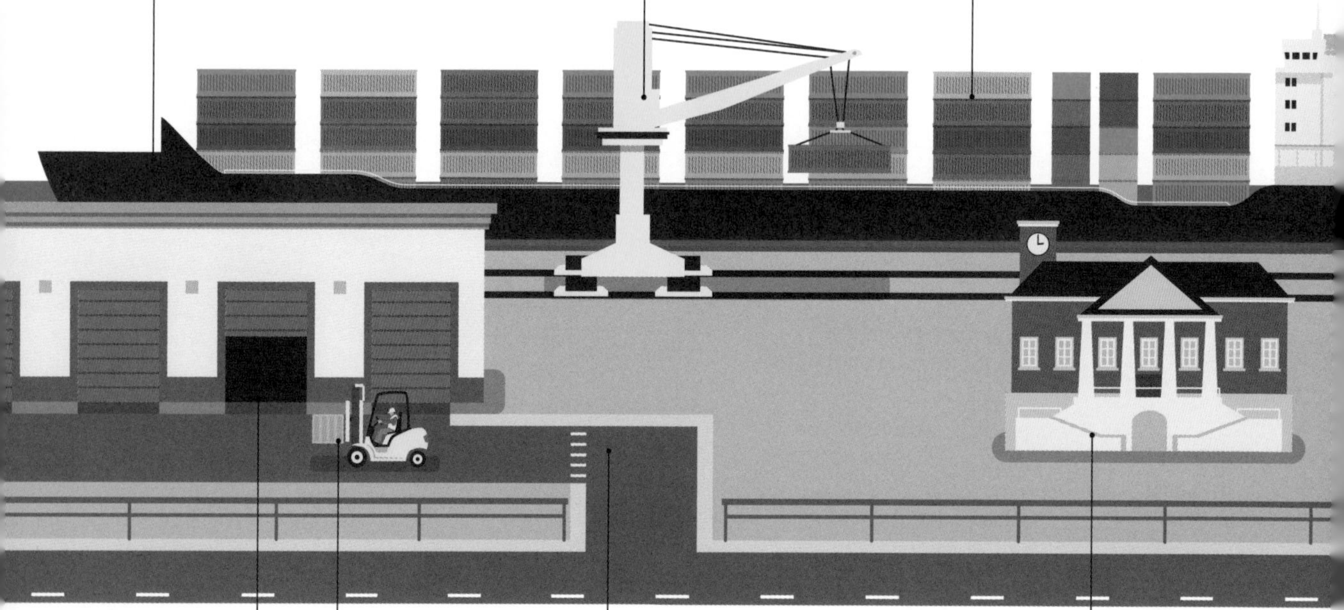

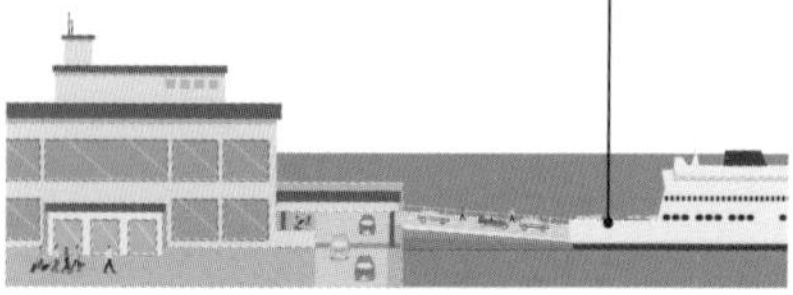

⑰ **la terminal de ferris**
ferry terminal

⑲ **el puerto de pasajeros**
passenger port

㉑ **el puerto pesquero**
fishing port

㉒ **la taquilla**
ticket office

㉗ **el amarradero**
mooring

㉘ **el puerto**
harbour

㉙ **el puerto deportivo**
marina

㉚ **el muelle**
pier

㉛ **el pantalán**
jetty

㉜ **el astillero**
shipyard

See also
96 Las carreteras • Roads **102** Los trenes • Trains
105 Los buques • Sea vessels

el atracadero
quay

⑩ **el embarcadero**
wharf

⑪ **la terminal petrolífera**
oil terminal

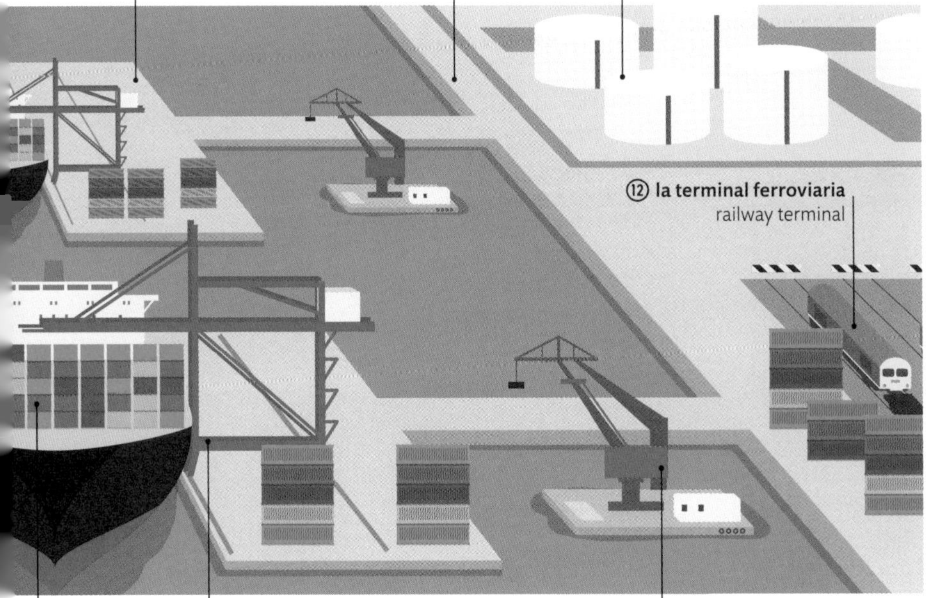

⑫ **la terminal ferroviaria**
railway terminal

⑬ **el cargamento**
cargo

⑭ **la grúa de puente**
bridge crane

⑮ **el puerto**
port

⑯ **la grúa flotante**
floating crane

㉓ **el dique seco**
dry dock

㉔ **la boya**
buoy

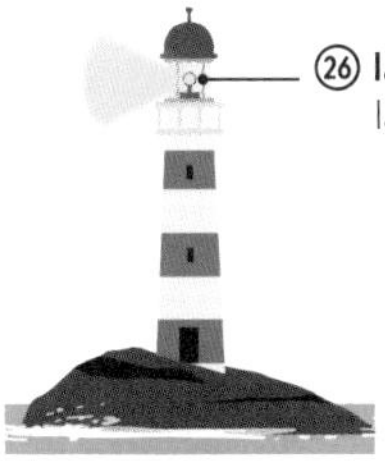

㉖ **la linterna**
lamp

㉕ **el faro**
lighthouse

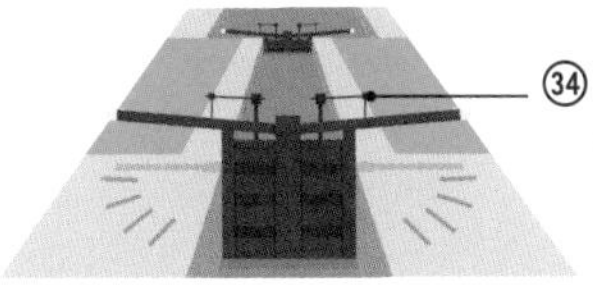

㉞ **la compuerta**
gate

㉝ **la esclusa**
lock

㉟ **el guardacostas** *m*
la guardacostas *f*
coastguard

㊱ **el capitán del puerto** *m*
la capitana del puerto *f*
harbour master

106.2 LOS VERBOS
VERBS

① **embarcar**
to board

② **amarrar**
to moor

③ **desembarcar**
to disembark

④ **echar el ancla**
to drop anchor

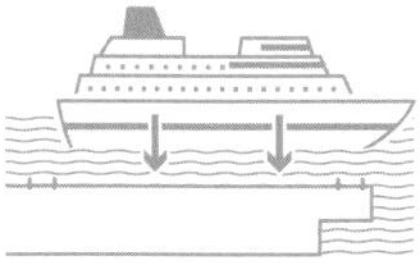

⑤ **atracar**
to dock

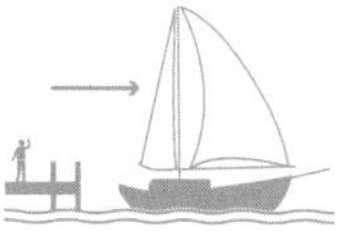

⑥ **zarpar**
to set sail

107 El fútbol americano

American football

107.1 EL FÚTBOL AMERICANO · AMERICAN FOOTBALL

① **el esquinero izquierdo** *m*
la esquinera izquierda *f*
left cornerback

② **el apoyador externo** *m*
la apoyadora externa *f*
outside linebacker

③ **el ala defensivo izquierdo** *m*
el ala defensiva izquierda *f*
left defensive end

④ **el profundo izquierdo** *m* **/ la profunda izquierda** *f*
left safety

⑤ **el tacle defensivo izquierdo** *m* **/ la tacle defensiva izquierda** *f*
left defensive tackle

⑥ **el apoyador medio** *m* **/ la apoyadora media** *f*
middle linebacker

⑦ **el ala defensivo derecho** *m* **/ el ala defensiva derecha** *f*
right defensive tackle

⑧ **el profundo derecho** *m* **/ la profunda derecha** *f*
right safety

⑨ **el tacle defensivo derecho** *m* **/ la tacle defensiva derecha** *f*
right defensive end

⑩ **el ala defensivo derecho** *m* **/ la ala defensiva derecha** *f*
outside linebacker

⑪ **el esquinero derecho** *m* **/ la esquinera derecha** *f*
right cornerback

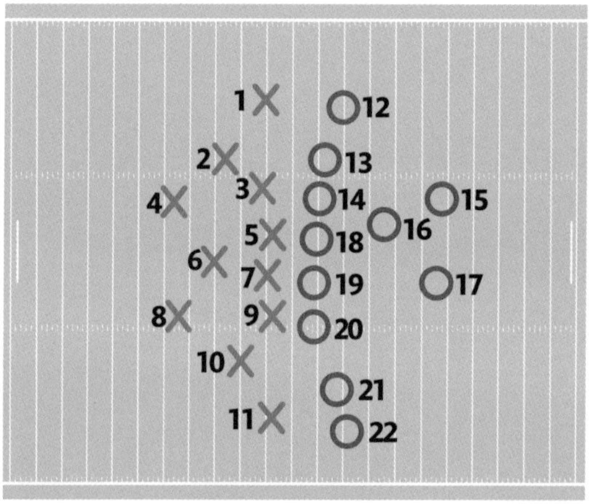

㉓ **las posiciones del fútbol americano**
American football positions

㉔ **la defensa**
defence

㉕ **el ataque**
offence

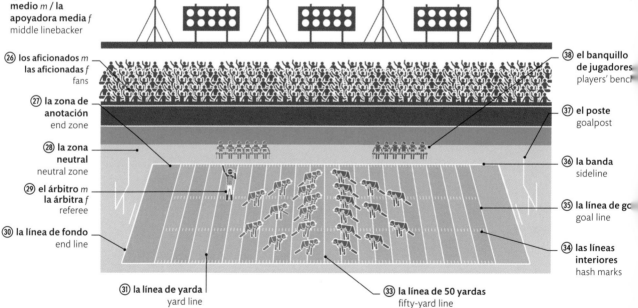

⑫ **el receptor** *m*
la receptora *f*
wide receiver

⑬ **el tacle derecho** *m* **/ la tacle derecha** *f*
right tackle

⑭ **el guardia derecho** *m* **/ la guardia derecha** *f*
right guard

⑮ **el corredor** *m*
la corredora *f*
running back / halfback

⑯ **el corredor de poder** *m*
la corredora de poder *f*
fullback

⑰ **el mariscal de campo** *m* **/ la maris de campo** *f*
quarterback

⑱ **el central m**
la central f
centre

⑲ **el guardia izquierdo** *m* **/ la guardia izquierda**
left guard

⑳ **el tacle izquier** *m* **/ la tacle izquier**
left tackle

㉑ **el receptor** *m*
la receptora *f*
wide receiver

㉒ **el receptor** *m*
la receptora *f*
wide receiver

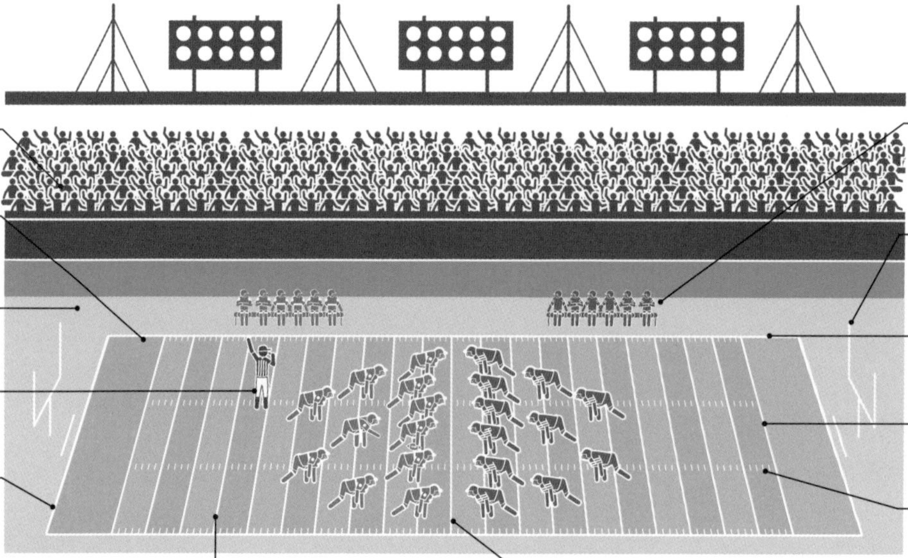

㉖ **los aficionados** *m*
las aficionadas *f*
fans

㉗ **la zona de anotación**
end zone

㉘ **la zona neutral**
neutral zone

㉙ **el árbitro** *m*
la árbitra *f*
referee

㉚ **la línea de fondo**
end line

㉛ **la línea de yarda**
yard line

㉜ **el campo**
field / pitch

㉝ **la línea de 50 yardas**
fifty-yard line

㉞ **las líneas interiores**
hash marks

㉟ **la línea de go**
goal line

㊱ **la banda**
sideline

㊲ **el poste**
goalpost

㊳ **el banquillo de jugadores**
players' bench

See also
108 El rugby • Rugby **109** El fútbol • Football
110 El hockey y el lacrosse • Hockey and lacrosse

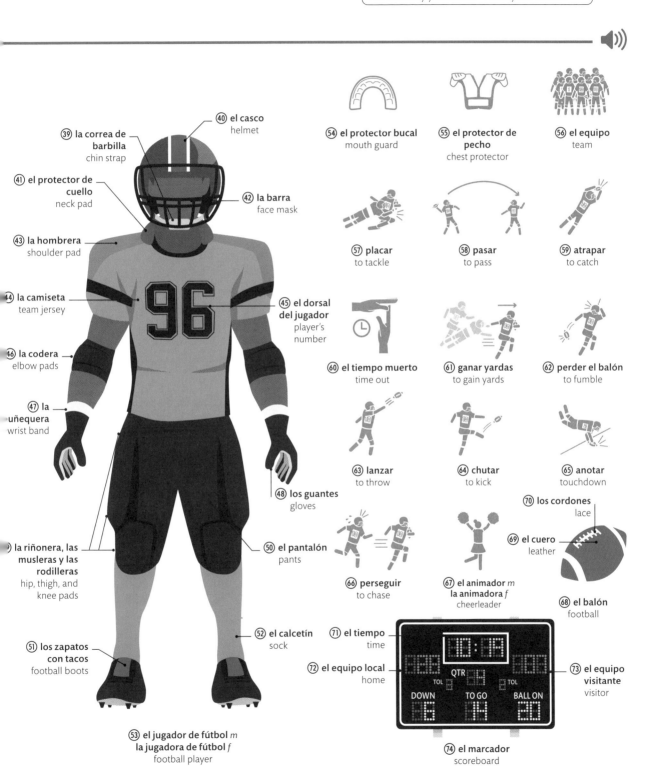

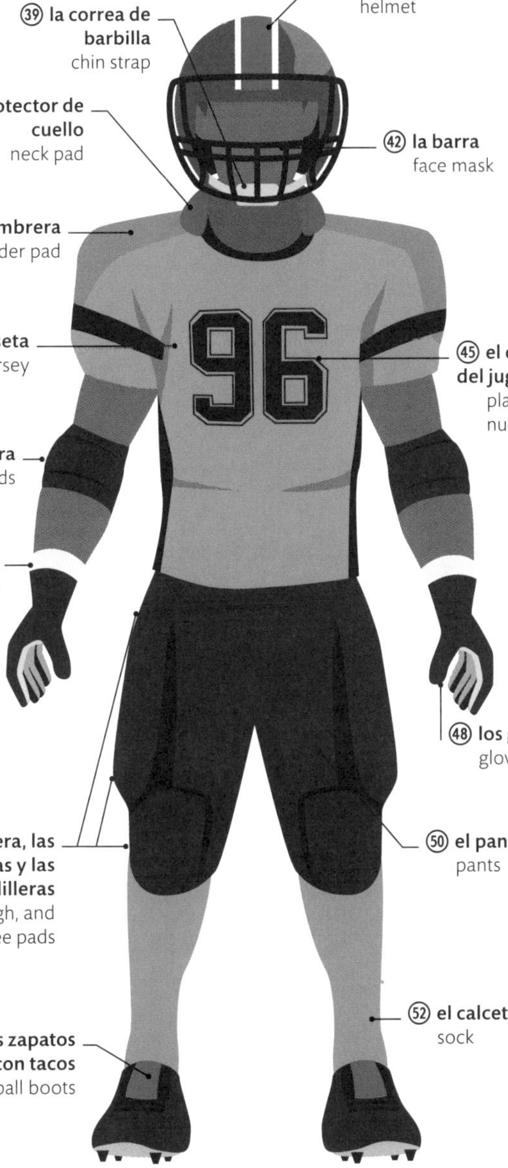

53 **el jugador de fútbol** *m*
la jugadora de fútbol *f*
football player

54 **el protector bucal**
mouth guard

55 **el protector de pecho**
chest protector

56 **el equipo**
team

57 **placar**
to tackle

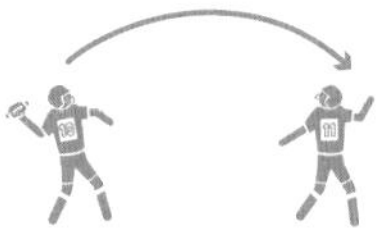

58 **pasar**
to pass

59 **atrapar**
to catch

60 **el tiempo muerto**
time out

61 **ganar yardas**
to gain yards

62 **perder el balón**
to fumble

63 **lanzar**
to throw

64 **chutar**
to kick

65 **anotar**
touchdown

66 **perseguir**
to chase

67 **el animador** *m*
la animadora *f*
cheerleader

68 **el balón**
football

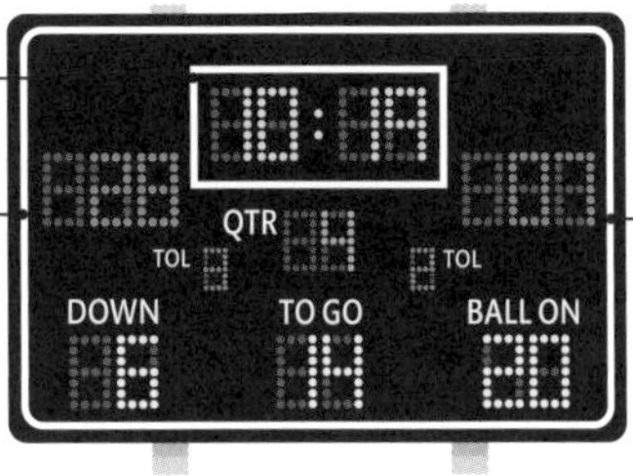

74 **el marcador**
scoreboard

108 El rugby
Rugby

108.1 EL RUGBY · RUGBY

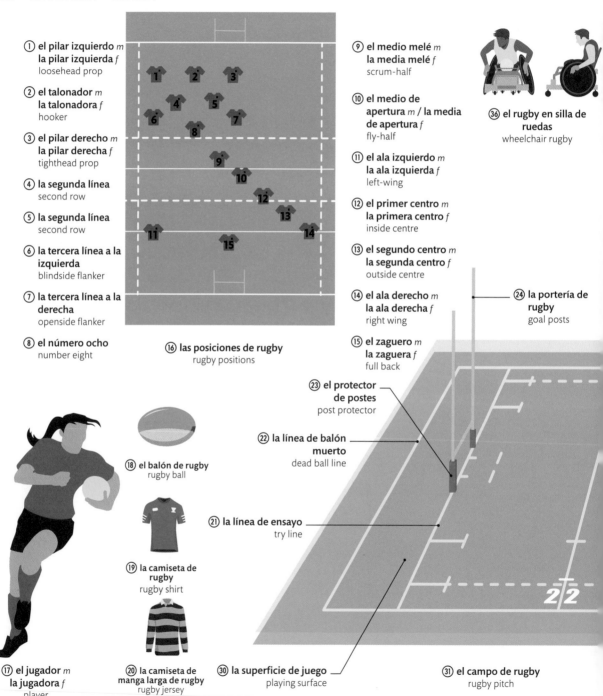

① **el pilar izquierdo** *m*
la pilar izquierda *f*
loosehead prop

② **el talonador** *m*
la talonadora *f*
hooker

③ **el pilar derecho** *m*
la pilar derecha *f*
tighthead prop

④ **la segunda línea**
second row

⑤ **la segunda línea**
second row

⑥ **la tercera línea a la izquierda**
blindside flanker

⑦ **la tercera línea a la derecha**
openside flanker

⑧ **el número ocho**
number eight

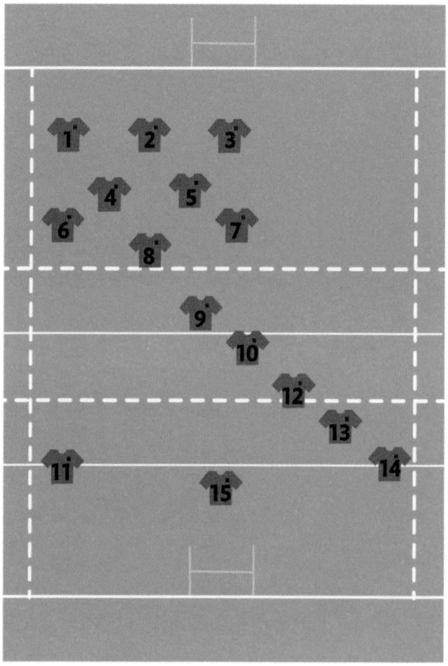

⑯ **las posiciones de rugby**
rugby positions

⑨ **el medio melé** *m*
la media melé *f*
scrum-half

⑩ **el medio de apertura** *m* / **la media de apertura** *f*
fly-half

⑪ **el ala izquierdo** *m*
la ala izquierda *f*
left-wing

⑫ **el primer centro** *m*
la primera centro *f*
inside centre

⑬ **el segundo centro** *m*
la segunda centro *f*
outside centre

⑭ **el ala derecho** *m*
la ala derecha *f*
right wing

⑮ **el zaguero** *m*
la zaguera *f*
full back

㊱ **el rugby en silla de ruedas**
wheelchair rugby

⑰ **el jugador** *m*
la jugadora *f*
player

⑱ **el balón de rugby**
rugby ball

⑲ **la camiseta de rugby**
rugby shirt

⑳ **la camiseta de manga larga de rugby**
rugby jersey

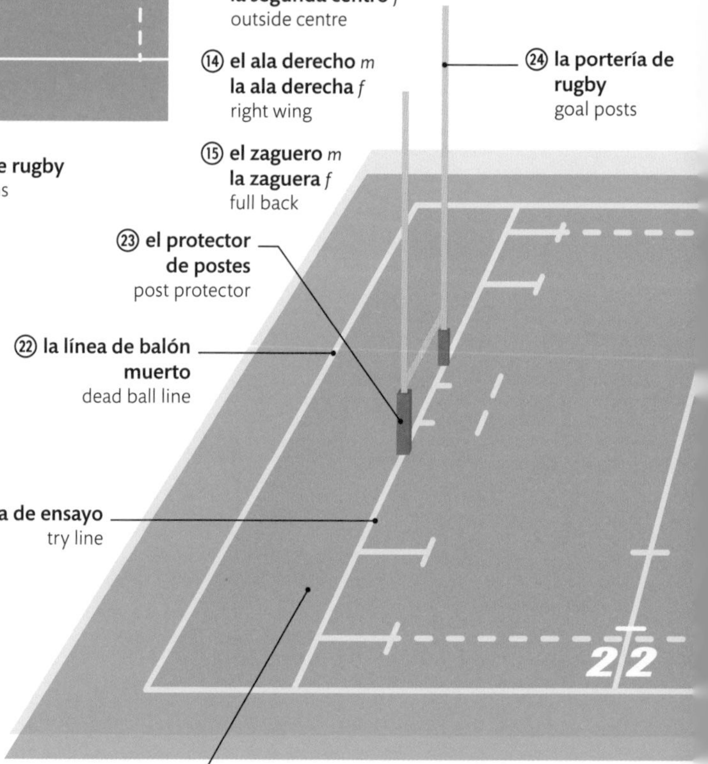

㉔ **la portería de rugby**
goal posts

㉓ **el protector de postes**
post protector

㉒ **la línea de balón muerto**
dead ball line

㉑ **la línea de ensayo**
try line

㉚ **la superficie de juego**
playing surface

㉛ **el campo de rugby**
rugby pitch

See also
107 El fútbol americano • American football **109** El fútbol • Football **110** El hockey y el lacrosse • Hockey and lacrosse **112** El baloncesto y el voleibol • Basketball and volleyball

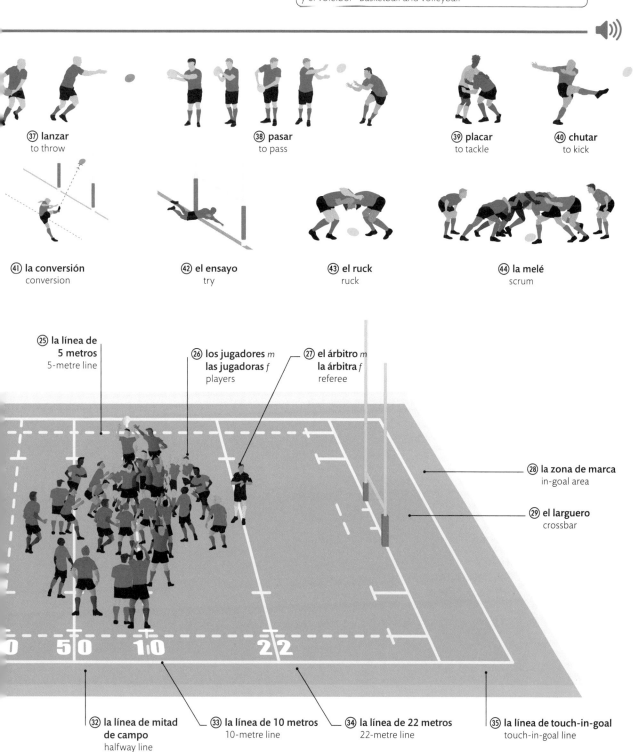

㊲ **lanzar**
to throw

㊳ **pasar**
to pass

㊴ **placar**
to tackle

㊵ **chutar**
to kick

㊶ **la conversión**
conversion

㊷ **el ensayo**
try

㊸ **el ruck**
ruck

㊹ **la melé**
scrum

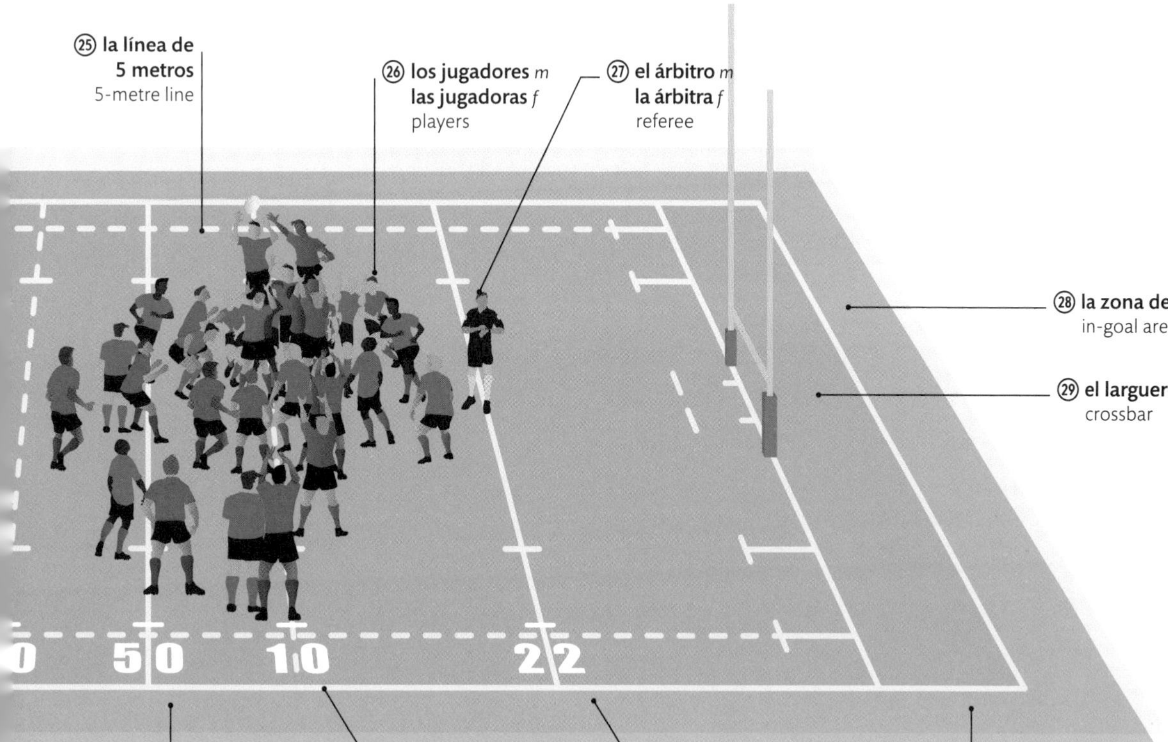

109 El fútbol
Football

109.1 EL PARTIDO DE FÚTBOL · FOOTBALL GAME

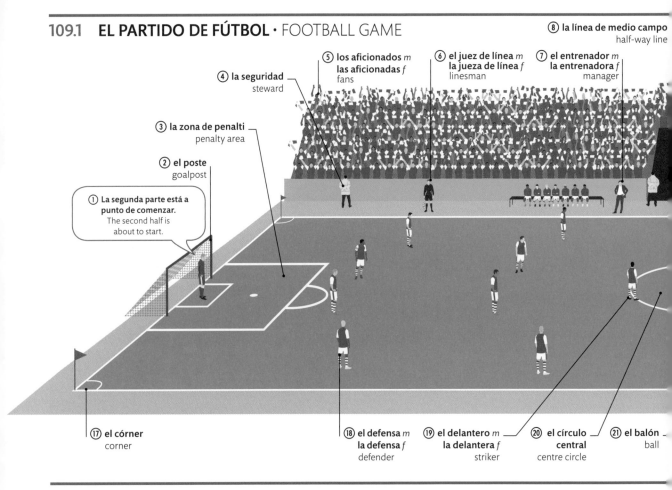

① La segunda parte está a punto de comenzar.
The second half is about to start.
② el poste
goalpost
③ la zona de penalti
penalty area
④ la seguridad
steward
⑤ los aficionados m
las aficionadas f
fans
⑥ el juez de línea m
la jueza de línea f
linesman
⑦ el entrenador m
la entrenadora f
manager
⑧ la línea de medio campo
half-way line
⑰ el córner
corner
⑱ el defensa m
la defensa f
defender
⑲ el delantero m
la delantera f
striker
⑳ el círculo central
centre circle
㉑ el balón
ball

109.2 LOS TIEMPOS Y LAS REGLAS · TIMING AND RULES

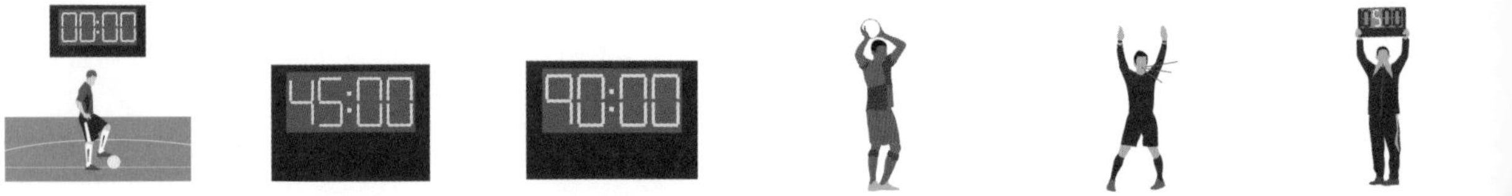

① el saque de centro
kickoff

② el descanso
half time

③ el final de partido
full time

④ el saque de banda
throw-in

⑤ el silbido final
final whistle

⑥ el tiempo añadid
injury time

⑨ el tiro de esquina
corner kick

⑩ la tarjeta amarilla
yellow card

⑪ la tarjeta roja
red card

⑫ ser expulsado m
ser expulsada f
to be sent off

⑬ empatar
to draw

⑭ perder
to lose

See also
107 El fútbol americano • American football **108** El rugby • Rugby **110** El hockey y el lacrosse • Hockey and lacrosse **112** El baloncesto y el voleibol • Basketball and volleyball

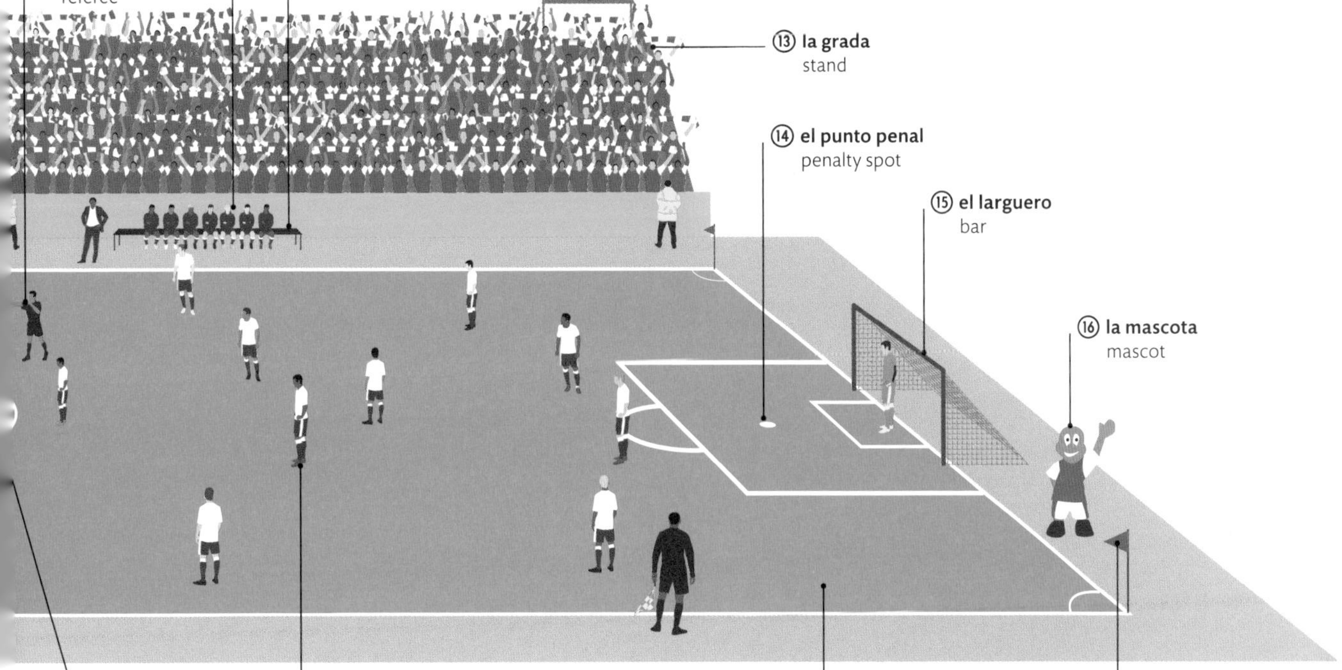
⑩ **los suplentes** *m*
las suplentes *f*
substitutes
⑪ **el banquillo de jugadores**
players' bench
⑫ **la pancarta**
banner
⑨ **el árbitro** *m*
la árbitra *f*
referee
⑬ **la grada**
stand
⑭ **el punto penal**
penalty spot
⑮ **el larguero**
bar
⑯ **la mascota**
mascot
㉒ **el túnel de entrada y salida**
players' entrance / exit
㉓ **el centrocampista** *m*
la centrocampista *f*
midfielder
㉔ **el campo de fútbol**
pitch
㉕ **el banderín de córner**
corner flag

⑦ **ganar**
to win

⑧ **la copa de campeones**
winners' cup

⑮ **la camiseta de fútbol**
football shirt

⑯ **las botas de fútbol**
football boots

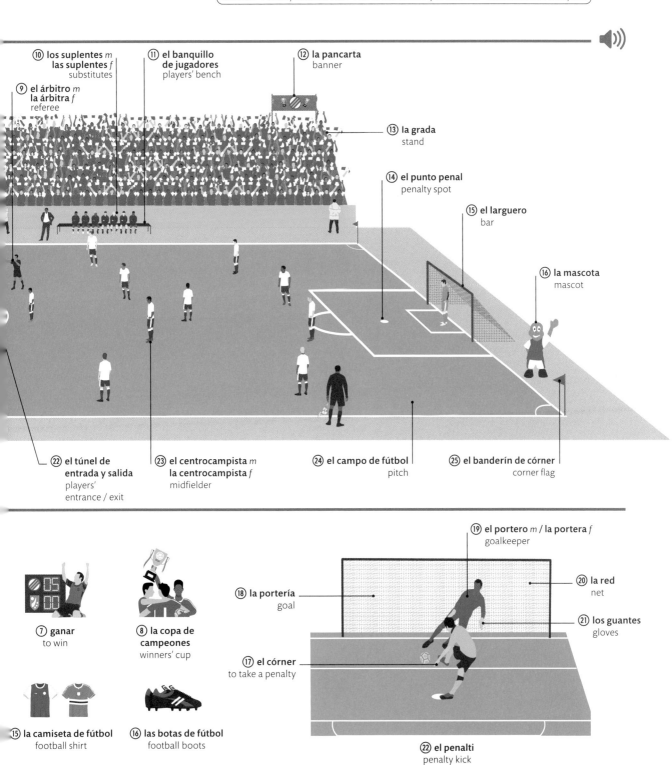

⑲ **el portero** *m* / **la portera** *f*
goalkeeper
⑱ **la portería**
goal
⑳ **la red**
net
㉑ **los guantes**
gloves
⑰ **el córner**
to take a penalty

㉒ **el penalti**
penalty kick

110 El hockey y el lacrosse
Hockey and lacrosse

110.1 EL HOCKEY SOBRE HIELO · ICE HOCKEY

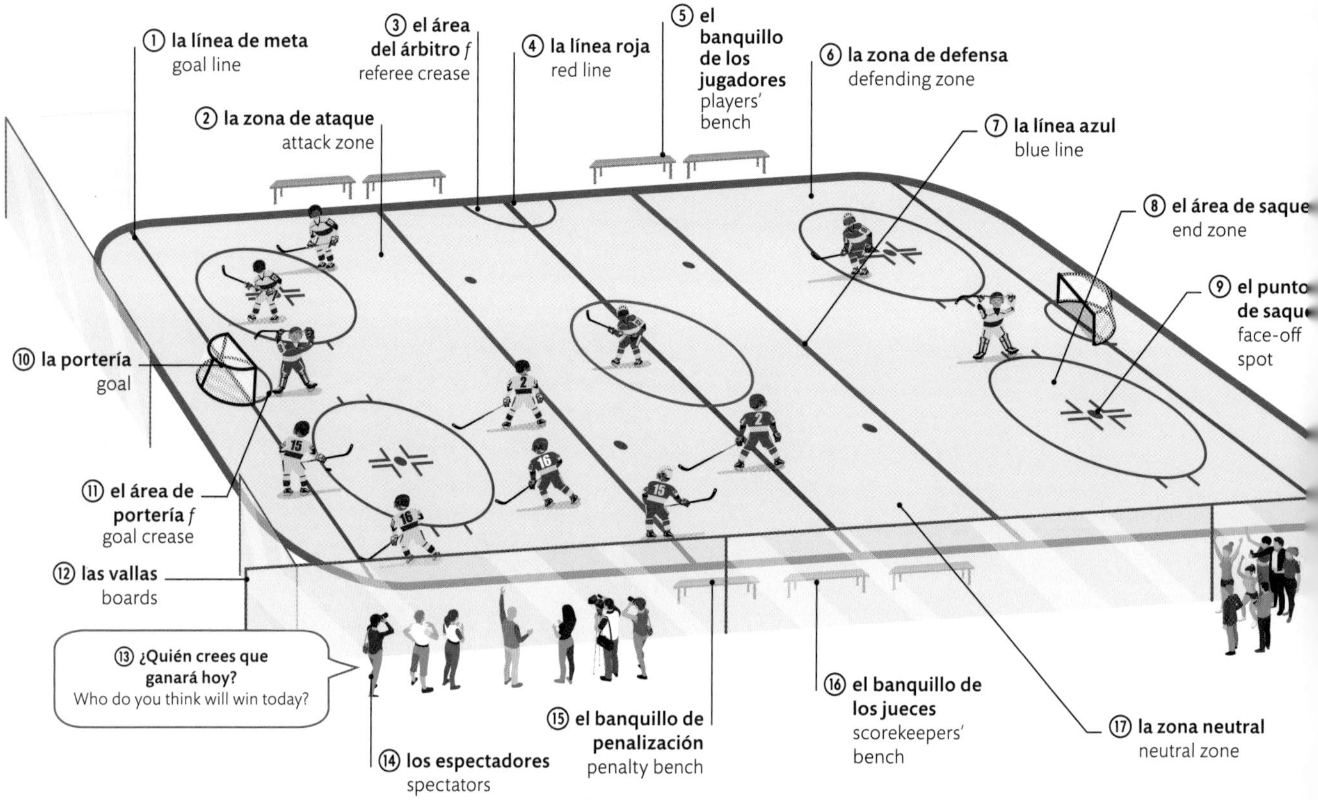

⑱ la pista de hockey sobre hielo
ice hockey rink

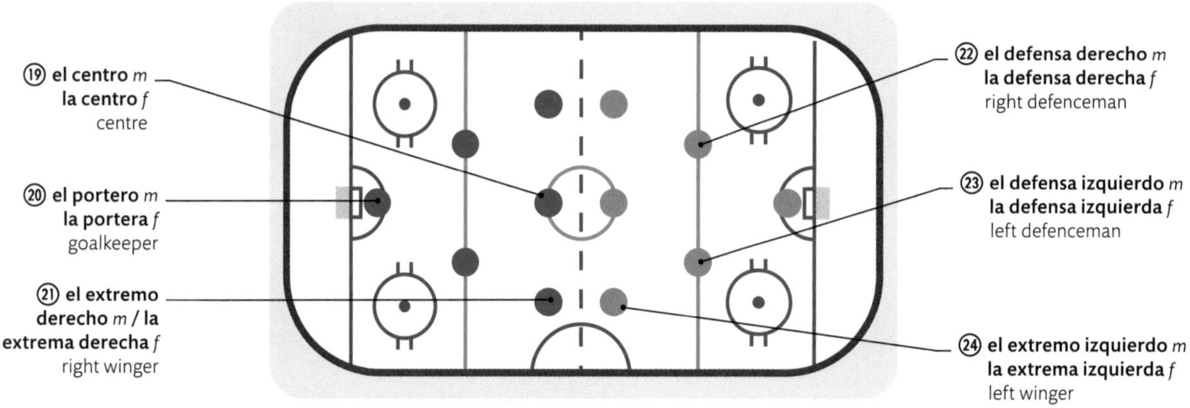

㉕ las posiciones de hockey sobre hielo
ice hockey positions

See also
107 El fútbol americano • American football **111** El críquet • Cricket **112** El baloncesto y el voleibol • Basketball and volleyball **113** El béisbol • Baseball **114** El tenis • Tennis

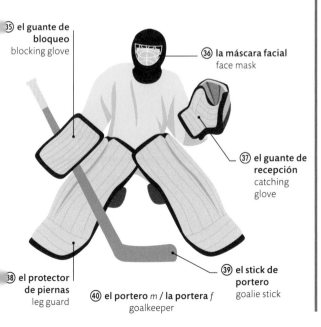

㉖ **patinar**
to skate

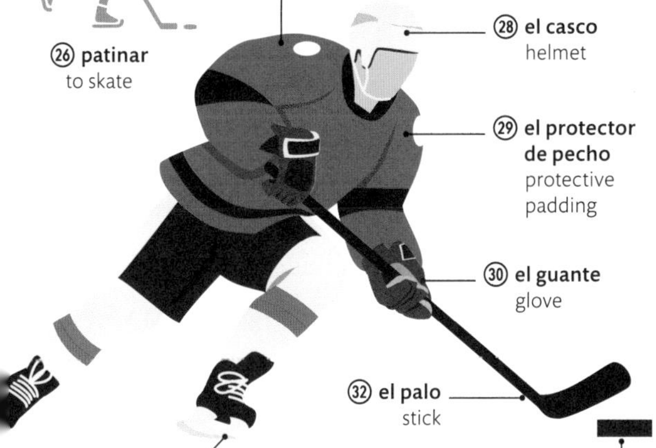

㉗ **la hombrera**
shoulder pad

㉘ **el casco**
helmet

㉙ **el protector de pecho**
protective padding

㉚ **el guante**
glove

㉜ **el palo**
stick

㉛ **el patín de hielo**
ice skate

㉝ **el disco**
puck

㉞ **el jugador de hockey sobre hielo** *m*
la jugadora de hockey sobre hielo *f*
ice hockey player

㉟ **el guante de bloqueo**
blocking glove

㊱ **la máscara facial**
face mask

㊲ **el guante de recepción**
catching glove

㊳ **el protector de piernas**
leg guard

㊴ **el stick de portero**
goalie stick

㊵ **el portero** *m* / **la portera** *f*
goalkeeper

110.2 EL HOCKEY SOBRE HIERBA • FIELD HOCKEY

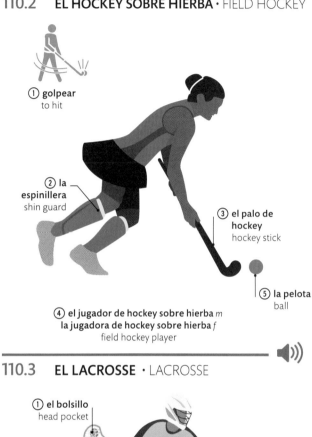

① **golpear**
to hit

② **la espinillera**
shin guard

③ **el palo de hockey**
hockey stick

⑤ **la pelota**
ball

④ **el jugador de hockey sobre hierba** *m*
la jugadora de hockey sobre hierba *f*
field hockey player

110.3 EL LACROSSE • LACROSSE

① **el bolsillo**
head pocket

② **el crosse**
crosse

③ **el protector de brazo**
arm protection

④ **el mango**
handle

⑤ **el jugador de lacrosse** *m* / **la jugadora de lacrosse** *f*
lacrosse player

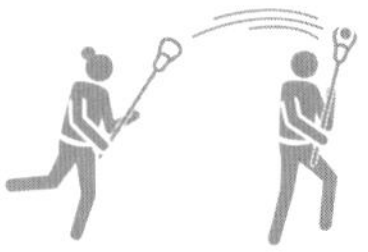

⑥ **pasar**
to pass

⑦ **recoger**
to scoop

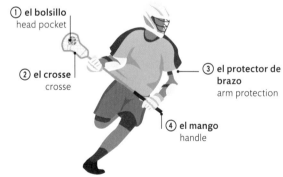

⑧ **el saque**
face-off

111 El críquet
Cricket

111.1 EL CAMPO DE CRÍQUET Y LAS POSICIONES
CRICKET PITCH AND POSITIONS

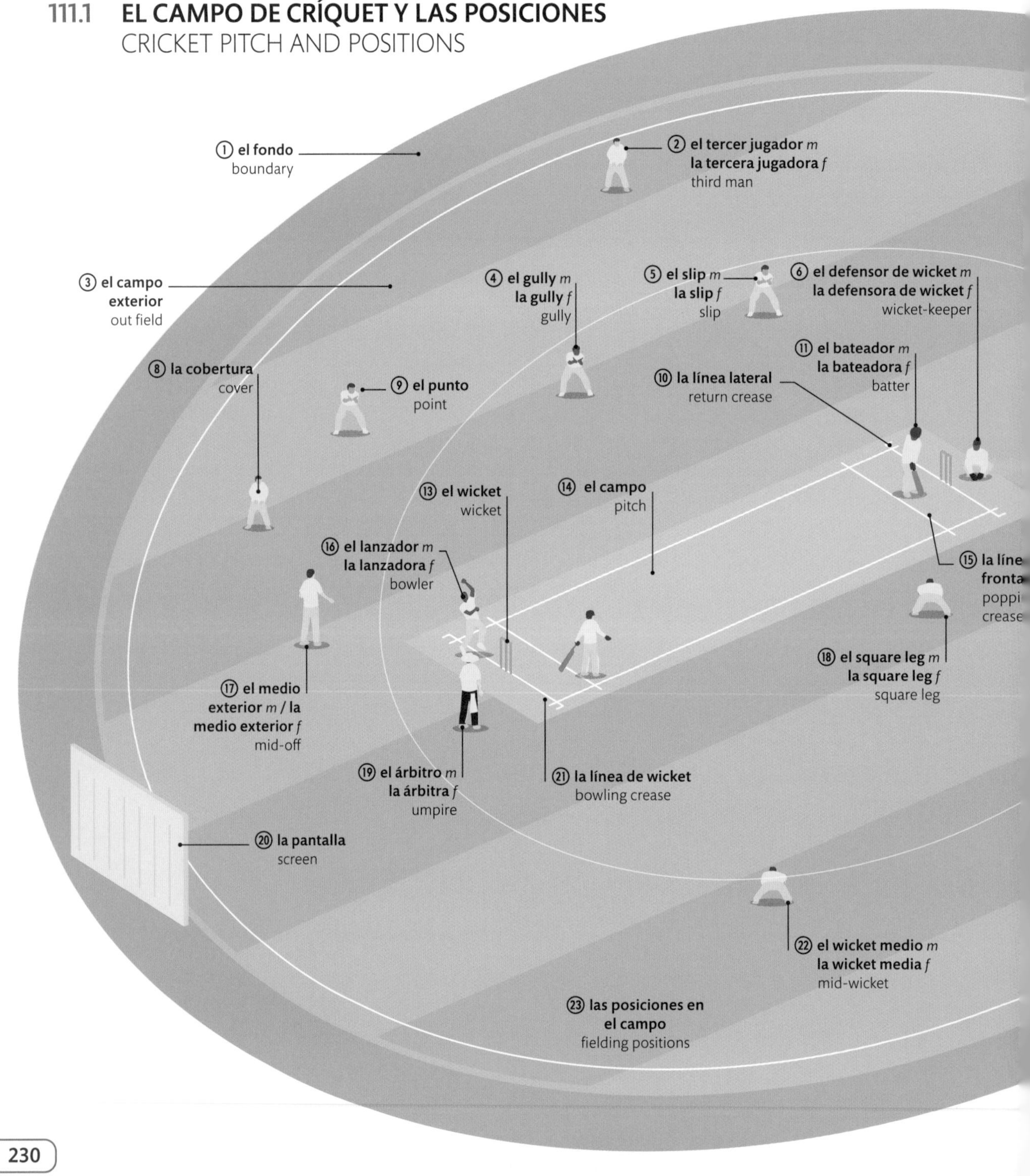

See also
109 El fútbol • Football **110** El hockey y el lacrosse
Hockey and lacrosse **113** El béisbol • Baseball **115** El golf • Golf

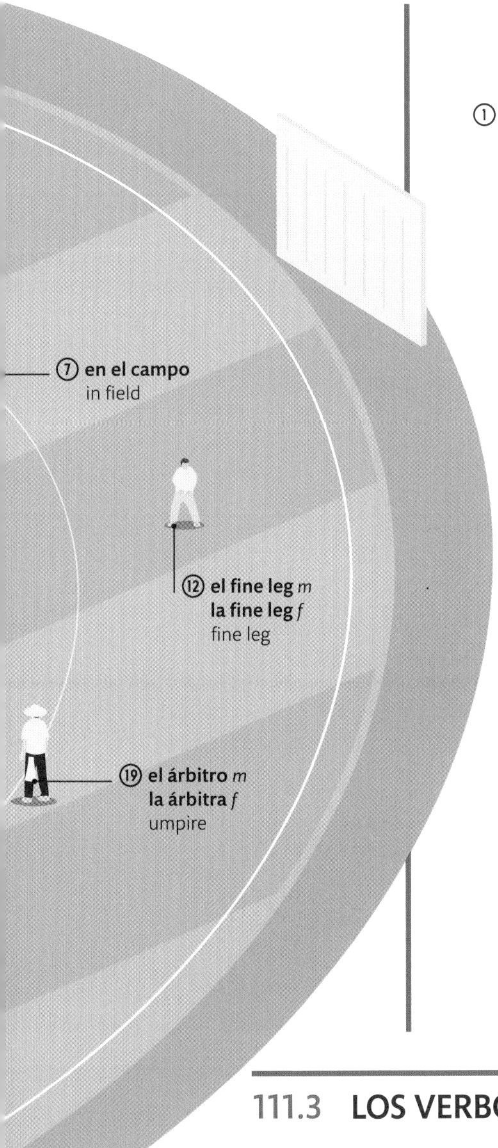

111.2 EL EQUIPO DE CRÍQUET • CRICKET EQUIPMENT

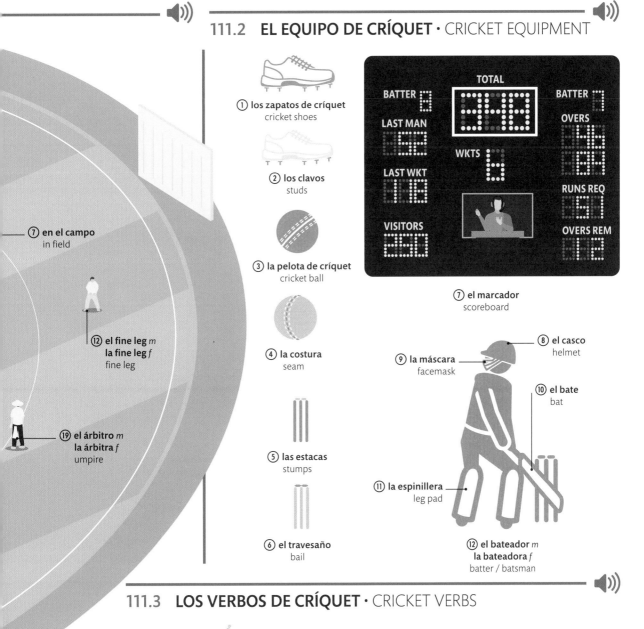

① **los zapatos de críquet**
cricket shoes

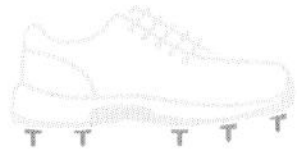

② **los clavos**
studs

③ **la pelota de críquet**
cricket ball

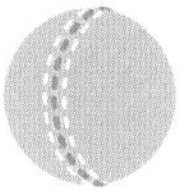

④ **la costura**
seam

⑤ **las estacas**
stumps

⑥ **el travesaño**
bail

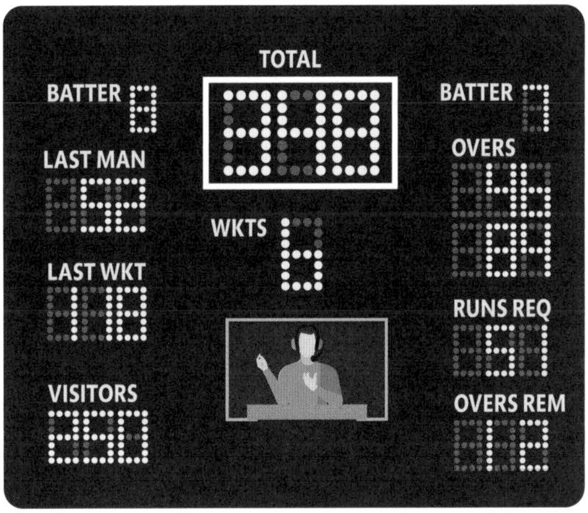

⑦ **el marcador**
scoreboard

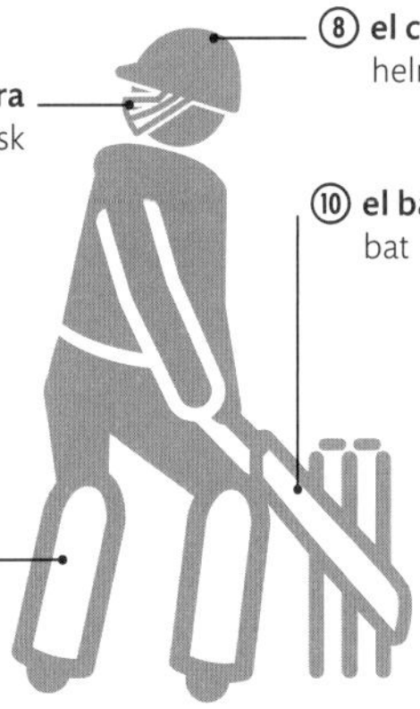

⑫ **el bateador** *m*
la bateadora *f*
batter / batsman

111.3 LOS VERBOS DE CRÍQUET • CRICKET VERBS

① **correr**
to run

② **lanzar**
to bowl

③ **batear**
to bat

④ **interceptar y devolver**
to field

⑤ **eliminar**
to strike out

⑥ **quedar eliminado** *m*
quedar eliminada *f*
to stump

112 El baloncesto y el voleibol
Basketball and volleyball

112.1 EL BALONCESTO · BASKETBALL

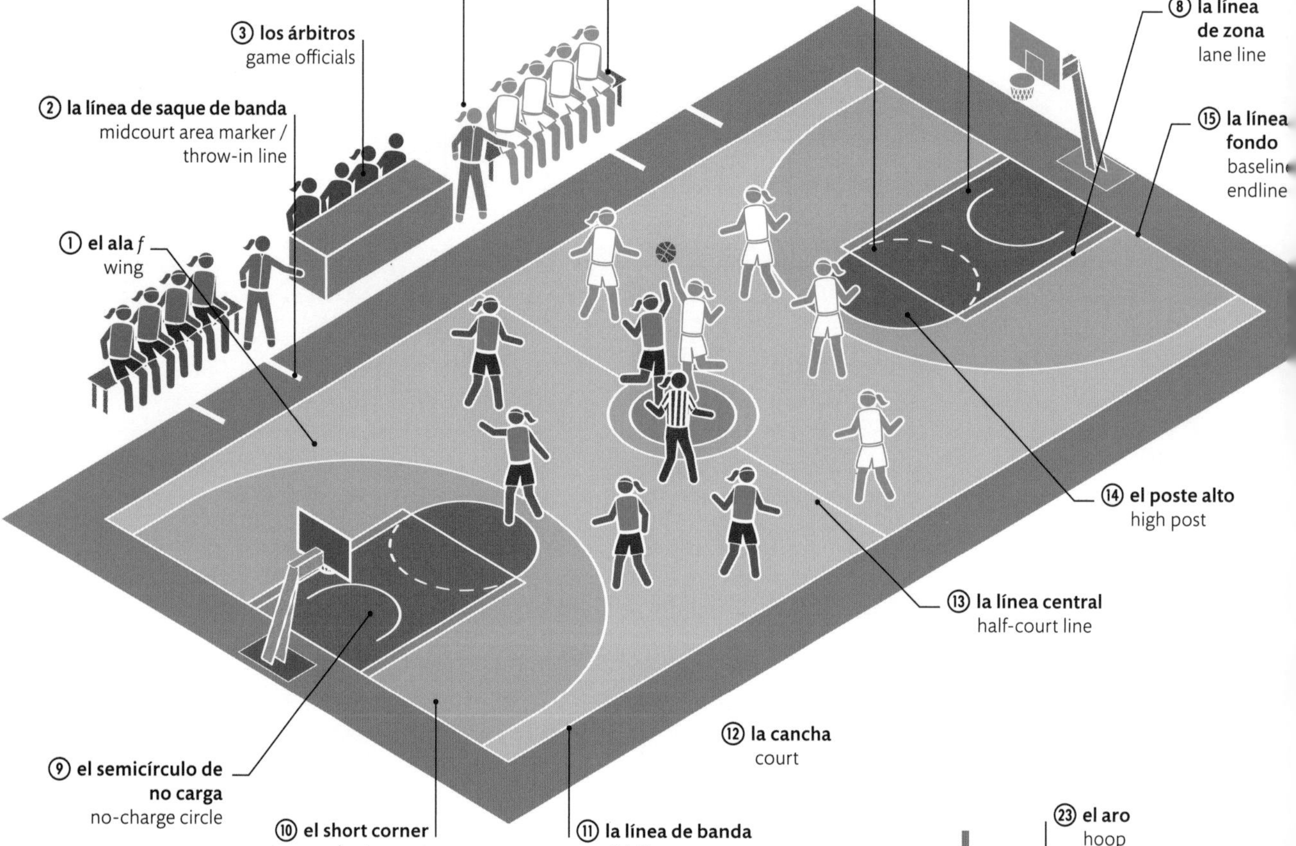

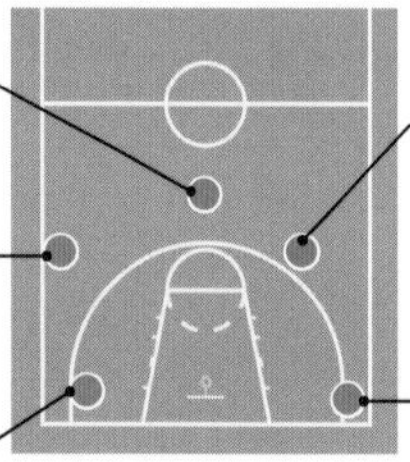

㉑ las cinco posiciones
five positions

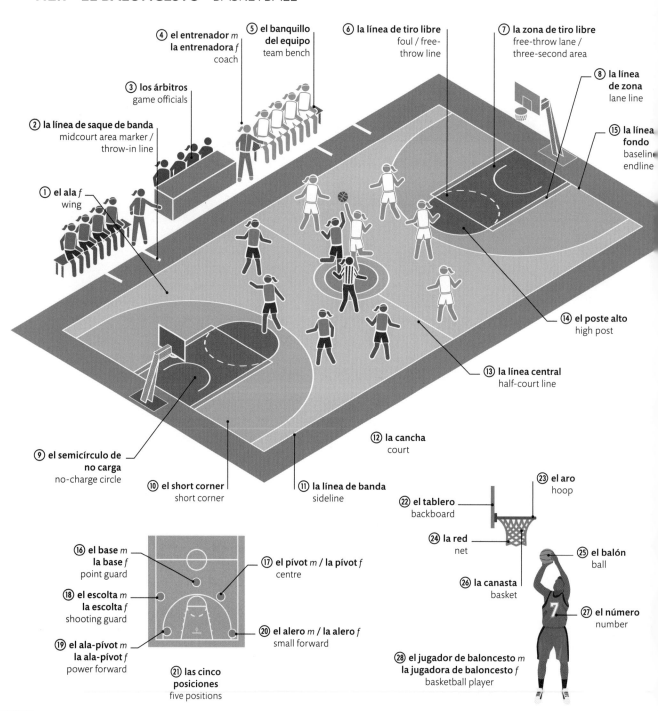

See also
107 El fútbol americano • American football **108** El rugby • Rugby
109 El fútbol • Football **124** En el gimnasio • At the gym
125 Otros deportes • Other sports

㉙ **pasar**
pass

㉚ **fuera de banda**
out of bounds

㉛ **el saque de banda**
throw-in

㉜ **el rebote**
rebound

㉝ **el tiro fallido**
airball

㉞ **el salto entre dos**
jump ball

㉟ **la falta**
foul

㊱ **marcar**
to mark

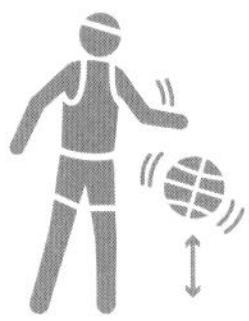

㊲ **botar**
to bounce

㊳ **hacer un mate**
to dunk

㊴ **tirar**
to shoot

㊵ **bloquear**
to block

112.2 **EL VOLEIBOL** • VOLLEYBALL

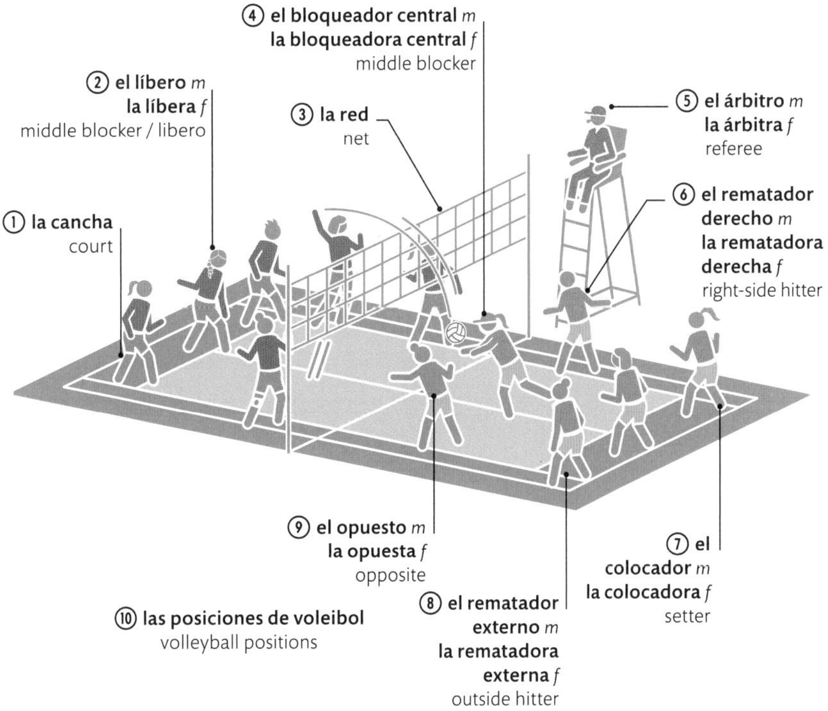

⑩ **las posiciones de voleibol**
volleyball positions

⑪ **recepcionar**
to bump

⑫ **hacer un pase bajo**
to dig

⑭ **bloquear**
to block

113 El béisbol
Baseball

113.1 EL PARTIDO DE BÉISBOL · BASEBALL GAME

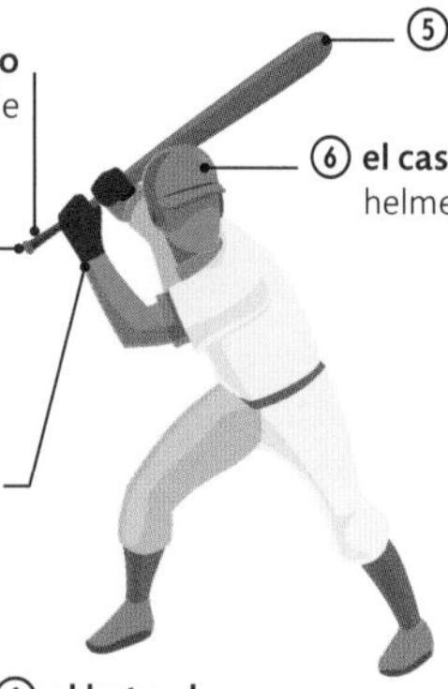

① **el mango** handle
② **el pomo** knob
③ **el guante de batear** batting glove
④ **el bateador** *m* **la bateadora** *f* batter
⑤ **el bate** bat
⑥ **el casco** helmet

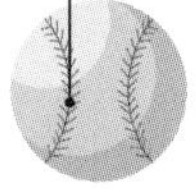

⑦ **las costuras** stitches
⑧ **la pelota de béisbol** baseball

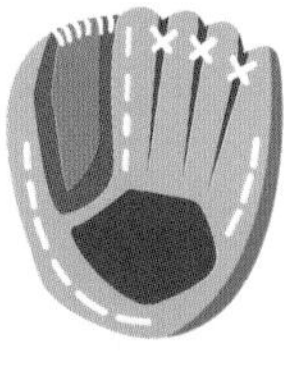

⑨ **el guante** mitt

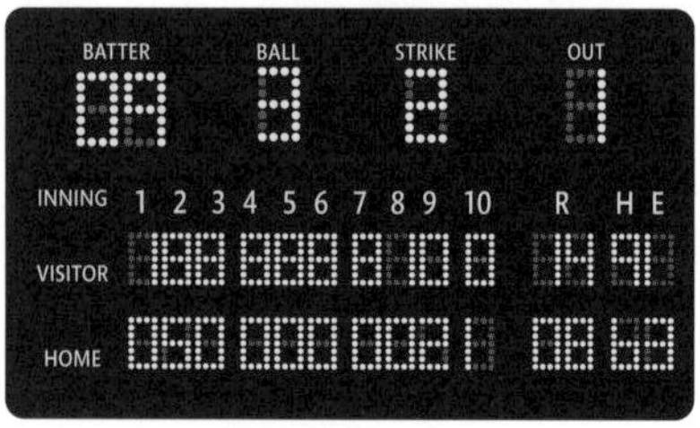

⑩ **la entrada** inning

⑪ **la máscara** mask

㉕ **el poste de foul** foul pole
㉖ **la línea de falta** foul line
㉗ **la franja de alerta** warning track
㉘ **el jardín** outfield

⑫ **el strike** strike
⑬ **fuera** out
⑭ **la falta** foul ball

⑮ **a salvo** safe
⑯ **hacer una jugada** to play
⑰ **lanzar** to throw
⑱ **atrapar** to catch

⑲ **batear** to bat
⑳ **resbalar** to slide
㉑ **lanzar** to pitch
㉒ **correr** to run
㉓ **perseguir** to tag
㉔ **interceptar y devolver** to field

See also
107 El fútbol americano • American football **110** El hockey y el lacrosse • Hockey and lacrosse
111 El críquet • Cricket **112** El baloncesto y el voleibol • Basketball and volleyball

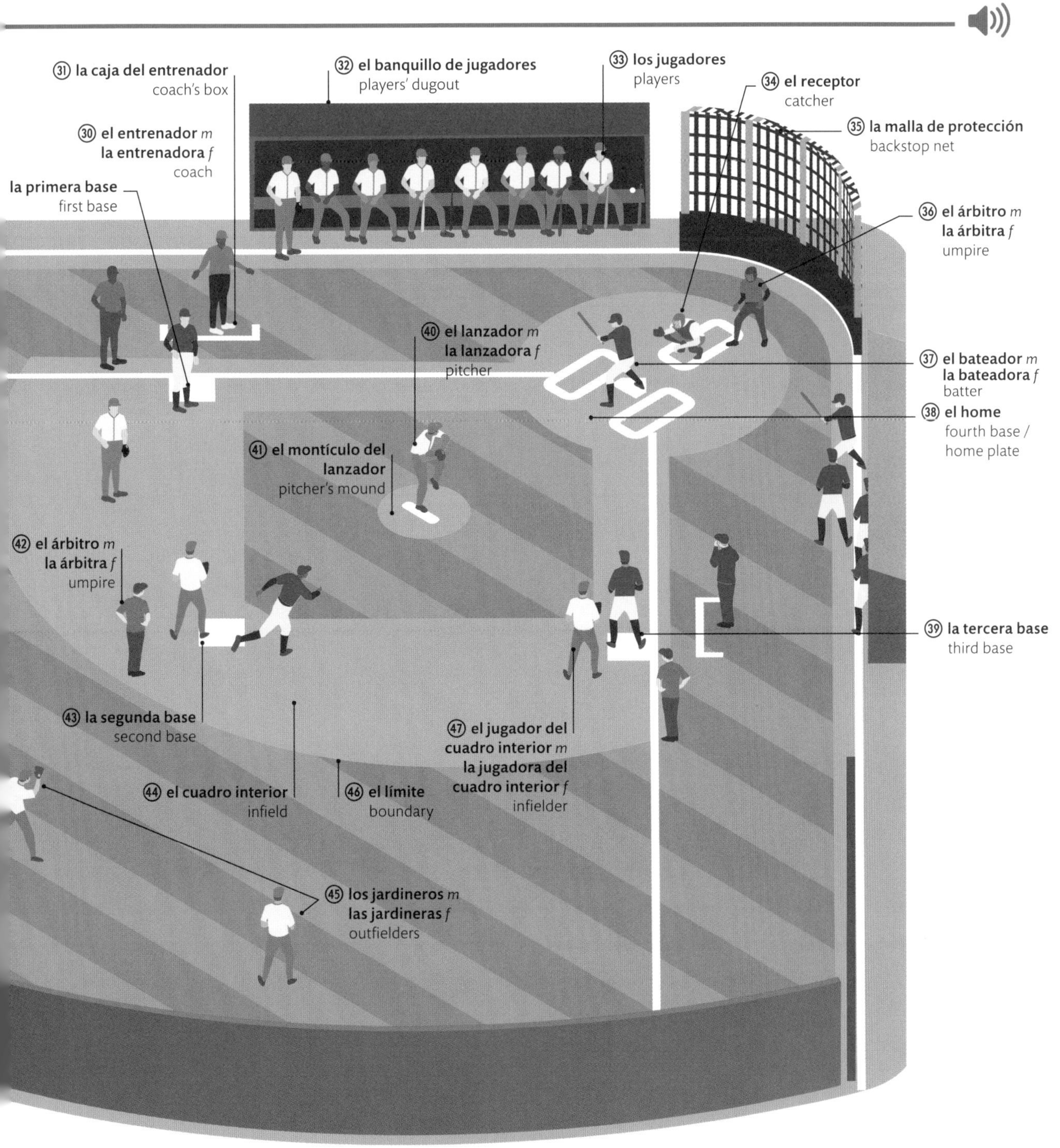

㊽ **el campo de béisbol**
baseball field

El tenis
Tennis

114.1 EL PARTIDO DE TENIS · TENNIS MATCH

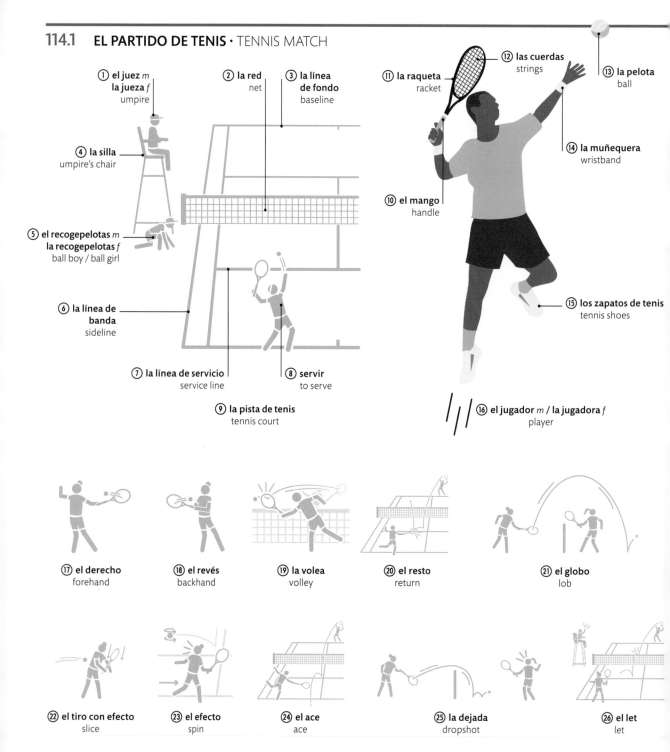

① **el juez** *m* **la jueza** *f* umpire

② **la red** net

③ **la línea de fondo** baseline

④ **la silla** umpire's chair

⑤ **el recogepelotas** *m* **la recogepelotas** *f* ball boy / ball girl

⑥ **la línea de banda** sideline

⑦ **la línea de servicio** service line

⑧ **servir** to serve

⑨ **la pista de tenis** tennis court

⑩ **el mango** handle

⑪ **la raqueta** racket

⑫ **las cuerdas** strings

⑬ **la pelota** ball

⑭ **la muñequera** wristband

⑮ **los zapatos de tenis** tennis shoes

⑯ **el jugador** *m* / **la jugadora** *f* player

⑰ **el derecho** forehand

⑱ **el revés** backhand

⑲ **la volea** volley

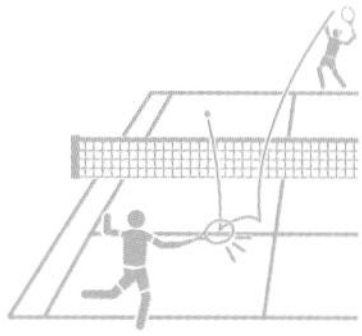

⑳ **el resto** return

㉑ **el globo** lob

㉒ **el tiro con efecto** slice

㉓ **el efecto** spin

㉔ **el ace** ace

㉕ **la dejada** dropshot

㉖ **el let** let

See also
111 El críquet • Cricket **113** El béisbol • Baseball
115 El golf • Golf **116** El atletismo • Athletics

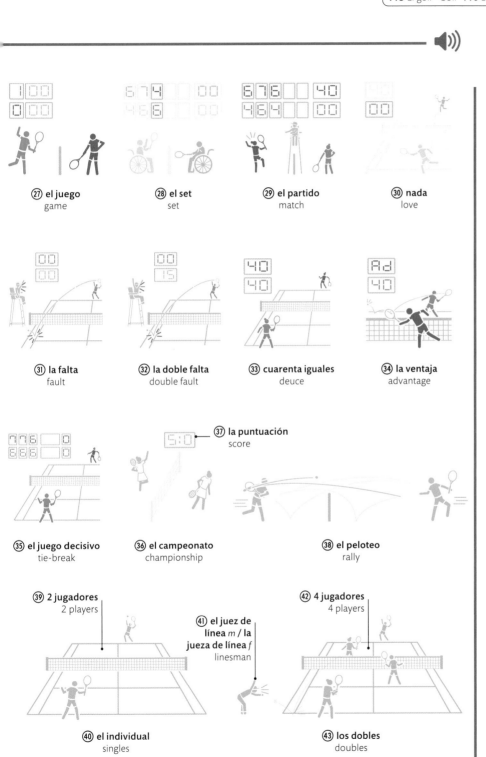

㉗ **el juego**
game

㉘ **el set**
set

㉙ **el partido**
match

㉚ **nada**
love

㉛ **la falta**
fault

㉜ **la doble falta**
double fault

㉝ **cuarenta iguales**
deuce

㉞ **la ventaja**
advantage

㉟ **el juego decisivo**
tie-break

㊲ **la puntuación**
score

㊱ **el campeonato**
championship

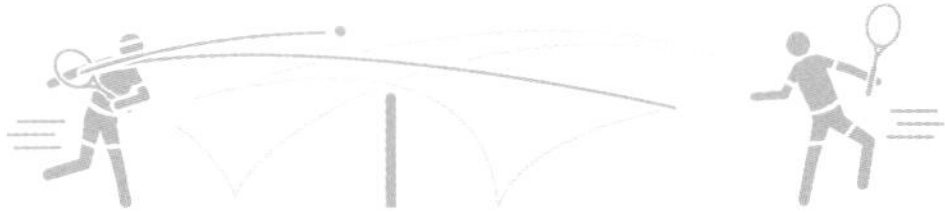

㊳ **el peloteo**
rally

㊴ **2 jugadores**
2 players

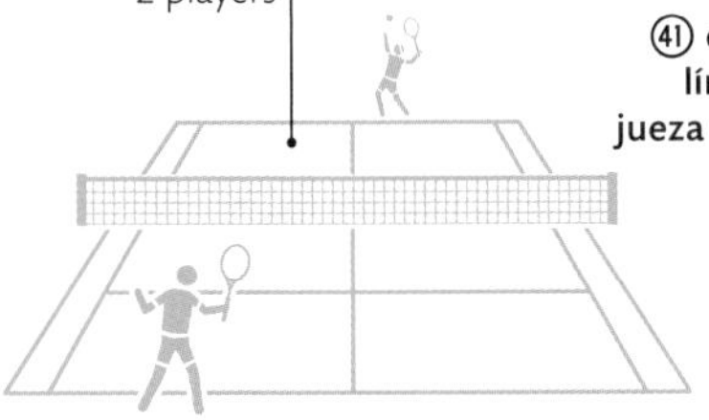

㊵ **el individual**
singles

㊶ **el juez de línea** *m* **/ la jueza de línea** *f*
linesman

㊷ **4 jugadores**
4 players

㊸ **los dobles**
doubles

114.2 LOS JUEGOS DE RAQUETA
RACKET GAMES

① **el squash**
squash

② **el racketball**
racquetball

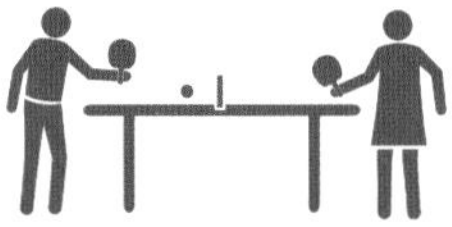

③ **el ping pong**
ping pong / table tennis

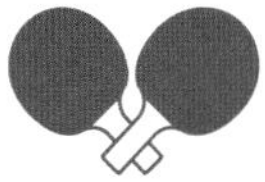

④ **el pádel**
bat

⑤ **el bádminton**
badminton

⑥ **el volante**
shuttlecock

115 El golf
Golf

115.1 EN EL CAMPO DE GOLF · ON THE GOLF COURSE

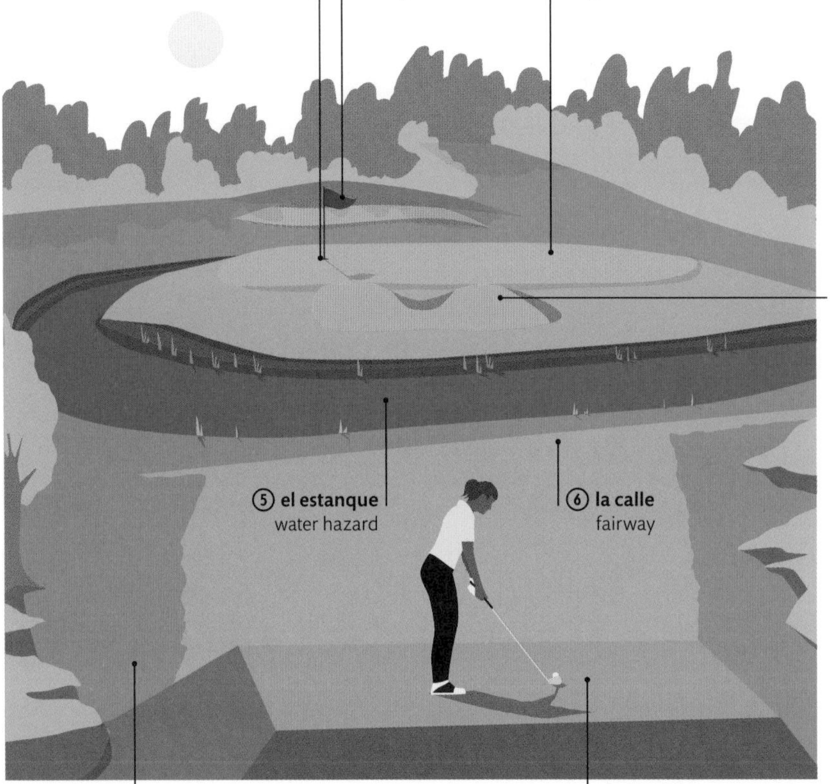

① **el hoyo**
hole

② **la banderola**
flag

③ **el green**
green

④ **el búnker**
bunker

⑤ **el estanque**
water hazard

⑥ **la calle**
fairway

⑦ **el rough**
rough

⑧ **el campo de golf**
golf course

⑨ **la salida**
teeing ground

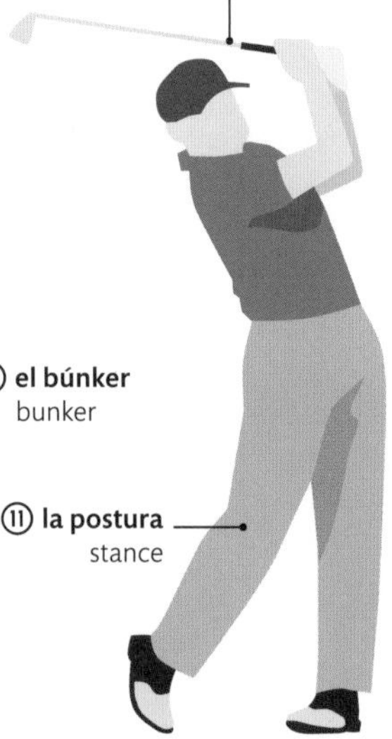

⑩ **el swing**
swing

⑪ **la postura**
stance

⑫ **el golfista** *m* / **la golfista** *f*
golfer

⑬ **el club**
clubhouse

⑭ **el buggy**
buggy

⑮ **el caddy**
caddy

⑯ **el par**
par

⑰ **el sobre par**
over par

⑱ **el bajo par**
under par

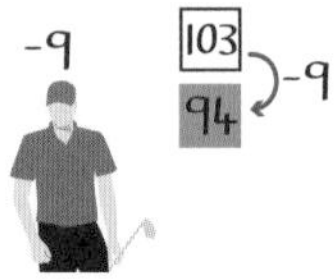

⑲ **el hándicap**
handicap

⑳ **la línea de juego**
line of play

㉑ **el swing de práctica**
practice swing

㉒ **el backswing**
backswing

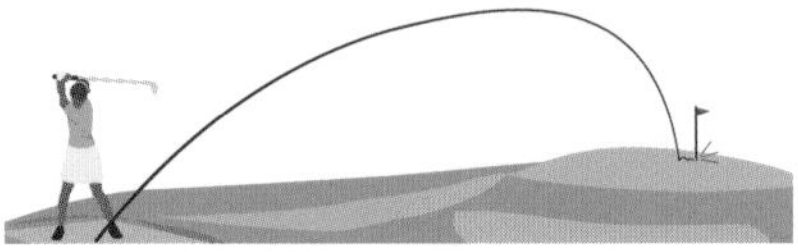

㉓ **el hoyo en uno**
hole in one

㉔ **el torneo**
tournament

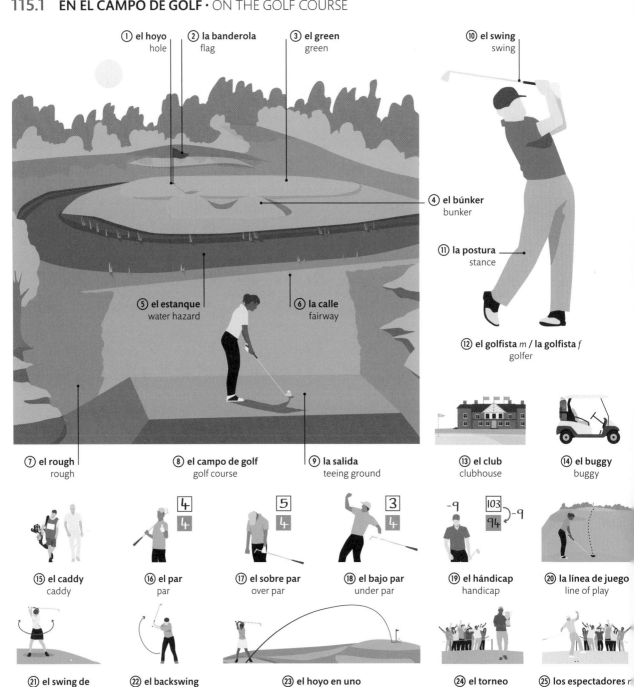

㉕ **los espectadores** *m* / **las espectadoras** *f*
spectators

See also
111 El críquet • Cricket **113** El béisbol
Baseball **114** El tenis • Tennis

115.2 EL EQUIPO DE GOLF
GOLF EQUIPMENT

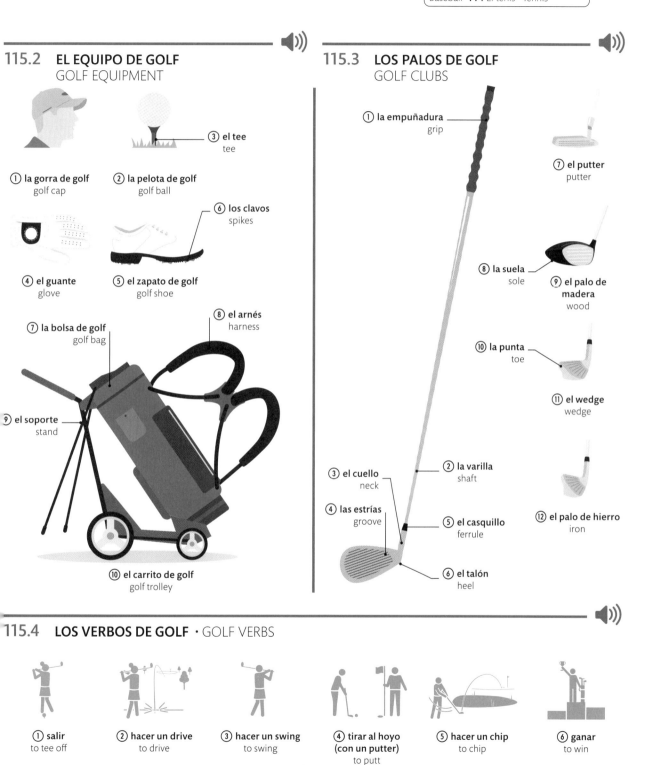

1. **la gorra de golf** golf cap
2. **la pelota de golf** golf ball
3. **el tee** tee
4. **el guante** glove
5. **el zapato de golf** golf shoe
6. **los clavos** spikes
7. **la bolsa de golf** golf bag
8. **el arnés** harness
9. **el soporte** stand
10. **el carrito de golf** golf trolley

115.3 LOS PALOS DE GOLF
GOLF CLUBS

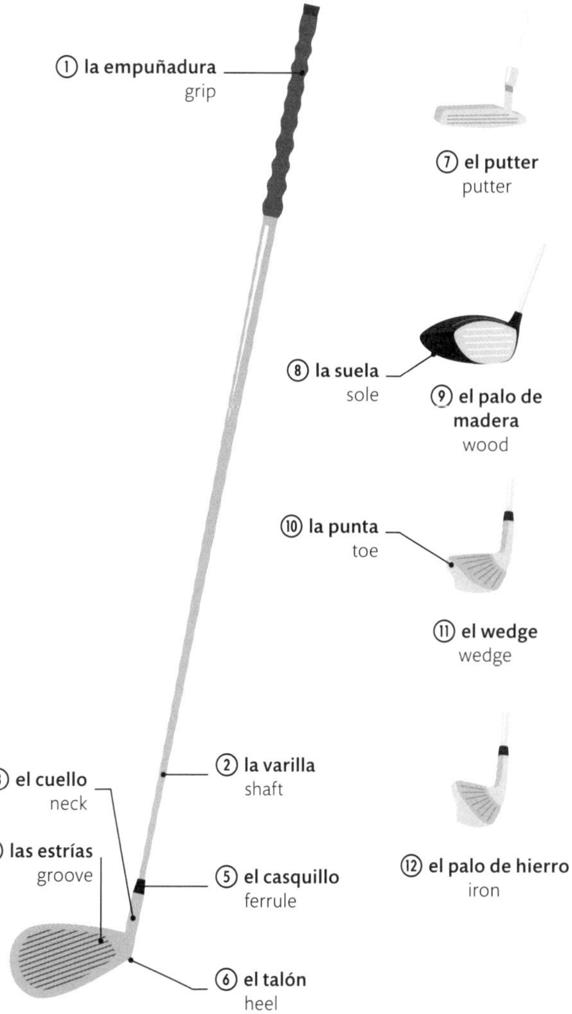

1. **la empuñadura** grip
2. **la varilla** shaft
3. **el cuello** neck
4. **las estrías** groove
5. **el casquillo** ferrule
6. **el talón** heel
7. **el putter** putter
8. **la suela** sole
9. **el palo de madera** wood
10. **la punta** toe
11. **el wedge** wedge
12. **el palo de hierro** iron

115.4 LOS VERBOS DE GOLF • GOLF VERBS

1. **salir** to tee off
2. **hacer un drive** to drive
3. **hacer un swing** to swing
4. **tirar al hoyo (con un putter)** to putt
5. **hacer un chip** to chip
6. **ganar** to win

116 El atletismo
Athletics

116.1 LA PISTA DE ATLETISMO • ATHLETICS TRACK

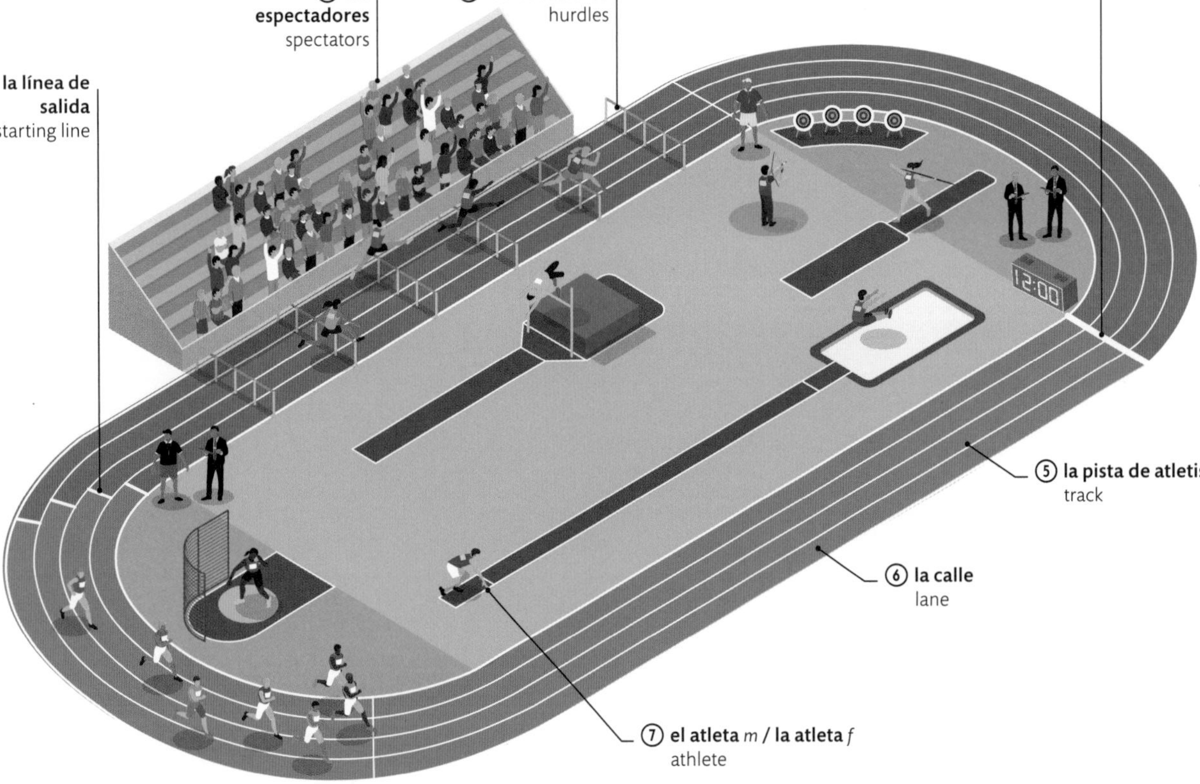

116.2 LAS CARRERAS • RACING EVENTS

① **la carrera**
race

② **el bloque de salida**
starting block

③ **el velocista** *m*
la velocista *f*
sprinter

④ **la carrera T11 (deportistas ciegos)**
T11 (visual impairment) race

⑤ **la carrera en silla de ruedas**
wheelchair race

⑥ **la carrera de relevos**
relay race

⑦ **el testigo**
baton

⑧ **la maratón**
marathon

⑨ **la foto finish**
photo finish

See also
117 Los deportes de combate • Combat sports **118** La natación • Swimming **119** La navegación y los deportes acuáticos • Sailing and watersports **120** la equitación • Horse riding **122** Los deportes de invierno • Winter sports **124** En el gimnasio • At the gym **125** Otros deportes • Other sports

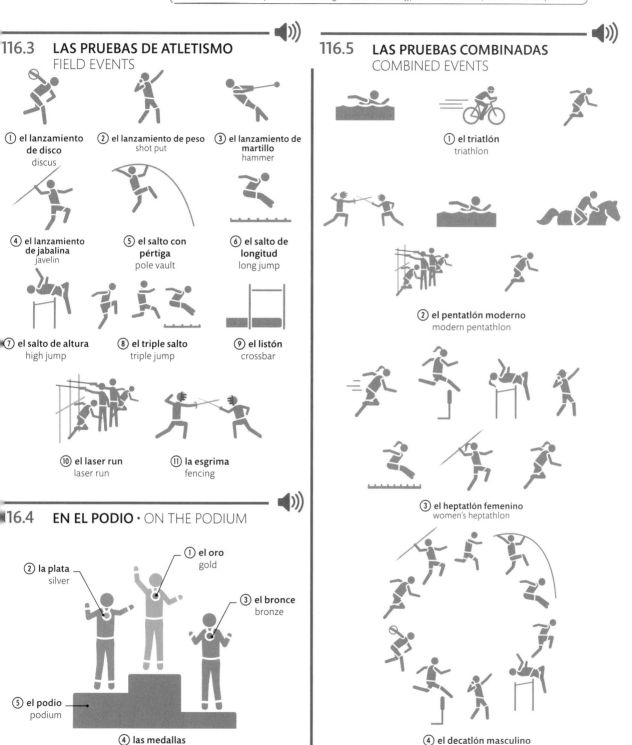

116.3 LAS PRUEBAS DE ATLETISMO
FIELD EVENTS

① **el lanzamiento de disco**
discus

② **el lanzamiento de peso**
shot put

③ **el lanzamiento de martillo**
hammer

④ **el lanzamiento de jabalina**
javelin

⑤ **el salto con pértiga**
pole vault

⑥ **el salto de longitud**
long jump

⑦ **el salto de altura**
high jump

⑧ **el triple salto**
triple jump

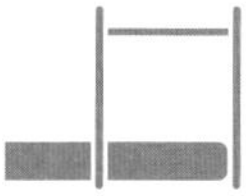
⑨ **el listón**
crossbar

⑩ **el laser run**
laser run

⑪ **la esgrima**
fencing

116.4 EN EL PODIO • ON THE PODIUM

① **el oro**
gold

② **la plata**
silver

③ **el bronce**
bronze

④ **las medallas**
medals

⑤ **el podio**
podium

116.5 LAS PRUEBAS COMBINADAS
COMBINED EVENTS

① **el triatlón**
triathlon

② **el pentatlón moderno**
modern pentathlon

③ **el heptatlón femenino**
women's heptathlon

④ **el decatlón masculino**
men's decathlon

117 Los deportes de combate
Combat sports

117.1 LAS ARTES MARCIALES · MARTIAL ARTS

① **la coquilla** groin protector
② **el guante** glove
③ **el cinturón** belt
④ **el casco** head guard
⑤ **el peto** chest protection
⑥ **el taekwondo** taekwondo

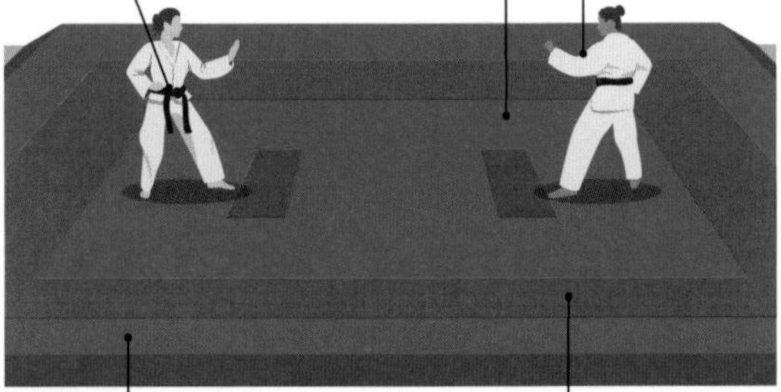

⑦ **el cinturón negro** black belt
⑧ **el tatami de kárate** karate mat
⑨ **el oponente** *m* **la oponente** *f* opponent
⑩ **la zona de seguridad** safety area
⑪ **el kárate** karate
⑫ **la zona de peligro** danger area

⑬ **el judo** judo

⑭ **el aikido** aikido
⑮ **el hakama** hakama

⑯ **el kung fu** kung fu

⑰ **el jiu jitsu** jujitsu

⑱ **la capoeira** capoeira

⑲ **el kickboxing** kickboxing

⑳ **el tai chi** tai chi

㉑ **la lucha libre** wrestling

㉒ **el sumo** sumo wrestling

㉓ **el casco** mask
㉔ **la espada** sword
㉕ **el kendo** kendo

117.2 LAS ACCIONES · ACTIONS

① **caer** to fall

② **agarrar** to hold

③ **derribar** to throw

④ **inmovilizar** to pin

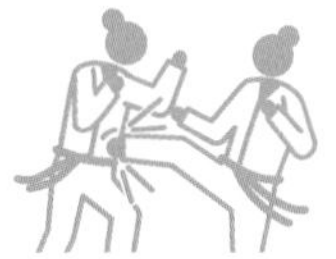

⑤ **la patada frontal** front kick

⑥ **la patada voladora** flying kick

See also
116 El atletismo • Athletics **124** En el gimnasio • At the gym
125 Otros deportes • Other sports

117.3 EL BOXEO • BOXING

① **el ring**
boxing ring

② **las cuerdas**
ropes

③ **el combate de boxeo**
boxing match

④ **la ronda**
round

⑤ **el noqueo**
knock out

⑥ **los guantes de boxeo**
boxing gloves

⑦ **el protector bucal**
mouth guard

⑧ **el saco de boxeo**
punchbag

117.4 LA ESGRIMA • FENCING

① **atacar**
to lunge

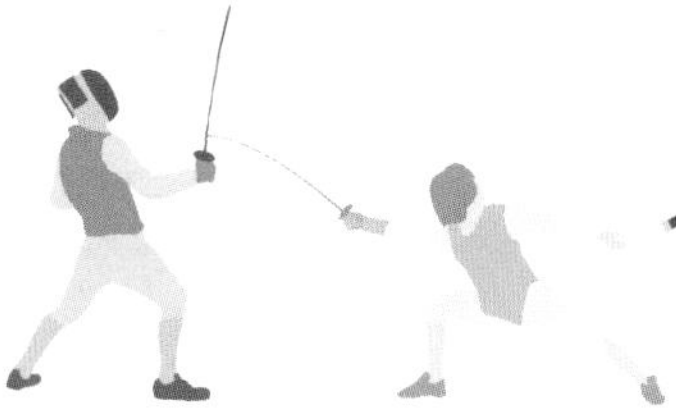

② **defender**
to parry

③ **la empuñadura**
hilt

⑤ **la hoja**
blade

④ **el florete**
foil

⑥ **la espada**
épée

⑦ **el sable**
sabre

⑦ **dar un puñetazo**
to punch

⑧ **golpear**
to strike

⑨ **bloquear**
to block

⑩ **saltar**
to jump

⑪ **el golpe de mano abierta**
to chop

118 La natación
Swimming

118.1 LA NATACIÓN · SWIMMING

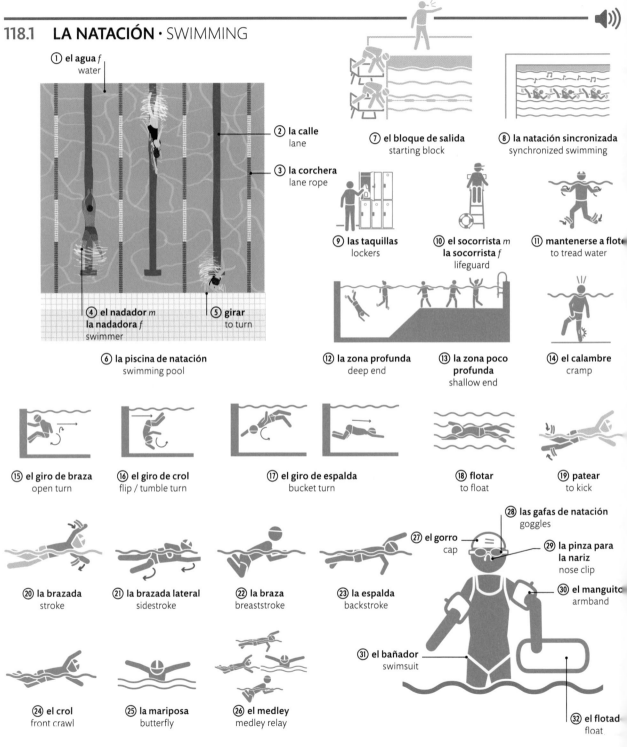

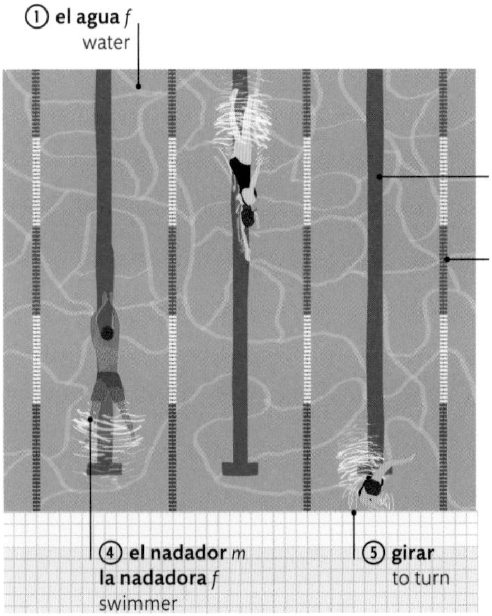

⑥ **la piscina de natación**
swimming pool

⑦ **el bloque de salida**
starting block

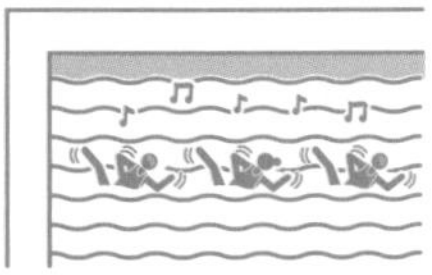

⑧ **la natación sincronizada**
synchronized swimming

⑨ **las taquillas**
lockers

⑩ **el socorrista** *m*
la socorrista *f*
lifeguard

⑪ **mantenerse a flot**
to tread water

⑫ **la zona profunda**
deep end

⑬ **la zona poco profunda**
shallow end

⑭ **el calambre**
cramp

⑮ **el giro de braza**
open turn

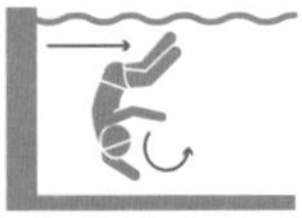

⑯ **el giro de crol**
flip / tumble turn

⑰ **el giro de espalda**
bucket turn

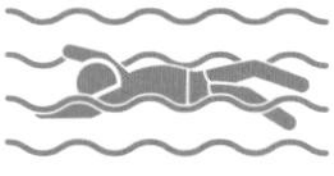

⑱ **flotar**
to float

⑲ **patear**
to kick

⑳ **la brazada**
stroke

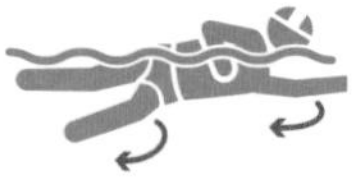

㉑ **la brazada lateral**
sidestroke

㉒ **la braza**
breaststroke

㉓ **la espalda**
backstroke

㉔ **el crol**
front crawl

㉕ **la mariposa**
butterfly

㉖ **el medley**
medley relay

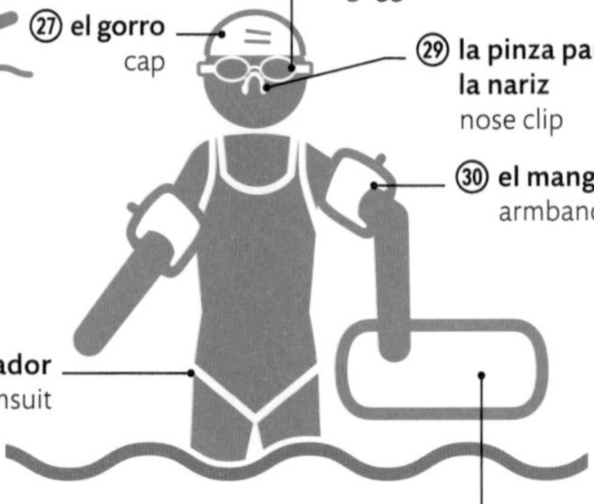

See also
119 La navegación y los deportes acuáticos • Sailing and watersports
134 En la playa • On the beach **166** La vida oceánica • Ocean life

118.2 EL SALTO
DIVING

118.3 EL BUCEO • UNDERWATER DIVING

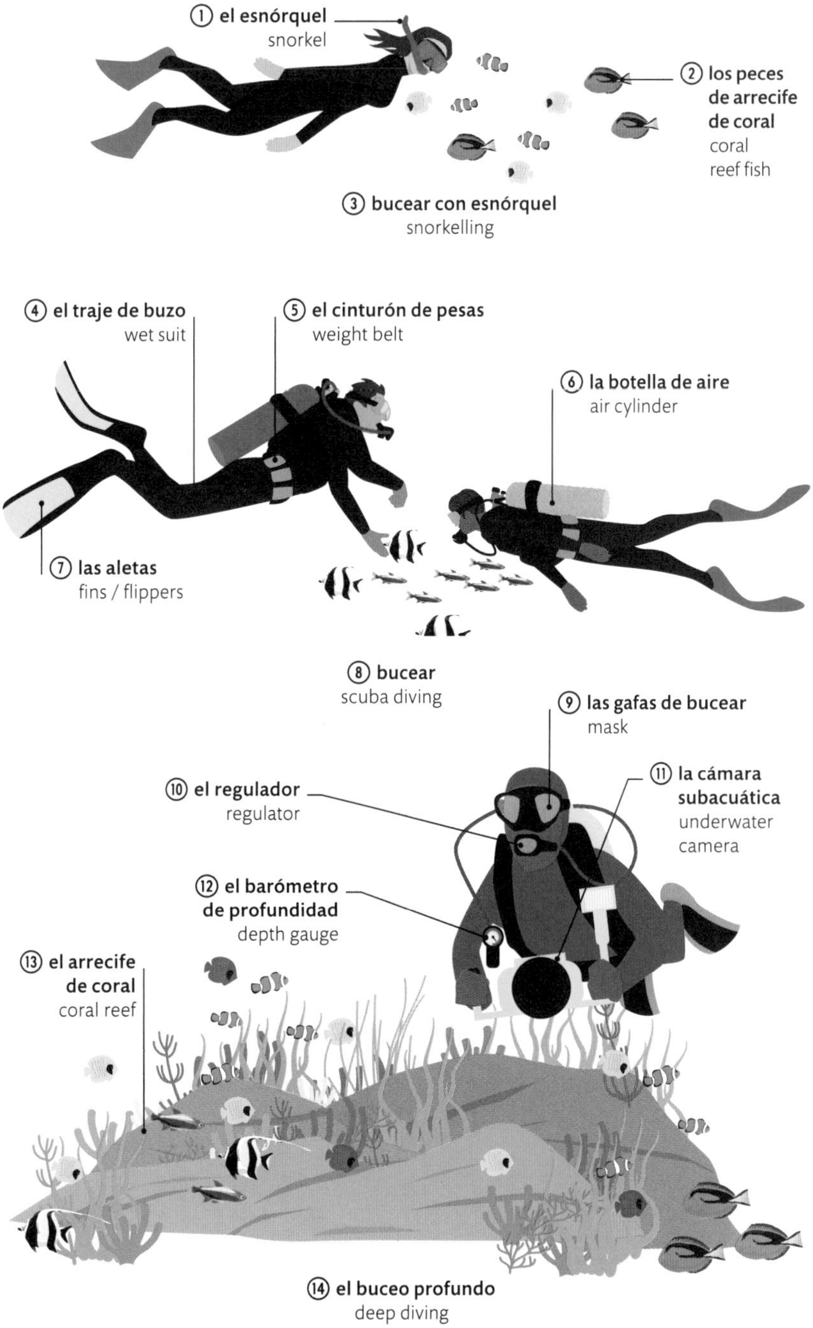

La navegación y los deportes acuáticos

Sailing and watersports

119.1 LA NAVEGACIÓN · SAILING

① **la tripulación**
crew

② **la brújula**
compass

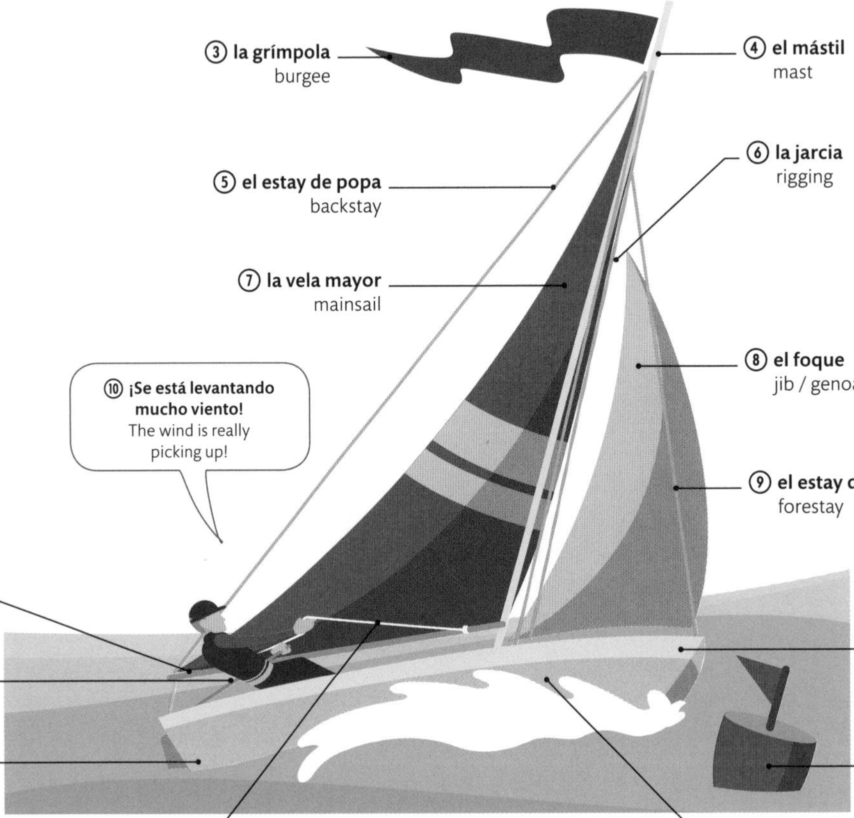

③ **la grímpola**
burgee

④ **el mástil**
mast

⑤ **el estay de popa**
backstay

⑥ **la jarcia**
rigging

⑦ **la vela mayor**
mainsail

⑧ **el foque**
jib / genoa

⑨ **el estay de proa**
forestay

⑩ **¡Se está levantando mucho viento!**
The wind is really picking up!

⑪ **la botavara**
boom

⑫ **la caña del timón**
tiller

⑬ **la popa**
stern

⑭ **la proa**
bow

⑮ **la boya**
buoy

⑯ **el cabo**
rope

⑰ **el yate de vela**
yacht

⑱ **el casco**
hull

⑲ **el ancla** *f*
anchor

⑳ **la escota**
sheet

㉑ **la escotera**
cleat

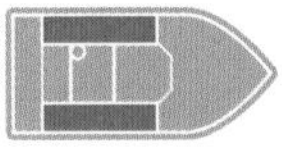

㉒ **la cubierta**
sidedeck

㉓ **la rueda del timón**
boat's wheel

㉔ **el timón**
helm

㉕ **la orza**
centreboard

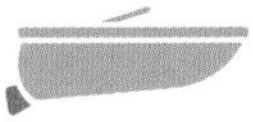

㉖ **la pala de timón**
rudder

㉗ **la quilla**
keel

㉘ **la bengala**
flare

㉙ **el aro salvavidas**
life ring

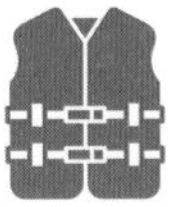

㉚ **el chaleco salvavidas**
life jacket

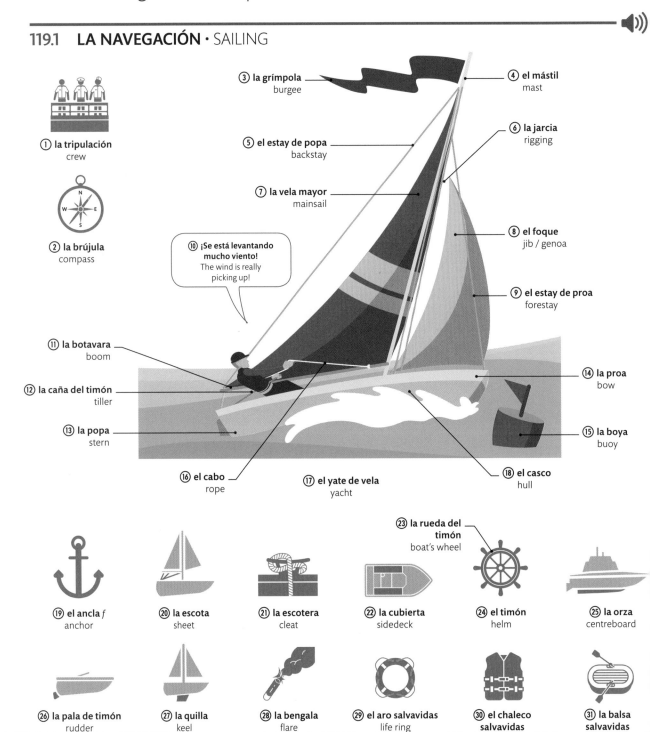

㉛ **la balsa salvavidas**
life raft

See also
105 Los buques • Sea vessels **106** El puerto • The port **118** La natación • Swimming **121** La pesca Fishing **134** En la playa • On the beach

119.2 LOS DEPORTES ACUÁTICOS • WATERSPORTS

remero *m*
a remera *f*
rower

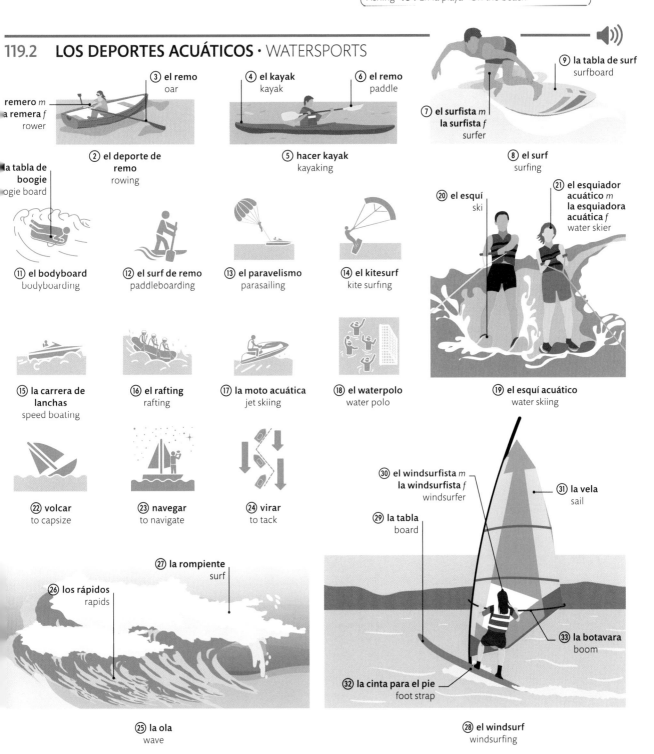

③ **el remo**
oar

② **el deporte de remo**
rowing

④ **el kayak**
kayak

⑥ **el remo**
paddle

⑤ **hacer kayak**
kayaking

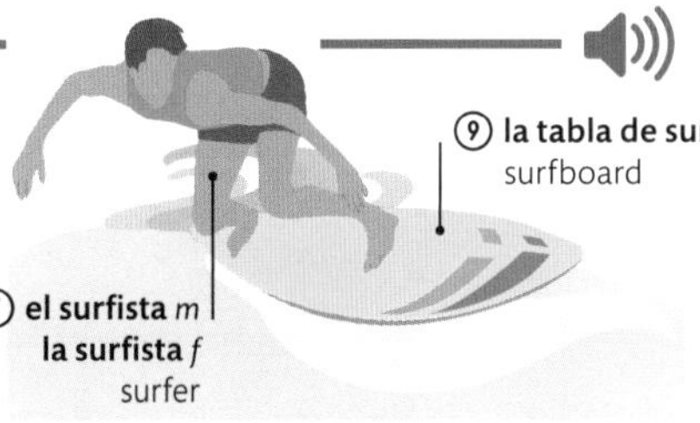

⑨ **la tabla de surf**
surfboard

⑦ **el surfista** *m*
la surfista *f*
surfer

⑧ **el surf**
surfing

la tabla de boogie
ogie board

⑪ **el bodyboard**
bodyboarding

⑫ **el surf de remo**
paddleboarding

⑬ **el paravelismo**
parasailing

⑭ **el kitesurf**
kite surfing

⑳ **el esquí**
ski

㉑ **el esquiador acuático** *m*
la esquiadora acuática *f*
water skier

⑲ **el esquí acuático**
water skiing

⑮ **la carrera de lanchas**
speed boating

⑯ **el rafting**
rafting

⑰ **la moto acuática**
jet skiing

⑱ **el waterpolo**
water polo

㉒ **volcar**
to capsize

㉓ **navegar**
to navigate

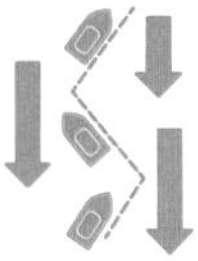

㉔ **virar**
to tack

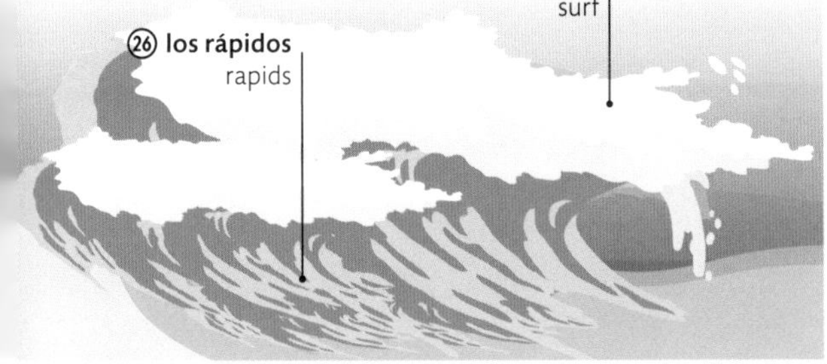

㉗ **la rompiente**
surf

㉖ **los rápidos**
rapids

㉕ **la ola**
wave

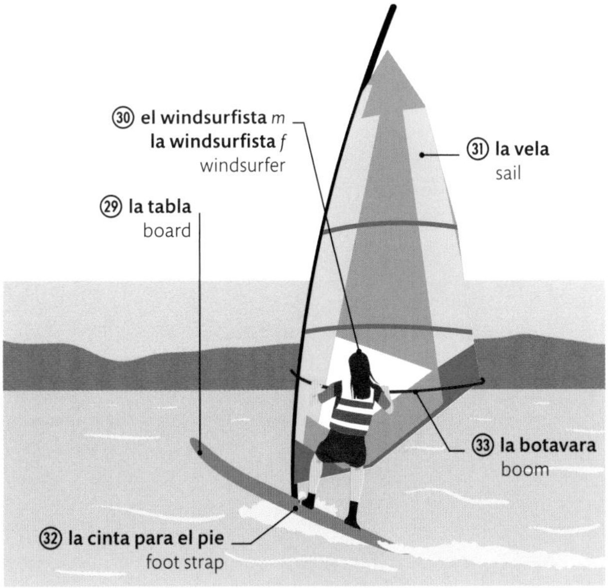

㉚ **el windsurfista** *m*
la windsurfista *f*
windsurfer

㉛ **la vela**
sail

㉙ **la tabla**
board

㉝ **la botavara**
boom

㉜ **la cinta para el pie**
foot strap

㉘ **el windsurf**
windsurfing

120 La equitación
Horse riding

120.1 LA EQUITACIÓN · HORSE RIDING

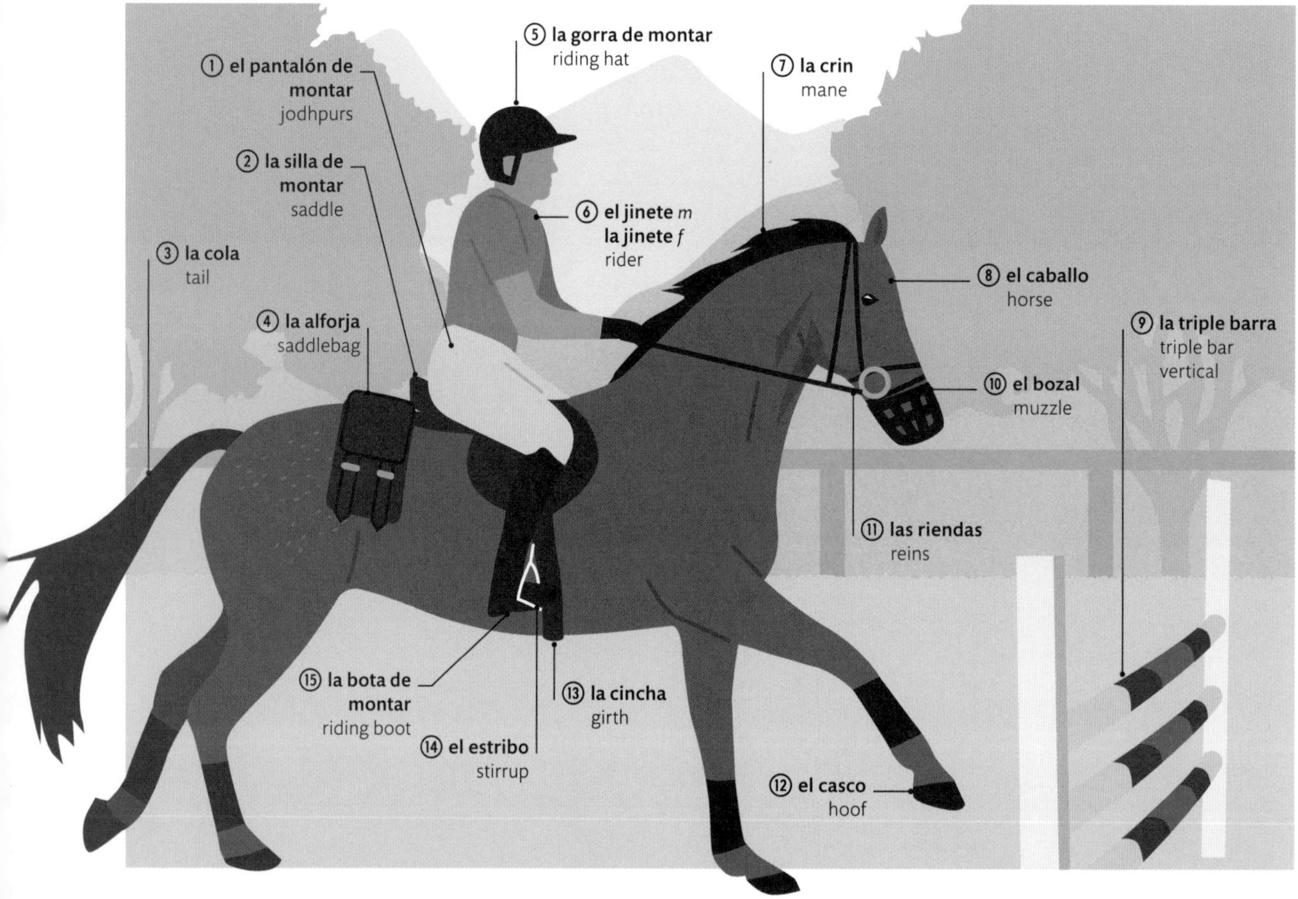

⑯ **la herradura**
horseshoe

⑰ **el cabestro**
halter

⑱ **la muserola**
noseband

⑲ **el bocado**
bit

⑳ **la frontalera**
browband

㉑ **la brida**
bridle

㉒ **el borrén**
pommel

㉓ **el sillín**
seat

㉔ **la fusta**
riding crop

㉕ **el jockey**
jockey

㉖ **el caballo de carreras**
racehorse

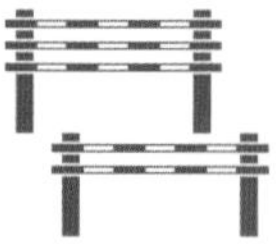
㉗ **los verticales**
verticals

See also
116 El atletismo • Athletics **125** Otros deportes • Other sports
133 Las actividades al aire libre • Outdoor activities

㉘ **la montura de amazona**
side-saddle

㉙ **la carrera de caballos**
horse race

㉚ **la carrera de trotones**
harness race

㉛ **la carrera sin obstáculos**
flat race

㉜ **la carrera de obstáculos**
steeplechase

㉝ **la carrera de enganches**
carriage race

㉞ **el concurso de saltos**
showjumping

㉟ **la doma y monta**
dressage

㊱ **el polo**
polo

㊲ **el rodeo**
rodeo

㊳ **el paseo**
trekking

㊴ **el ruedo**
arena

㊵ **el hipódromo**
racecourse

㊶ **el prado**
paddock

㊷ **el establo**
stable

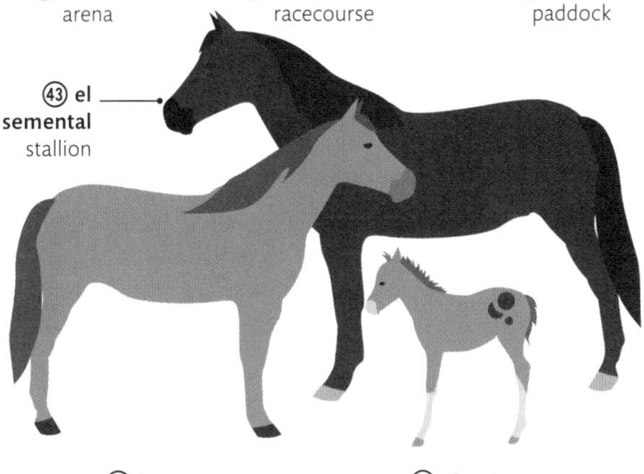

㊸ **el semental**
stallion

㊹ **la yegua**
mare

㊺ **el potro**
foal

120.2 LOS VERBOS • VERBS

① **cepillar**
to groom

② **ir al paso**
to walk

③ **trotar**
to trot

④ **ir a medio galope**
to canter

⑤ **galopar**
to gallop

⑥ **saltar**
to jump

⑦ **criar**
to breed

⑧ **limpiar**
to muck out

121 La pesca
Fishing

121.1 EL PESCADOR DE CAÑA · ANGLER

121.2 LA PESCA · FISHING

① **la caja de pesca**
tackle box

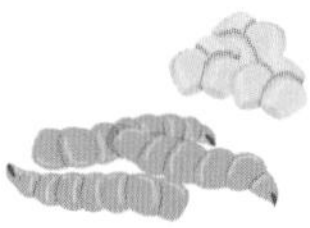

② **el cebo**
bait

③ **el flotador**
float

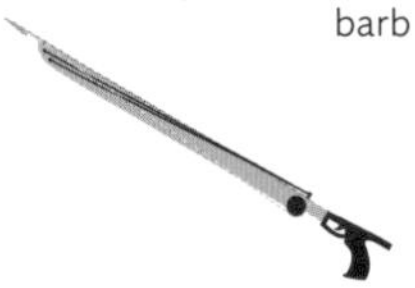

④ **el arpón**
harpoon

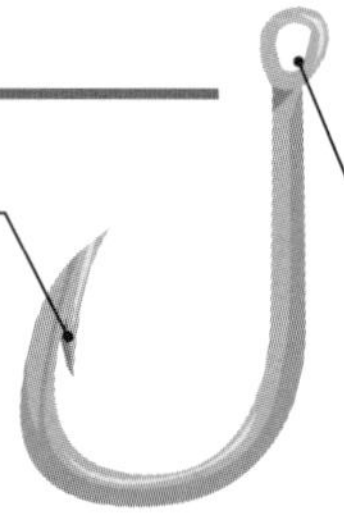

⑤ **el anzuelo**
fishhook

⑧ **el anzuelo triple**
treble fishhook

⑨ **el plomo**
weight

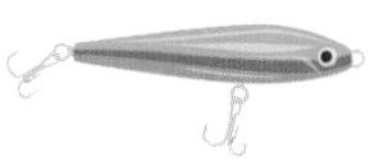

⑩ **el señuelo**
lure

⑪ **la mosca**
fly

⑫ **el carrete**
reel

⑬ **la sacadera**
landing net

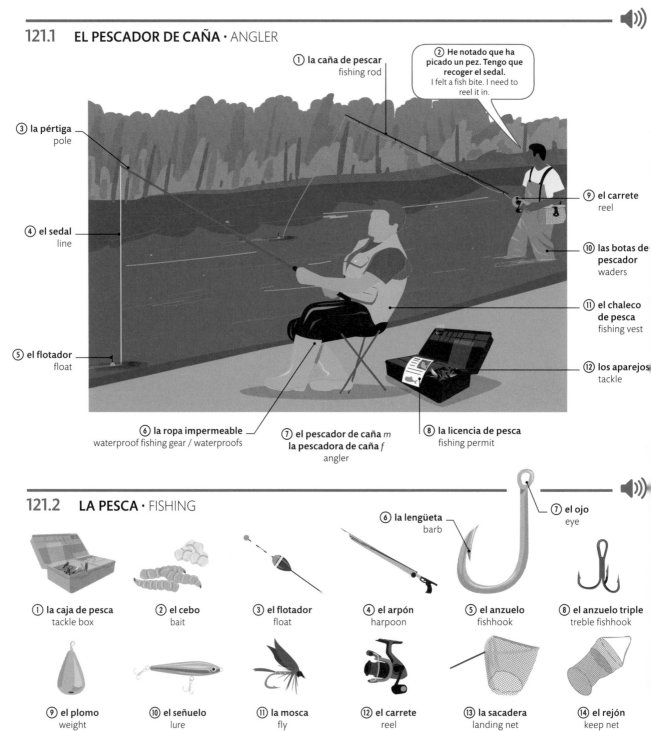

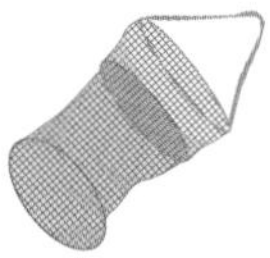

⑭ **el rejón**
keep net

See also
54 El pescado y el marisco • Fish and seafood **119** La navegación y los deportes acuáticos • Sailing and watersports **166** La vida oceánica • Ocean life

121.3 LOS TIPOS DE PESCA
TYPES OF FISHING

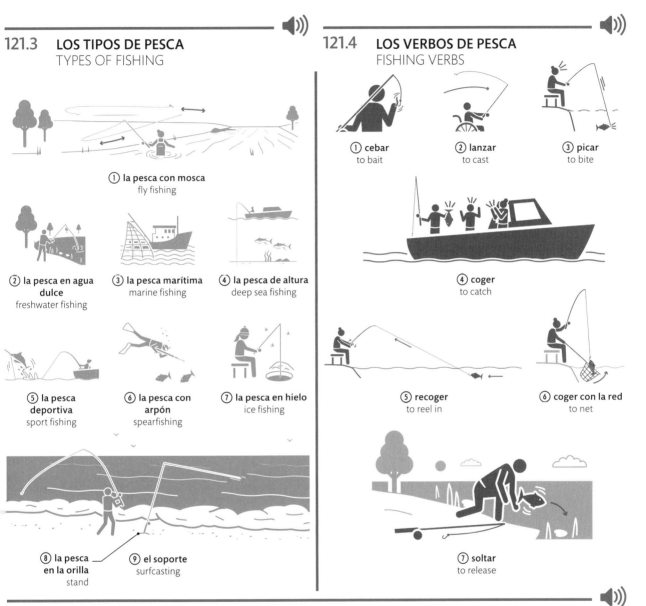

① **la pesca con mosca**
fly fishing

② **la pesca en agua dulce**
freshwater fishing

③ **la pesca marítima**
marine fishing

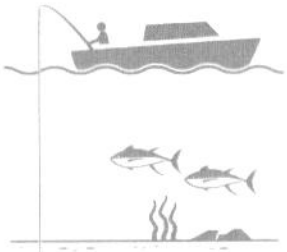

④ **la pesca de altura**
deep sea fishing

⑤ **la pesca deportiva**
sport fishing

⑥ **la pesca con arpón**
spearfishing

⑦ **la pesca en hielo**
ice fishing

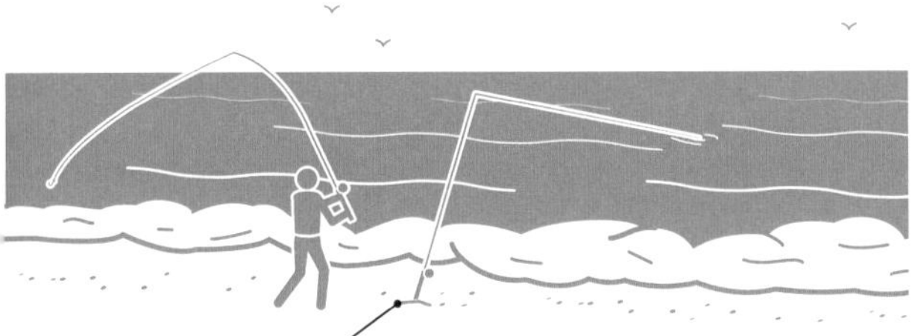

⑧ **la pesca en la orilla**
stand

⑨ **el soporte**
surfcasting

121.4 LOS VERBOS DE PESCA
FISHING VERBS

① **cebar**
to bait

② **lanzar**
to cast

③ **picar**
to bite

④ **coger**
to catch

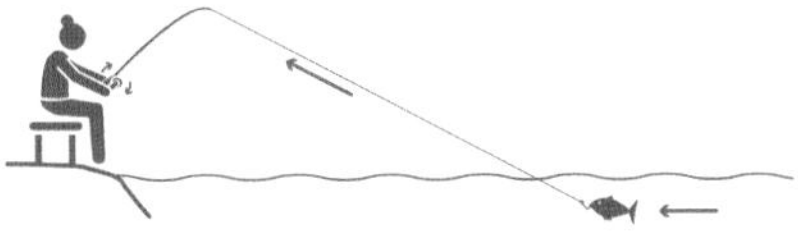

⑤ **recoger**
to reel in

⑥ **coger con la red**
to net

⑦ **soltar**
to release

121.5 LOS NUDOS • KNOTS

① **el nudo de pescador**
clinch knot

② **el nudo de sangre**
blood knot

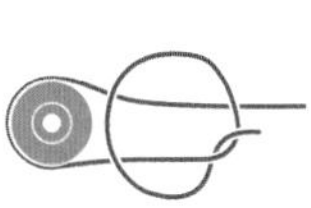

③ **el nudo arbor**
arbor knot

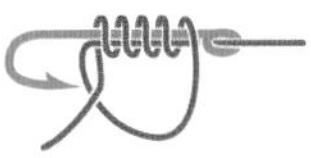

④ **el nudo snell**
snell knot

⑤ **el nudo turle**
turle knot

⑥ **el nudo palomar**
palomar knot

122 Los deportes de invierno
Winter sports

122.1 EL ESQUÍ · SKIING

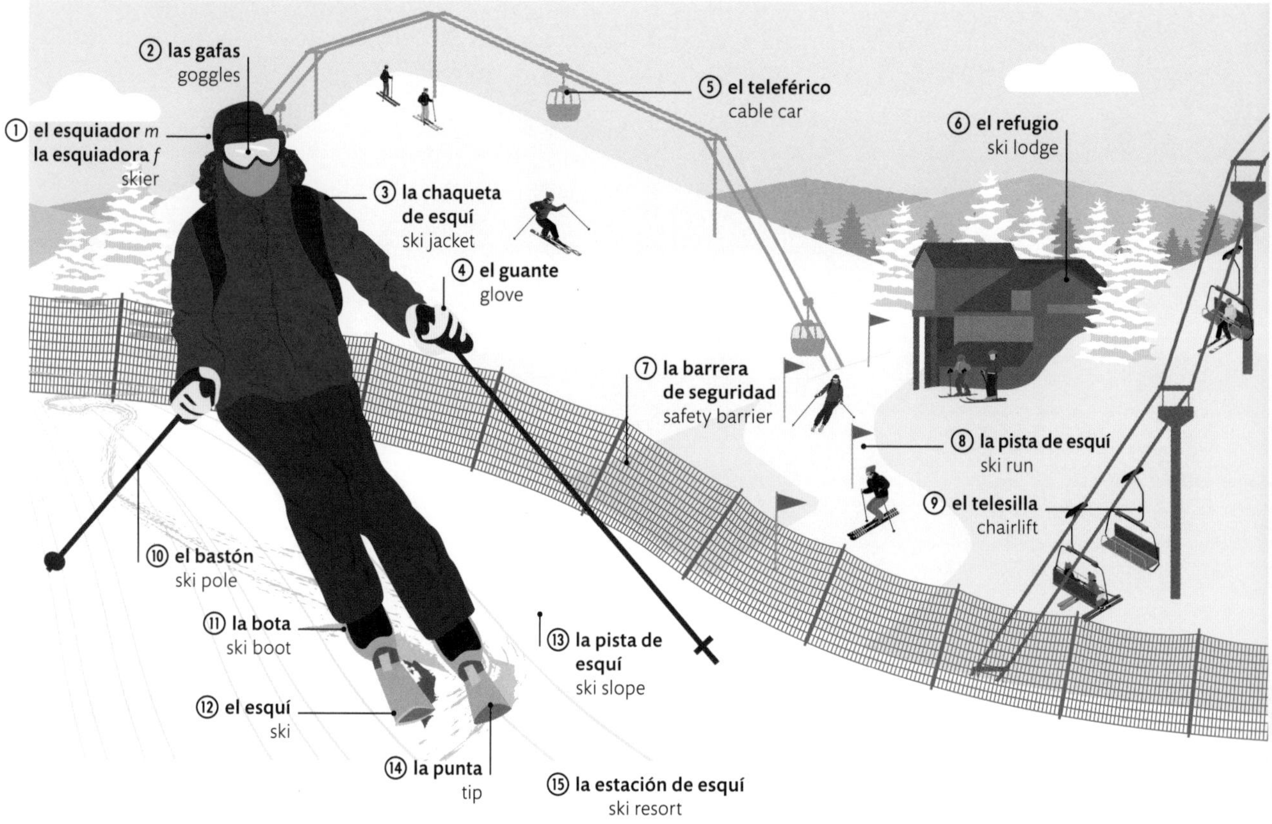

⑯ esquiar
to ski

⑰ el descenso
downhill skiing

⑱ el slalom
slalom

⑲ el slalom gigante
giant slalom

⑳ el esquí de fondo
cross-country skiing

㉑ fuera de pista
off-piste

㉒ el biatlón
biathlon

㉓ la avalancha
avalanche

㉔ la pendiente de aterrizaje
landing hill

㉕ la puerta
gate

㉖ el salto de esquí
ski jump

㉗ el trampolín de salto
jumping ramp

See also
116 El atletismo • Athletics **124** En el gimnasio At the gym **125** Otros deportes • Other sports

122.2 OTROS DEPORTES DE INVIERNO • OTHER WINTER SPORTS

① **los deportes de invierno**
winter sports

② **el patín**
skate

③ **el patinaje sobre hielo**
ice-skating

④ **la carrera de patinaje sobre hielo**
speed skating

⑤ **el patinaje artístico**
figure skating

⑥ **el snowboard**
snowboarding

⑦ **el luge**
luge

⑧ **el skeleton**
skeleton

⑨ **el trineo**
sledging

⑩ **el bobsleigh**
bobsleigh

⑪ **los corredores** *m*
las corredoras *f*
runners

⑫ **el trineo**
sleigh

⑬ **la escalada en hielo**
ice climbing

⑭ **la motonieve**
snowmobile

⑮ **el hockey sobre hielo paralímpico**
para ice hockey

⑯ **el curling en silla de ruedas**
wheelchair curling

⑰ **el curling**
curling

⑱ **la piedra de curling**
curling stone

⑲ **la escoba de curling**
curling brush

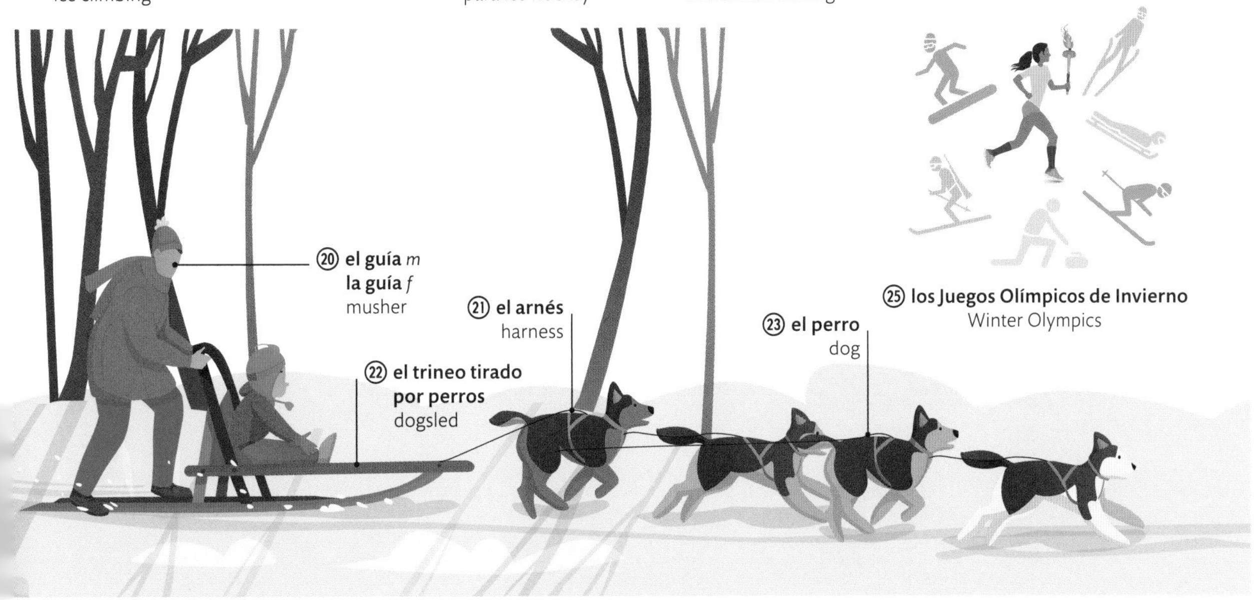

⑳ **el guía** *m*
la guía *f*
musher

㉑ **el arnés**
harness

㉒ **el trineo tirado por perros**
dogsled

㉓ **el perro**
dog

㉔ **el trineo tirado por perros**
dog sledding

㉕ **los Juegos Olímpicos de Invierno**
Winter Olympics

123 Los deportes de motor
Motorsports

123.1 EL COCHE DE CARRERAS · RACING CAR

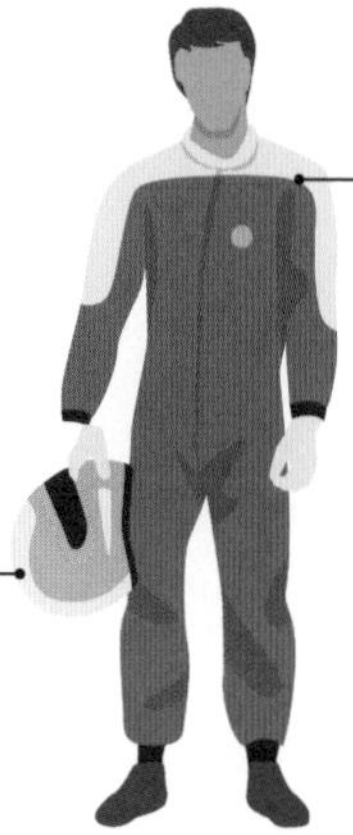

① **el mono de carreras**
racing overalls

② **el casco**
helmet

③ **el piloto de carreras**
racing driver

④ **la carrocería**
bodywork

⑤ **el chasis**
chassis

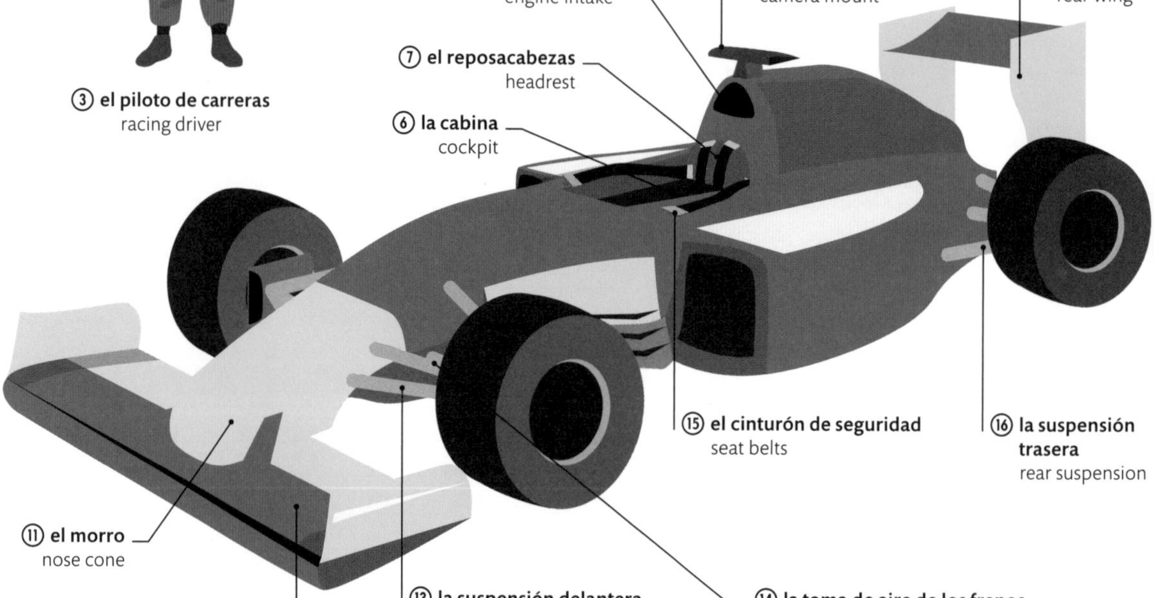

⑥ **la cabina**
cockpit

⑦ **el reposacabezas**
headrest

⑧ **la toma de aire**
engine intake

⑨ **el soporte de la cámara**
camera mount

⑩ **el alerón trasero**
rear wing

⑪ **el morro**
nose cone

⑫ **el alerón delantero**
front wing

⑬ **la suspensión delantera**
front suspension

⑭ **la toma de aire de los frenos**
brake cooling intake

⑮ **el cinturón de seguridad**
seat belts

⑯ **la suspensión trasera**
rear suspension

123.2 LOS TIPOS DE DEPORTES DE MOTOR · TYPES OF MOTORSPORTS

① **el automovilismo**
motor racing

② **el rally**
rally driving

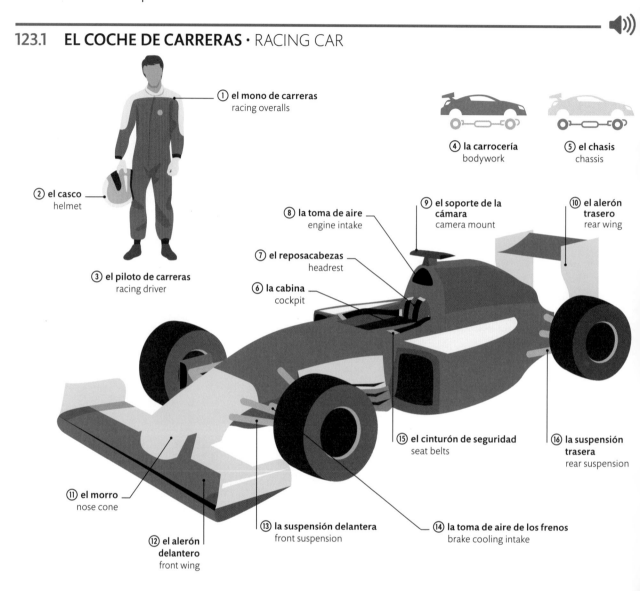

③ **la carrera de aceleración**
drag racing

See also
96 Las carreteras • Roads **97-98** Los coches • Cars **99** Los coches y los autobuses • Cars and buses **100** Las motocicletas • Motorcycles

123.3 **EL CIRCUITO DE CARRERAS** • RACE TRACK

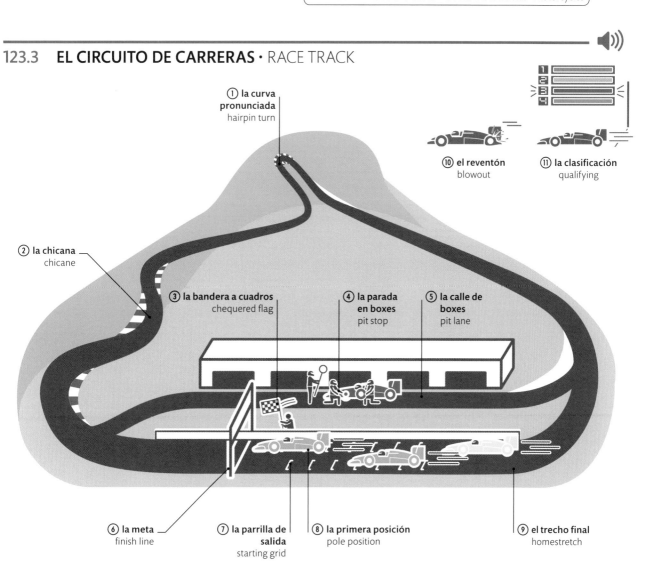

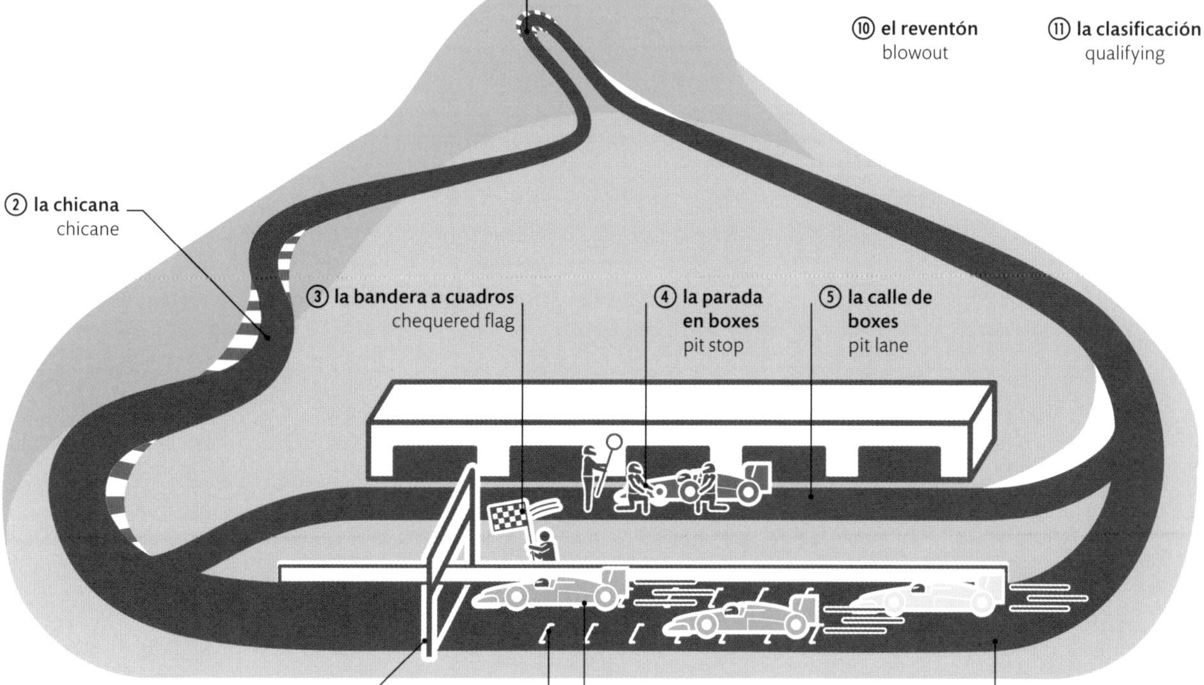

⑩ **el reventón**
blowout

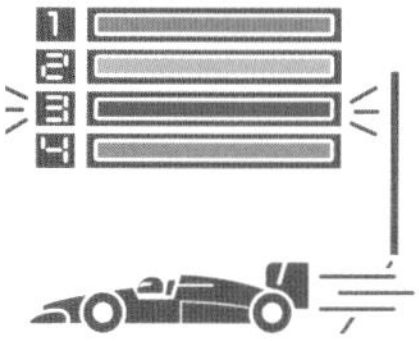

⑪ **la clasificación**
qualifying

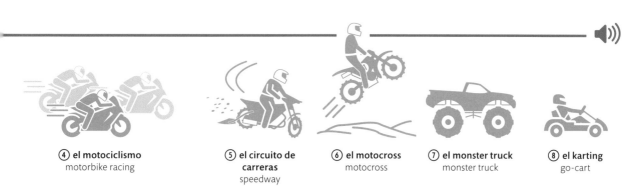

④ **el motociclismo**
motorbike racing

⑤ **el circuito de carreras**
speedway

⑥ **el motocross**
motocross

⑦ **el monster truck**
monster truck

⑧ **el karting**
go-cart

En el gimnasio
At the gym

124.1 LOS ENTRENAMIENTOS · WORKING OUT

② Entreno tres veces a la semana.
I exercise three times a week.
① ¿Con qué frecuencia haces ejercicio?
How often do you work out?
③ la elíptica
cross-trainer
④ el ejercicio
working out
⑤ la máquina de remo
rowing machine
⑥ la bicicleta estática
exercise bike
⑫ las máquinas de gimnasio
gym machines

⑬ los vestuarios
changing room
⑭ las taquillas
lockers
⑮ la clase de ejercicio
exercise class
⑯ el pilates
Pilates
⑰ el estiramiento
stretch
⑲ los ejercicios
exercises
⑱ el entrenamiento en circuito
circuit training
⑳ el aeróbic
aerobics
㉑ los saltos de tijera
star jumps
㉒ los círculos con los brazos
arm circles
㉓ el desplazamiento lateral
side shuffles
㉔ correr
running
㉕ la zancada
lunge
㉖ el curl de bíceps
bicep curl
㉗ la sentadilla
squat
㉘ el abdominal
sit-up
㉙ el boxercise
boxercise
㉚ saltar a la comba
to skip
㉛ flexionar
to flex
㉜ correr en parada
to jog on the spot
㉝ entrenar
to train
㉞ levantar
to pull up
㉟ extender
to extend
㊱ calentar
to warm up
㊲ enfriar
to cool down

See also
116 El atletismo • Athletics **117** Los deportes de combate • Combat sports **118** La natación
Swimming **122** Los deportes de invierno • Winter sports **125** Otros deportes • Other sports

㊳ **el abono**
membership

㊴ **los aparatos de gimnasia**
gym equipment

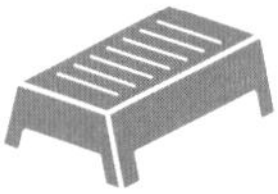
㊵ **el step**
aerobics step

㊶ **la mancuerna**
dumbbell

㊷ **las pinzas de mano**
hand grips

㊸ **la barra de pesas**
barbell / weight bar

㊹ **la barra**
bar

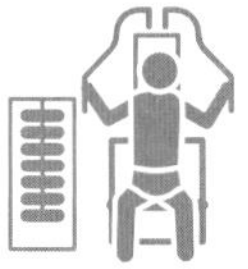
㊺ **la prensa de pecho**
chest press

㊻ **la comba**
skipping rope

㊼ **el balón de gimnasia**
exercise ball

㊽ **el bastón de giro**
twist bar

㊾ **las pesas de muñeca / de tobillo**
ankle weights / wrist weights

㊿ **el ejercicio de piernas**
leg press

(51) **el expansor de pecho**
chest expander

(52) **la rueda abdominal**
wheel roller

(53) **la cinta de correr**
running machine

(54) **el banco**
bench

(55) **la frecuencia cardíaca**
heart rate

(56) **la sauna**
sauna

(57) **el jacuzzi**
hot tub

(58) **el entrenador personal** *m*
la entrenadora personal *f*
personal trainer

125 Otros deportes

Other sports

125.1 LA GIMNASIA · GYMNASTICS

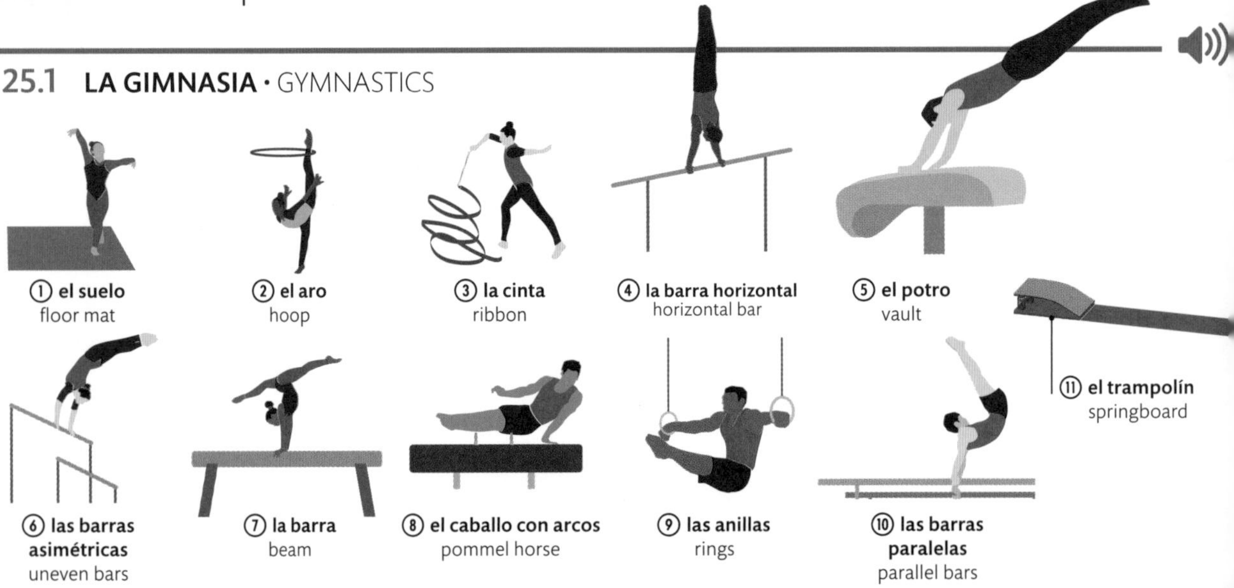

125.2 OTROS DEPORTES · OTHER SPORTS

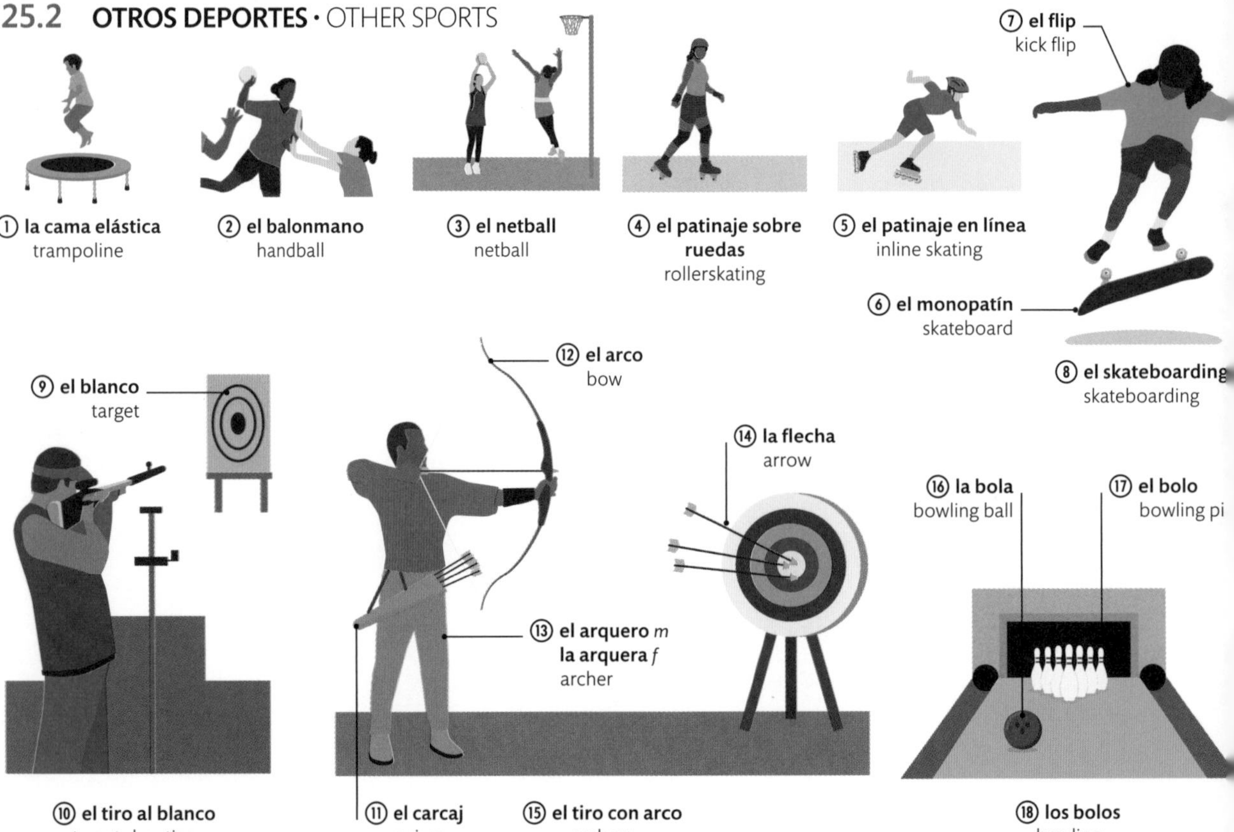

See also
116 El atletismo • Athletics 117 Los deportes de combate • Combat sports 118 La natación • Swimming
120 La equitación • Horse riding 122 Los deportes de invierno • Winter sports 124 En el gimnasio • At the gym

125.3 LOS DEPORTES ADAPTADOS • PARASPORTS

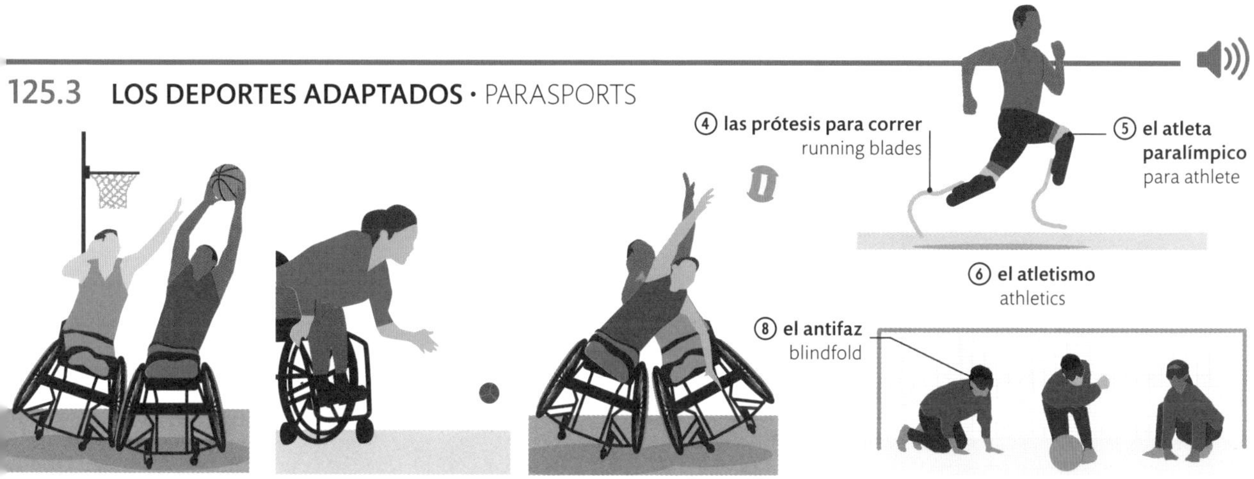

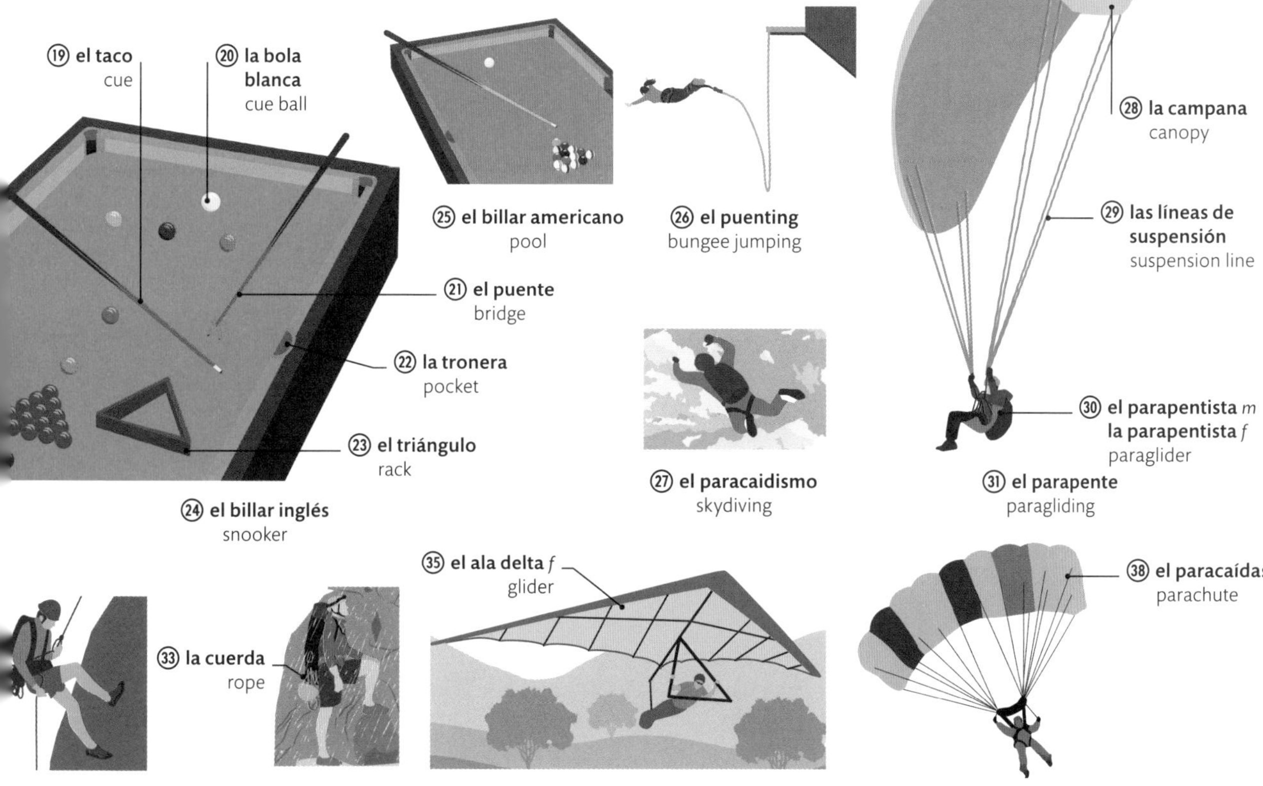

126 Sobre el escenario
On stage

126.1 **EL TEATRO** • THEATRE

⑯ **la obra**
play

⑰ **el vestuario**
costumes

⑱ **el atrezo**
props

⑲ **los decorados**
sets

⑳ **el telón de fondo**
backdrop

㉑ **el guion**
script

㉒ **el productor** *m*
la productora *f*
producer

㉓ **el director** *m*
la directora *f*
director

㉔ **el actor** *m*
la actriz *f*
actor

㉕ **el reparto**
cast

㉖ **la noche de estreno**
opening night

㉗ **el intermedio**
interval

See also
127 La películas • Films **128-129** La música • Music
139 La fantasía y los mitos • Fantasy and myth

(28) **el programa**
programme

(29) **el acomodador** *m*
la acomodadora *f*
usher

(30) **la tragedia**
tragedy

(31) **la comedia**
comedy

(32) **el musical**
musical

(33) **la ovación de pie**
standing ovation

126.2 EL BALLET • BALLET

(4) **hacer piruetas / girar**
to pirouette / to turn

(5) **hacer plié / flexionar**
to plié / to bend

(6) **el bailarín de ballet**
male ballet dancer

(7) **la bailarina**
ballerina

(8) **el tutú**
tutu

(9) **el leotardo**
ballet leotard

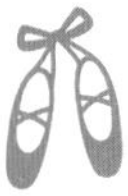

(10) **los zapatos de ballet**
ballet shoes

(11) **la actuación**
performance

(12) **el bis**
encore

(13) **el aplauso**
applause

126.3 LA ÓPERA • OPERA

(1) **el bajo**
bass

(2) **el barítono**
baritone

(3) **el tenor**
tenor

(4) **el teatro de ópera**
opera house

(5) **el contralto**
alto

(6) **la mezzosoprano**
mezzo-soprano

(7) **la soprano**
soprano

(8) **la prima donna**
prima donna

(9) **el libreto**
libretto

127 Las películas
Films

127.1 EN EL CINE • AT THE CINEMA

① **el drama**
drama

② **el musical**
musical

③ **la ciencia ficción**
science fiction

④ **el suspense**
thriller

⑤ **la comedia**
comedy

⑥ **la película de acció**
action movie

⑦ **el terror**
horror

⑧ **la animación**
animation

⑨ **la comedia romántica**
romantic comedy

⑩ **el drama policial**
crime drama

⑪ **la película de vaqueros**
western

⑫ **el drama de época**
historical drama

⑬ **la fantasía**
fantasy

⑭ **las artes marciales**
martial arts

⑮ **los efectos especiales**
special effects

⑯ **la taquilla**
box office

⑰ **los multicines**
multiplex

⑱ **las palomitas**
popcorn

⑲ **la estrella de cine**
film star

⑳ **la pantalla**
screen

㉑ **el público**
audience

㉒ **el cine**
cinema

㉓ **el protagonista** *m*
la protagonista *f*
main character

㉔ **el héroe** *m*
la heroína *f*
hero

㉕ **el villano** *m*
la villana *f*
villain

See also
126 Sobre el escenario • On stage **136** El ocio en el hogar
Home entertainment **137** La televisión • Television

127.2 EL ESTUDIO DE CINE • FILM STUDIO

① **el ingeniero de sonido** *m*
la ingeniera de sonido *f*
sound engineer

② **la lente**
lens

③ **el director de fotografía** *m*
la directora de fotografía *f*
cinematographer

④ **el cámara** *m*
la cámara *f*
camera operator

el director *m*
la directora *f*
director

⑥ **el productor** *m*
la productora *f*
producer

⑦ **la cámara de cine**
movie camera

⑧ **el plató**
film set

⑨ **los paparazzi** *m*
las paparazzi *f*
paparazzi

⑩ **la alfombra roja**
red carpet

⑪ **el famoso** *m*
la famosa *f*
celebrity

⑫ **el estreno**
premiere

⑬ **la audición**
audition

⑭ **el reparto**
cast

⑮ **los extras**
extras

⑯ **la escena de riesgo**
stunt

⑰ **el atrezo**
props

⑱ **el guion**
screenplay

⑲ **el vestuario**
costumes

⑳ **la banda sonora**
soundtrack

㉑ **el guionista** *m*
la guionista *f*
screenwriter

La música
Music

128.1 LOS INSTRUMENTOS DE ORQUESTA · ORCHESTRAL INSTRUMENTS

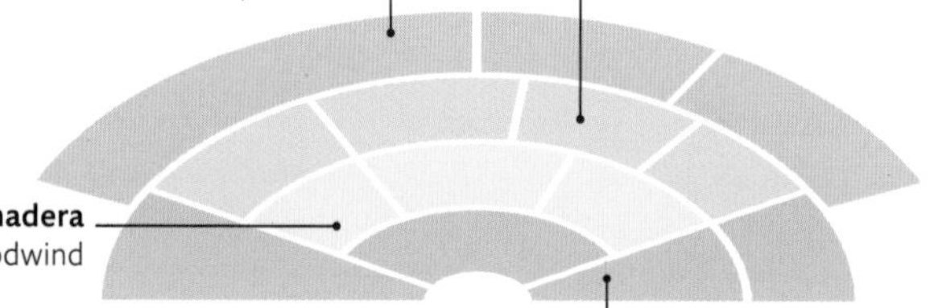

㉚ **el vibráfono**
vibraphone

㉛ **el bongó**
bongo drums

㉜ **las campanas tubulares**
tubular bells

㉝ **la pandereta**
tambourine

㉞ **el triángulo**
triangle

㉟ **las maracas**
maracas

㊱ **la corneta inglesa**
cor anglais

㊲ **el flautín**
piccolo

㊳ **el órgano**
pipe organ

㊴ **el solo**
solo

㊵ **el compositor** *m*
la compositora *f*
composer

㊶ **el coro**
choir

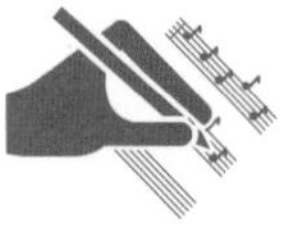

㊷ **componer**
to compose

㊸ **dirigir**
to conduct

㊹ **tocar (la trompeta)**
to play (the trumpet)

㊺ **la obertura para piano**
piano overture

㊻ **la sinfonía**
symphony

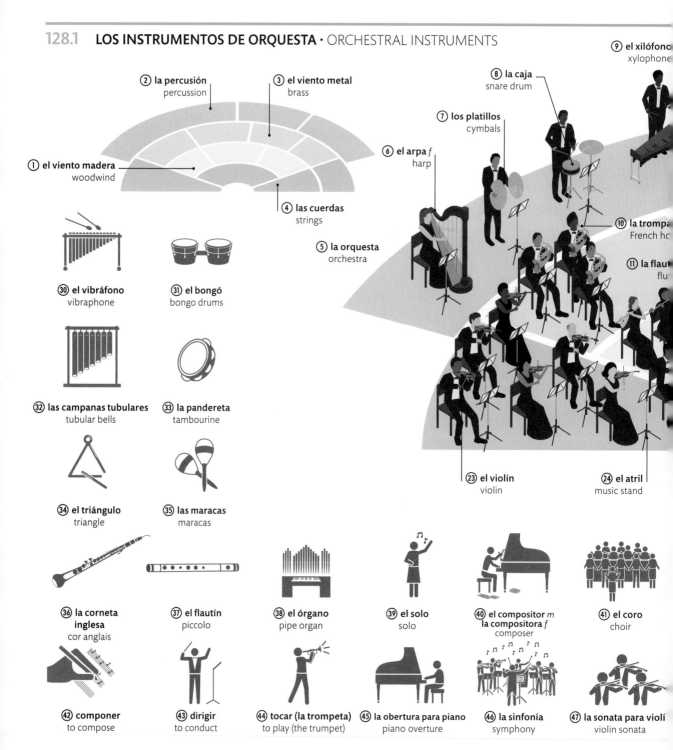

㊼ **la sonata para violí**
violin sonata

See also
126 Sobre el escenario • On stage **127** Las películas • Films **129** La música (continuación) • Music continued **136** El ocio en el hogar • Home entertainment

128.2 LA PARTITURA, LAS NOTAS Y LAS NOTACIONES • SCORE, NOTES, AND NOTATION

⑤ la partitura
score

⑥ el acorde
chord

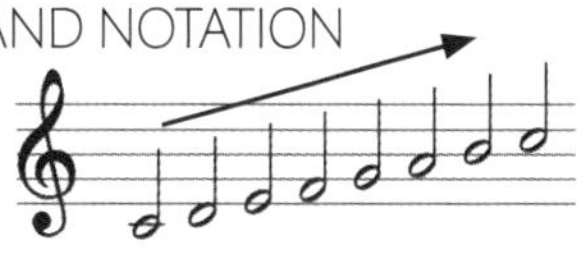

⑦ la escalada
scale

⑩ el tono
pitch

⑪ el sostenido
sharp

⑫ el bemol
flat

La música (continuación)

Music continued

129.1 LA MÚSICA POPULAR · POPULAR MUSIC

① **los aparejos** rig

② **el batería** *m* **la batería** *f* drummer

③ **el guitarrista acústico** *m* **la guitarrista acústica** *f* acoustic guitarist

④ **el cantante** *m* **la cantante** *f* lead singer

⑤ **el guitarrista eléctrico** *m* **la guitarrista eléctrica** *f* electric guitarist

⑥ **las luces del escenario** stage lights

⑦ **el bajista** *m* **la bajista** *f* bass guitarist

⑧ **los altavoces** speaker

⑨ **los fans** *m* / **las fans** *f* fans

⑩ **el concierto de pop** pop concert

⑪ **el amplificador** amplifier

⑫ **el tocadiscos** turntable

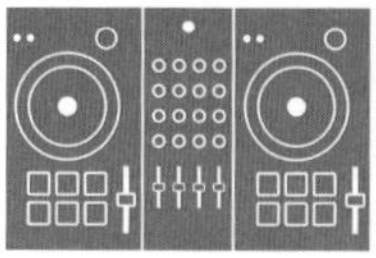

⑬ **el controlador de DJ** DJ console

⑭ **los discos de vinilo** vinyl records

⑮ **los coristas** *m* **las coristas** *f* backing singers

⑯ **la canción** song

⑰ **la melodía** melody

⑱ **el ritmo** beat

⑲ **la banda** band

⑳ **el álbum** album

㉑ **el jazz** jazz

㉒ **el blues** the blues

㉓ **el punk** punk

㉔ **el folk** folk

㉕ **el pop** pop

㉖ **el k-pop** K-pop

㉗ **el heavy metal** heavy metal

㉘ **el hip-hop** hip-hop

㉙ **el country** country

㉚ **el rock** rock

㉛ **el soul** soul

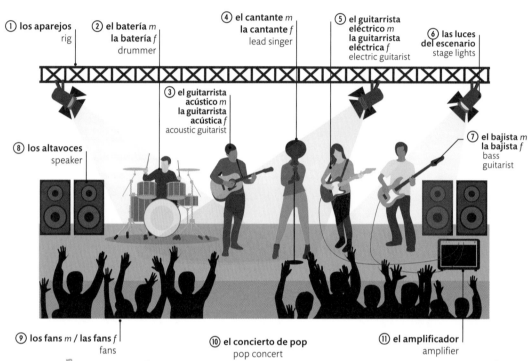

㉜ **la música latina** Latin

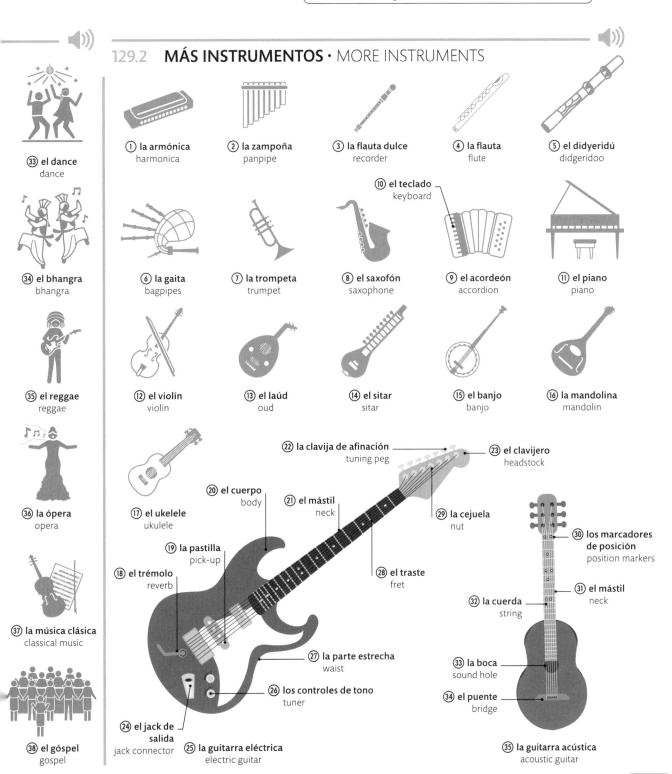

See also
126 Sobre el escenario • On stage **127** Las películas • Films
136 El ocio en el hogar • Home entertainment

129.2 MÁS INSTRUMENTOS • MORE INSTRUMENTS

(33) **el dance**
dance

(34) **el bhangra**
bhangra

(35) **el reggae**
reggae

(36) **la ópera**
opera

(37) **la música clásica**
classical music

(38) **el góspel**
gospel

(1) **la armónica**
harmonica

(2) **la zampoña**
panpipe

(3) **la flauta dulce**
recorder

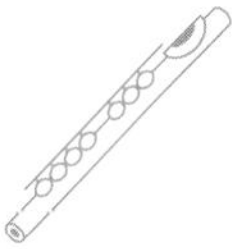
(4) **la flauta**
flute

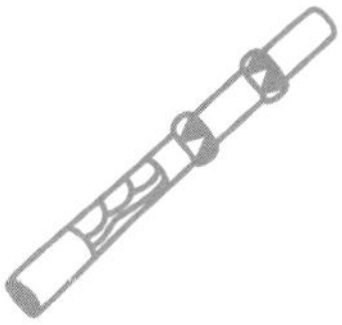
(5) **el didyeridú**
didgeridoo

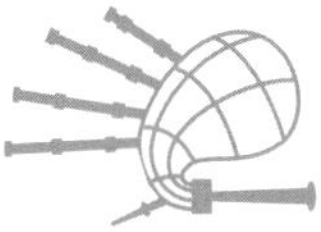
(6) **la gaita**
bagpipes

(7) **la trompeta**
trumpet

(8) **el saxofón**
saxophone

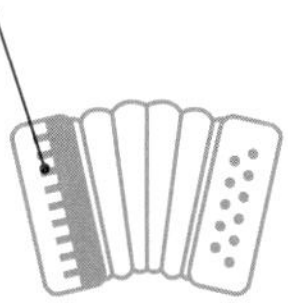

(9) **el acordeón**
accordion

(11) **el piano**
piano

(12) **el violín**
violin

(13) **el laúd**
oud

(14) **el sitar**
sitar

(15) **el banjo**
banjo

(16) **la mandolina**
mandolin

(17) **el ukelele**
ukulele

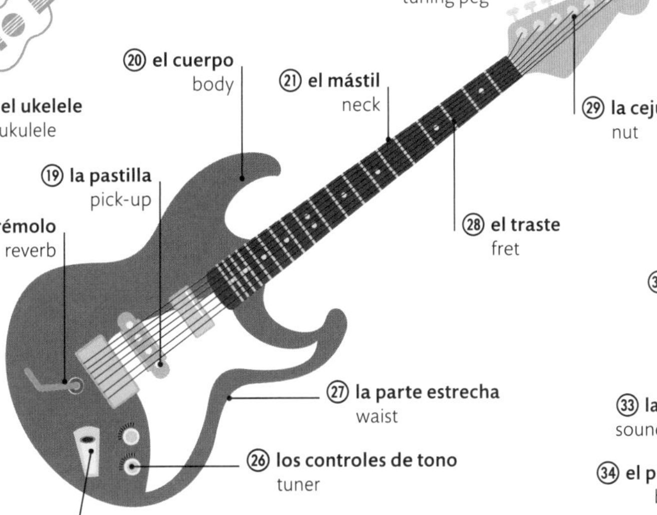

(25) **la guitarra eléctrica**
electric guitar

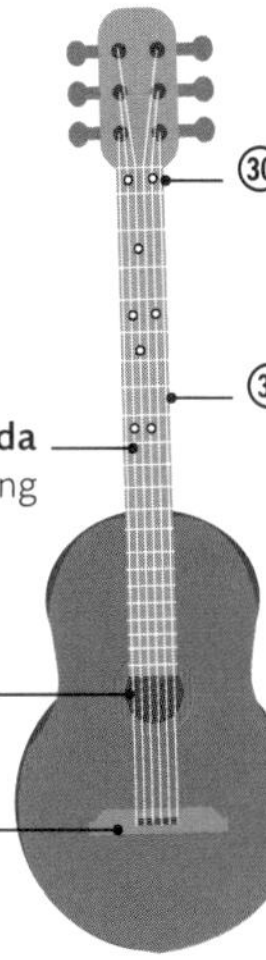

(35) **la guitarra acústica**
acoustic guitar

Los museos y las galerías
Museums and galleries

130.1 EN EL MUSEO Y LA GALERÍA DE ARTE · AT THE MUSEUM AND ART GALLERY

① **la galería**
gallery

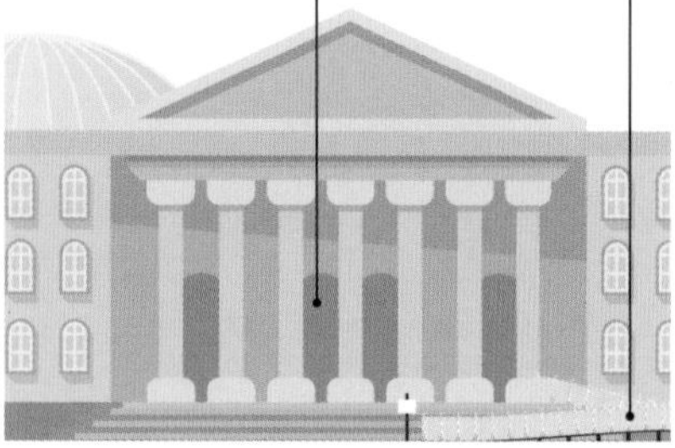

② **la entrada**
entrance

③ **la rampa de acceso**
wheelchair ramp

④ **el museo**
museum

⑤ **los aseos**
toilets

⑥ **el guardarropa**
cloakroom

⑦ **la tarifa de entrada**
admission fee

⑧ **la entrada**
ticket

⑨ **la taquilla**
ticket office

⑩ **los donativos**
donation

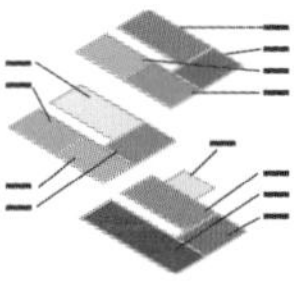

⑪ **el plano**
floor plan

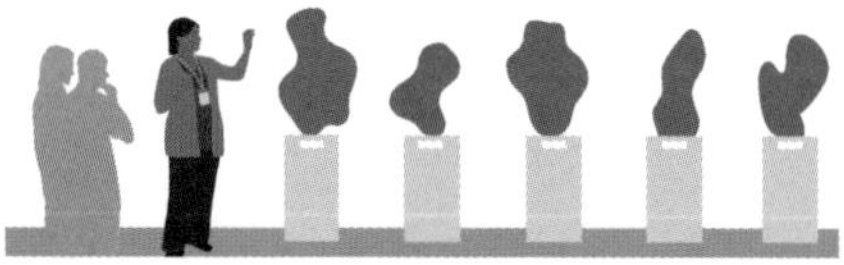

⑫ **el conservador** *m* **/ la conservadora** *f*
curator

⑬ **la exposición**
exhibition

⑭ **la pieza**
exhibit

⑮ **la exposición permanente**
permanent exhibition

⑯ **la exposición temporal**
temporary exhibition

⑰ **la obra**
installation

⑱ **la colección**
collection

⑲ **la restauración**
conservation

⑳ **el guía** *m* **/ la guía** *f*
tour guide

㉑ **la audioguía**
audio guide

㉒ **prohibido fotografiar**
no photography

㉓ **la tienda de regalos**
gift shop

See also
42-43 La ciudad • In town **132** La visita turística • Sightseeing
141-142 Las manualidades • Arts and crafts

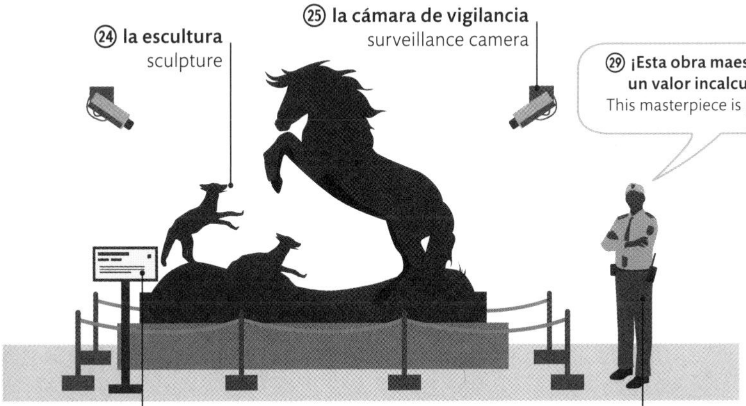
㉙ **¡Esta obra maestra tiene un valor incalculable!**
This masterpiece is priceless!

㉔ **la escultura**
sculpture

㉕ **la cámara de vigilancia**
surveillance camera

㉖ **el rótulo**
label

㉗ **la obra maestra**
masterpiece

㉘ **el guardia de seguridad** *m*
la guardia de seguridad *f*
security guard

㉚ **el marco**
frame

㉛ **la pintura**
painting

㉜ **la pintura al óleo**
oil painting

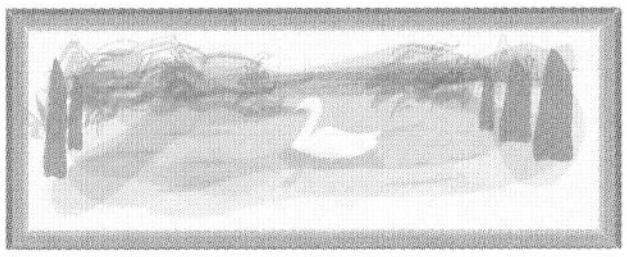

㉝ **la pintura de acuarela**
watercolour

㉞ **el clasicismo**
Classicism

㉟ **el impresionismo**
Impressionism

㊱ **el posimpresionismo**
Post-Impressionism

㊶ **el art déco**
Art Deco

㊷ **el art nouveau**
Art Nouveau

㊲ **el cubismo**
Cubism

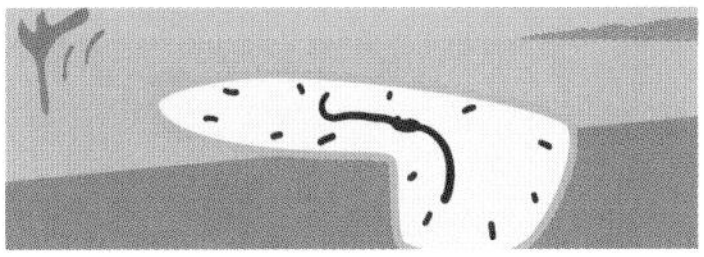

㊳ **el surrealismo**
Surrealism

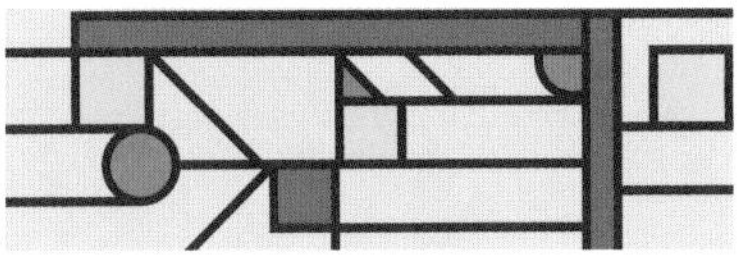

㊴ **el Bauhaus**
Bauhaus

㊵ **el arte pop**
Pop Art

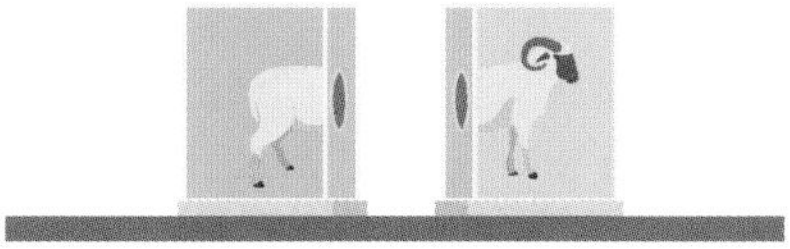

㊸ **el arte conceptual**
conceptual art

131 El viaje y el alojamiento
Travel and accommodation

131.1 EL VIAJE · TRAVEL

① **la guía turística**
guidebook

② **la guía de conversación**
phrasebook

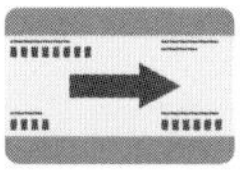
③ **el billete de ida**
one-way ticket

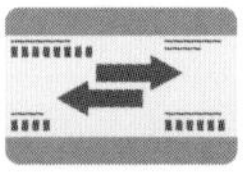
④ **el billete de ida y vuelta**
return ticket

⑤ **reservar unas vacaciones**
to book a holiday

⑥ **hacer la maleta**
to pack your bags

⑦ **irse de vacaciones**
to go on a holiday

⑧ **irse de crucero**
to go on a cruise

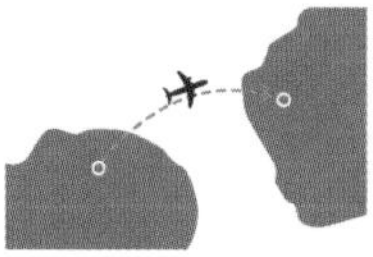
⑨ **viajar al extranjero**
to go abroad

⑩ **hacer una reserva**
to make a reservation

⑪ **alquilar una casa rural**
to rent a cottage

⑫ **irse de mochilero**
to go backpacking

⑬ **registrarse**
to check in

⑭ **dejar la habitación**
to check out

⑮ **quedarse en un hotel**
to stay in a hotel

131.2 EL ALOJAMIENTO · ACCOMMODAT

① **el hotel**
hotel

② **el apartamento**
apartment

③ **el hostal**
hostel

⑨ **la pensión**
guest house

⑩ **el bed and breakfast**
bed and breakfast

⑪ **la villa**
villa

131.3 LOS SERVICIOS · SERVICES

① **el restaurante**
restaurant

② **el gimnasio**
gym

③ **la piscina**
swimming pool

See also
104 En el aeropuerto • At the airport **132** La visita turística • Sightseeing
133 Las actividades al aire libre • Outdoor activities **134** En la playa • On the beach

4 **el chalet**
chalet

5 **la cabaña**
cabin

6 **el ecoturismo**
ecotourism

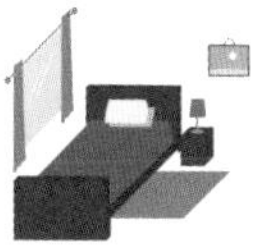

7 **la habitación individual**
single room

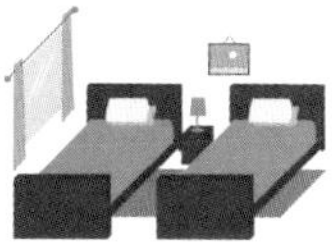

8 **la habitación con dos camas**
twin room

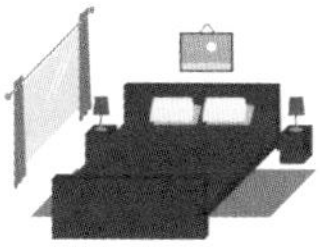

12 **la habitación doble**
double room

13 **el baño privado**
private bathroom / en suite bathroom

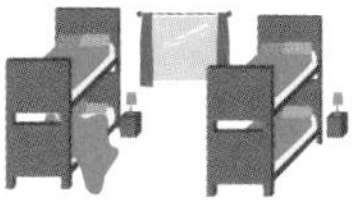

14 **la habitación compartida**
dorm

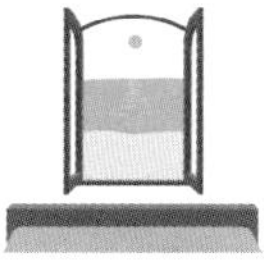

15 **la habitación con vistas**
room with a view

16 **con habitaciones libres**
vacancies

17 **completo**
no vacancies

20 **el recepcionista** *m*
la recepcionista *f*
receptionist

21 **la recepción**
reception

22 **los aseos**
toilets

23 **la salida de emergencia**
emergency exit

27 **el mostrador**
counter

28 **el vestíbulo del hotel**
hotel lobby

5 **la bandeja del desayuno**
breakfast tray

4 **el servicio de habitaciones**
room service

6 **el servicio de lavandería**
laundry service

7 **el servicio de limpieza**
maid service

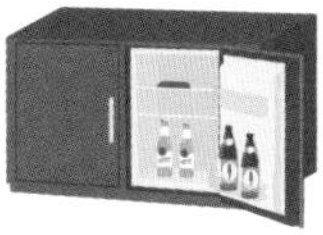

8 **el minibar**
minibar

9 **la caja fuerte**
safe

132 La visita turística
Sightseeing

132.1 LA ATRACCIÓN TURÍSTICA · TOURIST ATTRACTION

① **el autobús turístico**
tourist bus

② **ir de excursión**
to go on an excursion

③ **la visita guiada**
guided tour

⑥ **hacer una visita guiada**
to go on a tour

⑦ **el turista** *m*
la turista *f*
tourist

⑧ **el guía turístico** *m*
la guía turística *f*
tour guide

⑨ **la visita turística**
sightseeing

132.2 LAS ATRACCIONES · ATTRACTIONS

① **la galería de arte**
art gallery

② **el museo**
museum

③ **el monumento**
monument

④ **el palacio**
palace

⑤ **el edificio histórico**
historic building

⑥ **el jardín botánico**
botanical gardens

⑧ **el paisaje**
landscape

⑨ **pintoresco** *m*
pintoresca *f*
scenic

⑦ **el parque nacional**
national park

See also
99 Los coches y los autobuses • Cars and buses **130** Los museos y las galerías • Museums and galleries
131 El viaje y el alojamiento • Travel and accommodation **149-151** Los países • Countries

) ¿Tenemos que pagar una entrada?
Do we have to pay an admission fee?

④ **el yacimiento arqueológico**
archaeological site

⑩ **la cola**
queue

⑪ **el puesto de souvenirs**
souvenir stall

ADMISSION
$
$
$
$

⑫ **la tarifa de entrada**
entrance fee

OPEN

⑬ **abierto**
open

CLOSED

⑭ **cerrado**
closed

⑮ **la guía turística**
guidebook

⑯ **la postal**
postcard

⑰ **el souvenir**
souvenir

⑱ **el mapa turístico**
tourist map

⑲ **las indicaciones**
directions

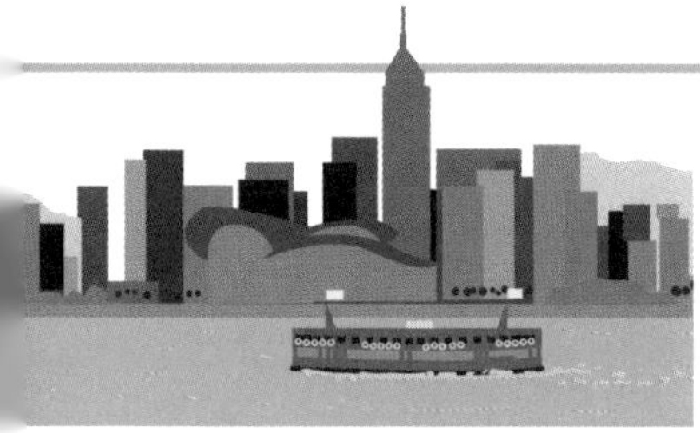

⑩ **el frente marítimo**
waterfront

⑪ **el mercado artesanal**
craft market

⑬ ¿Me puedes informar sobre los lugares de interés de la zona?
Can I have some information on the local sights?
i

⑫ **la oficina de turismo**
tourist information

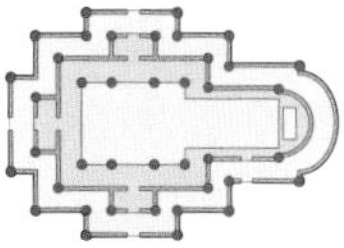

⑭ **la planta**
floor plan

⑮ **el mapa turístico**
map

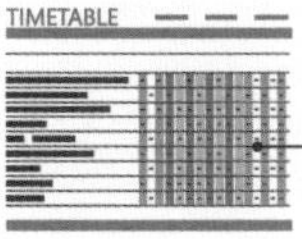
TIMETABLE

⑰ **las horas de apertura**
opening times

⑯ **el horario**
timetable

133 Las actividades al aire libre
Outdoor activities

133.1 LAS ACTIVIDADES AL AIRE LIBRE • OPEN-AIR ACTIVITIES

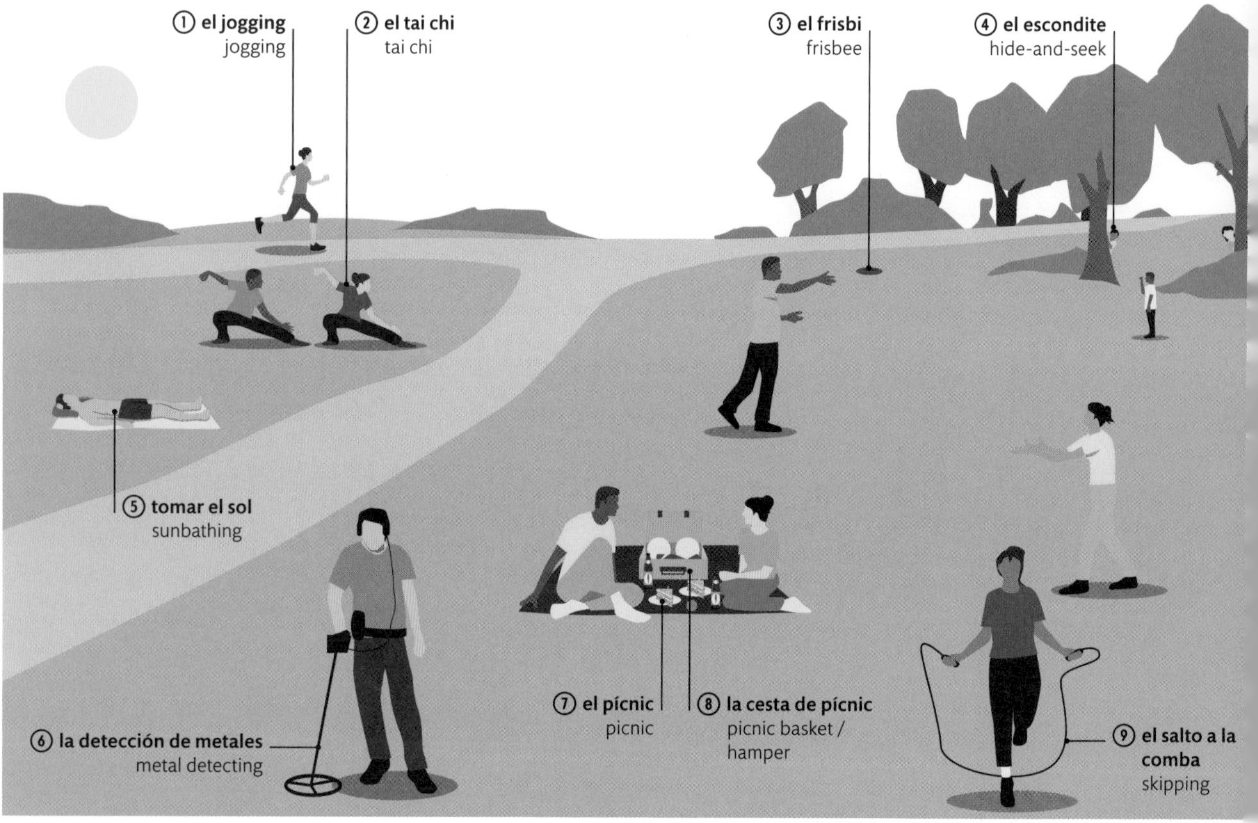

① **el jogging** jogging
② **el tai chi** tai chi
③ **el frisbi** frisbee
④ **el escondite** hide-and-seek
⑤ **tomar el sol** sunbathing
⑥ **la detección de metales** metal detecting
⑦ **el pícnic** picnic
⑧ **la cesta de pícnic** picnic basket / hamper
⑨ **el salto a la comba** skipping

⑩ **el parque**
park

㉓ **la casa del árbol** tree house
㉔ **el columpio** swing

㉒ **trepar a los árboles**
tree climbing

㉕ **la jardinería**
gardening

㉖ **el cróquet**
croquet

㉗ **la observación de aves**
bird-watching

㉘ **el paintball**
paintballing

㉛ **la piscina hinchable**
paddling pool

㉜ **el skateboarding**
skateboarding

㉝ **ir en patinete**
scootering

㉞ **el patinaje**
rollerblading

㉟ **el ciclismo**
cycling

㊱ **el parkour**
parkour

See also
11 Las habilidades y las acciones • Abilities and actions **134** En la playa • On the beach
135 La acampada • Camping **148** Los mapas y las indicaciones • Maps and directions

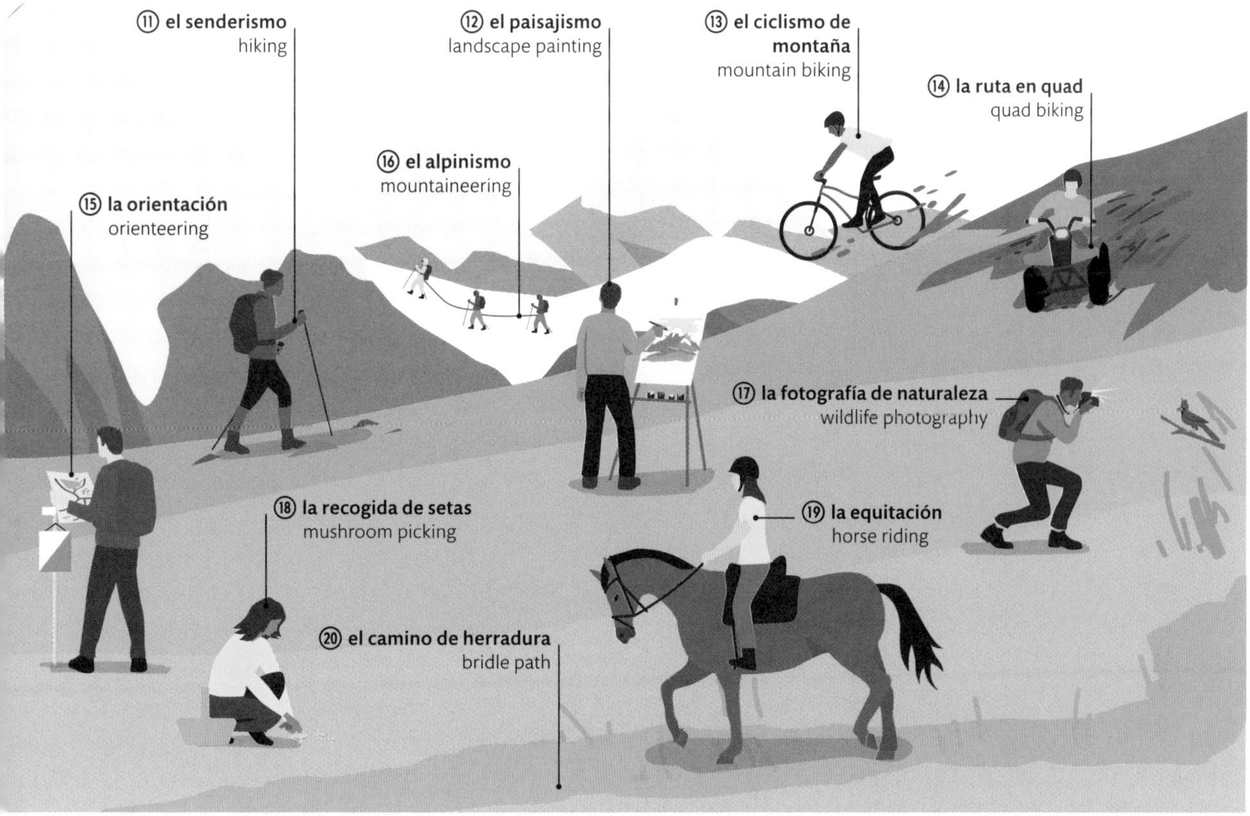

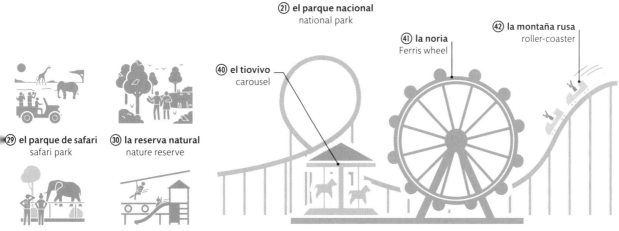

㉑ **el parque nacional**
national park

㉙ **el parque de safari**
safari park

㉚ **la reserva natural**
nature reserve

㊲ **el zoo**
zoo

㊳ **el parque de aventura**
adventure playground

㊴ **el parque de atracciones**
theme park

134 En la playa
On the beach

134.1 EN LA PLAYA • THE BEACH

㉖ el yate
yacht

㉗ la pasarela
boardwalk

㉘ el paseo marítimo
promenade

㉙ la caseta de playa
beach hut

See also
105 Los buques • Sea vessels **118** La natación • Swimming **119** La navegación y los deportes acuáticos • Sailing and watersports **121** La pesca • Fishing **133** Las actividades al aire libre • Outdoor activities **166** La vida oceánica • Ocean life

⑧ **el socorrista** *m*
la socorrista *f*
lifeguard

⑨ **el windsurf**
windsurfing

⑩ **el traje de neopreno**
wet suit

⑯ **la torre de vigilancia**
lifeguard tower

⑰ **el cangrejo**
crab

⑱ **el castillo de arena**
sandcastle

⑲ **las chanclas**
flip-flops

⑳ **tomar el sol**
sunbathing

㉔ **los shorts de baño**
swimming trunks

㉚ **el cangrejo ermitaño**
hermit crab

㉛ **la poza de marea**
rock pool

㉜ **la estrella de mar**
starfish

㉝ **el percebe**
barnacle

㉞ **las algas**
seaweed

㉟ **la lapa**
limpet

㊱ **la anémona**
anemone

㊲ **el buggy de playa**
beach buggy

㊳ **el cubo y la pala**
bucket and spade

㊴ **la sombrilla**
beach umbrella

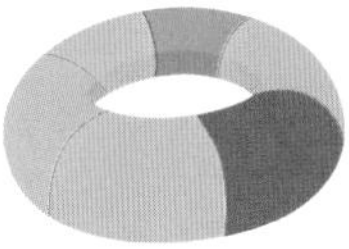

㊵ **el flotador**
rubber ring

㊶ **la gaviota**
gull

㊷ **el helado**
ice cream

㊸ **la boya**
buoy

㊹ **la tabla de surf**
surfboard

㊺ **la palmera**
palm tree

㊻ **el bikini**
bikini

㊼ **el bolso de playa**
beach bag

㊽ **la pamela**
sun hat

㊾ **las gafas de sol**
sunglasses

㊿ **el bloqueador solar**
sunblock

(51) **el protector solar**
sun cream

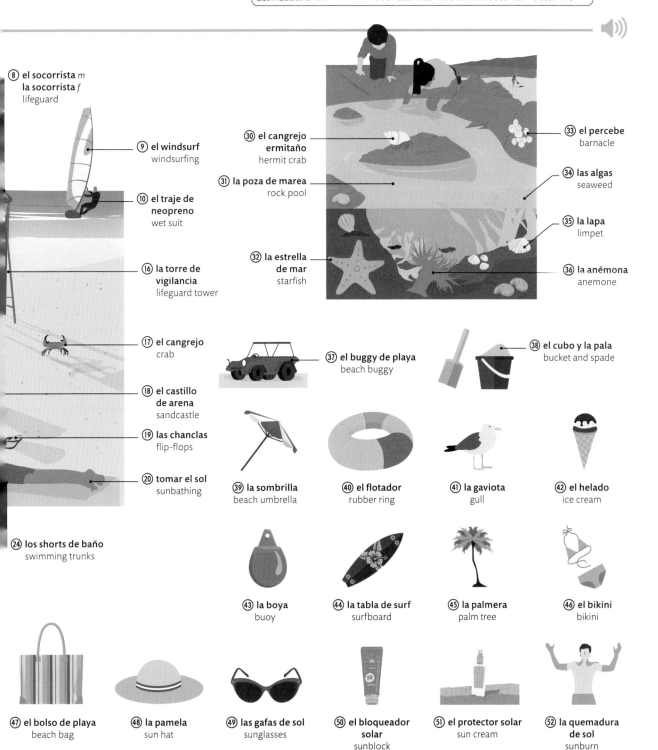

(52) **la quemadura de sol**
sunburn

135 La acampada
Camping

135.1 **EL EQUIPO DE CAMPING Y LAS INSTALACIONES** · CAMPING EQUIPMENT AND FACILITIES

① **acampar**
to camp

② **montar la tienda**
to pitch a tent

③ **la tienda para dos personas**
two-person tent

④ **la parcela**
pitch

⑤ **con parcelas disponibles**
pitches available

⑥ **completo**
full

⑧ **la conexión eléctrica**
electric hook-up

⑨ **el remolque**
trailer

⑩ **la autocaravana**
camper van

⑪ **la hamaca**
hammock

⑫ **la hoguera**
campfire

⑬ **encender una hoguera**
to light a fire

⑮ **el carbón**
charcoal

⑯ **la barbacoa**
barbecue

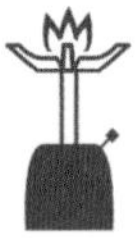

⑰ **el hornillo**
single-burner camping stove

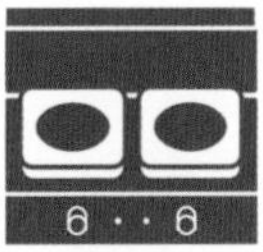

⑱ **el hornillo de dos fuegos**
double-burner camping stove

⑲ **la parrilla plegable**
folding grill

⑳ **la mesa de pícnic**
picnic bench

㉒ **las duchas**
shower block

㉓ **el bloque de aseos**
toilet block

㉔ **el contenedor de basura**
waste disposal

㉕ **la recepción**
site manager's office

㉖ **la mochila**
backpack / rucksack

㉗ **la linterna**
torch

㉙ **la brújula**
compass

㉚ **la ropa térmica**
thermals

㉛ **las botas de senderismo**
walking boots

㉜ **la ropa impermeable**
waterproofs

㉝ **la navaja multiusos**
multi-purpose knife

㉞ **el repelente de insectos**
insect repellent

㊱ **el saco de dormir**
sleeping bag

㊲ **la esterilla de dormir**
sleeping mat

㊳ **el catre**
camp bed

㊴ **el colchón autohinchable**
self-inflating mattress

㊵ **el colchón hinchable**
air bed / air mattress

㊶ **la bomba de aire**
air pump

See also
131 El viaje y el alojamiento • Travel and accommodation **133** Las actividades al aire libre • Outdoor activities **146-147** La geografía • Geography

135.2 EL CAMPAMENTO • CAMPSITE

⑦ **la caravana**
caravan

⑭ **las pastillas de encendido**
firelighter

㉑ **las botellas de agua**
water bottles

㉘ **la linterna frontal**
headlamp

㉟ **la mosquitera**
mosquito net

㊷ **la bomba eléctrica**
electric pump

① **la tienda de campaña familiar**
family tent

② **la estructura**
frame

③ **el poste**
tent pole

④ **la cuerda**
guy rope

⑤ **la tienda de campaña instantánea**
pop-up tent

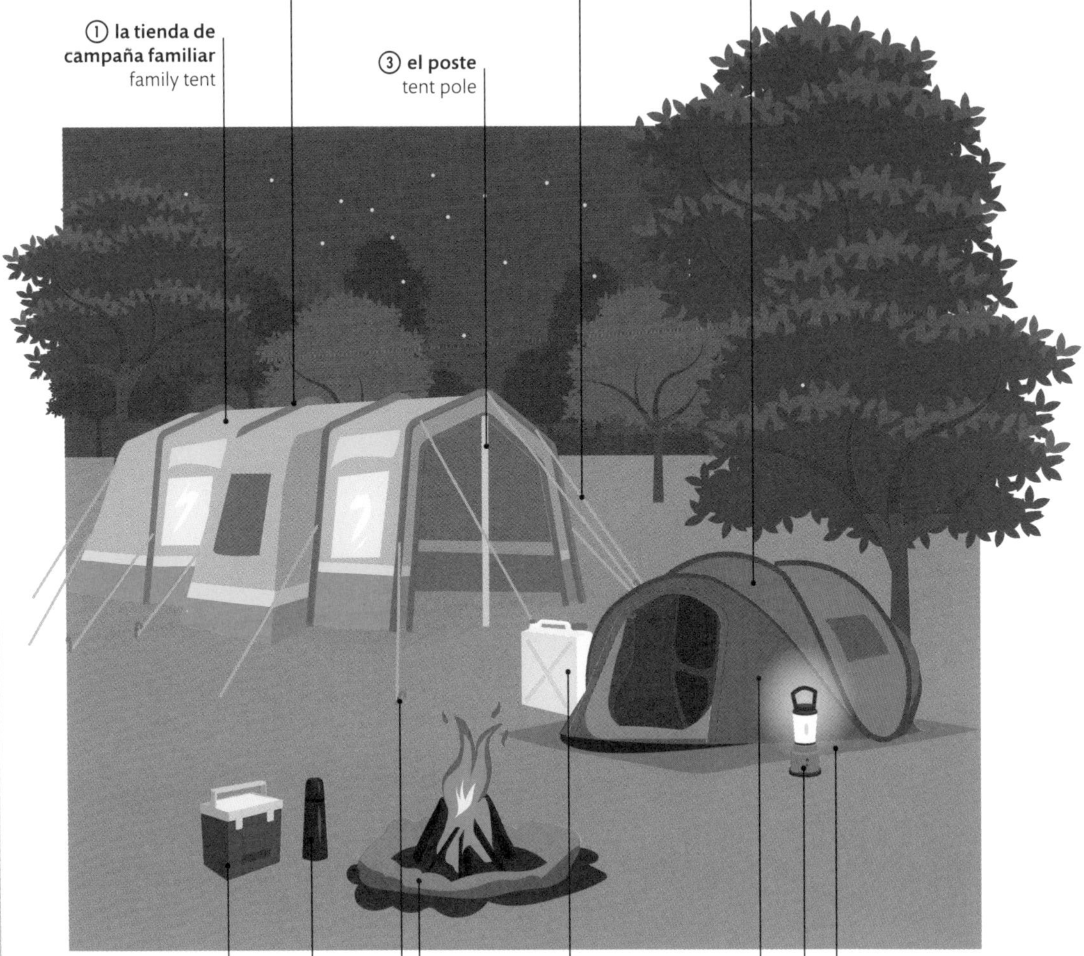

⑥ **la nevera**
cooler

⑦ **el termo**
thermal flask

⑧ **la piqueta**
tent peg

⑨ **el área para hogueras** *f*
firepit

⑩ **la garrafa de agua**
water carrier

⑪ **el doble techo**
flysheet

⑫ **el farol**
lamp / lantern

⑬ **la lona para el suelo**
groundsheet

El ocio en el hogar
Home entertainment

136.1 LA TELEVISIÓN Y EL AUDIO • TELEVISION AND AUDIO

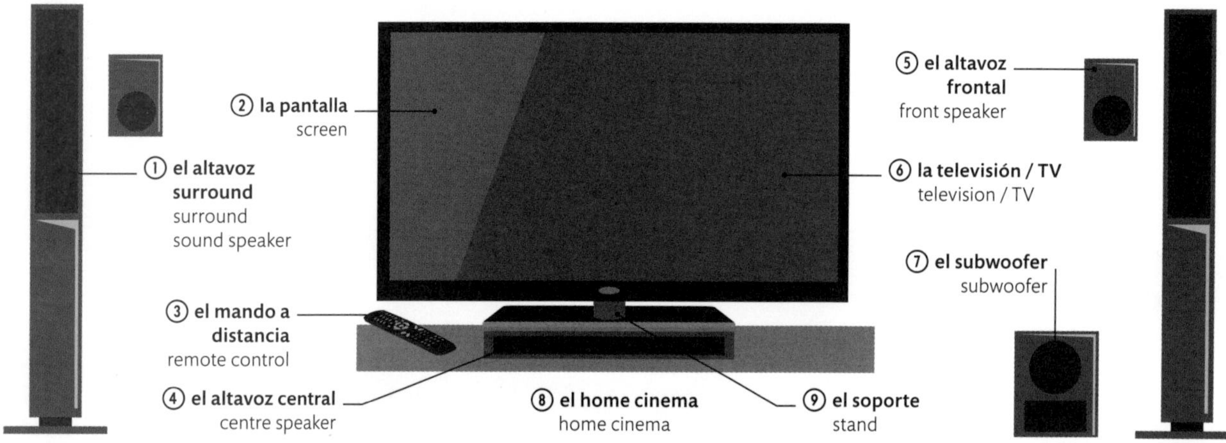

⑩ **la barra de sonido**
sound bar

⑪ **el CD**
CD

⑫ **el DVD**
DVD

⑮ **la radio**
radio

⑯ **los auriculares**
earphones

⑰ **los cascos**
headphones

⑱ **los cascos inalámbricos**
wireless headphones

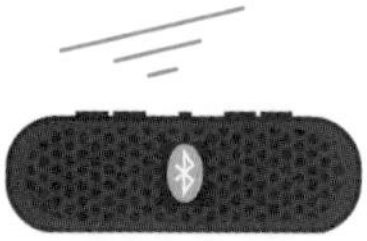
⑲ **el altavoz Bluetooth**
Bluetooth speaker

⑳ **el tocadiscos**
record player

㉑ **los discos**
records

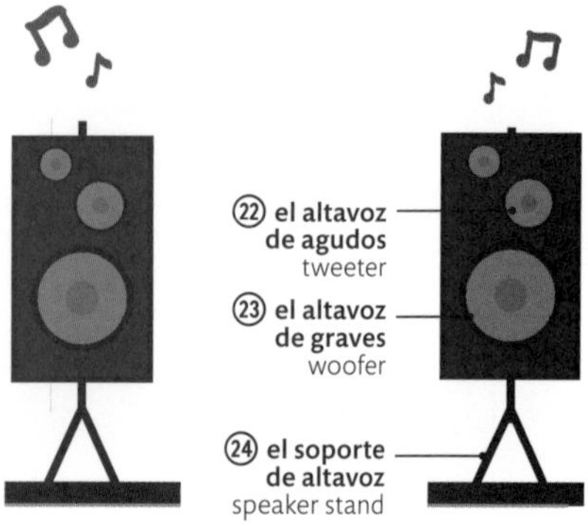

㉕ **los altavoces**
loudspeakers

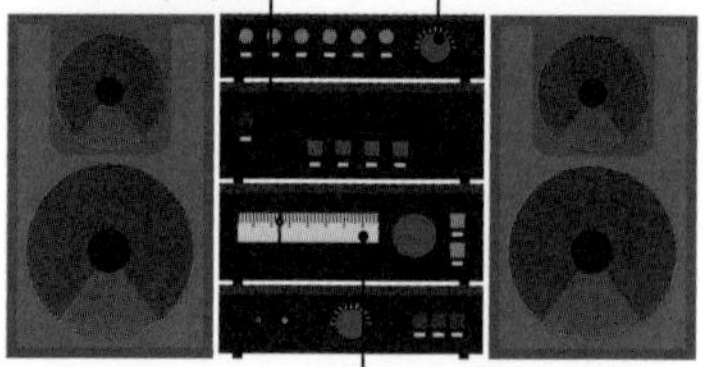

㉙ **el equipo de alta fidelidad**
hi-fi system

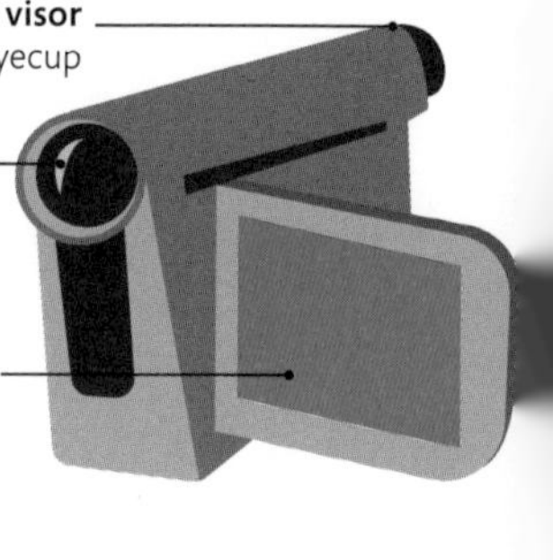

㉝ **la cámara de vídeo**
camcorder

See also
127 Las películas • Films **128-129** La música • Music
137 La televisión • Television **140** Los juegos • Games

(34) **estéreo**
stereo

(35) **mono**
mono

(36) **sintonizar**
to tune in

(37) **el volumen**
volume

(38) **subir el volumen**
to turn up

(39) **bajar el volumen**
to turn down

(40) **la antena parabólica**
satellite dish

(41) **el sintonizador digital**
digital box

(42) **el micrófono**
microphone

(43) **el karaoke**
karaoke

136.2 LOS VIDEOJUEGOS • VIDEO GAMES

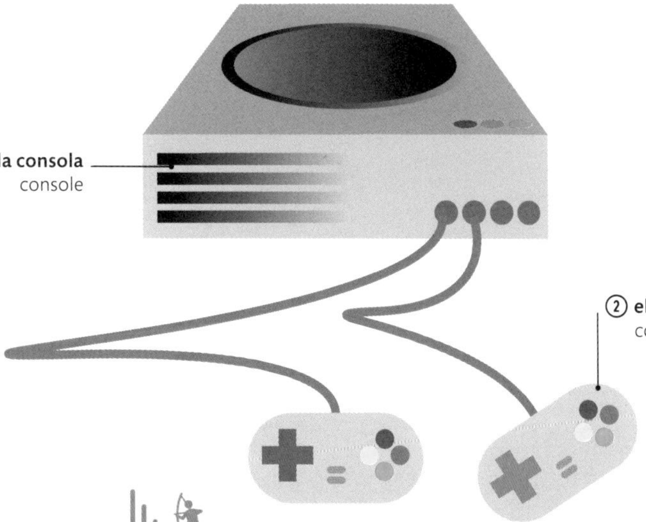
(1) **la consola**
console

(2) **el mando**
controller

(3) **el juego de estrategia**
strategy game

(4) **el juego de preguntas y respuestas**
trivia game

(5) **el juego de plataformas**
platform game

(6) **el juego de aventuras**
adventure game

(7) **el juego de rol**
role-playing game

(8) **el juego de acción**
action game

(9) **el juego multijugador**
multiplayergame

(10) **el juego de simulación**
simulation game

(11) **el juego de deportes**
sports game

(12) **el juego de puzles**
puzzle game

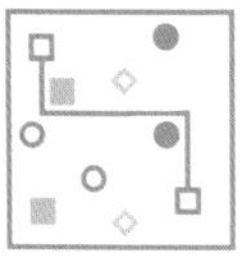
(13) **el juego de lógica**
logic game

137 La televisión

Television

137.1 VIENDO LA TELEVISIÓN • WATCHING TELEVISION

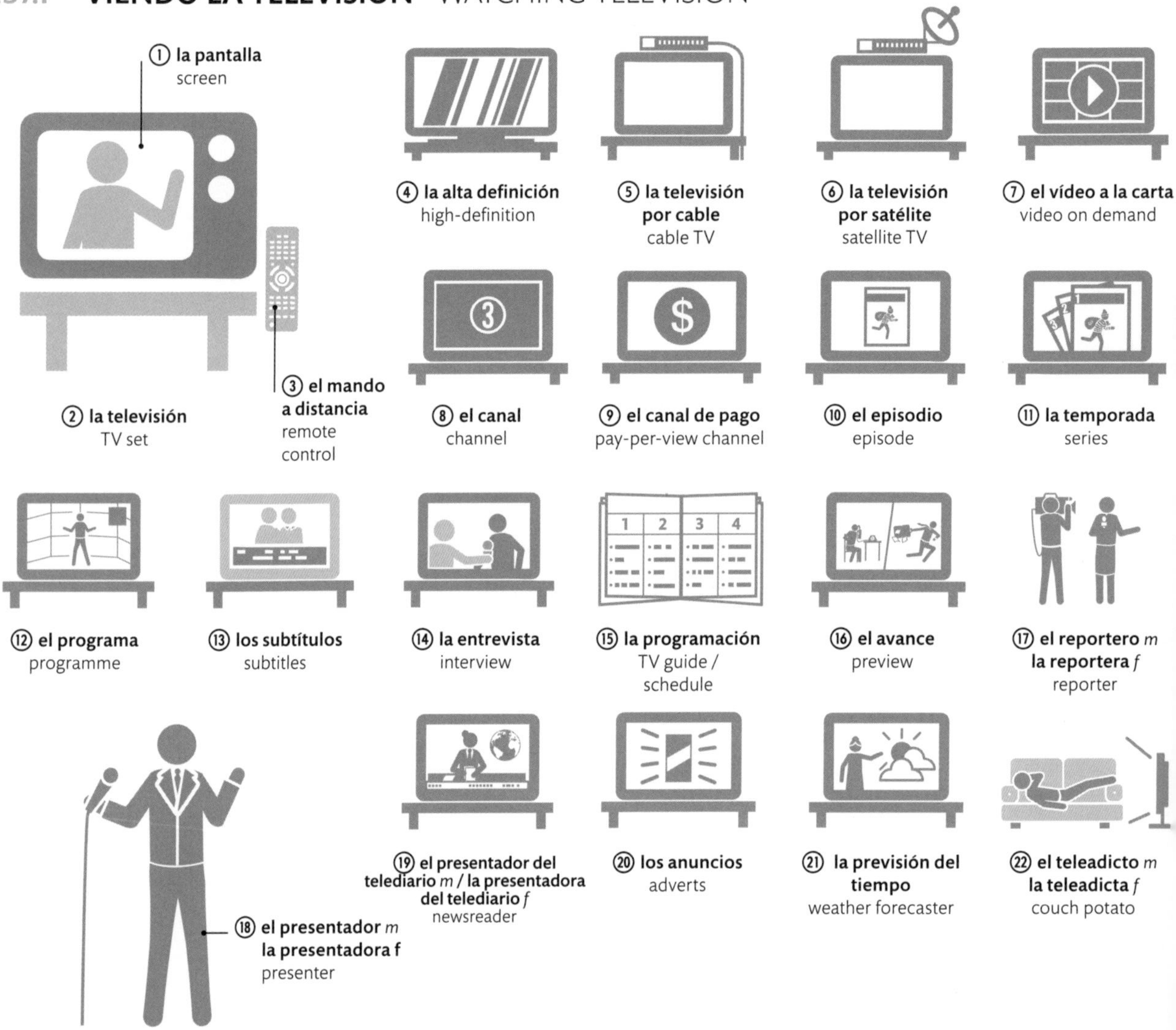

1. **la pantalla** screen
2. **la televisión** TV set
3. **el mando a distancia** remote control
4. **la alta definición** high-definition
5. **la televisión por cable** cable TV
6. **la televisión por satélite** satellite TV
7. **el vídeo a la carta** video on demand
8. **el canal** channel
9. **el canal de pago** pay-per-view channel
10. **el episodio** episode
11. **la temporada** series
12. **el programa** programme
13. **los subtítulos** subtitles
14. **la entrevista** interview
15. **la programación** TV guide / schedule
16. **el avance** preview
17. **el reportero** *m* **la reportera** *f* reporter
18. **el presentador** *m* **la presentadora f** presenter
19. **el presentador del telediario** *m* **/ la presentadora del telediario** *f* newsreader
20. **los anuncios** adverts
21. **la previsión del tiempo** weather forecaster
22. **el teleadicto** *m* **la teleadicta** *f* couch potato

137.2 LOS VERBOS DE LA TELEVISIÓN • TELEVISION VERBS

1. **encender** to turn on
2. **apagar** to turn off
3. **subir el volumen** to turn up the volume
4. **bajar el volumen** to turn down the volume
5. **cambiar de canal** to change the channel
6. **transmitir** to stream

See also
26 El salón y el comedor • Living room and dining room **84** Los medios de comunicación • Media **127** Las películas • Films **136** El ocio en el hogar • Home entertainment

137.3 LOS PROGRAMAS DE TV Y LOS CANALES • TV SHOWS AND CHANNELS

① **el programa de cocina**
cooking show

② **el programa de entrevistas**
chat show

③ **los deportes**
sports

④ **el documental**
documentary

⑤ **el documental de naturaleza**
nature documentary

⑥ **el drama de época**
period drama / costume drama

⑦ **la comedia de situación**
sitcom

⑧ **el concurso de preguntas y respuestas**
quiz show

⑨ **el programa de actualidad**
current affairs

⑩ **las noticias**
news

⑪ **el tiempo**
weather

⑫ **la telenovela**
soap opera

⑬ **el concurso**
game show

⑭ **la comedia**
comedy

⑮ **los dibujos animados**
cartoon

⑯ **el crimen**
crime

⑰ **el suspense**
thriller

⑱ **la sátira**
satire

⑲ **el programa infantil**
children's TV

⑳ **el programa matutino**
breakfast TV

㉑ **el reality show**
reality TV

㉒ **la televisión a la carta**
catch-up TV

㉓ **la teletienda**
shopping channel

㉔ **el canal de música**
music channel

⑦ **reproducir**
to play

⑧ **parar**
to stop

⑨ **pausar**
to pause

⑩ **rebobinar**
to rewind

⑪ **adelantar**
to fast forward

⑫ **grabar**
to record

Los libros y la lectura
Books and reading

138.1 **LOS LIBROS** · BOOKS

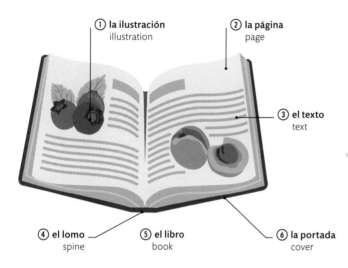

① **la ilustración** illustration
② **la página** page
③ **el texto** text
④ **el lomo** spine
⑤ **el libro** book
⑥ **la portada** cover

⑦ **el autor** *m* **la autora** *f*
author

⑧ **de tapa blanda**
paperback

⑨ **de tapa dura**
hardback

⑬ **la reseña**
review

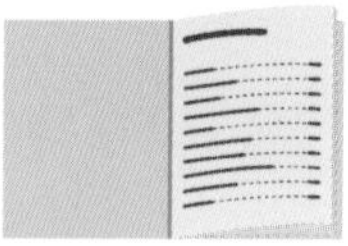

⑭ **la tabla de contenidos**
contents

⑮ **el capítulo**
chapter

138.2 **LA LECTURA Y LOS GÉNEROS** · READING AND GENRES

① **la no ficción**
non-fiction

② **el diccionario**
dictionary

③ **la enciclopedia**
encyclopedia

④ **el libro de jardinería**
gardening book

⑤ **la guía de televisión**
TV guide

⑥ **la autoayuda**
self-help

⑦ **la autobiografía**
autobiography

⑧ **la biografía**
biography

⑨ **el libro de cocina**
cookbook

⑩ **la guía turística**
guidebook

⑪ **el libro de naturaleza**
nature writing

⑫ **el libro de texto**
textbook / course book

⑬ **la ficción**
fiction

⑭ **la novela**
novel

⑮ **la ciencia ficción**
science fiction

⑯ **la fantasía**
fantasy

⑰ **el cómic**
comic

⑱ **el libro de viajes**
travel writing

See also
127 Las películas • Films **136** El ocio en el hogar • Home entertainment
139 La fantasía y los mitos • Fantasy and myth **175** La escritura • Writing

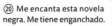

⑩ **el título**
title

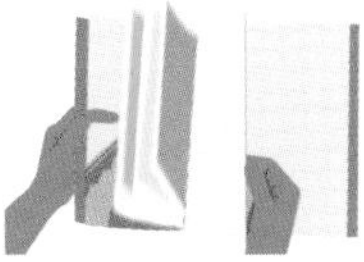

⑪ **hojear**
to flip through

⑫ **el libro electrónico**
e-reader

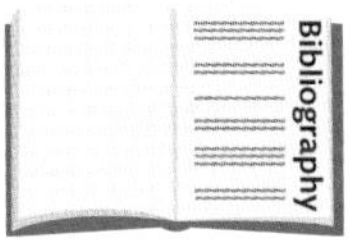

⑯ **la bibliografía**
bibliography

⑰ **el glosario**
glossary

⑱ **el índice**
index

⑳ **Me encanta esta novela negra. Me tiene enganchado.**
I love this crime novel. It's a real page-turner.

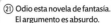

㉑ **Odio esta novela de fantasía. El argumento es absurdo.**
I hate this fantasy novel. The plot is ridiculous.

⑲ **la lectura**
reading

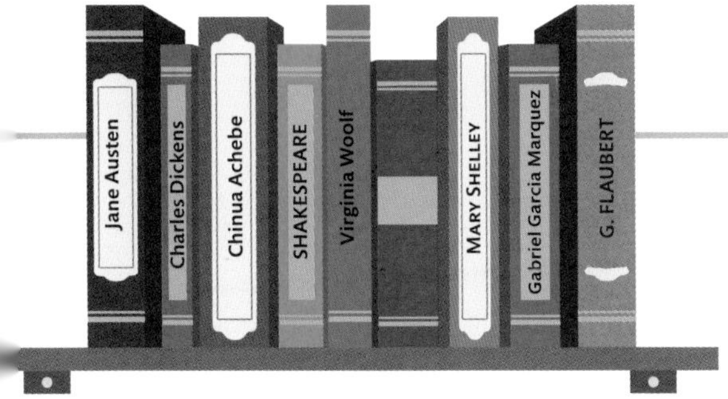

⑲ **la ficción literaria**
literary fiction

㉑ **el personaje**
character

⑳ **el libro infantil**
children's book

㉒ **el libro para colorear**
colouring book

㉓ **el cuento de hadas**
fairy tale

㉔ **el romance**
romance

㉕ **la novela policíaca**
crime fiction

㉖ **el humor**
humour

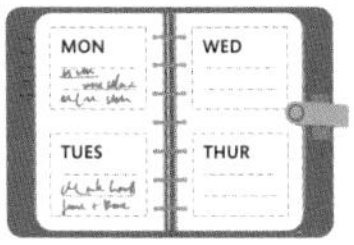

㉗ **la agenda**
diary

㉝ **el titular**
headline

㉞ **el artículo**
article

㉜ **el periódico**
newspaper

㉘ **el bestseller**
bestseller

㉙ **el horóscopo**
horoscope

㉚ **la revista del corazón**
gossip magazine

㉛ **los crucigramas**
puzzles

139 La fantasía y los mitos

Fantasy and myth

139.1 LOS MITOS, LAS HISTORIAS Y LAS CRIATURAS FANTÁSTICAS · MYTHS, STORIES, AND FANTASTIC CREATURES

② **Érase una vez, en un lugar muy lejano...**
Once upon a time in a land far away...

① **el cuento de hadas**
fairy tale

③ **el unicornio**
unicorn

⑥ **hechizar**
to cast a spell

⑤ **la varita**
wand

④ **el libro de hechizos**
spell book

⑧ **el brebaje de la bruja**
witches' brew

⑦ **el caldero**
cauldron

⑨ **la bola de cristal**
crystal ball

⑩ **la poción**
potion

⑪ **la magia de las velas**
candle magic

⑱ **el báculo**
staff

⑰ **el mago**
wizard

⑭ **el héroe**
hero

⑬ **el minotauro**
Minotaur

⑫ **la mitología griega**
Greek mythology

⑮ **el elixir**
elixir

⑯ **el amuleto**
amulet

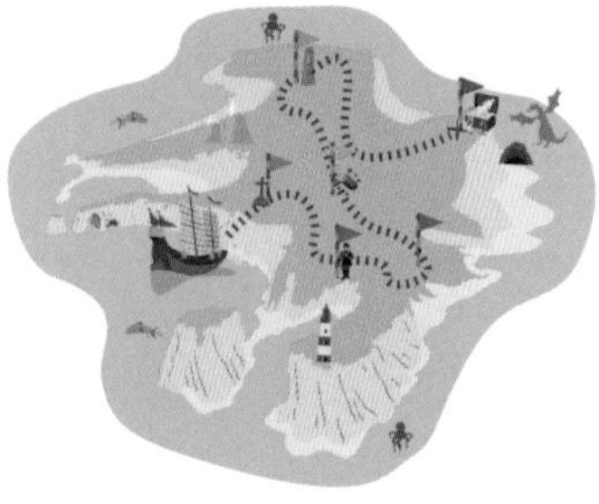

⑲ **la misión**
quest

⑳ **el tesoro**
treasure

㉑ **la alfombra mágica**
flying carpet

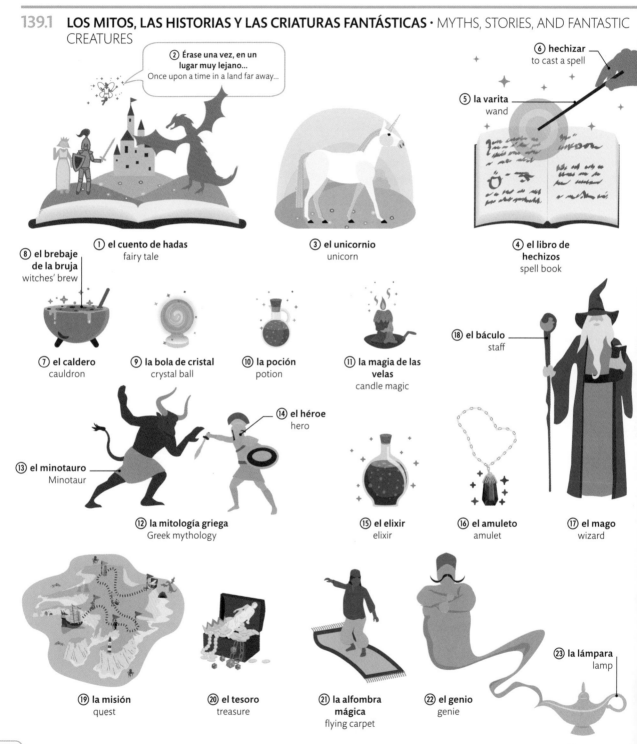

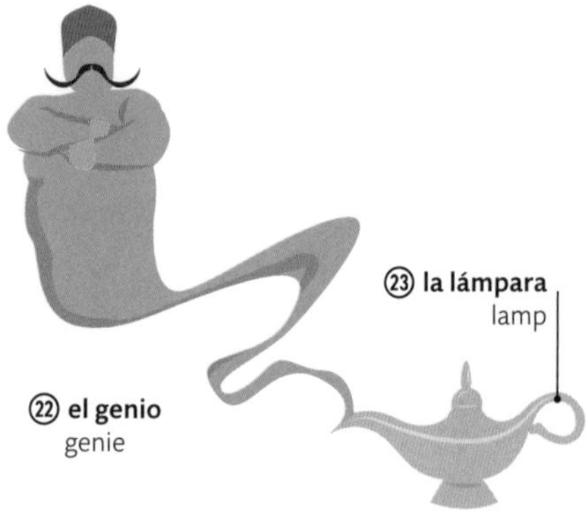

㉒ **el genio**
genie

㉓ **la lámpara**
lamp

See also
127 Las películas • Films **137** La televisión • Television
138 Los libros y la lectura • Books and reading

㉔ la serpiente de mar
sea serpent

㉕ Hugin y Munin
Hugin and Munin

㉖ las Dísir
the Disir

㉗ el monstruo
monster

㉘ el zombi
zombie

㉙ el hombre lobo
werewolf

㉚ el vampiro
vampire

㉛ el fantasma
ghost

㉜ la calabaza de Halloween
jack-o'-lantern

㉝ el dragón
dragon

㉞ el caballero
knight

㊱ la escoba
broomstick

㉟ la bruja
witch

㊲ el hada *f*
fairy

㊳ el duendecillo
pixie

㊴ el fauno
faun

㊵ el gnomo
gnome

㊶ el leprechaun
leprechaun

㊷ el diablillo
gremlin

㊸ el trasgo
goblin

㊹ el trol
troll

㊺ el ogro
ogre

㊻ el orco
orc

㊼ el gigante
giant

㊽ el elfo
elf

㊾ el enano
dwarf

㊿ la sirena
mermaid

51 el tritón
merman

52 el fénix
phoenix

53 el grifo
griffin

54 la hidra
hydra

55 el centauro
centaur

56 la esfinge
sphinx

57 Cerbero
Cerberus

58 el robot malvado
bad robot

59 el alienígena
alien

140 Los juegos
Games

140.1 EL AJEDREZ • CHESS

① **Voy a mover el caballo.**
I'm going to move my knight.

② **el tablero de ajedrez**
chessboard

③ **las piezas**
pieces

④ **el rey**
king

⑤ **el alfil**
bishop

⑥ **el caballo**
knight

⑦ **la casilla**
square

⑧ **las piezas blancas**
white

⑨ **la torre**
rook

⑩ **el peón**
pawn

⑪ **la reina**
queen

⑫ **las piezas negras**
black

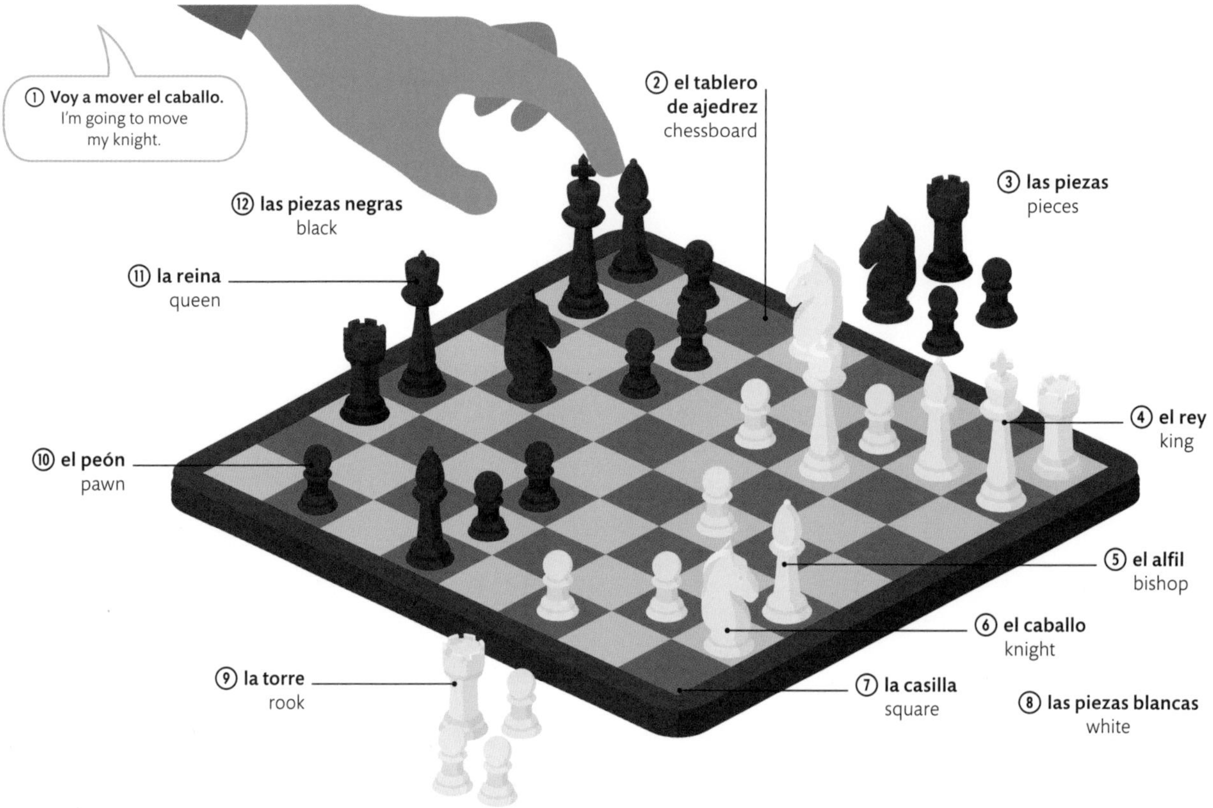

140.3 LOS JUEGOS • GAMES

① **los juegos de mesa**
board games

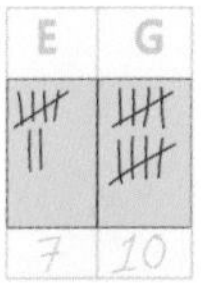

② **los puntos**
points

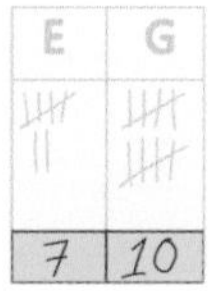

③ **la puntuación**
score

④ **el tres en raya**
noughts and crosses

⑤ **los dados**
dice

⑥ **el solitario**
solitaire

⑦ **las piezas**
pieces

⑧ **el puzle**
jigsaw puzzle

⑨ **el dominó**
dominoes

⑩ **los dardos**
darts

⑪ **la diana**
dartboard

⑫ **el centro de la diana**
bullseye

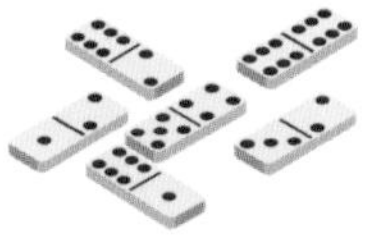

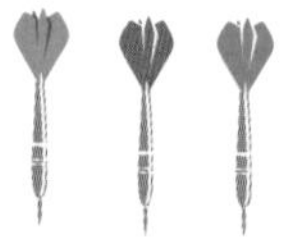

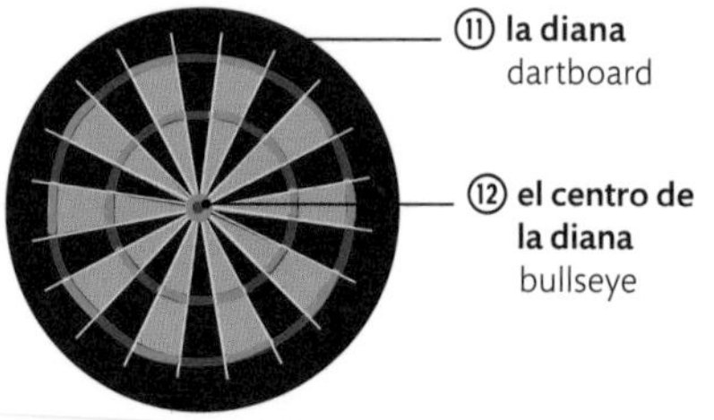

See also
136 El ocio en el hogar • Home entertainment **138** Los libros y la lectura • Books and reading **141-142** Las manualidades • Arts and crafts

140.2 **JUGANDO A LAS CARTAS** • PLAYING CARDS

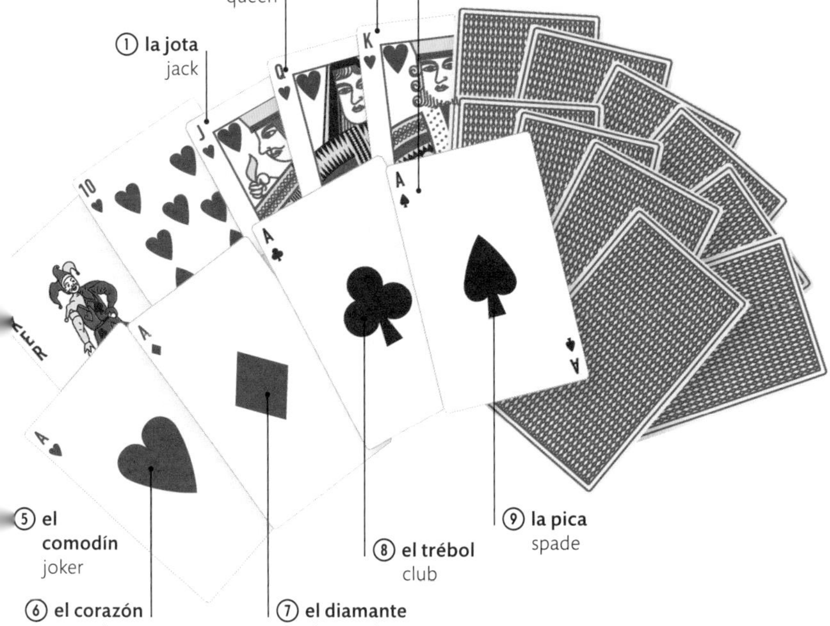

⑩ **barajar** to shuffle

⑪ **repartir** to deal

⑫ **la baraja de cartas** deck of cards / pack of cards

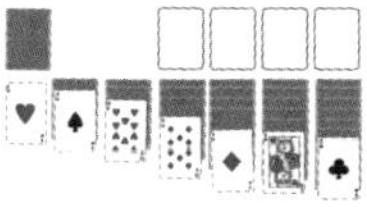

⑬ **el solitario** patience

⑭ **el bridge** bridge

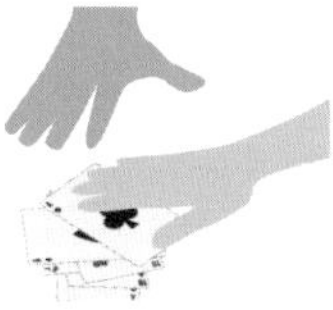

⑮ **el juego de pares** snap

⑭ **jugar** to play

⑯ **ganar** to win

⑰ **perder** to lose

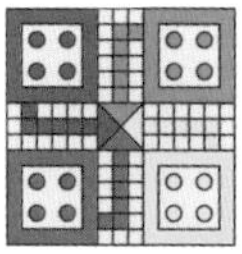

⑱ **el parchís** ludo

⑲ **coger** to take

⑳ **mover** to move

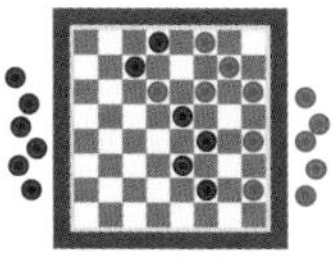

㉑ **las damas** draughts

㉒ **serpientes y escaleras** snakes and ladders

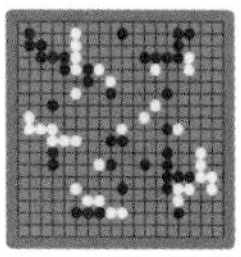

㉓ **el go** go

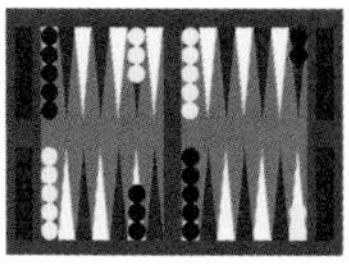

㉔ **el backgammon** backgammon

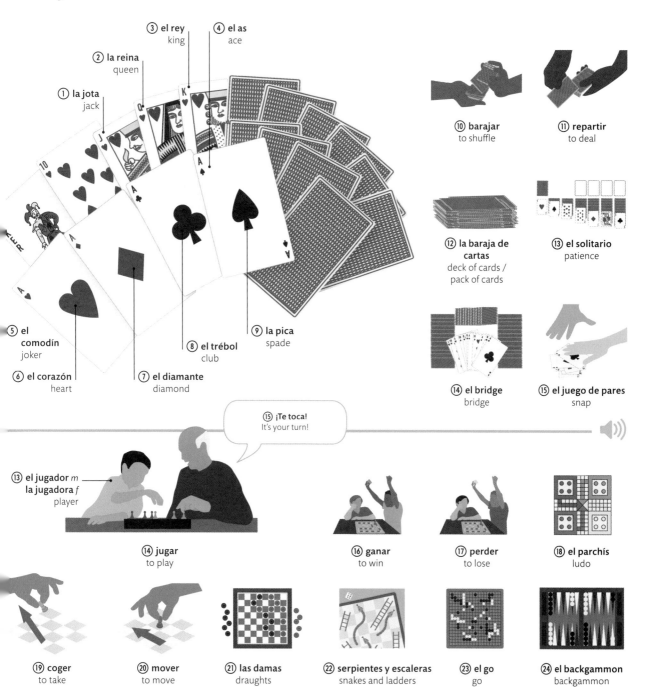

141 Las manualidades
Arts and crafts

141.1 LA PINTURA • PAINTING

⑨ **rojo**
red

⑩ **escarlata**
scarlet

⑪ **azul**
blue

⑫ **turquesa**
turquoise

⑬ **azul marino**
navy blue

⑭ **amarillo**
yellow

⑮ **verde**
green

⑯ **naranja**
orange

⑰ **morado**
purple

⑱ **añil**
indigo

⑲ **rosa**
pink

⑳ **marrón**
brown

㉑ **gris**
grey

㉒ **negro**
black

㉓ **blanco**
white

㉔ **la pintura al óleo**
oil paints

㉕ **la acuarela**
watercolour paints

㉖ **el pastel**
pastels

㉗ **la pintura acrílica**
acrylic paints

㉘ **la témpera**
poster paint

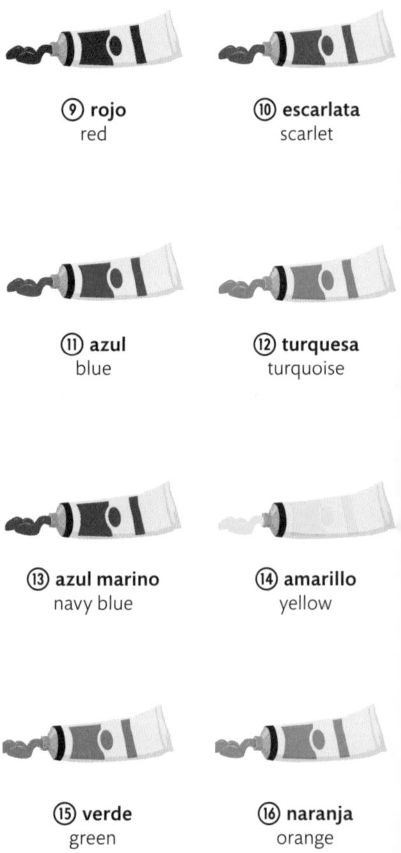

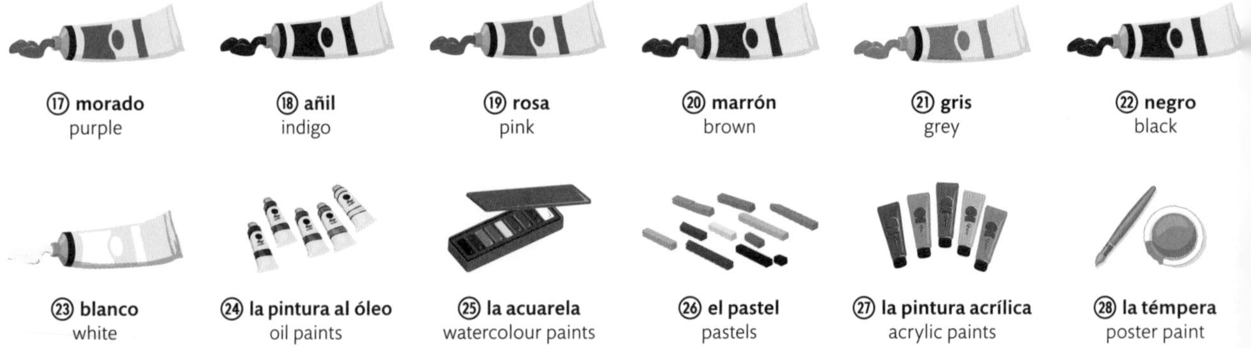

See also
37 La decoración • Decorating **130** Los museos y las galerías • Museums and galleries **142** Las manualidades (continuación) • Arts and crafts continued

141.2 OTRAS ARTES Y MANUALIDADES • OTHER ARTS AND CRAFTS

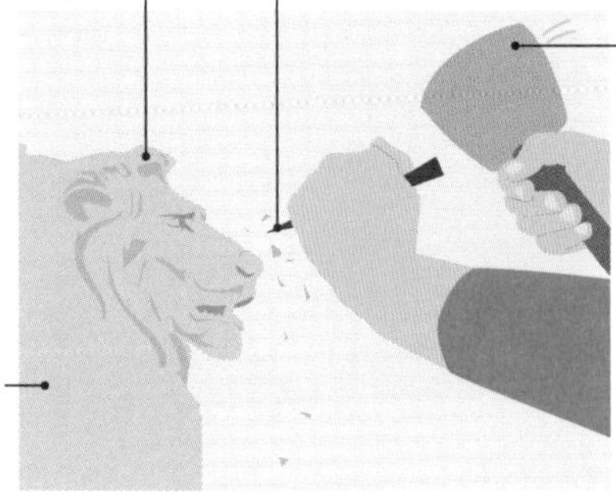

⑤ **la escultura**
sculpting

⑥ **el dibujo**
drawing

⑦ **el boceto**
sketch

⑧ **el carboncillo**
charcoal

⑨ **el lápiz**
pencil

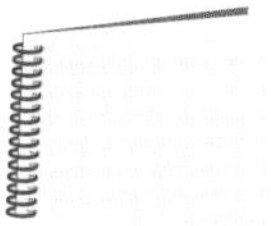

⑩ **el bloc de dibujo**
sketch pad

⑪ **la impresión**
printing

⑫ **la tinta**
ink

⑬ **el grabado**
engraving

⑭ **la talla en madera**
woodworking

⑯ **la cartulina**
card

⑰ **el collage**
collage

⑱ **el pegamento**
glue

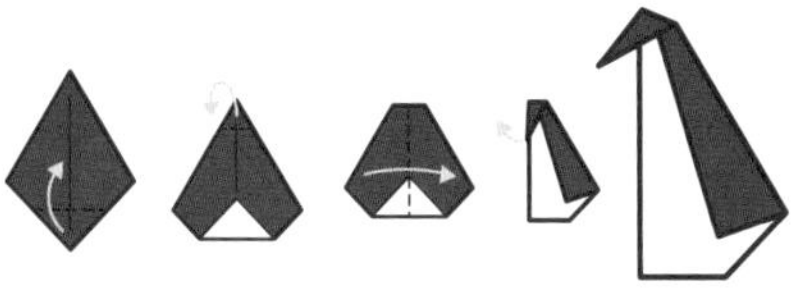

⑲ **el origami**
origami

⑳ **el modelismo**
model making

㉑ **el papel maché**
papier-mâché

㉒ **las herramientas para modelar**
modelling tool

㉓ **la orfebrería**
making jewellery

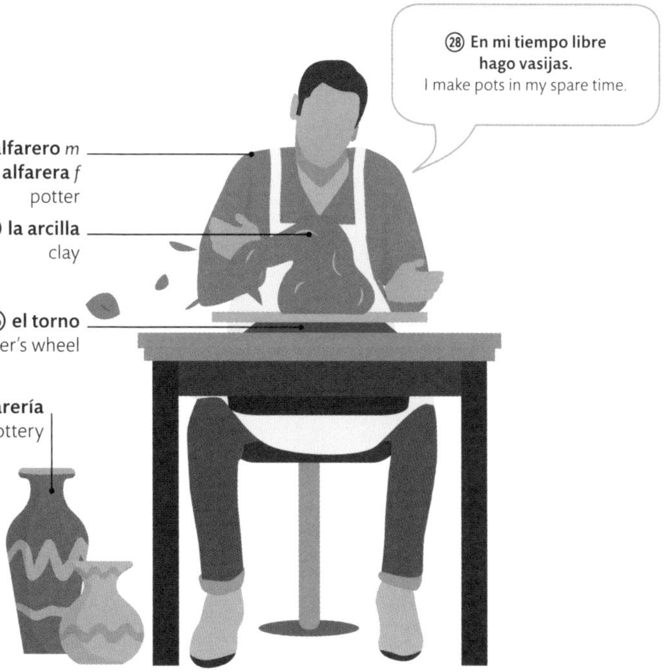

Las manualidades (continuación)

Arts and crafts continued

142.1 LA COSTURA · SEWING

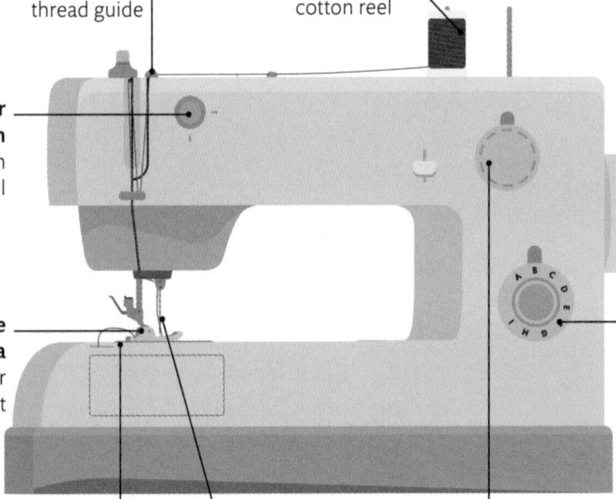

① **la guía del hilo**
thread guide

② **el carrete de hilo**
cotton reel

③ **la rueda de ajuste**
balance wheel

④ **el selector de tensión**
tension control

⑤ **el pie de la aguja**
presser foot

⑥ **el selector de puntada**
stitch selector

⑦ **la placa de la aguja**
needle plate

⑧ **la aguja para máquina de coser**
machine needle

⑨ **el selector de largo de puntada**
stitch length selector

⑩ **la máquina de coser**
sewing machine

⑪ **la cinta métrica**
tape measure

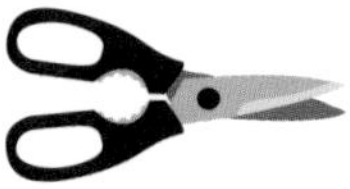

⑫ **las tijeras**
scissors

⑬ **las tijeras dentadas**
pinking scissors

⑭ **el maniquí de costura**
tailor's dummy

⑮ **el patrón vestido**
dress pat

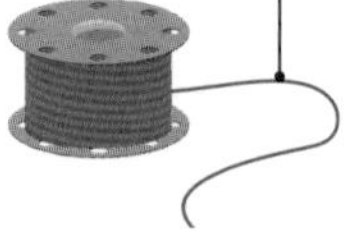

⑰ **el hilo**
thread

⑯ **el carrete**
bobbin

⑱ **la caja de costura**
sewing box

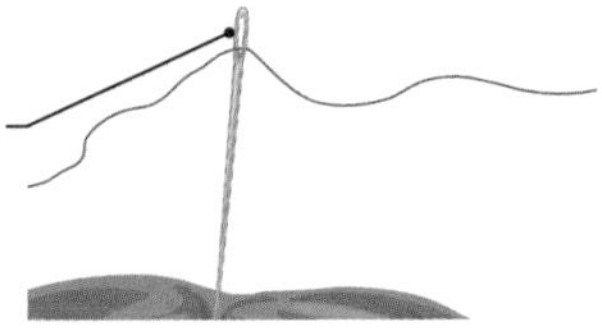

⑳ **el ojo**
eye

⑲ **la aguja de coser**
sewing needle

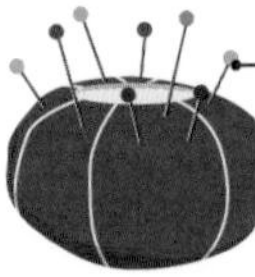

㉒ **el alfiler**
pin

㉑ **el alfiletero**
pincushion

㉓ **el dedal**
thimble

㉔ **confeccionar**
to tailor

㉕ **estrechar**
to take in

㉖ **agrandar**
to let out

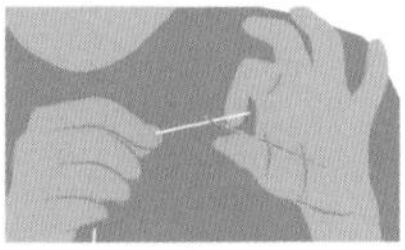

㉗ **enhebrar**
to thread

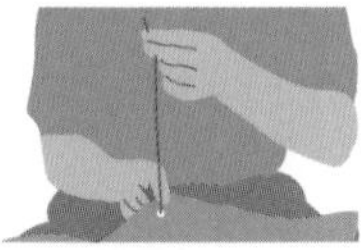

㉘ **coser**
to sew

㉙ **cortar**
to cut

㉚ **zurcir**
to darn

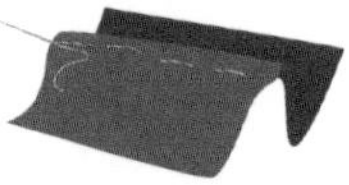

㉛ **hilvanar**
to tack

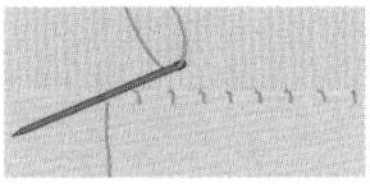

㉜ **la puntada**
stitch

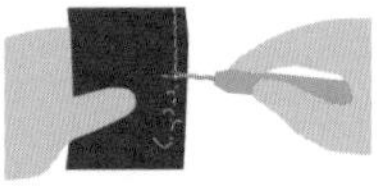

㉝ **descoser**
to unpick

㉞ **la cinta**
ribbon

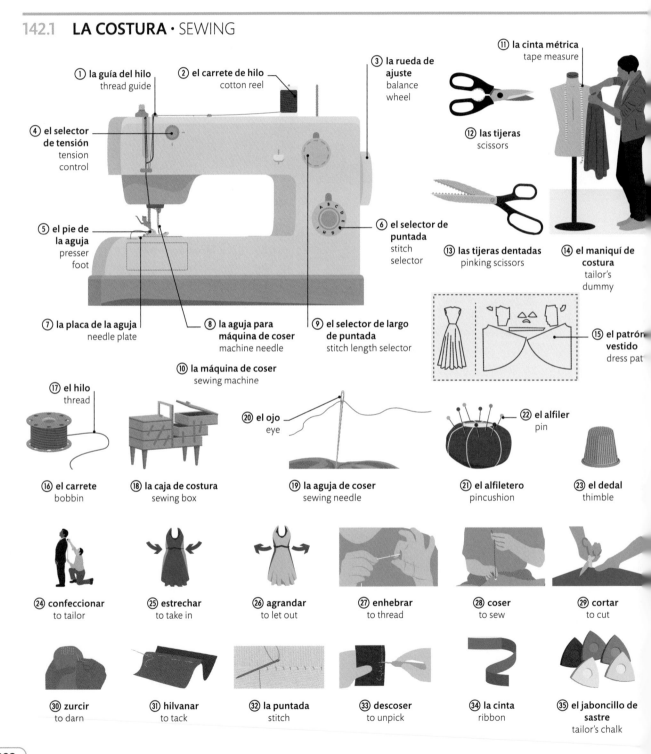

㉟ **el jaboncillo de sastre**
tailor's chalk

See also
11 Las habilidades y las acciones • Abilities and actions **13-15** La ropa • Clothes
37 La decoración • Decorating **39** La jardinería • Practical gardening

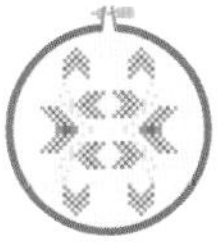

36 **el punto de aguja**
needlepoint

37 **el bordado**
embroidery

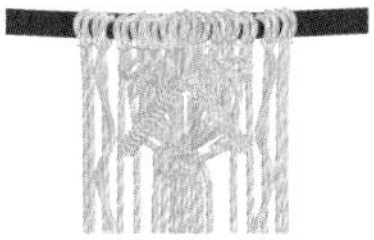

38 **el macramé**
macramé

39 **la confección de colchas**
quilting

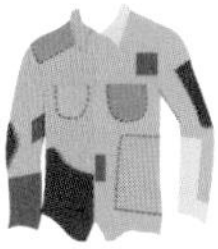

40 **el patchwork**
patchwork

41 **la tela**
fabric

42 **el encaje de bolillos**
lace-making

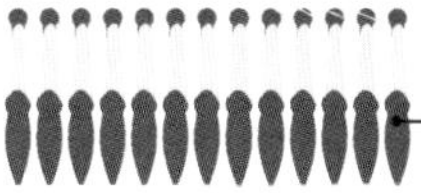

43 **el bolillo**
lace bobbin

44 **Vendo mis productos artesanales en las ferias de artesanía locales.**
I sell my handicrafts at local craft fairs.

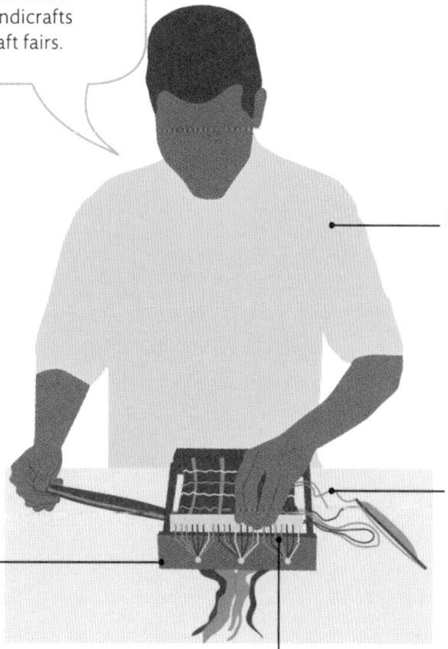

45 **el tejedor** *m*
la tejedora *f*
weaver

46 **el hilo de trama**
weft thread

47 **el telar**
loom

48 **el hilo de urdimbre**
warp thread

49 **la tejeduría**
weaving

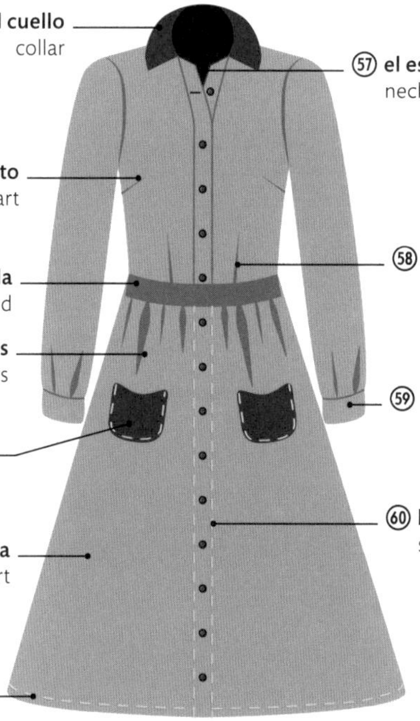

50 **el cuello**
collar

51 **la pinza del busto**
bust dart

52 **la cinturilla**
waistband

53 **los frunces**
gathers

54 **el bolsillo**
pocket

55 **la falda fruncida**
gathered skirt

56 **el bajo**
hem

57 **el escote**
neckline

58 **la pinza**
dart

59 **el puño**
cuff

60 **la costura**
seam

61 **el ganchillo**
crochet

62 **la aguja de ganchillo**
crochet hook

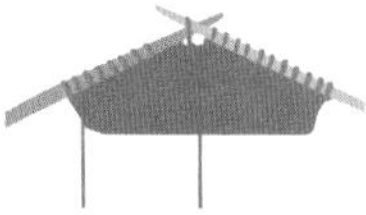

63 **el punto**
knitting

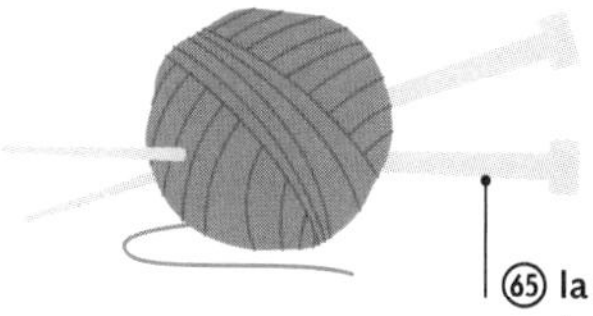

64 **la lana**
wool

65 **la aguja de hacer punto**
knitting needle

66 **la madeja**
skein

67 **los botones**
buttons

68 **la cremallera**
zip

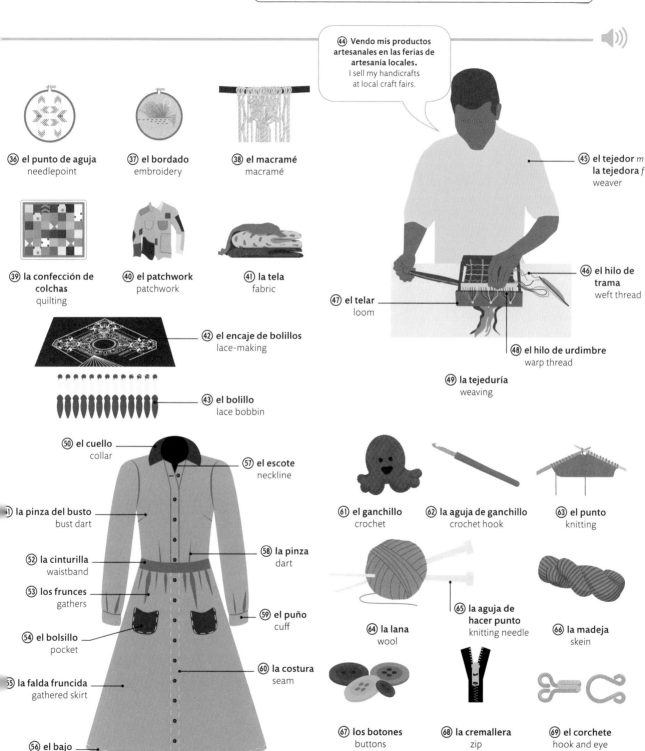

69 **el corchete**
hook and eye

143 El espacio
Space

143.1 EL SISTEMA SOLAR · THE SOLAR SYSTEM

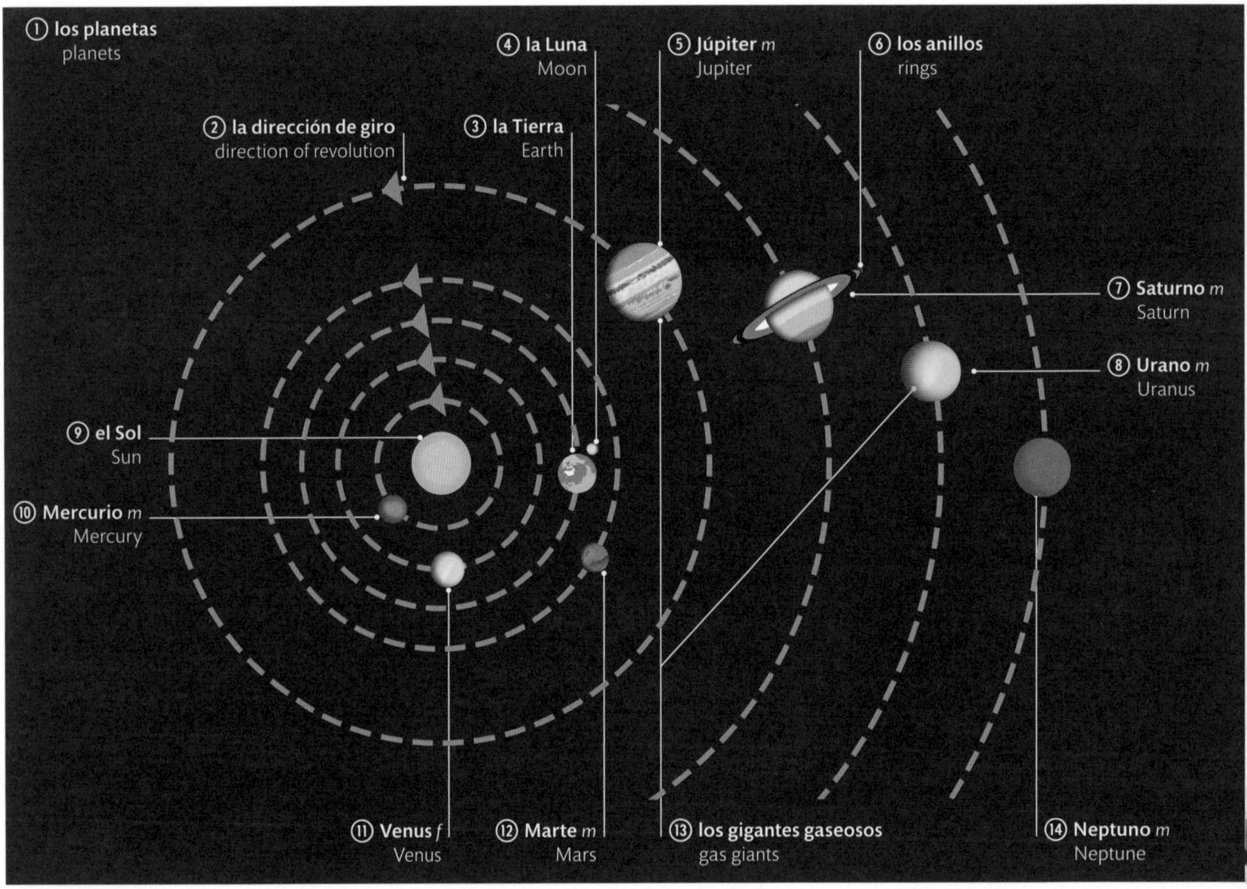

① los planetas
planets
② la dirección de giro
direction of revolution
③ la Tierra
Earth
④ la Luna
Moon
⑤ Júpiter m
Jupiter
⑥ los anillos
rings
⑦ Saturno m
Saturn
⑧ Urano m
Uranus
⑨ el Sol
Sun
⑩ Mercurio m
Mercury
⑪ Venus f
Venus
⑫ Marte m
Mars
⑬ los gigantes gaseosos
gas giants
⑭ Neptuno m
Neptune

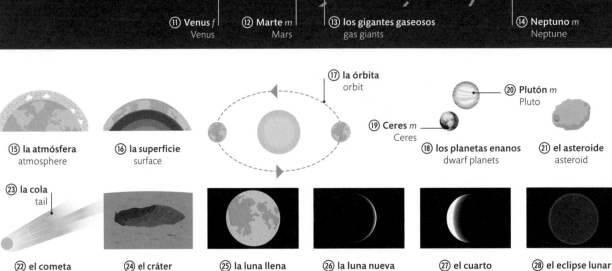

⑮ **la atmósfera**
atmosphere

⑯ **la superficie**
surface

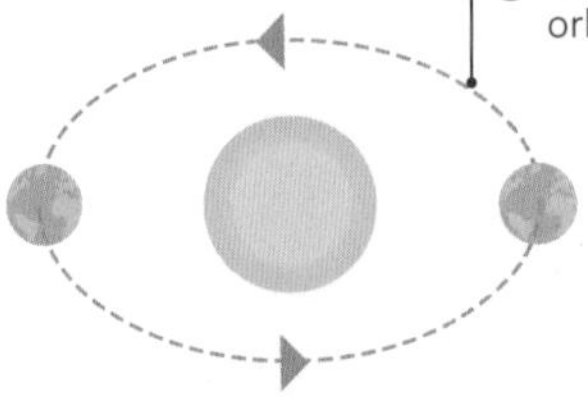

⑰ la órbita
orbit

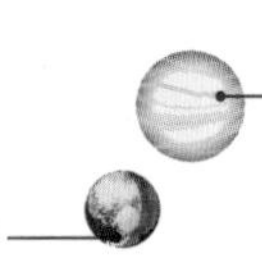

⑳ Plutón m
Pluto
⑲ Ceres m
Ceres

⑱ **los planetas enanos**
dwarf planets

㉑ **el asteroide**
asteroid

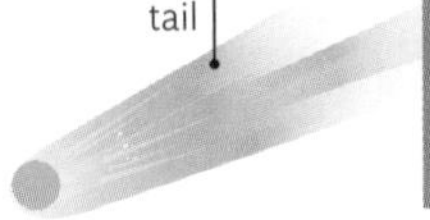

㉓ la cola
tail

㉒ **el cometa**
comet

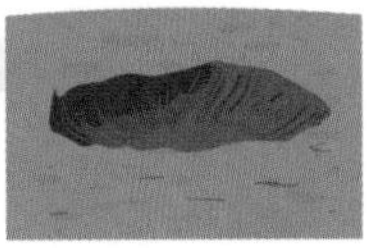

㉔ **el cráter**
crater

㉕ **la luna llena**
full moon

㉖ **la luna nueva**
new moon

㉗ **el cuarto creciente**
crescent moon

㉘ **el eclipse lunar**
lunar eclipse

See also
74 Las matemáticas • Mathematics **75** La física • Physics **83** Los ordenadores y la tecnología • Computers and technology **144** El espacio (continuación) • Space continued **145** El planeta Tierra • Planet Earth **156** Las rocas y los minerales • Rocks and minerals

143.2 LA EXPLORACIÓN ESPACIAL • SPACE EXPLORATION

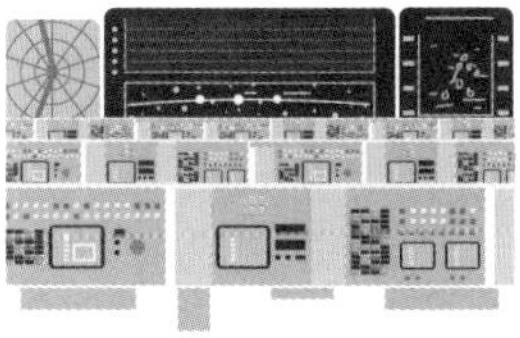

① **el centro de control**
mission control

② **el buggy lunar**
lunar rover

③ **el róver**
rover

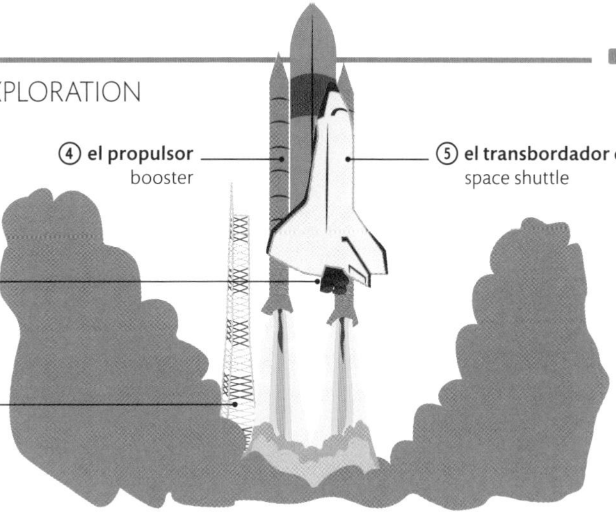

⑧ **el lanzamiento del transbordador espacial**
space shuttle launch

⑨ **el cohete**
rocket

⑩ **el satélite**
satellite

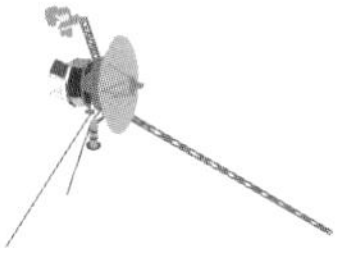

⑪ **la sonda espacial**
space probe

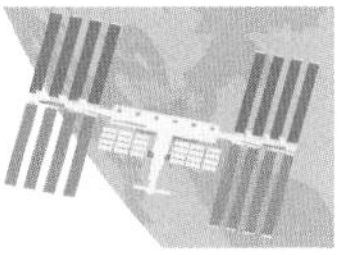

⑫ **la estación espacial**
space station

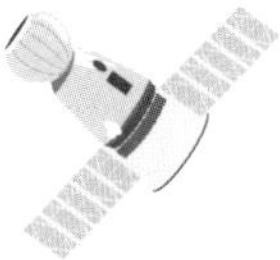

⑬ **la nave espacial**
spacecraft

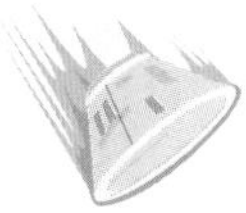

⑭ **el módulo de descenso**
descent module

㉑ **el astronauta** *m*
la astronauta *f*
astronaut

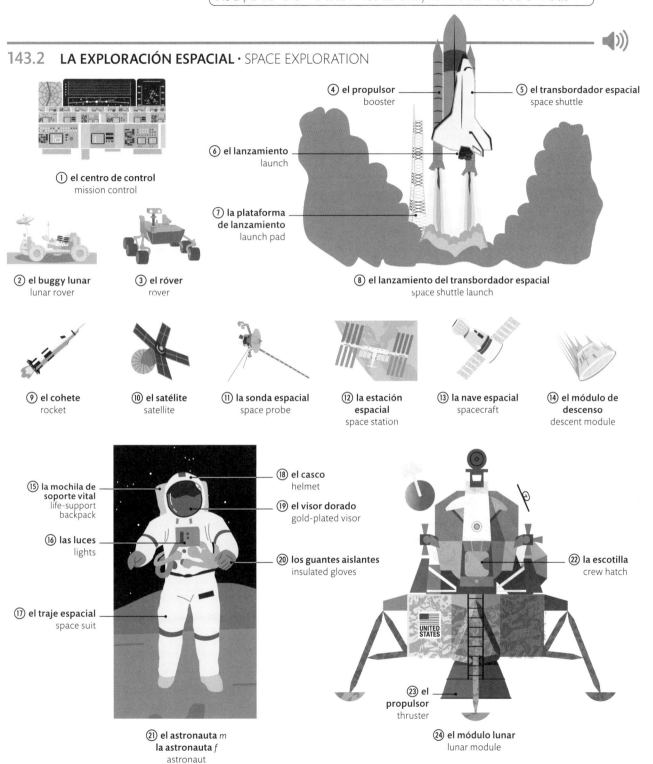

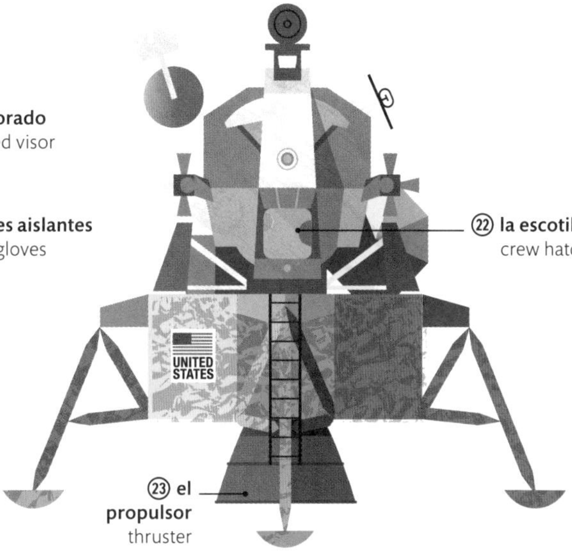

㉔ **el módulo lunar**
lunar module

144 El espacio (continuación)

Space continued

144.1 LA ASTRONOMÍA · ASTRONOMY

① **los prismáticos**
binoculars

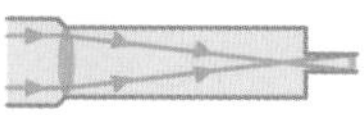

② **el telescopio refractor**
refractor telescope

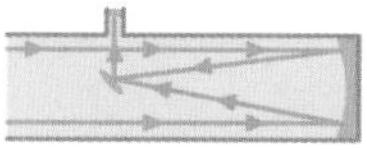

③ **el telescopio reflector**
reflector telescope

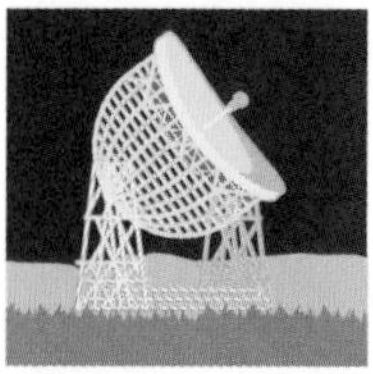

④ **el radiotelescopio**
radio telescope

⑤ **el observatorio**
observatory

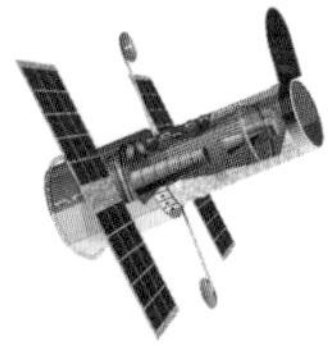

⑥ **el telescopio espacial**
space telescope

⑦ **la constelación**
constellation

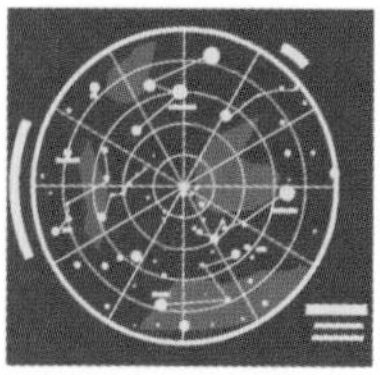

⑧ **el mapa celeste**
star chart

⑨ Acabo de avistar un cometa.
I've just spotted a comet.

⑩ **el ocular**
eyepiece

⑪ **el buscador**
finderscope

⑫ **el cometa**
comet

⑬ **el trípode**
tripod

⑭ **el tornillo de enfoque**
focusing knob

⑮ **el telescopio**
telescope

144.2 LAS ESTRELLAS Y CONSTELACIONES · STARS AND CONSTELLATIONS

① **la gravedad**
gravity

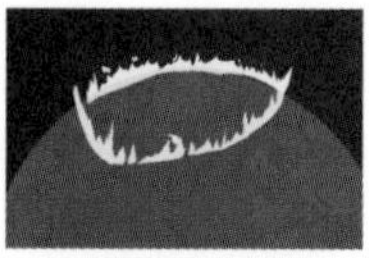

② **la aurora**
aurora

③ **la estrella**
star

④ **la estrella fulgurante**
flare

⑤ **la estrella doble**
double star

⑥ **la estrella de neutrones**
neutron star

⑬ **la Estrella Polar**
the Pole Star / Polaris

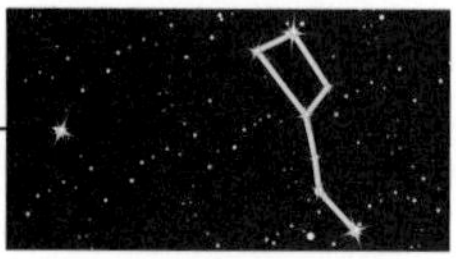

⑭ **la Osa Mayor**
the Plough

⑮ **la Cruz del Sur**
the Southern Cross

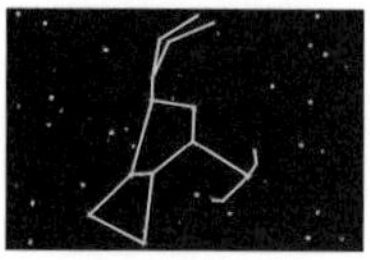

⑯ **Orión** *m*
Orion

⑰ **la gigante roja**
red giant

⑱ **la enana blanca**
white dwarf

See also
74 Las matemáticas • Mathematics **75** La física • Physics **83** Los ordenadores y la tecnología • Computers and technology **145** El planeta Tierra • Planet Earth **156** Las rocas y los minerales • Rocks and minerals

144.3 EL ZODÍACO • THE ZODIAC

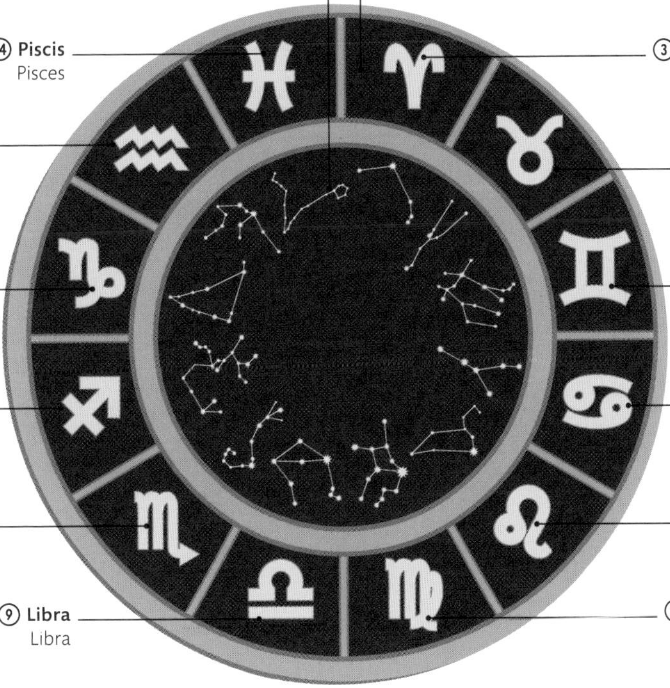

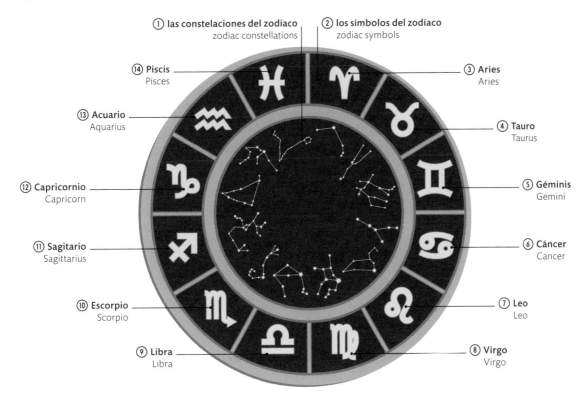

① **las constelaciones del zodíaco** zodiac constellations
② **los símbolos del zodíaco** zodiac symbols
③ **Aries** Aries
④ **Tauro** Taurus
⑤ **Géminis** Gemini
⑥ **Cáncer** Cancer
⑦ **Leo** Leo
⑧ **Virgo** Virgo
⑨ **Libra** Libra
⑩ **Escorpio** Scorpio
⑪ **Sagitario** Sagittarius
⑫ **Capricornio** Capricorn
⑬ **Acuario** Aquarius
⑭ **Piscis** Pisces

⑦ **la supernova** supernova

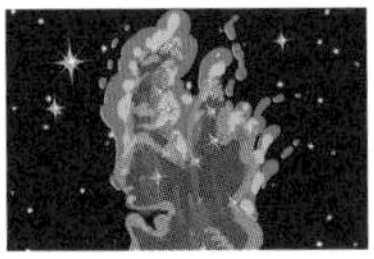

⑧ **la nebulosa** nebula

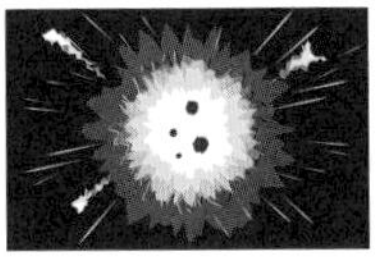

⑨ **el Big Bang** the Big Bang

⑩ **el cúmulo estelar** star cluster

⑪ **la galaxia elíptica** elliptical galaxy

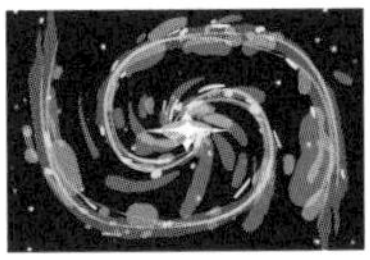

⑫ **la galaxia espiral** spiral galaxy

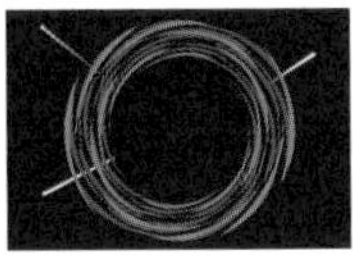

⑲ **el agujero negro** black hole

⑳ **el meteoro** meteor

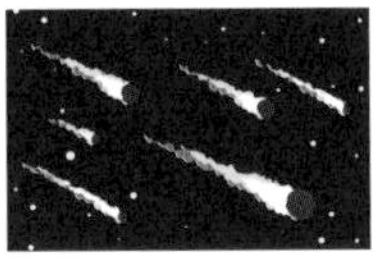

㉑ **la lluvia de meteoros** meteor shower

㉒ **la Vía Láctea** the Milky Way

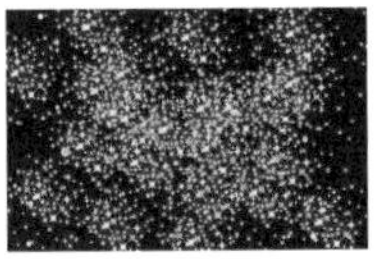

㉓ **el universo** the universe

145 El planeta Tierra
Planet Earth

145.1 LA TIERRA · THE EARTH

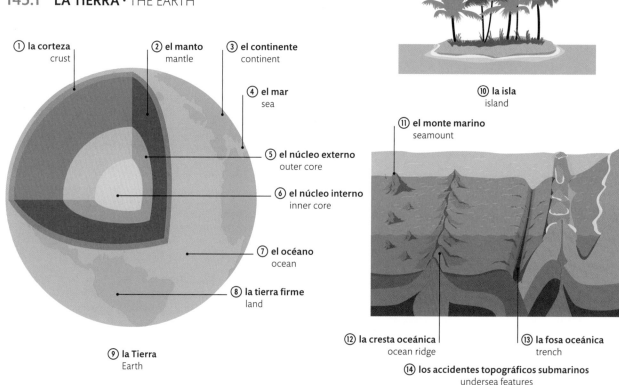

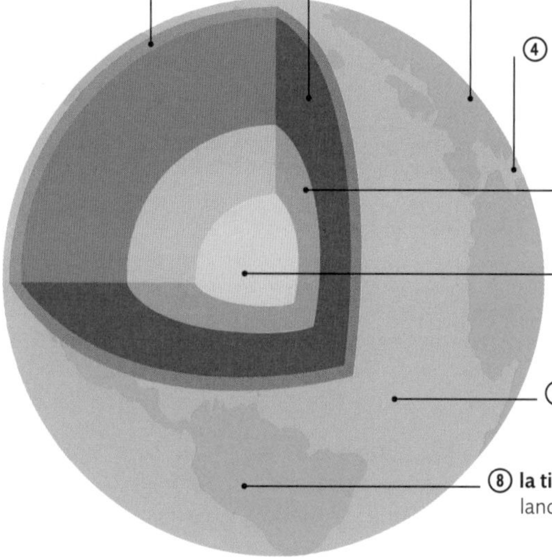

⑨ **la Tierra**
Earth

⑩ **la isla**
island

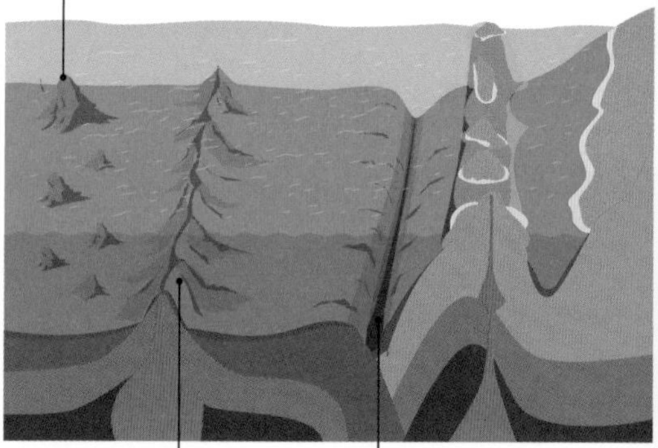

⑭ **los accidentes topográficos submarinos**
undersea features

145.2 LAS PLACAS TECTÓNICAS · PLATE TECTONICS

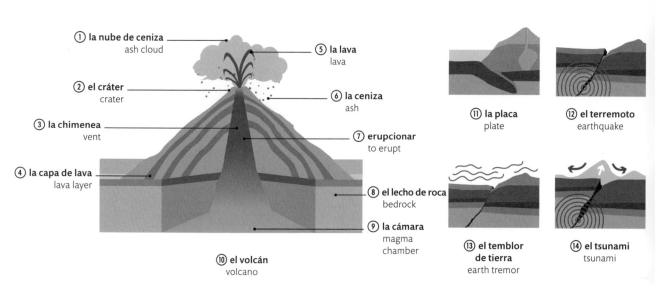

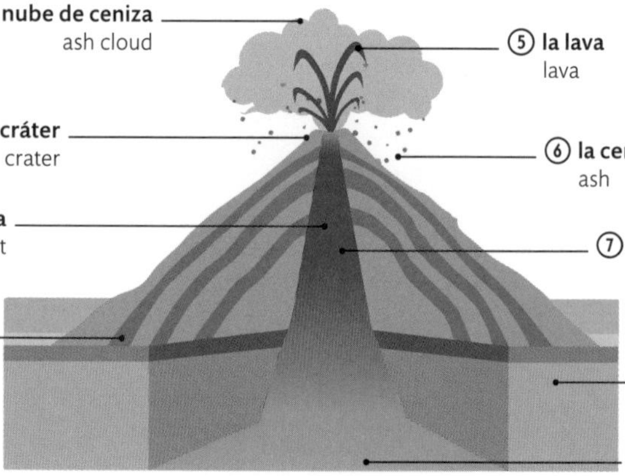

⑩ **el volcán**
volcano

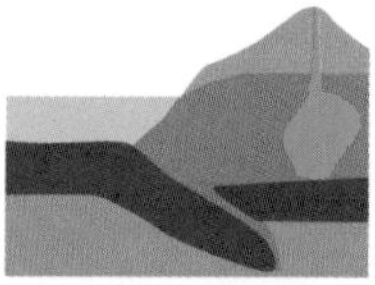

⑪ **la placa**
plate

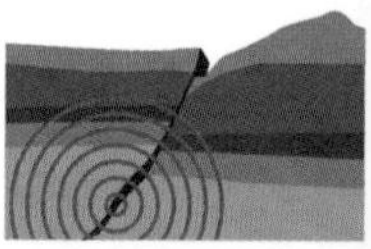

⑫ **el terremoto**
earthquake

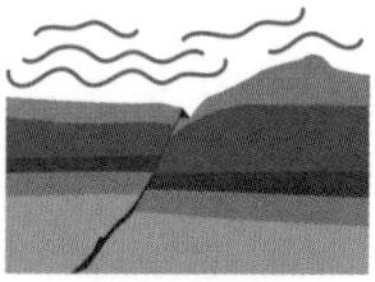

⑬ **el temblor de tierra**
earth tremor

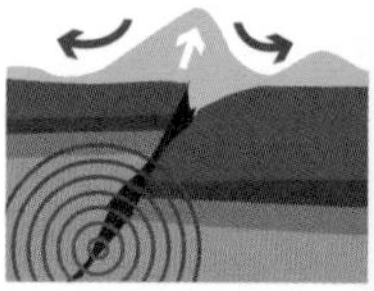

⑭ **el tsunami**
tsunami

See also
143-144 El espacio • Space **146-147** La geografía • Geography **148** Los mapas y las indicaciones • Maps and directions **149-151** Los países • Countries

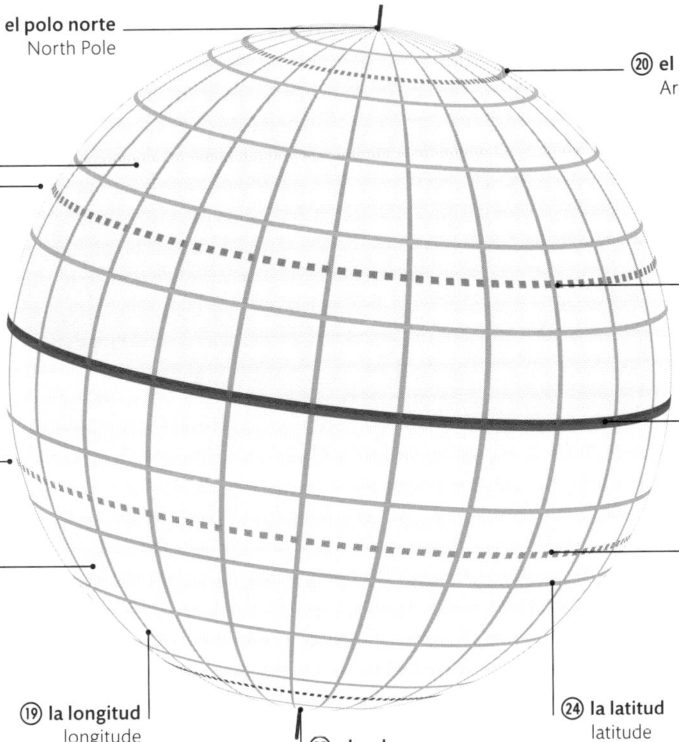

145.3 LOS ACCIDENTES Y FENÓMENOS HIDROLÓGICOS • WATER FEATURES AND PHENOMENA

① **las cataratas Victoria**
Victoria Falls

② **Hang Son Doong**
Hang Son Doong

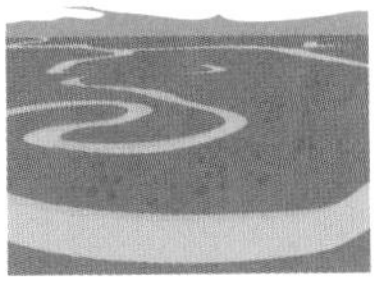
③ **el Amazonas**
the Amazon

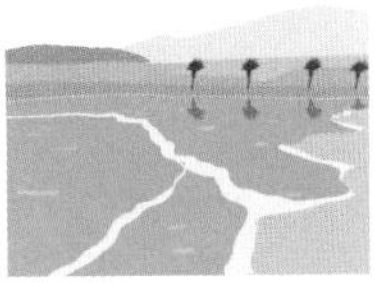
④ **el mar Muerto**
the Dead Sea

⑤ **Caño Cristales**
Caño Cristales

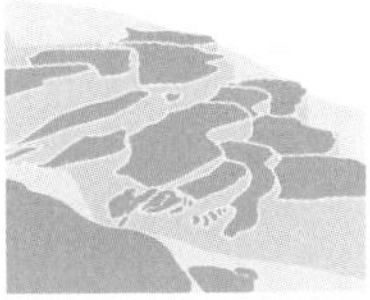
⑥ **Pamukkale**
Pamukkale

⑦ **la Gran Barrera de Coral**
the Barrier Reef

⑧ **el Ganges**
the Ganges

⑨ **Salto Ángel**
Angel Falls

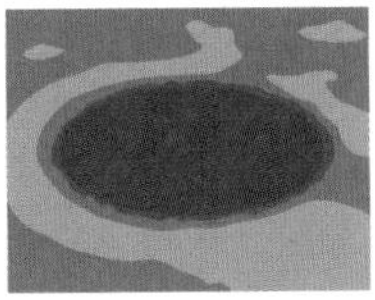
⑩ **el Gran Agujero Azul**
the Great Blue Hole

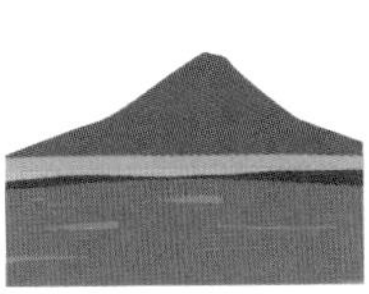
⑪ **el lago Natron**
Lake Natron

⑫ **el lago Moteado**
Spotted Lake

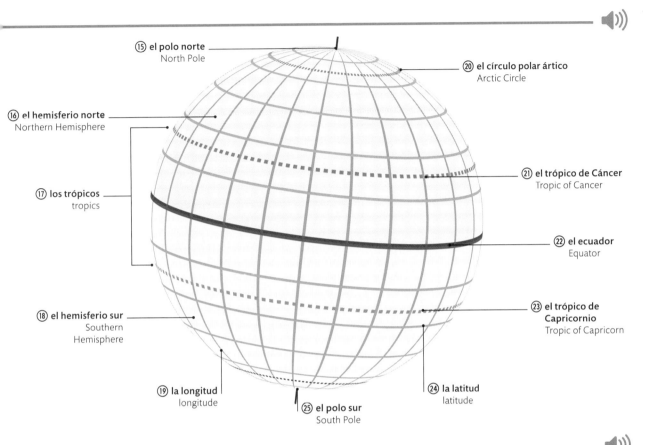

146 La geografía

Geography

146.1 LAS CARACTERÍSTICAS GEOGRÁFICAS Y EL PAISAJE · GEOGRAPHICAL FEATURES AND LANDSCAPE

① **el bosque**
wood

② **la selva tropical**
rain forest

③ **el bosque de coníferas**
coniferous forest

④ **el bosque caducifolio**
deciduous forest

⑤ **los rápidos**
rapids

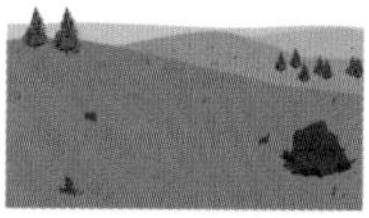

⑥ **la campiña**
countryside

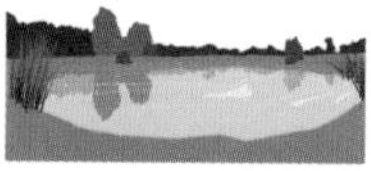

⑦ **el lago**
lake

⑧ **el pantano**
swamp

⑨ **la catarata**
waterfall

⑩ **el campo**
field

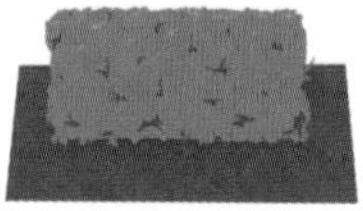

⑪ **el seto**
hedge

⑫ **el valle**
valley

⑬ **la tierra de labranza**
farmland

⑭ **el humedal**
wetlands

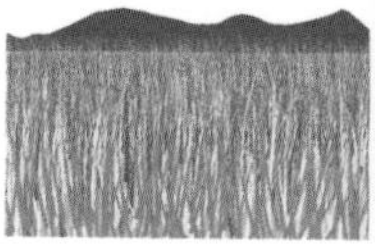

⑮ **el herbazal**
grassland

⑯ **la pradera**
prairie

⑰ **la estepa**
steppe

⑱ **la meseta**
mesa

⑲ **la zona montañosa**
highland

⑳ **la cresta**
ridge

㉑ **la cordillera**
mountain range

㉒ **la sabana**
savannah

㉓ **la cadena montañosa**
chain

㉔ **el géiser**
geyser

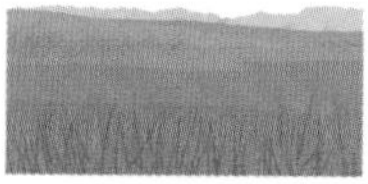

㉕ **la llanura**
plain

㉖ **el oasis**
oasis

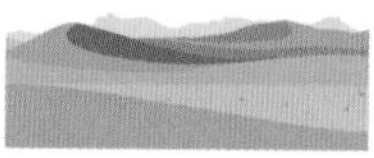

㉗ **el desierto**
desert

㉘ **la duna**
sand dune

See also
133 Las actividades al aire libre • Outdoor activites **145** El planeta Tierra • Planet Earth **147** La geografía (continuación) • Geography continued **148** Los mapas y las indicaciones • Maps and directions **149-151** Los países • Countries

(29) **el cañón**
canyon

(30) **el iceberg**
iceberg

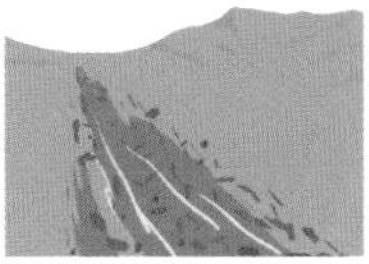

(31) **el flujo de lodo**
mudslide

(32) **el corrimiento de tierra**
landslide

(33) **el altiplano**
plateau

(34) **las regiones polares**
polar region

(35) **la tundra**
tundra

(36) **el glaciar**
glacier

146.2 LAS CUEVAS Y LA ESPELEOLOGÍA • CAVES AND CAVING

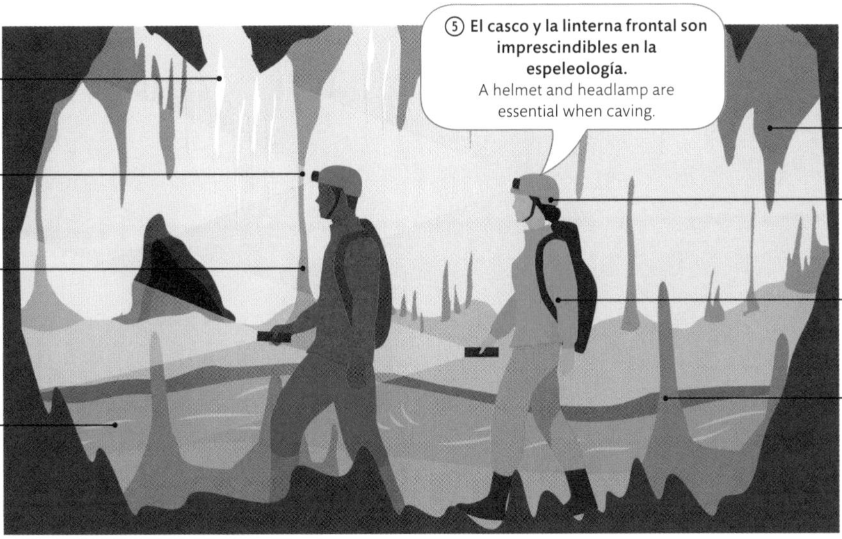
(1) el carámbano
icicle
(2) la linterna frontal
headlamp
(3) la columna
column
(4) el río subterráneo
subterranean stream
(5) El casco y la linterna frontal son imprescindibles en la espeleología.
A helmet and headlamp are essential when caving.
(6) la estalactita
stalactite
(7) el casco
helmet
(8) el espeleólogo m
la espeleóloga f
caver
(9) la estalagmita
stalagmite

147 La geografía (continuación)
Geography continued

147.1 **LOS ACCIDENTES COSTEROS** · COASTAL FEATURES

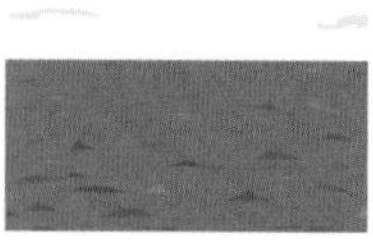

① **el océano**
ocean

② **la ola**
wave

③ **la duna**
dune

④ **la isla**
island

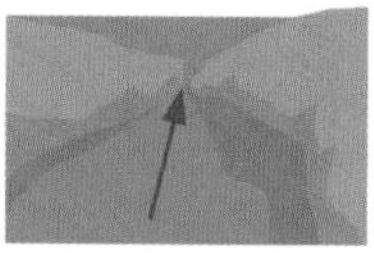

⑤ **el estrecho**
strait

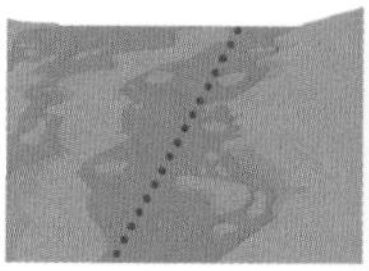

⑥ **el canal**
channel

⑦ **la marea alta**
high tide

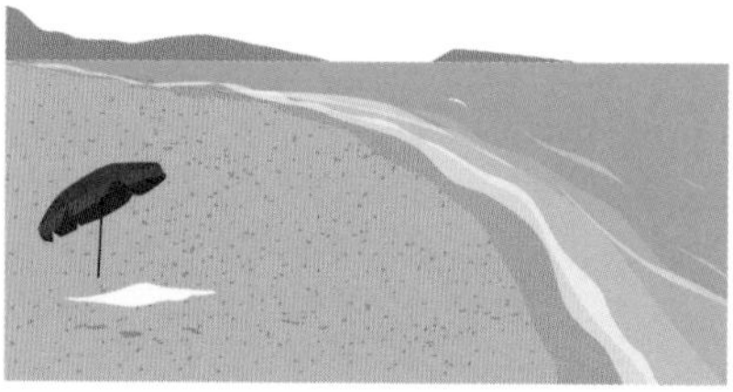

⑧ **la marea baja**
low tide

⑨ **el arrecife**
reef

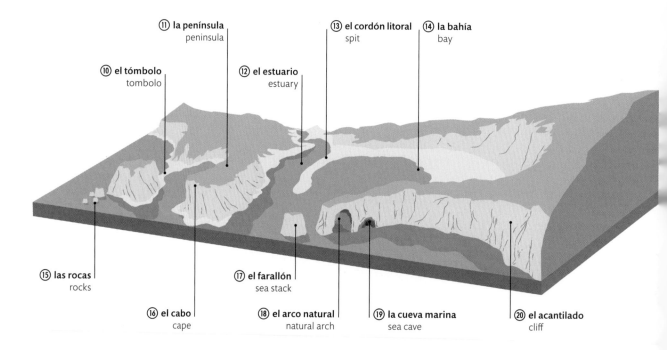

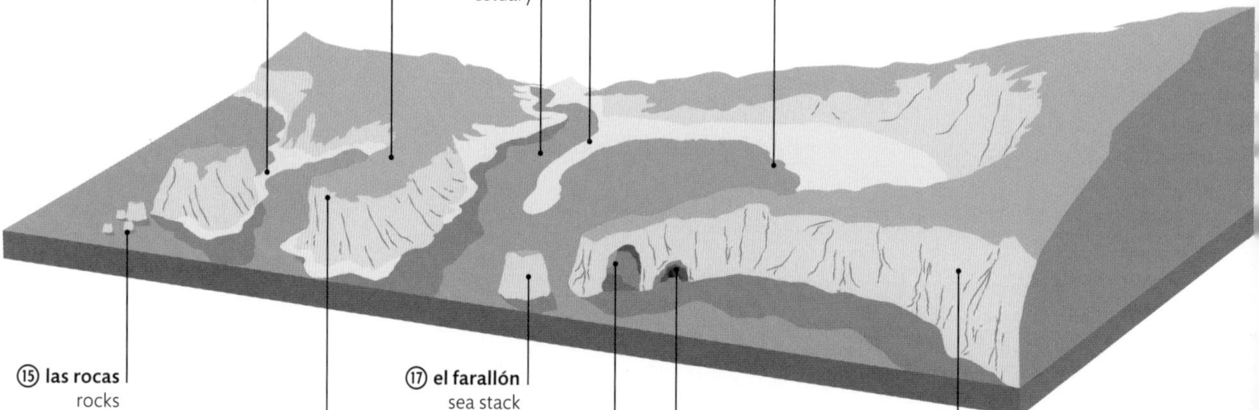

See also
133 Las actividades al aire libre • Outdoor activities **145** El planeta Tierra • Planet Earth
148 Los mapas y las indicaciones • Maps and directions **149-151** Los países • Countries

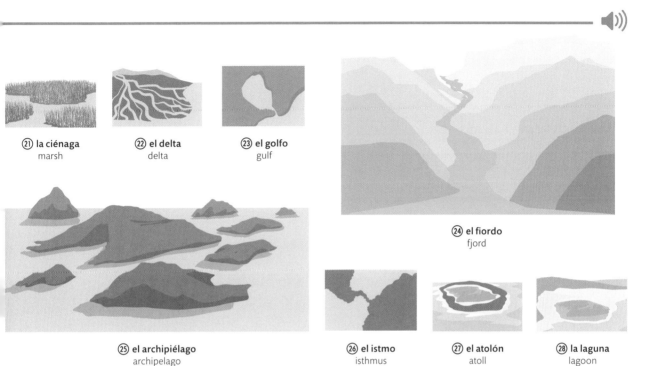

21 **la ciénaga**
marsh

22 **el delta**
delta

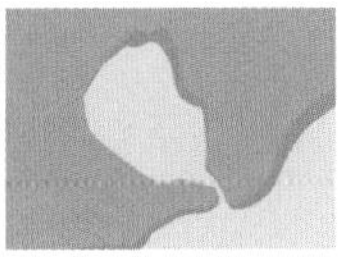

23 **el golfo**
gulf

24 **el fiordo**
fjord

25 **el archipiélago**
archipelago

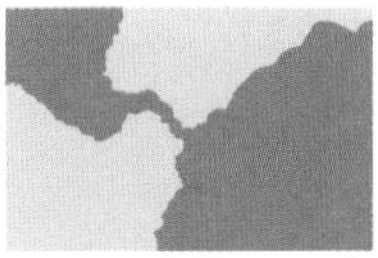

26 **el istmo**
isthmus

27 **el atolón**
atoll

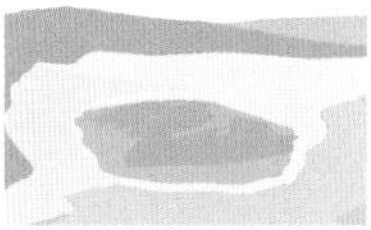

28 **la laguna**
lagoon

147.2 LAS CARACTERÍSTICAS DEL RÍO • RIVER FEATURES

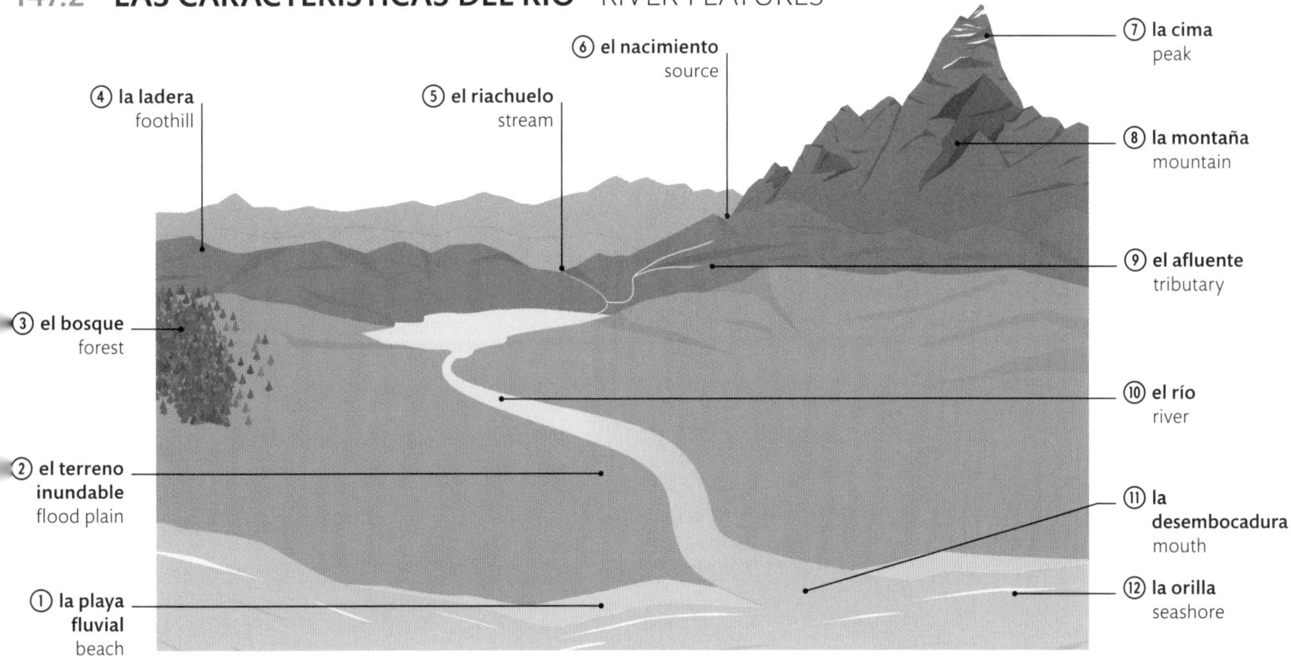

148 Los mapas y las indicaciones
Maps and directions

148.1 LEYENDO EL MAPA · READING A MAP

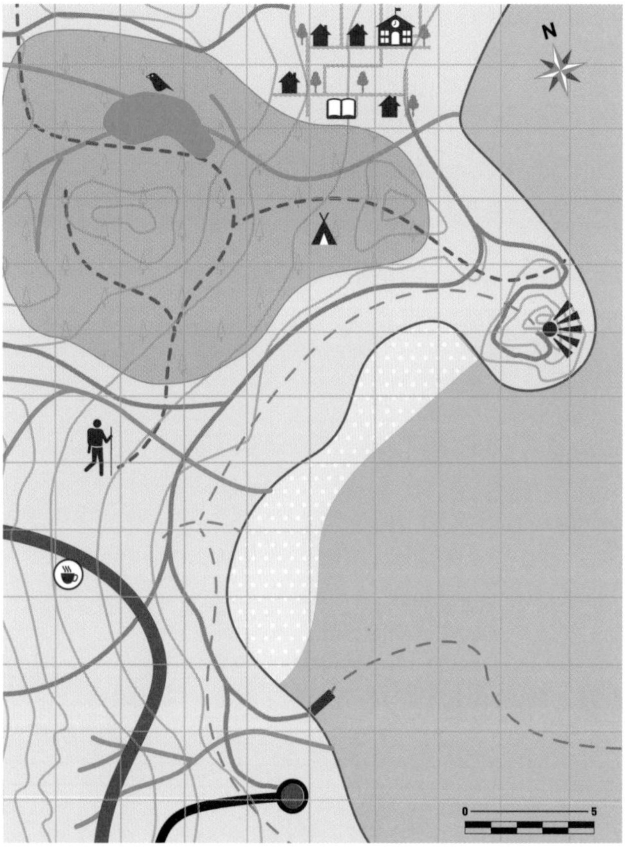

① **el mapa**
map

③ **el norte**
north

⑩ **el noroeste**
northwest

④ **el noreste**
northeast

⑨ **el oeste**
west

⑤ **el este**
east

⑧ **el suroeste**
southwest

⑥ **el sureste**
southeast

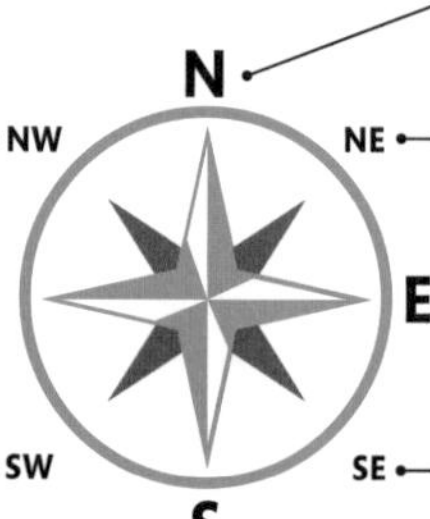

⑦ **el sur**
south

② **la brújula**
compass

⑪ **la carretera principal**
main road

⑫ **la carretera secundaria**
secondary road

⑬ **el sendero público**
public footpath

⑭ **la vía férrea**
railway

⑮ **la estación de tren**
train station

⑯ **el campamento**
campsite

⑰ **la estación de servicio**
service station

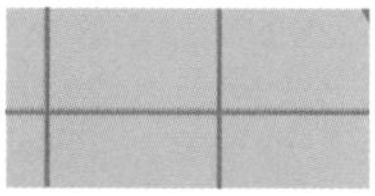

⑱ **la cuadrícula**
grid lines

⑲ **la reserva natural**
nature reserve

⑳ **el mirador**
viewpoint

㉑ **la ruta senderista**
walking trail

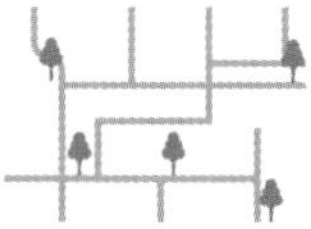

㉒ **el pueblo**
town

㉓ **la casa / el edificio**
house / building

㉔ **la escuela**
school

㉕ **la biblioteca**
library

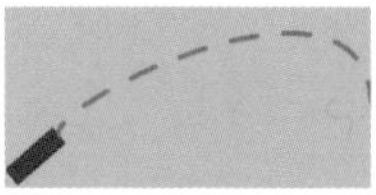

㉖ **la ruta de ferri**
ferry route

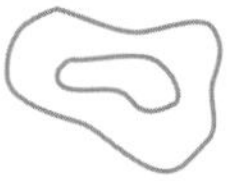

㉗ **la curva de nivel**
contours

㉘ **el río**
river

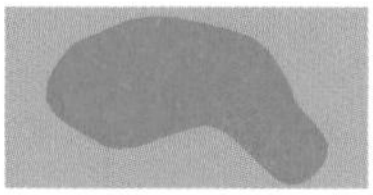

㉙ **el lago**
lake

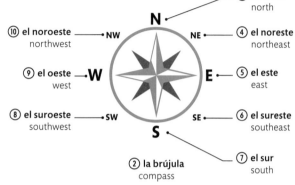

㉚ **el bosque**
forest

㉛ **la playa**
beach

See also
96 Las carreteras • Roads **133** Las actividades al aire libre • Outdoor activities **145** El planeta Tierra • Planet Earth **146-147** La geografía • Geography **150-153** Los países • Countries

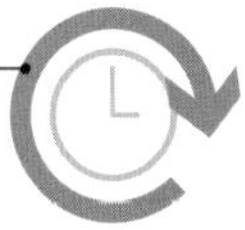

㉜ **en el sentido de las agujas del reloj**
clockwise

㉝ **en el sentido contrario a las agujas del reloj**
anticlockwise

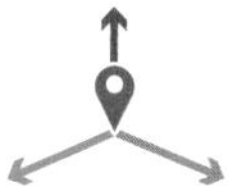

㉞ **las coordenadas**
coordinates

㉟ **la orientación**
orienteering

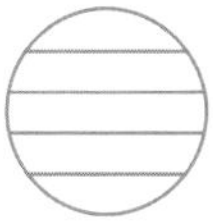

㊱ **la latitud**
latitude

㊲ **la longitud**
longitude

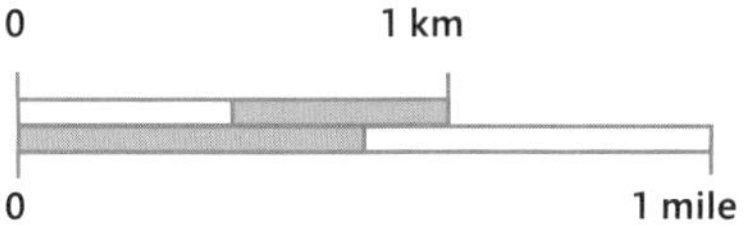

㊳ **la escala**
scale

㊴ **el cartógrafo** *m*
la cartógrafa *f*
cartographer

㊵ **el mapa en línea**
online map

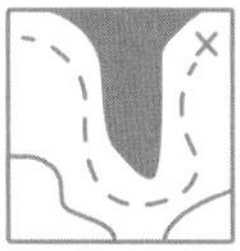

㊶ **el mapa de senderismo**
hiking map

㊷ **el mapa de carretera**
streetmap

148.2 LAS PREPOSICIONES DE LUGAR • PREPOSITIONS OF PLACE

① **junto a**
next to / beside

② **frente a**
opposite

③ **entre**
between

④ **en la esquina**
on the corner

⑤ **en frente de**
in front of

⑥ **detrás de**
behind

⑦ **a la izquierda**
on the left

⑧ **a la derecha**
on the right

148.3 LOS VERBOS DE DIRECCIÓN • DIRECTION VERBS

① **girar a la izquierda**
to go left / to turn left

② **girar a la derecha**
to go right / to turn right

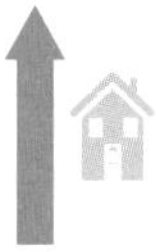

③ **seguir recto**
to go straight ahead / on

④ **dar media vuelta**
to go back

⑤ **pasar (el restaurante)**
to go past (the restaurant)

⑥ **girar en la primera calle a la izquierda**
to take the first left

⑦ **girar en la segunda calle a la derecha**
to take the second right

⑧ **parar en (el hotel)**
to stop at (the hotel)

⑨ **planificar la ruta**
to plan your route

⑩ **perderse**
to lose your way

⑪ **leer el mapa**
to read a map

⑫ **preguntar la dirección**
to ask directions

149 Los países
Countries

149.1 ÁFRICA • AFRICA

① **Marruecos** *m*
Morocco

② **Mauritania** *f*
Mauritania

③ **Cabo Verde** *m*
Cape Verde

④ **Senegal** *m*
Senegal

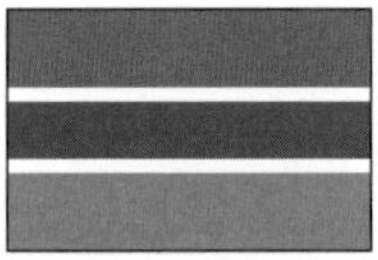
⑤ **Gambia** *f*
Gambia

⑥ **Guinea-Bisáu** *f*
Guinea-Bissau

⑦ **Guinea** *f*
Guinea

⑧ **Sierra Leona** *f*
Sierra Leone

⑨ **Liberia** *f*
Liberia

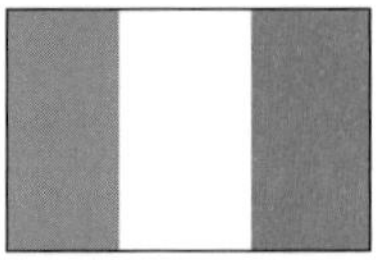
⑩ **Costa de Marfil** *f*
Ivory Coast

⑪ **Burkina Faso** *m*
Burkina Faso

⑫ **Mali** *m*
Mali

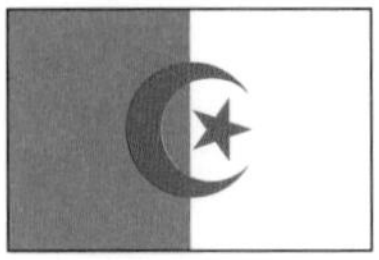
⑬ **Argelia** *f*
Algeria

⑭ **Túnez** *m*
Tunisia

⑮ **Libia** *f*
Libya

⑯ **Níger** *m*
Niger

⑰ **Ghana** *f*
Ghana

⑱ **Togo** *m*
Togo

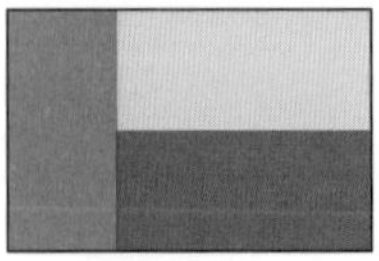
⑲ **Benín** *m*
Benin

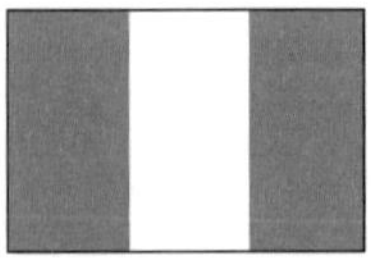
⑳ **Nigeria** *f*
Nigeria

㉑ **Santo Tomé y Príncipe** *m*
São Tomé and Príncipe

㉒ **Guinea Ecuatorial** *f*
Equatorial Guinea

㉓ **Gabón** *m*
Gabon

㉔ **Camerún** *m*
Cameroon

㉕ **Chad** *m*
Chad

㉖ **Ruanda** *f*
Rwanda

㉗ **Burundi** *m*
Burundi

㉘ **Tanzania** *f*
Tanzania

㉙ **Mozambique** *m*
Mozambique

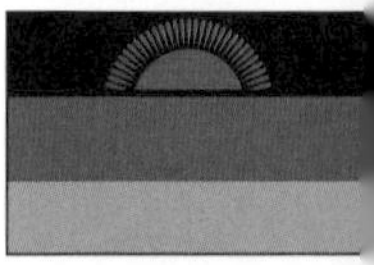
㉚ **Malaui** *m*
Malawi

㉛ **República del Congo** *f*
Republic of the Congo

㉜ **República Democrática del Congo** *f*
Democratic Republic of the Congo

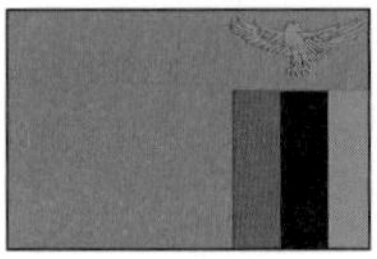
㉝ **Zambia** *f*
Zambia

㉞ **Angola** *f*
Angola

㉟ **Namibia** *f*
Namibia

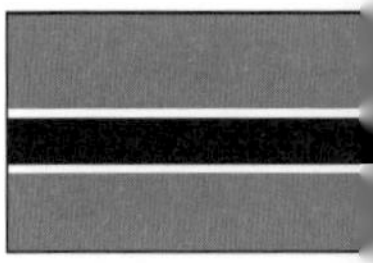
㊱ **Botsuana** *f*
Botswana

See also
145 El planeta Tierra • Planet Earth **146-147** La geografía • Geography **148** Los mapas y las indicaciones • Maps and directions **150-151** Los países (continuación) Countries continued **152-153** Las nacionalidades • Nationalities

㊲ **Zimbabue** *m*
Zimbabwe

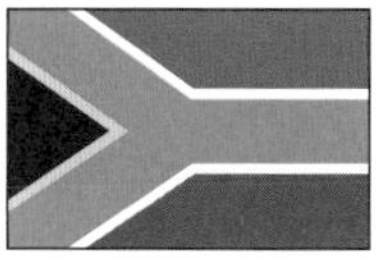

㊳ **Sudáfrica** *f*
South Africa

㊴ **Lesoto** *m*
Lesotho

㊵ **Comoras** *f, pl*
Comoros

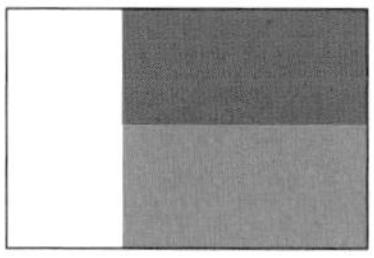

㊶ **Madagascar** *m*
Madagascar

㊷ **Egipto** *m*
Egypt

㊸ **Sudán** *m*
Sudan

㊹ **Sudán del Sur** *m*
South Sudan

㊺ **Etiopía** *f*
Ethiopia

㊻ **Eritrea** *f*
Eritrea

㊼ **Somalia** *f*
Somalia

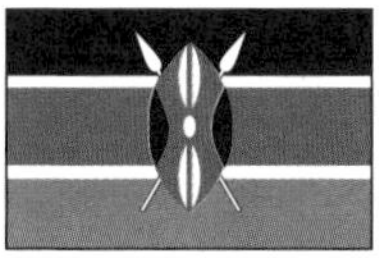

㊽ **Kenia** *f*
Kenya

㊾ **Uganda** *f*
Uganda

㊿ **Yibuti** *m*
Djibouti

(51) **Islas Seychelles** *f, pl*
Seychelles

(52) **Islas Mauricio** *f, pl*
Mauritius

(53) **República Centroafricana** *f*
Central African Republic

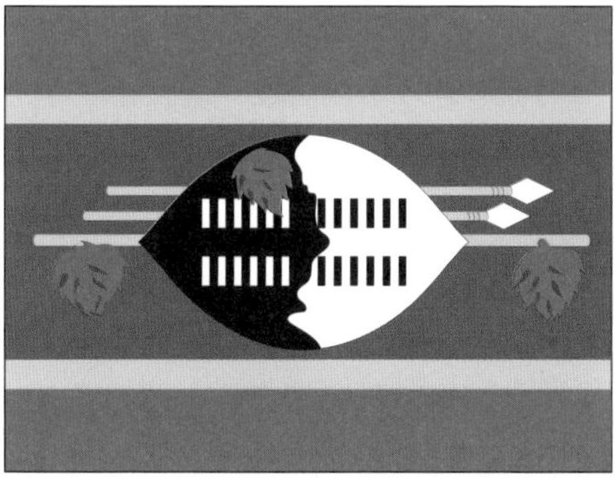

(54) **Suazilandia** *f*
Eswatini

149.2 SUDAMÉRICA
SOUTH AMERICA

① **Venezuela** *f*
Venezuela

② **Colombia** *f*
Colombia

③ **Brasil** *m*
Brazil

④ **Bolivia** *f*
Bolivia

⑤ **Ecuador** *m*
Ecuador

⑥ **Perú** *m*
Peru

⑦ **Chile** *m*
Chile

⑧ **Argentina** *f*
Argentina

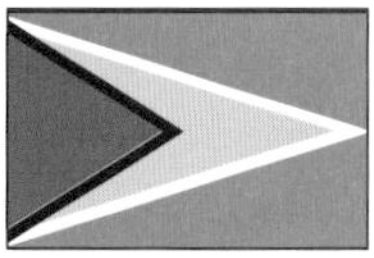

⑨ **Guyana** *f*
Guyana

⑩ **Surinam** *m*
Suriname

⑪ **Paraguay** *m*
Paraguay

⑫ **Uruguay** *m*
Uruguay

150 Los países (continuación)
Countries continued

150.1 AMÉRICA DEL NORTE, AMÉRICA CENTRAL Y EL CARIBE • NORTH AND CENTRAL AMERICA AND THE CARIBBEAN

① **Canadá** *m*
Canada

② **Estados Unidos de América** *m, pl*
United States of America

③ **México** *m*
Mexico

④ **Guatemala** *f*
Guatemala

⑤ **Belice** *m*
Belize

⑥ **El Salvador** *m*
El Salvador

⑧ **Honduras** *f*
Honduras

⑨ **Nicaragua** *f*
Nicaragua

⑩ **Costa Rica** *f*
Costa Rica

⑪ **Panamá** *f*
Panama

⑫ **Cuba** *f*
Cuba

⑬ **Islas Bahamas** *f, pl*
Bahamas

⑮ **Jamaica** *f*
Jamaica

⑯ **Haití** *m*
Haiti

⑰ **República Dominicana** *f*
Dominican Republic

⑱ **Barbados** *f*
Barbados

⑲ **Trinidad y Tobago** *f*
Trinidad and Tobago

⑳ **San Cristóbal y Nieves** *m*
St. Kitts and Nevis

㉒ **Dominica** *f*
Dominica

㉓ **Antigua y Barbuda** *f*
Antigua and Barbuda

150.2 OCEANÍA • OCEANIA

① **Papúa Nueva Guinea** *f*
Papua New Guinea

② **Australia** *f*
Australia

③ **Nueva Zelanda** *f*
New Zealand

④ **Islas Marshall** *f, pl*
Marshall Islands

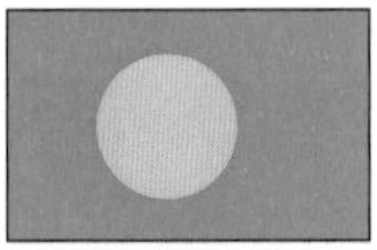
⑤ **Palaos** *m*
Palau

⑥ **Micronesia** *f*
Micronesia

⑧ **Nauru** *m*
Nauru

⑨ **Kiribati** *f, pl*
Kiribati

⑩ **Tuvalu** *m*
Tuvalu

⑪ **Samoa** *f*
Samoa

⑫ **Tonga** *f*
Tonga

⑬ **Vanuatu** *m*
Vanuatu

See also
145 El planeta Tierra • Planet Earth **146-147** La geografía • Geography **148** Los mapas y las indicaciones • Maps and directions **151** Los países (continuación) Countries continued **152-153** Las nacionalidades • Nationalities

⑦ **Granada** *f*
Grenada

⑭ **Santa Lucía** *f*
St Lucia

㉑ **San Vicente y las Granadinas** *f, pl*
St. Vincent and The Grenadines

⑦ **Islas Salomón** *f, pl*
Solomon Islands

⑭ **Islas Fiyi** *f, pl*
Fiji

150.3 ASIA • ASIA

① **Turquía** *f*
Türkiye

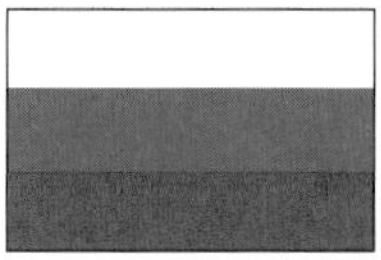
② **Federación Rusa** *f*
Russian Federation

③ **Georgia** *f*
Georgia

④ **Armenia** *f*
Armenia

⑤ **Azerbaiyán** *m*
Azerbaijan

⑥ **Irak** *m*
Iraq

⑦ **Siria** *f*
Syria

⑧ **Líbano** *m*
Lebanon

⑨ **Israel** *m*
Israel

⑩ **Jordania** *f*
Jordan

⑪ **Pakistán** *m*
Pakistan

⑫ **India** *f*
India

⑬ **Maldivas** *f, pl*
Maldives

⑭ **Sri Lanka** *f*
Sri Lanka

⑮ **China** *f*
China

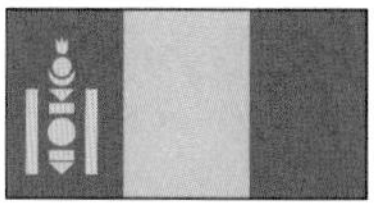
⑯ **Mongolia** *f*
Mongolia

⑰ **Corea del Norte** *f*
North Korea

⑱ **Corea del Sur** *f*
South Korea

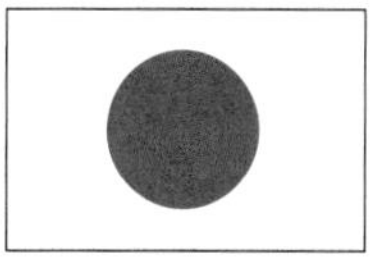
⑲ **Japón** *m*
Japan

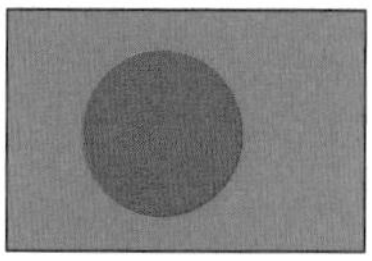
⑳ **Bangladés** *m*
Bangladesh

㉑ **Bután** *m*
Bhutan

㉒ **Birmania** *f*
Myanmar (Burma)

㉓ **Tailandia** *f*
Thailand

㉔ **Laos** *m*
Laos

㉕ **Vietnam** *m*
Vietnam

㉖ **Camboya** *f*
Cambodia

㉗ **Nepal** *m*
Nepal

151 Los países (continuación)

Countries continued

151.1 ASIA (CONTINUACIÓN) • ASIA CONTINUED

① **Singapur** *m*
Singapore

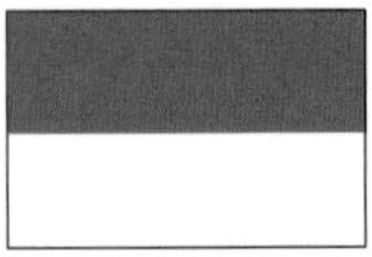

② **Indonesia** *f*
Indonesia

③ **Brunéi** *m*
Brunei

④ **Filipinas** *f, pl*
Philippines

⑤ **Timor Oriental** *m*
East Timor

⑥ **Malasia** *f*
Malaysia

⑦ **Emiratos Árabes Unidos** *m, pl*
United Arab Emirates

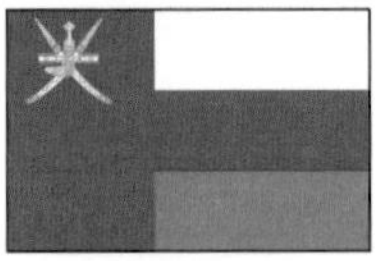

⑧ **Omán** *m*
Oman

⑨ **Baréin** *m*
Bahrain

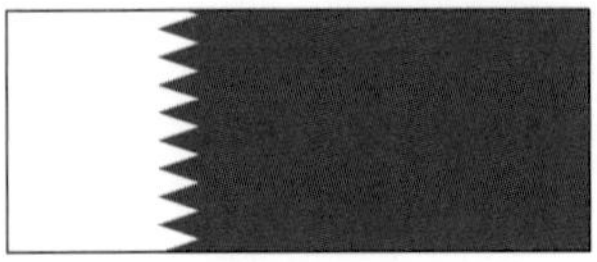

⑩ **Catar** *m*
Qatar

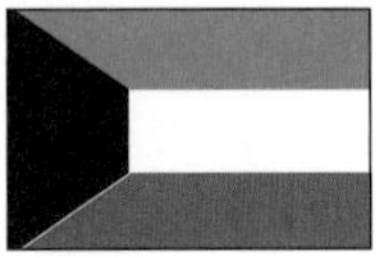

⑪ **Kuwait** *m*
Kuwait

⑫ **Irán** *m*
Iran

⑬ **Yemen** *m*
Yemen

⑭ **Arabia Saudí** *f*
Saudi Arabia

⑮ **Uzbekistán** *m*
Uzbekistan

⑯ **Turkmenistán** *m*
Turkmenistan

⑰ **Afganistán** *m*
Afghanistan

⑱ **Tayikistán** *m*
Tajikistan

⑲ **Kirguistán** *m*
Kyrgyzstan

⑳ **Kazajistán** *m*
Kazakhstan

151.2 EUROPA • EUROPE

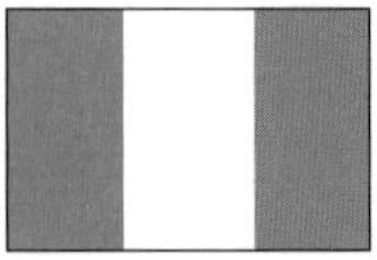

① **Irlanda** *f*
Ireland

② **Reino Unido** *m*
United Kingdom

⑨ **Bélgica** *f*
Belgium

⑩ **Países Bajos** *m, pl*
Netherlands

⑰ **Portugal** *m*
Portugal

⑱ **España** *f*
Spain

㉕ **Luxemburgo** *m*
Luxembourg

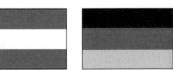

㉖ **Alemania** *f*
Germany

㉝ **Andorra** *f*
Andorra

㉞ **Francia** *f*
France

㊶ **Dinamarca** *f*
Denmark

㊷ **Noruega** *f*
Norway

See also
145 El planeta Tierra • Planet Earth **146-147** La geografía • Geography **148** Los mapas y las indicaciones • Maps and directions **152-153** Las nacionalidades • Nationalities

(3) **Suecia** *f*
Sweden

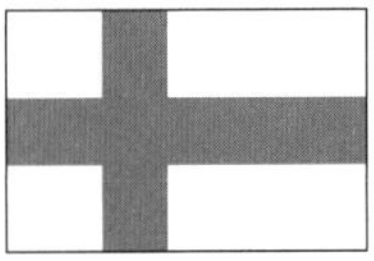

(4) **Finlandia** *f*
Finland

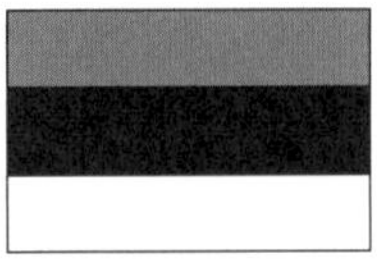

(5) **Estonia** *f*
Estonia

(6) **Letonia** *f*
Latvia

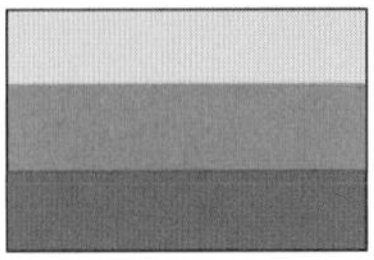

(7) **Lituania** *f*
Lithuania

(8) **Polonia** *f*
Poland

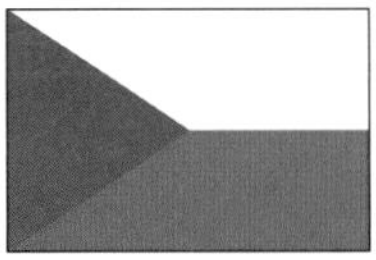

(11) **República Checa** *f*
Czech Republic

(12) **Austria** *f*
Austria

(13) **Liechtenstein** *m*
Liechtenstein

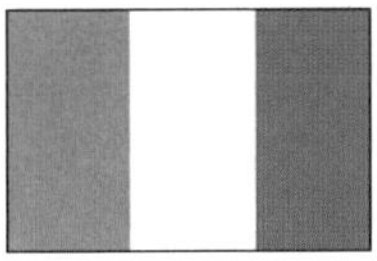

(14) **Italia** *f*
Italy

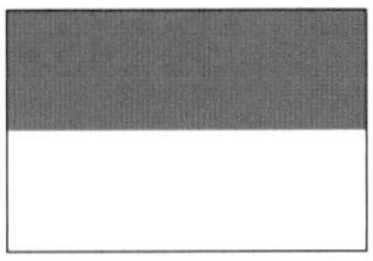

(15) **Mónaco** *m*
Monaco

(16) **San Marino** *m*
San Marino

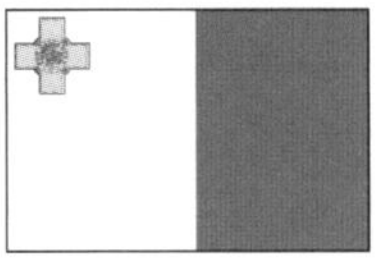

(19) **Malta** *f*
Malta

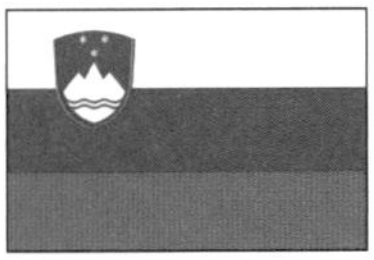

(20) **Eslovenia** *f*
Slovenia

(21) **Croacia** *f*
Croatia

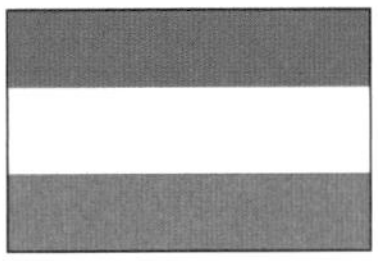

(22) **Hungría** *f*
Hungary

(23) **Eslovaquia** *f*
Slovakia

(24) **Ucrania** *f*
Ukraine

(27) **Bielorrusia** *f*
Belarus

(28) **Moldavia** *f*
Moldova

(29) **Rumanía** *f*
Romania

(30) **Serbia** *f*
Serbia

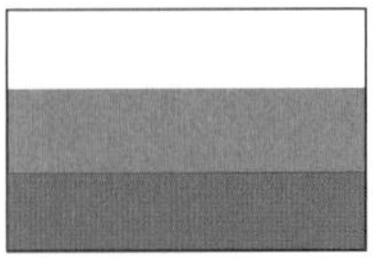

(31) **Bulgaria** *f*
Bulgaria

(32) **Albania** *f*
Albania

(35) **Grecia** *f*
Greece

(36) **Islandia** *f*
Iceland

(37) **Chipre** *m*
Cyprus

(38) **Montenegro** *m*
Montenegro

(39) **Ciudad del Vaticano** *f*
Vatican City

(40) **Turquía** *f*
Türkiye

(43) **Bosnia y Herzegovina** *f*
Bosnia and Herzegovina

(44) **Macedonia del Norte** *f*
North Macedonia

(45) **Suiza** *f*
Switzerland

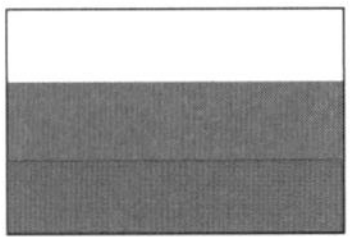

(46) **Federación Rusa** *f*
Russian Federation

Las nacionalidades
Nationalities

152.1 ÁFRICA · AFRICA

Country	Adjective	English Adjective
1 **Africa** Africa	**africano** *m* **africana** *f*	African
2 **Marruecos** Morocco	**marroquí** *m / f*	Moroccan
3 **Mauritania** Mauritania	**mauritano** *m* / **mauritana** *f*	Mauritanian
4 **Cabo Verde** Cape Verde	**caboverdiano** *m* **caboverdiana** *f*	Cape Verdean
5 **Senegal** Senegal	**senegalés** *m* / **senegalesa** *f*	Senegalese
6 **Gambia** Gambia	**gambiano** *m* / **gambiana** *f*	Gambian
7 **Guinea-Bisáu** Guinea-Bissau	**bisauguineano** *m* **bisauguineana** *f*	Bissau-Guinean
8 **Guinea** Guinea	**guineano** *m* / **guineana** *f*	Guinean
9 **Sierra Leona** Sierra Leone	**sierraleonés** *m* **sierraleonesa** *f*	Sierra Leonean
10 **Liberia** Liberia	**liberiano** *m* / **liberiano** *f*	Liberian
11 **Costa de Marfil** Ivory Coast	**marfileño** *m* / **marfileña** *f*	Ivorian
12 **Burkina Faso** Burkina Faso	**burkinés** *m* / **burkinesa** *f*	Burkinabe
13 **Mali** Mali	**maliense** *m / f*	Malian
14 **Argelia** Algeria	**argelino** *m* / **argelina** *f*	Algerian
15 **Túnez** Tunisia	**tunecino** *m* / **tunecina** *f*	Tunisian
16 **Libia** Libya	**libio** *m* / **libia** *f*	Libyan
17 **Níger** Niger	**nigerino** *m* / **nigerina** *f*	Nigerien
18 **Ghana** Ghana	**ghanés** *m* / **ghanesa** *f*	Ghanaian
19 **Togo** Togo	**togolés** *m* / **togolesa** *f*	Togolese
20 **Benín** Benin	**beninés** *m* / **beninesa** *f*	Beninese
21 **Nigeria** Nigeria	**nigeriano** *m* / **nigeriana** *f*	Nigerian
22 **Santo Tomé y Príncipe** São Tomé and Príncipe	**santotomense** *m / f*	São Toméan
23 **Guinea Ecuatorial** Equatorial Guinea	**ecuatoguineano** *m* **ecuatoguineana** *f*	Equatorial Guinean
24 **Camerún** Cameroon	**camerunés** *m* **camerunesa** *f*	Cameroonian
25 **Chad** Chad	**chadiano** *m* / **chadiana** *f*	Chadian
26 **Egipto** Egypt	**egipcio** *m* / **egipcia** *f*	Egyptian
27 **Sudán** Sudan	**sudanés** *m* / **sudanesa** *f*	Sudanese
28 **Sudán del Sur** South Sudan	**sursudanés** *m* **sursudanesa** *f*	South Sudanese
29 **Eritrea** Eritrea	**eritreo** *m* / **eritrea** *f*	Eritrean
30 **Yibuti** Djibouti	**yibutiano** *m* / **yibutiana** *f*	Djiboutian
31 **Etiopía** Ethiopia	**etíope** *m / f*	Ethiopian
32 **Somalia** Somalia	**somali** *m / f*	Somalian
33 **Kenia** Kenya	**keniano** *m* / **keniana** *f*	Kenyan
34 **Uganda** Uganda	**ugandés** *m* / **ugandesa** *f*	Ugandan
35 **República Centroafricana** Central African Republic	**centroafricano** *m* **centroafricana** *f*	Central African
36 **Gabón** Gabon	**gabonés** *m* / **gabonesa** *f*	Gabonese
37 **República del Congo** Republic of the Congo	**congoleño** *m* **congoleña** *f*	Congolese
38 **República Democrática del Congo** Democratic Republic of the Congo	**congoleño** *m* **congoleña** *f*	Congolese
39 **Ruanda** Rwanda	**ruandés** *m* / **ruandesa** *f*	Rwandan
40 **Burundi** Burundi	**burundés** *m* **burundesa** *f*	Burundian
41 **Tanzania** Tanzania	**tanzano** *m* / **tanzana** *f*	Tanzanian
42 **Mozambique** Mozambique	**mozambiqueño** *m* **mozambiqueña** *f*	Mozambican
43 **Malaui** Malawi	**malauí** *m / f*	Malawian
44 **Zambia** Zambia	**zambiano** *m* / **zambiana** *f*	Zambian
45 **Angola** Angola	**angoleño** *m* / **angoleña** *f*	Angolan
46 **Namibia** Namibia	**namibio** *m* / **namibia** *f*	Namibian
47 **Botsuana** Botswana	**botsuano** *m* / **botsuana** *f*	Botswanan
48 **Zimbabue** Zimbabwe	**zimbabuense** *m / f*	Zimbabwean
49 **Sudáfrica** South Africa	**sudafricano** *m* **sudafricana** *f*	South African
50 **Lesoto** Lesotho	**lesotense** *m / f*	Basotho
51 **Suazilandia** Eswatini	**suazi** *m / f*	Swazi
52 **Comoras** Comoros	**comorense** *m / f*	Comorans
53 **Madagascar** Madagascar	**malgache** *m / f*	Madagascan
54 **Seychelles** Seychelles	**seychellense**	Seychellois
55 **Mauricio** Mauritius	**mauriciano** *m* **mauriciana** *f*	Mauritian

See also
145 El planeta Tierra • Planet Earth **146-147** La geografía • Geography
148 Los mapas y las indicaciones • Maps and directions **149-151** Los países
Countries **153** Las nacionalidades (continuación) • Nationalities continued

152.2 SUDAMÉRICA • SOUTH AMERICA

Country	Adjective	English Adjective
① **Sudamérica** South America	**sudamericano** *m* **sudamericana** *f*	South American
② **Venezuela** Venezuela	**venezolano** *m* **venezolana** *f*	Venezuelan
③ **Colombia** Colombia	**colombiano** *m* **colombiana** *f*	Colombian
④ **Ecuador** Ecuador	**ecuatoriano** *m* **ecuatoriana** *f*	Ecuadorian
⑤ **Perú** Peru	**peruano** *m* / **peruana** *f*	Peruvian
⑥ **Guyana** Guyana	**guyaneso** *m* / **guyanesa** *f*	Guyanese
⑦ **Surinam** Suriname	**surinamés** *m* **surinamesa** *f*	Surinamese

Country	Adjective	English Adjective
⑧ **Brasil** Brazil	**brasileño** *m* / **brasileña** *f*	Brazilian
⑨ **Bolivia** Bolivia	**boliviano** *m* / **boliviana** *f*	Bolivian
⑩ **Chile** Chile	**chileno** *m* / **chilena** *f*	Chilean
⑪ **Argentina** Argentina	**argentino** *m* / **argentina** *f*	Argentinian
⑫ **Paraguay** Paraguay	**paraguayo** *m* **paraguaya** *f*	Paraguayan
⑬ **Uruguay** Uruguay	**uruguayo** *m* / **uruguaya** *f*	Uruguayan

152.3 AMÉRICA DEL NORTE, AMÉRICA CENTRAL Y EL CARIBE
NORTH AND CENTRAL AMERICA AND THE CARIBBEAN

Country	Adjective	English Adjective
① **América del Norte, América Central y el Caribe** North and Central America and the Caribbean	**norteamericano** *m* **norteamericana** *f* **centroamericano** *m* **centroamericana** *f* **caribeño** *m* / **caribeña** *f*	North American, Central American, and Caribbean
② **Canadá** Canada	**canadiense** *m* / *f*	Canadian
③ **Estados Unidos de América** United States of America	**estadounidense** *m* / *f*	American
④ **México** Mexico	**mexicano** *m* / **mexicana** *f*	Mexican
⑤ **Guatemala** Guatemala	**guatemalteco** *m* **guatemalteca** *f*	Guatemalan
⑥ **Belice** Belize	**beliceño** *m* / **beliceña** *f*	Belizean
⑦ **El Salvador** El Salvador	**salvadoreño** *m* **salvadoreña** *f*	Salvadoran
⑧ **Honduras** Honduras	**hondureño** *m* **hondureña** *f*	Honduran
⑨ **Nicaragua** Nicaragua	**nicaragüense** *m* / *f*	Nicaraguan
⑩ **Costa Rica** Costa Rica	**costarriqueño** *m* **costarriqueña** *f*	Costa Rican
⑪ **Panamá** Panama	**panameño** *m* **panameña** *f*	Panamanian
⑫ **Cuba** Cuba	**cubano** *m* / **cubana** *f*	Cuban
⑬ **Bahamas** Bahamas	**bahameño** *m* **bahameña** *f*	Bahamian

Country	Adjective	English Adjective
⑭ **Jamaica** Jamaica	**jamaicano** *m* **jamaicana** *f*	Jamaican
⑮ **Haití** Haiti	**haitiano** *m* / **haitiana** *f*	Haitian
⑯ **República Dominicana** Dominican Republic	**dominicano** *m* **dominicana** *f*	Dominican
⑰ **Barbados** Barbados	**barbadense** *m* / *f*	Barbadian
⑱ **Trinidad y Tobago** Trinidad and Tobago	**trinitense** *m* / *f*	Trinidadian or Tobagonian
⑲ **San Cristóbal y Nieves** St. Kitts and Nevis	**sancristobaleño** *m* **sancristobaleña** *f*	Kittitian or Nevisian
⑳ **Antigua y Barbuda** Antigua and Barbuda	**antiguano** *m* **antiguana** *f*	Antiguan or Barbudan
㉑ **Dominica** Dominica	**dominiqués** *m* **dominiquesa** *f*	Dominican
㉒ **Santa Lucía** St. Lucia	**santalucense** *m* / *f*	St. Lucian
㉓ **San Vicente y las Granadinas** St. Vincent and The Grenadines	**sanvicentino** *m* **sanvicentina** *f*	Vincentian
㉔ **Granada** Grenada	**granadino** *m* **granadina** *f*	Grenadian

153 Las nacionalidades (continuación)

Nationalities continued

153.1 OCEANÍA · OCEANIA

Country	Adjective	English Adjective
① **Oceanía** Oceania	**oceánico** *m* **oceánica** *f*	Oceanian
② **Papúa Nueva Guinea** Papua New Guinea	**papú** *m / f*	Papua New Guinean
③ **Australia** Australia	**australiano** *m* **australiana** *f*	Australian
④ **Nueva Zelanda** New Zealand	**neozelandés** *m* **neozelandesa** *f*	New Zealand
⑤ **Islas Marshall** Marshall Islands	**marshalés** *m* **marshalesa** *f*	Marshallese
⑥ **Palaos** Palau	**palauano** *m* / **palauana** *f*	Palauan
⑦ **Micronesia** Micronesia	**micronesio** *m* **micronesia** *f*	Micronesian
⑧ **Nauru** Nauru	**nauruano** *m* / **nauruana** *f*	Nauruan
⑨ **Kiribati** Kiribati	**kiribatiano** *m* **kiribatiana** *f*	Kiribati
⑩ **Tuvalu** Tuvalu	**tuvaluano** *m* / **tuvaluana** *f*	Tuvaluan
⑪ **Samoa** Samoa	**samoano** *m* / **samoana** *f*	Samoan
⑫ **Tonga** Tonga	**tongano** *m* / **tongana** *f*	Tongan
⑬ **Vanuatu** Vanuatu	**vanuatuense** *m / f*	Vanuatuan
⑭ **Islas Salomón** Solomon Islands	**salomonense** *m / f*	Solomon Island
⑮ **Fiyi** Fiji	**fiyiano** *m* / **fiyiana** *f*	Fijian

153.2 ASIA · ASIA

Country	Adjective	English Adjective
① **Asia** • Asia	**asiático** *m* / **asiática** *f*	Asian
② **Turquía** Türkiye	**turco** *m* / **turca** *f*	Turkish
③ **Federación Rusa** Russian Federation	**ruso** *m* / **rusa** *f*	Russian
④ **Georgia** Georgia	**georgiano** *m* / **georgiana** *f*	Georgian
⑤ **Armenia** Armenia	**armenio** *m* / **armenia** *f*	Armenian
⑥ **Azerbaiyán** Azerbaijan	**azerbaiyano** *m* **azerbaiyana** *f*	Azerbaijani
⑦ **Irán** Iran	**iraní** *m / f*	Iranian
⑧ **Irak** Iraq	**iraquí** *m / f*	Iraqi
⑨ **Siria** Syria	**sirio** *m* **siria** *f*	Syrian
⑩ **Líbano** Lebanon	**libanés** *m* / **libanesa** *f*	Lebanese
⑪ **Israel** Israel	**israelí** *m / f*	Israeli
⑫ **Jordania** Jordan	**jordano** *m* / **jordana** *f*	Jordanian
⑬ **Arabia Saudí** Saudi Arabia	**saudí** *m / f*	Saudi
⑭ **Kuwait** Kuwait	**kuwaití** *m / f*	Kuwaiti
⑮ **Baréin** Bahrain	**bareiní** *m / f*	Bahraini
⑯ **Catar** Qatar	**catarí** *m / f*	Qatari
⑰ **Emiratos Árabes Unidos** United Arab Emirates	**emiratí** *m / f*	Emirati
⑱ **Omán** Oman	**omaní** *m / f*	Omani
⑲ **Yemen** Yemen	**yemení** *m / f*	Yemeni
⑳ **Kazajistán** Kazakhstan	**kazajo** *m* / **kazaja** *f*	Kazakh
㉑ **Uzbekistán** Uzbekistan	**uzbeko** *m* / **uzbeka** *f*	Uzbek
㉒ **Turkmenistán** Turkmenistan	**turcomano** *m* **turcomana** *f*	Turkmen
㉓ **Afganistán** Afghanistan	**afgano** *m* / **afgana** *f*	Afghan
㉔ **Tayikistán** Tajikistan	**tayiko** *m* / **tayika** *f*	Tajikistani
㉕ **Kirguistán** Kyrgyzstan	**kirguís** *m / f*	Kyrgyz
㉖ **Pakistán** Pakistan	**pakistaní** *m / f*	Pakistani
㉗ **India** India	**indio** *m* / **india** *f*	Indian
㉘ **Las Islas Maldivas** Maldives	**maldivo** *m* / **maldiva** *f*	Maldivian
㉙ **Sri Lanka** Sri Lanka	**cingalés** *m* / **cingalesa** *f*	Sri Lankan
㉚ **China** China	**chino** *m* / **china** *f*	Chinese
㉛ **Mongolia** Mongolia	**mongol** *m* / **mongola** *f*	Mongolian
㉜ **Corea del Norte** North Korea	**norcoreano** *m* **norcoreana** *f*	North Korean
㉝ **Corea del Sur** South Korea	**surcoreano** *m* **surcoreana** *f*	South Korean
㉞ **Japón** Japan	**japonés** *m* / **japonesa** *f*	Japanese
㉟ **Nepal** Nepal	**nepalés** *m* / **nepalesa** *f*	Nepalese
㊱ **Bután** Bhutan	**butanés** *m* / **butanesa** *f*	Bhutanese
㊲ **Bangladés** Bangladesh	**bangladesí** *m / f*	Bangladeshi
㊳ **Birmania** Myanmar (Burma)	**birmano** *m* / **birmana** *f*	Burmese
㊴ **Tailandia** Thailand	**tailandés** *m* / **tailandesa** *f*	Thai

See also
145 El planeta Tierra • Planet Earth **146-147** La geografía • Geography **148** Los mapas y las indicaciones • Maps and directions **149-151** Los países • Countries

153.2 ASIA • ASIA CONTINUED

Country	Adjective	English Adjective
(40) **Laos** Laos	**laosiano** *m* **laosiana** *f*	Laotian
(41) **Vietnam** Vietnam	**vietnamita** *m / f*	Vietnamese
(42) **Camboya** Cambodia	**camboyano** *m* **camboyana** *f*	Cambodian
(43) **Malasia** Malaysia	**malasio** *m* / **malasia** *f*	Malaysian
(44) **Singapur** Singapore	**singapurense** *m / f*	Singaporean
(45) **Indonesia** Indonesia	**indonesio** *m* / **indonesia** *f*	Indonesian
(46) **Brunéi** Brunei	**bruneano** *m* / **bruneana** *f*	Bruneian
(47) **Filipinas** Philippines	**filipino** *m* / **filipina** *f*	Filipino
(48) **Timor Oriental** East Timor	**timorense** *m / f*	Timorese

153.3 EUROPA • EUROPE

Country	Adjective	English Adjective
(1) **Europa** • Europe	**europeo** *m* / **europea** *f*	European
(2) **Irlanda** Ireland	**irlandés** *m* / **irlandesa** *f*	Irish
(3) **Reino Unido** United Kingdom	**británico** *m* / **británica** *f*	British
(4) **Portugal** Portugal	**portugués** *m* **portuguesa** *f*	Portuguese
(5) **España** Spain	**español** *m* / **española** *f*	Spanish
(6) **Andorra** Andorra	**andorrano** *m* **andorrana** *f*	Andorran
(7) **Francia** France	**francés** *m* / **francesa** *f*	French
(8) **Bélgica** Belgium	**belga** *m / f*	Belgian
(9) **Países Bajos** Netherlands	**neerlandés** *m* **neerlandesa** *f*	Dutch
(10) **Luxemburgo** Luxembourg	**luxemburgués** *m* **luxemburguesa** *f*	Luxembourg
(11) **Alemania** Germany	**alemán** *m* / **alemana** *f*	German
(12) **Dinamarca** Denmark	**danés** *m* / **danesa** *f*	Danish
(13) **Noruega** Norway	**noruego** *m* / **noruega** *f*	Norwegian
(14) **Suecia** Sweden	**sueco** *m* / **sueca** *f*	Swedish
(15) **Finlandia** Finland	**finlandés** *m* / **finlandesa** *f*	Finnish
(16) **Estonia** Estonia	**estonio** *m* / **estonia** *f*	Estonian
(17) **Letonia** Latvia	**letón** *m* / **letona** *f*	Latvian
(18) **Lituania** Lithuania	**lituano** *m* / **lituana** *f*	Lithuanian
(19) **Polonia** Poland	**polaco** *m* / **polaca** *f*	Polish
(20) **República Checa** Czech Republic	**checo** *m* / **checa** *f*	Czech
(21) **Austria** Austria	**austríaco** *m* / **austríaca** *f*	Austrian
(22) **Liechtenstein** Liechtenstein	**liechtensteiniano** *m* **liechtensteiniana** *f*	Liechtensteiner
(23) **Suiza** Switzerland	**suizo** *m* / **suiza** *f*	Swiss
(24) **Italia** Italy	**italiano** *m* / **Italiana** *f*	Italian
(25) **Mónaco** Monaco	**monegasco** *m* **monegasca** *f*	Monacan
(26) **San Marino** San Marino	**sanmarinense** *m / f*	Sammarinese
(27) **Malta** Malta	**maltés** *m* / **maltesa** *f*	Maltese
(28) **Eslovenia** Slovenia	**esloveno** *m* / **eslovena** *f*	Slovenian
(29) **Croacia** Croatia	**croata** *m / f*	Croatian
(30) **Hungría** Hungary	**húngaro** *m* / **húngara** *f*	Hungarian
(31) **Eslovaquia** Slovakia	**eslovaco** *m* / **eslovaca** *f*	Slovakian
(32) **Ucrania** Ukraine	**ucraniano** *m* / **ucraniana** *f*	Ukrainian
(33) **Bielorrusia** Belarus	**bielorruso** *m* / **bielorrusa** *f*	Belarusian
(34) **Moldavia** Moldova	**moldavo** *m* / **moldava** *f*	Moldovan
(35) **Rumanía** Romania	**rumano** *m* / **rumana** *f*	Romanian
(36) **Serbia** Serbia	**serbio** *m* / **serbia** *f*	Serbian
(37) **Bosnia y Herzegovina** Bosnia and Herzegovina	**bosnio** *m* / **bosnia** *f*	Bosnian
(38) **Albania** Albania	**albanés** *m* / **albanesa** *f*	Albanian
(39) **Macedonia del Norte** North Macedonia	**macedonio** *m* **macedonia** *f*	North Macedonian
(40) **Bulgaria** Bulgaria	**búlgaro** *m* / **búlgara** *f*	Bulgarian
(41) **Grecia** Greece	**griego** *m* / **griega** *f*	Greek
(42) **Montenegro** Montenegro	**montenegrino** *m* **montenegrina** *f*	Montenegrin
(43) **Islandia** Iceland	**islandés** *m* / **islandesa** *f*	Icelandic
(44) **Chipre** Cyprus	**chipriota** *m / f*	Cypriot
(45) **Turquía** Türkiye	**turco** *m* / **turca** *f*	Turkish
(46) **Federación Rusa** Russian Federation	**ruso** *m* / **rusa** *f*	Russian

154 El tiempo
Weather

154.1 **EL TIEMPO** · WEATHER

① **la humedad**
humidity

② **la ola de calor**
heatwave

③ **la sequía**
drought

④ **seco**
dry

⑤ **mojado**
wet

⑥ **nublado**
overcast

⑦ **el esmog**
smog

⑧ **la gota de lluvia**
raindrop

⑨ **la lluvia ligera**
light shower

⑩ **la llovizna**
drizzle

⑪ **el chaparrón**
downpour

⑫ **la inundación**
flood

⑬ **la tormenta de arena**
sandstorm

⑭ **el vendaval**
gale

⑮ **la tormenta**
storm

⑯ **el trueno**
thunder

⑰ **el rayo**
lightning

⑱ **el arcoíris**
rainbow

⑲ **la aguanieve**
sleet

⑳ **el copo de nieve**
snowflake

㉑ **el banco de nieve**
snowdrift

㉒ **la ventisca**
blizzard

㉓ **la tormenta de nieve**
snowstorm

㉔ **el granizo**
hailstone

㉕ **el huracán**
hurricane

㉖ **el tornado**
tornado

㉘ **Hoy caen chuzos de punta.**
It's raining cats and dogs today.

㉗ **el charco**
puddle

See also
145 El planeta Tierra • Planet Earth **146-147** La geografía • Geography
155 El clima y el medio ambiente • Climate and the environment

154.2 LA TEMPERATURA • TEMPERATURE

① **gélido** *m* / **gélida** *f*
freezing

② **frío** *m* / **fría** *f*
cold

③ **fresco** *m* / **fresca** *f*
chilly

④ **cálido** *m* / **cálida** *f*
warm

⑤ **caluroso** *m*
calurosa *f*
hot

⑥ **sofocante**
stifling

⑦ **el punto de congelación**
freezing point

⑧ **el punto de ebullición**
boiling point

⑨ **10 grados bajo cero**
minus 10

⑩ **25 grados**
25 degrees

⑪ **Celsius**
Celsius

⑫ **Fahrenheit**
Fahrenheit

⑬ **fresquito** *m*
fresquita *f*
cool

⑭ **templado** *m*
templada *f*
mild

⑯ ¡Hace un calor asfixiante! Tengo que ponerme a la sombra.
It's boiling! I need to find some shade
⑮ **asfixiante**
boiling

154.3 LOS ADJETIVOS DEL TIEMPO • WEATHER ADJECTIVES

① **el sol ➜ soleado**
sun → sunny

② **la nube ➜ nublado**
cloud → cloudy

③ **la niebla ➜ neblinoso**
fog → foggy

④ **la lluvia ➜ lluvioso**
rain → rainy

⑤ **la nieve ➜ nevado**
snow → snowy

⑥ **el hielo ➜ helado**
ice → icy

⑦ **la escarcha ➜ escarchado**
frost → frosty

⑧ **el viento ➜ ventoso**
wind → windy

⑨ **la tormenta ➜ tormentoso**
storm → stormy

⑩ **el trueno ➜ tempestuoso**
thunder → thundery

⑪ **la neblina ➜ neblinoso**
mist → misty

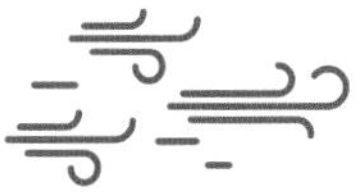
⑫ **la brisa ➜ ventoso**
breeze → breezy

155 El clima y el medio ambiente
Climate and the environment

155.1 LA ATMÓSFERA · ATMOSPHERE

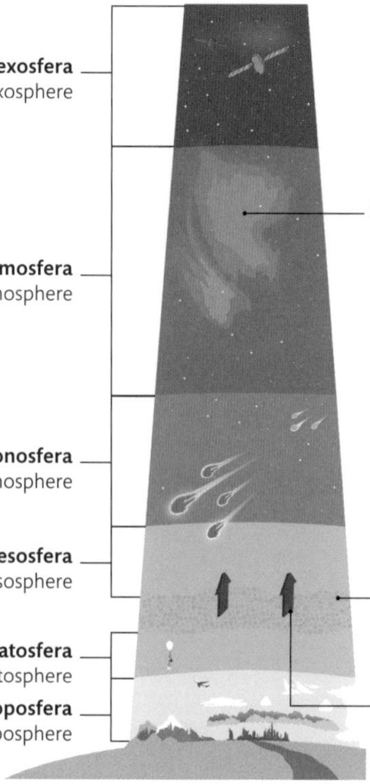

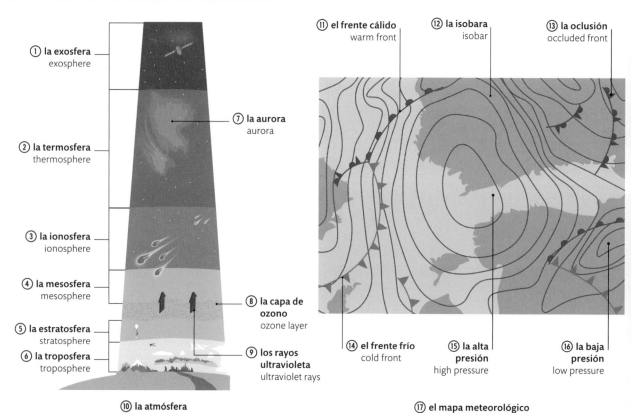

① **la exosfera** exosphere

② **la termosfera** thermosphere

③ **la ionosfera** ionosphere

④ **la mesosfera** mesosphere

⑤ **la estratosfera** stratosphere

⑥ **la troposfera** troposphere

⑦ **la aurora** aurora

⑧ **la capa de ozono** ozone layer

⑨ **los rayos ultravioleta** ultraviolet rays

⑩ **la atmósfera** atmosphere

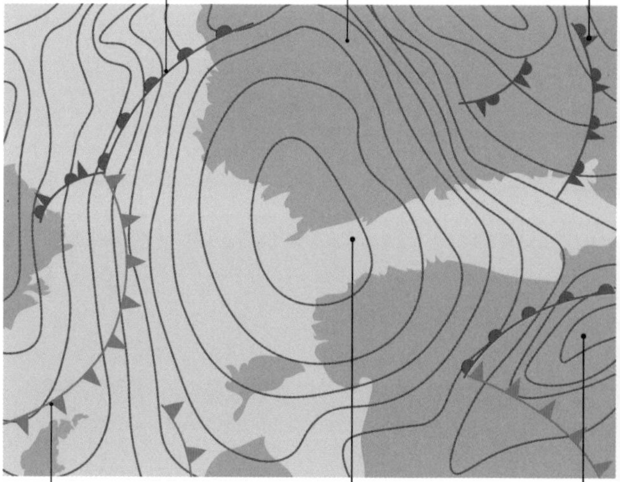

⑪ **el frente cálido** warm front

⑫ **la isobara** isobar

⑬ **la oclusión** occluded front

⑭ **el frente frío** cold front

⑮ **la alta presión** high pressure

⑯ **la baja presión** low pressure

⑰ **el mapa meteorológico** weather map

155.2 LOS PROBLEMAS MEDIOAMBIENTALES · ENVIRONMENTAL ISSUES

① **la deforestación** deforestation

② **la pérdida de hábitat** habitat loss

③ **las especies en peligro de extinción** endangered species

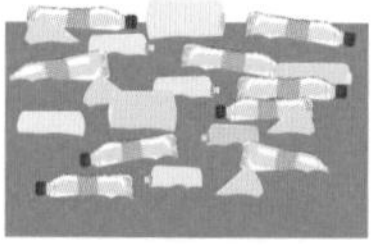

④ **los residuos plásticos** plastic waste

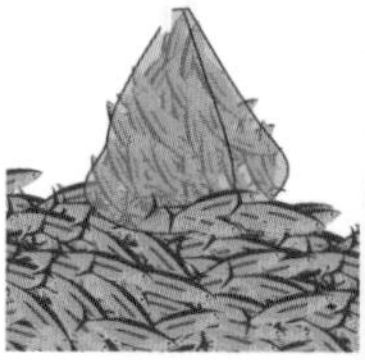

⑤ **la sobrepesca** overfishing

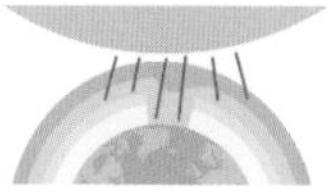

⑥ **el agotamiento de la capa de ozono** ozone depletion

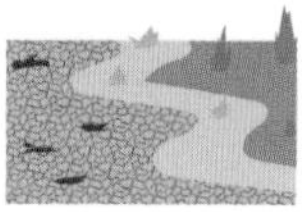

⑦ **la desertificación** desertification

⑧ **el derrame de petróleo** oil slick

⑨ **la lluvia ácida** acid rain

See also
145 El planeta Tierra • Planet Earth **146-147** La geografía • Geography
154 El tiempo • Weather

155.3 EL CAMBIO CLIMÁTICO • CLIMATE CHANGE

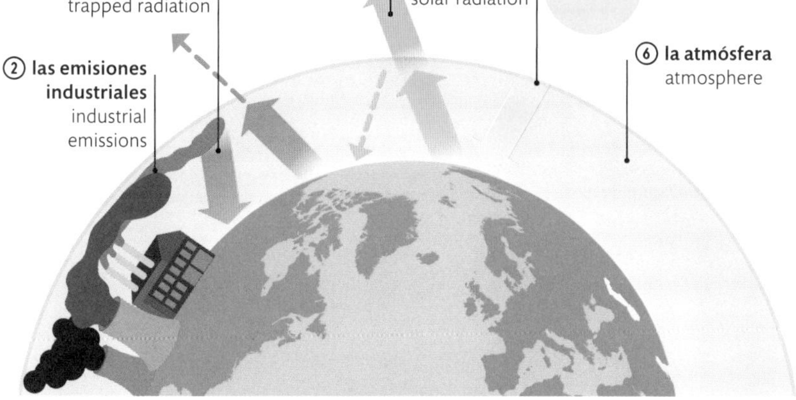

④ **la radiación reflejada**
reflected radiation

⑤ **la radiación solar**
solar radiation

③ **la radiación atrapada**
trapped radiation

② **las emisiones industriales**
industrial emissions

⑥ **la atmósfera**
atmosphere

① **el efecto invernadero**
greenhouse effect

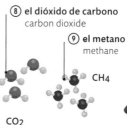

⑧ **el dióxido de carbono**
carbon dioxide

⑨ **el metano**
methane

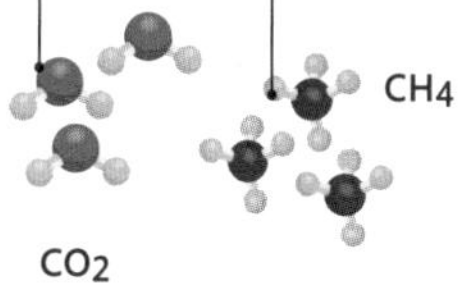

⑦ **los gases de efecto invernadero**
greenhouse gases

⑩ **los combustibles fósiles**
fossil fuels

⑪ **las emisiones**
emissions

⑫ **la contaminación**
pollution

⑬ **el ecosistema**
ecosystem

⑭ **el carbono cero**
zero carbon

⑮ **el retroceso de los glaciares**
shrinking glaciers

⑯ **el deshielo de los casquetes polares**
melting ice caps

155.4 LOS RESIDUOS Y EL RECICLAJE • WASTE AND RECYCLING

② **Intento reciclar el plástico y el papel lo máximo posible.**
I try to recycle plastic and paper as much as possible.

① **clasificar la basura**
to sort your rubbish

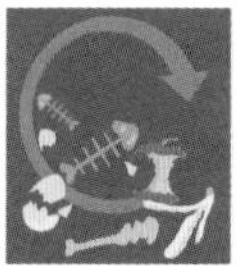

③ **los desechos alimenticios**
food waste

④ **el papel**
paper

⑤ **el plástico**
plastic

⑥ **el vidrio**
glass

⑦ **el metal**
metal

⑧ **las bolsas compostables**
compostable bags

⑨ **el vertedero**
landfill

156 Las rocas y los minerales

Rocks and minerals

156.1 LAS ROCAS · ROCKS

① **sedimentario** *m* **sedimentaria** *f*
sedimentary

② **la arenisca**
sandstone

③ **la caliza**
limestone

④ **la tiza**
chalk

⑤ **el sílex**
flint

⑥ **el conglomerado**
conglomerate

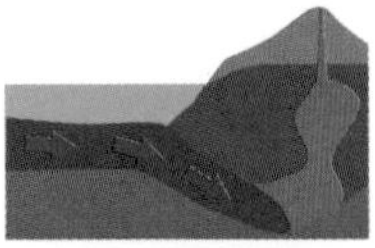
⑦ **metamórfico** *m* **metamórfica** *f*
metamorphic

⑧ **la pizarra**
slate

⑨ **el esquisto**
schist

⑩ **el gneis**
gneiss

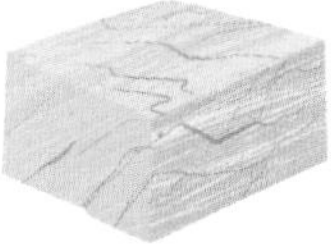
⑪ **el mármol**
marble

⑫ **la cuarcita**
quartzite

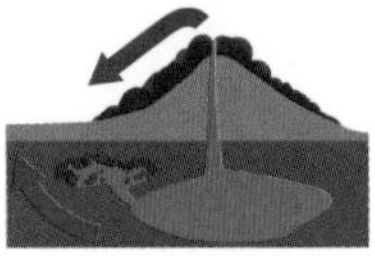
⑬ **ígneo** *m* / **ígnea** *f*
igneous

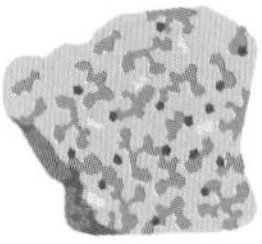
⑭ **el granito**
granite

⑮ **la obsidiana**
obsidian

⑯ **el basalto**
basalt

⑰ **la toba volcánica**
tuff

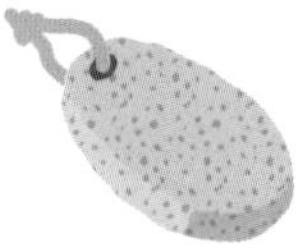
⑱ **la piedra pómez**
pumice

156.2 LOS MINERALES · MINERALS

① **el cuarzo**
quartz

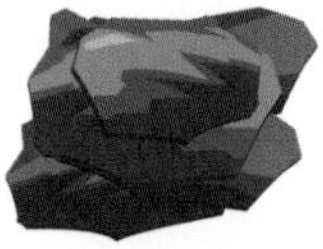
② **la mica**
mica

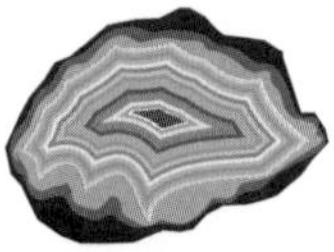
③ **el ágata** *f*
agate

④ **la hematita**
hematite

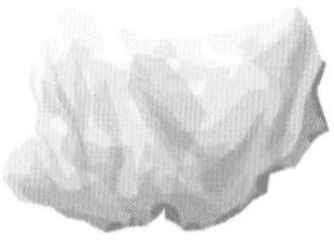
⑤ **la calcita**
calcite

⑥ **la malaquita**
malachite

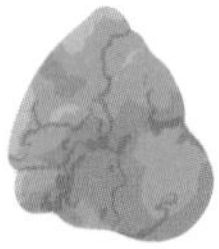
⑦ **la turquesa**
turquoise

⑧ **el ónix**
onyx

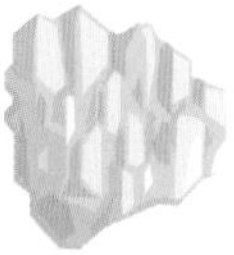
⑨ **el azufre**
sulphur

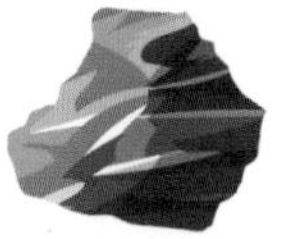
⑩ **el grafito**
graphite

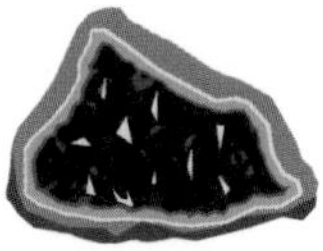
⑪ **la geoda**
geode

⑫ **la rosa del desierto**
sand rose

See also
76 La química • Chemistry **78** La tabla periódica • The periodic table
145 El planeta Tierra • Planet Earth **146-147** La geografía • Geography

156.3 **LAS GEMAS** • GEMS

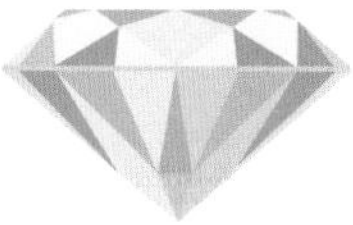
① **el diamante**
diamond

② **el zafiro**
sapphire

③ **la esmeralda**
emerald

④ **el rubí**
ruby

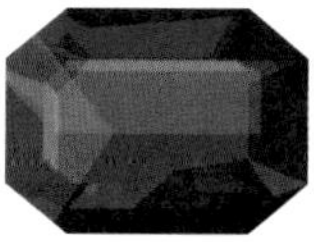
⑤ **la amatista**
amethyst

⑥ **el topacio**
topaz

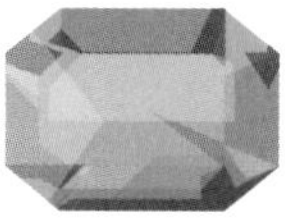
⑦ **la aguamarina**
aquamarine

⑧ **la piedra lunar**
moonstone

⑨ **el ópalo**
opal

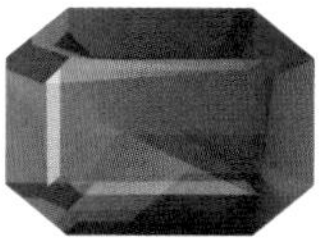
⑩ **la turmalina**
tourmaline

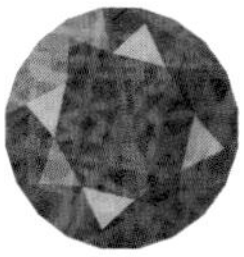
⑪ **el granate**
garnet

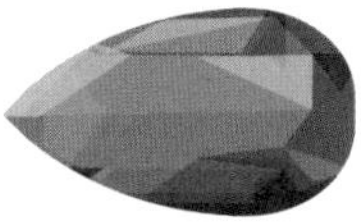
⑫ **el cuarzo**
citrine

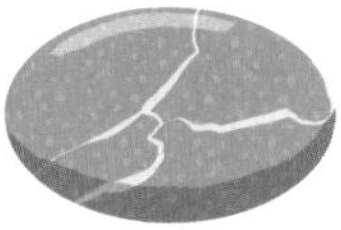
⑬ **el jade**
jade

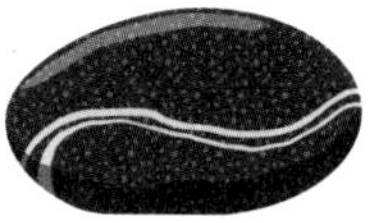
⑭ **el azabache**
jet

⑮ **el lapislázuli**
lapis lazuli

⑯ **el jaspe**
jasper

⑰ **el ojo de tigre**
tiger's eye

⑱ **la cornalina**
carnelian

156.4 **LOS METALES** • METALS

① **el oro**
gold

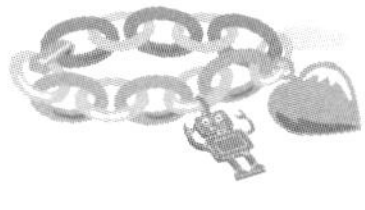
② **la plata**
silver

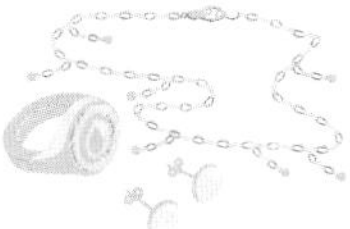
③ **el platino**
platinum

④ **el magnesio**
magnesium

⑤ **el hierro**
iron

⑥ **el cobre**
copper

⑦ **el estaño**
tin

⑧ **el aluminio**
aluminium

⑨ **el mercurio**
mercury

⑩ **el níquel**
nickel

⑪ **el zinc**
zinc

⑫ **el cromo**
chromium

157 La historia natural
Natural history

157.1 LOS PERÍODOS GEOLÓGICOS · GEOLOGICAL PERIODS

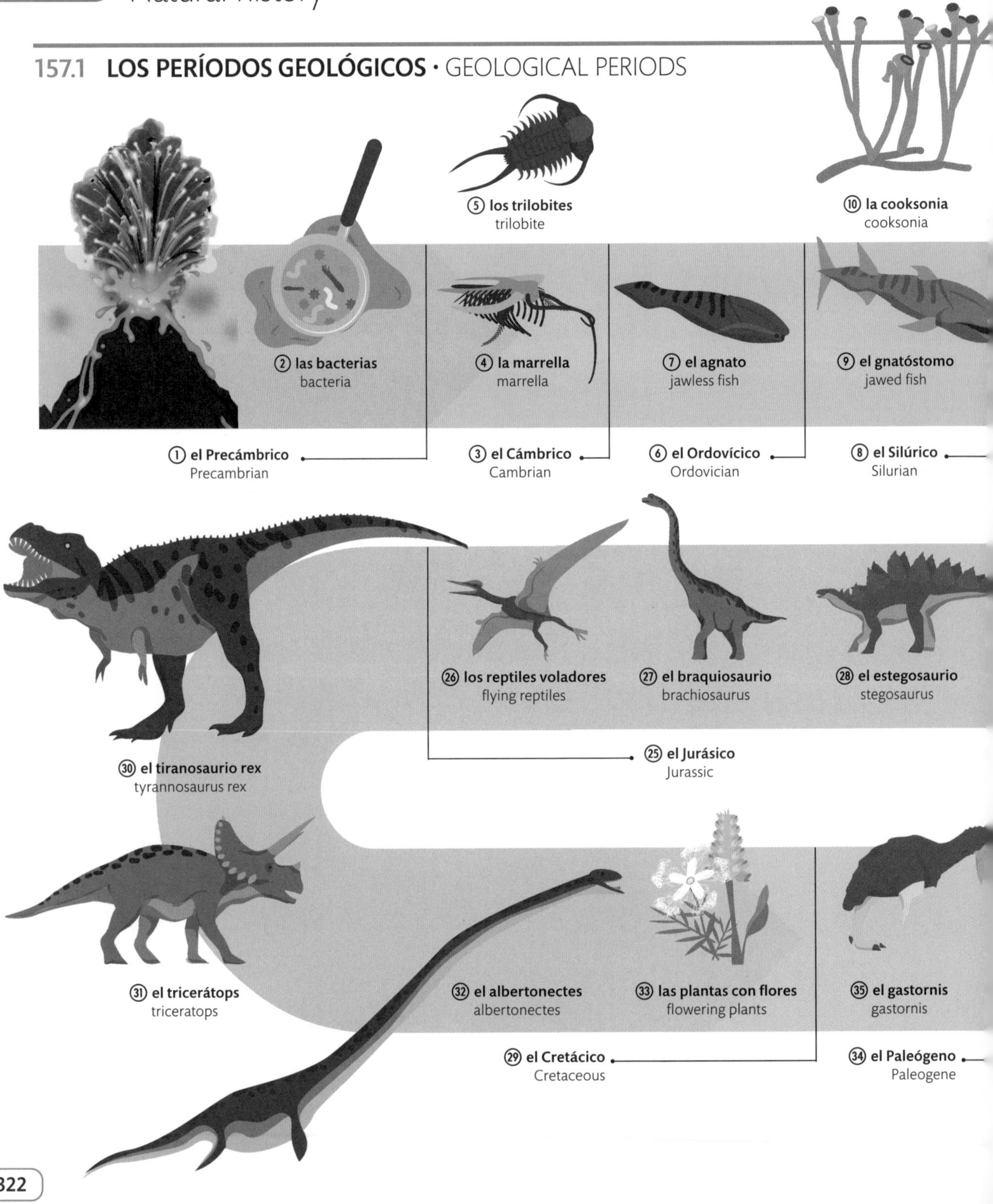

See also
145 El planeta Tierra • Planet Earth **158-159** Los mamíferos • Mammals **160-161** Las aves • Birds **162** Los insectos y los bichos • Insects and bugs **163** Los anfibios y los reptiles • Amphibians and reptiles **166** La vida oceánica • Ocean life **167-169** Las plantas y los árboles • Plants and trees

LAS ERAS • ERAS

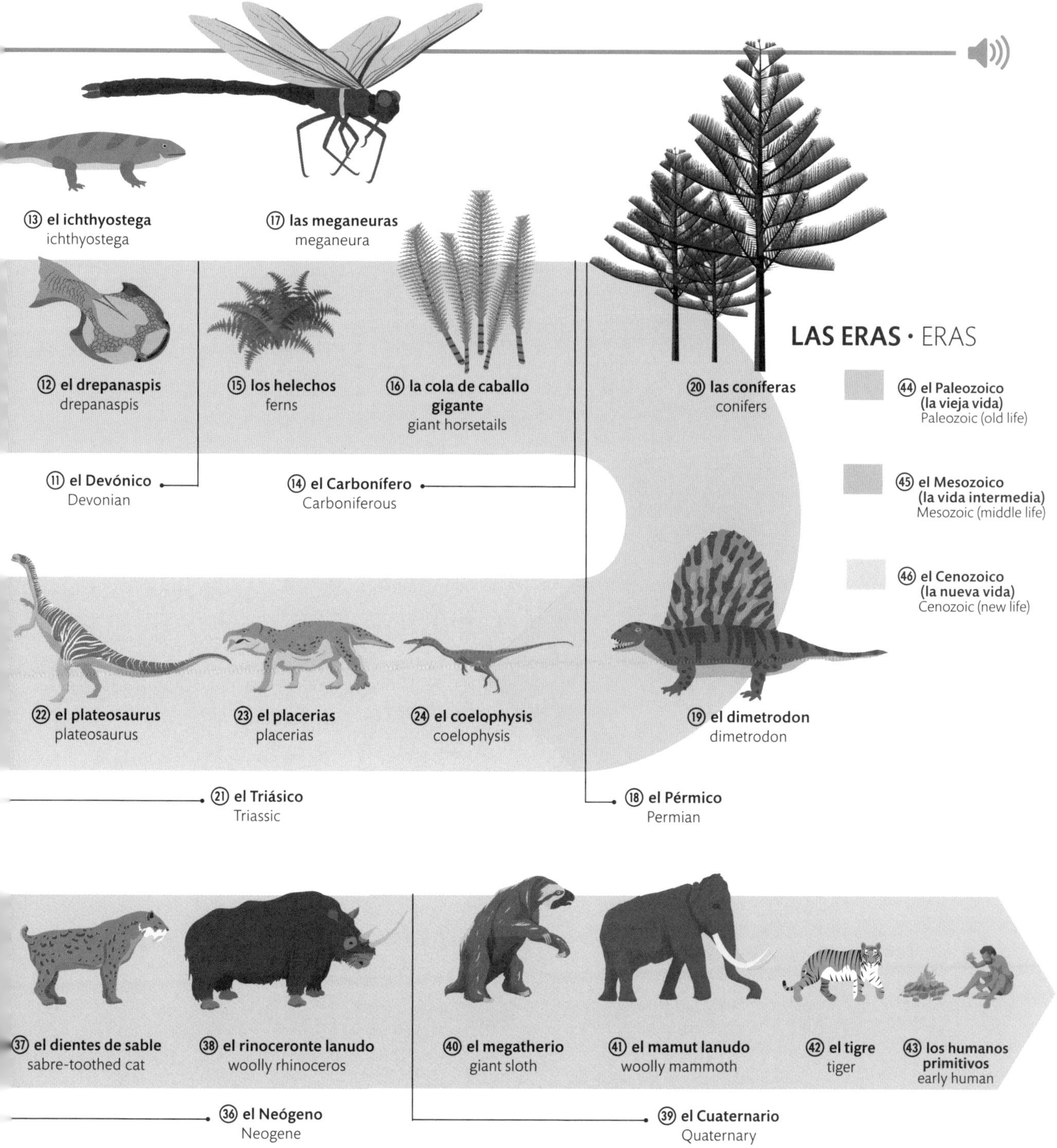

Los mamíferos
Mammals

158.1 LAS ESPECIES DE MAMÍFEROS · SPECIES OF MAMMALS

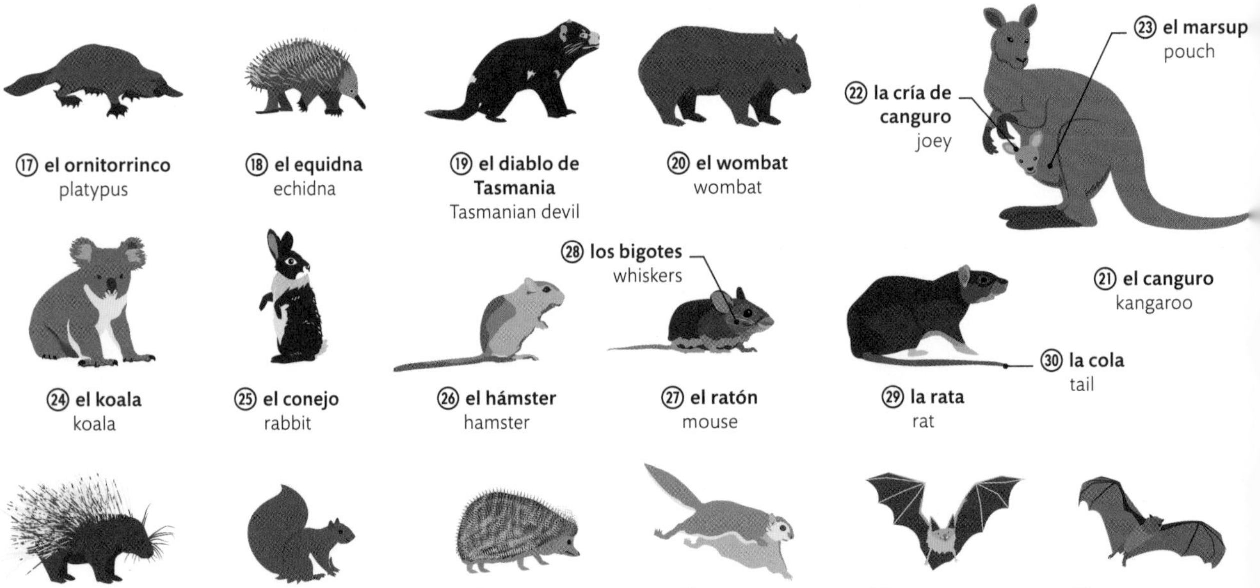

See also
157 La historia natural • Natural history **159** Los mamíferos (continuación) • Mammals continued
164 Las mascotas • Pets **165** Los animales de granja • Farm animals **166** La vida oceánica • Ocean life

㊲ **el mapache**
raccoon

㊳ **la mofeta**
skunk

㊴ **la comadreja**
weasel

㊵ **el tejón europeo**
European badger

㊶ **el ratel**
honey badger

㊷ **la nutria**
otter

㊸ **el fénec**
fennec fox

㊹ **el chacal**
jackal

㊺ **el corzo**
roe deer

㊻ **el ciervo**
red deer

㊼ **el gamo común**
fallow deer

㊽ **la gacela**
springbok

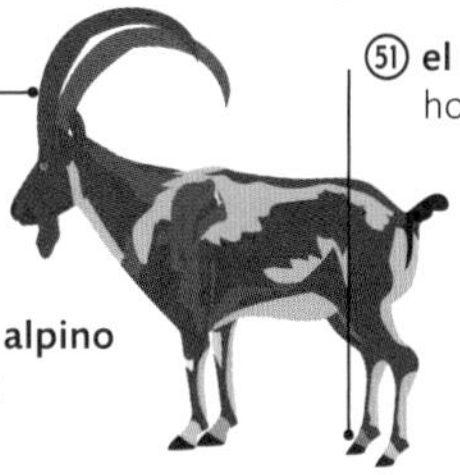

㊾ **el íbice alpino**
ibex

52 **el camello bactriano**
Bactrian camel

53 **el dromedario**
dromedary

55 **la vicuña**
vicuña

56 **la llama**
llama

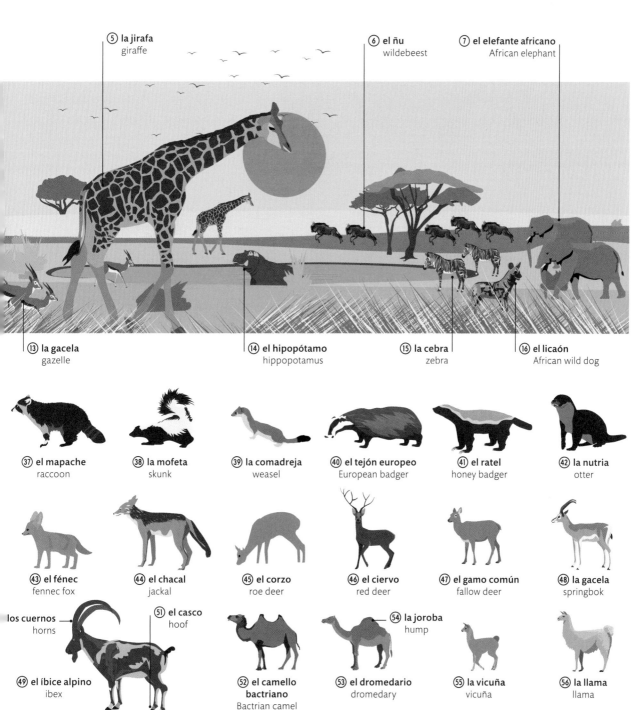

159 Los mamíferos (continuación)
Mammals continued

159.1 LAS ESPECIES DE MAMÍFEROS · SPECIES OF MAMMALS

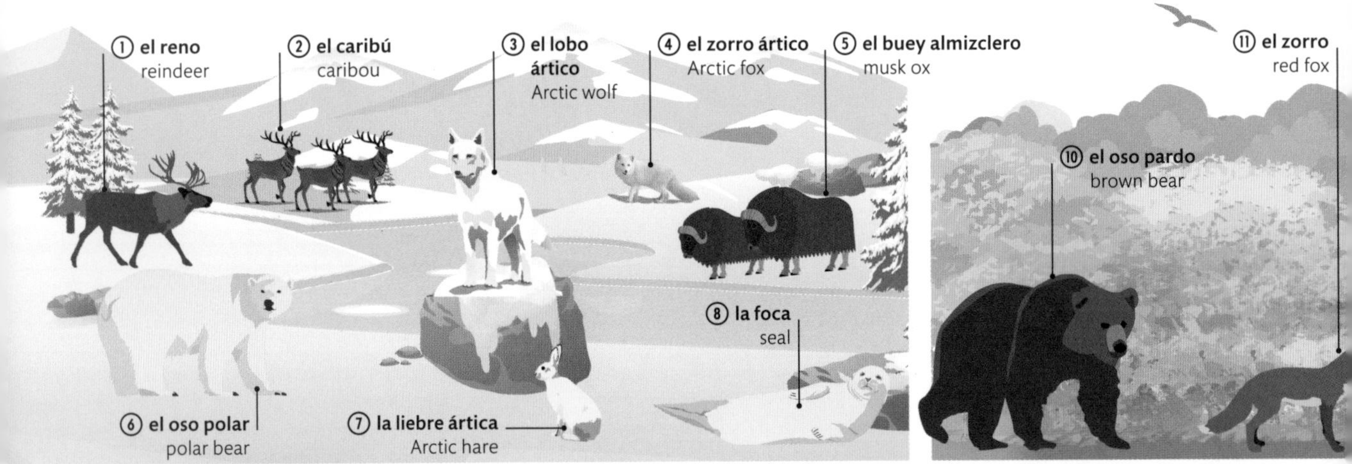

⑨ **el Ártico**
Arctic

⑮ **el bosque latifoliado**
broadleaf forest

㉓ **el elefante asiático**
Asian elephant

㉕ **el oso hormiguero**
anteater

㉖ **el tigre**
tiger

㉘ **el leopardo**
leopard

㉙ **el gato salvaje**
wildcat

㉚ **el gato montés**
bobcat

㉛ **el leopardo de las nieves**
snow leopard

㉜ **el lémur de cola anillada**
ring-tailed lemur

㉝ **el mono capuchino**
capuchin monkey

㉞ **el mono araña**
spider monkey

㊱ **el mono narigudo**
proboscis monkey

㊳ **el macaco**
macaque

㊴ **el mandril**
mandrill

㊵ **el tití**
marmoset

㊶ **el orangután**
orangutan

㊷ **el chimpancé**
chimpanzee

㊸ **el gibón**
gibbon

㊹ **el gorila**
gorilla

㊺ **el panda**
panda

See also
157 La historia natural • Natural history **164** Las mascotas • Pets
165 Los animales de granja • Farm animals **166** La vida oceánica • Ocean life

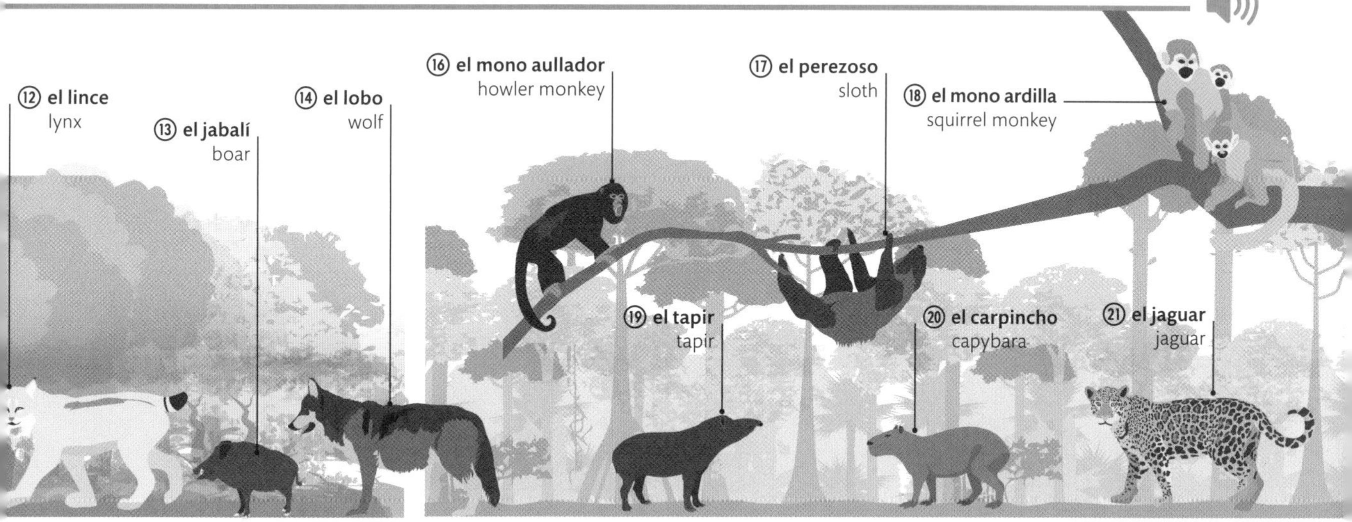

㉒ **el bosque pluvial**
rain forest

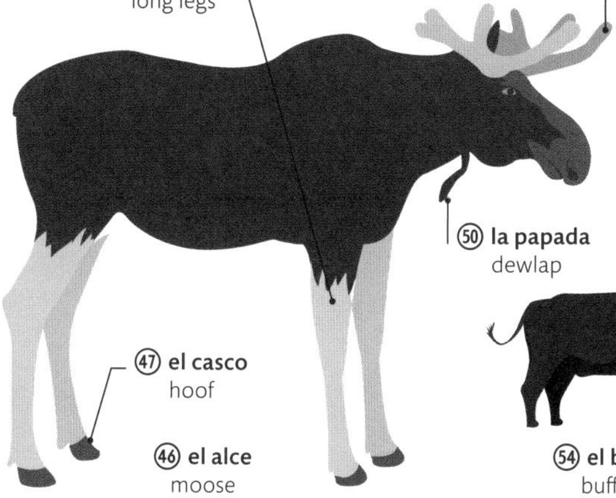

㊻ **el alce**
moose

51 **el pangolín**
pangolin

52 **el panda rojo**
red panda

53 **el jabalí verrugoso**
warthog

54 **el búfalo**
buffalo

55 **el yak**
yak

56 **el órix**
oryx

57 **la cabra de las Montañas Rocosas**
mountain goat

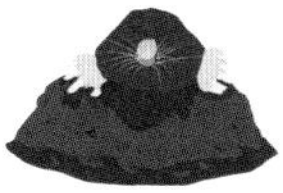

58 **el topo**
mole

59 **la ardilla rayada**
chipmunk

60 **la mangosta**
mongoose

61 **el armadillo**
armadillo

62 **la suricata**
meerkat

63 **cazar**
to hunt

64 **acechar**
to prowl

65 **rugir**
to roar

66 **balancearse**
to swing

67 **lanzarse**
to pounce

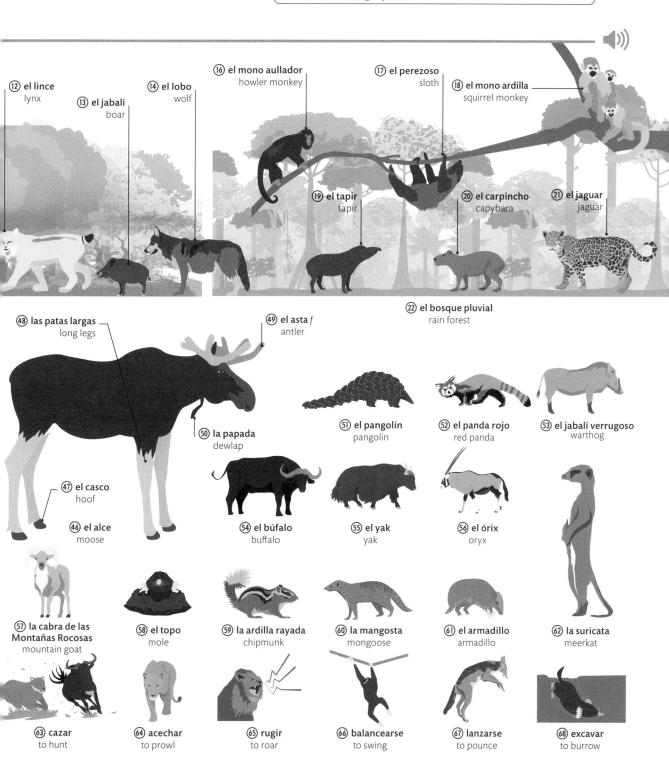

68 **excavar**
to burrow

160 Las aves
Birds

160.1 LAS ESPECIES DE AVES · SPECIES OF BIRDS

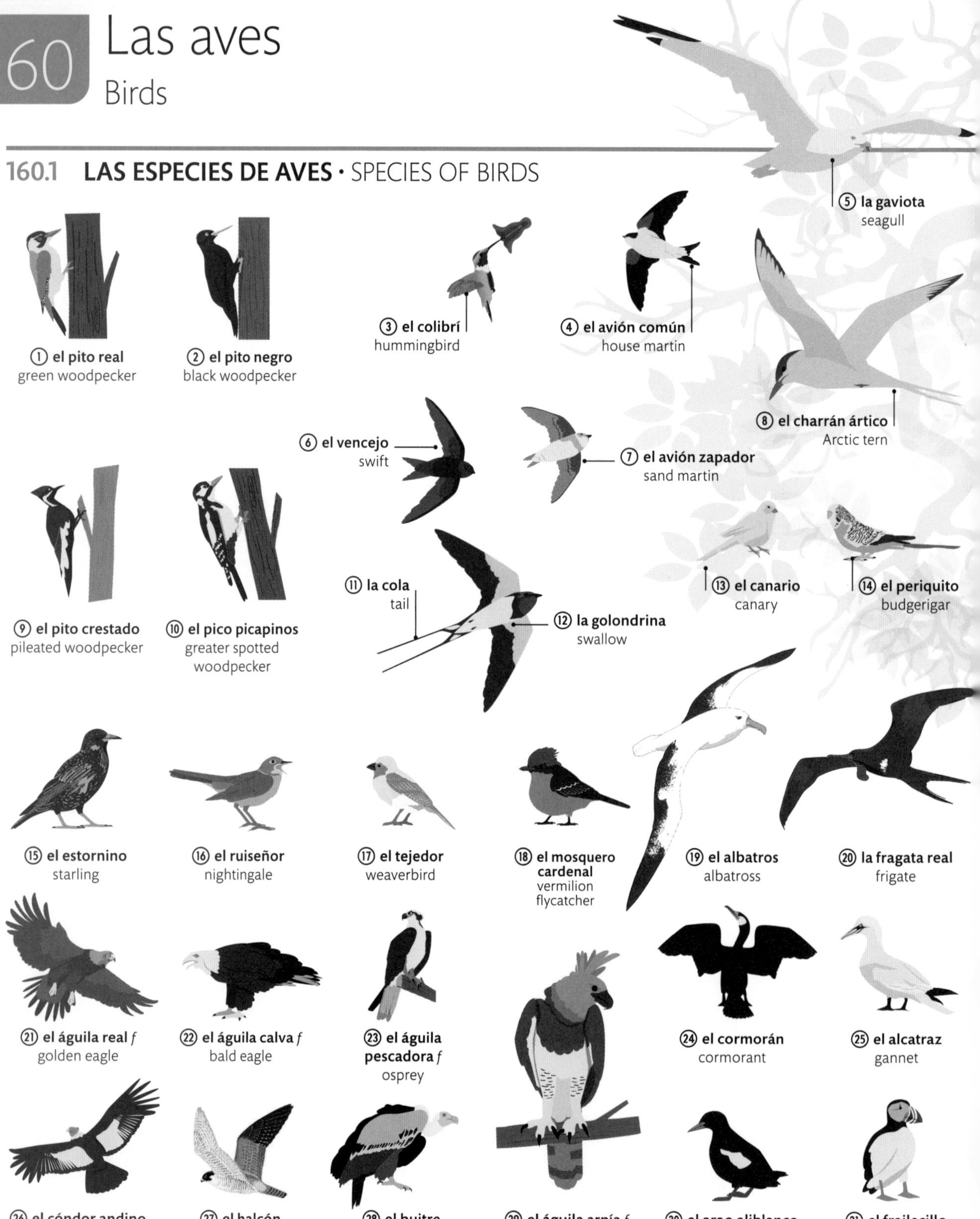

1. **el pito real** green woodpecker
2. **el pito negro** black woodpecker
3. **el colibrí** hummingbird
4. **el avión común** house martin
5. **la gaviota** seagull
6. **el vencejo** swift
7. **el avión zapador** sand martin
8. **el charrán ártico** Arctic tern
9. **el pito crestado** pileated woodpecker
10. **el pico picapinos** greater spotted woodpecker
11. **la cola** tail
12. **la golondrina** swallow
13. **el canario** canary
14. **el periquito** budgerigar
15. **el estornino** starling
16. **el ruiseñor** nightingale
17. **el tejedor** weaverbird
18. **el mosquero cardenal** vermilion flycatcher
19. **el albatros** albatross
20. **la fragata real** frigate
21. **el águila real** *f* golden eagle
22. **el águila calva** *f* bald eagle
23. **el águila pescadora** *f* osprey
24. **el cormorán** cormorant
25. **el alcatraz** gannet
26. **el cóndor andino** Andean condor
27. **el halcón peregrino** peregrine falcon
28. **el buitre** vulture
29. **el águila arpía** *f* harpy eagle
30. **el arao aliblanco** guillemot
31. **el frailecillo atlántico** Atlantic puffin

See also
157 La historia natural · Natural history **161** Las aves (continuación)
Birds continued **165** Los animales de granja · Farm animals

㉜ **el tucán esmeralda**
emerald toucan

㉝ **el tucán grande**
toco toucan

㉞ **el petirrojo europeo**
European robin

㉟ **el chochín**
wren

㊱ **el gorrión**
sparrow

㊲ **el nido**
nest

㊳ **el ibis escarlata**
scarlet ibis

㊴ **el ibis sagrado**
sacred ibis

㊶ **la paloma**
pigeon

㊷ **el mirlo**
blackbird

㊵ **el pinzón**
finch

㊸ **el grajo**
rook

㊹ **el cuervo
americano**
crow

㊺ **el tordo**
thrush

㊻ **el cuervo
común**
raven

㊼ **el ave del paraíso** *f*
bird of paradise

㊽ **el pelícano**
pelican

㊾ **el ostrero**
oystercatcher

㊿ **el martín
pescador**
kingfisher

(51) **la cucaburra**
kookaburra

(52) **la cigüeña**
stork

(53) **la garza**
heron

(54) **el ganso del Nilo**
Egyptian goose

(55) **la barnacla
canadiense**
Canada goose

(56) **el ánsar nival**
snow goose

(57) **la grulla**
crane

(58) **el flamenco**
flamingo

(59) **el avestruz**
ostrich

(60) **el kiwi**
kiwi

(61) **el casuario**
cassowary

(62) **el emú**
emu

161.1 LAS ESPECIES DE AVES · SPECIES OF BIRDS

① **la cacatúa Galah**
galah

② **el loro eclecto**
eclectus parrot

③ **la cotorra de Kramer**
rose-ringed parakeet

④ **el guacamayo escarlata**
scarlet macaw

⑤ **el lori arcoíris**
lorikeet

⑮ **ulular**
to hoot

⑩ **el búho nival**
snowy owl

⑪ **el búho real**
eagle owl

⑫ **el cárabo lapón**
great grey owl

⑬ **el búho corniblanco**
crested owl

⑭ **la lechuza común**
barn owl

㉒ **el cisne vulgar**
mute swan

㉓ **el cisne negro**
black swan

㉔ **el cisne cantor**
whooper swan

㉕ **la focha común**
coot

㉖ **el ánade real**
mallard

㉗ **el pato mandarín**
mandarin duck

㉘ **el zampullín**
grebe

㉙ **el pato joyuyo**
wood duck

㉚ **el rascón europeo**
water rail

㉛ **el zarapito**
curlew

㉜ **el faisán**
pheasan

㉝ **el pavo**
turkey

㉟ **el plumaje extendido**
feathers displayed

㊱ **el cuello**
neck

㉞ **el pavo real**
peacock

See also
157 La historia natural • Natural history
165 Los animales de granja • Farm animals

⑨ **¡Acabo de ver un águila real!**
I've just spotted a golden eagle!

⑥ **la cacatúa**
cockatoo

⑦ **el loro yaco**
African grey parrot

⑧ **el observador de aves** *m*
la observadora de aves *f*
bird-watcher

⑯ **el cárabo común**
tawny owl

⑰ **el mochuelo**
elf owl

⑱ **la cría**
hatchling

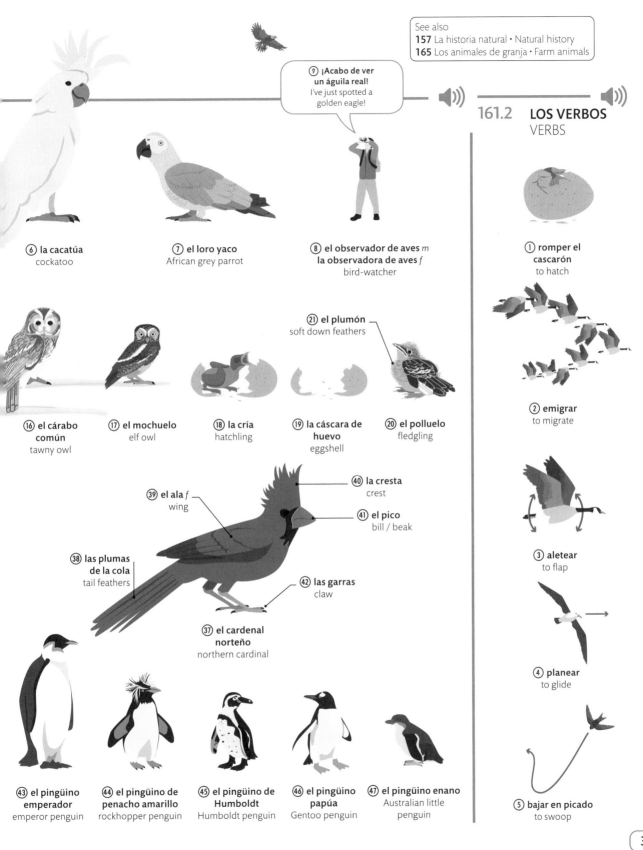

⑲ **la cáscara de huevo**
eggshell

㉑ **el plumón**
soft down feathers

⑳ **el polluelo**
fledgling

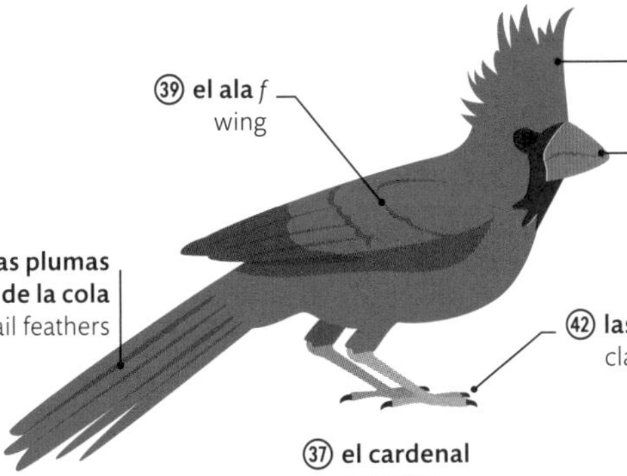

㊴ **el ala** *f*
wing

㊵ **la cresta**
crest

㊶ **el pico**
bill / beak

㊳ **las plumas de la cola**
tail feathers

㊷ **las garras**
claw

㊲ **el cardenal norteño**
northern cardinal

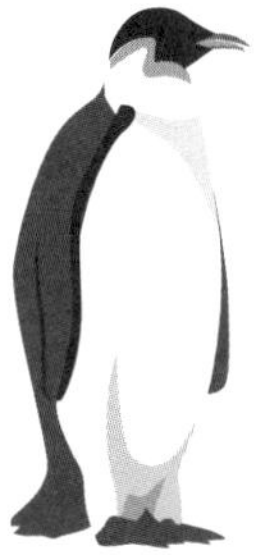

㊸ **el pingüino emperador**
emperor penguin

㊹ **el pingüino de penacho amarillo**
rockhopper penguin

㊺ **el pingüino de Humboldt**
Humboldt penguin

㊻ **el pingüino papúa**
Gentoo penguin

㊼ **el pingüino enano**
Australian little penguin

161.2 LOS VERBOS
VERBS

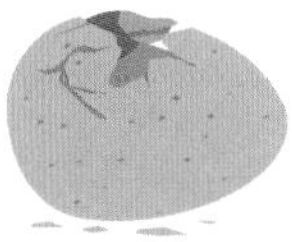

① **romper el cascarón**
to hatch

② **emigrar**
to migrate

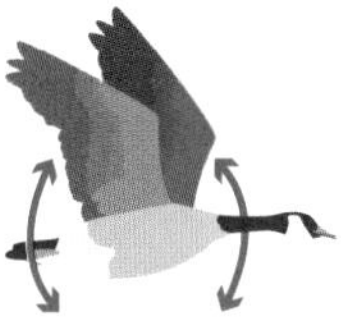

③ **aletear**
to flap

④ **planear**
to glide

⑤ **bajar en picado**
to swoop

162 Los insectos y los bichos
Insects and bugs

162.1 LAS MARIPOSAS Y LAS POLILLAS · BUTTERFLIES AND MOTHS

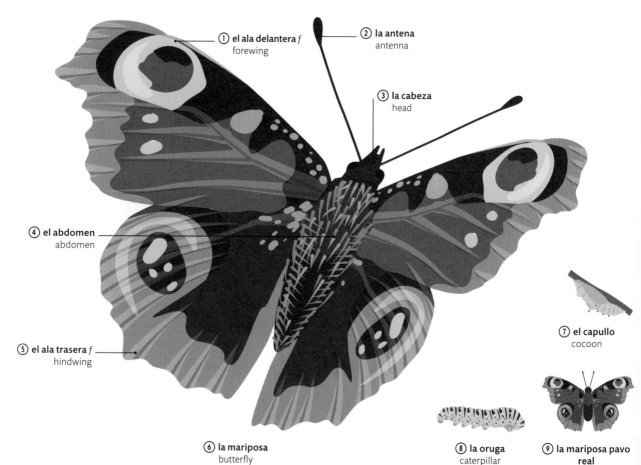

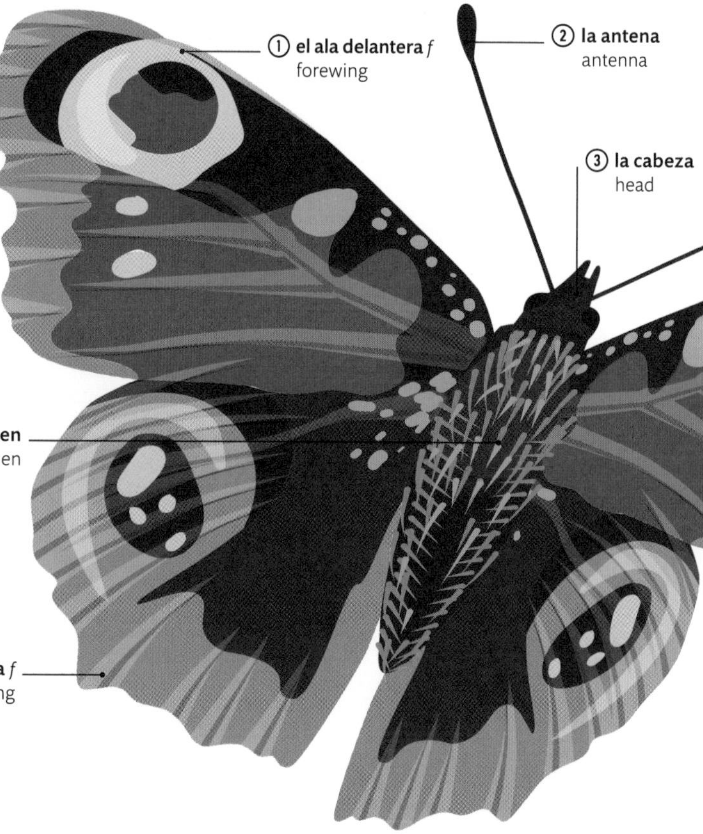

6 **la mariposa**
butterfly

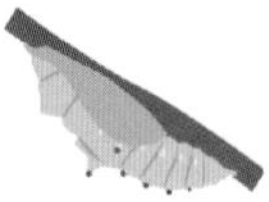

7 **el capullo**
cocoon

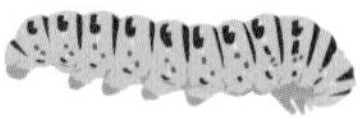

8 **la oruga**
caterpillar

9 **la mariposa pavo real**
peacock butterfly

10 **la mariposa monarca**
la mariposa monarca

11 **la vanesa de los cardos**
painted lady butterfly

12 **la mariposa cola de golondrina**
swallowtail butterfly

13 **la mariposa de cristal**
glasswing butterfly

14 **la mariposa blanquita de la col**
cabbage white butterfly

15 **la polilla moteada**
peppered moth

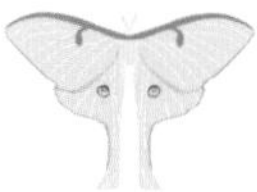

16 **la mariposa lunar**
luna moth

17 **la esfinge colibrí**
hummingbird hawksmoth

18 **la polilla emperador**
emperor moth

19 **la mariposa atlas**
atlas moth

20 **la polilla de la ropa**
clothes moth

21 **la polilla esfinge**
hawk moth

See also
157 La historia natural • Natural history **158-159** Los mamíferos • Mammals
160-161 Las aves • Birds **163** Los anfibios y los reptiles • Amphibians and reptiles

162.2 OTROS BICHOS E INVERTEBRADOS • OTHER BUGS AND INVERTEBRATES

① **el escarabajo rinoceronte**
rhinoceros beetle

② **el ciervo volante**
stag beetle

③ **el gorgojo**
weevil

④ **la cucaracha**
cockroach

⑤ **la mariquita**
ladybird

⑥ **la mosca**
fly

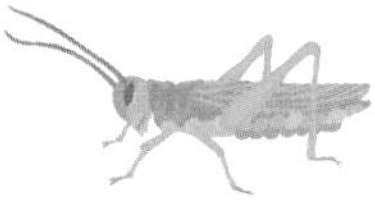

⑦ **el saltamontes**
grasshopper

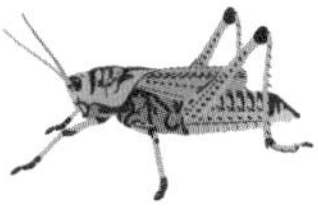

⑧ **la langosta**
locust

⑨ **el insecto hoja**
leaf insect

⑩ **la mantis religiosa**
praying mantis

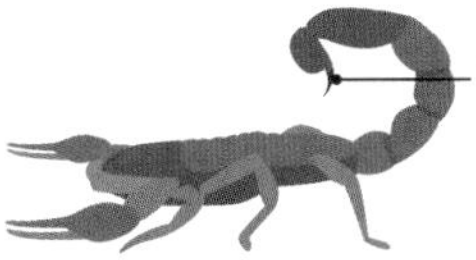

⑫ **el aguijón**
sting

⑪ **el escorpión**
scorpion

⑬ **el grillo**
cricket

⑭ **el ciempiés**
centipede

⑮ **el milpiés**
millipede

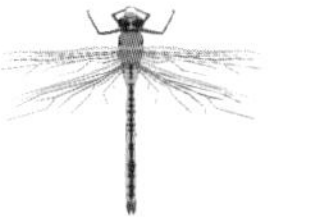

⑯ **la libélula**
dragonfly

⑰ **el mosquito**
mosquito

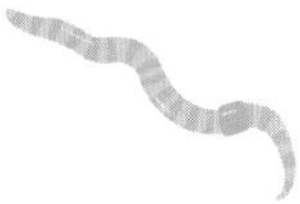

⑱ **el gusano**
worm

⑲ **la tarántula**
tarantula

⑳ **la viuda negra**
black widow spider

㉑ **la araña saltadora**
jumping spider

㉒ **la araña tejedora de orbes**
orb weaver

㉓ **la babosa**
slug

㉔ **el caracol**
snail

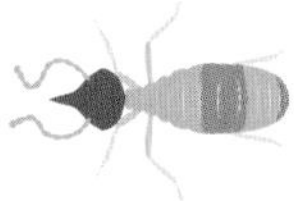

㉕ **la termita**
termite

㉖ **la hormiga**
ant

㉗ **el abejorro**
bumble bee

㉘ **la avispa**
wasp

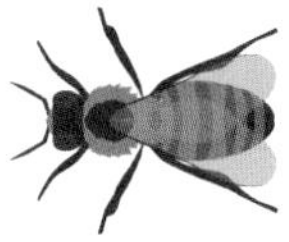

㉙ **la abeja melífera**
honey bee

㉚ **picar**
to sting

㉛ **volar**
to fly

㉜ **zumbar**
to buzz

㉝ **el avispero**
wasp nest

㉞ **la colmena**
beehive

㉟ **el enjambre**
swarm

163 Los anfibios y los reptiles

Amphibians and reptiles

163.1 LOS ANFIBIOS · AMPHIBIANS

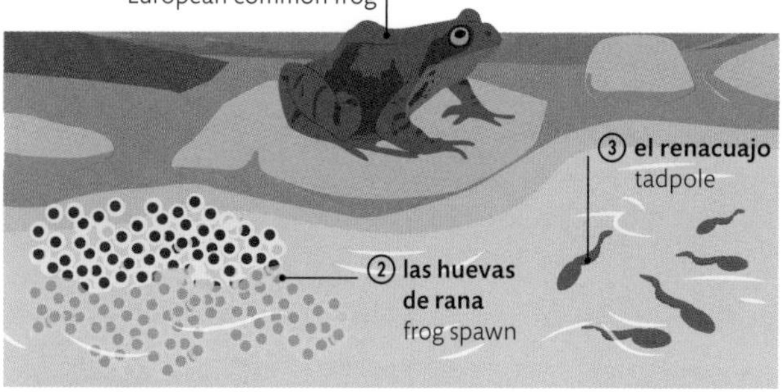

④ **la rana voladora de Wallace**
Wallace's flying frog

⑤ **la rana de dardo venenosa**
poison dart frog

⑥ **la rana de Darwin**
Darwin's frog

⑦ **la rana verde de ojos rojos**
red-eyed tree frog

⑧ **el sapo común**
common toad

⑨ **la rana toro africana**
African bullfrog

⑩ **el sapo de vientre de fuego oriental**
Oriental fire-bellied toad

⑪ **el sapo de las grandes planicies**
Great Plains toad

⑫ **la salamandra de fuego**
fire salamander

⑬ **el olm**
olm

⑭ **el ajolote mexicano**
Mexican axolotl

⑮ **el tritón crestado del norte**
great crested newt

⑯ **la salamandra roja**
red salamander

163.2 LOS REPTILES · REPTILES

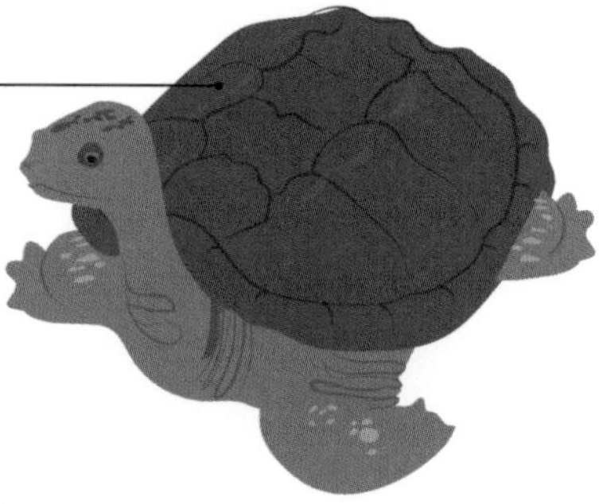

① **la tortuga de las Galápagos**
Galápagos turtle

③ **la tortuga estrellada**
radiated tortoise

④ **la tortuga matamata**
matamata

⑤ **la tortuga espalda de diamante**
diamond back terrapin

⑥ **la tortuga de cuello de serpiente**
common snake-necked turtle

⑦ **la tortuga verde**
green sea turtle

⑧ **la tortuga laúd**
leatherback sea turtle

⑨ **el camaleón de Parson**
parson's chameleon

⑩ **el camaleón pantera**
panther chameleon

⑪ **el camaleón de Jackson**
Jackson's chameleon

⑫ **el dragón de Komodo**
Komodo dragon

See also
77 La biología • Biology **157** La historia natural • Natural history **158-159** Los mamíferos Mammals **160-161** Las aves • Birds **162** Los insectos y los bichos • Bugs and insects

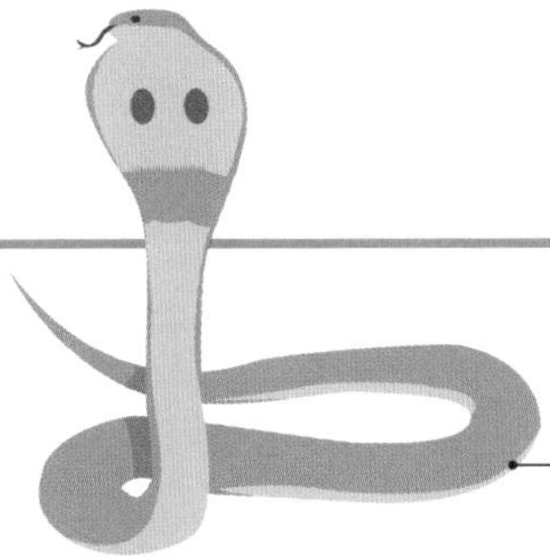

⑬ **la cobra india**
Indian cobra

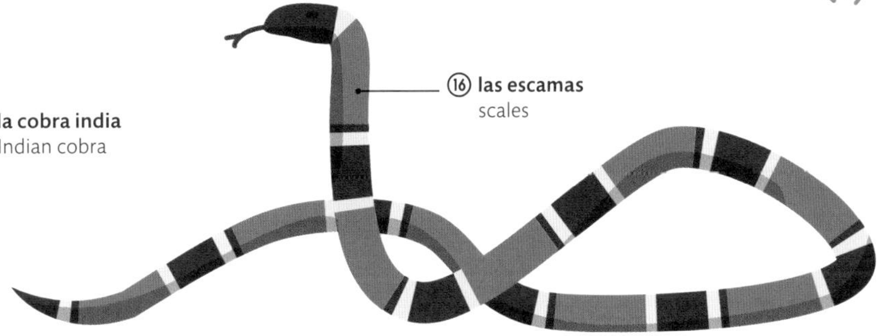

⑯ **las escamas**
scales

⑭ **la serpiente de cascabel**
rattlesnake

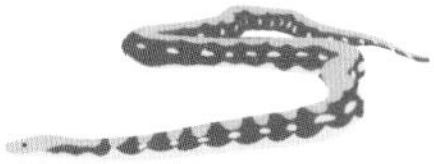

⑮ **la pitón reticulada**
reticulated python

⑰ **la serpiente de coral común**
eastern coral snake

⑱ **la boa esmeralda**
emerald tree boa

⑲ **la uropeltis macrolepis**
Bombay earth snake

⑳ **el crótalo cornudo**
sidewinder

㉑ **la serpiente liana verde**
Asian vine snake

㉒ **la cobra marina**
sea krait

㉓ **la serpiente comedora de huevos común**
common egg-eater

㉔ **la iguana marina**
marine iguana

㉕ **la iguana verde**
common green iguana

㉖ **el diablo espinoso**
thorny devil

㉗ **el basilisco verde**
green basilisk

㉘ **el escinco de lengua azul**
blue-tongued skink

㉙ **el monstruo de Gila**
gila monster

㉚ **el lagarto de cuello con volantes**
frill-necked lizard

㉛ **el gavial**
gharial

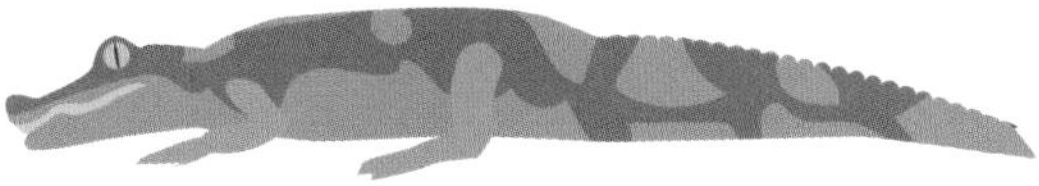

㉜ **el caimán de anteojos**
spectacled caiman

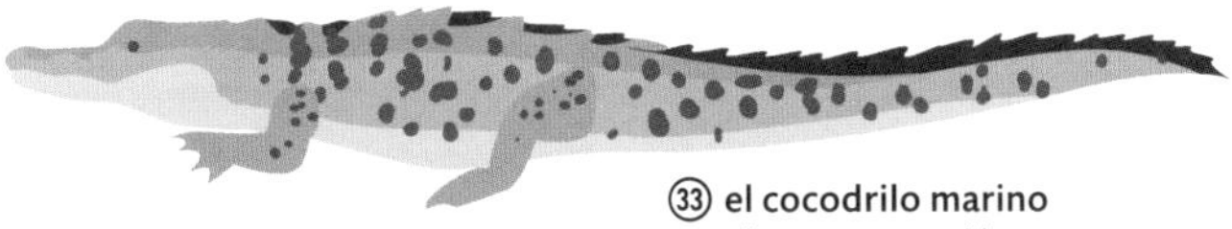

㉝ **el cocodrilo marino**
saltwater crocodile

㉞ **el cocodrilo del Nilo**
Nile crocodile

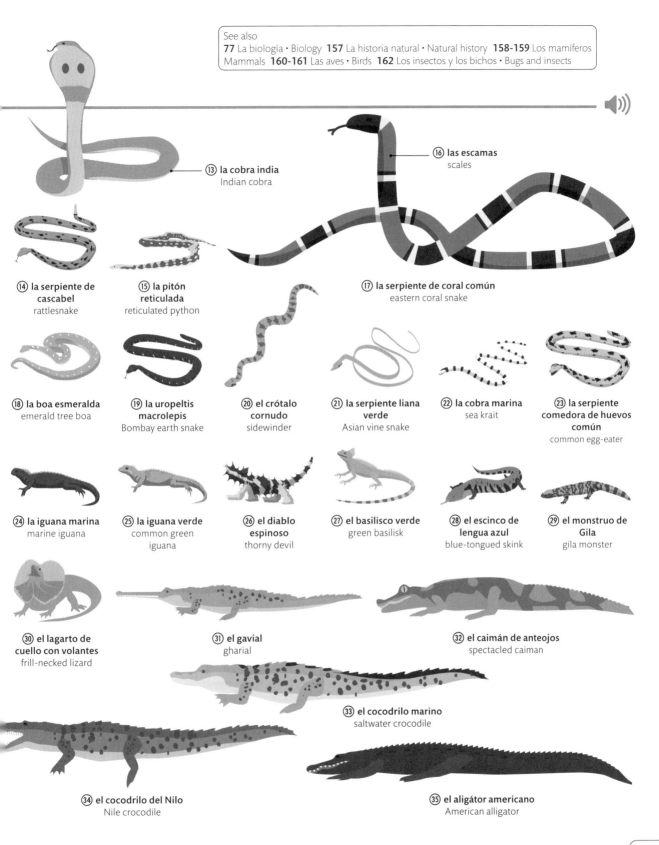

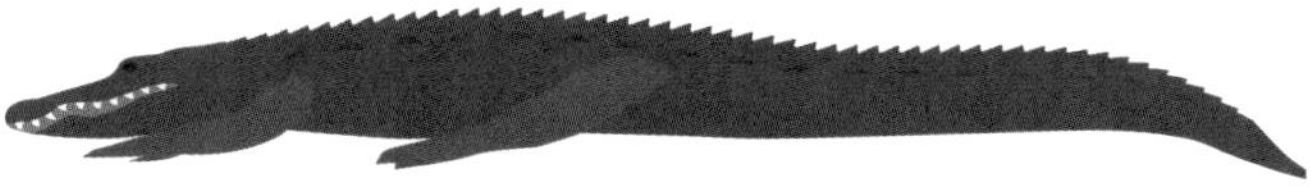

㉟ **el aligátor americano**
American alligator

164 Las mascotas
Pets

164.1 LAS RAZAS DE GATO · CAT BREEDS

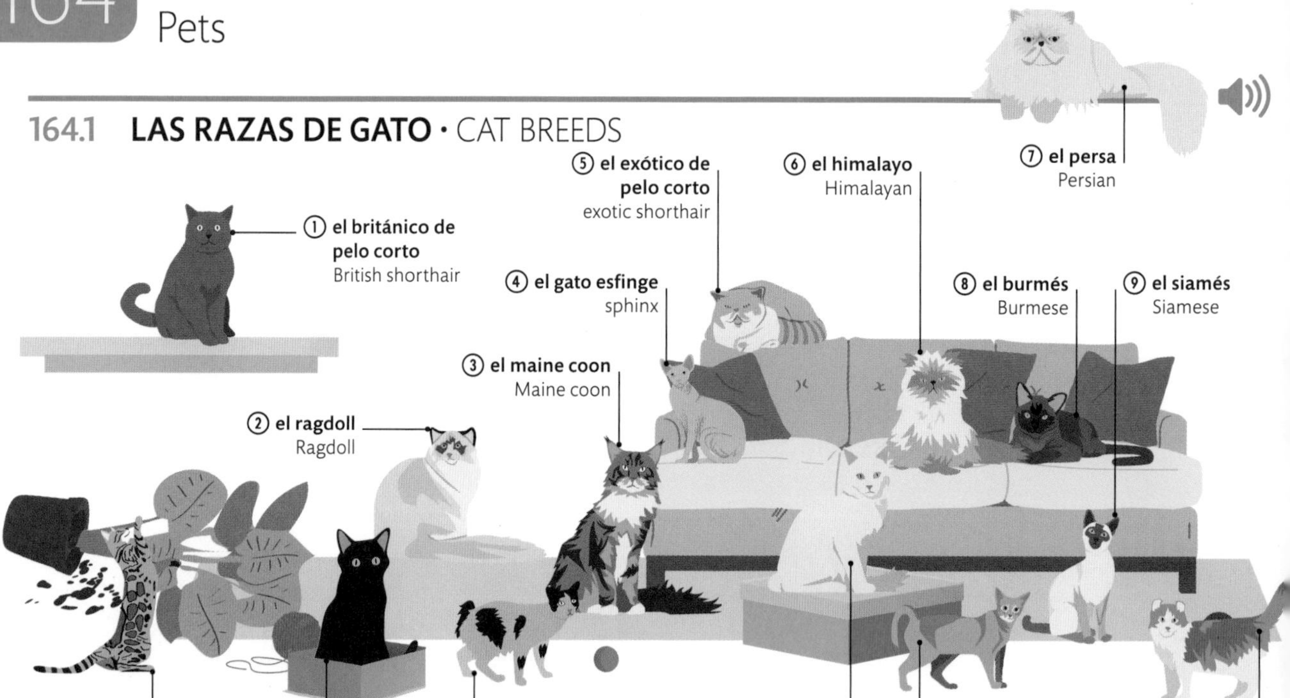

① **el británico de pelo corto**
British shorthair

② **el ragdoll**
Ragdoll

③ **el maine coon**
Maine coon

④ **el gato esfinge**
sphinx

⑤ **el exótico de pelo corto**
exotic shorthair

⑥ **el himalayo**
Himalayan

⑦ **el persa**
Persian

⑧ **el burmés**
Burmese

⑨ **el siamés**
Siamese

⑩ **el bengalí**
Bengal

⑪ **el bombay**
Bombay

⑫ **el bobtail japonés**
Japanese bobtail

⑬ **el angora**
Angora

⑭ **el abisinio**
Abyssinian

⑮ **el curl americano**
American curl

⑯ **maullar**
to meow

⑰ **ronronear**
to purr

⑱ **esconderse**
to hide

⑲ **mudar el pelo**
to moult

⑳ **el gatito**
kitten

164.3 OTRAS MASCOTAS · OTHER PETS

① **el hámster**
hamster

② **el jerbo**
gerbil

③ **el ratón**
mouse

④ **chillar**
to squeak

⑤ **el conejillo de indias**
guinea pig

⑥ **el conejo**
rabbit

⑦ **saltar**
to hop

⑧ **el hurón**
ferret

⑨ **el pez**
fish

⑩ **el lagarto**
lizard

⑪ **el insecto palo**
stick insect

⑫ **la tortuga**
tortoise

⑬ **el periquito**
budgerigar / budgie

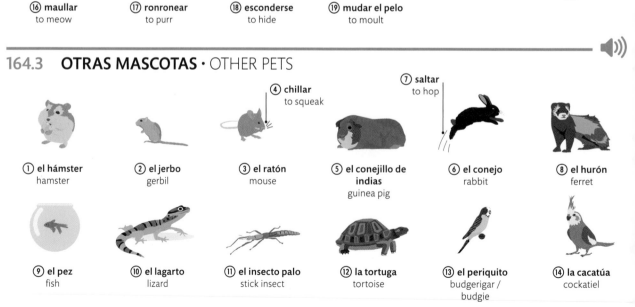

⑭ **la cacatúa**
cockatiel

See also
158-159 Los mamíferos • Mammals **160-161** Las aves • Birds **162** Los insectos y los bichos • Insects and bugs **163** Los anfibios y los reptiles • Amphibians and reptiles

164.2 LAS RAZAS DE PERRO • DOG BREEDS

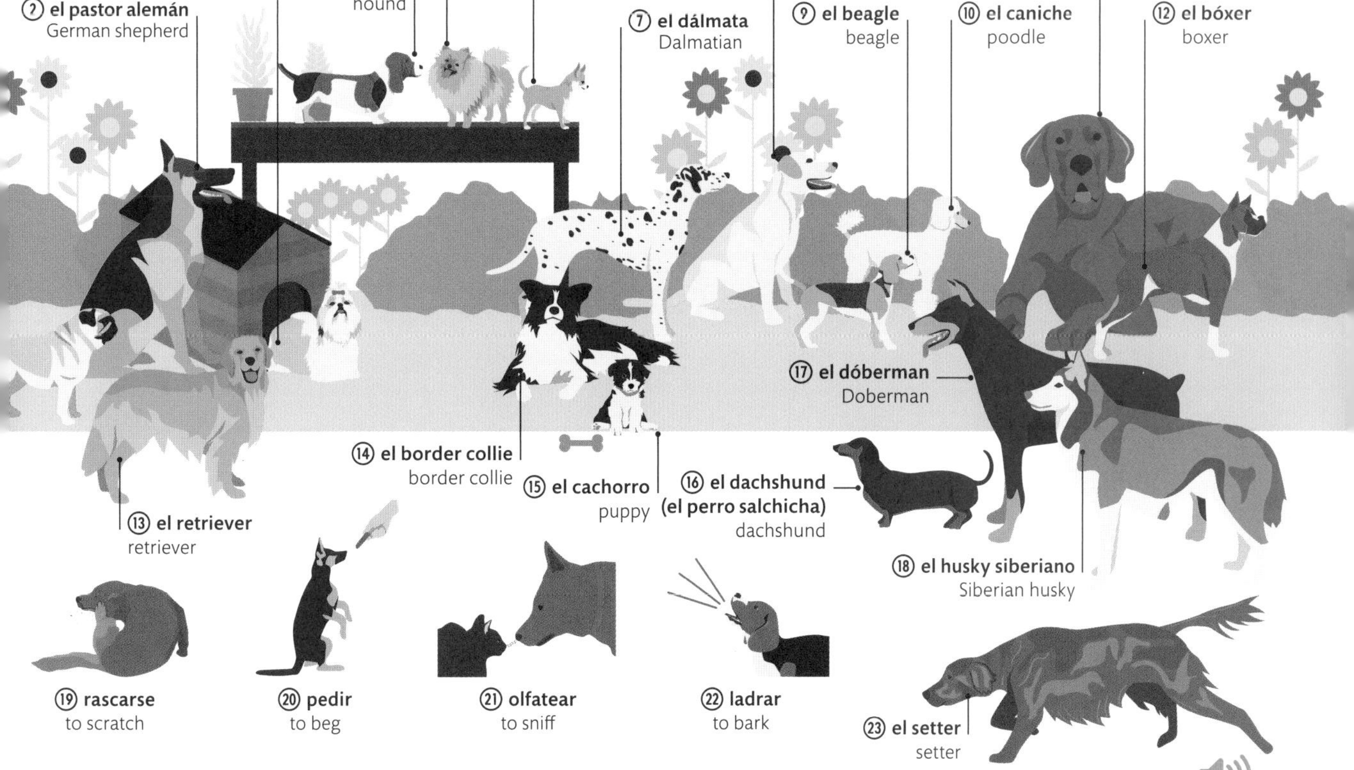

① **el carlino**
pug

② **el pastor alemán**
German shepherd

③ **el shih tzu**
shih tzu

④ **el basset hound**
basset hound

⑤ **el pomerania**
Pomeranian

⑥ **el chihuahua**
chihuahua

⑦ **el dálmata**
Dalmatian

⑧ **el labrador**
labrador

⑨ **el beagle**
beagle

⑩ **el caniche**
poodle

⑪ **el gran danés**
Great Dane

⑫ **el bóxer**
boxer

⑬ **el retriever**
retriever

⑭ **el border collie**
border collie

⑮ **el cachorro**
puppy

⑯ **el dachshund (el perro salchicha)**
dachshund

⑰ **el dóberman**
Doberman

⑱ **el husky siberiano**
Siberian husky

⑲ **rascarse**
to scratch

⑳ **pedir**
to beg

㉑ **olfatear**
to sniff

㉒ **ladrar**
to bark

㉓ **el setter**
setter

164.4 LOS PRODUCTOS PARA MASCOTAS • PET SUPPLIES

① **el acuario**
fish tank / aquarium

② **la cesta**
basket

③ **la caseta del perro**
kennel

④ **la jaula**
cage

⑤ **la conejera**
rabbit hutch

⑥ **el arenero**
litter tray

⑦ **la correa**
leash / lead

⑧ **el vivero**
vivarium

⑨ **el alpiste**
birdseed

⑩ **los premios**
treats

⑪ **los juguetes**
toys

165 Los animales de granja
Farm animals

165.1 **EN LA GRANJA** · ON THE FARM

② **Doy de comer a las gallinas dos veces al día.**
I feed the chickens twice a day.
① **la gallina**
chicken
③ **la oveja**
sheep
④ **el pollito**
chick
⑤ **la vaca**
cow
⑥ **el cordero**
lamb

⑭ **el gallo**
rooster / cockerel

⑮ **la gallina**
hen

⑯ **el pavo**
turkey

⑰ **las aves de corral**
poultry

㉑ **la abeja**
bee

㉒ **el rebaño de ovejas**
flock of sheep

⑱ **el carnero**
ram

⑲ **la oveja hembra**
ewe

⑳ **la colmena**
hive

㉓ **el rebaño de vacas**
herd of cows

㉔ **el toro**
bull

㉕ **el ternero**
calf

㉖ **el ganado**
cattle

㉗ **el burro**
donkey

See also
53 La carne • Meat **86** La agricultura • Farming
158-159 Los mamíferos • Mammals **164** Las mascotas • Pets

㉘ **el semental**
stallion

㉙ **la yegua**
mare

㉚ **el potro**
foal

㉛ **la cabra**
goat

㉜ **el cabrito**
kid

㉝ **el avestruz**
ostrich

㉞ **la llama**
llama

㉟ **la alpaca**
to shear

㊱ **esquilar**
to shear

㊲ **trotar**
to trot

㊳ **galopar**
to gallop

㊴ **cargar**
to charge

㊵ **cacarear**
to crow

㊶ **balar**
to bleat

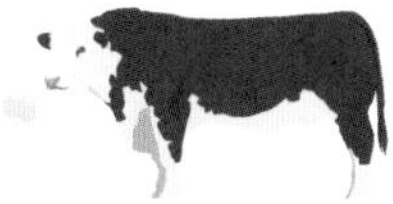
㊷ **resoplar**
to snort

㊸ **gruñir**
to grunt

㊹ **rebuznar**
to bray

㊺ **graznar**
to quack

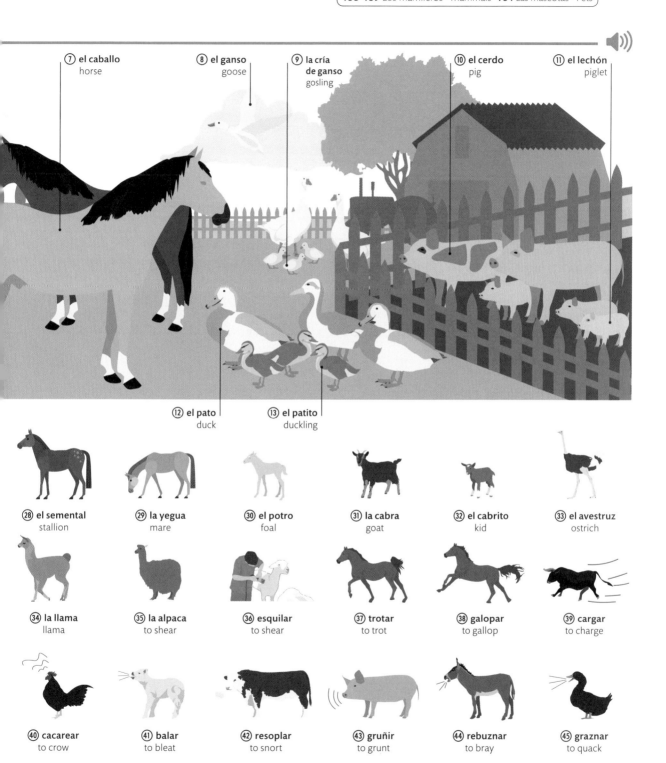

166 La vida oceánica
Ocean life

166.1 LAS ESPECIES MARINAS · MARINE SPECIES

① **el percebe** barnacle
② **la lapa** limpet
③ **la anémona** anemone
④ **el erizo de mar** sea urchin
⑤ **la estrella de mar** starfish
⑥ **el agujón** needlefish

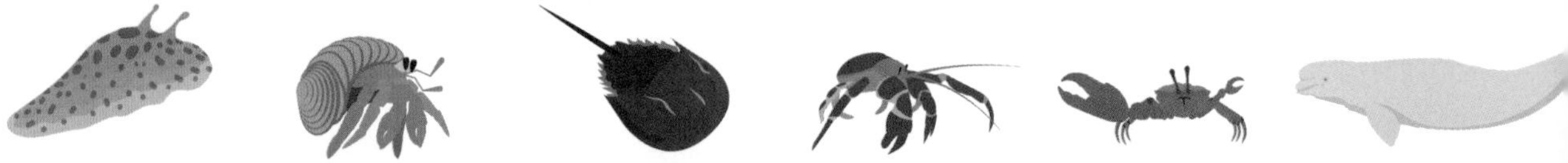

⑦ **el nudibranquio** sea slug
⑧ **el cangrejo ermitaño** hermit crab
⑨ **el cangrejo herradura** horseshoe crab
⑩ **el cangrejo cocotero** coconut crab
⑪ **el cangrejo violinista** fiddler crab
⑫ **la beluga** beluga

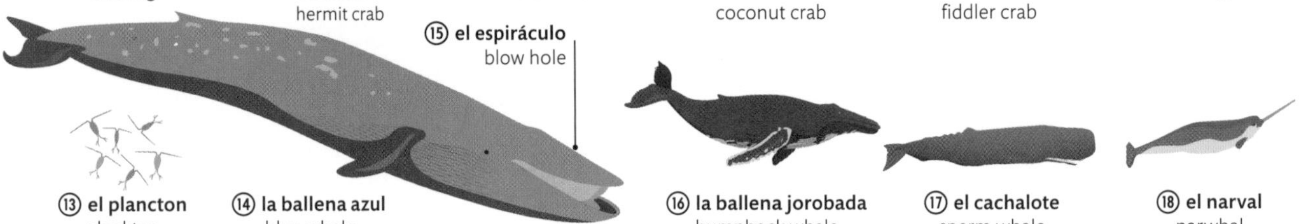

⑬ **el plancton** plankton
⑭ **la ballena azul** blue whale
⑯ **la ballena jorobada** humpback whale
⑰ **el cachalote** sperm whale
⑱ **el narval** narwhal

⑲ **la orca asesina** killer whale
⑳ **la marsopa** porpoise
㉑ **el delfín** dolphin
㉒ **la foca** seal
㉓ **el león marino** sea lion
㉔ **la morsa** walrus

166.2 EL ARRECIFE DE CORAL · CORAL REEF

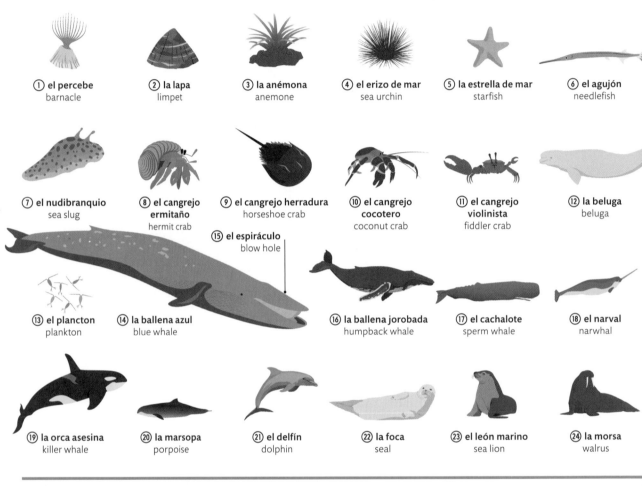

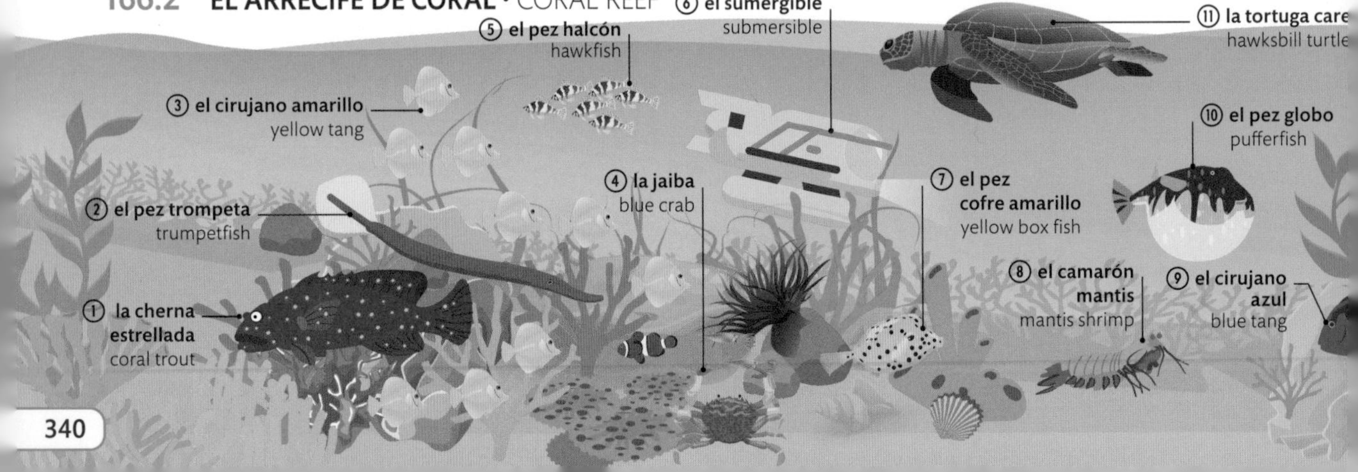

See also
54 El pescado y el marisco • Fish and seafood **121** La pesca Fishing **134** En la playa • On the beach **146-147** La geografía Geography **157** La historia natural • Natural history

㉕ **el nautilo**
nautilus

㉖ **la medusa**
jellyfish

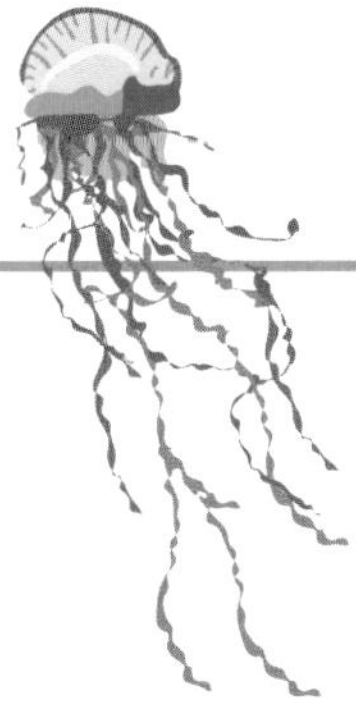

㉗ **la carabela portuguesa**
Portuguese man-of-war

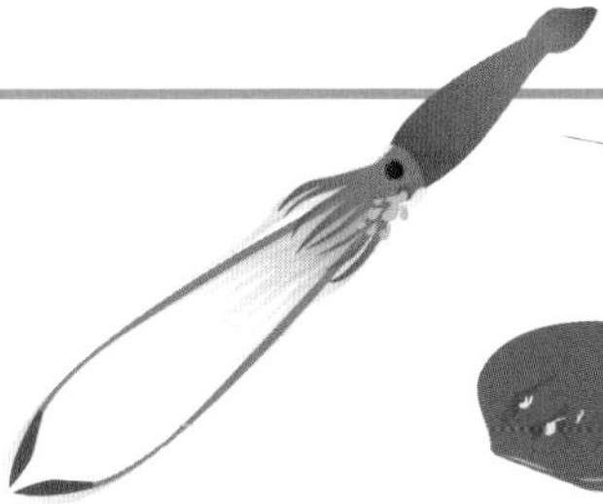

㉘ **el calamar gigante**
giant squid

㉙ **la raya**
ray

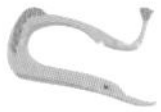

㉚ **el pez pipa**
pipefish

㉛ **el salmón del Atlántico**
Atlantic salmon

㉜ **el bacalao**
cod

㉝ **la barracuda**
barracuda

㉞ **el pez sierra**
sawfish

㉟ **el pez volador**
flying fish

㊱ **el pez vela**
sail fish

㊲ **el tiburón blanco**
great white shark

㊳ **el tiburón martillo**
hammerhead shark

㊴ **el tiburón peregrino**
basking shark

㊵ **el rape abisal**
angler fish

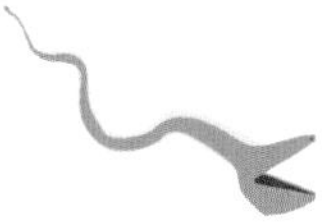

㊶ **el pez pelícano**
gulper eel

㊷ **el saltarín del fango**
mudskipper

㊸ **el alga** *f*
seaweed

㊹ **el alga parda** *f*
kelp

㊺ **la zona fótica**
sunlit zone

㊻ **la zona crepuscular**
twilight zone

㊼ **la zona de medianoche**
midnight zone

㊽ **la zona adal**
hadal zone

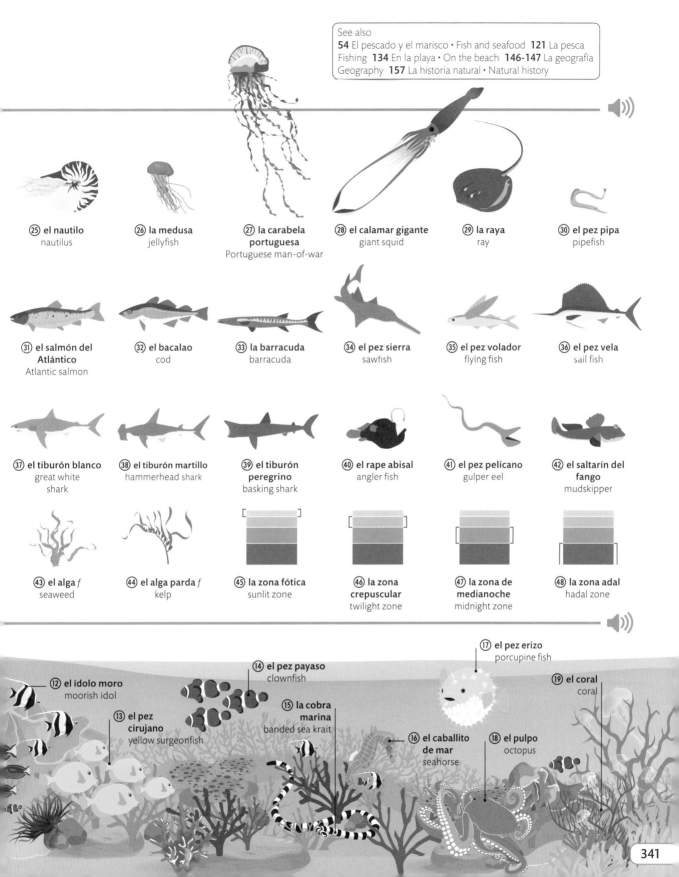

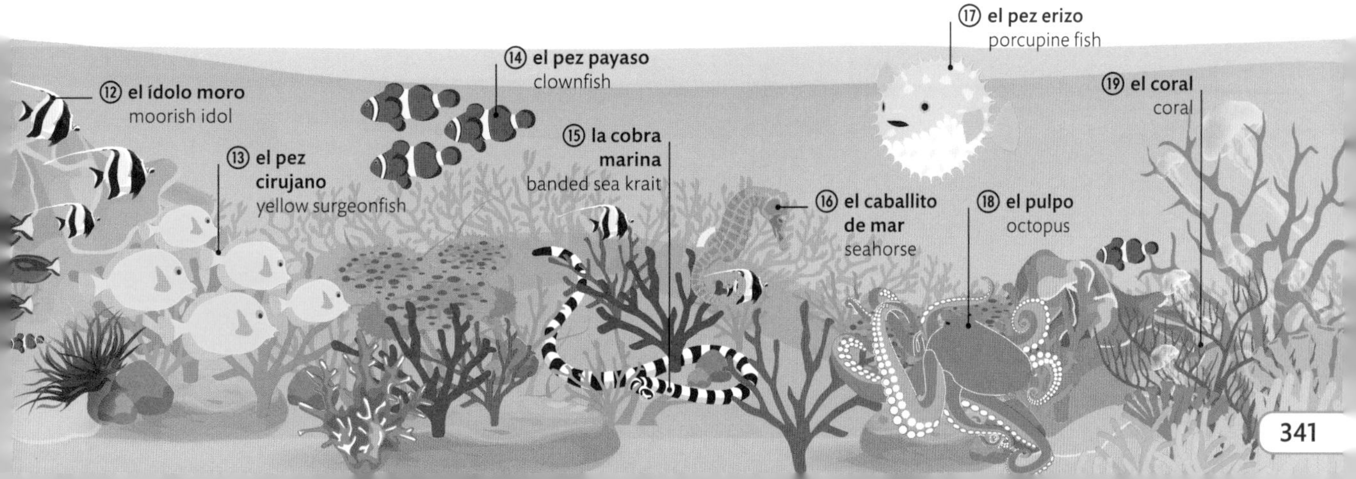

Las plantas y los árboles
Plants and trees

167.1 LAS PLANTAS Y LOS ÁRBOLES · PLANTS AND TREES

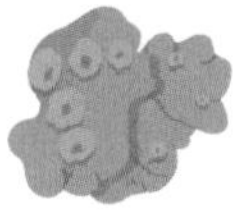

① **la hepática**
liverwort

② **el musgo**
moss

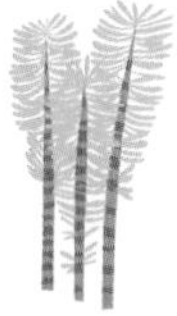

③ **la cola de caballo**
horsetail

④ **el helecho**
fern

⑤ **la cica**
cycad

⑥ **el ginkgo**
ginkgo

⑪ **las coníferas**
conifers

⑦ **la pícea**
spruce

⑧ **el abeto**
fir

⑨ **el árbol de cola de mono**
monkey puzzle

⑩ **el tejo**
yew

⑫ **el alerce**
larch

⑬ **el cedro del Líbano**
cedar of Lebanon

⑭ **el pino sombrilla**
umbrella pine

⑮ **el nenúfar**
water lily

⑯ **la magnolia**
magnolia

⑰ **el aguacatero**
avocado tree

⑱ **el laurel**
laurel

⑲ **la cala**
arum lily

⑳ **la secuoya gigante**
giant sequoia

㉑ **el árbol de Josué**
Joshua tree

㉒ **la amarilis**
amaryllis

㉓ **las orejas de burro**
cast-iron plant

㉔ **el árbol dragón**
dragon tree

㉕ **la campanilla azul**
English bluebell

㉖ **la campanilla de invierno**
snowdrop

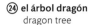

㉗ **el azafrán**
crocus

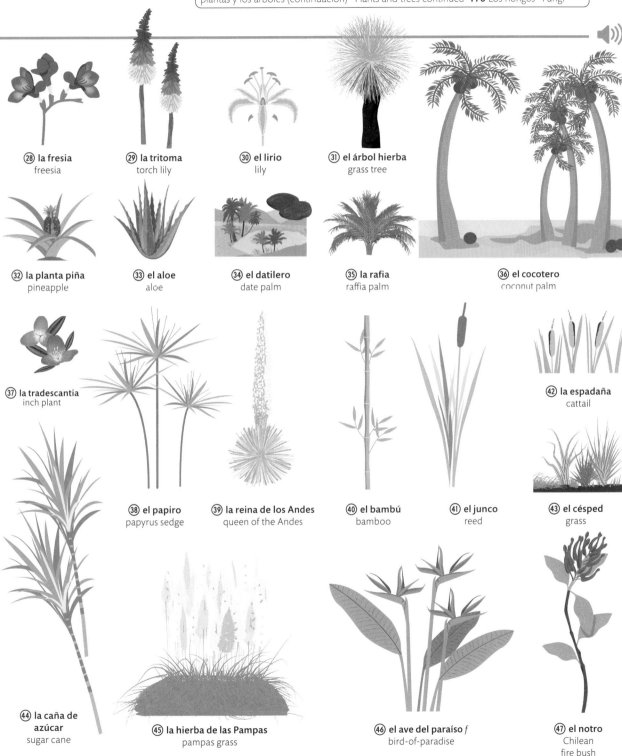

See also
38 Las plantas de interior y de jardín • Garden plants and houseplants **57** La fruta • Fruit
58 La fruta y los frutos secos • Fruit and nuts **157** La historia natural • Natural history **169** Las plantas y los árboles (continuación) • Plants and trees continued **170** Los hongos • Fungi

㉘ la fresia
freesia

㉙ la tritoma
torch lily

㉚ el lirio
lily

㉛ el árbol hierba
grass tree

㉜ la planta piña
pineapple

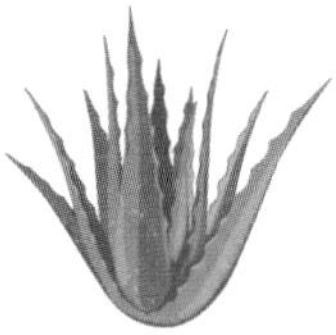

㉝ el aloe
aloe

㉞ el datilero
date palm

㉟ la rafia
raffia palm

㊱ el cocotero
coconut palm

㊲ la tradescantia
inch plant

㊳ el papiro
papyrus sedge

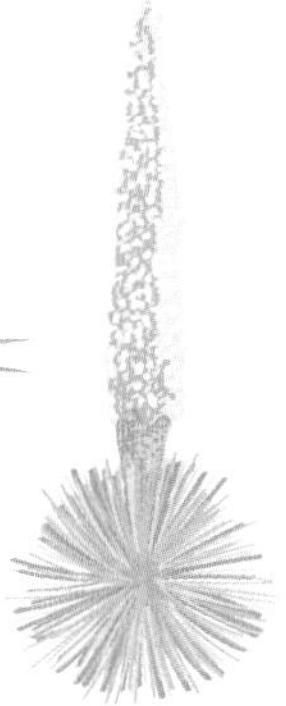

㊴ la reina de los Andes
queen of the Andes

㊵ el bambú
bamboo

㊶ el junco
reed

㊷ la espadaña
cattail

㊸ el césped
grass

㊹ la caña de azúcar
sugar cane

㊺ la hierba de las Pampas
pampas grass

㊻ el ave del paraíso *f*
bird-of-paradise

㊼ el notro
Chilean fire bush

Las plantas y los árboles (continuación)
Plants and trees continued

168.1 LAS PLANTAS Y LOS ÁRBOLES · PLANTS AND TREES

① **la celandina**
celandine

② **la amapola**
common poppy

③ **el agracejo**
barberry

④ **el plátano de sombra**
London plane

⑤ **el botón de oro**
buttercup

⑥ **la adormidera**
opium poppy

⑦ **el árbol del viajero**
traveller's tree

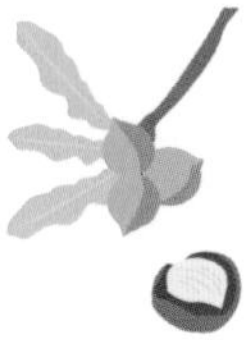

⑧ **la macadamia**
macadamia

⑨ **la enredadera amarilla**
golden guinea vine

⑩ **el ruibarbo gigante**
gunnera

⑪ **la aquilegia**
columbine

⑫ **la frítia**
fairy elephant's feet

⑬ **las piedras vivas**
living stones

⑭ **el cactus cabeza de viejo**
old man cactus

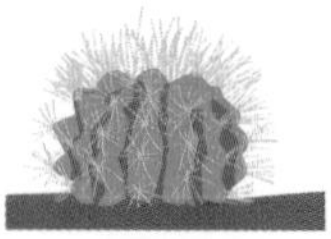

⑮ **el cactus barril dorado**
barrel cactus

⑯ **la chumbera**
prickly pear

⑰ **la juliana falsa**
campion

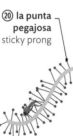

⑱ **la gloria de Texas**
glory of Texas

⑳ **la punta pegajosa**
sticky prong

㉑ **el insecto atrapado**
trapped insect

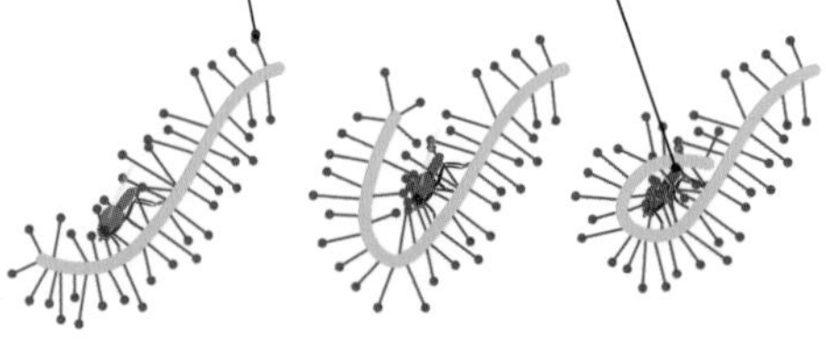

⑲ **el rocío del sol**
sundew

㉒ **la venus atrapamoscas**
Venus fly-trap

㉔ **la mosca**
fly

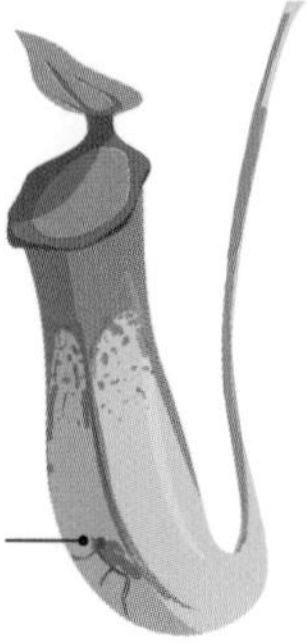

㉓ **la planta odre**
pitcher plant

See also
38 Las plantas de interior y de jardín • Garden plants and houseplants **57** La fruta • Fruit
58 La fruta y los frutos secos • Fruit and nuts **157** La historia natural • Natural history **169** Las plantas y los árboles (continuación) • Plants and trees continued **170** Los hongos • Fungi

㉕ **la buganvilla**
bougainvillea

㉖ **el flamboyán**
fire tree

㉗ **el muérdago**
mistletoe

㉘ **la siempreviva de los tejados**
common houseleek

㉙ **la parra**
grapevine

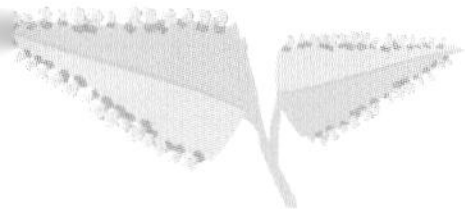

㉚ **el aranto**
mother of thousands

㉛ **la peonía**
peony

㉜ **la parra virgen**
Virginia creeper

㉝ **el mirto**
myrtle

㉞ **el granado**
pomegranate

㉟ **la arroyuella**
purple loosestrife

㊱ **la henna**
henna

㊲ **el árbol del cepillo**
Tonghi bottlebrush

㊳ **el guayabo**
guava

㊴ **la fucsia**
fuchsia

㊵ **la mimosa**
mimosa

㊶ **el árbol de la seda**
silk tree

㊷ **el hojarazo**
hornbeam

㊹ **las semillas**
seed

㊸ **el avellano**
hazel

㊺ **el nogal**
walnut

㊻ **el castaño**
Spanish chestnut

㊼ **el pecán**
pecan

㊽ **el haya** *f*
beech

㊾ **el abedul**
birch

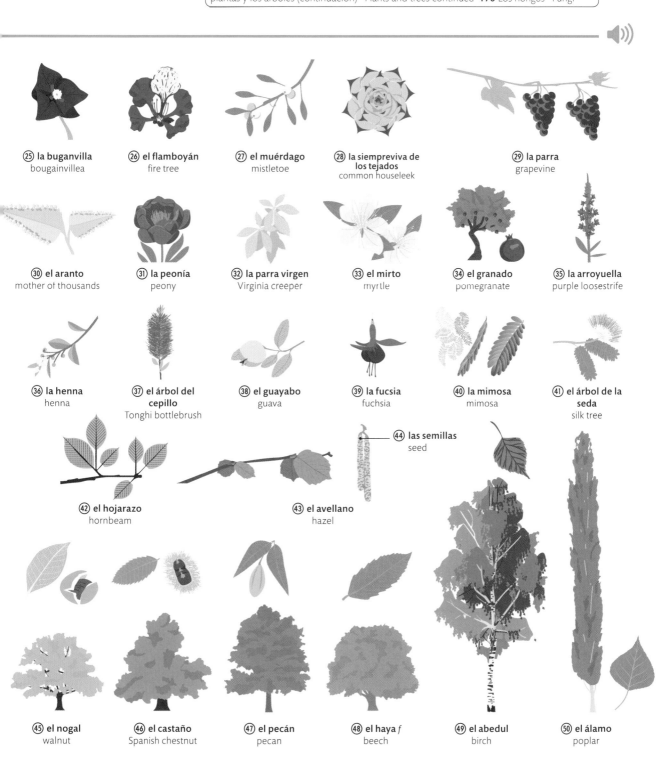

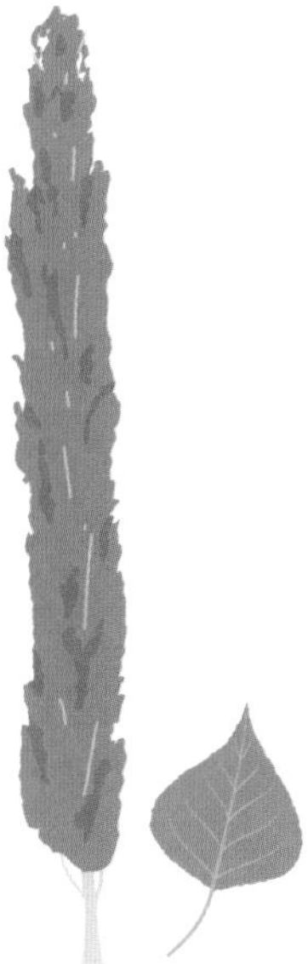

㊿ **el álamo**
poplar

169 Las plantas y los árboles (continuación)

Plants and trees continued

169.1 LAS PLANTAS Y LOS ÁRBOLES · PLANTS AND TREES

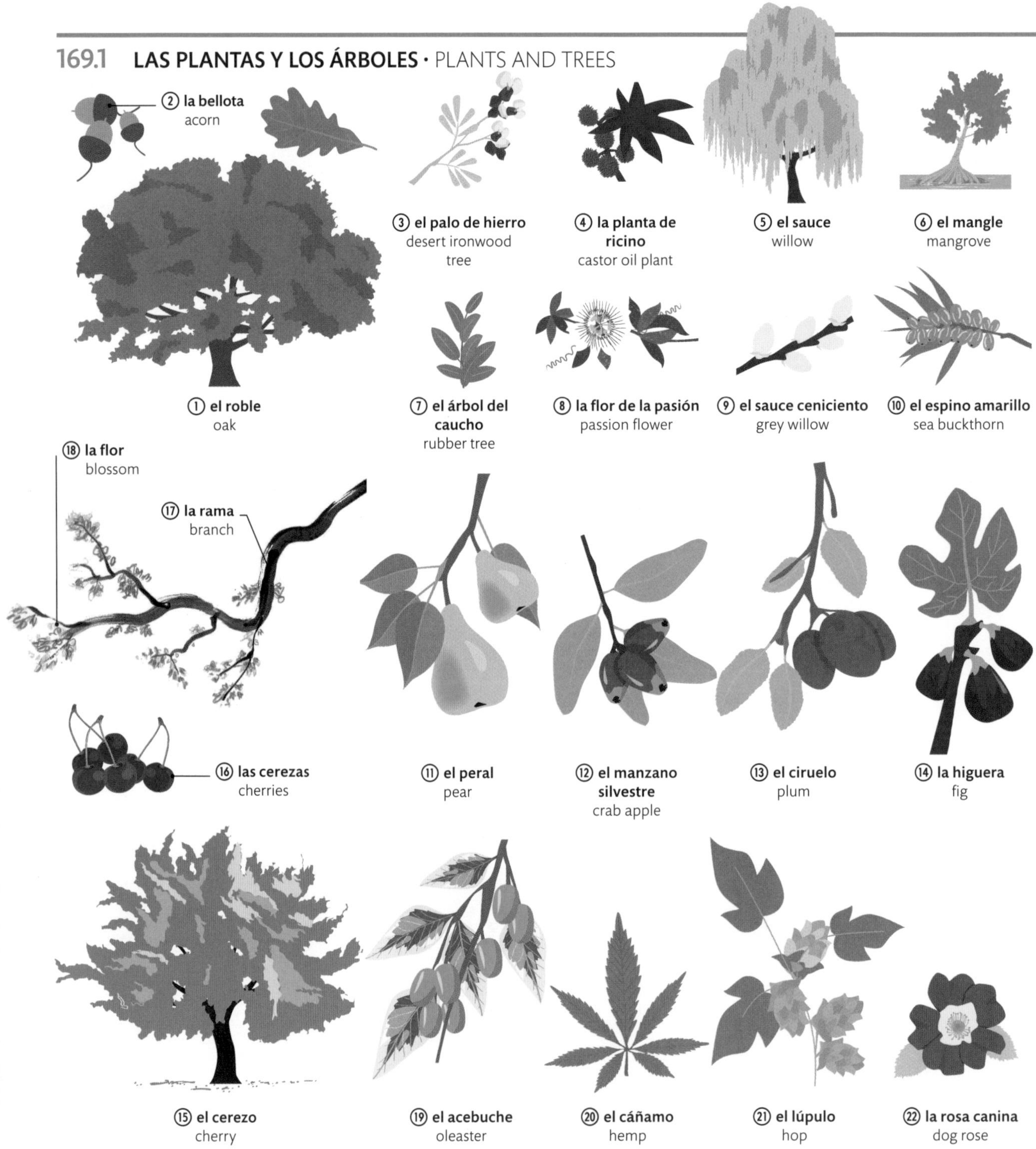

See also
38 Las plantas de interior y de jardín • Garden plants and houseplants **57** La fruta • Fruit **58** La fruta y los frutos secos • Fruit and nuts **157** La historia natural • Natural history **170** Los hongos • Fungi

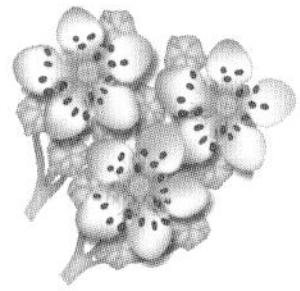
(23) **la griñolera**
cotoneaster

(24) **el serbal**
mountain ash

(25) **el níspero**
medlar

(26) **el espino**
hawthorn

(27) **el olmo**
elm

(28) **la ortiga**
nettle

(29) **la capuchina**
nasturtium

(30) **el alhelí**
wallflower

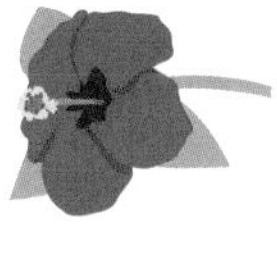
(31) **el hibisco**
Chinese hibiscus

(32) **el cacao**
cocoa

(43) **la sámara**
samara

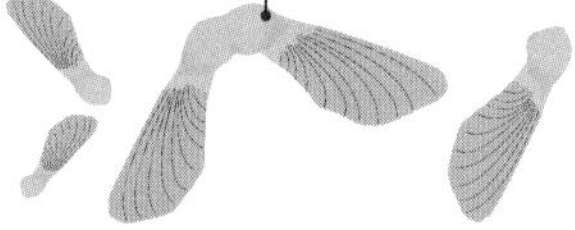

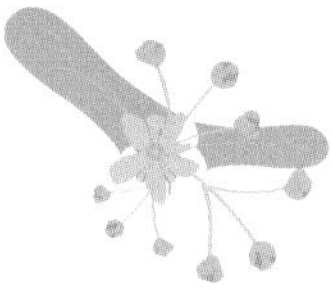
(33) **el tilo**
lime / linden

(34) **la prímula**
cowslip

(35) **el cedro chino**
Chinese mahogany

(36) **el baobab**
baobab tree

(42) **la hoja de verano**
summer leaf

(41) **el sicomoro**
sycamore

(44) **la hoja de otoño**
autumn leaf

(37) **el arce**
maple

(38) **el castaño de Indias**
horse chestnut

(39) **la adelfa**
oleander

(40) **el olivo**
olive

(45) **el dondiego de día**
morning glory

(46) **la belladona**
deadly nightshade

(47) **la cicuta**
hemlock

(48) **el cardo**
thistle

(49) **la hiedra**
ivy

(50) **la linterna china**
Chinese lantern

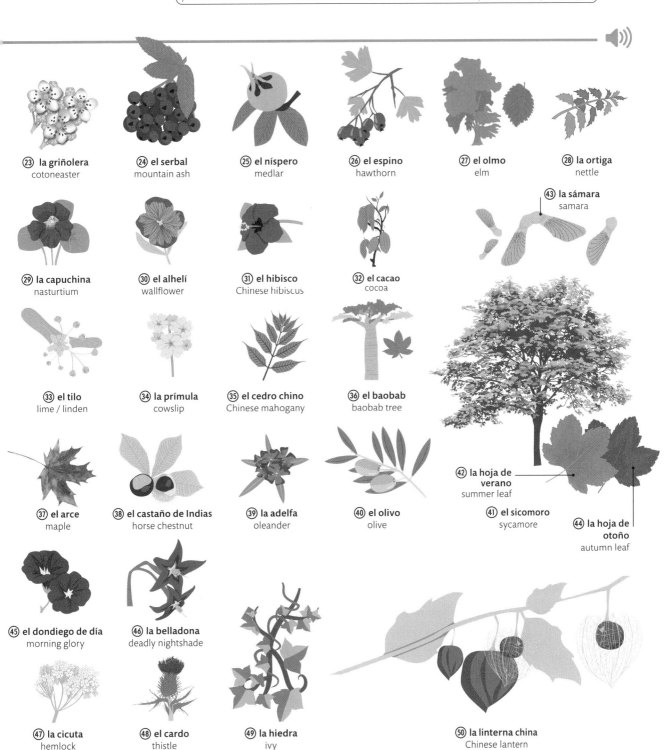

Los hongos
Fungi

170.1 LAS ESPECIES DE HONGOS · SPECIES OF FUNGI

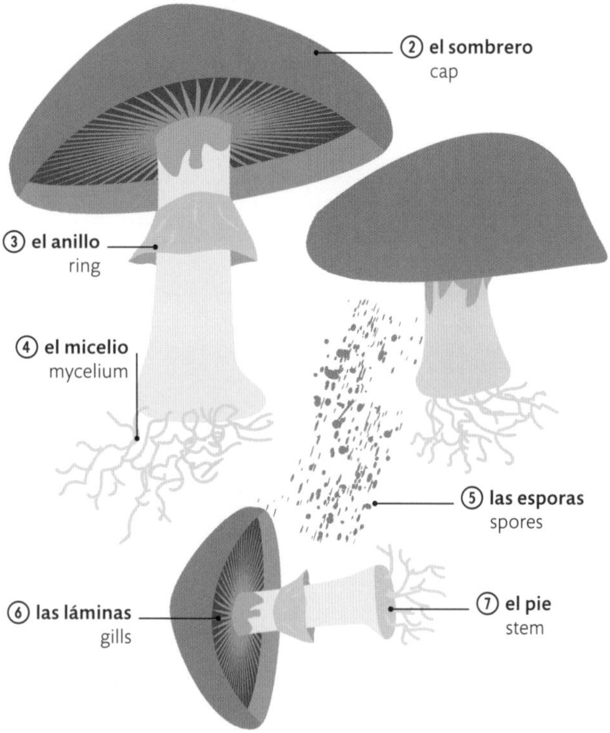

① **las setas**
mushrooms

⑧ **el yesquero erizado**
shaggy bracket fungus

⑨ **recoger setas**
to forage / to pick mushrooms

⑬ **el bejín**
common puffball

㉑ **las setas cultivadas**
cultivated mushrooms

㉒ **las setas venenosas**
toadstools

㉓ **el anillo de hadas**
fairy ring

㉔ **la seta ostra**
oyster mushroom

㉕ **la oronja**
orange-cap boletus

㉖ **el pollo del bosque**
chicken of the woods

㉗ **la lengua de gato**
hedgehog mushroom

㉘ **la melena de león**
bear's head tooth

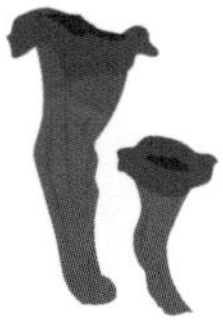

㉙ **la trompeta de la muerte**
black trumpet

㉚ **la seta barbuda**
shaggy mane mushroom

㉛ **la gallina del bosque**
hen of the wood

㉜ **el moho**
mold

See also
55-56 La verdura • Vegetables **133** Las actividades al aire libre • Outdoor activities
167-169 Las plantas y los árboles • Plants and trees

⑩ **el enoki**
enoki mushroom

⑪ **el shiitake**
shiitake mushroom

⑫ **el higróforo**
waxcap

⑮ **la colmenilla**
morel

⑯ **el bejín gigante**
giant puffball

⑰ **el champiñón silvestre**
field mushroom

⑱ **la trufa**
truffle

⑲ **el hongo blanco**
porcini

⑳ **el rebozuelo**
chanterelle

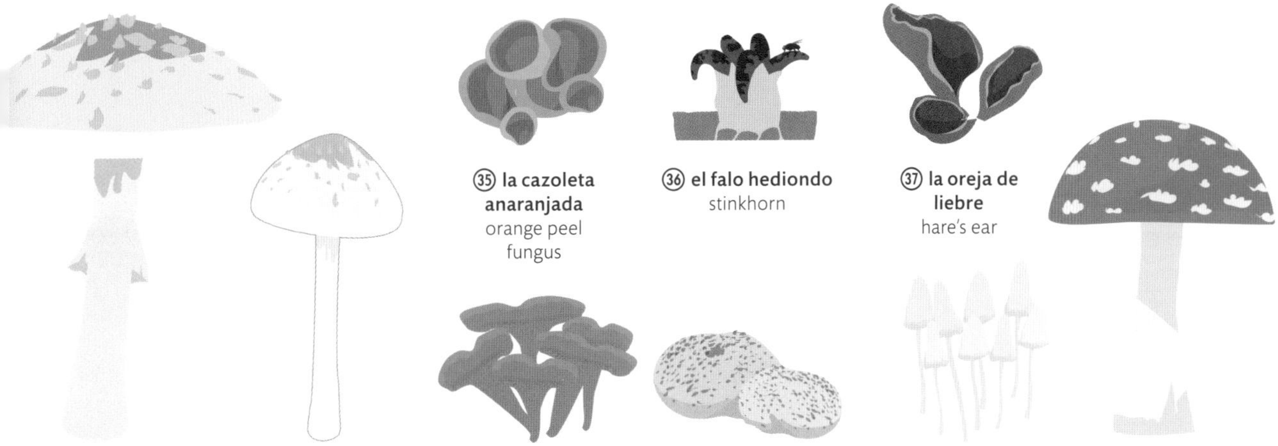

㉟ **la cazoleta anaranjada**
orange peel fungus

㊱ **el falo hediondo**
stinkhorn

㊲ **la oreja de liebre**
hare's ear

㉝ **la oronja verde**
death cap

㉞ **el ángel destructor**
death angel

㊳ **la seta de olivo**
jack-o'-lantern

㊴ **la bola de tierra común**
common earthball

㊵ **la seta de jardín**
milky conecap

㊶ **la matamoscas**
fly agaric

171 El tiempo
Time

171.1 DAR LA HORA · TELLING THE TIME

① ¿Qué hora es?
What time is it?
② Son las tres en punto.
It's three o'clock.

③ **la una en punto**
one o'clock

④ **la una y cinco**
five past one

⑤ **la una y diez**
ten past one

⑥ **la una y cuarto**
quarter past one

⑦ **la una y veinte**
twenty past one

⑧ **la una y veinticinco**
twenty-five past one

⑨ **la una y media**
one thirty / half past one

⑩ **las dos menos veinticinco**
twenty-five to two

⑪ **las dos menos veinte**
twenty to two

⑫ **las dos menos cuarto**
quarter to two

⑬ **las dos menos diez**
ten to two

⑭ **las dos menos cinco**
five to two

⑮ **las dos en punto**
two o'clock

⑯ **el segundo**
second

⑰ **el minuto**
minute

⑱ **el cuarto de hora**
quarter of an hour

171.2 LAS PARTES DEL DÍA · PARTS OF THE DAY

① **el alba** *f*
dawn

② **el amanecer**
sunrise

③ **la mañana**
morning

④ **el mediodía**
midday

⑤ **la tarde**
afternoon

See also
172 El calendario · The calendar **173** Los números · Numbers
174 Los pesos y las medidas · Weights and measures

⑲ **veinte minutos**
twenty minutes

⑳ **media hora**
half an hour

㉑ **cuarenta minutos**
forty minutes

㉒ **una hora**
an hour

㉓ **ahora**
now

㉔ **temprano**
early

㉕ **a tiempo**
on time

㉖ **tarde**
late

㉗ **después**
later

㉘ **cada hora**
hourly

㉙ **siempre**
always

㉚ **nunca**
never

㉜ **el minutero**
minute hand

㉝ **el reloj**
clock

㉛ **el segundero**
second hand

㉞ **el horario**
hour hand

㉟ **¿A qué hora empieza?**
What time does
it start?

㊱ **A las 6 p.m. ¡Vamos a
llegar tarde!**
At 6pm. We're going to
be late!

㊲ **llegar tarde**
to be late

⑥ **la tarde-noche**
evening

⑦ **el atardecer**
sunset

⑧ **el crepúsculo**
dusk

⑨ **la medianoche**
midnight

⑩ **la noche**
night

⑪ **el día**
day

172 El calendario

The calendar

172.1 EL CALENDARIO Y LAS ESTACIONES · CALENDAR AND SEASONS

① **el día** day | ② **la semana** week | ③ **la quincena** two weeks / fortnight | ④ **el fin de semana** weekend | ⑤ **el mes** month

⑥ **el año** year | ⑦ **la década** decade | ⑧ **el siglo** century | ⑨ **el milenio** millennium

⑩ **lunes** Monday | ⑪ **martes** Tuesday | ⑫ **miércoles** Wednesday | ⑬ **jueves** Thursday | ⑭ **viernes** Friday | ⑮ **sábado** Saturday | ⑯ **domingo** Sunday

⑰ **enero** *m* January | ⑱ **febrero** *m* February | ⑲ **marzo** *m* March | ⑳ **abril** *m* April | ㉑ **mayo** *m* May | ㉒ **junio** *m* June

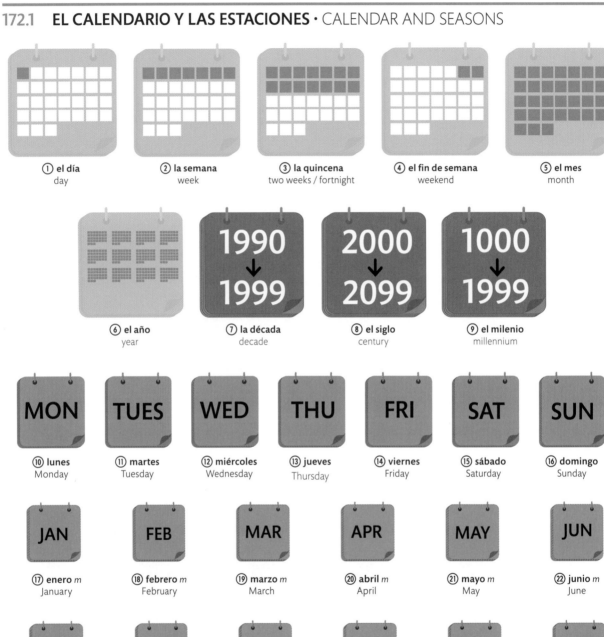

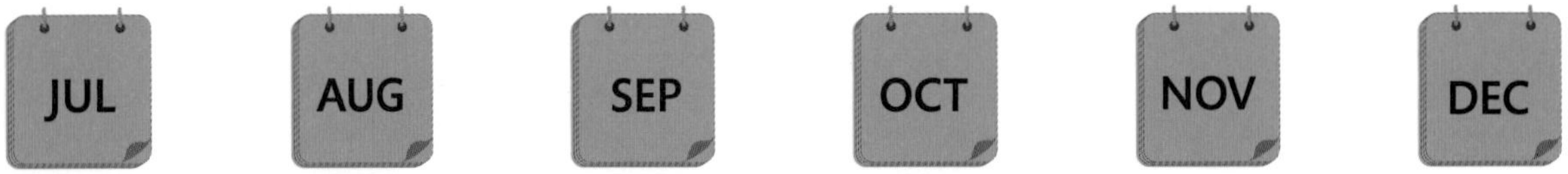

㉓ **julio** *m* July | ㉔ **agosto** *m* August | ㉕ **septiembre** *m* September | ㉖ **octubre** *m* October | ㉗ **noviembre** *m* November | ㉘ **diciembre** *m* December

See also
171 El tiempo • Time
173 Los números • Numbers

(29) mil novecientos
nineteen hundred

(30) mil novecientos uno
nineteen-oh-one

(31) mil novecientos diez
nineteen ten

(32) dos mil
two thousand

(33) dos mil uno
two thousand and one

(34) dos mil treinta y tres
twenty thirty-three

(35) una vez a la semana
once a week

(36) dos veces a la semana
twice a week

(37) tres veces a la semana
three times a week

(38) todos los días
every day

(39) cada dos días
every other day

(40) solo los fines de semana
only weekends

(41) cada hora
hourly

(42) cada día
daily

(43) cada semana
weekly

(44) cada mes
monthly

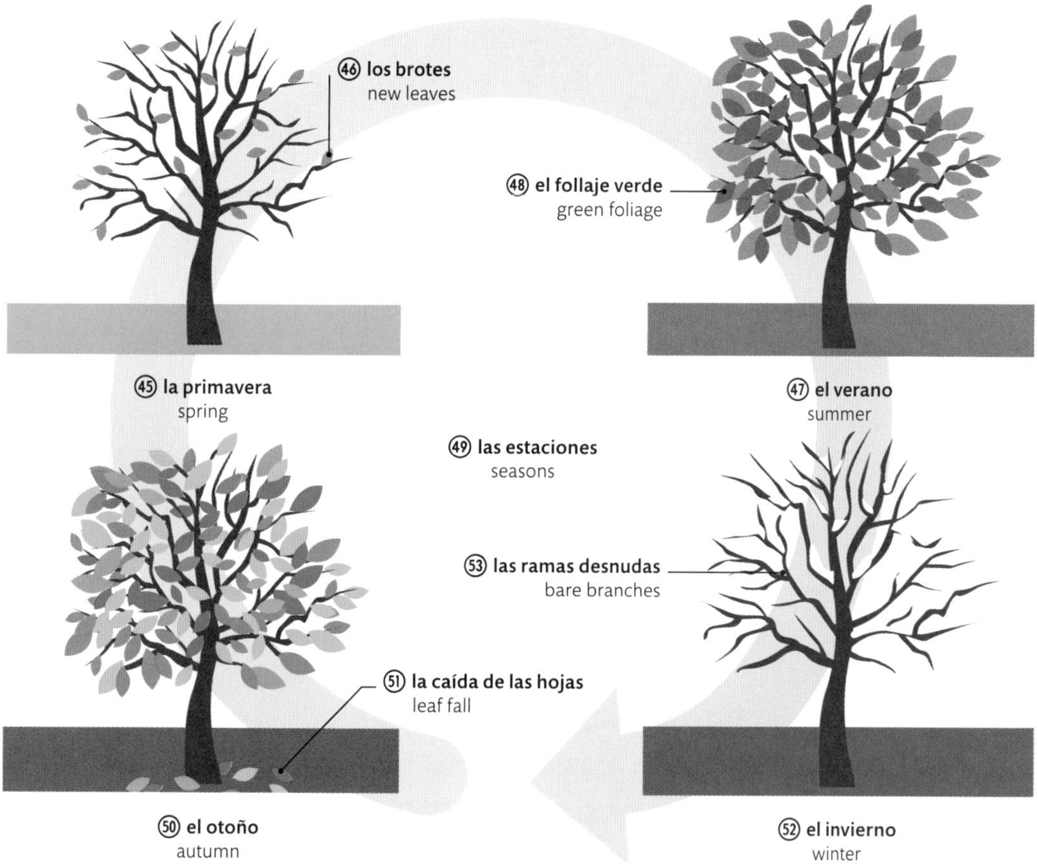

(46) los brotes
new leaves

(48) el follaje verde
green foliage

(45) la primavera
spring

(47) el verano
summer

(49) las estaciones
seasons

(53) las ramas desnudas
bare branches

(51) la caída de las hojas
leaf fall

(50) el otoño
autumn

(52) el invierno
winter

173 Los números
Numbers

173.1 LOS NÚMEROS CARDINALES · CARDINAL NUMBERS

1 ① **uno** one
2 ② **dos** two
3 ③ **tres** three
4 ④ **cuatro** four
5 ⑤ **cinco** five
6 ⑥ **seis** six
7 ⑦ **siete** seven
8 ⑧ **ocho** eight
9 ⑨ **nueve** nine
10 ⑩ **diez** ten
11 ⑪ **once** eleven
12 ⑫ **doce** twelve
13 ⑬ **trece** thirteen
14 ⑭ **catorce** fourteen
15 ⑮ **quince** fifteen
16 ⑯ **dieciséis** sixteen
17 ⑰ **diecisiete** seventeen
18 ⑱ **dieciocho** eighteen
19 ⑲ **diecinueve** nineteen
20 ⑳ **veinte** twenty
21 ㉑ **veintiuno** twenty-one
22 ㉒ **veintidós** twenty-two
30 ㉓ **treinta** thirty
40 ㉔ **cuarenta** forty
50 ㉕ **cincuenta** fifty
60 ㉖ **sesenta** sixty
70 ㉗ **setenta** seventy
80 ㉘ **ochenta** eighty
90 ㉙ **noventa** ninety
100 ㉚ **cien** one hundred
0 ㉛ **cero** zero

173.2 LOS NÚMEROS ORDINALES · ORDINAL NUMBERS

1st ① **primero** *m* **primera** *f* first
2nd ② **segundo** *m* **segunda** *f* second
3rd ③ **tercero** *m* **tercera** *f* third
4th ④ **cuarto** *m* **cuarta** *f* fourth
5th ⑤ **quinto** *m* **quinta** *f* fifth
6th ⑥ **sexto** *m* / **sexta** *f* sixth
7th ⑦ **séptimo** *m* **séptima** *f* seventh
8th ⑧ **octavo** *m* **octava** *f* eighth
9th ⑨ **noveno** *m* / **novena** *f* ninth
10th ⑩ **décimo** *m* **décima** *f* tenth
20th ⑪ **vigésimo** *m* **vigésima** *f* twentieth
21st ⑫ **vigésimo primero** **vigésima primera** *f* twenty-first

See also
74 Las matemáticas • Mathematics **171** El tiempo • Time **172** El calendario The calendar **174** Los pesos y las medidas • Weights and measures

173.3 LOS NÚMEROS GRANDES • LARGE NUMBERS

200
① **doscientos**
two hundred

250
② **doscientos cincuenta**
two hundred and fifty

500
③ **quinientos**
five hundred

750
④ **setecientos cincuenta**
seven hundred and fifty

1,000
⑤ **mil**
one thousand

1,200
⑥ **mil doscientos**
one thousand two hundred

10,000
⑦ **diez mil**
ten thousand

100,000
⑧ **cien mil**
one hundred thousand

1,000,000
⑨ **un millón**
one million

5,000,000
⑩ **cinco millones**
five million

500,000,000
⑪ **quinientos millones**
five hundred million / half a billion

1,000,000,000
⑫ **mil millones**
one billion

3,846
⑬ **tres mil ochocientos cuarenta y seis**
three thousand, eight hundred and forty-six

82,043
⑭ **ochenta y dos mil cuarenta y tres**
eighty-two thousand and forty-three

⑮ **¡He perdido la cuenta!**
I've lost count!

234,407
⑯ **doscientos treinta y cuatro mil cuatrocientos siete**
two hundred and thirty-four thousand, four hundred and seven

3,089,342
⑰ **tres millones ochenta y nueve mil trescientos cuarenta y dos**
three million, eighty-nine thousand, three hundred and forty-two

173.4 LAS FRACCIONES, LOS DECIMALES Y LOS PORCENTAJES • FRACTIONS, DECIMALS, AND PERCENTAGES

$\frac{1}{8}$
① **un octavo**
an eighth

$\frac{1}{4}$
② **un cuarto**
a quarter

$\frac{1}{3}$
③ **un tercio**
a third

$\frac{1}{2}$
④ **medio** *m* / **media** *f*
a half

$\frac{3}{5}$
⑤ **tres quintos**
three-fifths

$\frac{7}{8}$
⑥ **siete octavos**
seven-eighths

0.5
⑦ **cero coma cinco**
nought point five

1.7
⑧ **uno coma siete**
one point seven

3.97
⑨ **tres coma noventa y siete**
three point nine seven

1%
⑩ **uno por ciento**
one percent

99%
⑪ **noventa y nueve por ciento**
ninety-nine percent

100%
⑫ **cien por cien**
one hundred percent

174 Los pesos y las medidas
Weights and measures

174.1 EL PESO · WEIGHT

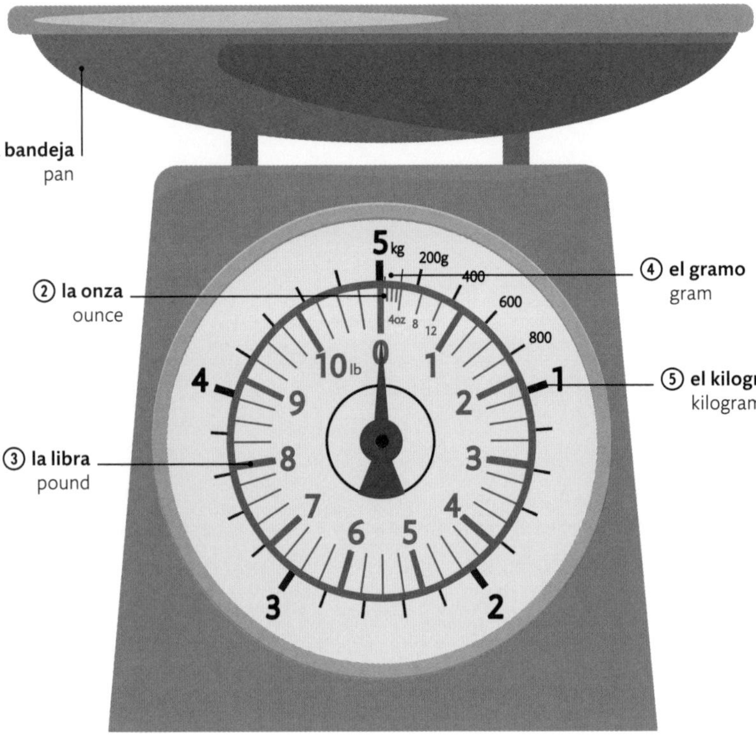

① la bandeja
pan

② la onza
ounce

③ la libra
pound

④ el gramo
gram

⑤ el kilogramo
kilogram

⑥ la balanza
scales

⑦ la tonelada
tonne / ton

⑧ el miligramo
milligram

⑨ pesar
to weigh

174.2 LA DISTANCIA, EL ÁREA Y LA LONGITUD · DISTANCE, AREA, AND LENGTH

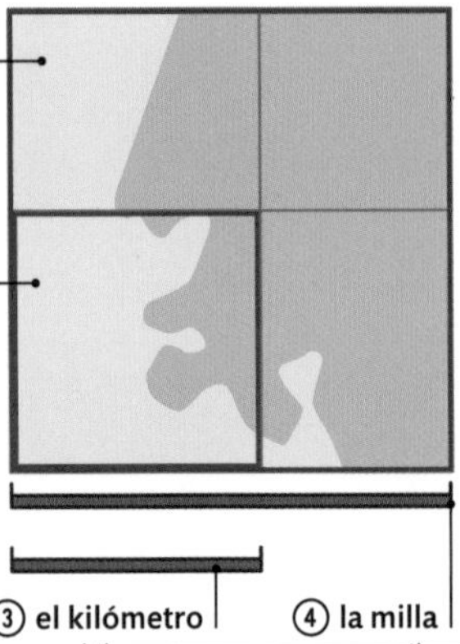

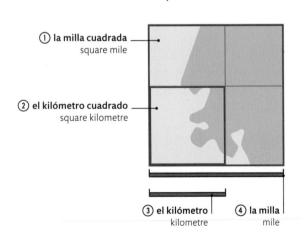

① la milla cuadrada
square mile

② el kilómetro cuadrado
square kilometre

③ el kilómetro
kilometre

④ la milla
mile

100 metros (32,8 pies)
100 metres (328 feet)

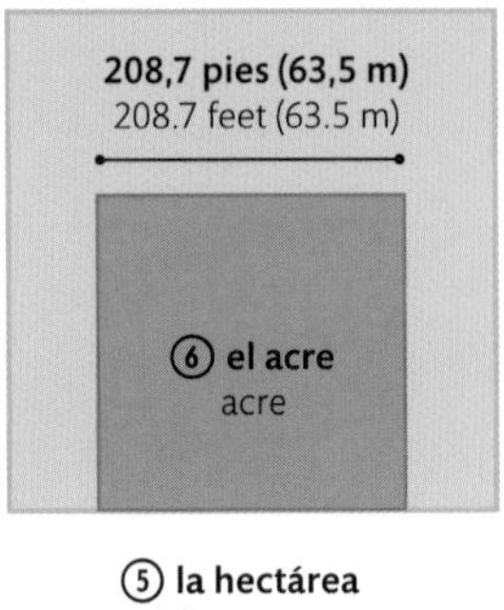

208,7 pies (63,5 m)
208.7 feet (63.5 m)

⑥ el acre
acre

⑤ la hectárea
hectare

⑧ el pie cuadrado
square foot

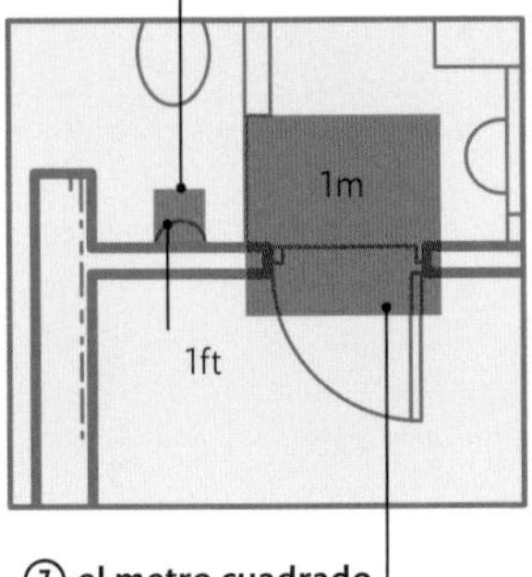

⑦ el metro cuadrado
sqaure metre

See also
29 La cocina • Cooking **35** El bricolaje • Home improvements
74 Las matemáticas • Mathematics **173** Los números • Numbers

174.3 LAS MEDIDAS DE CAPACIDAD Y VOLUMEN • LIQUID MEASUREMENTS / VOLUME

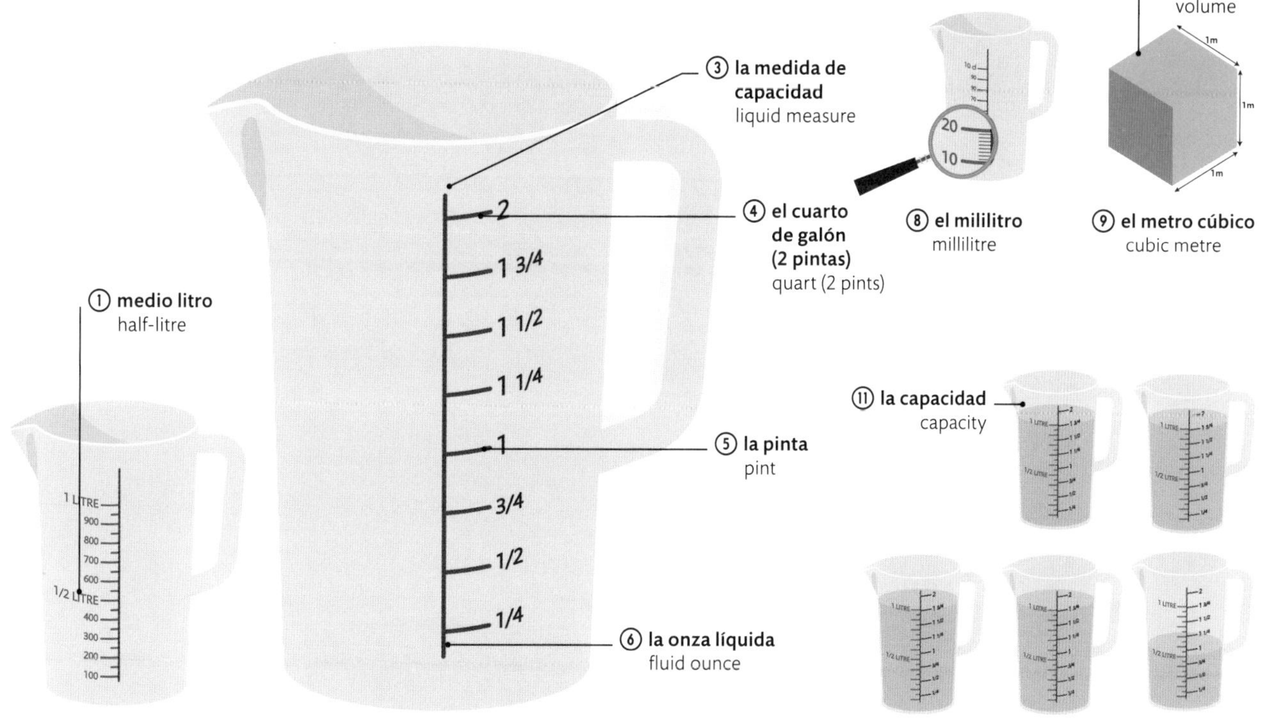

① **medio litro**
half-litre

② **el litro**
litre

③ **la medida de capacidad**
liquid measure

④ **el cuarto de galón (2 pintas)**
quart (2 pints)

⑤ **la pinta**
pint

⑥ **la onza líquida**
fluid ounce

⑦ **la jarra medidora**
measuring jug

⑧ **el mililitro**
millilitre

⑨ **el metro cúbico**
cubic metre

⑩ **el volumen**
volume

⑪ **la capacidad**
capacity

⑫ **el galón = 4,6 litros**
gallon = 4.6 litres

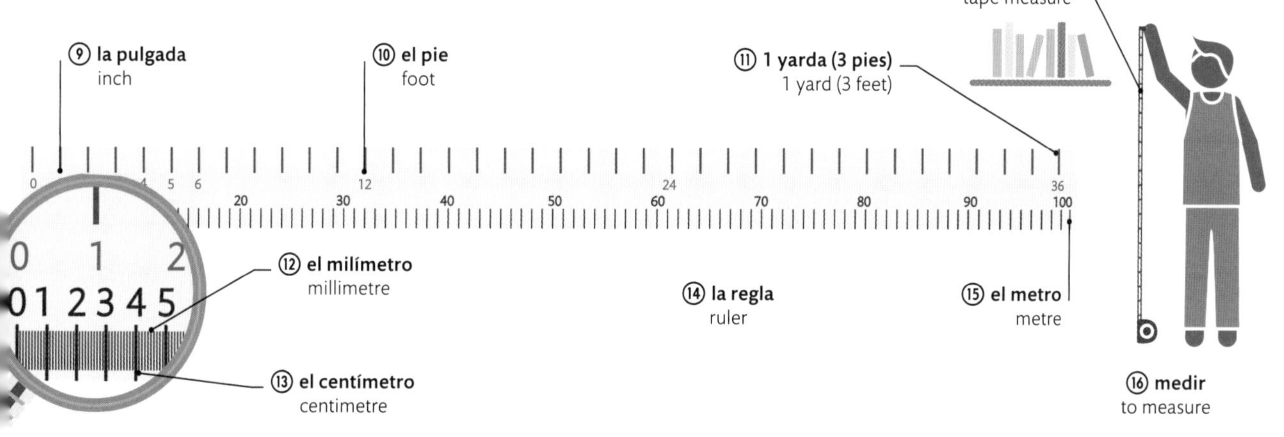

⑨ **la pulgada**
inch

⑩ **el pie**
foot

⑪ **1 yarda (3 pies)**
1 yard (3 feet)

⑫ **el milímetro**
millimetre

⑬ **el centímetro**
centimetre

⑭ **la regla**
ruler

⑮ **el metro**
metre

⑯ **medir**
to measure

⑰ **la cinta métrica**
tape measure

175 La escritura
Writing

175.1 LA ESCRITURA Y LOS MATERIALES DE ESCRITURA
WRITING AND WRITING EQUIPMENT

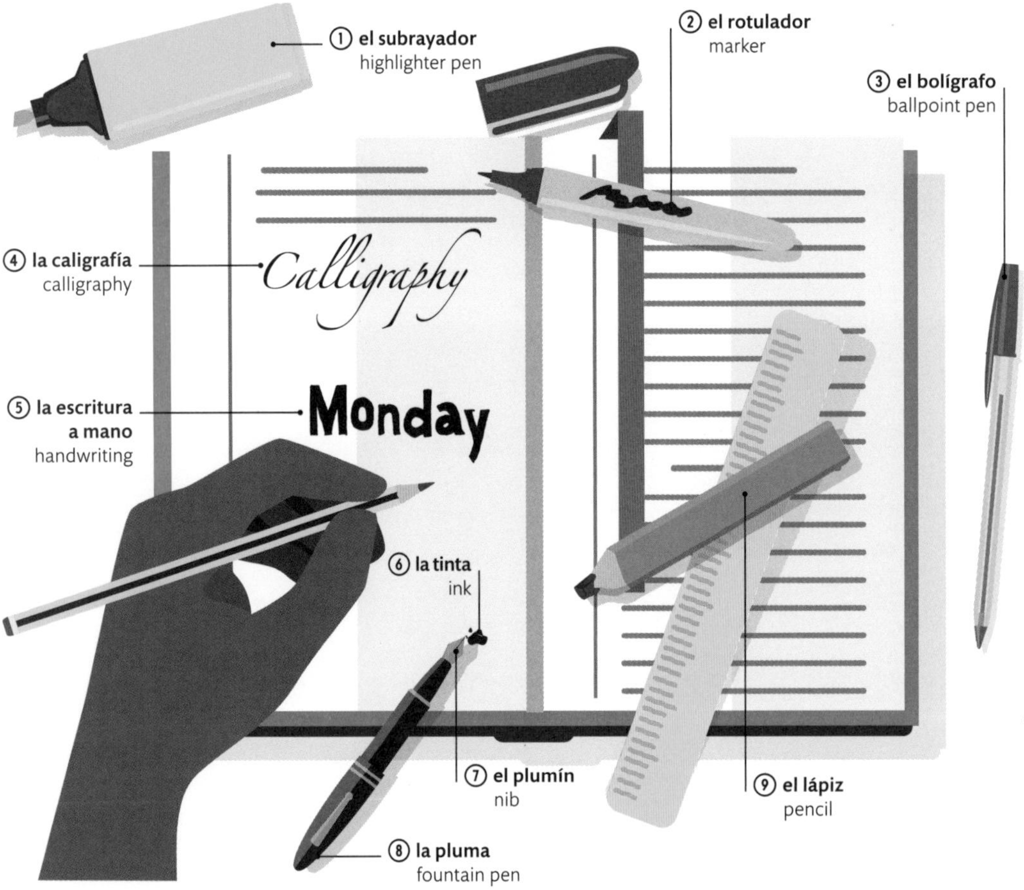

① **el subrayador**
highlighter pen

② **el rotulador**
marker

③ **el bolígrafo**
ballpoint pen

④ **la caligrafía**
calligraphy

⑤ **la escritura a mano**
handwriting

⑥ **la tinta**
ink

⑦ **el plumín**
nib

⑧ **la pluma**
fountain pen

⑨ **el lápiz**
pencil

⑩ **el pergamino**
parchment

⑪ **la impresión**
printing

⑫ **los emojis**
emojis

abcdefghijk
lmnopqrst
uvwxyz

⑬ **la tipografía**
typeface

Aa	ABC	abc	**abc**	*abc*	123
⑭ **las letras** letters	⑮ **las mayúsculas** uppercase / capital letters	⑯ **las minúsculas** lowercase	⑰ **la negrita** bold	⑱ **la cursiva** italic	⑲ **los números** numerals

ft	.	-	—	_	,
⑳ **la ligadura** ligature	㉑ **el punto** full stop	㉒ **el guion** hyphen	㉓ **la raya** dash	㉔ **el guion bajo** underscore	㉕ **la coma** comma

See also
73 En la escuela • At school
138 Los libros y la lectura • Books and reading

;
(26) el punto y coma
semicolon

:
(27) los dos puntos
colon

...
(28) los puntos suspensivos
ellipsis

!
(29) el signo de exclamación
exclamation mark

?
(30) el signo de interrogación
question mark

’
(31) el apóstrofo
apostrophe

‘
(32) las comillas simples
single quotation mark

“
(33) las comillas dobles
double quotation mark

*
(34) el asterisco
asterisk

@
(35) la arroba
at sign / at symbol

&
(36) el signo et
ampersand

ũ
(37) la virgulilla
tilde

é
(38) el acento agudo
acute accent

è
(39) el acento grave
grave accent

ü
(40) la diéresis
umlaut

ĉ
(41) el acento circunflejo
circumflex

ç
(42) la cedilla
cedilla

©
(43) el copyright
copyright

®
(44) la marca registrada
registered trademark

( )
(45) los paréntesis
brackets

#
(46) la almohadilla
hashtag

cat
(47) el alfabeto latino
Latin alphabet

Γάτα
(48) el alfabeto griego
Greek alphabet

кошка
(49) el alfabeto cirílico
Cyrillic alphabet

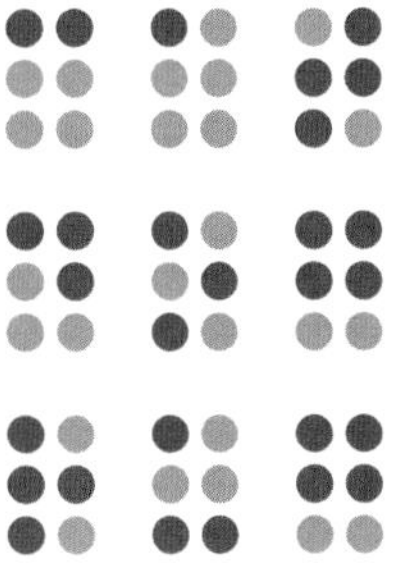
(50) el braille
Braille

قط
شجرة
ماء
(51) la escritura árabe
Arabic script

市
車両
道
(52) los caracteres japoneses
Japanese characters

桃
橘子
柠檬
(53) los caracteres chinos
Chinese characters

खेत
घोड़ा
नदी
(54) la escritura devanagari
Devanagari script

(55) los jeroglíficos egipcios
Ancient Egyptian hieroglyphs

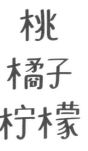

176 Describiendo las cosas

Describing things

176.1 LOS MATERIALES · MATERIALS

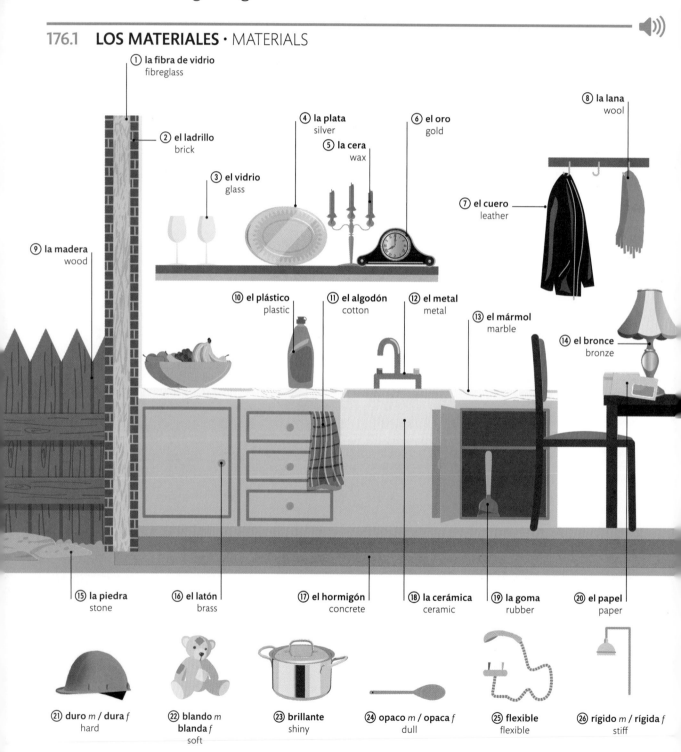

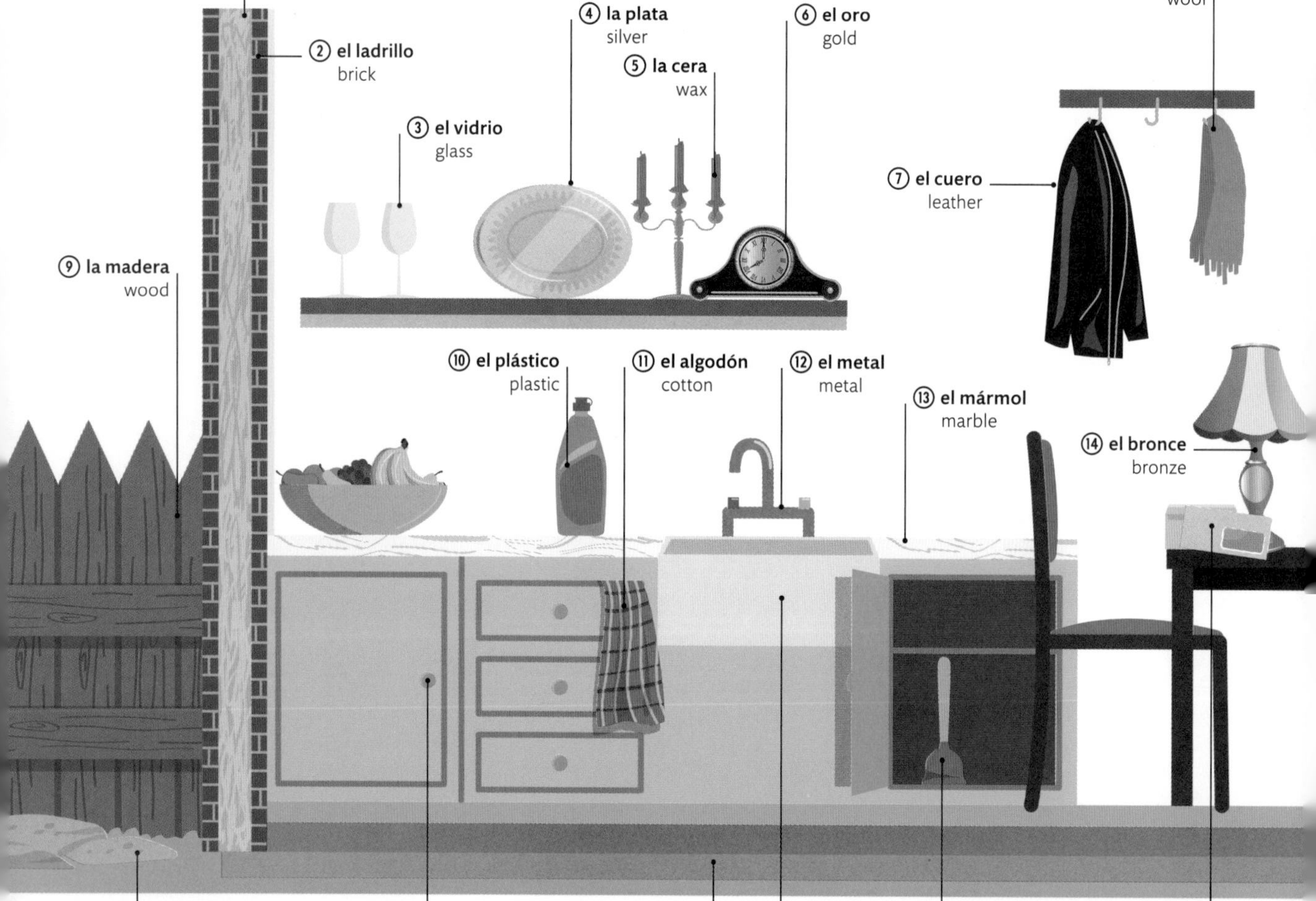

㉑ **duro** *m* / **dura** *f*
hard

㉒ **blando** *m*
blanda *f*
soft

㉓ **brillante**
shiny

㉔ **opaco** *m* / **opaca** *f*
dull

㉕ **flexible**
flexible

㉖ **rígido** *m* / **rígida** *f*
stiff

See also
32 La casa y el hogar • House and home **35** El bricolaje • Home improvements
37 La decoración • Decorating **87** La construcción • Construction
177 Describiendo las cosas (continuación) • Describing things continued

176.2 **LOS ADJETIVOS** • ADJECTIVES

① **grande**
big / large

② **pequeño** *m*
pequeña *f*
small / little

③ **ancho** *m* / **ancha** *f*
wide

④ **estrecho** *m*
estrecha *f*
narrow

⑤ **profundo** *m*
profunda *f*
deep

⑥ **superficial**
shallow

⑦ **alto** *m* / **alta** *f*
high

⑧ **bajo** *m* / **baja** *f*
low

⑨ **pesado** *m*
pesada *f*
heavy

⑩ **ligero** *m* / **ligera** *f*
light

⑪ **limpio** *m* / **limpia** *f*
clean

⑫ **sucio** *m* / **sucia** *f*
dirty

⑬ **caliente**
hot

⑭ **frío** *m* / **fría** *f*
cold

⑮ **largo** *m* / **larga** *f*
long

⑯ **corto** *m* / **corta** *f*
short

⑰ **flojo** *m* / **floja** *f*
loose

⑱ **apretado** *m*
apretada *f*
tight

⑲ **fino** *m* / **fina** *f*
thin

⑳ **grueso** *m* / **gruesa** *f*
thick

㉑ **cerca**
near

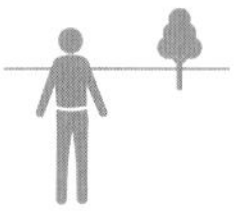
㉒ **lejos**
far

㉓ **lento** *m* / **lenta** *f*
slow

㉔ **rápido** *m* / **rápida** *f*
fast

㉕ **nuevo** *m* / **nueva** *f*
new

㉖ **viejo** *m* / **vieja** *f*
old

㉗ **vacío** *m* / **vacía** *f*
empty

㉘ **lleno** *m* / **llena** *f*
full

㉙ **ruidoso** *m*
ruidosa *f*
noisy

㉚ **silencioso** *m*
silenciosa *f*
quiet

㉛ **correcto** *m*
correcta *f*
correct

㉜ **incorrecto** *m*
incorrecta *f*
incorrect

㉝ **iluminado** *m*
iluminada *f*
light

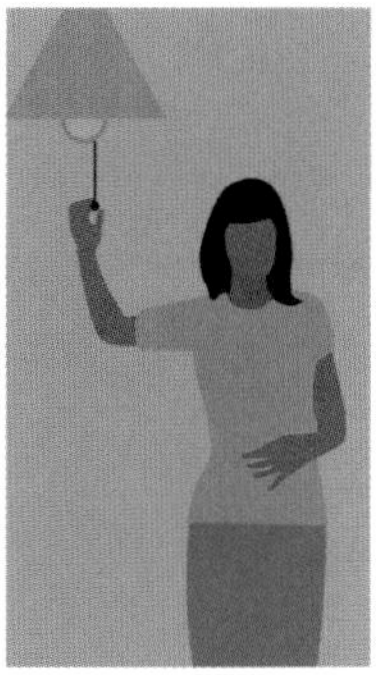
㉞ **oscuro** *m*
oscura *f*
dark

177 Describiendo las cosas (continuación)

Describing things continued

177.1 LAS OPINIONES • OPINIONS

② **Las vistas desde aquí son impresionantes.**
The view here is absolutely breathtaking.

① **impresionante**
breathtaking

③ **emocionante**
exciting

④ **bonito** *m* / **bonita** *f*
beautiful

⑤ **emocionante**
thrilling

⑥ **divertido** *m*
divertida *f*
fun

⑦ **romántico** *m*
romántica *f*
romantic

⑧ **asombroso** *m*
asombrosa *f*
stunning

⑨ **excelente**
great

10
10
10

⑩ **increíble**
incredible

⑪ **importante**
important

⑫ **adorable**
cute

⑬ **respetuoso** *m*
respetuosa *f*
respectful

⑭ **especial**
special

⑮ **grácil**
graceful

⑯ **destacable**
remarkable

⑰ **sobresaliente**
outstanding

⑱ **desternillante**
hilarious

⑲ **gracioso** *m*
graciosa *f*
funny

⑳ **extraordinario** *m*
extraordinaria *f*
extraordinary

㉑ **maravilloso** *m*
maravillosa *f*
wonderful

㉒ **inofensivo** *m*
inofensiva *f*
harmless

㉓ **anticuado** *m*
anticuada *f*
old-fashioned

See also
06 Los estados de ánimo • Feelings and moods **10** Los rasgos de personalidad • Personality traits **11** Las habilidades y las acciones • Abilities and actions **93** Las competencias laborales • Workplace skills

㉔ **bueno** *m* / **buena** *f*
good

㉕ **malo** *m* / **mala** *f*
bad

㉖ **fantástico** *m*
fantástica *f*
fantastic

㉗ **horrible**
terrible

㉘ **agradable**
pleasant

㉙ **desagradable**
unpleasant

㉚ **brillante**
brilliant

㉛ **espantoso** *m*
espantosa *f*
dreadful

㉜ **útil**
useful

㉝ **inútil**
useless

㉞ **delicioso** *m*
deliciosa *f*
delicious

㉟ **asqueroso** *m*
asquerosa *f*
disgusting

㊱ **bonito** *m* / **bonita** *f*
pretty

㊲ **feo** *m* / **fea** *f*
ugly

㊳ **interesante**
interesting

㊴ **aburrido** *m*
aburrida *f*
boring

㊵ **relajante**
relaxing

㊶ **agotador** *m*
agotadora *f*
exhausting

㊷ **magnífico** *m*
magnífica *f*
superb

㊸ **terrible**
awful

㊹ **simpático** *m*
simpática *f*
nice

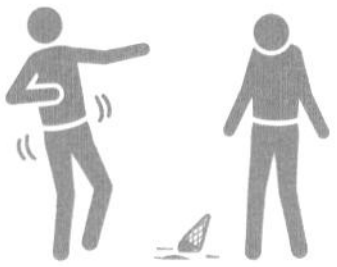

㊺ **cruel**
nasty

㊻ **asombroso** *m*
asombrosa *f*
amazing

㊼ **mediocre**
mediocre

㊽ **terrorífico** *m*
terrorífica *f*
frightening

㊾ **aterrador** *m*
aterradora *f*
terrifying

㊿ **extraño** *m*
extraña *f*
strange / odd

(51) **impactante**
shocking

(52) **fastidioso** *m*
fastidiosa *f*
annoying

(53) **horrible**
horrible

(54) **desastroso** *m*
desastrosa *f*
disastrous

(55) **confuso** *m*
confusa *f*
confusing

(56) **fatigoso** *m*
fatigosa *f*
tiring

(57) **irritante**
irritating

(58) **pésimo** *m*
pésima *f*
dire

(59) **decepcionante**
disappointing

Los verbos compuestos comunes
Common phrasal verbs

178.1 **LOS VERBOS DE LA VIDA COTIDIANA** · VERBS FOR DAILY LIFE

① **calmarse**
to calm down

② **relajarse**
to chill out

③ **buscar**
to look for

④ **crecer**
to grow up

⑨ **amontonar**
to pile up

⑤ **dar un toque**
to call up

⑥ **ponerse**
to put on

⑦ **vestirse elegante**
to dress up

⑧ **presumir**
to show off

⑩ **devolver**
to give back

⑪ **quedarse dormido** *m*
quedarse dormida *f*
to doze off

⑫ **dormir hasta tarde**
to sleep in

⑬ **levantarse**
to get up

⑭ **subir**
to go up

⑮ **bajar**
to go down

⑯ **alcanzar**
to catch up

⑰ **hacer el tonto**
to mess around

⑱ **colgar**
to hang up

⑲ **dejar entrar**
to let in

⑳ **arrancar**
to rip out

㉑ **quedarse sin**
to run out (of)

㉒ **activar**
to set off

㉓ **tropezarse**
to trip over

㉔ **medir**
to measure out

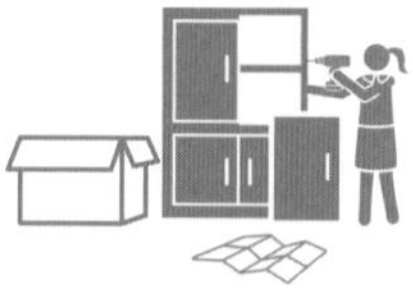
㉕ **montar**
to put together

㉖ **remodelar**
to do up

㉗ **guardar en su sitio**
to put away

㉙ ¡Llevo toda la noche esperando despierto!
I've been waiting up all night!
㉘ **esperar despierto** *m* / **esperar despierta** *f*
to wait up

㉚ **rellenar**
to fill out

㉛ **iniciar sesión**
to log in

㉜ **cerrar sesión**
to log out

See also
09 Las rutinas diarias • Daily routines **11** Las habilidades y las acciones • Abilities and actions **179-180** Las expresiones útiles • Useful expressions

33 despertarse
to wake up

34 pesar
to weigh out

35 encender
to turn on

36 apagar
to turn off

37 subir el volumen
to turn up

38 bajar el volumen
to turn down

39 averiarse
to break down

40 repostar
to fill up

41 registrarse
to check in

42 dejar la habitación
to check out

43 comer fuera
to eat out

44 atender
to wait on

45 subir a
to get on

46 bajar de
to get off

47 llover a cántaros
to pour down

48 irse fuera
to go away

49 señalar
to point out

50 cuidar de
to look after

51 mirar
to look at

52 regalar
to give away

53 repartir
to give out

54 desistir
to give up

60 ¡Hola! ¡Qué bien que has podido unirte!
Hi! So glad you could join us!

59 juntarse
to get together

55 romper con
to break up

56 suspender
to call off

57 reconciliarse
to make up

58 reunirse
to meet up

61 repartir
to hand out

62 limpiar
to clean up

63 recoger
to pick up

64 tirar
to throw away

65 huir
to run away

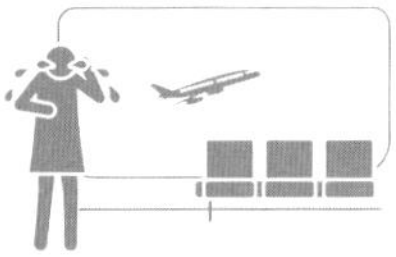
66 despegar
to take off

179 Las expresiones útiles
Useful expressions

179.1 LOS SALUDOS · GREETINGS

② ¡Hola!
Hi!
③ Hola.
Hello.

① **conocer alguien**
to meet

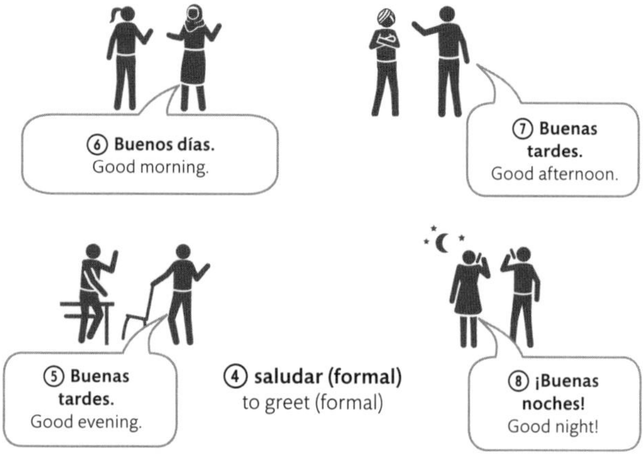
⑥ **Buenos días.**
Good morning.
⑦ **Buenas tardes.**
Good afternoon.
⑤ **Buenas tardes.**
Good evening.
⑧ **¡Buenas noches!**
Good night!

④ **saludar (formal)**
to greet (formal)

⑩ **¡Hola! ¿Cómo estáis?**
Hi! How are you?
⑪ **Bien, gracias.**
I'm fine, thanks.
⑫ **Me alegro de verte, Ed.**
Nice to see you, Ed.

⑨ **saludar (informal)**
to greet (informal)

⑭ **¡Adiós!**
Goodbye!
⑮ **¡Hasta luego!**
See you later!

⑬ **marcharse**
to leave

179.2 CONOCIENDO A ALGUIEN · GETTING TO KNOW SOMEONE

① **¿Cómo te llamas?**
What's your name?
② **Me llamo Sally.**
My name is Sally.

③ **¿Cuántos años tienes?**
How old are you?
④ **Tengo 25 años.**
I'm 25 years old.

⑤ **¿Dónde vives?**
Where do you live?
⑥ **Vivo en Edimburgo.**
I live in Edinburgh.

See also
09 Las rutinas diarias • Daily routines **07** Los acontecimientos • Life events **46** Las compras
Shopping **180** Las expresiones útiles (continuación) • Useful expressions (continued)

179.3 **COMPRANDO** • SHOPPING

① **¿Cuánto cuesta?** How much is this?
② **Son 15 dólares.** It's 15 dollars
③ **¿Puedo pagar aquí?** Can I pay here?
④ **¿Podrías alcanzarme la taza roja, por favor?** Could you get the red cup for me, please?

⑤ **¿Puedo ayudarla?** Can I help you?
⑥ **Gracias, pero solo estoy mirando.** I'm just browsing, thanks.
⑦ **¿Vendéis paraguas?** Do you sell umbrellas?
⑧ **¿Tiene este en una talla más pequeña?** Do you have this in a smaller size?
⑨ **Déjeme mirar** Let me check for you.

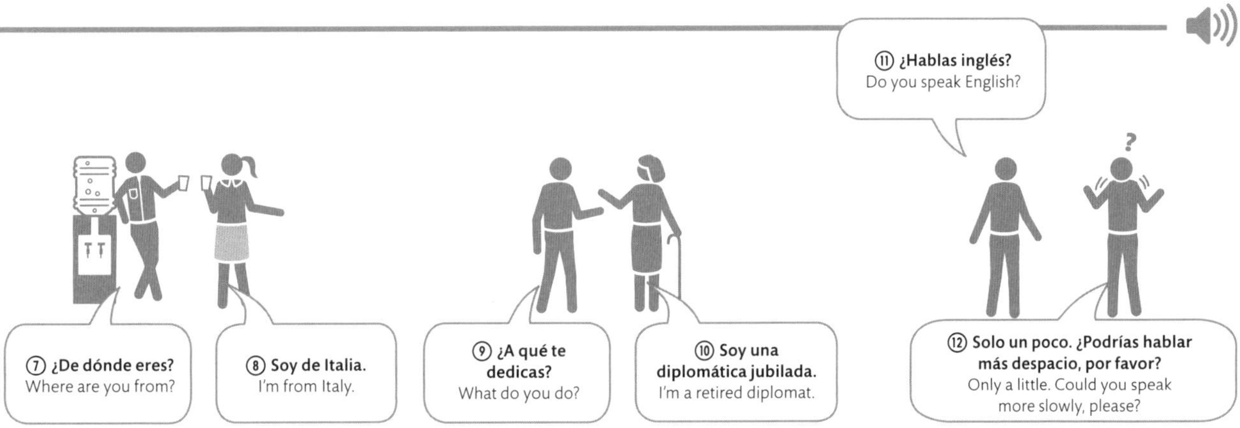
⑦ **¿De dónde eres?** Where are you from?
⑧ **Soy de Italia.** I'm from Italy.
⑨ **¿A qué te dedicas?** What do you do?
⑩ **Soy una diplomática jubilada.** I'm a retired diplomat.
⑪ **¿Hablas inglés?** Do you speak English?
⑫ **Solo un poco. ¿Podrías hablar más despacio, por favor?** Only a little. Could you speak more slowly, please?

180 Las expresiones útiles (continuación)

Useful expressions continued

180.1 LAS DIRECCIONES · DIRECTIONS

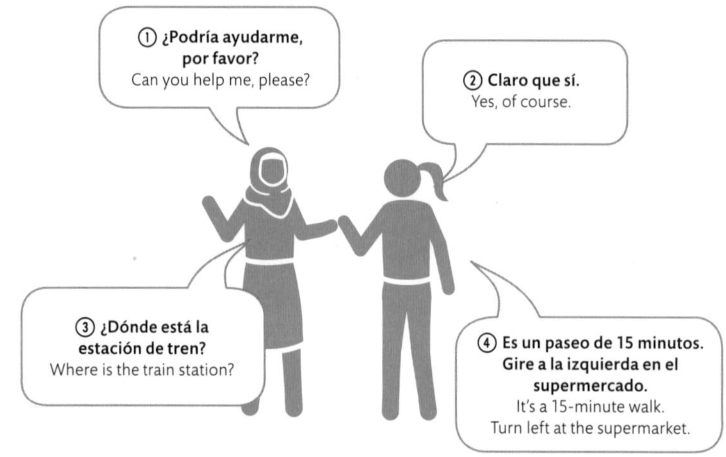

① **¿Podría ayudarme, por favor?** Can you help me, please?
② **Claro que sí.** Yes, of course.
③ **¿Dónde está la estación de tren?** Where is the train station?
④ **Es un paseo de 15 minutos. Gire a la izquierda en el supermercado.** It's a 15-minute walk. Turn left at the supermarket.

⑤ **¿A qué distancia está el hotel?** How far is it to the hotel?

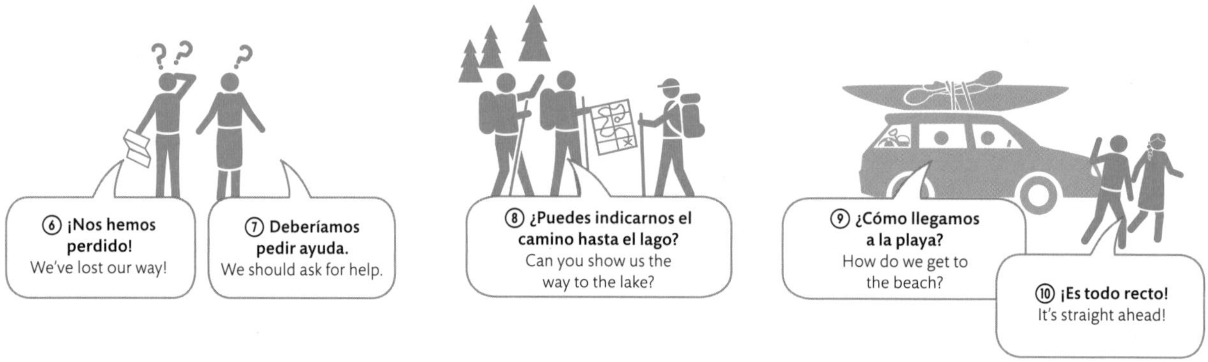

⑥ **¡Nos hemos perdido!** We've lost our way!
⑦ **Deberíamos pedir ayuda.** We should ask for help.
⑧ **¿Puedes indicarnos el camino hasta el lago?** Can you show us the way to the lake?
⑨ **¿Cómo llegamos a la playa?** How do we get to the beach?
⑩ **¡Es todo recto!** It's straight ahead!

⑪ **¿Dónde puedo encontrar un buen sitio para comer?** Where can I find a good place to eat?
⑫ **Prueba en la cafetería que hay junto a la oficina de correos.** Try the café next to the post office.

See also
42-43 La ciudad • In town
148 Los mapas y las indicaciones • Maps and directions

180.2 LAS PREPOSICIONES • PREPOSITIONS

① **en**
in

② **fuera**
out

③ **dentro**
inside

④ **fuera**
outside

⑤ **entre**
between

⑥ **debajo**
under

⑦ **encima**
on

⑧ **junto a**
next to / beside

⑨ **en frente de**
in front of

⑩ **detrás de**
behind

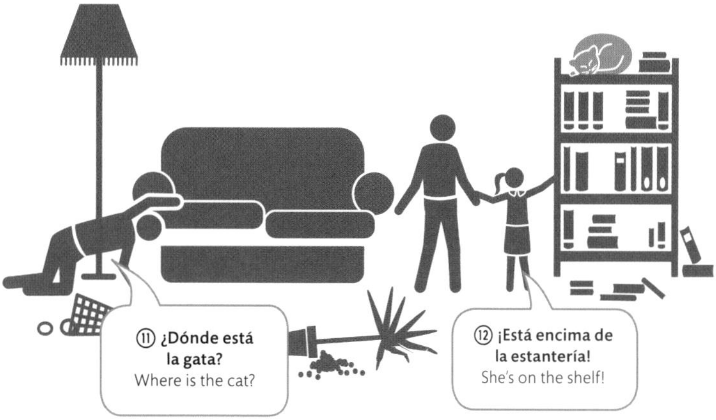
⑪ **¿Dónde está la gata?**
Where is the cat?
⑫ **¡Está encima de la estantería!**
She's on the shelf!

English word list

The numbers after each word or phrase refer to the units in which they can be found.

KEY
adj - adjective
adv - adverb
n - noun
num - number
phr - phrase
prep - preposition
v - verb

A

à la carte menu *n* **69**
A&E *n* **21, 50**
aardvark *n* **158**
abdomen *n* **01, 162**
abdominals *n* **03**
abilities *n* **11**
ability to drive *n* **93**
abseiling *n* **125**
Abyssinian *n* **164**
acacia *n* **47**
accelerator *n* **99**
access road *n* **106**
accessories *n* **16**
accident *n* **19**
accident and emergency *n* **50**
accommodation *n* **131**
accordion *n* **129**
account number *n* **45**
accountant *n* **90, 94**
accounts *n* **91**
accurate *adj* **93**
accused *n* **85**
ace *n* **114, 140**
ache *v* **20**
Achilles tendon *n* **03**
acid *n* **76**
acid rain *n* **51, 155**
acorn *n* **169**
acoustic guitar *n* **129**
acoustic guitarist *n* **129**
acquaintance *n* **07**
acquitted *adj* **85**
acre *n* **174**
acrylic paint *n* **141**
act *v* **11**
actinide series *n* **78**
actinium *n* **78**
action game *n* **136**
action movie *n* **127**
action points *n* **95**
actions *n* **11**
actor *n* **89, 126**
acupressure *n* **24**
acupuncture *n* **24**
acute accent *n* **175**
Adam's apple *n* **04**
adaptable *adj* **93**
add *v* **11, 29, 74**
add to cart *v* **46**
add to wishlist *v* **46**
additives *n* **23**
address *n* **45**
adhesive tape *n* **20**
administration *n* **91, 93**
admiral *n* **88**
admission fee *n* **130**
admissions *n* **80**
admit *v* **21**
adrenal gland *n* **04**
adult frog *n* **77**
adult teeth *n* **03**
adults *n* **05**
advantage *n* **114**
adventure game *n* **136**
adventure playground *n* **133**
adventurous *adj* **10**
advertising *n* **91**
adverts *n* **137**
aerate *v* **39**
aerial *n* **25, 97**
aerobics *n* **124**
aerobics step *n* **124**
aerospace *n* **91**
Afghan *adj* **153**
Afghanistan *n* **151, 153**
Africa *n* **149, 152**
African *adj* **152**
African bullfrog *n* **163**
African daisy *n* **38**
African elephant *n* **158**
African grey parrot *n* **161**
African wild dog *n* **158**
Afro *n* **12**
afternoon *n* **09, 171**
aftershave *n* **18, 31**
agate *n* **156**
agbada *n* **15**
agenda *n* **95**
agriculture *n* **91**
aikido *n* **117**
aileron *n* **103**
air ambulance *n* **50**
air bed *n* **135**
air cargo *n* **104**
air conditioning *n* **33, 99**
air control tower *n* **43**
air cylinder *n* **118**
air filter *n* **98, 100**
air mattress *n* **135**
air pump *n* **135**
air vent *n* **103**
airbag *n* **99**
airball *n* **112**
aircraft carrier *n* **88, 105**
aircraft *n* **103**
airforce *n* **88**
airline *n* **104**
airmail *n* **45**
airman *n* **88**
airport *n* **43, 104**
airship *n* **103**
airtight container *n* **52**
aisle, aisles *n* **48, 80, 103, 126**
alarm *n* **50**
alarm clock *n* **30**
alarm goes off *phr* **09**
Albania *n* **151, 153**
Albanian *adj* **153**
albatross *n* **160**
albertonectes *n* **157**
album *n* **129**
alcohol-free beer *n* **68**
ale *n* **68**
alfalfa *n* **86**
Algeria *n* **149, 152**
Algerian *adj* **152**
Alice band *n* **16**
alien *n* **139**
alkali *n* **76**
alkali metals *n* **78**
alkaline earth metals *n* **78**
all-terrain vehicle *n* **100**
Allen keys *n* **36**
allergic *adj* **23**
allergy *n* **19**
alley *n* **42**
alloy *n* **76**
allspice *n* **59**
almond milk *n* **61**
almond oil *n* **60**
almonds *n* **58, 68**
aloe *n* **167**
alpaca *n* **165**
alpine plants *n* **41**
alternating current *n* **33, 75**
alto *n* **126**
aluminium *n* **78, 156**
always *adj* **171**
amaryllis *n* **167**
amazed *adj* **06**
amazing *adj* **177**
Amazon *n* **145**
ambitious *adj* **10, 93**
ambulance *n* **21, 50**
ambulance stretcher *n* **50**
American *adj* **152**
American alligator *n* **163**
American curl *n* **164**
American football field *n* **107**
American football *n* **107**
American football positions *n* **107**
americium *n* **78**
amethyst *n* **156**
amount *n* **45**
amp *n* **33**
ampersand *n* **175**
amphibians *n* **163**
amphibious vehicle *n* **88**
amplifier *n* **129**
amulet *n* **139**
amused *adj* **06**
anaesthetist *n* **90**
analytics *n* **93**
anchor *n* **105, 119**
anchovies *n* **64**
Ancient Egyptian hieroglyphs *n* **175**
Ancient Greek temple *n* **44**
ancient ruins *n* **44**
Andean condor *n* **160**
Andorra *n* **151, 153**
Andorran *adj* **153**
anemone *n* **134, 166**
Angel Falls *n* **145**
angle *n* **74**
angler *n* **121**
angler fish *n* **166**
Angola *n* **149, 152**
Angolan *adj* **152**
Angora *n* **164**
angry *adj* **06**
animal cell *n* **77**
animation *n* **127**
anise *n* **59**
ankle *n* **01-02**
ankle boots *n* **17**
ankle strap heels *n* **17**
ankle weights *n* **124**
anklet *n* **16**
anniversary *n* **07**
annoyed *adj* **06**
annoying *adj* **177**
annual *n* **41**
annual general meeting (AGM) *n* **95**
annual leave *n* **81**
anorak *n* **15**
answer *v* **73**
ant *n* **162**
anteater *n* **159**
antenna *n* **162**
anther *n* **38**
anti-inflammatory *n* **49**
antibiotics *n* **49**
anticlockwise *adv* **148**
antifreeze *n* **97**
Antigua and Barbuda *n* **150, 152**
Antiguan *adj* **152**
antimony *n* **78**
antiques shop *n* **46**
antiseptic *n* **20**
antiseptic wipes *n* **20**
antler *n* **159**
anxious *adj* **06**
any other business *phr* **95**
apartment *n* **131**
apex *n* **74**
apostrophe *n* **175**
app developer *n* **89**
appeal *n* **85**
appearance *n* **12**
appendicitis *n* **19**
appendix *n* **04**
applause *n* **126**
apple *n* **58**
apple corer *n* **28**
apple juice *n* **65**
applicant *n* **81**
application form *n* **92**
apply for a job *v* **92**
applying for a job *n* **92**
appointment *n* **20, 81**
appreciative *adj* **06**
apprentice *n* **81, 92**
approachable *adj* **10**
apricot *n* **57**
April *n* **172**
apron *n* **13, 29**
aquamarine *n* **156**
aquarium *n* **164**
Aquarius *n* **144**
Arabic script *n* **175**
arable farm *n* **86**
arbor knot *n* **121**
arc *n* **74, 112**
arch *n* **02, 41, 44**
arch window *n* **32**
archaeological site *n* **132**
archaeology *n* **79**
archaeologist *n* **79**
archer *n* **125**
archery *n* **125**
archipelago *n* **147**
architect *n* **90**
architecture *n* **44**
archive *n* **79**
Arctic *n* **159**
Arctic Circle *n* **145**
Arctic fox *n* **159**
Arctic hare *n* **159**
Arctic tern *n* **160**
Arctic wolf *n* **159**
area *n* **74, 174**

arena *n* **120**
Argentina *n* **149, 152**
Argentinian *adj* **152**
argon *n* **78**
Aries *n* **144**
arm, arms *n* **01, 126**
arm circles *n* **124**
arm protection *n* **110**
armadillo *n* **159**
armband *n* **118**
armchair *n* **26**
armed drone *n* **88**
armed forces *n* **88**
Armenia *n* **150, 153**
Armenian *adj* **153**
armour *n* **79**
armoured vehicle *n* **88**
armpit *n* **01**
armrest *n* **99, 103**
army *n* **88**
aromatherapy *n* **24**
arrest *n* **50**
arrival *n* **43**
arrive *v* **09**
arrive early *v* **09**
arrive home *v* **09**
arrive late *v* **09**
arrive on time *v* **09**
arrogant *adj* **10**
arrow *n* **79, 125**
arrow slit *n* **44**
arsenic *n* **78**
art, arts *n* **73, 91, 141-142**
art college *n* **80**
Art Deco *n* **130**
art gallery *n* **43, 130, 132**
Art Nouveau *n* **130**
art school *n* **80**
art shop *n* **46**
art therapy *n* **24**
artery *n* **04**
artichoke *n* **56**
artichoke heart *n* **56**
article *n* **138**
articulated bus *n* **99**
artificial intelligence *n* **83**
artisan *n* **79**
artist *n* **90, 141**
arum lily *n* **167**
ash *n* **145**
ash cloud *n* **145**
Asia *n* **150, 153**
Asian *adj* **153**
Asian elephant *n* **159**
Asian vine snake *n* **163**
ask directions *v* **148**
asparagus *n* **56**
asparagus tip *n* **56**
assertive *adj* **10, 93**
astatine *n* **78**
asterisk *n* **175**
asteroid *n* **143**
asthma *n* **19**
astigmatism *n* **22**
astronaut *n* **143**
astronomy *n* **144**
at sign *n* **83, 175**
at symbol *n* **83, 175**
athlete *n* **116**
athletics *n* **116, 125**
athletics track *n* **116**
Atlantic puffin *n* **160**
Atlantic salmon *n* **166**
atlas moth *n* **162**
atlas *n* **73**
ATM *n* **45**
atmosphere *n* **143, 155**
atoll *n* **147**
atom *n* **76**
attachment *n* **83**
attack helicopter *n* **88**
attack zone *n* **110**
attend a meeting *v* **95**
attic *n* **25**
attractions *n* **132**
aubergine *n* **56**
auburn hair *n* **12**
audience *n* **126, 127**
audio *n* **136**
audio guide *n* **130**
audition *n* **127**
August *n* **172**
aunt *n* **05**
aurora *n* **144, 155**
Australia *n* **150, 153**
Australian *adj* **153**
Australian little penguin *n* **161**
Austria *n* **151, 153**
Austrian *adj* **153**
author *n* **138**
autobiography *n* **138**
autocue *n* **84**
automatic *n* **99**
automotive industry *n* **91**
autumn *n* **57, 172**
autumn leaf *n* **169**
avalanche *n* **122**
avatar *n* **84**
avenue *n* **43**
avocado *n* **56**
avocado toast *n* **71**
avocado tree *n* **167**
awful *adj* **177**
awning *n* **65**
axe *n* **36, 50, 79**
axle *n* **100**
ayran *n* **61**
ayurveda *n* **24**
azalea *n* **38**
Azerbaijan *n* **150, 153**
Azerbaijani *adj* **153**

B

babies' clothes *n* **13**
baboon *n* **158**
baby *n* **05**
baby bath *n* **08**
baby changing facilities *n* **47**
baby formula *n* **08**
baby monitor *n* **08, 30**
baby products *n* **48**
baby sweetcorn *n* **55**
babygro *n* **13**
back *adj* **03**
back *n* **26**
back bacon *n* **53**
back brush *n* **31**
back door *n* **97**
back seat *n* **99**
back up *v* **83**
back-flip *n* **118**
backache *n* **19**
backboard *n* **112**
backdrop *n* **126**
backgammon *n* **140**
backhand *n* **114**
backing singers *n* **129**
backpack *n* **16, 135**
backpack sprayer *n* **40**
backstay *n* **119**
backstop net *n* **113**
backstroke *n* **118**
backswing *n* **115**
bacon *n* **53, 71**
bacteria *n* **77, 157**
Bactrian camel *n* **158**
bad *adj* **52, 177**
bad robot *n* **139**
badge *n* **50**
badge *n* **16**
badminton *n* **114**
bag, bags *n* **16, 52**
bag store *n* **47**
bagel *n* **62, 71**
baggage claim *n* **104**
baggage trailer *n* **104**
bagpipes *n* **129**
baguette *n* **62**
baggy *adj* **13, 176**
Bahamas *n* **150, 162**
Bahamian *adj* **152**
Bahrain *n* **151, 153**
Bahraini *adj* **153**
bail *n* **85, 111**
Baisakhi *n* **07**
bait *n* **121**
bait *v* **121**
bake *v* **29, 62-63**
baked *adj* **72**
baked beans *n* **71**
baker *n* **62**
bakery *n* **46, 48, 62-63**
baking *n* **29**
baking tray *n* **29**
baklava *n* **63**
balance wheel *n* **142**
balanced diet *n* **23**
balcony *n* **25**
bald *adj* **12**
bald eagle *n* **160**
ball *n* **02, 08, 109-110, 112, 114**
ball boy *n* **114**
ball girl *n* **114**
ballerina *n* **126**
ballet *n* **126**
ballet flats *n* **17**
ballet leotard *n* **126**
ballet shoes *n* **126**
ballistic missile *n* **88**
balloon *n* **08**
ballpoint pen *n* **175**
balsamic vinegar *n* **60**
bamboo *n* **41, 55, 167**
banana *n* **58**
band *n* **129**
bandage *n* **20, 49**
banded sea krait *n* **166**
Bangladesh *n* **150, 153**
Bangladeshi *adj* **153**
bangle *n* **16**
banister *n* **25-26**
banjo *n* **129**
bank *n* **45, 94**
bank loan *n* **45**
bank statement *n* **45**
banking *n* **91**
banner *n* **109**
baobab tree *n* **169**
baptism *n* **07**
bar, bars *n* **30, 68, 109, 124**
bar chart *n* **95**
bar counter *n* **68**
bar mitzvah *n* **07**
bar snacks *n* **68**
bar stool *n* **68**
bar tender *n* **69**
barb *n* **121**
Barbadian *adj* **152**
Barbados *n* **150, 152**
barbecue *n* **41**
barbecue *n* **135**
barbell *n* **124**
barber *n* **89**
barberry *n* **168**
Barbudan *adj* **152**
barcode *n* **48**
bare branches *n* **172**
bargain *n* **48**
barista *n* **65, 89**
baritone *n* **126**
barium *n* **78**
bark *v* **164**
barley *n* **86**
barn *n* **86**
barn owl *n* **161**
barnacle *n* **134, 166**
barracuda *n* **166**
barrel cactus *n* **168**
Barrier Reef *n* **145**
bartender *n* **68, 89**
basa *n* **54**
basalt *n* **156**
base *n* **74, 76**
baseball *n* **113**
baseball cap *n* **16**
baseball cleats *n* **17**
baseball game *n* **113**
baseline *n* **114**
basement *n* **25, 47**
basil *n* **59**
basin *n* **22, 33**
basket *n* **48, 101, 103, 112, 164**
basket of fruit *n* **57**
basketball *n* **112**
basketball player *n* **112**
basking shark *n* **166**
Basotho *adj* **152**
basque *n* **14**
bass *n* **126**
bass clef *n* **128**
bass drum *n* **128**
bass guitarist *n* **129**
basset hound *n* **164**
bassoon *n* **128**
bat *n* **111, 113-114, 158**
bat *v* **111, 113**
bat mitzvah *n* **07**
bath towel *n* **31**
bath toys *n* **31**
bath tub *n* **31**
bathmat *n* **31**
bathroom *n* **31**
bathroom extractor fan *n* **31**
bathroom scales *n* **31**
baton *n* **116**
batsman *n* **111**
Battenburg markings *n* **50**
batter *n* **111, 113**
battering ram *n* **79**
battery *n* **75, 83, 98**
battery pack *n* **35**
batting glove *n* **113**
battle *n* **79, 88**
battlement *n* **44**
battleship *n* **105**
Bauhaus *n* **130**
bay *n* **147**
bay leaf *n* **59**
bay tree *n* **38**
bay window *n* **25**
bayonet base *n* **33**
be absent *v* **95**
be born *v* **07**
be delayed *v* **104**

be laid off *v* **81**
be late *v* **09, 171**
be promoted *v* **81**
be sent off *v* **109**
be unemployed *v* **81**
beach *n* **134, 147-148**
beach bag *n* **134**
beach ball *n* **134**
beach buggy *n* **97, 134**
beach hut *n* **134**
beach umbrella *n* **134**
bead maze *n* **08**
beagle *n* **164**
beak *n* **161**
beaker *n* **27, 76**
beam *n* **125**
bean *n* **56**
bean sprouts *n* **55**
beanie *n* **16**
bear's head tooth *n* **170**
beard *n* **12**
beat *n* **129**
beat eggs *v* **29**
beautiful *adj* **12, 177**
beauty *n* **18, 47**
beauty treatments *n* **18**
bed *n* **30**
bed and breakfast *n* **131**
bed linen *n* **30**
bedrock *n* **145**
bedroom *n* **30**
bedside lamp *n* **30**
bedside table *n* **30**
bedspring *n* **30**
bee *n* **165**
beech *n* **168**
beef *n* **53**
beehive *n* **86, 162**
beer *n* **52, 68**
beer tap *n* **68**
beet leaves *n* **55**
beetroot *n* **56**
beg *v* **164**
begonia *n* **38**
behind *prep* **148, 180**
being a fast learner *n* **93**
Belarus *n* **151, 153**
Belarusian *adj* **153**
Belgian *adj* **153**
Belgium *n* **151, 153**
Belize *n* **150, 152**
Belizean *adj* **152**
bell *n* **99**
bell tower *n* **44**
belt *n* **15-16, 117**
beluga *n* **166**
bench *n* **124**
bend *v* **126**
benefits *n* **81**
Bengal *n* **164**
Benin *n* **149, 152**
Beninese *adj* **152**
beret *n* **16**
berkelium *n* **78**
Bermuda shorts *n* **14**
berries *n* **57**
beryllium *n* **78**
beside *prep* **180**
best friend *n* **07**
bestseller *n* **138**
between *prep* **148, 180**
beverage,
beverages *n* **65, 69**
bhangra *n* **129**
Bhutan *n* **150, 153**
Bhutanese *adj* **153**
biathlon *n* **122**
bib *n* **13**
bibliography *n* **138**
bicep curl *n* **124**
biceps *n* **03**
bicycle *n* **101**
bidet *n* **31**
biennial *n* **41**
bifocal *n* **22**
big *adj* **176**
Big Bang *n* **144**
Big Ben *n* **44**
big toe *n* **02**
bike helmet *n* **101**
bike rack *n* **101**
bikini *n* **134**
bilberry *n* **57**
bill *n* **161, 32**
bill *n* **69**
bin *n* **82**
bin liner *n* **33, 34**
binder clip *n* **82**
binoculars *n* **144**
biochemistry *n* **76**
biodegradable waste *n* **33**
biography *n* **138**
biologist *n* **77**
biology *n* **73, 77, 80**
biomass energy *n* **51**
biometric passport *n* **104**
biotechnology *n* **91**
biplane *n* **103**
birch *n* **168**
bird of paradise *n* **160**
bird-of-paradise *n* **167**
bird seed *n* **164**
bird-watching *n* **133**
bird's eye chillies *n* **59**
birds *n* **160, 161**
birdwatcher *n* **161**
birth *n* **08**
birth certificate *n* **07**
birthday *n* **07**
birthday cake *n* **63**
birthday candles *n* **63**
birthday card *n* **07**
biscuits *n* **63**
bishop *n* **140**
bismuth *n* **78**
Bissau-Guinean *adj* **152**
bistro *n* **69**
bit *n* **120**
bite *n* **19**
bite *v* **52, 121**
bitter *adj* **52, 56**
black *adj* **140-141**
black *n* **140-141**
black belt *n* **117**
black coffee *n* **65**
black hair *n* **12**
black hole *n* **144**
black mustard *n* **59**
black olives *n* **64**
black pudding *n* **70**
black swan *n* **161**
black tea *n* **66**
black trumpet *n* **170**
black widow spider *n* **162**
black woodpecker *n* **160**
blackberry *n* **57**
blackbird *n* **160**
blackcurrant *n* **57**
blacksmith *n* **79**
blade *n* **33, 40, 51, 117**
blanket *n* **30**
bleach *n* **34**
bleat *v* **165**
bleed *v* **20**
blender *n* **27, 65**
blindfold *n* **125**
blindside flanker *n* **108**
blink *v* **02**
blister *n* **19**
blizzard *n* **154**
block *v* **84, 112, 117**
block of flats *n* **25, 43**
blocker *n* **112**
blocking glove *n* **110**
blog *n* **84**
blogger *n* **84**
blond hair *n* **12**
blonde hair *n* **12**
blood knot *n* **121**
blood orange *n* **57**
blood pressure *n* **20**
blood pressure
monitor *n* **21**
blood sausage *n* **71**
blood test *n* **20-21**
blossom *n* **169**
blouse *n* **14**
blow *v* **11**
blow hole *n* **166**
blow out *v* **63**
blowout *n* **123**
blue *adj* **01, 141**
blue *n* **01, 141**
blue cheese *n* **61**
blue crab *n* **166**
blue line *n* **110**
blue tang *n* **166**
blue whale *n* **166**
blue-tongued skink *n* **163**
blueberry *n* **57**
blues *n* **129**
Bluetooth headset *n* **83**
Bluetooth speaker *n* **136**
blush *v* **02**
blusher *n* **18**
boar *n* **53, 159**
board *n* **119**
board *v* **106**
board a plane *v* **104**
board game *n* **08**
board games *n* **140**
board of directors *n* **95**
boarding gate *n* **104**
boarding pass *n* **104**
boardroom *n* **95**
boards *n* **110**
boardwalk *n* **134**
boat shoes *n* **17**
boat's wheel *n* **119**
boater *n* **16**
boats *n* **105**
bob *n* **12**
bobbin *n* **142**
bobble hat *n* **16**
bobcat *n* **159**
bobsleigh *n* **122**
boccia *n* **125**
body *n* **129**
body lotion *n* **31**
body powder *n* **31**
body systems *n* **04**
bodyboarding *n* **119, 134**
bodyguard *n* **90**
bodywork *n* **98, 123**
bohrium *n* **78**
boil *v* **29**
boiled *adj* **72**
boiled egg *n* **61, 71**
boiled sweets *n* **67**
boiler *n* **33**
boiling *adj* **154**
boiling point *n* **154**
bold *adj* **175**
bold *n* **175**
Bolivia *n* **149, 152**
Bolivian *adj* **152**
bollard, bollards *n* **43, 105**
Bolognese sauce *n* **64**
bolt *n* **25, 36**
Bombay *n* **164**
Bombay earth snake *n* **163**
bomber *n* **88**
bomber jacket *n* **15**
bone *n* **03**
bone meal *n* **39**
boned *adj* **54**
bongo drums *n* **128**
bonnet *n* **97-98**
bonsai tree *n* **38**
bonus *n* **81**
boogie board *n* **119**
book, books *n* **26, 80, 138**
book a holiday *v* **131**
bookcase *n* **26**
bookshelf *n* **80**
bookshop *n* **46**
boom *n* **50, 119**
booster *n* **143**
boot *n* **97**
boot, boots *n* **17, 100**
boot shapers *n* **17**
booties *n* **13**
borage *n* **59**
border collie *n* **164**
bored *adj* **06**
boring *adj* **177**
boron *n* **78**
borrow *v* **80**
Bosnia and Herzegovina
n **151, 153**
Bosnian *adj* **153**
boss *n* **81**
botanical gardens *n* **132**
botanist *n* **77**
botany *n* **77**
Botswana *n* **149, 152**
Botswanan *adj* **152**
bottle *n* **08, 52**
bottle opener *n* **28, 68**
bottled oils *n* **60**
bougainvillea *n* **168**
bounce *v* **112**
bound ankle pose *n* **24**
boundary *n* **111, 113**
bouquet *n* **15, 47**
bouquet garni *n* **59**
boutique *n* **46**
bow *n* **79, 119, 125**
bow *v* **02**
bow pose *n* **24**
bow tie *n* **16**
bowl *n* **27, 33, 52**
bowl *v* **111**
bowler *n* **111**
bowling *n* **125**
bowling ball *n* **125**
bowling crease *n* **111**
bowling pin *n* **125, 08**
box, boxes *n* **32, 52, 126**
box office *n* **127**
boxer *n* **164**
boxer shorts *n* **14**
boxercise *n* **124**
boxing *n* **117**
boxing gloves *n* **117**
boxing match *n* **117**
boxing ring *n* **117**
boy *n* **05**
boyfriend *n* **05**
bra *n* **14**
brace *n* **35**
bracelet *n* **16**
braces *n* **22**
brachiosaurus *n* **157**
brackets *n* **175**
braids *n* **12**
Braille *n* **175**
brain *n* **04**
brake *n* **99-101**
brake cooling intake *n* **123**

brake disk *n* **100**
brake fluid reservoir *n* **98**
brake lever *n* **101**
brake pad *n* **101**
brake pedal *n* **100**
brake *v* **98, 101**
branch *n* **81, 169**
branch manager *n* **45**
brandy *n* **68**
brass *adj* **176**
brass *n* **128, 176**
brave *adj* **10**
bray *v* **165**
Brazil *n* **149, 152**
brazil nuts *n* **58**
Brazilian *adj* **152**
bread, breads *n* **62, 71**
bread basket *n* **71**
bread knife *n* **28**
breadfruit *n* **56**
break down *v* **98, 178**
break even *v* **94**
break in *n* **50**
break up *v* **178**
breakdown assistance *n* **98**
breakfast *n* **26, 71**
breakfast buffet *n* **71**
breakfast burrito *n* **71**
breakfast cereals *n* **48**
breakfast roll *n* **71**
breakfast tray *n* **131**
breakfast TV *n* **137**
breast *n* **01, 53**
breastbone *n* **03**
breaststroke *n* **118**
Breathalyzer *n* **50**
breathe *v* **02**
breathtaking *adj* **177**
breed *v* **120**
breeze *n* **154**
breeze block *n* **87**
breezy *adj* **154**
bribery *n* **85**
brick *adj* **176**
brick, bricks *n* **35, 87, 176**
bride *n* **07**
bridesmaid's dress *n* **15**
bridge crane *n* **106**
bridge *n* **02, 43, 105, 125, 129, 140**
bridge pose *n* **24**
bridle *n* **120**
bridle path *n* **133**
Brie *n* **64**
briefcase *n* **16**
brilliant *adj* **177**
bring *v* **11**
brioche *n* **62, 71**
British *adj* **153**
British shorthair *n* **164**
broad beans *n* **55**
broadcast *v* **84**
broadleaf forest *n* **159**
broccoli *n* **55-56**
brogues *n* **17**
broken bone *n* **19**
bromine *n* **78**
bronze *adj* **176**
bronze *n* **116, 176**
Bronze age *n* **79**
brooch *n* **16**
broom *n* **34, 40**
broomstick *n* **139**
broth *n* **72**
brother *n* **05**
brother-in-law *n* **05**
browband *n* **120**
brown *adj* **01**
brown *n* **01, 141**
brown bear *n* **159**
brown bread *n* **62**
brown flour *n* **62**
brown hair *n* **12**
bruise *n* **19**
brunch *n* **69**
Brunei *n* **151, 153**
Bruneian *adj* **153**
brush *n* **34, 141**
brush *v* **22**
brush your hair *v* **09**
brush your teeth *v* **09**
Brussels sprouts *n* **55**
bubble bath *n* **18, 31**
bucket *n* **34, 37, 40**
bucket and spade *n* **134**
bucket turn *n* **118**
buckle *n* **16**
buckled shoes *n* **17**
buckwheat flour *n* **62**
budgerigar *n* **160, 164**
budget *n* **94**
budgie *n* **160, 164**
buffalo *n* **159**
buffer *n* **102**
buffet *n* **69**
buggy *n* **08, 115**
bugs *n* **162**
build *v* **11, 87**
builder *n* **87**
building, buildings *n* **42-44, 148**
building blocks / bricks *n* **08**
building site *n* **87**
built-in wardrobe *n* **30**
bulb *n* **41**
Bulgaria *n* **151, 153**
Bulgarian *adj* **153**
bull *n* **165**
bull-nose pliers *n* **36**
bulldozer *n* **87**
bullet train *n* **102**
bullseye *n* **140**
bumble bee *n* **162**
bump *v* **112**
bumper *n* **97**
bumps *n* **96**
bun *n* **12**
bunch *n* **47**
bungalow *n* **32**
bungee jumping *n* **125**
bunker *n* **115**
Bunsen burner *n* **76**
buoy *n* **106, 119, 134**
bureau de change *n* **45**
burgee *n* **119**
burger *n* **70**
burger bar *n* **70**
burglar alarm *n* **25**
burglary *n* **85**
Burj Khalifa *n* **44**
Burkina Faso *n* **149, 152**
Burkinabe *adj* **152**
Burma (Myanmar) *n* **150, 153**
Burmese *adj* **153**
Burmese *n* **164**
burn *n* **19, 29**
burner *n* **27, 103**
burrow *v* **159**
Burundi *n* **149, 152**
Burundian *adj* **152**
bus, buses *n* **43, 99**
bus driver *n* **90**
bus shelter *n* **99**
bus station *n* **42, 99**
bus stop *n* **25**
bus ticket *n* **99**
bus transfer *n* **104**
business class *n* **103**
business deal *n* **81**
business lunch *n* **81**
business man *n* **81**
business trip *n* **81**
businesslike attitude *n* **93**
businessman *n* **90**
businesswoman *n* **81, 90**
bust dart *n* **142**
butcher *n* **46, 53, 89**
butter *n* **61, 71**
butter dish *n* **28**
butter knife *n* **27**
buttercup *n* **38, 168**
buttercup squash *n* **56**
butterfly, butterflies *n* **77, 118, 162**
buttermilk *n* **61**
butternut squash *n* **56**
buttock *n* **03**
button, buttons *n* **15, 142**
button acorn squash *n* **56**
button hole *n* **15**
buy *v* **32, 46**
buy groceries *v* **09, 34**
buying a house *n* **32**
buzz *v* **162**

C

cab *n* **50**
cabbage *n* **55**
cabbage white butterfly *n* **162**
cabin *n* **32, 103, 105, 131**
cabinet *n* **27**
cable *n* **101**
cable car *n* **122**
cable TV *n* **137**
cacti *n* **41**
caddy *n* **115**
caddy bin *n* **155**
cadmium *n* **78**
caesium *n* **78**
café *n* **42, 46, 65-66**
cafetière *n* **28**
cage *n* **164**
cake, cakes *n* **63**
cake shop *n* **46**
cake tin *n* **28-29**
cake topper *n* **63**
calamari *n* **54**
calcite *n* **156**
calcium *n* **23, 49, 78**
calculator *n* **73-74**
calendar *n* **82, 172**
calf *n* **01, 03, 165**
californium *n* **78**
call a friend *v* **09**
call a plumber *v* **33**
call in sick *v* **81**
call off *v* **178**
call up *v* **178**
call your family *v* **09**
calligraphy *n* **175**
calm *adj* **06, 10, 93**
calm down *v* **178**
calorie-controlled diet *n* **23**
calories *n* **23**
Cambodia *n* **150, 153**
Cambodian *adj* **153**
Cambrian *adj* **157**
Cambrian *n* **157**
camel pose *n* **24**
camellia *n* **38**
Camembert *n* **64**
camera *n* **83-84**
camera crane *n* **84**
camera mount *n* **123**
camera operator *n* **84, 127**
Cameroon *n* **149, 152**
Cameroonian *adj* **152**
camisole *n* **14**
camomile tea *n* **66**
camouflage *n* **88**
camp *v* **135**
camp bed *n* **135**
camper van *n* **135**
campfire *n* **135**
camping *n* **135**
camping equipment *n* **135**
camping facilities *n* **135**
campion *n* **168**
campsite *n* **135, 148**
campus *n* **80**
Canada *n* **150, 152**
Canada goose *n* **160**
Canadian *adj* **152**
canary *n* **160**
Canary melon *n* **58**
cancel *v* **69**
Cancer *n* **144**
candle *n* **26, 30**
candle magic *n* **139**
candlestick *n* **26**
candy cane *n* **67**
candy floss *n* **67**
canes *n* **40**
canines *n* **03**
canned drink *n* **70**
cannelloni *n* **64**
cannon *n* **79**
Caño Cristales *n* **145**
canoe *n* **105**
canola oil *n* **60**
canopy *n* **103, 125**
cantaloupe *n* **58**
canter *v* **120**
canvas *n* **141**
canyon *n* **146**
cap *n* **118, 170**
cap sleeve *n* **15**
capacity *n* **174**
cape *n* **147**
cape gooseberry *n* **57**
Cape Verde *n* **149, 152**
Cape Verdean *adj* **152**
capers *n* **64**
capital letters *n* **175**
capoeira *n* **117**
cappuccino *n* **65**
Capricorn *n* **144**
capsize *v* **119**
capsules *n* **49**
captain *n* **105**
capuchin monkey *n* **159**
capybara *n* **159**
cars *n* **97-99**
car exterior *n* **97**
car hire *n* **104**
car interior *n* **99**
car park *n* **42**
car stereo *n* **99**
car theft *n* **85**
car wash *n* **97**
caravan *n* **135**
caravan *n* **32**
caraway seeds *n* **59**
carbohydrates *n* **23**
carbon *n* **78**

carbon dioxide *n* **155**
carbonated *adj* **52**
Carboniferous *adj* **157**
Carboniferous *n* **157**
card *n* **141**
card machine *n* **45, 48**
cardamom *n* **59**
cardigan *n* **14**
cardinal numbers *n* **173**
cardiology *n* **21**
cardiovascular *n* **04**
cargo *n* **102, 106**
cargo plane *n* **103**
cargo trousers *n* **13**
Caribbean *n* **152**
Caribbean *adj* **152**
caribou *n* **159**
caring *adj* **10**
carnation *n* **38**
carnelian *n* **156**
carnival *n* **07**
carousel *n* **133**
carp *n* **54**
carpenter *n* **89**
carpentry bit *n* **36**
carpet *n* **30**
carriage *n* **102**
carriage race *n* **120**
carrier *n* **100**
carrier bag *n* **47, 48**
carrot *n* **56**
carry *v* **11**
cartilage *n* **03**
cartographer *n* **148**
carton *n* **52**
cartoon *n* **137**
carve *v* **29, 35**
carving fork *n* **28**
case *n* **22**
cash machine *n* **45**
cashew nut, cashew nuts *n* **58, 68**
cashier *n* **45, 48**
cassava *n* **56**
casserole dish *n* **28**
cassowary *n* **160**
cast *n* **126-127**
cast *v* **121**
cast a spell *v* **139**
cast-iron plant *n* **167**
castle *n* **44**
castor oil plant *n* **169**
casual clothes *n* **14**
casualty *n* **88**
cat breeds *n* **164**
catamaran *n* **105**
catapult *n* **79**
cataract *n* **22**
catch *v* **11, 107, 113, 121**
catch a train *v* **102**
catch the bus *v* **09**
catch the train *v* **09**
catch up *v* **178**
catch-up TV *n* **137**
catcher *n* **113**
catching glove *n* **110**
catering *n* **91**
caterpillar *n* **77, 162**
catfish *n* **54**
cattail *n* **167**
cattle *n* **165**
cauldron *n* **139**
cauliflower *n* **56**
caulk *n* **37**
cautious *adj* **10**
caver *n* **146**
caves *n* **146**
caving *n* **146**
cavity *n* **22**
cavolo nero *n* **55**
cayenne pepper *n* **59**
CD *n* **136**
CD player *n* **136**
cedar of Lebanon *n* **167**
cedilla *n* **175**
ceiling *n* **26**
ceiling fan *n* **33**
celandine *n* **168**
celebration cakes *n* **63**
celebrations *n* **07**
celebrity *n* **127**
celeriac *n* **56**
celery *n* **55**
celery allergy *n* **23**
cell *n* **85**
cell membrane *n* **77**
cell wall *n* **77**
cello *n* **128**
Celsius *n* **154**
cement *n* **87**
cement mixer *n* **87**
cemetery *n* **43**
Cenozoic (new life) *adj* **157**
Cenozoic (new life) *n* **157**
centaur *n* **139**
centimetre *n* **174**
centipede *n* **162**
Central African *adj* **152**
Central African Republic *n* **149, 152**
Central America *n* **150, 152**
Central American *adj* **152**
central reservation *n* **96**
centre *n* **74, 107, 110, 112**
centre circle *n* **109**
centre speaker *n* **136**
centre parting *n* **12**
centreboard *n* **119**
centrifugal force *n* **75**
centripetal force *n* **75**
century *n* **172**
CEO (chief executive officer) *n* **81**
ceramic *adj* **176**
ceramic *n* **176**
ceramic hob *n* **27**
Cerberus *n* **139**
cereal *n* **71**
cereal bowl *n* **71**
Ceres *n* **143**
cerium *n* **78**
cervical vertebrae *n* **03**
cervix *n* **04**
CFL (compact fluorescent lamp) bulb *n* **33**
Chad *n* **149, 152**
Chadian *adj* **152**
chain *n* **16, 101, 146**
chair *n* **26, 82**
chair pose *n* **24**
chairlift *n* **122**
chalet *n* **32, 131**
chalk *n* **39, 156**
challah *n* **62**
Champagne *n* **68**
championship *n* **114**
change *v* **14**
change a light bulb *v* **35**
change gear *v* **101**
change money *v* **45**
change the channel *v* **137**
change the sheets *v* **34**
change trains *v* **102**
changing bag *n* **08**
changing mat *n* **30**
changing room *n* **124**
changing rooms *n* **47**
changing table *n* **30**
channel *n* **137, 147**
chanterelle *n* **56, 170**
chapati *n* **62**
chapter *n* **138**
character *n* **138**
charcoal *n* **135, 141**
charentais *n* **58**
charge *n* **50, 75, 85**
charge *v* **165**
charging cable *n* **83**
chariot *n* **79**
chase *v* **107**
chassis *n* **123**
chat *n* **83**
chat online *v* **09**
chat show *n* **137**
chat with friends *v* **09**
check in *v* **131, 178**
check out *v* **131, 178**
check the oil *v* **98**
check the tyres *v* **98**
check your emails *v* **09**
check-in desk *n* **104**
check-up *n* **22**
checked *adj* **13**
checkout *n* **48**
cheddar *n* **64**
cheek *n* **01**
cheerful *adj* **06**
cheerleader *n* **107**
cheese, cheeses *n* **61, 64, 71**
cheese platter *n* **69**
cheeseburger *n* **70**
cheesecake *n* **63**
cheetah *n* **158**
chef *n* **69, 90**
chef's coat *n* **13**
chef's hat *n* **13**
chef's uniform *n* **13**
Chelsea boots *n* **17**
chemical equation *n* **76**
chemical formula *n* **76**
chemical industry *n* **91**
chemical symbol *n* **76**
chemist *n* **76**
chemistry *n* **73, 76, 80**
cheque *n* **45, 94**
chequered flag *n* **123**
cherry, cherries *n* **57, 169**
cherry tomatoes *n* **55**
chervil *n* **59**
chess *n* **140**
chessboard *n* **140**
chest *n* **01**
chest compressions *n* **20**
chest expander *n* **124**
chest of drawers *n* **30**
chest press *n* **124**
chest protection *n* **117**
chest protector *n* **107**
chestnuts *n* **58**
chew *v* **52**
chewing gum *n* **67**
chicane *n* **123**
chick *n* **165**
chicken *n* **53, 165**
chicken burger *n* **70**
chicken coop *n* **86**
chicken nuggets *n* **70**
chicken of the woods *n* **170**
chickenpox *n* **19**
chicory *n* **55**
chihuahua *n* **164**
child *n* **05**
child seat *n* **101**
childcare provider *n* **90**
child's meal *n* **69**
child's pose *n* **24**
childbirth *n* **08**
childhood *n* **08**
children's book *n* **138**
children's department *n* **47**
children's TV *n* **137**
children's ward *n* **21**
Chile *n* **149, 152**
Chilean *adj* **152**
Chilean fire bush *n* **167**
chill *n* **19**
chill out *v* **178**
chilled *adj* **52**
chilli *n* **56, 60, 64**
chilli flakes *n* **59**
chilly *adj* **154**
chimney *n* **25, 32, 87**
chimney pot *n* **25**
chimpanzee *n* **159**
chin *n* **01**
chin strap *n* **107**
China *n* **150, 153**
Chinese *adj* **153**
Chinese characters *n* **175**
Chinese hibiscus *n* **169**
Chinese hotpot *n* **72**
Chinese lantern *n* **169**
Chinese mahogany *n* **169**
Chinese money plant *n* **38**
chip *v* **115**
chipboard *n* **35**
chipmunk *n* **159**
chips *n* **70**
chiropractic *n* **24**
chisel *n* **36, 141**
chives *n* **59**
chlorine *n* **78**
chloroplast *n* **77**
chocolate bar *n* **67**
chocolate cake *n* **63**
chocolate chip cookie *n* **63**
chocolate doughnut *adj* **63**
chocolate milkshake *n* **61, 65**
chocolate spread *n* **60**
choir *n* **128**
choker *n* **16**
cholesterol *n* **23**
choose *v* **46**
chop *n* **53**
chop *v* **29, 39, 117**
chopped salad *n* **72**
chopping board *n* **28**
chopsticks *n* **27**
chord *n* **128**
chorizo *n* **53, 64**
choux pastry *n* **63**
christening *n* **07**
Christmas *n* **07**
chromium *n* **78, 156**
chromosome *n* **77**
chrysalis *n* **77**
chrysanthemum *n* **38**
chuck *n* **35**
chukka boots *n* **17**
church *n* **43-44**
chutney *n* **60, 72**
cider *n* **68**
cider vinegar *n* **60**
cinema *n* **42, 127**
cinematographer *n* **127**
cinnamon *n* **59**
cinnamon rolls *n* **71**
cinnamon stick *n* **59**
circle *n* **74**
circuit *n* **83**
circuit board *n* **75**
circuit training *n* **124**
circular saw *n* **35**
circumference *n* **74**

circumflex *n* **175**
cistern *n* **33**
citrine *n* **156**
citrus fruit *n* **57**
city centre *n* **42**
claimant *n* **85**
clam *n* **54**
clamp *n* **35, 76**
clap *v* **02**
clapper board *n* **84**
clarinet *n* **128**
class *n* **73**
classical *adj* **129**
Classicism *n* **130**
classroom *n* **73**
clavicle *n* **03**
claw *n* **161**
clay *n* **39, 141**
clean *adj* **176**
clean the bathroom *v* **34**
clean the car *v* **09**
clean the oven *v* **34**
clean the windows *v* **34**
clean up *v* **34, 178**
cleaned *adj* **54**
cleaner *n* **89**
cleaning *n* **34**
cleanser *n* **18**
clear the table *v* **09, 34**
cleat *n* **119**
cleaver *n* **28**
clementine *n* **57**
click *n* **83**
client, clients *n* **81, 85**
cliff *n* **147**
climate *n* **155**
climate change *n* **155**
climb *v* **11**
climber *n* **41**
climbing frame *n* **43**
clinch knot *n* **121**
clinic *n* **20**
clipboard *n* **82**
cloak *n* **15**
cloakroom *n* **130**
cloche *n* **16**
clock *n* **44, 171**
clock radio *n* **30**
clockwise *adv* **148**
clogs *n* **17**
closed *adj* **48, 132**
closed to bicycles *adj* **96**
closed to pedestrians *adj* **96**
cloth *n* **34**
clothes *n* **13-15**
clothes moth *n* **162**
clothes peg *n* **34**
clothesline *n* **34**
clothing *n* **100**
cloud, clouds *n* **51, 154**
cloudy *adj* **154**
cloves *n* **59**
clown *n* **89**
clownfish *n* **166**
club *n* **140**
club sandwich *n* **70**
clubhouse *n* **115**
clumsy *adj* **10**
clutch *n* **99-100**
CMS (content management system) *n* **84**
co-pilot *n* **103**
co-worker *n* **81**
CO_2 bubbles *n* **62**
coach *n* **99, 112-113**
coach's box *n* **113**
coal *n* **51**
coal mine *n* **51**
coastal features *n* **147**
coaster *n* **27, 68**
coastguard *n* **106**
coat hanger *n* **30**
coats *n* **15**
cobalt *n* **78**
cobra pose *n* **24**
coccyx *n* **03**
cockatiel *n* **164**
cockatoo *n* **161**
cockerel *n* **165**
cockle *n* **54**
cockpit *n* **103, 123**
cockroach *n* **162**
cocktail *n* **68**
cocktail glass *n* **68**
cocktail shaker *n* **68**
cocoa *n* **169**
cocoa powder *n* **65**
coconut *n* **58**
coconut crab *n* **166**
coconut oil *n* **60**
coconut palm *n* **167**
coconut shell *n* **57**
coconut water *n* **58, 65**
cocoon *n* **162**
cod *n* **166**
cod fillet *n* **54**
coelophysis *n* **157**
coffee *n* **52, 65, 69, 71, 86**
coffee cup *n* **27**
coffee machine *n* **65, 68**
coffee press *n* **28**
coffee shop *n* **46**
coffee table *n* **26**
coins *n* **45, 94**
cola *n* **52**
colander *n* **28**
cold *adj* **154, 176**
cold *n* **19**
cold frame *v* **39**
cold front *n* **155**
cold meats *n* **71**
cold water *n* **31**
collaborate *v* **92**
collage *n* **141**
collar *n* **15, 142**
collarbone *n* **03**
collards *n* **55**
colleague *n* **07, 81, 92**
collect *v* **11**
collection *n* **130**
college departments *n* **80**
college schools *n* **80**
Colombia *n* **149, 152**
Colombian *adj* **152**
colon *n* **175**
Colosseum *n* **44**
coloured pencils *n* **73**
colouring book *n* **138**
columbine *n* **168**
column *n* **44, 146**
comb *n* **12**
combat aircraft *n* **88**
combat sports *n* **117**
combination *adj* **18**
combine harvester *n* **86**
combined events *n* **116**
comedian *n* **89**
comedy *n* **126-127, 137**
comet *n* **143-144**
comic *n* **48, 138**
comma *n* **175**
commence *v* **95**
commercial district *n* **42**
commis chef *n* **69**
commission *n* **94**
common earthball *n* **170**
common egg-eater *n* **163**
common green iguana *n* **163**
common houseleek *n* **168**
common poppy *n* **168**
common puffball *n* **170**
common snake-necked turtle *n* **163**
common toad *n* **163**
community website *n* **84**
commuters *n* **102**
Comoran *adj* **152**
Comoros *n* **149, 152**
company *n* **81**
compartment *n* **102**
compass *n* **73-74, 119, 135, 148**
competitive *adj* **93**
complain *v* **46**
complaint *n* **50**
compose *v* **128**
composer *n* **128**
compost *n* **40**
compost bin *n* **40**
compost heap *n* **41**
compostable bags *n* **155**
composter *n* **40**
compound *n* **76**
compressed-air cylinder *n* **50**
computer, computers *n* **82-83**
computer desk *n* **83**
computer literacy *n* **93**
computing *n* **93**
concave lens *n* **75**
concealer *n* **18**
conceptual art *n* **130**
concert hall *n* **43**
conchiglie *n* **64**
concourse *n* **102**
concrete *adj* **176**
concrete *n* **35, 176**
concussion *n* **19**
condensed milk *n* **61**
condiments *n* **60, 71-72**
conduct *v* **128**
conductor *n* **75, 128**
cone *n* **74, 87**
confectionery *n* **48**
conference *n* **95**
confident *adj* **06, 10, 93**
confused *adj* **06**
confusing *adj* **177**
conglomerate *n* **156**
Congolese *adj* **152**
coniferous forest *n* **146**
conifers *n* **41, 157, 167**
connection *n* **104**
conning tower *n* **105**
conservation *n* **130**
considerate *adj* **10**
console *n* **136**
constellation, constellations *n* **144**
construction *n* **87, 91**
construction waste *n* **33**
contact *n* **83**
contact lens, contact lenses *n* **22, 49**
contact lens solution *n* **22**
container *n* **105**
container port *n* **106**
container ship *n* **105-106**
containers *n* **52**
contents *n* **138**
continent *n* **145**
contours *n* **148**
contract *n* **92**
control tower *n* **104**
controller *n* **136**
controls *n* **100, 136**
convenience food *n* **23, 48**
conversion *n* **108**
convert the attic *v* **35**
convert the loft *v* **35**
convertible *n* **97**
convex lens *n* **75**
conveyor belt *n* **48**
cook dinner *v* **09**
cookbook *n* **138**
cooked *adj* **56**
cooked breakfast *n* **71**
cooked meat *n* **53, 64**
cooked vegetables *n* **72**
cookie *n* **63, 84**
cooking *n* **29**
cooking show *n* **137**
cooksonia *n* **157**
cool *adj* **154**
cool down *v* **124**
coolant reservoir *n* **98**
cooler *n* **135**
cooling rack *n* **29**
cooling system *n* **98**
cooling tower *n* **51**
coordinate *v* **92**
coordinates *n* **148**
coot *n* **161**
copernicium *n* **78**
copper *n* **78, 156**
copy *v* **11**
copyright *n* **175**
cor anglais *n* **128**
coral *n* **166**
coral reef *n* **118, 166**
coral reef fish *n* **118**
coral trout *n* **166**
cordless drill *n* **35**
core *n* **57**
coriander *n* **59**
coriander seeds *n* **59**
cork *n* **60**
corkscrew *n* **28, 68**
cormorant *n* **160**
corn *n* **55, 86**
corn bread *n* **62**
corn oil *n* **60**
cornea *n* **22**
corner *n* **109**
corner flag *n* **109**
corner kick *n* **109**
cornerback *n* **107**
cornichons *n* **60**
cornrows *n* **12**
corpse pose *n* **24**
correct *adj* **176**
correction fluid *n* **82**
cortado *n* **65**
Costa Rica *n* **150, 152**
Costa Rican *adj* **152**
costume, costumes *n* **13, 126-127**
costume drama *n* **137**
cot *n* **30**
cotoneaster *n* **169**
cottage *n* **32**
cottage cheese *n* **61**
cottage garden *n* **41**
cotton *adj* **176**
cotton *n* **13, 86, 176**
cotton balls *n* **18**
cotton reel *n* **142**
cotton wool *n* **20**
couch *n* **26**
couch potato *n* **137**
cough *n* **19**
cough *v* **20**
cough medicine *n* **49**
counsellor *n* **24**
count *v* **11, 74**
counter *n* **45, 131**

counterclockwise *adv* **148**
counterfeit money *n* **94**
counterweight *n* **87**
country, countries *n* **129, 149-150**
countryside *n* **146**
couple *n* **07**
coupling rod *n* **102**
courgette *n* **56**
courier *n* **45**
course book *n* **138**
court *n* **85, 112**
court case *n* **85**
court date *n* **85**
court officer *n* **85**
court official *n* **85**
courtroom *n* **85**
courtyard *n* **25, 41**
cousin *n* **05**
cover *n* **111, 138**
cover letter *n* **92**
cow *n* **165**
cowcatcher *n* **102**
co-worker *n* **92**
cow's milk *n* **61**
cowboy boots *n* **17**
cowboy hat *n* **16**
cowslip *n* **169**
crab *n* **54, 134**
crab apple *n* **58, 169**
cradle *n* **50**
craft market *n* **132**
crafts *n* **141-142**
cramp, cramps *n* **19, 118**
cranberry *n* **57**
cranberry juice *n* **65**
crane *n* **106, 160**
crash barrier *n* **96**
crater *n* **143, 145**
crawl *v* **11**
crayfish *n* **54**
cream *n* **49, 61, 71**
cream cheese *n* **61**
creative *adj* **93**
credit card *n* **45, 94**
creep *v* **11**
creeper *n* **41**
crème pâtissière *n* **63**
crêpe *n* **70**
crescent moon *n* **143**
cress *n* **55**
crest *n* **161**
crested owl *n* **161**
Cretaceous *adj* **157**
Cretaceous *n* **157**
crew *n* **119**
crew cut *n* **12**
crew hatch *n* **143**
cricket *n* **111, 162**
cricket ball *n* **111**
cricket equipment *n* **111**
cricket pitch *n* **111**
cricket positions *n* **111**
cricket shoes *n* **111**
crime *n* **85, 137**
crime drama *n* **127**
crime fiction *n* **138**
crime scene *n* **50**
criminal *n* **85**
criminal record *n* **85**
crisp *adj* **57**
crispbread *n* **62, 71**
crisps *n* **48, 68**
critical *adj* **10**
Croatia *n* **151, 153**
Croatian *adj* **153**
crochet *n* **142**
crochet hook *n* **142**
crockery *n* **27**
crocodile clip *n* **75**
crocus *n* **38, 167**
croissant *n* **62, 71**
crop *n* **12**
cropped *adj* **13**
crops *n* **86**
croquet *n* **133**
cross-country skiing *n* **122**
cross-section of tooth *n* **03**
cross-trainer *n* **124**
crossbar *n* **101, 108, 116**
crosse *n* **110**
crossroads *n* **43**
crow *n* **160**
crow *v* **165**
crow pose *n* **24**
crown *n* **22**
crucible *n* **76**
crudités *n* **72**
cruise missile *n* **88**
cruise ship *n* **105**
cruiser *n* **88**
crumpled *adj* **13**
crunchy *adj* **52, 56**
crust *n* **62, 145**
crutches *n* **19**
cry *v* **02**
crystal *n* **76**
crystal ball *n* **139**
crystal healing *n* **24**
cub *n* **159**
Cuba *n* **150, 152**
Cuban *adj* **152**
cube *n* **74**
cubic metre *n* **174**
Cubism *n* **130**
cucumber *n* **55**
cue *n* **125**
cue ball *n* **125**
cuff *n* **15, 21, 142**
cufflinks *n* **16**
cultivate *v* **39**
cultivated mushrooms *n* **170**
cumin *n* **59**
cupcake *n* **63**
curator *n* **130**
cured *adj* **72**
cured meat *n* **53, 64**
curious *adj* **06, 93**
curium *n* **78**
curlew *n* **161**
curling *n* **122**
curling brush *n* **122**
curling stone *n* **122**
curly hair *n* **12**
currant *n* **58**
currency *n* **45, 94**
current account *n* **45**
current affairs *n* **137**
curry *n* **72**
curry powder *n* **59**
curtain, curtains *n* **26, 126**
curved *adj* **74**
cushion *n* **26**
custard *n* **63**
custard slice *n* **63**
customer, customers *n* **45, 48, 65, 69**
customer service *n* **47, 93**
customer-focused *adj* **93**
customs *n* **104**
customs house *n* **106**
cut *n* **19**
cut *v* **29, 35, 142**
cut down on *v* **23**
cute *adj* **177**
cuticle *n* **02**
cutlery *n* **26, 27**
cuts *n* **53**
cuts of meat *n* **53**
CV *n* **92**
cycad *n* **167**
cycle *v* **101**
cycle lane *n* **101**
cycle parking *n* **43**
cycle path *n* **43**
cycling *n* **101, 133**
cycling shoe *n* **17**
cylinder *n* **74**
cylinder head *n* **98**
cymbals *n* **128**
Cypriot *adj* **153**
Cyprus *n* **151, 153**
Cyrillic alphabet *n* **175**
cytoplasm *n* **77**
Czech *adj* **153**
Czech Republic *n* **151, 153**

D

dachshund *n* **164**
dad *n* **05**
daffodil *n* **38**
daily *adj* **172**
daily *adv* **172**
daily life *n* **178**
daily routines *n* **09**
dairy *n* **23, 48**
dairy allergy *n* **23**
dairy farm *n* **86**
dairy produce *n* **61**
dairy-free *adj* **23**
daisy *n* **38**
Dalmatian *n* **164**
dam *n* **51**
dance *n* **129**
dance *v* **11**
dance school *n* **80**
dancer *n* **89**
dandelion *n* **38, 55**
dandruff *n* **12**
danger area *n* **117**
Danish *adj* **153**
dark *adj* **60, 176**
dark chocolate *n* **67**
darmstadtium *n* **78**
darn *v* **142**
dart, darts *n* **140, 142**
dartboard *n* **140**
Darwin's frog *n* **163**
dash *n* **29, 175**
dashboard and controls *n* **99**
date *n* **57-58**
date palm *n* **167**
daughter *n* **05**
daughter-in-law *n* **05**
dawn *n* **171**
day *n* **171-172**
Day of the Dead *n* **07**
dead ball line *n* **108**
Dead sea *n* **145**
deadhead *v* **39**
deadly nightshade *n* **169**
deal *v* **140**
death angel *n* **170**
death cap *n* **170**
debit card *n* **45, 94**
decade *n* **172**
decay *n* **22**
December *n* **172**
decide *v* **11**
deciduous *n* **41**
decimals *n* **173**
decision-making *n* **93**
decisive *adj* **10**
deck *n* **105**
deck chair *n* **134**
deck of cards *n* **140**
decking *n* **41**
decorate *v* **29, 63**
decorating *n* **37**
decoration *n* **63**
decorator *n* **37**
deep *adj* **176**
deep diving *n* **118**
deep end *n* **118**
deep sea fishing *n* **121**
deep-fried *adj* **72**
deep-tread tyre *n* **100**
deer crossing *n* **96**
deerstalker *n* **16**
defence *n* **85, 107**
defender *n* **109**
defending zone *n* **110**
defensive specialist *n* **112**
defibrillator *n* **50**
deforestation *n* **155**
defrost the freezer *v* **34**
degree *n* **80**
degrees *n* **154**
delay *n* **102**
delete *v* **83**
deli *n* **48**
delicatessen *n* **46, 64**
delicious *adj* **52, 177**
delighted *adj* **06**
delivery *n* **45**
delivery man *n* **48**
delta *n* **147**
deltoid *n* **03**
Democratic Republic of the Congo *n* **149, 152**
denim *n* **13**
denim jacket *n* **15**
Denmark *n* **151, 153**
denomination *n* **74, 94**
dental care *n* **49**
dental floss *n* **22**
dental floss *n* **31**
dental history *n* **22**
dental hygienist *n* **22**
dental mirror *n* **22**
dental surgery *n* **22**
dental X-ray *n* **22**
dentist *n* **22, 89**
dentist chair *n* **22**
dentures *n* **22**
deodorant *n* **49**
department store *n* **47**
departments *n* **21, 91**
departure, departures *n* **43, 104**
departure board *n* **102**
departure lounge *n* **104**
deposit *n* **32**
deposit *v* **45**
depressed *adj* **06**
depth *n* **74**
depth gauge *n* **118**
Derby shoes *n* **17**

derelict building *n* **44**
dermatology *n* **21**
derrick *n* **51**
descaled *adj* **54**
descent module *n* **143**
describing abilities *n* **11**
describing actions *n* **11**
describing clothes *n* **13**
describing fruit *n* **57**
describing personalities *n* **10**
describing things *n* **176-177**
desert *n* **146**
desert boots *n* **17**
desert ironwood tree *n* **169**
desertification *n* **155**
design and technology *n* **73**
designer *n* **89**
designer labels *n* **47**
desk *n* **73, 82**
desktop computer *n* **83**
dessert, desserts *n* **63, 69**
destination *n* **104**
destroyer *n* **88**
detached house *n* **32**
detective *n* **50**
determined *adj* **93**
detox *n* **23**
deuce *n* **114**
Devanagari script *n* **175**
Devonian *adj* **157**
Devonian *n* **157**
dewlap *n* **159**
diabetes *n* **19**
diagonal *adj* **74**
diameter *n* **74**
diamond *n* **140, 156**
diamond back terrapin *n* **163**
diarrhoea *n* **19**
diary *n* **82, 138**
dice *n* **140**
dice *v* **29**
dictionary *n* **73, 138**
didgeridoo *n* **129**
die *v* **07**
diesel *n* **97**
diesel train *n* **102**
diffraction *n* **75**
diffusion *n* **76**
dig *n* **79**
dig *v* **11, 39, 112**
digestif *n* **69**
digestive *n* **04**
digger *n* **87**
digital *adj* **84**
digital box *n* **136**
digital currency *n* **94**
digital projector *n* **73, 82**
digital screen *n* **136**
digital wallet *n* **94**
Dijon mustard *n* **60**
dill *n* **59-60**
dimensions *n* **74**
dimetrodon *n* **157**
dimples *n* **12**
dine *v* **52**
dining car *n* **102**
dining room *n* **26**
dinner *n* **26, 72**
dinner party *n* **26**
dinner plate *n* **27**
diode *n* **75**
diploma *n* **80**
dipstick *n* **98**
dire *adj* **177**
direct current *n* **33, 75**
direct debit *n* **45**
direct flight *n* **104**
direction of revolution *n* **143**
direction to follow *n* **96**
directions *n* **132, 148, 180**
director *n* **84, 126-127**
director's chair *n* **84**
dirty *adj* **176**
dirty washing *n* **34**
disabled parking *n* **96**
disappointed *adj* **06, 177**
disastrous *adj* **177**
discharge *v* **21**
discount voucher *n* **48**
discus *n* **116**
discuss *v* **73**
disembark *v* **106**
disgusted *adj* **06**
disgusting *adj* **52, 177**
dish rack *n* **27**
dishes *n* **72**
dishonest *adj* **10**
dishwasher *n* **27, 34**
dishwasher tablets *n* **34**
Disir *n* **139**
dismount *v* **100**
dispensary *n* **49**
dispersion *n* **75**
display *n* **21, 136**
disposable razor *n* **31**
dissertation *n* **80**
distance *n* **174**
distracted *adj* **06**
distributor *n* **98**
districts *n* **42**
dive *v* **118**
diver *n* **118**
diversion *n* **96**
divide *v* **74**
dividends *n* **94**
divider *n* **96**
diving *n* **118**
diving board *n* **118**
diving tower *n* **118**
division sign *n* **74**
divorce *n* **07**
divorced *adj* **05**
Diwali *n* **07**
DIY (do it yourself) *n* **47**
DIY equipment *n* **35**
dizzy *adj* **19**
DJ *n* **84**
DJ console *n* **129**
Djibouti *n* **149, 152**
Djiboutian *adj* **152**
DM someone *v* **84**
DNA *n* **77**
do homework *v* **09, 11**
do not bend *phr* **45**
do the dishes *v* **34**
do the ironing *v* **34**
do the laundry *v* **34**
do the weeding *v* **39**
do up *v* **178**
Doberman *n* **164**
dock *v* **106**
docks *n* **106**
doctor *n* **19-21, 89**
doctor's surgery *n* **20**
doctorate *n* **80**
document *n* **79**
documentary *n* **137**
dog *n* **122**
dog breeds *n* **164**
dog rose *n* **169**
dog sledding *n* **122**
dogsled *n* **122**
doll *n* **08**
doll's house *n* **08**
dolphin *n* **166**
dolphin pose *n* **24**
dome *n* **44**
domestic flight *n* **104**
Dominica *n* **150, 152**
Dominican *adj* **152**
Dominican Republic *n* **150, 152**
dominoes *n* **140**
donation *n* **130**
donkey *n* **165**
door *n* **99, 102**
door buzzer *n* **25**
door chain *n* **25-26**
door handle *n* **25-26, 97, 99**
door knocker *n* **25**
door lock *n* **99**
doorbell *n* **25**
doormat *n* **25-26**
dorm *n* **131**
dormer *n* **25**
dosa *n* **72**
dosage *n* **49**
double *adj* **68**
double bass *n* **128**
double bed *n* **30**
double burner camping stove *n* **135**
double cream *n* **61**
double espresso *n* **65**
double fault *n* **114**
double quotation mark *n* **175**
double room *n* **131**
double star *n* **144**
double-decker bus *n* **99**
doubles *n* **114**
dough *n* **62**
doughnut *n* **63, 70**
downhill skiing *n* **122**
download *v* **83**
downpour *n* **154**
downstairs *adv, n* **25**
downward dog *n* **24**
doze off *v* **178**
draft *n* **83**
drag racing *n* **123**
dragon *n* **139**
dragon tree *n* **38, 167**
dragonfly *n* **162**
drain *n* **31, 33, 43**
drainage *n* **39**
drama *n* **73, 127**
draughts *n* **140**
draw *v* **73**
draw *v* **109**
drawbridge *n* **44**
drawer *n* **27, 30, 82**
drawing *n* **141**
drawing pin *n* **82**
dreadful *adj* **177**
dream *n* **30**
drepanaspis *n* **157**
dress *n* **14**
dress circle *n* **126**
dress pattern *n* **142**
dress up *v* **178**
dressage *n* **120**
dressed *adj* **72**
dressing *n* **20, 72**
dressing gown *n* **14**
dressing table *n* **30**
dried apricots *n* **58**
dried beans *n* **55**
dried fig *n* **58**
dried fruit *n* **58, 71**
dried yeast *n* **62**
drill *n* **22**
drill *v* **35**
drill bit, drill bits *n* **35-36**
drilling rig *n* **51**
drink *v* **52**
drink tea or coffee *v* **09**
drink water *v* **20**
drinking *n* **52**
drinks *n* **48, 52, 68**
drip *n* **21**
drip stand *n* **21**
drive *v* **09, 95, 115**
driver *n* **90, 99**
driver's cab *n* **102**
driver's seat *n* **99**
driveshaft *n* **98**
driving instructor *n* **89**
drizzle *n* **154**
dromedary *n* **158**
drop anchor *v* **106**
drop someone off *v* **98**
dropper *n* **76**
drops *n* **49**
dropshot *n* **114**
drought *n* **154**
drug dealing *n* **85**
drummer *n* **129**
dry *adj* **18, 154**
dry hair *n* **12**
dry-cleaner's *n* **46**
dry dock *n* **106**
dry the dishes *v* **34**
dry your hair *v* **09**
dry yourself *v* **31**
dry-cured meat *n* **64**
dual carriageway *n* **96**
dubnium *n* **78**
duck *n* **53, 165**
duck egg *n* **61**
duckling *n* **165**
due date *n* **08**
duffle coat *n* **15**
dull *adj* **176**
dumbbell *n* **124**
dummy *n* **08**
dumper truck *n* **87**
dumplings *n* **70, 72**
dune *n* **147**
dungarees *n* **13**
dunk *v* **112**
dusk *n* **171**
dust *v* **34**
dustbin *n* **25**
duster *n* **34**
dustpan *n* **34**
dustsheet *n* **37**
Dutch *adj* **153**
duty belt *n* **50**
duty-free shop *n* **104**
duvet *n* **30**
DVD *n* **136**
dwarf *n* **139**
dwarf planets *n* **143**
dynamo *n* **101**
dysprosium *n* **78**

E

e-reader *n* **83, 138**
eagle owl *n* **161**
ear *n* **01**
ear muffs *n* **87**
ear phone *n* **88**
ear protectors *n* **87**
ear thermometer *n* **20**

early *adj* **171**
early *adv* **171**
early human *n* **157**
earn *v* **81**
earphones *n* **136**
earrings *n* **16**
Earth *n* **143, 145**
earth tremor *n* **145**
earthing *n* **33**
earthquake *n* **145**
easel *n* **82, 141**
east *n* **148**
East Timor *n* **151, 153**
Easter *n* **07**
eastern coral snake *n* **163**
eat *v* **52**
eat breakfast *v* **09**
eat dinner *v* **09**
eat in *v* **70**
eat lunch *v* **09**
eat out *v* **69, 178**
eating *n* **52**
eccentric *adj* **10**
echidna *n* **158**
éclair *n* **63**
eclectus parrot *n* **161**
economic downturn *n* **94**
economics *n* **80**
economy class *n* **103**
ecosystem *n* **77, 155**
ecotourism *n* **131**
ecstatic *adj* **06**
Ecuador *n* **149, 152**
Ecuadorian *adj* **152**
eczema *n* **19**
Edam *n* **64**
editor *n* **89**
education *n* **91**
eel *n* **54**
efficient *adj* **93**
egg, eggs *n* **61, 77**
egg allergy *n* **23**
egg cup *n* **27, 61**
egg slicer *n* **28**
egg timer *n* **28**
egg white *n* **61, 71**
eggshell *n* **161**
Egypt *n* **149, 152**
Egyptian *adj* **152**
Egyptian goose *n* **160**
Eid al-Fitr *n* **07**
Eiffel Tower *n* **44**
eight *num* **173**
eighteen *num* **173**
eighth *num* **173**
eighty *num* **173**
einsteinium *n* **78**
El Salvador *n* **150, 152**
elbow *n* **01**
elbow pads *n* **107**
elderberry *n* **57**
elderly *adj* **05**
electric bike *n* **101**
electric blanket *n* **30**
electric car *n* **97**
electric charge point *n* **97**
electric drill *n* **35**
electric field *n* **75**
electric guitar *n* **129**
electric guitarist *n* **129**
electric hook-up *n* **135**
electric kettle *n* **27**
electric lines *n* **102**
electric motorcycle *n* **100**
electric pump *n* **135**
electric razor *n* **31**
electric scooter *n* **100**
electric shock *n* **19**
electric train *n* **102**
electrical appliances *n* **47**
electrical goods *n* **48**
electrical waste *n* **33**
electrician *n* **89**
electricity *n* **33, 51, 75**
electricity meter *n* **33**
electrics *n* **33**
electromagnetic spectrum *n* **75**
electron *n* **76**
electronics *n* **91**
electronics store *n* **46**
elements *n* **76**
eleven *num* **173**
elf *n* **139**
elf owl *n* **161**
elixir *n* **139**
ellipsis *n* **175**
elliptical galaxy *n* **144**
elm *n* **169**
email *n* **83**
embarrassed *adj* **06**
embroidery *n* **142**
embryo *n* **08**
emerald *n* **156**
emerald toucan *n* **160**
emerald tree boa *n* **163**
emergency department *n* **50**
emergency exit *n* **103, 131**
emergency lever *n* **102**
emergency phone *n* **96**
emergency room *n* **21**
emergency services *n* **50**
emergency vehicle beacon *n* **50**
emigrate *v* **07**
Emirati *adj* **153**
emissions *n* **51, 155**
emoji, emojis *n* **84, 175**
empanada *n* **70**
emperor *n* **79**
emperor moth *n* **162**
emperor penguin *n* **161**
empire *n* **79**
Empire State Building *n* **44**
employee *n* **81**
employer *n* **81**
employment *adj* **81**
empress *n* **79**
empty *adj* **176**
emu *n* **160**
emulsion *n* **37**
en suite bathroom *n* **131**
enamel *n* **03**
encore *n* **126**
encyclopedia *n* **73, 138**
end line *n* **107**
end zone *n* **107, 110**
endangered species *n* **155**
endive *n* **55**
endocrine *n* **04**
endocrinology *n* **21**
endoskeleton *n* **77**
energetic *adj* **93**
energy *n* **23, 51, 91**
energy drink *n* **52**
engaged couple *n* **07**
engine *n* **98, 100, 103**
engine intake *n* **123**
engine room *n* **105**
engineer *n* **90**
engineering *n* **80**
English *n* **73**
English bluebell *n* **167**
English mustard *n* **60**
engraving *n* **141**
Enlightenment *n* **79**
enoki mushroom *n* **56, 170**
ENT *n* **21**
enter *v* **11**
entertainment *n* **91**
enthusiastic *adj* **10**
entrance *n* **130**
entrance fee *n* **132**
envelope *n* **45, 82, 103**
environment *n* **155**
environmental issues *n* **155**
épée *n* **117**
epiglottis *n* **04**
episode *n* **137**
equals *n* **74**
equation *n* **74**
Equator *n* **145**
Equatorial Guinea *n* **149, 152**
Equatorial Guinean *adj* **152**
equity *n* **94**
erbium *n* **78**
Eritrea *n* **149, 152**
Eritrean *adj* **152**
erupt *v* **145**
escalator *n* **47, 104**
espadrilles *n* **17**
espresso *n* **65**
espresso maker *n* **27**
essay *n* **73**
essential oils *n* **24**
estate *n* **97**
estate agent *n* **32, 89**
Estonia *n* **151, 153**
Estonian *adj* **153**
estuary *n* **147**
Eswatini *n* **149, 152**
Ethiopia *n* **149, 152**
Ethiopian *adj* **152**
Europe *n* **151, 153**
European *adj* **153**
European badger *n* **158**
European common frog *n* **163**
European robin *n* **160**
europium *n* **78**
eave *n* **32, 44**
evening *n* **09, 171**
evening dress *n* **15**
evening menu *n* **69**
evening primrose *n* **38**
evergreen *n* **41**
every day *adv* **172**
every other day *adv* **172**
evidence *n* **50, 85**
evolution *n* **77**
ewe *n* **165**
ex-husband *n* **05**
ex-wife *n* **05**
exam *n* **73**
excavation *n* **79, 87**
excess baggage *n* **104**
exchange *v* **46**
exchange rate *n* **45, 94**
excited *adj* **06**
exciting *adj* **177**
exclamation mark *n* **175**
exercise *v* **09, 20**
exercise ball *n* **124**
exercise bike *n* **124**
exercise book *n* **73**
exercise class *n* **124**
exercise mat *n* **124**
exercises *n* **124**
exhaust pipe *n* **98, 100**
exhausted *adj* **06**
exhausting *adj* **177**
exhibit *n* **130**
exhibition *n* **130**
exit *n* **48**
exit *v* **11**
exit ramp *n* **96**
exoskeleton *n* **77**
exosphere *n* **155**
exotic shorthair *n* **164**
expenditure *n* **94**
experiment *n* **76**
expiry date *n* **49**
extend *v* **124**
extension lead *n* **35**
extra virgin *adj* **60**
extraction *n* **22**
extractor fan *n* **27**
extraordinary *adj* **177**
extras *n* **127**
eye, eyes *n* **01, 121, 142**
eye drops *n* **22**
eye mask *n* **14**
eyeball *n* **22**
eyebrow *n* **01**
eyebrow brush *n* **18**
eyebrow pencil *n* **18**
eyecup *n* **136**
eyelashes *n* **01**
eyelet *n* **17**
eyelid *n* **01**
eyeliner *n* **18**
eyepiece *n* **77, 144**
eyeshadow *n* **18**

F

fabric *n* **142**
fabric softener *n* **34**
face *n* **01**
face cream *n* **31**
face mask *n* **18**
face mask *n* **20, 107, 110**
face powder *n* **18**
face wash *n* **18**
face-off *n* **110**
face-off spot *n* **110**
facemask *n* **111**
facial *n* **18**
facial hair *n* **12**
facilities *n* **91**
factory *n* **42**
Fahrenheit *n* **154**
fail *v* **73**
faint *v* **20**
fairway *n* **115**
fairy *n* **139**
fairy elephant's feet *n* **168**
fairy ring *n* **170**
fairy tale *n* **138-139**
falafel *n* **70**
fall *v* **11, 117**
fall in love *v* **07**
fall leaf *n* **169**
fallopian tube *n* **04**
fallow deer *n* **158**
false teeth *n* **22**
family *n* **05**
family tent *n* **135**
famous buildings *n* **44**
fan *n* **33**
fan belt *n* **98**
fan space heater *n* **33**
fans *n* **107, 109, 129**
fantastic *adj* **177**
fantastic creatures *n* **139**
fantasy *n* **127, 138-139**
far *adj* **176**

fare *n* **99, 102**
farm *n* **86, 165**
farm animals *n* **165**
farmer *n* **79, 86, 89**
farmers' market *n* **23**
farmhouse *n* **86**
farming *n* **86, 91**
farming terms *n* **86**
farmland *n* **86, 146**
farmyard *n* **86**
fashion *n* **91**
fashion accessories *n* **16**
fashion designer *n* **90**
fashion store *n* **47**
fast *adj* **176**
fast food *n* **47, 70**
fast forward *v* **137**
fast-food restaurant *n* **70**
fasten *v* **14**
fastening *n* **16**
fat free *adj* **61**
father *n* **05**
father-in-law *n* **05**
fault *n* **114**
faun *n* **139**
feather duster *n* **34**
feather *n* **161**
feathers displayed *n* **161**
February *n* **172**
fedora *n* **16**
feed *v* **86**
feed the cat *v* **09**
feed the dog *v* **09**
feed the pets *v* **34**
feel better *v* **20**
feelings *n* **06**
feet *n* **02**
feet-first *adj* **118**
feijoa *n* **58**
female *n* **04**
feminine hygiene *n* **49**
femur *n* **03**
fence *n* **41, 86**
fencing *n* **116-117**
feng shui *n* **24**
fennec fox *n* **158**
fennel *n* **55, 59**
fennel seeds *n* **59**
fenugreek leaves *n* **59**
fermium *n* **78**
fern, ferns *n* **41, 156, 167**
ferret *n* **164**
ferris wheel *n* **133**
ferrule *n* **115**
ferry *n* **105-106**
ferry route *n* **148**
ferry terminal *n* **106**
fertilize *v* **39**
fertilizer *n* **39**
festivals *n* **07**
feta *n* **64**
fetus *n* **08**
fever *n* **19**
fez *n* **16**
fiancé *n* **07**
fiancée *n* **07**
fibre *n* **23, 57**
fibreglass *adj* **176**
fibreglass *n* **176**
fibula *n* **03**
fiction *n* **138**
fiddler crab *n* **166**
field *n* **107, 113, 146**
field *v* **111, 113**
field events *n* **116**
field hockey *n* **110**
field hockey player *n* **110**
field hospital *n* **88**
field mushroom *n* **170**
fielding positions *n* **111**
fifteen *num* **173**
fifth *num* **173**
fifty *num* **173**
fifty-yard line *n* **107**
fig *n* **169**
fighter *n* **88**
figure skating *n* **122**
Fiji *n* **150, 153**
Fijian *adj* **153**
filament *n* **38**
file, files *n* **36, 82**
filing cabinet *n* **82**
Filipino *adj* **153**
fill *v* **37**
fill out *v* **178**
fill out a form *v* **92**
fill up *v* **98, 178**
filler *n* **37**
fillet *n* **53**
fillet *n* **54**
filling *n* **22, 63, 70**
film set *n* **127**
film star *n* **127**
film studio *n* **127**
films *n* **127**
filo *n* **63**
filter coffee *n* **65**
filter paper *n* **76**
fin *n* **103**
final whistle *n* **109**
finance *n* **91, 94**
financial advisor *n* **94**
finch *n* **160**
finderscope *n* **144**
finds *n* **79**
fine *n* **85**
fine leg *n* **111**
fingernail *n* **02**
fingerprint *n* **50**
finish line *n* **116, 123**
finish work *v* **09**
Finland *n* **151, 153**
Finnish *adj* **153**
fins *n* **118, 134**
fir *n* **167**
fire *n* **50**
fire alarm *n* **50**
fire brigade *n* **50**
fire engine *n* **50**
fire escape *n* **50**
fire extinguisher *n* **50**
fire salamander *n* **163**
fire station *n* **42, 50**
fire tree *n* **168**
firefighter,
firefighters *n* **50, 89**
firefighter's uniform *n* **13**
firelighter *n* **135**
firepit *n* **135**
fireplace *n* **26**
first *num* **173**
first aid bag *n* **50**
first base *n* **113**
first floor *n* **25, 47**
first-aid kit *n* **20, 49**
fish *n* **48, 54, 164**
fish and chips *n* **70**
fish box *n* **54**
fish farm *n* **86**
fish sauce *n* **60**
fish slice *n* **28**
fish tank *n* **164**
fisherman *n* **89**
fishhook *n* **121**
fishing *n* **91, 121**
fishing permit *n* **121**
fishing port *n* **106**
fishing rod *n* **121**
fishing vest *n* **121**
fishmonger *n* **18, 54, 89**
fission *n* **75**
fissures *n* **51**
fist *n* **02**
fit *v* **14, 46**
fit a carpet *v* **35**
fitted *adj* **13**
five *num* **173**
five hundred *num* **173**
five past one *n* **171**
five positions *n* **112**
five spice *n* **59**
five to two *n* **171**
fix *v* **11**
fix a fence *v* **35**
fix a puncture *v* **101**
fizzy drink *n* **70**
fjord *n* **147**
flag *n* **115**
flagstone *n* **35**
flamenco dress *n* **15**
flamingo *n* **160**
flan *n* **64**
flan tin *n* **29**
flap *v* **161**
flare *n* **51, 119, 144**
flask *n* **52**
flask *n* **76**
flat *adj* **128**
flat *n* **25**
flat cap *n* **16**
flat-head screwdriver *n* **36**
flat race *n* **120**
flat tyre *n* **98**
flat white *n* **65**
flat wood bit *n* **36**
flatbed truck *n* **87**
flatbread *n* **62**
flats *n* **17**
flavoured oil *n* **60**
flax *n* **86**
fledgling *n* **161**
flerovium *n* **78**
flesh *n* **58**
flex *v* **124**
flexible *adj* **93, 176**
flexitime *n* **81**
flight attendant,
flight attendants *n* **90, 103-104**
flight instructor *n* **90**
flight number *n* **104**
flint *n* **156**
flint tools *n* **79**
flip *n* **118**
flip chart *n* **82, 95**
flip through *v* **138**
flip-flops *n* **17, 134**
flipper, flippers *n* **15, 118, 134**
float *n* **118, 121**
float *v* **118**
floating crane *n* **106**
flock of sheep *n* **165**
flood *n* **154**
flood plain *n* **147**
floor *n* **25-26, 30**
floor length *adj* **15**
floor mat *n* **125**
floor plan *n* **130, 132**
floorboards *n* **26**
Florentine *n* **63**
floret *n* **55**
florist *n* **46-47, 89**
floss *v* **22**
flours *n* **62**
flower anatomy *n* **38**
flower stall *n* **47**
flowerbed *n* **41**
flowering plants *n* **157**
flowering shrub *n* **41**
flu *n* **19**
fluent in languages *adj* **93**
fluid ounce *n* **174**
fluorine *n* **78**
flute *n* **128-129**
fly *n* **121, 162, 168**
fly *v* **11, 162**
fly agaric *n* **170**
fly fishing *n* **121**
fly-half *n* **108**
flying carpet *n* **139**
flying fish *n* **166**
flying kick *n* **117**
flying reptiles *n* **157**
flying squirrel *n* **158**
flyover *n* **96**
flysheet *n* **135**
FM *adj* **84**
foal *n* **120, 165**
focusing knob *n* **77, 144**
foetus *n* **08**
fog *n* **154**
foggy *adj* **154**
foil *n* **117**
fold *v* **14**
fold clothes *v* **34**
folders *n* **82**
folding grill *n* **135**
foliage *n* **47**
folk blouse *n* **15**
folk music *n* **129**
follow *v* **84**
follower *n* **84**
food *n* **65, 91**
food allergies *n* **23**
food bowl *n* **26**
food compost bin *n* **33**
food court *n* **47**
food poisoning *n* **19**
food preparation *n* **72**
food processor *n* **27**
food van *n* **70**
food waste *n* **155**
foot *n* **01, 174**
foot board *n* **30**
foot boot *n* **19**
foot pedals *n* **99**
foot stool *n* **26**
foot strap *n* **119**
football *n* **109**
football boots *n* **17, 107, 109**
football game *n* **109**
football player *n* **107**
football rules *n* **109**
football
shirt *n* **15, 109**
football timing *n* **109**
footbridge *n* **104**
foothill *n* **147**
footrest *n* **82**
forage mushrooms *v* **170**
Forbidden City *n* **44**
forearm *n* **01**
forecourt *n* **97**
forehand *n* **114**
forehead *n* **01**
foreperson *n* **85**
forest *n* **147-148**
forestay *n* **119**
forewing *n* **162**
forget *v* **11**
fork *n* **27, 40, 101**
fork-lift
truck *n* **87, 106**
formal garden *n* **41**
formal wear *n* **15**
fortnight *n* **172**
fortune cookies *n* **63**
forty *num* **173**

forty minutes *n* **171**
forward *v* **83**
fossil *n* **77**
fossil fuels *n* **51, 155**
foul *n* **112**
foul ball *n* **113**
foul line *n* **112-113**
foul pole *n* **113**
foundation *n* **18**
fountain *n* **41-42**
fountain pen *n* **175**
four *num* **173**
four-wheel drive *n* **97**
fourteen *num* **173**
fourth *num* **173**
fourth base *n* **113**
foxglove *n* **38**
fracking *n* **51**
fraction, fractions *n* **74, 173**
fracture *n* **19**
fragile *adj* **45**
frame *n* **26, 101, 130, 135**
France *n* **151, 153**
francium *n* **78**
fraud *n* **85**
freckles *n* **12**
free weights *n* **124**
free-range *adj* **53**
free-throw lane *n* **112**
free-throw line *n* **112**
freesia *n* **47, 167**
freeze *v* **29**
freezer *n* **27**
freezing *adj* **154**
freezing point *n* **154**
freight *n* **105**
freight train *n* **102**
freighter *n* **105**
French *adj* **153**
French beans *n* **55**
French doors *n* **25**
French horn *n* **128**
French plait *n* **12**
French toast *n* **71**
frequency *n* **84**
fresh *adj* **52, 54, 56**
fresh cheese *n* **61**
fresh chilli *n* **59**
fresh fruit *n* **71**
fresh yeast *n* **62**
freshwater fishing *n* **121**
fret *n* **129**
Friday *n* **172**
fridge *n* **27**
fried *adj* **72**
fried chicken *n* **70**
fried egg *n* **61, 71**
fried mushrooms *n* **71**
friend *n* **07**
friendly *adj* **10**
frigate *n* **88, 160**
frightened *adj* **06**
frightening *adj* **177**
frill-necked lizard *n* **163**
frisbee *n* **133**
frisée *n* **55**
frizzy hair *n* **12**
frog spawn *n* **77, 163**
front *adj* **03**
front *n* **88**
front crawl *n* **118**
front door *n* **25, 97**
front entrance *n* **25**
front kick *n* **117**
front loader *n* **87**
front speaker *n* **136**
front suspension *n* **123**
front view *n* **97**
front wheel *n* **99**
front wing *n* **97, 123**
front-flip *n* **118**
frontal *n* **03**
frost *n* **154**
frosty *adj* **154**
froth *n* **65**
frown *v* **02**
frozen *adj* **54, 56**
frozen food *n* **48**
frozen yoghurt *n* **61**
fruit *n* **48, 57-58**
fruit bat *n* **158**
fruit bowl *n* **26**
fruit bread *n* **62**
fruit farm *n* **86**
fruit gums *n* **67**
fruit juice *n* **71**
fruit tart *n* **63**
fruit yoghurt *n* **71**
fruitcake *n* **63**
frustrated *adj* **06**
fry *v* **29**
frying basket *n* **28**
frying pan *n* **28**
fuchsia *n* **168**
fuel rods *n* **51**
fuel tank *n* **100**
full *adj* **26, 135, 176**
full back *n* **108**
full moon *n* **143**
full stop *n* **175**
full time *n* **109**
fullback *n* **107**
fumble *v* **107**
fun *adj* **177**
funeral *n* **07**
fungi *n* **77, 170**
funnel *n* **76, 105**
funny *adj* **10, 177**
furious *adj* **06**
furnished *n* **32**
fuse box *n* **33, 98**
fusilli *n* **64**
fusion *n* **75**

G

Gabon *n* **149, 152**
Gabonese *adj* **152**
gada *n* **79**
gadgets *n* **83**
gadolinium *n* **78**
gain weight *v* **20**
gain yards *v* **107**
galah *n* **161**
Galápagos turtle *n* **163**
gale *n* **154**
galia *n* **58**
gall bladder *n* **04**
gallery *n* **105, 130**
gallium *n* **78**
gallon *n* **174**
gallop *v* **120, 165**
Gambia *n* **149, 152**
Gambian *adj* **152**
game, games *n* **08, 53, 114, 140**
game officials *n* **112**
game show *n* **137**
gaming *n* **91**
gamma radiation *n* **75**
Ganges *n* **145**
gangway *n* **105**
gannet *n* **160**
garage *n* **25**
garage *n* **98**
garden centre *n* **46**
garden features *n* **41**
garden flowers *n* **38**
garden gloves *n* **40**
garden hose *n* **40**
garden peas *n* **55**
garden plants *n* **38**
garden tools *n* **40**
garden types *n* **41**
gardener *n* **89**
gardenia *n* **38**
gardening *n* **39, 133**
gardening basket *n* **40**
gardening book *n* **138**
gardening features *n* **41**
garland *n* **47**
garlic *n* **56**
garlic press *n* **28**
garnet *n* **156**
garnish *v* **29**
garter *n* **14**
gas *n* **51, 76**
gas giants *n* **143**
gas space heater *n* **33**
gastornis *n* **157**
gastroenterology *n* **21**
gate *n* **32, 41, 86, 106, 122**
gate number *n* **104**
gateau *n* **63**
gathered skirt *n* **142**
gathers *n* **142**
gauze *n* **20**
gazelle *n* **158**
gear lever *n* **101**
gear stick *n* **99**
gearbox *n* **98, 100**
gears *n* **101**
gel *n* **49**
Gemini *n* **144**
gems *n* **156**
gene *n* **77**
general *n* **88**
general appearance *n* **12**
generator *n* **33, 51**
generous *adj* **10**
genie *n* **139**
genitals *n* **01**
genoa *n* **119**
genres *n* **138**
Gentoo penguin *n* **161**
geode *n* **156**
geographical features *n* **146**
geography *n* **73, 146-147**
geological periods *n* **157**
geometry *n* **74**
Georgia *n* **150, 153**
Georgian *adj* **153**
geothermal energy *n* **51**
geothermal power station *n* **51**
geranium *n* **38**
gerbera *n* **47**
gerbil *n* **164**
German *adj* **153**
German shepherd *n* **164**
germanium *n* **78**
Germany *n* **151, 153**
get a job *v* **07**
get changed *v* **14**
get dressed *v* **09**
get fired *v* **81**
get into debt *v* **94**
get married *v* **07**
get off *v* **100, 178**
get off a bike *v* **101**
get on *v* **100, 178**
get on a bike *v* **101**
get the job *v* **92**
get together *v* **178**
get up *v* **09, 178**
get your hair cut *v* **12**
getting to know someone *n* **179**
geyser *n* **146**
Ghana *n* **149, 152**
Ghanaian *adj* **152**
gharial *n* **163**
ghee *n* **61**
gherkin *n* **60**
ghost *n* **139**
giant *n* **139**
giant horsetails *n* **157**
giant puffball *n* **170**
giant sequoia *n* **167**
giant slalom *n* **122**
giant sloth *n* **157**
giant squid *n* **166**
gibbon *n* **159**
gift shop *n* **46, 130**
gila monster *n* **163**
gills *n* **170**
gin and tonic *n* **68**
ginger *n* **59**
gingerbread man *n* **63**
ginkgo *n* **167**
ginkgo nuts *n* **58**
giraffe *n* **158**
girder *n* **87**
girl *n* **05**
girlfriend *n* **05**
girth *n* **120**
give a presentation *v* **95**
give away *v* **178**
give back *v* **178**
give notice *v* **32**
give out *v* **178**
give up *v* **23, 178**
give way *v* **96**
glacier *n* **146**
gladiator sandals *n* **17**
gladiolus *n* **47**
glass *adj* **176**
glass, glasses *n* **27, 52, 68, 155, 176**
glass baking dish *n* **28**
glass bottle *n* **76**
glass rod *n* **76**
glasses *n* **22**
glassware *n* **27**
glasswing butterfly *n* **162**
glaze *v* **62-63**
glide *v* **161**
glider *n* **103, 125**
glory of Texas *n* **168**
gloss *n* **37**
glossary *n* **138**
glove, gloves *n* **16, 100, 110, 115, 117, 122, 107, 109**
glue *n* **82, 101, 141**
glue gun *n* **35**
gluten intolerant *adj* **23**
gluten-free *adj* **23**
gluten-free flour *n* **62**
gluteus maximus *n* **03**
gneiss *n* **156**
gnocchi *n* **64**
gnome *n* **139**
go *n* **140**
go abroad *v* **104, 141**
go away *v* **178**
go back *v* **148**
go backpacking *v* **131**
go down *v* **178**
go on a cruise *v* **131**
go on a diet *v* **23**

go on a holiday *v* **131**
go on an excursion *v* **132**
go on a tour *v* **132**
go on Hajj *v* **07**
go on maternity leave *v* **81**
go out of business *v* **94**
go out with friends *v* **09**
go past (the restaurant) *v* **148**
go straight on *v* **96, 148**
go to a café *v* **09**
go to bed *v* **09**
go to nursery *v* **07**
go to school *v* **09**
go to sleep *v* **09**
go to work *v* **09**
go up *v* **178**
go viral *v* **84**
go-cart *n* **123**
goal *n* **108-110**
goal crease *n* **110**
goal line *n* **107, 110**
goal posts *n* **108**
goalball *n* **125**
goalie stick *n* **110**
goalkeeper *n* **109-110**
goalpost *n* **107-09**
goat *n* **53, 165**
goat's cheese *n* **61**
goat's milk *n* **61**
goatee *n* **12**
goblin *n* **139**
goggles *n* **15, 118, 122**
goji berry *n* **57**
gold *adj* **176**
gold *n* **78, 116, 156, 176**
gold-plated visor *n* **143**
golden eagle *n* **160**
golden guinea vine *n* **168**
golf *n* **115**
golf bag *n* **115**
golf ball *n* **115**
golf cap *n* **115**
golf clubs *n* **115**
golf course *n* **115**
golf equipment *n* **115**
golf shoe, golf shoes *n* **17, 115**
golf trolley *n* **115**
golfer *n* **115**
gong *n* **128**
good *adj* **177**
good afternoon *phr* **179**
good evening *phr* **179**
good listener *n* **93**
good morning *phr* **179**
good night *phr* **179**
goodbye *phr* **179**
goose *n* **53, 165**
goose egg *n* **61**
gooseberry *n* **57**
gorilla *n* **159**
gosling *n* **165**
gospel *n* **129**
gossip magazine *n* **138**
government building *n* **43**
GPS *n* **99**
grab bar *n* **31**
graceful *adj* **177**
grade *n* **73**
grader *n* **87**
graduate *n* **80**
graduate *v* **07**
graduation ceremony *n* **80**
graffiti *n* **85**
graft *v* **39**
gram *n* **174**
granary bread *n* **62**
granddaughter *n* **05**
grandfather *n* **05**
grandmother *n* **05**
grandparents *n* **05**
grandson *n* **05**
granite *n* **156**
grapefruit *n* **57**
grapes *n* **57**
grapeseed oil *n* **60**
grapevine *n* **168**
graphite *n* **156**
grass, grasses *n* **25, 41, 167**
grass collector *n* **40**
grass tree *n* **167**
grasshopper *n* **162**
grassland *n* **146**
grate *v* **29**
grated cheese *n* **61**
grateful *adj* **06**
grater *n* **28**
grave accent *n* **175**
gravel *n* **35, 40**
gravity *n* **144**
graze *n* **19**
grease *v* **29**
greasy hair *n* **12**
great *adj* **177**
Great Blue Hole *n* **145**
great crested newt *n* **163**
Great Dane *n* **164**
great grey owl *n* **161**
Great Mosque of Djenné *n* **44**
Great Plains toad *n* **163**
great white shark *n* **166**
greater spotted woodpecker *n* **160**
grebe *n* **161**
Greece *n* **151, 153**
Greek *adj* **153**
Greek alphabet *n* **175**
Greek mythology *n* **139**
Greek salad *n* **72**
green *adj* **01, 141**
green *n* **115, 141**
green basilisk *n* **163**
green beans *n* **55**
green energy *n* **51**
green foliage *n* **172**
green olives *n* **64**
green sea turtle *n* **163**
green tea *n* **66**
green woodpecker *n* **160**
greengrocer *n* **89**
greengrocers *n* **46, 56**
greenhouse *n* **39**
greenhouse effect *n* **155**
greenhouse gases *n* **155**
greet *v* **179**
greetings *n* **179**
gremlin *n* **139**
Grenada *n* **150, 152**
grenade *n* **88**
grenade launcher *n* **88**
Grenadian *adj* **152**
grey *adj* **01, 141**
grey *n* **01, 141**
grey hair *n* **12**
grey willow *n* **169**
grid lines *n* **148**
griddle pan *n* **28**
griffin *n* **139**
grill *v* **29**
grilled *adj* **72**
grilled tomato *n* **71**
grin *v* **02**
grip *n* **115**
groin *n* **01**
groin protector *n* **117**
groom *n* **07**
groom *v* **120**
groove *n* **115**
ground chilli *n* **59**
ground cinnamon *n* **59**
ground cover *n* **41**
ground floor *n* **25, 47**
ground level *n* **47**
ground maintenance *n* **89**
ground mince *n* **53**
ground sheet *n* **135**
groundnut oil *n* **60**
group therapy *n* **24**
grout *n* **37**
grow up *v* **178**
grow your hair *v* **12**
growing up *n* **05**
grunt *v* **165**
guarantee *n* **47**
Guatemala *n* **150, 152**
Guatemalan *adj* **152**
guava *n* **58, 168**
guest *n* **26**
guest house *n* **131**
guest speaker *n* **95**
guests *n* **131**
guidebook *n* **131-132, 138**
guided tour *n* **132**
guillemot *n* **160**
guilty *adj* **06, 85**
Guinea *n* **149, 152**
guinea pig *n* **164**
Guinea-Bissau *n* **149, 152**
Guinean *adj* **152**
gulf *n* **147**
gull *n* **134**
gully *n* **111**
gulp *v* **52**
gulper eel *n* **166**
gum *n* **03**
gun, guns *n* **88**
gunfire *n* **88**
gunnera *n* **168**
gutter *n* **25, 43**
guy rope *n* **135**
Guyana *n* **149, 152**
Guyanese *adj* **152**
gym *n* **124, 131**
gym equipment *n* **124**
gym machines *n* **124**
gymnastics *n* **125**
gynaecology *n* **21**
gypsophila *n* **47**
gyrocopter *n* **103**

H

habitat loss *n* **155**
hacking *n* **85**
hacksaw *n* **36**
hadal zone *n* **166**
haddock tail *n* **54**
haemorrhage *n* **19**
hafnium *n* **78**
haggle *v* **46**
hailstone *n* **154**
hair *n* **01, 12**
hair band *n* **16**
hair curler *n* **12**
hair dryer *n* **12**
hair dye *n* **18**
hair gel *n* **12**
hair salon *n* **47**
hair scissors *n* **12**
hair spray *n* **12**
hair straightener *n* **12**
hair towel wrap *n* **18**
hairbrush *n* **12**
hairdresser *n* **89**
hairpin turn *n* **123**
Haiti *n* **150, 152**
Haitian *adj* **152**
hakama *n* **117**
halal *adj* **72**
half *num* **173**
half an hour *n* **171**
half moon pose *n* **24**
half time *n* **109**
half-court line *n* **112**
half-litre *n* **174**
half-way line *n* **109**
halfback *n* **107**
halfway line *n* **108**
halibut *n* **54**
halloumi *n* **64**
Halloween *n* **07**
halls of residence *n* **80**
hallway *n* **25-26**
halogens *n* **78**
halter *n* **120**
halter neck *n* **15**
halva *n* **67**
ham *n* **53, 71**
hamburger *n* **70**
hammer *n* **36, 116**
hammer *v* **35**
hammerhead shark *n* **166**
hammock *n* **135**
hamper *n* **133, 134**
hamster *n* **158, 164**
hamstrings *n* **03**
hand, hands *n* **01-02**
hand cream *n* **18**
hand drill *n* **36**
hand fork *n* **40**
hand grips *n* **124**
hand in your notice *v* **81**
hand luggage *n* **103-104**
hand out *v* **178**
hand towel *n* **31**
handbag *n* **16**
handball *n* **125**
handbrake *n* **99**
handcuffs *n* **50**
handful *n* **29**
handicap *n* **115**
handkerchief *n* **16**
handle *n* **16, 28, 40, 87, 110, 113-114**
handle with care *phr* **45**
handlebar *n* **101**
handouts *n* **95**
handrail *n* **25, 99**
handsaw *n* **36**
handsome *adj* **12**
handwriting *n* **175**
hang *v* **37**
hang glider *n* **125**
hang out clothes *v* **34**
Hang Son Doong *n* **145**
hang up *v* **14, 178**
hang-gliding *n* **125**
hangar *n* **104**
hanging basket *n* **41**
hangman *n* **140**
Hanukkah *n* **07**
happy *adj* **06**
harbour *n* **106**
harbour master *n* **106**
hard *adj* **57, 176**

hard cheese *n* **61**
hard drive *n* **83**
hard hat *n* **87**
hard shoulder *n* **96**
hard-working *adj* **93**
hardback *n* **138**
hardboard *n* **35**
hardware store *n* **46**
hardwood *n* **35**
hare's ear *n* **170**
harissa *n* **60**
harmless *adj* **177**
harmonica *n* **129**
harness *n* **115, 122**
harness race *n* **120**
harp *n* **128**
harpoon *n* **121**
harpy eagle *n* **160**
harvest *v* **39, 86**
hash browns *n* **70-71**
hash marks *n* **107**
hashtag *n* **83-84, 175**
hassium *n* **78**
hatch *v* **161**
hatchback *n* **97**
hatchling *n* **161**
have a baby *v* **07, 09**
have a break *v* **09**
have a car accident *v* **98**
have a conference call *v* **95**
have a day off *v* **81**
have a shower *v* **09**
have an interview *v* **92**
have breakfast *v* **09**
have dinner *v* **09**
have lunch *v* **09**
have tea or coffee *v* **09**
have your hair cut *v* **12**
hawk moth *n* **162**
hawkfish *n* **166**
hawksbill turtle *n* **166**
hawthorn *n* **169**
hay *n* **86**
hay fever *n* **19**
hazard *n* **96**
hazard lights *n* **99**
hazardous waste *n* **33**
hazel *adj* **01**
hazel *n* **01, 168**
hazelnut *n* **58**
hazelnut oil *n* **60**
HDMI cable *n* **95**
head *n* **01, 04, 162**
head guard *n* **117**
head injury *n* **19**
head pocket *n* **110**
head teacher *n* **73**
head-first *adj* **118**
headache *n* **19**
headboard *n* **30**
headlamp *n* **135, 146**
headlight, headlights *n* **50, 97, 100**
headlight controls *n* **99**
headline *n* **138**
headphones *n* **84, 95, 136**
headquarters *n* **81**
headrest *n* **99, 123**
headset *n* **82**
headstand *n* **24**
headstock *n* **129**
headwear *n* **16**
heal *v* **20**
health food shop *n* **23, 46-47**
healthcare *n* **91**
healthy body *n* **24**
healthy living *n* **23**
healthy mind *n* **24**
heart *n* **04, 53, 140**
heart rate *n* **124**
heater controls *n* **99**
heather *n* **38, 41**
heatwave *n* **154**
heavy *adj* **176**
heavy metal *n* **129**
hectare *n* **174**
hedge *n* **41, 86, 146**
hedgehog *n* **158**
hedgehog mushroom *n* **170**
heel *n* **01-02, 17, 115**
height *n* **74**
helicopter *n* **103**
helipad *n* **51**
helium *n* **78**
hello *phr* **179**
helm *n* **119**
helmet *n* **50, 100, 107, 111, 113, 123, 143, 146**
help *v* **11**
hem *n* **14, 142**
hematite *n* **156**
hemlock *n* **169**
hemp *n* **169**
hen *n* **165**
hen of the wood *n* **170**
hen's egg *n* **61**
henna *n* **168**
herb garden *n* **41**
herbaceous border *n* **41**
herbal remedies *n* **49**
herbal tea *n* **52, 66**
herbalism *n* **24**
herbicide *n* **86**
herbs *n* **41, 59**
herd *n* **86**
herd of cows *n* **165**
hermit crab *n* **134, 166**
hero *n* **127, 139**
heron *n* **160**
herring *n* **54**
Herzegovinian *adj* **153**
hex keys *n* **36**
hexagon *n* **74**
hi *phr* **179**
hi-fi system *n* **136**
hibernation *n* **77**
hibiscus *n* **38**
hide *v* **164**
hide-and-seek *n* **133**
high *adj* **176**
high blood pressure *n* **19**
high calorie *adj* **23**
high chair *n* **08**
high dive *n* **118**
high jump *n* **116**
high pressure *n* **155**
high street *n* **46**
high tide *n* **147**
high-definition *adj* **137**
high-heeled shoes *n* **17**
high-speed train *n* **102**
high-tops *n* **17**
high-visibility jacket *n* **13**
high-visibility vest *n* **87**
higher pitch *n* **128**
highland *n* **146**
highlighter *n* **73, 82**
highlighter pen *n* **175**
highlights *n* **12**
hijab *n* **16**
hiking *n* **133**
hiking boots *n* **17**
hiking map *n* **148**
hilarious *adj* **177**
hilt *n* **117**
Himalayan *n* **164**
Himeji Castle *n* **44**
hindwing *n* **162**
hip *n* **01**
hip-hop *n* **129**
hip pads *n* **107**
hippopotamus *n* **158**
historian *n* **79**
historic building *n* **44, 132**
historic quarter *n* **43**
historical drama *n* **127**
historical site *n* **79**
history *n* **73, 79-80**
hit *v* **11, 110**
hive *n* **165**
hob *n* **27**
hobby horse *n* **08**
hockey *n* **110**
hockey stick *n* **110**
hoe *n* **40**
hold *v* **11, 117**
hold your breath *v* **02**
holdall *n* **16**
hole *n* **115**
hole in one *n* **115**
hole punch *n* **82**
Holi *n* **07**
holiday *n* **104**
holmium *n* **78**
holy water *n* **07**
home *n* **32, 107**
home button *n* **83**
home cinema *n* **136**
home delivery *n* **48, 70**
home entertainment *n* **136**
home furnishings *n* **47**
home improvements *n* **35**
home plate *n* **113**
homeopathy *n* **24**
homestretch *n* **123**
homework *n* **73**
homogenized *adj* **61**
Honduran *adj* **152**
Honduras *n* **150, 152**
honest *adj* **10, 93**
honey *n* **60, 71**
honey badger *n* **158**
honey bee *n* **162**
honey dipper *n* **60**
honeycomb *n* **60**
honeydew melon *n* **58**
honeymoon *n* **07**
honeysuckle *n* **38**
hood *n* **13, 15**
hoof *n* **120, 158-159**
hook *n* **87**
hook and eye *n* **142**
hooker *n* **108**
hooliganism *n* **85**
hoop *n* **16, 112, 125**
hoot *v* **161**
hop *n* **169**
hop *v* **11, 164**
hopeful *adj* **06**
horizontal bar *n* **125**
horn, horns *n* **99, 100, 158**
hornbeam *n* **168**
horoscope *n* **138**
horrible *adj* **177**
horror *n* **127**
horse *n* **120, 165**
horse chestnut *n* **169**
horse race *n* **120**
horse riding *n* **120, 133**
horseradish *n* **56**
horseshoe *n* **120**
horseshoe crab *n* **166**
horsetail *n* **167**
hose *n* **50**
hose reel *n* **40**
hospital *n* **21, 42**
hospital bed *n* **21**
hospitality *n* **91**
host *n* **26**
hostel *n* **131**
hostess *n* **26**
hot *adj* **52, 56, 154, 176**
hot chocolate *n* **52**
hot dog *n* **70**
hot sauce *n* **60**
hot tub *n* **124**
hot water *n* **31**
hot-air balloon *n* **103**
hot-water bottle *n* **30**
hotel *n* **42, 131**
hotel lobby *n* **131**
hour *n* **171**
hour hand *n* **171**
hourly *adj, adv* **171-172**
hourly rate *n* **81**
house, houses *n* **25, 32, 148**
house martin *n* **160**
houseboat *n* **32**
household chores *n* **34**
household products *n* **48**
household renovation *n* **37**
household tasks *n* **34**
housekeeper *n* **89**
housemate *n* **32**
houseplants *n* **38**
hovercraft *n* **105**
howler monkey *n* **159**
hub *n* **51, 101**
hubcap *n* **98**
Hugin and Munin *n* **139**
hula hoop *n* **08**
hull *n* **105, 119**
human body *n* **01**
human resources (HR) *n* **91**
humanities *n* **80**
Humboldt penguin *n* **161**
humerus *n* **03**
humidity *n* **154**
hummingbird *n* **160**
hummingbird hawksmoth *n* **162**
hummus *n* **72**
humour *n* **138**
hump *n* **158**
humpback whale *n* **166**
Hungarian *adj* **153**
Hungary *n* **151, 153**
hungry *adj* **26**
hunt *v* **159**
hurdles *n* **116**
hurricane *n* **154**
hurt *v* **20**
husband *n* **05**
hut *n* **32**
hybrid *n* **97**
Hydra *n* **139**
hydrangea *n* **38**
hydrant *n* **50**
hydroelectric energy *n* **51**
hydroelectric power station *n* **51**
hydrofoil *n* **105**
hydrogen *n* **78**
hydrotherapy *n* **24**
hyena *n* **158**
hyphen *n* **175**
hypnotherapy *n* **24**
hypotenuse *n* **74**
hyssop *n* **59**

I

Iberian ham *n* **64**
ibex *n* **158**
ice *n* **68, 154**
ice and lemon *n* **68**
ice bucket *n* **68**
ice climbing *n* **122**
ice cream *n* **61, 70, 134**
ice cream cone *n* **65**
ice cream scoop *n* **65**
ice cream sundae *n* **63**
ice fishing *n* **121**
ice hockey *n* **110**
ice hockey player *n* **110**
ice hockey rink *n* **110**
ice maker *n* **27**
ice skate *n* **110**
ice-skating *n* **122**
iceberg lettuce *n* **55**
iceberg *n* **146**
iced *adj* **52**
iced bun *n* **63**
iced coffee *n* **65**
iced tea *n* **52, 66**
Iceland *n* **151, 153**
Icelandic *adj* **153**
ichthyostega *n* **157**
icicle *n* **146**
icing *n* **29, 63**
icy *adj* **154**
igloo *n* **32**
igneous *adj* **156**
ignition *n* **99**
illness *n* **19**
illustration *n* **138**
imaginative *adj* **93**
immature *adj* **10**
immigration *n* **104**
impala *n* **158**
impatient *adj* **10**
important *adj* **177**
Impressionism *n* **130**
impulsive *adj* **10**
in brine *phr* **64**
in credit *phr* **45**
in debt *phr* **45**
in field *n* **111**
in front of *prep* **148, 180**
in oil *phr* **64**
in *prep* **180**
in sauce *phr* **72**
in the black *phr* **45**
in the red *phr* **45**
in town *n* **42**
in-goal area *n* **108**
inbox *n* **83**
incandescent bulb *n* **33**
inch *n* **174**
inch plant *n* **167**
incisors *n* **03**
income *n* **94**
incontinence pads *n* **49**
incorrect *adj* **176**
incredible *adj* **177**
incubator *n* **08**
independent *adj* **93**
index *n* **138**
index finger *n* **02**
India *n* **150, 153**
Indian *adj* **153**
Indian cobra *n* **163**
Indian pale ale (IPA) *n* **68**
indicate *v* **98**
indicator *n* **97, 100**
indifferent *adj* **06**
indigo *n* **141**
indium *n* **78**
Indonesia *n* **151, 153**
Indonesian *adj* **153**
industrial emissions *n* **155**
industrial estate *n* **42**
industrial revolution *n* **79**
industries *n* **91**
infection *n* **19**
infield *n* **113**
infielders *n* **113**
inflatable boat *n* **134**
inflatable dinghy *n* **105**
influencer *n* **84, 93**
information age *n* **79**
information chart *n* **49**
information screen *n* **104**
information technology (IT) *n* **73, 91**
infrared *n* **75**
inhaler *n* **20, 49**
initiative *n* **93**
injera *n* **62**
injury *n* **19**
injury time *n* **109**
ink *n* **141, 175**
inline skating *n* **125**
inner core *n* **145**
inner tube *n* **101**
inning *n* **113**
innocent *adj* **85**
innovative *adj* **93**
inoculation *n* **20**
insect repellent *n* **49, 135**
insects *n* **162**
insensitive *adj* **10**
inside *prep* **180**
inside centre *n* **108**
inside lane *n* **96**
insoles *n* **17, 49**
insomnia *n* **19, 30**
inspector *n* **50**
install *v* **33**
installation *n* **130**
instep *n* **02**
instruments *n* **129**
insulated gloves *n* **143**
insulating tape *n* **36**
insulation *n* **35**
insulin *n* **49**
intelligent *adj* **10**
intensive care unit *n* **21**
intercity train *n* **102**
intercom *n* **25**
intercostal *n* **03**
interdental brush *n* **22**
interest rate *n* **45**
interested *adj* **06**
interesting *adj* **177**
intern *n* **81**
internal organs *n* **04**
international flight *n* **104**
interpersonal skills *n* **93**
interrogation room *n* **50**
interrupt *v* **95**
interval *n* **126**
interview *n* **81, 137**
interviewer *n* **81**
intolerant *adj* **23**
intrigued *adj* **06**
invertebrate *n* **77**
investigation *n* **50**
investment *n* **94**
invoice *n* **94**
iodine *n* **78**
ionosphere *n* **155**
Iran *n* **151, 153**
Iranian *adj* **153**
Iraq *n* **150, 153**
Iraqi *adj* **153**
Ireland *n* **151, 153**
iridium *n* **78**
iris *n* **01, 38**
Irish *adj* **153**
Irish coffee *n* **65**
iron *n* **23, 34, 49, 78, 115, 156**
iron a shirt *v* **09**
Iron age *n* **79**
ironing board *n* **34**
irritated *adj* **06**
irritating *adj* **177**
Islamic Golden Age *n* **79**
island *n* **88, 145, 147**
isobar *n* **155**
Israel *n* **150, 153**
Israeli *adj* **153**
isthmus *n* **147**
IT manager *n* **89**
Italian *adj* **153**
italic *adj* **175**
italic *n* **175**
Italy *n* **151, 153**
Ivorian *adj* **152**
Ivory Coast *n* **149, 152**
ivy *n* **169**

J

jack *n* **98, 140**
jack connector *n* **129**
jack-o'-lantern *n* **139, 170**
jackal *n* **158**
jacket *n* **15**
jackfruit *n* **58**
Jackson's chameleon *n* **163**
jacuzzi *n* **25**
jade *n* **156**
jade pothos *n* **38**
jaguar *n* **159**
jalapeños *n* **59**
jam *n* **71**
jam doughnut *n* **63**
Jamaica *n* **150, 152**
Jamaican *adj* **152**
janitor *n* **90**
January *n* **172**
Japan *n* **150, 153**
Japanese *adj* **153**
Japanese bobtail *n* **164**
Japanese characters *n* **175**
jar *n* **27, 52, 60**
jasper *n* **156**
javelin *n* **116**
jaw *n* **01, 03**
jawed fish *n* **157**
jawless fish *n* **157**
jazz *n* **129**
jealous *adj* **06**
jeans *n* **14**
jelly beans *n* **67**
jelly sandals *n* **17**
jellyfish *n* **166**
Jerusalem artichoke *n* **56**
jester *n* **79**
jet *n* **156**
jet engine *n* **103**
Jet Ski *n* **134**
jet skiing *n* **119**
jetty *n* **106**
jetway *n* **104**
jeweller *n* **46, 89**
jeweller's *n* **46**
jewellery *n* **16**
jewellery box *n* **16**
jewellery making *n* **141**
jib *n* **87, 119**
jigsaw *n* **35**
jigsaw puzzle *n* **08, 140**
job ads *n* **92**
job applications *n* **92**
job sheet *n* **92**
job skills *n* **92**
jobs *n* **89-90**
jockey *n* **120**
jockey pants *n* **14**
jodhpurs *n* **120**
joey *n* **158**
jog on the spot *v* **124**
jogging *n* **133**
joint *n* **53**
joker *n* **140**
Jordan *n* **150, 153**
Jordanian *adj* **153**
Joshua tree *n* **167**
journal *n* **80**
journalism *n* **91**
journalist *n* **90**
judge *n* **85, 90**
judo *n* **117**
jug, jugs *n* **27-29**
juggle *v* **11**
juice, juices *n* **52, 65**
juicy *adj* **52**
jujitsu *n* **117**
July *n* **172**
jumbo jet *n* **103**
jump *v* **11, 117, 120**
jump ball *n* **112**
jumper *n* **14**
jumping ramp *n* **122**
jumping spider *n* **162**
junction *n* **96**
June *n* **172**
junk mail *n* **83**
Jupiter *n* **143**
Jurassic *adj* **157**
Jurassic *n* **157**
jury *n* **85**
jury box *n* **85**
jury deliberation *n* **85**

K

K-pop *n* **129**
kale *n* **55**
kangaroo *n* **158**
karaoke *n* **136**
karate *n* **117**
karate mat *n* **117**
kayak *n* **105, 119**
kayaking *n* **119**
Kazakhstan *n* **151, 153**
kebab *n* **70, 72**
keel *n* **105, 119**
keep *n* **44**
keep net *n* **121**
kefir *n* **61**
kelp *n* **166**

kendo *n* **117**
kennel *n* **164**
Kenya *n* **149, 152**
Kenyan *adj* **152**
kerb *n* **43**
kernel *n* **55**
ketchup *n* **60, 70**
kettledrum *n* **128**
key, keys *n* **25, 32**
key cutting shop *n* **46**
keyboard *n* **83, 129**
keyhole *n* **25-26**
keypad *n* **45**
kick *n* **108, 118**
kick *v* **11, 107**
kick flip *n* **125**
kickboxing *n* **117**
kickoff *n* **109**
kickstand *n* **101**
kid *n* **165**
kidney,
kidneys *n* **04, 53, 71**
kids' clothes *n* **13**
kids' shoes *n* **17**
killer whale *n* **166**
kilogram *n* **174**
kilometre *n* **174**
kilt *n* **15**
kimchi *n* **60**
kimono *n* **15**
kind *adj* **10**
king *n* **79, 140**
kingdom *n* **79**
kingfisher *n* **160**
kiosk *n* **46-48**
kippers *n* **71**
Kiribati *adj* **153**
Kiribati *n* **150, 153**
kitchen *n* **27, 69**
kitchen appliances *n* **27**
kitchen equipment *n* **28**
kitchen fitter *n* **90**
kitchen installer *n* **90**
kitchen knife *n* **28**
kitchen scissors *n* **28**
kitchenware *n* **28**
kite *n* **08**
kite surfing *n* **119**
kitten *n* **164**
kitten heels *n* **17**
Kittitian *adj* **152**
kiwi *n* **160**
kiwi /
kiwi fruit *n* **58**
knead *v* **62**
knee *n* **01, 126**
knee joint *n* **03**
knee pad *n* **107, 100**
knee-high boots *n*
kneecap *n* **03**
kneeler *n* **40**
kneeling chair *n* **82**
knickers *n* **14**
knife *n* **27**
knife sharpener *n* **28**
knife stand *n* **28**
knight *n* **79, 139-140**
knitting *n* **142**
knitting needle *n* **142**
knob *n* **25-26, 113**
knock down
a wall *v* **35**
knock out *n* **117**
knots *n* **121**
knuckle *n* **02**
koala *n* **158**
kohlrabi *n* **55**
kola nuts *n* **58**
Komodo dragon *n* **163**
kookaburra *n* **160**
kosher *adj* **72**
krypton *n* **78**
kumquat *n* **57**
kung fu *n* **117**
Kuwait *n* **151, 153**
Kuwaiti *adj* **153**
Kwanzaa *n* **07**
Kyrgyz *adj* **153**
Kyrgyzstan *n* **151, 153**

L

lab *n* **76**
lab coat *n* **13**
label, labels *n* **40, 130**
laboratory *n* **76**
labrador *n* **164**
lace *n* **17, 107**
lace bobbin *n* **142**
lace-making *n* **142**
lace-up boots *n* **17**
lacrosse *n* **110**
lacrosse player *n* **110**
lactose free *adj* **61**
lactose intolerant *adj* **23**
ladder *n* **36, 50, 87**
ladle *n* **27**
lady *n* **79**
ladybird *n* **162**
lager *n* **68**
lagoon *n* **147**
laid-back *adj* **10**
lake *n* **146, 148**
Lake Natron *n* **145**
lamb *n* **53, 165**
lamp *n* **26, 82, 101, 106, 135, 139**
lampshade *n* **26**
land *n* **145**
land *v* **104**
landfill *n* **155**
landing gear *n* **103**
landing hill *n* **122**
landing net *n* **121**
landlord *n* **32**
landscape *n* **132**
landscape *v* **39**
landscape painting *n* **133**
landslide *n* **146**
lane *n* **116, 118**
lane line *n* **112**
lane rope *n* **118**
languages *n* **73, 80**
lantern *n* **135**
lanthanum *n* **78**
lanthanide series *n* **78**
Laos *n* **150, 153**
Laotian *adj* **153**
lapel *n* **15**
lapis lazuli *n* **156**
laptop *n* **82-83**
larch *n* **167**
large *adj* **176**
large intestine *n* **04**
larynx *n* **04**
lasagna *n* **64, 72**
laser *n* **75**
laser run *n* **116**
late *adj* **171**
later *adj* **171**
later *adv* **171**
Latin *n* **129**
Latin alphabet *n* **175**
latissimus dorsi *n* **03**
latitude *n* **145, 148**
Latvia *n* **151, 153**
Latvian *adj* **153**
laugh *v* **02**
launch *n* **143**
launch pad *n* **143**
Launderette *n* **46**
laundry *n* **34**
laundry
basket *n* **31, 34**
laundry detergent *n* **34**
laundry service *n* **131**
laurel *n* **167**
lava *n* **145**
lava layer *n* **145**
lavender *n* **38**
law *n* **80, 85**
law court *n* **43, 85**
lawn *n* **41**
lawn rake *n* **40**
lawnmower *n* **40**
lawrencium *n* **78**
lawyer *n* **85, 90**
lawyer's office *n* **85**
laxative *n* **49**
lay bricks *v* **35**
lay turf *v* **39**
layer cake *n* **63**
lazy *adj* **10**
leaching *n* **39**
lead *n* **78**
lead *n* **164**
lead singer *n* **129**
leaded *n* **97**
leader *n* **81**
leadership *n* **93**
leaf *n* **55**
leaf blower *n* **40**
leaf fall *n* **172**
leafy *adj* **56**
lean meat *n* **53**
Leaning Tower
of Pisa *n* **44**
learn *v* **73**
lease *n* **32**
leash *n* **164**
leather *adj* **176**
leather *n* **13, 107, 176**
leatherback
sea turtle *n* **163**
leathers *n* **100**
leave *v* **179**
leave the house *v* **09**
leave work *v* **09**
Lebanese *adj* **153**
Lebanon *n* **150, 153**
lecture theatre *n* **80**
lecturer *n* **80, 89**
LED (light emitting diode)
bulb *n* **33**
lederhosen *n* **15**
leek *n* **56**
left defenceman *n* **110**
left defensive end *n* **107**
left defensive tackle *n* **107**
left guard *n* **107**
left safety *n* **107**
left tackle *n* **107**
left winger *n* **110**
left-wing *n* **108**
leg *n* **01, 26, 53**
leg guard *n* **110**
leg pad *n* **111**
leg press *n* **124**
legal *n* **91**
legal advice *n* **85**
legal system *n* **85**
leggings *n* **14**
lemon *n* **57**
lemon balm *n* **59**
lemon curd *n* **60**
lemon squeezer *n* **28**
lemonade *n* **52**
lemongrass *n* **59**
length *n* **74, 174**
lens *n* **22, 75, 127, 136**
lens case *n* **22**
lens cleaning cloth *n* **22**
lens solution *n* **49**
Leo *n* **144**
leopard *n* **159**
leotard *n* **15**
leprechaun *n* **139**
Lesotho *n* **149, 152**
lesson *n* **73**
let *n* **114**
let in *v* **178**
let out *v* **142**
letter *n* **45, 82**
letterbox *n* **25, 45**
letters *n* **175**
lettuce *n* **55**
Liberia *n* **149, 152**
Liberian *adj* **152**
libero *n* **112**
Libra *n* **144**
librarian *n* **80, 90**
library *n* **43, 80, 148**
library card *n* **80**
libretto *n* **126**
Libya *n* **149, 152**
Libyan *adj* **152**
licence plate *n* **97**
lick *v* **02, 11**
lid *n* **28**
lie down *v* **20**
Liechtenstein *n* **151, 153**
Liechtensteiner *adj* **153**
life cycle *n* **77**
life events *n* **07**
life jacket *n* **105, 119**
life raft *n* **119**
life ring *n* **105, 119, 134**
life-support
backpack *n* **143**
lifeboat *n* **105**
lifeguard *n* **118, 134**
lifeguard tower *n* **134**
lift *n* **25, 47, 131**
lift *v* **11**
ligament *n* **03**
ligature *n* **175**
light *adj* **60, 176**
light, lights *n* **32, 50, 84, 101, 143**
light a fire *v* **135**
light aircraft *n* **103**
light bulbs *n* **33**
light shower *n* **154**
light switch *n* **33**
lighthouse *n* **44, 106**
lighting *n* **47**
lightning *n* **154**
like *v* **84**
lilac *n* **38**
lily *n* **38, 167**
lily of the valley *n* **38**
lime *n* **57, 169**
lime pickle *n* **60**
limestone *n* **156**
limousine *n* **97**
limpet *n* **134, 166**
linden *n* **169**
line, lines *n* **74, 121**
line of play *n* **115**
linen chest *n* **30**
linesman *n* **109, 114**

lingerie *n* **47**
lining *n* **15**
lining paper *n* **37**
lintel *n* **87**
lion *n* **158**
lioness *n* **158**
lip balm *n* **18**
lip brush *n* **18**
lip liner *n* **18**
lips *n* **01**
lipstick *n* **18**
liqueur *n* **68**
liquid *n* **76**
liquid measure *n* **174**
liquid measurements *n* **174**
liquorice *n* **67**
listen *v* **11**
listen to the radio *v* **09**
literary fiction *n* **138**
literature *n* **73, 80**
lithium *n* **78**
Lithuania *n* **151, 153**
Lithuanian *adj* **153**
litre *n* **174**
litter tray *n* **164**
little finger *n* **02**
little gem *n* **55**
little toe *n* **02**
live *n* **33**
live rail *n* **102**
liver *n* **04, 53**
livermorium *n* **78**
liverwort *n* **167**
living room *n* **26**
living stones *n* **168**
lizard *n* **164**
llama *n* **158, 165**
load the dishwasher *v* **34**
loaf *n* **62**
loafers *n* **17**
loam *n* **39**
loans desk *n* **80**
lob *n* **114**
lobster *n* **54**
local produce *n* **23**
lock *n* **101, 106**
lockers *n* **118, 124**
locksmith *n* **90**
locust *n* **162**
lodger *n* **32**
log in *v* **83, 178**
log out *v* **83, 178**
loganberry *n* **57**
logic game *n* **136**
loin *n* **54**
lollipop *n* **67**
London plane *n* **168**
lonely *adj* **06**
long *adj* **176**
long hair *n* **12**
long jump *n* **116**
long legs *n* **159**
long-handled shears *n* **40**
long-sighted *adj* **22**
longitude *n* **145, 148**
look after *v* **178**
look at *v* **178**
look for *v* **178**
loom *n* **142**
loose *adj* **13, 176**
loosehead prop *n* **108**
loppers *n* **40**
lord *n* **79**
lorikeet *n* **161**
lorry driver *n* **90**
lose *v* **109, 140**
lose weight *v* **20, 23**
lose your way *v* **148**
lost and found *n* **104**
lost property office *n* **102**
lotus *n* **38**
loudspeakers *n* **136**
lovage *n* **59**
love *n* **114**
low *adj* **176**
low calorie *adj* **23**
low pressure *n* **155**
low tide *n* **147**
lower deck *n* **99**
lower pitch *n* **128**
lowercase *n* **175**
loyalty card *n* **47**
lucky *adj* **06**
ludo *n* **140**
luge *n* **122**
luggage *n* **104, 131**
luggage hold *n* **99**
luggage rack *n* **102**
luggage storage *n* **102**
lumbar vertebrae *n* **03**
luna moth *n* **162**
lunar eclipse *n* **143**
lunar module *n* **143**
lunar rover *n* **143**
lunch *n* **26, 72**
lunch menu *n* **69**
lung *n* **04**
lunge *n* **117, 124**
lupin *n* **38**
lure *n* **121**
lutetium *n* **78**
Luxembourg *adj* **153**
Luxembourg *n* **151, 153**
lychee *n* **57**
lymphatic *n* **04**
lynx *n* **159**

M

macadamia, macadamias *n* **58, 168**
macaque *n* **159**
macaron *n* **63**
macaroni *n* **64**
mace *n* **59, 78**
machine gun *n* **88**
machine needle *n* **142**
machinery *n* **87**
mackerel *n* **54**
macramé *n* **142**
Madagascan *adj* **152**
Madagascar *n* **149, 152**
magazine website *n* **84**
maglev *n* **102**
magma chamber *n* **145**
magnesium *n* **49, 78, 156**
magnet *n* **75**
magnetic field *n* **75**
magnolia *n* **167**
maid *n* **89**
maid service *n* **131**
main character *n* **127**
main course *n* **69**
main road *n* **148**
Maine coon *n* **164**
mains supply *n* **33**
mainsail *n* **119**
maize *n* **86**
make *v* **11**
make a loss *v* **94**
make a profit *v* **94**
make a reservation *v* **69, 131**
make a will *v* **07**
make curtains *v* **35**
make friends *v* **07**
make the bed *v* **09, 34**
make up *v* **178**
makeup *n* **18**
makeup bag *n* **18**
malachite *n* **156**
Malawi *n* **149, 152**
Malawian *adj* **152**
Malaysia *n* **151, 153**
Malaysian *adj* **153**
Maldives *n* **150, 153**
Maldivian *adj* **153**
male *n* **04**
Mali *n* **149, 152**
Malian *adj* **152**
mallard *n* **161**
mallet *n* **36, 141**
malt vinegar *n* **60**
Malta *n* **151, 153**
Maltese *adj* **153**
mammals *n* **158, 159**
man *n* **05**
manage *v* **92**
manager *n* **81, 109**
managing director *n* **81**
manchego *n* **64**
mandarin duck *n* **161**
mandolin *n* **28**
mandolin *n* **129**
mandrill *n* **159**
mane *n* **120**
manganese *n* **78**
mangetout *n* **55**
mango *n* **57**
mango juice *n* **65**
mangosteen *n* **58**
mangrove *n* **169**
manhole *n* **43**
manicure *n* **18**
mansion *n* **32**
mantis shrimp *n* **166**
mantle *n* **145**
mantlepiece *n* **26**
manual *n* **99**
manufacturing *n* **91**
map *n* **132**
maple *n* **169**
maple syrup *n* **60**
maps *n* **148**
maracas *n* **128**
marathon *n* **116**
marble *adj* **176**
marble *n* **156, 176**
marble queen *n* **38**
March *n* **172**
mare *n* **120, 165**
margarine *n* **61**
marigold *n* **38**
marina *n* **106**
marinated *adj* **64, 72**
marinated fish *n* **64**
marine *n* **88**
marine fishing *n* **121**
marine iguana *n* **163**
marine species *n* **166**
marjoram *n* **59**
mark *v* **112**
marker *n* **175**
market researcher *n* **89**
marketing *n* **91**
marmalade *n* **60, 71**
marmoset *n* **159**
marrella *n* **157**
married *n* **05**
married couple *n* **07**
marrow *n* **56**
Mars *n* **143**
marsh *n* **147**
Marshall Islands *n* **150, 153**
Marshallese *adj* **153**
marshmallow *n* **67**
martial arts *n* **117, 127**
Martini *n* **68**
Mary Janes *n* **17**
marzipan *n* **63**
mascara *n* **18**
mascot *n* **109**
mash *v* **29**
mashed *adj* **72**
masher *n* **28**
mask *n* **113, 117-118**
masking tape *n* **37**
Mason jar *n* **52**
masonry bit *n* **36**
massage *n* **24**
mast *n* **105, 119**
master's degree *n* **80**
masterpiece *n* **130**
mat *n* **24**
matamata *n* **163**
match *n* **114**
materials *n* **35, 176**
maternity *n* **21**
maternity ward *n* **21**
mathematical equipment *n* **74**
mathematics *n* **74**
maths *n* **73**
matte *n* **37**
mattress *n* **30**
mature *adj* **10**
matzo *n* **62**
Mauritania *n* **149, 152**
Mauritanian *adj* **152**
Mauritian *adj* **152**
Mauritius *n* **149, 152**
May *n* **172**
mayonnaise *n* **60**
MDF *n* **35**
meal deal *n* **70**
meals *n* **72**
mean *adj* **10**
measles *n* **19**
measure *n* **68**
measure *v* **174**
measure out *v* **178**
measurements *n* **74**
measures *n* **174**
measuring jug *n* **27-29, 174**
measuring spoon *n* **28, 49**
meat *n* **48, 53**
meat hook *n* **53**
meat pie *n* **72**
meat pies *n* **64**
meat tenderizer *n* **28**
meat thermometer *n* **28**
meatballs *n* **72**
mechanic *n* **89, 98**
mechanics *n* **98**
medal *n* **88, 116**
media *n* **84, 91**
medical chart *n* **21**
medical examination *n* **20**
medication *n* **20, 49**
medicine *n* **20, 49, 80**
mediocre *adj* **177**
meditation *n* **24**

medium height *adj* **12**
medlar *n* **169**
medley relay *n* **118**
meerkat *n* **159**
meet *v* **179**
meet a deadline *v* **92**
meet up *v* **178**
meeting *n* **81, 82, 95**
meeting-room equipment *n* **82**
meganeura *n* **157**
megaphone *n* **50**
meitnerium *n* **78**
melody *n* **129**
melons *n* **58**
melt butter *v* **29**
melting ice caps *n* **155**
membership *n* **124**
memory card *n* **83**
mendelevium *n* **78**
men's decathlon *n* **116**
menswear *n* **47**
menu *n* **65, 70**
meow *v* **164**
merchant *n* **79**
Mercury *n* **143**
mercury *n* **78, 156**
meringue *n* **63**
mermaid *n* **139**
merman *n* **139**
mesa *n* **146**
mesosphere *n* **155**
Mesozoic (middle life) *adj* **157**
Mesozoic (middle life) *n* **157**
mess *n* **88**
mess around *v* **178**
metacarpals *n* **03**
metal *adj* **176**
metal, metals *n* **35, 155, 156, 176**
metal bit *n* **36**
metal detecting *n* **133**
metamorphic *adj* **156**
metamorphosis *n* **77**
metatarsals *n* **03**
meteor *n* **144**
meteor shower *n* **144**
methane *n* **155**
meticulous *adj* **10**
metre *n* **174**
metre line *n* **108**
Mexican *adj* **152**
Mexican axolotl *n* **163**
Mexico *n* **150, 152**
mezzo-soprano *n* **126**
mica *n* **156**
microbiologist *n* **77**
microbiology *n* **77**
microlight *n* **103**
Micronesia *n* **150, 153**
Micronesian *adj* **153**
microphone *n* **84, 95, 136**
microscope *n* **77**
microwave *v* **29**
microwave oven *n* **27**
microwaves *n* **75**
mid-off *n* **111**
mid-wicket *n* **111**
midcourt area marker *n* **112**
midday *n* **171**
middle blocker *n* **112**
middle finger *n* **02**
middle lane *n* **96**
middle level *n* **47**
middle linebacker *n* **107**
middle-aged *adj* **12**
midfielder *n* **109**
midnight *n* **171**
midnight zone *n* **166**
midwife *n* **08**
migraine *n* **19**
migrate *v* **161**
mild *adj* **154**
mile *n* **174**
military *n* **88, 91**
military ambulance *n* **88**
military transport aircraft *n* **88**
military truck *n* **88**
military uniform *n* **13**
military vehicles *n* **88**
milk *n* **61, 65, 71**
milk *v* **86**
milk carton *n* **61**
milk chocolate *n* **67**
milk products *n* **61**
milk teeth *n* **22**
milkshake *n* **52, 65, 70**
milky conecap *n* **170**
Milky Way *n* **144**
millennium *n* **172**
millet *n* **86**
milligram *n* **174**
millilitre *n* **174**
millimetre *n* **174**
millipede *n* **162**
mimosa *n* **168**
minaret *n* **44**
mince *v* **29**
mindfulness *n* **24**
mine shaft *n* **51**
miner, miners *n* **51, 89**
mineral water *n* **52, 68**
minerals *n* **23, 156**
minibar *n* **131**
minibus *n* **99**
mining *n* **91**
Minotaur *n* **139**
minstrel *n* **79**
mint *n* **59, 67**
mint tea *n* **66**
minus sign *n* **74**
minute *n* **82, 171**
minute hand *n* **171**
mirror *n* **18, 30, 77**
miserable *adj* **06**
miss a train *v* **102**
mission control *n* **143**
mist *n* **154**
mistletoe *n* **168**
misty *adj* **154**
mitochondria *n* **77**
mitt *n* **113**
mittens *n* **13**
mix *v* **29, 62**
mixed salad *n* **72**
mixing bowl *n* **28**
mixing desk *n* **84**
moat *n* **44**
mobile *n* **30**
mobile banking *n* **94**
mobile phone *n* **82**
moccasins *n* **17**
mochi *n* **63**
mocktail *n* **68**
model making *n* **141**
modelling tool *n* **141**
modern building *n* **44**
modern pentathlon *n* **116**
moisturizer *n* **18**
molars *n* **03**
mold *n* **170**
Moldova *n* **151, 153**
Moldovan *adj* **153**
mole *n* **12, 159**
molecule *n* **76**
molybdenum *n* **78**
Monacan *adj* **153**
Monaco *n* **151, 153**
monarch butterfly *n* **162**
monastery *n* **44**
Monday *n* **172**
money *n* **45, 94**
Mongolia *n* **150, 153**
Mongolian *adj* **153**
mongoose *n* **159**
monkey puzzle *n* **167**
monkey wrench *n* **36**
monkfish *n* **54**
mono *adj* **136**
monocle *n* **22**
monoplane *n* **103**
monorail *n* **102**
monster *n* **139**
monster truck *n* **123**
Montenegrin *adj* **153**
Montenegro *n* **151, 153**
month *n* **172**
monthly *adj* **172**
monthly *adv* **172**
monument *n* **42, 44, 132**
moods *n* **06**
Moon *n* **143**
moonstone *n* **156**
moor *v* **106**
mooring *n* **106**
moorish idol *n* **166**
moose *n* **159**
mop *n* **34**
mop the floor *v* **34**
morel *n* **170**
morning *n* **09, 171**
morning glory *n* **169**
Moroccan *adj* **152**
Morocco *n* **149, 152**
mortar *n* **28, 35, 76, 87**
mortar and pestle *n* **28**
mortarboard *n* **80**
mortgage *n* **32, 45**
moscovium *n* **78**
Moses basket *n* **08, 30**
mosque *n* **44**
mosquito *n* **162**
mosquito net *n* **135**
moss *n* **167**
mother *n* **05**
mother-in-law *n* **05**
mother of thousands *n* **168**
moths *n* **162**
motivated *adj* **93**
motor racing *n* **123**
motor scooter *n* **100**
motorbike *n* **100**
motorbike racing *n* **123**
motocross *n* **123**
motorcycle officer *n* **50**
motorsports *n* **123**
motorway *n* **96**
moulding *n* **26**
moult *v* **164**
mount *v* **100**
mountain *n* **147**
mountain ash *n* **169**
mountain bike *n* **101**
mountain biking *n* **133**
mountain goat *n* **159**
mountain pose *n* **24**
mountain range *n* **146**
mountaineering *n* **133**
mouse *n* **83, 158, 164**
mouse mat *n* **83**
moustache *n* **12**
mouth *n* **01, 147**
mouth guard *n* **107, 117**
mouthwash *n* **31**
movable panel *n* **82**
move *v* **11, 140**
move in *v* **32**
move out *v* **32**
movie camera *n* **127**
mow the lawn *v* **09, 39**
Mozambican *adj* **152**
Mozambique *n* **149, 152**
mozzarella *n* **64**
muck out *v* **120**
mudguard *n* **100**
mudskipper *n* **166**
mudslide *n* **146**
muesli *n* **71**
muffin *n* **63, 70**
muffin tray *n* **29**
mug *n* **27**
mugging *n* **85**
mulberry *n* **57**
mulch *v* **39**
mules *n* **17**
multi-purpose knife *n* **135**
multi-vitamins *n* **49**
multiplayer game *n* **136**
multiplex *n* **127**
multiplication sign *n* **74**
multiply *v* **74**
mum *n* **05**
mumps *n* **19**
muscles *n* **03**
museum *n* **43, 130, 132**
museum curator *n* **89**
musher *n* **122**
mushroom picking *n* **133**
mushroom, mushrooms *n* **56, 170**
music *n* **73, 128, 129**
music channel *n* **137**
music school *n* **80**
music stand *n* **128**
music teacher *n* **90**
music therapy *n* **24**
musical *n* **126, 127**
musician *n* **90**
musk ox *n* **159**
mussel *n* **54**
mustard *n* **70**
mustard allergy *n* **23**
mustard seeds *n* **60**
mute swan *n* **161**
muzzle *n* **120**
Myanmar (Burma) *n* **150, 153**
mycelium *n* **170**
myrtle *n* **168**
myths *n* **139**

N

nacelle *n* **51**
nachos *n* **70**
nail *n* **36**
nail clippers *n* **18, 49**
nail file *n* **18**
nail polish *n* **18**
nail polish remover *n* **18**
nail scissors *n* **18**
nail varnish *n* **18**
Namibia *n* **149, 152**
Namibian *adj* **152**
napkin *n* **27, 72**

napkin ring *n* **27**
nappy *n* **08**
nappy rash cream *n* **08**
narrow *adj* **176**
narwhal *n* **166**
nasal spray *n* **20**
nasturtium *n* **169**
nasty *adj* **177**
national park *n* **132, 133**
nationalities *n* **152, 153**
natural arch *n* **147**
natural history *n* **157**
nature documentary *n* **137**
nature reserve *n* **133, 148**
nature therapy *n* **24**
nature writing *n* **138**
naturopathy *n* **24**
Nauru *n* **150, 153**
Nauruan *adj* **153**
nausea *n* **19**
nautilus *n* **166**
navel *n* **01**
navigate *v* **119**
navy *n* **88**
navy blue *n* **141**
navy vessels *n* **88**
near *adj* **176**
nebula *n* **144**
neck *n* **01, 115, 129, 161**
neck brace *n* **19**
neck pad *n* **107**
necklace *n* **16**
neckline *n* **142**
nectarine *n* **57**
needle *n* **20**
needlefish *n* **166**
needle-nose pliers *n* **36**
needle plate *n* **142**
needlepoint *n* **142**
negative *adj* **75**
negative electrode *n* **75**
negotiate *v* **92**
negotiating *n* **93**
neighbour *n* **07**
neodymium *n* **78**
Neogene *adj* **157**
Neogene *n* **157**
neon *n* **78**
Nepal *n* **150, 153**
Nepalese *adj* **153**
nephew *n* **05**
Neptune *n* **143**
neptunium *n* **78**
nerve *n* **03, 22**
nervous *adj* **04, 06, 10**
nest *n* **160**
net *n* **109, 112, 114**
net *v* **121**
net curtain *n* **26**
netball *n* **125**
Netherlands *n* **151, 153**
nettle *n* **169**
neurology *n* **21**
neutral *n* **33**
neutral zone *n* **107, 110**
neutron *n* **76**
neutron star *n* **144**
never *adv* **171, 172**
Nevisian *adj* **152**
new *adj* **176**
new leaves *n* **172**
new moon *n* **143**
new potato *n* **56**
New Year *n* **07**
New Zealand *adj* **153**
New Zealand *n* **150, 153**
newborn baby *n* **08**
news *n* **137**
news website *n* **84**
newsboy cap *n* **16**
newsfeed *n* **84**
newspaper *n* **48, 138**
newsreader *n* **89, 137**
newsstand *n* **46, 48**
next to *prep* **148, 180**
nib *n* **73, 175**
nibble *v* **52**
Nicaragua *n* **150, 152**
Nicaraguan *adj* **152**
nice *adj* **177**
nickel *n* **78, 156**
niece *n* **05**
nigella seeds *n* **59**
Niger *n* **149, 152**
Nigeria *n* **149, 152**
Nigerian *adj* **152**
Nigerien *adj* **152**
night *n* **171**
night light *n* **30**
nightclub *n* **42**
nightgown *n* **14**
nightie *n* **14**
nightingale *n* **160**
nightmare *n* **30**
nightwear *n* **14**
nihonium *n* **78**
Nile crocodile *n* **163**
nine *num* **173**
nine-to-five job *n* **81**
nineteen *num* **173**
ninety *num* **173**
ninth *num* **173**
niobium *n* **78**
nipple *n* **01, 08**
nitrogen *n* **78**
no entry *n* **96**
no overtaking *phr* **96**
no photography *phr* **130**
no right turn *phr* **96**
no U-turn *phr* **96**
no vacancies *phr* **131**
no-charge semi-circle *n* **112**
nobelium *n* **78**
noble gases *n* **78**
nobles *n* **79**
nod *v* **02**
noisy *adj* **176**
non-blood relative *n* **05**
non-carbonated *adj* **52**
non-fiction *n* **138**
non-metals *n* **78**
noodle soup *n* **72**
noodles *n* **64, 70, 72**
normal *adj* **18**
normal hair *n* **12**
north *n* **148**
North America *n* **150, 152**
North American *adj* **152**
North Korea *n* **150, 153**
North Korean *adj* **153**
North Macedonia *n* **151, 153**
North Macedonian *adj* **153**
North Pole *n* **75, 145**
northeast *n* **148**
northern cardinal *n* **161**
Northern Hemisphere *n* **145**
northwest *n* **148**
Norway *n* **151, 153**
Norwegian *adj* **153**
nose *n* **01, 103**
nose clip *n* **118**
nose cone *n* **123**
noseband *n* **120**
nosebleed *n* **19**
nosewheel *n* **103**
nostrils *n* **01**
notation *n* **128**
notebook *n* **73, 95**
notepad *n* **82**
notes *n* **45, 94**
notes *n* **95, 128**
notice board *n* **82**
nougat *n* **67**
nought point five *num* **173**
noughts and crosses *n* **140**
novel *n* **138**
November *n* **172**
now *adv* **171**
nozzle *n* **40**
nuclear energy *n* **51**
nuclear power station *n* **51**
nuclear waste *n* **51**
nucleus *n* **76, 77**
number *n* **112**
number eight *n* **108**
numbers *n* **173**
numeracy *n* **93**
numerals *n* **175**
numerator *n* **74**
nurse *n* **20, 21, 89**
nursery *n* **30**
nursing *n* **80**
nut allergy *n* **23**
nut, nuts *n* **36, 58, 68, 129**
nutmeg *n* **59**
nutrition *n* **23**

O

oak *n* **169**
oar *n* **119**
oasis *n* **146**
objective lens *n* **77**
obliques *n* **03**
oboe *n* **128**
observatory *n* **144**
obsidian *n* **156**
obstetrician *n* **08**
occupations *n* **89-90**
occluded front *n* **155**
ocean *n* **145, 147**
ocean life *n* **166**
ocean ridge *n* **145**
Oceania *n* **150, 153**
Oceanian *adj* **153**
octagon *n* **74**
October *n* **172**
octopus *n* **54, 166**
odd *adj* **177**
odometer *n* **99**
oesophagus *n* **04**
off *adj* **52**
off licence *n* **46**
off the shoulder *adj* **15**
off-piste *n* **122**
off-road motorcycle *n* **100**
offal *n* **53**
offence *n* **107**
office *n* **82**
office building *n* **42**
office equipment *n* **82**
office manager *n* **81**
office reception *n* **81**
office services *n* **91**
office work *n* **81**
often *adv* **172**
oganesson *n* **78**
ogre *n* **139**
oil *n* **51, 60, 64, 97**
oil field *n* **51**
oil painting *n* **130**
oil paints *n* **141**
oil slick *n* **155**
oil tank *n* **100**
oil tanker *n* **105**
oil terminal *n* **106**
oil-filled radiator *n* **33**
oily *adj* **18**
ointment *n* **20, 49**
okra *n* **55**
old *adj* **12, 176**
old man cactus *n* **168**
old-fashioned *adj* **177**
oleander *n* **169**
oleaster *n* **169**
olive *n* **68, 169**
olive oil *n* **60**
olm *n* **163**
Oman *n* **151, 153**
Omani *adj* **153**
omelette *n* **61, 71, 72**
on *prep* **180**
on stage *adj* **126**
on the corner *phr* **148**
on the left *phr* **148**
on the right *phr* **148**
on time *adj* **171**
once a week *adv* **172**
oncology *n* **21**
one *num* **173**
one billion *num* **173**
one hundred *num* **173**
one million *num* **173**
one o'clock *n* **171**
one thirty *n* **171**
one thousand *num* **173**
one-way street *n* **96**
one-way system *n* **42**
one-way ticket *n* **131**
onesie *n* **13**
onion *n* **56**
onion dome *n* **44**
online banking *n* **45, 94**
online check-in *n* **104**
online communication *n* **83**
online delivery *n* **91**
online map *n* **148**
online media *n* **84**
online retail *n* **91**
online shopping *n* **48**
only child *n* **05**
only weekends *adv* **172**
onyx *n* **156**
opal *n* **156**
open *adj* **48, 132**
open sandwich *n* **70**
open turn *n* **118**
open-air activities *n* **133**
open-air hobbies *n* **133**
open-cast mining *n* **51**
open-plan *n* **32**
opening night *n* **126**
opening times *n* **132**
openside flanker *n* **108**

opera *n* **126, 129**
opera glasses *n* **22**
opera house *n* **126**
operating table *n* **21**
operating theatre *n* **21**
operation *n* **21**
ophthalmology *n* **21**
opinions *n* **177**
opium poppy *n* **168**
opponent *n* **117**
opposite *prep* **112, 148**
optician *n* **22, 46, 89**
optics *n* **75**
optimistic *adj* **10**
optometrist *n* **22**
orange *n* **57, 141**
orange juice
with pulp *n* **65**
orange peel fungus *n* **170**
orange-cap boletus *n* **170**
orangeade *n* **52**
orangutan *n* **159**
orb weaver *n* **162**
orbit *n* **143**
orc *n* **139**
orchestra *n* **128**
orchestra pit *n* **126**
orchestral
instruments *n* **128**
orchid *n* **38, 47**
order *v* **46, 69**
ordering online *n* **46**
ordinal numbers *n* **173**
Ordovician *adj* **157**
Ordovician *n* **157**
oregano *n* **59**
organic *adj* **23, 39, 53**
organic food section *n* **23**
organic vegetables *n* **55**
organization *n* **93**
organize *v* **92**
organized *adj* **93**
oriental fire-bellied toad *n* **163**
orienteering *n* **133, 148**
origami *n* **141**
original *adj* **93**
Orion *n* **144**
ornamental plants *n* **41**
orthodontist *n* **89**
Orthodox church *n* **44**
orthopaedics *n* **21**
oryx *n* **159**
osmium *n* **78**
osprey *n* **160**
osteopathy *n* **24**
ostrich *n* **160, 165**
otter *n* **158**
Ottoman *n* **30**
oud *n* **129**
ounce *n* **174**
out *adj* **113**
out *adv* **180**
out field *n* **111**
out of bounds *adj* **112**
outboard motor *n* **105**
outbox *n* **83**
outdoor activities *n* **133**
outer core *n* **145**
outfield *adj* **113**
outfielders *n* **113**
outgoing *adj* **10**
outlay *n* **94**
outpatient *n* **21**
outside *adv, prep* **180**
outside centre *n* **108**
outside hitter *n* **112**
outside lane *n* **96**
outside linebacker *n* **107**
outstanding *adj* **177**
oval *n* **74**
ovary *n* **04, 38**
oven *n* **27**
oven glove *n* **29**
over par *adj* **115**
overhanging eaves *n* **44**
over-the-counter
drugs *n* **49**
overalls *n* **13, 37**
overcast *adj* **154**
overdraft *n* **45, 94**
overeat *v* **23**
overfishing *n* **155**
overhead
compartment *n* **103**
overpass *n* **102**
overtake *v* **98**
overtime *n* **81**
own *v* **32**
Oxfords *n* **17**
oxygen *n* **78**
oxygen mask *n* **21, 50**
oyster *n* **54**
oyster mushroom *n* **56, 170**
oyster sauce *n* **60**
oystercatcher *n* **160**
ozone depletion *n* **155**
ozone layer *n* **155**

P

PA (personal assistant) *n* **81**
pack *v* **11, 32**
pack your bags *v* **131**
pack your lunch *v* **09**
package *n* **45**
packet *n* **52**
paddle *n* **114, 119**
paddleboarding *n* **119**
paddling pool *n* **25, 133**
paddock *n* **120**
paediatrics *n* **21**
paella *n* **72**
page *n* **138**
pain au chocolat *n* **62**
pain *n* **19**
painkillers *n* **20, 49**
paint *n* **37**
paint *v* **37**
paint a wall *v* **35**
paint kettle *n* **37**
paint stripper *n* **37**
paint tray *n* **37**
paint tube *n* **141**
paintballing *n* **133**
paintbrush *n* **37**
painted lady
butterfly *n* **162**
painter *n* **89**
painting *n* **26, 130, 141**
paisley *adj* **13**
pak-choi *n* **55**
Pakistan *n* **150, 153**
Pakistani *adj* **153**
palace *n* **132**
palate *n* **04**
Palau *n* **150, 153**
Palauan *adj* **153**
Paleogene *adj* **157**
Paleogene *n* **157**
paleontologist *n* **77**
Paleozoic
(old life) *adj* **157**
Paleozoic
(old life) *n* **157**
palette *n* **141**
palette knife *n* **141**
palladium *n* **78**
pallet *n* **87**
palm *n* **02, 41**
palm hearts *n* **55**
palm oil *n* **60**
palm tree *n* **134**
palomar knot *n* **121**
pampas grass *n* **38, 167**
Pamukkale *n* **145**
pan *n* **174**
panama *n* **16**
Panama *n* **150, 152**
Panamanian *adj* **152**
pancake *n* **65, 71**
pancreas *n* **04**
panda *n* **159**
paneer *n* **64**
pangolin *n* **159**
panpipe *n* **129**
pansy *n* **38**
panther chameleon *n* **163**
pantograph *n* **102**
pantry *n* **27**
panty liner *n* **49**
paparazzi *n* **127**
papaya *n* **58**
paper *adj* **176**
paper *n* **82, 155, 176**
paper clip,
paper clips *n* **73, 82**
paper napkin *n* **70**
paperback *n* **138**
papier-mâché *n* **141**
paprika *n* **59**
Papua New
Guinea *n* **150, 153**
Papua New
Guinean *adj* **153**
papyrus sedge *n* **167**
par *n* **115**
para athlete *n* **125**
para ice hockey *n* **122**
parachute *n* **125**
parachuting *n* **125**
paragliding *n* **125**
Paraguay *n* **149, 152**
Paraguayan *adj* **152**
parallel *adj* **74**
parallel bars *n* **125**
parallelogram *n* **74**
paramedic *n* **21, 50, 90**
paramotor *n* **103**
parasailing *n* **119**
parasol *n* **65**
parasports *n* **125**
parcel *n* **45**
parchment *n* **175**
parents *n* **05**
park *n* **42, 133**
park *v* **98**
parking attendant *n* **96**
parking meter *n* **96**
parking space *n* **32**
parkour *n* **133**
Parmesan *n* **64**
parole *n* **85**
parry *v* **117**
parsley *n* **59**
parsnip *n* **56**
parson's chameleon *n* **163**
particle accelerator *n* **75**
particle *n* **75**
partner *n* **05, 07**
parts of the body *n* **01**
parts of the day *n* **171**
pass *n* **112**
pass *v* **73, 98, 107, 108, 110**
passenger
aeroplane *n* **103**
passenger port *n* **106**
passengers *n* **102, 106**
passion flower *n* **169**
passion fruit *n* **58**
passionate *adj* **10**
Passover *n* **07**
passport *n* **104**
passport control *n* **104**
password *n* **83**
pasta *n* **64, 72**
pasta shells *n* **64**
pastels *n* **141**
pasteurized *adj* **61**
pasting table *n* **37**
pastrami *n* **64**
pastry *n* **63**
pastry brush *n* **29**
pasture *n* **86**
patch *n* **101**
patchwork *n* **142**
pâté *n* **64, 71**
patella *n* **03**
path *n* **41**
pathology *n* **21**
patience *n* **140**
patient *adj* **10, 93**
patient *n* **19, 20, 21**
patio *n* **25**
patio doors *n* **25**
patio garden *n* **41**
patio umbrella *n* **65**
patty pan *n* **56**
pause *v* **137**
pavement *n* **25, 43, 65**
paving *n* **41**
pavlova *n* **63**
pawn *n* **140**
pay *n* **81**
pay *v* **46**
pay by card *v* **94**
pay cut *n* **81**
pay in *v* **45**
pay-per-view channel *n* **137**
pay separately *v* **69**
pay slip *n* **81**
pay the bills *v* **09**
pay with cash *v* **94**
paying attention
to detail *n* **93**
pea *n* **55**
peace lily *n* **38**
peach *n* **57**
peacock butterfly *n* **162**
peacock *n* **161**
peak *n* **147**
peanut *n* **58, 68**
peanut allergy *n* **23**
peanut butter *n* **60**
pear *n* **58, 169**
peasants *n* **79**
peat *n* **39**
peat bog *n* **79**
pecan *n* **58, 168**
pectoral *n* **03**
pedal *n* **101**
pedal *v* **101**
pedestrian crossing *n* **96**
pedestrian zone *n* **42**
pedicure *n* **18**
pediment *n* **44**
peel *v* **29**
peeled prawn *n* **54**

peeler *n* **28**
peep toes *n* **17**
pelican *n* **160**
pelvis *n* **03**
pen *n* **73, 82, 86**
penalty area *n* **109**
penalty bench *n* **110**
penalty kick *n* **109**
penalty spot *n* **109**
pencil *n* **73, 82, 141, 175**
pencil case *n* **73**
pencil sharpener *n* **73, 82**
pendant *n* **16**
pendulous nose *n* **159**
peninsula *n* **147**
penis *n* **04**
penne *n* **64**
pen pal *n* **07**
penstock *n* **51**
pentagon *n* **74**
peony *n* **47, 168**
people carrier *n* **97**
pepper *n* **26, 56**
peppercorns *n* **59**
peppered moth *n* **162**
pepperoni *n* **64**
percent *n* **173**
percentage,
percentages *n* **74, 173**
perch *n* **54**
percussion *n* **128**
peregrine falcon *n* **160**
perennial *n* **41**
performance *n* **126**
performer *n* **126**
performing arts *n* **91**
perfume *n* **18**
perfumery *n* **47**
pergola *n* **41**
period drama *n* **137**
periodic table *n* **78**
periodical *n* **80**
permanent *adj* **81**
permanent
exhibition *n* **130**
Permian *adj* **157**
Permian *n* **157**
perpendicular *n* **74**
Persian *n* **164**
persimmon *n* **58**
personal assistant
(PA) *n* **90**
personal services *n* **91**
personal trainer *n* **124**
personality traits *n* **10**
perspire *v* **02**
Peru *n* **149, 152**
Peruvian *adj* **152**
pescatarian *adj* **23**
pescatarian *n* **23**
pesticide *n* **40, 55, 86**
pestle *n* **28, 76**
pet *n* **164**
pet food *n* **48**
pet services *n* **91**
pet shop *n* **46**
pet supplies *n* **164**
pet therapy *n* **24**
petal *n* **38**
petri dish *n* **77**
petrol *n* **97**
petrol pump *n* **97**
petrol station *n* **42, 97**
petroleum
engineering *n* **91**
pH level *n* **76**
pharmaceuticals *n* **91**
pharmacist *n* **49, 89**
pharmacy *n* **42, 49**
pharynx *n* **04**
pheasant *n* **53, 161**
Philippines *n* **151, 153**
Phillips screwdriver *n* **36**
philosopher *n* **79**
philosophy *n* **80**
phoenix *n* **139**
phone *n* **82**
phoropter *n* **22**
phosphorus *n* **78**
photo booth *v* **46**
photo finish *n* **116**
photocopier *n* **82**
photofit *n* **85**
photographer *n* **89**
photosynthesis *n* **77**
phrasal verbs *n* **178**
phrasebook *n* **131**
physical education *n* **73**
physical therapist *n* **89**
physics *n* **73, 75, 80**
physiotherapist *n* **89**
physiotherapy *n* **21**
piano *n* **128, 129**
piano overture *n* **128**
piccalilli *n* **60**
piccolo *n* **128**
pick *v* **57**
pick 'n' mix *n* **67**
pick mushrooms *v* **170**
pick someone up *v* **98**
pick up *v* **11, 178**
pick-up *n* **129**
pickaxe *n* **87**
pickled *adj* **72**
pickled beetroot *n* **60**
pickled onions *n* **60**
pickles *n* **60, 72**
pickpocketing *n* **85**
picnic *n* **133**
picnic basket *n* **133, 134**
picnic bench *n* **135**
pie dish *n* **29**
pieces *n* **140**
pier *n* **106**
pig *n* **165**
pig farm *n* **86**
pigeon *n* **160**
pigeon pose *n* **24**
piglet *n* **165**
pigtails *n* **12**
pike perch *n* **54**
Pilates *n* **124**
pile up *v* **178**
pileated
woodpecker *n* **160**
pillion *n* **100**
pillow *n* **26, 30**
pillowcase *n* **30**
pills *n* **20, 49**
pilot *n* **90, 103**
Pilsner *n* **68**
pin *n* **16, 33, 142**
PIN *n* **45**
pin *v* **117**
pinch *n* **29**
pincushion *n* **142**
pine nuts *n* **58**
pineapple *n* **58, 167**
pineapple juice *n* **65**
ping pong *n* **114**
pink *n* **141**
pinking scissors *n* **142**
pint *n* **174**
pint glass *n* **27**
pipe cutter *n* **36**
pipe *n* **33, 87, 98**
pipe organ *n* **128**
pipefish *n* **166**
pipette *n* **76**
piping bag *n* **29**
pirouette *v* **126**
Pisces *n* **144**
pistachio *n* **58**
pistol *n* **88**
pit lane *n* **123**
pit stop *n* **123**
pitch *n* **107, 109, 111, 128**
pitch *n* **109, 135**
pitch a tent *v* **135**
pitch *v* **113**
pitcher *n* **113**
pitcher plant *n* **168**
pitcher's mound *n* **113**
pitches
available *phr* **135**
pitta bread *n* **62, 72**
pixie *n* **139**
pizza *n* **70**
pizza cutter *n* **28**
pizza oven *n* **70**
pizzeria *n* **70**
place mat *n* **26**
place setting *n* **27**
place to live *n* **25**
placenta *n* **08**
placerias *n* **157**
plaice *n* **54**
plaid *adj* **13**
plain *n* **146**
plain *adj* **13**
plain flour *n* **62**
plait *n* **12**
plan your route *v* **148**
plane *n* **36**
plane *v* **35**
planets *n* **143**
plank pose *n* **24**
plankton *n* **77, 166**
plant cell *n* **77**
plant cutting *n* **39**
plant food *n* **39**
plant *n* **77, 167-169**
plant pot *n* **40**
plant *v* **39, 86**
plantains *n* **86**
plaque *n* **22**
plaster *n* **37, 49**
plaster *v* **37**
plaster *n* **20**
plastic *adj* **155, 176**
plastic *n* **155, 176**
plastic surgery *n* **21**
plastic waste *n* **155**
plate *n* **145**
plate tectonics *n* **145**
plateau *n* **146**
plateosaurus *n* **157**
platform *n* **84, 102, 118**
platforms *n* **17**
platform game *n* **136**
platform number *n* **102**
platinum *n* **78, 156**
platypus *n* **158**
play *n* **126**
play *v* **11, 113, 137, 140**
play a musical
instrument *v* **09**
play suit *n* **13**
play (the trumpet) *v* **128**
play with your kids *v* **09**
player *n* **108, 113, 114, 140**
player's number *n* **107**
players' bench *n*
107, 109, 110
players' dugout *n* **113**
players' entrance /
exit *n* **109**
playground *n* **43**
playing cards *n* **140**
playing surface *n* **108**
playpen *n* **08**
plead *v* **85**
pleasant *adj* **177**
pleased *adj* **06**
pleat *n* **14**
plié *v* **126**
Plimsoll line *n* **105**
plough *n* **86**
Plough *n* **144**
plug *n* **31, 33, 83**
plug in *v* **83**
plug-in hybrid *n* **97**
plughole *n* **31**
plum *n* **57, 169**
plum tomato *n* **56**
plumb line *n* **37**
plumber *n* **89**
plumbing *n* **33**
plunger *n* **31, 36**
plus sign *n* **74**
Pluto *n* **143**
plutonium *n* **78**
plywood *n* **35**
pneumatic drill *n* **87**
poach *v* **29**
poached *adj* **72**
poached egg *n* **61, 71**
pocket *n* **15, 125, 142**
pod *n* **55**
podcast *n* **84**
podium *n* **116, 128**
poetry therapy *n* **24**
point *n* **111**
point *v* **11**
point guard *n* **112**
point out *v* **178**
points *n* **140**
poison dart frog *n* **163**
poisoning *n* **19**
Poland *n* **151, 153**
polar bear *n* **159**
polar region *n* **146**
Polaris *n* **144**
pole *n* **121**
pole position *n* **123**
Pole Star *n* **144**
pole stretcher *n* **50**
pole vault *n* **116**
police *n* **50**
police bike *n* **50**
police car *n* **50**
police cell *n* **50**
police dog *n* **50**
police hat *n* **50**
police officer *n* **50, 89**
police station *n* **42, 50**
Polish *adj* **153**
polish *n* **34**
polite *adj* **10**
politics *n* **80**
polka dot plant *n* **38**
pollock *n* **54**
pollution *n* **155**
polo *n* **120**
polo shirt *n* **14**
polonium *n* **78**
pomegranate *n* **58, 168**
pomelo *n* **57**
Pomeranian *n* **164**
pommel *n* **120**
pommel horse *n* **125**
poncho *n* **15**
pond *n* **41, 86**
ponytail *n* **12**
poodle *n* **164**
pool *n* **125**
pop *n* **129**
Pop Art *n* **130**
pop concert *n* **129**
pop-up *n* **84**

pop-up tent *n* **135**
popcorn *n* **127**
poplar *n* **168**
popper *n* **13**
popping crease *n* **111**
poppy *n* **38**
poppy seeds *n* **59**
popular music *n* **129**
porch *n* **25**
porch light *n* **25**
porcini *n* **170**
porcupine *n* **158**
porcupine fish *n* **166**
pores *n* **12**
pork *n* **53**
porpoise *n* **166**
porridge *n* **71**
port *n* **68, 106**
portable speakers *n* **95**
portcullis *n* **44**
porter *n* **21, 131**
portfolio *n* **92, 94**
portion *n* **26**
Portugal *n* **151, 153**
Portuguese *adj* **153**
Portuguese man-of-war *n* **166**
position markers *n* **129**
positive *adj* **75**
positive electrode *n* **75**
post *v* **84**
post office *n* **42, 45**
Post-Impressionism *n* **130**
postal worker *n* **45**
postbox *n* **45**
postcard *n* **48, 132**
postcode *n* **45**
poster paint *n* **141**
postgraduate *n* **80**
postman *n* **45, 90**
postmark *n* **45**
postwoman *n* **45, 90**
pot plant *n* **47**
pot up *v* **39**
potassium *n* **78**
potato *n* **56, 86**
potato cakes *n* **71**
potato fork *n* **40**
pothole *n* **101**
potion *n* **139**
potted plant *n* **41**
potter *n* **141**
potter's wheel *n* **141**
pottery *n* **141**
potting shed *n* **39**
potty *n* **08**
pouch *n* **158**
poultry *n* **48, 53, 165**
poultry farm *n* **86**
pounce *v* **159**
pound *n* **174**
pour *v* **29**
pour down *v* **178**
powder *n* **49**
powder puff *n* **18**
powdered milk *n* **61**
power *n* **33**
power cut *n* **33**
power forward *n* **112**
power lead *n* **83**
power station *n* **44**
power supply *n* **51**
practical *adj* **93**
practice swing *n* **115**
prairie *n* **146**
pram *n* **08**
praseodymium *n* **78**
praying mantis *n* **162**
Precambrian *adj* **157**
Precambrian *n* **157**
prefab house *n* **32**
pregnancy *n* **08**
pregnancy test *n* **08**
pregnant *adj* **08**
premiere *n* **127**
premolars *n* **03**
preparation *n* **54**
prepositions *n* **148, 180**
prescription *n* **20, 49**
present *n* **07**
presentation *n* **82, 95**
presenter *n* **84, 137**
presenter remote *n* **95**
presenting *n* **95**
preserved fruit *n* **60**
preserving jar *n* **60**
press ups *n* **124**
presser foot *n* **142**
pressure cooker *n* **28**
pressure gauge *n* **33**
pretty *adj* **177**
pretzel *n* **62**
preview *n* **137**
price *n* **69**
price list *n* **70**
price tag *n* **47**
prickly pear *n* **58, 168**
prima donna *n* **126**
primer *n* **37**
prince *n* **79**
princess *n* **79**
principal *n* **73**
print *v* **83**
printer *n* **82**
printing *n* **141, 175**
priority traffic *n* **96**
prism *n* **75**
prison *n* **85**
prison guards *n* **85**
prisoners *n* **85**
private bathroom *n* **131**
private investigator *n* **89**
private jet *n* **103**
private room *n* **21**
probe *n* **22**
problem-solving *n* **93**
proboscis monkey *n* **159**
proceed to checkout *v* **46**
processed food *n* **23**
producer *n* **126, 127**
production *n* **91**
professional *adj* **93**
professional attributes *n* **93**
professional expertise *n* **93**
programme *n* **126, 137**
project management *n* **93**
projector *n* **82, 95**
promenade *n* **134**
promethium *n* **78**
propagate *v* **39**
propeller *n* **103, 105**
property *n* **32, 91**
proposal *n* **82**
props *n* **126, 127**
prosciutto *n* **64**
prosecution *n* **85**
prosecutor *n* **85**
prostate gland *n* **04**
protactinium *n* **78**
protea *n* **38**
protective padding *n* **110**
protein *n* **23**
proton *n* **76**
protractor *n* **73, 74**
proud *adj* **06**
prove *v* **62**
prow *n* **105**
prowl *v* **159**
prune *v* **39**
prunes *n* **58**
pruning knife *n* **40**
pruning saw *n* **40**
psychiatry *n* **21**
psychologist *n* **90**
psychotherapy *n* **24**
public address system *n* **102**
public footpath *n* **148**
public relations (PR) *n* **91**
public speaking *n* **93**
puck *n* **110**
pudding *n* **69**
puddle *n* **154**
puff pastry *n* **63**
pufferfish *n* **166**
pug *n* **164**
pull *v* **11**
pull-along toy *n* **08**
pulp *n* **03, 57**
pulses *n* **23**
pumice *n* **156**
pumice stone *n* **31**
pump *n* **101**
pumpkin *n* **56**
punch *v* **117**
punchbag *n* **117**
punctual *adj* **93**
puncture *n* **101**
puncture repair kit *n* **101**
punk *n* **129**
pupil *n* **01, 73**
puppet *n* **08**
puppy *n* **164**
purchasing *n* **91**
purple *n, adj* **141**
purple loosestrife *n* **168**
purr *v* **164**
purse *n* **16, 94**
push ups *n* **124**
push *v* **11**
put away *v* **178**
put on *v* **14, 178**
put on makeup *v* **09**
put the children to bed *v* **09**
put together *v* **178**
put up shelves *v* **35**
putt *v* **115**
putter *n* **115**
puzzle game *n* **136**
puzzles *n* **138**
pyjamas *n* **14**
pylon *n* **51**
pyramid *n* **74**
pyramids of Giza *n* **44**

Q

Qatar *n* **151, 153**
Qatari *adj* **153**
qibla prayer wall *n* **44**
quack *v* **165**
quad bike *n* **100**
quad biking *n* **133**
quadriceps *n* **03**
quail *n* **53**
quail egg *n* **61**
qualifying *n* **123**
quart *n* **174**
quarter *num* **173**
quarter of an hour *n* **171**
quarter past one *n* **171**
quarter to two *n* **171**
quarterback *n* **107**
quarterdeck *n* **105**
quartz *n* **156**
quartzite *n* **156**
Quaternary *adj* **157**
Quaternary *n* **157**
quay *n* **106**
queen *n* **79, 140**
queen of the Andes *n* **167**
quest *n* **139**
question *v* **73**
question mark *n* **175**
queue *n* **48, 104, 132**
queue *v* **104**
quiet *adj* **176**
quilt *n* **30**
quilted jacket *n* **15**
quilting *n* **142**
quince *n* **58**
quiver *n* **125**
quiz show *n* **137**

R

rabbit *n* **53, 158, 164**
rabbit hutch *n* **164**
raccoon *n* **158**
race *n* **116**
race number *n* **100**
race track *n* **123**
racecourse *n* **120**
racehorse *n* **120**
racing bike *n* **100, 101**
racing car *n* **97, 123**
racing dive *n* **118**
racing driver *n* **123**
racing events *n* **116**
racing overalls *n* **123**
rack *n* **125**
racket *n* **114**
racket games *n* **114**
racquetball *n* **114**
radar *n* **105**
radar speed gun *n* **50**
radiated tortoise *n* **163**
radiator *n* **33, 98**
radicchio *n* **55**
radio antenna *n* **105**
radio *n* **50, 84, 88, 136**
radio DJ *n* **90**
radio station *n* **84**
radio telescope *n* **144**
radio waves *n* **75**
radioactivity *n* **75**
radiology *n* **21**
radish *n* **56**
radium *n* **78**
radius *n* **03, 74**
radon *n* **78**
raffia palm *n* **167**
rafter *n* **87**
rafting *n* **119**

Ragdoll *n* **164**
rail network *n* **102**
railing *n* **65**
railway *n* **148**
railway terminal *n* **106**
rain *n* **51, 154**
rain forest *n* **146, 159**
rainbow *n* **154**
rainbow trout *n* **54**
raincoat *n* **15**
raindrop *n* **154**
rainy *adj* **154**
raise *n* **81**
raise *v* **11**
raised mudguard *n* **100**
raisin *n* **58**
rake *n* **40**
rake (leaves) *v* **39**
rake (soil) *v* **39**
rally *n* **114**
rally driving *n* **123**
ram *n* **165**
ramekin *n* **28**
ramen *n* **64, 72**
rapeseed *n* **86**
rapeseed oil *n* **60**
rapids *n* **119, 146**
ras el hanout *n* **59**
rash *n* **19**
raspberry *n* **57**
raspberry jam *n* **60**
rat *n* **158**
rattle *n* **08**
rattlesnake *n* **163**
raven *n* **160**
raw *adj* **56**
raw meat *n* **53**
ray *n* **166**
razor blade *n* **31**
razor-shell *n* **54**
reach a consensus *v* **95**
reach an agreement *v* **95**
reaction *n* **76**
reaction direction *n* **76**
reactor *n* **51**
read *v* **73**
read a map *v* **148**
read a newspaper *v* **09**
reading *n* **138**
reading a map *n* **148**
reading glasses *n* **22, 49**
reading light *n* **103**
reading list *n* **80**
reading room *n* **80**
reality TV *n* **137**
reamer *n* **36**
rear light *n* **101**
rear suspension *n* **123**
rear wheel *n* **99**
rear wing *n* **97, 123**
reasonable *adj* **10**
rebound *n* **112**
receipt *n* **48, 69, 94**
receptacle *n* **38**
reception *n* **131**
receptionist *n* **81, 90, 131**
reconnaissance aircraft *n* **88**
reconnaissance vehicle *n* **88**
record player *n* **136**
record shop *n* **46**
record *v* **137**
recorder *n* **129**
recording studio *n* **84**
records *n* **136**
recover *v* **20**
recovery room *n* **21**
recruitment agency *n* **92**
rectangle *n* **74**
recycling *n* **91, 155**
recycling bin *n* **33, 34**
red *n* **141**
red blood cell *n* **77**
red cabbage *n* **55**
red card *n* **109**
red carpet *n* **127**
red deer *n* **158**
red fox *n* **159**
red giant *n* **144**
red hair *n* **12**
red line *n* **110**
red meat *n* **53**
red mullet *n* **54**
red panda *n* **159**
red salamander *n* **163**
red wine *n* **52, 68**
red-eyed tree frog *n* **163**
redcurrant *n* **57**
reed *n* **167**
reef *n* **147**
reel *n* **121**
reel in *v* **121**
refectory *n* **80**
referee *n* **107-109, 112**
referee crease *n* **110**
reflected radiation *n* **155**
reflection *n* **75**
reflector *n* **100, 101**
reflector strap *n* **100**
reflector telescope *n* **144**
reflexology *n* **24**
refraction *n* **75**
refractor telescope *n* **144**
refrigerator *n* **27**
refund *v* **46**
reggae *n* **129**
registered mail *n* **45**
registered trademark *n* **175**
regulator *n* **118**
reiki *n* **24**
reindeer *n* **159**
reins *n* **120**
relationships *n* **05, 07**
relaxation *n* **24**
relaxed *adj* **06**
relaxing *adj* **177**
relay race *n* **116**
release *v* **121**
reliable *adj* **10, 93**
remains *n* **79**
remarkable *adj* **177**
remember *v* **11**
remote *n* **137**
remote control *n* **26, 83, 136**
removal van *n* **32**
renew *v* **80**
renewable energy *n* **51**
rent *v* **32**
rent a cottage *v* **131**
rent out *v* **32**
renting a house *n* **32**
repair *v* **11, 33**
reply *v* **83**
reply to all *v* **83**
report *n* **82**
reporter *n* **137**
reproduction *n* **77**
reproductive *n* **04**
reproductive organs *n* **04**
reptiles *n* **163**
Republic of the Congo *n* **149, 152**
research *n* **91, 93**
research and development (R&D) *n* **91**
reserve *v* **80**
reservoir *n* **51**
residential area *n* **32**
residential buildings *n* **44**
residential district *n* **42**
resign *v* **81**
resit *v* **73**
respectful *adj* **177**
respiratory *n* **04**
responsible *adj* **93**
rest *v* **20**
restaurant *n* **42, 69, 131**
restaurant manager *n* **69**
restricted area *n* **112**
resurfacing *n* **87**
resuscitate *v* **20**
retail *n* **91**
reticulated python *n* **163**
retina *n* **22**
retinal camera *n* **22**
retire *v* **07, 81**
retriever *n* **164**
return *n* **114**
return *v* **46, 80**
return crease *n* **111**
return ticket *n* **131**
reusable cup *n* **70**
rev counter *n* **99**
reverb *n* **129**
reverse *v* **96**
reversible direction *n* **76**
review *n* **138**
revise *v* **73**
rewind *v* **137**
rewire the house *v* **35**
rhenium *n* **78**
rhinoceros *n* **158**
rhinoceros beetle *n* **162**
rhodium *n* **78**
rhododendron *n* **38**
rhombus *n* **74**
rhubarb *n* **58**
rib *n* **03, 53**
rib cage *n* **03**
ribs *n* **70**
ribbon *n* **63, 125, 142**
rice *n* **72, 86**
rice bowl *n* **27**
rice noodles *n* **64**
rice pudding *n* **63**
rich *adj* **52**
ride *v* **11**
ride pillion *v* **100**
rider *n* **100, 120**
ridge *n* **146**
ridge beam *n* **87**
riding boot *n* **17, 120**
riding crop *n* **120**
riding hat *n* **120**
rifle *n* **88**
rig *n* **129**
rigging *n* **119**
right angle *n* **74**
right bend *n* **96**
right cornerback *n* **107**
right defenceman *n* **110**
right defensive end *n* **107**
right defensive tackle *n* **107**
right guard *n* **107**
right safety *n* **107**
right side *n* **112**
right tackle *n* **107**
right wing *n* **108**
right winger *n* **110**
rim *n* **101**
rind *n* **61, 64**
ring *n* **16, 170**
ring binder *n* **82**
ring finger *n* **02**
ring ties *n* **40**
ring-tailed lemur *n* **159**
rings *n* **125, 143**
rinse *v* **22**
rip out *v* **178**
ripe *adj* **57**
rise *v* **62**
risotto *n* **72**
river *n* **147, 148**
river features *n* **147, 148**
road *n* **96**
road bike *n* **101**
road markings *n* **96**
road signs *n* **96**
roadmap *n* **95**
roadworks *n* **87, 96**
roadworks ahead *n* **96**
roar *v* **159**
roast *n* **29, 72**
robbers *n* **50**
robbery *n* **50, 85**
robe *n* **80**
rock *n* **129**
rock climbing *n* **125**
rock garden *n* **41**
rock pool *n* **134**
rock star *n* **90**
rocket *n* **143**
rocket *n* **55**
rockhopper penguin *n* **161**
rocks *n* **147, 156**
rocking chair *n* **26**
rocking horse *n* **08**
rodeo *n* **120**
roe deer *n* **158**
roentgenium *n* **78**
role-playing game *n* **136**
roll *n* **62**
roll *v* **29**
roller *n* **37, 87**
roller bar *n* **97**
roller blind *n* **26**
roller coaster *n* **133**
roller extension pole *n* **37**
rollerblading *n* **133**
rollerskating *n* **125**
rolling pin *n* **29**
romaine lettuce *n* **55**
romance *n* **138**
Romania *n* **151, 153**
Romanian *adj* **153**
romantic *adj* **10, 177**
romantic comedy *n* **127**
romper suit *n* **13**
roof *n* **25, 98**
roof garden *n* **41**
roof ladder *n* **50**
roof rack *n* **97**
roof tiles *n* **87**
rook *n* **140, 160**
room service *n* **131**
room with a view *n* **131**
rooster *n* **165**
root *n* **03**
rope *n* **117, 119, 125**
rose *n* **38**
rosé *n* **68, 52**
rose of Sharon *n* **38**
rose-ringed parakeet *n* **161**
rosemary *n* **38, 59**
rotor *n* **51**
rotor blade *n* **103**
rotten *adj* **57**
rough *n* **115**
round *n* **117**
round neck *n* **14**
roundabout *n* **96**
route number *n* **99**
router *n* **35, 83**

rover *n* **143**
row *n* **103, 126**
rower *n* **119**
rowing *n* **119**
rowing boat *n* **105**
rowing machine *n* **124**
royal circle *n* **126**
rubber *n* **73, 82**
rubber *adj* **176**
rubber *n* **176**
rubber bands *n* **82**
rubber gloves *n* **34**
rubber plant *n* **38**
rubber ring *n* **134**
rubber tree *n* **169**
rubbish bin *n* **27, 33**
rubidium *n* **78**
ruby *n* **156**
ruck *n* **108**
rucksack *n* **16, 135**
rudder *n* **103, 119**
rude *adj* **10**
rug *n* **26**
rugby *n* **108**
rugby ball *n* **108**
rugby jersey *n* **108**
rugby pitch *n* **108**
rugby positions *n* **108**
rugby shirt *n* **108**
ruler *n* **73, 74, 72, 174**
rum *n* **68**
rum and cola *n* **68**
rump steak *n* **53**
run away *v* **178**
run out (of) *v* **178**
run out of time *v* **95**
run *v* **11, 111, 113**
rung *n* **36**
runner beans *n* **55**
runners *n* **122**
running *n* **124**
running back *n* **107**
running blades *n* **125**
running machine *n* **124**
running shoes *n* **17**
running spikes *n* **17**
runny nose *n* **19**
runway *n* **104**
rush hour *n* **42, 102**
rushes *n* **41**
Russian *adj* **153**
Russian Federation *n* **150, 151, 153**
rustic baguette *n* **62**
ruthenium *n* **78**
rutherfordium *n* **78**
Rwanda *n* **149, 152**
Rwandan *adj* **152**
rye bread *n* **62**

S

sabre *n* **117**
sabre-toothed cat *n* **157**
sacred ibis *n* **160**
sad *adj* **06**
saddle *n* **101, 120**
saddlebag *n* **120**
safari park *n* **133**
safe *adj* **113**
safe *n* **131**
safety area *n* **117**
safety barrier *n* **122**
safety glasses *n* **87**
safety gloves *n* **87**
safety goggles *n* **36, 76**
safety notice board *n* **87**
safety pin *n* **20**
saffron *n* **59**
sage *n* **59**
Sagittarius *n* **144**
sail *n* **119, 134**
sail fish *n* **166**
sailing *n* **119**
sailing boat *n* **105**
sailor, sailors *n* **88, 99**
sake cup *n* **27**
salad *n* **55, 65**
salad drawer *n* **27**
salad vegetables *n* **55**
salami *n* **53, 64**
salary *n* **81**
sale *n* **47**
sale sign *n* **47**
sales *n* **91**
sales assistant *n* **89**
salmon fillet *n* **54**
saloon *n* **97**
salt *n* **23, 26**
salt beef *n* **64**
salted *adj* **54, 61, 64**
saltwater crocodile *n* **163**
salty *adj* **52**
Salvadoran *adj* **152**
samara *n* **169**
samarium *n* **78**
Sammarinese *adj* **153**
Samoa *n* **150, 153**
Samoan *adj* **153**
San Marino *n* **151, 153**
sand *n* **35, 39, 134**
sand *v* **37**
sand dune *n* **146**
sand martin *n* **160**
sand rose *n* **156**
sandals *n* **17**
sandcastle *n* **134**
sander *n* **35**
sandpaper *n* **36-37**
sandpit *n* **43**
sandstone *n* **156**
sandstorm *n* **154**
sandwich *n* **65, 70, 72**
sandwich pickle *n* **60**
sanitary towel *n* **49**
São Tomé and Príncipe *n* **149, 152**
São Toméan *adj* **152**
sapphire *n* **156**
sardines *n* **54, 64**
sari *n* **15**
sarong *n* **15**
sash window *n* **25**
satellite *n* **143**
satellite dish *n* **25, 136**
satellite TV *n* **137**
satire *n* **137**
satnav *n* **99**
satsuma *n* **57**
saturated fat *n* **23**
Saturday *n* **172**
Saturn *n* **143**
sauce, sauces *n* **60, 64, 70**
saucepan *n* **28**
Saudi *adj* **153**
Saudi Arabia *n* **151, 153**
sauerkraut *n* **60**
sauna *n* **124**
sausage, sausages *n* **53, 71**
sausage patties *n* **71**
sauté *v* **29**
savannah *n* **146, 158**
save up *v* **32**
savings *n* **45**
savings account *n* **45**
savoy cabbage *n* **55**
savoury *adj* **52**
saw *v* **35**
sawfish *n* **166**
saxophone *n* **128-129**
scale *n* **54, 104, 128, 148**
scales *n* **20, 29, 45, 76, 163, 174**
scallop *n* **54**
scalpel *n* **21, 77**
scan *n* **21**
scandium *n* **78**
scanner *n* **48, 82, 104**
scapula *n* **03**
scarecrow *n* **86**
scared *adj* **06**
scarf *n* **16**
scarlet *n* **141**
scarlet ibis *n* **160**
scarlet macaw *n* **161**
scenic *adj* **132**
schist *n* **156**
scholarship *n* **80**
school *n* **43, 73, 148**
school bag *n* **73**
school bus *n* **99**
school equipment *n* **73**
school shirt *n* **13**
school students *n* **73**
school tie *n* **13**
school uniform *n* **13**
school zone *n* **96**
science, sciences *n* **73, 80**
science fiction *n* **127, 138**
scientist *n* **90**
scimitar *n* **79**
scissors *n* **20, 37, 82**
scissors *n* **142**
scoop *n* **28**
scoop *v* **110**
scootering *n* **133**
score *n* **114, 128, 140**
scoreboard *n* **107, 111**
scorekeepers bench *n* **110**
Scorpio *n* **144**
scorpion *n* **162**
Scotch and water *n* **68**
scouring pad *n* **34**
scrambled eggs *n* **61, 71**
scraper *n* **37**
scratch *v* **164**
screen *n* **45, 83, 111, 127, 136-137**
screen wash *n* **97**
screen wash reservoir *n* **98**
screenplay *n* **127**
screenwriter *n* **127**
screw *n* **36**
screw base *n* **33**
scribe *n* **79**
script *n* **126**
scroll *n* **79**
scrotum *n* **04**
scrub the floor *v* **34**
scrubbing brush *n* **34**
scrubs *n* **13, 21**
scrum *n* **108**
scrum-half *n* **108**
scuba diving *n* **118**
sculpting *n* **141**
sculptor *n* **89**
sculpture *n* **130, 141**
sea *n* **134, 145**
sea bass *n* **54**
sea bed *n* **51**
sea bream *n* **54**
sea buckthorn *n* **169**
sea cave *n* **147**
sea krait *n* **163**
sea lion *n* **166**
sea serpent *n* **139**
sea slug *n* **166**
sea stack *n* **147**
sea urchin *n* **166**
sea vessels *n* **105**
seaborgium *n* **78**
seafood *n* **54**
seafood allergy *n* **23**
seafood platter *n* **54**
seagull *n* **160**
seahorse *n* **166**
seal *n* **159, 166**
sealant *n* **37**
seam *n* **111, 142**
seamount *n* **145**
seaplane *n* **103**
seashore *n* **147**
seasonal fruit *n* **57**
seasons *n* **172**
seat *n* **26, 33, 100, 102-103, 120**
seat back *n* **103**
seat belt, seat belts *n* **103, 123**
seat post *n* **101**
seated forward fold *n* **24**
seated twist *n* **24**
seating *n* **47, 126**
seaweed *n* **134, 166**
secateurs *n* **40**
second *n* **171**
second *num* **173**
second base *n* **113**
second hand *n* **171**
second row *n* **108**
second-hand shop *n* **46**
secondary road *n* **148**
secretary *n* **90**
secretive *adj* **10**
sections *n* **48**
security *n* **104**
security bit *n* **36**
security guard *n* **89-90, 130**
sedative *n* **49**
sedimentary *adj* **156**
see *v* **11**
seed, seeds *n* **40, 58 168**
seed tray *n* **40**
seeded bread *n* **62**
seedless *adj* **57**
seesaw *n* **43**
segment *n* **57**
selenium *n* **78**
self checkout *n* **48**
self management *n* **93**
self-help *n* **138**
self-inflating mattress *n* **135**
self-raising flour *n* **62**
self-tanning lotion *n* **18**
selfish *adj* **10**
sell *v* **46**
semi-detached *n* **32**
semi-hard cheese *n* **61**
semi-metals *n* **78**
semi-skimmed milk *n* **61**
semi-soft cheese *n* **61**
semicolon *n* **175**
semiconductor *n* **75**
seminal gland *n* **04**

send *v* **83**
send a parcel *v* **09**
Senegal *n* **149, 152**
Senegalese *adj* **152**
sensitive *adj* **10, 18**
sentence *n* **85**
sepal *n* **38**
September *n* **172**
Serbia *n* **151, 153**
Serbian *adj* **153**
series *n* **137**
serious *adj* **06, 10**
serve *v* **65, 114**
service charge *n* **69**
service focused *adj* **93**
service included *phr* **69**
service line *n* **114**
service not included *phr* **69**
service station *n* **148**
service the car *v* **98**
service vehicle *n* **104**
services *n* **131**
serving spoon *n* **27**
sesame allergy *n* **23**
sesame seed oil *n* **60**
set *n* **114, 126**
set honey *n* **60**
set menu *n* **69**
set off *v* **98, 178**
set sail *v* **106**
set square *n* **73-74**
set the alarm *v* **09**
set the table *v* **26, 34**
sets *n* **126**
setter *n* **112, 164**
seven *num* **173**
seventeen *num* **173**
seventh *num* **173**
seventy *num* **173**
sew *v* **142**
sewing *n* **142**
sewing box *n* **142**
sewing machine *n* **142**
sewing needle *n* **142**
Seychelles *n* **149, 152**
Seychellois *adj* **152**
shade plants *n* **41**
shaft *n* **115**
shaggy bracket fungus *n* **170**
shaggy mane mushroom *n* **170**
shake *v* **11**
shake hands *v* **92**
shake your head *v* **02**
shale *n* **51**
shale gas *n* **51**
shallot *n* **56**
shallow *adj* **176**
shallow end *n* **118**
shaobing *n* **62**
shapes *n* **74**
share *v* **84**
share price *n* **94**
share your screen *v* **95**
shares *n* **94**
sharp *adj* **128**
sharpening stone *n* **36**
shave *v* **09, 12, 31**
shaved head *n* **12**
shaving foam *n* **31**
shears *n* **40**
shed *n* **25, 39**
sheep *n* **165**
sheep farm *n* **86**
sheep's milk *n* **61**
sheep's milk cheese *n* **61**
sheer *v* **165**
sheet *n* **30, 119**
shelf *n* **26-27**
shell *n* **58, 61, 163**
shelter *n* **44**
shelves *n* **27, 48**
sherry *n* **68**
shiatsu *n* **24**
shield *n* **40, 79**
shih tzu *n* **164**
shiitake mushroom *n* **56, 170**
shin *n* **01**
shin guard *n* **110**
shiny *adj* **176**
ship's captain *n* **89**
shipping *n* **91**
shipping container *n* **106**
ships *n* **105**
shipyard *n* **106**
shirt *n* **15**
shiver *v* **02**
shocked *adj* **06**
shocking *adj* **177**
shoe accessories *n* **17**
shoe brush *n* **17**
shoe polish *n* **17**
shoe shop *n* **46**
shoe trees *n* **17**
shoelaces *n* **17**
shoes *n* **17**
shoe accessories *n* **17**
shoot *v* **112**
shooting guard *n* **112**
shop *n* **42**
shop window *n* **25**
shoplifting *n* **85**
shopper *n* **47**
shopping *n* **46, 179**
shopping centre *n* **42, 47**
shopping channel *n* **137**
shopping list *n* **46**
shopping mall *n* **42, 47**
shopping spree *n* **46**
short *adj* **12, 176**
short corner *n* **112**
short hair *n* **12**
short-sighted *adj* **22**
short-sleeved shirt *n* **14**
shortbread *n* **63**
shorts *n* **14**
shot *n* **68**
shot put *n* **116**
shotgun *n* **88**
shoulder *n* **01**
shoulder bag *n* **16**
shoulder blade *n* **03**
shoulder pad *n* **15, 107, 110**
shoulder strap *n* **16**
shoulder-launched missile *n* **88**
shoulder-length hair *n* **12**
shout *v* **11**
shovel *n* **40, 87**
show of hands *n* **95**
show off *v* **178**
shower *n* **31**
shower block *n* **135**
shower curtain *n* **31**
shower door *n* **31**
shower gel *n* **31**
showjumping *n* **120**
shredder *n* **82**
shrinking glaciers *n* **155**
shrubs *n* **41**
shrug *v* **02**
shuffle *v* **140**
shutoff valve *n* **33**
shutter *n* **25**
shuttle bus *n* **99**
shuttlecock *n* **114**
shy *adj* **10**
Siamese *n* **164**
Siberian husky *n* **164**
siblings *n* **05**
side *n* **69, 74**
side car *n* **100**
side dishes *n* **72**
side effects *n* **49**
side order *n* **69**
side parting *n* **12**
side plate *n* **27**
side shuffles *n* **124**
side street *n* **42**
side view *n* **97**
side-saddle *n* **120**
sideboard *n* **26**
sideburns *n* **12**
sidedeck *n* **119**
sideline *n* **107, 112, 114**
sidestroke *n* **118**
sidewinder *n* **163**
Sierra Leone *n* **149, 152**
Sierra Leonean *adj* **152**
sieve *n* **28**
sieve *v* **39**
sift *v* **62**
sigh *v* **02**
sightseeing *n* **99, 132**
sign *n* **104**
sign a contract *v* **92**
signal *n* **102**
signature *n* **45, 83**
signet ring *n* **16**
silencer *n* **98, 100**
silicon *n* **78**
silk *n* **13**
silk tree *n* **168**
silly *adj* **10**
silo *n* **86**
silt *n* **39**
Silurian *adj* **157**
Silurian *n* **157**
silver *adj* **176**
silver *n* **78, 116, 156, 176**
sim card *n* **48**
simmer *v* **29**
simulation game *n* **136**
sing *v* **11**
Singapore *n* **151, 153**
Singaporean *adj* **153**
singer *n* **89**
single *adj* **68**
single bed *n* **30**
single cream *n* **61**
single parent *n* **05**
single quotation mark *n* **175**
single room *n* **131**
single-burner camping stove *n* **135**
singles *n* **114**
sink *n* **27**
sink *n* **33**
sinus *n* **04**
sip *v* **52**
sirloin steak *n* **53**
sister *n* **05**
sister-in-law *n* **05**
sit down *v* **11**
sit-up *n* **124**
sitar *n* **129**
sitcom *n* **137**
site manager *n* **89**
site manager's office *n* **135**
six *num* **173**
sixteen *num* **173**
sixth *num* **173**
sixty *num* **173**
skate *n* **54, 122**
skate *v* **110**
skate wing *n* **54**
skateboard *n* **125**
skateboarding *n* **125, 133**
skein *n* **142**
skeleton *n* **03, 122**
sketch *n* **141**
sketch pad *n* **141**
skewer *n* **28**
ski *n* **119, 122**
ski boot *n* **17, 122**
ski instructor *n* **89**
ski jacket *n* **122**
ski jump *n* **122**
ski lodge *n* **122**
ski pole *n* **122**
ski resort *n* **122**
ski run *n* **122**
ski slope *n* **122**
skier *n* **122**
skiing *n* **122**
skillet *n* **28**
skimmed milk *n* **61**
skin *n* **01, 58**
skin care *n* **49**
skin type *n* **18**
skip *v* **124**
skipping *n* **133**
skipping rope *n* **08, 124**
skirt *n* **14**
skirting board *n* **30**
skittles *n* **08**
skull *n* **03**
skunk *n* **158**
skydiving *n* **125**
skyscraper *n* **42**
slalom *n* **122**
slate *n* **156**
sledgehammer *n* **87**
sledging *n* **122**
sleep in *v* **178**
sleeping bag *n* **135**
sleeping compartment *n* **102**
sleeping mat *n* **135**
sleeping pills *n* **49**
sleepsuit *n* **13**
sleet *n* **154**
sleeve *n* **15**
sleeveless *adj* **15**
sleigh *n* **122**
slice *n* **53, 114**
slice *v* **29, 62**
sliced bread *n* **62**
slicer *n* **62**
slide *n* **43, 77, 95**
slide *v* **113**
slides *n* **17**
sling *n* **19-20**
slingback heels *n* **17**
slip *n* **14, 111**
slip road *n* **96**
slip-ons *n* **17**
slippers *n* **14, 17**
slit skirt *n* **15**
sloth *n* **159**
slotted spoon *n* **28**
Slovakia *n* **151, 153**
Slovakian *adj* **153**
Slovenia *n* **151, 153**
Slovenian *adj* **153**
slow *adj* **176**
slow down *v* **98**
slug *n* **162**
sluice gates *n* **51**
small *adj* **176**
small creatures *n* **162**
small forward *n* **112**
small intestine *n* **04**

smartpen *n* **95**
smartphone *n* **83**
smartwatch *n* **83**
smell *v* **11**
smile *v* **02**
smog *n* **154**
smoke *n* **50**
smoke alarm *n* **50**
smoked *adj* **54, 72**
smoked fish *n* **64**
smoked haddock *n* **64**
smoked mackerel *n* **64, 71**
smoked meat *n* **53**
smoked salmon *n* **64, 71**
smooth orange juice *n* **65**
smoothie *n* **52**
smuggling *n* **85**
snack bar *n* **48, 65**
snacks *n* **65**
snail *n* **162**
snake plant *n* **38**
snakes and ladders *n* **140**
snap *n* **140**
snare drum *n* **128**
sneeze *v* **02, 20**
snell knot *n* **121**
Snellen chart *n* **22**
sniff *v* **164**
snooker *n* **125**
snore *v* **02, 30**
snorkel *n* **118**
snorkel and mask *n* **15, 134**
snorkelling *n* **118**
snort *v* **165**
snow *n* **154**
snow goose *n* **160**
snow leopard *n* **159**
snow tyres *n* **97**
snowboarding *n* **122**
snowdrift *n* **154**
snowdrop *n* **167**
snowflake *n* **154**
snowmobile *n* **122**
snowstorm *n* **154**
snowsuit *n* **13**
snowy *adj* **154**
snowy owl *n* **161**
soap *n* **31**
soap dish *n* **31**
soap opera *n* **137**
social media *n* **84**
social sciences *n* **80**
sociologist *n* **89**
sociology *n* **80**
sock, socks *n* **14, 107**
socket *n* **33**
socket wrench *n* **36**
soda bread *n* **62**
sodium *n* **78**
sofa *n* **26**
sofa bed *n* **26**
soft *adj* **57, 176**
soft cheese *n* **61**
soft down feathers *n* **161**
soft drink *n* **70**
soft sweets *n* **67**
soft toy *n* **08**
softwood *n* **35**
soil *n* **39**
soil tiller *n* **40**
soil types *n* **39**
solar charger *n* **83**
solar energy *n* **51**
solar farm *n* **51**
solar panel *n* **51**
solar radiation *n* **155**
solar system *n* **143**
solar water heating *n* **51**
solder *n* **35-36**
solder *v* **35**
soldering iron *n* **35-36**
soldier *n* **88-89**
sole *n* **02, 17, 54, 115**
solid, solids *n* **74, 76**
solo *n* **128**
Solomon Island *adj* **153**
Solomon Islands *n* **150, 153**
soluble *adj* **49**
solvent *n* **37**
Somalia *n* **149, 152**
Somalian *adj* **152**
sombrero *n* **16**
sometimes *adj* **172**
sommelier *n* **69**
son *n* **05**
son-in-law *n* **05**
song *n* **129**
soprano *n* **126**
sore throat *n* **19**
sorrel *n* **55, 59**
sort your rubbish *v* **155**
sorting unit *n* **33**
soufflé *n* **72**
soufflé dish *n* **28**
soul *n* **129**
sound bar *n* **136**
sound boom *n* **84**
sound engineer *n* **127**
sound hole *n* **129**
sound technician *n* **84**
soundtrack *n* **127**
soup *n* **69, 72**
soup bowl *n* **27**
soup spoon *n* **27**
sour *adj* **52, 57**
source *n* **147**
sources *n* **79**
sourdough bread *n* **62**
sourdough starter *n* **62**
south *n* **148**
South Africa *n* **149, 152**
South African *adj* **152**
South America *n* **149, 152**
South American *adj* **152**
South Korea *n* **150, 153**
South Korean *adj* **153**
South Pole *n* **75, 145**
South Sudan *n* **149, 152**
South Sudanese *adj* **152**
southeast *n* **148**
Southern Cross *n* **144**
Southern Hemisphere *n* **145**
southwest *n* **148**
souvenir *n* **132**
souvenir stall *n* **132**
sow *v* **39, 86**
soy sauce *n* **60**
soy sauce dip *n* **72**
soya allergy *n* **23**
soya milk *n* **61**
soybean oil *n* **60**
space *n* **143-144**
space exploration *n* **143**
space probe *n* **143**
space shuttle *n* **143**
space shuttle launch *n* **143**
space station *n* **143**
space suit *n* **143**
space telescope *n* **144**
spacecraft *n* **143**
spade *n* **40, 140**
spaghetti *n* **64, 72**
Spain *n* **151, 153**
spam *n* **83**
Spanish *adj* **153**
Spanish chestnut *n* **168**
spanner *n* **36**
spare tyre *n* **98**
spark plug *n* **98**
sparkling *adj* **52**
sparkling wine *n* **68**
sparrow *n* **160**
spatula *n* **28, 76**
speak *v* **11**
speaker, speakers *n* **83, 129**
speaker stand *n* **136**
spear *n* **79**
spearfishing *n* **121**
special *adj* **177**
special effects *n* **127**
special offer *n* **48**
specials *n* **69**
species *n* **77**
species of birds *n* **160-161**
species of fungi *n* **170**
species of mammals *n* **158-159**
spectacled caiman *n* **163**
spectators *n* **110, 115-116**
speed boating *n* **119**
speed camera *n* **96**
speed limit *n* **96**
speed skating *n* **122**
speed up *v* **98**
speedboat *n* **105**
speeding *n* **85**
speedometer *n* **99-100**
speedway *n* **123**
spell *v* **11, 73**
spell book *n* **139**
sperm whale *n* **166**
sphere *n* **74**
sphinx *n* **139, 164**
spices *n* **59**
spicy *adj* **52, 56**
spicy sausage *n* **64**
spider monkey *n* **159**
spider plant *n* **38**
spikes *n* **115**
spin *n* **114**
spinach *n* **55**
spinal cord *n* **04**
spine *n* **03, 138**
spinning top *n* **08**
spiral galaxy *n* **144**
spirit dispenser *n* **68**
spirit level *n* **35-36, 87**
spit *n* **147**
splashback *n* **27**
spleen *n* **04**
splinter *n* **19**
split the bill *v* **69**
spoiler *n* **97**
spoke *n* **101**
sponge *n* **31, 34, 37**
sponge cake *n* **63**
spontaneous *adj* **10**
spores *n* **170**
sport fishing *n* **121**
sports bra *n* **15**
sports car *n* **97**
sports centre *n* **43**
sports drink *n* **52**
sports field *n* **80**
sports game *n* **136**
sports jacket *n* **15**
sports programme *n* **137**
sports shoes *n* **17**
sportsperson *n* **89**
sportswear *n* **15**
spotted *adj* **13**
Spotted Lake *n* **145**
sprain *n* **19**
spray *n* **49**
spray *v* **39**
spray nozzle *n* **40**
sprayer *n* **40**
spring *n* **57, 172**
spring a leak *v* **33**
spring greens *n* **55**
spring onion *n* **55**
spring roll *n* **72**
springboard *n* **118, 125**
springbok *n* **158**
sprinkle *v* **29**
sprinkler *n* **40**
sprinter *n* **116**
sprocket *n* **101**
spruce *n* **167**
spy *n* **89**
square *n* **42, 74, 140**
square foot *n* **174**
square kilometre *n* **174**
square leg *n* **111**
square metre *n* **174**
square mile *n* **174**
squash *n* **114**
squat *n* **124**
squeak *v* **164**
squeegee *n* **34**
squid *n* **54**
squirrel *n* **158**
squirrel monkey *n* **159**
Sri Lanka *n* **150, 153**
Sri Lankan *adj* **153**
St. Basil's cathedral *n* **44**
St. Kitts and Nevis *n* **150, 152**
St. Lucia *n* **150, 152**
St. Lucian *adj* **152**
St. Vincent and The Grenadines *n* **150, 152**
stabilizers *n* **101**
stable *n* **86, 120**
staff *n* **81, 139**
stag beetle *n* **162**
stage *n* **126**
stage lights *n* **129**
stained glass window *n* **44**
stair gate *n* **08**
staircase *n* **25**
stairs *n* **25**
stake *v* **39**
stalactite *n* **146**
stalagmite *n* **146**
stalk *n* **55**
stall *n* **47**
stallion *n* **120, 165**
stalls *n* **126**
stamen *n* **38**
stamp, stamps *n* **45, 48**
stance *n* **115**
stand *n* **40, 109, 115, 121, 136**
stand up *v* **11**
standing ovation *n* **126**
stapler *n* **73, 82**
staples *n* **82**
star, stars *n* **144**
star anise *n* **59**
star chart *n* **144**
star cluster *n* **144**
star jumps *n* **124**
Star of David *n* **44**
starfish *n* **134, 166**
starfruit *n* **58**

starling *n* **160**
start school *v* **07**
starter *n* **69**
starting block *n* **116, 118**
starting grid *n* **123**
starting line *n* **116**
statement *n* **85**
stationery *n* **82**
status *n* **104**
status update *n* **84**
stay in a hotel *v* **131**
steam *v* **29**
steam dome *n* **102**
steam train *n* **102**
steamed *adj* **72**
steeplechase *n* **120**
steering wheel *n* **99**
stegosaurus *n* **157**
stem *n* **38, 170**
stemware *n* **27**
stencil *n* **37**
stenographer *n* **85**
stepbrother *n* **05**
stepladder *n* **37**
stepmother *n* **05**
stepmum *n* **05**
steppe *n* **146**
steps *n* **25**
stepsister *n* **05**
stereo *adj* **136**
stern *n* **105, 119**
sternum *n* **03**
stethoscope *n* **20**
stew *n* **72**
steward *n* **109**
stick *n* **110**
stick insect *n* **164**
sticky notes *n* **82**
sticky prong *n* **168**
stiff *adj* **176**
stifling *adj* **154**
stigma *n* **38**
stilettos *n* **17**
still *adj* **52**
stilt house *n* **32**
sting *n* **19, 162**
sting *v* **162**
stinkhorn *n* **170**
stir *v* **29**
stir-fry *n* **29, 72**
stir-fried *adj* **72**
stirrer *n* **68**
stirrup *n* **120**
stitch *n* **142**
stitches *n* **21, 113**
stitch length selector *n* **142**
stitch selector *n* **142**
stock exchange *n* **94**
stockbroker *n* **94**
stockings *n* **14**
stocks *n* **47, 94**
stomach *n* **04**
stomach ache *n* **19**
stone *adj* **176**
stone *n* **16, 141, 176**
Stone age *n* **79**
stone fruit *n* **57**
stool *n* **65**
stop *v* **96, 137**
stop at (the hotel) *v* **148**
stop button *n* **99**
stop light ahead *n* **96**
stopper *n* **76**
storage *n* **32**
stories *n* **139**
stork *n* **160**
storm *n* **154**
storm drain *n* **43**
stormy *adj* **154**
stout *n* **68**
straight *adj* **74**
straight hair *n* **12**
strainer *n* **28**
strait *n* **147**
strange *adj* **177**
strapless *adj* **15**
strategy game *n* **136**
stratosphere *n* **155**
straw *n* **70**
strawberry *n* **57**
strawberry jam *n* **60**
strawberry milkshake *n* **61, 65**
strawberry smoothie *n* **65**
streaky bacon *n* **53**
stream *n* **137, 147**
street *n* **42**
street corner *n* **42**
street market *n* **46**
street sign *n* **43**
street stall *n* **70**
streetlight *n* **25, 43**
streetmap *n* **148**
stress *n* **19**
stressed *adj* **06**
stretch *n* **124**
stretcher *n* **21**
strike *n* **113**
strike *v* **117**
strike out *v* **111**
striker *n* **109**
string *n* **129**
string of pearls *n* **16**
strings *n* **114, 128**
strip *v* **37**
striped *n* **13**
stripes *n* **14**
stroke *n* **118**
strong *adj* **52**
strong flour *n* **62**
strontium *n* **78**
stubble *n* **12**
studs *n* **16, 111**
study *n* **26**
study *n* **73**
studying the past *n* **79**
stuffed *adj* **72**
stuffed olives *n* **64**
stuffed vine leaves *n* **64**
stump *v* **111**
stumps *n* **111**
stunning *adj* **177**
stunt *n* **127**
style *n* **38**
style your hair *v* **12**
stylist *n* **89**
subject *n* **83**
submarine *n* **88, 105**
submersible *n* **166**
subscript *n* **76**
subsoil *n* **39**
substitutes *n* **109**
subterranean stream *n* **146**
subtitles *n* **137**
subtract *v* **11, 74**
suburb *n* **42**
subwoofer *n* **136**
succulents *n* **38, 41**
suck *v* **02**
suction hose *n* **34**
Sudan *n* **149, 152**
Sudanese *adj* **152**
sugar *n* **23**
sugar cane *n* **86, 167**
sugar-snap peas *n* **55**
suit *n* **15**
suit (someone) *v* **14**
suitcase *n* **16, 104**
sulphite allergy *n* **23**
sulphur *n* **78, 156**
sultana *n* **58**
sum up *v* **95**
sumac *n* **59**
summer *n* **57, 172**
summer leaf *n* **169**
summer roll *n* **72**
summons *n* **85**
sumo wrestling *n* **117**
Sun *n* **143**
sun *n* **154**
sun bed *n* **18**
sun cream *n* **134**
sun hat *n* **14, 16, 134**
sunbathing *n* **133-134**
sunblock *n* **49, 134**
sunburn *n* **19, 134**
Sunday *n* **172**
sundew *n* **168**
sunflower, sunflowers *n* **38, 86**
sunflower oil *n* **60**
sunglasses *n* **22, 134**
sunlit zone *n* **166**
sunny *adj* **154**
sunrise *n* **171**
sunroof *n* **98**
sunset *n* **171**
superb *adj* **177**
superfoods *n* **23**
supermarket *n* **48**
supernova *n* **144**
supervise *v* **92**
supervisor *n* **81, 92**
supplement *n* **23, 49**
support *n* **87**
support cane *n* **39**
supportive *adj* **10**
suppository *n* **49**
surf *n* **119**
surface *n* **39, 143**
surface cleaner *n* **34**
surface-to-air missile *n* **88**
surfboard *n* **119, 134**
surfcasting *n* **121**
surfer *n* **119**
surfing *n* **119, 134**
surgeon *n* **21, 90**
surgery *n* **21**
surgical mask *n* **21**
Suriname *n* **149, 152**
Surinamese *adj* **152**
surprised *adj* **06**
Surrealism *n* **130**
surround sound speaker *n* **136**
surveillance camera *n* **130**
surveyor *n* **90**
sushi *n* **54**
sushi set *n* **27**
suspect *n* **50, 85**
suspenders *n* **14**
suspension *n* **98, 100**
suspension line *n* **125**
swallow *n* **160**
swallow *v* **52**
swallowtail butterfly *n* **162**
swamp *n* **146**
swarm *n* **162**
Swazi *adj* **152**
sweat *v* **02**
sweatpants *n* **15**
sweater *n* **14**
sweatshirt *n* **14**
swede *n* **56**
Sweden *n* **151, 153**
Swedish *adj* **153**
sweep the floor *v* **34**
sweet *adj* **52, 56-57**
sweet chilli *n* **60**
sweet potato *n* **56**
sweet shop *n* **67**
sweet spreads *n* **60**
sweet trolley *n* **63, 69**
sweetcorn *n* **55**
sweets *n* **67**
swift *n* **160**
swimmer *n* **118**
swimming *n* **118**
swimming pool *n* **118, 131**
swimming trunks *n* **15, 134**
swimsuit *n* **15, 118, 134**
swing *n* **43, 115, 133**
swing *v* **115, 159**
Swiss *adj* **153**
Swiss chard *n* **55**
Swiss cheese plant *n* **38**
Switzerland *n* **151, 153**
swoop *v* **161**
sword *n* **79, 117**
swordfish *n* **54**
sycamore *n* **169**
Sydney Opera House *n* **44**
sympathetic *adj* **06**
symphony *n* **128**
symptoms *n* **19**
synagogue *n* **44**
synchronized swimming *n* **118**
synthetic *n* **13**
Syria *n* **150, 153**
Syrian *adj* **153**
syringe *n* **20, 49, 77**
syrup *n* **49**

T

T-shirt *n* **14**
T-strap heels *n* **17**
T11 (visual impairment) race *n* **116**
tabard *n* **13**
tabi boots *n* **17**
table *n* **26, 65**
table setting *n* **69**
table tennis *n* **114**
tablecloth *n* **26**
tablespoon *n* **27**
tablet *n* **83**
tablets *n* **20, 49**
tableware *n* **27**
tack *v* **119, 142**
tackle *n* **108, 121**
tackle *v* **107**
tackle box *n* **121**
taco *n* **70**
tadpole *n* **77, 163**
taekwondo *n* **117**
tag *v* **113**
tagine *n* **28**
tai chi *n* **117, 133**
tail *n* **54, 103, 120, 143, 158-160**
tail feathers *n* **161**
tail light *n* **100**
tailbone sacrum *n* **03**
tailgate *n* **97**
tailor *n* **46, 89**
tailor *v* **142**
tailor's chalk *n* **142**

tailor's dummy *n* **142**
tailored *adj* **15**
tailplane *n* **103**
Taj Mahal *n* **44**
Tajikistan *n* **151, 153**
Tajikistani *adj* **153**
take *v* **11, 140**
take a bath *v* **09, 31**
take a nap *v* **09**
take a penalty *v* **109**
take a shower *v* **09, 31**
take an exam *v* **73**
take in *v* **142**
take minutes *v* **95**
take notes *v* **73**
take off *v* **14, 98, 104, 178**
take on *v* **81**
take out the rubbish *v* **09, 34**
take questions *v* **95**
take the first left *v* **96, 148**
take the second right *v* **96, 148**
take-away *n* **70**
talented *adj* **10**
talk *v* **11**
talkative *adj* **10**
tall *adj* **12**
tamarillo *n* **58**
tambourine *n* **128**
tampon *n* **49**
tandem *n* **101**
tank *n* **88**
tank top *n* **14**
tanning goggles *n* **18**
tanning mitt *n* **18**
tantalum *n* **78**
Tanzania *n* **149, 152**
Tanzanian *adj* **152**
tap *n* **27, 31, 33**
tap *n* **33**
tap water *n* **52**
tape *n* **20, 32, 82**
tape measure *n* **36, 142**
tapir *n* **159**
tarantula *n* **162**
target *n* **125**
target shooting *n* **125**
taro root *n* **56**
tarragon *n* **59**
Tasmanian devil *n* **158**
taste *v* **11, 29, 52**
tasty *adj* **52**
Taurus *n* **144**
tawny owl *n* **161**
taxi driver *n* **90**
taxi rank *n* **104**
tea *n* **52, 66, 71, 86**
tea infuser *n* **66**
tea strainer *n* **66**
tea towel *n* **28**
tea with lemon *n* **66**
tea with milk *n* **66**
teacher *n* **73, 90**
teacup *n* **27**
team *n* **107**
team bench *n* **112**
team jersey *n* **107**
team leader *n* **92**
team player *n* **93**
teamwork *n* **92-93**
teapot *n* **27, 66**
tear *n* **22**
tear duct *n* **01**
tearful *adj* **06**
teaspoon *n* **27**
teat *n* **08**
technetium *n* **78**
technological revolution *n* **79**
technology *n* **83**
technology literate *adj* **93**
teddy bear *n* **30**
tee *n* **115**
tee off *v* **115**
teeing ground *n* **115**
teenagers *n* **05**
teepee *n* **32**
teeth *n* **01, 03**
telephone *n* **82**
telephone banking *n* **94**
telephone manner *n* **93**
teleprompter *n* **84**
telescope *n* **144**
television *n* **26, 136-137**
television studio *n* **84**
telling the time *n* **171**
tellurium *n* **78**
temperate forest *n* **146**
temperature *n* **154**
temperature display *n* **33**
temperature gauge *n* **99**
temple *n* **01, 44**
temporary *adj* **81**
temporary exhibition *n* **130**
ten *num* **173**
ten past one *n* **171**
ten to two *n* **171**
tenancy agreement *n* **32**
tenant *n* **32**
tend *v* **39**
tendon *n* **03**
tennessine *n* **78**
tennis *n* **114**
tennis court *n* **114**
tennis match *n* **114**
tennis shoes *n* **114**
tenon saw *n* **36**
tenor *n* **126**
tension control *n* **142**
tent peg *n* **135**
tent pole *n* **135**
tenth *num* **173**
terbium *n* **78**
terminal *n* **104**
termite *n* **162**
terrace *n* **25, 65**
terraced house *n* **32**
terrible *adj* **177**
terrified *adj* **06**
terrifying *adj* **177**
test *n* **73**
test results *n* **20**
test tube *n* **76**
test tube rack *n* **76**
testicle *n* **04**
text *n* **138**
textbook *n* **73, 138**
textiles *n* **91**
Thai *adj* **153**
thallium *n* **78**
Thanksgiving *n* **07**
thatched cottage *n* **32**
thatched roof *n* **32**
thawb *n* **15**
theatre *n* **42, 126**
theme park *n* **133**
therapy *n* **24**
thermal flask *n* **135**
thermals *n* **135**
thermometer *n* **20, 76**
thermosphere *n* **155**
thesis *n* **80**
thick *adj* **176**
thigh *n* **01, 53**
thigh-high boot *n* **17**
thimble *n* **142**
thin *adj* **176**
think *v* **11**
third *num* **173**
third base *n* **113**
third man *n* **111**
thirteen *num* **173**
thirty *num* **173**
this way up *phr* **45**
thistle *n* **38, 169**
thoracic vertebrae *n* **03**
thorium *n* **78**
thorny devil *n* **163**
thoughtless *adj* **10**
thread *n* **84, 142**
thread *v* **142**
thread guide *n* **142**
three *num* **173**
three times a week *adv* **172**
three-course meal *n* **69**
three-second area *n* **112**
three-wheeler *n* **100**
thrilled *adj* **06**
thriller *n* **127, 137**
thrilling *adj* **177**
throat *n* **04**
throat lozenge *n* **49**
throttle *n* **100**
throw *n* **26, 30**
throw *v* **11, 107-108, 113, 117**
throw away *v* **178**
throw-in *n* **109, 112**
throw-in line *n* **112**
thrush *n* **160**
thruster *n* **143**
thulium *n* **78**
thumb *n* **02**
thunder *n* **154**
thundery *adj* **154**
Thursday *n* **172**
thyme *n* **59**
thyroid gland *n* **04**
tiara *n* **16**
tibia *n* **03**
ticket *n* **102, 104, 130**
ticket barrier *n* **102**
ticket inspector *n* **102**
ticket office *n* **102, 102, 130**
tidal barrage *n* **51**
tidal energy *n* **51**
tidy *v* **34**
tie *n* **15-16**
tie your hair back *v* **12**
tie-break *n* **114**
tie-pin *n* **16**
tiger *n* **157, 159**
tiger's eye *n* **156**
tight *adj* **13, 176**
tighthead prop *n* **108**
tights *n* **14**
tilde *n* **175**
tile, tiles *n* **25, 35**
tile *v* **35, 37**
till *n* **48, 68, 94**
tiller *n* **119**
timber *n* **87**
time *n* **104, 107, 171**
time management *n* **93**
time out *n* **107**
timer *n* **28, 76, 95**
timetable *n* **102, 132**
Timorese *adj* **153**
tin *n* **78, 156**
tin *n* **52**
tin opener *n* **28**
tinned *adj* **56**
tinned food *n* **48**
tinned tomato *n* **71**
tip *n* **69, 122**
tiramisu *n* **63**
tired *adj* **06**
tiring *adj* **177**
tissue *n* **49**
tissue box *n* **30**
titanium *n* **78**
title *n* **138**
toadstools *n* **170**
toast *n* **71**
toasted sandwich *n* **71**
toaster *n* **27**
tobacco *n* **86**
Tobagonian *adj* **152**
toco toucan *n* **160**
toddler *n* **05, 08**
toe *n* **02, 115**
toe box *n* **126**
toe clip *n* **101**
toe strap *n* **101**
toenail *n* **02**
toffee *n* **67**
Togo *n* **149, 152**
Togolese *adj* **152**
toilet *n* **31, 33**
toilet block *n* **34, 135**
toilet brush *n* **31**
toilet cleaner *n* **34**
toilet float *n* **33**
toilet paper *n* **31**
toilet paper holder *n* **31**
toilet seat *n* **31**
toiletries *n* **18, 48**
toilets *n* **47, 130-131**
tollbooth *n* **96**
tomato *n* **56**
tomato juice *n* **65**
tomato sauce *n* **70**
tomb *n* **79**
tombolo *n* **147**
ton *n* **174**
toner *n* **18**
Tonga *n* **150, 153**
Tongan *adj* **153**
Tonghi bottlebrush *n* **168**
tongs *n* **28, 68, 76**
tongue *n* **04, 17, 53**
tonne *n* **174**
tonsillitis *n* **19**
tool belt *n* **36, 87**
tool rack *n* **35**
toolbox *n* **36**
tools *n* **35-36, 40, 87**
toothache *n* **22**
toothbrush *n* **31**
toothpaste *n* **31**
top dress *v* **39**
top tier *n* **63**
topaz *n* **156**
topiary *n* **41**
topping *n* **70**
topsoil *n* **39**
torc *n* **16**
torch *n* **135**
torch lily *n* **167**
tornado *n* **154**
tortellini *n* **64**
tortilla *n* **62**
tortoise *n* **164**
touch-in goal line *n* **108**
touchdown *n* **107**
tour guide *n* **90, 130, 132**
tourer *n* **100**
touring bike *n* **101**
tourism *n* **91**
tourist *n* **132**
tourist attraction *n* **132**
tourist bus *n* **99, 132**
tourist information *n* **42, 132**
tourist map *n* **48, 132**
tourmaline *n* **156**

tournament n 115
tow away v 96
tow truck n 98
towel rail n 31
towels n 31
tower n 44, 51
tower crane n 87
town n 43, 148
town features n 42-43
town house n 32, 43
toy car n 08
toy shop n 46
toybox n 08
toys n 08, 164
trachea n 04
track n 102, 116
track your order v 46
tracksuit n 15
tractor n 86
traditional clothes n 15
traffic n 96
traffic jam n 43, 96
traffic light n 43, 96
traffic light ahead n 96
traffic warden n 96
tragedy n 126
trailer n 135
train, trains n 15, 102
train v 39, 124
train driver n 90
train set n 08
train station n 42, 102, 148
trainer n 17
training cane n 39
tram n 99, 102
trampoline n 08, 125
transfer money v 45
transformer n 33, 75
transition metals n 78
translator n 89
transmission n 98
transplant v 39
transport helicopter n 88
transportation n 91
trap n 33
trapezium n 74
trapezius n 03
trapped insect n 168
trapped radiation n 155
trash n 83
33, 82
travel n 131
travel agent n 46, 90
travel card n 48
travel writing n 138
travel-sickness
pills n 49
traveller's tree n 168
trawler n 105
tray n 69-70
tray table n 103
trays n 82
tread n 101
tread water v 118
treadmill n 124
treasure n 139
treatment n 20-21
treatments n 24
treats n 164
treble clef n 128
treble fishhook n 121
tree, trees n 41, 167-169
tree climbing n 133
tree house n 32, 133
tree pose n 24
tree pruner n 40
trekking n 120
trellis n 41
trench n 145
trench coat n 15
trend v 84
trial n 85
triangle n 74, 128
triangle pose n 24
Triassic adj n 157
Triassic n 157
triathlon n 116
tributary n 147
triceratops n 157
trilobite n 157
trim v 39
trimmer n 40
Trinidad and Tobago n
150, 152
Trinidadian adj 152
trip over v 178
trip switch n 33
triple bar vertical n 120
triple jump n 116
triplets n 05
tripod n 76, 144
trivia game n 136
troll n 139
troll v 84
trolley n 48, 102, 104
trolley n 102, 104, 131
trolley bus n 99
trolling n 84
trombone n 128
Tropic of Cancer n 145
Tropic of Capricorn n 145
tropics n 145
troposphere n 155
trot v 120, 165
trousers n 15
trout n 54
trowel n 40, 87
truck-mounted crane n 87
truffle n 56, 170
trug n 40
trumpet n 128-129
trumpetfish n 166
truncheon n 50
trunk n 159
try n 108
try line n 108
try on v 46
try something on v 14
tsunami n 145
tuba n 128
tubular bells n 128
Tuesday n 172
tuff n 156
tugboat n 105
tulip n 38
tumble dryer n 34
tumble turn n 118
tumbler n 27
turmeric n 59
tuna n 54
tundra n 146
tune in v 136
tuner n 129, 136
tungsten n 78
tuning buttons n 136
tuning peg n 129
Tunisia n 149, 152
Tunisian adj 152
turban n 16
turbine n 51
turbot n 54
turkey n 53, 161, 165
Turkish adj 153
Turkish delight n 67
Türkiye n 150, 151, 153
Turkmen adj 153
Turkmenistan n 151, 153
turle knot n 121
turn v 35, 118, 126
turn down v 136, 178
turn down the
volume v 137
turn left v 96, 148
turn off v 83, 137, 178
turn on v 83, 137, 178
turn right v 96, 148
turn up v 14, 136, 178
turn up the volume v 137
turner n 28
turnip n 56
turntable n 129
turquoise n 141, 156
turret n 44
tutu n 126
Tuvalu n 150, 153
Tuvaluan adj 153
tuxedo n 15
TV n 26, 136
TV channels n 137
TV guide n 137-138
TV schedule n 137
TV set n 137
TV shows n 137
tweeter n 136
tweezers n 18, 20, 77
twelve num 173
twentieth num 173
twenty num 173
twenty-five past one n 171
twenty-five to two n 171
twenty minutes n 171
twenty past one n 171
twenty thirty-three n 172
twenty to two n 171
twenty-first num 173
twenty-one num 173
twenty-two num 173
twice a week adv 172
twilight zone n 166
twin room n 131
twine n 40
twins n 05
twist bar n 124
twist ties n 40
two num 173
two hundred num 173
two o'clock n 171
two weeks n 172
two-person tent n 135
typeface n 175
types of aircraft n 103
types of buildings n 44
types of buses n 99
types of cars n 97
types of fishing n 121
types of houses n 32
types of meat n 53
types of motorcycles n 100
types of motorsports n
123
types of plants n 41
types of soil n 39
types of trains n 102
tyrannosaurus rex n 157
tyre n 97, 100-101
tyre lever n 101

U

udon n 64
Uganda n 149, 152
Ugandan adj 152
ugli fruit n 57
ugly adj 177
Ukraine n 151, 152
Ukrainian adj 153
ukulele n 129
ulna n 03
ultrasound n 08
ultraviolet n 75
ultraviolet rays n 155
umbilical cord n 08
umbrella n 16
umbrella pine n 167
umbrella plant n 38
umlaut n 175
umpire n 111, 113-114
umpire's chair n 114
unanimous vote n 95
unapproachable adj 10
unblock the
sink v 35
unblock the
toilet v 35
uncle n 05
under prep 180
under par adj 115
undercoat n 37
undergraduate n 80
underground
map n 102
underground
train n 102
underpass n 96, 102
underscore n 175
undersea features n 145
undershirt n 14
understand v 11
underwater camera n 118
underwater diving n 118
underwear n 14
unemployment benefit n
81
unenthusiastic adj 06
uneven bars n 125
unfasten v 14
unfriendly adj 10
unfurnished adj 32
unhappy adj 06
unicorn n 139
unicycle n 101
uniform,
uniforms n 13, 50, 88
unimpressed adj 06
United Arab
Emirates n 151, 153
United Kingdom n 151,
153
United States
of America n 150, 152
universe n 144
university n 43, 80
university
departments n 80
university schools n 80
unkind adj 10
unleaded n 97
unload the
dishwasher v 34
unpack v 11, 32
unpasteurized adj 61
unpeeled prawn n 54
unpick v 142
unpleasant adj 177
unreasonable adj 10
unreliable adj 10
unsalted adj 61
unsaturated fat n 23
upload v 83
upmarket adj 47
upper deck n 99

upper level *n* **47**
uppercase *n* **175**
upset *adj* **06**
upstairs *adv, n* **25**
uranium *n* **78**
Uranus *n* **143**
urinary *n* **04**
urology *n* **21**
Uruguay *n* **149, 152**
Uruguayan *adj* **152**
USB drive *n* **83**
useful *adj* **177**
useful expressions *n* **179-180**
useless *adj* **177**
usher *n* **126**
uterus *n* **04, 08**
utility knife *n* **36-37**
UV tubes *n* **18**
Uzbek *adj* **153**
Uzbekistan *n* **151, 153**

V

V-neck *n* **14**
vacancies *n* **92, 131**
vaccination *n* **08, 20**
vacuole *n* **77**
vacuum *n* **75**
vacuum cleaner *n* **34**
vacuum the carpet *v* **34**
vagina *n* **04**
Vaisakhi *n* **07**
valance *n* **30**
valley *n* **146**
valve *n* **101**
vampire *n* **139**
vanadium *n* **78**
vandalism *n* **85**
vanilla milkshake *n* **61**
Vanuatu *n* **150, 153**
Vanuatuan *adj* **153**
varnish *n* **37**
vase *n* **26**
Vatican City *n* **151**
vault *n* **125**
veal *n* **53**
vegan *adj* **23**
vegan *n* **23**
vegetable garden *n* **41, 86**
vegetable plot *n* **86**
vegetables *n* **48, 55-56**
vegetarian *adj* **23**
vegetarian *n* **23**
veggie burger *n* **70**
veil *n* **15**
vein *n* **04**
Venetian blinds *n* **26**
Venezuela *n* **149, 152**
Venezuelan *adj* **152**
venison *n* **53**
vent *n* **145**
Venus *n* **143**
Venus fly-trap *n* **168**
verdict *n* **85**
vermilion flycatcher *n* **160**
vertebrate *n* **77**
verticals *n* **120**
vest *n* **14**
vet *n* **89**
veteran *n* **88**
vial *n* **36**
vibraphone *n* **128**
Victoria Falls *n* **145**
vicuña *n* **158**
video chat *n* **83**
video conference *n* **83**
video games *n* **136**
video on demand *n* **137**
Vietnam *n* **150, 153**
Vietnamese *adj* **153**
view a house *v* **32**
viewing platform *n* **44**
viewpoint *n* **148**
villa *n* **32, 131**
village *n* **43**
villain *n* **127**
Vincentian *adj* **152**
vinegar *n* **60, 64**
vineyard *n* **86**
vintage *adj* **13**
vintage *n* **97**
vinyl records *n* **129**
viola *n* **128**
violet *n* **38**
violin *n* **128-29**
violin sonata *n* **128**
Virginia creeper *n* **168**
Virgo *n* **144**
virus *n* **19, 77**
visa *n* **104**
visible light *n* **75**
vision *n* **22**
visitor *n* **107**
visor *n* **100**
vitamins *n* **23, 49**
vivarium *n* **164**
vlog *n* **84**
vlogger *n* **84**
vocal cords *n* **04**
vodka *n* **68**
vodka and orange *n* **68**
voice recorder *n* **83**
volcano *n* **145**
volley *n* **114**
volleyball *n* **112**
volleyball positions *n* **112**
volt *n* **75**
voltage *n* **33**
volume *n* **74, 136, 174**
volunteer *v* **92**
vomit *v* **20**
vote *n* **85**
vulture *n* **160**

W

waders *n* **121**
waffle, waffles *n* **65, 70-71**
wages *n* **81**
waist *n* **01, 129**
waistband *n* **15, 142**
waistcoat *n* **15**
wait on *v* **178**
wait up *v* **178**
waiter *n* **69, 89**
waiting room *n* **20, 102**
waitress *n* **65, 69, 89**
wake up *v* **09, 178**
walk *v* **120**
walk the dog *v* **09**
walkie-talkie *n* **50**
walking boots *n* **135**
walking trail *n* **148**
wall *n* **25, 44, 87**
wall light *n* **26**
Wallace's flying frog *n* **163**
wallet *n* **94**
wallflower *n* **169**
wallpaper *n* **37**
wallpaper *v* **37**
wallpaper border *n* **37**
wallpaper brush *n* **37**
wallpaper paste *n* **37**
wallpaper roll *n* **37**
wallpaper stripper *n* **37**
walnut *n* **58, 168**
walnut oil *n* **60**
walrus *n* **166**
wand *n* **139**
want *v* **46**
war *n* **79, 88**
war elephant *n* **79**
ward *n* **21**
wardrobe *n* **30**
warehouse *n* **44, 106**
warfare *n* **79**
warhorse *n* **79**
warm *adj* **154**
warm front *n* **155**
warning track *n* **113**
warp thread *n* **142**
warrant *n* **85**
warrior *n* **79**
warrior pose *n* **24**
warthog *n* **159**
wasabi *n* **60**
wash the car *v* **34**
wash up *v* **09**
wash your face *v* **09**
wash your hair *v* **09, 12**
washer *n* **36**
washing line *n* **34**
washing machine *n* **34**
washing-up liquid *n* **34**
wasp *n* **162**
wasp nest *n* **162**
waste *n* **33**
waste disposal *n* **135**
waste pipe *n* **33**
watch *n* **16**
watch TV *v* **09**
watching television *n* **137**
water *n* **48, 91, 118**
water *v* **39**
water bottle, water bottles *n* **101, 135**
water carrier *n* **135**
water chestnut *n* **56**
water cooler *n* **82**
water features *n* **145**
water garden *n* **41**
water hazard *n* **115**
water jet *n* **50**
water lilies *n* **167**
water phenomena *n* **145**
water plants *n* **41**
water polo *n* **119**
water rail *n* **161**
water shoes *n* **17**
water skier *n* **119**
water skiing *n* **119**
water sports *n* **119**
water the plants *v* **09, 34**
water vapour *n* **51**
watercolour *n* **130**
watercolour paints *n* **141**
watercress *n* **55**
waterfall *n* **146**
waterfront *n* **132**
watering *n* **40**
watering can *n* **40**
watermark *n* **94**
watermelon *n* **58**
waterproof fishing gear *n* **121**
waterproofs *n* **121, 135**
wave *n* **75, 119, 134, 147**
wave *v* **02**
wavelength *n* **75**
wavy hair *n* **12**
wax *adj* **176**
wax *n* **18, 176**
waxcap *n* **170**
weapons *n* **79, 88**
wear *v* **14**
weasel *n* **158**
weather *n* **137, 154**
weather forecaster *n* **137**
weather map *n* **155**
weaver *n* **142**
weaverbird *n* **160**
weaving *n* **142**
webcam *n* **83**
wedding *n* **07**
wedding cake *n* **63**
wedding dress *n* **15**
wedge *n* **115**
wedge sandals *n* **17**
Wednesday *n* **172**
weedkiller *n* **39**
weeds *n* **41**
week *n* **172**
weekends *n* **172**
weekly *adj* **172**
weekly *adv* **172**
weevil *n* **162**
weft thread *n* **142**
weigh *v* **174**
weigh out *v* **178**
weight, weights *n* **121, 174**
weight bar *n* **124**
weight belt *n* **118**
weight training *n* **124**
well-qualified *adj* **93**
wellies *n* **40**
wellington boots *n* **17**
werewolf *n* **139**
west *n* **148**
western *n* **127**
wet *adj* **154**
wet suit *n* **118, 134**
wet wipe, wet wipes *n* **08, 49**
wetlands *n* **146**
wharf *n* **106**
wheat allergy *n* **23**
wheat beer *n* **68**
wheel *n* **97, 101**
wheel nuts *n* **98**
wheel pose *n* **24**
wheel roller *n* **124**
wheelbarrow *n* **40**
wheelchair *n* **21**
wheelchair access *n* **99**
wheelchair basketball *n* **125**
wheelchair curling *n* **122**
wheelchair race *n* **116**
wheelchair ramp *n* **130**
wheelchair rugby *n* **108, 125**
wheelie bin *n* **25**
whiplash *n* **19**
whipped cream *n* **61**
whisk *n* **28**
whisk *v* **29**

whiskers *n* **158**
whisky *n* **68**
whisper *v* **11**
white *adj* **140-141**
white *n* **140-141**
white blood cell *n* **77**
white bread *n* **62**
white chocolate *n* **67**
white coffee *n* **65**
white currant *n* **57**
white dwarf *n* **144**
white flour *n* **62**
White House *n* **44**
white meat *n* **53**
white mustard *n* **59**
white spirit *n* **37**
white tea *n* **66**
white vinegar *n* **34**
white wine *n* **52, 68**
whiteboard *n* **73, 95**
whitening *n* **22**
whiting *n* **54**
whole milk *n* **61**
wholegrain mustard *n* **60**
wholemeal flour *n* **62**
whooper swan *n* **161**
Wi-Fi *n* **83**
wicket *n* **111**
wicket-keeper *n* **111**
wide *adj* **176**
wide range *n* **48**
wide receiver *n* **107**
widow *n* **05**
width *n* **74**
wife *n* **05**
wig *n* **12**
wigwam *n* **32**
wildcat *n* **159**
wildebeest *n* **158**
wildlife photography *n* **133**
willow *n* **169**
win *v* **11, 109, 115, 140**
win a prize *v* **07**
wind *n* **51, 154**
wind energy *n* **51**
wind farm *n* **51**
wind turbine *n* **51**
windbreak *n* **134**
windlass *n* **105**
windmill *n* **44**
window cleaner *n* **90**
window shopping *n* **46**
windscreen *n* **97, 100**
windsurfer *n* **119**
windsurfing *n* **119, 134**
windy *adj* **154**
wine *n* **68**
wine list *n* **69**
wine vinegar *n* **60**
wineglass *n* **27**
wing *n* **53, 103, 112, 161**
wing mirror *n* **97**
wings *n* **49, 126**
wink *v* **02**
winners' cup *n* **109**
winter *n* **172**
Winter Olympics *n* **122**
winter sports *n* **122**
wipe the surfaces *v* **34**
wiper *n* **97**
wire *n* **35, 83**
wire cutters *n* **36**
wire strippers *n* **36**
wire wool *n* **36**
wireless *adj* **83**
wireless headphones *n* **136**
wires *n* **33**
wiring *n* **33**
wisteria *n* **38**
witch *n* **139**
witches' brew *n* **139**
with ice *adj* **68**
withdraw money *v* **45**
without ice *adj* **68**
witness *n* **85**
wizard *n* **139**
wok *n* **28**
wolf *n* **159**
woman *n* **05**
womb *n* **04, 08**
wombat *n* **158**
women's heptathlon *n* **116**
womenswear *n* **47**
wonderful *adj* **177**
wood *adj* **176**
wood *n* **35, 115, 141, 146, 176**
woods *n* **176**
wood duck *n* **161**
wood glue *n* **35**
wood preserver *n* **37**
wooden spoon *n* **28**
woodwind *n* **128**
woodworking *n* **141**
woofer *n* **136**
wool *adj* **176**
wool *n* **142, 176**
woollen *n* **13**
woolly mammoth *n* **157**
woolly rhinoceros *n* **157**
work *n* **81**
work *v* **11**
work bench *n* **35**
work boots *n* **17**
work from home *v* **81**
work full-time *v* **81**
work part-time *v* **81**
work shifts *v* **81**
workclothes *n* **13**
worker *n* **81**
working out *n* **124**
working well under pressure *n* **93**
workplace skills *n* **93**
workstation *n* **82**
worktop *n* **27**
worm *n* **162**
worried *adj* **06**
wound *n* **19**
wrap *n* **70**
wrap up the meeting *v* **95**
wren *n* **160**
wrestling *n* **117**
wrinkles *n* **12**
wrist *n* **01-02**
wrist band *n* **107**
wrist weights *n* **124**
wristband *n* **114**
writ *n* **85**
write *v* **73**
writer *n* **90**
writing *n* **175**
writing equipment *n* **175**
written communication *n* **93**

XY

X-ray, X-rays *n* **19, 21, 75**
X-ray machine *n* **104**
xenon *n* **78**
xylophone *n* **128**
yacht *n* **105, 119, 134**
yak *n* **159**
yam *n* **56, 86**
yard *n* **174**
yard line *n* **107**
yarmulke *n* **16**
yawn *v* **02**
year *n* **172**
yellow *n* **141**
yellow box fish *n* **166**
yellow card *n* **109**
yellow mustard *n* **60**
yellow surgeonfish *n* **166**
yellow tang *n* **166**
Yemen *n* **151, 153**
Yemeni *adj* **153**
yew *n* **167**
yo-yo *n* **08**
yoga *n* **24**
yoga class *n* **24**
yoga pants *n* **24**
yoga teacher *n* **90**
yoghurt *n* **61**
yolk *n* **61, 71**
young *adj* **12**
young frog *n* **77**
ytterbium *n* **78**
yttrium *n* **78**
yucca *n* **38**
yurt *n* **32**

Z

Zambia *n* **149, 152**
Zambian *adj* **152**
zebra *n* **158**
zero carbon *adj* **155**
zest *n* **57**
ziggurat *n* **44**
Zimbabwe *n* **149, 152**
Zimbabwean *adj* **152**
zinc *n* **78, 156**
zip *n* **17, 142**
zirconium *n* **78**
zodiac *n* **144**
zodiac constellations *n* **144**
zodiac symbols *n* **144**
zombie *n* **139**
zoo *n* **133**
zookeeper *n* **90**
zoologist *n* **77**
zoology *n* **77, 80**

Spanish word list

The numbers after each word or phrase refer to the units in which they can be found.

A

a domicilio **70**
a la derecha **148**
a la izquierda **148**
a la parrilla **72**
a medida **15**
a rayas **13**
a salvo **113**
a tiempo **171**
abadejo **54**
abadejo ahumado **64**
abatido / abatida **06**
abdomen **01, 162**
abdominal, abdominales **03, 124**
abedul **168**
abeja **165**
abeja melífera **162**
abejorro **162**
abeto **167**
abierto **48, 132**
abisinio **164**
abogado / abogada **85, 90**
abogar **85**
abonar **39**
abono **124**
abrazadera **35, 76**
abrebotellas **28, 68**
abrelatas **28**
abrigos **15**
abril **172**
abrillantador **34**
abuela / abuelo **05**
abuelos **05**
aburrido / aburrida **06, 177**
acacia **47**
acampada **135**
acampar **135**
acantilado **147**
accesorios **16**
accidente **19**
accidentes costeros **147**
accidentes hidrológicos**145**
accidentes topográficos submarinos **145**
accidentes y emergencias **50**
acciones **11, 94**
ace **114**
acebuche **169**
acechar **159**
acedera **55, 59**
aceite **60, 64, 97**
aceite aromatizado **60**
aceite de almendras **60**
aceite de avellana **60**
aceite de cacahuete **60**
aceite de coco **60**
aceite de colza **60**
aceite de girasol **60**
aceite de maíz **60**
aceite de nuez **60**
aceite de oliva **60**
aceite de palma **60**
aceite de semilla de uva **60**
aceite de sésamo **60**
aceite de soja **60**
aceites esenciales **24**
aceitunas **68**
aceitunas negras **64**
aceitunas rellenas **64**
aceitunas verdes **64**
acelerador **99, 100**
acelerador de partículas **75**
acelerar **98**
acelga china **55**
acelga suiza roja **55**
acento agudo **175**
acento circunflejo **175**
acento grave **175**
acera **25, 43, 65**
achicoria **55**
achicoria roja **55**
ácido **76**
acomodador / acomodadora **126**
acontecimientos de la vida **07**
acorde **128**
acordeón **129**
acostar a los niños **09**
acre **174**
acta **82**
actínidos **78**
actinio **78**
actitud profesional **93**
activar **178**
actividades al aire libre **133**
actor / actriz **89, 126**
actuación **126**
actualización de estado **84**
actuar **11**
acuarela **141**
Acuario **144, 164**
acuerdo comercial **81**
acupresión **24**
acupuntura **24**
acusación **85**
acusado / acusada **85**
adaptable **93**
adelantar **98, 137**
adelfa **169**
aderezar **29**
adiós **179**
aditivos **23**
administración **93**
adn **77**
adolescentes **05**
adorable **177**
adormidera **168**
aduana **104, 106**
adultos **05**
aeróbic **124**
aerodeslizador **105**
aerogenerador **51**
aerolínea **104**
aeropuerto **43, 104**
afeitadora eléctrica **31**
afeitarse **09, 12, 31**
Afganistán **151, 153**
afgano / afgana **153**
aficionados / aficionadas **107, 109**
afilador **28**
afluente **147**
afortunado / afortunada **06**
África **149, 152**
africano / africana **152**
afueras **42**
agarrar **117**
ágata **156**
agbada **15**
agencia de viajes **46**
agenda **82, 138**
agente de bolsa **94**
agente de policía **50**
agente de viajes **90**
agente inmobiliario / agente inmobiliaria **32, 89**
agitador **68**
agitar **11**
aglomerado **35**
agnato **157**
agosto **172**
agotador / agotadora **177**
agotamiento de la capa de ozono **155**
agracejo **168**
agradable **177**
agradecido / agradecida **06**
agrandar **142**
agricultura **86, 91**
agrio / agria **52, 57**
agua **48, 118**
agua bendita **07**
agua caliente **31**
agua caliente solar **51**
agua de coco **58, 65**
agua del grifo **52**
agua fría **31**
agua mineral **52, 68**
aguacate **56**
aguacatero **167**
aguamarina **156**
aguanieve **154**
aguantar la respiración **02**
aguarrás mineral **37**
aguijón **162**
águila arpía **160**
águila calva **160**
águila pescadora **160**
águila real **160**
aguja **20**
aguja de coser **142**
aguja de ganchillo **142**
aguja de hacer punto **142**
aguja para máquina de coser **142**
agujero negro **144**
agujón **166**
ahora **171**
ahorrar **32**
ahorros **45**
ahumado / ahumada **54, 74**
aikido **117**
airbag **99**
aire acondicionado **33, 99**
airear **39**
aislamiento **35**
ajedrez **140**
ajo **56**
ajolote mexicano **163**
ajustado / ajustada **13**
ajustar **14**
al vapor **72**
ala, alas **49, 53, 103, 112, 161**
ala defensivo derecho / ala defensiva derecha **107**
ala defensivo izquierdo / ala defensiva izquierda **107**
ala delantera **162**
ala delta **125**
ala derecho / ala derecha **108**
ala izquierdo / ala izquierda **108**
ala trasera **162**
ala-pívot **112**
alambre **35, 40**
álamo **168**
alargador **35**
alargador de rodillo **37**
alarma **50**
alarma antirrobo **25**
alarma de incendios **50**
alba **171**
albahaca **59**
albanés / albanesa **153**
Albania **151, 153**
albaricoque **57**
albatros **160**
albertonectes **157**
albóndigas **72**
albornoz **31**
álbum **129**
alcachofa **56**
alcalino **76**
alcantarilla **43**
alcanzar **178**
alcaparras **64**
alcaravea **59**
alcatraz **160**
alcázar **105**
alce **159**
alcoholímetro **50**
aldaba **25**
aleación **76**
alegre **06**
alemán / alemana **153**
Alemania **151, 153**
alentador / alentadora **10**
alerce **167**
alergia **19**
alergia a la leche **23**
alergia a la mostaza **23**
alergia a la soja **23**
alergia a los cacahuetes **23**
alergia a los frutos secos **23**
alergia al apio **23**
alergia al huevo **23**

alergia al marisco **23**
alergia al polen **19**
alergia al sésamo **23**
alergia al sulfito **23**
alergia al trigo **23**
alergias alimentarias **23**
alérgico / alérgica **23**
alero **32, 44, 112**
alerón **97, 103**
alerón delantero **97, 123**
alerón trasero **97, 123**
aleta, aletas **15, 103, 118, 134**
aletear **161**
alfabetización informática **93**
alfabetización tecnológica **93**
alfabeto cirílico **175**
alfabeto griego **175**
alfabeto latino **175**
alfalfa **86**
alfarería **141**
alfarero / alfarera **141**
alfil **140**
alfiler **16, 142**
alfiletero **142**
alfombra **26**
alfombra mágica **139**
alfombra roja **127**
alfombrilla de baño **31**
alfombrilla para el ratón **83**
alforja **120**
alga, algas **134, 166**
alga parda **166**
algodón **13, 86, 176**
algodón de azúcar **67**
alguacil **85**
alhelí **47, 169**
alicatar **35, 37**
alicates **36**
alicates de punta **36**
alienígena **139**
aligátor americano **163**
alimentar a las mascotas **34**
alimentos **52–72**
alimentos ecológicos **23**
alimentos precocinados **23**
alimentos procesados **23**
aliñado / aliñada **72**
aliño **72**
alisar **35**
almacén **44, 106**
almeja **54**
almena **44**
almendras **58, 68**
almirante **88**
almohada **30**
almohadilla **175**
almorzar **09**
almuerzo **26, 69, 72**
aloe **167**
alojamiento **131**
alpaca **165**
alpargatas **17**
alpinismo **133**
alpiste **164**
alquilar **32**
alquilar una casa rural **131**
alquiler de coches **104**
alquiler de una casa **32**
alta definición **137**
alta presión **155**
altavoces **83, 129, 136**
altavoces portátiles **95**
altavoz bluetooth **136**
altavoz central **136**
altavoz de agudos **136**
altavoz de graves **136**
altavoz frontal **136**
altavoz surround **136**
altiplano **146**
alto / alta **12, 176**
altramuz **38**
altura **74**
alubias con tomate **71**
aluminio **78, 156**
alumno / alumna **73**
alzar **11**
amable **10**
amanecer **171**
amapola **38, 168**
amargo / amarga **52, 56**
amarilis **167**
amarillo **141**
amarradero **106**
amarrar **106**
amasar **62**
amatista **156**
Amazonas **145**
ambicioso / ambiciosa **10, 93**
ambulancia **21, 50**
ambulancia aérea **50**
ambulancia militar **88**
ambulatorio **20**
América Central **150**
América del Norte **150**
americio **78**
ametralladora **88**
amigdalitis **19**
amigo / amiga **07**
amigo por correspondencia / amiga por correspondencia **07**
amistoso / amistosa **10**
amontonar **178**
amperio **33**
amplificador **129**
ampolla **19**
amueblado / amueblada **32**
amuleto **139**
anacardo, anacardos **58, 68**
ánade real **161**
analgésicos **20, 49**
análisis de sangre **20, 21**
analítica **93**
anatomía de la flor **38**
ancho / ancha **74, 176**
anchoas **64**
anciano / anciana **05**
ancla **105, 109**
andén **102**
Andorra **151, 153**
andorrano / andorrana **153**
anémona **134, 166**
anestesista **90**
anfibios **163**
anfitrión / anfitriona **26**
ángel destructor **170**
Angola **149, 152**
angoleño / angoleña **152**
angora **164**
anguila **54**
ángulo **74**
ángulo recto **74**
anillas **40, 125**
anillo, anillos **16, 143, 170**
anillo de hadas **170**
anillo de sello **16**
animación **127**
animador / animadora **107**
animales de granja **165**
anís **59**
anís estrellado **59**
aniversario **07**
anorak **15**
anotar **107**
ánsar nival **160**
ansioso / ansiosa **06**
antebrazo **01**
antecedentes penales **85**
antena **25, 97, 162**
antena de radio **105**
antena parabólica **25, 136**
antera **38**
antibióticos **49**
anticongelante **97**
anticuado / anticuada **177**
antifaz **14, 125**
Antigua y Barbuda **150, 152**
antiguano / antiguana **152**
antiinflamatorio **49**
antimonio **78**
antipático / antipática **10**
anual **41**
anular **02**
anuncios **137**
anzuelo **121**
anzuelo triple **121**
añadir **29**
añadir a la lista de deseos **46**
añadir al carrito **46**
añil **141**
año **172**
año nuevo **07**
apagar **83, 137, 178**
apagar el despertador **09**
aparador **26**
aparatos **35**
aparatos de gimnasia **124**
aparatos electrónicos **47**
aparcabicicletas **43, 101**
aparcar **98**
aparejos **121, 129**
apariencia **12–18**
apartamento **131**
apasionado / apasionada **10**
apelar **85**
apéndice **04**
apendicitis **19**
aperitivos **68**
ápice **74**
apio **55**
apio del monte **59**
apisonadora **87**
aplaudir **02**
aplauso **126**
aplicado / aplicada **93**
aplique **26**
apóstrofe **175**
apoyador externo / apoyadora externa **107**
apoyador medio / apoyadora media **107**
apreciativo / apreciativa **06**
aprender **73**
aprendiz **81, 92**
aprendizaje rápido **93**
apretado / apretada **176**
aprobar **73**
apuesto **12**
aquilegia **168**
Arabia Saudí **151, 153**
arado **40**
arándano azul **57**
arándano rojo **57**
arandela **36**
aranto **168**
araña saltadora **162**
araña tejedora de orbes **162**
arao aliblanco **160**
arar **86**
árbitro / árbitra **107, 108, 109, 111, 112, 113**
árbitros **112**
árbol, árboles **24, 41, 167, 168, 169**
árbol de cola de mono **167**
árbol de josué **167**
árbol de la seda **168**
árbol del caucho **169**
árbol del cepillo **168**
árbol del viajero **168**
árbol dragón **167**
árbol hierba **167**
arbusto de flor **41**
arbustos **41**
arce **169**
arcén **96**
archipiélago **147**
archivo **79, 82**
arcilla **39, 141**
arco **02, 24, 41, 44, 74, 79, 125**
arco natural **147**
arcoíris **154**
ardilla **158**
ardilla rayada **159**
ardilla voladora **158**
área **74, 174**
área de portería **110**
área de saque **110**
área del árbitro **110**
área para hogueras **135**
área residencial **32**
arena **35, 39, 134**
arenero **43, 164**
arenisca **156**
arenque **54**
arenque ahumado **71**
argamasa **35**
argelia **149, 152**
argelino / argelina **152**
Argentina **149, 152**
argentino / argentina **152**
argón **78**
Aries **144**
ariete **79**
armada **88**
armadillo **159**
armadura **79**
armario **27, 30**
armario empotrado **30**
armas **79, 88**

Armenia **150, 153**
armenio / armenia **153**
armónica **129**
arnés **115, 122**
aro **112, 125**
aro salvavidas **105, 119, 134**
aromaterapia **24**
arpa **128**
arpón **121**
arqueología **79**
arqueólogo / arqueóloga **79**
arquero / arquera **125**
arquitecto / arquitecta **90**
arquitectura **44**
arrancar **178**
arrecife **147**
arrecife de coral **118, 166**
arreglar **11**
arreglar un pinchazo **101**
arriate de plantas herbáceas **41**
arroba **83, 175**
arrodrigar **39**
arrogante **10**
arroyuella **168**
arroz **72, 86**
arroz con leche **63**
arrugado / arrugada **13**
arrugas **12**
arsénico **78**
art déco **130**
art nouveau **130**
arte **73**
arte conceptual **130**
arte pop **130**
arteria **04**
artes **91**
artes escénicas **91**
artes marciales **117, 127**
artesano / artesana **79**
arteterapia **24**
ártico **159**
articulación **03**
artículo **138**
artículo de aseo **48**
artículo para el bebé **48**
artista **90, 141**
as **140**
asa **16, 40**
asamblea general anual **95**
asar **29**
asar a la parrilla **29**
ascender **81**
ascensor **25, 47, 131**
asentir **02**
aseos **47, 130, 131**
asertivo / asertiva **10, 93**
asesor financiero / asesora financiera **94**
asesoría legal **85**
asfixiante **154**
Asia **150, 151, 153**
asiático / asiática **153**
asidero **31**
asiento, asientos **26, 33, 47, 100, 102, 103, 126**
asiento del conductor **99**
asiento del váter **31**
asiento trasero **99, 100**
asistencia en carretera **98**
asistente personal / asistenta personal **81, 90**
asistir a una reunión **95**
asma **19**
asombrado / asombrada **06, 177**
aspa **103**
aspersor **40**
aspiradora **34**
aspirar la moqueta **34**
asqueado / asqueada **06**
asqueroso / asquerosa **52, 177**
asta **159**
astato **78**
asterisco **175**
asteroide **143**
astigmatismo **22**
astilla **19**
astillero **106**
astronauta **143**
astronomía **144**
asunto **83**
asustado / asustada **06**
atacar **117**
ataque **107**
atar **14**
atardecer **171**
atasco **43, 96**
atemorizado / atemorizada **06**
atención a los detalles **93**
atención al cliente **47, 93**
atención plena **24**
atender **178**
aterrado / aterrada **06**
aterrador / aterradora **177**
aterrizaje **43**
aterrizar **104**
ático **25**
atlas **73**
atleta **116**
atleta paralímpico / atleta paralímpica **125**
atletismo **116, 125**
atmósfera **143, 155**
atolón **147**
atomizador **40**
átomo **76**
atracadero **106**
atracar **106**
atracarse **23**
atracción turística **132**
atraco **85**
atrapar **11, 107, 113**
atrezo **126, 127**
atributos profesionales **93**
atril **128**
atún **54**
audición **127**
audio **136**
audioguía **130**
auditorio **80**
aula **73**
aumento salarial **81**
auricular **88**
auricular bluetooth **83**
auriculares **136**
aurora **144, 155**
ausentarse **95**
ausentarse por enfermedad **81**
Australia **150, 153**
australiano / australiana **153**
Austria **151, 153**
austríaco / austríaca **153**
autoayuda **138**
autobiografía **138**
autobús **43, 99**
autobús articulado **99**
autobús de dos pisos **99**
autobús de transbordo **99**
autobús escolar **99**
autobús turístico **99, 132**
autocar **99**
autocaravana **135**
autogestión **93**
autogiro **103**
automático **99**
automovilismo **123**
autopago **48**
autopista **96**
autor / autora **138**
autovía **96**
avalancha **122**
avance **137**
avatar **84**
ave del paraíso **160, 167**
avellana **01, 58**
avellano **168**
avenida **43**
aventurero / aventurera **10**
avergonzado / avergonzada **06**
averiarse **98, 178**
aves **48, 160, 161**
aves de corral **165**
avestruz **160, 165**
avión **103**
avión común **160**
avión de carga **103**
avión de pasajeros **103**
avión de reconocimiento **88**
avión de transporte militar **88**
avión zapador **160**
aviones de combate **88**
avioneta **103**
avispa **162**
avispero **162**
axila **01**
ayran **61**
ayudante del chef **69**
ayudar **11**
ayurveda **24**
azabache **156**
azada **40**
azafato / azafata, azafatos / azafatas **90, 103, 104**
azafrán **38, 59, 167**
azalea **38**
Azerbaiyán **150, 153**
azerbaiyano / azerbaiyana **153**
azúcar **23**
azufre **78, 156**
azul, azules **01, 141**
azul marino **141**
azulejos **35**

B

babero **13**
babosa **162**
babuino **158**
baca **97**
bacalao **166**
bache, baches **96, 101**
backgammon **140**
backswing **115**
bacteria, bacterias **77, 157**
báculo **139**
bádminton **114**
baguette **62**
bahamas **152**
bahameño / bahameña **152**
bahía **147**
bailar **11**
bailarín / bailarina **89, 126**
bailarín de ballet **126**
bailarinas **17**
baisakhi **07**
baja **88**
baja presión **155**
bajar **178**
bajar de **178**
bajar el volumen **136, 137, 178**
bajar en picado **161**
bajarse **100**
bajarse de la bici **101**
bajista **129**
bajo / baja **12, 14, 126, 142, 176**
bajo en calorías **23**
bajo par **115**
baklava **63**
balancearse **159**
balancín **43**
balanza **29, 76, 174**
balar **165**
balcón **25**
ballena azul **166**
ballena jorobada **166**
ballet **126**
balón **107, 109, 112**
balón de gimnasia **124**
balón de rugby **108**
baloncesto **112**
baloncesto en silla de ruedas **125**
balonmano **125**
balsa hinchable **134**
balsa salvavidas **119**
bálsamo labial **18**
bambú **41, 55, 167**
banca **91**
banca digital **45, 94**
banca móvil **94**
banca telefónica **94**
banco **45, 94, 124**
banco de nieve **154**
banco de trabajo **35**
banda **107, 129**
banda de rodadura **101**
banda sonora **127**
bandas elásticas **82**
bandeja **69, 70, 103, 174**
bandeja de entrada **83**
bandeja de horno **29**
bandeja de pintura **37**
bandeja de salida **83**

bandeja del desayuno **131**
bandejas **82**
bandera a cuadros **123**
banderín de córner **109**
banderola **115**
Bangladés **150, 153**
bangladesí **153**
banjo **129**
banquete **26**
banquillo de jugadores **107, 109, 110, 113**
banquillo de los jueces **110**
banquillo de penalización **110**
banquillo dequipo **112**
bañador **15, 118, 134**
bañador de hombre **15**
bañarse **09, 31**
bañera **31**
bañera para bebés **08**
baño privado **131**
baobab **169**
bar **68**
bar mitzvá **07**
baraja de cartas **140**
barajar **140**
barandilla **25, 65, 99**
barba **12**
barba incipiente **12**
barbacoa **41, 135**
barbadense **152**
Barbados **150, 152**
barbero **89**
barbilla **01**
barbo **54**
barcos **105**
Baréin **151, 153**
bareiní **153**
bario **78**
barista **65, 89**
barítono **126**
barman **69, 89**
barnacla canadiense **160**
barniz **37**
barómetro de profundidad **118**
barquilla **103**
barra **68, 107, 124, 125**
barra antivuelco **97**
barra de labios **18**
barra de pesas **124**
barra de sonido **136**
barra horizontal **125**
barracuda **166**
barras asimétricas **125**
barras de combustible **51**
barras paralelas **125**
barrer **34**
barrera **102**
barrera de seguridad **08, 122**
barrera de tráfico **96**
barrio residencial **42**
barrios **42**
barrita **48**
barrita de chocolate **67**
barrotes **30**
basalto **156**
báscula **20, 31, 45, 104**
base **74, 76, 112**
base de maquillaje **18**
basilisco verde **163**
basset hound **164**
bastidores **126**
bastón **122**
bastón de caramelo **67**
bastón de giro **124**
bat mitzvá **07**
bata **13**
batalla **56, 88**
batata **56, 86**
bate **111, 113**
bateador / bateadora **111, 113**
batear **111, 113**
batería **35, 98, 129**
batido, batidos **52, 70, 65**
batido de chocolate **61, 65**
batido de fresa **61, 65**
batido de vainilla **61**
batidor de mano **28**
batidora **27, 65**
batín **14**
batir huevos **29**
bauhaus **130**
baúl **30**
baúl de juguetes **08**
bautismo **07**
baya del saúco **57**
baya goji **57**
bayas **57**
bazo **04**
beagle **164**
bebé **05**
beber **52**
beber agua **20**
beber té o café **09**
bebida, bebidas **48, 52, 65, 68, 69**
bebida en lata **70**
bebida energética **52**
beca **80**
becario / becaria **81**
bed and breakfast **131**
begonia **38**
beicon **53, 71**
béisbol **113**
bejín **170**
bejín gigante **170**
belga **153**
Bélgica **151, 153**
Belice **150, 152**
beliceño / beliceña **152**
belladona **169**
belleza **18**
bellota **169**
beluga **166**
bemol **128**
bengala **119**
bengalí **164**
benín **149, 152**
beninés / beninesa **152**
berberecho **54**
berenjena **56**
berilio **78**
berkelio **78**
bermudas **14**
berro **55**
berro de agua **55**
berza **55**
bestseller **138**
betún **17**
bhangra **129**
biatlón **122**
biberón **08**
bibliografía **138**
biblioteca **43, 80, 148**
bibliotecario / bibliotecaria **80, 90**
bíceps **03**
bichos **162**
bicicleta **101**
bicicleta de carreras **101**
bicicleta de carretera **101**
bicicleta de montaña **101**
bicicleta de paseo **101**
bicicleta eléctrica **101**
bicicleta estática **124**
bidé **31**
biela de acoplamiento **102**
Bielorrusia **151, 153**
bielorruso / bielorrusa **153**
bien cualificado / bien cualificada **93**
bienal **41**
big bang **144**
Big Ben **44**
bigote, bigotes **12, 158**
bikini **134**
billar americano **125**
billar inglés **125**
billete **102, 104**
billete de autobús **99**
billete de ida **131**
billete de ida y vuelta **131**
billetera digital **94**
billetes **45, 94**
biografía **138**
biología **73, 77, 80**
biólogo / bióloga **77**
bioquímica **76**
biotecnología **91**
biplano **103**
Birmania **150, 153**
birmano / birmana **153**
birrete **80**
bis **126**
bisauguineano / bisauguineana **152**
biscote, biscotes **62, 71**
bismuto **78**
bistró **69**
bisturí **21, 77**
bizcocho **63**
blanco **125, 141**
blando / blanda **176**
blanqueamiento dental **22**
bloc de dibujo **141**
bloc de notas **82**
blog **84**
blogger **84**
bloque de aseos **135**
bloque de hormigón **87**
bloque de pisos **25, 43**
bloque de salida **116, 118**
bloqueador central / bloqueadora central **112**
bloqueador solar **49, 134**
bloquear **84, 112, 117**
bloques de construcción **08**
blues **129**
blusa **14**
blusa tradicional **15**
boa esmeralda **163**
bobsleigh **122**
bobtail japonés **164**
boca **01, 129**
boca de incendios **50**
bocadillo **65, 70, 72**
bocado **120**
boccia **125**
boceto **141**
bocina **99, 100**
boda **07**
bodyboard **119, 134**
boeing 747 **103**
bohrio **78**
boina **16**
bol **27, 28, 52**
bol de sopa **27**
bol de arroz **27**
bol de cereales **71**
bola **02, 125**
bola blanca **125**
bola de algodón **18**
bola de cristal **139**
bola de helado **65**
bola de tierra común **170**
bolardo, bolardos **43, 105**
bolígrafo **73, 82, 175**
bolillo **142**
bolivia **149, 152**
boliviano / boliviana **152**
bolo **125**
bolos **08, 125**
bolsa **52**
bolsa de agua caliente **30**
bolsa de basura **33, 34**
bolsa de golf **115**
bolsa de la compra **47, 48**
bolsa de valores **94**
bolsa de viaje **16**
bolsas compostables **155**
bolsillo **15, 110, 142**
bolso cambiador **08**
bolso de hombro **16**
bolso de mano **16**
bolso de playa **134**
bolsos **16**
bomba **101**
bomba de aire **135**
bomba eléctrica **135**
bombardero **88**
bombay **164**
bombero / bombera **89**
bomberos **50**
bombilla incandescente **33**
bombilla led **33**
bombillas **33**
bombo **128**
bondadoso / bondadosa **10**
bongó **128**
boniato **56**
bonificación **81**
bonito / bonita **177**
bonsái **38**
boquilla **40**
boquilla pulverizadora **40**
bordado **142**
border collie **164**
bordillo **43**
boro **78**
borrador **83**
borraja **59**
borrén **120**
Bosnia y Herzegovina **151, 153**
bosnio / bosnia **153**
bosque **146, 147, 148**

bosque caducifolio **146**
bosque de coníferas **146**
bosque latifoliado **159**
bosque pluvial **159**
bostezar **02**
bota, botas **17, 100, 122**
bota de esquí **17**
bota de montar, botas de montar **17, 120**
bota ortopédica **19**
bota por encima de la rodilla **17**
botánico / botánica **77**
botar **112**
botas chelsea **17**
botas de cordones **17**
botas de fútbol **17, 109**
botas de goma **40**
botas de lluvia **17**
botas de montaña **17**
botas de pescador **121**
botas de senderismo **135**
botas de trabajo **17**
botas hasta el muslo **17**
botas safari **17**
botas vaqueras **17**
botavara **119**
bote de remos **105**
bote inflable **105**
bote salvavidas **105**
botella **52**
botella de aceite **60**
botella de agua **101, 135**
botella de aire **118**
botella de aire comprimido **50**
botines **17**
botiquín de primeros auxilios **20, 49, 50**
botón, botones **15, 131, 142**
botón de inicio **83**
botón de oro **168**
botón de parada **99**
botones de mando **136**
botones de presión **13**
botsuana **149, 152**
botsuano / botsuana **152**
bouquet garni **59**
boxeo **117**
bóxer **164**
boxercise **124**
bóxers **14**
boya **106, 119, 134**
bozal **120**
braguitas **14**
braille **175**
brandy **68**
braquiosaurio **157**
brasil **149, 152**
brasileño / brasileña **152**
braza **118**
brazada **118**
brazada lateral **118**
brazalete **16, 21**
brazo **01, 50, 126**
brebaje de la bruja **139**
bretzel **62**
brezo **38, 41**
bricolaje **35, 47**
brida **120**
bridge **140**
brie **64**
brillante **37, 176, 177**
brincar **11**
brioche **62, 71**
brisa **154**
británico / británica **153**
británico de pelo corto **164**
broca, brocas **35, 36**
broca de seguridad **36**
broca para hormigón **36**
broca para madera **36**
broca para metal **36**
broca plana para madera **36**
brocha **18, 37**
broche **16**
brócoli **55, 56**
brogues **17**
bromo **78**
bronce **116, 176**
brotes **172**
brotes de soja **55**
bruja **139**
brújula **119, 135, 148**
brunch **69**
bruneano / bruneana **153**
Brunéi **151, 153**
bucear **118**
bucear con esnórquel **118**
buceo **118**
buceo profundo **118**
buenas noches **179**
buenas tardes **179**
bueno / buena **177**
buenos días **179**
buey almizclero **159**
búfalo **159**
bufanda **16**
bufét **69**
bufét de desayuno **71**
bufete de abogados **85**
bufón **79**
buganvilla **168**
buggy **97, 115**
buggy de playa **134**
buggy lunar **143**
buhardilla **25**
búho corniblanco **161**
búho nival **161**
búho real **161**
buitre **160**
buje **51**
bujía **98**
bulbo **41**
buldócer **87**
Bulgaria **151, 153**
búlgaro / búlgara **153**
bungalow **32**
búnker **115**
buque **105**
buque de guerra **105**
buques de la armada **88**
burbuja **36**
burbujas de co2 **62**
Burj Khalifa **44**
Burkina Faso **149, 152**
burkinés / burkinesa **152**
burmés **164**
burrito de desayuno **71**
burro **165**
burundés / burundesa **152**
burundi **149, 152**
buscador **144**
buscar **178**
Bután **150, 153**
butanés / butanesa **153**
buzón **25, 45**

C

caballa **54**
caballa ahumada **64, 71**
caballero **79, 139**
caballete **82, 101, 141**
caballito de juguete **08**
caballito de mar **166**
caballo **120, 140, 165**
caballo balancín **08**
caballo con arcos **125**
caballo de carreras **120**
caballo de guerra **79**
cabaña **32, 131**
cabecero **30**
cabello graso **12**
cabello normal **12**
cabello seco **12**
cabestrillo **19, 20**
cabestro **120**
cabeza **01, 04, 162**
cabeza rapada **12**
cabezuela **55**
cabina **50, 103, 123**
cabina de bronceado **18**
cabina del conductor **102**
cabina del piloto **103**
cable, cables **33, 83, 101**
cable de alimentación **83**
cable de carga **83**
cable hdmi **95**
cableado **33**
cabo **119, 147**
cabo verde **149, 152**
caboverdiano / caboverdiana **152**
cabra **53, 165**
cabra de las Montañas Rocosas **159**
cabrito **165**
cacahuete **58, 68**
cacao **169**
cacao en polvo **65**
cacarear **165**
cacatúa **161, 164**
cacatúa galah **161**
cachalote **166**
cachorro **159, 164**
cactus **41**
cactus barril dorado **168**
cactus cabeza de viejo **168**
cada día **172**
cada dos días **172**
cada hora **171, 172**
cada mes **172**
cada semana **172**
cadáver **24**
caddy **115**
cadena **16, 101**
cadena de la puerta **25**
cadena montañosa **146**
cadera **01**
cadmio **78**
caer **117**
caerse **11**
café **52, 65, 69, 71, 86**
café con hielo **65**
café con leche **65**
café cortado **65**
café de filtro **65**
café expreso **65**
café expreso doble **65**
café irlandés **65**
café solo **65**
cafetera **27, 65, 68**
cafetera francesa **28**
cafetería **42, 46, 65**
caída de las hojas **172**
caimán de anteojos **163**
caja, cajas **32, 48, 52, 128**
caja de cambios **98, 100**
caja de costura **142**
caja de fusibles **33, 98**
caja de herramientas **36**
caja de pañuelos **30**
caja de pesca **121**
caja de pescado **54**
caja del entrenador **113**
caja fuerte **131**
caja registradora **48, 68, 94**
caja torácica **03**
cajero / cajera **45, 48**
cajero automático **45**
cajón **27, 30, 82**
cajón para verduras **27**
cajonera **39**
cala **167**
calabacín **56**
calabaza **56**
calabaza bellota **56**
calabaza bonetera **56**
calabaza de halloween **139**
calabaza de invierno **56**
calabaza violín **56**
calabozo **50**
calamar **54**
calamar gigante **166**
calambre **19, 118**
calapiés **101**
calcetín, calcetines **14, 107**
calcio **23, 49, 78**
calcita **156**
calculadora **73, 74**
caldero **139**
caldo **72**
calendario **82, 172**
caléndula **38**
calentador **33**
calentar **124**
calentar en el microondas **29**
cálido / cálida **154**
caliente **176**
californio **78**
caligrafía **175**
caliza **39, 156**
calle **42, 115, 116, 118**
calle de boxes **123**
calle principal **46**
calle secundaria **42**
callejón **42**
calmado / calmada **06, 10, 93**
calmantes **49**
calmarse **178**
calorías **23**
caluroso / calurosa **154**

calvicie **12**
calzado **17**
calzado deportivo **17**
calzoncillos **14**
cama **30**
cama de hospital **21**
cama de matrimonio **30**
cama elástica **08, 125**
cama individual **30**
camaleón de jackson **163**
camaleón de parson **163**
camaleón pantera **163**
cámara **83, 84, 101, 127, 145**
cámara de cine **127**
cámara de vídeo **83, 136**
cámara de vigilancia **130**
cámara retinal **22**
cámara subacuática **118**
cámara web **83**
camarero / camarera **65, 68, 69, 89**
camarón mantis **166**
camarote **105**
cambiador de bebés **47**
cambiar **46**
cambiar de canal **137**
cambiar de marcha **101**
cambiar de tren **102**
cambiar dinero **45**
cambiar la instalación eléctrica **35**
cambiar las sábanas **34**
cambiar una bombilla **35**
cambiarse **14**
cambio climático **155**
cambio de divisa **104**
Camboya **150, 153**
camboyano / camboyana **153**
cámbrico **157**
camelia **38**
camello **24**
camello bactriano **158**
camembert **64**
camerún **149, 152**
camerunés / camerunesa **152**
camilla **21**
camilla de ambulancia **50**
camilla de lona **50**
camino **41**
camino de herradura **133**
camión de bomberos **50**
camión de la mudanza **32**
camión de plataforma **87**
camión grúa **87**
camión militar **88**
camionero / camionera **90**
camisa **15**
camisa de manga corta **14**
camisa escolar **13**
camiseta **14, 107**
camiseta de fútbol **15, 109**
camiseta de manga larga de rugby **108**
camiseta de rugby **108**
camiseta de tirantes **14**
camiseta interior **14**
camisola **14**
camisón **14**
campamento **135, 148**
campana **103, 125**
campana extractora **27**
campanario **44**
campanas tubulares **128**
campanilla azul **167**
campanilla de invierno **167**
campeonato **114**
campesinos **79**
campiña **146**
campo **107, 111, 146**
campo de béisbol **113**
campo de críquet **111**
campo de fútbol **109**
campo de golf **115**
campo de rugby **108**
campo deportivo **80**
campo eléctrico **75**
campo exterior **111**
campo magnético **75**
campo petrolífero **51**
campus **80**
camuflaje **88**
Canadá **150, 152**
canadiense **152**
canal **137, 147**
canal de música **137**
canal de pago **137**
canales de tv **137**
canalón **25**
cáñamo **169**
canario **160**
canasta **112**
cancelar **69**
Cáncer **144**
cancha **112**
canción **129**
candado **101**
candelabro **26**
candidato / candidata **81**
canela **59**
canela en polvo **59**
canela en rama **59**
canelones **64**
cangrejeras **17**
cangrejo **54, 134**
cangrejo cocotero **166**
cangrejo ermitaño **134, 166**
cangrejo herradura **166**
cangrejo violinista **166**
canguro **158**
caniche **164**
caninos **03**
canoa **105**
canotier **16**
cansado / cansada **06**
cantante **89, 129**
cantar **11**
caña **40**
caña de azúcar **86, 167**
caña de pescar **121**
caña del timón **119**
Caño Cristales **145**
cañón **79, 88, 146**
capa **15**
capa de lava **145**
capa de ozono **155**
capacidad **174**
capacidad de trabajo bajo presión **93**
capacidad para conducir **93**
caparazón **163**
capitán / capitana **89, 105**
capitán del puerto / capitana del puerto **106**
capítulo **138**
capó **97, 98**
capoeira **117**
Capricornio **144**
cápsulas **49**
capucha **13, 15**
capuchina **169**
capuchino **65**
capullo **162**
caqui **58**
carabela portuguesa **166**
cárabo común **161**
cárabo lapón **161**
caracol **162**
caracteres chinos **175**
caracteres japoneses **175**
características del río **147**
características geográficas **146**
carámbano **146**
carambola **58**
caramelos blandos **67**
caramelos de menta **67**
caramelos duros **67**
caravana **32, 135**
carbohidratos **23**
carbón **51, 135**
carboncillo **141**
carbonífero **157**
carbono **78**
carbono cero **155**
carcaj **125**
carceleros / carceleras **85**
cardamomo **59**
cardenal norteño **161**
cardiología **21**
cardiovascular **04**
cardo **38, 169**
carga **75, 105**
carga aérea **104**
cargador solar **83**
cargamento **102, 106**
cargar **11, 165**
cargo **50, 85**
carguero **105**
Caribe **150**
caribeño / caribeña **152**
caribú **159**
caries **22**
carlino **164**
carnaval **07**
carne **53**
carne ahumada **53**
carne blanca **53**
carne cocinada **53**
carne cruda **53**
carne curada **53, 64**
carne de ave **53**
carne de caza **53**
carne en conserva **64**
carne magra **53**
carne picada **53**
carne roja **53**
carnero **165**
carnet de biblioteca **80**
carnicería **46, 48**
carnicero / carnicera **53, 89**
carpa **54**
carpetas **82**
carpincho **159**
carpintero / carpintera **89**
carpo **03**
carrera **116**
carrera de aceleración **123**
carrera de caballos **120**
carrera de enganches **120**
carrera de lanchas **119**
carrera de obstáculos **120**
carrera de patinaje sobre hielo **122**
carrera de relevos **116**
carrera de trotones **120**
carrera en silla de ruedas **116**
carrera sin obstáculos **120**
carrera t11 (deportistas ciegos) **116**
carrete **121, 142**
carrete de hilo **142**
carretera principal **148**
carretera secundaria **148**
carreteras **96**
carretilla **40**
carretilla elevadora **87, 106**
carril bici **43, 101**
carril central **96**
carril exterior **96**
carril interior **96**
carrito **102, 104, 131**
carrito de golf **115**
carrito de la compra **48**
carrito de los postres **63, 69**
carro de bebé **08**
carrocería **98, 123**
carta **45, 82**
carta de presentación **92**
cartabón **73, 74**
cartel de información **49**
cartel de rebajas **47**
cartel de seguridad **87**
cartera **16, 94**
cartera de valores **94**
carterismo **85**
cartero / cartera **45, 90**
cartílago **03**
cartógrafo / cartógrafa **148**
cartón **52**
cartón de leche **61**
cartulina **141**
casa **32, 148**
casa adosada, casas adosadas **32, 43**
Casa Blanca **44**
casa de campo **32**
casa de labranza **86**
casa de muñecas **08**
casa del árbol **32, 133**
casa flotante **32**
casa pareada **32**
casa prefabricada **32**
casa rústica con tejado de paja **32**
casa unifamiliar **32**
casaca sanitaria **13, 21**
casados **05**
casarse **07**
cáscara **58, 61**
cáscara de coco **57**
cáscara de huevo **161**
casco **50, 87, 100, 101, 105, 107, 110, 111, 113, 117, 119, 120, 123, 143, 146, 158, 159**
casco viejo **43**

cascos **82, 84, 95, 136**
cascos inalámbricos **136**
caseta de peaje **96**
caseta de playa **134**
caseta del perro **164**
casilla **140**
caspa **12**
casquillo **33, 115**
castaña de agua **56**
castañas **58**
castaño **168**
castaño de indias **169**
castillo **44**
castillo de arena **134**
Castillo Himeji **44**
casuario **160**
catamarán **105**
catapulta **79**
Catar **151, 153**
catarata **22, 146**
cataratas victoria **145**
catarí **153**
Catedral de San Basilio **44**
catenaria **102**
catering **91**
catorce **173**
catre **135**
cauteloso / cautelosa **10**
cavar **11, 39**
cavidad **22**
cayena **59**
caza **88**
cazadora **15**
cazar **159**
cazo **28**
cazoleta anaranjada **170**
cazuela **28**
cd **136**
cebada **86**
cebar **121**
cebo **121**
cebolla **56**
cebolleta **55**
cebollino **59**
cebollitas en vinagre **60**
cebra **158**
ceda el paso **96**
cedilla **175**
cedro chino **169**
cedro del líbano **167**
ceja **01**
cejuela **129**
celador / celadora **21**
celandina **168**
celda **85**
celebraciones **07**
celiaquía **23**
celoso / celosa **06**
celsius **154**
célula animal **77**
célula vegetal **77**
cementerio **43**
cemento **87**
cena **26, 72,**
cenar **09, 52**
cenefa **37**
ceniza **145**
cenozoico **157**
centauro **139**
centímetro **174**
central **107**
central eléctrica **44**
central geotérmica **51**
central hidroeléctrica **51**
central nuclear **51**
centro **42, 74, 110**
centro comercial **42, 47**
centro de control **143**
centro de la diana **140**
centroafricano / centroafricana **152**
centroamericano / centroamericana **152**
centrocampista **109**
cepillar **120**
cepillarse el pelo **09**
cepillarse los dientes **09, 22**
cepillo **12, 36**
cepillo barrendero **40**
cepillo de dientes **31**
cepillo de empapelar **37**
cepillo de fregar **34**
cepillo interdental **22**
cepillo para cejas **18**
cepillo para la espalda **31**
cepillo para zapatos **17**
cera **18, 176**
cerámica **176**
cerbero **139**
cerca **176**
cerdo **53, 165**
cerdo hormiguero **158**
cereales **48, 71**
cerebro **04**
ceremonia de graduación **80**
Ceres **143**
cereza, cerezas **57, 169**
cerezo **169**
cerio **78**
cero **173**
cerrado **48, 132**
cerrajería **46**
cerrajero / cerrajera **90**
cerrar sesión **83, 178**
cerrojo **25**
certificado de nacimiento **07**
cerveza **52, 68**
cerveza ale **68**
cerveza de trigo **68**
cerveza ipa **68**
cerveza lager **68**
cerveza negra **68**
cerveza pilsener **68**
cerveza sin alcohol **68**
cesio **78**
césped **25, 41, 167**
cesta **48, 50, 101, 164**
cesta colgante **41**
cesta de frutas **57**
cesta de jardinero **40**
cesta de la ropa **34**
cesta de pan **71**
cesta de pícnic **133, 134**
cesta freidora **28**
cesto de la ropa sucia **31**
chacal **158**
chad **149, 152**
chadiano / chadiana **152**
chaleco **15**
chaleco de pesca **121**
chaleco reflectante **13, 87**
chaleco salvavidas **105, 119**
chalet **32, 131**
chalota **56**
champán **68**
champiñon **56**
champiñón silvestre **170**
champiñones salteados **71**
chanclas **17, 134**
chándal **15**
chapa de madera **35**
chaparrón **154**
chapati **62**
chaqueta **15**
chaqueta acolchada **15**
chaqueta bomber **15**
chaqueta de cocinero **13**
chaqueta de esquí **122**
chaqueta vaquera **15**
charco **154**
charcutería **48**
charlar con amigos **09**
charrán ártico **160**
chasis **123**
chat **83**
chatear en línea **09**
checo / checa **153**
cheddar **64**
chef **69, 90**
cheflera **38**
cheque **45, 94**
cherna estrellada **166**
chicana **123**
chicle **67**
chihuahua **164**
chile **56, 59, 60, 64, 149, 152**
chile en polvo **59**
chile ojo de pájaro **59**
chileno / chilena **152**
chillar **164**
chimenea **25, 26, 32, 87, 105, 145**
chimpancé **159**
China **150, 153**
chincheta **82**
chinelas **17**
chino / china **153**
Chipre **151, 153**
chipriota **153**
chiringuito **65**
chirivía **56**
chochín **160**
chocolate blanco **67**
chocolate caliente **52**
chocolate con leche **67**
chocolate negro **67**
chollo **48**
chorizo **53**
chorizo picante **64**
chorro de agua **50**
choza **32**
chubasquero **15**
chucrut **60**
chuleta **53**
chumbera **168**
chupete **08**
chupito **68**
chutar **107, 108**
chutney **60, 72**
cica **167**
ciclismo **101, 133**
ciclismo de montaña **133**
ciclo de vida de la mariposa **77**
ciclo de vida de la rana **77**
cicuta **169**
ciempiés **162**
cien **173**
ciénaga **147**
ciencia **73**
ciencia ficción **127, 138**
ciencias **80**
ciencias sociales **80**
cieno **39**
científico / científica **90**
cierre **16**
cierre de bayoneta **33**
ciervo **158**
ciervo volante **162**
cigala **54**
cigüeña **160**
cilantro **59**
cilindro **74**
cima **147**
cimitarra **79**
cinc **78**
cincel **36, 141**
cincha **120**
cinco **173**
cinco posiciones **112**
cincuenta **173**
cine **42, 127**
cingalés / cingalesa **153**
cinta **32, 125, 142**
cinta adhesiva **82**
cinta aislante **36**
cinta de carrocero **37**
cinta de correr **124**
cinta de lomo **53**
cinta métrica **36, 142, 174**
cinta para el pie **119**
cinta reflectante **100**
cinta transportadora **48**
cintura **01**
cinturilla **15, 142**
cinturón **15, 16, 103, 117**
cinturón de herramientas **36, 87**
cinturón de pesas **118**
cinturón de seguridad **123**
cinturón negro **117**
cinturón policial **50**
circonio **78**
circuito **83**
circuito de carreras **123**
círculo **74**
círculo central **109**
círculo polar ártico **145**
círculos con los brazos **124**
circunferencia **74**
ciruela **57**
ciruelas pasas **58**
ciruelo **169**
cirugía **21**
cirugía plástica **21**
cirujano / cirujana **21, 90**
cirujano amarillo **166**
cirujano azul **166**
cisne cantor **161**
cisne negro **161**
cisne vulgar **161**
cisterna **33**
cita **81**
cita médica **20**
citación **85**
citoplasma **77**
cítricos **57**
ciudad **42, 43**

Ciudad del Vaticano **151**
Ciudad Prohibida **44**
cizalla **40**
claqueta **84**
clara **60, 61, 71**
clarinete **128**
clase **73**
clase de ejercicio **124**
clase de yoga **24**
clase ejecutiva **103**
clase turista **103**
clasicismo **130**
clásico / clásica **13**
clasificación **123**
clasificador **82**
clasificar la basura **155**
clave de fa **128**
clave de sol **128**
clavel **38**
clavícula **03**
clavija **33, 83**
clavija de afinación **129**
clavijero **129**
clavo, clavos **36, 59, 111, 115**
clementina **57**
cliente / clienta **45, 48, 65, 85**
clientes **69, 81**
clima **155**
clínica dental **22**
clip, clips **73, 82**
cloro **78**
cloroplasto **77**
club **115**
cms (sistema de gestión de contenidos) **84**
cobalto **78**
cobertizo **25, 39**
cobertizo de jardín **39**
cobertura **111**
cobra **24**
cobra india **163**
cobra marina **163, 166**
cobre **78, 156**
cocer a fuego lento **29**
coche cama **102**
coche de carreras **97, 123**
coche de cinco puertas **97**
coche de época **97**
coche de juguete **08**
coche de policía **50**
coche deportivo **97**
coche eléctrico **97**
coche híbrido **97**
coche híbrido enchufable **97**
coches **97, 98, 99**
cocina **27, 29, 69, 105**
cocinado / cocinada **56**
cocinar al vapor **29**
coco **58**
cocodrilo del nilo **163**
cocodrilo marino **163**
cocotero **167**
cóctel **68**
cóctel sin alcohol **68**
coctelera **68**
codera **107**
código de barras **48**
código postal **45**
codo **01**
codorniz **53**
coelophysis **157**
coger **11, 121, 140**
coger con la red **121**
coger el autobús **09**
coger el tren **09, 102**
coger la baja por maternidad **81**
cogollo **55**
cohete **143**
cojín **26**
col **55**
col de saboya **55**
col lombarda **55**
col negra **55**
col rizada **55**
cola **15, 48, 54, 103, 120, 132, 143, 158, 159, 160**
cola de abadejo **54**
cola de caballo **167**
cola de caballo gigante **157**
cola para empapelar **37**
colaborador / colaboradora **93**
colaborar **92**
colada **34**
colador **28**
colador de té **66**
colcha **30**
colchón **30**
colchón autohinchable **135**
colchón hinchable **135**
colección **130**
coles de bruselas **55**
colesterol **23**
coleta **12**
colgante **16**
colgar **14, 37, 178**
colgar una estantería **35**
colibrí **160**
coliflor **56**
colinabo **55**
colirio **22**
Coliseo **44**
collage **141**
collar **16**
collar de perlas **16**
collarín cervical **19**
colmena **82, 162, 165**
colmenilla **170**
colocador / colocadora **112**
colombia **149, 152**
colombiano / colombiana **152**
columna **44, 146**
columna vertebral **03**
columpio **43, 133**
colza **86**
coma **175**
comadreja **158**
comba **08, 124**
combate de boxeo **117**
combinación **14**
combo **70**
combustibles fósiles **51, 155**
comedero **26**
comedia **126, 127, 137**
comedia de situación **137**
comedia romántica **127**
comedor **26, 80, 88**
comenzar **95**
comer **52**
comer en el local **70**
comer fuera **69, 178**
comerciante **79**
comercio **91**
comercio en línea **91**
cometa **08, 143, 144**
cómic **48, 138**
cómico / cómica **89**
comida **65**
comida de negocios **81**
comida de tres platos **69**
comida para mascotas **48**
comida precocinada **48**
comida rápida **47, 70**
comidas **72**
comillas dobles **175**
comillas simples **175**
comino **59**
comisaría de policía **42, 50**
comisión **94**
cómoda **30**
comodín **140**
comoras **149, 152**
comorense **152**
compañero de piso / compañera de piso **32**
compañero de trabajo / compañera de trabajo **07, 81, 92**
compartimento **102**
compartimento portaequipajes **103**
compartir **84**
compartir la pantalla **95**
compás **73, 74**
compasivo / compasiva **06**
competencias laborales **93**
competitivo / competitiva **93**
completo **131, 135**
componer **128**
compositor / compositora **128**
compost **40**
compostador **33, 40**
compra de una casa **32**
compra en línea **48**
comprador / compradora **47**
comprando **179**
comprar **32, 46**
compras **46**
compras en línea **46**
compresa **49**
compresiones torácicas **20**
comprobar el nivel de aceite **98**
comprobar los neumáticos **98**
compuerta **106**
compuerta de esclusa **51**
compuesto **76**
comunicación en línea **83**
comunicación escrita **93**
con gas **52**
con habitaciones libres **131**
con hielo **68**
con hombros descubiertos **15**
con parcelas disponibles **135**
con plomo **97**
conchiglie **64**
concierto de pop **129**
concluir la reunión **95**
concurso **137**
concurso de preguntas y respuestas **137**
concurso de saltos **120**
condenar **85**
condimentos **60, 71, 72**
cóndor andino **160**
conducir **09, 96**
conducto lacrimal **01**
conductor / conductora **75, 90, 99**
conductor de autobús / conductora de autobús **90**
conejera **164**
conejillo de indias **164**
conejo **53, 158, 164**
conexión eléctrica **135**
confección de colchas **142**
confeccionar **142**
conferencia **95**
confitura **60**
confundido / confundida **06**
confuso / confusa **177**
congelado / congelada **54, 56**
congelador **27**
congelados **48**
congelar **29**
conglomerado **156**
congoleño / congoleña **152**
coníferas **41, 157, 167**
conmoción cerebral **19**
cono **74, 87**
cono de chimenea **25**
conocer alguien **179**
conocido / conocida **07**
conseguir el empleo **92**
conserje **90**
conservador / conservadora **130**
conservador del museo / conservadora del museo **89**
conservante de madera **37**
conservas **48**
conservatorio **80**
considerado / considerada **10**
consigna **102**
consola **136**
constelación **144**
construcción **87, 91**
construir **11, 87**
contable **90, 94**
contacto **83**
contador de la luz **33**
contaminación **155**
contar **11, 74**
contenedor **105, 106**
contenedor de basura **25, 135**
contento / contenta **06**
continente **145**
contrabajo **128**
contrabando **85**
contrachapado **35**
contralto **126**

contrapeso **87**
contraseña **83**
contrato **92**
contrato de alquiler **32**
control de pasaportes **104**
controlador de dj **129**
controles **99, 100, 136**
controles de la calefacción **99**
controles de tono **129**
conversión **108**
cónyuge **07**
cookies **84**
cooksonia **157**
coordenadas **148**
coordinar **92**
copa de campeones **109**
copa de cóctel **68**
copa de vino **27**
copa helada **63**
copas **27**
copernicio **78**
copiar **11**
copiloto **103**
copo de nieve **154**
copos de chile **59**
copyright **175**
coquilla **117**
coral **166**
corazón **04, 53, 57, 140**
corazón de alcachofa **56**
corbata **15, 16**
corbata escolar **13**
corchera **118**
corchete **142**
corcho **60**
cordero **53, 165**
cordillera **146**
cordón litoral **147**
cordón umbilical **08**
cordones **17, 107**
Corea del Norte **150, 153**
Corea del Sur **150, 153**
coristas **129**
cormorán **160**
cornalina **156**
córnea **22**
córner **109**
corneta inglesa **128**
coro **128**
corona **22**
corral **86**
correa **16, 164**
correa de barbilla **107**
correa del calapiés **101**
correa del ventilador **98**
correcto / correcta **176**
corrector **18**
corredor / corredora **107**
corredor de poder / corredora de poder **107**
corredores / corredoras **122**
correo aéreo **45**
correo certificado **45**
correo electrónico **83**
correr **11, 111, 113, 124**
correr en parada **124**
corriente alterna **33, 75**
corriente continua **33, 75**
corrimiento de tierra **146**
corsé **14**
cortaalambres **36**
cortabordes **40**
cortacésped **40**
cortadera **38**
cortador de pizza **28**
cortadora de pan **62**
cortahuevos **28**
cortar **29, 35, 142**
cortar el césped **09, 39**
cortarse el pelo **12**
cortasetos **40**
cortatubos **36**
cortaúñas **18, 49**
corte, cortes **19, 53**
corte bob **12**
corte de luz **33**
corte de pelo militar **12**
cortes de carne **53**
corteza **61, 62, 64, 145**
cortina de ducha **31**
cortinas **26**
corto / corta **13, 176**
corzo **158**
cosechadora **86**
cosechar **39, 86**
coser **142**
cosmética **18**
costa de marfil **149, 152**
Costa rica **150, 152**
costarriqueño / costarriqueña **152**
costilla, costillas **03, 53, 70**
costura, costuras **111, 113, 142**
cotización **94**
cotorra de kramer **161**
country **129**
coxis **03**
cráneo **03**
cráter **143, 145**
creativo / creativa **93**
crecer **178**
crecimiento **05**
crema **49, 63**
crema bronceadora **18**
crema de afeitar **31**
crema de chocolate **60**
crema de limón **60**
crema de manos **18**
crema de pañal **08**
crema facial **31**
crema hidratante **18**
crema pastelera **63**
cremallera **17, 142**
crepe **70**
crepúsculo **171**
cresta **146, 161**
cresta oceánica **145**
cretácico **157**
cría **161**
cría de canguro **158**
cría de ganso **165**
criar **120**
criaturas fantásticas **139**
cribar **39, 62**
crimen **85, 137**
criminal **85**
crin **120**
críquet **111**
crisálida **77**
crisantemo **38**
crisol **76**
cristal **35, 76**
cristalería **27**
cristalino **22**
crítico / crítica **10**
Croacia **151, 153**
croata **153**
crol **118**
cromo **78, 156**
cromosoma **77**
cronología **84**
cróquet **133**
crosse **110**
crótalo cornudo **163**
cruasán **62, 71**
cruce **96**
crucero **88, 105**
crucigramas **138**
cruda **61**
crudités **72**
crudo / cruda **51, 56**
cruel **177**
crujiente **52, 56**
cruz del sur **144**
cuadrado **74**
cuádriceps **03**
cuadrícula **148**
cuadriga **79**
cuadro **26, 101**
cuadro interior **113**
cuarcita **156**
cuarenta **173**
cuarenta iguales **114**
cuarenta minutos **171**
cuarto / cuarta **173**
cuarto creciente **143**
cuarto de baño **31**
cuarto de galón **174**
cuarto de hora **171**
cuarzo **156**
cuaternario **157**
cuatro **173**
Cuba **150, 152**
cubano / cubana **152**
cubertería **26**
cubeta **37**
cubierta **101, 105, 119**
cubiertos **27, 69**
cubismo **130**
cubitera **68**
cúbito **03**
cubo **34, 37, 40, 74, 134**
cubo de basura **25**
cubo de compostaje **40**
cubo de reciclaje **34**
cubrecanapé **30**
cubrir la tierra **39**
cubrir pérdidas **94**
cucaburra **160**
cucaracha **162**
cuchara **27**
cuchara de helado **28**
cuchara de madera **28**
cuchara de servir **27**
cuchara medidora, cucharas medidoras **28, 49**
cuchara mielera **60**
cuchara sopera **27**
cucharilla **27**
cucharón **27**
cuchilla **31**
cuchillo **27, 28**
cuchillo de carnicero **28**
cuchillo de podar **40**
cuchillo del pan **28**
cuchillo para la mantequilla **27**
cucurucho de helado **65**
cuello **01, 15, 115, 142, 161**
cuello de pico **14**
cuello halter **15**
cuello redondo **14**
cuello uterino **04**
cuenta **69**
cuenta corriente **45**
cuenta de ahorros **45**
cuentagotas **76**
cuentakilómetros **99**
cuentarrevoluciones **99**
cuento de hadas **138, 139**
cuerda, cuerdas **114, 117, 125, 128, 129, 135**
cuerdas vocales **04**
cuernos **158**
cuero **13, 107, 176**
cuerpo **129**
cuerpo de bomberos **50**
cuerpo humano **01**
cuervo **24**
cuervo americano **160**
cuervo común **160**
cueva marina **147**
cuevas **146**
cuidado de la piel **49**
cuidar **39**
cuidar de **178**
culata **98**
culpable **06, 85**
cultivar **39**
cumpleaños **07**
cumplir el plazo de entrega **92**
cúmulo estelar **144**
cuna **30**
cuneta **43**
cuñada / cuñado **05**
cupcake **63**
cupón **48**
cúpula **44**
cúpula bulbosa **44**
curado / curada **72**
curar **20**
cúrcuma **59**
curio **78**
curioso / curiosa **06, 93**
curl americano **164**
curl de bíceps **124**
curling **122**
curling en silla de ruedas **122**
currículum **92**
curry **72**
curry en polvo **59**
cursiva **175**
curva **74**
curva de nivel **148**
curva peligrosa hacia la derecha **96**
curva pronunciada **123**
cúter **36, 37**
cutícula **02**

D

dachshund 164
dados 140
dálmata 164
damas 140
dance 129
danés / danesa 153
dar a me gusta 84
dar aviso 32
dar de alta 21
dar de comer 86
dar de comer al gato 09
dar de comer al perro 09
dar el preaviso de baja voluntaria 81
dar la hora 171
dar la mano 92
dar marcha atrás 96
dar media vuelta 148
dar un puñetazo 117
dar un toque 178
dar un trago 52
dar una presentación 95
dardos 140
darmstatio 78
dársena 106
datáfono 45, 48
dátil 57, 58
datilero 167
de alta gama 47
de cachemir 13
de cuadros 13
de cuadros escoceses 13
de granja 53
de hoja 56
de hoja caduca 41
de hoja perenne 41
de lunares 13
de mediana edad 12
de otoño 57
de planta abierta 32
de primavera 57
de verano 57
debajo 180
deberes 73
década 172
decapante 37
decatlón masculino 116
decepcionado / decepcionada 06
decepcionante 177
decidido / decidida 10
decidir 11
decimales 173
décimo / décima 173
decir 11
declaración 85
decoración 37, 63
decorado 126
decorador / decoradora 37
decorados 126
decorar 29, 63
dedal 142
dedalera 38
dedo 02
dedo corazón 02
dedo gordo 02
defender 117
defensa 85, 107, 109
defensa derecho / defensa derecha 110
defensa izquierdo / defensa izquierda 110
defensor de wicket / defensora de wicket 111
deforestación 155
dejada 114
dejar a alguien 98
dejar de tomar 23
dejar entrar 178
dejar la habitación 131, 178
dejarse crecer el pelo 12
delantal 13, 29
delante 03
delantero / delantera. 109
deletrear 11, 73
delfín 24, 166
deliberación del jurado 85
delicatessen 46, 64
delicias turcas 67
delicioso / deliciosa 52, 177
delta 147
deltoide 03
demandante 85
denominador 74
dentadura postiza 22
dentista 22, 89
dentro 180
denuncia 50
departamento de administración 91
departamento de compras 91
departamento de investigación y desarrollo (i+d) 91
departamento de mantenimiento 91
departamento de marketing 91
departamento de producción 91
departamento de recursos humanos 91
departamento de relaciones públicas 91
departamento de ventas 91
departamento financiero 91
departamento infantil 47
departamento informático 91
departamento jurídico 91
departamentos 21, 80, 91
dependiente / dependienta 89
deporte de remo 119
deportes 107-125, 137
deportes acuáticos 119
deportes adaptados 125
deportes de combate 117
deportes de invierno 122
deportes de motor 123
deportista 89
depósito 32
depósito de aceite 100
depósito del líquido de frenos 98
depósito del líquido limpiaparabrisas 98
depósito del líquido refrigerante 98
deprimido / deprimida 06
derecho 80, 85, 114
dermatología 21
derrame de petróleo 155
derretir la mantequilla 29
derribar 117
derribar una pared 35
desagradable 10, 177
desagüe 31, 33
desarrollador de aplicaciones / desarrolladora de aplicaciones 89
desastroso / desastrosa 177
desatar 14
desatascador 31, 36
desatascar el lavabo 35
desatascar el váter 35
desayunar 09
desayuno 26, 71
desayuno cocinado 71
descamado / descamada 54
descansar 20
descanso 109
descapotable 97
descarga eléctrica 19
descargar 83
descendencia 05
descenso 122
descongelar el congelador 34
desconsiderado / desconsiderada 10
descorazonador 28
descoser 142
describir acciones 11
describir habilidades 11
descubierto 94
descubierto bancario 45
descubrimiento 79
desechos alimenticios 155
desembarcar 106
desembocadura 147
desempaquetar 11, 32
desertificación 155
desfibrilador 50
desganado / desganada 06
deshielo de los casquetes polares 155
deshonesto / deshonesta 10
desierto 146
desinfectante 20
desinfectante de váter 34
desistir 178
desmayarse 20
desnatada 61
desodorante 49
despacho 26
despegar 43, 104, 178
despensa 27, 60
despertador 30
despertarse 09, 178
desplazamiento lateral 124
desplazarse 96-106
desprendedor de papel pintado 37
despreocupado / despreocupada 10
después 171
destacable 177
desternillante 177
destino 104
destornillador de estrella 36
destornillador plano 36
destructor 88
desvío 96
detección de metales 133
detective 50
detective privado / detective privada 89
detector de humo 50
detención 50
detergente de ropa 34
detrás 03
detrás de 148, 180
devolver 46, 80, 178
devónico 157
día 171, 172
día de acción de gracias 07
día de los muertos 07
diabetes 19
diablillo 139
diablo de tasmania 158
diablo espinoso 163
diadema 16
diagonal 74
diamante 140, 156
diámetro 74
diana 140
diapositiva 95
diarrea 19
dibujar 73
dibujo 141
dibujos animados 137
diccionario 73, 138
diciembre 172
didyeridú 129
diecinueve 173
dieciocho 173
dieciséis 173
diecisiete 173
diente, dientes 01, 03
diente de león 38, 55
dientes de leche 22
dientes de sable 157
diéresis 175
diésel 97
dieta 23
dieta baja en calorías 23
dieta detox 23
dieta equilibrada 23
diez 173
difracción 75
difusión 76
digestivo 04, 69
digital 84
dimensiones 74
dimetrodon 157
dimitir 81
Dinamarca 151, 153
dinamo 101
dinero 45, 94
dinero falso 94
dintel 87
diodo 75
dióxido de carbono 155
dique 51
dique seco 106
dirección 45

dirección de giro **143**
dirección de la reacción **76**
direcciones **180**
director / directora **73, 81, 84, 126, 127**
director de fotografía / directora de fotografía **127**
director de la sucursal / directora de la sucursal **45**
director de orquesta / directora de orquesta **128**
dirigible **103**
dirigir **92, 128**
disco **110**
disco de freno **100**
disco duro **83**
discos **136**
discos de algodón **20**
discos de vinilo **129**
discoteca **42**
discutir **73**
diseñador / diseñadora **89**
diseñador de moda / diseñadora de moda **90**
diseñar el jardín **39**
diseño y tecnología **73**
disertación **80**
disfraz **13**
disgustado / disgustada **06**
dísir **139**
disolvente **37**
disparos **88**
dispensador de agua **82**
dispensador de hielo **27**
dispensador de licores **68**
dispensario **49**
dispersión **75**
disposición de la mesa **27**
dispositivo inalámbrico **83**
dispositivos **83**
disprosio **78**
distancia **174**
distraído / distraída **06**
distribuidor **98**
distrito comercial **42**
divertido / divertida **06, 177**
dividendos **94**
dividir **74**
divisa **94**
divorciados **05**
divorciarse **07**
divorcio **05**
diwali **07**
DJ **84**
dj de radio **90**
dóberman **164**
doblar **14**
doblar la ropa **34**
doble **68**
doble falta **114**
doble techo **135**
dobles **114**
doce **173**
doctor / doctora **19, 20, 21, 89**
doctorado **80**
documental **137**
documental de naturaleza **137**
documento **79**
documento adjunto **83**
doler **20**
dolor **19**
dolor de cabeza **19**
dolor de espalda **19**
dolor de estómago **19**
dolor de garganta **19**
dolor de muelas **22**
doma y monta **120**
domiciliación bancaria **45**
domingo **172**
Dominica **150, 152**
dominicano / dominicana **152**
dominio de los idiomas **93**
dominiqués / dominiquesa **152**
dominó **140**
domo de vapor **102**
donativos **130**
dondiego de día **169**
dónut **63, 70**
dónut de chocolate **63**
dónut relleno de mermelada **63**
dormir hasta tarde **178**
dormir la siesta **09**
dormitorio **30**
dorsal ancho **03**
dos **173**
dos coletas **12**
dos puntos **175**
dos veces a la semana **172**
dosa **72**
doscientos **173**
dosis **49**
drácena **38**
dragón **139**
dragón de komodo **163**
drama **127**
drama de época **127, 137**
drama policial **127**
drenaje **39**
drepanaspis **157**
dromedario **158**
dron armado **88**
dubnio **78**
ducha, duchas **31, 135**
ducharse **09, 31**
duendecillo **139**
dulce **52, 56, 57**
dumplings **70, 72**
duna **146, 147**
duro / dura **57, 176**
dvd **136**

E

echar el ancla **106**
eclipse lunar **143**
ecografía **08**
economía **80**
ecosistema **77, 155**
ecoterapia **24**
ecoturismo **131**
ecuación **74**
ecuación química **76**
ecuador **145, 149, 152**
ecuatoguineano / ecuatoguineana **152**
ecuatoriano / ecuatoriana **152**
eczema **19**
edad de bronce **79**
edad de hierro **79**
edad de oro islámica **79**
edad de piedra **79**
edam **64**
edificio, edificios **42, 43, 44, 148**
edificio abandonado **44**
edificio de oficinas **42**
edificio de viviendas **44**
edificio del gobierno **43**
edificio histórico **44, 132**
edificio moderno **44**
edificios famosos **44**
editor / editora **89**
edredón **30**
educación **91**
educación física **73**
educado / educada **10**
efectivo **45**
efecto **114**
efecto invernadero **155**
efectos especiales **127**
efectos secundarios **49**
efervescente **49**
eficiente **93**
egipcio / egipcia **152**
egipto **149, 152**
egoísta **10**
eid al-fitr **07**
einstenio **78**
eje **100, 101**
eje de transmisión **98**
ejercicio **124**
ejercicio de piernas **124**
ejercicios **124**
ejército **88**
El salvador **150, 152**
electricidad **33, 51, 75**
electricista **89**
electrodo negativo **75**
electrodo positivo **75**
electrodomésticos **27, 48**
electrón **76**
electrónica **91**
elefante africano **158**
elefante asiático **159**
elefante de guerra **79**
elegir **46**
elementos **76**
elementos del jardín **41**
elfo / elfa **139**
eliminar **83, 111**
elíptica **124**
elixir **139**
embalse **51**
embarazo / embarazada **08**
embarcadero **106**
embarcar **104, 106**
embrague **99, 100**
embrión **08**
embudo **76**
embutidos **64**
emigrar **07, 161**
emiratí **153**
Emiratos Árabes Unidos **151, 153**
emisiones **51, 155**
emisiones industriales **155**
emisora de radio **84**
emitir **84**
emocionado / emocionada **06**
emocionante **177**
emoji, emojis **84, 175**
empanada **70**
empapelar **37**
empaquetar **11, 32**
empaste **22**
empatar **109**
empeine **02**
emperador / emperatriz **79**
Empire State Building **44**
empleado / empleada **81**
empleado de correos / empleada de correos **45**
empleado doméstico / empleada doméstica **89**
empleador / empleadora **81**
empleo **81**
empresa **81**
empresa de selección de personal **92**
empresario / empresaria **81, 90**
empujar **11**
empuñadura **115, 117**
emú **160**
en **180**
en aceite **64**
en el campo **111**
en el piso de abajo **25**
en el piso de arriba **25**
en el sentido contrario a las agujas del reloj **148**
en el sentido de las agujas del reloj **148**
en escabeche **64**
en frente de **148, 180**
en la esquina **148**
en la playa **134**
en números rojos **45**
en polvo **61**
en sal **54**
en salsa **72**
en vinagre **72**
enamorarse **07**
enana blanca **144**
enano / enana **139**
encaje de bolillos **142**
encantado / encantada **06**
encargado de mantenimiento / encargada de mantenimiento **89**
encender **83, 137, 178**

encender una hoguera **135**
encendido **99**
enchufar **83**
enchufe **33**
encía **03**
enciclopedia **73, 138**
encima **180**
encimera **27**
encogerse de hombros **02**
encontrar trabajo **07**
encurtidos **60, 72**
endeudarse **94**
endivia **55**
endocrino **04**
endocrinología **21**
endoesqueleto **77**
eneldo **59, 60**
energético / energética **93**
energía **33, 51, 91**
energía de biomasa **51**
energía eólica **51**
energía geotérmica **51**
energía hidroeléctrica **51**
energía mareomotriz **51**
energía nuclear **51**
energía renovable **51**
energía solar **51**
energía verde **51**
enero **172**
enfadado / enfadada **06**
enfermedades **19**
enfermería **80**
enfermero / enfermera **20, 21, 89**
enfriar **124**
engrasar **29**
enhebrar **142**
enjambre **162**
enjuagarse **22**
enjuague bucal **31**
enlatado / enlatada **56**
enoki **56, 170**
enredadera amarilla **168**
enrollar **29**
ensalada **55, 65**
ensalada griega **72**
ensalada mixta **72**
ensalada picada **72**
ensayo **108**
entallado / entallada **13**
entarimado **26, 41**
entender **11**
entorno **143-156**
entrada **113, 130**
entrada principal **25**
entrada prohibida a peatones **96**
entrante **69**
entrar **11**
entrar por la fuerza **50**
entre **148, 180**
entrega **45**
entrega a domicilio **48, 91**
entrenador / entrenadora **109, 112, 113**
entrenador personal / entrenadora personal **124**
entrenamiento con pesas **124**
entrenamiento en circuito **124**
entrenamientos **124**
entrenar **124**
entretenimiento **91**
entrevista **81, 137**
entrevistador / entrevistadora **81**
entusiasmado / entusiasmada **06**
entusiasta **10**
envenenamiento **19**
enviar **83**
enviar dinero **45**
enviar un md **84**
enviar un paquete **09**
envoltura **103**
enyesar **37**
epiglotis **04**
episodio **137**
equidna **158**
equipaje **104, 131**
equipaje de mano **103, 104**
equipo **107**
equipo de alta fidelidad **136**
equipo de la sala de reuniones **82**
equipo local **107**
equipo visitante **107**
equitación **120, 131**
era de la información **79**
eras **157**
erbio **78**
eritrea **149, 152**
eritreo / eritrea **152**
erizo **158**
erizo de mar **166**
erupcionar **145**
escala **104, 148**
escala de ph **76**
escalada **125, 128**
escalada en hielo **122**
escalar **11**
escalera, escaleras **25, 36, 50, 87**
escalera de incendios **50**
escalera de mano **37**
escalera del camión **50**
escalera mecánica **47, 104**
escalfado / escalfada **72**
escalofríos **19**
escalones **25**
escama, escamas **54, 163**
escandio **78**
escáner **21, 42, 82, 104**
escaparate **25**
escarabajo rinoceronte **162**
escarcha **154**
escarchado **154**
escardar **39**
escariador **36**
escarlata **141**
escarola **55**
escarpines **17**
escena de riesgo **127**
escena del crimen **50**
escenario **126**
escinco de lengua azul **163**
esclusa, esclusas **51, 106**
escoba **34, 40, 139**
escoba de curling **122**
escobilla **31, 34**
escobilla limpiacristales **34**
escolta **112**
escombros **33**
esconderse **164**
escondite **133**
escopeta **88**
Escorpio **144**
escorpión **162**
escota **119**
escote **142**
escotera **119**
escotilla **143**
escriba **79**
escribir **73**
escritor / escritora **90**
escritorio **73, 82**
escritura **175**
escritura a mano **175**
escritura árabe **175**
escritura devanagari **175**
escroto **04**
escuchar **11**
escuchar la radio **09**
escudo **79**
escuela **43, 73, 148**
escuela de arte **80**
escuela de danza **80**
escultor / escultora **89**
escultura **130, 141**
escupidera **22**
escurreplatos **27**
escurridor **28**
esfera **74**
esfinge **139**
esfinge colibrí **162**
esgrima **116, 117**
esguince **19**
eslovaco / eslovaca **153**
Eslovaquia **151, 153**
Eslovenia **151, 153**
esloveno / eslovena **153**
esmalte **03**
esmeralda **156**
esmog **154**
esmoquin **15**
esnórquel **118**
esnórquel y gafas de buceo **15, 134**
esófago **04**
espacio **143, 144**
espada **79, 117**
espadaña **167**
espaguetis **64, 72**
espalda **118**
espaldera **41**
espantapájaros **86**
espantoso / espantosa **177**
España **151, 153**
español / española **153**
esparadrapo **20**
espárragos **56**
espárragos trigueros **56**
espátula **28, 76, 141**
especial **177**
especias **59**
especies **77**
especies de aves **160, 161**
especies de mamíferos **158, 159**
especies en peligro de extinción **155**
especies marinas **166**
espectadores **110, 116**
espectadores / espectadoras **115**
espectro electromagnético **75**
espectro visible **75**
espejo **18, 22, 30, 77**
espeleología **146**
espeleólogo / espeleóloga **146**
esperar despierto / esperar despierta **178**
espía **89**
espinaca **55**
espinilla **01**
espinillera **110, 111**
espino **169**
espino amarillo **169**
espiráculo **166**
espolvorear **29**
esponja **31, 34, 37**
esponja para polvos **18**
espontáneo / espontánea **10**
esporas **170**
esposas **50**
espray **49**
espray nasal **20**
espuma **65**
espuma de baño **18, 31**
espumadera **28**
esqueje **39**
esqueleto **03**
esquí **119, 122**
esquí acuático **119**
esquí de fondo **122**
esquiador / esquiadora **122**
esquiador acuático / esquiadora acuática **119**
esquiar **122**
esquilar **165**
esquina **42**
esquinero derecho / esquinera derecha **107**
esquinero izquierdo / esquinera izquierda **107**
esquisto **51, 156**
esta tubería tiene una fuga **89**
estabilizador **103**
establo **86, 120**
estacas **111**
estación de autobús **42, 99**
estación de bomberos **42, 50**
estación de esquí **122**
estación de servicio **148**
estación de tren **42, 102, 148**
estación espacial **143**
estaciones **172**
estado **104**
estados de ánimo **06**
Estados unidos de américa **150, 152**
estadounidense / estadounidense **152**
estalactita **146**
estalagmita **146**
estambre **38**
estaño **78, 156**
estanque **41, 86, 115**
estante **26, 27**
estantería, estanterías **26, 48, 80**

estantes **27**
estar desempleado / estar desempleada **81**
estar lleno / estar llena **26**
estatura media **12**
estay de popa **119**
estay de proa **119**
este **148**
este lado hacia arriba **45**
estegosaurio **157**
estepa **146**
estéreo **136**
esterilla **24, 124**
esterilla de dormir **135**
esternón **03**
estetoscopio **20**
estigma **38**
estilo **38**
estiramiento **124**
estofado **72**
estómago **04**
Estonia **151, 153**
estonio / estonia **153**
estornino **160**
estornudar **02, 20**
estragón **59**
estratosfera **155**
estrechar **142**
estrecho **147**
estrecho / estrecha **176**
estrella **144**
estrella de cine **127**
estrella de david **44**
estrella de mar **134, 166**
estrella de neutrones **144**
estrella del rock **90**
estrella doble **144**
estrella fulgurante **144**
estrella polar **144**
estreno **127**
estrés **19**
estresado / estresada **06**
estrías **115**
estribo **120**
estroncio **78**
estropajo **34**
estropajo de aluminio **36**
estructura **135**
estuario **147**
estuche **22, 73**
estuche de lentillas **22**
estudiante de grado **80**
estudiante de posgrado **80**
estudiantes **73**
estudio de cine **127**
estudio de grabación **84**
estudio de televisión **84**
estudios **73-80**
estufa de gas **33**
etíope **152**
etiopía **149, 152**
etiqueta del precio **47**
etiquetas **40**
eufórico / eufórica **06**
Europa **151, 153**
europeo / europea **153**
europio **78**
evolución **77**
examen **73**
examen médico **20**
excavación **79**
excavadora **87**
excavar **159**
excelente **177**
excéntrico / excéntrica **10**
exceso de equipaje **104**
exceso de velocidad **85**
exhausto / exhausta **06**
exmarido **05**
exmujer **05**
exoesqueleto **77**
exosfera **155**
exótico de pelo corto **164**
expansor de pecho **124**
experimento **76**
exploración espacial **143**
exposición **130**
exposición permanente **130**
exposición temporal **130**
expresiones útiles **179, 180**
exprimidor de limones **28**
extender **124**
extintor **50**
extracción **22**
extracto **45**
extractor de aire **31**
extraño / extraña **177**
extraordinario / extraordinaria **177**
extras **127**
extremo derecho / extrema derecha **110**
extremo izquierdo / extrema izquierda **110**

F

fábrica **42**
factura, facturas **32, 94**
facturación en línea **104**
facultades **80**
fagot **128**
fahrenheit **154**
faisán **53, 161**
falafel **03, 70**
falda **14**
falda con abertura **15**
falda fruncida **142**
falo hediondo **170**
falta **112, 113, 114**
familia **05**
famoso **127**
fans **129**
fantasía **127, 138**
fantasía y mitos **139**
fantasma **139**
fantástico / fantástica **177**
farallón **147**
faringe **04**
farmacéutico / farmacéutica **49, 89**
farmacia **42, 49**
faro, faros **44, 50, 97, 100, 101, 106**
faro trasero **101**
farol **135**
farola **25, 43**
fase **33**
fastidioso / fastidiosa **177**
fatigoso / fatigosa **177**
fauno **139**
febrero **172**
fecha de caducidad **49**
fecha de parto **08**
fecha del juicio **85**
Federación Rusa **150, 151, 154**
feijoa **58**
feliz **06**
felpudo **25**
femenino / feminina **04**
fémur **03**
fénec **158**
feng shui **24**
fénix **139**
fenogreco **59**
feo / fea **177**
fermio **78**
ferretería **46**
ferri **105, 106**
fertilizante **39**
fertilizar **39**
feta **64**
feto **08**
fez **16**
fiambre **64, 71**
fianza **85**
fibra **23, 57**
fibra de vidrio **176**
fibra sintética **13**
ficción **138**
ficción literaria **138**
ficus **38**
fidedigno / fidedigna **93**
fideos **64, 70, 72**
fideos de arroz **64**
fiebre **19**
fiesta del fin del ayuno **07**
fiestas **07**
figuras **63**
figuras espaciales **74**
fijo / fija **81**
fila **103, 126**
filamento **38**
filete **53, 54**
filete de bacalao **54**
filete de cadera **53**
filete de salmón **54**
filete de solomillo **53**
Filipinas **151, 153**
filipino / filipina **153**
filosofía **80**
filósofo **79**
filtración **39**
filtro de aire **98, 100**
fin de la vía para ciclistas **96**
fin de semana **172**
final de partido **109**
finanzas **91, 94**
fine leg **111**
finlandés / finlandesa **153**
Finlandia **151, 153**
fino / fina **176**
fiordo **147**
firma **45, 83**
firmar un contrato **92**
fiscal **85**
física **73, 75, 80**
fisión **75**
fisioterapeuta **89**
fisuras **51**
Fiyi **153**
fiyiano / fiyiana **153**
flamboyán **168**
flamenco **160**
flan **64**
flat white **65**
flauta **62, 128, 129**
flauta dulce **129**
flautín **128**
flecha **79, 125**
flerovio **78**
fletán **54**
flexible **93, 176**
flexionar **124, 126**
flexiones **124**
flip **125**
flojo / floja **176**
flor, flores **38, 169**
flor de la pasión **169**
florete **117**
florista **47, 89**
floristería **46**
flotador **118, 121, 134**
flotador de la cisterna **33**
flotar **118**
flujo de lodo **146**
flúor **78**
fm **84**
foca **159, 166**
focha común **161**
folk **129**
follaje verde **172**
folletos **95**
fondo **111**
fondo marino **51**
fondue china **72**
fontanería **33**
fontanero / fontanera **89**
food truck **70**
foque **119**
formal **10**
formas **74**
formulario de solicitud **92**
fórmuquímica **76**
foróptero **22**
forro **15**
fosa oceánica **145**
fosas nasales **01**
fósforo **78**
fósil **77**
foso **44**
foso de la orquesta **126**
foto finish **116**
fotocopiadora **82**
fotografía de naturaleza **133**
fotógrafo / fotógrafa **89**
fotomatón **46**
fotosíntesis **77**
fracción **74**
fracciones **173**
fractura **19**
fracturación hidráulica **51**
fragata **88**
fragata real **160**
frágil **45**
frailecillo atlántico **160**
frambuesa **57**
francés / francesa **153**
Francia **151, 153**
francio **78**
franja de alerta **113**
frasco **27, 52**
fraude **85**
frecuencia **84**

frecuencia cardíaca **124**
fregadero **27**
fregar **34**
fregar el suelo **34**
fregona **34**
freír **29**
frenar **98, 101**
freno **99, 100, 101**
freno de mano **99**
frenos **101**
frente **01, 88**
frente a **148**
frente cálido **155**
frente frío **155**
frente marítimo **132**
fresa **22, 57**
fresadora **35**
fresco / fresca **52, 56, 57, 154**
fresia **47, 167**
fresquito / fresquita **154**
frigorífico **27**
frío / fría **52, 154, 176**
frisbi **133**
fritia **168**
frito / frita **72**
frito con mucho aceite **72**
frontal **03**
frontalera **120**
frontón **44**
frunces **142**
fruncir el ceño **02**
frustrado / frustrada **06**
fruta **48, 57, 58**
fruta de la pasión **58**
fruta de temporada **57**
fruta deshidratada **58, 71**
fruta en conserva **60**
fruta fresca **71**
frutas con hueso **57**
frutería **46**
frutero **26**
frutipán **56**
frutos secos **58, 68**
fucsia **168**
fuego **50**
fuente, fuentes **41, 42, 79**
fuente de vidrio **28**
fuera **113, 180**
fuera de banda **112**
fuera de pista **122**
fuerte **52**
fuerza aérea **88**
fuerza centrífuga **75**
fuerza centrípeta **75**
fuerzas armadas **88, 91**
funcionario judicial / funcionaria judicial **85**
funda de almohada **30**
funeral **07**
furgoneta de comida **70**
furioso / furiosa **06**
fusilli **64**
fusión **75**
fusta **120**
fútbol **109**
fútbol americano **107**

G

gabardina **15**
Gabón **149, 152**
gabonés / gabonesa **152**
gacela **158**
gachas **71**
gada **79**
gadolinio **78**
gafas **122**
gafas de bronceado **18**
gafas de bucear **118**
gafas de lectura **22, 49**
gafas de natación **15, 118**
gafas de seguridad **36, 76, 87**
gafas de sol **22, 134**
gaita **129**
gajo **57**
galaxia elíptica **144**
galaxia espiral **144**
galería **130**
galería de arte **43, 132**
galio **78**
galleta con trocitos de chocolate **63**
galleta de mantequilla **63**
Galleta de la suerte **63**
galleta florentina **63**
galletas **63**
gallina **165**
gallina del bosque **170**
gallinero **86, 126**
gallo **165**
galón **174**
galopar **120, 165**
gamba pelada **54**
gamba sin pelar **54**
gamberrismo **85**
Gambia **149, 152**
gambiano / gambiana **152**
gamo común **158**
gamuza para gafas **22**
ganado **165**
ganar **11, 81, 115, 109, 140**
ganar peso **20**
ganar un premio **07**
ganar yardas **107**
ganchillo **142**
gancho **53, 87**
Ganges **145**
ganso **53, 165**
ganso del nilo **160**
garaje **25**
garantía **47**
gardenia **38**
garganta **04**
gargantilla **16**
garrafa de agua **135**
garras **161**
garza **160**
gas **51, 76**
gas de esquisto **51**
gasa **20**
gases de efecto invernadero **155**
gases nobles **78**
gasolina **97**
gasolinera **42, 97**
gasto **94**
gastornis **157**
gastroenterología **21**
gatear **11**
gatito **164**
gato esfinge **164**
gato hidráulico **98**
gato montés **159**
gato salvaje **159**
gavial **163**
gaviota **134, 160**
géiser **146**
gel **49**
gel de baño **31**
gel para el cabello **12**
gélido / gélida **154**
gemas **156**
gemelo **03**
gemelos **16**
gemelos / gemelas **05**
Géminis **144**
gen **77**
generador **33, 51**
general **88**
géneros **138**
generoso / generosa **10**
genio **139**
genitales **01**
geoda **156**
geografía **73, 146, 147**
Georgia **150, 153**
georgiano / georgiana **153**
geranio **38**
gerbera **47**
gerente **81**
gerente del restaurante **69**
germanio **78**
gestión de proyectos **93**
gestión del tiempo **93**
Ghana **149, 152**
ghanés / ghanesa **152**
ghee **61**
gibón **159**
gigante / giganta **139**
gigante roja **144**
gigantes gaseosos **143**
gimnasia **125**
gimnasio **124, 131**
gin-tonic **68**
ginecología **21**
ginkgo **167**
girar **118, 126**
girar a la derecha **148**
girar a la izquierda **148**
girar en la primera calle a la izquierda **96, 148**
girar en la segunda calle a la derecha **96, 148**
girar hacia la derecha **96**
girar hacia la izquierda **96**
girasol, girasoles **38, 86**
giro de braza **118**
giro de crol **118**
giro de espalda **118**
gisófila **47**
glaciar **146**
gladiolos **47**
glándula suprarrenal **04**
glaseado **29, 63**
glasear **62, 63**
glicinia **38**
globo **08, 114**
globo aerostático **103**
globo ocular **22**
glóbulo rojo **77**
gloria de texas **168**
glosario **138**
glúteo **03**
gnatóstomo **157**
gneis **156**
gnomo **139**
go **140**
gofre, gofres **65, 70, 71**
golbol **125**
golf **115**
golfista / golfista **115**
golfo **147**
golondrina **160**
golosinas **48, 67**
golpe de mano abierta **117**
golpear **11, 110, 117**
goma **176**
goma de borrar **73, 82**
gominola **67**
góndola **51**
gong **128**
gorgojo **162**
gorila **159**
gorra de béisbol **16**
gorra de cazador **16**
gorra de golf **115**
gorra de montar **120**
gorra de policía **50**
gorra de repartidor de periódicos **16**
gorra inglesa **16**
gorrión **160**
gorro **118**
gorro con pompón **16**
gorro de cocinero **13**
gorro de punto **16**
góspel **129**
gota de lluvia **154**
gotas **49**
gotero **21**
gps **99**
grabado **141**
grabadora de voz **83**
grabar **137**
grácil **177**
gracioso / graciosa **10, 177**
grada **109**
gradilla **76**
grado **80**
grados **154**
graduado / graduada **80**
graduarse **07**
gráfico de barras **95**
grafiti **85**
grafito **156**
grageas **67**
grajo **160**
gramo **174**
Gran Agujero Azul **145**
Gran Barrera de Coral **145**
gran danés **164**
Gran Mezquita de Djenné **44**
Granada **58, 88, 150, 152**
granadino / granadina **152**
granado **168**
granate **156**
grande **176**
grandes almacenes **47**
granero **86**
granito **156**
granizo **154**
granja **86, 165**
granja avícola **86**

granja frutícola **86**
granja lechera **86**
granja ovina **86**
granja porcina **86**
granjero / granjera **79, 86, 89**
grano de maíz **55**
grapadora **73, 82**
grapas **82**
grasa **18**
grasas insaturadas **23**
grasas saturadas **23**
grava **35, 40**
gravedad **144**
graznar **165**
Grecia **151, 153**
green **115**
griego / griega **153**
grifo **27, 31, 33, 139**
grifo de cerveza **68**
grillo **162**
grímpola **119**
griñolera **169**
gripe **19**
gris, grises **01, 141**
gritar **11**
grosella blanca **57**
grosella negra **57**
grosella roja **57**
grúa **98, 106**
grúa de la cámara **84**
grúa de puente **106**
grúa flotante **106**
grúa torre **87**
grueso / gruesa **176**
grulla **160**
gruñir **165**
guacamayo escarlata **161**
guante **100, 110, 113, 115, 117, 122**
guante autobronceador **18**
guante de batear **113**
guante de bloqueo **110**
guante de recepción **110**
guantes **16, 107, 109**
guantes aislantes **143**
guantes de boxeo **117**
guantes de goma **34**
guantes de jardinería **40**
guantes de seguridad **87**
guapo **12**
guardabarros **100**
guardabarros alto **100**
guardacoches **96**
guardacostas **106**
guardaespalda **90**
guardar en su sitio **178**
guardarropa **130**
guardia de seguridad **89, 90, 130**
guardia de tráfico **96**
guardia derecho / guardia derecha **107**
guardia izquierdo / guardia izquierda **107**
guardián del zoo / guardiana del zoo **90**
guarnición **69, 72**
Guatemala **150, 152**
guatemalteco / guatemalteca **152**
guayaba **58**
guayabo **168**
guepardo **158**
guerra **79, 88**
guerrero **24, 79**
guía **122, 130**
guía de conversación **131**
guía de televisión **138**
guía del hilo **142**
guía turístico / guía turística **90, 131, 132, 138**
guiar **39**
Guinea **149, 152**
Guinea Ecuatorial **149, 152**
Guinea-Bisáu **149, 152**
guineano / guineana **152**
guiñar **02**
guion **126, 127, 175**
guion bajo **175**
guionista **127**
guirnalda **47**
guisante, guisantes **55**
guitarra acústica **129**
guitarra eléctrica **129**
guitarrista acústico / guitarrista acústica **129**
gully **111**
gusano **162**
Guyana **149, 152**
guyanés / guyanesa **152**

H

habas **55**
habilidades **11**
habilidades interpersonales **93**
habilidades numéricas **93**
habilidades profesionales **93**
habitación compartida **131**
habitación con dos camas **131**
habitación con vistas **131**
habitación del bebé **30**
habitación doble **131**
habitación individual **131**
habitación privada **21**
hablador / habladora **10**
hablar **11**
hacer (los deberes) **11**
hacer (un muñeco de nieve) **11**
hacer amigos **07**
hacer clic **83**
hacer cola **104**
hacer ejercicio **09, 20**
hacer el seguimiento del pedido **46**
hacer el tonto **178**
hacer kayak **119**
hacer la cama **09, 34**
hacer la cena **09**
hacer la compra **09, 34**
hacer la maleta **131**
hacer los deberes **09**
hacer malabares **11**
hacer piruetas **126**
hacer plié **126**
hacer testamento **07**
hacer un chip **115**
hacer un examen **73**
hacer un mate **112**
hacer un pase bajo **112**
hacer un drive **115**
hacer un swing **115**
hacer una copia de seguridad **83**
hacer una entrevista **92**
hacer una jugada **113**
hacer una pausa **09**
hacer una reserva **131**
hacer una reverencia **02**
hacer una teleconferencia **95**
hacer una visita guiada **132**
hacer unas cortinas **35**
hacerse viral **84**
hacha **36, 50, 79**
hada **139**
hafnio **78**
Haití **150, 152**
haitiano / haitiana **152**
hajj **07**
hakama **117**
halal **72**
halcón peregrino **160**
halloumi **64**
halloween **07**
halógenos **78**
halva **67**
hamaca **135**
hamburguesa **70**
hamburguesa con queso **70**
hamburguesa de pollo **70**
hamburguesa de salchicha **71**
hamburguesa vegetal **70**
hamburguesería **70**
hámster **158, 164**
hándicap **115**
Hang Son Doong **145**
hangar **104**
harina blanca **62**
harina con levadura **62**
harina de fuerza **62**
harina de huesos **39**
harina de trigo integral **62**
harina de trigo sarraceno **62**
harina morena **62**
harina sin gluten **62**
harina sin levadura **62**
harinas **62**
harissa **60**
hashtag **83, 84**
hasio **78**
haya **168**
heavy metal **129**
hebilla **16**
hechizar **139**
hectárea **174**
helado **61, 70, 134, 154**
helecho, helechos **41, 157, 167**
hélice **103, 105**
helicóptero **103**
helicóptero de ataque **88**
helicóptero de transporte **88**
helio **78**
helipuerto **51**
hematita **156**
hemisferio norte **145**
hemisferio sur **145**
hemorragia **19**
hemorragia nasal **19**
henna **168**
heno **86**
hepática **167**
heptatlón femenino **116**
herbazal **146**
herbicida **39, 86**
herbología **24**
herida **19**
herida en la cabeza **19**
hermana / hermano **05**
hermanastro / hermanastra **05**
hermanos **05**
héroe / heroína **127, 139**
herradura **120**
herramientas **35, 36, 87**
herramientas de jardinería **40**
herramientas de sílex **79**
herramientas para modelar **141**
herrero / herrera **79**
hervido / hervida **72**
hervidor eléctrico **27**
hervir **29**
hexágono **74**
hibernación **77**
hibisco **38, 169**
hidra **139**
hidroala **105**
hidroavión **103**
hidrógeno **78**
hidroterapia **24**
hiedra **169**
hielo **68, 154**
hielo y limón **68**
hiena **158**
hierba, hierbas **41, 59**
hierba de las pampas **167**
hierbas medicinales **49**
hierro **23, 49, 78, 156**
hígado **04, 53**
higiene femenina **49**
higienista dental **22**
higo chumbo **58**
higo seco **58**
higróforo **170**
higuera **169**
hijab **16**
hijo / hija **05**
hijo único / hija única **05**
hilo **84, 142**
hilo bramante **40**
hilo de trama **142**
hilo de urdimbre **142**
hilo dental **22, 31**
hilvanar **142**
himalayo **164**
hinojo **55, 59**
hip-hop **129**
hipermetropía **22**
hipertensión **19**
hipnoterapia **24**
hipódromo **120**
hipopótamo **158**
hipoteca **32, 45**

hipotenusa **74**
hisopo **59**
historia **73, 79, 80**
historia natural **157**
historiador / historiadora **79**
historial dental **22**
historial médico **21**
historias **139**
hockey sobre hielo **110**
hockey sobre hielo paralímpico **122**
hockey sobre hierba **110**
hogar **25-41, 32**
hogaza **62**
hoguera **135**
hoja **40, 55, 117**
hoja de otoño **169**
hoja de ruta **95**
hoja de sangre **38**
hoja de verano **169**
hojaldre **63**
hojarazo **168**
hojas de parra rellenas **64**
hojas de remolacha **55**
hojear **138**
hola **179**
holgado / holgada **13**
holi **07**
holmio **78**
hombre **05**
hombre de jengibre **63**
hombre lobo **139**
hombrera, hombreras **15, 107, 110**
hombro **01**
home **113**
home cinema **136**
homeopatía **24**
homogeneizada **61**
Honduras **150, 152**
hondureño / hondureña **152**
hongo blanco **170**
hongos **77, 170**
honrado / honrada **10, 93**
hora **104**
hora punta **42, 102**
horario **132, 171**
horario flexible **81**
horas de apertura **132**
horas extra **81**
horca **40**
horca para patatas **40**
hormas para botas **17**
hormas para zapatos **17**
hormiga **162**
hormigón **35, 176**
hormigonera **87**
horneado / horneada **72**
hornear **29, 62, 63**
hornillo **135**
hornillo de dos fuegos **135**
horno **27**
horno de pizza **70**
horóscopo **138**
horquilla **40, 101**
horrible **177**
hortensia **38**
hospital **21, 42**
hospital de campaña **88**
hostal **131**
hotel **42, 131**
hoyo **115**
hoyo en uno **115**
hoyuelos **12**
huellas dactilares **50**
huerto **41, 86**
hueso **03**
hueso roto **19**
huéspedes **131**
huevas de rana **77, 163**
huevera **27, 61**
huevo, huevos **61, 77**
huevo cocido **61, 71**
huevo de codorniz **61**
huevo de gallina **61**
huevo de ganso **61**
huevo de pato **61**
huevo escalfado **61, 71**
huevo frito **61, 71**
huevos revueltos **61, 71**
hugin y munin **139**
huir **178**
hula-hop **08**
humanidades **80**
humanos primitivos **157**
humedad **154**
humedal **146**
húmero **03**
hummus **72**
humo **50**
humor **138**
húngaro / húngara **153**
Hungría **151, 153**
huracán **154**
hurón **164**
husky siberiano **164**

I

íbice alpino **158**
ibis escarlata **160**
ibis sagrado **160**
iceberg **146**
ichthyostega **157**
idiomas **73, 80**
ídolo moro **166**
iglesia **43, 44**
iglesia ortodoxa **44**
iglú **32**
ígneo / ígnea **156**
iguana marina **163**
iguana verde **163**
iluminación **47, 84**
iluminado / iluminada **176**
ilustración **79, 138**
imaginativo / imaginativa **93**
imán **75**
imbornal **43**
impaciente **10**
impactado / impactada **06**
impactante **177**
impala **158**
imperdible **20**
imperio **79**
importante **177**
importe **45**
impresión **141, 175**
impresionante **177**
impresionismo **130**
impresora **82**
imprimación **37**
imprimir **83**
impulsivo / impulsiva **10**
incisivos **03**
incorrecto / incorrecta **176**
increíble **177**
incubadora **08**
independiente **93**
India **150, 153**
indicaciones **132**
indicador de temperatura **33, 99**
índice **02, 138**
indiferente **06**
indio / india **78, 153**
individual **114**
Indonesia **151, 153**
indonesio / indonesia **153**
industria aeroespacial **91**
industria automovilística **91**
industria del agua **91**
industria farmacéutica **91**
industria hotelera **91**
industria química **91**
industria textil **91**
industrias **91**
infancia **08**
infección **19**
infeliz **06**
influencer **84**
influyente **93**
informal **10**
informática **73, 93**
informático / informática **89**
informe **82**
infrarrojos **75**
infusión **52**
infusor **66**
ingeniería **80**
ingeniería petrolífera **91**
ingeniero / ingeniera **90**
ingeniero de sonido / ingeniera de sonido **127**
ingle **01**
inglés **73**
ingredientes **70**
ingresar **21, 45**
ingresos **94**
inhalador **20, 49**
iniciar sesión **83, 178**
iniciativa **93**
injera **62**
injertar **39**
inmaduro / inmadura **10**
inmigración **104**
inmobiliaria **32**
inmovilizar **117**
innovador / innovadora **93**
inocente **85**
inofensivo / inofensiva **177**
inquilino / inquilina **32**
insecto atrapado **168**
insecto hoja **162**
insecto palo **164**
insectos **162**
insensible **10**
insomnio **19, 30**
inspector / inspectora **50**
instalar **33**
instalar el césped artificial **39**
instructor de esquí / instructora de esquí **89**
instructor de vuelo / instructora de vuelo **90**
instrumentos **129**
instrumentos de orquesta **128**
instrumentos matemáticos **74**
insulina **49**
inteligencia artificial **83**
inteligente **10**
interceptar y devolver **111, 113**
interesado / interesada **06**
interesante **177**
interfono **25**
interior del coche **99**
intermedio **126**
intermitente **97, 100**
intérprete **89, 126**
interrumpir **95**
interruptor **33**
interruptor de fusibles **33**
intersección **43**
intestino delgado **04**
intestino grueso **04**
intolerancia a la lactosa **23**
intolerante **23**
intoxicación alimenticia **19**
intratable **10**
intrigado / intrigada **06**
inundación **154**
inútil **177**
invernadero **39**
inversión **94**
invertebrados **77**
investigación **50, 91, 93**
investigador de mercado / investigadora de mercado **89**
invierno **172**
invitado / invitada **26**
ionosfera **155**
ir a la escuela **07, 09**
ir a la guardería **07**
ir a medio galope **120**
ir a trabajar **09**
ir al paso **120**
ir de compras **46**
ir de excursión **132**
ir de pasajero **100**
ir en bicicleta **101**
ir en patinete **133**
Irak **150, 153**
Irán **151, 153**
iraní **153**
iraquí **153**
iridio **78**
iris **01, 38**

Irlanda 151, 153
irlandés / irlandesa 153
Islas Marshall 153
irracional 10
irritado / irritada 06
irritante 177
irse 98
irse a dormir 09
irse a la cama 09
irse de crucero 131
irse de mochilero 131
irse de vacaciones 131
irse fuera 178
isla 88, 145, 147
islandés / islandesa 153
Islandia 151, 153
Islas bahamas 150
Islas fiyi 150
Islas maldivas 153
Islas marshall 150
Islas mauricio 149
Islas salomón 150, 153
Islas seychelles 149
isobara 155
isquiotibiales 03
Israel 150, 153
israelí 153
istmo 147
Italia 151, 153
italiano / italiana 153
iterbio 78
itrio 78

J

jabalí 53, 159
jabalí verrugoso 159
jabón 31
jabón facial 18
jaboncillo de sastre 142
jabonera 31
jaca 58
jack de salida 129
jacuzzi 25, 124
jade 156
jaguar 159
jaiba 166
jalá 62
jalapeño 59
Jamaica 150, 152
jamaicano / jamaicana 152
jamón 53, 64, 71
jamón ibérico 64
janucá 07
Japón 150, 153
japonés / japonesa 153
jarabe 49
jarcia 119
jardín 113
jardín acuático 41
jardín botánico 132
jardín campestre 41
jardín clásico 41
jardín de la azotea 41
jardín de plantas herbáceas 41
jardinería 39, 133
jardinero / jardinera, jardineros / jardineras 89, 113
jarra medidora, jarras medidoras 27, 28, 174
jarrón 26
jaspe 156
jaula 164
jazz 129
jefe de equipo / jefa de equipo 92
jefe de obra / jefa de obra 89
jefe de personal / jefa de personal 81
jengibre 59
jerbo 164
jerez 68
jeringuilla 20, 49, 77
jeroglíficos egipcios 175
jersey 14
jet privado 103
jinete 120
jirafa 158
jiu jitsu 117
jockey 120
jogging 133
Jordania 150, 153
jordano / jordana 153
joroba 158
jota 140
joven 12
joyería 16, 46
joyero / joyera 16, 89
jubilarse 07, 81
judías 56
judías planas 55
judías secas 55
judías verdes 55
judo 117
juego, juegos 08, 114, 140
juego de acción 136
juego de aventuras 136
juego de deportes 136
juego de estrategia 136
juego de lógica 136
juego de mesa 08
juego de pares 140
juego de plataformas 136
juego de preguntas y respuestas 136
juego de puzles 136
juego de rol 136
juego de simulación 136
juego decisivo 114
juego multijugador 136
juegos de mesa 140
juegos de raqueta 114
juegos olímpicos de invierno 122
jueves 172
juez / jueza 85, 90, 114
juez de línea / jueza de línea 109, 114
jugador / jugadora 108, 114, 140
jugador de baloncesto / jugadora de baloncesto 112
jugador de fútbol / jugadora de fútbol 107
jugador de hockey sobre hielo / jugadora de hockey sobre hielo 110
jugador de hockey sobre hierba / jugadora de hockey sobre hierba 110
jugador de lacrosse / jugadora de lacrosse 110
jugador del cuadro interior / jugadora del cuadro interior 113
jugadores / jugadoras 108, 113
jugando a las cartas 140
jugar 11, 40
jugar con tus hijos 09
jugoso / jugosa 52
juguete de arrastre 08
juguetería 46
juguetes 08, 164
juguetes de baño 31
juicio 85
juliana falsa 168
julio 172
junco, juncos 41, 167
junio 172
junta directiva 95
juntarse 178
junto a 148, 180
Júpiter 143
jurado 85
jurásico 157
juzgado 43

K

k-pop 129
karaoke 136
kárate 117
karting 123
kayak 105, 119
Kazajistán 151, 153
kazajo / kazaja 153
kebab 70, 72
kéfir 61
kendo 117
Kenia 149, 152
keniano / keniana 152
kétchup 60, 70
kickboxing 117
kilogramo 174
kilómetro 174
kilómetro cuadrado 174
kilt 15
kimchi 60
kimono 15
kiosco 46, 48
kipá 16
kirguís 153
Kirguistán 151, 153
Kiribati 150, 153
kiribatiano / kiribatiana 153
kit de reparación de pinchazos 101
kitesurf 119
kiwi 58, 160
koala 158
kosher 72
kriptón 78
kumquat 57
kung fu 117
Kuwait 151, 153
kuwaití 153
kwanzaa 07

L

laberinto de cuentas 08
labios 01
laboratorio 76
labrador 164
laca 12
lacrosse 110
lácteos 23, 48
ladera 147
lado 74
ladrar 164
ladrillo, ladrillos 35, 87, 176
ladrones 50
lagarto 164
lagarto de cuello con volantes 163
lago 146, 148
lago Moteado 145
lago Natron 145
lágrima 22
laguna 147
lamer 02, 11
láminas 170
lámpara 26, 82, 139
lámpara de la mesita de noche 30
lámpara de noche 30
lámpara fluorescente compacta (lfc) 33
lana 13, 142, 176
lancha rápida 105
langosta 54, 162
lantánidos 78
lantano 78
lanza 79
lanzador / lanzadora 111, 113
lanzagranadas 88
lanzamiento 143
lanzamiento de disco 116
lanzamiento de jabalina 116
lanzamiento de martillo 116
lanzamiento de peso 116
lanzamiento del transbordador espacial 143
lanzamisiles portátil 88
lanzar 11, 107, 108, 111, 113, 121
lanzarse 159
Laos 150, 153
laosiano / laosiana 153

lapa **134, 166**
lápices de colores **73**
lapislázuli **156**
lápiz **73, 82, 141, 175**
lápiz de ojos **18**
lápiz para cejas **18**
largo / larga **74, 176**
largo hasta el suelo **15**
larguero **108, 109**
laringe **04**
las dos en punto **171**
las dos menos cinco **171**
las dos menos cuarto **171**
las dos menos diez **171**
las dos menos veinte **171**
las dos menos veinticinco **171**
lasaña **64, 72**
láser **75**
laser run **116**
lata **52**
latigazo cervical **19**
latitud **145, 148**
latón **176**
laúd **129**
laurel **38, 59, 167**
laurencio **78**
lava **145**
lavabo **33**
lavadero de coches **97**
lavadora **34**
lavanda **38**
lavandería **46**
lavar el coche **09, 34**
lavar la ropa **34**
lavar los platos **09, 34**
lavarse el pelo **09, 12**
lavarse la cara **09**
lavavajillas **27, 34**
laxante **49**
lazo **63**
lección **73**
lechada **37**
leche **61, 65, 71**
leche condensada **61**
leche de almendra **61**
leche de cabra **61**
leche de oveja **61**
leche de soja **61**
leche de vaca **61**
leche desnatada **61**
leche en polvo **08**
leche entera **61**
leche semidesnatada **61**
lecho de roca **145**
lechón **165**
lechuga **55**
lechuga iceberg **55**
lechuga romana **55**
lechuza común **161**
lectura **138**
lederhosen **15**
leer **73**
leer el correo electrónico **09**
leer el mapa **148**
leer el periódico **09**
legumbres **23**
lejía **34**
lejos **176**
lemongrass **59**
lémur de cola anillada **159**
lencería **47**
lengua **04, 53**
lengua de gato **170**
lenguado **54**
lengüeta **17, 121**
lente **75, 127, 136**
lente cóncava **75**
lente convexa **75**
lentes bifocales **22**
lentillas **22, 49**
lento / lenta **176**
Leo **144**
león **158**
león marino **166**
leona **158**
leopardo **159**
leopardo de las nieves **159**
leotardo **15, 126**
leprechaun **139**
lesiones **19**
lesotense **152**
Lesoto **149, 152**
let **114**
letón / letona **153**
Letonia **151, 153**
letras **175**
leucocito **77**
leudar **62**
levadura en polvo **62**
levadura fresca **62**
levantar **11, 124**
levantar un muro de ladrillos **35**
levantarse **09, 11, 178**
leyendo el mapa **148**
libanés / libanesa **153**
Líbano **150, 153**
libélula **162**
Liberia **149, 152**
liberiano / liberiana **152**
líbero / líbera **112**
libertad condicional **85**
Libia **149, 152**
libio / libia **152**
Libra **144, 174**
librería **46**
libreta **73, 95**
libreto **126**
libro, libros **26, 80, 138**
libro de cocina **138**
libro de hechizos **139**
libro de jardinería **138**
libro de naturaleza **138**
libro de texto **73, 138**
libro de viajes **138**
libro electrónico **83, 138**
libro infantil **138**
libro para colorear **138**
licaón **158**
licencia de pesca **121**
lichi **57**
licor **68**
licorería **46**
licuadora **27**
líder **81**
liderazgo **93**
liebre **53**
liebre ártica **159**
Liechtenstein **151, 153**
liechtensteiniano / liechtensteiniana **153**
lienzo **141**
liga **14**
ligadura **175**
ligamento **03**
ligero / ligera **176**
liguero **14**
lijadora **35**
lijar **37**
lila **38**
lima **18, 36, 57**
lima encurtida **60**
límite **113**
límite de velocidad **96**
limón **57**
limonada **52**
limpiador **18**
limpiador / impiadora **89**
limpiador de baños **34**
limpiador de cristales / limpiadora de cristales **90**
limpiador de superficies **34**
limpiaparabrisas **97**
limpiar **120, 178**
limpiar el baño **34**
limpiar el horno **34**
limpiar las superficies **34**
limpiar las ventanas **34**
limpiarse los dientes con hilo dental **22**
limpieza **34**
limpio / limpia **54, 176**
limusina **97**
lince **159**
línea azul **110**
línea central **112**
línea de **10** metros **108**
línea de **22** metros **108**
línea de **5** metros **108**
línea de **50** yardas **107**
línea de balón muerto **108**
línea de banda **112, 114**
línea de ensayo **108**
línea de falta **113**
línea de flotación **105**
línea de fondo **107, 112, 114**
línea de gol **107**
línea de juego **115**
línea de medio campo **109**
línea de meta **110, 116**
línea de mitad de campo **108**
línea de salida **116**
línea de saque de banda **112**
línea de servicio **114**
línea de tiro libre **112**
línea de touch-in-goal **108**
línea de wicket **111**
línea de yarda **107**
línea de zona **112**
línea divisoria **96**
línea frontal **111**
línea lateral **111**
línea roja **110**
líneas **74**
líneas de suspensión **125**
líneas interiores **107**
linfático **04**
lino **86**
linterna **106, 135**
linterna china **169**
linterna frontal **135, 146**
líquido **76**
líquido corrector **82**
líquido de lavavajillas **34**
líquido de lentillas **22, 49**
líquido limpiaparabrisas **97**
lirio **38, 167**
lirio de la paz **38**
lirio de los valles **38**
liso / lisa **13**
lista de la compra **46**
lista de lectura **80**
lista de precios **70**
lista de vinos **69**
listón **116**
literatura **73, 80**
litio **78**
litro **174**
Lituania **151, 153**
lituano / lituana **153**
livermorio **78**
llama **51, 158, 165**
llamar a un amigo **09**
llamar a un familiar **09**
llamar al fontanero **33**
llanta **101**
llanura **146**
llave, llaves **25, 32**
llave alen **36**
llave de vaso **36**
llave fija **36, 98**
llave inglesa **36**
llegar **09**
llegar a casa **09**
llegar a tiempo **09**
llegar a un acuerdo **95**
llegar a un consenso **95**
llegar tarde **09, 171**
llegar temprano **09**
llenar el lavavajillas **34**
lleno / llena **176**
llevar **14**
llorar **02**
lloroso / llorosa **06**
llover a cántaros **178**
llovizna **154**
lluvia **51, 154**
lluvia ácida **51, 155**
lluvia de meteoros **144**
lluvia ligera **154**
lluvioso / lluviosa **154**
lobo **159**
lobo ártico **159**
loción corporal **31**
loción de afeitar **18, 31**
lomo **54, 138**
lona para el suelo **135**
longitud **145, 148, 174**
longitud de onda **75**
lori arcoíris **161**
loro eclecto **161**
loro yaco **161**
losa **35**
loto **24, 38**
lubina **54**
luces **50, 143**
luces de emergencia **99**
luces del escenario **129**
lucha libre **117**
lucioperca **54**
lugar histórico **79**
luge **122**
luna **143**
luna de miel **07**
luna llena **143**
luna nueva **143**

lunar 12
lunes 172
lúpulo 169
lutecio 78
Luxemburgo 151, 153
luxemburgués / luxemburguesa 153
luz 32, 101
luz de lectura 103
luz del porche 25
luz roja 96
luz trasera 100
luz ultravioleta 75

M

macaco 159
macadamia 168
macarrón, macarrones 63, 64
macarrones penne 64
Macedonia del Norte 151, 153
macedonio / macedonia 153
maceta 40
machacado / machacada 72
machacador de patatas 28
machacar 29
macis 59
macramé 142
Madagascar 149, 152
madeja 142
madera 35, 87, 141, 176
madera blanda 35
madera dura 35
madrastra 05
madre 05
madreselva 38
maduro / madura 10, 57
magdalena 63, 70
magia de las velas 139
magnesio 49, 78, 156
magnífico / magnífica 177
magnolia 167
mago 139
maine coon 164
maíz 86
malaquita 156
malas hierbas 41
Malasia 151, 153
malasio / malasia 153
Malaui 149, 152
Maldivas 150
maldivo / maldiva 153
maleducado / maleducada 10
maleta 16, 104
maletero 97
maletín 16
malgache 152
Mali 149, 152
maliense 152
malla de protección 113
mallas 14
mallas de yoga 24
malo / mala 177
Malta 151, 153
maltés / maltesa 153
mamá 05
mamíferos 158, 159
mampara de la ducha 31
mamut lanudo 157
manchego 64
mancuerna 124
mandíbula 01, 03
mandioca 56
mando 136
mando a distancia 26, 83, 136, 13
mando de luces 99
mando para presentaciones 95
mandolina 28
mandril 159
manejar con cuidado 45
manga 15
manga de casquillo 15
manga pastelera 29
manganeso 78
mangle 169
mango 28, 57, 87, 110, 113, 114
mango del paraguas 16
mangosta 159
mangostino 58
manguera 40, 50
manguera de succión 34
manguito 118
manicura 18
manillar 101
maniquí de costura 142
mano, manos 01, 02
mano de mortero 28, 76
manómetro 33
manoplas 13, 29
mansión 32
manta 26, 30
manta eléctrica 30
mantel 26
mantenerse a flote 118
mantequera 28
mantequilla 61, 71
mantequilla con sal 61
mantequilla de cacahuete 60
mantequilla sin sal 61
mantillo 39
mantis religiosa 162
manto 145
manual 99
manualidades 141, 142
manufactura 91
manzana 58
manzana silvestre 58
mañana 09, 171
manzanilla 66
manzano silvestre 169
mapa 48, 148
mapa celeste 144
mapa de carretera 148
mapa de senderismo 148
mapa del metro 102
mapa en línea 148
mapa meteorológico 155
mapa turístico 132
mapache 158
maquillaje 18
maquillarse 09
máquina de coser 142
máquina de rayos x 104
máquina de remo 124
maquinaria 87
máquinas de gimnasio 124
maquinilla de afeitar desechable 31
maquinista 90
mar 134, 145
mar Muerto 145
maracas 128
maratón 116
maravilloso / maravillosa 177
marca de agua 94
marca registrada 175
marcador 107, 111
marcadores de posición 129
marcar 112
marcas de diseño 47
marcas viales 96
marcharse 179
marchas 101
marco 26, 130
marea alta 147
marea baja 147
mareo 19
marfileño / marfileña 152
margarina 61
margarita 38
margarita africana 38
marido 05
marinado / marinada 64, 72
marinero / marinera, marineros / marineras 88, 89
marioneta 08
mariposa, mariposas 77, 118, 162
mariposa atlas 162
mariposa blanquita de la col 162
mariposa cola de golondrina 162
mariposa de cristal 162
mariposa lunar 162
mariposa monarca 162
mariposa pavo real 162
mariquita 162
mariscada 54
mariscal de campo 107
marisco 54
mármol 156, 176
marquesina 99
marrella 157
marrón, marrones 01, 141
marroquí 152
marruecos 149, 12
marshalés / marshalesa 153
marsopa 166
marsupio 158
Marte 143
martes 172
martillear 35
martillo 36
martillo ablandador 28
martillo neumático 87
martín pescador 160
martini 68
marzo 172
masa de profiteroles 63
masa filo 63
masa madre 62
masaje 24
máscara 111, 113
máscara facial 110
mascarilla 18, 20
mascarilla de oxígeno 21, 50
mascarilla quirúrgica 21
mascota, mascotas 109, 164
masculino 04
masilla 37
máster 80
masticar 52
mástil 105, 119, 129
matamoscas 170
matasellos 45
mate 37
matemáticas 73, 74
material de papelería 82
materiales 35, 176
materiales de escritura 175
materiales de oficina 82
maternidad 21
matraz 76
matraz aforado 76
matrícula 97
matrimonio 05, 07
matrón / matrona 08
maullar 164
mauriciano / mauriciana 152
Mauricio 152
Mauritania 149, 152
mauritano / mauritana 152
mayo 172
mayonesa 60
mayúsculas 175
mazapán 63
mazo 36, 87, 141
mazorca 55
mazorquitas 55
me encanta esta novela negra. me tiene enganchado 138
mecánico / mecánica 89, 98
mecedora 26
mechas 12
mechero bunsen 76
medalla, medallas 88, 116
media hora 171
media luna 24
media melena 12
media torsión sentada 24
mediana 96
medianoche 171
medias 14
medicación 20, 49
medicamento 49
medicamento para la tos 49
medicamentos sin receta 49
medicina 80
medida, medidas 68, 174
medida de capacidad, medidas de capacidad 174
medidas de volumen 174
medio / media 173

medio ambiente **155**
medio de apertura / media de apertura **108**
medio exterior **111**
medio melé / media melé **108**
mediocre **177**
mediodía **171**
medios **91**
medios de comunicación **84**
medios en línea y redes sociales **84**
medir **174**, **178**
meditación **24**
medley **118**
médula espinal **04**
medusa **166**
megáfono **50**
meganeuras **157**
megaterio **157**
meitnerio **78**
mejilla **01**
mejillón **54**
mejor amigo / mejor amiga **07**
mejorana **59**
melé **108**
melena de león **170**
melisa **59**
melocotón **57**
melodía **129**
melón amarillo **58**
melón cantalupo **58**
melón charentais **58**
melón galia **58**
melón verde **58**
melones **58**
membrana celular **77**
membrillo **58**
menaje de cocina **28**
mendelevio **78**
meñique **02**
mensajero / mensajería **45**
menta **59**
menta poleo **66**
menú **65**, **70**
menú a la carta **69**
menú de cena **69**
menú del día **69**
menú infantil **69**
mercadillo **46**
mercadillo agrícola **23**
mercado de valores **94**
mercado artesanal **132**
mercado inmobiliario **91**
merceditas **17**
Mercurio **78**, **143**, **156**
merengue **63**
mermelada **60**, **71**
mermelada de cítricos **71**
mermelada de frambuesa **60**
mermelada de fresa **60**
mes **172**
mesa **26**, **65**
mesa de centro **26**
mesa de encolar **37**
mesa de mezclas **84**
mesa de operaciones **21**
mesa de ordenador **83**
mesa de pícnic **135**
meseta **146**
mesita de noche **30**
mesosfera **155**
mesozoico **157**
meta **123**
metacarpo **03**
metal, metales **35**, **155**, **156**, **176**
metales alcalinos **78**
metales alcalinotérreos **78**
metales de transición **78**
metaloides **78**
metamórfico / metamórfica **156**
metamorfosis **77**
metano **155**
metatarso **03**
meteoro **144**
meticuloso / meticulosa **10**
metro **102**, **174**
metro cúbico **174**
mexicano / mexicana **152**
México **150**, **152**
mezclar **29**, **2**
mezquino / mezquina **10**
mezquita **44**
mezzosoprano **126**
mica **156**
micelio **170**
microbiología **77**
microbiólogo / microbióloga **77**
micrófono **84**, **95**, **136**
Micronesia **150**, **153**
micronesio / micronesia **153**
microondas **27**, **75**
microscopio **77**
miel **60**, **71**
miel pura **60**
miércoles **172**
migraña **19**
mijo **86**
mil **173**
mil millones **173**
milenio **172**
milhojas **63**
miligramo **174**
mililitro **174**
milla **174**
milla cuadrada **174**
milpiés **162**
mimosa **168**
mina a cielo abierto **51**
mina de carbón **51**
minarete **44**
minerales **23**, **156**
minería **91**
minero / minera, mineros / Mineras **51**, **89**
minibar **131**
minibús **99**
minifurgoneta **97**
minotauro **139**
minúsculas **175**
minutero **171**
minuto **171**
miopía **22**
mirador **44**, **148**
mirar **178**
mirar escaparates **46**
mirlo **160**
mirtilo **57**
mirto **168**
misil antiaéreo **88**
misil balístico **88**
misil teledirigido **88**
misión **139**
mitocondria **77**
mitología griega **139**
mitos **139**
mixta **18**
mobiliario **47**
mocasines con bridón **17**
mocasines indios **17**
mochi **63**
mochila **16**, **73**, **135**
mochila de soporte vital **143**
mochuelo **161**
moda **91**
modales por teléfono **93**
modelismo **141**
módulo de descenso **143**
módulo lunar **143**
mofeta **158**
moho **170**
moisés **08**, **30**
mojado / mojada **154**
molares **03**
Moldavia **151**, **153**
moldavo / moldava **153**
molde de hornear **29**
molde de magdalenas **29**
molde de suflé **28**
molde individual **28**
molde para bizcochos **28**, **29**
molde para tartaletas **29**
moldura **26**
molécula **76**
molesto / molesta **06**
molibdeno **78**
molinete **105**
molino **44**
Mónaco **151**, **153**
monasterio **44**
moneda digital **94**
monedas **45**, **94**
monedero **94**
monegasco / monegasca **153**
mongol / mongola **153**
Mongolia **150**, **153**
mono **37**, **136**
mono araña **159**
mono ardilla **159**
mono aullador **159**
mono capuchino **159**
mono corto **13**
mono de carreras **123**
mono de trabajo **13**
mono narigudo **159**
monociclo **101**
monóculo **22**
monopatín **125**
monoplano **103**
monorraíl **102**
monster truck **123**
monstera **38**
monstruo **139**
monstruo de gila **163**
montador de cocinas / montadora de cocinas **90**
montaña **24**, **147**
montaña rusa **133**
montar **11**, **178**
montar la tienda **135**
monte marino **145**
montenegrino / montenegrina **153**
Montenegro **151**, **153**
montículo del lanzador **113**
montón de composta **41**
montura de amazona **120**
monumento **42**, **132**
moño **12**
moqueo **19**
moqueta **30**
mora **57**
mora roja **57**
morado **141**
moratón **19**
morcilla **71**
morder **52**
mordisco **19**
mordisquear **52**
morirse **07**
morro **103**, **123**
morsa **166**
mortero **28**, **76**
mosca **121**, **162**, **168**
moscovio **78**
mosquero cardenal **160**
mosquitera **135**
mosquito **162**
mostaza **60**, **70**
mostaza antigua **60**
mostaza blanca **59**
mostaza de dijon **60**
mostaza inglesa **60**
mostaza negra **59**
mostrador **45**, **131**
mostrador de facturación **104**
mostrador de préstamos **80**
motivado / motivada **93**
moto **100**
moto acuática **119**
moto de agua **134**
moto de carreras **100**
moto de policía **50**
moto de turismo **100**
moto eléctrica **100**
moto todoterreno **100**
motocicletas **100**
motociclismo **123**
motocross **123**
motonieve **122**
motoniveladora **87**
motor **98**, **100**, **103**
motor del avión **103**
motor fueraborda **105**
motorista **100**
mover **11**, **140**
moverse sigilosamente **11**
móvil de cuna **30**
Mozambique **149**, **152**
mozambiqueño / mozambiqueña **152**
mozzarella **64**
mudar el pelo **164**
mudarse a **32**
mudarse de **32**
mueble cambiador **30**
muelle **106**
muérdago **168**
muesli **71**
mujer **05**

muletas **19**
multa **85**
multicines **127**
multiplicar **74**
multivitamínico **49**
mundo natural **157-170**
muñeca **01, 02, 08**
muñequera **107, 114**
murciélago **158**
murciélago de la fruta **158**
muro **44**
músculos **03**
músculos intercostales **03**
museo **43, 130, 132**
muserola **120**
musgo **167**
música **73, 128, 129**
música clásica **129**
música latina **129**
música popular **129**
musical **126, 127**
músico / música **90**
musicoterapia **24**
muslo **01, 53**

N

nabo **56**
nacer **07**
nachos **70**
nacimiento **147**
nacionalidades **152, 153**
nada **114**
nadador / nadadora **118**
Namibia **149, 152**
namibio / namibia **152**
napolitana de chocolate **62**
naranja **57, 141**
naranja sanguina **57**
naranjada **52**
narciso **38**
nariz **01**
nariz colgante **159**
narval **166**
nata **61, 71**
nata montada **61**
nata para cocinar **61**
nata para montar **61**
natación **118**
natación sincronizada **118**
naturopatía **24**
Nauru **150, 153**
nauruano / nauruana **153**
náuseas **19**
náuticos **17**
nautilo **166**
navaja **54**
navaja multiusos **135**
nave espacial **143**
navegación **119**
navegar **119**
navidad **07**
neblina **154**
neblinoso **154**
nebulosa **144**
neceser **18**
nectarina **57**
neerlandés / neerlandesa **153**
negar **02**
negativo **75**
negociación **93**
negociar **92**
negrita **175**
negro **141**
nenúfar **167**
neodimio **78**
neógeno **157**
neón **78**
neozelandés / neozelandesa **153**
Nepal **150, 153**
nepalés / nepalesa **153**
neptunio **78**
Neptuno **143**
nervio **03, 22**
nervioso / nerviosa **04, 06, 10**
netball **125**
neumático **97, 100**
neumático con dibujo profundo **100**
neumáticos de invierno **97**
neurología **21**
neutro **33**
neutrón **76**
nevado **154**
nevera **27, 135**
Nicaragua **150, 152**
nicaragüense **152**
nido **160**
nieb **154**
nieto / nieta **05**
nietos **05**
nieve **154**
Níger **149, 152**
Nigeria **149, 152**
nigeriano / nigeriana **152**
nigerino / nigerina **152**
nihonio **78**
niñero / niñera **90**
niño / niña, niños / niñas **05, 24**
niño pequeño / niña pequeña **05, 08**
niobio **78**
níquel **78, 156**
níspero **169**
nitrógeno **78**
nivel **35, 36, 87**
no doblar **45**
no ficción **138**
no girar a la derecha **96**
no metales **78**
nobelio **78**
nobles **79**
noche **09, 171**
noche de estreno **126**
nogal **168**
nómina **81**
noqueo **117**
norcoreano / norcoreana **153**
noreste **148**
noria **133**
normal **18**
noroeste **148**
norte **148**
norteamericano / norteamericana **152**
Noruega **151, 153**
noruego / noruega **153**
nota, notas **73, 95, 128**
notación **128**
notas adhesivas **82**
noticias **137**
notro **167**
novela **138**
novela policíaca **138**
noveno / novena **173**
noventa **173**
noviembre **172**
novio / novia **05, 07**
nube, nubes **51, 67, 154**
nube de ceniza **145**
nublado **154**
núcleo **76, 77**
núcleo externo **145**
núcleo interno **145**
nudibranquio **166**
nudillo **02**
nudo arbor **121**
nudo de pescador **121**
nudo de sangre **121**
nudo palomar **121**
nudo snell **121**
nudo turle **121**
nudos **121**
nueces de brasil **58**
nueces de cola **58**
nueces de ginkgo **58**
nueces de macadamia **58**
nueces pecanas **58**
nuera **05**
Nueva Zelanda **150, 153**
nueve **173**
nuevo / nueva **176**
nuez **04, 58**
nuez moscada **59**
nuggets de pollo **70**
numerador **74**
número, números **112, 173, 175**
número del jugador **107**
número de andén **102**
número de corredor **100**
número de cuenta **45**
número de puerta de embarque **104**
número de ruta **99**
número de vuelo **104**
número ocho **108**
números cardinales **173**
números ordinales **173**
nunca **171**
nutria **158**
nutrición **23**

Ñ

ñoquis **64**
ñu **158**

O

oasis **146**
obertura para piano **128**
objetivo **77**
oblicuos **03**
oboe **128**
obra **87, 126, 130**
obra maestra **130**
obras **96**
obras en la carretera **87, 96**
obrero / obrera **87, 90**
observación de aves **133**
observador de aves / observadora de aves **161**
observatorio **144**
obsidiana **156**
obstáculos **116**
obstetra **08**
obtener beneficios **94**
Oceanía **150, 153**
oceánico / oceánica **153**
océano **145, 147**
ochenta **173**
ocho **173**
oclusión **155**
octágono **74**
octavo / octava **173**
octubre **172**
ocular **77, 144**
oculista **22**
odio esta novela de fantasía. el argumento es absurdo **138**
oeste **148**
oferta especial **48**
ofertas de empleo **92**
oficina **82**
oficina central **81**
oficina de acceso **80**
oficina de cambio **45**
oficina de correos **42, 45**
oficina de objetos perdidos **102, 104**
oficina de turismo **42, 132**
oficina del director / oficina de la directora **81**
ofrecerse voluntario / ofrecerse voluntaria **92**
oftalmología **21**
ogro **139**
ojal, ojales **15, 17**
ojo, ojos **01,121, 142**
ojo de la cerradura **25**
ojo de tigre **156**
okra **55**
ola **119, 134, 147**
ola de calor **154**
oler **11**
olfatear **164**
olivo **169**
olla a presión **28**
olla arrocera **27**
olm **163**
olmo **169**
olvidar **11**

Omán **151**, **153**
omaní **153**
ombligo **01**
omóplato **03**
onagra **38**
once **173**
oncología **21**
onda **75**
ondas de radio **75**
onesie **13**
ónix **156**
onza **174**
onza líquida **174**
opaco / opaca **176**
ópalo **156**
ópera **126**, **129**
Ópera de Sídney **44**
operación, operaciones **21**, **74**
opiniones **177**
oponente **117**
oporto **68**
óptica **46**, **75**
óptico / óptica **89**
optimista **06**, **10**
optometrista **22**
opuesto / opuesta **112**
orangután **159**
oratoria **93**
órbita **143**
orca asesina **166**
orco / orca **139**
orden del día **95**
orden judicial **85**
ordenador, ordenadores **82**, **83**
ordenador de sobremesa **83**
ordenador portátil **82**, **83**
ordeñar **86**
ordovícico **157**
orégano **59**
oreja **01**
oreja de liebre **170**
orejas de burro **167**
orejeras **87**
orejones **58**
orfebrería **141**
organesón **78**
orgánico / orgánica **23**, **39**, **53**
organización **93**
organizado / organizada **93**
organizador de herramientas **35**
organizar **92**
órgano **128**
órganos internos **04**
órganos reproductores **04**
orgulloso / orgullosa **06**
orientación **133**, **148**
orientado al cliente / orientada al cliente **93**
orientador / orientadora **24**
origami **141**
original **93**
orilla **147**
orinal **08**
orión **144**
órix **159**
ornitorrinco **158**
oro **78**, **116**, **156**, **176**
oronja **170**
oronja verde **170**
orquesta **128**
orquídea **38**, **47**
ortiga **169**
ortodoncia **22**
ortodoncista **89**
oruga **77**, **162**
orza **119**
osa mayor **144**
oscuro / oscura **60**, **176**
osmio **78**
oso de peluche **08**, **30**
oso hormiguero **159**
oso pardo **159**
oso polar **159**
osteopatía **24**
ostra **54**
ostrero **160**
otomana **30**
otoño **172**
otorrinolaringología **21**
otros asuntos **95**
otros metales **78**
ovación de pie **126**
óvalo **74**
ovario **04**, **38**
oveja **165**
oveja hembra **165**
oxígeno **78**

P

paciente **10**, **19**, **20**, **21**, **93**
paciente externo **21**
pádel **114**
padre **05**
padre soltero / madre soltera **05**
padres **05**
paella **72**
pagar **46**
pagar a medias **69**
pagar con tarjeta **94**
pagar el alquiler **32**
pagar en efectivo **94**
pagar las facturas **09**
pagar por separado **69**
página **138**
paintball **133**
paisaje **132**, **146**
paisajismo **133**
países **149**, **150**, **151**
Países Bajos **151**, **153**
pajarita **16**
pajita **70**
Pakistán **153**
pakistaní **153**
pala **28**, **33**, **40**, **51**, **87**, **134**
pala cuadrada **40**
pala de timón **119**
palacio **132**
paladar **04**
paladio **78**
palafito **32**
palanca de cambio **101**
palanca de cambios **99**
palanca de emergencia **102**
palanca de la llanta **101**
Palaos **150**, **153**
palauano / palauana **153**
palco **126**
palé **87**
paleógeno **157**
paleontólogo / paleontóloga **77**
paleozoico **157**
paleta **40**, **87**, **141**
palillos **27**
palma **02**
palmera, palmeras **41**, **134**
palmitos **55**
palo **110**
palo de golf **115**
palo de hierro **115**, **169**
palo de hockey **110**
palo de madera **115**
paloma **24**, **160**
palomitas **127**
pamela **16**, **134**
Pamukkale **145**
pan **71**
pan ácimo **62**
pan blanco **62**
pan con semillas **62**
pan de centeno **62**
pan de cereales **62**
pan de frutas **62**
pan de maíz **62**
pan de masa madre **62**
pan de molde **62**
pan de pita **62**, **72**
pan de soda **62**
pan integral **62**
pan sin levadura **62**
panadería **46**, **48**, **62**, **63**
panadero / panadera **62**
panal **60**
Panamá **150**, **152**
panameño / panameña **152**
pancarta **109**
páncreas **04**
panda **159**
panda rojo **159**
pandereta **128**
panecillo **62**
panecillo de desayuno **71**
paneer **64**
panel móvil **82**
panel solar **51**
panes **62**
panga **54**
pangolín **159**
paño **34**
paño de cocina **28**
pantalán **106**
pantalla **21**, **45**, **83**, **111**, **127**, **136**, **137**
pantalla de información **104**
pantalla de lámpara **26**
pantalla de salidas **102**
pantalla digital **136**
pantalla protectora **40**
pantalón, pantalones **15**, **107**
pantalón cargo **13**
pantalón de montar **120**
pantalones cortos **14**
pantalones de gimnasia **15**
pantano **146**
pantis **14**
pantógrafo **102**
pantorrilla **01**
pantuflas **14**, **17**
pañal **08**
pañuelo **16**, **49**
papá **05**
papada **159**
paparazzi **127**
papaya **58**
papel **82**, **155**, **176**
papel de filtro **76**
papel de lija **36**, **37**
papel higiénico **31**
papel maché **141**
papel pintado **37**
papelera **27**, **33**, **82**, **83**
papelera de reciclaje **33**
paperas **19**
papiro **167**
papú **153**
Papúa Nueva Guinea **150**, **153**
paquete **45**, **52**
par **115**
para llevar **70**
parabrisas **97**, **100**
paracaídas **125**
paracaidismo **125**
parachoques **97**
parada de autobús **25**
parada de cabeza **24**
parada de taxis **104**
parada en boxes **123**
paraguas **16**
Paraguay **149**, **152**
paraguayo / paraguaya **152**
paralela **74**
paralelogramo **74**
paramédico / paramédica **21**, **50**, **90**
paramotor **103**
parapente **125**
parapentista **125**
parar **96**, **137**
parar en (el hotel) **148**
paravelismo **119**
paravientos **134**
parcela **135**
parche **101**
parchís **140**
pared **25**, **87**
pared celular **77**
pareja **05**, **07**
pareja comprometida **07**
paréntesis **175**
pargo **54**
pariente afín **05**
parking **42**
parking para minusválidos **96**
parking subterráneo **47**
parkour **133**
parmesano **64**
parpadear **02**
párpado **01**
parque **42**, **133**
parque de atracciones **133**

parque de aventura **133**
parque de safari **133**
parque eólico **51**
parque infantil **43**
parque nacional **132**, **133**
parque para bebés **08**
parque solar **51**
parquímetro **96**
parra **168**
parra virgen **168**
parrilla de salida **123**
parrilla plegable **135**
parte de trabajo **92**
parte estrecha **129**
parterre **41**
partes del cuerpo **01**
partícula **75**
partido **114**
partido de fútbol **109**
partido de tenis **114**
partitura **128**
parto **08**
pasa **58**
pasa de corinto **58**
pasa sultana **58**
pasado / pasada **52**
pasajeros **102**, **106**
pasamanos **25**
pasaporte **104**
pasaporte biométrico **104**
pasar **107**, **108**, **110**, **112**
pasar (el restaurante) **148**
pasar la revisión al coche **98**
pasarela **104**, **105**, **134**
pascua judía **07**
paseo **120**
paseo marítimo **134**
pasil **48**
pasillo **80**, **103**, **126**
paso de animales salvajes **96**
paso de peatones **96**
paso elevado **96**, **102**
paso subterráneo **96**, **102**
pasta **63**, **64**, **72**
pasta de dientes **31**
pastel **63**, **72**, **141**
pastelería **46**
pasteles de carne **64**, **72**
pastelitos de patata **71**
pasteurizada **61**
pastilde encendido **135**
pastilde lavavajillas **34**
pastilla, pastillas **20**, **49**, **129**
pastilla de encendido **135**
pastilla de frenos **101**
pastilla de lavavajillas **34**
pastilla para dormir **49**
pastilla para el mareo **49**
pastilla para la garganta **49**
pasto **86**
pastor alemán **164**
pastrami **64**
pata **26**
patada frontal **117**
patada voladora **117**
patas largas **159**
patata, patatas **56**, **86**
patata nueva **56**
patatas fritas **48**, **68**, **70**
patchwork **142**
paté **64**, **71**
patear **11**, **118**
patillas **12**
patín **122**
patín de hielo **110**
patinaje **133**
patinaje artístico **122**
patinaje en línea **125**
patinaje sobre hielo **122**
patinaje sobre ruedas **125**
patinar **110**
patinete eléctrico **100**
patio **25**, **41**
patito **165**
pato **53**, **165**
pato joyuyo **161**
pato mandarín **161**
patología **21**
patrimonio neto **94**
patrón Battenburg **50**
patrón del vestido **142**
patucos **13**
pausar **137**
pavimento **41**
pavlova **63**
pavo **53**, **161**, **165**
pavo real **161**
payaso / payasa **89**
pecán **168**
pecas **12**
peces de arrecife de coral **118**
pecho **01**
pechuga **53**
pectoral **03**
pedal, pedales **99**, **101**
pedal de freno **100**
pedalear **101**
pediatría **21**
pedicura **18**
pedir **46**, **69**, **164**
pegamento **82**, **101**, **141**
pegamento para madera **35**
peinarse **12**
peine **12**
pelacables **36**
pelador **28**
pelar **29**
peldaño **36**
pelele **13**
pelícano **160**
película de acción **127**
película de vaqueros **127**
películas **127**
peligro **96**
peligro por semáforos **96**
pelo **01**, **12**
pelo afro **12**
pelo canoso **12**
pelo castaño **12**
pelo cobrizo **12**
pelo corto **12**
pelo encrespado **12**
pelo largo **12**
pelo liso **12**
pelo muy corto **12**
pelo negro **12**
pelo ondulado **12**
pelo pelirrojo **12**
pelo rizado **12**
pelo rubio **12**
pelota **08**, **110**, **114**
pelota de béisbol **113**
pelota de críquet **111**
pelota de golf **115**
pelota de playa **134**
peloteo **114**
peluca **12**
peluquería **47**
peluquero / peluquera **89**
pelvis **03**
penalti **109**
pendiente de aterrizaje **122**
pendientes **16**
pendientes de aro **16**
pendientes de botón **16**
pene **04**
península **147**
pensamiento **38**
pensar **11**
pensión **131**
pentágono **74**
pentatlón moderno **116**
peón **140**
peonía **47**, **168**
peonza **08**
pepinillo **60**
pepino **55**
pepperoni **64**
pequeño / pequeña **176**
pera **58**
peral **169**
perca **54**
percebe **134**, **166**
percha **30**
percusión **128**
perder **140**
perder el balón **107**, **109**
perder el tren **102**
perder peso **20**, **23**
perderse **148**
pérdida de hábitat **155**
peregrinar a la meca **07**
perejil **59**
perenne **41**
perezoso **159**
perfilador de labios **18**
perforadora **82**
perfume **18**
perfumería **47**
pergamino **79**, **175**
pérgola **41**
perifollo **59**
perilla **12**
periódico **48**, **138**
periodismo **91**
periodista **90**
períodos geológicos **157**
periquito **160**, **164**
pérmico **157**
perno **36**
peroné **03**
perpendicular **74**
perrito caliente **70**
perro **122**
perro boca abajo **24**
perro policía **50**
perro salchicha **164**
persa **164**
perseguir **107**, **113**
persiana **25**
persiana enrollable **26**
persiana veneciana **26**
personaje **138**
personal **81**
personas **1-11**
personas que se desplazan al trabajo **102**
pértiga **121**
pértiga para micrófono **84**
Perú **149**, **152**
peruano / peruana **152**
pesadilla **30**
pesado / pesada **52**, **176**
pesar **174**, **178**
pesas **124**
pesas de muñeca **124**
pesas de tobillo **124**
pesca **91**, **121**
pesca con arpón **121**
pesca con mosca **121**
pesca de altura **121**
pesca deportiva **121**
pesca en agua dulce **121**
pesca en hielo **121**
pesca en la orilla **121**
pesca marítima **121**
pescadería **46**, **48**
pescadero / pescadera **54**, **89**
pescadilla **54**
pescado **54**
pescado ahumado **64**
pescado frito con patatas **70**
pescado marinado **64**
pescador / pescadora **89**
pescador de caña / pescadora de caña **121**
pescetariano **23**
pésimo / pésima **177**
peso **174**
pesquero de arrastre **105**
pestañas **01**
pesticida, pesticidas **40**, **86**, **55**
pestillo **99**
pétalo **38**
petirrojo europeo **160**
petisú de chocolate **63**
petisú de crema **63**
peto **13**
petróleo **51**
petrolero **105**
pez **164**
pez cirujano **166**
pez cofre amarillo **166**
pez erizo **166**
pez espada **54**
pez globo **166**
pez halcón **166**
pez payaso **166**
pez pelícano **166**
pez pipa **166**
pez sierra **166**
pez trompeta **166**
pez vela **166**
pez volador **166**
pezón **01**
piano **128**, **129**
pica **140**
picadura **19**
picante **52**, **56**
picar **29**, **121**, **162**
picar carne **29**
pícea **167**
pícnic **133**
pico **87**, **161**
pico picapinos **160**
pie, pies **01**, **02**, **170**, **174**

pie de cama **30**
pie de la aguja **142**
piedra **16**, **141**, **176**
piedra de afilar **36**
piedra de curling **122**
piedra lunar **156**
piedra pómez **31**, **156**
piedras vivas **168**
piel **01**, **58**
pierna **01**, **53**
pieza, piezas **53**, **140**
piezas blancas **140**
piezas negras **140**
pijama **14**
pijama de bebé **13**
pila **75**, **83**
pilar derecho / pilar derecha **108**
pilar izquierdo / pilar izquierda **108**
pilates **124**
piloto **88**, **90**, **103**
piloto de carreras **123**
pimentón **59**
pimienta **26**
pimienta de jamaica **59**
pimienta en grano **59**
pimiento **56**
pin **16**, **33**, **45**

pincel **141**
pincel de cocina **29**
pinchazo **98**, **101**
pincho **28**
pincel para labios **18**
ping pong **114**
pingüino de humboldt **161**
pingüino de penacho amarillo **161**
pingüino emperador **161**
pingüino enano **161**
pingüino papúa **161**
pino sombrilla **167**
pinta **174**
pintar **37**
pintar una pared **35**
pintaúñas **18**
pintor / pintora **89**
pintoresco / pintoresca **132**
pintura **37**, **130**, **141**
pintura acrílica **141**
pintura al óleo **130**, **141**
pintura de acuarela **130**
pintura de emulsión **37**
pinza, pinzas **18**, **20**, **24**, **28**, **34**, **68**, **76**, **77**, **142**
pinza del busto **142**
pinza para la nariz **118**
pinza sujetapapeles **82**
pinzas de cocodrilo **75**
pinzas de mano **124**
pinzón **160**
piña **58**
piñón **101**
piñones **58**
pipeta **76**
piqueta **135**
pirámide **74**
Pirámides de Guiza **44**
piratería informática **85**
piruleta **67**
piscifactoría **86**
piscina **131**
piscina de natación **118**
piscina hinchable **25**, **133**
Piscis **144**
piso **25**
piso inferior **99**
piso principal **126**
piso superior **99**
pista de aterrizaje **104**
pista de atletismo **116**
pista de esquí **122**
pista de hockey sobre hielo **110**
pista de tenis **114**
pistacho **58**
pistola de pegamento **35**
pistola **88**
pito crestado **160**
pito negro **160**
pito real **160**
pitón reticulada **163**
pívot **112**
pizarra **73**, **95**, **156**
pizza **70**
pizzería **70**
placa **50**, **145**
placa de circuito impreso **75**
placa de la aguja **142**
placa de petri **77**
placar **107**, **108**
placas tectónicas **145**
placenta **08**
placerias **157**
plancha **12**, **24**, **28**, **34**
planchar **34**
planchar una camisa **09**
plancton **77**, **166**
planeador **103**
planear **161**
planeta tierra **145**
planetas **143**
planetas enanos **143**
planificar la ruta **148**
plano **130**
planta, plantas **41**, **77**, **132**, **167**, **168**, **169**
planta (del pie) **02**
planta alta **47**
planta araña **38**
planta baja **25**, **47**
planta de maceta **41**
planta de ricino **169**
planta del dinero china **38**
planta en maceta **47**
planta intermedia **47**
planta odre **168**
planta para cubrir el suelo **41**
planta piña **167**
planta serpiente **38**
planta trepadora **41**
plantar **39**, **86**
plantar en una maceta **39**
plantas acuáticas **41**
plantas alpinas **41**
plantas con flores **157**
plantas de interior **38**
plantas de jardín **38**
plantas de sombra **41**
plantas ornamentales **41**
plantilla, plantillas **37**, **17**, **49**
plástico **155**, **176**
plata **78**, **116**, **156**, **176**
plataforma **84**
plataforma de clavados **118**
plataforma de lanzamiento **143**
plataforma petrolífera **51**
plátano **58**, **86**
plátano de sombra **168**
platea **126**
plateosaurus **157**
platija **54**
platillos **128**
platina **77**
platino **78**, **156**
plató **127**
plato de postre **27**
plato llano **27**
plato principal **69**
platos **72**
platos del día **69**
playa **148**
playa fluvial **147**
plaza **42**
plaza de garaje **32**
pliegue **14**
plomada **37**
plomo **78**, **121**
pluma **87**, **175**
plumaje extendido **161**
plumas de la cola **161**
plumero **34**
plumín **73**, **175**
plumón **161**
Plutón **143**
plutonio **78**
pochar **29**
pocilga **86**
poción **139**
poco impresionado / poco impresionada **06**
podadera de brazo largo **40**
podadora de altura **40**
podar **39**
pódcast **84**
podio **116**, **128**
podrido / podrida **57**
poesía terapéutica **24**
polaco / polaca **153**
policía **50**, **89**
policía en moto **50**
polideportivo **43**
polígono industrial **42**
polilla de la ropa **162**
polilla emperador **162**
polilla esfinge **162**
polilla moteada **162**
polillas **162**
política **80**
pollito **165**
pollo **53**
pollo asado **72**
pollo del bosque **170**
pollo frito **70**
polluelo **161**
polo **14**, **120**
polo norte **75**, **145**
polo sur **75**, **145**
Polonia **151**, **153**
polonio **78**
polvo de cinco especias **59**
polvos **49**
polvos corporales **31**
polvos de maquillaje **18**
pomada **20**, **49**
pomelo **57**
pomerania **164**
pomo **113**
pomo de la puerta **25**
poncho **15**
ponente invitado / ponente invitada **95**
poner el intermitente **98**
poner la alarma **09**
poner la mesa **26**, **34**
poner una moqueta **35**
ponerse **14**, **178**
ponerse a dieta **23**
pop **129**
popa **105**, **119**
porcentaje, porcentajes **74**, **173**
porche **25**
porción **26**
poros **12**
porra **50**
portabrocas **35**
portacontenedores **105**, **106**
portada **138**
portaequipaje, portaequipajes **99**,**100**, **102**
portafolio **92**
portamangueras **40**
portarrollos **31**
portaviones **88**, **105**
portería **109**, **110**
portería de rugby **108**
portero / portera **109**, **110**
portero automático **25**
Portugal **151**, **153**
portugués / portuguesa **153**
posavasos **27**, **68**
posiciones de hockey sobre hielo **110**
posiciones de rugby **108**
posiciones de voleibol **112**
posiciones del fútbol americano **107**
posiciones en el campo **111**
posimpresionismo **130**
positivo **75**
postal **48**, **132**
poste **107**, **109**, **135**
poste alto **112**
poste de foul **113**
postre, postres **63**, **69**
postura **115**
potasio **78**
poto **38**
potro **120**, **125**, **165**
poza de marea **134**
pozo minero **51**
práctico / práctica **93**
pradera **146**
prado **120**
praseodimio **78**
precámbrico **157**
precio **69**
preciso / precisa **93**
preguntar **73**

preguntar la dirección **148**
premios **164**
premolares **03**
prensa de ajos **28**
prensa de pecho **124**
preocupado / preocupada **06**
preparación de los alimentos **72**
preparar el almuerzo **09**
preposiciones **180**
preposiciones de lugar **148**
presa de marea **51**
presentación **82, 95**
presentador / presentadora **84, 89, 137**
presentador del telediario / presentadora del telediario **137**
presentando **95**
presentarse para un puesto de trabajo **92**
presidente del jurado / presidenta del jurado **85**
presos / presas **85**
prestación por desempleo **81**
prestaciones **81**
préstamo **45**
presumir **178**
presupuesto **94**
pretz **62**
previsión del tiempo **137**
prima donna **126**
primavera **172**
primer centro / primera centro **108**
primera base **113**
primera mano **37**
primera planta **25, 47**
primera posición **123**
primero / primera **173**
primo / prima **05**
prímula **169**
príncipe / princesa **79**
prisión **85**
prisma **75**
prismáticos **144**
prismáticos de ópera **22**
proa **105, 119**
probadores **47**
probar **29, 52**
probarse **14, 46**
productor / productora **126, 127**
productos de belleza **47**
productos de limpieza **48**
productos lácteos **48, 61**
productos locales **23**
productos para mascotas **164**
profesional **93**
profesiones **89, 90**
profesor / profesora **73, 80, 89, 90**
profesor de autoescuela / profesora de autoescuela **89**
profesor de música / profesora de música **90**
profesor de yoga / profesora de yoga **90**
profundidad **74**
profundo / profunda **176**
profundo derecho / profunda derecha **107**
profundo izquierdo / profunda izquierda **107**
programa **126, 137**
programa de actualidad **137**
programa de cocina **137**
programa de entrevistas **137**
programa infantil **137**
programa matutino **137**
programación **137**
programas de tv **137**
prohibido cambiar de sentido **96**
prohibido el adelantamiento **96**
prohibido el paso **96**
prohibido fotografiar **130**
prometida / prometido **07**
prometio **78**
propagar **39**
propietario / propietaria **32**
propina **69**
propuesta **82**
propulsor **143**
próstata **04**
protactinio **78**
protagonista **127**
protea **38**
protector **37**
protector bucal **107, 117**
protector de brazo **110**
protector de cuello **107**
protector de pecho **107, 110**
protector de piernas **110**
protector de postes **108**
protector solar **49, 134**
protegeslip **49**
proteínas **23**
prótesis para correr **125**
protón **76**
proyector **82, 95**
proyector digital **73, 82**
prueba **50, 85**
pruebas de atletismo **116**
psicólogo / psicóloga **90**
psicoterapia **24**
psiquiatría **21**
publicar **84**
publicidad **91**
público **126, 127**
pueblo **43, 148**
puente **02, 24, 43, 105, 125, 129**
puente levadizo **44**
puenting **125**
puercoespín **158**
puerro **56**
puerta **41, 99, 102, 122**
puerta de embarque **104**
puerta de terraza **25**
puerta del maletero **97**
puerta delantera **97**
puerta principal **25**
puerta trasera **97**
puerto **106**
puerto de pasajeros **106**
puerto deportivo **106**
puerto pesquero **106**
puesto **47**
puesto callejero **70**
puesto de flores **47**
puesto de souvenirs **132**
puesto de trabajo **82**
pulgada **174**
pulgar **02**
pulmón **04**
pulpa **03, 57, 58**
pulpo **54, 166**
pulsera **16**
pulverizador **40**
punk **129**
punta **115, 122**
punta pegajosa **168**
puntada **142**
puntera **126**
puntero láser **95**
punto, puntos **21, 111, 140, 142, 175**
punto de aguja **142**
punto de congelación **154**
punto de ebullición **154**
punto de recarga **97**
punto de saque **110**
punto penal **109**
punto y coma **175**
puntos de acción **95**
puntos suspensivos **175**
puntuación **114, 140**
puntual **93**
puño **02, 142**
puños **15**
pupila **01**
putter **115**
puzle **140**

Q

quad **100**
que sabe escuchar **93**
quebrar **94**
quedar bien **46**
quedar bien (a alguien) **14**
quedar eliminado / quedar eliminada **111**
quedarse dormido / quedarse dormida **178**
quedarse en un hotel **131**
quedarse sin **178**
quedarse sin tiempo **95**
quemador **27, 103**
quemadura **19**
quemadura de sol **134**
quemadura solar **19**
quemar **29**
querer **46**
queso, quesos **61, 64, 71**
queso azul **61**
queso cottage **61**
queso cremoso **61**
queso cremoso semicurado **61**
queso curado **61**
queso de cabra **61**
queso de oveja **61**
queso de untar **61**
queso fresco **61**
queso rallado **61**
queso semicurado **61**
quibla **44**
quilla **105, 119**
química **73, 76, 80**
químico / química **76**
quince **173**
quincena **172**
quinientos **173**
quinto / quinta **173**
quirófano **21**
quiropráctica **24**
quitaesmalte **18**
quitapiedras **102**
quitar **37**
quitar el polvo **34**
quitar las flores muertas **39**
quitarse **14**

R

rábano **56**
rábano picante **56**
rabas **54**
racketball **114**
radar **105**
radar de velocidad **50, 96**
radiación atrapada **155**
radiación gamma **75**
radiación reflejada **155**
radiación solar **155**
radiador **33, 98**
radiador de aceite **33**
radio **03, 50, 74, 78, 84, 88, 101, 136**
radio del coche **99**
radioactividad **75**
radiodespertador **30**
radiografía **19, 21**
radiografía dental **22**
radiología **21**
radiotelescopio **144**
radón **78**
rafia **167**
rafting **119**
ragdoll **164**
raíl electrificado **102**
raíz **03**
raíz de apio **56**
raíz de taro **56**
rallador **28**
ralladura **57**
rallar **29**
rally **123**
rama **169**
ramaje **47**
ramas desnudas **172**
ramen **64, 72**

ramo **15**, **47**
ramo de flores **47**
rampa de acceso **130**
rampa para sillas de ruedas **99**
rana adulta **77**
rana bermeja **163**
rana de dardo venenosa **163**
rana de darwin **163**
rana joven **77**
rana toro africana **163**
rana verde de ojos rojos **163**
rana voladora de wallace **163**
ranchera **97**
ranúnculo **38**
ranura del correo **25**, **45**
rape **54**
rape abisal **166**
rápel **125**
rápido / rápida **176**
rápidos **119**, **146**
raqueta **114**
ras el hanout **59**
rascacielos **42**
rascarse **164**
rascón europeo **161**
rasgos de personalidad **10**
rasguño **19**
raspador **37**
rastrillar **39**
rastrillar las hojas **39**
rastrillo **40**, **44**
rata **158**
ratel **158**
ratón **83**, **158**, **164**
raya **54**, **166**, **175**
raya al lado **12**
raya en medio **12**
rayas **14**
rayo **154**
rayos ultravioleta **155**
rayos x **75**
razas de gato **164**
razas de perro **164**
razonable **10**
reacción **76**
reacción reversible **76**
reactor **51**
reality show **137**
reanimar **20**
rebaja **47**
rebanar **29**, **62**
rebaño **86**
rebaño de ovejas **165**
rebaño de vacas **165**
rebeca **14**
rebobinar **137**
rebote **112**
rebozuelo **56**, **170**
rebuznar **165**
recepción **131**, **135**
recepción de la oficina **81**
recepcionar **112**
recepcionista **81**, **90**, **131**
receptáculo **38**
receptor **113**
receptor / receptora **107**
recesión **94**
receta **20**, **49**
recibo **48**, **69**, **94**
reciclaje **91**, **155**
recién nacido / recién nacida **08**
recipiente **28**
recipiente hermético **52**
recipientes **52**
reclamar **46**
reclinatorio de jardín **40**
recogedor **34**
recogedor de césped **40**
recogepelotas **114**
recoger **11**, **34**, **110**, **121**, **178**
recoger a alguien **98**
recoger la mesa **09**
recoger setas **170**
recogerse el pelo **12**
recogida de equipajes **104**
recogida de setas **133**
recolectar **57**
reconciliarse **178**
recordar **11**
recortar **39**
recorte salarial **81**
recta **74**
rectángulo **74**
recuperarse **20**
red **109**, **112**, **114**
red eléctrica **33**
red ferroviaria **102**
redacción **73**
redactar el acta **95**
reducir el consumo **23**
reducir la velocidad **98**
reembolsar **46**
reenviar **83**
reflectante **100**, **101**
reflexión **75**
reflexología **24**
reformar el ático **35**
reformas **37**
refracción **75**
refresco **70**
refresco de cola **52**
refugio **44**, **122**
regadera **40**
regalar **178**
regaliz **67**
regalo **07**
regar **39**
regar las plantas **09**, **34**
regatear **46**
reggae **129**
regiones polares **146**
registrarse **131**, **178**
regla, reglas **73**, **74**, **82**,**109**, **174**
regulador **118**
rehabilitación **21**
reiki **24**
reina **79**, **140**
reina de los andes **167**
reina de mármol **38**
reino **79**
Reino Unido **151**, **153**
reír **02**
rejilla **29**
rejón **121**
relaciones **05**, **07**
relajación **24**
relajado / relajada **06**
relajante **177**
relajarse **178**
rellano **25**
rellenar **37**, **178**
rellenar un formulario **92**
relleno / rellena **63**, **70**, **72**
reloj **16**, **44**, **171**
reloj de cocina **28**
reloj inteligente **83**
remangar **14**
rematador derecho / rematadora derecha **112**
rematador externo / rematadora externa **112**
remero / remera **119**
remo **119**
remodelar **178**
remolacha **56**
remolacha encurtida **60**
remolcador **105**
remolcar **96**
remolque **135**
remolque del equipaje **104**
remover **29**
renacuajo **77**, **163**
renio **78**
reno **159**
renovar **80**
reparar **11**, **33**
reparar una valla **35**
repartidor **48**
repartidor de comida a domicilio **70**
repartir **140**, **178**
reparto **126**, **127**
repasar **73**
repavimentación **87**
repelente de insectos **49**, **135**
repetir **73**
repisa **26**
reportero / reportera **137**
reposabrazos **99**, **103**
reposacabezas **99**, **123**
reposapiés **26**, **82**
repostar **98**, **178**
reproducción **77**
reproducir **137**
reproductor **04**
reproductor de cd **136**
reptiles **163**
reptiles voladores **157**
República Centroafricana **149**, **152**
República Checa **151**, **153**
República del Congo **149**, **152**
República Democrática del Congo **149**, **152**
República Dominicana **150**, **152**
resbalar **113**
reseña **138**
reserva natural **133**, **148**
reservado / reservada **10**
reservar **69**, **80**
reservar unas vacaciones **131**
resfriado **19**
residencia de estudiantes **80**
residuos **33**, **155**
residuos biodegradables **33**
residuos electrónicos **33**
residuos nucleares **51**
residuos plásticos **155**
residuos tóxicos **33**
resolución de problemas **93**
resolución judicial **85**
resoplar **165**
respaldo **26**, **103**
respetuoso / respetuosa **177**
respirar **02**
respiratorio **04**
responder **73**, **83**
responder a todos **83**
responder preguntas **95**
responsable **93**
restar **11**, **74**
restauración **130**
restaurante **42**
resto, restos **79**, **114**
resuelto / resuelta **93**
resultados **20**
resumir **95**
retina **22**
retirar la mesa **34**
retrasarse **104**
retraso **102**
retrato robot **85**
retriever **164**
retroceso de los glaciares **155**
retrovisor **97**
reuniéndose **95**
reunión **81**, **82**
reunirse **178**
reventón **123**
revés **114**
revestimiento de papel **37**
revisión **22**
revisor / revisora **102**
revista **48**, **80**
revista del corazón **138**
revista en línea **84**
revolución industrial **79**
revolución tecnológica **79**
rey **79**, **140**
riachuelo **147**
rico en calorías **23**
riego **40**
riendas **120**
rifle **88**
rígido / rígida **176**
rímel **18**
ring **117**
rinoceronte **158**
rinoceronte lanudo **157**
riñón, riñones **04**, **53**, **71**
riñonera musleras y rodilleras **107**
río **147**, **148**
río subterráneo **146**
risotto **72**
ritmo **129**
rizador de pelo **12**
roble **169**
robo **50**, **85**
robo de vehículos **85**
robo en una tienda **85**
robot malvado **139**
rocalla **41**
rocas **147**, **156**
rociar **39**
rocío del sol **168**
rock **129**
rodaballo **54**
rodaja **53**
rodapié **30**

rodeo **120**
rodilla **01, 126**
rodillera **100**
rodillo **29, 37**
rodio **78**
rododendro **38**
roentgenio **78**
rojo **141**
rollitos de canela **71**
rollitos de primavera **72**
rollo de papel pintado **37**
rollo de verano **72**
romance **138**
romántico / romántica **10, 177**
rombo **74**
romero **38, 59**
rompecabezas **08**
romper con **178**
romper el cascarón **161**
rompiente **119**
ron **68**
ron con cola **68**
roncar **02, 30**
ronda **117**
ronronear **164**
ropa **13, 14, 15, 100**
ropa de bebé **13**
ropa de cama **30**
ropa de dormir **14**
ropa de hombre **47**
ropa de mujer **47**
ropa de niño **13**
ropa deportiva **15**
ropa formal **15**
ropa impermeable **121, 135**
ropa informal **14**
ropa interior **14**
ropa interior absorbente **49**
ropa sucia **34**
ropa térmica **135**
ropa tradicional **15**
rosa **38, 141**
rosa canina **169**
rosa del desierto **156**
rosca **62, 71**
rostro **01**
rotafolio **82, 95**
rotonda **96**
rotor **51**
rótula **03**
rotulador **175**
rótulo **130**
rough **115**
router **83**
róver **143**
Ruanda **149, 152**
ruandés / ruandesa **152**
rubí **156**
rubidio **78**
ruborizarse **02**
ruck **108**
rúcula **55**
rueda **24, 97, 101**
rueda abdominal **124**
rueda de ajuste **142**
rueda de repuesto **98**
rueda del timón **119**
rueda delantera **99**
rueda trasera **99**
ruedas de apoyo **101**
ruedo **120**
rugby **108**
rugby en silla de ruedas **108, 125**
rugir **159**
ruibarbo **58**
ruibarbo gigante **168**
ruidoso / ruidosa **176**
ruinas **44**
ruiseñor **160**
Rumanía **151, 153**
rumano / rumana **153**
ruso / rusa **153**
ruta de ferri **148**
ruta en quad **133**
ruta senderista **148**
rutabaga **56**
rutenio **78**
rutherfordio **78**
rutinas diarias **09**

S

sábado **172**
sabana **146, 158**
sábana **30**
sable **117**
saborear **11**
sabroso / sabrosa **52**
sacacorchos **28, 68**
sacadera **121**
sacapuntas **73, 82**
sacar al perro **09**
sacar dinero **45**
sacar en préstamo **80**
sacar la basura **09, 34**
saco de boxeo **117**
saco de dormir **135**
sacro **03**
Sagitario **144**
sal **23, 26**
sala de conciertos **43**
sala de embarque **104**
sala de espera **20, 102**
sala de hospital **21**
sala de interrogatorios **50**
sala de juntas **95**
sala de lectura **80**
sala de máquinas **105**
sala de maternidad **21**
sala de pediatría **21**
sala de reanimación **21**
sala de urgencias **21**
sala del tribunal **85**
salado / salada **52**
salamandra de fuego **163**
salamandra roja **163**
salami **53, 64**
salario **81**
salario fijo **81**
salario por hora **81**
salario variable **81**
salchicha, salchichas **53, 71**
saldo positivo **45**
salida, salidas **48, 104, 115**
salida de emergencia **103, 131**
salir **11, 115**
salir con amigos **09**
salir de casa **09**
salir del trabajo **09**
salmón ahumado **64, 71**
salmón del atlántico **166**
salmonete **54**
salomonense **153**
salón **26**
salpicadero **27, 99**
salsa, salsas **60, 64, 70**
salsa boloñesa **64**
salsa de chile dulce **60**
salsa de ostras **60**
salsa de pescado **60**
salsa de sándwich **60**
salsa de soja **60, 72**
salsa de tomate **70**
salsa picante **60**
salsa piccalilli **60**
saltador / saltadora **118**
saltamontes **162**
saltar **11, 117, 118, 120, 164**
saltar a la comba **124**
saltarín del fango **166**
salteado / salteada **72**
saltear **29**
salto **118**
salto a la comba **133**
Salto Ángel **145**
salto con pértiga **116**
salto de altura **116**
salto de cabeza **118**
salto de esquí **122**
salto de gran altura **118**
salto de longitud **116**
salto de pie **118**
salto de salida **118**
salto entre dos **112**
salto hacia atrás **118**
salto hacia delante **118**
saltos de tijera **124**
salud **19–24**
salud dental **49**
saludar **02, 179**
saludos **179**
salvadoreño / salvadoreña **152**
salvamanteles **26**
salvia **59**
sámara **169**
samario **78**
Samoa **150, 153**
samoano / samoana **153**
San Cristóbal y Nieves **150, 152**
San Marino **151, 153**
San Vicente y las Granadinas **150, 152**
Sanación con cristales **24**
sancristobaleño / sancristobaleña **152**
sandalias **17**
sandalias con cuña **17**
sandalias gladiadoras **17**
sandía **58**
sándwich **65, 70, 72**
sándwich club **70**
sándwich tostado **71**
sangrar **20**
sanidad **91**
sanmarinense **153**
Santa Lucía **150, 152**
santalucense **152**
Santo Tomé y Príncipe **149, 152**
santotomense / santototomense **152**
sanvicentino / sanvicentina **152**
sapo común **163**
sapo de las grandes planicies **163**
sapo de vientre de fuego oriental **163**
saque **110**
saque de banda **109, 112**
saque de centro **109**
sarampión **19**
sardinas **54, 64**
sari **15**
sarong **15**
sarpullido **19**
sarro **22**
sartén **28**
sartén de hierro fundido **28**
sastre modista **89**
sastrería **46**
satélite **143**
sátira **137**
satsuma **57**
Saturno **143**
sauce **169**
sauce ceniciento **169**
saudí **153**
sauna **124**
saxofón **128, 129**
sazonado / sazonada **64**
scooter **100**
scooter de tres ruedas **100**
seaborgio **78**
seca **18**
secador de pelo **12**
secadora **34**
secar los platos **34**
secarse **31**
secarse el pelo **09**
secciones **48**
seco **154**
secretario / secretaria **90**
secuoya gigante **167**
seda **13**
sedal **121**
sedán **97**
sedimentario / sedimentaria **156**
seguidor / seguidora **84**
seguir **84**
seguir recto **96, 148**
segunda base **113**
segunda línea **108**
segundero **171**
segundo / segunda **171, 173**
segundo centro / segunda centro **108**
seguridad **104, 109**
seguro / segura **06, 10, 93**
seis **173**
selector de largo de puntada **142**
selector de tensión **142**
selenio **78**
sellador **37**

sello, sellos **45, 48**
selva tropical **146**
semáforos **43**
semana **172**
semana santa **07**
sembrar **39, 86**
semental **120, 165**
semicírculo de no carga **112**
semiconductor **75**
semilla de amapola **59**
semilla de cilantro **59**
semilla de hinojo **59**
semilla de mostaza **60**
semilla de nigella **59**
semillas **40, 58, 168**
semillero **40**
sencillo **68**
senderismo **133**
sendero público **148**
Senegal **149, 152**
senegalés / senegalesa **152**
seno nasal **04**
sensible **10, 18**
sentadilla **124**
sentarse **11**
sentido obligatorio **96**
sentirse mejor **20**
señal **102, 104**
señal de la calle **43**
señal de prioridad **96**
señalar **11, 178**
señales de tráfico **96**
señor / señora **79**
señuelo **121**
sépalo **38**
septiembre **172**
séptimo / séptima **173**
sequía **154**
ser absuelto / ser absuelta **85**
ser cesado / ser cesada **81**
ser despedido / ser despedida **81**
ser expulsado / ser expulsada **109**
ser tendencia **84**
serbal **169**
Serbia **151, 153**
serbio / serbia **153**
serio / seria **06, 10**
serpiente comedora de huevos común **163**
serpiente de cascabel **163**
serpiente de coral común **163**
serpiente de mar **139**
serpiente liana verde **163**
serpientes y escaleras **140**
serrar **35**
serrucho **36**
servicial **93**
servicio **69**
servicio de habitaciones **131**
servicio de lavandería **131**
servicio de limpieza **131**
servicio de urgencias **50**
servicio incluido **69**
servicio no incluido **69**
servicios de emergencias **50**
servicios personales **91**
servicios veterinarios **91**
servilleta **27, 72**
servilleta de papel **70**
servilletero **27**
servir **65, 114**
sesenta **173**
set **114**
seta barbuda **170**
seta de jardín **170**
seta de olivo **170**
seta ostra **56, 170**
setas **170**
setas cultivadas **170**
setas venenosas **170**
setenta **173**
seto **41, 86, 146**
setter **164**
sexto / sexta **173**
seychellense **152**
Seychelles **152**
shaobing **62**
shiatsu **24**
shih tzu **164**
shiitake **56, 170**
short corner **112**
shorts de baño **134**
siamés **164**
sicomoro **169**
sidecar **100**
sidra **68**
siempre **171**
siempreviva de los tejados **168**
sien **01**
sierra circular **35**
sierra de arco **36**
sierra de calar **35**
sierra de mano **36**
sierra de podar **40**
Sierra Leona **149, 152**
sierraleonés / sierraleonesa **152**
siete **173**
sifón **33**
siglo **172**
signo de división **74**
signo de exclamación **175**
signo de igual **74**
signo de interrogación **175**
signo de multiplicación **74**
signo et **175**
signo más **74**
signo menos **74**
silbido final **109**
silenciador **98, 100**
silencioso / silenciosa **176**
sílex **156**
silicio **78**
silla **24, 26, 82, 114**
silla de montar **120**
silla de niños **101**
silla de paseo **08**
silla de playa **134**
silla de rodillas **82**
silla de ruedas **21**
silla del director **84**
sillín **101, 120**
sillón **26**
sillón dental **22**
silo **86**
silúrico **157**
símbolo del zodíaco **144**
símbolo químico **76**
simpático / simpática **177**
sin amueblar **32**
sin espinas **54**
sin gas **52**
sin gluten **23**
sin hielo **68**
sin lactosa **23, 61**
sin mangas **15**
sin plomo **97**
sin semillas **57**
sin tirantes **15**
sinagoga **44**
sinfonía **128**
Singapur **151, 153**
singapurense **153**
síntomas **19**
sintonizador **136**
sintonizador digital **136**
sintonizar **136**
sirena **139**
sirena de la ambulancia **50**
Siria **150, 153**
sirio / siria **153**
sirope de arce **60**
sistema de clasificación de basura **33**
sistema de megafonía **102**
sistema de refrigeración **98**
sistema judicial **85**
sistema solar **143**
sistemas corporales **04**
sitar **129**
skateboarding **125, 133**
skeleton **122**
slalom **122**
slalom gigante **122**
slip **111**
smoothie **52**
snowboard **122**
soborno **85**
sobre **45, 82**
sobre par **115**
sobrepesca **155**
sobresaliente **177**
sobrino / sobrina **05**
sociable **10**
sociología **80**
sociólogo / socióloga **89**
socorrista **118, 134**
sodio **78**
sofá **26**
sofá cama **26**
sofocante **154**
sofreír **29**
sol **143, 154**
solapa **15**
soldado / soldado **88, 89**
soldado de marina **88**
soldador / soldadura **35, 36**
soldar **35**
sole **115**
soleado **154**
solicitud de empleo **92**
sólido **76**
solitario **140**
solitario / solitaria **06**
solo **128**
solo los fines de semana **172**
soltar **121**
somalí **152**
Somalia **149, 152**
sombra de ojos **18**
sombrero, sombreros **14, 16, 170**
sombrero de campana **16**
sombrero de fieltro **16**
sombrero de panamá **16**
sombrero de vaquero **16**
sombrero mexicano **16**
sombrilla **65, 134**
somier de muelles **30**
sonajero **08**
sonata para violín **128**
sonda **22**
sonda espacial **143**
sonreír **02**
sonreír de oreja a oreja **02**
sopa **69, 72**
sopa de fideos **72**
soplador **40**
soplar **11, 63**
soporte **40, 87, 115, 121, 136**
soporte de altavoz **136**
soporte de la cámara **123**
soporte del sillín **101**
soporte para cuchillos **28**
soporte para gotero **21**
soprano **126**
sorber **02, 52**
sorprendido / sorprendida **06**
sospechoso **50**
sospechoso / sospechosa **85**
sostenido **128**
sótano **25**
soul **129**
souvenir **132**
spam **83**
square leg **111**
squash **114**
Sri Lanka **150, 153**
step **124**
stick de portero **110**
strike **113**
suave **57**
suavizante de ropa **34**
Suazilandia **149, 152**
subíndice **76**
subir **62, 83, 178**
subir a **178**
subir el volumen **136, 137, 178**
subirse **100**
subirse en la bici **101**
submarino **88, 105**
subrayador **73, 82, 175**
subsuelo **39**
subtítulos **137**
subwoofer **136**
sucio / sucia **176**
suculentas **38, 41**
sucursal **81**
sudadera **14**
Sudáfrica **149, 152**
sudafricano / sudafricana **152**
Sudamérica **149, 152**
sudamericano / sudamericana **152**
Sudán **149, 152**
Sudán del Sur **149, 152**
sudanés / sudanesa **152**

sudar **02**
Suecia **151, 153**
sueco / sueca **153**
suegro / suegra **05**
suela **17**
suelo **25, 30, 125**
sueño **30**
suero de mantequilla **61**
suflé **72**
Suiza **151, 153**
suizo / suiza **153**
sujetador **14**
sujetador deportivo **15**
sujetapapeles **82**
sujetar **11**
sumar **11, 74**
sumergible **166**
sumiller **69**
suministro eléctrico **51**
sumo **117**
superalimentos **23**
superficial **176**
superficie **39, 143**
superficie de juego **108**
supermercado **48**
supernova **144**
supervisar **92**
supervisor / supervisora **81, 92**
suplemento, suplementos **49, 23**
suplemento para plantas **39**
suplentes **109**
supositorio **49**
sur **148**
surcoreano / surcoreana **153**
sureste **148**
surf **119, 134**
surf de remo **119**
surfista **119**
suricata **159**
Surinam **149, 152**
surinamés / surinamesa **152**
suroeste **148**
surrealismo **130**
sursudanés / sursudanesa **152**
surtido de gominolas **67**
surtidor **97**
sushi **54**
suspender **73, 178**
suspense **127, 137**
suspensión **98, 100**
suspensión delantera **123**
suspensión trasera **123**
suspirar **02**
susurrar **11**
swing **115**
swing de práctica **115**

T

tabaco **86**
tabardo **13**
tabi **17**
tabla **119**
tabla de boogie **119**
tabla de contenidos **138**
tabla de cortar **28**
tabla de planchar **34**
tabla de quesos **69**
tabla de surf **119, 134**
tabla periódica **78**
tablero **112**
tablero de ajedrez **140**
tablero mdf **35**
tableta **83**
tablón de anuncios **82**
taburete **65, 68**
tacle defensivo derecho / tacle defensiva derecha **107**
tacle defensivo izquierdo / tacle defensiva izquierda **107**
tacle derecho / tacle derecha **107**
tacle izquierdo / tacle izquierda **107**
taco **70, 125**
tacón, tacones **17**
tacones bajos **17**
tacones con puntera abierta **17**
tacones con tira en t **17**
tacones con tira talonera **17**
tacones con tira tobillera **17**
tacones de aguja **17**
tacos de béisbol **17**
taekwondo **117**
tai chi **117, 133**
tailandés / tailandesa **153**
Tailandia **150, 153**
Taj mahal **44**
taladrar **35**
taladro de mano **36**
taladro eléctrico **35**
taladro inalámbrico **35**
taladro manual **35**
talar **39**
talentoso / talentosa **10**
talio **78**
talla en madera **141**
tallar **35**
taller mecánico **98**
tallo, tallos **38, 55**
talón **01, 02, 115**
talonador / talonadora **108**
tamarillo **58**
tampón **49**
tándem **101**
tanque **88**
tanque de gasolina **100**
tántalo **78**
Tanzania **149, 152**
tanzano / tanzana **152**
tapa **28**
tapa blanda **138**
tapa dura **138**
tapacubos **98**
tapir **159**
tapón **31, 76**
taquígrafo / taquígrafa **85**
taquilla, taquillas **102, 106, 118, 124, 127, 130**
tarántula **162**
tarde **09, 171**
tarde-noche **171**
tareas de casa **34**
tareas domésticas **34**
tarifa **99, 102**
tarifa de entrada **130, 132**
tarjeta amarilla **109**
tarjeta de crédito **45, 94**
tarjeta de cumpleaños **07**
tarjeta de débito **45, 94**
tarjeta de embarque **104**
tarjeta de fidelización **47**
tarjeta de memoria **83**
tarjeta de transporte **48**
tarjeta roja **109**
tarjeta sim **48**
tarro **52, 60**
tarro de conservas **60**
tarso **03**
tarta de boda **63**
tarta de chocolate **63**
tarta de cumpleaños **63**
tarta de frutas **63**
tarta de queso **63**
tarta rellena **63**
tartas **63**
tasa de cambio **45, 94**
tasa de interés **45**
tatami de kárate **117**
Tauro **144**
taxista **90**
Tayikistán **151, 153**
tayiko / tayika **153**
tayín **28**
taza **27, 33**
taza de café **27**
taza de té **27**
taza medidora **29**
té **52, 66, 71, 86**
té blanco **66**
té con hielo **66**
té con leche **66**
té con limón **66**
té de hierbas **66**
té helado **52**
té negro **66**
té verde **66**
teatro **42, 73, 126**
teatro de ópera **126**
techo **26, 98**
techo corredizo **98**
teclado **83, 129**
teclado numérico **45**
tecnecio **78**
técnico de sonido / técnica de sonido **84**
tecnología **83**
tee **115**
teja, tejas **25, 87**
tejado **25**
tejado de paja **32**
tejedor **160**
tejedor / tejedora **142**
tejeduría **142**
tejo **167**
tejón europeo **158**
tela **142**
tela vaquera **13**
telar **142**
teleadicto / teleadicta **137**
teleférico **122**
teléfono **82**
teléfono de emergencia **96**
teléfono inteligente **83**
teléfono móvil **82**
telenovela **137**
teleprompter **84**
telescopio **144**
telescopio espacial **144**
telescopio reflector **144**
telescopio refractor **144**
telesilla **122**
teletienda **137**
televisión **26, 136, 137**
televisión a la carta **137**
televisión por cable **137**
televisión por satélite **137**
telón **126**
telón de fondo **126**
teluro **78**
temblor de tierra **145**
témpera **141**
temperatura **154**
tempestuoso **154**
templado / templada **154**
templo **44**
templo griego **44**
temporada **137**
temporal **81**
temporizador **28, 76, 95**
temprano **171**
tendedero **34**
tender la ropa **34**
tendón **03**
tendón de aquiles **03**
tenedor **27**
tenedor de trinchar **28**
tener en propiedad **32**
tener hambre **26**
tener pérdidas **94**
tener un accidente de coche **98**
tener un bebé **07**
tener un día libre **81**
tener una fuga **33**
teneso **78**
tenis **114**
tenor **126**
tensiómetro **21**
tensión arterial **20**
tentempiés **65**
terapia asistida con animales **24**
terapia de grupo **24**
terapias **24**
terbio **78**
tercer jugador / tercera jugadora **111**
tercera base **113**
tercera línea a la derecha **108**
tercera línea a la izquierda **108**
tercero / tercera **173**
tercio / tercia **173**
terminal **104**
terminal de ferris **106**
terminal ferroviaria **106**
terminal petrolífera **106**
terminar el trabajo **09**
termita **162**
termo **52, 135**
termómetro **20, 76**
termómetro de carne **28**
termómetro de oído **20**

termosfera **155**
ternera **53**
ternero **165**
terraza **25**, **65**
terraza ajardinada **41**
terremoto **145**
terreno inundable **147**
terrible **177**
terror **127**
terrorífico / terrorífica **177**
tesis **80**
tesoro **139**
test de embarazo **08**
test de snellen **22**
testículo **04**
testigo **85**, **116**
tetera **27**, **66**
tetina **08**
texto **138**
thawb **15**
tía / tío **05**
tiara **16**
tibia **03**
tiburón blanco **166**
tiburón martillo **166**
tiburón peregrino **166**
tiempo **107**, **137**, **154**, **171**
tiempo añadido **109**
tiempo libre **126–142**
tiempo muerto **107**
tienda **42**
tienda de antigüedades **46**
tienda de arte **46**
tienda de bolsos **47**
tienda de campaña familiar **135**
tienda de campaña instantánea **135**
tienda de discos **46**
tienda de electrónica **46**
tienda de golosinas **67**
tienda de mascotas **46**
tienda de moda **46**
tienda de regalos **46**, **130**
tienda de ropa **47**
tienda de segunda mano **46**
tienda ecológica **23**, **46**, **47**
tienda india **32**
tienda libre de impuestos **104**
tienda para dos personas **135**
tierra **39**, **143**, **145**
tierra de labranza **146**
tierra fértil **39**
tierra firme **145**
tierras de cultivo **86**
tigre **157**, **159**
tijeras **28**, **37**, **82**, **142**
tijeras de peluquería **12**
tijeras de podar **40**
tijeras de uñas **18**, **20**
tijeras dentadas **142**
tilo **169**
timbal **128**
timbre **25**, **99**
tímido / tímida **110**
timón **103**, **119**
Timor Oriental **151**, **153**
timorense **153**
tinta **141**, **175**
tinte de pelo **18**
tintorería **46**
tiovivo **133**
tipi **32**
tipografía **175**
tipos de piel **18**
tipos de suelo **39**
tirabeque **55**
tirador **97**, **99**
tiramisú **63**
tirar **11**, **112**, **178**
tirar al hoyo (con un putter) **115**
tirita **20**, **49**
tiritar **02**
tiro al blanco **125**
tiro con arco **125**
tiro con efecto **114**
tiro de esquina **109**
tiro fallido **112**
tiroides **04**
titanio **78**
tití **159**
titular **138**
título **80**, **138**
tiza **156**
toalla de baño **31**
toalla de mano **31**
toalla del pelo **18**
toallas **31**
toallero **31**
toallitas **08**, **49**
toallitas desinfectantes **20**
toba volcánica **156**
tobillera **16**
tobillo **01**, **02**
tobogán **43**
tocadiscos **129**, **136**
tocador **30**
tocar (la trompeta) **128**
tocar un instrumento **09**
todos los días **172**
todoterreno **97**
tofe **67**
toga **80**
Togo **149**, **152**
togolés / togolesa **152**
toldo **65**
toma de aire **123**
toma de aire de los frenos **123**
toma de decisiones **93**
toma de tierra **33**
tomar apuntes **73**
tomar el sol **133**, **134**
tomar un café **09**
tomate **56**
tomate a la parrilla **71**
tomate en conserva **71**
tomate pera **56**
tomates cherry **55**
tómbolo **147**
tomillo **59**
tonelada **174**
Tonga **150**, **153**
tongano / tongana **153**
tónico **18**
tono **128**
tonos altos **128**
tonos bajos **128**
tonto / tonta **10**
topacio **156**
tope **102**
topiarios **41**
topo **159**
topógrafo / topógrafa **90**
tordo **160**
torio **78**
tormenta **154**
tormenta de arena **154**
tormenta de nieve **154**
tormentoso **154**
tornado **154**
tornear **35**
torneo **115**
tornillo **36**
tornillo de enfoque **77**, **144**
torno **141**
toro **165**
toronja **57**
torpe **10**
torque **16**
torre **44**, **51**, **118**, **140**
torre de control **104**
torre de control del tráfico aéreo **43**
torre de mando **105**
torre de perforación **51**
Torre de Pisa **44**
torre de refrigeración **51**
torre de vigilancia **134**
torre del homenaje **44**
Torre Eiffel **44**
torreón **44**
tortellini **64**
tortilla **61**, **62**, **71**, **72**
tortita, tortitas **65**, **71**
tortitas de patata **70**, **71**
tortuga **164**
tortuga carey **166**
tortuga de cuello de serpiente **163**
tortuga de las galápagos **163**
tortuga espalda de diamante **163**
tortuga estrellada **163**
tortuga laúd **163**
tortuga matamata **163**
tortuga verde **163**
tos **19**
toser **20**
tosta **70**
tostada **71**
tostada con aguacate **71**
tostada francesa **71**
tostadora **27**
trabajador / trabajadora **81**
trabajar a jornada completa **81**
trabajar a media jornada **81**
trabajar a turnos **81**
trabajar desde casa **81**
trabajar horas extras **09**, **11**
trabajo, trabajos **81–95**, **89**, **90**
trabajo de nueve a cinco **81**
trabajo de oficina **81**
trabajo en equipo **92**, **93**
tractor **86**
tradescantia **167**
traer **11**
tráfico **96**
tráfico de drogas **85**
tragar **52**
tragedia **126**
traje **15**
traje de buzo **118**
traje de cuero **100**
traje de invierno **13**
traje de neopreno **134**
traje espacial **143**
tramitar el pedido **46**
trampolín **118**, **125**
trampolín de salto **122**
transbordador espacial **143**
transformador **33**, **75**
transmisión **98**
transmitir **137**
transportador **73**, **74**
transporte **91**
transporte marítimo **91**
tranvía **99**, **102**
trapecio **03**, **74**
trapo del polvo **34**
tráquea **04**
trasgo **139**
traslado en autobús **104**
trasplantar **39**
traste **129**
trastero **32**
tratable **10**
tratamiento, tratamientos **20**, **21**, **24**
tratamiento facial **18**
tratamientos de belleza **18**
traumatología **21**
travesaño **111**
trébol **140**
trece **173**
trecho final **123**
treinta **173**
trémolo **129**
tren, trenes **102**
tren bala **102**
tren de alta velocidad **102**
tren de aterrizaje **103**
tren de cercanías **102**
tren de juguete **08**
tren de levitación magnética **102**
tren de mercancías **102**
tren de vapor **102**
tren delantero **103**
tren diésel **102**
tren eléctrico **102**
trenca **15**
trenza **12**
trenza francesa **12**
trenzas africanas **12**
trenzas apretadas **12**
trepar a los árboles **133**
tres **173**
tres en raya **140**
tres veces a la semana **172**
triángulo **24**, **74**, **125**, **128**
triásico **157**
triatlón **116**
tribuna del jurado **85**
tribunal de justicia **85**
tríceps **03**
tricerátops **157**
trigo **86**
trillizos / trillizas **05**
trilobites **157**
trinchar **29**
trineo **122**
trineo tirado por perros **122**

Trinidad y Tobago **150, 152**
trinitense **152**
triple barra **120**
triple salto **116**
trípode **76, 144**
tripulación **119**
triste **06**
tritoma **167**
tritón **139**
tritón crestado del norte **163**
trituradora de papeles **82**
trol **139**
trolear **84**
trolebús **99**
trombón **128**
trompa **128, 159**
trompa de falopio **04**
trompeta **128, 129**
trompeta de la muerte **170**
trona **08**
tronco **55**
tronera **44, 125**
tropezarse **178**
trópico de cáncer **145**
trópico de capricornio **145**
trópicos **145**
troposfera **155**
trotar **120, 165**
trovador **79**
trucha **54**
trucha arco iris **54**
trueno **154**
trufa **56, 170**
tsunami **145**
tu pedido está de camino **70**
tuba **128**
tubería **33, 87**
tubo **98**
tubo de ensayo **76**
tubo de escape **98, 100**
tubo de pintura **141**
tubo superior **101**
tubos de rayos uva **18**
tucán esmeralda **160**
tucán grande **160**
tuerca **36**
tuercas de llanta **98**
tulio **78**
tulipán **38**
tumba **79**
tumbarse **20**
túnde entrada y salida **109**
tundra **146**
tunecino / tunecina **152**
túnez **149, 152**
tungsteno **78**
tupinambo **56**
turba **39**
turbante **16**
turbera **79**
turbina **51**
turco / turca **153**
turcomano / turcomana **153**
turismo **91**
turista **132**
Turkmenistán **151, 153**
turmalina **156**
turquesa **141, 156**
Turquía **150, 151, 153**
turrón **67**
tutor **39**
tutú **126**
Tuvalu **150, 153**
tuvaluano / tuvaluana **153**
tv **26, 136**
tiranosaurio rex **157**

U

uchuva **57**
Ucrania **151, 153**
ucraniano / ucraniana **153**
udon **64**
Uganda **149, 152**
ugandés / ugandesa **152**
ugli **57**
ukelele **129**
último piso **63**
ultraligero **103**
ulular **161**
un chorro **29**
un millón **173**
un puñado **29**
una en punto **171**
una gran variedad **48**
una hora **171**
una pizca **29**
una vez a la semana **172**
una y cinco **171**
una y cuarto **171**
una y diez **171**
una y media **171**
una y veinte **171**
una y veinticinco **171**
unicornio **139**
unidad de cuidados intensivos **21**
unidad usb **83**
unidades de medida **74**
uniforme **50, 88**
uniforme de bombero **13**
uniforme de cocinero **13**
uniforme de trabajo **13**
uniforme escolar **13**
uniforme militar **13**
universidad **43, 80**
universo **144**
uno **173**
uno por ciento **173**
uña **02**
uranio **78**
Urano **143**
urinario **04**
urología **21**
uropeltis macrolepis **163**
Uruguay **149, 152**
uruguayo / uruguaya **152**
utensilios de cocina **28**
útero **04, 08**
útil **177**
útiles de jardinería **40**
uva espina **57**
uvas **57**
Uzbekistán **151, 153**
uzbeko / uzbeka **153**

V

vaca **165**
vacaciones **81, 104**
vacante **92**
vaciar el lavavajillas **34**
vacío / vacía **75, 176**
vacuno / vacuna **08, 20, 53**
vacuola **77**
vagina **04**
vago / vaga **10**
vagón **102**
vagón restaurante **102**
vaina **55**
vainilla **59**
vaisakhi **07**
vajilla **27**
vajilla de sushi **27**
valiente **10**
valla, vallas **41, 86, 110**
valle **146**
valor **94**
válvula **101**
válvula de desagüe **33**
vampiro **139**
vanadio **78**
vandalismo **85**
vanesa de los cardos **162**
Vanuatu **150, 153**
vanuatuense **153**
vapor de agua **51**
vaqueros **14**
varicela **19**
varilla **115**
varilla de vidrio **76**
varilla del nivel de aceite **98**
varita **139**
vaso, vasos **52, 68**
vaso con boquilla **27**
vaso de pinta **27**
vaso de precipitado **76**
vaso de sake **27**
vaso de whisky **27**
vaso reutilizable **70**
váter **31, 33**
vecino / vecina **07**
vegano **23**
vegetariano **23**
vehículo anfibio **88**
vehículo blindado **88**
vehículo de exploración **88**
vehículo de servicio **104**
vehículos militares **88**
veinte **173**
veinte minutos **171**
veintidós **173**
veintiuno **173**
vela **26, 119, 134**
vela mayor **119**
velas de cumpleaños **63**
velero **105**
vello facial **12**
velo **15**
velocímetro **99, 100**
velocista **116**
vena **04**
venado **53**
vencejo **160**
venda **20, 49**
vendaje **20**
vendaval **154**
vender **46**
venezolano / venezolana **152**
Venezuela **149, 152**
ventaja **114**
ventana **25, 87,99, 102**
ventana de guillotina **25**
ventana emergente **84**
ventana en arco **32**
ventana mirador **25**
ventanilla **103**
ventilador **33, 103**
ventilador calefactor **33**
ventilador de techo **33**
ventisca **154**
ventoso **154**
Venus **143**
venus atrapamoscas **168**
ver **11**
ver la tele **09**
verano **172**
verde, verdes **01, 141**
verdulería **46, 56**
verdulero / verdulera **89**
verdura **48, 55, 56**
verduras cocidas **72**
verduras orgánicas **55**
verduras para ensalada **55**
veredicto **85**
verja **32, 86**
vertebrados **77**
vértebras cervicales **03**
vértebras lumbares **03**
vértebras torácicas **03**
vertedero **155**
verter **29**
verticales **120**
vesícula biliar **04**
vesícula seminal **04**
vestíbulo **102**
vestíbulo del hotel **131**
vestido **14**
vestido de dama de honor **15**
vestido de flamenca **15**
vestido de noche **15**
vestido de novia **15**
vestirse **09**
vestirse elegante **178**
vestuario, vestuarios **124, 126, 127**
veterano / veterana **88**
veterinario / veterinaria **89**
vía **102**
vía de acceso **96, 106**
vía de salida **96**
vía de un solo sentido **42, 96**
vía férrea **148**
vía láctea **144**

viajar al extranjero **104**, **131**
viaje **131**
viaje de trabajo **81**
vibráfono **128**
vicuña **158**
vida en ciudad **42–51**
vida oceánica **166**
vida sana **23**
vídeo a la carta **137**
videoconferencia **83**
videojuegos **91**, **136**
videollamada **83**
vidriera **44**
vidrio **155**, **176**
vieira **54**
viejo / vieja **12**, **176**
viento **51**, **154**
viento madera **128**
viento metal **128**
viernes **172**
Vietnam **150**, **153**
vietnamita **153**
viga **87**
viga de cumbrera **87**
viga maestra **87**
vigésimo primero / vigésima primera **173**
vigésimo / vigésima **173**
vigilabebés **08**, **30**
villa **32**, **131**
villano / villana **127**
vinagre **60**, **64**
vinagre balsámico **60**
vinagre blanco **34**
vinagre de malta **60**
vinagre de manzana **60**
vinagre de vino **60**
vino **68**
vino blanco **52**, **68**
vino espumoso **68**
vino rosado **52**, **68**
vino tinto **52**, **68**
viñedo **86**
viola **128**
violeta **38**
violín **128**, **129**
violonchelo **128**
virar **119**
virgen extra **60**
Virgo **144**
virgulilla **175**
virus **19**, **77**
visado **104**
vísceras **53**
visera **100**
visillo **26**
visión **22**
visita guiada **132**
visita turística **99**, **132**
visitar una casa **32**
visor **136**
visor teñido de dorado **143**
vista frontal **97**
vista lateral **97**
vitaminas **23**, **49**
vitrocerámica **27**
viuda **05**
viuda negra **162**
vivero **46**, **164**
vivienda **25**
vivienda urbana **32**
vlog **84**
vlogger **84**
vodka **68**
vodka con naranja **68**
volante **99**, **114**
volar **11**, **162**
volcán **145**
volcar **119**
volea **114**
voleibol **112**
volquete **87**
voltaje **33**
voltio **75**
volumen **74**, **136**, **174**
vomitar **20**
votación **85**
votación a mano alzada **95**
voto unánime **95**
vuelo directo **104**
vuelo internacional **104**
vuelo nacional **104**

W

walkie-talkie **50**
wasabi **60**
waterpolo **119**
web comunitaria **84**
web de noticias **84**
wedge **115**
whisky **68**
whisky escocés con agua **68**
wicket **111**
wicket medio / wicket media **111**
wifi **83**
windsurf **119**, **134**
windsurfista **119**
wok **28**
wombat **158**
wrap **70**

XY

xenón **78**
xilófono **128**
yacimiento arqueológico **132**
yak **159**
yarda **174**
yate **105**, **134**
yate de vela **119**
yegua **120**, **165**
yema **61**, **71**
Yemen **151**, **153**
yemení **153**
yerno **05**
yeso **37**
yesquero erizado **170**
Yibuti **149**, **152**
yibutiano / yibutiana **152**
yodo **78**
yoga **24**
yogur **61**
yogur de frutas **71**
yogur helado **61**
yoyó **08**
yuca **38**
yurta **32**

Z

zafiro **156**
zaguero / zaguera **108**
Zambia **149**, **152**
zambiano / zambiana **152**
zampoña **129**
zampullín **161**
zanahoria **56**
zancada **124**
zapatería **46**
zapatilla de ciclismo **17**
zapatillas de clavos **17**
zapatilla deportiva **17**
zapatillas para correr **17**
zapatos abotinados **17**
zapatos con hebilla **17**
zapatos con plataforma **17**
zapatos con tacos **107**
zapatos de ballet **126**
zapatos de críquet **111**
zapatos de golf **17**, **115**
zapatos de niño **17**
zapatos de tenis **114**
zapatos derby **17**
zapatos oxford **17**
zapatos planos **17**
zapatos sin cierres **17**
zarapito **161**
zarpar **106**
zigurat **44**
Zimbabue **149**, **152**
zimbabuense **152**
zinc **156**
zodíaco **144**
zombi **139**
zona adal **166**
zona crepuscular **166**
zona de abastecimiento **97**
zona de anotación **107**
zona de ataque **110**
zona de defensa **110**
zona de espera **81**
zona de marca **108**
zona de medianoche **166**
zona de peligro **117**
zona de penalti **109**
zona de restaurantes **47**
zona de seguridad **117**
zona de tiro libre **112**
zona escolar **96**
zona fótica **166**
zona montañosa **146**
zona neutral **107**, **110**
zona peatonal **42**
zona poco profunda **118**
zona profunda **118**
zoo **133**
zoología **77**, **80**
zoólogo / zoóloga **77**
zorro **159**
zorro ártico **159**
zuecos **17**
zumaque **59**
zumbar **162**
zumo, zumos **52**, **65**
zumo de arándanos **65**
zumo de fresa **65**
zumo de fruta **71**
zumo de mango **65**
zumo de manzana **65**
zumo de naranja con pulpa **65**
zumo de naranja sin pulpa **65**
zumo de piña **65**
zumo de tomate **65**
zurcir **142**

Acknowledgments

The publisher would like to thank:
Dr. Steven Snape for his assistance with hieroglyphs. Elizabeth Blakemore for editorial assistance; Mark Lloyd, Charlotte Johnson, and Anna Scully for design assistance; Simon Mumford for national flags; Sunita Gahir and Ali Jayne Scrivens for additional illustration; Adam Brackenbury for art colour correction; Claire Ashby and Romaine Werblow for images; William Collins for fonts; Lori Hand, Kayla Dugger, and Jane Perlmutter for Americanization; Justine Willis for proofreading; Elizabeth Blakemore for indexing; Helen Peters for the wordlists; Christine Stroyan for audio recording management and ID Audio for audio recording and production.

DK India
Senior Art Editors Vikas Sachdeva, Ira Sharma; **Art Editor** Anukriti Arora;
Assistant Art Editors Ankita Das, Adhithi Priya; **Editors** Hina Jain, Saumya Agarwal;
DTP Designer Manish Upreti

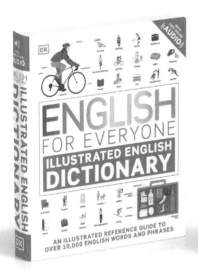

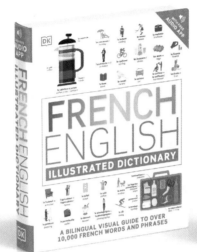

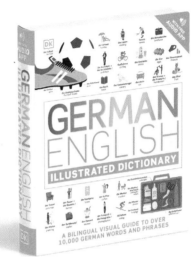

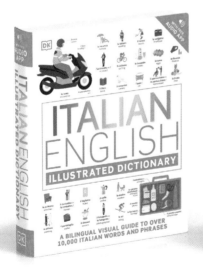

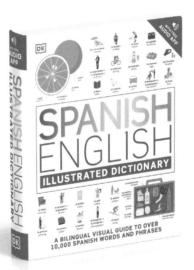